INTRODUCTION TO SOCIAL PSYCHOLOGY

Introduction to Social Psychology

Richard A. Lippa
California State University, Fullerton

Wadsworth Publishing Company
Belmont, California
A Division of Wadsworth, Inc.

A study guide has been specially designed to help students master the concepts presented in this textbook. Order from your bookstore.

Psychology Editor: Kenneth King
Development Editors: Mary Arbogast, John Bergez
Editorial Assistant: Michelle L. Palacio
Production Editor: Donna Linden
Print Buyer: Barbara Britton
Designer: Andrew H. Ogus
Design Assistant: Jill Turney
Copy Editor: Alan Titche
Photo Researcher: Stephen Forsling
Technical Illustrator: Judith Ogus/Random Arts
Compositor: Thompson Type, San Diego, California
Cover Photograph: © 1988 Richard Pasley/Stock, Boston:
Mirrored wall at the Epcot Center

Acknowledgments appear on pages A-51, A-52.

Printed in the United States of America 48

3 4 5 6 7 8 9 10 — 94 93 92

Library of Congress Cataloging-in-Publication Data

Lippa, Richard A.
    Introduction to social psychology / Richard A. Lippa.
        p.   cm.
    Includes bibliographical references.
    ISBN 0-534-11772-4
    1. Social psychology.   I. Title.
    [DNLM: 1. Psychology, Social.   HM 251 L765i]
HM251.L49   1990
302 — dc20
DNLM/DLC
for Library of Congress   89-22738
                                                                    CIP

To Ann Litvin, a special person who, among many other things, taught me the Yiddish expression *oyf tsulokhes*.

To my mother and father, Alice and Leo Lippa, my sister Janet, and brother Edward — all of whom saw much too little of me during the time I worked on this book.

And in loving memory of my aunt, Laura Weinstein.

Brief Contents

CHAPTER 1   What Is Social Psychology?   3

CHAPTER 2   Social Psychological Research   23

CHAPTER 3   Person Perception   61

CHAPTER 4   Attribution   97

CHAPTER 5   Social Cognition   133

CHAPTER 6   Personality and the Self   171

CHAPTER 7   Attitudes and Beliefs   219

CHAPTER 8   Persuasion and Attitude Change   257

CHAPTER 9   Prejudice   301

CHAPTER 10   Gender and Social Behavior   343

CHAPTER 11   Liking, Loving, and Close Relationships   387

CHAPTER 12   Aggression   433

CHAPTER 13   Altruism and Prosocial Behavior   477

CHAPTER 14   Conformity, Compliance, and Obedience   521

CHAPTER 15   Group Behavior   567

CHAPTER 16   Applying Social Psychology   613

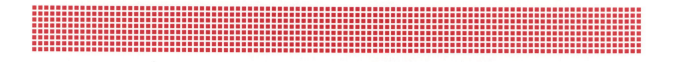

Detailed Contents

List of Applied Topics   xv

Preface   xviii

CHAPTER 1

What Is Social Psychology?   3

The Nature of Social Psychology   6

Social Psychology Studies Influence on Social Behavior ■ Social Psychology Explains Social Behavior ■ Social Psychology Studies Social Behavior ■ The Self in Social Psychology ■ Differences Between Social Psychology and Related Fields

Theories in Social Psychology   11

The Functions of Social Psychological Theories ■ Four Theoretical Perspectives

Applying Social Psychology   17

The Two Faces of Applied Social Psychology ■ The Profession of Social Psychology

Summary   20

Glossary   20

CHAPTER 2

Social Psychological Research   *23*

Issues in Social Psychological Research   25

Theories in Social Psychology ▪ Operational Definitions in Social Psychology ▪ Reliability and Validity of Measures ▪ Kinds of Social Psychological Studies ▪ Generalizing from the Results of Research Studies ▪ Statistics and Social Psychology Research ▪ Bias in Social Psychological Research

Ethics in Social Psychological Research   49

Ethical Problems ▪ Measures to Reduce Ethical Problems — APA Guidelines

The Social Relevance of Social Psychological Research   55

Summary   56

Glossary   57

CHAPTER 3

Person Perception   *61*

The Nature of Person Perception ▪ Differences Between Person Perception and Object Perception ▪ Research Topics in Person Perception

First Impressions   65

Physical Characteristics ▪ Nonverbal Behaviors ▪ The Power of First Impressions

Accuracy of Direct Judgments   73

Judging Personality ▪ Judging Emotions ▪ Detecting Deception

Direct Judgments: A Postscript   93

Summary   93

Glossary   94

CHAPTER 4

Attribution   *97*

Attribution Processes: Internal and External Causes   98

Our Preference for Internal Explanations

Theories of Attribution   103

Jones and Davis's Theory of Correspondent Inferences ▪ Kelley's Cube Model of Attribution ▪ Causal Schemas

Attribution Errors and Biases   116

The Fundamental Attribution Error ▪ *The Actor-Observer Effect* ▪ *Salience Effects in Attribution* ▪ *Motivational Biases in Attribution*

Applying Attribution Theory   126

Treating Depression ▪ *Improving Academic Performance*

Summary   129

Glossary   130

CHAPTER 5
▪▪▪▪▪▪▪▪▪▪▪▪▪▪

Social Cognition   133

Putting Information Together: Impression Formation   134

Asch's Gestalt Model ▪ *Anderson's Weighted Averaging Model*

Schemas and Social Perception   139

The Nature of Schemas ▪ *Kinds of Schemas in Social Cognition* ▪ *Effects of Schemas on Social Cognition* ▪ *The Persistence of Schemas* ▪ *Illusory Correlations in Social Perception*

Social Inference and Decision Making   156

The Effects of Sampling Errors on Inferences ▪ *The Underutilization of Baserate Information* ▪ *Heuristics — Shortcuts to Social Inference* ▪ *Framing Effects in Decision Making*

Social Cognition: A Final Thought   166

Summary   167

Glossary   168

CHAPTER 6
▪▪▪▪▪▪▪▪▪▪▪▪▪▪

Personality and the Self   171

Personality and Social Behavior   172

Trait Theories: Personality as Stable Internal Dispositions ▪ *Social Learning Theories: Personality as Learned Behavior* ▪ *Research on Personality Theories*

The Self   189

Classic Views of the Self ▪ *Self-Knowledge — Research on the "Me"* ▪ *Self-Awareness Theory* ▪ *Public and Private Selves* ▪ *The Self and Mental Health*

Summary   213

Glossary   216

CHAPTER 7

Attitudes and Beliefs 219

What Are Attitudes? 220
Characteristics of Attitudes ■ *A Functional Approach to Attitudes* ■ *Attitude Measurement*

Attitude Formation 229
Learning Theories of Attitude Formation ■ *Personality and Attitude Formation* ■ *Logical Inference Theories*

Attitudes and Behavior 243
Difficulties in Predicting Behavior from Attitudes ■ *Fishbein and Ajzen's Theory of Reasoned Action*

Beliefs and Attitudes: A Final Comment 251

Summary 252

Glossary 254

CHAPTER 8

Persuasion and Attitude Change 257

A Communication Model of Persuasion: The Yale Research 257
Communicator Variables ■ *Message Variables* ■ *Channel Variables* ■ *Target or Audience Variables* ■ *Interactions Among Persuasion Variables*

Dissonance Theory and Research 269
Festinger's Theory of Cognitive Dissonance ■ *The Festinger and Carlsmith (1959) Study* ■ *The Psychology of Insufficient Justification* ■ *Variations on a Dissonance Theme* ■ *Qualifications on Dissonance Theory* ■ *Self-Perception Theory: An Alternate Explanation* ■ *Evaluating Dissonance Theory and Self-Perception Theory*

Cognitive Responses and Attitude Change 288
Forewarning Effects ■ *Attitudes as Schemas*

The Elaboration Likelihood Model of Persuasion 293

Summary 297

Glossary 299

CHAPTER 9

Prejudice   301

What is Prejudice?   302
Analyzing Prejudice

Stereotypes   307
Measuring Stereotypes ▪ The Formation of Stereotypes ▪ Consequences of Stereotypes

Social Causes of Prejudice   318
The Authoritarian Personality ▪ Social Ideologies and Prejudice ▪ Social Groups and Prejudice ▪ Intergroup Competition and Prejudice

Reducing Prejudice: The Intergroup Contact Hypothesis   331
Contact Between Groups in Schools ▪ The Effect of Contact on Intergroup Attitudes ▪ Residential Contact ▪ Vicarious Contact Through the Mass Media

Summary   339

Glossary   341

CHAPTER 10

Gender and Social Behavior   343

The Changing Roles of Women and Men   343

Psychological Research on Sex and Gender   347

Stereotypes About Women and Men   347
Personality Stereotypes ▪ Broader Stereotypes About Gender ▪ Gender and the Perception of Ability

Sex Differences   354
The Study of Sex Differences ▪ The Meaning of Sex Differences

Theories of Gender and Sex-Typing   363
Biological Theories ▪ Freudian Theory ▪ Social Learning Theories ▪ Cognitive Approaches to Gender ▪ Social Role Theory ▪ Self-Presentation Theory of Gender

Masculinity, Femininity, and Androgyny   378
Masculinity and Femininity as Separate Dimensions ▪ Beyond Masculinity, Femininity, and Androgyny

A Final Comment on Gender   382

Summary   383

Glossary   384

CHAPTER 11
■■■■■■■■■■■■■■■

Liking, Loving, and Close Relationships 387

Trends in the Scientific Study of Attraction 388

The Beginnings of Attraction 389

Affiliation and Anxiety: The "Dr. Zilstein Experiment" ■ From Affiliation to Attraction

Theories of Attraction 401

Learning Theories ■ Exchange and Equity Theories ■ Cognitive Consistency Theories

Love 407

The Sociobiological Perspective ■ The History of Love in Western Culture ■ The Social Psychology of Love ■ How Do You Know You're in Love?

The Life Cycle of Close Relationships 421

Initial Attraction and Beginnings ■ Building a Relationship ■ Continuation and Consolidation ■ Deterioration and Decline ■ Endings

Summary 428

Glossary 430

CHAPTER 12
■■■■■■■■■■■■■■■

Aggression 433

Defining Aggression ■ Measuring Aggression

Factors that Influence Human Aggression 437

Biological Groups, Instincts, and Aggression ■ Cultural Influences on Aggression ■ Individual Differences in Aggression ■ The Environment, Internal Psychological Processes, and Aggression ■ Social Learning and Aggression

Reducing Aggression 464

Catharsis ■ Punishing Aggression ■ Creating Responses Incompatible with Aggression ■ Providing Social Restraints ■ Cognitive Strategies for Controlling Aggression ■ A Concluding Word on Controlling Aggression

Summary 474

Glossary 475

CHAPTER 13
▪▪▪▪▪▪▪▪▪▪▪▪▪▪▪▪

Altruism and Prosocial Behavior   477

Defining and Measuring Prosocial Behavior   478

Major Approaches to the Study of Prosocial Behavior   480
Sociobiological Theory and Prosocial Behavior ▪ *Cultural Norms of Prosocial Behavior*

The Psychology of Prosocial Behavior   487
Is There a Prosocial Personality? ▪ *The Psychology of Emergency Intervention* ▪ *Guilt, Moods, and Helping*

Helping People to Help   513
Exhortation ▪ *Modeling* ▪ *Assuming Responsibility* ▪ *Humanizing the Victim Who Needs Help* ▪ *Education About Helping*

Summary   517

Glossary   519

CHAPTER 14
▪▪▪▪▪▪▪▪▪▪▪▪▪▪▪▪

Conformity, Compliance, and Obedience   521

Kinds of Social Influence ▪ *Levels of Social Influence*

Conformity   524
Research on Conformity ▪ *Factors That Influence Conformity*

Compliance   545
Positive Moods and Compliance ▪ *Reciprocity and Compliance* ▪ *Commitment and Compliance* ▪ *Psychological Reactance and Compliance*

Obedience   552
The Nature of Obedience ▪ *The Milgram Studies in Perspective* ▪ *Obedience Studies Since Milgram's*

Summary   562

Glossary   564

CHAPTER 15
▪▪▪▪▪▪▪▪▪▪▪▪▪▪▪▪

Group Behavior   567

What Is a Group?   568

Studying Group Behavior   569
Dimensions of Group Behavior

Groups at Work   571

Social Facilitation ▪ Individual Versus Group Performance ▪ Decision Making in Groups ▪ Groupthink

Leadership in Groups   588

What Is Leadership? ▪ Theories of Leadership

The Good and Bad of Groups   593

Deindividuation

Competition and Cooperation in Groups   602

Groups: A Final Word   607

Summary   607

Glossary   609

CHAPTER 16

▪▪▪▪▪▪▪▪▪▪▪▪▪▪

Applying Social Psychology   613

Answering Social Questions ▪ Designing Social Interventions ▪ Evaluating Social Programs

Social Psychological Factors in Health   615

Stress, Social Support, and Health ▪ Personality, Health, and Illness

Using Social Psychology to Make People Healthier   630

Personal Control and Health ▪ Helplessness in the Elderly ▪ The Age of Prevention

Cultivating Our Garden   639

Summary   641

Glossary   642

References   A-1

Name Index   A-34

Subject Index   A-42

List of Applied Topics

Chapter 1

Discussion of applied social psychology in the context of
the overall field of social psychology   17

Chapter 2

Quasi-experimental designs   36
Laboratory versus field studies   36
Internal and external validity in experiments   39
Mundane and experimental realism   40

Chapter 3

First impressions in the courtroom   70
Perceived and actual cues of deception   88
Detecting deception in real life   89

Chapter 4

The discounting principle, worker supervision, and
supervisors' trust of workers   111
The over-justification effect and intrinsic motivation in real life   111
The fundamental attribution error in clinical settings   116
Misattribution therapies and attributional retraining therapies   126

Chapter 5

The effects of schemas on everyday evaluations of others   144

The complexity of in-group and out-group schemas and how it affects the evaluations of in-groups and out-groups   148

Illusory correlations in clinical judgments   155

Decision-making rules in everyday life   159

Framing effects in everyday decisions and in business negotiations   163

Chapter 6

Self-monitoring in everyday life: effects on consumer behavior, close relationships, and mental health   186

Self-awareness and depression   210

Self-complexity, emotional volatility, and depression   213

Chapter 7

Developing an attitude scale   228

How best to predict behavior from attitudes   247

Applying Fishbein and Ajzen's theory of reasoned action to applied domains   251

Chapter 8

Communicator, message, channel, and audience variables in advertising and public information campaigns   258

Fear appeals and persuasion   261

Severity of initiation effects in real life   279

Inoculation to persuasion   290

Chapter 9

Sherif's work on reducing intergroup conflict   328

The intergroup contact hypothesis   331

Classroom integration and cooperative classrooms   332

Residential integration and its effects on racial attitudes   337

The mass media and prejudice: using enlightened media programming to reduce prejudice   338

Chapter 10

Gender stereotypes and real-life evaluations of individuals   353

Attributions about the work of men and women   354

Applying meta-analysis   357

Chapter 11

Effects of physical attractiveness in everyday life   398

Life cycle of close relationships   421

The dissolution of close relationships   424

Chapter 12

Economic frustration and societal violence and revolutions   446

TV violence and aggression   453

Research on pornography and aggression against women   456

Techniques to reduce aggression: catharsis, punishment, incompatible responses, and cognitive skills training   464

Predicting and reducing family violence   468

Chapter 13

Child-rearing practices and prosocial behavior   489

Effects of prosocial TV programming on prosocial behavior   490

Techniques to foster prosocial behavior: modeling, assigning responsibility   513

Chapter 14

Ingratiation and compliance   546

Compliance techniques and ways to resist them: door-in-the-face, the foot-in-the-door, low-ball, and that's-not-all techniques   548

Psychological reactance and compliance   550

Brainwashing   552

Chapter 15

Steiner's analysis of work groups   577

Brainstorming   582

Group polarization in real-life groups such as juries   583

Groupthink and decision making in government policy-making groups   585

Leadership effectiveness   592

Mass psychogenic illness   598

Chapter 16

Stress and health   616

Social support and health   620

Hardiness as a buffer against stress   625

Optimism, negative affectivity, and health   627

Type A behavior pattern and coronary heart disease   629

Personal control and health   631

Social psychology of doctor-patient interactions   634

Social psychology is an engaging yet difficult field to survey in an introductory text. Its central topics — social perception, attitudes and attitude change, attraction, aggression, prosocial behavior, influence, and group behavior — are highly relevant to everyday life and of great interest to students. At the same time, social psychology embraces a sometimes bewildering collection of topics, theories, and informationally dense empirical studies. The challenge facing a survey text is to maintain the intrinsic interest of the material while providing complete coverage of a complex field. Such a text must be well-organized, cohesive, comprehensive, clear, and engrossing. Does this text meet the challenge? I invite you to read a chapter and be the judge. In the process you will encounter the following features that serve to organize the book's content, to capture and maintain the reader's interest, and most important, to teach social psychology.

Integrative Themes and Emphases

Each chapter, and indeed the entire book, begins with a conceptual overview that "tills the soil" and prepares the student for what is to follow.

Levels of explanation. To locate social-psychological explanations within the broader context of scientific understanding, Chapter 1 discusses levels of explanation that can be applied to social behavior and illustrates them with a conceptual diagram. For example, Chapter 1 notes that aggression can be explained in terms of group-level explanations (biological groups, cultural groups), individual-level explanations (the individual's unique physiology, past environment, and current setting), and internal mediating variables (attitudes, traits, emotions). The notion of different levels of explanation is used repeatedly in subsequent chapters to remind students of the "big picture" and underscore the complexity of social behavior. The levels-

Preface

of-explanation diagram serves to organize and summarize research on prejudice (Chapter 9), attraction (Chapter 11), aggression (Chapter 12), and prosocial behavior (Chapter 13).

Historical context. This text continually links social psychological research to the history of the field and to the history of the world at large. In the pursuit of up-to-date citations, recent texts have too often jettisoned important older research. This book contains a good mix of both classic and contemporary studies. When appropriate, I describe the historical development of a research topic so that the reader understands why social psychologists study certain topics and how research evolves. Thus, for example, I discuss in some detail the vicissitudes of research on the accuracy of person perception (Chapter 3), classic and contemporary work on the functions of attitudes (Chapter 7), research on the authoritarian personality (Chapter 9), Sherif's classic contributions to conformity research (Chapter 14), and early work on dimensions of group behavior and styles of leadership (Chapter 15).

Complete treatment of theory and methodological issues. Chapter 1 provides a brief account of four major theoretical perspectives in social psychology and prepares the student for more detailed accounts in later chapters. Both Chapters 1 and 2 discuss the role of theory in social psychological research. Chapter 2 includes a number of topics not typically found in introductory-level chapters on research methods: meta-analysis, internal and external validity in experiments, quasi-experimental designs, and a nontechnical discussion of the "statistical significance" of research findings.

Methodological issues introduced in Chapter 2 reappear in later chapters. For example, Chapter 6 (Personality and the Self) and Chapter 7 (Attitudes and Beliefs) *xix* elaborate on the concepts of reliability and validity. Later chapters reinforce the distinction between correlational and experimental studies with substantive research examples. Chapter 10 (Gender and Social Behavior) includes a readable presentation of the meta-analytic techniques used in research on sex differences.

Integration of applied social psychology.   Students want to know how social psychological theories and research apply to real life. Fortunately, much theory and research in social psychology addresses applied topics, and each chapter of this text presents varied applied content. Because applied social psychology is woven into all chapters, this text solves a pedagogical problem faced by many instructors of social psychology: applied topics are frequently slighted because they are tacked on as the final chapters of most texts and thus taught (or simply not taught) during the rushed final days of the academic semester or quarter.

The applied social psychology in each chapter of this text takes two forms. First, each chapter provides real-life examples that illustrate social psychological theories and principles. For example, Chapter 3 applies research on first impressions to the impressions formed by lawyers and jurors in the courtroom. Chapter 5 illustrates illusory correlations with examples of errors in clinical judgment. Chapter 8 links research on attitude change to commercial advertising.

The second form: Research frequently attempts to answer pressing social questions (Does TV violence contribute to aggression?) or to find ways of ameliorating social problems (Do cooperative integrated classrooms reduce prejudice?). Each chapter includes a section that addresses such applied topics. Chapter 3 (Person Perception) concludes, for example, with a discussion of detecting deception in real-life settings, Chapter 4 (Attribution) with a description of "attributional retraining" therapies for depression and test anxiety, and Chapter 12 (Aggression) with a discussion of ways to reduce aggression.

The treatment of applied topics culminates in Chapter 16 (Applying Social Psychology). Because applied social psychology is an integral part of all chapters, this final chapter focuses on one particular applied domain — health psychology — and describes three ways of applying social psychology to it: answering social questions, evaluating social programs, and designing social interventions. Thus Chapter 16 describes the *process* of applying social psychology to one substantive research area instead of reviewing a motley collection of applied topics. While learning about the process, the reader learns much about social psychological factors in health as well.

Facilitating Understanding: Pedagogical Aids

A consistent and coherent program of pedagogy is employed throughout the text. In addition to such usual features as itemized chapter summaries and complete chapter glossaries, the text includes a number of noteworthy and innovative pedagogical aids.

Examples that open and organize chapters.   Each chapter begins with a quotation that captures the reader's attention. For example, Chapter 11 (Liking, Loving, and Close Relationships) opens with a passage from *Anna Karenina* on the nature of romantic love. Other passages from *Anna Karenina* appear throughout the chapter and serve to sustain the narrative flow.

Sources quoted in other chapters include the *Man of La Mancha* (Chapter 4), Hermann Hesse's *Steppenwolf* (Chapter 6), Adolf Hitler's *Mein Kampf* (Chapter 7),

William Shakespeare's *Julius Caesar* (Chapter 8), Toni Morrison's *The Bluest Eye* (Chapter 9), Ursula K. LeGuin's *The Left Hand of Darkness* (Chapter 10), William Golding's *Lord of the Flies* (Chapter 12), Fyodor Dostoevsky's *The Brothers Karamazov* (Chapter 13), and George Orwell's *1984* (Chapter 14). These excerpts are brilliant, for they are written by brilliant people. (The one exception is the material from *Mein Kampf*, which, if not brilliant, is morbidly fascinating.) Do these excerpts work? Again, I invite you to read a chapter. I think they serve extremely well to illustrate social psychological concepts.

Summary tables.   All chapters contain summary tables that gather research findings and present students with a grand overview of a particular research area. These summary tables serve several pedagogical functions. They reiterate important terms and concepts, organize material conceptually, and serve as convenient study aids. They also serve to familiarize students with the numerous technical terms used by social psychologists. For example, the summary table for Chapter 4 reinforces students' understanding of various concepts in attribution theory: correspondent inferences, Kelley's cube model, the discounting principle, the fundamental attribution error, the actor-observer effect, self-handicapping strategies, and so on.

Figures, tables, and graphs.   The figures and tables in this text are more than window dressing; they are valuable learning aids. Each chapter contains a number of conceptual diagrams as well as the usual graphs and tables of experimental results. For example, the conceptual diagrams in Chapter 2 (Social Psychological Research) provide clear illustrations of correlational and experimental studies and highlight what each kind of study can tell us about cause-effect relationships. Chapter 2 also presents a thorough graphic depiction of correlations and correlation coefficients — concepts that are often incompletely understood by students.

Because many students have difficulty extracting appropriate information from tables and graphs, the figures in this book have been carefully designed to stimulate critical thinking and lead students to meaningful conclusions. The typical figure begins by posing a question. The remainder of the figure recapitulates the general research procedure used to answer the question, presents results, and often concludes with a comment that elaborates on the research findings or hypotheses. Students are thereby encouraged to think about research findings repeatedly and creatively.

Photo essays.   Four varied, dramatic photo essays grace this text. In keeping with the overall philosophy of the book, the essays are linked to important recurring themes. The first illustrates the concept of levels of explanation discussed in Chapter 1 and used throughout the text to organize research findings. The second shows the many faces of applied social psychology. The third illustrates the variety of social influences that occur through the life cycle. The last essay ties social psychological research to broader cultural and moral concerns by discussing the "good and evil" of social behavior. Each essay was carefully developed to complement material in the text.

Boxed material.   Chapters contain boxes that elaborate on important research topics (such as the Schachter-Singer theory of emotion, box 1 of Chapter 4), examine specific applied domains (predicting and treating family violence, box 2 of Chapter

11), or take stock of a research area (the legacy of the Yale research on persuasion, box 1 of Chapter 8). Unlike the boxed material in most texts, these are not intended to be asides; they are part of the ongoing narrative flow.

Supplementary materials.   The text is accompanied by an Instructor's Manual prepared by Gloria Cowan, a Study Guide prepared by Gary S. Nickell, a 1,100-item test bank, and color transparencies. In writing the test items, I have striven to provide a balanced pool of both conceptual and informational questions. These items are based on years of experience teaching social psychology to thousands of students.

Acknowledgments

Writing a textbook is a bit like having a baby — painful at the time but rewarding in retrospect. Now that the labor is over and I have had some time to examine the final product, I can say without embarrassment that I am proud of my offspring. Of course, like all babies, this one had more than one parent.

When I began working on *Introduction to Social Psychology* I had little conception of how much the writing of a comprehensive textbook is a team effort. Despite my naïveté, I was blessed with one of the best teams in the business.

Psychology Editor Ken King kept the project on target. Senior Development Editor Mary Arbogast read my manuscript with an astonishing attention to detail. Her clarity of thought and expression shows throughout the book. John Bergez assisted in the development of the many figures and tables with unfailing creativity. In the process, he offered many useful suggestions about the text and photography program.

Andrew Ogus supervised the design, art, and photography programs and Stephen Forsling served as photo researcher. Together, I think we have created a book that is visually pleasing and exciting. Michael Oates launched my book into production with a firm hand, and Donna Linden brought the book to safe harbor. Thanks to each of them.

The quality of any text depends on the quality of its reviewers. Mine generously shared their critical acumen and expert knowledge. I have given my reviewers what I consider the ultimate compliment — incorporating their ideas and suggestions into the text. To each of the following reviewers, thanks: Donald M. Amoroso, University of Waterloo; Nancy Brekke, University of Virginia; Jerry M. Burger, Santa Clara University; Gloria Cowan, California State University, San Bernardino; Robert T. Croyle, University of Utah; Frederick Gibbons, Iowa State University; Ralph Juhnke, Claremont McKenna College; Eric Knowles, University of Arkansas; Mark R. Leary, Wake Forest University; Diane M. Mackie, University of California, Santa Barbara; Paul R. Nail, Southwestern Oklahoma State University; Paul B. Paulus, University of Texas at Arlington; R. E. Petty, Ohio State University; Fred Rodewalt, University of Utah; Steve Slane, Cleveland State University; Robin R. Vallacher, Florida Atlantic University; Russell Veitch, Bowling Green State University; Linda A. Wood, University of Guelph.

Ann Litvin read original drafts of most chapters and provided the much-needed perspective of an intelligent lay person.

For their exceptional secretarial skills, I wish to thank my two personal computers. They accepted without protest the crudest prose and the most uninspired first drafts.

Finally, I must acknowledge my two dogs, Seymour (a dachshund) and Puccini (a collie). As I spent interminable hours before my computer working on this book, Seymour would often sleep curled on my lap and Puccini would lie near my feet with his nose resting on the books and articles inevitably scattered over the floor. These two were wise enough not to let a social psychology text interfere with the simpler pleasures of life.

Richard Lippa
California State University, Fullerton

INTRODUCTION TO SOCIAL PSYCHOLOGY

New York, Dec. 8 — Mikhail S. Gorbachev, the Soviet leader, left here for Moscow today, cutting short a triumphant diplomatic mission to deal with the aftermath of an earthquake reported to have killed tens of thousands in Soviet Armenia.

Mr. Gorbachev, speaking to reporters at an isolated runway of Kennedy International Airport, expressed gratitude for . . . [the U.S.] offer of aid and confidence that his visit had assured a continuing warming of Soviet-American relations.

Moscow, Dec. 8 — Extensive physical damage and overwhelming human tragedy were described by rescue workers sifting through the debris for signs of life and treating the injured. Relief aid and workers rushed to the area. . . .

The evening news program "Vremya" said tonight that hundreds of thousands of people were homeless, severely straining the resources of a republic that is already struggling to place more than 117,000 refugees from ethnic strife with neighboring Azerbaijan.

A spokesman . . . said the quake tragedy appeared to have brought the recent violent ethnic clashes to a halt. . . .

—— excerpts from the *New York Times*,
December 9, 1988

CHAPTER 1

What Is Social Psychology?

The Armenian earthquake of December 8, 1988, quickly captured the world's attention. Mikhail Gorbachev ended a summit meeting in the United States early because of the earthquake. Assistance poured in to Soviet Armenia from countries throughout the world. The centralized government of the Soviet Union tried, often unsuccessfully, to coordinate rescue and relief efforts. Ethnic unrest in Armenia subsided, then flared again. In the area devastated by the earthquake, survivors searched desperately for relatives and friends. Many found that they had lost their loved ones, homes, and possessions.

Thus the news of the earthquake was largely news about people interacting with people. The following newspaper items prompt numerous questions about these human interactions:

> From Los Angeles and New York, from Argentina and Cuba, from Britain, Scandinavia, Israel and Japan, people around the world have sent food, medical supplies and rescue equipment to victims of the earthquake. . . .
>
> —— *New York Times*, Dec. 12, 1988

> **Chicago**, Dec. 12 —. . . All through the day, people . . . made their way across town to this building on the city's far North Side, bringing bundles of clothing and boxes of food and donations of money. . . .
>
> Some, like Gwen Levine, who drove an hour from suburban Flossmoor to deliver a check for $75, said they were moved by pity after watching grim television footage from the region. "I couldn't rest until I got here and did something," she said.
>
> —— *New York Times*, Dec. 13, 1988

Questions: When do people help others? What leads people to assume responsibility for others' welfare? Are people ever truly altruistic?

3

Soviet newspapers and television asserted today that rescue efforts were hampered by poor preparedness and disorganization.

—— *New York Times*, Dec. 13, 1988

Especially in the first few days, rescue and relief efforts were plagued by confusion and inefficiency, according to relief workers and residents interviewed throughout the region.

Foreigners said they were frequently frustrated by a bureaucracy that still awaits orders from the top.

A British rescue team had to go all the way to the commanding general to get clearance to use an army truck, and then had to negotiate for diesel fuel to run it.

—— *New York Times*, Dec. 18, 1988

Questions: What is the nature of social influence? Why do people obey orders "from the top"? What is the nature of leadership? When are groups of people effective and ineffective in carrying out tasks?

Armenians across the United States flooded the New York headquarters of the Armenian Apostolic Church in America yesterday with offers of medical aid, supplies, food and other emergency assistance for their homeland.

—— *New York Times*, Dec. 9, 1988

Moscow, Dec. 10 —. . . People were talking loudly, nearly shouting at airline agents in the hopes of getting an elusive seat on a plane. Their pleas were much the same:

"I have a sister."
"I have a brother and my father."
"I need to get to Armenia."

—— *New York Times*, Dec. 11, 1988

Questions: What leads individuals to be attracted to other people? What is the nature of liking and loving? Why are people particularly attracted to blood relatives and those who share their ethnic heritage?

Ethnic tension between Armenia and neighboring Azerbaijan has caused dozens of deaths in the last year, and the army newspaper *Krasnaya Zvezda* reported that on the day of the earthquake, three people were killed by militia forces after gangs rampaged through a town in Azerbaijan.

—— *New York Times*, Dec. 10, 1988

In both Armenia and Azerbaijan, troops from the Soviet Interior Ministry have apparently been held back from rescue efforts in order to police cities where ethnic tensions have sporatically erupted since February.

—— *New York Times*, Dec. 12, 1988

Questions: What leads to intergroup hostility and aggression? What creates hostile attitudes between ethnic groups? How can ethnic tensions be reduced?

The Soviet Union today accepted an offer of United States assistance in coping with the earthquake in Armenia, marking the first time that large-scale American aid will be sent to the Soviet Union since the two countries were allies in World War II.

—— *New York Times*, Dec. 10, 1988

Workers trying to rescue Armenian earthquake victims trapped in rubble.

Robert Legvold, director of the Harriman Institute for Soviet studies at Columbia University, said he saw political significance in Moscow's decision to [accept foreign assistance].

"For the average Soviet citizen, the outside world, often seen as hostile, turns out to be compassionate," Mr. Legvold said.

— *New York Times*, Dec. 12, 1988

Marshall I. Goldman of the Russian Research Center at Harvard University said Mr. Gorbachev . . . had helped engender an especially sympathetic and emotional reaction among Americans.

. . . "By asking for our help, our reaction is almost one of relief. We are thinking, so they are vulnerable, they are human after all, just like us."

Roger E. Kanet, . . . a Soviet specialist at the University of Illinois, said, "If there had not been this shift in perceptions, I cannot believe there would have been this kind of outpouring of help."

— *New York Times*, Dec. 13, 1988

Questions: What determines how we perceive other people and other groups? What leads to conflict and competition among groups, and what leads to peace and cooperation?

The human drama of the Armenian earthquake provides a microcosm of social life in general. The questions raised by people's behavior after the Armenian earthquake are exactly those posed by the field of social psychology: How do people influence other people? What is the nature of social perception, social influence, altruism, attraction, aggression, prejudice, and group behavior? Social psychology is a field that develops theories and gathers facts about just such questions.

The Nature of Social Psychology

Social Psychology Studies Influences on Social Behavior

Social psychology, according to one classic definition, represents "an attempt to understand and explain how the thought, feeling, and behavior of individuals are influenced by the actual, imagined, or implied presence of others" (Allport, 1985). The core of this definition is that social psychology studies how people influence people. The topics of conformity, obedience, persuasion and attitude change, and group processes all address interpersonal influence. Many of the questions we posed about people's behavior after the Armenian earthquake focused on different varieties of social influence.

Social psychologists study not only social influences on behavior, but non-social influences on social behavior as well. For example, emergencies and anxiety-provoking events like the Armenian earthquake can lead people to seek out others (see Chapter 11). The physical environment can affect friendships (for example, we're more likely to be friends with someone who lives near us; see Chapter 11) or aggression (we're more likely to be aggressive when we're confined in a hot, noisy room; see Chapter 12). Note that these findings lie in the realm of social psychology because they study influences on *social* behavior, even though these influences do not come from other people.

Social Psychology Explains Social Behavior

There is yet another way to define social psychology—through the kinds of explanations it offers for social behaviors. Examine Figure 1.1, which visually presents the factors that a social scientist might use to explain human behavior, including broad explanations (such as evolutionary and cultural factors), individual-level explanations (such as individual rearing and family history), and internal factors (such as personality traits and attitudes). Social psychologists tend to emphasize some of these explanations more than others. To illustrate, let's consider a particular kind of social behavior—aggression. What leads people to be aggressive? Even more specifically, what led to violence between Armenians and the peoples of Azerbaijan? Let's begin providing possible answers to these questions by looking first at the top level of Figure 1.1—"group-level" explanations.

To understand human aggression, it may be useful to examine the *biological groups* to which humans belong—mammals, primates, and our species, *Homo sapiens*. Clearly, Siamese fighting fish and laboratory rats show different patterns of aggression than do human beings; some of these differences are biologically based. Could the ethnic unrest in the Soviet Union be due in part to evolutionary factors? For example, is it possible that people have evolved with a tendency to be more aggressive to "outsiders" than to "our own kind"?

Human aggression is also influenced by *cultural and social groups*. Some societies, like that of the Arapesh of New Guinea, are reported to be quite peaceful and cooperative, whereas others, like that of the Mundugumor (also of New Guinea), are reported to be dominating and aggressive (Mead, 1935). Although most societies show some degree of violence and aggression, absolute levels can vary dramatically

FIGURE 1.1   Levels of explanation of social behavior.

Which of the many ways of explaining behavior are emphasized in social psychology?

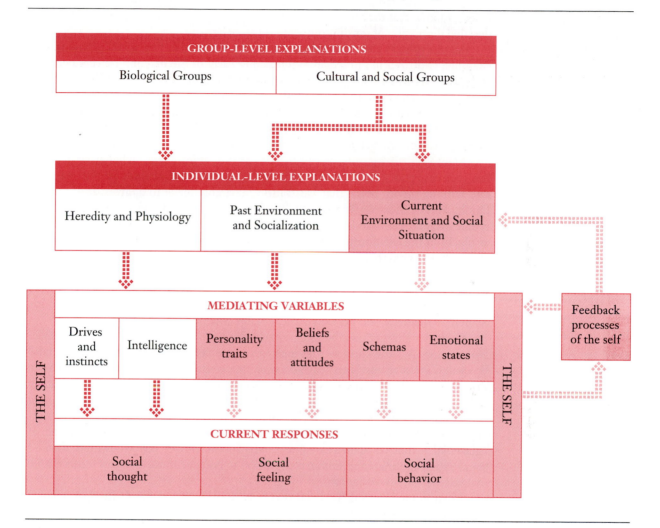

Social behaviors (such as love, prejudice, and aggression) can be analyzed at many different levels. Social psychology focuses on the kinds of explanations highlighted in this diagram. Different explanations may complement rather than contradict one another.

across different cultures. In the mid-1980s the United States reported 8.5 homicides per 100,000 people, Canada reported 2.3, and Great Britain reported only .7 (Demographic Yearbook of the United Nations, 1986). Why these differences? It seems likely that cultural and sociological factors, not biology, are responsible. To return to our example of aggression in Armenia and Azerbaijan, we might study cultural attitudes toward aggression in each of these Soviet republics.

Each individual's unique *heredity and physiology* (Figure 1.1) may influence aggression. For example, there is some evidence that males, perhaps in part because of the effects of male hormones, are on average more aggressive than females (Maccoby & Jacklin, 1974; Eagly & Steffen, 1986b). Although the news reports from Armenia and Azerbaijan contain no reference to the gender of the warring "gangs," it seems likely that they were largely composed of males (see Chapter 10 for a more detailed discussion of sex differences in social behavior).

An individual's *past environment* can exert a potent effect on social behavior. For example, child-rearing practices and learning early in life may influence a person's aggressiveness later in life. One explanation for the observed tendency for women to be less aggressive than men is that girls and women are consistently taught to be less aggressive by family members, their peers, and the mass media. In Armenia and Azerbaijan, residents may have learned during their childhoods ethnic prejudices that later fostered aggressive behaviors.

A person's *current situation* can also exert a potent influence on behavior. Indeed, this type of explanation is particularly emphasized in social psychology. For example, one famous theory holds that frustration inevitably leads to aggression (Dollard, Doob, Miller, Mowrer, & Sears, 1939). In a classic study Hovland & Sears (1940) found a significant correlation between the health of the economy and the lynching of blacks in the old South. Presumably, as whites were frustrated by economic bad times, they vented their resulting hostility on "safe" targets, namely blacks. According to the frustration-aggression hypothesis, factors in the current situation — specifically, anything that thwarts achievement of a desired goal — lead to aggression. Armenians living in Azerbaijan presumably felt frustrated and harrassed by the non-Armenian majority, and perhaps these feelings contributed to ethnic violence.

Consider another possible situational influence on aggression — media violence. Do violent TV shows and movies lead to aggressive behavior in some individuals? We will discuss research evidence on this important topic in Chapter 12. For now we'll simply note that this question focuses on how the past environment (watching "Miami Vice" reruns over the past year) and the current environment (watching a video of *Rambo* right now) may affect a person's level of aggressiveness. It is interesting to note that ethnic unrest in the Soviet Union was preceded by a period of "glasnost" — that is, of increased openness in the Soviet media — which allowed people striving for greater ethnic recognition to become more aware of other ethnic struggles in the Soviet Union.

Many topics central to social psychology deal with the influence of current situational pressures on individuals' behavior: Research on conformity investigates how pressures from groups of people induce individuals to shift their stated attitudes and beliefs, research on attitude change examines how persuasive messages can change people's opinions, and research on group processes probes how being in a group affects individuals' performance and decision making. Because social psychology often focuses on social influence, it makes sense that the social setting should be seen as an important explanatory variable in social psychology.

When we consider the third level of boxes in Figure 1.1, *mediating variables*, we seem to slip inside the skin of the individual. Such explanatory variables cannot be directly observed, but rather must be inferred from behavior. For example, we may infer that our friend has the trait of aggressiveness because he always gets into fights. We might further explain that his high level of aggression is due to his aggressive "drives" or his strong aggressive "instincts." Perhaps we might observe

Explanations of Social Behavior

Social scientists explain social behaviors in many different ways (see Chapter 1). *Group-level explanations* focus on the biological and social groups to which individuals belong. *Individual-level* explanations focus on variables that influence individuals — their unique heredity and physiology, their past environments, and their current environments. *Mediating variables* are inferred internal variables, such as attitudes, personality traits, and emotions that influence behavior. Any complex social behavior, such as aggression, can be analyzed at each of these levels.

Aggression occurs in many species and may be adaptive when it fosters individual or genetic survival. Human aggression has an evolutionary past. Aggression varies considerably across cultures and subcultures. Some preliterate cultures are peaceful, whereas others are warlike.

The United States comprises subcultures that are violent, such as the Hell's Angels motorcycle gang, and others that are non-violent, such as the Amish.

An individual's physiology may influence aggression. Many studies suggest that men, on average, are more physically aggressive than women. This may be due in part to physiological differences between men and women.

Environmental influences exert a profound influence on human aggression through learning. Many children imitate aggressive behaviors they see on TV. Others may learn aggressive behaviors while participating in sports.

Frustrating situations can foster aggressive behavior.

The immediate social setting strongly influences human aggression. Lynch mobs in the old South encouraged wanton acts of violence.

Mediating variables such as attitudes and personality traits may also influence an individual's aggressiveness. Adolf Hitler's bellicose and bigoted attitudes led to the deaths of millions of people.

Martin Luther King Jr.'s philosophy of nonviolence profoundly influenced the attitudes and behavior of civil-rights activists and supporters.

also that his "attitude" that it is good for men to be strong and aggressive leads him to be aggressive in many settings. In Soviet Armenia and Azerbaijan, prejudiced attitudes undoubtedly contributed to the reported aggression.

Social psychologists tend to study some of these mediating variables more than others. *Beliefs and attitudes* have traditionally been among those most studied by social psychologists (Allport, 1935; McGuire, 1985). Beliefs comprise the cognitive information people hold about various people and things. Attitudes are evaluative responses (that is, reactions of liking or disliking) to people and things. Beliefs and attitudes have always intrigued social psychologists because of these concepts' presumed close relation to a host of important social behaviors, including aggression, discrimination, altruism, and attraction (see Chapters 7, 8, and 9).

In recent years, social psychologists have studied intensively a number of cognitive mediators of social behavior (such mediators focus on thought processes and information processing; see Chapters 4 and 5). For example, the concept of cognitive *schemas* (Hastie, 1981; Taylor & Crocker, 1981) has recently been at the forefront of social psychological theory and research. A schema — a kind of mental model or theory that people hold — contains the information we have about social groups and social settings, and even about ourselves.

Social psychologists have frequently studied *emotional states* and *personality traits*. Emotions are transient states of arousal and cognition that motivate and direct behavior, particularly in novel situations demanding quick action (Mandler, 1975). Examples are anger, fear, and elation. Social psychologists particularly study emotions that relate to social behavior. Love and attraction, for example, are eminently social forms of emotion.

Personality traits are stable dispositions that influence broad domains of behavior. The personality traits most studied by social psychologists are those affecting interpersonal relations and social behavior (see Chapter 6). For example, social psychologists have studied such varied traits as locus-of-control (Rotter, 1966) — how much individuals feel their behaviors are controlled by themselves rather than by external factors; authoritarianism (Adorno, Frenkel-Brunswick, Levinson, & Sanford, 1950) — the degree to which an individual possesses a prejudiced, defensive personality; and self-monitoring (Snyder, 1979) — the degree to which individuals look to their inner feelings and attitudes or to others to decide how to behave.

Levels of explanation.   In Figure 1.1 all levels of explanation are interconnected by arrows, which represent causal relations among different kinds of explanations. Thus, our biological group influences the heredity and physiology of each of us, the culture we belong to influences the way our parents reared us (our past environment), and so on. When viewed as interlocked levels of explanation, Figure 1.1 points to an important fact about social behavior: A single level of explanation is rarely sufficient. A question such as "What is the cause of human aggression?" is overly simplistic because it ignores the complexity of human behavior and the multiple levels of explanation that inevitably must be applied.

Similarly, there are no single answers to such commonsense questions as "What is the cause of obedience?" or "What is the cause of prejudiced attitudes?" or "What is the cause of romantic love?" When more precisely and specifically framed, however, such questions are worth asking, and indeed, most of this book will be devoted to answering such questions. From Figure 1.1 it is apparent that social scientists can apply many kinds of explanations in their attempts to understand social behavior.

And by emphasizing some of these explanations more than others, social psychology sheds its unique light on the complex tapestry of social thoughts, feelings, and behavior.

Responses to be explained.   At the bottom of Figure 1.1 are the *responses* that social psychologists hope to explain: individuals' thoughts, feelings, and observable behaviors. Please note the following subtle point: Some of the boxes in Figure 1.1 (emotional states, for example) are both mediating variables *and* responses to be explained. That is, social psychologists may focus on emotion as an explanation of some other social behavior (for example, anger leads to aggression), or they may focus on emotion as something that *results* from other variables (for example, emotions are influenced by a person's social setting). Thus emotion can be seen as both a cause and an effect. We should view the boxes at the bottom of Figure 1.1 — thought, feeling, and behavior — as current responses that are affected by other variables, that is, as things we're trying to explain.

Social Psychology Studies *Social* Behavior

Of course, the thoughts, feelings, and behaviors of greatest interest to social psychologists are *social* thoughts, feelings, and behaviors. Research on social cognition examines how we process information about other people, and thus such investigations study social forms of thought. Research on interpersonal attraction investigates why people like and love others; liking and loving are decidedly social forms of emotion. And the observable behaviors of greatest interest to social psychologists are interpersonal forms of behavior, such as aggression (when people hurt others), altruism (when people help others), group behavior and processes (how individuals act in concert with others), conformity, obedience, attitude change, and bargaining. Note the common thread tying all these diverse topics together — they all deal with people interacting with other people.

The Self in Social Psychology

Let's turn our attention to the area in Figure 1.1 labeled "the self." The self comprises our current thoughts, feelings, and behavior, as well as mediating variables (see Chapter 6). Psychologists since the time of William James (1890) have often considered the self to have two aspects: what James called the "me" and the "I."

The "me," or the self as an object of knowledge and contemplation, consists of all the knowledge each of us has about ourselves. This is why schemas, beliefs, and attitudes are considered part of the self. The "I," or the self as an active agent, is the "executive" inside us who makes decisions and choices; it is also our ongoing stream of consciousness. In keeping with recent social psychological theories (for example, Carver & Scheier, 1981; see Chapter 6), the active self is conceptualized here, at least in part, as some kind of decision-making process that has the interesting quality of at times "going back" and influencing the other levels of explanation we've already discussed, a quality represented in Figure 1.1 by the arrows labeled "feedback processes of the self."

To return to the example of aggression, suppose you note one day that you are so frustrated at work that you are about to "explode," and as a result you decide to take a week's vacation and go on a cruise to "unwind." In other words, you consciously decide to change your environment in order to avoid an outburst of aggression. In such ways, the self monitors behavior and inner states, evaluates them, and then alters them by influencing other levels in the chain of explanations depicted in Figure 1.1.

In recent years social psychologists have intensely studied the "self" and its processes (for example, Wegner & Vallacher, 1980). The "self" is a topic in social psychology because there are many important links between the self and social behavior. The knowledge we have about ourselves often comes from other people. Social psychologists study self-perception—how we know our own feelings, attitudes, and emotions—and how such self-perception is influenced by other people. Social psychologists also study self-presentation—the images of ourselves that we present to others.

Differences Between Social Psychology and Related Fields

Many disciplines other than social psychology study social behavior, among them anthropology, sociology, political science, and economics. Why, then, is social psychology a distinct field? One reason is that social psychology has its own preferred set of theoretical explanations that tends to differ from those of other fields. For example, an anthropologist would focus more on the concept of "culture" (a "group-level explanation" in Figure 1.1) as a cause of behavior. Sociology often deals with such "group-level" concepts as social classes and strata. Social psychology, in contrast, generally offers explanations that focus on the *individual* as its unit of analysis.

Social psychology also differs from related fields in its research methods, a topic we'll consider in much greater detail in Chapter 2. For now, it is sufficient to note that social psychologists often prefer to conduct controlled experiments using precise, quantified measures. Contrast this preference with that of classical anthropologists, for example, who use the technique of naturalistic observation—watching people in their natural settings and recording their behaviors, often anecdotally. Summary Table 1.1 highlights the main features that distinguish social psychology as a discipline, including some of its applications (to be discussed later in the chapter).

Theories in Social Psychology

Before social psychology became an empirical science in the twentieth century, many social theorists and philosophers speculated about the causes of social behavior. Often these early theories attempted to propose simple encompassing principles that would explain virtually all aspects of society and social interaction (see Allport, 1985). Different philosophers, for example, invoked each of the following as universal principles: hedonism (people seek to gain pleasure and avoid pain in their dealings with others), imitation (people, from childhood on, look to others to guide their social behavior), and instincts (people behave in accordance with innate social motives—instincts—for gregariousness, sex, aggression, and so on).

The Functions of Social Psychological Theories

In general, modern social psychology has eschewed such grand unitary theories of social behavior in favor of "middle range" theories designed to explain and predict limited aspects of social behavior (Jones, 1985). What are the main functions of these theories?

Summary Table 1.1   An Overview of Social Psychology

What distinguishes social psychology as a discipline?

	Characteristic Emphases	Examples
Subject matter	Social behaviors and social influences on behavior.	What personal traits are associated with aggressive behavior? What effect does punishment have on aggression?
Preferred level of explanation	Individual, situational, with certain mediating variables such as beliefs and attitudes.	Focus on the social setting (e.g., aggressive models) as a cause of individuals' aggression.
Preferred type of research strategy	Experimental, but also correlational and quasi-experimental.	Manipulating amount of TV violence seen by children and observing effects on aggression.
Applications	Applying theories to practical issues. Answering important social questions. Designing social programs.	Do learning theories predict that TV influences aggression? How? Does TV violence influence aggression? How can children's programming best be developed to encourage helpful behavior and discourage aggressive behavior?

Social psychology is a varied field, and there are exceptions to the general picture provided here. For example, although social psychologists generally don't study "nonsocial" variables such as intelligence, an attitude researcher might study whether intelligence is related to persuasion.

Theories explain social behavior.   First, social psychological theories provide systematic ways of explaining and predicting social behavior. A useful theory embodies a relatively cohesive set of basic concepts and principles that allows us to make specific predictions about a particular kind of social behavior.

Theories help to organize empirical findings.   Not only do theories help explain and predict social behavior, but they also serve to organize and give meaning to the many varied empirical findings of social psychology. For example, research on interpersonal attraction (see Chapter 11) has provided a number of well-documented findings: People tend to like others more when they hold similar attitudes, people are more likely to be friends or lovers with people who live nearby, and people typically like people who are physically attractive more than those who are unattractive. How are we to understand such findings? Theories help social psychologists to organize and conceptualize large bodies of research findings such as those on attraction.

Theories focus and direct research.   Finally, theories not only serve to explain behavior and organize research findings; they also suggest new research hypotheses and directions. Although social psychologists can study a virtually infinite number of social psychological processes and variables, theories help to focus empirical research on specific questions. Whether they are eventually supported or refuted, theories help set the research agendas of social psychologists (Shaw & Costanzo, 1970). We'll examine in greater detail the relation between theory and research in Chapter 2.

▪▪▪▪▪▪▪▪▪▪▪▪▪▪▪▪▪▪▪▪▪▪▪▪▪

Four Theoretical Perspectives

Social psychological theories come in many varieties, but in this book we'll refer repeatedly to the following classes of theories: (1) learning theories, (2) cognitive consistency theories, (3) attribution and other cognitive information-processing theories, and (4) equity and exchange theories. Each of these meets the three criteria of a good social psychological theory: It has proven ability to help predict and explain social behavior, to organize large bodies of data, and to guide significant programs of research.

Let's examine a thumbnail sketch of each of these theoretical approaches (see Summary Table 1.2 for an overview). It is important that we recognize that these four theoretical perspectives are not necessarily mutually exclusive. Each may have a valid, overlapping range of application to the complexity of human social behavior. To make each of these perspectives a bit more clear and concrete, let's apply each to the following question: Why do we like and love the people we do?

Learning theories.   Social psychology has borrowed from a long and rich tradition of research on learning processes (Lott & Lott, 1985). For example, research on classical conditioning, operant conditioning, and observational learning can be applied to social behavior. Perhaps friendships are partly a matter of operant conditioning — we like and seek out people who are rewarding, and we dislike and avoid people who are punishing. Attraction may also be influenced by classical conditioning. Perhaps, all other things being equal, we come to dislike people who are associated with pain or unpleasant events (for example, a teacher who lectures to you in a hot, crowded room), and you come to like people associated with pleasant events (the students who sit next to you in a fun class).

Note that learning theories are in a sense "content-free." They describe basic processes that occur in all people (and animals) and which can apply to many different kinds of social behavior. Variations of conditioning and learning theories have been used in social psychology to explain attitude formation and change, aspects of interpersonal attraction, the effects of groups on individual performance, and aspects of morality (Lott & Lott, 1985).

Cognitive consistency theories.   Social psychology has long studied people's thought processes. In the 1950s a number of theories were developed, all of which emphasized that people strive for consistency in their thoughts (that is, among their beliefs, attitudes, and feelings). Perhaps the two most famous consistency theories are Festinger's (1957) theory of cognitive dissonance and Heider's (1946, 1958) balance theory, which was elaborated by Newcomb (1953). Dissonance theory postulates that when people hold inconsistent beliefs they experience an unpleasant motivational state that can, in certain circumstances, motivate an attitude change

SUMMARY TABLE 1.2   Theoretical Perspectives in Social Psychology

How are the four major theoretical perspectives in social psychology different from one another? How are they similar?

THEORETICAL APPROACH	BASIC ASSUMPTIONS	IMAGE OF HUMAN SOCIAL BEHAVIOR	TOPICS IN SOCIAL PSYCHOLOGY TO WHICH THEORIES APPLY
Learning theories	Human social behavior can be explained by applying research and theory on basic learning processes such as classical and operant conditioning.	People are seen as conditioned organisms under the influence of environmental contingencies; animal learning experiments used as models.	Attitudes and attitude change Group influences Aggression Prosocial behavior Prejudice Attraction
Cognitive-consistency theories	People strive for consistency among their beliefs and feelings.	People strive for mental peace and quiet; mental inconsistency is uncomfortable, and people strive to reduce it.	Attitudes and attitude change Attraction Prejudice
Attribution and information-processing theories	People strive to understand the world around them.	People are seen as *social computers*, noticing, encoding, and organizing social information.	Social perception Attitudes Prejudice Prosocial behavior Aggression Group decision making
Equity and exchange theories	Human interactions are governed by their *costs, rewards*, and *profits*. People strive for fair or equitable exchanges in social interaction.	Economic model of social relations; includes elements of learning theories, consistency theories, and cognitive theories.	Attraction Prejudice and group conflict Bargaining and negotiation Organizational and industrial behavior

You may have noticed that social-psychological theories often emphasize individuals' thought processes. Except for some learning theories, all the perspectives listed here deal with internal processes.

(see Chapter 8). For example, if you believe that cigarettes are very unhealthy and also acknowledge that you smoke several packs each day, this uncomfortable and inconsistent knowledge may lead you to change your attitude toward cigarettes — maybe they're *not* so unhealthy.

Balance theory focuses on the consistency or inconsistency of our likes and dislikes. Some patterns of likes and dislikes are cognitively consistent (or "balanced," to use the language of balance theory). For example, if you and your new romantic partner both love cats, then your likes are "balanced"—you both like the same things. On the other hand, if you love cats but your new beloved detests them, your pattern of attractions is unharmonious or "unbalanced." A basic assumption of balance theory is that because unbalanced patterns of likes or attitudes are jarring and uncomfortable, people will change their attitudes to create balance. Thus, you may decide that because your beloved hates your cat, then you can no longer be lovers—that is, you change your attitude toward your lover to restore cognitive balance. (See Chapter 11 for a more detailed presentation of balance theory.)

Notice that consistency theories are "cognitive" to the extent they focus on our mental representations of beliefs and attitudes. And these theories are "motivational" to the extent they postulate that unpleasant mental states must be resolved when we hold inconsistent beliefs, likes, and dislikes. Although consistency theories have been applied most often to the topics of attitudes and attitude change, they have also yielded insights into psychological processes that influence attraction, prejudice, and aggression.

Attribution and other cognitive information-processing theories.   Simple learning theories and cognitive consistency theories fail to acknowledge much of the complexity of everyday social thought and behavior. For example, in evaluating people and forming likes and dislikes, we often try to figure out *why* people behave as they do. If Sam constantly compliments you and expresses interest in your life because he's truly concerned with your well-being, that should lead you to like him. But if he compliments you merely because he hopes to sell you a piece of real estate, you may justifiably dislike him. Attribution theories (Heider, 1958; Jones & Davis, 1965; Kelley, 1967, 1972) focus on the thought processes that people use to figure out the causes of others' behavior. Note that within this theoretical perspective we are no longer just the conditioned organisms that learning theories portray or merely people striving for mental peace and quiet (that is, consistency); instead we are actively thinking information processors who sift through the "facts" of the social world around us and try to understand what those "facts" are all about.

Cognitive theories (of which attribution theory is just one example) have played a dominant role in social psychology in recent years (Markus & Zajonc, 1985). Considerable recent research has been devoted to understanding how people notice, encode (that is, represent in their memory), process, and retrieve (recover from memory) social information. According to this recent theoretical perspective, each of us is a kind of "social computer" instead of a blindly conditioned social animal or a single-minded seeker of consistency.

Cognitive theories have been applied most directly to the study of social perception—how we perceive and remember information about other people. Cognitive theories have also yielded major insights into the nature of prejudice, aggression, altruism, and even such clinical disorders as depression.

Equity and exchange theories.   Learning theories, consistency theories, and attribution theories all largely seek to explain the individual's social thought and behavior. Social psychology has always faced the problem of linking the individual to a broader social context. It is not enough to account for just the individual's behavior; we must also describe how the individual relates to others.

Equity and exchange theories (for example, Adams, 1965; Homans, 1974; Thibaut & Kelley, 1959; Walster, Walster, & Berscheid, 1978) are economic theories of social behavior that attempt to explain social relations in terms of the give-and-take of social life. These theoretical approaches analyze social relations in terms of their "costs," "rewards," and "profits." Let's return to our example of interpersonal attraction: Suppose two people ask you out for a date on Saturday night. Which date do you decide to accept? A cold-blooded (but pragmatic) approach might be to mentally tally the potential rewards and costs of each date. For example, you might note that Date #1 is attractive and has a good sense of humor but is quite sarcastic and inconsiderate. Date #2, on the other hand, is kind, intelligent, and loyal, but also average looking and rather boring. Somehow you must compute the "profit" from each potential date and make your choice accordingly.

In a sense, equity and exchange theories extend certain notions of learning theories to the social domain: People are seen as pursuing rewards and avoiding punishments in their relations with others. But equity and exchange theories are more complex than simple learning theories. For one thing, they allow for the existence of cognitive processes that can tally up "rewards" and "costs" over an extended period of time. For example, in deciding whether or not a marriage is "equitable," a person may consider what he or she "gave" and "got" over many years. Furthermore, equity and exchange theories, in contrast to simple learning theories, acknowledge the existence of social rules or norms. The *norm of reciprocity* (Gouldner, 1960), for example, holds that we should give as we get from others: If someone does us a favor, we should be willing to do a favor in return.

Equity and exchange theories are "cognitive" in the sense that they emphasize how people mentally represent and think about the rewards and costs of social life. They incorporate aspects of learning theory to the extent that they focus on rewards and punishments in social relations. And finally, they borrow some aspects of consistency theory when they argue that people strive for "reciprocity" or "equity" in their relations. In other words, there are cognitively comfortable and cognitively uncomfortable kinds of social exchange. Indeed, a major goal of these theories is to predict precisely when social exchanges are seen as "fair" and comfortable, and when they are not. Equity and exchange theories have been profitably applied to the topics of interpersonal attraction, perception of social justice and injustice, competition and bargaining, behavior in industrial and organizational settings, and prosocial behavior and altruism.

■■

Applying Social Psychology

Social psychologists, like all scientists, want to formulate general theories that can explain empirical findings. Indeed, many studies in social psychology are designed specifically to test particular theories and hypotheses derived from those theories; the goal is to advance science, not necessarily to solve social problems. Still, social psychologists have traditionally combined a strong focus on basic theory and research with an equally strong concern for real-life, applied topics. Throughout its relatively brief history, social psychology has been concerned with topics of great social relevance — persuasion and attitude change, prejudice, obedience, aggression, and altruism and helping.

The history of social psychology has intimate ties to the larger political and cultural history of the world (Gergen, 1973; Jones, 1985; Sampson, 1977). The horrors of World War II, for example, stimulated research on the nature of prejudice. The U.S. government's interest in issues of propaganda and persuasion led social psychologists to begin modern research on attitude change in the 1940s and 1950s. The civil rights movement of the 1950s and 1960s led social psychologists to study anew prejudice, stereotypes, and social conflict. Social violence and higher crime rates in the 1960s and 1970s stimulated new research on aggression and its causes. In the 1980s, skyrocketing health-care costs and growing awareness of behaviors that contribute to disease led to new research on social psychological factors in health.

Social psychology has and continues to address questions of great social import: Does TV violence contribute to aggression in our society? What are the best ways for hostile groups to negotiate nonviolent solutions to their conflicts? Does pornography lead to aggression and foster prejudice against women?

■■■■■■■■■■■■■■■■■■■■■■■■■■

The Two Faces of Applied Social Psychology

In the chapters that follow we will weave together the "pure science" of social psychology with the application of research topics. In some studies the theories and principles of social psychology can be applied to real-life events and behavior. Thus, for example, research on attitude change and persuasion (see Chapter 8) has applications to commercial advertising and consumer behavior. Other studies apply social psychological principles and research methods to real-life domains with the specific intent of ameliorating a social problem or providing answers to pressing social questions. Thus, in Chapter 9 we'll examine research on prejudice and conclude by discussing research on school and residential integration and some ways of reducing prejudice. These two aspects of applied social psychology — linking the theory and

research of social psychology to real-life events and seeking to answer questions about real-life topics and social issues — are both an integral part of this book.

The topic of applying social psychology brings us back to the example with which we began this chapter — the Armenian earthquake. We noted earlier that people's behavior after the earthquake suggested many social psychological questions: When do people help others? Why are people aggressive? What leads to intergroup conflict? To a scientist, each of these questions is interesting in its own right. However, answering these questions carries a practical as well as a scientific

FIGURE 1.2   The profession of social psychology.

Where do social psychologists work, and what do they do?

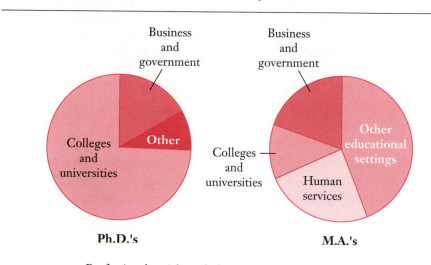

Ph.D.'s   M.A.'s

Professional social psychologists generally have earned a
graduate degree; they frequently work in educational
settings. Smaller numbers of social psychologists
work in government, business, and human services.

bonus: By understanding the nature of helping, we may be able to induce people to
be more helpful. By understanding the causes of aggression, we may be able to reduce
aggression. And by understanding the dynamics of group conflict, we may more
successfully negotiate peaceful settlements between contending groups.

**The Profession
of Social Psychology**

What is it like to be a social psychologist — where do social psychologists work, and
what do social psychologists do? As shown in Figure 1.2, 75 percent of social psychologists with Ph.D.'s work at colleges or universities; however, a significant minority (17 percent) find employment in business and government settings (Stapp &
Fulcher, 1981). Social psychologists with Master's degrees enjoy greater job diversity: 12 percent work at four-year colleges; 44 percent work in other, nonuniversity
academic settings; 20 percent work in business and government; and an additional
24 percent work in human-services fields (for example, clinics, public-health agencies, probation departments).

It seems likely that in the near future new areas of applied research in social
psychology will lead to new kinds of employment for social psychologists. For example, the recent increase in research on health psychology, on the social psychology
of the legal system, and on social psychological factors in such clinical disorders as
depression (see Rodin, 1985) promises employment for social psychologists in the
domains of medicine, law, and clinical psychology.

The skills of a good social psychologist can be applied to many kinds of work: marketing research, opinion polling, evaluation research in business and government (that is, research that assesses the effects of new programs), and statistical analysis of behavioral data.

The many social psychologists who work in academic settings often divide their time among teaching, staying abreast of new research, and conducting research. The focus of all this teaching, study, and research is, of course, the subject that social psychologists consider one of the most fascinating in the world: human social behavior.

Summary

1. Social psychology investigates social behavior and social influences on behavior.

2. Social scientists offer many different explanations for social behavior. Social psychologists in particular emphasize the current social setting and such mediating variables as beliefs, attitudes, schemas, emotional states, and personality traits. Social psychology examines the self as both a cause and an effect of social behavior.

3. Social psychology differs from related fields in its explanations of social behavior, its focus on the individual as the unit of analysis, and its research methods.

4. Social psychologists develop theories to explain and predict social behavior, to organize empirical findings, and to suggest hypotheses to guide future research.

5. Four important theoretical approaches in social psychology are 1) learning theories, 2) cognitive consistency theories, 3) attribution and cognitive information-processing theories, and 4) equity and exchange theories.

6. Social psychology combines a strong interest in both pure and applied science. Most social psychologists work in academic settings, but a significant minority work in business, government, and human services settings.

Glossary

Applied social psychology: Social psychological theory and research used to answer practical questions or to design and implement programs in real-life domains

Attitude: An evaluative response (a like or a dislike) directed at an object; a mediating variable studied in social psychology

Attribution theories: Theories that explain the thought processes people use to explain the causes of others' behavior

Belief: Cognitive knowledge about an object; a mediating variable studied in social psychology

Cognitive consistency theories: Theories that hold that people strive for consistency in their thoughts and feelings; dissonance theory and balance theory are the most famous examples

Cognitive theories: Theories that emphasize human information processing and its effects on social behavior

Emotion: A transient state of arousal and cognition that motivates and directs behavior, particularly in novel settings that demand quick action; a mediating variable studied in social psychology

Exchange and equity theories: Economic theories of social interaction that hold that people monitor the costs, rewards, and profits of their social relations and strive for fair or equitable exchanges of social "goods"

Group-level explanation: An explanation of social behavior that focuses on the individual's membership in social or biological groups

Individual-level explanation: An explanation of social behavior that focuses on factors unique to the individual (such as heredity and physiology), on the individual's past environment, and on the individual's current environment

Learning theories: Theories that use principles of learning (such as those supported by research on classical and operant conditioning) to explain aspects of social behavior

Mediating variable: A hypothetical internal variable that cannot be directly observed and that is used to explain an individual's behavior; examples are attitudes, personality traits, and schemas

Personality trait: A stable disposition that influences broad domains of an individual's behavior; a mediating variable studied in social psychology

Schema: A cognitive model or theory that an individual holds about people, groups, events, or things; a mediating variable studied in social psychology

Social psychology: The scientific study of social behavior and social influences on behavior; it focuses on the individual as its unit of analysis and emphasizes situational variables and certain mediating variables as explanations of social behavior

Unitary theories: Theories that offer simple encompassing principles (such as hedonism) to explain a broad range of human social behavior

Simplicity is the key to effective scientific inquiry. This is especially true in the case of subject matter with a psychological content. Psychological matter, by its nature, is difficult to get at and likely to have many more sides to it than appear at first glance. Complicated procedures only get in the way of clear scrutiny of the phenomenon itself. To study obedience most simply, we must create a situation in which one person orders another person to perform an observable action and we must note when obedience to the imperative occurs and when it fails to occur.

. . . The precise mode of acting against the victim is not of central importance. For technical reasons, the delivery of electric shock was chosen for the study. It seemed suitable, first, because it would be easy for the subject to understand the notion that shocks can be graded in intensity; second, its use would be consistent with the general scientific aura of the laboratory; and finally, it would be relatively easy to simulate the administration of shock in the laboratory.

—— from *Obedience to Authority*
by Stanley Milgram, pp. 13–14

CHAPTER 2

Social Psychological Research

*I*n the early 1960s, Stanley Milgram, a Yale social psychologist, wanted to understand why Germans had obeyed the vicious commands issued by their leaders during World War II. Like most researchers, Milgram began with a hypothesis: that the blind obedience of Germans during World War II resulted from some aspect of the "German character." Milgram intended to conduct his research in Germany, but first he had to develop an objective experimental procedure for measuring obedience precisely. The procedure Milgram developed was relatively straightforward: In the guise of conducting a learning experiment, an experimenter would order subjects to deliver increasingly intense electrical shocks—up to 450 volts—to an innocent victim. The subject's level of obedience would be defined as the highest level of shock delivered by the subject upon command from the experimenter.

In testing his procedure Milgram discovered, to his dismay, that all of his Yale subjects obeyed completely. "I'll tell you quite frankly," Milgram stated in one interview (Meyer, 1970), "before I began this experiment . . . I thought that most people would break off. . . . You would get only a very small proportion of people going . . . to the end [to 450 volts], and they would constitute a pathological fringe." But in his pilot studies Milgram's "pathological fringe" turned out to be all of his subjects.

Because his subjects obeyed so readily, Milgram modified and elaborated his procedure to create for subjects additional pressures to disobey. Imagine you are a subject in this modified study: You come to a laboratory at Yale University, and the experimenter—a stern-looking man in a white coat—informs you that he is conducting research on the effects of punishment on learning. The experimenter describes the procedure: You will be a "teacher" who reads lists of words to another subject—a pleasant-looking, middle-aged man. You will then test this "learner" to see whether he correctly remembers the words. Every time he makes a mistake, you are to deliver a punishment to him—an electric shock.

Before the trials begin, the learner tells the experimenter in your presence that he's a bit afraid to receive electric shocks because he's been diagnosed as having a slight heart condition. The experimenter assures the learner that although the shocks may be painful, they will not harm him. While you watch, the experimenter takes the learner to the next room, where he is strapped into an apparatus that looks like an electric chair. The experimenter returns to the main room and seats you at a console that appears to be a shock generator. The machine has a row of levers marked in 15-volt increments, from 15 volts to 450 volts. The voltage levels also have labels ranging from "slight shock" through "strong shock," "intense shock," and "danger: severe shock," followed by "X X X" beyond 435 volts. Your instructions are to read the lists of words over a microphone to the learner in the next room. Periodically you will test his recall of these words. Every time the learner remembers a word incorrectly you are to deliver a shock as punishment. And with each successive incorrect response, you are to increase the level of shock one step (that is, 15 volts).

The experiment begins uneventfully. You read lists of words and then test the learner periodically. Occasionally he makes a mistake, and you deliver his punishment. Once you have reached the lever marked 75 volts, the learner in the next room begins to grunt in pain with each shock. At 120 volts the learner starts to complain verbally. As you progress to higher levels of shock, the victim shouts out, "I can't stand the pain. Let me out of here! . . . My heart's bothering me. Let me out!" At still higher levels of shock the learner screams in agony and desperately pleads for his release. Finally, at the highest levels of shock, approaching 450 volts, the learner stops responding entirely. You hear nothing from the next room. For all you know, your victim is dead of a heart attack, sprawled out in the "electric chair."

To what extent did subjects on average obey the experimenter in this new version of the study; that is, how far did subjects proceed in shocking the learner? Would any normal person now administer shocks all the way to 450 volts? Milgram (1974) found that *62 percent* of his subjects—a clear majority—proceeded all the way to 450 volts and delivered what they thought to be excruciatingly painful electric shocks to the learner upon command from the experimenter.

It should be emphasized that Milgram's subjects did not enjoy inflicting pain on their victim. Indeed, most subjects were horribly distressed and agitated; they stopped periodically and virtually begged the experimenter to check in on the learner. But the experimenter always responded with prompts like, "Please continue. The experiment requires that you continue." Sadly and surprisingly, although most subjects felt morally upset about inflicting terrible pain on the learner, they nonetheless followed the experimenter's orders to the end.

It is important to note at this point that no learner in the Milgram study was actually shocked. The learner was in fact a confederate in the experiment, not a real subject. And the "screams" from the next room were in fact tape recordings (so that the situation was totally standardized for all subjects).

Clearly, Milgram's initial hypothesis was wrong. Destructive obedience doesn't occur just in certain countries, or among a "pathological fringe." When placed in the proper situation, average Americans displayed startling levels of obedience. Based on this discovery, Milgram conducted an influential series of landmark experiments investigating the social factors that lead normal people to obey grossly unethical commands issued by authority figures.

Milgram's research is interesting on a number of different levels: It provides important information about the nature of obedience in particular and about the power of social pressures in general, and it also poses important questions about the

Milgram's experiment on obedience: *upper:* the shock generator used in his study; *lower:* the "learner" is strapped into a chair and a shock electrode is attached to his arm.

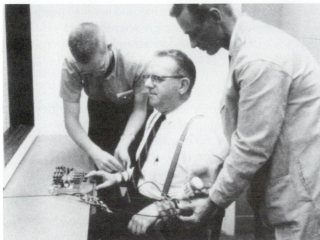

methods and ethics of social psychological research. For now, think about Milgram's study in terms of its scientific merit. Was this study "scientific"? What possible flaws existed in Milgram's research methods? Can Milgram's results be generalized to real-life settings? If you were Milgram and had completed your first obedience experiment, what would be your next step in studying obedience?

The laboratory situation gives us a framework in which to study the subject's reactions to the principal conflict of the experiment. Again, this conflict is between the experimenter's demands that he continue to administer the electric shock and the learner's demands, which become increasingly insistent, that the experiment be stopped. The crux of the study is to vary systematically the factors believed to alter the degree of obedience. . . .

—— *Obedience to Authority*, p. 26

Issues in Social Psychological Research

Social psychology is a relatively young science. The first experimental study in social psychology is thought to be Triplett's (1897) study on social facilitation (how the presence of others influences an individual's performance), and the first textbooks in this emerging discipline were written in the early years of the twentieth century.

In some ways social psychology is like other sciences; it attempts to gather knowledge by testing theories against empirical (that is, measured) data. In other ways, social psychology differs from other sciences. Unlike the natural sciences, social psychology studies topics (for example, obedience, attraction, and persuasion) that are the subject both of strong everyday beliefs and of formal scientific theories as well. Furthermore, social psychology often seeks answers to questions ("Does TV violence lead to aggression?" "Does integration change racial attitudes?") that are highly relevant to public policy and passions. Social psychological research, compared to research in some sciences, is complicated by the fact that its subjects—human beings—consciously think and may be aware that they are subjects in a research study. Because of this, social psychological research may suffer from some unique kinds of bias.

Let's examine more closely the role of the scientific method in social psychology and the special problems social psychology poses for the scientific method. What kinds of theories do social psychologists develop, and what kinds of research studies do they conduct?

Theories in Social Psychology

Social psychologists, like all scientists, develop theories—sets of propositions that are used to explain, predict, and organize empirical data (Shaw & Costanzo, 1970). Social psychological theories help to explain, for example, why people change their attitudes, begin and end intimate relationships, and obey authority figures.

Typically, social psychological theories are designed to be general enough to apply to a broad range of specific social behaviors. For example, equity theory, a set of propositions about the costs and rewards in social relationships, has been used to understand relationships between employees and bosses, between close friends, and between spouses. This theory, like other theories, can generate a host of hypotheses—specific, testable propositions derived from the theory. Thus, equity theory might suggest the hypotheses that workers who feel they are not receiving pay commensurate with their efforts will either demand more pay or work less, or that a wife who believes she "puts more into" her marriage than she receives from her husband will try to get more rewards from her husband, create more costs for him, or if these fail, end the relationship.

In Chapter 1 we sketched out four main theoretical approaches in social psychology: learning theories, cognitive consistency theories, attribution and other cognitive information-processing theories, and equity and exchange theories. Some of these theories are expressed in terms of mathematical propositions. For example, versions of equity theory (Walster, Walster, & Berscheid, 1978) offer precise mathematical statements to explain how certain patterns of "costs," "rewards," and "investments" result in equitable or inequitable relationships. Other theories in social psychology are sets of verbal propositions. Festinger's (1957) theory of cognitive dissonance, for example, proposes that when people hold inconsistent beliefs they experience an unpleasant state of arousal; furthermore, under certain conditions people will shift their beliefs to reduce this arousal. Social psychological theories help to focus researchers' attention on crucial variables and to suggest hypotheses that can be proven correct or incorrect by empirical data. Useful theories typically are logically consistent, relatively simple, and capable of being disproved.

Although data may prove a theory (and the hypotheses derived from that theory) incorrect, they never truly "prove" that a theory is correct. Rather, confirming data increase the *likelihood* that theories are correct. Think back to Milgram's obedience research. If Milgram had traveled to Germany and found that German subjects showed high levels of obedience, this evidence would have provided data consistent with his hypothesis that obedience in Germans resulted from their "national character." However, such data would not prove the hypothesis. Instead, the obedience data Milgram collected in the United States made his hypothesis about a unique link between German national character and obedience less plausible.

The development of theories proceeds hand-in-hand with the gathering of empirical data: Empirical data suggest theoretical generalizations (see Figure 2.1). Often, a theory must be modified or elaborated as empirical findings that are inconsistent with the theory emerge. Although it might seem that the ideal study is one that lends perfect support for a theory, some of the most important advances in science have resulted from jarring contradictions between theoretical hypotheses and the data collected to test them. Stanley Milgram's obedience research provides a good example of such a study — his data did not support his initial hypotheses, and our understanding of obedience advanced as a result.

■■■■■■■■■■■■■■■■■■■■■■■■■
Operational Definitions in Social Psychology

> The main measure for any subject is the maximum shock he administers before he refuses to go any farther. In principle this may vary from 0 (for a subject who refuses to administer even the first shock) to 30 (for a subject who administers the highest shock on the generator).
>
> —— *Obedience to Authority*, p. 24

The core scientific assumptions of social psychology are that social reality can be measured and that the test of all theories and hypotheses lies in empirical data. Social psychologists, like all scientists, must decide how to measure concretely the variables they wish to study. An *operational definition* is a definition of some concept (like obedience, love, or an attitude) in terms of the procedures or methods used to measure the concept. Sometimes it is difficult for researchers to agree on operational definitions. How, for example, are we to operationally define such concepts as "obedience," "attitudes," "romantic love," or "anxiety"?

Social psychologists typically use two different kinds of operational definitions: subjective reports and behavioral measures (Aronson, Brewer, & Carlsmith, 1985). In *subjective reports* people are asked to report their own experiences, sometimes through direct questioning but more commonly through questionnaires and rating scales. *Behavioral measures*, on the other hand, represent direct observations of behavior that are not filtered through the individual's subjective experience.

Suppose, for example, that I wish to operationally define subjects' "anxiety." Using subjective measures I could ask them to rate themselves on a scale from "1 — totally calm, relaxed, and free of anxiety" to "10 — nervous, tense, and anxious." Or, I could administer a standard anxiety questionnaire — for example, the Taylor Manifest Anxiety Scale (Taylor, 1953), which includes such true-false items as "I worry over money and business," "I have diarrhea once a month or more," "I have had periods in which I lost sleep over worry," and "Life is a strain for me much of the time."

FIGURE 2.1   Theory, hypothesis, and research in social psychology.

How are theories in social psychology tested scientifically?

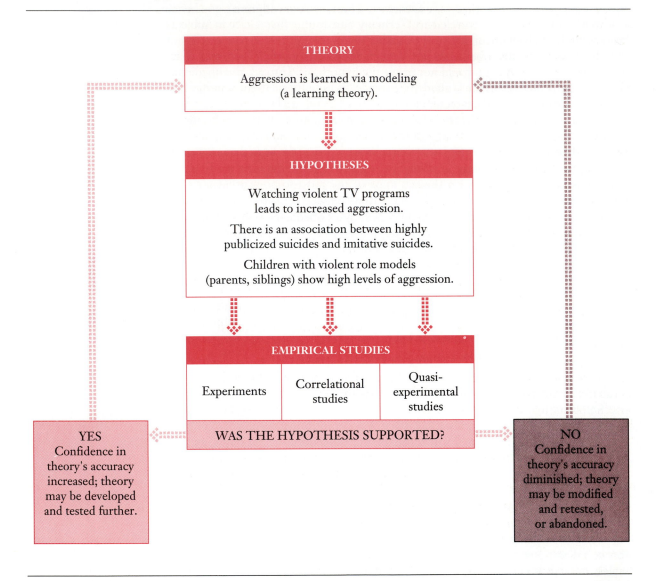

Theories are sets of propositions that generate testable hypotheses. As the diagram suggests, the relationship between theory and research is reciprocal: Theories lead to studies, and the results of studies lead to the modification of theories.

To obtain behavioral measures of anxiety, I could measure subjects' heart rate, breathing, and Galvanic Skin Response (a measure of electrical skin conductivity and, indirectly, of perspiration). Presumably, anxious people show more physiological arousal than do less anxious people. I could also observe and measure such mannerisms as twitching, fidgeting, and speech nonfluencies. In his experiments Stanley Milgram used a behavioral measure of obedience — a subject's obedience was the highest level of shock used in punishing the learner.

Let's consider another, very different social psychological concept — romantic love. How might we operationally define this concept? To obtain subjective reports, I could have subjects rate on a ten-point scale how much they love a particular person. Or I could have them complete a "love scale" developed by rigorous principles of test construction (see Rubin, 1970). But can we always rely on what people say about themselves? Some individuals may lie about such personal emotions as love or anxiety; some may not be fully aware of their emotions. Perhaps, then, we should also obtain behavioral measures. For example, in one research study on romantic love (Rubin, 1970), dating couples were placed together in a room while researchers unobtrusively measured their mutual eye contact and how close together they sat on a couch. In recent years it has even become acceptable to measure directly subjects' levels of sexual arousal.

Perhaps social psychologists can be most confident in their data if they obtain multiple, corroborating measures. For example, we would strongly believe that John indeed passionately loves Joan if he says he loves her strongly, scores very high on Rubin's Love Scale, constantly gazes into her eyes, sits right next to her on the couch, and displays measurable sexual arousal. Agreement of results obtained by multiple operationalizations increases our confidence in measurements. On the other hand, when the various measures of a concept are not consistent with one another, then the measures are flawed because they are more a function of the particular operational definition than of the concept we're trying to measure (Campbell & Fiske, 1959). For example, if none of the measures of love just described correlate with one another, we might reasonably doubt that they are all truly measuring "love."

Reliability and Validity of Measures

Whenever social psychologists use either subjective or behavioral measures, they must demonstrate that their measures have two important properties: *reliability* and *validity*. A reliable measure is repeatable and consistently obtained. A valid measure assesses what it is designed to measure. For example, an attitude scale is reliable if it yields highly consistent scores for given subjects when administered at two or more different times. (This kind of reliability, called "test-retest reliability," is one of several different varieties of reliability.) An attitude scale is valid if it truly measures the attitude it is designed to measure and if it predicts relevant criteria. For example, a valid measure of voters' attitudes toward a political candidate might predict whether they will vote for the candidate.

In general, reliability is a prerequisite to validity. That is, a measure cannot validly assess some conceptual variable if it is not measuring *something* consistently.

Kinds of Social Psychological Studies

Social psychological studies generally come in two forms: experiments and correlational studies. What are the defining characteristics of these two types of studies, and what are their relative advantages and disadvantages?

FIGURE 2.2   Schematic diagram of an experiment.

What are the two essential elements of an experiment?

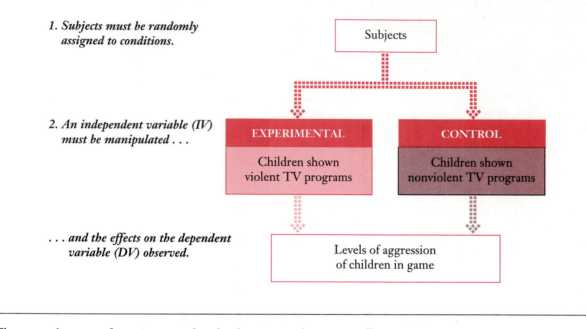

1. Subjects must be randomly assigned to conditions.

Subjects

2. An independent variable (IV) must be manipulated . . .

EXPERIMENTAL

Children shown violent TV programs

CONTROL

Children shown nonviolent TV programs

. . . and the effects on the dependent variable (DV) observed.

Levels of aggression of children in game

The great advantage of experiments is that they let scientists draw cause-effect conclusions.

Experiments.   In an experiment, the social psychologist manipulates (that is, intentionally alters or varies) a variable, termed the *independent variable* (IV), and observes its influence on a second variable, termed the *dependent variable* (DV). For example, in an experiment testing the effects of TV violence on children's aggression we might show some children a violent TV show and others a nonviolent show (the violence of the show would constitute the independent variable) and then observe whether the two kinds of programs have any effect on the children's aggressiveness (the dependent variable).

   Random assignment is an essential element of an experiment. Subjects have been randomly assigned to experimental conditions whenever any given subject had an equal probability of being assigned to any experimental condition. In an experiment on TV violence and aggression, random assignment of subjects would require that the experimenter decide (by a procedure such as the flip of a coin) whether a particular child watches a violent TV show or a nonviolent TV show (see Figure 2.2).

   Random assignment in experiments is not the same thing as random sampling in a survey. Random assignment refers to subjects' equal likelihood of being assigned by an experimenter to different experimental conditions; random sampling is a process in which each member of a population (such as registered voters) has the same probability of being surveyed as does anyone else in that population. The goal of an experiment is to determine whether an experimental manipulation—the in-

dependent variable — has an effect on the dependent variable. The goal of a probability sample in survey research, on the other hand, is to measure a small group of people (a sample, for example, 2,000 U.S. voters) in order to reliably generalize to a larger population (the U.S. electorate).

To understand better the logic of experiments, let's consider an actual experiment on TV violence and aggression conducted by Liebert and Baron (1972). One hundred thirty-six children individually came to a "waiting room" and watched TV programming controlled by the experimenters. Half of the children were randomly assigned to see a very violent TV segment (containing two fistfights, two shootings, and a knifing) from the old show, "The Untouchables." The remaining children viewed a part of a track meet with lots of activity, but no violence. Viewing or not viewing the violent TV segment constituted the independent variable in this experiment.

Stated a bit differently, one group of subjects was exposed to the experimental treatment (watching violent TV), whereas the other group — the control group — was not. The control group provided a baseline measure of the dependent measure (children's aggressiveness) to compare with the aggressiveness of the children who viewed violent TV. In general, a *control group* in an experiment is a group that does not receive the experimental treatment (see Figure 2.3).

After watching television for a few minutes, the children in Liebert and Baron's experiment participated in a "game" in which they thought they could either help or hurt another child in an adjacent room by pressing buttons on a machine. Finally, the children were allowed to play in a room that contained both aggressive and nonaggressive toys (for example, guns and knives vs. a slinky, a space station, and dolls). The children's aggressiveness in the game and in play served as the dependent measures. Liebert and Baron found that children who watched the violent TV

How can we determine experimentally whether watching violent programs on television causes heightened aggression in children?

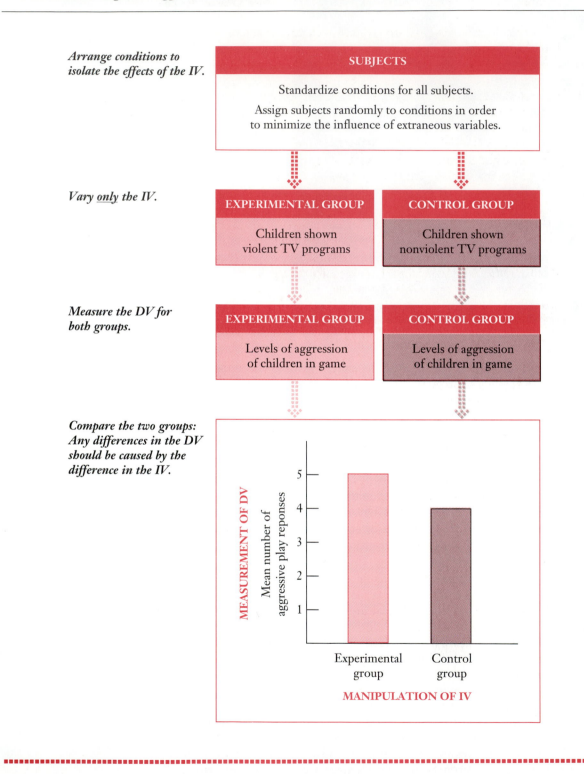

Arrange conditions to isolate the effects of the IV.

SUBJECTS

Standardize conditions for all subjects.

Assign subjects randomly to conditions in order to minimize the influence of extraneous variables.

Vary only the IV.

EXPERIMENTAL GROUP

Children shown violent TV programs

CONTROL GROUP

Children shown nonviolent TV programs

Measure the DV for both groups.

EXPERIMENTAL GROUP

Levels of aggression of children in game

CONTROL GROUP

Levels of aggression of children in game

Compare the two groups: Any differences in the DV should be caused by the difference in the IV.

MEASUREMENT OF DV

Mean number of aggressive play reponses

Experimental group

Control group

MANIPULATION OF IV

segment hurt other children more in their "game" and played more aggressively than did children who watched the sports segment. This effect was present for both boys and girls.

From these results, Liebert and Baron could conclude that watching violent TV *caused* children to behave more aggressively in their experiment. One major strength of experiments is that they allow researchers to infer cause-effect relationships between independent and dependent variables (Aronson, Brewer, & Carlsmith, 1985). Why are such inferences possible? The key lies in the random assignment of subjects, which essentially rules out all possible causal explanations other than the experimental manipulation itself.

Let's describe how this worked in Liebert and Baron's experiment. Many variables may influence children's aggressiveness, among them personality traits (perhaps extraverts are more aggressive than introverts), social class (perhaps lower-class children are more aggressive than middle-class children), religion, and ethnic background. But because subjects were *randomly assigned* to experimental conditions, all of these extraneous variables were balanced out; that is, on average there were as many introverts, lower-class children, and so on in the experimental group as in the control group. Thus, if we obtain a significant difference in the aggressiveness between the children in the two groups, that difference must be due to the manipulation (that is, to viewing a violent TV segment vs. viewing a track event), not to extraneous variables.

Correlational studies.   In a correlational study there is neither random assignment of subjects nor manipulation of independent variables. Instead, the researcher measures variables as they naturally occur in some setting and observes whether they are related (see Figure 2.4).

Let's consider two more studies on TV violence and aggression. McLeod, Atkin, and Chaffee (1972a, 1972b) measured the TV watching habits and aggressiveness of 473 teenagers in Maryland and 151 teenagers in Wisconsin. Specifically, they asked the teenagers to rate how often they watched 65 different prime-time TV shows that had been independently rated on their degree of violent content. The teens also completed various self-report measures that asked them to rate their own levels of aggressiveness and delinquency. In the Wisconsin study (1972b), the researchers also asked the teenagers' mothers and peers to rate them on aggressiveness. (Note that in this study no independent variable was manipulated and no random assignment of subjects occurred; therefore it is correlational, not experimental.) The teenagers who watched more violent TV shows in this study tended to describe themselves as more aggressive, and their parents and friends tended to rate them as more aggressive as well.

What's the difference between Liebert and Baron's experiment on TV violence and aggression and McLeod, Atkin, and Chaffee's 1972 correlational studies? One major difference is that whereas a cause-effect conclusion can be drawn from the experiment, it cannot necessarily be drawn from the correlational study. Psychologists and statisticians are fond of noting that correlation does not equal causation— it's true, and worth remembering. McLeod, Atkin, and Chaffee's correlational studies indicate that viewing violent TV goes along with real-life aggressiveness. This is not the same, however, as saying that watching violent TV *causes* aggression, for other interpretations are possible (see Figure 2.5). For example, perhaps innate aggressiveness in children causes a preference for violent TV programs—that is, the arrow of causation points in the opposite direction from what we might intuitively

FIGURE 2.4   Comparing experimental and correlational studies.

What information is provided by experiments and correlational studies?

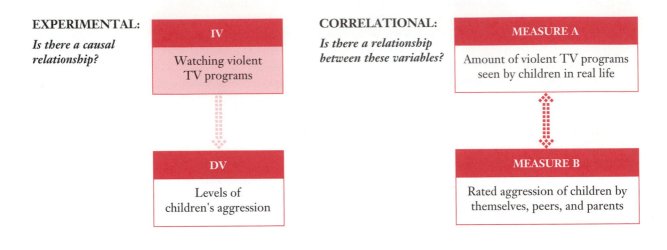

EXPERIMENTAL:

Is there a causal relationship?

IV

Watching violent TV programs

DV

Levels of children's aggression

CORRELATIONAL:

Is there a relationship between these variables?

MEASURE A

Amount of violent TV programs seen by children in real life

MEASURE B

Rated aggression of children by themselves, peers, and parents

Experiments demonstrate cause-effect relationships between variables; correlational studies can show only that two variables are related.

hypothesize. Or perhaps there is some third variable that accounts for the relationship between viewed TV violence and aggression in children. For example, perhaps the real cause of aggression in children is parental aggressiveness — perhaps hostile, aggressive parents produce hostile, aggressive children. And such parents might also have a preference for violent TV programs, which of course their children watch too because they live in the same house. None of these alternate interpretations can be ruled out in a correlational study.

Sophisticated correlational studies can sometimes provide *suggestive* information about causal relationships. For example, Lefkowitz, Eron, Walder, and Huesmann (1972) measured the television viewing habits and aggressiveness of 211 boys at age 9 and then again ten years later at age 19. These researchers found that not only did TV violence correlate with aggressiveness in the nine-year-old subjects, but the amount of violent TV boys viewed at age 9 predicted the boys' aggressiveness at age 19 as well. In other words, the correlation of TV viewing habits at one time with aggressiveness at a later time suggested (but did not prove!) a cause-effect relationship between the two.

In addition to providing different information about cause-effect relationships, these experimental and correlational studies on TV violence and aggression differed in another important way as well: The correlational study was somewhat more "realistic" in that it measured patterns of *real* TV viewing and also obtained measures of real-life aggression. The experimental study, on the other hand, used a very brief and perhaps somewhat unrealistic manipulation of TV violence; in real life,

FIGURE 2.5   Possible causal relationships among correlated variables.

Why is a correlation insufficient to establish causation?

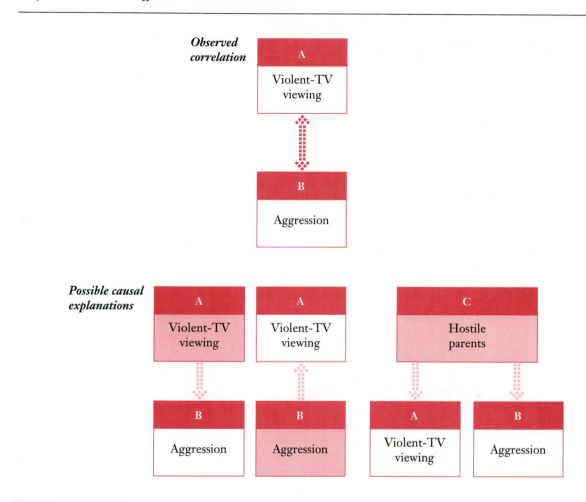

When two variables are correlated, it is not clear which variable causes the other — or whether they are both caused by a third variable.

after all, children don't watch shows for just a few minutes, but rather for hours and hours. Similarly, children's performance in the "game" that allowed them to "hurt" or "help" another child seems to be a somewhat contrived and artificial measure of aggression.

Both correlational and experimental studies are important, and in an important sense they are complementary. Because experimental studies are often better controlled and standardized, they produce data that are less affected by extraneous variables than do correlational studies. Experiments, as we have noted, can support strong causal inferences. Correlational studies, on the other hand, may be more true-to-life than experiments.

Sometimes researchers must conduct correlational studies when true experiments are not possible for practical or ethical reasons. For example, we could carry out a hypothetical experiment in which we randomly assign some children at a boarding school to watch many violent TV programs every day over a three-year period. Other children — those in the control group — would watch no violent TV programs. Aside from being impractical (no one, including parents, has perfect control over what TV shows children watch over a long period of time), this study is also unethical. If you were a parent, would you want your child to be exposed to three years of violent TV programming for the sake of contributing to interesting social psychological research?

Quasi-experimental designs.   Our discussion up to this point would seem to suggest that a social psychology study must be either an experiment or a correlational study. Some studies combine features of both experiments and correlational studies; such designs are referred to as *quasi-experimental designs* (Campbell & Stanley, 1966; Cook & Campbell, 1979). In a quasi-experimental study there is a manipulation (as in an experiment), but there is no truly random assignment of subjects.

A study by Hennigan and her colleagues (1982) on the relationship between TV viewing and crime provides a good example of a quasi-experimental design. This study investigated crime statistics in various cities in the United States during the late 1940s and early 1950s, when television broadcasting was first introduced in the United States. The Federal Communications Commission inadvertently helped these researchers by ordering a freeze on new TV broadcasting licenses between late 1949 and mid-1952. Thus some communities were introduced to television and others were not, and this constituted a kind of "manipulation," as might occur in an experiment. (Note, however, that communities were not randomly assigned to "conditions" and that the Federal Communications Commission, not the researchers, had control over which cities got TV stations.) This quasi-experimental study showed that the introduction of TV to communities was accompanied by increased rates of thefts (stealing of property without violence or force) but not of homicides or forcible robberies. Thus we have evidence from yet a different kind of study for some link between TV viewing and criminal behavior. As the Hennigan study makes clear, quasi-experimental designs are quite useful in studying the effects of changes in social policy — interventions over which researchers have no control. (For an overview of the three main types of research design, see Summary Table 2.1.)

Generalizing from the Results of Research Studies

In discussing the differences among correlational, experimental, and quasi-experimental studies, we touched on the notion of "realism" in social psychological research. Often, correlational and quasi-experimental studies seem more "true-to-life" than experiments. Does this mean that such studies can be more easily generalized to real-life settings than can experiments? Under what circumstances can research studies be generalized to other settings, behaviors, and populations?

Laboratory versus field studies.   Laboratory studies are conducted, reasonably enough, in laboratories, often in university settings. Field studies, on the other hand,

---

SUMMARY TABLE 2.1   Research Methods in Social Psychology

What distinguishes the principal research methods in social psychology?

	EXPERIMENTAL	QUASI-EXPERIMENTAL	CORRELATIONAL
Type of question addressed	Is there a causal relationship between the variables?	Does a manipulation that the researcher does not control seem to affect the dependent variable?	Are the variables related? To what degree?
Independent variable manipulated?	Yes.	Yes, but it is not under the researcher's control.	No.
Establish causation?	Yes.	No, but may suggest causation.	No.
Advantages	Control. Ability to demonstrate causation.	Useful for study of real-life interventions over which the researcher has no control.	Can study realistic variables; useful when experiments would be impractical or unethical.
Disadvantages	May be artificial; some questions not amenable to experimental study.	Lacks control; does not permit strong causal inferences.	Cannot demonstrate cause-effect relations.
Examples	Milgram obedience studies.	Hennigan et al. study of larceny rates and introduction of TV to U.S. cities.	McLeod et al. study of TV viewing and aggression in teenagers.

Social psychologists must study statistics and research design as well as social psychology. To gather useful data, social psychologists must devote much time and thought to the design of their studies.

---

are carried out in real-life settings, and thus their results must apply to at least one real-life setting. Field research, although more difficult to control and standardize than laboratory research, effectively complements laboratory research. Although in practice laboratory research is more likely to be experimental and field research is more likely to be correlational, both kinds of studies can be conducted in either the field or the laboratory.

Research on altruism and bystander intervention provides a good example of the usefulness of both field and laboratory research in social psychology. In one famous laboratory experiment, Darley and Latané (1968) had college subjects talk to another student in a nearby cubicle via a microphone and earphones. Partway through the conversation, the other student seemed to suffer an epileptic seizure. The experimenters wanted to know when subjects would help in emergencies and

Piliavin, Rodin, and Piliavin (1969) conducted a field experiment on bystander intervention in New York City subway cars.

when they wouldn't, and in particular they wanted to study how the number of people present during an emergency affects helping behavior. Strangely, it turned out that "more was less" in this experiment — that is, a given subject was less likely to help the epileptic victim when other subjects were present than when he or she was alone. (This, by the way, shows that social psychology is not always just "common sense." Sometimes, a study may yield unexpected, counterintuitive results.)

In another well-known study on helping in emergencies, Piliavin, Rodin, & Piliavin (1969) arranged for confederates to collapse in New York subway cars in order to identify variables that influence whether or not bystanders help the "victim." This experiment showed, for instance, that "victims" who appeared to be drunk were helped less often than were victims who appeared to be disabled.

Both the epileptic seizure study (which was conducted in the laboratory) and the subway study (which was conducted in the field) were experiments — each manipulated an independent variable (the number of bystanders present or the drunkenness of the victim) and randomly assigned subjects to experimental conditions. The distinction between correlational and experimental studies clearly is conceptually independent of the distinction between field and laboratory studies.

Field studies possess one definite advantage over laboratory studies: They are more natural and thus necessarily apply to real-life settings. When the goal of a social psychologist is to answer a question relevant to actual social policies (for example, "What effect does forced school integration have on racial attitudes?"), field research is often appropriate.

At the same time, field studies suffer from the messiness of real-life in which many variables interact in extremely complex ways. Field data are often influenced by factors irrelevant to the variables with which the study is truly concerned. (For example, whether or not subjects helped the collapsed confederate in Piliavin, Rodin, and Piliavin's subway experiment could depend on a host of uncontrollable variables — the number of people in the subway, the ethnic mix of people on the subway, the dirtiness of the particular subway, and so on.) Laboratory studies, on the other hand, permit maximal standardization and control of extraneous variables. (Recall Milgram's laboratory experiment on obedience in which all subjects received exactly the same instructions and heard exactly the same screams from the same apparent victim, in exactly the same environment.)

Traditionally, social psychology has emphasized laboratory experiments (Higbee, Millard, & Folkman, 1982). For this reason, social psychological research is sometimes accused of being artificial, contrived, and lacking in generalizability to the real world (Gergen, 1978; Gilmore & Duck, 1980). Furthermore, the subjects of social psychology experiments are often college students, which may limit the degree to which such social psychology experiments generalize to broader populations (Sears, 1986).

Internal and external validity.   If their results are to be generalized to broader settings and populations, experiments must demonstrate two important characteristics: internal and external validity (Campbell & Stanley, 1963; Cook & Campbell, 1979; Crano & Brewer, 1986).

An experiment possesses *internal validity* if the independent variable manipulates what it's supposed to and if the observed experimental effects are truly caused by the independent variable. For example, Liebert and Baron's experiment on TV violence and aggression possesses internal validity if it truly manipulated the "amount of violence" in the TV segments and if this manipulation was indeed the cause of the observed differences in the children's aggressiveness.

An experiment possesses *external validity* when its findings apply to broader populations or settings. Liebert and Baron's experiment possesses external validity if its results apply to children other than those in the experiment, to different kinds of violent TV, to children playing at home, and so on. Internal validity is a necessary but not sufficient precondition for external validity; in other words, experimental findings cannot be generalized to broader populations if the variables in the experiment were not manipulated properly in the first place.

The internal validity of an experiment is threatened whenever the independent variable is confounded with another variable. Two variables are said to be *confounded* when they occur together and when it then becomes impossible to tell whether an experimental effect was due to one or the other variable. For example, in Liebert and Baron's experiment on TV violence and aggression, what caused the differences in aggression between the experimental and control groups? Was it the difference between a "violent" and a "nonviolent" TV segment, or was it perhaps instead the difference between a "sports" and a "nonsports" TV segment? Notice that in the Liebert and Baron experiment, these variables were perfectly confounded.

Replication.   To increase our confidence in the generalizability of Liebert and Baron's experimental findings on TV violence and aggression in children and to assure ourselves that these results were not due to the presence of confounded variables in that particular experiment, we could conduct several *replications*, or repetitions of the study. Successful replications are those that produce the same or

The Issue of Realism in Social Psychology Experiments

Must experimental settings be like real-life settings in order to yield valid findings? Aronson and Carlsmith (1968) have distinguished between two different kinds of realism in social psychological studies — what they term mundane and experimental realism.

Mundane realism is probably quite similar to your common-sense notion of realism. It refers to how much a study reflects what goes on in real-life settings. For example, in many ways the Milgram obedience study is quite low in mundane realism: Most of us, in the course of our everyday lives, are not asked to deliver excruciatingly painful electric shocks to innocent victims in the course of participating in a learning experiment.

Experimental realism, on the other hand, focuses on quite a different issue: Regardless of whether or not the study is like "real life," do the subjects nonetheless take it seriously? Are they emotionally and mentally involved in what's going on? Most observers agree that the Milgram study was quite high in experimental realism — subjects truly believed what was occurring and were quite emotionally involved. We can think of mundane realism as referring to the study's similarity to the outside world, whereas experimental realism refers more to realism within the closed world of the study itself.

Aronson and Carlsmith argue that experimental realism is more important than mundane realism: If subjects do not believe what is occurring in a study and do not take their participation in it seriously, it does not matter how much the study reflects real life — the study is a failure. Imagine a study on persuasive messages and attitude change in which I ask subjects to read newspaper editorials that either support or oppose a new U.S. defense program. Subjects then complete a questionnaire that assesses their attitude toward the program. This study is quite high on mundane realism — in real life people do read newspaper editorials that sometimes influence their attitudes. But, on the other hand, the study may not be very high on experimental realism; subjects may not take it seriously. They may be bored with the editorials, read their questionnaires carelessly, or fill in answers as quickly as possible just to be done with the study. To the extent the subjects don't take the study seriously, the data collected are worthless.

Students of social psychology are often concerned whenever experiments lack mundane realism. Their concerns seem valid: If an experiment is not like real life, how can it inform us about real life? Real life is complex and messy! But because experiments create a kind of artificial simplicity, social psychologists can isolate variables and thus carefully and systematically examine variables' effects in a way that would be impossible in real life. In this way laboratory studies can give us valuable information about processes that occur outside the laboratory. Thus Milgram's obedience studies may further our theoretical understanding of the conditions under which obedience is either likely or unlikely to occur, and we can then apply this knowledge to real-life settings.

It is also a mistake to assume that the primary purpose of all social psychology experiments is to make generalizations to the real world. Rather, social psychologists, like all scientists, often design experiments *to test theories* (Mook, 1983). A theory that is supported by many laboratory experiments may be applicable to real-life settings even if the experiments themselves are not exactly like real life. Mundane realism, although desirable, is not necessarily of paramount importance in an experiment.

similar results each time; they demonstrate repeatability. Furthermore, replications reduce the likelihood that the confoundings of any particular experiment are responsible for results, which helps to establish the external validity of experimental results.

Replications can take three important forms: exact, conceptual, and systematic (Carlsmith, Ellsworth, & Aronson, 1976). An *exact replication* tries to reproduce as precisely as possible the procedures, equipment, and design of a previous study. (Of

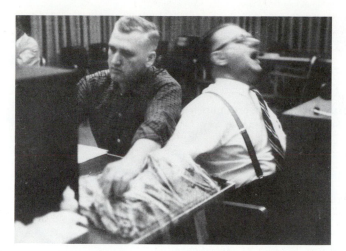

In this replication of Milgram's experiment the teacher must force the learner's hand onto the shock plate against his will.

course, this is impossible in the most literal sense. After all, the new study often takes place in a new setting, with different subject populations, and with different experimenters.) A *conceptual replication* manipulates the same conceptual variables as the initial study, but uses different procedures and operationalizations. Finally, a *systematic replication* tries to theoretically extend the findings of the original study, often by including new variables or conditions in the replication.

Let's return to the Milgram study for an illustration. If I wished to test the reliability and repeatability of the findings of Milgram's study, then I would carry out an exact replication at my university. I would in effect be asking whether the results of the Milgram study were "for real," or whether they were merely some sort of unreliable statistical fluke. If another researcher also carries out an exact replication of the Milgram study and obtains the same results, we can be more confident that the original results were "for real," whatever their cause. Milgram's results, by the way, have been successfully replicated by other researchers (Miller, 1986), which increases our confidence that Milgram's results are robust and repeatable.

In conceptual replication of Milgram's results researchers would measure obedience using procedures different from those used by Milgram. For example, one study measured obedience by having a doctor call 22 nurses and order each of them to administer an obviously dangerous overdose of a drug to a patient (Hofling, Brotzman, Dalrymple, Graves, & Pierce, 1966). Twenty-one out of 22 nurses in this study immediately proceeded to deliver the deadly dose. (The nurses were stopped before they could carry out their orders.) This study could be considered a conceptual replication of Milgram's study because the conceptual focus of the study—destructive obedience—is the same, but it is measured in a different way. Conceptual replications help to establish the generalizability of a finding by ruling out the procedures, operational definitions, and confoundings of a particular study as the cause of the results.

Ultimately, of course, social psychologists want to understand the processes that account for the behaviors they observe. For example, what caused subjects to obey to the extent observed in the Milgram study? Systematic replications help answer such questions by adding new variables and manipulations to the study design.

FIGURE 2.6   Milgram conducts a systematic replication of his obedience experiment.

What is a systematic replication?

In this replication by Milgram, proximity had
a pronounced effect on obedience.

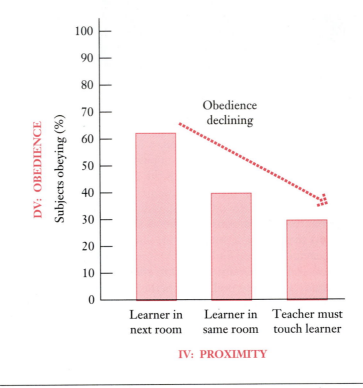

*In this study, Milgram added a new variable — proximity to the victim — to his experiment
on obedience, thus making this a systematic replication. An exact replication would have
exactly repeated the previous study, and a conceptual replication would have attempted
to measure obedience in a different way.*

Milgram in fact carried out numerous systematic replications of his own study. In
one set of replications, he varied the proximity of the learner to the subject: In one
condition the learner was in the next room; in another condition, the learner sat in
the same room with the teacher and displayed convincing facial expressions of pain;
in a third condition, the teacher was required to sit next to the learner and actually
force his hand down onto a shock plate in order to "punish" him. As shown in Figure
2.6, Milgram found that obedience decreased as the victim was moved closer to the

subject: 63 percent of the subjects obeyed fully when the victim was in the next room, 40 percent obeyed when the victim was in the same room, and 30 percent obeyed when they had to touch the victim. Clearly Milgram had identified a variable — proximity to the victim — that had a strong effect on obedience, and his systematic replications increased our understanding of the factors that led to obedience in his experiment.

Combining the results of many studies.   We began this chapter with an account of a single provocative study — the Milgram obedience experiment. The popular press often presents dramatic reports about the findings of single published studies in psychology, biology, medicine, and other sciences. Important scientific questions are rarely resolved by a single experiment or study, however. Rather, evidence is cumulative and is supplied by many research reports. If, for example, a social psychologist wants to identify the circumstances under which TV violence leads to aggression in viewers, then he or she must consider all the research that addresses this question. (This particular topic, by the way, is still being debated — see Friedrich-Coffer & Huston, 1986; Freedman, 1984; still, considerable research suggests some link between TV viewing and violence, as we have already seen — see Chapter 12.)

Similarly, if a social psychologist wants to know whether men are more aggressive than women, then he or she must review all the literature on this topic. No single study can provide a definitive answer; rather, it is the weight of evidence accumulated from many studies that suggests a valid scientific generalization. A recently developed statistical technique called *meta-analysis* allows researchers to combine the results of many studies and to decide objectively which findings are reliable and which are not (Glass, McGraw, & Smith, 1981; Rosenthal, 1984). Eagly and Steffen (1986b) used meta-analysis to examine the results of dozens of studies on gender and aggression, and they concluded that based on all the research evidence, men are on average somewhat more aggressive than women, particularly when the kind of aggression measured is physical rather than verbal or psychological.

Earlier we suggested that sometimes the results of social psychological studies may be "statistical flukes." How do we know whether the differences we observe in an experimental study are meaningful? In Liebert and Baron's experiment on TV violence and aggression, for example, how much would the measured aggressiveness of children in the violent TV group have to differ from the measured aggressiveness of children in the control group for us to be sure that there was a true difference between the groups? Answering questions of this sort is one of the main topics of *inferential statistics*, the branch of statistics that deals with making inferences from data and testing hypotheses. A detailed discussion of statistical analysis is beyond the scope of this book, but we can discuss some basic principles here.

Statistics and Social Psychological Research

Significance levels.   The next time you're in the library at your college or university, take a look at some academic journals that publish social psychological research. (Two prominent journals in the field are the *Journal of Personality and Social Psychology* and the *Journal of Experimental Social Psychology*.) Generally, when papers in these journals present an empirical result they also present a *significance level*, in the form of a probability — for example, $p < .05$. In Liebert and Baron's experiment on TV violence and aggression, the children who viewed violent TV played more aggressively than the children who viewed the televised track meet, and this difference was reported to be statistically significant at the level, $p < .01$.

In commonsense terms this means the probability is less than 1 in 100 that the observed differences are due to chance alone. In other words, a low value for p means that it is likely the results are "for real" and not due to the chance fluctuations that occur in all measurements. How small must the probability level be to be "significant"? In psychology a probability level less than .05 is generally regarded as significant, whereas a larger probability value is not. Note that a "significant" effect is not necessarily a large effect; it is simply an effect that is unlikely to occur by chance alone. Generally, the results reported in this book are significant in the sense just described.

The mean and median.   When summarizing results social psychologists often compute measures of the typical or average behavior of people in a group. The mean and median are two statistics frequently used for this purpose. The *mean* is simply the arithmetic average of the values in a group, while the *median* is the value of the middle observation in the group. By *middle* we mean the observations for which there are an equal number of observations with either higher or lower values. Suppose we observe three children as they play and count the number of times each child hits another child. The first child hits another child once, the second hits three times, and the third hits eight times. The mean number of times these children hit others is thus 4; however, the median is 3, the value of the middle child in the distribution.

Correlation coefficients.   Correlational studies typically make use of a statistical measure called the *correlation coefficient*, which measures how much two variables are related or "go together" (for an explanation of correlation, see Figure 2.7). This statistic can range from -1 (a perfect negative or inverse correlation) through 0 (no correlation) up to $+1$ (a perfect positive correlation). For example, in the previously described correlational study on TV viewing and aggression by Lefkowitz and his colleagues (1972), the correlation beween the amount of violent TV boys watched in third grade with their level of aggressiveness ten years later was computed to be .31. This means there was a positive, but by no means perfect, relationship between TV viewing and future aggressiveness.

Suppose the correlation coefficient turned out to be a different value. (See Figure 2.8 for graphic illustrations of different correlation coefficients.) If the correlation were, say, $-.7$, then this would indicate a negative, or inverse, relation between watching violent TV and aggression—that is, as children view *more* violent TV they are *less* aggressive. (Certainly, this would be an unexpected finding.) If the correlation coefficient turned out to be 0, then our study would show *no systematic relationship* between viewing violent TV and aggressiveness. Finally, if the correlation coefficient were 1.0 or -1.0 (which almost never occurs in real research data), then our study would show a perfect relationship between viewing TV violence and aggression.

Why do perfect positive (1.0) and negative (-1.0) correlations almost never occur in research studies? Consider the studies on viewing violent TV and aggression as a case in point. Clearly, in real life there are many factors that influence aggres-

FIGURE 2.7   **Types of correlation.**

What is the meaning of positive, negative, and zero correlation?

Each point on the graphs below represents a pairing of two measures (such as level of aggression and hours of violent-TV viewing per week) for a given subject. The point is plotted where the two values intersect on the graph.

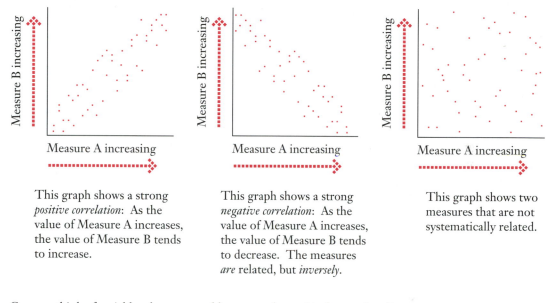

This graph shows a strong *positive correlation*: As the value of Measure A increases, the value of Measure B tends to increase.

This graph shows a strong *negative correlation*: As the value of Measure A increases, the value of Measure B tends to decrease. The measures *are* related, but *inversely*.

This graph shows two measures that are not systematically related.

Can you think of variables that you would expect to be positively correlated? Negatively correlated? Uncorrelated?

We have already described two variables that are positively correlated: TV viewing and aggression. Two variables that tend to be negatively correlated are the distance people live from friends and the strength of the friendships. Two variables that probably are uncorrelated are aggression and the size of one's spleen.

sion — personality traits, social class, parental rearing, and so on. TV viewing is just one variable among many that influences aggression, and thus it is unrealistic to expect it to perfectly predict people's aggressiveness. Furthermore, even if TV viewing were the only variable to influence aggression, we would not be able to measure with perfect reliability either TV viewing or aggression. In other words, all operational definitions and measures are subject to some error, and such errors alone would prevent measures from showing a perfect correlation.

Correlations need not be perfect to provide useful information about how variables are related. Correlations, like other kinds of statistical results, can be tested for

FIGURE 2.8   Correlations of different magnitudes.

What do correlation coefficients signify?

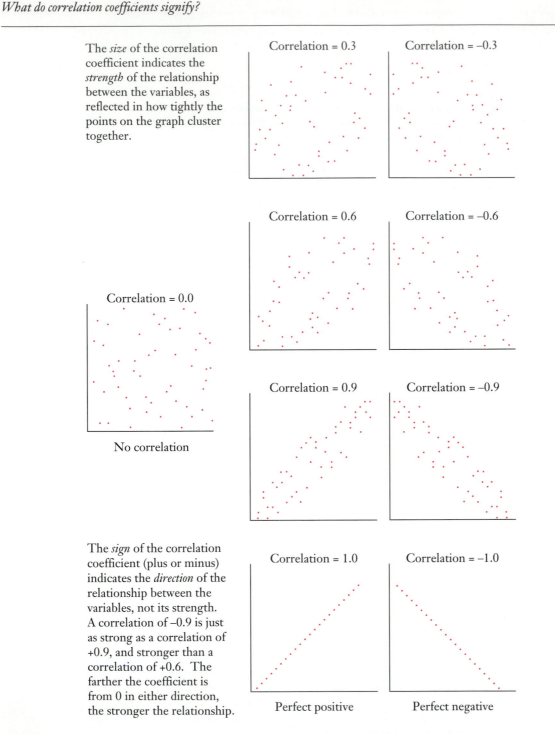

The *size* of the correlation coefficient indicates the *strength* of the relationship between the variables, as reflected in how tightly the points on the graph cluster together.

Correlation = 0.3

Correlation = −0.3

Correlation = 0.6

Correlation = −0.6

Correlation = 0.0

No correlation

Correlation = 0.9

Correlation = −0.9

The *sign* of the correlation coefficient (plus or minus) indicates the *direction* of the relationship between the variables, not its strength. A correlation of −0.9 is just as strong as a correlation of +0.9, and stronger than a correlation of +0.6. The farther the coefficient is from 0 in either direction, the stronger the relationship.

Correlation = 1.0

Correlation = −1.0

Perfect positive

Perfect negative

Correlation coefficients show the degree of relationship between two variables. As the text notes, correlations do not have to be perfect (+ 1.0 or − 1.0) to provide useful information.

statistical significance. A correlation is statistically significant if the correlation coefficient is sufficiently different from 0 and the occurrence of this difference is sufficiently unlikely to be due to chance alone.

> Misinformation is employed in the experiment; illusion is used when necessary in order to set the stage for the revelation of certain difficult-to-get-at truths. . . .
>
> —— *Obedience to Authority*, p. 198

Social psychologists face certain research problems that physicists and chemists, for example, do not — namely, their subjects think, may try to discover the purpose of the experiment, and may pick up subtle cues from the experimenter and from the experiment. When designing an experiment on, say, elementary particles, a physicist does not worry about what the particles are thinking. However, social psychologists *must* concern themselves with what human subjects are thinking during the course of an experiment. Experimenters who communicate their expectations to subjects, or subjects who develop on their own hypotheses about the experiment, can bias experimental results. Let's consider each of these kinds of bias in turn.

Experimenter bias.   Experimenters can sometimes subtly influence their subjects' behavior. In one investigation of this phenomenon, Rosenthal and Fode (1963) conducted a study in which student experimenters instructed their subjects to rate photographed faces. Specifically, the subjects were to rate on a scale ranging from -10 (failure) to $+10$ (success) whether the people in the photographs were experiencing success or failure at the time the photograph was taken. Rosenthal and Fode led half of the student experimenters to believe that subjects tended to rate the faces as showing success, and led the other half to believe the opposite: that subjects tended to rate the faces as showing failure. Thus, the independent variable in this study was the expectations of the student experimenters.

Each of the student experimenters was told to read standard instructions informing their subjects how to carry out the rating task. The results showed a clear experimenter-bias effect: Those experimenters who expected subjects to rate the faces as showing success did indeed have subjects who tended to rate the faces as successful, whereas those experimenters who expected subjects to rate the faces as showing failure did indeed have subjects who so rated the faces. Somehow, the experimenters communicated their hypotheses and expectations to their subjects. Rosenthal (1966) has documented many other cases in which experimenters inadvertently biased the results of their experiments.

On the surface it seems that experimenter bias should make us skeptical about all social psychological research. Where is the objectivity of scientific social psychology if researchers' hypotheses and expectations can so easily influence subjects' behavior?

Experimenter bias is a serious but not hopeless problem. The careful researcher can reduce and often eliminate the possibility of such bias (Carlsmith, Ellsworth, & Aronson, 1976). One solution is to standardize the experiment, including the experimenter's words and behavior, as much as possible. In a social psychology experiment, the researcher must try to treat all subjects the same. The experimenter should use the same language and demeanor with all subjects. The Milgram obedience experiment provides a good example of standardization: The experimenter always gave the

■■■■■■■■■■■■■■■■■■■■■■■■■

**Bias in Social
Psychological
Research**

same instructions to all subjects, subjects sat at the same shock machine and heard exactly the same tape-recorded screams, and so on. Such standardization reduced the possibility that the experimenter treated different subjects differently. Mechanization is perhaps the ultimate guarantee of a totally standardized experiment. If a videotape or computer gives the subject instructions, then there is absolutely no possibility of treating subjects differently; there can be no experimenter bias because no human experimenter is present.

Of course, it is neither possible nor desirable to mechanize all social psychology experiments. Another way to eliminate experimenter bias is to keep the experimenter *blind* to experimental conditions—the experimenter does not know which experimental condition the subject is in. For example, in a blind experiment on TV violence and aggression in children, the experimenter would not know whether the child saw a violent or nonviolent TV segment. How could the experimenter be kept blind in this experiment? One possibility is that the experimenter could create two unlabeled videotapes—one containing the violent TV segment, the other containing the nonviolent segment. After leaving the room where the child watches TV, the experimenter would insert one of the tapes in a VCR machine, show the recorded segment to the child, and then return to observe the child's aggressiveness. After a particular child is observed, the experimenter would note which tape had been played and record that fact.

In some social psychology experiments, the experimenter cannot help but know what condition a subject is in after the experimental manipulation takes place. Consider Liebert and Baron's (1972) experiment on TV violence and aggression, for example: As the experimenter showed a given child one of the TV segments (violent or sports), she watched the child from behind a one-way mirror, and thus she knew the experimental condition the child was in. One way to avoid experimenter bias in this study would be to switch experimenters after the manipulation was completed. A different experimenter—one who had no idea which TV segment the child just viewed—would then observe and record the child's level of aggressiveness. With careful forethought, it is usually possible to greatly reduce or even eliminate experimenter bias in studies.

Subject bias.   Subjects often try to "see through" a study, and once they figure out the apparent purpose of a study, they can choose to be cooperative or uncooperative. If you were in an experiment in which I showed you a violent movie and then asked you to deliver shocks to another subject, do you think you might guess that the purpose of the study was to determine whether there is a relationship between media violence and aggressive behavior? To aid the experimenter a cooperative subject might behave aggressively in such an experiment. On the other hand, an uncooperative subject might behave unaggressively to defy the experimenter. Whether the subject tries either to help or to hinder the experimenter, to the extent the subject has correctly perceived the purpose of the study, the study is hopelessly biased.

Subject bias occurs particularly when a study possesses strong *demand characteristics*—that is, salient cues that inappropriately suggest how the subject should behave (Orne, 1962). What's the difference between experimenter bias and subject bias resulting from demand characteristics? Experimenter bias occurs when the experimenter inadvertently provides cues to the subject about how to behave; demand characteristics refer to inappropriate cues *in the experimental setting itself* that may lead the subject to behave consistently with the experimenter's hypotheses.

There are several ways to avoid subject bias. One solution is to deceive subjects so they don't know the true purpose of the study. In Milgram's obedience research, subjects thought they were participating in a learning experiment (a lie — it was really a study on obedience). They believed the middle-aged man to be another subject (a lie — he was really a confederate). They believed the other subject was receiving excruciating electric shocks (a lie — he actually received none), and so on. To the extent the subjects believed all the lies, there was little possibility for subject bias.

The Milgram study was so well disguised that subjects probably had very little chance to discover its true purpose. Even if subjects could have discovered it, the experiment was so emotionally gripping that they had very little time or attention to devote to thinking about anything other than the painful dilemma they faced. This is yet another reason for placing a high premium on "experimental realism." Could the Milgram study have been carried out without deception? Probably not. If subjects knew at the start that they were participating in a study on obedience, would they have behaved as they did? Deception, although it entails potential ethical problems, seems to be methodologically essential to this study.

Milgram's research used repeated, profound deceptions that led to considerable upset in subjects. Although most social psychology experiments don't use deception as extreme as that in Milgram's work, a majority of social psychological research entails some deception, such as "cover stories" designed to mislead subjects about the true purpose of the study (Adair, Dushenko, & Lindsay, 1985; Gross & Fleming, 1982).

A second solution to subject bias is to measure subjects without their awareness — in other words, to use *nonreactive measures* (sometimes also referred to as *unobtrusive measures*). The subject who doesn't realize that he or she is being studied cannot systematically bias results. Nonreactive measures can take many forms (Webb, Campbell, Schwartz, Sechrest, & Grove, 1981): archival data (for example, marriage licenses), trace data (for example, how worn particular books are in a library), audio and video recordings of subjects without their knowledge, and so on. Nonreactive measures sometimes give a "Candid Camera" flavor to social psychological research.

To illustrate, suppose we want to conduct a survey on alcohol consumption in our community. We could walk door-to-door interviewing local residents, but many of our subjects might not answer our questions honestly. We might measure alcohol consumption more accurately by visiting homes on trash collection day and searching through trash cans, literally counting the number of beer cans, whiskey bottles, and so on. Nutrition studies sometimes use such "trash can" data as a means of more honestly assessing what people *really* eat. Each of us could be a subject in such a research study without ever knowing it.

▪▪▪

The central moral justification for allowing a procedure of the sort used in my experiment is that it is judged acceptable by those who have taken part in it. Moreover, it is the salience of this fact that constituted the chief moral warrant for the continuation of the experiments.

—— *Obedience to Authority,* p. 199

Ethics in Social Psychological Research

The Milgram Experiments: Ethically Acceptable or Unacceptable?

Stanley Milgram's obedience experiments created a storm of controversy that continues to the present (Miller, 1986). Is it ethically acceptable to expose subjects to pain, upset, and possible long-term psychological changes in order to carry out interesting scientific research? In response to Milgram's research, Diana Baumrind (1964) wrote a paper severely criticizing the ethics of obedience experiments.

Baumrind's critique was multifaceted. First, she argued that Milgram's procedures created unacceptable levels of stress in subjects. Indeed, according to Milgram's own descriptions, his subjects were frequently extremely upset:

In a large number of cases the degree of tension reached extremes that are rarely seen in sociopsychological laboratory studies. Subjects were observed to sweat, tremble, stutter, bite their lips, groan, and dig their fingernails into their flesh. These were characteristic rather than exceptional responses to the experiment.

One sight of tension was the regular occurrence of nervous laughing fits.

Fourteen of the 40 subjects showed definite signs of nervous laughing and smiling. The laughter seemed entirely out of place, even bizarre. Full-blown, uncontrollable seizures were observed for 3 subjects. On one occasion we observed a seizure so violently convulsive that it was necessary to call halt to the experiment. . . . (Milgram, 1963, p. 375)

Baumrind further argued that Milgram's study potentially had lasting negative effects on subjects: When the "hoax" was revealed to subjects at the end of the study, they would feel foolish and "used" by the experimenter. Obedient subjects would know that they had not actually shocked the victim, but they would still realize that they *would have* shocked the victim if the procedure had been for real. More generally, the embarrassing experience of being duped by the experimenter might leave subjects alienated and suspicious of psychologists in particular and of legitimate authorities in general.

Finally, Baumrind questioned the scientific merit of Milgram's studies. If Milgram's studies yielded insights about real-life obedience,

this might help justify a procedure that was somewhat traumatic to subjects. However, according to Baumrind, obedience in the laboratory is unlike obedience in real life. Subjects have a dependent, trusting relationship with an experimenter that they do not necessarily have with real-life authority figures. The laboratory is an unfamiliar and ambiguous setting to subjects, thus leading them to be more easily influenced.

Milgram (1964) responded to all of Baumrind's criticisms. He noted that subjects' extreme levels of obedience and their accompanying upset became apparent only after the first studies were run. No one could have predicted the ethical dilemmas created by the research before it was actually conducted. Once it became clear that his procedure produced great distress in subjects, Milgram had to choose whether or not to continue his experiments.

Milgram decided that although his procedures created "momentary excitement," they did not produce long-term negative effects in the huge majority of subjects. This conclusion was based partly on

Many social psychology studies are straightforward and benign. However, research that uses deception and causes distress (as Milgram's studies did) or that invades someone's privacy (as "trash can" studies may) can create a conflict for social psychologists — a dilemma between conducting methodologically sound, unbiased research and treating subjects ethically. How can social psychologists conduct research that is both ethical and scientifically rigorous?

Ethical Problems

The use of nonreactive measures points to one important ethical problem that some social psychological studies face — they constitute an *invasion of privacy*. What right questionnaires subjects completed after participating in his experiments (see the accompanying table). In general, subjects reported that they were glad to have participated in the obedience experiment, and in addition approximately three-fourths of them stated that they had learned important things about themselves by being in the study. Note, however, that the data in the accompanying table show that a small minority of subjects were in fact "sorry" or "very sorry" to have been in the experiment.

Milgram conducted careful debriefings of his subjects, and a year after his initial experiment was completed, he asked a psychiatrist to interview 40 of his experimental subjects to determine whether his study had "possible injurious effects." This follow-up revealed no indications of long-term distress or traumatic reactions among subjects.

Milgram reversed Baumrind's argument that his experiments might lead subjects to be less trusting of authorities: ". . . the experimenter is not just any authority: He is an authority who tells the subject to act harshly and inhumanely against another man. I would consider it of the highest value if participation in the experiment could . . . inculcate a skepticism of this kind of authority" (p. 852).

In response to Baumrind's observation that psychology experiments are special settings in which subjects are particularly under the influence of the experimenter, Milgram pointed out that about a third of his subjects successfully rebelled against the destructive commands of the experimenter. Milgram argued that a "person who comes to the laboratory is an active, choosing adult, capable of accepting or rejecting the prescriptions for action addressed to him" (p. 852).

Many social psychologists have viewed Milgram's obedience research as a classic demonstration of the power of social settings to overwhelm an individual's freedom of choice and inner values (Miller, 1986). It is thus ironic that Milgram justified his obedience experiments by appealing to the subject's "free choice."

What then is the answer to the question we started with: Were Milgram's studies ethically acceptable? You must be the final judge.

How Glad or Sorry Subjects Were to Have Participated in Milgram's Obedience Study

Now that I have read the report, and all things considered . . .	Defiant (%)	Obedient (%)	All (%)
1. I am very glad to have been in the experiment.	40.0	47.8	43.5
2. I am glad to have been in the experiment.	43.8	35.7	40.2
3. I am neither sorry nor glad to have been in the experiment.	15.3	14.8	15.1
4. I am sorry to have been in the experiment.	0.8	0.7	0.8
5. I am very sorry to have been in the experiment.	0.0	1.0	0.5

do social psychologists have to measure subjects without their awareness? Isn't it unethical to observe people without their consent?

Other studies create *physical and psychological discomfort* in subjects. For example, many of the subjects in Milgram's studies were tense and upset during the course of their participation. Imagine you were one of Milgram's subjects who obeyed fully. Wouldn't you emerge from this experience with some very upsetting conclusions about yourself, including "I am willing to inflict horrible pain on another human being merely because someone ordered me to do so"? Even if you had eventually disobeyed, you would still have been exposed to psychological discomfort. How would *you* feel if you were delivering shocks to a person who shrieked in pain in the next room?

FIGURE 2.9   Ethical principles established by the American Psychological Association.

What are some of the ethical principles psychologists are expected to observe when conducting research on human subjects?

1. The researcher has the personal responsibility to make a careful ethical evaluation of his or her research.
2. The researcher must determine if subjects are placed at any physical or psychological risk.
3. The researcher is responsible for the treatment of subjects by employees, research assistants, and student researchers.
4. The research must establish a clear and fair agreement with subjects before the study (principle of informed consent).
5. Deception is to be employed only when absolutely necessary and when adequate debriefing is provided.
6. Subjects always have the right to decline to participate in a study and to withdraw from a study at any time.
7. The researcher must protect the subject from physical or psychological harm. This includes informing the subject of risk ahead of time, and providing means by which the subject can contact the researcher after the study is over.
8. Whenever possible, research results and hypotheses should be explained to subjects after they participate in a study.
9. The researcher has the responsibility to detect and remove any lasting negative effects of a study on subjects.
10. Information about a subject obtained in a study is confidential. Subjects should be informed who will see data and how the confidentiality of data will be protected.

As the text notes, observance of these APA guidelines is reinforced by careful institutional (university and government) review of research projects.

Deception constitutes yet another ethical dilemma in social psychological research. As we noted earlier, many social psychology studies use varying degrees of deception in order to reduce subject bias. But isn't it unethical to lie to people, even to advance scientific knowledge?

Measures to Reduce Ethical Problems — APA Guidelines

There are no absolute solutions to the ethical dilemmas of social psychological research. To some extent, each researcher must decide what is ethically acceptable and what is not. Today, studies tend to be much more carefully monitored for potential ethical problems than when Milgram conducted his studies in the 1960s. The controversy provoked by such studies led psychologists to develop procedures to monitor the ethical propriety of research, and it prompted the federal government to require that each university receiving federal research funds review its research for possible ethical problems. Further, the excesses of some research pointed to the necessity of institutional guidelines and control. As a result, the American Psychological Association (APA, 1982) developed rigorous ethical guidelines for research on human subjects (see Figure 2.9).

Peer review.   Typically, a proposed social psychology study is reviewed by members of a psychology department or a university committee. If the study is judged by the

"ACCORDING TO THE AGENDA TODAY WE START NEGOTIATING WITH THE GUINEA PIGS' LAWYER."

researcher's peers to be at all ethically questionable, it may be rejected, or the researcher may be asked to alter certain procedures or to provide greater safeguards to ensure subjects' well-being.

An ethics committee reviewing a proposal for Milgram's study today, for example, might ask the researcher to "tone down" the experimental procedures, provide subjects with a guaranteed right to quit the study at any time, and have a clinical psychologist on duty at all times to deal with potential psychological problems. Many ethics committees might even reject the proposal. Because of peer review, researchers generally think hard to minimize deception, discomfort, and invasion of privacy in their studies.

Informed consent.   Still, it is impossible to eliminate deceptive or uncomfortable procedures from all research studies. Whenever studies involve any procedure capable of producing distress or discomfort in subjects, it is essential that researchers obtain each subject's informed consent. Basically, this means that each subject is told, at least in rough terms, what the experimental procedure entails, and furthermore, that he or she may decide to cease participation in the study at any time without penalty. Subjects need not necessarily know the full details or hypotheses of the study at the start, but subjects should be informed of important procedures. For example, if subjects are to receive painful electric shocks, they should be informed of that in advance. Clearly, when subjects are minors (for example, infants or school children) the notion of consent includes obtaining permission from each child's parents or guardian.

Although clear-cut in theory, the notion of informed consent becomes somewhat fuzzy in practice. Sometimes it seems necessary to conduct certain procedures without the subject's awareness; thus the subject cannot be fully informed at the time he or she consents to participate in the study. How complete a description is complete enough to be ethically acceptable, yet incomplete enough to avoid biasing the study? If you were conducting the Milgram experiment, what would and wouldn't you tell the subjects at the start?

Debriefing.   Informed consent focuses on providing information to subjects before they participate in a study. After the study is completed, information must also be provided in the form of a debriefing, or postexperimental interview. In a debriefing, which is an essential part of any carefully conducted social psychology experiment, the experimenter carefully explains any deception that occurred and determines whether the subject was upset by any experimental procedure. Debriefings also serve an important methodological purpose: The experimenter learns what subjects were thinking during the experiment, whether or not they "saw through" the study, and whether experimental manipulations worked as planned.

Of course, any study that causes distress in subjects (such as Milgram's) should carry out a particularly careful and thorough debriefing. In such studies, the researcher may even employ clinical psychologists or psychiatrists to interview subjects after the study is completed. Ideally, a subject should leave an experiment in a positive mood, unaltered in any lasting way by the experimental procedures.

Some social psychology experiments intentionally give subjects false information about themselves as part of the experimental manipulation. Consider, for example, a study on the effects of self-esteem on romantic attraction. Walster (1965) first gave female college students a fake personality test and then falsely told some of the women that they had well-adjusted personalities and others that they had poorly adjusted personalities. (This experiment, by the way, found that the women with lowered self-esteem were more romantically attracted to a handsome male confederate than were the women with elevated self-esteem.) As part of the debriefing in this experiment, the researcher had to inform the subjects that the personality test results they received were contrived. The debriefing of the women with lowered self-esteem required particular care so that they would not leave the experiment feeling bad about themselves.

A number of recent research studies suggest that subjects often continue to believe false information about themselves presented in experiments, even after being informed of the deception (Ross, Lepper, & Hubbard, 1975; Jennings, Lepper, & Ross, 1981). In the context of Walster's study, this finding would suggest that even though the women with lowered self-esteem were told at the end of the experiment that the negative feedback about their personality was contrived, they still may have continued to experience lowered self-esteem. Apparently, subjects convince themselves during the course of the experiment that false information is really true. (We will consider the perseverance of false beliefs more fully in Chapter 5.) The ethical implication for social psychological research is clear: Any study that provides subjects with false information about themselves must include especially careful and thorough debriefing procedures.

Please note that we have discussed several dramatic studies to illustrate ethical issues in social psychological research. Although some social psychology studies raise serious ethical questions, many others use little or no deception, invade no one's privacy, and create no discomfort. The ethical problems described here thus pertain to only some social psychological research.

The results, as seen and felt in the laboratory, are to this author disturbing. They raise the possibility that human nature, or — more specifically — the kind of character produced in American democratic society, cannot be counted on to insulate its citizens from brutality and inhumane treatment at the direction of malevolent authority.

—— *Obedience to Authority*, p. 189

Our discussion of ethics cannot be complete without acknowledging the practical and applied contributions social psychological research makes to science and to society. The topics investigated by social psychologists often have great relevance to everyday life (for example, person perception, interpersonal attraction, bargaining, negotiating) as well as to society at large (for example, aggression, mass persuasion, prejudice, intergroup relations). The research discussed earlier on TV violence and aggression obviously possesses great social significance. And while Milgram's research extends our theoretical understanding of the factors that influence obedience, it also relates to a pressing real-life issue: When will people obey malevolent authority and commit atrocities against other human beings? Milgram (1974) draws parallels between the behavior of his subjects and the Nazis who "just followed orders" when they murdered millions of innocent people during World War II.

Certainly, we cannot justify unethical treatment of subjects simply because the knowledge gained is valuable, but in evaluating the ethical pluses and minuses of social psychological research, we should acknowledge as a definite plus the potential of social psychological data to help us understand, evaluate, and design solutions to social problems. Since its beginnings in the early part of this century, social psychology has often probed important topics: the causes of aggression, the nature of prejudice, the dynamics of propaganda and persuasion, and the good and bad ways in which groups influence individuals. Recently, social psychology has turned to other applied topics as well, including the social psychology of the legal system, health psychology, and environmental psychology (Rodin, 1985). To the extent it addresses both socially relevant issues and basic theoretical questions about social behavior, social psychology will continue to challenge the ingenuity of its best researchers and the ethics of its best moral thinkers. It will also continue to be a lively, exciting, and provocative field.

Summary

1. Stanley Milgram's obedience experiments provide a dramatic example of the methods, concepts, and ethics of social psychological research.

2. The scientific method holds that empirical measurement is necessary to test hypotheses and theories. Theories are sets of propositions that help to explain, predict, and organize empirical data.

3. Scientists use operational definitions that define concepts in terms of the procedures used to measure them. Both subjective reports and behavioral measures serve as operational definitions in social psychology.

4. Scientific measures should be both reliable and valid. A reliable measure is consistent and repeatable; a valid measure assesses what it is supposed to and relates to real-life criteria.

5. Social psychologists conduct experiments, correlational studies, and quasi-experimental studies. In experiments, researchers manipulate independent variables and observe their effects on dependent variables, and they randomly assign subjects to experimental conditions. In correlational studies, researchers observe naturally occurring relationships between variables. In quasi-experimental studies, a variable is manipulated, but subjects are not randomly assigned to conditions.

6. Laboratory studies are conducted in controlled, laboratory environments, whereas field studies are conducted in natural settings.

7. Mundane realism refers to how well a study approximates real-life settings and behavior. Experimental realism refers to the extent to which a study cognitively and emotionally involves subjects.

8. An experiment possesses internal validity when its variables are measured and manipulated properly. The confounding, or co-occurrence, of variables can be a threat to internal validity. An experiment possesses external validity when its results can be generalized to broader settings and populations.

9. Our confidence in scientific results is increased by replication. Exact replications attempt to reproduce previous studies as precisely as possible. Conceptual replications attempt to measure the same conceptual variables studied in previous studies, but use different operationalizations. Systematic replications add new variables or conditions to a previous study. Meta-analysis is a statistical technique that combines the results of many studies to determine whether those results are reliable.

10. Results are considered statistically significant when they are sufficiently unlikely to be due to chance. The mean and median are statistics used to measure the average score in a group. The correlation coefficient measures the degree of association between two variables.

11. Experimenter bias occurs when experimenters inappropriately communicate their hypotheses to subjects. Blind experiments, as well as standardization and mechanization of experiments, can be used to reduce or eliminate experimenter bias.

12. Subject bias occurs when subjects "see through" the purpose of a study or respond to demand characteristics (inappropriate cues in the experimental setting) in a study. Deception and nonreactive (unobtrusive) measures can be used to reduce or eliminate subject bias.

13. The subjects in social psychology studies sometimes suffer from discomfort, deception, and invasion of privacy as a result of their participation in those studies. Professional guidelines, institutional peer review, informed consent, and careful debriefing help to guarantee that researchers treat subjects in ethically acceptable ways.

14. Social psychological research projects often address socially important topics; such investigations constitute a positive contribution to society.

Glossary

Behavioral data: Direct observations or measurements of subjects' behavior that do not rely on subjects' reports about themselves

Blind experiments: Experiments in which experimenters do not know what conditions subjects are in; in *double blind* experiments, both subjects and experimenters don't know what conditions subjects are in

Conceptual replication: A study in which a previous study is repeated, but the variables are measured in different ways from those used in the previous study

Confounding: A description of variables in certain instances; variables are said to be confounded in a study when they co-occur, and thus it is impossible to tell if effects are due to one or the other variable

Construct: A theoretical concept or variable; constructs are hypothetical variables; operational definitions provide ways of measuring hypothetical constructs

Control group: A group of subjects in an experiment that is not exposed to the experimental treatment; thus the control group is characterized by the *absence* of the experimental treatment and serves as a comparison group

Correlation coefficient: A statistical measure of the degree of relationship between two variables; can range from -1 to 1

Correlational study: A study in which the relation between naturally occurring variables is observed; no variables are manipulated, and subjects are not randomly assigned to conditions

Debriefing: A post-experimental interview between experimenter and subject in which the experimenter learns about the subject's reactions to the experiment, reveals any deception, and explains the purpose of the study

Deception: Providing false information to subjects in experiments in order to eliminate subject bias

Dependent variable: The variable that is influenced by the independent variable in an experiment

Demand characteristics: Cues in experimental settings that inappropriately influence subjects' behavior and thus bias results

Exact replication: An attempt to repeat another study exactly

Experiment: A study in which a variable is manipulated (the independent variable) to observe its effect on another (dependent) variable; in an experiment subjects are randomly assigned to experimental conditions

Experimental realism: The degree to which a study cognitively and emotionally involves subjects

Experimenter bias: Bias that occurs in studies when experimenters inappropriately communicate their hypotheses and expectations to subjects

External validity: The degree to which the results of an experiment generalize to broader settings and populations

Field study: A study conducted in a natural environment outside of the laboratory

Independent variable: The variable that the researcher controls and manipulates in an experiment

Inferential statistics: The branch of statistics that deals with making inferences from data and testing hypotheses

Informed consent: The process of informing subjects of the general procedures used in a study and obtaining their consent to participate as subjects

Internal validity: A property possessed by an experiment when variables are measured and manipulated properly

Laboratory study: A study (usually carefully controlled and standardized) that is carried out in a laboratory environment

Mean: The arithmetic average of a set of numbers

Median: The value or score of the "middle" observation in a distribution

Meta-analysis: A statistical technique to combine the findings of many studies on the same topic in order to determine whether findings are reliable

Mundane realism: The degree to which a study is similar to real-life situations

Nonreactive measures: Also known as *unobtrusive measures*; measures of subjects' behavior obtained without subjects' knowledge

Operational definition: A definition of a concept in terms of the specific procedures or methods used to measure the concept

Quasi-experimental study: A study in which a variable is manipulated, but subjects are not randomly assigned to conditions

Random assignment: Occurs when a subject has an equal probability of being assigned to any experimental condition

Reliability: The repeatability and consistency of a measure

Statistical significance: The probability that research findings are due to chance; in psychology, results are considered significant if the probability is less than .05 that the results are due to chance alone

Subject bias: Bias that occurs when subjects inappropriately pick up cues from the experimental setting or "see through" the purpose of the study

Subjective reports: Data that consist of subjects' reports of their own behavior or mental states; typically collected via rating scales, questionnaires, or interviews

Systematic replication: Repeating a study, but adding new variables in order to increase understanding of the phenomenon being studied

Theory: A set of propositions about constructs that helps to explain, predict, and organize empirical data

Validity: The ability of a measure to predict real-life criteria; a measure is valid when it measures the construct it is supposed to measure

Two of the people he had never seen before, and the others consisted of Ernest Harrowden, one of those middle-aged mediocrities so common in London clubs who have no enemies, but are thoroughly disliked by their friends; Lady Ruxton, an over-dressed woman of forty-seven, with a hooked nose, who was always trying to get herself compromised, but was so peculiarly plain that to her great disappointment no one would ever believe anything against her; Mrs. Erlynne, a pushing nobody, with a delightful lisp, and Venetian-red hair; Lady Alice Chapman, his hostess's daughter, a dowdy dull girl, with one of those characteristic British faces, that, once seen, are never remembered; and her husband, a red-cheeked, white-whiskered creature who, like so many of his class, was under the impression that inordinate joviality can atone for an entire lack of ideas.

—— from *The Picture of Dorian Gray*, by Oscar Wilde, pp. 176–177

CHAPTER 3

Person Perception

Like Dorian Gray describing guests at a party, most of us make detailed observations and inferences about others, sometimes based on little information. *Person perception* — the process by which we judge the traits and characteristics of others — is an essential part of everyday social interaction. Although commonplace, person perception is also complex and multifaceted. Consider, for example, that even as you read Dorian Gray's perceptions of others, you've probably begun to form an impression of Dorian Gray (he's cruel and patronizing), and perhaps even some perceptions of the author who created Dorian Gray (he's British).

How do we know what we know about others? Research on person perception attempts to answer this question by carefully studying the ways in which people observe and mentally process information about other people.

The study of person perception is but one part of the study of perception in general. The psychologist studying object perception asks, "How well can people perceive depth, colors, sound frequencies, and tastes?" Perhaps the most basic question a psychologist studying perception asks is, "How do people know reality?" Social psychologists too are concerned with how people know reality — in particular, social reality. The social psychologist studying person perception asks, "How accurately can people judge personality and emotions?" and "How well can people detect when others lie?"

The goal of both object and person perception is to abstract stable qualities from inconsistent sensory information. After viewing a table, we may judge its shape and

The Nature of Person Perception

size. After observing a woman, we may judge her friendliness, intelligence, and age. Although we receive varied and often inconsistent information about people, we still generally perceive them to possess traits — that is, stable internal dispositions. If I ask you to describe your best friend, a considerable part of your description will probably be devoted to the traits that your friend possesses, just as in the passage at the beginning of this chapter Dorian Gray describes various people as "pushing," "dowdy," or "dull," among other things. In one recent study (Park, 1986), college students were asked to describe other students in their seminar class. Sixty-five percent of all their statements contained what could be classified as traits. In light of how often their behavior is inconsistent, it is interesting (and a little puzzling) that we consider others to be so stable and constant (that is, to possess traits).

Differences Between Person Perception and Object Perception

Although person perception and object perception study many of the same general issues, person perception is more complex in certain key ways:

First, person perception is more susceptible than object perception to errors and biases. One reason for this is that we frequently try to perceive intangible qualities in people — personality traits, motives, attitudes, and intelligence — that cannot be directly observed but rather must be inferred from behavior. For example, during the 1988 presidential campaign people may have perceived George Bush to have been a "conservative" candidate because he supported strong defense programs and opposed legalized abortion, higher taxes, and the American Civil Liberties Union. Judging a person's "conservatism" seems to involve more inference than judging, say, the color of a book.

A second way in which person perception is more complex than object perception is that we generally perceive people, but not objects, as *causal agents* — that is, as conscious, self-directing entities possessing wishes, motives, and intentions. A Zen parable captures this difference between person perception and object perception:

> Suppose a boat is crossing a river and another boat, an empty one, is about to collide with it. Even an irritable man would not lose his temper. But suppose there was someone in the second boat? Then the occupant of the first would shout to him to keep clear. And if he did not hear the first time, nor even when called to three times, bad language would inevitably follow . . .
>
> —— *The Gospel According to Zen*, p. 119

If struck by the occupied boat, you might decide that its captain was careless or malicious, but you probably would not impute such traits or intentions to an empty boat. Thus person perception is intrinsically more complicated than object perception because we must try to perceive people's underlying intentions and motivations in addition to their surface behavior.

Unlike objects, people may try to deceive us or mislead us with false information. A used-car dealer may appear friendly, honest, and concerned and still sell you a lemon. Thus one goal of person perception is to break through possibly deceptive surface information to discern the "real truth" about a person. This is generally *not* an issue in object perception; if a table looks brown, you generally do not ask yourself whether it is really red and only trying to put on a false front of brownness.

A final, rather subtle, difference between person perception and object perception is that our perception of a person can sometimes change that person's behavior. One well-known study demonstrated this effect in the classroom (Rosenthal &

Jacobson, 1968). Teachers were led to believe by fake IQ-test results that some of their elementary school students were bright "late bloomers" whereas others were not. Later those children who had been labeled "bright" did indeed perform better on an achievement test than did control children. Numerous studies have replicated these findings (Babad, Inbar, & Rosenthal, 1982). Apparently, when teachers *perceive* students to be bright, they start treating those students differently and thereby ultimately encourage them to be "brighter" than other children.

Similarly, if you perceive a person to be "cold and distant," perhaps you'll treat the person accordingly, which will have the net effect of proving you right: The other person will in fact be cold and distant in response to your "cold shoulder" (Curtis & Miller, 1986). In other words, person perception can have a "self-fulfilling" quality that object perception does not.

Research Topics in Person Perception

Person perception comprises many different and at times overlapping processes (Schneider, Hastorf, & Ellsworth, 1979). These processes can be classified into three general research topics: direct judgments, attribution, and social cognition.

Direct judgments.   When we meet a person, we often make very rapid judgments based on surface cues like physical appearance, dress, and mannerisms. Dorian Gray, for example, noticed that Lady Ruxton was "over-dressed" and "peculiarly plain." Direct judgments may at times be correct, but they also may reflect biased, stereotypical thinking. On the basis of very scant information we may make judgments that greatly influence our future interactions with a person.

In this chapter we'll explore direct judgments in person perception. We begin by first considering the raw material upon which first impressions and direct judgments are based, such as physical appearance and nonverbal behaviors. Then we turn to the accuracy of direct judgment of personality traits and emotions. We conclude by examining people's ability to detect deception—another kind of direct judgment that has practical implications for everyday life.

Attribution.   As we noted earlier, person perception differs from object perception in that it frequently entails attempts to discern the *causes* of people's behavior. For example, if an acquaintance frowns at you for no apparent reason, you might wonder why—did you unknowingly offend her or is she simply a sullen person? Attribution theories (the topic of Chapter 4) deal with the thought processes people use to infer the causes of others' behavior. Attribution often requires more involved thought processes than do direct judgments; it also requires that we observe people more than once and compare their behavior with broader social knowledge. Accordingly, if your acquaintance frequently frowns regardless of who she's with and in unexpected settings (for example, at comedy movies), you'll probably attribute her frown to some trait in her and not to your behavior.

Social cognition.   The field of social cognition (the focus of Chapter 5) studies person perception from the vantage point of modern research on the ways humans process information. Thus it studies how people store information about others in their memories, how they combine information to form overall impressions, and how they apply mental rules-of-thumb to form judgments about others. Like attribution research, social cognition research focuses on the inferences we make from information about others; however, social cognition research does not focus solely

SUMMARY TABLE 3.1   Three Topic Areas in the Study of Person Perception

What general areas have social psychologists studied in research on person perception?

AREA	DESCRIPTION	EXAMPLES
Direct judgments (*Chapter 3*)	How we arrive at first impressions; how we judge personality traits and emotions; how successful we are in detecting deception.	How do you decide that a new acquaintance is outgoing? How accurate are judgments of emotions? What nonverbal cues are associated with deception?
Attributions (*Chapter 4*)	How we infer the causes of behavior.	Do we tend to explain behavior in terms of personal traits or situational causes? Do we explain others' behavior in the same way that we explain our own?
Social cognition (*Chapter 5*)	How we store, combine, and process information about others.	What processes underlie the complex inferences we make about others? What shortcuts do we use in arriving at social judgments?

Perception of persons, of course, involves an interaction of all the processes studied in these three topic areas.

on causal inferences, but on all kinds of social inferences. So, for example, social cognition research might examine how people remember and evaluate the information contained in clinical transcripts or how people combine and process information to make such practical decisions as hiring employees.

Our division of person perception research into studies on direct judgments, attribution, and social cognition is not absolutely clear-cut. In part, these topic areas reflect the historical development of the field. Research on the judgment of emotional expressions and personality traits appeared first, in the late nineteenth and early twentieth centuries. Attribution became the central topic of person perception research from the late 1960s through the 1970s, and it gave rise to the broader field of social cognition in the 1980s. Each topic area tends to center upon certain key issues: Research on direct judgments examines the link between stimuli (for example, facial expressions) and perception, and it addresses the question of accuracy in person perception; research on attribution deals with the perceived causes of behavior; and social cognition research addresses the broad question of how information about others is organized and remembered. By focusing on different aspects of person perception, each area complements the others. (See Summary Table 3.1 for an overview.)

Person perception is not a single, instantaneous event. Rather, it comprises many ongoing processes, some that take a few seconds (for example, forming a first impression of a stranger on the street) and others that take years (for example, forming an increasingly subtle and detailed portrait of a lifelong friend). In spite of its complexity, person perception is well worth studying, for few skills are as important to us as knowing and understanding other human beings.

Yes, he was certainly wonderfully handsome, with his finely-curved scarlet lips, his frank blue eyes, his crisp gold hair. There was something in his face that made one trust him at once. All the candour of youth was there, as well as all youth's passionate purity. One felt that he had kept himself unspotted from the world.

—— *The Picture of Dorian Gray*, p. 15

Folk wisdom advises us not to judge a book by its cover, but in our everyday dealings with people, it's difficult not to. *The Picture of Dorian Gray* is a complex parable about the human tendency to believe that a person's inner nature reveals itself in surface appearances. After observing his "wonderfully handsome" image in a newly painted portrait, Dorian observes, "How sad it is! I shall grow old, and horrible, and dreadful. But this picture will remain always young. . . . If it were only the other way! If it were I who was to be always young, and the picture that was to grow old! . . . I would give my soul for that!" (pp. 25–26). Dorian has his wish: As age and moral decline corrupt his portrait, his body remains unchanged. Dorian stays forever young and innocent-looking. Unfortunately, Dorian's acquaintances mistakenly assume that his physical beauty reflects a spiritual beauty.

Let's turn our attention to two important kinds of raw material of first impressions: physical characteristics and nonverbal behaviors.

Physical Characteristics

" . . . You have a wonderfully beautiful face, Mr. Gray. Don't frown. You have. And Beauty is a form of Genius — is higher, indeed . . . as it needs no explanation. . . . It cannot be questioned. It has its divine right of sovereignty. It makes princes of those who have it."

—— *The Picture of Dorian Gray*, p. 21

Numerous studies have shown that we judge traits from facial and body features. Perhaps you believe that people with high foreheads and clear eyes are intelligent, that very muscular men are gregarious but stupid, and that blondes do indeed have more fun. Berry & McArthur (1986) reported that adults with childlike facial features are perceived to be more submissive, honest, and naive than other adults. (For other research on presumed relationships between physical and psychological traits, see Secord, Dukes, & Bevan, 1954; Bradshaw, 1969; Dibiase & Hjelle, 1968.)

When we first meet people we often judge how attractive they are. Many people seem to agree with Dorian Gray's admirer that attractive people are "better" than unattractive people (Hatfield & Sprecher, 1986). For instance, subjects in one study judged attractive people to be more "sensitive, kind, interesting, poised, modest, and sociable" than unattractive people (Dion, Berscheid, & Walster, 1972). They also judged attractive people to have better romantic relationships and job prospects than less attractive people. (Chapter 11 presents a more detailed discussion of the relation between attractiveness and liking.)

One of the first things we learn from a person's appearance is his or her gender, and once we know that we immediately make inferences about other characteristics. Considerable research indicates the existence of gender stereotypes — that is, people ascribe different traits to women than they ascribe to men. For example, Broverman and her colleagues (1972) found that college students tend to think that women are "talkative," "tactful," and "gentle," whereas men are "aggressive," "independent," and "competitive" (see Chapter 10 for a more detailed discussion of gender stereotypes).

We often use physical characteristics such as skin color and facial appearance to judge others' racial and ethnic backgrounds. Once we so categorize a person, a host of further inferences typically follow. One early study on ethnic stereotypes (Katz & Braly, 1933) found that Princeton students in the 1930s thought that Italians were "artistic, impulsive, and passionate"; the English were "sportsmanlike, intelligent, and conventional." Blacks were thought to be "superstitious, lazy, and happy-go-lucky," whereas Turks were "cruel, very religious, and treacherous." More recent studies indicate that in our society people with dark skin are often judged to have less desirable traits than those with lighter skin (Brigham, 1971). Clearly, such inferences from ethnicity are frequently wrong. However, once we've judged people's ethnicity, we *think* we know other information about them as well. (See Chapter 9 for a detailed discussion of research on stereotypes and prejudice.)

Nonverbal Behaviors

Dorian Gray frowned and turned his head away. He could not help liking the tall, graceful young man who was standing by him. His romantic, olive-coloured face and worn expression interested him. There was something in his low, languid voice that was absolutely fascinating. His cool, white, flower-like hands, even, had a curious charm. They moved, as he spoke, like music, and seemed to have a language of their own.

—— *The Picture of Dorian Gray*, pp. 20–21

In forming first impressions, we attend not only to relatively static cues like appearance and attractiveness, but also to the more dynamic, stylistic aspects of a person's behavior. We may notice, for example, whether a person's gestures are expansive or constricted, nervous or relaxed. Or we may notice whether a person talks slowly or quickly. Recent research suggests that we readily infer personality traits from stylistic, nonverbal cues (Lippa, 1983). For instance, we may decide that someone with expansive gestures and a loud voice is "extroverted," whereas a person who fidgets, twitches, and stutters is "neurotic."

The significance of nonverbal information.   How important are nonverbal behaviors in creating first impressions? Suppose you meet someone who says he's cool-headed and calm, but as he speaks he fidgets, twitches, and his voice cracks with nervous tremors. Which information would influence your impression more — his words or his nonverbal behaviors? Many studies that ask subjects to judge conflicting verbal and nonverbal cues have found that people weight nonverbal information more heavily (see, for example, Mehrabian & Wiener, 1967). Apparently, we often

■■■■■■■■■■■■■■■■■■■■■■■
Winston Churchill flashes an emblem — his famous "V-for-victory" sign — at sailors during World War II.

assume that nonverbal information is more "honest" and less controlled than verbal information. These studies *do not* imply that nonverbal behaviors carry "more information" than verbal behavior, but rather that when verbal and nonverbal behaviors are inconsistent, we are more likely to believe the nonverbal "message."

Kinds of nonverbal behavior.   Ekman and Friesen (1969b) have suggested a classification of nonverbal behaviors that points to their diversity. We'll restrict our discussion to physical movements of some part of the body. Ekman and Friesen identified five varieties of body movement: emblems, affect displays, illustrators, regulators, and adaptors.

Emblems are fixed, culturally learned and defined gestures for which dictionary definitions could be given within a specific culture. For example, in our society the "V-for-victory" sign, the "A-okay" sign, and "the finger" are all emblems. By definition, emblems can vary across cultures. Thus whereas we might form a circle with a thumb and forefinger to say "Okay," in other societies this same gesture, particularly if lowered a bit, may be considered obscene.

Affect displays are emotional expressions. Facial expressions of anger, sadness, or happiness are all affect displays. Later in this chapter we'll discuss research on how accurately people can judge emotions from emotional expressions.

Illustrators, as the term suggests, nonverbally illustrate physical events or thought processes. Think of illustrators as nonverbal pictures, metaphors, or analogies. For example, I might hold my hands two feet apart when I tell you about the fish that just got away, or when you say "on the one hand," you gesture with one hand.

Regulators help lend structure to social interaction. In a sense, they are the nonverbal oil that lubricates the flow of social life. For example, as I talk to you, my head nods up and down, we establish eye contact, my eyebrows move up and down, and I gesture to emphasize points and to take turns in conversation. Such nonverbal cues serve to signal attention and to help segment and emphasize the verbal flow. Often we are unconscious of regulators in ourselves and others.

Adaptors are self-directed gestures that occur when a person is not paying attention to himself or herself, or when a person is in conflict or distracted. When you glance around the classroom during a test, you may see one student twirling a piece of hair with her finger, another pulling at his beard, and a third rubbing her hand on her thigh. All three movements are adaptors. Such gestures have sometimes been interpreted by clinicians to be reflections of the individual's personality. For example, Mahl (1968) interviewed a woman who constantly slipped her wedding ring off and on her finger during the interview. Mahl interpreted this adaptor as expressing the woman's ambivalence about her husband and marriage.

Ekman and Friesen's classification scheme suggests the great variety of nonverbal behaviors. Some nonverbal cues seem to be at least partly biologically innate (for example, affect displays), whereas others are not (for example, illustrators). Some are clearly culturally learned (for example, emblems), whereas others are not (for example, affect displays). Some represent conscious, intentional communications (for example, an emblem like "the finger"), whereas others are largely unconscious (for example, many regulators). Given their diversity, it is amazing that we form impressions so quickly and readily from nonverbal behaviors.

Nonverbal behavior, power, and preference.   Despite the variety of nonverbal behaviors, we often use them to infer two main characteristics of people and social relations: power and preference. Power refers to status and dominance in social life, whereas preference refers to our degree of liking for or intimacy with others. Perhaps these themes occur so often in nonverbal communication because they are basic to social life itself (Foa, 1961; Leary, 1957; Triandis, 1977). Thus nonverbal cues seem particularly good at conveying the emotional messages of interpersonal relations. To see the themes of power and preference in action, let's consider three specific nonverbal behaviors: eye contact, personal space, and touching.

Eye contact frequently signals either intimacy or dominance (Exline, 1972). Research indicates, for example, that the more couples report to be in love, the more time they spend gazing into each other's eyes (Rubin, 1970). On the other hand, in competitive settings eye contact is often seen as challenging and aggressive. Low-status people typically engage in less eye contact than high-status people, and furthermore, highly competitive people increase eye contact in competitive settings (Exline, 1972). Very likely, the total context of a particular setting determines whether eye contact signals power or preference (Ellsworth & Carlsmith, 1968). Thus eye contact with your date means something very different from eye contact with a potential mugger.

Personal space, like eye contact, often conveys information about intimacy and dominance. Americans act as if they have an 18-inch "bubble" of personal space around them that demarks "intimate distance" and "personal distance" (Hall, 1966). Generally, close friends, family, or romantic relations may enter our 18-inch bubble, but others tend to stay outside.

■■■■■■■■■■■■■■■■■■■■■■■
**Nonverbal behaviors
provide information
about status and inti-
macy in social relation-
ships. What do you
think the relationship
is between these two
people? On what cues
are you basing your
judgment?**

Not only do we maintain our personal space with others on the basis of intimacy, but we also pay careful attention to such distances in judging others' relationships. For example, if you saw a couple standing an inch apart while they talked together in the cafeteria, you would probably assume they had a very different relationship than if they stood two feet apart.

Like eye contact, personal space can signal power as well as intimacy. Imagine, for example, that you are called to your boss's office: You enter and stand in front of the desk, probably at a respectful distance. Now reverse the situation. When your boss comes to your desk, he or she will probably feel comfortable stepping right up beside your chair. Low-status people tend to respect the personal space of high-status people; the reverse is not true. Theodore White described a dramatic example of this in *The Making of the President, 1960*: Once it became clear late on election night that John Kennedy was the next President of the United States, associates and friends stood farther from him.

Touching is a third nonverbal behavior that signals intimacy and power in social life (Frank, 1957; Jourard & Rubin, 1968; Goffman, 1967). We tend to touch those we like and those we're intimate with more than those we dislike. Furthermore, we touch those of lower status more than those of higher status. A boss, for example, might ask an assistant to retrieve a file and might touch the assistant's shoulder at the same time. However, when the assistant returns with the file, it is quite unlikely that the assistant will touch the boss in return.

First Impressions in the Courtroom

First impressions can have important consequences in everyday life, and nowhere is this more apparent than in the courtroom. A standard procedure in American jury trials is *voir dire*, a pretrial interview of prospective jurors during which attorneys ask questions, form impressions of potential jurors, and eliminate those they feel may be prejudiced against their case or client.

How do attorneys form impressions of jurors, and what evidence do they use to approve or eliminate prospective jurors? Attorneys' accounts of their selection criteria and books on trial practice provide a rich source of information about factors influencing lawyers' first impressions of jurors. Like people in general, attorneys often subscribe to unvalidated and questionable stereotypes. The famous American criminal lawyer, Clarence Darrow, offered the following advice:

I try to get a jury with little education but with much human emotion. The Irish are always the best jurymen for the defense. I don't want a Scotchman, for he has too little human feelings; I don't want a Scandinavian, for he has too strong a respect for law as law. In general, I don't want a religious person, for he believes in sin and punishment. The defense should avoid rich men who have regard for the law, as they make and use it. The smug and ultra-respectable think they are the guardians of society, and they believe the law is for them (quoted in Sutherland & Cressey, 1966).

In discussing *voir dire*, a president of the Trial Lawyers of America stated, "Trial attorneys are acutely attuned to the nuances of human behavior, which enables them to detect the minutest traces of bias or inability to reach an appropriate decision" (Begam, 1977). Is it possible that this attorney overestimates his colleagues' ability to form accurate impressions of jurors and thereby select sympathetic juries?

In one careful study addressing this question, Zeisel and Diamond (1978) asked prospective jurors who were rejected by attorneys in 12 actual criminal trials to attend the trials as spectators and report how they would have voted as jurors. The researchers could then compare the verdicts of the actual juries with verdicts arrived at by the rejected jurors. Lawyers' selection of jurors seemed to have a major impact on trial outcomes in only 3 of the 12 trials. These results support other studies indicating that jury decisions are generally influenced more by the actual evidence of the case than by juror biases (Myers, 1979; Kassin & Wrightsman, 1988). By implication, jury selection is most important in cases entailing difficult decisions concerning ambiguous evidence. Not surprisingly, some lawyers seem to be more astute than others in selecting sympathetic jurors (Bermant, 1977; Zeisel & Diamond, 1978).

First impressions enter the courtroom in another important way; not only must attorneys form impressions of jurors, but jurors

---

Thus research on eye contact, personal space, and touching suggests that we can use these nonverbal cues to figure out emotional and social relations between people. Nonverbal cues can provide important information about intimacy, power, and status in individuals and in social relationships.

The Power of First Impressions

" . . . You are really wonderful, Dorian. You have never looked more charming than you do to-night. You remind me of the day I saw you first. You were rather cheeky, very shy, and absolutely extraordinary. You have changed, of course, but not in appearance."

—— *The Picture of Dorian Gray*, p. 216

First impressions can be based on many different kinds of information. Because they are based on superficial information and rely on stereotypes about physical appear-

must form impressions of defendants and witnesses. Many of the variables that we've already discussed play a role in jurors' impressions of defendants. Mock jury experiments suggest that jurors often treat physically attractive defendants more leniently than they treat unattractive defendants (Baumeister & Darley, 1982); however, these effects are not always corroborated in observational studies of actual court trials (Stewart, 1980). Judges as well as jurors are sometimes swayed by a defendant's physical appearance. In a study that rated the physical attractiveness of 74 male defendants in Pennsylvania courts, Stewart (1980) found that attractive convicted defendants tended to receive lighter sentences from judges than did unattractive defendants, and attractive defendants were considerably less likely to serve prison sentences.

Facial features play a role in jurors' impressions of defendants. In a simulated trial Berry and McArthur (1986) found that defen-dants with "babyish" faces were more likely to be found guilty of negligence (for selling products without adequately warning consumers of their dangers), whereas defendants with mature-looking faces were more likely to be found guilty of the crime of deliberately misinforming their customers about the products. Apparently, jurors intuitively felt that babyish faces matched the "immature" crime of negligence, whereas mature faces matched the calculated crime of intentional and malicious deceit.

Defendants' verbal and nonverbal behaviors are another powerful influence on jurors' first impressions. Parkinson (1979) studied 38 actual trials to determine the effects of a defendant's style of speech on jurors' decision to convict or acquit. In general, jurors were more likely to acquit defendants who were polite and deferential, who spoke in complete, grammatical sentences, and who made fewer self-references in their testimony.

Jurors also look to the nonverbal behaviors of witnesses to decide whether they are telling the truth. We shall examine research on the detection of deception in more detail later in this chapter, but for now it's sufficient to note that although judges often instruct jurors to pay careful attention to witnesses' demeanor, research suggests that people are not very good at telling who is lying and who is telling the truth from nonverbal cues (Kassin & Wrightsman, 1988). Of course, this inability does not stop jurors from forming strong impressions about a witness's believability.

In sum, first impressions in the courtroom can influence who serves on juries, whose testimony is believed, and, ultimately, which defendants are found guilty and innocent.

ance and social groups, first impressions are often wrong. However, even when wrong, first impressions are often lasting impressions. Studies investigating the temporal order of information in person perception often find strong evidence for a *primacy effect* — that is, the first information carries more weight than later information.

The primacy effect and personality judgments.   Consider an early study by Luchins (1957) in which subjects read a story about a character named "Jim." Here's the story:

> Jim left the house to get some stationery. He walked out into the sun-filled street with two of his friends, basking in the sun as he walked. Jim entered the stationery store which was full of people. Jim talked with an acquaintance while he waited for the clerk to catch his eye. On his way out, he stopped to chat

with a school friend who was just coming into the store. Leaving the store, he walked toward school. On his way out he met the girl to whom he had been introduced the night before. They talked for a short while, and then Jim left for school.

After reading this story, subjects were asked to describe Jim's personality and looks (even his posture). They also answered some standardized questions (for example, "Is Jim: (a) shy, (b) more shy than forward, (c) more forward than shy, (d) forward, or (e) none of these?") In general, subjects described Jim as friendly, forward, and sociable. Furthermore, he was often judged to be muscular, athletic, and assertive and to have good posture.

Luchins wrote a second story that creates a different impression of Jim:

After school Jim left the classroom alone. Leaving the school, he started on his long walk home. The street was brilliantly filled with sunshine. Jim walked down the street on the shady side. Coming down the street toward him, he saw the pretty girl whom he had met on the previous evening. Jim crossed the street and entered a candy store. The store was crowded with students, and he noticed a few familiar faces. Jim waited quietly until the counterman caught his eye and then gave his order. Taking his drink, he sat down at a side table. When he had finished his drink he went home.

After reading this story, subjects typically described Jim as shy, reserved, quiet, and introverted. They also imagined him to be thin, weak, and unassertive and to have poor posture.

Perhaps you noticed that the two paragraphs about Jim can be "hooked" together to read as a single story. Luchins used this combined story to study how people combine information. This study could have turned out in one of three ways. Subjects could weight the first information most heavily, perceiving Jim to be predominantly extroverted. This would be an example of a primacy effect. Or subjects could weight the last information most heavily and perceive Jim to be predominantly introverted. This is a *recency effect*. Or subjects could weight the two paragraphs equally and average them, judging Jim to be halfway between extroverted and introverted.

What did the data in fact suggest? Luchins found strong evidence for a primacy effect—subjects weighted early information most heavily in forming an impression of Jim's personality. Although specific manipulations can alter and at times reverse the primacy effect (for example, if we warn subjects to pay careful attention to later information, or if we create a large time delay between early and later information), in general primacy effects tend to be more common than recency effects (Jones & Goethals, 1972).

The primacy effect and judgments of ability.   The primacy effect may also function in judgments of ability. In one well-known study, Jones and his colleagues (1968) had subjects observe how a person performed on a 30-question "intelligence test." Some subjects saw the test taker answer many of the first questions correctly and then answer more and more later questions incorrectly. Other subjects saw the test taker answer many questions incorrectly at first and then answer more and more correctly.

In both conditions, the test taker got the same total score—15 correct out of 30. However, subjects who saw the test taker "start off strong" tended to rate the person as more intelligent than did subjects who saw the person "start off weak." Furthermore, on average, subjects falsely remembered that the test taker who "started off strong" answered 21 questions correctly and that the test taker who had "started off weak" answered only 13 questions correctly. Here again we have evidence for a primacy effect.

Recent research suggests that the primacy effect is particularly strong when people have little time to make judgments and are not under great pressure to be correct (Kruglanski & Freund, 1983). Thus we might expect the primacy effect to be weakest when we can ponder information about others in depth. Often, though, we don't have the time or motivation. If primacy effects occur regularly in person perception, then our first impressions become all the more important, simply because they are first.

Accuracy of Direct Judgments

"I shall stay with the real Dorian," he said. . . .

"Is it the real Dorian?" cried the original of the portrait, strolling across to him. "Am I really like that?"

"Yes; you are just like that."

—— *The Picture of Dorian Gray*, p. 29

In general, how accurate are people in judging others? Are some people (clinical psychologists, for example) better judges than others? Is social perceptiveness a general trait or ability, as is intelligence?

Although such questions are both seemingly obvious and intriguing, the research concerning them provides answers that are not as simple as you might expect. First, the questions just posed about the accuracy of person perception are too broad. Researchers have tended both conceptually and historically to separate them into two questions: How accurately can people judge *personality traits* in others, and how accurately can people judge *emotions* in others? The first question focuses on the perception of long-term, stable characteristics, whereas the second focuses more on the perception of short-term, transient states. Both questions are important.

Judging Personality

"Sin is a thing that writes itself across a man's face. It cannot be concealed. People talk sometimes of secret vices. There are no such things. If a wretched man has a vice, it shows itself in the lines of his mouth, the droop of his eyelids, the moulding of his hands even."

—— *The Picture of Dorian Gray*, p. 150

Can you tell moral people from immoral people? Can you distinguish introverts from extroverts, neurotics from stable individuals, or assertive people from passive people? Put simply, can you accurately judge another's personality? Studies that attempt to answer such questions face two important methodological problems.

First, what *criteria of accuracy* should we use? Different studies have used personality test scores, ratings by intimates and peers, and even the judgments of clinical psychologists, but each of these criteria has potential problems. Personality tests are not always valid (Mischel, 1968). Intimates and peers may provide biased ratings or possess incomplete knowledge. Nor is clinical judgment always accurate — sometimes clinicians don't agree with one another in assessing clients (Crow & Hammond, 1957). No perfect criterion of accuracy exists. In this regard, it's worth comparing person perception to object perception again. If I want to determine how accurately a subject perceives color or brightness, I can objectively measure these attributes and compare the measurements to the subject's perceptions, but if I want to determine how accurately a subject perceives "personality," no such objective criteria exist.

The second important methodological problem relates to the *kinds of behavior* on which subjects base their judgments. Should subjects judge others after watching them in a brief film? Should they talk to people for half an hour before judging them? Should they judge only friends they've known for years? Subjects' accuracy in judging strangers after a few minutes may reflect their skill at interpreting physical characteristics and nonverbal cues, whereas accuracy in judgments about long-term acquaintances might reflect their ability to cognitively process complex social information.

Early research and problems with statistical measures of accuracy.   Early research on personality judgment focused on quick judgments of others based on brief exposure to limited information. Dymond (1949, 1950) devised a clever technique to sidestep the criterion problems mentioned earlier. As a part of her procedure, she asked subjects to use a 5-point scale to rate themselves on six traits: "superior-inferior," "friendly-unfriendly," "leader-follower," "shy–self-assured," "sympathetic-unsympathetic," and "secure-insecure." After briefly interacting with these subjects, judges were asked to predict how they had rated themselves on the six traits. Note that the judges did not evaluate a subject's "true" personality, but rather "put themselves into another's shoes" and filled in rating scales as they thought the actual subjects completed them.

Dymond believed she had devised a technique to measure empathy — the ability to take the role of someone else. She found that some judges were more accurate at predicting subjects' ratings on the rating scales than were others and that such accuracy correlated with general intelligence and such personality traits as extroversion and warmth. By 1955, 50 similar studies had been published (Taft, 1955). However, the evidence on whether accuracy is a general trait that correlates with other personality and intelligence measures remains inconclusive.

To understand why, we must look a little more carefully at the statistical measures of accuracy these researchers used. Their technique was to find the difference between a judge's prediction for a subject and that subject's self-rating, square this difference to remove minus signs, and then to add up these numbers over the different traits and over the different subjects being judged. The result was an overall index of accuracy for each judge. The larger the index (or score), the farther "off" were the judge's estimated ratings from the subjects' self ratings; the closer to zero the score, the more accurate were the judge's estimated ratings.

This overall accuracy score provided a simple, comprehensive measure, but it was obtained at the cost of considerable underlying complexity. In a detailed mathematical analysis of such accuracy scores, Cronbach (1955) showed that these seemingly simple measures contained many different components. In addition, they were influenced by judges' *response sets* — their habitual ways of filling in rating scales. Without presenting the mathematical detail, let's examine some of the problems Cronbach uncovered.

One common response set is to assume that others answer questions similarly to the way we answer them. In fact, we often assume that others' opinions and behavioral choices are more similar to ours than they actually are (Ross, Greene, & House, 1977; Mullen, Atkins, Champion, Edwards, Hardy, Story, & Vanderklok, 1985; Campbell, 1986). For example, people who rate themselves as shy are likely to overestimate the number of other people who also describe themselves as shy. This tendency is known as the *false consensus effect*.

If people are fairly typical, then their assumption that others are similar to them will help their accuracy; if they are eccentric, then their assumption that others are similar will hurt their accuracy. Note that this increase or decrease in accuracy has little to do with true "perceptiveness" but instead merely reflects the influence of assumed similarity. Recent research suggests that a person's assumption that others are similar can lead to accurate predictions of others' attitudes, particularly when the others are in fact demographically similar to that person (Hoch, 1987).

Even if we could eliminate response sets, Cronbach's analysis showed that accuracy scores include several additional components. Two that are particularly important are stereotype accuracy and differential accuracy. *Stereotype accuracy* is that component of accuracy resulting from a judge's sense of how people in general fill in their rating scales, rather than the judge's ability to perceive true personality differences among subjects. For example, you may feel that people in general rate themselves as low on "anxiety" and high on "honesty." If you're right, this assumption will help your accuracy, not because you're sensitive to people's personality traits, but rather because you're knowledgeable about how people on average rate themselves. *Differential accuracy*, on the other hand, refers to a judge's ability to predict the differences in how people rate themselves (for example, Mary rates herself as more extroverted than John and less anxious than Seymour). This is probably the kind of accuracy in which the original researchers were most likely interested.

New directions in accuracy research.   Cronbach's (1955) statistical critique of accuracy scores meant that valid interpretations of previous accuracy score data were not possible. What had seemed to be a simple accuracy score was in fact quite complicated. Because of the statistical difficulties, many researchers stopped conducting studies on the accuracy of personality judgments after the 1950s.

There were a few notable exceptions. In one careful study, Cline and Richards (1960) filmed various people as they answered interview questions, gave them a variety of personality tests, and then asked judges to view the films and rate the stimulus persons on trait scales and personality tests. Cline and Richards conducted complex statistical analyses to separate out various components of accuracy, including stereotype accuracy and differential accuracy. Interestingly, they found that both of these components contributed to subjects' overall accuracy; furthermore, the two components were largely uncorrelated. In other words, a person's ability to judge how people *in general* rate themselves on personality scales bears little relationship to a person's ability to judge differences among individual's personalities. Even though Cline and Richards's study produced some evidence that accuracy in judging personality is a general ability (that is, one that would be consistent over various traits, people, and settings), the evidence on this research topic remains complex.

For a time, Cronbach's analysis chilled researchers' enthusiasm for investigating the accuracy of personality judgments, but interest in the question seems to be reviving (DePaulo, Kenny, Hoover, Webb, & Oliver, 1987; Funder, 1987; Kenny & Albright, 1987). In the future, accuracy research may have to pose more specific sorts of questions: How good are certain kinds of people (for example, clinical psychologists) at judging specific traits (for example, dominance) based on specific sorts of information (for example, after watching a half-hour clinical interview)? Funder (1987) mentions the need for more real-life criteria of accuracy. For example, it's not sufficient to assess judges' accuracy solely by their ratings on trait scales; we must also determine whether they can accurately predict real-life outcomes and behaviors. Thus, can people accurately predict, after briefly observing people, whether they would make good friends, or reliable employees, or successful college students?

Early studies on accuracy, including Dymond's, were quite artificial. Judges rated others in laboratory settings on traits scales provided by the researchers. In everyday life, people judge others on traits that are personally relevant to them. A recent study by Wright and Dawson (1988) showed that people can more accurately infer the trait of aggressiveness from others' behavior than they can infer the trait of withdrawal from others' behavior. This makes sense, for perceiving aggressiveness is important; it enables us to avoid aggressive people. Thus research on accuracy must address the purposes of person perception in everyday life.

Recently, researchers have proposed new statistical techniques for measuring accuracy. For example, the *social relations model* (Kenny & La Voie, 1984; Kenny & Albright, 1987) holds that when judges rate stimulus persons, the ratings are determined partly by the judges, partly by the stimulus persons, and partly by the unique relationship between the two. To illustrate, if everyone in your family rated everyone else on a scale of "likability," these ratings would in part be determined by the particular rater — perhaps your mother is a Pollyanna who tends to rate everyone as being quite likable. The ratings would be determined in part by characteristics of the people being rated — perhaps everyone tends to agree that your sister is unlikable. Finally, ratings would be determined in part by unique relationships between people — you might rate your favorite brother as likable, although no one else does. The social relations model represents an advance in that it acknowledges that perceived traits have reality only within the context of particular social relationships.

Albright, Kenny, and Malloy (1988) used the social relations model in a study that asked small groups of unacquainted college students to rate one another on five traits: "sociable," "good-natured," "responsible," "calm," and "intellectual." Interestingly, students showed moderately good agreement in their ratings of two of the traits, "sociable" and "responsible," suggesting that there are reliable physical cues from which these two traits may be inferred. Furthermore, judges agreed moderately well with subjects' self-ratings on these traits, suggesting some degree of accuracy in their first impressions. Thus some personality traits seem to be more accurately judged than others.

Dimensions of perceived personality.   In research on the accuracy of personality judgments, researchers typically select the traits on which subjects judge others. But in real life, nobody gives us a scale and asks us to rate another person on "extroversion" or "insecurity." Rather, we judge and categorize people in ways that seem relevant to us. In *The Picture of Dorian Gray*, Oscar Wilde repeatedly describes his characters in terms of their physical beauty, wittiness, and moral virtue. Do you think that people evaluate others on nearly the same attributes, or does each person have unique ways of evaluating others? And are these dimensions of person perception dictated more by the perceiver or by those being perceived?

Dornbusch and his colleagues (1965) investigated how much the categories of person perception are "in the eye of the beholder" and how much they are dictated by the object of perception. Specifically, children at summer camp were asked to describe their tentmates. These descriptions were content-analyzed; that is, each description was coded as falling into one of 69 categories that described attributes in other children such as "humor," "interpersonal skill," or "physical ability."

On average, this study found more overlap in the categories used when one child described two other children than when two children described the same stimulus child. In other words, the categories of person perception seemed to be more a function of the perceiver than of the person perceived. Thus one child may be likely to perceive almost everyone on "sports ability," but when two children describe little Tommy, one might mention his "sports ability" and the other his "school ability."

Park (1986) conducted a similar study on seven college students in the same seminar class. Each week for seven weeks these students wrote a detailed description of every other student in the class. As in the Dornbusch study, Park found more overlap in the descriptions made by one student of two other students than in the descriptions made by two students of any single student. Again, the categories of person perception seemed to be "projected" by the perceiver more than dictated by the stimulus person.

Initially, Park computed overlap of descriptions simply by determining whether a given category, such as intelligence, occurred in more than one written description of a student. In a second analysis, however, she looked also at the valence, or positivity or negativity, of the description. (Thus, for example, "Jane is intelligent" and "Jennie is stupid" are both descriptions about the same attribute, intelligence, but they are opposite in valence.) In her second analysis, Park considered an attribute to overlap in two descriptions if the same attribute, with the same valence, was mentioned in both. In this analysis she found more overlap in two students' descriptions of a given third student than in one student's descriptions of two other students. In other words, our perceptions of others are not just determined by our own evaluative categories; sometimes our evaluative categories coincide with those of other perceivers and are dictated by real characteristics of the stimulus person.

In the studies just described, subjects were free to describe others in any terms they chose. If we consider personality traits alone, do people choose the same standard personality dimensions in judging others?

To answer this question, Rosenburg, Nelson, and Vivekanathan (1968) provided subjects with a list of 60 varied traits ("serious," "shrewd," "boring," "submissive," "honest," and so on) and asked them to group those traits that "go together" in actual people. The data from this grouping task were analyzed by a statistical technique called multidimensional scaling, which plots the traits in two-dimensional space. Traits that subjects tend to group together are close to one another in space, whereas traits that are rarely grouped together are far apart.

Using multidimensional scaling, Rosenburg and colleagues identified two basic underlying dimensions along which subjects grouped traits: good versus bad intellectual traits and good versus bad social traits (see Figure 3.1). We seem to judge others' personalities along these two fundamental dimensions.

Other researchers have used statistical techniques that can identify multiple dimensions of person perception (see, for example, Norman, 1963; Conley, 1985; Goldberg, 1981; McCrae & Costa, 1985). Such studies regularly find five dimensions of personality in subjects' ratings of actual people: (1) extroversion, (2) agreeableness, (3) conscientiousness, (4) anxiety, and (5) intelligence-culturedness. Factors 1, 2, and 4 seem to load highly on what Rosenburg and his colleagues (1968) called "good and bad social traits," whereas factors 3 and 5 load highly on "good and bad

FIGURE 3.1   Two main dimensions of person perception.

What dimensions underlie our impressions of others?

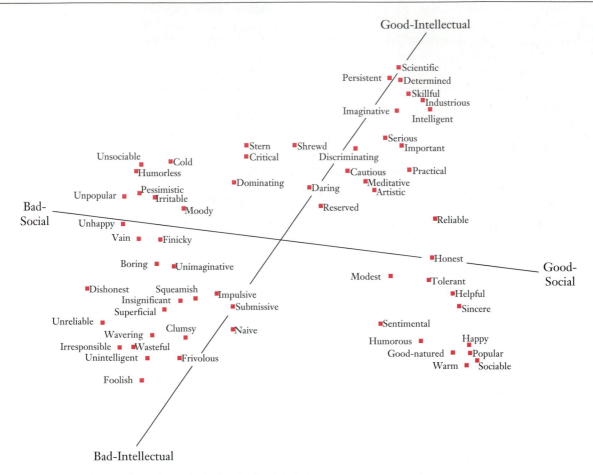

SOURCE: Rosenburg et al. (1968). Copyright 1968 by the American Psychological Association. Used by permission of the author.

You may have noticed that the two axes of this space (good versus bad intellectual traits and good versus bad social traits) are not at right angles. This means that good intellectual traits are perceived to be somewhat correlated with good social traits, and bad intellectual traits are perceived to be somewhat correlated with bad social traits. Thus, there is one super *dimension underlying our impressions of others — good versus bad.*

intellectual traits." In other words, this five-factor model is a more fine-grained analysis of the dimensions of perceived personality than the two-dimension model.

Do these five basic trait dimensions reflect the true underlying dimensions of personality, or do they simply exist "in the mind of the beholder"? Psychologists have

Based on their facial expressions, what are these people looking at? *Answer:* **They are looking at photographs of their village and family members taken years earlier. As this photo illustrates, emotional expressions in real-life settings may sometimes be complex, ambiguous, and hard to interpret.**

argued both positions (see Passini & Norman, 1966; Powell & Juhnke, 1983; Block, Weiss, & Thorne, 1979; Shweder, 1982). Because McCrae and Costa (1987) found that subjects' self-ratings on the five basic dimensions of personality correlated quite strongly with peers' ratings on the same dimensions, they argue for the psychological reality of the five dimensions.

Judging Emotions

> He looked at Dorian Gray in absolute amazement. He had never seen him like this before. The lad was actually pallid with rage. His hands were clenched, and the pupils of his eyes were like discs of blue fire. He was trembling all over.
> —— *The Picture of Dorian Gray*, p. 112

How accurately can people judge emotions in others? Modern work on the judgment of emotion is generally traced back to the work of Charles Darwin.

Darwin's legacy.   Most famous for his monumental *The Origin of the Species* (1859), Darwin is also well known to psychologists for his seminal work, *The Expression of Emotions in Man and Animals* (1872), in which he sought to uncover the evolutionary origins of emotional expression. Darwin argued that emotional expressions evolved because of their survival value. For example, members of a species who can communicate fear to one another have a better chance of escaping from predators.

Darwin attempted to explain how emotional expressions evolved originally. His "principle of serviceable associated habits" held that evolution "borrowed" already-existent behaviors for the new purpose of emotional expression. To illustrate this principle, consider how people often show disgust by wrinkling their noses and

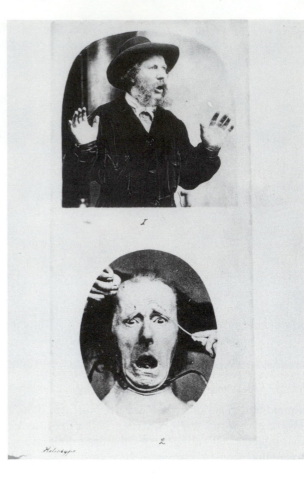

■■■■■■■■■■■■■■■■■■■■■■■■
**Photographs from
Darwin's *The Expres-
sion of Emotion in Man
and Animals*. What
emotions do you think
are being expressed
here?**

pulling back their upper lips. According to Darwin, this expression evolved from a
more primitive vomit response. A second principle — "antithesis" — held that once
an emotional expression is established, the opposite emotion will be signaled (reasonably enough) by the opposite expression or body position. For example, if people
display angry dominance by staring hostilely, showing their teeth, hunching their
shoulders forward, and clenching their fists, then they should show docile submission
with the opposite expressions — averted gaze, closed mouth, slumped shoulders, and
open hands.

Darwin's evolutionary theory suggested that emotional expression is innate and
therefore cross-culturally universal. If emotional expressions are biologically "wired
in," as Darwin suggested, then we should see a definite correspondence between
emotions and expressions, and people should be relatively good at identifying emotions from expressions. Thus Darwin's writings led to several testable propositions.

Early research on Darwin's theories was relatively unsophisticated (Ekman,
Friesen, & Ellsworth, 1972). For example, in early research, Landis (1924, 1929)
attempted to determine how well subjects could match facial expressions with the
situations that elicited them. He photographed subjects' faces while they listened to
a Wagnerian opera, looked at erotic pictures, and — believe it or not — decapitated a
rat. (Each activity was designed to create a different emotion.) Next, Landis showed

the photos to judges and in essence asked them, "In which of these photos do you think the subject is listening to an opera? Or looking at erotic pictures? Or decapitating a rat?" Landis found that judges were not very good at such matching, and later researchers concluded from his findings that people cannot accurately recognize emotions from facial expressions.

This conclusion was premature, however, for Landis's study suffered from many flaws. First, it's not clear what emotions Landis created in his subjects — a prude might be disgusted by erotic pictures, whereas a libertine might be delighted. Second, the judges in Landis's study were not really asked to judge emotions from facial expressions; rather, they were asked to match situations with expressions. Finally, Landis's subjects were aware that they were being photographed, so they may well have been controlling their expressions.

Recent research.   Given all these methodological problems, it's not surprising that Landis's findings have been superseded by recent, well-controlled research, which indicates that subjects are able to recognize six *primary* emotions — happiness, sadness, surprise, fear, anger, and disgust — from posed facial expressions (Ekman, Friesen, & Ellsworth, 1982b). Outside the laboratory, judging people's emotions from their expressions is undoubtedly more complex. In everyday life we try to judge more complex emotions: What does an expression of "love" or "jealousy" look like? Furthermore, in real life, emotional expressions occur in complex mixtures and vary rapidly over time. Finally, in everyday life people often control their emotional expressions to varying degrees for both personal and cultural reasons.

Ekman and Friesen (1969b) use the term *display rules* to refer to cultural norms that govern emotional expressions. An average American woman who is feeling happy may display a full, toothy smile. In contrast, because Japanese culture seems to require that women inhibit certain expressions, a traditional Japanese woman may show only a tiny, inhibited smile. Various groups within a culture may also have different display rules. In our society, for example, it is more acceptable for women to show grief openly than it is for men. The innate display of grief is probably the same for men and women, but men have learned to inhibit that display more. Conversely, women in our society seem to control their displays of hostility and aggression more than do men.

Cross-cultural universality.   Despite the mitigating influence of display rules, recent research suggests that the recognition and display of primary facial emotions is universal across cultures (Ekman, Friesen, & Ellsworth, 1982b); that is, people the world over seem to recognize and show the six basic emotions in the same ways. This finding supports Darwin's hypothesis that emotional expressions are to some degree biologically innate.

Studies by Dickey and Knower (1941), Izard (1969), and Ekman and his colleagues (Ekman, Friesen, & Ellsworth, 1982a; Ekman et al., 1987) all indicate that members of various literate cultures (for example, Japan, the United States, France, Brazil) substantially agree on the emotions displayed in facial photographs. Although this evidence does not conclusively prove that people the world over *display* emotions with the same expressions, it does suggest that various cultures *interpret* facial expressions in the same way. Of course, the cultures included in these studies all have considerable exposure to one another. Perhaps cultural contamination explains why

Is this expression of emotion universal across cultures?

these cultures share conventions about facial expressions; maybe the Japanese have seen so many "I Love Lucy" and "Dynasty" reruns that they have learned to recognize and interpret our most common facial expressions.

Ekman and Friesen (1971) attempted to circumvent the problem of cultural contamination by studying a preliterate tribe in New Guinea that had had no contact with Western civilization. In one study, they told natives stories that depicted a specific emotion—for example, "A man's child died and he felt sad." Then, they showed the natives a set of photographs, which were similar to those shown in Figure 3.2, and asked the natives to pick the photograph that best represented the emotion in the story. Interestingly, the New Guinea natives generally picked the same photographs that westerners selected. In other words, the two groups agreed that certain conventional facial expressions represented certain emotions.

Ekman and Friesen (cited in Ekman, 1972) also photographed posed New Guinea natives expressing various emotions. The researchers again told the natives stories (for example, "You are standing in the forest, and suddenly you see a wild boar about to attack you. You are afraid") and asked them to make an appropriate facial expression. Study participants in the United States later judged which of the

FIGURE 3.2   Photographic examples of four primary emotions. Which primary emotion do you think is being portrayed in each photograph?

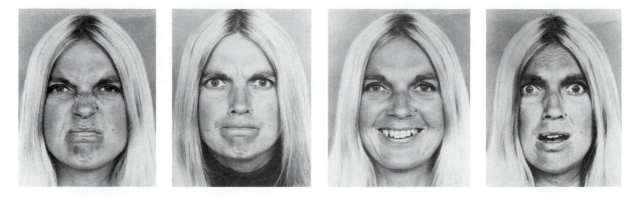

Answers: from left: disgust; anger; happiness; fear.

SOURCE: Ekman and Friesen (1975).

six primary emotions the person in the photograph intended to express. In general, these U.S. participants were able to categorize correctly the intended emotions of the New Guinea natives (see Figure 3.3).

Facial scoring systems.   The research we just discussed indicates that people can accurately judge primary emotions from facial expressions, but it cannot tell us how people accomplish this task. What facial expressions display each of the six primary emotions? In order to study more precisely the relation between facial expressions and emotions, researchers have developed objective facial scoring systems.

The *Facial Affect Scoring Technique* (FAST), developed by Ekman, Friesen, and Tompkins (1971), requires coders to score movements in each of three main areas of the face: the brow/forehead, the eyes/eyelids, and the lower face (cheeks, nose, mouth, and chin). Figure 3.4 provides some photographic examples of reference expressions in each facial area. The goal of FAST is to identify and distinguish among each of the six primary emotions in terms of the specific components of their facial expressions.

When using the FAST system, coders examine a photographed face, block out all but one facial area, and then compare the remaining exposed area (the eyes/eyelids, for example) with standard, sample photos illustrating the six primary emotions. The coder selects the standard photo in the FAST system that best matches the face being coded. Research shows that FAST scoring can reliably distinguish among different facial expressions. In one study, the FAST coding system was able to distinguish between photographed faces of people undergoing stress and those of people not undergoing stress (Ekman, Friesen, & Ellsworth, 1982b).

FIGURE 3.3   U.S. subjects' recognition of posed facial expressions of New Guinea natives.

Is the display of emotional expressions the same across cultures?

In this study, U.S. judges were asked to identify the primary emotion being displayed in photographs of facial expressions posed by New Guinea natives. The graph shows the percentage of correct judgments for each of the posed emotions.

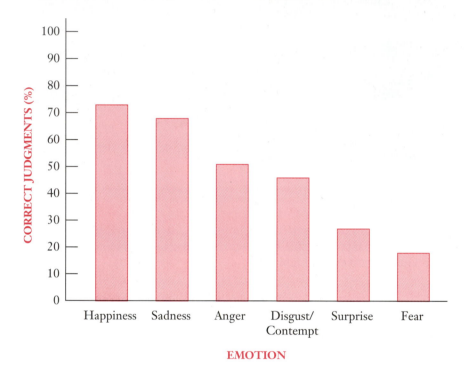

SOURCE: Based on Ekman and Friesen (1971), in Ekman (1972).

Clearly U.S. subjects were better at identifying some emotions (for example, happiness and sadness) than others (surprise and fear). New Guinea natives tended to confuse expressions of surprise and fear more than Americans, perhaps because in their lives the two tend to go together. Maybe this explains why their posed expressions of surprise and fear were judged rather poorly.

More recently, Ekman and Friesen (1982) have developed an even more microscopic approach to measuring facial movements—the *Facial Action Coding System* (FACS). This system codes very specific facial movements like "raising the inner brow," "raising the outer brow," and "lowering the brows." Often, a single muscle controls these movements. FACS is intended to measure any kind of facial move-

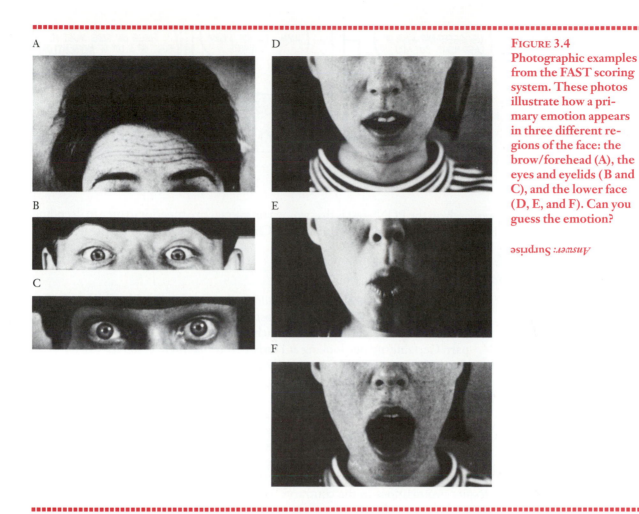

FIGURE 3.4
Photographic examples from the FAST scoring system. These photos illustrate how a primary emotion appears in three different regions of the face: the brow/forehead (A), the eyes and eyelids (B and C), and the lower face (D, E, and F). Can you guess the emotion?

Answer: Surprise

ment, not just emotional expressions. A number of studies suggest that the FACS system may be capable of validly identifying different emotions in the face (Ekman, Friesen, & Ancoli, 1980; Ekman & Friesen, 1982; Ekman, Hagar, & Friesen, 1981). Thus research that started with global judgments of emotion based on facial expressions has progressed in recent years to very precise and specific measurement of facial movement. Such precise measurements may lead to a better understanding of the relation between emotion and facial expression.

Besides measuring facial expressions more precisely, social psychologists have also begun to measure people's ability to decode (that is, perceive correctly) emotional expressions. The *Profile of Nonverbal Sensitivity*, or PONS test, presents videotaped samples of emotional expressions for subjects to identify (Rosenthal, Hall, DiMatteo, Rogers, & Archer, 1979). The PONS test is analogous to an intelligence test; both tests try to reliably assess individual differences, one in how "nonverbally perceptive" people are, the other in how "smart" people are. Research using the PONS test suggests that perceiving emotions may indeed be a general ability (Rosenthal et al., 1979; Funder & Harris, 1986). One reliable finding emerging from

Which do you believe more, Rose's words or her facial expressions?

research on the PONS test is that women on average are superior to men in decoding emotional expressions (Hall, 1984; see Chapter 10 for a broader discussion of sex differences).

Detecting Deception

His forehead was throbbing with maddened nerves, and he felt wildly excited, but his manner as he bent over his hostess' hand was as easy and graceful as ever. Perhaps one never seems so much at one's ease as when one has to play a part. Certainly no one looking at Dorian Gray that night could have believed that he had passed through a tragedy as horrible as any tragedy of our age.

—— *The Picture of Dorian Gray*, p. 175

Being able to detect deceptions is an important skill in social life. Deception and its detection affect social interactions ranging from intimate relations to international negotiations. As noted earlier, deception is a major complication in person perception that is absent in object perception. Can you tell when your friends *really* like your new haircut? Can you detect when your romantic partner is unfaithful, despite protestations to the contrary? And do you know when a politician is lying about his or her policies?

Recent research has focused on several important questions: How accurately do people detect deceptions in others? What cues give liars away? And what cues do people *think* (whether correctly or not) give liars away? (See Ekman, 1985; DePaulo, Stone, & Lassiter, 1985; and Zuckerman, DePaulo, & Rosenthal, 1981.) Note that we are addressing yet another accuracy question in person perception, but one more specific than those posed earlier.

Studies investigating deception and its detection take many forms. In one series of experiments, for example, after nurses viewed either a pleasant or a disturbing film they were asked to convince an interviewer that they had just viewed the pleasant film (Ekman & Friesen, 1974; Ekman, Friesen, O'Sullivan, & Scherer, 1980). Judges looking at videotapes of the nurses then tried to detect when the nurses were lying and when they were not. Other studies have asked subjects to pretend to like someone they in fact dislike and then see how well judges can detect this deception (for example, DePaulo, Lassiter, & Stone, 1982; DePaulo & Rosenthal, 1979).

How successful are people at detecting such deceptions? In general, the answer seems to be slightly better than chance, but not by much (DePaulo, Stone, & Lassiter, 1985). For example, suppose you see videotapes of 20 people, ten of whom are lying and ten of whom are telling the truth. If you randomly guess who is lying and who is telling the truth, then by chance alone you should be correct about 50 percent of the time. In studies of this kind, the overall accuracy of subjects who are trying to detect deception ranges from 45 percent to 60 percent—that is, just slightly above the accuracy level subjects would be expected to achieve by chance alone (Kraut, 1980).

Nonverbal cues of deception. Do some kinds of nonverbal cues reveal deception more accurately than others? Ekman and Friesen (1969a, 1974) hypothesized that in general the body (the limbs and torso) provides more valid nonverbal cues to deception than does the face. This might be so for two reasons: First, the face plays a central role in displaying emotions, and because others pay so much attention to it, we may devote considerable effort to its control. Second, physiological evidence suggests that we have finer muscular control over our faces than over other parts of the body.

A number of studies support the proposition that the body "leaks" more information about deception than the face. In one of these studies, Ekman & Friesen (1969a) had subjects view a filmed psychiatric interview. The woman in the film pretended to be happy and feeling well, when in fact she was quite distressed and had been recently hospitalized with schizophrenic symptoms. How well could judges see through the woman's facade after viewing the films? Interestingly, judges seemed to perceive the woman's tension and distress more accurately when they viewed films of her body alone; those who viewed only the woman's face were more taken in by her attempt to appear well.

In another carefully controlled study, Ekman and Friesen (1974) showed student nurses either a pleasant or a gruesome (for example, an amputation operation) film and asked them to act in all cases as if they were seeing something pleasant. The nurses were videotaped while watching these films. Clearly, the nurses who viewed the upsetting film were engaging in deception by pretending that the film was pleasant. Later, judges viewed tapes of either the nurses' faces or bodies and tried to determine when the nurses were lying. Again, judges more accurately detected deception from the nurses' bodies than from their faces (see Figure 3.5).

Vocal cues of deception. Ekman and Friesen's hypothesis focuses on nonverbal face and body cues, but other cues may also provide information about deception. For example, a person's spoken words contain both verbal information and *paralinguistic* cues (nonverbal qualities of speech such as tone of voice, speech nonfluencies, and pauses), which may offer cues to deception. Many studies have investigated how well people can detect deception from verbal content and voice quality.

A review of more than 30 such studies suggests several conclusions (DePaulo, Stone, & Lassiter, 1985). People more accurately detect deception from body or voice cues than from facial cues. Indeed, when subjects view only the face, they detect deception at a level that is not significantly better than what would be expected to occur by chance alone. Furthermore, subjects detect deception more accurately from the combination of body and voice cues than from the combination of body, voice, and face cues. Apparently, facial cues are misleading and including them actually makes people less accurate.

Another (perhaps surprising) conclusion is that the words people speak, even independent of tone of voice, convey accurate information about deception. Although we might think that people control the verbal content of their lies, this does not always seem to be the case.

FIGURE 3.5   **Detecting student nurses' deception from face or body.**

Which provides better cues for deception, the face or the body?

In this study by Ekman and Friesen (1974), subjects attempted to determine by viewing either face or body cues only whether student nurses' reactions were honest or deceptive. The graph shows the results for both kinds of cues in each of the two conditions.

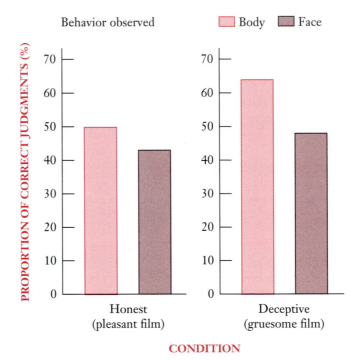

CONDITION

SOURCE: Based on Ekman and Friesen (1974).

Subjects were more accurate detecting honesty and deception when viewing bodies rather than faces. Note, however, that even when attending to body cues, subjects did not achieve high levels of accuracy.

Actual versus perceived cues of deception.   Many people think that "shifty eyes" and "stuttering" are valid cues to deception. Researchers have examined these and similar beliefs to determine which cues are in fact associated with deception and which cues are *perceived* to be associated with deception. Such research has identified a number of reliable cues to lying: speech hesitations, voice pitch, pupil dilation, and adaptors (self-directed gestures). Alas, as Figure 3.6 shows, these cues are not nec-

FIGURE 3.6   Nonverbal cues and deception.

What nonverbal cues actually are associated with deception?
What cues do people perceive *to be associated with deception?*

KIND OF CUE	ARE CUES ASSOCIATED WITH *ACTUAL* DECEPTION?	ARE CUES ASSOCIATED WITH *PERCEIVED* DECEPTION?
VOCAL		
Speech hesitations	YES: Liars hesitate more.	YES
Voice pitch	YES: Liars speak with higher pitch.	YES
Speech errors (stutters, stammers)	YES: Liars make more errors.	YES
Speech latency (pause before starting to speak or answer)	NO	YES: People think liars pause more.
Speech rate	NO	YES: People think liars talk slower.
Response length	YES: Liars give shorter answers.	NO
VISUAL		
Pupil dilation	YES: Liars show more dilation.	(No research data)
Adaptors (self-directed gestures)	YES: Liars touch themselves more.	NO
Blinking	YES: Liars blink more.	(No research data)
Postural shifts	NO	YES: People think liars shift more.
Smiling	NO	YES: People think liars smile less.
Gaze (eye contact)	NO	YES: People think liars engage in less eye contact.

SOURCE: Adapted from DePaulo, Stone, and Lassiter (1985).

The results presented in this table are based upon meta-analysis, a statistical procedure that combines the results of many studies and determines which findings are reliably obtained.

essarily the cues people in fact use in judging whether someone is lying (DePaulo, Stone, & Lassiter, 1985). For example, judges attend to speech hesitations and voice pitch as cues to deception, but not to pupil dilation and adaptors.

Detecting deception in real life.   Judging deception accurately is a skill most of us would like to possess in our personal relationships. For some, however, detecting deception is a professional duty. Customs inspectors and narcotics investigators, for example, must routinely detect and interview "suspicious-looking characters."

Deceptive Smiles

Because people have relatively good control over their faces, broad expressions such as smiles seem to have no consistent relationship to deception (DePaulo, Stone, & Lassiter, 1985; Zuckerman, DePaulo, & Rosenthal, 1981); on average people do not seem to smile more or less when they are lying. However, Ekman, Friesen, and O'Sullivan (1988) have recently argued that when researchers analyze smiles more carefully, they can demonstrate a difference between the smiles of truth tellers and liars. Specifically, the "masking smiles" of liars (smiles used to mask other expressions) may be held too long and may be mixed with traces of other facial expressions that belie a liar's true feelings.

To test their hypotheses, Ekman, Friesen, and O'Sullivan analyzed videotapes from earlier research in which student nurses were interviewed as they viewed either pleasant or upsetting films. The nurses were instructed to act as if they were always viewing a pleasant film, and thus they were attempting to deceive viewers each time they watched the upsetting films.

Ekman, Friesen, and O'Sullivan used the Facial Action Coding System described earlier to measure the movements occurring in the student nurses' faces. A student nurse was rated as showing an honest smile when she smiled without showing facial movements characteristic of negative emotions

(like sadness or disgust); she was rated as showing a masking smile when her smile was accompanied by other facial movements characteristic of negative emotions (see the accompanying photographic illustrations). The total number of honest and masking smiles was tallied for each subject during both honest and deceptive interviews.

The results of these observations showed that although student nurses did not show any differences in their overall degree of smiling during honest and deceptive interviews, they did show different kinds of smiling. Specifically, when student nurses lied, they showed fewer honest smiles and more masking smiles (see the accompanying bar chart).

How well did the kind of smile displayed predict when nurses were lying? Ekman, Friesen, and O'Sullivan were able to correctly classify the deceptive vs. honest interviews of 13 out of 31 student nurses based on their differential display of honest and masking smiles. The deceptive vs. honest interviews of two nurses were incorrectly classified based on their smiles, whereas the interviews of the remaining 16 nurses did not show sufficient differences in smiling patterns to permit classification. Thus honest and masking smiles were moderately good indicators of whether student nurses were lying or telling the truth.

Some of the student nurses originally videotaped were not able to

maintain their composure while viewing the upsetting films. About a fourth "confessed" part way through the interview and acknowledged they were viewing highly upsetting material. Thus the subjects studied by Ekman, Friesen, and O'Sullivan were a group of relatively able liars, which makes it all the more impressive that the researchers were able to identify nonverbal expressions that differentiated between honest and deceptive interviews.

Ekman, Friesen, and O'Sullivan believe that people can be trained to be more sensitive to the differences between honest and masking smiles. In addition to providing useful information that may enable people to detect deception better, their research demonstrates the worth of such methods as the Facial Action Coding System.

Photographs of real and masking smiles. The top left photograph shows a real happy smile. The other photographs show deceptive masking smiles (the subject was trying to appear happy while viewing disgusting or upsetting films). How are these smiles different?

The face with the real smile contains no hints of other emotions. In the lower left and upper right photos of masking smiles, a hint of disgust is displayed by the slightly raised upper lip. In the lower right photo, a hint of sadness is displayed by slightly pulled down lip corners.

SOURCE: Ekman, Friesen, and O'Sullivan (1988).

Real and masking smiles shown during honest and deceptive interviews. Is the display of real versus masking smiles a perfect indicator of deception? No, but on average, the pattern of smiling was different in student nurses' deceptive and honest interviews. Smiling was measured using the Facial Action Coding System.

SOURCE: Based on Ekman, Friesen, and O'Sullivan (1988).

They must also decide which people are not answering their interview questions honestly. Have such professionals honed their skills at detecting deception so that they are significantly superior to lay people?

In one study designed to answer this question, Kraut and Poe (1980) asked real airline passengers to try smuggling contraband (small packages of white powder that looked like illegal drugs) past a mock customs inspection conducted by a real U.S. Customs inspector at an airport. Other passengers did not smuggle contraband, and they told the truth when they went through Customs, whereas the "smugglers" lied. Both the lying "smugglers" and the truthful subjects were videotaped during the customs interview, and the videotapes were then shown to both experienced customs inspectors and to lay people, who were asked to decide which videotaped people should be physically inspected and which should not. Judges were informed that about half the videotaped subjects were attempting to smuggle contraband.

Were the judges accurate in identifying the "smugglers"? No. In fact, the smugglers were chosen slightly *less* often for inspection than the nonsmugglers! Were Customs officers better than lay people? No, both groups were equally poor. Interestingly, while neither Customs officers nor lay judges were very good at identifying smugglers, they generally agreed about who the guilty-looking people were. In particular, people with poor nonverbal comportment (including nervous mannerisms, poor eye contact, and speech hesitations) were more likely to be chosen for inspection, as were younger people and people of lower social status. This research again provides evidence that the cues people use to perceive deception in others are not necessarily valid ones.

Research by DePaulo and Pfeifer (1986) delivers yet another blow to presumed "experts" in detecting lies. Two groups — experienced federal law enforcement officers and undergraduates — were asked to detect deception in videotaped interviews. In these interviews, videotaped subjects answered questions about their attitudes on various topics; they lied in half their answers and told the truth in the other half. Were the officers better than the students at detecting lies? No, if anything they were slightly worse — students showed a mean accuracy of 54.3 percent correct identifications, whereas the officers showed a mean of 52.3 percent. But for both groups the results were just slightly above the level expected to occur by chance alone (50 percent).

Although the officers were no better than students at detecting deception, they expressed more confidence in their judgments than did students. Furthermore, they showed increasing confidence in their judgment as the trials progressed, whereas students did not. But clearly, the officers' confidence was unwarranted — they were no more accurate than the students, and they showed no increase in accuracy over time. DePaulo and Pfeifer suggest that the officers suffered from the mistaken belief that they could accurately detect deception in part because they never received adequate feedback about their successes and failures at detecting deception in their professional work.

Thus research suggests that such professional "lie detectors," like lay people, are not terribly good at detecting deception. Can people be trained to be better detectors of deception? Yes, at least to a degree. In order to improve people's accuracy in detecting deception, it may be necessary to both tell them explicitly what cues they should attend to and give them frequent and immediate feedback about their accuracy. For example, DePaulo, Lassiter, & Stone (1982) instructed some subjects to pay particular attention to voice tone (a valid cue of deception) in order to judge whether videotaped people were lying. Subjects who received these instructions were more accurate than a control group given no special instructions. Apparently, with proper instruction, we may be able to profit from social psychological research and become better detectors of deception. Such research may ultimately suggest ways to improve the skills of such people as Customs inspectors and law enforcement officers.

Direct Judgments: A Postscript

"... you must not say these extravagant things to me. You don't know everything about me. I think that if you did, even you would turn from me."

—— *The Picture of Dorian Gray*, p. 217

We began with a question: How do we know what we know about other people? The answer turns out to be complex, even for direct judgments of personality and emotion. Research on first impressions and on judgments of personality, emotion, and deception documents both accuracy and inaccuracy in person perception. Social psychological research, like *The Picture of Dorian Gray*, reveals that we are at best a step removed from those we perceive; surface appearances do not always reveal the truth about a person. It is perhaps a miracle of everyday life that we manage as well as we do in judging the people about us.

Summary

1. Research on person perception investigates how people judge the characteristics of others, the accuracy of those judgments, and the ways in which people form stable impressions of others from varied information.

2. Person perception differs from object perception in four ways: Person perception is more susceptible to inferential errors, people (but not objects) are perceived as causal agents, people (but not objects) sometimes attempt to deceive us, and person perception is more reactive than object perception.

3. First impressions are often based on physical appearances and nonverbal cues. People tend to consider nonverbal information to be more honest than verbal information. Five important kinds of nonverbal cues are emblems, illustrators, affect displays, regulators, and adaptors. Nonverbal behaviors frequently provide information about power and intimacy.

4. Judgments of personality and ability often show the primacy effect — the tendency for first information to carry more weight than later information.

5. The accuracy of personality judgments depends on the criteria of accuracy used, the behavior observed by judges, the statistical measure of accuracy used, and the specific traits being judged.

6. The categories of person perception are dictated by the perceiver as well as the perceived person. Good vs. bad social traits and good vs. bad intellectual traits are two fundamental dimensions along which we perceive others. Five more

specific dimensions of person perception often found in studies are extroversion, agreeableness, conscientiousness, anxiety, and intelligence.

7. Charles Darwin argued that emotional expressions are products of biological evolution, and thus such expressions are biologically innate and cross-culturally universal.

8. People can accurately recognize six primary emotions — happiness, sadness, surprise, fear, anger, and disgust — from facial expressions.

9. People in different cultures tend to show agreement in recognizing and displaying primary emotions.

10. The Facial Affect Scoring Technique (FAST) measures expressions in three areas of the face by comparing expressions with standard photographic examples of the six primary emotions. The Facial Action Coding System (FACS) measures specific facial movements, often resulting from the movements of single muscles. The Profile of Nonverbal Sensitivity, or PONS test, assesses people's ability to accurately recognize emotional expressions.

11. People are able to detect deception in others at levels only slightly better than those expected to occur by chance alone. People can detect deception better from body cues and voice cues than from facial expressions. The cues that actually relate to deception are not necessarily the ones people attend to in judging deception.

12. Experts such as Customs officers prove to be no better than lay people at detecting deception. Research may provide ways to train people to be better at detecting deception.

Glossary

Adaptors: Nonverbal behaviors consisting of self-directed movements and gestures

Affect displays: Nonverbal expressions of emotion

Attribution: The process by which people infer the *causes* of other peoples' behavior

Differential accuracy: The ability of judges to ascertain differences in others' personality traits; one component of accuracy in judging personality

Direct judgments: Quick judgments of others based on their surface appearance and behavior

Display rules: Cultural rules that regulate the display of emotions

Emblems: Nonverbal behaviors (like the "okay" sign) that are learned, cultural conventions and thus can be assigned specific meanings

Facial Action Coding System (FACS): A system for measuring small facial movements that often result from the movement of single muscles

Facial Affect Scoring Technique (FAST): A system for coding expressions in three areas of the face by comparing expressions to standard photographs illustrating the six primary emotions

False consensus effect: The tendency for individuals to assume that other people behave more similarly to them than they do in fact

Illustrators: Nonverbal gestures, like showing the size of an object, that physically illustrate a concept

Nonverbal behavior: Behavior other than linguistic speech that often conveys information about others; examples include gestures, eye contact, personal space, and touching

Paralinguistic cues: Cues in speech (such as tone of voice) other than the linguistic content that may provide information about the speaker

Person perception: The process by which people judge the traits and characteristics of others

Primacy effect: Occurs when initial information is weighted more heavily than later information in forming impressions about others

Primary emotions: The basic emotions that can be accurately judged from facial expressions — happiness, sadness, surprise, fear, anger, and disgust

Profile of Nonverbal Sensitivity (PONS test): A test designed to measure people's ability to accurately judge emotional expressions

Regulators: Nonverbal behaviors, such as gestures accompanying conversations, that serve to structure social interactions

Social cognition: The subfield of person perception research that focuses on how people encode, process, organize, and remember information about others

Social Relations Model: A statistical approach to assessing the accuracy of judgments about others that assumes that judgments are a function of the rater, the person being judged, and the unique relationship between the two

Stereotype accuracy: Accuracy in judging others' self-ratings that is due to the judge's knowledge of how people in general rate themselves

Voir dire: The pretrial interview during which attorneys question prospective jurors in order to eliminate jurors who may be prejudiced against their client or case

Why do you think President Lyndon Johnson is howling with his dog? What do you think his grandson thinks about his strange behavior?

Why do you do the things you do?
Why do you do these things?
Why do you rush at the world all alone,
    fighting mad battles that aren't your own?

Why do you do the things you do?
Why do you do these things?
Why do you batter at walls that won't break?
Why do you give when it's natural to take?
Where do you see all the good that you see?
And what do you want of me?
What do you want of me?

—— lyrics from "What Do You Want of Me?"
in *Man of La Mancha*

CHAPTER 4

Attribution

*I*n the song "What Do You Want of Me?" the serving wench, Aldonza, puzzles over the strange behavior of Don Quixote, the Man of La Mancha. Is he a lunatic, a harmless eccentric, or a saint? Why does Don Quixote charge about the world fighting imaginary evil? Why does he follow the rules of a quaint but outdated chivalry? Ultimately, of course, Aldonza wants to understand how Don Quixote's strange behavior will affect her.

Like Aldonza, most of us want to understand why other people behave as they do. We do not passively observe others' behavior, but rather ponder it and speculate about the causes of what we observe. *Attribution theories* focus on the thought processes that people use to explain their own and others' behavior. Such thought processes are fundamentally important in everyday life: If Aldonza decides that Don Quixote's strange behavior is due to insanity, she may decide to keep her distance, but if his behavior is due to saintliness, she may decide to follow him on his quest.

Like Aldonza, you likely respond to people's behavior based on the perceived causes of that behavior. You are angrier when you perceive that someone injures you "on purpose" than when you perceive that someone injures you accidentally. You are more likely to help a man who collapses if you perceive his collapse to be due to sickness rather than to drunkenness. And you will probably admire someone who makes a large charitable donation more if you perceive the cause of the donation to be compassion rather than a big tax deduction. In everyday life it's important to understand *why* people do what they do.

97

Attribution Processes: Internal and External Causes

Fritz Heider initiated the modern social psychological study of attribution processes. In his influential book, *The Psychology of Interpersonal Relations* (1958), Heider attempted to analyze philosophically the "naive psychology" that people use every day in thinking about others; he was not so much interested in the true causes of human behavior as in its perceived causes. Heider argued that an important part of the attribution process is deciding whether behavior is internally or externally caused. For example, if you decide that Don Quixote runs around in tin armor because he's insane, then you are offering an *internal* explanation for his behavior — the cause is a trait or characteristic inside him. If you conclude instead that he engages in battle to gain riches, then you are offering an *external* explanation for his behavior — the cause is outside of him, in the environment or social setting.

Consider another, less exotic example: Suppose your classmate Jim just flunked his first social psychology exam. If you decide that he flunked because of problems with his girlfriend, lack of sleep, and his mother's recent illness, you are offering *external* explanations (that is, environmental or situational causes) for his behavior. If you decide that Jim is simply stupid, then you are offering an *internal* explanation for his behavior (his failure is due to an internal trait). Attribution theories often try to answer the question, "When do we make internal attributions and when do we make external attributions?"

We may also try to answer other important attributional questions about people's behavior (Wimer & Kelley, 1982; Ross & Fletcher, 1985; Weiner, Frieze, Kukla, Reed, Rest, & Rosenbaum, 1972). For example, we often want to know whether behavior results from *stable* or *unstable* causes. Stable causes are permanent and enduring, whereas unstable causes are temporary and fluctuating. The distinction between perceived stable and unstable causes is independent of the distinction between perceived internal and external causes: Some causes are perceived to be both internal and stable ("Jim flunked because he is stupid"). Such stable, internal causes are often referred to as *dispositional* causes. Other causes may be perceived to be internal but unstable (for example, a person's effort — "Jim didn't study for the last test, but he may for the next one"). Similarly, some causes are perceived to be external and stable (for example, task difficulty — "Social psychology is a very difficult class, and that's why Jim did poorly on the test"), whereas others are perceived to be external and unstable (for example, transient situational factors — "The student sitting next to Jim during his exam kept sneezing, which distracted him"). These four kinds of causal attributions are summarized in Figure 4.1.

Although there are many ways we can explain others' behavior, the distinction between perceived internal and external causes has been central to attribution re-

Does Peppermint Patty's teacher explain her behavior internally or externally?

FIGURE 4.1   Two dimensions of causal attribution.

What dimensions underlie our explanations of behavior?

Each quadrant in Weiner's two-dimensional classification produces a distinct type of causal explanation. Think of a time when you succeeded at some task and of a time when you failed. How do you explain your success? Your failure? Place your explanations in the table below.

STABLE/UNSTABLE DIMENSION

INTERNAL/EXTERNAL DIMENSION		Stable	Unstable
	Internal	Dispositions; traits; level of ability or intelligence; physical characteristics	Effort; mood; physical state
	External	Degree of task difficulty; environmental helps and hindrances	Good or bad luck; opportunity; transient situational factors

SOURCE: Adapted from Weiner et al. (1972). Copyright 1972 by General Learning Corporation. Used with permission of Silver Burdett Company.

The two dimensions of attribution presented here often have been used to analyze the explanations people offer for their successes and failures. As we'll see later in this chapter, depressed people tend to attribute their failures to stable internal causes ("I'm stupid") and their successes to unstable external causes ("I was lucky"). Such attributions often aggravate their depression.

search, and this distinction cannot be overemphasized. The perception of internal and external causes is important in everyday life as well as in attribution theories: Did the new senatorial candidate come out against legalized abortion because she really believes in this position (internal explanation) or because she was pressured to do so by special interest groups (external explanation)? Your answers may determine whether or not you vote for her.

Attributions and Emotion

Attribution processes can influence how people perceive their emotions. In an influential theory, Stanley Schachter and Jerome Singer (1962) argued that for emotional experience to occur, a person must experience physiological arousal (such as increased heart rate, perspiration, or trembling) and consider that arousal to result from an emotion. The second requirement thus suggests that emotional experience depends in part on how we attribute our arousal (London & Nisbett, 1974).

In a classic experiment, Schachter and Singer (1962) attempted to manipulate separately subjects' physiological arousal and their emotional attributions. Under the guise that they were studying the effects of a new vitamin on vision, the researchers administered injections to subjects. Some subjects received epinephrine (also known as adrenaline), a stimulant. Control subjects received injections of saline solution. Subjects receiving epinephrine were either correctly informed of the side effects of the drug (". . . your hands will start to shake, your heart will start to pound") or were misinformed

(". . . your feet will feel numb, you will have an itching sensation over parts of your body"). Schachter and Singer hypothesized that subjects with unexplained arousal (the misinformed subjects) would be particularly likely to experience strong emotions, for they would falsely attribute their drug-induced arousal to their emotions.

After administering the injections, the researchers manipulated subjects' emotional attributions by placing them either in a setting designed to elicit anger or in one designed to elicit euphoria. In the anger-eliciting condition, subjects sat in a room with another subject (actually a confederate), and both completed annoying questionnaires, which asked subjects, among other things, to nominate members of their family who "need psychiatric care" and "do not bathe or wash regularly." As he filled in his questionnaire, the confederate became increasingly angry and finally ripped up his questionnaire and stomped out of the room. In the euphoria-eliciting condition, subjects waited with a confederate in a messy room containing papers, folders, and a hula

hoop. The confederate crumpled pieces of paper and "shot" them like basketballs into a trash can. He then made paper airplanes and threw them across the room, built towers out of manila folders, and finally twirled the hula hoop. In other words, he acted silly and happy.

Subjects' angry and euphoric behaviors were measured while they waited with the confederate (for example, did they make angry comments in the anger-eliciting condition or join in the confederate's play in the euphoria-eliciting condition?), and afterwards subjects rated their anger and happiness on 5-point scales. In the anger-eliciting condition, misinformed subjects showed a tendency to report being more angry and to show more angry behaviors than did informed subjects. In the euphoria-eliciting condition, misinformed subjects tended to report being happier and to show more play behaviors than informed subjects. It is important to note, however, that these observed effects were rather weak and inconsistent and that the total pattern of findings was complex. The

Our Preference for Internal Explanations

All other things being equal, people often prefer internal over external explanations of behavior (Heider, 1958; Ross, 1977). For example, we're more likely to believe that Don Quixote behaves strangely because he's "crazy" than because of external pressures.

Consider another example: You come to your social psychology class one day and observe your instructor dancing alone at the front of the room. How would you explain this strange behavior? Perhaps you decide that your teacher is conducting a classroom experiment to see how students react to unusual behavior in teachers. Or maybe you decide instead that your teacher has had a mental breakdown and that you'd better call the mental health authorities. Notice that both of these explanations postulate *internal* causes (either your teacher's intention to conduct an experiment data provided some support for the hypothesis that unexplained arousal (for example, arousal caused by injected epinephrine) can intensify the experience of situationally induced emotions.

The Schachter and Singer experiment has been controversial (Reisenzein, 1983), and a number of studies have failed to replicate its findings (Marshall & Zimbardo, 1979; Maslach, 1979). Despite this, it remains a classic study that contributed to the development of attribution theory and stimulated research on a number of important topics. Today, it is viewed as the first of many studies on *misattribution*, which occurs when subjects are led to attribute their behavior (often arousal) incorrectly. For example, Schachter and Singer's "misinformed" subjects misattributed their arousal insofar as they decided it was due to the emotional setting and not to the injection they received.

Misattribution research has since proceeded along two complementary lines. Some studies intensify emotional experience by creating extraneous arousal (for example, through drugs or physical exercise)

and then inducing subjects to misattribute this arousal to emotions. Others reduce the perceived intensity of emotions by leading subjects to misattribute real emotional arousal to external sources.

Research by Zillmann and Bryant (1974) provides a good example of the first kind of study. Subjects were aroused through physical exercise (for example, riding an exercise bicycle) and then placed in an experiment in which they could aggress against a confederate who had earlier attacked them. Interestingly, subjects aroused through exercise were more aggressive than unaroused control subjects. Apparently, lingering arousal from one source can intensify emotional responses in an unrelated setting. (This example also illustrates that misattribution studies can shed light on other topics in social psychology, in this case aggression.)

A recent study by Olson (1988) provides a good example of the second kind of misattribution study. Canadian college students were asked to perform a somewhat anxiety-provoking task—deliver a speech before a video camera.

Some subjects were falsely informed that the purpose of the study was to investigate the effects of "subliminal noise." Some were further informed that during their speech they would be exposed to subliminal noise that "makes a person feel unpleasantly aroused." Thus these subjects could attribute the anxiety they felt while speaking to be due to the "subliminal noise." After videotaping subjects' speeches, researchers counted their nervous speech errors (stutters, stammers, "ahs"). Subjects induced to misattribute their arousal to the "subliminal noise" showed fewer anxious errors in the speeches. In other words, anxious people may be somewhat calmed if they can misattribute their arousal to an external cause.

There are undoubtedly limits to how much we can lead people to misattribute their upsets and anxieties in everyday life (Försterling, 1985; Reisenzein, 1983). However, as we shall see later in this chapter, redirecting people's attributions can sometimes serve therapeutic ends.

or your teacher's "insanity"). You would probably offer an external explanation for your teacher's dancing only if you perceived an overwhelmingly obvious external cause. For example, if you saw an irate student pointing a gun at your teacher and saying, "Dance, or I'll fill you full of lead," you would have an obvious external explanation for your teacher's behavior.

Why do we often prefer internal to external explanations of behavior? Heider (1958) offered one possible answer: We frequently fail to distinguish adequately between behaviors and their underlying causes, and this failure leads us to make internal attributions. In Heider's words, we show a tendency to "assimilate acts to people." It is very easy for us to move from a behavioral observation ("Don Quixote does crazy things") to inferred internal traits ("Don Quixote is crazy"). Notice that

Lt. Colonel Oliver North was charged with diverting government funds and destroying government documents. Do you think he behaved as he did for internal reasons (his political attitudes) or for external reasons (he was ordered to do so by "higher-ups")?

the first statement is about Don Quixote's *behavior*, whereas the second is about his internal *disposition*. Although we may know intellectually that behavior doesn't always reflect a person's traits, attitudes, wishes, or intentions, nonetheless we often assume that it does.

For example, when we view TV shows, movies, or plays, we generally attribute actors' behaviors to their characters, not to the fact that they're playing a role. Our bias in favor of internal explanations is illustrated even more dramatically when we assume that actors have traits similar to those of the characters they portray. For example, is Leonard Nimoy, the actor who plays Mr. Spock in "Star Trek," cold, logical, and unemotional in real life? Many of us falsely assume so.

Heider offered another reason why we emphasize internal explanations so much: We perceptually focus more on people and their behavior than on the surrounding situation. In Heider's words, "behavior engulfs the field." Let's return to the example of your teacher dancing in front of the class. If this were to happen, you'd probably focus most of your attention on your teacher's strange behavior rather than on the surrounding situation. Heider argued that behavior is generally more salient and "attention-grabbing" than the situation, and because our attention is usually focused on people, we tend to see them, rather than the setting, as the cause of their behavior.

Heider (1958) posed many philosophical questions about attribution: What are the important dimensions of attribution (such as internal vs. external explanations)? Do people show errors and biases in attributing the causes of others' behavior (for example, do they prefer internal over external explanations)? How do people perceive the ways in which different causes combine? And how do people make attributions about specific domains of behavior (such as attributions of responsibility)? However, although he carefully analyzed how people actively interpret their social world and attribute causes to others' behavior, Heider did not propose general theories of attribution that could be proved or disproved by experimental research. It remained for later theorists to flesh out theories of attribution into more testable sorts of propositions.

SANCHO:	*(Patiently)* My master calls you Dulcinea.
ALDONZA:	*(Glowering)* Why?
SANCHO:	I don't know, but I can tell you from experience that knights have their own language for everything, and it's better not to ask questions because it only gets you into trouble. . . .
ALDONZA:	Well, what's he *want*?
SANCHO:	I'm getting to it!
	"—And send to me a token of thy fair esteem that I may carry as my standard into battle."
ALDONZA:	What kind of a token?
SANCHO:	He says generally it's a silken scarf.
ALDONZA:	Your master's a crackbrain!

—— *Man of La Mancha*, pp. 33–34

In *Man of La Mancha*, Don Quixote is actually Alonso Quijana, a Spanish nobleman suffering from delusions that he is a knight-errant. Sancho is his faithful "squire" and sidekick who accompanies him on his misadventures. When Don Quixote arrives at Aldonza's "castle" (actually an inn where Aldonza works as serving wench and whore), he perceives her as the lady "Dulcinea," who embodies all that is noble and virtuous in women. Aldonza faces an attributional choice concerning the reason Don Quixote treats her with so much deference and respect: Either he wants something from her or he's crazy. Aldonza quickly decides that Don Quixote is a "crackbrain"—that is, she offers an internal, dispositional explanation for his behavior.

How does she arrive at this conclusion? This is exactly the kind of question addressed by attribution theories. Two particularly important theories of attribution emerged in the 1960s: Jones and Davis's (1965) theory of correspondent inferences, and Kelley's (1967) cube model of attribution. Let's discuss each of these approaches in detail so that we may better understand some of the thought processes Aldonza used to reach her conclusion about Don Quixote.

Jones and Davis's Theory of Correspondent Inferences

Suppose you observe Susan donate $1,000 to the American Cancer Society; will you infer an internal trait from this behavior—for example, that Susan is "generous"? If you indeed decide Susan is generous, you are making a *correspondent inference* (Jones & Davis, 1965)—the inference that her behavior (donating money) corresponds to some underlying disposition or trait (generosity).

Jones and Davis (1965) identified several logical rules of thumb that people use to make correspondent inferences—that is, to infer dispositions from behavior. (Remember, we can never directly observe dispositions—such as attitudes and traits—in other people; the best we can do is observe behavior and its effects.) These

The principle of social desirability. This Chinese student single-handedly stopped a line of tanks. Because his behavior is so unexpected, we are likely to attribute his behavior to an internal disposition — he is "courageous" or "crazy."

rules of thumb help to explain how we make the inferential leap from observing behavior to inferring underlying dispositions.

Social desirability.   Jones and Davis argued that when we try to infer dispositions from behavior, we tend to consider socially undesirable behavior to be more informative than socially desirable behavior. (In this context, "socially desirable" means "normative" or "expected in this situation.") For example, we typically expect people to be somber at funerals, friendly and talkative at parties, and studious and attentive in classrooms. Such behavior is socially desirable. Thus a smile at a funeral is more informative about a person's traits than is a smile at a party.

Jones and Davis noted that we are more likely to make strong dispositional conclusions about behavior that is unexpected or socially undesirable in a given setting. This principle of social desirability is implicit in the song lyrics at the beginning of this chapter. Aldonza asks Don Quixote, "Why do you batter at walls that won't break? Why do you give when it's natural to take?" Because such behavior is atypical, it demands explanation. Numerous studies suggest that people are most likely to try spontaneously to figure out the causes of behavior when that behavior is unexpected (Weiner, 1985).

∎∎∎∎∎∎∎∎∎∎∎∎∎∎∎∎∎∎∎∎∎∎∎∎∎

The principle of social desirability. Does this woman's strange and unexpected appearance lead you to strongly attribute internal traits to her?

Jones and McGillis (1976) point out that our expectations about what is socially desirable may come from two sources. *Category-based expectancies* are kinds of expectations we associate with groups of people. For example, we would probably be surprised if a member of the Republican National Committee espoused legalized marijuana, free love, and socialism. *Target-based expectancies* are expectations based on knowledge gathered about a particular person. Thus we'd likely be quite surprised if Queen Elizabeth announced she was forming a new rock group. However we form our expectancies, the principle remains that unexpected behaviors seem more informative about a person than expected ones.

This principle was demonstrated nicely by a study in which subjects listened to tapes of a man applying for the job of "astronaut" or "submarine crew member" (Jones, Davis, & Gergen, 1961). In some tapes, the applicant described himself as having traits that matched the job, whereas in other tapes he described himself as having traits inappropriate for the job. For example, an astronaut (at least in the early 1960s, when space capsules carried just one person) should possess "inner-directed" traits that enable him to work well by himself. A submarine crew member, on the other hand, must be "outer-directed" — able to relate well to others in a confined space. The job candidate described himself as possessing either inner-directed or outer-directed traits. Subjects believed the applicants' self-descriptions more when they were inappropriate for the job—that is, when they were socially undesirable. An applicant for the job of astronaut who says he "needs to be around other people" must really mean it, for that's such an unexpected thing to say. On the other hand, if the applicant says he "works well in isolation," you're not sure if he's really being truthful or if he's just saying that because it's what the situation calls for.

Common and noncommon effects.   According to Jones and Davis, not only do we observe the social desirability of behaviors, we also analyze their consequences or *effects*. Then we try to infer something about the person's dispositions by working backward. When different behaviors (for example, reading books and going to school) have the same effects (they educate you), they are said to have *common effects*. When different behaviors (reading books and going to parties) have different effects (one educates you, the other improves your social life), they are said to have *noncommon effects*. Jones and Davis argued that behaviors with unique noncommon effects lead to stronger inferences about a person's dispositions than do behaviors with common effects.

To illustrate, suppose your friend Ralph is shopping for a new car. He has been looking at models made by Toyota, Volkswagen, and Mercedes. Some effects are common to the purchase of any of these cars—for example, whichever he buys, Ralph will probably get a reliable car, and he will definitely get a foreign car. However, only one of these three makes is a very high-status car. This conferral of status, then, is a unique noncommon effect that occurs only if Ralph buys a Mercedes. And if Ralph indeed buys a Mercedes, you may then say to yourself, "Aha, I knew it! Ralph is a status-seeker!" In drawing that conclusion, you used the unique noncommon effect of Ralph's behavior to infer his personality traits.

Jones and Davis argue that correspondent inferences are strongest when behavior has only a few noncommon effects; that is, a behavior is perceived to be most "diagnostic" of an underlying trait when that behavior has a small number of noncommon effects. These general propositions have been supported by research (see, for example, Newtson, 1974).

In general, Jones and Davis's model holds that people carry out a kind of logical information-processing procedure. We observe behavior and its effects, and then we try to work back and figure out what traits led to these behaviors. Jones and Davis's principles of social desirability and of common and noncommon effects both assume that people possess a considerable amount of hidden social knowledge. The only way you can decide whether a behavior is socially desirable, for example, is to know a lot about individuals and groups in various settings. Similarly, before you can make correspondent inferences based on the principle of common and noncommon effects, you must know the plausible effects of many different behaviors. In order for these theories to be complete, then, they must address both the nature of the social knowledge that feeds into your thought processes and describe the thought processes as well.

Hedonic relevance and personalism.   Jones and Davis describe two principles that might be thought of as biases in the way we infer dispositions from behavior. The first, the notion of *hedonic relevance*, holds that we tend to make stronger dispositional attributions when behavior affects us directly, such as causing us pleasure or pain.

More broadly, this could be taken to mean that behavior that inflames our passions leads to stronger dispositional attributions than behavior that does not. For example, if Ralph, a born-again Christian, and Robert, an agnostic not much concerned with religion, happen upon a street demonstration in which a woman burns a Bible, Robert might shrug his shoulders and say, "Well that's interesting—another demonstration," whereas Ralph might scream, "Look at that demented criminal, burning a Bible!" Ralph clearly comes to a stronger dispositional conclusion about the woman than does Robert.

The second principle, *personalism*, holds that behavior targeted at you or intended to affect you will lead to stronger dispositional attributions than behavior that is not. Kids who throw eggs at your neighbor's car are just bad kids, but kids who throw eggs at *your* car are "juvenile delinquents."

Kelley's Cube Model of Attribution

Jones and Davis's principles of attribution specify some of the thought processes that people use to infer dispositional (that is, stable internal) causes of behavior. However, these principles generally apply only to *single* observations of behavior. In real life we see not only isolated episodes of behaviors but also repeated instances of people's behavior at different times and places. For example, your sense of what causes a close relative's behavior is based on many, many experiences. Similarly, your notions about the personality of the President of the United States are based on repeated observations. A model of attribution developed by Harold Kelley (1967) helps us analyze how people mentally process multiple observations of behavior.

Consistency, consensus, and distinctiveness information.

Kelley argued that three kinds of information are crucial in determining our attributions: consistency, consensus, and distinctiveness information. *Consistency* refers to how behavior varies across situations and time (for example, does Cathy talk a lot at home, at parties, and in seminar classes?). *Consensus* refers to how a person's behavior compares with other people's behavior (is Cathy more or less talkative than Charles, Sally, or Robin?). Finally, *distinctiveness* refers to how behavior varies as a function of its target (for example, does Cathy's talkativeness vary when she talks with her professor, her boyfriend, or her mother?).

The covariation principle.

How do we decide what "causes" a behavior? According to Kelley's *covariation principle*, we attribute a behavior to the cause with which it covaries over time. This rather abstract statement is one answer to a question that has occupied philosophers' attention for some time: How do we know when one thing "causes" another? Some philosophers have argued that we can never directly observe cause and effect; all we can really observe is correlation, or "covariation" (Einhorn & Hogarth, 1986). For example, we think that clouds "cause" rain because the two go together—whenever it rains, it is also cloudy. Kelley applies this same notion—that observed covariation of two occurrences is often perceived as causation—to attribution. He argues that when we observe situations, people, or targets correlated with behavior, we tend to see them as being the "cause" of the behavior.

Let's make the covariation principle more concrete with an example. Suppose you observe Seymour make a pass at Lolita in a local singles' bar. Why do you think Seymour behaved as he did? Perhaps it's something about Seymour; perhaps

Seymour is "lecherous." (This is an internal attribution.) Perhaps Lolita is an irre-sistible woman (an external attribution). Or perhaps all men act that way in singles' bars (an external, situational attribution).

According to Kelley, in order to decide on a cause for Seymour's behavior, you must look at consistency, consensus, and distinctiveness information. Each of these three kinds of information can be pictorially represented on the sides of a cube (see Figure 4.2). To acquire consistency information, you look at Seymour in situations in addition to the singles' bar—in the classroom, at parties, and at work. To collect consensus information, you compare Seymour's behavior with that of other men—for example, the behavior of Tom, Dick, and Harry. And, finally, to gather dis-tinctiveness information, you look at several "targets" of Seymour's behavior (in this case, women)—namely, Susie, Marcie, Lolita, and (just for variety) Sister Mary Teresa.

Kelley's covariation principle now becomes simple to understand. If Seymour's behavior varies with situations (for example, Seymour often makes passes in singles' bars, less frequently at parties, and not at all in classes or at work), then you will likely conclude that the situation "caused" his behavior. If, however, the behavior of "making passes at women" seems to covary systematically across people (Seymour makes lots of passes, but Tom, Dick, and Harry don't), then you are more likely to attribute his behavior to an internal cause—you might decide that Seymour is "highly sexed." Finally, if behavior covaries with targets (for example, Seymour always makes passes at Lolita, sometimes at Susie and Marcie, and never at Sister Mary Teresa), then you are more likely to attribute his behavior to an external cause—the women.

Internal versus external attributions in Kelley's model.   Kelley argues that certain patterns of consistency, consensus, and distinctiveness information induce us to make internal attributions, whereas other patterns induce us to make external attributions. For example, high consistency, low consensus, and low distinctiveness information leads to internal attributions. To return to our example, suppose you learn that: (1) Seymour is always making passes at women—at bars, at parties, and even in class-rooms and at work, (2) Seymour makes more passes at women than does Tom or Dick or Harry, and (3) it doesn't matter who the woman is—he makes passes at Susie, Marcie, Lolita, and once even made a pass at Sister Mary Teresa! On the basis of this information it seems quite reasonable to attribute Seymour's behavior to a strong internal cause: Seymour is a "lecherous" person.

Other patterns of data in Kelley's attributional cube induce us to make external attributions. For example, high consistency over a given target, high consensus, and high distinctiveness lead to an external, "target" attribution. This time, suppose you learn that: (1) Seymour makes a pass at Lolita whenever he sees her and in whatever setting he sees her, (2) Tom, Dick, and Harry also makes passes at Lolita, and (3) the men aren't interested in other women—they yawn at Marcie and Susie, ignore Sister Mary Teresa, but go crazy with Lolita. Now it seems quite reasonable to attribute Seymour's behavior to Lolita's "sex appeal."

Perhaps we can understand now why Aldonza decided that Don Quixote was a "crackbrain." Don Quixote engaged in strange behaviors in many different settings (he attacked windmills that he thought were "giants," he imagined a simple wash basin to be the "Golden Helmet of Mambrino," and he treated a serving wench as if she were a "noblewoman"). He was more eccentric than anyone else Aldonza knew.

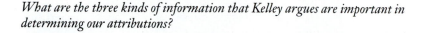

FIGURE 4.2   Kelley's cube model of attribution.

What are the three kinds of information that Kelley argues are important in determining our attributions?

The behavior to be explained: Seymour makes a pass at Lolita

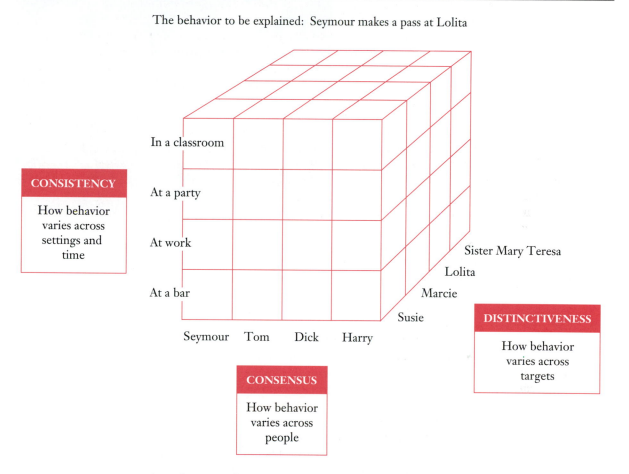

CONSISTENCY

How behavior varies across settings and time

In a classroom

At a party

At work

At a bar

Sister Mary Teresa

Lolita

Marcie

Susie

DISTINCTIVENESS

How behavior varies across targets

Seymour   Tom   Dick   Harry

CONSENSUS

How behavior varies across people

According to Kelley, the kind of explanation we give for a behavior depends on a combination of consistency, consensus, and distinctiveness information.

Note that to have complete information in this case, you would have to observe every man in every setting and with every woman. Of course, in everyday life we rarely have such complete information about people's behavior. Kelley's model is thus an idealized version of real-life attribution processes.

Don Quixote, the Man of La Mancha, and his manservant, Sancho.

And finally, Don Quixote displayed his peculiar behaviors around all the people with whom he interacted — Aldonza, Sancho, the innkeeper, and so on. Clearly his strange behavior must be due to something inside him; he must be deranged.

Kelley's model tested.   Kelley's model of attribution depicts human beings as highly rational and as logical information processors. In this regard, his model is an idealized version of the attribution process. In a sense, it describes how a good statistician might analyze behavioral information in order to determine whether behavior is "caused" by situations, personal traits, or targets.

Do people actually process information in the way Kelley's model suggests? McArthur (1972) attempted to answer this question by presenting subjects with stories in which consistency, consensus, and distinctiveness information varied systematically. For example, first a subject was given a brief description of a behavior: "John laughed at the comedian." Then the subject received consistency, consensus, and distinctiveness information: "John has almost always laughed at this comedian" (high consistency), "Other people also laugh at this comedian" (high consensus), and "John also laughs a lot at other comedians" (low distinctiveness).

Various subjects received all the possible combinations of low and high consistency, consensus, and distinctiveness information, and then they were asked to explain why John laughed at the comedian. The results of McArthur's study suggest several interesting conclusions. First, over all possible combinations of information, subjects tended to prefer internal attributions (John's laughter was due to some trait of John's). These were followed in overall frequency by unstable external attributions (that is, John's laughter was due to some unique occurrence, such as "John was drunk") and finally by external, stimulus attributions ("John's laughter was due to the comedian, who was hilarious"). This preference for internal attributions provides research support for Heider's speculation that people tend to prefer internal explanations of behavior to external ones.

McArthur's data also showed that, at least in general terms, people do seem to process information in the way Kelley's model suggests. That is, patterns of information that the model predicted should produce internal attributions did in fact lead subjects more often to make internal attributions, whereas patterns expected to produce external attributions did in fact lead subjects more often to make external attributions.

Besides showing that subjects' attributions followed Kelley's model, McArthur's data also pointed to important ways in which subjects' attributions differed from the model's predictions. For example, Kelley's model seems to assume that subjects consider consistency, consensus, and distinctiveness information equally in arriving at their attributions. But McArthur's data suggested that subjects use consensus information *less* than consistency and distinctiveness information. In terms of our example, this means that in trying to figure out why Seymour made a pass at Lolita you pay attention to how Seymour behaves in various situations and with various women, but you don't care as much about how Tom, Dick, or Harry behaves. Other studies have tended to confirm McArthur's findings (Karaz & Perlman, 1975; Zuckerman, 1978; Ruble & Feldman, 1976).

▪▪▪▪▪▪▪▪▪▪▪▪▪▪▪▪▪▪▪▪▪▪▪▪▪
Causal Schemas

In figuring out the causes of others' behavior we do not always ponder consistency, consensus, and distinctiveness information in detail; sometimes we use mental shortcuts. Kelley (1972) referred to such shortcuts as *causal schemas* — simple mental models of causality that allow us to make attributions without fully analyzing all the data available to us. Causal schemas also embody our hidden assumptions about how different kinds of attributed causes combine to influence behavior.

The discounting principle. One pervasive causal schema is the *discounting principle*, which holds that we assign less weight to a given cause of a behavior if another plausible cause is also present (Kelley, 1972). A concrete example should help clarify this principle. In *Man of La Mancha*, Don Quixote's niece, Antonia, wants her befuddled uncle pursued and restrained. She claims that she's acting out of the highest altruistic motives (thus, she offers an internal explanation for her behavior). But we learn that her upcoming marriage and the receipt of a large inheritance depends on her restoring Alonso Quijuana (who thinks he's Don Quixote) to sanity. Because of the obvious (external) explanation we have for her behavior (she really wants the large inheritance from her uncle), we are likely to discount her (internal) explanation that she is acting out of only altruistic motives.

Conversely, when no apparent external reason exists for a behavior, we do not discount internal causes. This is illustrated nicely when Aldonza asks Sancho why he follows Don Quixote on his painful misadventures:

SANCHO: Well, that's easy to explain, I . . . I . . .
ALDONZA: Why?
    . . . It doesn't make any sense!
SANCHO: That's because you're not a squire.
ALDONZA: All right, you're a squire. How does a squire squire?
SANCHO: Well, I ride behind him . . . and he fights. Then I pick him
    up off the ground . . .
ALDONZA: But what do *you* get out of it?

SANCHO: What do *I* get? Plenty! Why, already I've gotten . . .
ALDONZA: You've gotten nothing! So why do you *do* it?
SANCHO: . . . I like him.
   I really like him.

—— *Man of La Mancha*, pp. 34–35

After forcing Sancho to acknowledge that there is no external reason for his following Don Quixote, Aldonza forces him to accept the only logical alternative: his behavior is due to an internal disposition — he *likes* Don Quixote.

Many studies have provided evidence for the discounting principle (see, for example, Thibaut & Rieken, 1955; Kruglanski, 1970). In one classic experiment, Strickland (1958) asked subjects to supervise two workers, A and B, on a simulated assembly line at which both workers performed a boring task for ten trials. Each "supervisor" was allowed to supervise worker A on nine out of ten trials but could supervise B on only two out of ten trials. At the end of the ten trials, each "supervisor" received a record of the workers' performance. Both workers showed nearly identical, high performances. The "supervisors" were then asked to indicate *why* workers had performed so well and to rate how motivated each was. Interestingly, "supervisors" said they trusted worker B (whom they had supervised *least*) more and saw his performance as more internally motivated than worker A's.

This finding can readily be interpreted in terms of Kelley's discounting principle: Because subjects had strong evidence of an external cause for worker A's performance ("He did it because I was looking over his shoulder all the time"), they discounted internal causes ("He did it because he's a highly motivated, hard worker"). Beyond its theoretical implications, this study points to an important and unfortunate practical fact — the more you supervise a person, the less you may come to trust him or her.

Reward and intrinsic motivation.   The discounting principle applies to attributions we make about ourselves as well as to attributions we make about others. Imagine, for example, that you have been working for some years at a job that's not very stimulating but pays a high salary. You might reasonably decide that you are working hard not because of any real interest, but rather for the money. In other words, you may *discount* your internal interest and motivation because of an obvious strong external cause.

Research shows that rewards can sometimes undermine intrinsic motivation, even for tasks that are relatively enjoyable to begin with. This phenomenon is called the *over-justification effect*. Lepper, Greene, and Nisbett (1973) demonstrated this effect in a study in which nursery school children were allowed to draw with magic markers on blank sheets of paper, an activity the children found fun and interesting. Some children were informed ahead of time that they would receive an award for playing with the magic markers, others unexpectedly received an award after playing, and a third (control) group received no awards. When the children were given an opportunity to play freely with the magic markers a week or so later, children who had received expected awards played less than either of the other two groups (see Figure 4.3). The expectation of awards appeared to undermine the children's intrinsic motivation in the task; the same undermining effect of expected rewards (like money) has been demonstrated for adult subjects as well (Deci, 1975; Lepper & Greene, 1978; Wilson, Hull, & Johnson, 1981; Deci & Ryan, 1980, 1985). These

··

FIGURE 4.3   Effects of expected and unexpected rewards on children's play.

What effect do rewards have on intrinsic motivation?

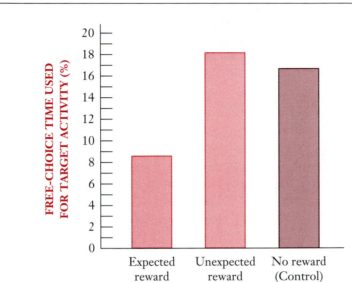

Children who learned to expect rewards when they chose to play with magic markers spent less free-choice time on this activity when rewards were discontinued than did children who had received no rewards or children who had received rewards unexpectedly.

SOURCE: Data from Lepper, Greene, and Nisbett (1973).

Rewards can undermine intrinsic motivation, particularly when they are expected and when they do not signal competence.

··

results are particularly intriguing because they seem to contradict a basic principle of operant conditioning — that rewards *increase* the probability of the responses they follow.

Kelley's discounting principle provides an explanation for the over-justification effect. In attributing the cause of our own behavior, we discount internal interest when salient and anticipated external incentives are present. A number of studies show that expected external rewards seem to undermine intrinsic motivation, particularly when the rewards are automatic and not related to competence or performance (Deci & Ryan, 1985).

It is interesting here to speculate about grades, external rewards that are probably highly relevant to you. Do grades ever undermine students' intrinsic motivation in their school work? If you consider grades to be signs of competence, then they need not destroy your interest in the subject matter. However, if you regard grades as commodities that don't really signal competence ("I've got to get 40 passing grades and then, thank God, I'll be able to graduate and get a job"), then they may undermine your intrinsic interest; then you become a student who completes course work "to get a passing grade" rather than because you're interested in the material.

The over-justification effect *does not* imply that rewards have no direct influence on behavior. Rather, it suggests that although they maintain behavior, rewards may also undermine intrinsic motivation. If your mother pays you $100 for every "A" you receive, you may work very hard to get "A's." But what happens if your mother can no longer pay you? You may slack off academically because you infer that you were working for the money, not because you were truly interested in your studies.

When discounting fails.   Although research on discounting demonstrates that subjects become less confident of internal causes of behavior when strong external causes are present, it is important to note that such discounting is not always complete. Indeed, as we discussed earlier, attribution theorists from Heider on have argued that internal explanations tend to be preferred over external explanations. Thus it seems reasonable to predict that people will be reluctant to discount their favored internal explanations for behavior unless overwhelmingly salient external causes are present.

In fact, the discounting of internal causes may be partial at best, even when strong external causes are evident. Jones and Harris (1967) carried out a particularly influential study that demonstrated partial discounting of internal causes. Subjects were asked to read another student's speech either praising or criticizing Fidel Castro, and their task was to guess the writer's *real* attitude toward Castro. Without any other information, subjects could reasonably assume that someone who writes a speech in favor of Castro is indeed pro-Castro, whereas someone who writes a speech against Castro is indeed anti-Castro.

Now let's add a complicating factor: In one condition subjects were told that the writer *freely chose* the speech topic, whereas subjects in another condition were told that the speech topic was assigned—that the writer had no choice of topic. Now it makes sense for subjects to assume that the student's speech reflects his or her real attitude only if he or she freely chose the speech's topic. Clearly, if a student was forced to write on a particular topic, subjects should discount the internal cause (that the student wrote the speech because he or she really believed in its content).

Figure 4.4 shows the findings of Jones and Harris's study. The numbers in the graph represent subjects' ratings of the speech-writer's attitude on a scale that ranged from "10—extremely anti-Castro" to "70—extremely pro-Castro." Note that discounting did indeed take place. When they thought that the writer freely chose his or her speech topic, subjects assumed that the speech strongly reflected the writer's real attitude. Subjects made such an assumption less in the "No choice" condition.

But—and this is a truly startling finding—the discounting was not complete. Even in the "No choice" condition, subjects still perceived a significant difference between the attitudes of the writers of pro- and anti-Castro speeches. That is, even with a strong external explanation for the speech-writer's behavior ("He was forced to write on this topic"), subjects still assumed that the writers' attitudes to some degree matched their speeches. This failure to discount internal causes completely

▪▪

**FIGURE 4.4   Subjects' attribution of attitudes from speeches that were either freely
chosen or assigned.**

*Generally we assume that people's stated and written opinions reflect their actual attitudes.
When would you* not *make this assumption?*

Jones and Harris (1967) asked subjects to rate the true attitudes of student
speech-writers toward Fidel Castro on the basis of "freely written"
speeches (choice condition) and "assigned" speeches (no-choice condition).
The graph shows the subjects' average attributions for both conditions.

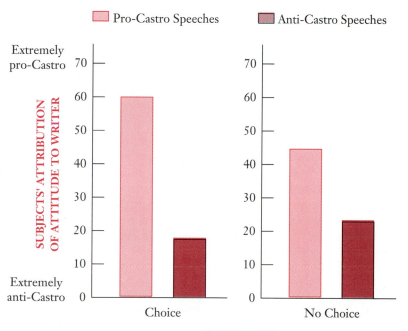

In the choice condition, writers of pro-Castro speeches were rated as
significantly more pro-Castro than writers of anti-Castro speeches. Thus,
subjects assumed that the speeches reflected the writers' true attitudes.
Although this difference was smaller in the no-choice condition, it did not
disappear. In other words, even when subjects thought that writers were
forced to write their speeches, they continued to assume that to some degree
the speeches reflected the writers' true attitudes.

SOURCE: Based on Jones and Harris (1967).

▪▪

in the face of obvious external causes is a highly reliable finding that has been
replicated in many different studies. (Jones, 1979, reviews many studies on this
topic.)

Attribution Errors and Biases

DON QUIXOTE: Sancho, Sancho, always thine eye sees evil in preference to good.

SANCHO: (*Stubbornly*) There's no use blaming my eye; it doesn't make the world, it only sees it. (*A band of Moors appears*) Anyway, there's something my eye sees truly enough. Moors! Let's make a wide track around them, for they're a scurvy lot. . . .

DON QUIXOTE: There, thou fallest into the trap of thy peasant mind again.

SANCHO: They're *not* thieves and murderers?

DON QUIXOTE: Do not condemn before thou knowest! (*The Moorish Girl undulates toward them*) Sh-h-h — a young innocent approaches. (*The Girl dances lasciviously as her Pimp encourages her. . . .*) . . .

DON QUIXOTE: . . . Sweet maiden, what wilt thou?

SANCHO: I think *I* know what she wilt! (*The Girl seizes one of Quixote's hands and presses it to her right breast*)

DON QUIXOTE: She wishes me to feel the beating of her heart. And such is her innocence she does not even know where it is.

—— *Man of La Mancha*, pp. 62–66

Don Quixote's noble but ridiculous attributions are a source of humor and pathos in *Man of La Mancha*. As outside observers we smile at the naive idealism that leads Don Quixote always to attribute others' behavior to noble intentions, and we wince at the realization that these overly optimistic attributions will lead others to take advantage of him. Like Don Quixote, we too at times make unrealistic, even false, attributions. Let's examine the most common kinds of errors that occur in attributing the causes of behavior.

The Fundamental Attribution Error

We've already discussed one important attribution error — that people seem to prefer internal, dispositional explanations of behavior over external, situational explanations. As the Jones and Harris study demonstrated, people may hold tenaciously to their preferred internal explanations even in the face of obvious external causes. This tendency to overemphasize internal causes and underemphasize external causes has been labeled "the fundamental attribution error" (Ross, 1977). Stated somewhat differently, the fundamental attribution error holds that the average person is more of a personality psychologist than a social psychologist; in our everyday thinking, most of us attribute behavior more to *traits in the person* than to situations or environmental pressures.

Like people in general, clinical psychologists often fall prey to the fundamental attribution error. Traditional "insight" therapists are likely to label their clients' problems dispositionally and thus believe that something's wrong with the person, rather than with the person's behavior or environment (Langer & Abelson, 1974). Furthermore, mental health services often focus treatment on personal, dispositional problems (the client is a depressed person) rather than on situational problems (a bad family situation and poor work conditions are leading to the client's depression) (see Caplan & Nelson, 1973; Halleck, 1971). Behavior problems may be diagnosed dispositionally to tailor diagnoses to available treatments; that is, clinical

Ignoring the Power of Social Roles: Another Example of the Fundamental Attribution Error

People's behavior is often constrained by social roles. For example, traditional sex roles assign child care to women and full-time work to men. If I ask you to explain why Martha stays home to care for her children and why her husband, George, goes to work each day, you can explain their behavior either in terms of their roles (an external explanation) or in terms of their traits (an internal, dispositional explanation). If you say that Martha takes care of the children because she's "nurturant" and "loves children" and George goes to work because he's "competitive" and "achievement-oriented," you are clearly offering internal explanations for their behavior. You may also be committing a subtle form of the fundamental attribution error; that is, you may be explaining women's and men's behavior too much in terms of their presumed traits while ignoring the overwhelming impact of their social roles.

Ross, Amabile, and Steinmetz (1977) conducted a clever experiment that clearly demonstrated subjects' failure to perceive the power of social roles. Pairs of college students played a "quiz game"

in which one student was randomly chosen to be the "quiz master" who asked questions and the other was the "contestant" who answered questions. Quiz masters generated "challenging but not impossible" questions on topics they were familiar with (for example, sports, music, science, and so on). Each quiz master posed ten questions.

The questions in fact turned out to be rather difficult: Contestants on average answered only four out of ten correctly. After the quiz game was over, subjects rated their own and their partners' level of general knowledge on a 100-point scale. Intriguingly, contestants viewed quiz masters as being considerably more knowledgeable than themselves, whereas quiz masters viewed both themselves and the contestants to be about equally knowledgeable (see the accompanying bar chart). In other words, contestants attributed both their own behavior ("I didn't get many answers right" and the quiz masters' behavior ("she sure asked some tough questions") to internal traits, whereas quiz masters did not. Were quiz masters in fact more knowledgeable than contes-

tants? No—the researchers administered a general knowledge test to all subjects, and it showed no difference between the two groups. Thus the contestants were in error when they assumed themselves to be less knowledgeable than the quiz masters.

What caused the contestants' mistaken perception? Clearly, subjects' experimentally assigned roles were biased in favor of the quiz masters, who could generate questions in their own areas of expertise. The quiz masters thus ended up appearing intelligent, and the contestants rather unintelligent. Because they were aware of how they selectively generated the questions, the quiz masters realized the hidden advantage conferred by their privileged role and thus did not attribute their difficult questions or contestants' often incorrect answers to internal traits.

In a second study, Ross, Amabile, and Steinmetz asked some observers to watch a simulated quiz game, and these observers, like the contestants, judged the quiz master to be more knowledgeable than the contestant. Thus they too showed the fundamental attribution error and failed adequately to

psychologists have developed more techniques to treat troubled people than those to treat problematic life settings (Batson, Jones, & Cochran, 1979).

Some classic studies in social psychology are fascinating and counterintuitive precisely because we make the fundamental attribution error when attempting to understand them (Ross, 1977). Thus many people are surprised when they first hear the results of Milgram's (1974) famous obedience studies—for example, that over 60 percent of "normal" subjects will obey an experimenter fully and deliver excruciatingly painful electric shocks to a screaming victim (see Chapter 2). Apparently most of us expect internal factors (like the subject's "conscience" or "empathy") to be stronger than they in fact are, and we grossly underestimate the power of the social situation created in the experiment.

Ignoring the Power of Social Roles (continued)

take into account the influence of the assigned roles in the experiment.

The quiz game experiment may apply to another, quite familiar situation—teachers' interactions with students. Teachers are like quiz masters—they can put students on the spot by asking questions in their areas of expertise. Students are like contestants—they must respond to whatever peculiar questions teachers come up with. In other words, the social roles are stacked against the student, who often appears less intelligent than the teacher.

More broadly, people's failure to acknowledge the power of social roles may help to explain how negative stereotypes develop about disadvantaged groups (Pettigrew, 1979). People often explain the behavior of such groups in terms of members' traits ("they're stupid and lazy") rather than in terms of members' environments and constrained roles ("they have little power; poverty, poor medical care, and malnutrition limit their opportunities"). Here is yet another example of the fundamental attribution error.

Subjects fail to take into account the power of social roles when making attributions.

SOURCE: Based on Ross, Amabile, and Steinmetz (1977).

<hr style="width:30%">

The Actor-Observer Effect

The tendency to overemphasize internal explanations of behavior seems to be stronger when we explain others' behavior (when we're an "observer" of others) than when we explain our own behavior (when we're the "actor"). Jones and Nisbett (1972) stated this *actor-observer hypothesis* as follows: ". . . there is a pervasive tendency for actors to attribute their actions to situational requirements, whereas observers tend to attribute the same actions to stable personal dispositions" (p. 80).

To illustrate, imagine you and I are walking across campus one day, and you clumsily trip and drop all your books. I say to myself, "What a klutz!" I've offered a dispositional cause for your behavior—your inner trait of "klutziness." Let's reverse the scenario now: Suppose this time *I* trip and scatter my books. Now I might say,

"Humph, there's a pothole in the sidewalk back there." I explain the same behavior in situational terms when it's my behavior. Of course, it is probably less bruising to my ego to explain my tripping in external terms. However, Jones and Nisbett argue that the tendency to explain our own behavior differently from the way we explain others' behavior is a broader phenomenon than the simple defense of our egos.

Research on the actor-observer effect.   Nisbett and his colleagues (1973) found evidence for the actor-observer effect in several studies. In one of these, subjects were asked to rate themselves, a friend, their father, and TV newscaster Walter Cronkite on a number of traits. Subjects could check one of three alternatives: (1) that the person possessed a given trait (for example, "lenient"), (2) that the person possessed the opposite trait ("firm"), or (3) that the subject didn't have either trait, but rather "it depends on the situation." Subjects checked "depends on the situation" most when rating themselves, less often for their friend and father, and least when rating Walter Cronkite. These findings support the basic hypothesis of the actor-observer effect; that is, subjects explained themselves more in situational terms and others more in dispositional terms (see Figure 4.5). This study points to a rather strange conclusion: Subjects were most willing to attribute traits to the person they know least (Walter Cronkite) and least willing to attribute traits to the person they know best (themselves).

In another demonstration of the actor-observer effect, Nisbett and his colleagues (1973) asked college students to write brief essays stating why they chose their college majors. These subjects were also asked to write similar essays describing why their best friends had chosen *their* majors. These essays were then content-analyzed to see how many external reasons (for example, "I chose Chemistry because it's a high-paying field") as compared to internal reasons ("I chose Chemistry because I'm good at science") were offered in each essay. In keeping with the actor-observer hypothesis, subjects gave more external reasons for their own behavior and more dispositional reasons for their friends' behavior. Actor-observer differences have been found in other studies as well (for example, Goldberg, 1978; West, Gunn, & Chernicky, 1975; see Watson, 1982).

Studies that support the actor-observer effect *do not* find that we *never* make dispositional attributions about ourselves. Rather, they suggest that we make *more* dispositional attributions about others than about ourselves. In a review of many actor-observer studies, Watson (1982) noted that both actors and observers tend to emphasize dispositional explanations more than situational explanations. (Here's our old friend, the fundamental attribution error, yet again.) However, our relative preference for dispositional over situational explanations is *greater* when we explain others' behavior than when we explain our own behavior.

Reasons for the actor-observer effect.   Why should we explain our own behavior differently from others? Jones and Nisbett (1972) proposed two possible explanations. First, we generally possess more information about ourselves than about others. In terms of Kelley's cube model, we possess greater consistency and distinctiveness information about ourselves than about others. For example, you know that you vary in how friendly you are in various situations and with different people, and thus you realize that your friendliness "depends on the situation." On the other hand, you've seen a TV personality like Walter Cronkite only in a limited, role-constrained situation. In a sense, you overgeneralize from his TV behavior and assume he must be "friendly" in general.

FIGURE 4.5   Trait versus situational attributions for self and others.

Do we tend to explain other people's behavior differently from the way we explain our own?

For each person shown, subjects in the Nisbett et al. (1973) study could give either "trait" or "situational" attributions on a number of traits. The graph shows the average number of trait (internal) attributions given for each person.

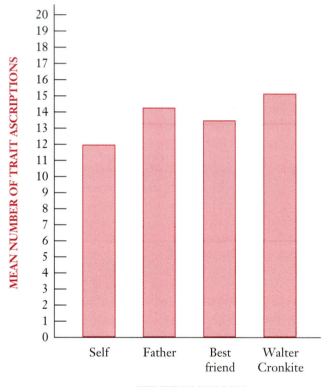

In keeping with the actor-observer hypothesis, subjects attributed fewer traits to themselves than to others, and rated their own behaviors as "depending on the situation" more than others' behaviors. Thus, subjects were most willing to attribute traits to the persons they knew least (Walter Cronkite) and least willing to attribute traits to the person they knew best (themselves).

SOURCE: Based on Nisbett et al. (1973).

Second, because of the structure of our perceptual systems, we focus on different things when explaining ourselves and when explaining others. Our sensory systems point "outward." For example, you are generally not an object in your own visual field (unless you're watching yourself in a mirror). Thus when we consider our own behavior, our perceptual systems are focused on the external environment. Other people, though, *are* objects in our perceptual field. We see them as salient, behaving objects, and thus we are more likely to attribute behavior to their inner dispositions. (This statement is reminiscent of Heider's observation that "behavior engulfs the field.")

Is there any evidence for this perceptual explanation of the actor-observer effect? Yes. In one study, Storms (1973) videotaped two subjects as they engaged in a "get acquainted" conversation. Two other subjects served as observers: They watched the conversation but did not participate. Storms found evidence for actor-observer effects in his study; that is, actors (people who were talking) attributed their own behavior more to the situation, whereas observers considered behavior to be more internally controlled. Later, Storms showed some of the subjects videotapes of their conversation; that is, he made them objects in their perceptual fields, just as another person would be! Such video feedback "undid" the actor-observer effect: After seeing a videotape of themselves, the actors attributed their behavior more to internal, dispositional causes, just as the outside observers did.

Salience Effects in Attribution

At least part of the actor-observer effect seems to result from perceptual salience — others' behavior is noticed more than is one's own. Others' behavior forms a perceptual "figure" against the less noticeable "background" of the environment. This illustrates a more general point: People and behavior that are perceptually salient (colorful, loud, novel, or deviant in some way) are seen to be more causally central and influential in general (Taylor & Fiske, 1978).

The effects of perceptual salience on causal attributions were demonstrated particularly clearly in a study by Taylor and Fiske (1975). Two actors engaged in a conversation while actual subjects sat around them in different positions, observing the conversation. Some observers faced the front of one actor and the back of the second. Other observers could see the faces of both actors. See Figure 4.6 for a sketch of subjects' seating arrangement in this study.

After the conversation, the observing subjects were asked how much each actor had set the tone and guided the course of the conversation. The results were quite clear: Observers assigned greater causal impact to the speaker who was perceptually salient. That is, an observer who faced one speaker but not the other tended to view the speaker he or she faced as the more influential in the conversation. Other studies suggest that a person who "stands out" in a group — for example, a woman in an all-male group or a black in an all-white group — is also seen by outside observers as more influential in guiding group discussions and decisions (Taylor, 1981; Taylor & Fiske, 1978).

Motivational Biases in Attribution

I've been told he's chasing dragons and I fear it may be true.
If my groom should hear about it, heaven knows what he will do!
Oh, I dearly love my uncle but for what he's done to me

■■■■■■■■■■■■■■■■■■■■■■■■■
Salience effects in attribution. Which person is the most influential member of this group? Why do you think so?

I would like to take and lock him up and throw away the key!
But if I do . . .
There is one thing I swear will still be true . . .
I'm only thinking of him;
I'm only thinking of him;
I'm only thinking and worrying about him.

—— lyrics from "I'm Only Thinking of Him,"
in *Man of La Mancha*

Don Quixote's niece, Antonia, is quite worried: If her uncle continues roaming the countryside as a knight-errant, she may lose both her fiancé and her inheritance. Thus she would like to find him and lock him up. But if she does, she assures everyone around her, it's because she's "only thinking of him." To maintain her self-esteem and the positive regard of others, Antonia attributes her behavior to altruistic impulses rather than to monetary and marital incentives.

Self-serving biases. So far, we have investigated ways in which perceptual orientation and the availability of information may potentially bias the attribution process. But as Antonia's words suggest, there are other, more motivational sources of attri-

FIGURE 4.6   The seating arrangement and results of the Taylor and Fiske (1975) study.

What effect does perceptual salience have on our attributions?

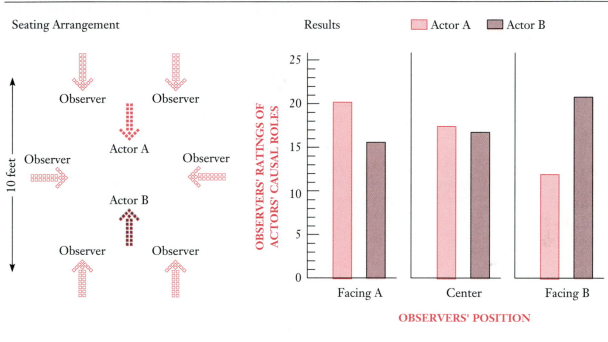

Seating arrangement for actors and observers, with arrows indicating visual orientation

How the subjects rated the actors' causal role

SOURCE: Adapted from Taylor and Fiske (1975). Copyright 1975 by the American Psychological Association. Used with permission of Shelley Taylor.

People who are perceptually salient are often perceived to be more causally influential. Imagine that a baseball comes crashing through your window. One of the boys playing ball outside has dyed red hair and the rest don't. Who do you think will catch your attention first? Will your first impression be that the boy with the dyed hair is likely to be responsible for the misdeed?

butional bias as well. We may at times distort the attributions we make about our own behavior in order to "look good" and to protect or enhance our self-esteem. Such *self-serving biases* in attribution seem to be fairly common. For example, imagine you just received an "A" on a test. What would make you feel better, attributing your performance to your intelligence (an internal trait) or to luck (an unstable, external factor). You'll probably agree that your self-esteem seems more enhanced if you attribute your successes to internal causes ("I'm smart") and your failures to external causes ("my dog kept me up the night before the exam").

A number of studies have found evidence for such self-serving biases in attributions (Miller & Ross, 1975; Carver, DeGregorio, & Gillis, 1980; Van Der Pligt & Eiser, 1983). Interestingly, people seem more willing to inflate their responsibility for successes than to deny their responsibility for failures (Miller & Ross, 1975). Perhaps it would make more sense for us to be more realistic about our failures, for then we could take corrective action. If you receive a bad test score and blame it on bad luck (when the real cause was inadequate study), you will only set yourself up for future failure. Furthermore, if you flunk your next three tests, it may strain even your own credulity to continue attributing your performance to "bad luck."

Miller (1978) points out that self-serving attributions serve two purposes: they may make us feel better about ourselves and they may make us appear better to others. In other words, Miller suggests that in addition to protecting our egos, self-serving attributions may serve a *self-presentational* purpose. Greenberg, Pyszczynski, and Solomon (1982) tried to distinguish between these two explanations by asking subjects to explain their successes and failures on an experimental task in two different conditions: when only they knew how they performed and when an outside observer also knew how they performed. Interestingly, subjects made self-serving attributions even when they alone knew their level of performance, which clearly suggests that self-serving attributions are motivated in part by a desire to "look good" to ourselves as well as to manage appearances for others.

Self-handicapping strategies.   Research on self-serving attributions has documented that people sometimes "fudge" their attributions to protect their self-esteem. Another way to protect ourselves from painful attributions is through *self-handicapping strategies*, which entail creating new apparent causes of our behavior, usually to protect us from painful internal attributions. For example, imagine that tomorrow you are to take a chemistry test, and deep down you doubt that you'll do well. Tonight your roommate asks if you want to go out drinking, and you accept the invitation. In fact, you stay out all night carousing. When you take the exam and do poorly, you can now attribute your bad performance to your carousing rather than to your lack of ability in chemistry. Stated more abstractly, you may seek to create powerful and salient external causes for poor performance so you can avoid attributing your failure to unflattering dispositional causes.

Berglas and Jones (1978; Jones & Berglas, 1978) demonstrated such self-handicapping strategies in a clever experiment. Subjects (college students) were first asked to solve a number of problems. One group received problems that were in fact impossible to solve, whereas another group received solvable problems. Both groups of subjects were told they had performed well. Subjects in the "impossible problem" group probably concluded that they had performed well because of luck, not skill, whereas subjects in the "solvable problem" group were more likely to conclude that their skill had enabled them to do well.

Subjects were then informed (falsely) that the purpose of the study was to investigate the effect of two new drugs — "Actavil," a drug reputed to improve intellectual performance, and "Pandocrin," a drug reputed to debilitate performance. Subjects were asked which drug they wanted to receive before attempting to solve new problems like those they had just worked on. The results: Subjects who had worked on impossible problems were relatively more likely to choose "Pandocrin" (the supposedly debilitating drug), whereas subjects who had worked on solvable problems were more likely to choose "Actavil" (see Figure 4.7).

●●●

FIGURE 4.7   **Self-handicapping strategies.**

Do we engage in self-handicapping behavior when we anticipate failure?

Berglas and Jones (1978) asked subjects who had just worked
on either solvable or insoluble problems to choose between drugs
that supposedly either inhibited or enhanced performance
before working on new problems.

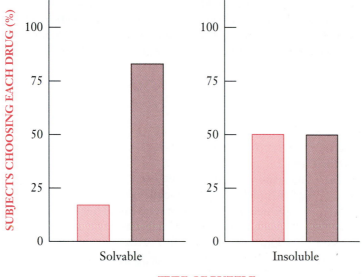

Whereas subjects who had worked on solvable problems tended to choose
the "performance-enhancing drug," subjects who had worked on insoluble
problems were more likely to engage in self-handicapping by selecting
the "debilitating" drug.

SOURCE: Data from Berglas and Jones (1978).

*In Berglas and Jones's study, men engaged in self-handicapping strategies, but women did
not. Why do you think this was so?*

●●●

Berglas and Jones interpreted these results to mean that the subjects in the
"impossible problem" condition engaged in a self-handicapping strategy; because
they expected to do badly the second time around, they chose more often to take the

debilitating drug. At least then they could blame their poor performance on the drug, rather than on their own lack of ability. Evidence for self-handicapping strategies has emerged in other studies as well (Arkin & Baumgardner, 1985).

Self-handicapping strategies may occur in everyday life when people anticipate poor performance in the future. For example, imagine a student who gets admitted to a top university because of his family's money and "connections," rather than because he's an able student. Such a student may reasonably expect to do poorly at school compared to his better-qualified classmates. One way for him to deal with this painful situation would be to behave in a way that will provide an excuse for his poor performance (for example, to overcommit himself to extracurricular activities). Then, at least, he can blame his bad grades on his many activities rather than make the painful admission that he lacks academic ability.

Thus, research on self-handicapping strategies indicates that not only do we sometimes directly shift our attributions to protect our self-esteem (as suggested by research on self-serving biases), but we also may seek to make certain "decoy" causes salient when we wish to discount other, more painful causes. Self-handicapping adds yet another dimension to the complex phenomenon of attribution. The principal concepts we have encountered in this chapter are reviewed in Summary Table 4.1.

Applying Attribution Theory

ALDONZA:	. . . You spoke to me and everything was — different!
DON QUIXOTE:	I . . . spoke to you?
ALDONZA:	And you looked at me! And you called me by another name! Dulcinea . . . Dulcinea . . .
	Once you found a girl and called her Dulcinea,
	When you spoke the name an angel seemed to whisper —
	Dulcinea . . . Dulcinea . . .

—— dialogue and lyrics from *Man of La Mancha*, p. 77

Toward the end of *Man of La Mancha*, Don Quixote is returned for a time to "sanity." He becomes the old and defeated Señor Quijana instead of the energetic and ever-optimistic Don Quixote. As he lies on his sick bed, Don Quixote is startled when Aldonza forces her way into his room to tell him an amazing story — that he has transformed her life. By attributing her behavior differently from anyone else, Don Quixote led Aldonza to think differently about herself. As a result, she has lifted herself out of squalor and become a respectable woman. Can altering people's attributions about themselves have positive therapeutic effects in real life as well as in the theater?

Treating Depression

And yet how lovely life would seem
If every man could weave a dream
To keep him from despair.

—— lyrics from "To Each His Dulcinea,"
in *Man of La Mancha*

What are the principal concepts in attribution theory and research?

CONCEPT	OBJECT OF ATTRIBUTION	FACTORS AFFECTING ATTRIBUTION	COMMENT
General Correspondent inference theory	Behavior of others (usually single instances)	Social desirability Common and noncommon effects Hedonic relevance Personalism	The theory tries to explain when we make dispositional attributions.
Kelley cube model	Behavior of others (multiple observations)	Covariation of consistency, consensus, and distinctiveness information with behavior	The theory tries to specify when we make internal or external attributions.
Causal schemas Discounting	Behavior of self and others	Presence of one salient cause leads us to discount other causes.	The over-justification effect is an example: Rewards (the salient external cause) can undermine intrinsic motivation.
Attributional biases Fundamental attribution error	Behavior of self and others	Salience of behavior Lack of complete information about the situation	We tend to prefer internal over external attributions.
Actor-observer effect	Behavior of self *versus* behavior of others	Greater information about self Greater perceptual salience of others' behavior	We tend to explain our own behavior more in external terms, and others' behavior more in terms of dispositions.
Salience effects	Behavior of others	Perceptual distinctiveness or vividness	Perceptually salient others are seen as more causally influential.
Motivational biases Self-serving biases	Behavior of self	Degree to which attribution is flattering or unflattering	We tend to attribute our successes to stable, internal factors and our failures to temporary, external factors.
Self-handicapping	Behavior of self	Anticipated failure and lowered self-esteem	When we anticipate failure, we may provide a "decoy" external explanation to avoid a painful internal attribution.

Attribution processes are complex. Though it is challenging for social psychologists to analyze all the factors that affect our attributions, in everyday life we make causal attributions all the time quite effortlessly.

In recent years researchers have investigated applications of attribution theories to such clinical problems as depression (Abramson, Seligman, & Teasdale, 1978; Coyne & Gotlieb, 1983; Försterling, 1985). Many studies suggest that clinically depressed people attribute the causes of their behavior differently than do nondepressed people. For example, depressed people attribute their failures more to stable internal traits ("I'm stupid and worthless") and their successes more to temporary, uncontrollable, external factors ("I was lucky").

Interestingly, in experimental tasks depressed people show a phenomenon called *depressive realism*: They often estimate the degree to which they are responsible for their successes and failures more accurately than do nondepressed people (Alloy & Abramson, 1979). How are nondepressed people in error? They tend to view their performance through rose-colored glasses—they overestimate their responsibility for successes and underestimate their responsibility for failures (that is, they show self-serving biases). Although they don't lead to accurate self-attributions, such biases may be psychologically healthy insofar as they protect us a bit from "the slings and arrows of outrageous fortune."

Does depression lead to self-deprecating attributions or do negative attributions cause depression? The answer seems to be "Both" (Lewinsohn, Hoberman, Teri, & Hautziner, 1986). Depression may be sustained by a vicious circle of events: Unexpected failures (a failed course, a failed marriage) may lead to negative emotions and self-defeating attributions, which then feed the negative emotions. Once a depressed person begins showing this depressive pattern of attributions, almost no event can relieve it. If the depressed person fails a test, it's because he's "stupid," which provides further proof of his worthlessness; but if he passes the test, he was simply "lucky." Only negative information about the self is viewed as valid.

One way to break the vicious circle of depression may be through attributional retraining. If we could somehow induce depressed people to take personal credit for their successes and happiness, and to attribute their failures and unhappiness more to external circumstances, perhaps we could guide them into an upward rather than downward emotional cycle. Layden (1982) describes just such a therapeutic intervention. She instructed depressed people to keep detailed, daily diaries in which they explained how they were personally responsible for their successes and how their environment had led to their failures. This attributional retraining worked: After a month, subjects showed less depression, higher self-esteem, and a more normal attributional style (that is, one more like that of nondepressed people).

■■■■■■■■■■■■■■■■■■■■■■■■■

Improving Academic Performance

College students may also at times benefit from attributional retraining. Imagine, for example, that you just completed your freshman year at college with a 2.5 grade point average, considerably lower than you had hoped. You could attribute your disappointing performance to internal causes ("I'm not very intelligent") or to external causes ("My first year away from home was very disruptive, and the freshman dorms were distracting").

The internal attribution is more likely to disrupt your future academic performance. If you think you're stupid, you will probably experience anxiety in future academic settings; that is, your negative attributions will trigger additional negative emotions. On the other hand, if you decide your lackluster freshman performance was due to external and temporary circumstances, you can start your sophomore year with a clean slate—now you're used to living away from home, and you can move out of the freshman dorm.

To determine whether students' attributions do in fact influence academic performance, Wilson and Linville (1982, 1985) conducted several clever studies. First they identified (via questionnaires) college freshman whose grade point averages were relatively low and who worried a lot about their academic performance. Next, they gave these subjects information designed to affect their attributions about their academic performance: Half the subjects were informed that students' grades are typically low in their freshman year and improve thereafter; the other half—the control subjects—were given no information about freshman grades. Thus, subjects in the first group were given information that allowed them to attribute their relatively poor grades to transient circumstances rather than to their internal ability.

This simple attributional manipulation affected students' later performance in two measurable ways. Subjects who were provided with external attributions performed better than control subjects on a scholastic aptitude test administered soon after the study, and, even more significantly, they tended to obtain higher grades than control subjects during the following semester. Apparently, learning to attribute failure to external factors can help anxious college students as well as clinically depressed people.

Thus, like Aldonza, we may sometimes benefit from changing the ways we explain our own behavior. Attributional retraining promises to be a useful therapeutic technique that can be applied to a number of real-life problems.

Summary

1. Attribution theories describe the thought processes people use to explain the causes of their own and others' behavior.

2. Fritz Heider, the father of modern attribution theory, argued that people often try to decide whether behavior is internally or externally caused. He also noted that people seem to prefer internal explanations of behavior to external ones.

3. Schachter and Singer's theory of emotion argued that emotional experience is influenced by physiological arousal and cognitive attributions. Their theory stimulated misattribution research, which induces subjects to falsely attribute the causes of their arousal.

4. Jones and Davis's theory of correspondent inferences offers four principles people use to infer dispositions from behavior: social desirability, common and noncommon effects, hedonic relevance, and personalism.

5. Kelley's cube model of attribution was formulated to explain how people infer internal or external causes from multiple observations of behavior. Kelley's model argues that people observe consistency, consensus, and distinctiveness information. Behavior is then attributed to the apparent cause with which it covaries over time.

6. Causal schemas are mental models of causality. The discounting principle is a causal schema in which people assign less weight to a given cause when another plausible cause is present. The over-justification effect occurs when people

discount their internal interest in a task after receiving an expected reward for performing the task.

7. The fundamental attribution error occurs when people overemphasize internal explanations and underemphasize external explanations. Jones and Harris's pro- and anti-Castro essay experiment shows that people will sometimes explain behavior internally even when highly salient external causes are present.

8. The actor-observer effect occurs when people attribute their own behavior relatively more to situational causes and attribute others' behavior more to dispositional causes. The effect may occur because people have more knowledge about the situational variability of their own behavior and because they have different perceptual perspectives when viewing their own and others' behavior.

9. People and behavior that are perceptually salient tend to be perceived as more causally influential.

10. Self-serving biases occur in attribution when people too strongly explain their successes internally and their failures externally. Such biases serve both self-presentational and ego-defensive functions.

11. People engage in self-handicapping strategies when they create apparent external causes of failures to protect themselves from painful internal attributions.

12. Depressed people tend to explain their failures internally and their successes externally. Attributional retraining can help break the link between depressive attributions and depression.

13. Students' academic anxiety may be reduced by inducing them to attribute their academic failures to external causes.

Glossary

Actor-observer effect: The tendency for people to attribute their own behavior relatively more to situational causes and others' behavior more to dispositional causes

Attribution: The processes by which people infer the causes of their own and others' behavior

Attribution theories: Social psychological theories that attempt to explain the thought processes people use to explain their own and others' behavior

Attributional retraining: A therapeutic technique that teaches people new ways to attribute the causes of their behavior; has been applied to the treatment of depression

Causal schemas: Mental models of causality and of how causes combine to influence behavior

Common and noncommon effects: Different behaviors have common effects when they have the same effects and noncommon effects when they have different effects; correspondent inference theory holds that behaviors with unique noncommon effects lead to stronger dispositional attributions

Consensus information: The degree to which behavior varies among different people who engage in the behavior; an important dimension of information in Kelley's cube model of attribution

Consistency information: The degree to which behavior varies over time or settings; an important dimension of information in Kelley's cube model of attribution

Correspondent inference: An inference of a disposition from a behavior

Covariation principle: Behavior is attributed to the cause with which it systematically varies over time; the basic principle of Kelley's cube model of attribution

Depressive realism: The tendency of depressed people to perceive more realistically than nondepressed people their control over successes and failures in experimental studies

Discounting principle: The principle that we assign less weight to a given cause of behavior if another plausible cause is also present; an example of a causal schema

Dispositions: Stable internal causes

Distinctiveness information: The degree to which behavior varies as a function of its object or target; an important dimension of information in Kelley's cube model of attribution

External explanations: Causal explanations of behavior that place the cause outside of the person — in the setting or in the environment

Fundamental attribution error: The tendency found in many studies for people to overemphasize internal explanations of behavior and underemphasize external explanations

Hedonic relevance: The degree to which a behavior affects a person's pleasure, pain, or emotions; correspondent inference theory holds that behavior that has high hedonic relevance leads to stronger dispositional inferences

Internal explanations: Causal explanations of behavior that place the cause inside the person

Kelley's cube model: A model of attribution that holds that people observe consistency, consensus, and distinctiveness information; people then attribute behavior to the cause with which it systematically varies over time

Misattribution: Occurs when a person attributes arousal to a source that is not the true source

Over-justification effect: The undermining effect of expected rewards on intrinsic motivation

Personalism: The degree to which a behavior is targeted at or intended for a person; correspondent inference theory holds that behaviors with high degrees of personalism lead to stronger dispositional inferences

Salience effect: The tendency for perceptually salient people and behavior to be perceived as more causally influential

Schachter-Singer theory of emotion: Also known as the two-component theory of emotion; this theory holds that the subjective experience of emotion depends on two factors: physiological arousal and cognitive attributions of the arousal

Self-handicapping strategies: Occur when people create salient but false external "causes" of their failures to avoid making painful internal attributions

Self-serving bias: The tendency for people to explain too strongly their successes internally and their failure externally; a motivational bias in attribution

Social desirability: A principle of correspondent inference theory that holds that people are more likely to attribute dispositions from behavior that is socially undesirable (that is, unexpected or nonnormative)

Stable causes: Causes that are perceived to be permanent and enduring

Unstable causes: Causes that are perceived to be fluctuating and transient

[SHERLOCK HOLMES:] " . . . You appeared to be surprised when I told you, on our first meeting, that you had come from Afghanistan."

[DR. WATSON:] "You were told, no doubt."

[HOLMES:] "Nothing of the sort. I *knew* you came from Afghanistan. From long habit the train of thoughts ran so swiftly through my mind that I arrived at the conclusion without being conscious of intermediate steps. There were such steps, however. The train of reasoning ran, 'Here is a gentleman of a medical type, but with the air of a military man. Clearly an army doctor, then. He has just come from the tropics, for his face is dark, and that is not the natural tint of his skin, for his wrists are fair. He has undergone hardship and sickness, as his haggard face says clearly. His left arm has been injured. He holds it in a stiff and unnatural manner. Where in the tropics could an English army doctor have seen much hardship and got his arm wounded? Clearly in Afghanistan.' The whole train of thought did not occupy a second. I then remarked that you came from Afghanistan, and you were astonished."

[WATSON:] "It's simple enough as you explain it. . . ."

—— from "A Study in Scarlet,"
by Sir Arthur Conan Doyle

CHAPTER 5

Social Cognition

*F*ew of us can match Sherlock Holmes's prowess in deducing facts about other people. But despite our limitations, we are all amateur sleuths who constantly gather, process, and integrate information to arrive at reasonable decisions about others. Imagine, for example, that you've placed an ad for a roommate, and you are interviewing people who've responded to your ad. How will you decide whom to accept? You must first gather information — look the latest applicant over, ask questions, and perhaps gather references. Then you must organize the information and try to figure out what traits this person has ("Is she reliable and tidy, loud and raucous?"). Finally, you must reach a decision based on your inferences ("No, she's no good — barely makes enough money to cover the rent, seems flighty; one reference said she wrote a bad check").

We constantly ponder information about others. How do such thought processes work? What do we remember about others and what do we forget? How do we organize our information? And how do we make judgments and decisions based on our knowledge? These are exactly the kinds of questions addressed by research on *social cognition*, the study of how people process information about other people.

Research on social cognition has occupied center stage in American social psychology in recent years (Markus & Zajonc, 1985; Sherman, Judd, & Park, 1989). In part this reflects the growth of cognitive psychology in general; an explosion of research on human knowledge, memory, and inference has provided social psychologists with new research methods and theoretical perspectives to apply to classic issues in person perception. (See Chapter 1 for a brief discussion of cognitive information-processing theories in social psychology and cognitive variables as explanations of social behavior.)

This chapter will focus on three main topics in social cognition: impression formation, schemas and social perception, and social inference and decision making. Let's briefly consider each of these important research areas.

133

Suppose you just interviewed a prospective roommate, Mary Smith, who tells you she's "neat," "clean," "responsible," and "quiet." Assuming this information is credible, how do you organize it into an overall impression? Do you simply mentally "add" or "average" information, or do more subtle and complex cognitive processes take place? Do you weight some kinds of information more than others in arriving at your decision? Research on *impression formation* deals with just these kinds of questions.

Recent research in social cognition suggests that the way we organize new information depends in part on our prior knowledge. We do not approach each new person and each new judgment from scratch. For example, perhaps you believe that Mary Smith is "neat," "clean," and "responsible," but you don't believe your next candidate, Peter Jones, who describes himself with the same list of traits. Maybe you find Mary more credible than Peter because you believe that women are more likely than men to be "neat" and "clean." Your *schemas*, or organized prior knowledge, about women and men may color how you perceive, remember, and evaluate information about specific women and men.

Once you have interviewed all your potential roommates and reviewed the "facts" in your memory, you must make *inferences, social judgments*, and *decisions* based on your limited knowledge. You must choose one of the applicants. Social cognition ultimately influences our social behavior.

Like Sherlock Holmes, we must often go beyond the given facts and fill in gaps in our knowledge to make decisions in everyday life. Unlike Holmes, most of us cannot tell from a glance and some brilliant deduction that an absolute stranger just came from Afghanistan. But we do gather information, infer what we think is likely to be true of the people and groups around us, and then decide whom to hire, befriend, marry, or accept as a roommate.

The previous chapter described how people infer the *causes* of behavior, the central concern of attribution theory. This chapter will describe additional kinds of social judgment and inference. For example, how do people infer how frequently a person or a group displays a given behavior? (Does your mother behave more aggressively than you? Do some ethnic groups behave more aggressively than others?) And how do people infer that social events are correlated? (Do you think there is a relationship between gender and driving ability? If so, how did you reach this conclusion?) In the process of describing research on social judgments, inference, and decision making, we shall see that people often use relatively simple thought processes to deal quickly with the complex information of everyday life. Summary Table 5.1, at the end of this chapter, summarizes these thought processes.

Putting Information Together: Impression Formation

"You have probably never heard of Professor Moriarity?" said [Holmes].
"Never." . . .

"His career has been an extraordinary one. He is a man of good birth and excellent education, endowed by nature with a phenomenal mathematical faculty. . . . But the man had hereditary tendencies of the most diabolical kind. A criminal strain ran in his blood, which, instead of being modified, was increased and rendered infinitely more dangerous by his extraordinary mental powers. . . .

**What can you infer
about the men in this
photo? How do you
form overall impres-
sions of each man?
How does your prior
social knowledge influ-
ence your judgments?**

"He is the Napoleon of crime, Watson. He is the organizer of half that
is evil and of nearly all that is undetected in this great city. He is a genius, a
philosopher, an abstract thinker. He has a brain of the first order. He sits mo-
tionless, like a spider in the centre of its web, but that web has a thousand
radiations, and he knows well every quiver of each of them. . . ."

—— from "The Final Problem,"
by Sir Arthur Conan Doyle

You just read some positive facts about Professor Moriarity (he is a "genius"), as
well as some very negative ones (he is "the Napoleon of crime"). Although you
probably don't remember all the specific facts, you have formed an overall impression of Professor Moriarity. How?

Information about people can come from many sources. Sometimes we hear or
read facts about them, and sometimes we form first impressions based on their
appearance, ethnic background, gender, or certain nonverbal cues (see Chapter 3).
If we are thoughtful and have the luxury of time, we may logically infer a person's traits via various attribution processes (see Chapter 4). However we acquire
pieces of information, in the end we must combine them all, for in our minds a person is generally more than a collection of behavior and traits. How we organize information into meaningful wholes is the basic concern of research on impression
formation.

Asch's Gestalt Model

Solomon Asch (1946) conducted a classic study that set the tone for later research on
this topic. He presented subjects with a list of traits describing a person (for example,
"Jim is intelligent, skillful, industrious, warm, determined, practical, and cautious").
Subjects then wrote a brief description of Jim and indicated whether he also possessed other specified traits (whether, for example, Jim is "generous," "wise," or
"happy").

How did subjects form their overall impressions from the initial trait list? Asch argued that they could use either "algebraic" or "Gestalt" processes in combining information. To illustrate these processes, let's focus on a specific judgment a subject might make: how "likable" is Jim? If the subject answers this question through an algebraic thought process, then he or she in some sense assigns a degree of likability to each trait and then mentally "adds" or "averages" these individual pieces of information. Algebraic theories argue that the whole impression is simply the sum (or average) of its parts.

According to Gestalt theory, however, more complex and "configurational" integration processes occur—the whole may be greater than the sum of its parts. For example, Asch suggested that the meanings of certain traits might literally change depending on other traits occurring with them. Didn't your interpretation of Professor Moriarity's "extraordinary mental powers" change somewhat when you learned he was "the Napoleon of crime"? Intelligence—normally a highly desirable and positive trait—takes on a dark and malevolent connotation here.

Asch argued that our impression of another person is not formed algebraically, but rather in an emergent pattern that may vary depending on the total context of information. Asch further hypothesized that certain pieces of information are more important than others in influencing the total impression. Thus Sherlock Holmes's description of Professor Moriarity as the "Napoleon of crime" is probably central to our interpretation of much of the remaining information.

In his research Asch suggested that "warm" and "cold" are *central traits* that dramatically influence how the remaining traits in the list are interpreted. When Asch substituted "cold" for "warm" in his list of stimulus traits, subjects' impressions were drastically altered; however, using "blunt" and "polite" in the initial list instead of either "warm" or "cold" had very little effect on subjects' impressions (see Figure 5.1).

Since Asch's work, many researchers have criticized his Gestalt approach to impression formation. Wishner (1960), for example, argued that "warm" and "cold" were central traits in Asch's study simply because the traits carried semantically different information from the other traits in the list; this argument subsequently was elaborated by Zanna and Hamilton (1972). You'll recall from Chapter 3 that two main dimensions of person perception are good vs. bad intellectual traits and good vs. bad social traits. (Note, by the way, that Professor Moriarity is described as possessing good intellectual traits but very bad social traits.) The traits in Asch's initial list—"intelligent," "skillful," "industrious," "determined," "practical," and "cautious"—all tend to be intellectual traits, not social traits. On the other hand, "warm" (or "cold") are social traits and thus carry distinctly different information from those in the initial list. Thus "warm" (or "cold") may be central traits in Asch's experiment because of the particular traits he chose for his list.

Furthermore, the traits that Asch's subjects checked to indicate their overall impression ("generous," "wise," "happy," and "good-natured") tended to be social traits; that is, they were traits semantically related to "warm" or "cold" but not to the surrounding six intellectual traits in the list. This helped ensure that the addition of "warm" or "cold" would strongly affect the traits subjects checked. Thus both Asch's initial trait list and his checklist were predisposed to showing that "warm" and "cold" had a large effect on impressions. Despite methodological problems in his study, Asch's notion of "central traits" was quite influential. As we shall see, Asch's work is related to more recent research on schemas.

....

FIGURE 5.1   **Asch's study of impression formation.**

Are "warm" and "cold" central traits?

Asch (1946) presented subjects with the following list of traits:

intelligent, skillful, industrious, _____, determined, practical, cautious

The blank was filled with the words "warm," "cold," "polite," or "blunt" to see whether each word was a central trait—that is, whether each strongly influenced the subjects' perceptions of *other* traits the described person might have. The following table contains the percentages of subjects who thought the person described by the list of traits also possessed certain additional traits:

| | *Traits inserted into list* | | | |
Additional traits	*"warm"*	*"cold"*	*"polite"*	*"blunt"*
Generous	91%	8%	56%	58%
Wise	65	25	30	50
Happy	90	34	75	65
Good-natured	94	17	87	56
Reliable	94	99	95	100

In general, "warm" and "cold" produced more widely differing associations, indicating that these traits had a powerful impact on subjects' overall impressions of the person described.

....

....
Anderson's Weighted Averaging Model

Since Asch's research, social psychologists have refined various algebraic models of impression formation. One of the most influential of these—the weighted averaging model—was developed by Norman Anderson. In Anderson's research (1974), a typical subject might be asked to judge how likable an "intelligent, neurotic, loyal, and proud" person would be. Anderson found that each subject's overall impression of the person's likability seemed to be a *weighted average* of the likability of the individual traits and an "initial impression" factor reflecting a subject's general tendency to rate people either positively or negatively. The weighting of information implies that some traits have a greater effect on impressions than others, and the addition of weighted items implies that each trait's effect is additive (that is, it does not shift the meanings of other traits). See Figure 5.2 for an illustration of Anderson's weighted averaging model.

What determines how information is weighted? In forming an impression of likability, subjects often weight *negative* information more heavily than positive information (Kanouse & Hanson, 1972). Thus, in forming an impression of Professor Moriarty, you probably weighted his criminal tendencies more highly than his genius, thus forming a rather negative overall impression of him. Perhaps the tendency to weight negative information highly is another instance of the principle of *social desirability* (see Chapter 4). That is, because it is unexpected and socially undesirable, negative information is perceived to be more diagnostic of the person's true personality than is positive information. Consistent with this perspective, extreme

FIGURE 5.2   Anderson's weighted averaging model.

How do people combine trait information according to Anderson's weighted averaging model?

Suppose Sherlock Holmes tells Dr. Watson that Professor Moriarty is "brilliant" and "evil." How does Anderson's weighted averaging model explain Watson's overall impression of Moriarty?

The full equation is as follows:

$$\text{Overall evaluation} = \frac{w_0 I_0 + w_1 I_1 + w_2 I_2 + \ldots}{w_0 + w_1 + w_2 + \ldots}$$

where: I_0 = Watson's initial impression
w_0 = how much Watson weights his initial impression
I_1 = Watson's evaluation of trait #1
w_1 = how much Watson weights the first trait
I_2 = Watson's evaluation of trait #2, and so on

Let's assume that on a 100-point scale of "likability," Watson's initial impression of Moriarty (I_0) is neutral — that is, "50" on the scale — and that he rates the likability of "brilliant" to be "80" and "evil" to be "10." Now suppose that Watson weights the trait "evil" .5 — twice as much as he weights "brilliant" and his initial impression (both weighted .25). Then Watson's overall impression of Moriarty's likability is:

$$\frac{(.25 \times 50) + (.25 \times 80) + (.5 \times 10)}{.25 + .25 + .5} = 37.5$$

In Anderson's model, a central trait would be a highly weighted trait, but it would not shift the meanings of other traits.

information of any sort usually carries more weight in impression formation (Skowronski & Carlston, 1987). Almost by definition, extreme information is also somewhat unexpected.

The primacy effect (weighting early information more heavily than later information; see Chapter 3) frequently occurs in impression formation studies. In both Asch's and Anderson's research, subjects' impressions were influenced more by the first traits in lists than by later traits. This seems to result from at least two different processes: Early traits influence how subjects interpret later traits, and subjects simply pay more attention to early traits than to later traits (Anderson & Hubert, 1963; Belmore, 1987; Jones & Goethals, 1972; Zanna & Hamilton, 1977).

In a way, Anderson's averaging model allows for a kind of "central trait" — a trait that is very heavily weighted in forming an overall impression. However — and this is the crucial point — Anderson's analysis of why a particular trait is central is quite different from Asch's. Anderson simply considers the "central trait" to be a particularly heavily weighted or salient piece of information, whereas Asch argued that a "central trait" literally shifts the meanings of surrounding traits and reorganizes the way we perceive the entire body of information.

Both Gestalt and algebraic models may be valid accounts of certain kinds of impression formation. It is important to note that typically Anderson's weighted averaging model has been applied to relatively simple one-dimensional judgments — "How likable is a person with these traits?" However, the averaging model is more a description of such judgments than it is an explanation of them; it does not inform us much about the thought processes people use in making their judgments. As we shall see in the next section, the organized information we possess about others is often quite complex, and thus processes of impression formation are unlikely to be described fully by research techniques that assess only single dimensions such as likability.

In recent years, social psychologists have focused anew on Asch's hypothesis that central pieces of information can serve to organize impressions. However, Asch's concept of "central traits" has been supplanted by the more general concept of cognitive schemas (Fiske & Taylor, 1984).

Schemas and Social Perception

[Lestrade] struck a match on his boot and held it up against the wall.

"Look at that!" he said, triumphantly. . . .

. . . Across this bare space there was scrawled in blood-red letters a single word—

RACHE

. . . "And what does it mean now that you *have* found it?" . . .

"Mean? Why, it means that the writer was going to put the female name Rachel, but was disturbed before he or she had time to finish. You mark my words, when this case comes to be cleared up, you will find that a woman named Rachel has something to do with it. It's all very well for you to laugh, Mr. Sherlock Holmes. . . ."

"Come along, Doctor," [Holmes] said. . . . "There has been murder done, and the murderer was a man. He was more than six feet high, was in the prime of life, had small feet for his height, wore coarse, square-toed boots and smoked a Trichinopoly cigar. He came here with his victim in a four-wheeled cab. . . ."

Lestrade and Gregson glanced at each other with an incredulous smile.

"If this man was murdered, how was it done?" asked the former.

"Poison," said Sherlock Holmes curtly, and strode off. "One other thing, Lestrade," he added, turning round at the door: " 'Rache' is the German for 'revenge'; so don't lose your time looking for Miss Rachel."

—— "A Study in Scarlet," by Sir Arthur Conan Doyle

The bumbling Lestrade is the perfect foil to the master detective, Sherlock Holmes. In "A Study in Scarlet," Lestrade makes a common mistake — his prior knowledge (in this case, of the English language) leads him to misinterpret a clue. Perceiving a person (or a word) is not simply a matter of adding up all the pieces of information;

**Dr. Watson and
Sherlock Holmes
study a clue.**

it consists also of relating the information to prior knowledge — that is, to cognitive schemas. *Schemas* are hypothetical cognitive structures comprising organized knowledge; they influence how we perceive, organize, and remember information (Fiske & Taylor, 1984).

The effect of such prior knowledge on the perception and organization of new knowledge is the subject of considerable recent research in cognitive psychology. In an early and classic study, Bartlett (1932) demonstrated that people distort their memories of stories to make them more consistent with their cultural preconceptions. Bartlett's subjects read an Eskimo folk tale describing a battle in which the protagonist, shot by an arrow, dies at sundown after a mysterious black thing passes from his mouth. According to Eskimo folklore, a dying person's soul (the black object) departs through the mouth at sunset; this, of course, is the intended meaning of the story. However, when British subjects were asked to recount the story, they either forgot to mention the black object or interpreted it to be something understandable to them, such as some sickly discharge of fluid. In other words, they didn't literally remember the facts of the story; rather, they assimilated those facts into their existing cultural schemas.

Schematic processing of information is not exotic and unusual, but rather is characteristic of much everyday thought. It would be difficult for us to interpret new information without relating it to prior knowledge. For example, when you see a new color television set, you inevitably relate it to your previous experience with TV sets. You might say to yourself, "Where's the off-on switch? I know all TVs have off-on switches. . . ." Similarly, when you meet a new classmate from Texas, you probably perceive this person's traits and behaviors in light of your previous experience with Texans ("he's sort of brash, but I won't be offended — Texans are like that").

Knowledge that is obvious and trivial when organized by a schema might be quite incomprehensible without the schema. Try to figure out the subject of the following paragraph:

> The procedure is actually quite simple. First you arrange things into different groups. Of course, one pile may be sufficient depending on how much there is to do. If you have to go somewhere else due to lack of facilities that is the next step; otherwise you are pretty well set. It is important not to overdo things. That is, it is better to do too few things at once than too many. In the short run this may not seem important, but complications can easily arise. A mistake can be expensive as well. At first the whole procedure will seem complicated. Soon, however, it will become just another facet of life. It is difficult to foresee any end to the necessity for this task in the immediate future, but then, one can never tell. After the procedure is completed one arranges the materials into different groups again. . . . (Bransford & Johnson, 1972, p. 722)

As an experiment, take a minute or two and write down as much of the previous paragraph as you can recall. Now let me inform you that the title of the paragraph is "Washing Clothes." Reread the paragraph and see if it makes more sense. Not surprisingly, Bransford and Johnson (1972) found that subjects could recall more than twice as much information from this paragraph when they knew the title first — that is, when they had a schema with which to organize the information.

The Nature of Schemas

Schemas may influence what we perceive, how we perceive it, and what we remember, and thus they are not static bundles of "facts." Rather, they are dynamic mental categories, presumably based on experience, that we use to perceive and remember new information. This new information can be either consistent with a schema (for example, you might learn that your professor likes opera, which is probably consistent with your schema for professors), or inconsistent with a schema (your professor is a member of a heavy-metal rock band), or irrelevant to a schema (your professor is left-handed). A schema leads you to expect certain kinds of information but not others (Hastie, 1981).

Recent research indicates that our schemas for objects and people in everyday life do not have clear-cut boundaries (Anderson, 1980; Rosch, Mervis, Gray, Johnson, & Boyes-Braem, 1976; Rosch, 1978). For example, the difference between "triangles" and "squares" may be absolute and sharply defined, but the difference between "trees" and "shrubs" or between "introverts" and "extroverts" may be much less clear.

Theorists suggest that natural categories, like "trees" and "extroverts," are defined by sets of typical *features* (McCloskey & Glucksberg, 1978; Rosch, 1978). For example, some features of "trees" include "very tall," "have bark," and "have trunks without foliage." Some features of extroverts include "talk a lot," "go to many parties," "have lots of friends," and so on. Note that any given tree or any given extrovert may not have all of the features associated with its category, but the more "tree" features a tree possesses, the more "tree-like" it is. Similarly, the more "extrovert" features a person has, the more "extrovert-like" he or she is. Objects or mental examples that constitute an ideal, perfect example of a category are called *prototypes* (Anderson, 1980; Cantor & Mischel, 1977). A stately maple is a more prototypical tree than a dwarf palm, for it possesses more features considered to be characteristic of trees.

Schemas for social stimuli are like natural categories in that they comprise the features or attributes of certain objects or people (like college professors). Often they are not clear-cut, absolute categories, and they suggest prototypical examples (like the forgetful professor who wears tweed jackets and black horn-rim glasses, smokes a pipe, and carries Dostoyevsky novels under his arm during walks across campus).

Kinds of Schemas in Social Cognition

Taylor and Crocker (1981) distinguish among four main kinds of schemas of interest to social psychologists: person schemas, self-schemas, role schemas, and event schemas (sometimes also referred to as "scripts").

A *person schema* is a mental category that describes typical or specific individuals. For example, you may have schemas for "extrovert," "neurotic," and "intellectual," and you probably have schemas for specific individuals, such as your parents, Queen Elizabeth, or Joan Rivers.

Self-schemas, as the term suggests, refer to ways in which we classify and describe ourselves (Markus, 1977; Markus & Smith, 1981; Markus & Sentis, 1982). For example, your self-schema may include the attributes "intelligent," "independent," and "sensitive to criticism." People who strongly and readily categorize their behavior along a certain dimension are said to be "schematic" along that dimension. For example, a "macho" male may often perceive his behavior in terms of its masculinity (Bem, 1981).

Role-schemas are mental categories describing broad social groups and roles. In a sense, they are similar to our everyday term *stereotype*. Each of us may hold schemas about genders, races, religious groups, social classes, and professional groups. For example, a person might hold that women are "emotional" and "soft-hearted," that Asians are "hard-working" and "technically oriented," that Protestants are "industrious" and "moralistic," and so on.

Finally, *event schemas* (or *scripts*) refer to our mental categorization of social events like "going on a date," "going to a doctor's appointment," or "going to a restaurant" (Schank & Abelson, 1977; Bower, Black, & Turner, 1979). Event schemas contain the standard attributes of social events along with their expected order and causal relationships. For example, "going on a date" may typically include "picking up date at apartment," "going out to eat at restaurant," "going to movie," "going out for dessert," "coming home to apartment," "kissing date goodnight," and so on. Clearly such social events have a prescribed order—we don't eat dessert before dinner. Like all schemas, event schemas suggest what is expected in social events (for example, going out to dinner on a date) and what is unexpected (for example, having your blood pressure tested on a date).

Effects of Schemas on Social Cognition

Social psychologists have studied intensively how schemas affect (1) our perception of social information, (2) our memory for social information, (3) the inferences we make from social information, and (4) social behavior (Markus & Zajonc, 1985). Let's look at some research examples of each of these possible effects of schemas.

FIGURE 5.3   Illustration used in Allport and Postman's (1947/1965) study on rumor transmission.

SOURCE: Gordon Allport and Leo Postman, *The Psychology of Rumor.* Copyright 1947, renewed 1975 by Holt, Rinehart and Winston, Inc. Reprinted by permission of the publisher.

Schemas can influence perception.   A study by Allport and Postman (1947/1965) dramatically demonstrates how preconceptions (that is, schemas) can influence our perception of events. As part of a study on rumor transmission, Allport and Postman asked subjects to look at a drawing of a scene in a New York subway and then to describe the scene to other subjects, who in turn described what they heard to yet other subjects. The original drawing (Figure 5.3) was rich with information. The scene included two standing men, one black, the other white, engaged in conversation. The black man held both hands open during the conversation. The white man held an open straight razor in his left hand.

When Allport and Postman's subjects passed the information along to others, their descriptions often shifted the razor to the black man's hand. In other words, subjects' preconceptions — their schemas about blacks and whites — influenced what they perceived and later described. Many subjects did not accurately describe reality; rather, they described what they expected. Interestingly, children serving as subjects in this same study *did not* tend to shift the razor to the black man's hand. Perhaps they had not yet developed schemas about race. Allport and Postman's study suggests

When Do Schemas Influence Perception?

When are schemas most likely to influence our perceptions and judgments, and how can we avoid their more negative consequences? Schematic thinking is often "lazy" thinking: Research indicates that the more ambiguous, fleeting, or rushed social information is, the more schemas tend to influence impressions (Kruglanski & Freund, 1983; Lord, Ross, & Lepper, 1979; White & Carlston, 1983). Stated in reverse, the less "real" information we have to go on and the less time we have to think about that information, the more we will rely on our preconceptions in interpreting social data. For instance, if you become roommates with a student of another race, wouldn't your race schemas influence your impression of your roommate more the first day you move in together than after six months of interaction?

People often think more about facts that contradict their schemas than about facts that fit their schemas (Brewer, Dull, & Lui, 1981). By implication, a schema may influence our judgments more when the "facts" generally fit that schema and less when the "facts" contradict it. Finally, the effects of schemas seem to vary depending on our perceptual goals. In particular, schemas tend to influence our perceptions more when we strive to form general impressions than when we evaluate people on specific dimensions (Cohen & Ebbesen, 1979).

A study by Gibbons and Kassin (1987) illustrates the variable effects of schemas on perception. College students evaluated three high-quality pictures and three low-quality pictures that were supposedly painted by junior high school students. One group of subjects was informed that the student-artists were mentally retarded; a second group was not so informed. Some subjects were asked to rate the "overall quality" of the paintings, whereas others were asked to evaluate several specific characteristics of the paintings, such as theme, use of color, and quality of design.

Did the label "mentally retarded" influence how subjects perceived the paintings? Sometimes. Subjects were most likely to derogate paintings by "retarded" students when the paintings were of low quality (that is, the information was consistent with their schema for "mentally retarded") and when they were instructed to form an impression of "overall quality." And this derogation occurred most for the first low-quality painting subjects viewed.

In a second part of the study, Gibbons and Kassin observed that when subjects could control the amount of time they spent viewing each painting, they spent more time studying high-quality paintings by "retarded" painters; that is, they attended more to information that contradicted their schemas. Furthermore, subjects who spent more time studying the high-quality paintings by "retarded" students tended to evaluate them more positively and thus were less influenced by the label "retarded."

In everyday life, people constantly perceive and evaluate others: Teachers grade students, college admissions officials judge applicants, and personnel officers review employment applications and make hiring decisions. How can such professionals reduce the likelihood that their schemas (for race, gender, and so on) influence their judgments? The research just reviewed offers some suggestions. Evaluators must give themselves adequate time to review and carefully examine their information. They should strive to evaluate specific attributes (previous work experience, grades, clarity of writing) rather than form overall impressions. And, of course, they should acknowledge the possibility of schematic bias and pay careful attention to facts that do not match their preconceptions.

that although we "know" more as adults, this "knowledge" may sometimes bias our perception of reality.

A more recent study by Duncan (1976) shows a similar effect of race schemas on the immediate perception of social events. Duncan asked 104 white college students in California to watch a videotape of two students in discussion. At one point the discussion became rather heated and one student shoved the other. The viewing subjects were asked to categorize the two discussants' behaviors using a standardized coding system. The key independent variable in this study was the race of the two videotaped students. One group of subjects saw a black student shove a white student, whereas another group saw a white student shove a black student (see Figure 5.4).

How did the subjects perceive the shove? Interestingly, when a black student shoved a white student, 75 percent of the subjects rated this behavior as "violent." However, when a white student shoved a black student, only 17 percent rated the same behavior as "violent." Instead, 42 percent of the subjects perceived the white student's shove as "playing around" or "dramatizing," but only 6 percent described the black's shove that way. A more recent study has shown similar effects in grade school students' perceptions of drawings that portrayed interactions between black and white students. For example, one student bumping into a second student was perceived as more threatening and aggressive when the first student was black (Sagar & Schofield, 1980). Thus, rather than perceiving "reality," we sometimes perceive what we expect.

Schemas can influence memory.   Considerable evidence indicates that it is easier for us to remember information that is consistent with our schemas. For example, Cohen (1981) investigated the effects of role schemas on memory by asking subjects to view a videotape of a woman celebrating her birthday by having dinner with her husband. Subjects were informed that the woman was either a waitress or a librarian.

Cohen's videotape portrayed many behaviors considered typical of either a waitress or librarian. (These stereotypical behaviors were identified through extensive pretesting.) For example, the videotaped woman wore glasses, liked classical music, spent the day reading, and had traveled in Europe—all stereotypical "librarian" behaviors. However, she also drank beer, liked pop music, had a bowling ball, and was openly affectionate with her husband—all "waitress" behaviors.

All subjects viewed the same videotape, which contained an equal number of "waitress" and "librarian" behaviors. Yet, subjects were more likely to remember accurately features that were consistent with the given occupational labels. In a forced-choice questionnaire that measured memory (for example, "Did the woman drink beer or did she drink wine?"), subjects showed 88 percent accuracy in remembering schema-consistent facts, but only 78 percent accuracy for schema-inconsistent facts. In other words, it's easier to remember that a waitress "drinks beer" than that she "likes classical music," even if both are true. The first fact fits our expectations; the second does not.

In another manipulation in her study, Cohen presented the occupation labels to some subjects *before* they viewed the videotapes and to others *after* viewing. The question addressed by this manipulation is quite interesting: Do schemas influence primarily the immediate perception and encoding of information (the "label before" condition) or can they also influence later retrieval of information (the "label after" condition). The results of Cohen's experiment are presented in Figure 5.5.

First, note that schema-consistent information is easier to remember, regardless of the timing. Apparently schemas can influence both encoding and retrieval of information. Furthermore, Cohen's data indicate that having a schema (that is, an occupational label) at the start enhanced subjects' memory in general, for both schema-consistent and schema-inconsistent information. Apparently, having *any* schema available for early use in organizing and assimilating the wealth of information in the videotape was a general aid to memory (think back to the paragraph called "Washing Clothes").

FIGURE 5.4   Design and results of the Duncan (1976) study.

Do schemas affect our perception of social events?

Duncan (1976) showed white college students a videotape in which either a black student shoved a white student or vice versa. Subjects coded this behavior as it occurred.

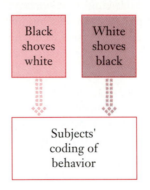

Subjects' coding of the shove was markedly different depending on whether it was the black or white student who did the shoving.

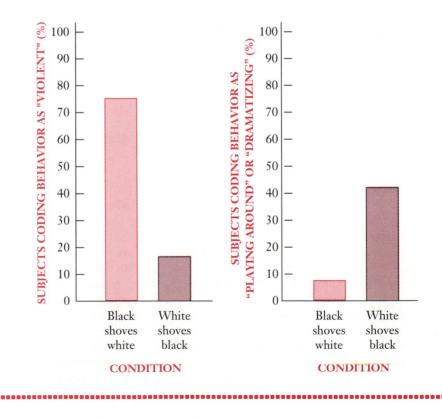

Is memory better for facts that are consistent with schemas?

Cohen (1981) tested the effects of a role schema on subjects' memory for
social facts by presenting occupational information about the woman
shown in the videotape either before or after subjects viewed the tape.
Memory was tested for facts that were either consistent or inconsistent
with the occupational information.

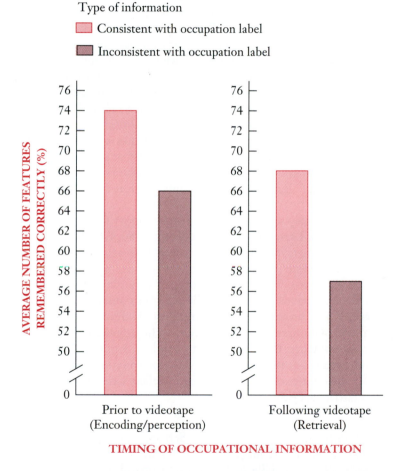

Type of information

▢ Consistent with occupation label

▢ Inconsistent with occupation label

Subjects remembered facts better that were consistent with occupation
labels. They also remembered facts better when occupation labels were
presented before rather than after the videotapes.

■■■

A study by Snyder and Uranowitz (1978) also suggests that a schema invoked *after* information is received may influence memory for that information. Two hundred twelve college students were asked to read the "case history of Betty K."; afterward, they were informed that Betty K. was either a lesbian or a heterosexual woman. Then, subjects were given multiple-choice questions to test their memory of facts in the case history. In general, the results indicated that subjects tended to remember "facts" consistent with Betty K.'s labeled sexuality, even to the point of falsely remembering some "facts" that hadn't been in the case history. For example, if Betty K. had been labeled as a "lesbian," subjects were more likely to remember that she "never went out with men" in high school, even though the case history reported that she "occasionally dated men" in high school. This research again suggests that we tend to remember facts consistent with our schemas, even to the point of reconstructing our memory to fit the schema. It is worth noting that two published studies (Clark & Woll, 1981; Belleza & Bower, 1981) failed to replicate the findings of the "Betty K." study, and thus future research must determine when "after-the-fact" schemas distort memory and when they do not.

Although research seems to confirm that subjects remember schema-consistent information better, the way subjects deal with schema-inconsistent information is less clear. Suppose you read a news story about Sister Felicia Philanthropy, a nun who rises daily at 5:30 a.m., ministers to the poor in a local soup kitchen, and prays one or two hours daily, but who also occasionally drinks whisky and tells off-color jokes. The research we've discussed so far suggests that your schema for "nuns" should help you to remember that Sister Felicia "ministers to the poor" and "prays one or two hours daily." But what about the information that Sister Felicia "drinks whisky"?

Interestingly, we may sometimes show good memory for inconsistent information (Fiske, Kinder, & Larter, 1983; Judd & Kulik, 1980; Graesser, Woll, Kowalski, & Smith, 1980). Hastie (1981) has suggested that if people have enough time, they ponder schema-inconsistent information and try to fit it into their preexisting schemas. This extra cognitive work may help explain why some studies find enhanced memory for schema-inconsistent information. For example, perhaps when you first read that Sister Felicia drinks whisky, this unexpected information might lead you to search for an explanation, such as "Well, she must be exposed to so many depressing cases in the soup kitchen that she needs to drink as a release." Such heightened attention and extra cognitive work occurs only for truly inconsistent information, not for irrelevant information (such as "Sister Felicia likes chocolate ice cream"), which we tend to forget easily.

Schemas can influence social inference.   Schemas may also influence how we "move beyond" given facts to make social judgments and evaluations. For example, Linville (1982a, 1982b; Linville & Jones, 1980) provides evidence that the more complex our schemas about groups are, the less extreme are our evaluations of people in those groups.

In one study, Linville and Jones (1980) asked white college students to evaluate a law-school applicant whose application was either quite strong (graduated Magna Cum Laude, received an Outstanding Senior Thesis Award, participated in important extracurricular activities, and had strong letters of recommendation) or rather

FIGURE 5.6 **Evaluations of weak and strong, white and black applicants to law school.**

Do we evaluate members of in-groups and out-groups differently?

Linville and Jones (1980) asked subjects to rate white and black applicants to law school who had either strong or weak credentials. The graph shows the subjects' ratings of the "applicants'" ability.

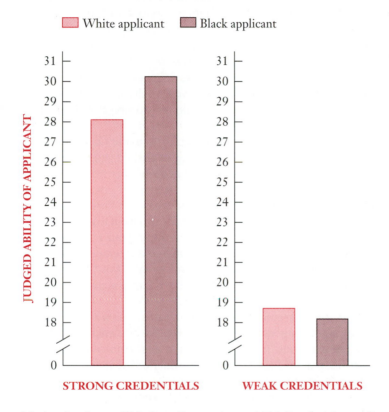

Notice that "strong" black applicants were rated higher than "strong" white applicants, but "weak" black applicants were rated lower than "weak" white applicants.

SOURCE: Data from Linville and Jones (1980).

Linville and Jones hypothesized that white subjects evaluated black law school applicants more extremely than white applicants because they held more complex schemas for in-groups (whites) than for out-groups (blacks).

weak (only minor honors and extracurricular activities). The applicant was also described as being either black or white. Interestingly, this experiment indicated that a weak black applicant was evaluated more negatively than a weak white applicant, but a strong black applicant was evaluated *more positively* than a strong white applicant. Some of the data from this study are presented in Figure 5.6.

These results do not show a simple pattern of direct prejudice against minority groups—the white applicant was not always evaluated more highly than the black applicant. Rather, Linville and Jones demonstrated that race *interacted* with the strength of the application in influencing subjects' evaluations. Why did this interaction occur? Linville and Jones suggest that white subjects' evaluations of black applicants are more extreme than their judgments of white applicants because schemas for "out-groups" tend to be less complex than schemas for "in-groups." That is, schemas for groups to which we belong are richer and have more features and cognitive dimensions than schemas for groups to which we do not belong. Linville's (1982) research further indicates that the polarizing effect of out-group schemas also holds for age (college students have less complex schemas for the elderly than they have for themselves) and for gender (we hold less complex schemas for the "opposite" sex than we have for our own).

Perhaps an analogy will help you appreciate Linville's hypothesis that complex schemas lead to less extreme judgments. Imagine I asked you to rate the intelligence of two people: your best friend and a stranger who sits near you in class. In one experimental condition I tell you that the stranger just got an "A+" on an exam, whereas in another condition I tell you that he received a "D." Wouldn't your rating of your friend be less influenced by the grade information than would your rating of the stranger? After all, you have a rich schema about your friend—you have lots of information and previous experience with him—and it tempers the effect of a single new piece of information. However, the grade—"A+" or "D"—may be the only thing you know about the stranger; as a result, that information will disproportionately influence your rating of his intelligence.

In Linville's studies, subjects could form evaluations while they examined "applications." But what happens when subjects receive information with an organizing schema and then *later* must make judgments or evaluations based on this information? Are their judgments based on their memory of the raw information or on the original organizing schema?

A study by Lingle and his colleagues (1979) shows quite clearly that we sometimes base judgments on evoked schemas rather than actual information. In one experiment, these researchers gave subjects a list of traits describing a hypothetical target person and asked these subjects to make one of two judgments: how well the person would perform in an occupation requiring intelligence ("Would this person make a good physicist?") or how well the person would perform in an occupation requiring friendliness ("Would this person make a good waiter?"). Then, without reviewing the initial traits, subjects were asked to rate the same person on intelligence and friendliness.

The results suggested that the target person was rated to be more intelligent when the subject had previously judged his suitability for being a physicist and to be more friendly when the subject had judged his suitability for being a waiter. In other words, judgments were influenced by the schema evoked by an "innocent" question as well as by the actual traits. The very act of making one judgment can influence later memory-based judgments (Lingle & Ostrom, 1979; Schul & Burnstein, 1985; Wyer, Srull, & Gordon, 1984).

The effects of schemas on such *memory-based inferences* were illustrated dramatically in research conducted by Loftus and Palmer (1974) on the accuracy of eyewitness testimony. In one intriguing experiment, after subjects viewed a brief film of a traffic accident in which two cars collided they were asked to report on the accident. The main independent variable was the *wording* of questions about the accident. Some subjects were asked how fast the cars were going when they "smashed" into each other; other subjects were asked how fast the cars were going when they "hit" each other. Surprisingly, subjects judged the cars' speed to be significantly greater (41 miles per hour) when questioned with the word "smashed" than when questioned with the word "hit" (34 miles per hour). In other words, the schema provided by words used in the questioning influenced subjects' memory of the event.

This study also suggested that an evoked schema may cause people to reconstruct their memories after the fact. Subjects were asked new questions about the filmed accident a week after seeing it. For example, they were asked whether they remembered seeing broken glass at the accident scene. Although there was no broken glass in the film, twice as many subjects reported "seeing" glass when previously questioned with the word "smash" than when questioned with the word "hit." Clearly, the "memory" of these subjects included "filled-in" information based on their schemas as well as accurately recalled facts. This study raises the disturbing possibility that crafty lawyers and interrogators can bias the memory of eyewitnesses through the clever use of language.

Schemas can influence behavior.
Thus far we have reviewed evidence that schemas (cognitive structures) can influence our perceptions, memories, and inferences (cognitive processes). Do schemas have only cognitive effects, or can they affect our actions as well?

Several kinds of research suggest that schemas do indeed influence behavior. Remember, schemas are mental classifications that lead us to expect certain things to be true—for example, that professors will be "smart," that librarians will be "quiet," that the elderly will be "absent-minded," and so on. It is perhaps a small step from expecting behavior in others to actually *eliciting* that behavior from them.

The sociologist Robert Merton (1948) coined the phrase "self-fulfilling prophecy" to refer to the process by which people's expectations become reality. We've already mentioned a well-known study by Rosenthal and Jacobson (1968) that showed that a teacher's expectations can influence students' behavior—that if a teacher thinks a child is smart, then the child will actually perform better in school. Similarly, Rosenthal demonstrated that experimenters' expectations could affect the behavior of their subjects (Rosenthal, 1966; see Chapter 2). Clearly, people can communicate their expectations in ways that can influence others' behavior. And, of course, our expectations are often derived from our schemas.

A clever study by Snyder, Tanke, and Berscheid (1977) showed how college subjects' schemas about physical attractiveness not only influence how they treat other students, but ultimately how these students behave in return; in other words, it showed a self-fulfilling prophecy in operation. In this study male subjects talked by telephone to females who they were led to believe were either attractive or unattractive. (The women's actual attractiveness was unrelated to what the men were told.)

Predictably, the men behaved in a warmer and friendlier manner to women they thought were attractive. But surprisingly, the women who had been labeled attractive were in fact warmer, more poised, and more humorous in their conversations; that is, the men's treatment influenced the women's behavior. Are attractive people really warmer, friendlier, and more poised? Regardless of the answer to this question, our schemas probably hold that they are true. To the extent they do, we may create what we expect.

One subtle way we can initiate a self-fulfilling prophecy is by selectively seeking out (and even creating) information that is consistent with our schemas. Snyder and his colleagues (Snyder & Swann, 1978; Snyder & Campbell, 1980; Snyder, 1981) found, for example, that subjects often ask questions that tend to confirm their expectations. For example, Snyder and Swann (1978) assigned college women the task of interviewing a partner about her personality. For some subjects, the goal of the interview was to determine whether the partner was an extrovert; for others the goal was to determine whether she was an introvert. Subjects chose their interview questions from a prepared list that included questions about extroverted behaviors ("What would you do if you wanted to liven things up at a party?"), questions about introverted behaviors ("What factors make it difficult for you to really open up to people?"), and neutral questions ("What kinds of charities do you like to contribute to?").

Interestingly, subjects trying to diagnose their partners' extroversion asked more "extroverted" questions, whereas subjects trying to diagnose introversion asked more "introverted" questions. Their partners' answers were tape-recorded, and judges then rated how extroverted or introverted partners seemed from their responses. Intriguingly, the partners of women trying to diagnose extroversion were in fact judged to be more extroverted from their interview responses, whereas the partners of women diagnosing introversion were judged to be more introverted. By attempting to diagnose a trait, subjects unknowingly asked leading questions and thus encouraged answers consistent with the trait. Do professional questioners do the same? For example, in examining patients suspected to have "mental illness," do psychologists and psychiatrists tend to ask questions that will confirm their hunches? If so, they may be guilty of creating the evidence on which they base their diagnoses.

Selective questioning undoubtedly occurs in many everyday settings. After talking to your professor about difficulties you're having with her class, is she more likely to ask "Are you having problems in any other classes?" or "Are you doing well in all your other classes?" If the first question sounds more probable, the professor may be asking questions that tend to confirm her "bad student" schema.

Priming effects.   Suppose you start a conversation with a woman sitting next to you in class. What schema will you use to organize information you learn about her? Do you perceive new facts in terms of, say, her gender, her ethnic background, or her age? One possibility is that you will classify her on the most salient dimension, the one that "sticks out" in the situation (McGuire, McGuire, Child, & Fujioka, 1978; McGuire & Padawer-Singer, 1976). If she is the only woman in an engineering class, a gender schema is likely to be evoked. If she is the only elderly person in a class of 20-year-olds, then an age schema may be evoked.

Another possibility is that a schema you have used in the recent past may "prime" you (that is, make you more likely) to use that schema for new information. Suppose you have just served on a college admissions committee reviewing the intelligence and scholastic aptitude of prospective students. When you next meet a high school senior, you may be more likely to assess this person's behavior in terms of intelligence and suitability to attend college as a result of your recent experience on the committee.

One study (Higgins, Rholes, & Jones, 1977) demonstrated such a *priming effect* by first having subjects read a list of either positive or negative traits (for example, "adventurous" vs. "reckless"). Later, in a seemingly unrelated study, these same subjects read about a man named Donald who engaged in a number of risk-taking activities like skydiving and racing. Interestingly, subjects rated Donald's behavior more negatively when they had already been primed with negative traits (like "reckless").

Apparently a schema that has been recently used is more readily available for subsequent use. An early study by Murray (1933) demonstrated this effect in a different context. Schoolgirls were asked to play a scary game called "Murder" (all the girls but one hid scattered throughout a darkened house while the remaining girl—the "murderer"—searched for them and "murdered" them by sneaking up and tagging them in their hiding places). Before and after the game, the girls were asked to rate people in photographs on various characteristics. In general they perceived the people in the photographs to be more cruel, malicious, and evil after playing the game. Put another way, after the game girls applied a "Murder" schema to their perceptions of people.

The more frequently a schema has been activated in the past, the more likely it is to be applied to new situations (Wyer & Srull, 1980; Higgins & King, 1981). In a sense, a much-used schema may become permanently primed. So police officers, for example, may be permanently primed to interpret other people's behavior in terms of criminality; they may possess a chronically primed "Murder" schema.

Do schemas ever change? If we receive enough contradictory evidence, we may alter a schema, particularly if the contradictory information observed is "spread out" among many members of the category rather than concentrated in a small number of very deviant members (Crocker & Weber, 1983; Weber & Crocker, 1983). For example, many people seem to think that waitresses like pop music, drink beer, go bowling, and read only romantic novels. Suppose I introduce you to five waitresses. One of them likes classical music, another drinks fine French wines, and yet another reads complex Russian novels in her spare time. Meeting these three waitresses is more likely to change your schema for waitresses than would meeting one waitress who likes classical music, drinks French wines, and reads Russian novels. One very deviant case is less damaging to your schema than many less extreme exceptions because it is easier to explain away as an exceptional case: "She's not a *real* waitress; she's actually a graduate student temporarily earning some extra money as a waitress. . . ."

Although change is possible, schemas are often remarkably stable. We have already provided some reasons why this is so: People often perceive ambiguous data in ways that are consistent with their schemas; they tend to remember better those facts that are consistent with their schemas; and they often induce others to behave in ways that are consistent with their schemas.

There is yet another reason for the inertia of schemas: They foster supporting cognitions and causal explanations that lead us to continue to believe in them, even in the face of subsequent contradictory evidence (Anderson, Lepper, & Ross, 1980; Anderson, 1983). For example, suppose you learn that little Simon was accused of stealing money from other children's lockers at school. You might say to yourself "Well, little wonder—Simon's parents are divorced, and his mother's an alcoholic. He's left alone all day. No wonder he's gotten in with a bad crowd." Based on one

What schema will you use to organize your perceptions of this woman? One answer is that you'll classify her on the dimension that "sticks out" in this situation. Thus, you are more likely to apply an age schema than a gender or "student" schema.

accusation you've constructed an elaborate "bad boy" schema complete with causal explanations. Now suppose you learn that Simon didn't really steal the money — another student confessed to the crime. Do you totally revise your opinion of Simon's criminality? No. You've spent so much cognitive work explaining and justifying Simon's crime that you've convinced yourself of his criminal tendencies, even though the original evidence has evaporated. If I asked you to rate the likelihood that Simon would steal something, you'd probably rate it higher than you should.

Such a *perseverance effect* — the maintenance of beliefs in the face of discrediting evidence — has been demonstrated in many experiments. In one of these Ross, Lepper, and Hubbard (1975) falsely informed subjects that a new personality test indicated that they were extremely socially sensitive and good at judging other people's traits. Later the subjects were informed that the personality test was invalid and completely worthless in assessing their social sensitivity. Subjects were then asked to rate their actual social sensitivity and perceptiveness. Interestingly, subjects who had been told they were sensitive rated themselves as being significantly more sensitive than did control subjects, even though they knew the initial information to be bogus. Apparently, once these subjects were (falsely) informed that they were socially sensitive, they constructed explanations for this "fact" that remained compelling even when the "fact" was invalidated (Anderson, Lepper, & Ross, 1980).

The perseverance effect is highly relevant to an ethical issue that we considered in Chapter 2: Can debriefing truly remove the negative effects of intrusive experimental manipulations? Suppose as part of an experiment on self-esteem we give subjects a fake personality test, and then falsely inform some of them that they have a "troubled, maladjusted personality." This manipulation does in fact produce lowered self-esteem in subjects (see Walster, 1965), and it also raises a serious ethical question: Can the experimenter completely remove the experimentally produced negative effects on self-esteem through debriefing? Studies on the perseverance effect show that this may be a fairly difficult task that requires careful debriefing procedures (Ross & Anderson, 1982).

▪▪▪▪▪▪▪▪▪▪▪▪▪▪▪▪▪▪▪▪▪▪▪▪▪

Illusory Correlations in Social Perception

Central to all schemas is the assumption that certain traits or features are associated with a particular category of people or events. How do we know when one variable is correlated with another? For example, is "criminality" correlated with certain ethnic groups? Is bigotry associated with certain religious sects? Is personality associated with hair color—do blondes have more fun? Each of these questions asks whether one variable is in some way related to another variable.

An important set of studies by Chapman and Chapman (1967, 1969, 1982) demonstrated that people may falsely see correlations between variables based on their preconceptions, rather than on real occurrences. In one study, Chapman and Chapman (1969) asked subjects to examine clinical information about "psychological patients" with various problems. In particular, the subjects looked at human figures supposedly drawn by patients and read a list of the corresponding patient's psychological symptoms. Subjects were asked to discern whether any features in the drawings (for example, big eyes) were correlated with specific psychological disorders (for example, paranoid thoughts). Some drawings and symptoms similar to those used in the Chapman and Chapman study are presented in Figure 5.7.

In fact *no correlation* existed between any of the drawings' features and patients' symptoms; the pictures and the lists of symptoms were constructed by the researchers, who randomly paired picture features with psychological conditions. Nonetheless, subjects perceived correlations that confirmed their preconceptions. For example, subjects felt there was a correlation between "big eyes" in drawn figures and "paranoia" and between "missing hands" and "psychological withdrawal."

Results like these may help to explain why some clinicians believe in the value of certain tests, even when research suggests that they are invalid. For example, many clinical psychologists use the Rorschach Ink Blot Test to assess personality, even though considerable research casts doubt on this test's reliability and validity (Chapman & Chapman, 1982). Clinicians often argue that they know "from clinical experience" that such tests are valid, but the Chapman and Chapman research indicates that we must be very careful in accepting the validity of intuitive correlations without more rigorous, scientific evidence.

Research on illusory correlations suggests yet again that schemas are difficult to change because people have a pervasive bias for perceiving reality according to their schemas.

FIGURE 5.7   Material similar to that used in Chapman and Chapman's (1969) study of illusory correlations.

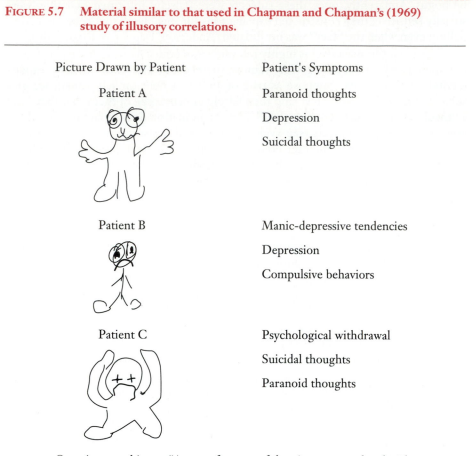

Picture Drawn by Patient

Patient A

Patient B

Patient C

Patient's Symptoms

Paranoid thoughts

Depression

Suicidal thoughts

Manic-depressive tendencies

Depression

Compulsive behaviors

Psychological withdrawal

Suicidal thoughts

Paranoid thoughts

Question to subjects: "Are any features of the pictures correlated with specific disorders?"

Social Inference and Decision Making

. . . "Beyond the obvious facts that he has at some time done manual labor, that he takes snuff, that he is a Freemason, that he has been in China, and that he has done a considerable amount of writing lately, I can deduce nothing else."

Mr. Jabez Wilson started up in his chair, with his forefinger upon the paper, but his eyes upon my companion.

"How, in the name of good-fortune, did you know all that, Mr. Holmes?" he asked. "How did you know, for example, that I did manual labor? . . ."

"Your hands, my dear sir. Your right hand is quite a size larger than your left. You have worked with it. . . ."

"Well, the snuff, then, and the Freemasonry?"

"I won't insult your intelligence by telling you how I read that, especially as, rather against the strict rules of your order, you use an arc-and-compass breastpin."

Even in the simplest social settings, people engage in complex chains of reasoning about others.

"Ah, of course, I forgot that. But the writing?"

"What else can be indicated by that right cuff so very shiny for five inches? . . ."

"Well, but China?"

"The fish that you have tattooed immediately above your right wrist could only have been done in China. . . ."

. . . "Well, I never!" said he. "I thought at first that you had done something clever. . . ."

—— from "The Red-Headed League,"
by Sir Arthur Conan Doyle

Social cognition often entails inferences; we go beyond the given facts to reach new judgments and conclusions. We've already touched upon issues of inference in several contexts. For example, the previous section examined some of the effects of schemas upon inferences and evaluations, and our discussion of impression formation described how people combine traits to form overall evaluations. None of these research areas, however, deals directly with such questions as: Where do we get the information upon which we base our inferences? How do we sample information from the external world or from our memories when making inferences? And how do we use this information to make decisions? Let's turn to these basic questions about social cognition.

The Effects of Sampling Errors on Inferences

The first stage in making an inference based on social information is getting the information. For example, if you want to decide whether Asian students are more industrious than Caucasian students, then somehow you must observe some Asian students or retrieve memories of Asian students. Or, if you want to decide how widespread drunk driving is, you must observe drivers or remember instances of drunk driving.

One common error people make in estimating the occurrence of social events is to place too much reliance on small samples (Nisbett & Ross, 1980; Tversky & Kahneman, 1974). For example, you might say, "Yes, the Chinese woman in my class always scores near the top. Asian students *are* more industrious." Or, "My cousin was seriously injured by a drunk driver. It's happening all the time."

Statistical sampling theory shows that small samples are highly unreliable. Would you believe that men are more intelligent than women if I told you that I carried out a study in which two men proved to have higher IQ scores than two

FIGURE 5.8   Subjects' judgments of a group based on a single member.

Do we sometimes ignore sampling information when making judgments about groups of people?

The table shows subjects' attitudes toward prison guards in general after they had observed a single guard who was described as either "typical" or "atypical." (Higher numbers indicate more positive ratings.)

	Description of Guard	
Type of Guard Observed	*Typical*	*Atypical*
Compassionate	12.56	11.94
Cruel	9.44	10.11

In both the "typical" and "atypical" conditions, the subjects' attitudes toward guards in general were more positive if they had observed the "compassionate" guard.

SOURCE: Data from Hamill, Wilson, and Nisbett (1980).

In this study, subjects' judgments of a group were strongly influenced by their experience with a single example, even when they knew that the person they had observed was not representative of the group.

women? Although concluding anything on the basis of such a limited sample seems ludicrous, we are apparently willing to make everyday inferences on the basis of equally limited samples. For example, do you think Libyans are "fanatical"? On how large a sample of Libyans do you base your judgment?

Not only are people inordinately influenced by small samples, but they fail to realize that their samples are often quite biased (Nisbett & Ross, 1980). For example, if I asked you whether college students these days are generally liberal or conservative, how would you decide on an answer? You might think of all the college students you know — for example, your friends — and count up how many of them are liberal and how many are conservative. The problem with this process, of course, is that your friends are far from a random sample of college students. Students at Oral Roberts University might answer my question quite differently from students at San Francisco State.

Even when given clear information about how typical and representative a sample is, subjects often seem to ignore this information. For example, in one interesting study (Hamill, Wilson, and Nisbett, 1980) subjects saw a videotaped interview of a prison guard, who was described as being either quite typical of most guards or quite atypical. In one version of the tape, the guard appeared cruel and inhumane, whereas in another version he seemed quite compassionate. After viewing one of the tapes, subjects were asked to rate how positive they felt about prison guards in general. The results of this study are presented in Figure 5.8.

How Do People Combine Information When Making Decisions?

Suppose you are a personnel executive who must hire a new manager for a store. The latest applicant is of Japanese descent, dresses well, and has a B.A. with average grades in economics from State University. She has good letters of recommendation and three years of work experience at Amalgamated Department Stores. How do you combine information to decide whether you will hire her?

We've already dealt with one kind of information integration—impression formation, the process by which people combine trait information to form impressions of others' personalities. The current question is a bit broader: How do people combine information in general to make decisions?

Perhaps the simplest possible decision rule is based on a *linear model*, in which you make decisions by simply adding or averaging each piece of information. This process is reminiscent of algebraic models of impression formation. For example, in hiring a new employee you might rate pieces of information about job applicants (such as educational background, G.P.A., previous work experience) on a ten-point scale and simply add or average them. (You might use a *weighted average* in which some information counts more heavily in your decision—perhaps you think previous job experience should be weighted twice as much as G.P.A.) Then you could use one of many possible decision rules. For example, you might decide to hire the person with the highest

average or the first applicant who exceeds some minimum threshold. If applicants are being evaluated on a number of quantifiable dimensions (such as test scores, G.P.A., or years of work experience), then you could easily program a computer to execute such a linear decision rule.

Nonlinear decision rules are also possible. Indeed, many decision makers pride themselves on being flexible and nonmechanical in evaluating data. Suppose that in evaluating job applicants for a new art designer for your company, you decide to weight all information equally in making your hiring decision. But then you interview Paula Picasso, who has won several graphic design awards and has a breathtaking portfolio. You decide not to count her college G.P.A. (a disappointing 2.00) at all—after all, creative artists don't need good grades. In other words, how you weighted one of the variables changed in light of other information, a situation reminiscent of Asch's Gestalt view of impression formation.

How do human decision makers in fact combine and integrate information? And how do mechanical decision rules compare to human decision making in consistency and quality? The answers provided by psychological research (Abelson & Levi, 1985; Dawes, 1988) are often surprising.

Although people pride themselves on applying subtle nonlinear judgments to complex information, in fact most people make

decisions simply by weighting a very small number of dimensions (Dawes, 1976, 1980, 1988). For example, when employers hire people they may think they sift through and weigh all the information, but when we statistically analyze who they hired and who they didn't, it often turns out that only two pieces of information—such as G.P.A. and years of work experience—really affected their decisions.

Second, all studies to date that pit mechanical (sometimes computerized), linear decision rules against human decision makers show that "mechanical" decision making is consistently as good or better than human judgments (Dawes & Corrigan, 1974; Dawes, 1988; Meehl, 1954; Sawyer, 1966; Wiggins, 1973). Perhaps one advantage of the mechanical decision rules is that they are applied more consistently and reliably than the variable strategies of fallible human beings.

To the extent that these research findings are true, they point to some interesting recommendations. Of course, human decision makers must choose the variables on which to base a decision, such as hiring personnel, admitting students to college, or diagnosing mental disorders. But once we choose these variables and decide how they are to be weighted, we should let an unbiased and consistent computer program make the decision.

Interestingly, the only significant result was that after viewing the compassionate guard, subjects rated guards in general more positively, whereas after viewing the cruel guard, they rated guards in general more negatively. Although subjects' ratings were slightly less extreme when they thought the videotaped guard to be "atypical," this effect was not statistically significant. Notice that subjects were willing to draw conclusions about prison guards in general on the basis of the smallest possible sample—a sample of one! In addition, subjects drew these conclusions regardless of whether they were told that the sample was "typical" or "atypical" of guards in general.

The Underutilization of Baserate Information

In the "guard" study, subjects' judgments were influenced too much by one concrete instance. They didn't seem much influenced by *baserate information* (broad, often statistical information about how groups or categories behave in general). Subjects received baserate information when they learned that guards in general either were or were not like the one they observed.

The underutilization of baserate information is quite common. Suppose you want to buy a popular new Italian sports car, a Primavera Tortellini. All the consumer and automobile magazines say the Tortellini is a superb machine with admirable performance and repair records. Then your best friend says to you, "No, don't buy a Tortellini! My mother bought one and it's been the biggest lemon—carburetor problems, a faulty steering column. . . ." What will influence you more—the highly positive statistical baserate information or the one concrete, vivid example from your friend?

Numerous research studies (for example, Bar-Hillel & Fischoff, 1981; Ginosar & Trope, 1980; Nisbett & Ross, 1980; Taylor & Thompson, 1982) suggest that people tend to pay more attention to a single concrete instance than to valid baserate information (which, because it represents a much better sample, is much more reliable). Some researchers have assumed that concrete instances are more attended to because they are vivid and salient and thus more compelling (Nisbett & Ross, 1980; see the discussion of salience effects in attribution, Chapter 4). Whatever the correct explanation, people often fail to weight baserate information as heavily as they should.

Actually, we've already encountered people's failure to use baserate information adequately, but in a slightly different context. Empirical tests of Kelley's cube model of attribution (McArthur, 1972; Kruglanski, Hamel, Maides, & Schwartz, 1978; Major, 1980; see Chapter 4) indicated that when they are deciding on the causes of others' behavior, people attend *least* to consensus information. If you want to know why Joan laughed at a comedian, you're not that interested in knowing whether Tom, Dick, and Harriet also laughed. In other words, subjects do not seem to attend strongly to statistical baserate information in making causal attributions.

Heuristics— Shortcuts to Social Inference

Everyday social life entails an extraordinary amount of cognitive "work." We must figure out the causes of people's behavior; we must perceive, encode, and retrieve information and fit it into our preexisting knowledge; and we must form organized impressions of others, integrate information, and somehow arrive at adaptive decisions and judgments.

With our cognitive "computer" so loaded with various duties, it is no wonder that we sometimes use mental shortcuts to answer certain questions. Rather than

How dangerous do you think air travel is today? One way to estimate the frequency of events (for example, airplane accidents) is to use the *availability heuristic:* recall as many instances as you can. Because the mass media highly publicize air disasters and because such disasters are vivid and memorable, we probably tend to remember many instances and thus overestimate their frequency.

San Francisco Examiner

★ ★
Friday afternoon
FEBRUARY 24, 1989
HOME EDITION
TWENTY-FIVE CENTS

AS MANY AS 11 PEOPLE LOST IN MIDAIR OFF HAWAII
747 rips open in sky

Tower: Bush's loyalties face test

By Christopher Matthews
EXAMINER WASHINGTON BUREAU CHIEF

WASHINGTON — The Senate Armed Services Committee's vote against John Tower promises an uphill, if not hopeless, battle for confirmation before the entire Senate. It creates the strong possibility that President Bush's choice to be Defense secretary will become only the ninth cabinet nominee ever to be rejected for confirma-

COMMENTARY

ASSOCIATED PRESS PHOTOS
A hole estimated at 10 by 40 feet *shows in the side of a Boeing 747 belonging to United Airlines after its return to Honolulu airport early Friday.*

Crippled plane struggles to safety despite gaping hole

FROM EXAMINER STAFF AND WIRE REPORTS

HONOLULU — As many as 11 passengers were apparently sucked from a United Airlines jumbo jet 20,000 feet over the Pacific Ocean Friday after the plane's fuselage was ripped open shortly after take-off, federal aviation officials said.

The damaged airliner, which was carrying 354 people, returned to Honolulu for an emergency landing. At least 11 other passengers were injured.

Initial reports had referred to an explosion aboard Flight 811, which originated in San Francisco, but investigators later said it appeared that the Boeing 747's cargo door had ripped off, puncturing the aircraft's fuselage and damaging the plane's engines. They did not, however, rule out sabotage.

National Transportation Safety Board spokeswoman Drucella Andersen said the jet had departed Honolulu International Airport

exhaustively analyze a particular problem, we may instead apply less time-consuming mental strategies to give us "quick and dirty" answers to pressing questions. Kahneman and Tversky (1973; Tversky & Kahneman, 1973; Tversky & Kahneman, 1982) have described several such cognitive *heuristics,* or shortcut cognitive processes, that yield quick estimates or answers. We will focus on two particularly important ones: the availability heuristic and the representativeness heuristic.

The availability heuristic.   In considering how serious a social problem drunk driving is, you might recall as many drunk driving accidents as you can. The more cases you can recall, the more likely you are to judge the problem to be serious. Kahneman and Tversky (1973) call this process of estimating the frequency of some event by the ease with which you can bring instances to mind the *availability heuristic.*

Although cognitive availability seems like a fairly reasonable process, it can sometimes lead to consequential errors. For example, we may overestimate the frequency of events that are easy to remember (Slovic, Fischoff, & Lichtenstein, 1977). Research suggests that people tend to overestimate the frequency of violent deaths caused by fire, murder, and accident and tend to underestimate the frequency of death from heart disease, strokes, and cancer. Apparently violent deaths are easier to recall (probably because of media coverage of them), and thus people overestimate their frequency. Similarly, because newspaper articles much more frequently mention the race of murderers when they are black, it is probably easier to recall murders committed by blacks and as a result to overestimate the proportion of murderers who are black. In subtle yet pernicious ways the availability heuristic may contribute to stereotyping and prejudice (Hamilton, 1981).

The availability heuristic may combine with other cognitive processes to make our beliefs quite resistant to change. Earlier we discussed a number of studies suggesting that we have better memory for schema-consistent information. The combination of this finding and the availability heuristic produces a vicious cycle of belief. If, for example, you possess a gender schema that men are more competent than women, you can probably remember more examples of competent men than competent women. Using the availability heuristic, you estimate the frequency of competent men and women by the ease with which you can recall specific examples. Because your memory is biased by your schema, the availability heuristic leads you to a conclusion that is comfortably consistent with your schema — namely, there *are* a lot more competent men than competent women.

The representativeness heuristic.
Sherlock Holmes masterfully assigned people to social groups (Freemasons, laborers) based on subtle diagnostic clues, and he was usually quite sure of his conclusions. But in everyday life we often face more ambiguous clues. How do we decide whether a person is likely to be a member of a group when we have suggestive but inconclusive evidence? For example, suppose I say that Jill is "conservative," "moralistic," "against abortion," and "in favor of prayer in the schools." How likely is she to be a fundamentalist Christian? Or suppose I say that Jack is "sensitive," "artistic," and "interested in interior design." How likely is it that Jack is gay?

One statistically correct but quite laborious approach to answering these questions would be to determine the probability that each trait is diagnostic of the category, and then mathematically combine the probabilities. For our question about Jill, we could estimate the probability that a fundamentalist Christian is "conservative," "moralistic," and so on, and then mathematically combine the probabilities to reach a conclusion.

In everyday life, we generally opt for a much simpler thought process: We simply see how well the information matches some imagined average or typical person in the category, and the closer the person is to the prototype, the more likely we are to judge the person to be in the category. Because Jill's traits seem to match those of the "typical" fundamentalist Christian, we are likely to judge that she is a fundamentalist Christian. Similarly, because Jack's traits match those of the "typical" gay man, we are very likely to judge him to be gay.

Kahneman and Tversky (1973) label this thought process the *representativeness heuristic* — we decide on any example's probability of class membership by assessing how similar the example's features are to the "typical" case. Like the availability heuristic, this seems like a quick and reasonable (if somewhat rough) way of making such judgments. But the representativeness heuristic can also produce biased judgments.

For example, using the representativeness heuristic can be particularly misleading if baserate information is also available. For example, if we learn that Jill is "moralistic," "conservative," "against abortion," "in favor of prayer in schools," *and* lives in the Crown Heights section of Brooklyn, it probably would not be wise for us to decide that Jill is a fundamentalist Christian because Crown Heights is inhabited largely by orthodox Jews. Regardless of how well other concrete "facts" fit our stereotype of a fundamentalist Christian, in this case the baseline odds are not good that our judgment is indeed correct.

The representativeness heuristic may also lead us astray when nondiagnostic and diagnostic information is mixed. Suppose we learn that Jack "drives a Toyota," "is sensitive," "lives in a house," "is artistic," "works as a lawyer," "is interested in interior design," and "plays tennis." Are we more or less likely to judge him to be gay now? In experimental tasks like this, most subjects judge Jack *less* likely to be gay, even though the added "facts" are truly irrelevant to being gay. (The earlier facts may be irrelevant too, but they reflect the typical stereotypes about gays. Whereas many people believe that being "interested in interior design" is diagnostic of being gay, almost everyone would agree that "living in a house" is unrelated to being gay.)

This finding — that nondiagnostic information mixed in with diagnostic information leads to more conservative inferences — is called the *dilution effect* (Nisbett, Zuckier, & Lemley, 1981; Zuckier, 1982). The representativeness heuristic provides one explanation for why the dilution effect occurs. When people learn facts that are unrelated to their image of the typical category member, those facts are considered to be less representative of the category. The logical error, of course, results from assuming that nondiagnostic information says anything at all about category membership.

The dilution effect may either increase or decrease the accuracy of inferences (Zuckier, 1982). When we hold strong and incorrect stereotypes, then dilution will lead to greater accuracy, for we will be less sure of our incorrect inferences. On the other hand, when diagnostic cues are valid, dilution will lead us to place less confidence in our valid inferences.

Framing Effects in Decision Making

The way a question is posed (or "framed") can have important effects on social judgments and decisions. Over the past ten years social psychologists have begun to study *framing effects* in social judgments and decisions, particularly those involving elements of risk (Tversky & Kahneman, 1984). Such studies often present subjects with a choice between two risk-taking alternatives. For example, imagine that a new strain of flu has appeared, and medical researchers have developed two new vaccines to combat it. Because of financial limitations, only one vaccine can be used for mass public inoculations. Medical experts have estimated that:

If vaccine A is chosen, 200 people will be saved.

If vaccine B is chosen, there is a ⅓ probability that 600 people will be saved and a ⅔ probability that no people will be saved.

SUMMARY TABLE 5.1   Social Cognition Research

TOPICS AND PROCESSES STUDIED	EXAMPLES	RESEARCH FINDINGS
Impression formation (How do people combine information about others?)	Gestalt models	Effects of central traits.
	Algebraic models	Early, negative, and extreme information is weighted heavily in judgments of likability.
Schematic processing of information (Effects of prior knowledge)	Effects on perception	Schematic biases in perception.
	Effects on memory	Better memory for schema-consistent information; mixed results for schema-inconsistent information.
	Effects on inferences	Out-groups evaluated more extremely than in-groups because schemas for out-groups are less complex than schemas for in-groups.
	Effects on behavior	Self-fulfilling prophecies; confirming schemas through selective questioning.
	Priming effects	Evoked schemas affect later judgments.
	Belief perseverence	Schemas resistant to change even in the face of disconfirming information.
	Illusory correlations	Schemas lead people to perceive correlations between variables when none exist.
Social judgment and inference (How do people "go beyond" given information?)	Sampling errors	People base inferences too much on small and biased samples.
	Underutilization of baserate information	People attend too much to concrete examples and too little on reliable statistical information.
	Cognitive heuristics	
	Availability	People judge an event's frequency by the ease with which they can bring examples to mind.
	Representativeness	People judge likelihood of group membership by comparing features of particular case to prototype.
	Dilution effect	Nondiagnostic information mixed in with diagnostic information leads to more conservative inferences.
	Framing effects	The way questions are framed influences decisions.
	Prospect theory	Perceived aversiveness of a negative event is greater than the perceived value of an equivalent positive event.

Which vaccine would you choose if you were in charge of vaccinating the public? If you are like a majority of subjects, you chose vaccine A (Tversky & Kahneman, 1981). Now consider this second scenario concerning flu vaccinations:

If vaccine C is chosen, 400 people will die.

If vaccine D is chosen, there is a ⅓ probability that nobody will die and a ⅔ probability that 600 will die.

Which vaccine would you choose now? If you are like most subjects, you chose vaccine D.

These results are intriguing because the first scenario is logically identical to the second scenario; all that differs is that the first scenario describes the decision's consequences in terms of "lives saved," whereas the second describes consequences in terms of "deaths." For example, the ⅓ chance that 600 people "will be saved" in the first scenario is logically identical to the ⅓ chance that "nobody will die" in the second.

In general, framing studies show that people are more likely to avoid risks and opt instead for a "sure thing" when decisions are framed in positive terms ("lives saved") and more likely to take risks when decisions are framed in negative terms ("deaths"). Thus in the first scenario the "sure thing" of saving 200 lives seems better than the "riskier" alternative that entails the possibility that no lives will be saved; in the second scenario, the "sure thing" of 400 deaths seems worse than the "riskier" alternative that entails the possibility that no deaths will result.

The way a choice is framed affects decisions in part because the frame provides a standard of reference and associative connotations to use in interpreting information. In one recent study (Levin, Schnittjer, & Thee, 1988), subjects were informed that a new cancer treatment had either a "50 percent success rate" or a "50 percent failure rate." Though logically equivalent, these two different frames led to quite different judgments. Subjects in the "50 percent success" group rated the treatment to be significantly more effective and stated that they would be more likely to advise a close family member with cancer to seek the treatment than did subjects in the "50 percent failure" group. Clearly, "success" conjures up more positive connotations than does "failure," and it implicitly leads subjects to compare 50 percent success with *less* successful treatment rates.

More fundamentally, the way a choice is framed affects decisions because people psychologically assign *value* to positive events to a lesser extent than they assign *costs* to negative events. Kahneman and Tversky's (1979) *prospect theory* describes this phenomenon. In commonsense terms, prospect theory implies that a given positive occurrence (say, receiving $5) is perceived somewhat differently than is a negative occurrence of equivalent magnitude (losing $5) — receiving $5 is less psychologically rewarding than losing $5 is punishing. Graphically, prospect theory is described by a curve in which the slope of perceived costs of increasingly negative events is steeper than the slope of perceived *values* of increasingly positive events (see Figure 5.9). Thus, because people perceive positive outcomes differently than they perceive negative outcomes, they tend to take risks when faced with a choice that includes a negative "sure thing" and avoid risks when faced with a choice that includes a positive "sure thing."

Framing can affect many social decisions and behaviors. For example, the ways in which situations are framed can influence how people negotiate in business relationships. In one study, Bazerman, Magliozzi, and Neale (1985) asked students at Boston University and at the University of Arizona to be "buyers" for retail stores and "sellers" for refrigerator manufacturers in simulated business negotiations. Many buyers and sellers simultaneously tried to arrive at agreements that would maximize profits and minimize expenses for their companies. Subjects' negotiations were "framed" in memos that emphasized one of two goals: that negotiators not exceed a certain level of costs in a deal or that they not accept less than a certain level

FIGURE 5.9   Prospect theory: The perceived value received from a given positive event is less than the perceived cost incurred by a negative event of the same magnitude.

How does prospect theory help to explain framing effects?

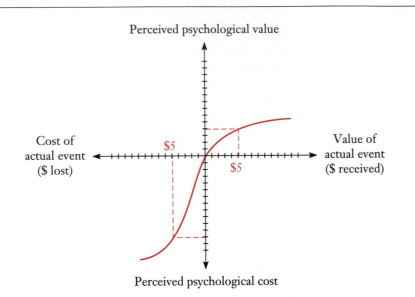

SOURCE: Adapted from Kahneman and Tversky (1979).

Prospect theory has a precise mathematical formulation. However, it is possible to understand some of the implications of prospect theory without a formal mathematical treatment.

of profit. Interestingly, subjects whose negotiations were framed in terms of "profits" rather than "costs" tended to complete more deals. Thus, the outcomes of negotiations may depend in part on how negotiation goals are framed.

Social Cognition:
A Final Thought

"Has anything escaped me?" I asked with some self-importance. "I trust there is nothing of consequence that I have overlooked?"

"I'm afraid, my dear Watson, that most of your conclusions were erroneous. When I said that you stimulated me I meant, to be frank, that in noting your fallacies I was occasionally guided towards the truth."

—— from "The Hound of the Baskervilles,"
by Sir Arthur Conan Doyle

Social cognition research has often focused on the ways we go wrong in thinking about others. For example, in this chapter we have seen that we are subject to schematic biases in perception, memory, and social inference. We sometimes maintain discredited beliefs and perceive illusory correlations between variables. In assessing social reality, we often sample information in limited and biased ways and use simplistic decision rules and heuristics to reach quick and sometimes biased conclusions. Our decisions and behavior may be strongly (and illogically) influenced by how information is framed.

Should these findings lead us to be disillusioned with the human "computer"? Clearly, the answer is no. Despite the many cognitive errors documented in this chapter, most of us process information well enough to be reasonably successful in everyday social life. In order to achieve more rational thought and better decision making, we must first understand how our thinking can go wrong (Dawes, 1988). In this way, research on social cognition can lead to better social cognition in such real-life situations as business negotiations, personnel decisions, and college admissions.

Sherlock Holmes was fond of paradoxes. Here is one we all should ponder: Human cognitive processes, the failings of which are studied in social cognition research, also design and interpret that research.

Summary

1. Social cognition research examines how people process information about other people.

2. Impression formation is the process by which people combine information about others to form overall judgments. Solomon Asch proposed a Gestalt model of impression formation and argued that central traits can both exert a strong influence on total impressions and shift the meanings of other traits. Norman Anderson developed a weighted averaging model of impression formation.

3. Research on impression formation often shows that early, negative, and extreme information tends to be weighted heavily.

4. Schemas are cognitive structures comprising organized knowledge about people, social roles, social events, and ourselves.

5. People often perceive social information in ways that are consistent with their schemas. Such effects are strongest when information is ambiguous and judgments are rushed.

6. People remember information better when it is consistent with their schemas. Information that is inconsistent with schemas may be remembered well if people have time to think about it.

7. Schemas for in-groups are often more complex than schemas for out-groups. This leads people to evaluate members of out-groups more extremely than they evaluate members of in-groups.

8. People often elicit in others behavior that confirms their expectations. Schemas may thus lead to self-fulfilling prophecies.

9. Once schemas are primed, they often affect subsequent perceptions and judgments.

10. Schemas are often resistant to change. The perseverance effect occurs when people maintain false beliefs in the face of discrediting evidence. Illusory correlations occur when people's expectations lead them to perceive a correlation between variables when none exists.

11. People often base social judgments on samples that are too small and biased, and they tend to underutilize baserate information when making judgments and decisions.

12. When people make decisions based on many dimensions of information, their decisions are usually a function of only a small number of these dimensions. Studies that pit mechanical, linear decision rules against human decision makers show those rules to be as good or better than humans.

13. Heuristics are shortcut cognitive processes that yield quick, rough estimates or answers. The availability heuristic refers to estimating the frequency of an event according to the ease with which we can call instances to mind. The representativeness heuristic refers to estimating the likelihood that a person is a member of a social category by assessing how well his or her traits match the group prototype. Both of these heuristics can lead to biased estimates.

14. Framing effects occur when social judgments and decisions are influenced by the wording used to describe the situation. In general, when decision outcomes are framed in terms of positive consequences, people tend to avoid risk; when outcomes are framed in negative terms, people tend to take risks.

Glossary

Availability heuristic: The practice of estimating the frequency of an event according to the ease with which instances of the event can be brought to mind

Baserate information: Broad, often statistical information about groups or categories of objects; people often underutilize such information in making judgments and decisions

Central traits: According to Asch's gestalt model of impression formation, central traits are highly important pieces of information that serve to organize a total impression and that influence the meanings of other traits

Dilution effect: The phenomenon in which people make more conservative inferences when undiagnostic information is mixed in with diagnostic information

Event schemas: Also known as scripts; schemas for social events

Framing effects: Occur when decisions are influenced by the wording of the decision outcomes

Heuristics: Shortcut cognitive processes that yield quick estimates or answers

Illusory correlations: Perceived correlations between uncorrelated events; when people expect events to be correlated they are subject to illusory correlations

Impression formation: The study of how people combine information about others to form overall judgments or evaluations of them

APPLYING SOCIAL PSYCHOLOGY

Throughout its relatively brief history, social psychology has combined an interest in pure and applied science. Applied social psychologists *answer social questions* ("Is there a link between violence and viewing of violent TV?"), *evaluate social interventions* ("What have been the effects of court-ordered school integration?"), and *design social programs* ("How should homes for the elderly be run to maximize the health and well-being of their residents?").

Answering social questions:
Federal troops enforce court-ordered school integration in Little Rock, Arkansas, in 1957. Chapter 9 discusses social psychological research on the effects of classroom and residential integration on racial attitudes. How do groups and crowds influence individuals' behavior? Chapters 13, 14, and 15 discuss different aspects of this question. Are employers biased against women and minority groups? Chapters 9 and 10 present research findings on prejudice and stereotypes. How do juries arrive at decisions? Chapter 15 presents research on group decision making.

Evaluating social programs:

What kinds of integrated classrooms are most effective in reducing prejudice? See Chapter 9 for an answer based upon social psychological research.

How do personnel managers decide whom to hire? Research on social cognition (Chapter 5) addresses this and many other questions about the thought processes people use in evaluating others.
How effective are customs inspectors at detecting deception? See Chapter 3.

*Designing programs
and interventions:*

A therapist talks with a client. Chapters 4 and 6 discuss how social psychological research has contributed to the treatment of clinical depression.

How effective are public advertising campaigns in encouraging intravenous drug users to stop sharing needes and smokers to stop smoking? Chapters 7 and 8 discuss the many applied sides of research on attitudes and attitude change.

Chapter 16 describes how assigning everyday responsibilities to nursing home residents can significantly improve their health and well-being. Research on attitude change (Chapter 8), compliance (Chapter 14), and group behavior (Chapter 15) offers guidance on how to encourage people to conserve resources through such efforts as recycling.

Linear decision models: Decision rules that add up or average the information used to make the decision

Nonlinear decision models: "Configural" decision rules that allow the possibility of changing the weight given to one kind of information depending on other information

Perseverance effect: The tendency for false beliefs to be maintained in the face of discrediting evidence

Person schema: A schema for specific individuals

Priming: Occurs when a schema activated in one setting affects judgments made in another setting

Prospect theory: A theory developed by Kahneman and Tversky that explains framing effects in decision making; it holds that people psychologically assign value to positive events and costs to negative events differently, which leads people to seek risks when decision outcomes are framed in terms of their negative outcomes but leads them to avoid risks when outcomes are framed in terms of their positive outcomes

Prototype: An ideal example of a category; a prototype possesses all the features that define the category

Representativeness heuristic: The practice of deciding on the probability of class membership (for example, whether a person belongs to a social group) by assessing how similar the features of the concrete instance are to the prototypical case; thus, if a man possesses all the traits of a "typical" gay, you will decide he is gay

Role schema: A schema for social groups

Schema: Cognitive structure comprising organized knowledge about people, social roles, events, and oneself

Self-fulfilling prophecy: The process whereby people's expectations become reality through their own actions

Self-schema: The schema one possesses about oneself

Social cognition: The study of how people process information about other people

Weighted averaging model: Norman Anderson's algebraic model of impression formation; it holds that a judge's impression of a person's likability is determined by a weighted average of the likability of individual traits, plus an "initial impression" factor reflecting the judge's tendency to rate people positively or negatively in general

. . . [I]t appears to be an inborn and imperative need of all men to regard the self as a unit. However often and however grievously this illusion is shattered, it always mends again. The judge who sits over the murderer and looks into his face, and at one moment recognizes all the emotions and potentialities and possibilities of the murderer in his own soul and hears the murderer's voice as his own, is at the next moment one and indivisible as the judge, and scuttles back into the shell of his cultivated self and does his duty and condemns the murderer to death. . . . In reality, however, every ego, so far from being a unity is in the highest degree a manifold world, a constellated heaven, a chaos of forms, of states and stages, of inheritances and potentialities.

—— from *Steppenwolf*, by Hermann Hesse, pp. 66–67

CHAPTER 6

Personality and the Self

Harry Haller, the protagonist of Hermann Hesse's strange and compelling novel, *Steppenwolf*, believed himself to have two parts or personalities: one a man, the other a wolf. The human part of Harry contained "a world of thoughts and feelings, of culture," whereas the wolf within him comprised "a dark world of instinct, of savagery and cruelty, of unsublimated raw nature." One self was the socialized product of bourgeois convention; the other was a natural, unfettered, and sensual self.

What about you? Do you have only one self, only one personality? Or perhaps two, like the Steppenwolf? Or maybe even more? Hesse suggested that Harry Haller's two-self view of himself was overly simplistic: "His life oscillates, as everyone's does, not merely between two poles, such as the body and the spirit, the saint and the sinner, but between thousands and thousands" (p. 66). Hesse argued that the unity of the self is an illusion that "rests upon a false analogy. As a body everyone is single, as a soul never."

Even if the unity of the self and of individual personality is an illusion, it is nonetheless a compelling one. Indeed, the "self" and "personality" constitute two of the most intuitively appealing explanations we can offer for our own and others' behavior (see Chapters 3 and 4). For example, Harry Haller may explain that his reluctance to talk to people is due to his introversion and shyness (personality traits). And you may explain your volunteer charity work by noting that it is consistent with your self-concept — that you are a helpful person. You may even state that you *choose* to engage in charitable activities.

As the previous examples illustrate, the concepts of personality and the self refer to processes *within* individuals that influence their behavior. Although it traditionally focuses more on *situational* explanations of behavior (see Chapter 1), social psychology has in recent years devoted considerable research to understanding the effects

171

of personality and the self on social behavior (Snyder & Ickes, 1985; Suls & Greenwald, 1986).

Social psychologists have studied certain personality traits because these traits directly relate to specific social behaviors, such as discrimination, bargaining, aggression, affiliation, altruism, and persuasion. The traits of introversion and shyness, for example, may influence the degree to which people affiliate with others and form friendships. Social psychologists have studied other personality traits because those traits *moderate* the effects of situational and personality variables on social behavior. For example, as we shall see later in this chapter, some kinds of people (termed high self-monitoring individuals) may be influenced more by their social setting, whereas others (low self-monitoring individuals) may be influenced more by their inner traits and values. Self-monitoring, then, is a trait that moderates the impact that situations and other traits have on behavior.

The self is an important topic in social psychology because it conceptually links the individual, social influences, and social behavior (Greenwald, 1982). The self contains the internalized rules and standards of society, and thus it leads us to behave (at least at times) in a manner that is consistent with such standards. Paradoxically, the self—perhaps the most private and individual aspect of each of us—has social origins and social consequences.

Social psychologists have posed some questions about the fundamental nature of personality and the self: Do people possess consistent unitary selves, or (as Hermann Hesse suggests) do they have many selves? Do people in general possess stable personality traits that lead them to behave consistently (for example, in an introverted fashion) across settings and over time, or do people behave more variably?

Social psychologists have also posed many questions about social influences on personality and the self: Do we change our self-concept and our self-presentation (the way we try to appear to others), depending on the people we're with? How do we negotiate our identities (our consensual beliefs about our personality and self) with the people around us?

We'll begin this chapter by considering the topic of personality. After discussing two major approaches to personality—trait theories and social learning theories—we'll turn to research generated by these two approaches. Next we'll consider some classic theories concerning the related topic of the self. Then we'll address a number of fundamental empirical questions: How does the self develop? How is knowledge about the self stored, and how does this knowledge influence the processing of information about the self and others? How does the self regulate social behavior? Is the public self different from the private self? And how is the self related to mental health?

Now that you have some idea of the topics we'll explore, let's turn to some psychological research and theory on that "chaos of forms, of states and stages, of inheritances and potentialities" that constitutes each individual human personality and each individual self.

Personality and Social Behavior

The word *personality* derives from the Latin word *persona*, which means an actor's mask. In ancient Greece and Rome, actors' masks symbolized the kind of characters they portrayed—a grinning mask for a comic character, a sneering mask for a mali-

Laurence Olivier as Hamlet. Do people have consistent traits, like characters in a play?

cious character, and so on. Characters in a play typically have distinctive and consistent traits. Shakespeare's Macbeth, for example, possessed unprincipled ambition; Othello, uncontrollable jealousy; and Hamlet, chronic melancholy and indecisiveness. Do real people show such consistent traits? Over the years, *persona* came to mean not only the roles that actors played, but also the consistent traits and characteristics that people display (Burnham, 1968). The term *personality*, then, traditionally has referred to the consistent, stable, and distinctive traits and behaviors that characterize individuals.

The scientific study of personality has often focused on a variety of *internal* processes that influence people's behavior. For example, various personality theories have focused on traits (Allport, 1937, 1961; Eysenck, 1952; Cattell, 1965), psychological needs (Murray, 1962), expectancies (Rotter, 1954; Bandura, 1986; Mischel, 1973), and the ways in which people process information (Kelly, 1955; Cantor & Kihlstrom, 1987). Traits, needs, expectancies, and cognition processes are all *mediating variables* (see Figure 6.1) that are presumed to reside within the person and that exert a general influence on behavior.

Personality psychologists generally study the ways in which people differ from one another. For example, some individuals are extroverted, some introverted; some are dominant, some submissive; some are anxious and nervous, and others calm

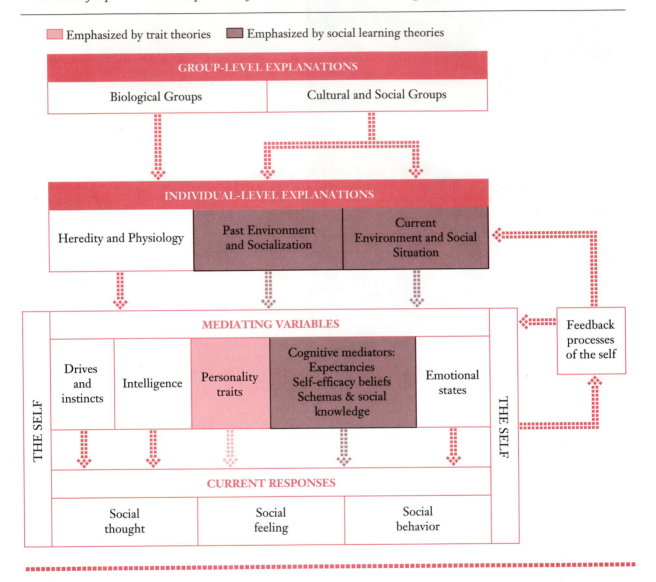

FIGURE 6.1   **Personality theories as explanations of behavior.**

What kinds of explanations are emphasized by trait theories and social learning theories?

☐ Emphasized by trait theories   ☐ Emphasized by social learning theories

GROUP-LEVEL EXPLANATIONS

Biological Groups	Cultural and Social Groups

INDIVIDUAL-LEVEL EXPLANATIONS

Heredity and Physiology	Past Environment and Socialization	Current Environment and Social Situation

MEDIATING VARIABLES

THE SELF

Drives and instincts	Intelligence	Personality traits	Cognitive mediators: Expectancies Self-efficacy beliefs Schemas & social knowledge	Emotional states

THE SELF

Feedback processes of the self

CURRENT RESPONSES

Social thought	Social feeling	Social behavior

and relaxed. Personality theories try to explain and understand such individual differences.

Implicit in the traditional concept of personality is the idea that people show behavioral consistency, both across settings and over time (Allport, 1937; Mischel, 1968; Mischel & Peake, 1983). If Louise is an "extroverted" person, she presumably displays extroverted behaviors frequently and in many situations—she has a lot of friends at school, she talks a lot with other people wherever she is, and she often goes places to be with others (for example, to parties). Furthermore, if she is an extroverted person today, she is likely to be so a month from today as well.

These central issues of personality psychology — internal causes of behavior, individual differences, and the consistency of behavior — have been addressed by two different theoretical approaches: trait theories and social learning theories (see Figure 6.1). Other approaches to personality exist as well, such as psychoanalytic and humanistic theories (see Liebert & Spiegler, 1987; Maddi, 1976), but trait theories and social learning theories have generated the most empirical research in contemporary social psychology. Furthermore, these approaches are important because they address a theoretical question that is central to social psychology: How much is behavior determined by stable internal traits, and how much is it determined by situational factors?

▪▪▪▪▪▪▪▪▪▪▪▪▪▪▪▪▪▪▪▪▪▪▪▪▪

Trait Theories:
Personality as Stable
Internal Dispositions

Trait theories make the basic assumption that people possess consistent internal dispositions (for example extroversion, shyness, or honesty) that have a general influence on behavior. Famous trait theorists include Gordon Allport (1937, 1961), Raymond Cattell (1965), and Hans Eysenck (1952). Most of us, as naive everyday personality psychologists, are trait theorists. Indeed, we saw in Chapter 3 that traits often constitute the largest single category of terms we use to describe other people.

Trait theories hold that people show consistent behavior across time and settings, and that behavior shows a direct relationship with its underlying trait. Thus if you have a high degree of the trait "extroversion," for example, you should consistently show extroverted behaviors in many settings and at different times, and the stronger the trait is, the more you should behave in extroverted ways.

One major challenge and potential dilemma for trait theories is cataloging the basic traits in human personality. In a monumental compilation, Allport and Odbert (1936) identified some 18,000 trait words used in the English language. Clearly, to possess practical utility, trait theories must focus on considerably fewer fundamental traits.

Studies that ask subjects to rate themselves on large numbers of traits (or on behaviors that reflect various traits) find considerable redundancy in such ratings. For example, the traits "introverted," "reserved," and "outgoing" may all describe the same thing ("outgoing," of course, is simply the reverse of the first two). Indeed, complex statistical analyses show that subjects' ratings of themselves on many different traits often boil down to just a small number of underlying "factors," or cohesive trait dimensions.

Five basic trait dimensions are repeatedly found in personality research: sociability, likability, conscientiousness, emotional adjustment, and intelligence/culturedness (Hogan, 1983; McCrae & Costa, 1987). These trait dimensions are quite similar to the basic dimensions of person perception we discussed in Chapter 3. (Note that in Chapter 3 we were concerned with the basic traits that people use *to describe others*. Here we are concerned with the basic traits people use *to describe themselves*. Clearly these are related issues.)

The measurement of personality traits. Psychologists often measure traits with standardized personality questionnaires that ask subjects to rate themselves on specific traits (such as "aggressive" or "extroverted") or to answer questions (such as "I enjoy going to parties often") by choosing a fixed response ("Yes/No" or "True/

False") or by checking a five-point scale ranging from "Agree" to "Disagree"). A good personality test is carefully developed; its questions or items are selected by rigorous statistical analysis and test-development procedures (Anastase, 1976; Cronbach, 1984). Generally, test items are administered to large groups of people, and only those items that successfully discriminate among people with respect to the trait under examination are used in the test. For example, only those questions that on average are answered differently by anxious and nonanxious people (so designated by, say, clinical psychologists) will be used in an anxiety scale.

A good personality test demonstrates two important properties: *reliability* and *validity* (see Chapter 2). A reliable test measures a trait consistently. How can psychologists ascertain whether or not a test is reliable? One way is to administer the test at two different times to the same people; if test scores remain relatively stable, the test possesses *test-retest reliability*. Another measure of reliability focuses on the consistency of items within a test. A test possesses *internal reliability* when individuals' responses to individual items tend to correlate with one another and with the overall test scores. High internal reliability implies that all the items on a personality scale are measuring the same underlying trait.

A valid personality test truly measures the trait it's intended to measure. A test has *predictive validity* when it can predict relevant criteria. Thus, for example, an extroversion test with high predictive validity might predict the number of parties subjects will attend during the three months following the administration of the test.

A well-conceived personality test should also yield scores that correlate with theoretically related variables, a concept called *construct validity*. For example, to test hypotheses derived from a theory about the nature of extroversion, a psychologist might conduct studies to determine whether extroversion correlates with certain kinds of mental illness—whether, for example, extroverts are more likely to be hysterics, whereas introverts are more likely to be obsessive-compulsives (Wilson, 1977). Stated another way, construct validity is concerned with whether the relation between test scores and other variables makes theoretical sense.

Finally, a good personality test should be able to discriminate between scores produced for traits it measures and scores resulting from tests of other traits. This is called *discriminant validity*. For instance, the finding that subjects' scores on an extroversion test correlate strongly with their scores on an intelligence test implies that the extroversion test may really measure intelligence, not extroversion.

For personality tests to be valid, they must first be reliable. If they are not reliable measures in the first place, personality test scores can neither predict useful criteria nor correlate in theoretically meaningful ways with other variables.

Social Learning Theories: Personality as Learned Behavior

Social learning theories (see, for example, Miller & Dollard, 1941; Rotter, 1954; Bandura, 1977, 1986; Mischel, 1973) consider the environment, rather than stable internal traits, to be the source of the individual differences we call "personality." A basic assumption of social learning theories is that individual differences in behavior are *learned* through such processes as classical conditioning, operant conditioning, and observational learning. For example, boys may come to show "masculine" behaviors and girls "feminine" behaviors because they have been rewarded by their parents for showing such behaviors (operant conditioning) and because they have learned such behaviors from models such as their peers or TV actors (observational learning). (See Chapter 10 for a more complete discussion of the relation of traits and social learning to gender-related behaviors.)

Social learning theories hold that behavior is not necessarily consistent across settings and over time. For example, Louise might be extroverted with her close friends, who always respond warmly to her, but introverted at the Ritz Country Club, where people tend to snub her. Think about your own behavior. Are you consistently "extroverted," "anxious," or "masculine" or "feminine" in all situations, or does your behavior vary considerably depending on who you are with and where you are?

Research based on social learning theories relies more on actual observation of subjects' behavior and on subjects' reports of their own behavior than on standardized personality tests. Thus if we wanted to study Louise's "anxiety," we might measure her heart rate in different situations or ask her to keep a diary of her anxious feelings at different times and places throughout the day. Social learning researchers are typically interested in studying the environments that elicit behavior (Mischel, 1982). According to social learning theories, the individuality of personality resides in each person's unique *pattern of behavior and learning history*, rather than in the person's pattern of traits.

What, then, do social learning theories say about the three central issues of personality psychology — internal causes of behavior, stable individual differences, and behavioral consistency? More than trait theories, social learning theories question all three assumptions (see Figure 6.2). Certainly, social learning theories do not consider behavior to necessarily reflect stable internal traits, although modern social learning theories do postulate the existence of inner cognitive variables such as expectancies, social knowledge, and self-efficacy beliefs (beliefs about our ability to perform certain behaviors). Because people are observed to differ from one another in highly idiosyncratic ways, social learning theories do not expect behavior necessarily to be consistent across settings; rather, different environments often elicit different behaviors. However, behavior may show consistency *over time* in the same setting because the same environmental factors are present (Mischel & Peake, 1983; Wright & Mischel, 1987). Thus, for example, the coarseness of your language may vary considerably — you might curse when with your friends but not in the presence of your parents. (Thus, your coarseness is not a consistent trait.) However, you may show consistency over time when in the presence of your parents — you *never* curse.

▪▪▪▪▪▪▪▪▪▪▪▪▪▪▪▪▪▪▪▪▪▪▪▪▪▪▪▪

**Research on
Personality Theories**

Social learning theories clearly emphasize different causal factors than those emphasized by trait theories (see Figure 6.1). Still, the two approaches are not necessarily contradictory. As we noted before, some traits (such as masculinity and femininity) may represent learned consistencies in behavior. Thus, social learning theories emphasize learning processes that may lead to consistency (and in some cases, inconsistency) in behavior. Let's consider some empirical research that investigates the utility and limits of trait theories and social learning theories.

Research on the assumptions of trait theories.   Several major reviews of personality research in the 1960s (Mischel, 1968; Peterson, 1968; Vernon, 1964) suggested that traits are not particularly good predictors of behavior. In his landmark book, *Personality and Assessment*, Walter Mischel (1968) noted that the correlation coefficients for the association between trait measures of personality and behavioral criteria are typically quite small, rarely exceeding .3. (Recall that 0 represents no correlation and 1 a perfect correlation; see Chapter 2.)

How has trait theory's assumption that behavior is consistent across situations fared in research studies? Personality psychologists have studied the cross-situational consistency of behavior for over half a century. In one classic study, Hartshorne and May (1928, 1929; Hartshorne, May, & Shuttleworth, 1930) measured the "morality" of school children in a number of different settings. For example, they measured how much the children cheated on tests, stole party favors, broke rules in athletic contests, and so on. Surprisingly, they found little consistency in the children's moral behavior; a given child might cheat on tests but never steal. Such findings clearly contradict the hypothesis that children possess a general trait of "morality" or "immorality." Other studies have shown that people are frequently inconsistent with respect to degrees of extroversion, punctuality, and conscientiousness (Dudycha, 1936; Newcomb, 1929; Mischel & Peake, 1982, 1983).

Does this evidence suggest that trait theory, although intuitively appealing, is simply wrong? Not necessarily. Some researchers have argued that their inability to demonstrate consistencies among behaviors, and between traits and behaviors, is in part due to research methodology. For example, Epstein (1980, 1983) argues that in order to measure behavior *reliably*, researchers must "aggregate" behaviors — that is, obtain a sum of many measures of behavior — rather than assess single behaviors. Remember, reliability is a prerequisite to validity: In order for trait measures to predict behavior and for behavior to show consistency, both behavior and traits must be measured reliably.

In research that provided empirical support for this point, Jaccard (1974) reported a correlation coefficient of .10 for the association between a trait measure of dominance and subjects' self-reports of single dominant behaviors (like "controlling conversations"); however, the correlation coefficient increased to .60 when trait scores were used to predict a summed measure of 40 different dominant behaviors. And Epstein and O'Brien (1985) reported that when classic studies such as Hartshorne and May's research on morality in children are reanalyzed using *summed* measures of behavior, behavior proves to be much more "trait-like" and consistent.

Bem (1983; Bem & Allen, 1974) has offered another remedy for the poor performance of traits in predicting behavior. He argued that specific traits may have predictive utility for only some people; to predict a person's behavior from his or her traits, we must first determine whether the trait is even relevant to that individual. Indeed, Bem and Allen (1974) found that people who rated themselves as consistent on a trait showed more consistent, "trait-like" behavior. These findings have been replicated in other studies as well (see, for example, Kenrick & Stringfield, 1980; Zuckerman, Koestner, DeBoy, Garcia, Maresca, & Sartoris, 1988).

Similarly, Mischel and Peake (1982; also see Buss & Craik, 1980) noted that people may show trait-like consistency among some behaviors but not others. In particular, behaviors that a person views as *prototypical* of a trait (that is, an ideal example) will be more likely to reflect that person's trait score and to show consistency. For example, if we think that "turning in assignments on time" is a good example of "conscientiousness" but that "dressing neatly" is not, then a trait measure of conscientiousness should predict punctuality about assignments better than should a measure of personal neatness.

In sum, to increase the ability of trait measures to predict behavior, researchers must ask several questions: Has the behavior under study been measured reliably? Are only some subjects consistent on the trait under study? What behaviors do subjects perceive to be prototypical for the trait? When traits are measured and conceptualized properly, they can lead to significant predictions of relevant behaviors (Kenrick & Funder, 1988).

The interaction between traits and situations.   Even when researchers use optimal methodologies and proper assessment of traits, people may still show inconsistency in behavior across settings (Mischel & Peake, 1983). To the social psychologist this inconsistency is not necessarily surprising, for social psychology has long assumed that the social setting has a profound impact on individuals' behavior. We learned in Chapter 4 that attribution theorists have postulated that people are prone to a "fundamental attribution error" — a tendency to overemphasize the internal causes of behavior (such as personality traits) and to underemphasize the external causes of behavior (situational pressures). In other words, recent attribution research and theory argue that traits may often be more "in the eye of the beholder" than in people's actual behavior.

Although we may sometimes believe in the influence of traits more than the scientific evidence warrants, to some degree traits do predict people's behavior. It is simplistic to believe that behavior results *solely* from either external factors (such as social pressures) or internal factors (such as personality traits). In fact, behavior is determined by the complex interactions of traits and situations (Lewin, 1935, 1936; Endler, 1981, 1983; Mischel, 1977; Snyder & Ickes, 1985).

Suppose I asked three people — Jane, John, and Joan — to report about their anxiety in three different settings — while taking an exam, while going out on a date, and while eating in a fancy restaurant. Would anxiety depend most on people's traits (Jane is never anxious, but John is always anxious), on the situation (everyone is anxious taking a test, but no one is anxious eating in a restaurant), or on idiosyncratic interactions between people and situations (Jane, a social misfit, is most anxious on dates; John, a dunce, is most anxious taking exams)? In a series of studies on self-reports of anxiety, Endler and Hunt (1966, 1969) found that the evidence lent greatest support to the third possibility; that is, they found that interactions between people's traits and the situations were considerably more important in accounting for anxiety than were either people's traits or the situations alone. Typically the interactions between traits and settings accounted for more than twice as much variance in self-reported anxiety as did either traits or situations alone. This finding, which has been replicated in many other studies (Bowers, 1973), provides evidence that people vary in anxiety across situations, each in his or her own idiosyncratic way.

Moderator variables.   As the previous research makes clear, both personality and situational variables can influence behavior, sometimes through complex interactions with one another. Other kinds of interaction effects are also possible. The moderator variable approach seeks to identify situations that are either powerful or weak in influencing behavior and to distinguish "trait-like" people from "non–trait-like" people (Snyder & Ickes, 1985.) A *moderator variable* is a variable that determines the effect one variable (for example, a personality trait) has on another variable (say, behavior).

FIGURE 6.2   Trait theories versus social learning theories.

How do trait and social learning theories differ in their predictions of individual behavior?

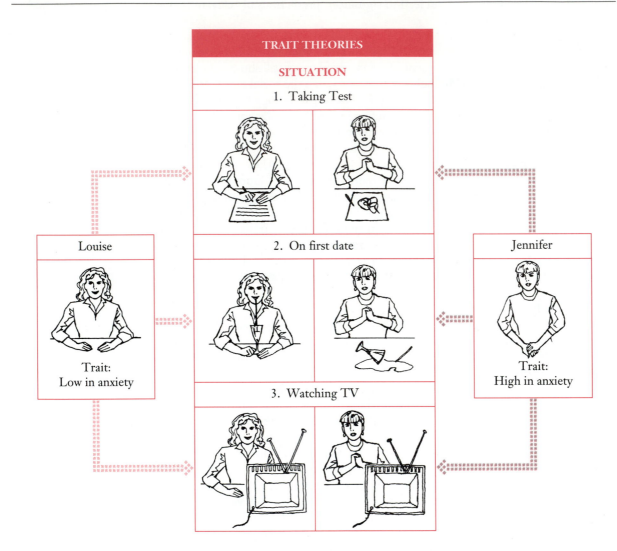

Individuals can be differentiated by their traits and will tend to behave consistently across situations.

■■■

FIGURE 6.2   Trait theories versus social learning theories. (continued)

How do trait and social learning theories differ in their predictions of individual behavior?

SOCIAL LEARNING THEORIES
SITUATION

Behavior results from the interaction of past learning and current situational factors.
Individuals differ in idiosyncratic ways and may not behave consistently across situations.

■■■

Let's consider situational moderator variables first. Some situations are powerful, compelling, and unambiguously interpreted by most people. A church service is an example of a setting that powerfully constrains most people's behavior. At church Jennifer and Louise tend to be quiet, sober, and reserved, and they generally do not yell, tell off-color jokes, or giggle. Behavior at church is highly scripted—that is, strong social rules govern such behavior. On the other hand, some settings are less scripted and permit more variability in people's behavior. When Jennifer and Louise go to the park, they can choose to talk with other people or to be alone. They can choose to sleep under a tree or to jog. Their behavior is not as rigidly constrained as when they are at church (although there are certainly some rules that govern behavior in parks). Thus a situation's "strength" or "weakness" may moderate the effect of personality traits on behavior, as diagrammed in Figure 6.3 (Mischel, 1977).

Monson, Hesley, and Chernick (1981) effectively demonstrated the moderating effects of strong and weak situations by studying the relationship between subjects' self-reported extroversion and actual extroversion in a conversation with two confederates. These researchers created one "weak" situation and two "strong" situations. In the "weak" situation, confederates engaged in natural, unconstrained conversation with subjects. In the two "strong" situations, the confederates either encouraged extroverted behaviors by constantly asking questions of the subjects or encouraged introverted behaviors by ignoring the subjects. The correlation between trait extroversion and behavioral extroversion was much stronger in the "weak" situation (a correlation coefficient of .63) than in the "strong" situations (.25 and .36, respectively). Furthermore, subjects' degree of extroversion was more varied in the "weak" situation than in the "strong" situations. In other words, subjects' behavior reflected their personality traits in the "weak" situation but not in the "strong" situations.

Often, social psychologists create "strong" (rather than "weak") situations in their experiments. That is, the independent variables in many social psychology experiments (recall Milgram's obedience studies described in Chapter 2) are powerful situational manipulations. Because social psychologists tend to study "strong" situations (those that produce obedience, conformity, and aggression), they may inadvertently ensure that personality traits have little influence on the behaviors they study.

Unlike "strong" situations, "weak" situations do not limit and constrain behavior, and thus they allow personality traits to have a larger impact on behavior. Some situations not only allow the display of personality but actually facilitate it as well. According to Snyder and Ickes (1985), such *precipitating situations* are relevant to a particular trait, make the trait salient, and provide behavioral options relevant to the trait.

What situations precipitate the expression of, say, the traits of "masculinity" and "femininity" possessed by some people? Some situations (for example, going on a first date) are highly relevant to "masculinity" and "femininity," make these traits highly salient, and provide a clear choice between "masculine" or "feminine" behaviors (Deaux & Major, 1987). Bem and Lenney (1976) conducted a study in which subjects were asked to engage in both stereotypically "masculine" activities (hammering a nail) and "feminine" activities (baking a cake). Thus "masculinity" and "femininity" were made quite salient to the subjects. On certain trials, subjects could choose between a "masculine" and a "feminine" task; thus clear behavioral options

FIGURE 6.3 The situation as a moderator variable.

How might a situation act as a moderator variable to determine the effects traits have on behavior?

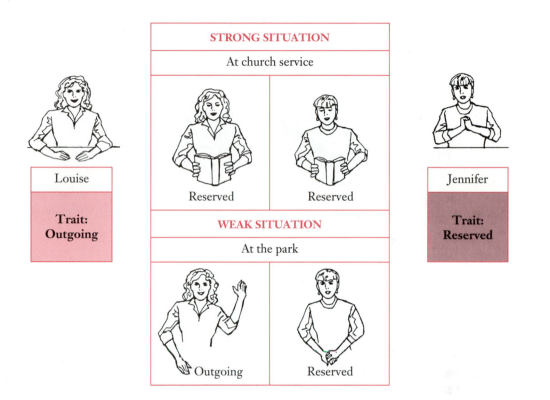

Jennifer and Louise may have different traits, but a strong situation can overwhelm the effects of traits on behavior. A weak situation, on the other hand, allows Jennifer and Louise to display their traits.

relating to "masculinity" and "femininity" were open to subjects. This study found a significant relationship between subjects' assessed traits of "masculinity" and "femininity" and their behavioral choices, perhaps in part because it created a precipitating situation.

Self-monitoring. Just as some kinds of situations are more likely than others to foster the display of personality, so are some kinds of people more likely than others to display consistent personalities. Snyder (1979, 1987) has argued that some people — low self-monitoring individuals — act in a manner consistent with their internal traits, whereas others — high self-monitoring individuals — act more in accordance

FIGURE 6.4   Self-monitoring as a moderator variable.

Why are some people more consistent than others in their behavior?

High on self-monitoring		*Low on self-monitoring*

John, who is reserved and low on self-monitoring, shows trait-like behavior: He is *always* reserved, regardless of what is appropriate for the situation. Louis, who is high on self-monitoring, exhibits behavior that varies according to the demands of the setting.

with the demands of their social setting (see Figure 6.4). (The "monitoring" in self-monitoring refers to regulating one's behavior to fit social demands or situational norms.)

According to Snyder (1987), low self-monitoring individuals have a *principled* concept of the self — they define themselves in terms of their inner values, beliefs, and traits ("I am liberal, free-thinking, honest, reserved . . ."). In contrast, high self-monitoring individuals have a *pragmatic* concept of the self — they define themselves in terms of their roles and behaviors in different social settings ("I am treasurer of my sorority, a social organizer at family gatherings, the second violin in the university orchestra. . . .").

Snyder (1974) developed the *Self-Monitoring Scale* to measure individual differences in self-monitoring (see Figure 6.5). It includes a variety of true-false items,

▪▪▪

FIGURE 6.5   A short, 18-item version of the self-monitoring scale.

Are you a high self-monitoring person or a low self-monitoring person?

To rate yourself on self-monitoring, complete the following scale. If a statement is true or mostly true as it applies to you, check the space in the "T" column. If a statement is false or not usually true as it applies to you, check the space in the "F" column.

T   F

☐ ☐   1. I find it hard to imitate the behavior of other people.

☐ ☐   2. At parties and social gatherings, I do not attempt to do or say things that others will like.

☐ ☐   3. I can only argue for ideas which I already believe.

☐ ☐   4. I can make impromptu speeches even on topics about which I have almost no information.

☐ ☐   5. I guess I put on a show to impress or entertain others.

☐ ☐   6. I would probably make a good actor.

☐ ☐   7. In a group of people I am rarely the center of attention.

☐ ☐   8. In different situations and with different people, I often act like very different persons.

☐ ☐   9. I am not particularly good at making other people like me.

☐ ☐   10. I'm not always the person I appear to be.

☐ ☐   11. I would not change my opinions (or the way I do things) in order to please someone or win their favor.

☐ ☐   12. I have considered being an entertainer.

☐ ☐   13. I have never been good at games like charades or improvisational acting.

☐ ☐   14. I have trouble changing my behavior to suit different people and different situations.

☐ ☐   15. At a party I let others keep the jokes and stories going.

☐ ☐   16. I feel a bit awkward in company and do not show up quite as well as I should.

☐ ☐   17. I can look anyone in the eye and tell a lie with a straight face (if for a right end).

☐ ☐   18. I may deceive people by being friendly when I really dislike them.

The answer key is printed below. If your answer matches the key's answer, give yourself one point for that item. Otherwise, give yourself no points. Add up your points over all 18 items.

1(F); 2(F); 3(F); 4(T); 5(T); 6(T); 7(F); 8(T); 9(F); 10(T); 11(F); 12(T); 13(F); 14(F); 15(F); 16(F); 17(T); 18(T).

SOURCE: Adapted from Snyder (1987).

Snyder (1987) reports that college students with scores of 11 or greater tend to be high self-monitoring individuals, whereas students with scores of 10 or lower tend to be low self-monitoring individuals. A score of 13 or greater places you among the upper 25 percent of college students on self-monitoring, whereas a score of 7 or lower places you among the lowest 25 percent.

▪▪▪

such as "I find it hard to imitate the behavior of other people," "My behavior is usually an expression of my true inner feelings, attitudes, and beliefs," and "In different situations and with different people, I often act like very different persons."

Self-Monitoring in Everyday Life

Most of us spend at least 40 hours a week working, and much of our sense of worth (not to mention our standards-of-living) is tied to our choice of career. How do people choose their careers? Recent research indicates that low and high self-monitoring people approach such choices very differently. In a laboratory simulation of job searching, Snyder and Gangestad (1982) "hired" students to serve as confederates in an upcoming experiment that would require them to play the role of an extrovert in a group discussion. Low self-monitoring applicants were more interested in the job when it matched their personalities (that is, when they were in fact extroverted) and less interested when it did not. On the other hand, high self-monitoring applicants were more interested in the job when they were given many details (including nonverbal gestures) useful in portraying "extroversion," and they were less interested when the job was more vaguely described. Put another way, high self-monitoring subjects preferred a job in which their "job performance" was spelled out in great detail.

Related research suggests that high self-monitoring individuals perform better in "boundary-spanning" jobs—jobs that require them to interact with different kinds of people and be comfortable in different roles and settings (Caldwell & O'Reilly, 1982). Such jobs are well suited to the high self-monitoring person's skill at changing his or her behavior to suit the setting. One of the most extreme examples of a "boundary-spanning" profession is politics. The skilled politician must act quite differently with different constituents. Former New York mayor Fiorello La Guardia was reputed to be a master at changing his style of speech and gestures when addressing different ethnic groups. La Guardia was most likely a high self-monitoring individual.

High and low self-monitoring individuals also show interesting differences in consumer behavior. For example, a low self-monitoring consumer is more likely to buy a car because it's reliable, fuel-efficient, and durable, whereas a high self-monitoring consumer is more likely to buy a car because it's stylish, "sexy," and has a high-status image (Snyder & DeBono, 1985, 1987; Snyder, 1987). Put another way, the low self-monitoring consumer seems attracted to a product because of its intrinsic quality and capacity to express his or her values, whereas the high self-monitoring consumer is more attracted to a product because it conveys the right image to a social audience.

Similarly, the low self-monitoring individual is attracted to *other people* more on the basis of their inner characteristics (attitudes, values, traits), whereas the high self-monitoring individual is attracted more on the basis of external appearances (Snyder, Berscheid, & Glick, 1985; Snyder, Berscheid, & Matwychuk, 1988). In intimate romantic relationships, low self-monitoring people tend to be more committed and to strive to find one partner to satisfy all their needs, whereas high self-monitoring people tend to be less committed and to seek varied partners (Snyder & Simpson, 1984). In friendships as well, low self-monitoring individuals seek close committed friends with whom they share basic attitudes, values, and interests. In contrast, high self-monitoring individuals tend to have many "special purpose" friends and acquaintances with whom they share specific activities—for example, a tennis-playing friend, a theater-going friend, and so on (Jamieson, Lydon, & Zanna, 1987; Snyder, Gangestad, & Simpson, 1983).

Even the personal problems of low and high self-monitoring individuals are significantly different. Low self-monitoring people report being more depressed by events that injure their sense of who they are—for instance, being accused of hypocrisy. High self-monitoring people, on the other hand, report being more depressed by events that injure their public image or sense of social skill—for instance, failing at a play audition or a job interview. Once they are depressed, low and high self-monitoring individuals report different strategies for coping with their "blues." Low self-monitoring people are more likely to seek out friends and vent their feelings, whereas high self-monitoring people are more likely to change their setting and "act" in a better mood (Snyder, 1987).

In sum, the trait-like behavior of low self-monitoring people and the situationally variable behavior of high self-monitoring people show up in everyday life as well as in the social psychology laboratory. Research on self-monitoring may help us to better understand career choices, consumer behavior, the nature of friendships and romantic relationships, the processes of psychological adjustment, and even the very nature of human personality.

New York Mayor
Fiorello La Guardia
changed his gestures
and style of speech de-
pending on the ethnic
group he was address-
ing. Thus he was
most likely a high self-
monitoring individual.

High self-monitoring individuals report that they have good control of their expressive behaviors, that they decide how to behave based on their social setting, and that they change their behavior depending on social cues. In contrast, low self-monitoring individuals say that they're not good actors and that they behave according to their inner traits and feelings, rather than the social setting.

Research shows that high self-monitoring people are indeed more sensitive to situational demands than are low self-monitoring people, and that their behavior is more variable across situations. For example, Snyder and Monson (1975) measured the conformity of psychology students participating in a group discussion. For some groups the discussion took place in private; for others the discussion was videotaped, supposedly to be shown to the students' psychology class. High self-monitoring subjects were extremely sensitive to the conditions of the discussion. In private discussions they tended to conform (presumably to get along with others), whereas in the videotaped condition they tended not to conform (presumably to display their independence to the larger audience of their classmates). Low self-monitoring subjects maintained a relatively stable degree of conformity in the two situations (see

FIGURE 6.6   Self-monitoring and responsiveness to the social setting.

*Does the social setting exert greater influence on the behavior of low
self-monitoring subjects or high self-monitoring subjects?*

Snyder and Monson (1975) measured conformity in situations they believed encourage either autonomy (videotaped discussion) or conformity (private discussion).

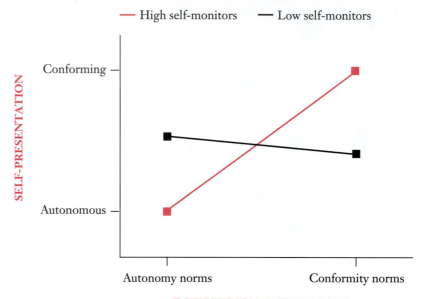

Whereas low self-monitoring subjects showed little change in their behavior in the
two situations, high self-monitoring subjects changed their behavior to suit the
interpersonal situation.

SOURCE: Adapted from Snyder and Monson (1975). Copyright 1975 by the
American Psychological Association. Used with permission of Mark Snyder.

*In this study, self-monitoring serves as a moderator variable that identifies
people who are and are not influenced by the social situation.*

Figure 6.6). In other words, high self-monitoring people seem to be "social chame-
leons" who change their behavior to suit their audience and to fit the norms of the
situation (Danheiser & Graziano, 1982; Lippa, 1976, 1978); low self-monitoring
people are more "true to themselves" and behave in a manner that is more consistent
with their inner traits, attitudes, and beliefs (Snyder & Swann, 1976; Snyder &
Tanke, 1976; Tunnell, 1980). Summary Table 6.1 identifies general principles in the
relationship between traits and behavior.

SUMMARY TABLE 6.1 The Relationship Between Traits and Behavior

When do traits predict behavior?

MODERATOR VARIABLE	EXAMPLE	GENERAL PRINCIPLE
Behaviors being predicted	Aggregated behaviors	Trait measures predict aggregated behaviors better than single behaviors.
	Prototypical behaviors	Behaviors that are prototypical of a trait are better predicted by trait measures.
Situational factors	Strong versus weak situations	Strong situations overwhelm the influence of traits; weak situations allow traits to express themselves.
	Precipitating situations	Precipitating situations encourage the display of traits by making them salient and providing behavioral options relevant to the trait.
Person variables	Self-reported consistency	Some people are consistent on some traits; to predict behavior, the researcher must determine whether the trait is relevant to an individual.
	Self-monitoring	Low self-monitoring individuals behave more consistently with their traits; high self-monitoring individuals respond more to the social setting and thus are more variable.

The Self

. . . I faced the gigantic mirror on the wall. There I saw myself.

I saw myself for a brief instant as my usual self, except that I looked unusually good-humored, bright and laughing. But I had scarcely had time to recognize myself before the reflection fell to pieces. A second, a third, a tenth, a twentieth figure sprang from it till the whole gigantic mirror was full of nothing but Harrys or bits of him, each of which I saw only for the instant of recognition. Some of these multitudinous Harrys were as old as I, some older, some very old. Others were young. There were youths, boys, schoolboys, scamps, children. Fifty-year-olds and twenty-year-olds, solemn and merry, worthy and comic, well-dressed and unpredictable, and even quite naked, long haired, and hairless, all were I and all were seen for a flash, recognized and gone.

—— *Steppenwolf*, p. 204

Research on self-monitoring poses the question "Do some people look more to their 'inner self' when deciding how to behave, and do others look more to their social setting?" But what is the "self"? Is it different from "personality"?

Before answering these basic questions, let's first pose a simpler question: Does a dog have a "self"? Dogs can have personality traits—stable, internal dispositions that lead to consistent behaviors that are different from those of other dogs. A pit bull may be very "aggressive," consistently attacking other dogs and people. The

▪▪▪▪▪▪▪▪▪▪▪▪▪▪▪▪▪▪▪▪▪▪▪
**Can chimpanzees rec-
ognize themselves in
reflected images?**

neighborhood collie, on the other hand, may be "sweet" and "friendly." But does either have a "self"? Probably not. The concept of "self" implies a conscious, aware "actor within" that initiates behavior and also knowledge about one's feelings, traits, thoughts, and behaviors, both present and past. To have a "self" you must be a conscious, self-reflective organism (Gergen, 1971). Thus people have selves; dogs do not.

Some clever research has investigated the degree to which various kinds of animals possess a sense of self (Gallup & Suarez, 1986). In one experiment, Gallup (1977) let a number of chimpanzees observe themselves in mirrors. He then anesthetized the chimps and dyed one eyebrow and one ear of each chimp bright red. After regaining consciousness, the chimps were again allowed to observe themselves in a mirror. Interestingly, many of them began touching their scarlet ears and eyebrows, a clear indication that they recognized themselves and were curious about their altered appearance. Human infants begin to show similar self-recognition in mirrors at about two years of age (Bertenthal & Fisher, 1978; Lewis, 1986; Lewis & Brooks, 1978). Orangutans show self-recognition in mirrors (using the "dye test" method), but lower primates (such as rhesus monkeys and macaques) and lower mammals (dogs, rats) do not and thus seem to lack even a primitive physical sense of self.

▪▪▪▪▪▪▪▪▪▪▪▪▪▪▪▪▪▪▪▪▪▪▪

**Classic Views
of the Self**

Gallup's experiments with chimps yielded another fascinating result: Chimps reared in social isolation did not learn to recognize themselves in mirrors, whereas those whose rearing included social interaction with other chimps did. This finding is particularly interesting because several famous theorists have argued that the self develops in humans because of social feedback and participation in social roles.

The self and social feedback.   William James (1890), the preeminent American psychologist of the late nineteenth century and perhaps the first great modern "self" theorist, argued that our sense of self embraces not just our inner values, interests, and traits, but also our friends, intimate relationships, and even our possessions. The social nature of the self was further emphasized by Charles Horton Cooley (1902) and George Herbert Mead (1934), both of whom argued that people develop selves only by incorporating the perspectives of other people. Cooley invoked the metaphor of a social mirror, which he called the "looking glass self" — the vision of the self that is reflected to us from symbolic (for example, linguistic) communication with other people. Mead offered his related concept of "the generalized other" — the "organized community or group which gives to the individual his unity of self" (Mead, 1934, p. 154). James, Cooley, and Mead all seemed to argue that the self is a social construction; a person growing up alone on a desert island could not develop a self, for a self requires social experience and feedback.

The "I" versus the "me."   William James introduced another important idea that was to have a lasting impact on later theory when he argued that the self has two quite different aspects: the "I" and the "me." The "I" is the active self, the ongoing stream of consciousness; the "me" is the self as an object of thought and includes all the knowledge and beliefs one holds about one's self. "I" am writing this paragraph right now, but when I stop and think about my work, I start thinking about "me" — about my writing skills, my past writing, and my feelings of fatigue.

For Mead (1934), the distinction between the "I" and the "me" was partly a matter of memory: "The 'I' of this moment is present in the 'me' of the next moment" (p. 174). In other words, the "I" is the spontaneous actor of the current instant, whereas the "me" consists of self-reflective knowledge. Social psychological research on self-concepts, self-knowledge, and self-schemas (to be described shortly) has focused primarily on the "me" rather than the "I," in part because the "me" is more accessible to empirical study (Kihlstrom & Cantor, 1984). Figure 6.7 highlights the variables of most interest to social psychologists when studying the self.

Development of the self.   Both Sigmund Freud (1961a), the founder of psychoanalytic theory, and Jean Piaget (1966), one of the most influential developmental psychologists of the twentieth century, held that when people are born they do not possess selves. Freud speculated that the feeling of mystical oneness that we sometimes experience as adults (for example, during transcendental religious experiences) represents a return to our infantile experience of selflessness, when we didn't know we were separate from our mother (or indeed from the rest of the universe). We are born unconscious, and the conscious ego (that is, the self) does not develop until later. In his landmark descriptions of cognitive development, Piaget argued that the young child is quite egocentric and does not fully realize the distinction between private experiences (the self) and other people's experiences. For example, a four-year-old child may expect his parents to know about a dream he had the previous night.

Duval and Wicklund (1972) later argued that awareness of self develops largely as a result of social conflicts. (Here again we hear echoes of the arguments first proposed by James, Cooley, and Mead that the self has social origins.) For example, little Billy becomes aware of his "aggressiveness" when his mother scolds him for hitting his little brother so often. Even as adults we may become conscious of new

FIGURE 6.7   **The self as an explanation of behavior.**

What kinds of explanations are emphasized in concepts of the "self"?

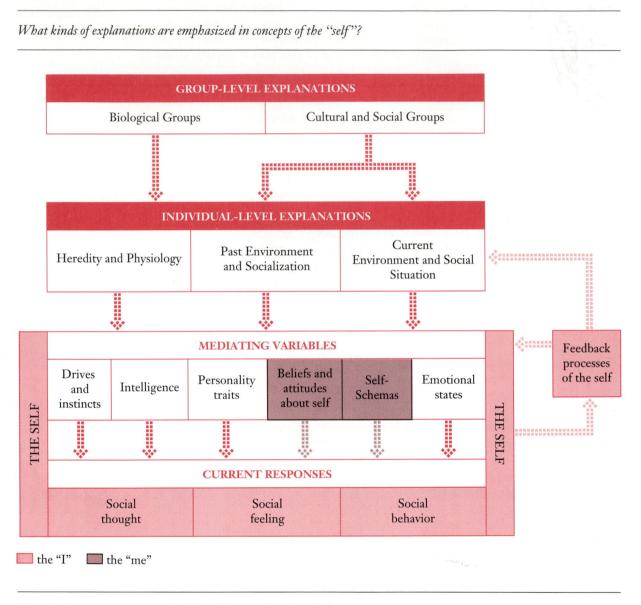

Note the distinction between the "I" and the "me" in this diagram.

aspects of ourselves through social conflict and disagreement. For example, when you first visit a foreign country with different customs, you may suddenly become aware of behavior that you had never thought about before. When all the people around you use their forks in their left hands when cutting and eating a piece of meat, you suddenly become aware that in the same situation you switch the fork to

At what age do human beings recognize themselves in reflected images?

your right hand. And when everybody else stands eight inches away from you, you realize quite painfully that you really prefer to stand 18 inches away. Unawareness is the original human condition; self-awareness develops only with experience.

Duval and Wicklund's argument suggests that people will be more aware of, and more likely to describe themselves in terms of, characteristics on which they "stand out" from others. This hypothesis has been supported by empirical research. McGuire and his colleagues (McGuire, McGuire, Child, & Fujioka, 1978; McGuire & Padawer-Singer, 1976; McGuire & McGuire, 1982, 1988) found that school children were more likely to describe themselves using traits, physical characteristics, or demographic information that distinguished them from others. For example, red-haired children were more likely to mention their hair color in self-descriptions, black children in a mostly white school were more likely to list their race, and so on.

As children grow older, their self-descriptions become more abstract and sophisticated. A number of studies (Livesly & Bromly, 1973; Montemayor & Eisen, 1977) have asked children of different ages to answer the question "Who am I?" Young children describe themselves in concrete, physical terms, whereas older children are more likely to include abstract traits, values, and interests in their self-descriptions.

To illustrate, here's a self-description from a fourth-grade boy:

My name is Bruce C. I have brown eyes. I have brown hair. I have brown eyebrows. I'm nine years old. I LOVE sports! I have seven people in my family. I have great! eye site [sic]. I have lots! of friends. I live on 1923 Pinecrest Drive. I'm going on 10 in September. I'm a boy. I have an uncle that is almost 7 feet tall. My school is Pinecrest. My teacher is Mrs. V. I play Hockey! I am almost the smartest boy in the class. I LOVE! food. I love fresh air. I LOVE school. (Montemayor & Eisen, 1977, p. 317)

Contrast Bruce's self-portrait with that of a 17-year-old girl in the twelfth grade:

I am a human being. I am a girl. I am an individual. I don't know who I am. I am a Pisces. I am a moody person. I am an indecisive person. I am an ambitious person. I am a very curious person. I am not an individual. I am a loner. I am an American (God help me), I am a Democrat. I am a liberal person. I am a radical, I am a conservative. I am a pseudoliberal. I am an atheist. I am not a classifiable person (i.e., I don't want to be). (p. 318)

Clearly, as an individual progresses from childhood to adulthood, he or she develops a "me" that is complex, subtle, elaborated, abstract, and even contradictory.

Hart and Damon (1986) describe four fundamental aspects of a child's self-concept: the physical self ("I am tall"), the active or behaving self ("I am good at baseball"), the social self ("I am friendly to others"), and the psychological self ("I believe in world peace"). These researchers propose that as children progress from early to late childhood, the emphasis on these four aspects of self shifts more toward the latter aspects. Interestingly, recent research suggests that children as young as three years of age have the ability to describe some of their psychological characteristics (Eder, Gerlach, & Perlmutter, 1987).

▪▪▪▪▪▪▪▪▪▪▪▪▪▪▪▪▪▪▪▪▪▪▪▪▪

**Self-Knowledge —
Research on
the "Me"**

Asked to describe himself, Lyndon Johnson, who would later become President of the United States, responded, "I am a free man, an American, a United States Senator and a Democrat, in that order. I am also a liberal, a conservative, a Texan, a taxpayer, a rancher, a businessman, a consumer, a parent, a voter, and not as young as I used to be nor as old as I expect to be — and I am all those things in no fixed order" (cited in Gordon, 1968, p. 123). The concept of "self" implies that people possess knowledge about themselves. The self, from this perspective, is "a theory of oneself . . . containing the organized, relatively stable contents of our personal experience. . . ." (Schlenker, 1985).

The self as a schema.   In Chapter 5 we defined schemas as knowledge structures that have a profound influence on how people perceive social events, remember information, and infer new facts. People may hold schemas about groups of people (librarians), about specific people (Queen Elizabeth), about social events (going on a date), or about themselves. Like any other schema, a *self-schema*, a schema we hold about ourselves, can influence our perceptions, memory, and inferences about ourselves and about others.

In a series of experiments, Hazel Markus (1977) examined how self-schemas affect the ways in which people process information about themselves. In one study she identified groups of college women who both described themselves as quite high on the traits of "independence" or "dependence" and rated these traits as very important to their self-descriptions. These women were assumed to be *schematic* on the respective traits — that is, to possess rich and well-developed self-schemas related to either independence or dependence. Markus also identified another group of women who were *aschematic* on independence and dependence — that is, they neither rated themselves highly on these traits nor viewed these traits to be very important to their self-description.

All subjects then participated in an experiment in which a series of adjectives were displayed on a screen; subjects then pressed one of two buttons to indicate whether a given adjective did or did not describe them. Measuring the speed with which subjects responded, Markus found that subjects who were schematic on independence responded much more quickly to adjectives relating to independence ("individualistic," "outspoken") than to adjectives related to dependence ("timid," "submissive"). Subjects who described themselves as schematic on dependence showed just the opposite pattern, and aschematic subjects showed no difference in response speed between the two kinds of adjectives (see Figure 6.8).

Schematic subjects also were better able to list examples of behavior relevant to their schemas than were aschematics; thus, for example, a woman who was schematic on independence could list many ways in which she was independent. Schematic subjects also more strongly resisted information from a bogus personality inventory

FIGURE 6.8 **Time required by schematic and aschematic people to judge whether traits are self-descriptive.**

Do self-schemas affect how quickly we process information about ourselves?

Markus (1977) measured how quickly subjects answered whether traits related to independence or dependence were self-descriptive. The graph shows response latency–that is, how long subjects took to respond.

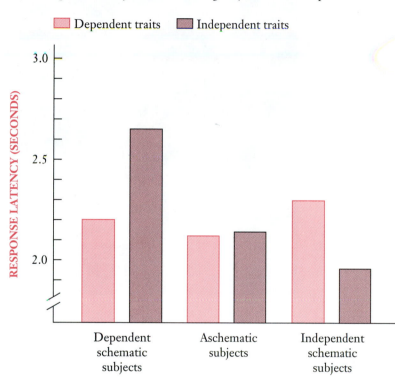

Subjects who were schematic on dependence or independence responded more quickly to traits that fit their schemas, whereas subjects who were aschematic for these traits responded to both types of traits at about the same speed.

SOURCE: Data from Markus (1977).

that contradicted their self-schemas. Markus, Crane, Bernstein, & Siladi (1982) report similar effects for self-schemas related to masculinity and femininity.

Schematic people as experts on the self. Experts readily recognize information relevant to their area of expertise and are able to "chunk" such information more effectively than novices. For example, when confronted with a musical score that to a novice looks like a thousand random notes, an expert musician can chunk it into harmonies, phrases, and themes. And an expert chess player can chunk several moves

■■■■■■■■■■■■■■■■■■■■■■■■■

The self-schema comprises a complex mix of beliefs, aspirations, and fantasies.

together into a meaningful strategic pattern that would be meaningless to a chess novice (Chase & Simon, 1973).

A person who is strongly schematic on a given dimension (such as "independence" or "masculinity") is a kind of expert about that particular domain of his or her behavior. Markus, Smith, and Moreland (1985) hypothesized that just as a chess expert chunks chess moves into higher-order units, so schematic people chunk others' behaviors into higher-order units when those behaviors are relevant to their self-schemas. To test this, Markus and her colleagues identified men who were schematic or aschematic on masculinity (using the same methods as those in the "independence" study described above). Subjects viewed two films, one depicting a man engaged in stereotypically masculine activities (lifting weights, watching a baseball game) and another depicting a man engaged in activities irrelevant to masculinity (playing records, eating an apple). Subjects were asked to press a button whenever they saw what they considered to be a "meaningful unit of action." Markus and her colleagues were interested in seeing how subjects would chunk the behaviors they observed.

The results were consistent with the hypothesis that subjects who were schematic on masculinity were "experts" in the domain of masculinity. When they viewed stereotypically masculine behaviors, the schematic men chunked behavior

■■

FIGURE 6.9 "Chunking" of schema-relevant information.

Do self-schemas affect how we process information about others?

Markus, Smith, and Moreland (1985) studied the effects of self-schemas on subjects' "chunking" of information about men viewed in a videotape.

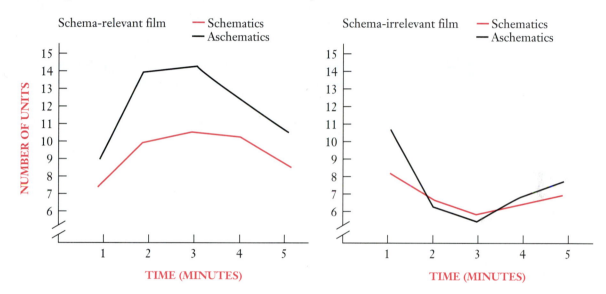

Schematic subjects "chunked" schema-relevant behavior (left panel) into fewer units that did aschematic subjects. Schematic subjects did not chunk behavior differently from aschematic subjects when behavior was irrelevant to their self-schemas (right panel).

SOURCE: Adapted from Markus, Smith, and Moreland (1985).

Schematic subjects behave like "experts" in that they organize behaviors relevant to their self-schema into meaningful higher-order perceptual units.

■■

into larger units than did aschematic men, thus producing fewer total units. However, when viewing behavior that was irrelevant to masculinity, men who were schematic and aschematic on masculinity did not differ in the number of units they produced (see Figure 6.9). Thus self-schemas can influence not only how we process information about ourselves but how we perceive *other's behavior* as well.

The complexity of the self-schema. It should hardly surprise you to learn that the self-schema is probably among the most complex schemas people possess. One reason for the complexity of self-knowledge is that we simply have a lot more information about ourselves than we do about other people or other concepts (Kihlstrom, Cantor, Albright, Chew, Klein, & Niedenthal, 1988). We "see" ourselves every day, and except perhaps for the respite of sleep (and even dreams offer a kind of information about the self), we are constantly awash in our thoughts, feelings, and behaviors. Also, unlike other sorts of knowledge, self-knowledge possesses a narrative continuity, an unbroken thread of observation through time (Gergen & Gergen, 1983, 1988; Cantor & Kihlstrom, 1987). Each of us tries to make sense of our own life histories, and we constantly interpret and reinterpret the self (Linton, 1978). And to make matters even more complex, people not only possess information about their past selves and their current selves, but they also have images of "future selves" (Markus & Nurius, 1986). Clearly the contents of "the self" is a complex mix of facts, interpretations, fantasies, and aspirations.

The complexity of self-knowledge has been demonstrated indirectly through its effect on memory: People often remember information that is related to the self better than they remember other kinds of information. In one study, Rogers, Kuiper, and Kirker (1977) showed subjects 40 adjectives, one at a time, and asked them to make one of four kinds of judgments about each adjective: (1) was it printed in big letters? (2) did it rhyme with another word? (3) did it mean the same thing as another word? or (4) did the adjective describe the subject? For example, if the adjective was "NEAT," subjects would be asked one of the following questions: "Is it printed in big letters?" or "Does it rhyme with 'heat'?" or "Does it mean the same as 'clean'?" or "Are you neat?" Each kind of judgment was made for 10 of the 40 adjectives. Note that a subject's self-schema was involved only when a subject was asked whether the adjective applied to the self.

After they judged adjectives and without prior warning, subjects were asked to recall as many of the 40 adjectives as they could. The results showed a marked *self-reference effect*; that is, subjects' recall was much superior for adjectives that had been judged in relation to the self. This effect was most marked for adjectives that subjects said did in fact describe them (see Figure 6.10).

Presumably, words processed for self-reference are remembered better in part because they become associated with the rich knowledge contained in the self-schema. The more that new knowledge is related to prior knowledge, the better we tend to remember it. The richly elaborated self-schema provides more retrieval cues for self-referring words—more paths that lead into memory, allowing us to locate information (Keenan & Baillet, 1980).

When subjects are asked whether words are true of themselves, they sometimes recall them better than when they're asked whether the words are true of other people, even people they know well (Lord, 1980). Thus our self-schema seems more complex than our schemas for other people. In general, the self-reference effect proves to be quite robust (Brown, Keenan, & Potts, 1986), and researchers continue to explore why and when it occurs (Klein & Loftus, 1988; Kihlstrom et al., 1988).

The self's resistance to change.   Thoreau once wrote in his *Journal* (1906), "For an impenetrable shield, stand inside yourself." Self-knowledge is often more resistant to change than other kinds of knowledge. This may in part be due to its complexity — the huge self-schema has a lot of "inertia" to it. But the self-conserving nature of the self is also motivated; people maintain the integrity of their selves through active effort and a kind of defensiveness. Indeed, Greenwald (1980) compares the self to a totalitarian dictator that needs to control information and revise history for his or her personal benefit. According to this point of view, the self—an organization of knowledge and beliefs — is conservative and defensive and does not change easily or lightly. In fact, the self will at times distort or forget facts in order to preserve itself.

FIGURE 6.10 **The self-reference effect.**

Do we remember information better when it has been processed for self-reference?

Rogers, Kuiper, and Kirker (1977) measured subjects' recall of adjectives that were cognitively processed in different ways (physical structure, sound, meaning, or self-reference).

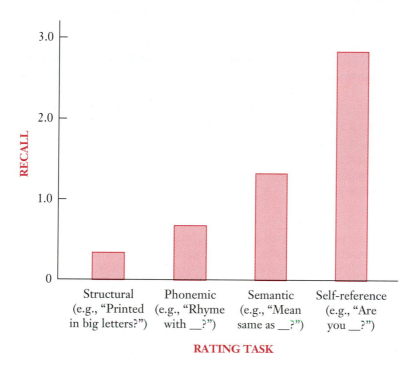

Subjects' recall was best for adjectives they judged in relation to themselves.

SOURCE: Data from Rogers, Kuiper, and Kirker (1977).

Research continues to explore why the self-reference effect occurs. One theory holds that because the self-schema is so rich and complex, it provides many "paths" through memory to information that is associated with the self.

This enforced stability may be quite useful, for if the self readily changed with each new piece of information, then life would become quite chaotic; our sense of the unity of the self would quickly be shattered.

How does the self maintain itself and prove to itself that self-knowledge is "true" knowledge? Swann and Read (1981) argue that people often engage in *self-verification*; that is, they engage in behaviors and thoughts that serve to prove the validity of their self-concept. People can verify their self-concepts in three specific ways: (1) they can selectively seek out from others feedback that confirms their self-concepts, (2) they can selectively remember feedback that confirms their self-concept, and (3) they can actively try to prove to others the truth of their self-concepts.

Swann and Read have found evidence for all three processes. In one experiment female subjects rated themselves as either likable or unlikable and then reviewed statements made about them by another person. Some subjects were led to believe that the other person probably liked them; others were led to believe that the person probably disliked them. Women who thought themselves to be "unlikable" spent more time looking at the statements when they thought the other person disliked them, whereas subjects who thought themselves "likable" spent more time looking at the statements when they thought the other person liked them. In other words, subjects attended more to information that seemed likely to confirm their self-concept.

These results are particularly intriguing because they indicate that the "unlikable" subjects actually attended more to potentially painful information—that is, information verifying their unlikability. In a related experiment, Swann and Read found that subjects recalled more statements made by another person when they believed that person shared their self-concept. Thus, not only do we attend more to self-verifying information, but we remember it better as well.

How do people respond when others threaten their self-concept? To answer this question, Swann and Read extended their experimental procedure a step further. College men who had rated themselves as either likable or unlikable engaged in a nine-minute conversation with a college woman. The men were told ahead of time either that the woman was likely to like them or was likely to dislike them. After the conversation, the women were asked to rate how much in fact they liked their conversation partners. As Figure 6.11 indicates, men who regarded themselves as unlikable were particularly unlikable when they thought their partner would like them! And men who regarded themselves as likable were particularly likable when they thought their partner would dislike them. Apparently, when their partner seemed about to challenge their self-concept, the men tried harder to prove the truth of their self-concept.

Self-verification versus self-enhancement.

Many psychologists have been proponents of this seemingly obvious proposition: People like to view themselves in the best possible light, and they will choose to boost their self-worth and self-esteem whenever possible (Epstein, 1973; Jones, 1973). Such self-enhancement has been documented in many studies (Greenwald, 1980; Shrauger, 1975). For example, people tend to rate themselves in unrealistically positive ways (Roth, Snyder, & Pace, 1986) and tend to remember their personal strengths better than their weaknesses (Mischel, Ebbesen, & Zeiss, 1973).

However, studies on self-verification show that not all people strive to make themselves look good! Recall that in Swann and Read's study, subjects who thought themselves unlikable actually attended more to information they expected to be unflattering. Furthermore, when they thought others would like them, they tried particularly hard to prove their unlikability. In other research, Swann and Pelham (1987) found that people who regard themselves as unlikable prefer friends and intimates who agree that they're unlikable! In other words, people with negative self-concepts often prefer negative information that is consistent with their negative self-view to positive but inconsistent information.

━━

FIGURE 6.11   Self-verification.

Do we change our behavior to maintain our self-concepts?

Swann and Read (1981) challenged subjects' self-concepts by telling them that their conversation partners were likely either to like or to dislike them. The table indicates how much subjects with different self-concepts were in fact liked by their partners after the discussion (higher numbers indicate greater likability).

PARTNERS' IMPRESSIONS OF SUBJECTS' LIKABILITY
(higher numbers = more likable)

Subjects' Self-Concept	Partner Likely to Like Subject	Partner Likely to Dislike Subject
Unlikable	39.9	42.4
Likable	43.9	49.4

SOURCE: Data from Swann and Read (1981).

Both groups of subjects responded to challenges to their self-concepts by intensifying behavior consistent with their self-concepts: "Likable" subjects were more likable when they thought their partners would dislike them, and "unlikable" subjects were particularly unlikable when they thought their partners would like them.

━━

In an attempt to understand this apparent paradox a bit better, Swann, Griffin, Predmore, and Gaines (1987) gathered data that suggest that people *cognitively* seek out self-verification (that is, information that is consistent with their self-concept) but *emotionally* respond to the positivity or negativity of information (see also Shrauger, 1975). More concretely, if I believe I'm quite unlikable, I may feel terrible that someone doesn't like me, but at the same time I feel this reaction is justified, and I may even seek out such a reaction. Emotionally I'm devastated, but cognitively I'm satisfied that the other person has responded in a predictable, expected, and valid way. The cognitive and emotional needs of such a person with low self-esteem are in conflict. (Fortunately, only a relatively small minority of people possess strongly negative self-concepts and thus face this mental tug-of-war.) People with high self-esteem, of course, do not experience any conflict between self-enhancement and self-verification because information verifying their self-concept ("You're a wonderful person") is also positive and self-enhancing.

Self-Awareness Theory

When do our self-schemas influence our everyday behavior? When do we act consistently with our selves, and when don't we? Shelly Duval and Robert Wicklund (1972) proposed a theory of self-awareness that argues that the contents of the self (the knowledge and standards stored in the self-schema) influences our behavior, particularly when we *pay attention* to the self. Conscious attention, according to Wicklund and Duval's theory, can be directed either toward the self or toward the external environment. When attention is self-focused, we think consciously about who we are—about our beliefs, values, and traits. When attention is externally focused (for example, on a football game), we are not in touch with our selves.

In research studies, self-awareness is triggered by a number of simple methods, including placing subjects in front of a mirror, tape-recording and videotaping them, and having others watch and evaluate them. All of these techniques make people "self-conscious" in the sense that they start attending to themselves.

In everyday life, self-awareness may be triggered by the scrutiny of others or by eye-contact, or when others explicitly ask us to think about ourselves and our behavior (Wicklund, 1982). When a father stares at his son, who just broke a vase, and says, "What do you have to say about this, young man?", the boy is very likely pushed into a state of self-directed attention.

The consequences of self-directed attention.   According to Duval and Wicklund, when people direct their attention to themselves, they begin to compare their behavior to internal standards (which may be internalized from society). For example, if you take a social psychology test and you start thinking consciously about yourself, you'll probably wonder if you're performing as well as you would like. If you don't match your internal standards, you become uncomfortable (as when you receive a "C" on your test when you had hoped for an "A").

When you become aware of a discrepancy between your actual behavior and internal standards, you have two ways of reducing the resulting discomfort: You can change your behavior to be more consistent with your internal standards ("I'm going to study twice as hard for the next test and get an 'A'!"). Or, if matching standards is unrealistic (when the tests are simply too difficult), you can try to avoid self-awareness ("I'm going to get drunk and forget all about my grades").

Many studies have provided support for the basic propositions of self-awareness theory. For example, Duval, Wicklund, and Fine (described in Duval & Wicklund, 1972) have demonstrated that people do in fact avoid self-awareness after irredeemable failure. In their experiment, college women took a bogus IQ test and were informed that they had performed either quite well or quite poorly. The women were then sent to another experiment with these instructions: "If the experimenter doesn't show up within five minutes, you can leave." Sometimes the room in which the women waited contained a mirror and a TV camera pointing at them; sometimes it did not. The researchers assumed, of course, that women who waited in the room with the mirror and camera would be more self-aware.

The researchers hypothesized that women who failed to do well and who were also self-aware would be most uncomfortable, and indeed these women waited a significantly shorter time in the room than did other women (see Figure 6.12). (Would you have wanted to spend a lot of time looking at yourself in a mirror after having "failed" the test?)

Self-awareness and internal standards.   Most college students report that they are honest, but most will cheat on a timed IQ test (by working past the time limit) if given the opportunity (Diener & Wallbom, 1976). When do people behave in a manner that is consistent with their internal "morals," and when don't they? One possible answer is that people behave "morally" particularly when they are in a state of self-focused attention. Beaman, Klentz, Diener, & Svanum (1979) demonstrated this in a clever experiment that showed that children "trick-or-treating" on Halloween were less likely to steal candy from an unattended bowl when a big mirror was placed behind it.

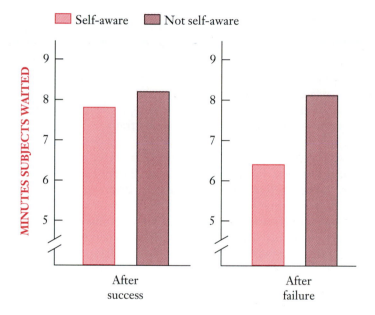

FIGURE 6.12   **The aversiveness of self-awareness after failure.**

Do we avoid self-awareness after failure?

Duval, Wicklund, and Fine (1971) measured how long female subjects waited for a "tardy" experimenter after being told they had performed either well or poorly on an IQ test. In one condition, subjects were made self-aware by the presence of a mirror and a TV camera.

Those women who had "failed" the IQ test and were made self-aware waited the shortest time.

SOURCE: Adapted from Duval and Wicklund (1972).

In everyday life we can avoid self-awareness in many ways — by distracting ourselves with external stimuli (TV, movies, physical exercise), by blurring our thoughts with drugs or alcohol, or by avoiding situations in which we're likely to "stand out" in any way.

Other studies in which subjects were placed in the presence of a mirror (that is, in a state of self-awareness) showed that subjects delivered electric shocks to victims to a degree that was more consistent with their attitudes toward aggression (Carver, 1975); that subjects responded to pornography in a manner that was more consistent with their self-reported attitudes (via a questionnaire) to pornography (Gibbons, 1978); and finally, that subjects' sociability in a conversation better reflected their self-reported sociability (Pryor, Gibbons, Wicklund, Fazio, & Hood, 1977). Thus self-awareness serves as a *moderator variable* that influences when people do and do not behave in ways that are consistent with their personalities and attitudes.

In addition, research suggests that by heightening awareness of internal arousal and inner feelings, self-focused attention intensifies a person's current mood or emotion (Scheier & Carver, 1977; Scheier, Carver, & Gibbons, 1979, 1981). If you're happy, focusing attention on yourself will make you feel happier; if you're sad, it will make you feel sadder.

Some people are more likely to engage in self-focused attention than others. For them, self-awareness can be viewed as a personality trait. Fenigstein, Scheier, and Buss (1975) developed a scale of *private self-consciousness* that measures how much people attend to their inner thoughts and feelings and internal states (sample item: "I reflect about myself a lot"). Many studies indicate that people who have a high degree of private self-consciousness behave in ways that are more consistent with their inner traits, attitudes, and values. In one study Scheier, Buss, & Buss (1978) found that subjects with high degrees of private self-consciousness behaved in ways that were more consistent with their self-described level of aggressiveness than did people low on private self-consciousness. Thus private self-consciousness also serves as a moderator variable that helps to predict when people do and do not engage in behaviors that are consistent with their personality traits.

A control model of self.   Carver and Scheier (1981) have elaborated some of the insights of self-awareness theory into a general theory based on cybernetics, or control theory (Wiener, 1948; Miller, Galanter, & Pribram, 1960). Control theory describes how a system (such as a heater with a thermostat) exerts control to maintain some desired state (a constant temperature). The basic unit of a control system is a *feedback loop* (see Figure 6.13), in which the control system tests current conditions or "input" against some standard. For example, a thermostat tests current room temperature against the setting of the thermostat. If the standard is met ("It's warm enough in the house"), the furnace is turned off or kept off. If the standard is not met ("It's too cold!"), the control system initiates a process (turning on the furnace) that will produce some change in the system so that the standard is matched. Thus, the control system "acts" whenever its standard is not met, and it keeps checking current conditions and acting until the standard is met.

By analogy, when it is in a state of self-awareness the self acts as a control system (again, see Figure 6.13). When you think about your grades, the control system that is your self asks, "Am I matching my standards?" If the answer is "Yes" (you're a 4.00 student), you feel happy, and you do not have to change your behavior. You can "exit" self-awareness now—that is, stop consciously thinking about your grades and turn your attention to other things. If you are not matching your standards (suppose you're a 1.50 student), then the control system poses another question: "Can I change my behavior to match my standards?" If the answer is "Yes," then you will study harder to try for better grades. However, if you're studying as hard as you can and you still don't get the grades you desire, then you're in a quandary. You probably feel guilty, ashamed, and upset, so you strive to avoid self-awareness. This mental "avoidance" can take different forms: You can distract yourself (shift your attention to external events and, for example, watch TV), blur your self-awareness with drugs or alcohol (Hull, 1981; Hull, Young, & Jouriles, 1986), or deny the existence of the problem. When a person is not in a state of self-awareness, behavior is "mindless"— unthinking, habitual, and in a sense "on automatic pilot" (Langer, 1978).

FIGURE 6.13   Two control systems.

Can the self be conceptualized as a control system?

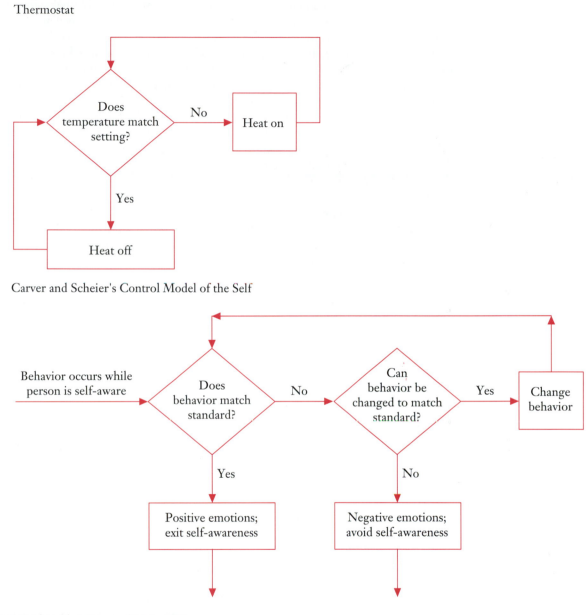

Thermostat

Carver and Scheier's Control Model of the Self

SOURCE: Adapted from Carver and Scheier (1981).

Notice that according to the model presented here, the self differs from a thermostat in several important ways: First, the control system of the self operates only when the individual is in a state of self-awareness. Second, the control processes of the self have emotional and motivational consequences (such as happiness, upset, or guilt). Finally, when behavior cannot be matched to standards, the self may try to avoid the pain of self-awareness and exit from the control "loop." (In contrast, a thermostat controlling a heater that is inadequate for the task will not become "upset" and decide to "give up"!)

Self-discrepancy.   Duval and Wicklund (1972) and Carver and Scheier (1981) suggest that the self regulates behavior by assessing the discrepancy between overt behavior and internal standards. But to which of the many possible behaviors and standards do we choose to attend? In their original formulation, Duval and Wicklund (1972) argued that some standards are particularly salient in a given situation. For example, when taking a test, your standard of behavior will be intellectual excellence, whereas at a party it may be physical attractiveness and personal charm.

Higgins (1987) argues that people hold four major kinds of inner standards. Standards can either be your own ("I want to be a straight-A student") or other peoples' ("My mother wants me to be a straight-A student"). Furthermore, standards can represent either your ideals and personal goals ("I want to be a concert pianist") or your duties and obligations (a kind of moral conscience, as in "I must not cheat"). Thus you can experience four kinds of discrepancy between yourself and your standards: (1) You may not match your own ideals, (2) you may not match another's ideals, (3) you may not match your own moral "oughts," and (4) you may not match another's moral "oughts."

Higgins's research shows that different kinds of self-discrepancy produce different kinds of negative emotions (Higgins, Klein, & Strauman, 1985; Strauman & Higgins, 1987). If you don't match your own ideals, then you feel disappointment and dissatisfaction ("All my life I wanted to be a concert pianist, but I'm not going to make it — drats!"). If you don't match another's ideals, then you feel shame or embarrassment ("All my life Mother wanted me to be a concert pianist. . . ."). If you don't live up to your own moral conscience, then you feel guilt and self-contempt ("I cheated on my test. . . ."). If you don't live up to another's moral standards, then you feel agitated, threatened, and perhaps even fearful ("If Mother finds out about my cheating she'll kill me!")

Why do people focus on a particular kind of self-discrepancy at a given moment? Higgins (1987) argues that this depends in part on how recently and frequently we have been aware of such discrepancies in the past. For example, if we've often thought about ways in which we've violated our moral standards in the past, then we are likely to evaluate new behaviors in that way. Some kinds of self-discrepancies are "primed," ready to be applied to new situations. (See Chapter 5 for a broader discussion of priming effects; Summary Table 6.2 discusses research findings regarding the self.)

Public and Private Selves

So far we've described the self both as a schema and as a control process that regulates behavior to keep it consistent with internal standards. The self, whether a schema or a control process, seems to be internal and private. However, the self has a public face as well: It is a collection of roles and public performances as well as certain internal processes (Baumeister, 1986; Schlenker, 1980). William James described this view particularly well:

> . . . we may practically say that [a man] has as many different social selves as there are distinct groups of persons about whose opinions he cares. He generally shows a different side of himself to each of these different groups. Many a youth who is demure enough before his parents and teachers swears and swaggers like a pirate among his "tough" young friends. We do not show ourselves to our children as to our club companions, to our masters and employers as to our intimate friends. (1890, vol. 1, p. 294)

SUMMARY TABLE 6.2   Research on the Self

What processes are studied when researching the self?

	TOPIC OF RESEARCH	PROCESSES STUDIED
The "Me"	Self-schemas	Ease of processing self-relevant information; schematic individuals as experts; self-reference effect — information processed for self-reference is remembered better.
	Self-verification	How people act to prove the validity of their self-concept: For low self-esteem people, self-verification may conflict with self-enhancement (trying to gain positive information about self).
Self-directed attention (aspects of the "I")	Self-awareness theory	Self-directed attention leads to comparison of behavior with standards. Behavior is changed when possible to match standards; otherwise, self-directed attention is avoided.
	Control model of self	The self as a cybernetic feedback loop; an elaboration of self-awareness theory.
The public self	Self-presentational strategies	Ingratiation; intimidation; self-promotion; basking in reflected glory.
Applied topics	Self-awareness and depression	Reactive depression as a feedback loop without an exit; the vicious cycle of depression.
	Self-complexity	People with complex self-concepts tend to be less emotionally volatile and less susceptible to depression.

Impression management: The self as an actor.   The most extreme view of the "public self" is that it is a facade. The sociologist Erving Goffman (1959) argued just this point by using a theater metaphor to describe human social interaction: People enact roles just like actors on stage. To stay "in character" people speak the right words, display convincing nonverbal behaviors, and use appropriate props. It's not good enough, for example, that a minister be a brilliant theologian; he must also speak in an inspiring tone of voice, fold his hands in a pious manner, and wear a clerical collar. In *The Presentation of Self in Everyday Life*, Goffman (1959) argued that con artists, used-car dealers, and professional actors are not the only ones who manage their appearances. Everyone does!

Consider this doctor's account of the "theater" of modern medicine:

> . . . And so I resort to theater. I stage a dazzlingly detailed neurologic exam. There are props: a reflex hammer and an ophthalmoscope, each of which I move about in carefully choreographed patterns. There are dramatic asides — thoughtful "hmm's" — and flourishes, too, like the motions I put my patient through to test for rare, abnormal reflexes. . . . Throughout it all, I'm careful to concentrate on my delivery, timing my words, smiles and gestures for best effect.

Private versus public selves. Despite his public image of piety and probity, Jimmy Swaggart was forced to resign his ministry due to allegations of sexual misconduct. In this photo, Swaggart confesses his misdeeds and asks for his followers' forgiveness. Do you think Swaggart is truly contrite, or is he engaged in a public "act"?

. . . In offices, clinics and hospitals, we give performances to make people feel better. . . . When we perform physical exams, we resort to the ritual laying on of hands. Dialogue is another useful device. A doctor often moves his patient through an artful soliloquy or by conferring a fancy attribution on an ailment either because it's common and we don't want the patient to feel unimportant, or because we don't have a name for it, and we don't want to deprive it of legitimacy.

For sheer healing power, nothing can match the theater. Just as a person will suspend disbelief during a play, so will he place his spirit momentarily in the hands of a doctor — so transcendent is the wish to believe and be healed. And though too much drama can be dangerous . . . medicine thrives on a healthy dose of it. Good bedside manner, in fact, is good theater.

—— from "The Doctor as Dramatist," by Stephen A. Hoffman, *Newsweek*, February 1, 1988

This doctor agrees with Goffman that life is a stage, with "on stage" and "backstage" areas and well-defined scripts for different settings. Most jobs require some degree of *impression management* — that is, control of the appearances we present to others. Imagine, for example, that you wait on tables in a restaurant. While serving your customers, you are "on stage"; you must smile, maintain your posture, and carry and serve food with care. When you walk through the swinging doors into the kitchen, however, you are "off stage" — out of view of your "audience." There you can slouch, or yawn, or complain to the cook about how much your feet hurt. We literally become different people with different audiences.

Reflected Glory: Another Self-Presentational Strategy

People make themselves look better in others' eyes not merely by saying what others want to hear, but also by associating themselves with "winners" and disassociating themselves from "losers" (Schlenker, 1980; Tesser & Rosen, 1975). Have you ever noticed that when the local football team wins, everyone says that "we" won, but when the team loses, it becomes "they" lost? This shift in pronouns has been documented in research studies (Cialdini, Borden, Thorne, Walker, Freeman, & Sloan, 1976). Similarly, college students are more likely to wear shirts, jackets, and buttons that identify their school after their football team wins than after a loss (Cialdini et al., 1976). Apparently, one way we make ourselves look good is by "basking in the reflected glory" of successful people with whom we're associated.

There's a paradox, however, to basking in reflected glory. Suppose everyone at your school is a great athlete. By basking in their reflected glory, you should feel good about yourself. But if you are a poor athlete, you have reason to feel bad about yourself, too — in comparison to your group, your performance is inferior. When do we bask in the reflected glory of people we're associated with, and when do we directly compare ourselves with those people? Tesser (1986; Tesser & Moore, 1986) argues that people bask in reflected glory in matters that are not highly relevant to their own self-concepts and for which they don't have high aspirations. If being an athlete isn't vital to my self-concept, then I can readily bask in reflected glory if my friends are great athletes. However, people do compare themselves with closely associated oth-

ers in highly self-relevant areas. If I aspire to be a great scholar, for example, I'm likely to compare my scholastic performance with my friends' (and to feel bad about myself if they all score higher than I do on an important test).

Tesser, Campbell, & Smith (1984) found evidence for these hypotheses in a study that asked 270 fifth- and sixth-grade students to list the activities (for example, academics, sports, art, or music) that were most and least important to them. The children also rated their own and other students' performances in these activities. The results indicated that children tended to choose friends who were superior to them in irrelevant activities (presumably to bask in reflected glory) but inferior to them in highly relevant activities (presumably to yield favorable comparison with others.)

Social psychologists have documented many strategies that people use to create favorable or powerful images of themselves for others' benefit (Jones & Wortman, 1973; Jones & Pittman, 1982). Among these strategies are ingratiation (saying or doing things to be liked by others), intimidation (presenting an image of power or competence to increase influence over others), and self-promotion (saying positive things about one's self, often in order to be viewed as able and competent). Generally, we engage in such self-presentational strategies to gain rewards and power and to avoid costs, or any negative occurrence, in a social relationship.

One common strategy used in self-presentation is simply telling others what they want to hear. In a clever study, Zanna and Pack (1975) led female undergraduates at Princeton University to believe that they would interact either with a very desirable man (a tall Princeton man who was looking for a girlfriend) or a not-so-desirable man (a very short non-Princeton man who already had a girlfriend). These women were also told that the man liked either very traditional women (women who were "emotional," "passive," and "soft") or nontraditional women (women who were "independent," "competitive," and "dominant"). The women then completed an attitude questionnaire and a so-called "intelligence test."

Women who believed they would interact with the highly desirable man molded their questionnaire responses to match the man's preferences. When they thought that the man liked "traditional" women, they described themselves in more traditional terms; when they thought the man liked nontraditional women, they described themselves as relatively more nontraditional. Interestingly, the women who thought they would interact with an "undesirable" man did not change their self-presentation in either direction—he apparently was not worth the effort. Perhaps the most startling finding of this experiment, however, was that the women who expected to interact with a desirable man who liked "traditional" women also performed significantly worse on their "intelligence tests" than did other women. In other words, in hopes of appearing "traditional" and "feminine," the women actually undermined their own intellectual performance. Such is the power of impression management!

The Self and Mental Health

"... Do you wish for instruction in the building up of the personality?"

"Yes, please."

"Then be so kind as to place a few dozen of your pieces at my disposal."

"My pieces—?"

"Of the pieces into which you saw your so-called personality broken up. I can't play without pieces."

He held up a glass to me and again I saw the unity of my personality broken up into many selves whose number seemed even to have increased. The pieces were now ... very small, about the size of chessmen. The player took a dozen or so of them in his sure and quiet fingers and placed them on the ground near the board.

"... We demonstrate to anyone whose soul has fallen to pieces that he can rearrange these pieces of a previous self in what order he pleases, and so attain to an endless multiplicity of moves in the game of life. As the playwright shapes a drama from a handful of characters, so do we from the pieces of the disintegrated self build up ever new groups, with ever new interplay and suspense, and new situations that are eternally inexhaustible. Look!"

—— *Steppenwolf*, pp. 218–219

Our sense of self is related to our mental health in many complex and subtle ways. Perhaps the most dramatic example of a "pathological" self is the multiple personality syndrome, in which an individual possesses several seemingly discrete personalities within the same body. The self is then literally like the shattered mirror in *Steppenwolf* (American Psychiatric Association, 1987; Osgood, Luria, Jeans, & Smith, 1976). Multiple personalities, although dramatic, are also quite rare. A more common mental disorder involving the self is depression. Recently social psychologists have used research on the self to understand and help alleviate this common problem (Lewinsohn, Hoberman, Teri, & Hautziner, 1985; Pyszczynski & Greenberg, 1987; Linville, 1985, 1987). Let's examine some of the links between the self and depression.

Self-awareness and depression.   Pyszczynski and Greenberg (1987; see also Lewinsohn et al., 1985) argue that depression is intimately tied to self-awareness. Let's explore this relationship in greater detail.

Certain kinds of depression, known as "reactive depressions," are most likely to occur after a major loss, such as the death of a loved one or the end of an important romantic relationship or job. For most people, having intimate relationships and doing meaningful work are two of life's most important goals. Recall that according to self-awareness theory, if you do not match your goal, then you try to change your behavior to achieve a better match. If that is impossible, you give up the goal and try to avoid self-awareness.

Most people find it possible to give up small goals (like getting an "A" in a class), but suffering a major loss (like the death of a loved one) prevents achievement of a "goal" that is difficult to relinquish. Self-directed attention is triggered (you focus a lot on yourself and your misery). The discrepancy between your goal (having a relationship with your deceased loved one) and your current situation (a horrible loss) is impossible to remedy. You feel the anguish of this discrepancy, and your state of self-focused attention makes you even more aware of your pain. You are in a "control loop" from which you cannot exit—you can't resolve the discrepancy between your current state and a major goal, and the goal is simply too important to abandon.

This conflict is the beginning of depression. Because the depressed person is self-focused, he or she begins to explain events in terms of the self (as predicted by salience effects in attribution; see Chapter 4). So the self seems to be the cause of the misery. The depressed person begins to develop depressive attributions in which the self is blamed (Abramson, Seligman, & Teasdale, 1978) and a depressive self-schema that characterizes the self as worthless and responsible for these negative events.

Paradoxically, once a depressive self-schema is established, the depressed person begins to maintain his or her misery. (Many of us have known depressed people who actually seemed to prefer misery to happiness.) This behavior is an example of a self-verification process; people act to verify their self-concepts even when such actions make them unhappy (Swann & Read, 1981). Although painful, a depressive self-schema at least makes the world understandable and predictable to a depressed person ("bad things happen to me because I am worthless and deserve them"), and it helps the person avoid being "burned" again by painful losses in the future (Pyszczynski, 1982). Figure 6.14 schematically summarizes the link between self-awareness and depression.

Breaking the cycle of depression.   This analysis of a link between depression and self-awareness has suggested some new ideas for research. For example, depressed people do in fact prove to be highly self-focused: Private self-consciousness correlates with depression (Ingram & Smith, 1984; Smith, Ingram, & Roth, 1985), and clinical descriptions of depressed people note their chronic preoccupation with themselves (Beck, 1976; Brown & Harris, 1978). Not only do depressed people show higher self-awareness in general, but they show the particularly self-defeating pattern of seeking self-awareness after negative events. Experimental studies indicate that depressed people, unlike nondepressed people, prefer sitting in front of a mirror (that is, being in a self-focused state) after failure and actually dislike self-focused attention after success (Pyszczynski & Greenberg, 1985).

If heightened self-awareness is one component of depression, then one goal of therapy should be to induce depressed people to focus on themselves less, especially after negative events (just as when we are mildly depressed it helps to "take our minds off ourselves" by going out with friends or to a movie). Interestingly, Schmitt (1983) has noted that insight therapies, in which subjects focus on themselves, tend to be less effective in treating depression than cognitive or behavioral therapies, which focus more on rechanneling the depressed person's thought processes or

FIGURE 6.14   Self-awareness and the vicious cycle of depression.

How does self-awareness contribute to depression?

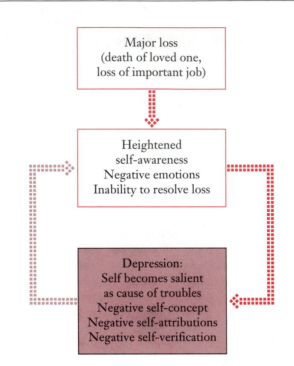

According to Pyszczynski and Greenberg (1987), depression often begins when a person suffers a profound loss that triggers negative emotions and heightened self-awareness. Self-awareness makes the self salient as a cause for the individual's misery. As the vicious cycle progresses, the depressed person develops a negative self-concept and negative self-attributions. Self-verification leads the depressed person to elicit negative responses from his or her social environment, which leads to more negative emotions and heightened self-awareness, and the cycle continues.

behavior. The last thing depressed people may need is therapy that induces them to contemplate their pain and loss in yet more agonizing detail.

If inappropriate self-focus is another component of depression—for example, choosing self-focus after failures but not after successes—then another goal of therapy should be to train depressed people to pay more attention to their successes and positive experiences and less attention to their failures and negative experiences. (This suggestion is closely related to some attributional therapies for depression discussed in Chapter 4.)

Cognitive complexity and depression. Another way to help people deal with profound losses is to encourage new and varied ways of seeing themselves. Recent research suggests that people who have varied self-concepts are more resistant to depression than are people whose entire identities are linked to one relationship (for example, with a spouse) or to one role (for example, success at school). Apparently, to avoid depression you shouldn't "put all of your eggs in one cognitive basket" (Linville, 1985).

To evaluate this hypothesis, Linville (1985) assessed 59 college men on the complexity of their self-concepts. Specifically, she asked them to sort 33 traits, each typed on a separate card, into any number of groups that described aspects of themselves. A subject might sort "relaxed," "reflective," "lazy," and "quiet" into a pile reflecting the "solitary self," and "lazy," "impulsive," "unorganized," and "not studious" into a pile representing the "bad self." The more groupings subjects produced, the more complex their self-concept was considered to be. Subjects were also rated more highly on self-complexity when traits were not placed in more than one pile.

After completing the trait sorting task, subjects took a bogus test of "analytical ability." Half the men were told they had performed very well on the test, whereas the other half were informed that they had performed poorly. After receiving this feedback, the men rated their mood and how "creative" they felt. The men with less complex self-concepts were more affected by feedback — that is, they felt worse after failure and more elated after success. In a second study, Linville (1985) found that college women with simpler self-concepts experienced wider mood swings over a two-week period than did women with more complex self-concepts. Thus people with simpler self-concepts seem to display more volatile emotions than people with more complex self-concepts. By implication, then, people who are low on self-complexity are more likely to become depressed after receiving negative information about themselves.

In research that directly tested the hypothesis that self-complexity buffers people against depression, Linville (1987) measured the self-complexity of 106 college students and also obtained measures of their stress levels, physical symptoms of stress (colds, stomach pains, headaches), and psychological symptoms (depression, perceived stress). These data provided clear evidence that high levels of stress lead to more severe physical and psychological symptoms in subjects low in self-complexity than in subjects with greater self-complexity.

Taken as a whole, Linville's research suggests that people who are prone to depression may need to be taught to see themselves in many different ways, for people with varied self-concepts seem less susceptible to a loss in any given realm of life. According to Linville's research, then, we should all aspire to self-complexity and, like the Steppenwolf, count ourselves lucky to have a multiplicity of selves.

▪▪▪

Summary

1. Both "personality" and the "self" refer to processes within individuals that influence their social behavior.

2. Personality research examines internal causes of behavior, individual differences in behavior, and the consistency of behavior over time and settings.

3. Trait theories of personality argue for the existence within people of stable internal dispositions that lead to consistent behavior across settings and over time. Personality traits are often measured by standardized tests. Five basic dimensions of personality found in many studies are sociability, likability, conscientiousness, emotional adjustment, and intelligence/culturedness.

4. Social learning theories argue that behavior is learned and often varies across situations. Social learning researchers often study the environments that elicit behavior.

5. Early research, like Hartshorne and May's work on morality in children, suggested that behavior is often quite inconsistent across settings. Reviews published in the 1960s argued that trait measures often do not correlate strongly with related behaviors.

6. More recent research indicates that aggregated behaviors often show trait-like consistency, whereas single behaviors do not. People may show trait-like consistency in some domains of behavior but not others. Finally, traits best predict behaviors that are prototypical of the trait.

7. Traits, situations, and their interactions all influence behavior. Research on moderator variables seeks to identify variables that determine when behavior is and is not influenced by situations and when it is and is not influenced by traits.

8. People in "strong" situations behave more as the situation dictates, whereas people in "weak" situations behave in ways that are more consistent with their traits. Precipitating situations encourage the display of personality traits by making specific traits salient and by permitting behavioral choices related to the traits.

9. Low self-monitoring individuals are people who are more trait-like in their behavior, whereas because high self-monitoring individuals are more responsive to their social settings, their behavior varies more with the situation.

10. The concept of "self" implies conscious, self-reflective knowledge. Research using mirrors suggests that only higher primates show self-recognition.

11. The classic self theories of James, Cooley, and Mead emphasize the social origins of the self. James distinguished between the "I," or the self as active agent, and the "me," or the self as an object of thought and a body of self-reflective knowledge.

12. People are not born with selves; the self develops as a result of feedback from a social environment. Distinctive characteristics are often salient in people's self-descriptions. The self-concept grows more complex and abstract as people grow older.

13. The self-schema comprises the organized knowledge people possess about themselves. People who are schematic on a given trait possess an elaborate self-schema concerning behavior relevant to that trait. Schematic people quickly answer whether they possess schema-relevant traits, and they behave like "experts" in that they "chunk" other people's behavior into large, meaningful units when it is relevant to their self-schemas.

14. Self-knowledge differs from other kinds of knowledge in that it is very complex and highly defended. People often remember information better when that information is judged in terms of its relevance to the self. Research on self-

verification shows that people try to prove the validity of their self-concepts by selectively seeking and remembering information that is consistent with their self-concept, and by proving the validity of their self-concepts to others through their behavior.

15. People are most likely to behave consistently with their self-concepts when in a state of self-directed attention. When people focus attention on themselves, they behave more consistently with their traits, attitudes, and values, and they experience emotions more intensely. Self-awareness is in part a function of situational factors and is in part a function of personality. In terms of control theory, the self can be conceived as a control system that strives to match behavior to internal standards when the self is in a state of self-directed attention.

16. The public self is a collection of varied roles. Erving Goffman offered a theater metaphor of the public self: Everyone is an actor who plays different roles depending on the social setting. Research demonstrates that people often display themselves differently to different social audiences.

17. One way people may boost their public image is by "basking in reflected glory" — that is, by publicly associating themselves with successful others. People are most likely to bask in reflected glory on dimensions that are not very important to them and are most likely to compare themselves directly to others on important dimensions.

18. Self-awareness theory has been used to understand the causes of depression. When a person suffers a major loss, self-directed attention is triggered and cannot readily be stopped. Incessant self-directed attention leads to self-blame, negative attributions about the self, and destructive self-verification processes.

19. People with simple self-concepts are more emotionally responsive to information about their successes or failures, are more emotionally volatile, and suffer more depression in response to real-life stress than do people with complex self-concepts.

Glossary

Cognitive complexity: The degree to which people have varied and independent facets to their self-concept; cognitive complexity is related to emotional volatility and susceptibility to depression

Construct validity: Possessed by a personality test when its scores correlate in theoretically meaningful ways with other variables

Control theory: Also known as cybernetic theory; describes how systems (such as thermostats) regulate themselves to maintain some state of equilibrium; the basic mechanism of a control system is a feedback loop, in which the system tests to see if some standard is met, and when it is not, it institutes corrective action; the self in a state of self-awareness acts as a control system

Discriminant validity: Possessed by a personality test when it measures something different from other tests

Impression management: Controlling the appearances we present to others to create a desired image for a social audience

Internal reliability: Possessed by a personality test when all of its items correlate with one another and thus measure the same trait

Moderator variables: Variables that influence the relation between two other variables; in personality research, situational moderator variables (such as "weak" vs. "strong" situations) specify in what situations traits are and are not likely to influence behavior; personality moderator variables (such as self-monitoring) identify people who tend to behave in a manner that is consistent with their traits and those who tend to behave more according to situational pressures

Personality: Traditionally, this term refers to the consistent, stable, distinctive traits and behaviors that characterize individuals; see *trait theories* and *social learning theories* for two different approaches to personality

Precipitating situation: A situation that encourages the behavioral display of a trait by making the trait relevant and salient and by providing behavioral options related to the trait

Predictive validity: The ability of a personality test to predict relevant criteria; for example, the ability of an extroversion test to predict the number of friends people have

Private self-consciousness: A trait that assesses the degree to which people engage in self-focused attention

Reflected glory: Occurs when we improve our own image by associating with successful, competent, or attractive people

Reliability: Possessed by a personality test when it measures some trait consistently

Self: According to different theories, the self is (1) the organized, self-reflective knowledge we hold about ourselves, (2) the active agent that monitors and chooses behavior, and (3) a collection of social roles and self-presentational strategies

Self-awareness theory: A theory that holds that people can focus attention either on themselves or on the external environment; when attention is self-focused, people think about their internal standards and try to match their behavior to these standards; if it is not possible to match behavior to standards, self-awareness is painful and people strive to avoid it

Self-discrepancy: Occurs when we do not behave in a manner that is consistent with internal standards; Higgins describes four kinds of self-discrepancy: violations of one's own ideals, of others' ideals, of one's own moral "oughts," or of others' moral "oughts"; each kind of violation leads to different negative emotions

Self-monitoring: A personality trait that assesses the degree to which an individual behaves consistently with inner traits, attitudes, and values or with the demands of the social setting; self-monitoring serves as a moderator variable in personality research

Self-reference effect: The tendency for people to remember information better that is judged in terms of its relevance to the self

Self-schema: The organized knowledge we have about ourselves; like other kinds of schemas, the self-schema can influence perception, memory, and inference about ourself and others

Self-verification: The tendency for people to engage in behaviors and thoughts that serve to prove the validity of their self-concept

Social learning theories: Personality theories that argue that individual differences in behavior are learned through classical conditioning, operant conditioning, and observational learning; such theories hold that behavior is not necessarily consistent across situations

Test-retest reliability: Possessed by a personality test when respondents' scores remain relatively stable over time

Trait theories: Theories of personality that assume that people possess consistent internal dispositions (such as extroversion or honesty) that exert a broad influence on their behavior; such theories predict that behavior should be relatively consistent across situations

Validity: Possessed by a personality test when it measures the trait it is supposed to measure; see *construct validity* and *predictive validity*

Approximately one and one-half million of the six million Jews killed during Hitler's "final solution" were children.

I was repelled by the conglomeration of races . . . by this whole mixture of Czechs, Poles, Hungarians, Ruthenians, Serbs, Croats, and everywhere, the eternal mushroom of humanity — Jews and more Jews (p. 123).

. . . The inexorable mortal enemy of the German people is and remains France (p. 619).

Never forget that the rulers of present-day Russia are common blood-stained criminals; they are the scum of humanity. . . (p. 660).

—— passages from *Mein Kampf*, by Adolf Hitler
(originally published 1925)

CHAPTER 7

Attitudes and Beliefs

Did the beliefs and attitudes of one man plunge the world into the most destructive war in recorded history? Were the wild prejudices of that same man responsible for the horrors of the Nazi holocaust? Can beliefs and attitudes so profoundly affect the course of human events?

Since World War II a huge amount of social psychological research has been devoted to understanding beliefs and attitudes — their formation, their organization, the ways they can be altered, and, of course, their effects on behavior. There are several reasons for the prominence of attitude research in social psychology: First, social psychologists have hoped that attitudes might serve as an organizing concept that is useful in predicting a host of important social behaviors, such as discrimination, aggression, interpersonal attraction, voting patterns, and religious activities. Second, as rigorous scaling techniques were first developed in the 1920s and 1930s (for example, Thurstone, 1928; Likert, 1932), the measurement of attitudes seemed both scientific and practical. Methodological advances transformed an intuitively appealing concept into a scientifically respectable topic with easily implemented operational definitions (see Chapter 2).

Finally, beyond its theoretical and methodological appeal, attitude research held the promise of having many real-life applications. The first major United States laboratory investigating attitude change (at Yale University) was created during World War II partly because of the government's growing list of questions about propaganda and persuasion (see Hovland, Lumsdaine, & Sheffield, 1949; Hovland, Janis, & Kelley, 1953). Was "Tokyo Rose" truly successful in demoralizing American troops in the Pacific? How could the Allies most effectively demoralize the enemy with propaganda leaflets and radio broadcasts? How could the military successfully indoctrinate soldiers, and how could the government best persuade civilians to support the war effort? These practical questions led to an explosion of research on attitudes and attitude change in the 1940s and 1950s.

The U.S. government's concern about propaganda and persuasion during World War II stimulated social psychological research on attitude change.

Of course, governments at war are not the only institutions interested in the formation, alteration, and behavioral consequences of attitudes. In the United States, advertisers currently spend over $50 billion a year to influence consumers' attitudes, and political candidates spend another one-half billion dollars to persuade the American electorate (McGuire, 1985). The American Cancer Society tells us that cigarettes are bad; tobacco company ads imply that cigarettes are chic. The National Safety Council states that seat belts save lives. The gas company advises us to conserve energy. And the Coca Cola Company continually informs us that Coke is "the real thing." Given our society's obsession with persuasion, it is not surprising that social psychologists have conducted so much research on the ever-relevant topic of attitudes.

What Are Attitudes?

The people in their overwhelming majority are so feminine by nature and attitude that sober reasoning determines their thoughts and actions far less than emotion and feeling.

> And this sentiment is not complicated, but very simple and all of a piece. It does not have multiple shadings; it has a positive and a negative; love or hate, right or wrong, truth or lie, never half this way and half that way. . . .
>
> —— *Mein Kampf*, p. 183

Attitudes are "mediating variables"—not tangible objects, but rather hypothetical constructs that can be inferred but not directly observed (see Chapter 1). We can observe the *effects* of an attitude, but not the attitude itself, when a political partisan votes for a chosen candidate, when someone buys a favorite soap at the supermarket, or when a bigot like Adolf Hitler attacks the objects of his prejudices.

Characteristics of Attitudes

An attitude is a learned evaluative response, directed at specific objects, which is relatively enduring and influences behavior in a generally motivating way (Allport, 1935; Bem, 1970; Oskamp, 1977; Petty & Cacioppo, 1981). Let's consider in turn each of the key characteristics listed in this definition.

First, according to most modern theorists, an attitude is *evaluative* (Bem, 1970; Oskamp, 1977; Fishbein & Ajzen, 1975); it involves a like or a dislike. Central to the notion of attitude is the assumption that people show some kind of emotional *response* when they hold an attitude.

But an attitude is different from just a mood or an emotion. Emotions may be broad and diffuse; you may feel happy for no particular reason, or you may suffer from "free-floating" anxiety. An attitude, however, is *directed at some object or target*. You may hold attitudes toward the President of the United States, the Soviet Union, your college, legalized abortion, and so on. The concept of attitude generally entails the placement of an object or concept on some mental dimension, usually a like-dislike continuum (McGuire, 1985).

An attitude is relatively *enduring*. Emotions can come and go in seconds, but attitudes are more stable; in this sense, attitudes are similar to personality traits (Ajzen, 1987; see Chapter 6). If you are violently opposed to capital punishment today, chances are that you will still be so a week from now. People's attitudes can change, but such change may not be quick or easy. Anyone who has tried to change the attitude of a "pig-headed" acquaintance can attest to the enduring nature of many attitudes.

Most of us believe that attitudes *influence behavior*. This assumption has not always been easy to demonstrate in research studies; nevertheless, attitude theorists have generally assumed that attitudes somehow mediate behavioral responses. Here are a few commonsense examples: Prejudiced attitudes lead to discrimination; positive attitudes toward political candidates lead us to vote for those candidates; negative attitudes toward a consumer product lead us not to buy that product; and so on.

Of course, other variables—habits, reflexes, instincts, and drives—influence behavior as well. How are attitudes different from these other mediating variables? Attitudes are *more generally motivating* than simple habits or reflexes. An attitude does not lead to a single, rigid behavioral response, but instead is reflected in many different behaviors. For example, if you are prejudiced against college professors, you might move to the other side of a bus whenever a college professor enters and sits down, refuse to sell your house to a college professor, and avoid sending your children to schools that accept the children of college professors. If a college professor brushes against you in a public place, you might pull away and break into a cold

▪▪▪▪▪▪▪▪▪▪▪▪▪▪▪▪▪▪▪▪▪▪▪▪▪

Do attitudes predict behavior? Outraged by the Chinese government's massacre of student demonstrators in Tianamen Square, these San Francisco marchers are translating their attitudes into action.

sweat. (Although this is a somewhat silly example, I'm sure you'll agree that real-life prejudices produce many behavioral consequences. Tragically, the attitudes Hitler expressed in *Mein Kampf* continued to motivate his behavior for some twenty years.)

Finally, attitudes are *learned*. As an infant you were not much concerned with the presidency, communism, the arms race, abortion, or capital punishment, but by now you have probably acquired attitudes about all of these topics. We'll consider the interesting and important theoretical question of how people acquire attitudes later.

▪▪▪▪▪▪▪▪▪▪▪▪▪▪▪▪▪▪▪▪▪▪▪▪▪

A Functional Approach to Attitudes

Why do people hold attitudes? What purposes do attitudes serve? In an influential paper Katz (1960) argued that attitudes may serve several different purposes in our lives. An attitude may serve (1) the *instrumental* function of helping us gain rewards and avoid punishments, (2) the *ego-defensive* function of helping us to avoid personality conflicts and anxiety, (3) a *knowledge* function by helping us to order and assimilate complex information, and (4) the *value-expressive* function of reflecting deeper values and ideals. Let's examine each of these functions in greater detail.

Sometimes we hold attitudes for eminently practical reasons — they bring us rewards or help us avoid punishments. Such attitudes are said to serve an instrumental function. For example, many people feel quite positively about the religion in which they were reared, in part because their parents rewarded them for expressing positive feelings about that religion and punished them when they criticized it.

Indeed, often the best predictors of individuals' religious and political attitudes are their parents' attitudes (Sears, 1975; Berger, 1980; Jessop, 1982).

An attitude is ego-defensive when it helps us to resolve personality conflicts or to guard against anxiety. Prejudiced attitudes provide a good example of ego-defensiveness (see Chapter 9 for a more complete discussion). Imagine that you've just flunked several exams and are worried that you might be intellectually inferior to others. Believing that members of various minorities have low IQ's may allow you to feel intellectually superior to them and therefore better about yourself.

Attitudes may serve a knowledge function by creating a cohesive and comprehensible social world. Adolf Hitler explained the reason for Germany's defeat in World War I and its subsequent economic hardships in terms that were consistent with his prejudices against labor unions, Social Democrats, Bolsheviks, foreigners, and, of course, Jews: "If we pass all the causes of the German collapse in review, the ultimate and most decisive remains the failure to recognize the racial problem and especially the Jewish menace" (*Mein Kampf*, p. 327). The "facts" we possess about current politics are very likely organized around our political attitudes. Attitudes give meaning and coherence to the flood of political information to which we are constantly exposed. In this sense, attitudes may serve as *schemas* (see Chapter 5) that influence how we perceive and remember information (Judd & Kulik, 1980; Tesser, 1978).

Finally, attitudes may be value-expressive—rationally thought out to express deeper underlying values. For example, some people may oppose legalized abortion because of their religious values; others may be "pro-choice" because of their libertarian political values.

In recent research Herek (1986, 1987) used a functional analysis to understand attitudes towards homosexuals. In one study he asked college students in California to write essays explaining why they held generally positive or negative attitudes toward homosexuals. Statistical analyses of the coded content of these essays indicated that students' attitudes served three different functions: ego-defensive, value-expressive, and a combination instrumental/knowledge function based on their actual experiences with homosexuals (see Figure 7.1 for excerpts from actual essays). Sixty-four percent of students' essays contained a single attitude function, whereas 36 percent combined two or more functions in the same essay. Thus a given attitude may serve more than one function simultaneously.

How are attitudes operationally defined? Since the 1920s and 1930s social psychologists have developed rigorous scaling techniques to assess people's attitudes. Let's consider the most prominent methods.

Attitude Measurement

Thurstone scales.   The first statistically adequate attitude scaling technique was developed by Thurstone (1928). His "equal appearing interval" method was fairly complicated—it entailed developing a range of attitude statements that varied in their positivity or negativity with respect to the attitude object.

For example, Thurstone and Chave (1929) developed statements to measure people's attitudes toward the church. Their scale included items that were quite negative toward organized religion, items that were more neutral, and items that were quite positive toward organized religion. Each statement was rated by many

FIGURE 7.1   College students explain why they hold their attitudes toward homosexuals.

What functions do attitudes serve?

The following examples of college students' explanations of their attitudes toward homosexuals illustrate several functions of attitudes.

FUNCTION SERVED

Knowledge/instrumental	[I have generally positive attitudes because] I have come to know some of these people and find them no different from any other people. This has not always been the case. In junior high and high school I didn't condemn so to speak but I held strong opinions against them. This was an attitude formed without any knowledge of homosexuality or homosexuals. When I first came to [college] I still had some of the same attitudes. Little did I know that the guy in the next room was gay. We became good friends and did things together all the time. Eventually he told me and it was then that I realized that homosexuals only differ in sexual preference.
Ego-defensive	[I have generally negative attitudes because] I feel homosexuality is not a normal lifestyle. I do, however, feel more comfortable with a male homosexual than with a lesbian. Male homosexuals may have a different lifestyle but they are not physically dangerous to me as a woman, and I feel casual friendships between myself and male homosexuals are less tense. Lesbianism, however, is disgusting to me. . . .
Value-expressive	[I have generally positive attitudes because] I don't think sexual preferences are a basis of judgment of someone's character or personality. Sexual preferences are a personal matter, and as long as a homosexual doesn't offend anyone or force his/her temptations on someone who is unwilling, there is no reason to condemn him/her. Homosexual tendencies aren't a deficit in someone's upbringing. I have these attitudes because of my own upbringing to be open-minded and nonstereotypical or nonjudgmental. . . .
	[I have generally negative attitudes because] in the Bible it clearly states that homosexuality is a SIN. I believe that no one can be a Christian if he/she is a homosexual. I believe the Bible is correct, and I follow its beliefs word for word. I am a Christian.

SOURCE: From Herek (1987). Reprinted by permission.

judges on how positive or negative it was toward the church, and the researchers then selected statements that were equal scale intervals apart—hence the name "equal appearing interval scaling." Figure 7.2 lists 12 items from Thurstone and Chave's scale and their respective scale values.

How then do we measure subjects' attitudes with a Thurstone scale? After developing a set of statements (like those in Figure 7.2), we ask subjects to check only those statements they agree with. The mean (or median) scale value of each subject's checked items is that subject's attitude "score."

Likert scales.   Because they require cumbersome multistage development, Thurstone scales are rarely used today. *Likert scales*, or *summated rating scales*, are much more common now (Likert, 1932; Murphy & Likert, 1938). Most of us have probably

FIGURE 7.2   Items from a Thurstone scale assessing attitudes toward the church.

How are attitudes measured in a Thurstone scale?

To develop the following Thurstone scale assessing attitudes toward the church, the researchers first had subjects rate how negative or positive items were toward the church. Final scale items were selected to represent a broad range of negative and positive attitudes. Ideally, each successive item in a Thurstone scale shows about the same amount of change in positivity from the previous item. People who complete the final attitude scale check only those items they agree with (the items appear in a random order without their scale values). Their attitude score is the mean (or median) scale value of the items they have checked.

SCALE VALUE*	ITEM
0.2	I believe the church is the greatest institution in America today.
1.2	I believe the church is a powerful agency for promoting both individual and social righteousness.
2.2	I like to go to church for I get something worthwhile to think about and it keeps my mind filled with right thoughts.
3.3	I enjoy my church because there is a spirit of friendliness there.
4.5	I believe in what the church teaches but with mental reservations.
5.6	Sometimes I feel that the church and religion are necessary and sometimes I doubt it.
6.7	I believe in sincerity and goodness without any church ceremonies.
7.5	I think too much money is being spent on the church for the benefit that is being derived.
8.3	I think the teaching of the church is altogether too superficial to have much social significance.
9.2	I think the church seeks to impose a lot of worn-out dogmas and medieval superstitions.
10.4	The church represents shallowness, hypocrisy, and prejudice.
11.0	I think the church is a parasite on society.

*The scale reflects how positive or negative the item is toward the church. Higher values represent more negative attitudes.

SOURCE: From Thurstone & Chave (1929). Reprinted by permission.

filled out many Likert scales in our lives. These questionnaires typically contain a number of attitude statements, and subjects are asked to rate how much they agree or disagree with each statement. The score on the scale is the sum of a subject's numeric responses on all items — hence the name "summated rating scale." (Contrast this with a Thurstone scale, in which subjects check only those statements they agree with.) Likert scales tend to be easier to develop than Thurstone scales and are just as reliable, and it is this practical advantage that accounts for their current popularity among researchers (Murphy & Likert, 1938; McNemar, 1946; Poppleton & Pilkington, 1964). Figure 7.3 presents a recently developed Likert scale for assessing attitudes toward homosexuals (Kite & Deaux, 1986).

Semantic differential scales.   If the core of an attitude is its *evaluative* component, then it makes sense to assess attitudes by measuring how "good" or "bad" we feel about a particular object (thing or person). Since the 1950s researchers have attempted to measure the connotative meanings of concepts (for example, "Iran," "Mother Teresa," "AIDS," "social security") by having subjects rate them on *semantic differential scales* (Osgood, Suci, & Tannenbaum, 1957). Subjects might be asked to rate concepts on dimensions like "good–bad," "smooth–rough," "beautiful–ugly," and "fast–slow."

Research consistently shows that the dimension of meaning that accounts for most of the variation in such ratings is one of *evaluation* — that is, how "good" or "bad" the concept is judged to be. This evaluative dimension is measured by such scales as "good–bad," "beautiful–ugly," and "worthy–unworthy." It seems likely that a concept like "AIDS" would be rated as quite "bad" and "ugly," indicating that raters hold negative attitudes towards AIDS, whereas "Mother Teresa" would be rated as "good" and "worthy," indicating raters' positive attitudes toward Mother Teresa.

Evaluative scales seem ideally suited to measure attitudes. Subjects rate a given attitude object (say, the President of the United States) on a number of evaluative semantic differential scales, and each subject's mean rating is considered to be a measure of his or her attitude. This approach has been used recently in some major research projects on attitudes (see, for example, Fishbein & Ajzen, 1975; Ajzen & Fishbein, 1980).

The validity of attitude scales.   Traditional attitude scaling techniques assume that people are willing and able to report honestly on their attitudes. However, this assumption may not always be valid. Subjects can usually figure out what attitude a scale is designed to measure (see Figures 7.2 and 7.3, for example), and they sometimes distort their responses to present themselves in ways that are socially more desirable or to satisfy the demand characteristics of the study (see Chapter 2). For example, many truly prejudiced people are unlikely to report their attitudes honestly on a prejudice scale because they feel either that such attitudes are undesirable or that the researcher might disapprove of them. (Adolf Hitler apparently was an exception, for he quite freely expressed his virulent prejudices in *Mein Kampf*. It seems safe to assume that he would have expressed his prejudices on an attitude scale as well.)

In recent years researchers have devised some clever techniques for inducing subjects to rate scale items more honestly. For example, in the *bogus pipeline method* (Jones & Sigal, 1971), subjects are led to believe that the researchers can accurately

FIGURE 7.3   A Likert scale for assessing attitudes toward homosexuals.

Why are Likert scales also known as "summated rating scales"?

Likert scales are commonly used in attitude research. Subjects rate the degree to which they agree or disagree with items that are preselected to be clear and to measure the same attitude. A subject's score on a Likert scale is the sum of his or her responses, thus the term *summated rating scale*.

Please indicate your level of agreement with the items below using the following scale:

1	2	3	4	5
Strongly agree		*Neutral*		*Strongly disagree*

1. I would not mind having homosexual friends.
2. Finding out that an artist was gay would have no effect on my appreciation of his/her work.
3. I won't associate with known homosexuals if I can help it.
4. I would look for a new place to live if I found out my roommate was gay.
5. Homosexuality is a mental illness.
6. I would not be afraid for my child to have a homosexual teacher.
7. Gays dislike members of the opposite sex.
8. I do not really find the thought of homosexual acts disgusting.
9. Homosexuals are more likely to commit deviant sexual acts, such as child molestation, rape, and voyeurism (Peeping Toms), than are heterosexuals.
10. Homosexuals should be kept separate from the rest of society (i.e., separate housing, restricted employment).
11. Two individuals of the same sex holding hands or displaying affection in public is revolting.
12. The love between two males or two females is quite different from the love between two persons of the opposite sex.
13. I see the gay movement as a positive thing.
14. Homosexuality, as far as I'm concerned, is not sinful.
15. I would not mind being employed by a homosexual.
16. Homosexuals should be forced to have psychological treatment.
17. The increasing acceptance of homosexuality in our society is aiding in the deterioration of morals.
18. I would not decline membership in an organization just because it had homosexual members.
19. I would vote for a homosexual in an election for public office.
20. If I knew someone were gay, I would still go ahead and form a friendship with that individual.
21. If I were a parent, I could accept my son or daughter being gay.

Note: Items 1, 2, 6, 8, 13, 14, 15, 18, 19, 20, and 21 are reverse-scored.

SOURCE: From Kite and Deaux (1986). Used by permission.

Developing an Attitude Scale

How is a Likert scale developed? In general terms, attitude items are generated and then the best are selected by rigorous statistical techniques that guarantee that the items correlate well with one another (Crano & Brewster, 1986). To make these processes more concrete, let's use the scale in Figure 7.3 as an example.

Kite and Deaux (1986) created their scale items by listening to questions about homosexuality that college students posed to gay rights speakers and by noting what "seemed to be the most common stereotypes, misconceptions, and anxieties about homosexuals" (p. 139). They also used common beliefs about homosexuals expressed in the mass media and in psychology textbooks to generate items. From these varied sources, they created an initial pool of 40 scale items.

These items were then administered to a group of 40 college students. Statistical analyses showed that some of the items did not correlate well with other items, sometimes because they did not adequately assess attitudes toward homosexuals and sometimes because they were worded unclearly. Fifteen of the worst items were dropped from the scale. About half of the remaining 25 items were positively worded (that is, positive attitudes toward homosexuals were expressed by agreeing with the statements) and the others were negatively worded (positive attitudes were expressed by disagreeing with items). This variety in wording guaranteed that the scale was not influenced by people's general preference simply to agree or disagree with items.

The improved 25-item scale was then administered to 317 students at the University of Texas and 252 students at Purdue University. Again the researchers conducted statistical analyses, and four additional items were dropped because they didn't correlate well with other items. The final result was the highly reliable and internally consistent 21-item scale shown in Figure 7.3.

We learned in Chapters 2 and 6 that good self-report measures are both reliable and valid. A *reliable* attitude scale measures a given attitude consistently, and a *valid* scale measures the attitude it's supposed to measure and thus predicts real-life criteria. Psychometricians (experts in test construction and psychological measurement) emphasize that reliability is a prerequisite to validity. In other words, for an attitude scale to predict anything in real life, it first must be measuring *something* consistently. The reason an attitude scale (or any test) contains many items is to create high reliability. Psychometric theory holds that all single items are imperfect measures and that the only way to develop a reliable test is to add up responses over many items, which is exactly what a Likert scale does.

Kite and Deaux's careful scale development processes yielded an attitude measure that was reliable. But was it also valid? To answer this question, the researchers administered their scale to a large number of college students and then selected 72 men who expressed negative attitudes toward homosexuals and 72 men who expressed positive attitudes. Each of these men interacted via written

communications with another male subject in the next room. Sometimes subjects were informed that their partner was homosexual; sometimes subjects were given no such information at all. In general, men liked their partner less when he was labeled homosexual than when he was given no label, and this negative feeling was particularly pronounced for the men with negative attitudes toward homosexuals. Attitudes also influenced the content of subjects' communications. For example, men with negative attitudes toward homosexuals were more likely than men with more positive attitudes to communicate their "traditionally masculine" hobbies to their partners. Thus, Kite and Deaux's attitude scale predicted subjects' feelings and behaviors in social interactions.

In yet another attempt to assess the validity of their attitude scale, Kite and Deaux examined how well it correlated with other psychological measures. For example, data collected from 630 students at Purdue University showed that people possessing negative attitudes toward homosexuals tend also to have more traditional attitudes toward the roles of men and women in general. Of course, such research is just the first step in establishing this relatively new scale's validity. As the authors note, additional research will be necessary to understand more precisely the nature of the attitudes measured by their scale.

assess their attitudes through some physiological measure (by, for instance, attaching recording electrodes to the arm). If we ask subjects to rate various minority groups on an attitude rating scale while they are hooked up to the electrodes, they will probably answer more honestly because they believe we know the truth anyway.

Indeed, Jones, Bell, and Aronson (1972) demonstrated that subjects expressed more negative attitudes toward blacks when attached to the "bogus pipeline" than when not. Presumably subjects answered more honestly — by expressing a greater degree of prejudice — when they thought they were being monitored physiologically.

Behavioral measures of attitude.   Although less common than self-report measures, behavioral measures have at times been used in attitude research. Theoretically we can assess attitudes by measuring behaviors just as well as we can by using self-report questions (Fishbein & Ajzen, 1975; Ajzen, 1987), although in practice an "attitude" is generally equated with questionnaire measures, whereas behavioral measures are considered to be dependent variables, or criteria to predict.

Some researchers have tried to use relatively subtle physiological measures as indices of attitudes. For example, physiological arousal as assessed by the Galvanic Skin Response (a measure of skin conductivity related to perspiration) may be associated with prejudice. One study indicated that subjects who were prejudiced against blacks tended to show a greater Galvanic Skin Response when touched by a black research assistant than did nonprejudiced subjects (Porier & Lott, 1967). Pupil dilation may also be an unobtrusive physiological measure of attitude (Hess, 1975). When exposed to people or things toward which they hold strong attitudes, subjects often show pupil dilation.

Unfortunately, such physiological measures can indicate the presence of some "attitude" (or more precisely, an emotional response to an object), but not its "direction" (whether the subject likes or dislikes it). Furthermore, physiological measures are often less reliable than self-report measures, and self-report measures are simply easier to obtain. For these reasons, social psychologists commonly rely on scales to operationally define attitudes.

Newly developed physiological measures may overcome some of these problems, though. Some recent studies have attempted to measure attitudes by recording the electrical activity in facial muscles that are responsible for the display of emotion in humans (Cacioppo, Petty, Losch, & Kim, 1986; Cacioppo & Petty, 1987; see Chapter 3). Electrodes are attached to various locations on subjects' faces so that electrical activity can be measured, even when no facial movement is visible. Such methods hold the promise of both reliably measuring subtle emotional responses and assessing the *kind* of emotional reaction by identifying the specific pattern of muscle responses.

Attitude Formation

Today it is difficult, if not impossible, for me to say when the word "Jew" first gave me ground for special thoughts. At home I do not remember having heard the word during my father's lifetime. I believe the old gentleman would have regarded any special emphasis on this term as cultural backwardness. . . .

Not until my fourteenth or fifteenth year did I begin to come across the word "Jew," with any frequency, partly in connection with political discussions.

This filled me with a mild distaste, and I could not rid myself of an unpleasant feeling that always came over me whenever religious quarrels occurred in my presence. . . .

As in all such cases, I now began to try to relieve my doubts by books. For a few hellers I bought the first anti-Semitic pamphlets of my life.

—— *Mein Kampf*, pp. 51–56

Where do attitudes come from? Three general sorts of answers that correspond roughly to Katz's (1960) functional classification of attitudes can be offered to this question: (1) attitudes are formed through standard learning processes, (2) attitudes are formed as a result of personality dynamics, and (3) attitudes are logically derived from other beliefs and attitudes. The idea that learning theories can explain the formation of some attitudes relates to Katz's notion of instrumental attitudes. Similarly, the view that attitudes result from personality dynamics relates to Katz's description of ego-defensive attitudes. Finally, the idea that attitudes may be formed through logical inferential processes is consistent with both the value-expressive and knowledge functions of some attitudes.

Learning Theories of Attitude Formation

Traditional learning theories can help explain how some attitudes are formed. We will focus in particular on three varieties of learning: classical conditioning, operant conditioning, and observational learning (also known as modeling).

Classical conditioning.   Classical conditioning was first studied systematically by the Russian physiologist Ivan Pavlov, and thus it is sometimes referred to as "Pavlovian conditioning" (for more details, see Schwartz, 1978). In a typical classical conditioning study, we present the subject (a hungry dog) with an *unconditioned stimulus* (food), which automatically produces the *unconditioned response* (salivation). By repeatedly pairing the unconditioned stimulus (the food) with a *conditioned stimulus* (a ringing bell, for example), the dog acquires a *conditioned response*. The dog is classically conditioned when it salivates at the sound of the bell, even when food is not present. The key elements of classical conditioning are diagrammed in Figure 7.4.

Generally, classical conditioning occurs for involuntary responses such as salivation. Other involuntary responses that can be classically conditioned include changes in heart rate, perspiration, vasoconstriction (narrowing of blood vessels), and gastric motility. How do these involuntary responses relate to attitudes? Remember that an emotional response to some object is central to the notion of an attitude. Emotions are often characterized by physiological arousal (increased heart rate, blood pressure, perspiration), and it is exactly these kinds of "emotional" responses that can be classically conditioned. Thus some attitudes may be viewed as classically conditioned emotional responses to specific objects.

In the quote from *Mein Kampf* at the beginning of this section, Adolf Hitler seems to suggest that he underwent a process of classical conditioning when he came "across the word 'Jew' . . . in connection with political discussions" that were unpleasant. In a similar manner, you might acquire prejudiced attitudes through a process of classical conditioning. If whenever you saw a member of a minority group your mother pulled you away and warned you to stay away from "those people," your mother was in essence conditioning fear and arousal to "those people."

FIGURE 7.4   Classical conditioning of attitudes.

How can classical conditioning explain how we acquire some of our attitudes?

In classical conditioning, an originally neutral stimulus (such as a bell) comes to elicit a response (such as salivation) by being paired with a stimulus (such as food) that naturally elicits the response.

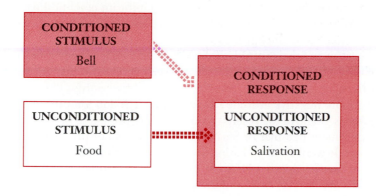

Some attitudes might be acquired (learned) in a similar way, if the object of the attitude (originally a neutral stimulus) is paired with a stimulus that naturally elicits a certain response.

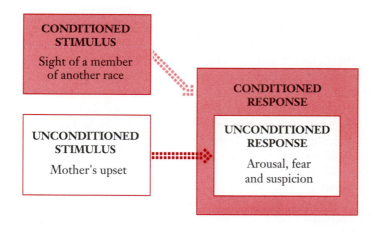

Classical conditioning best explains how we acquire the "gut" emotional components of an attitude.

In an early study demonstrating the classical conditioning of attitudes, Staats and Staats (1958) asked subjects to remember words paired with various nationality names, such as "French–*blue*," "Dutch–*gift*," "German–*table*," and "Swedish–*pain*." One target nationality—"Dutch," for example—was always paired with words having pleasant emotional connotations (like *gift*, *beauty*, or *romance*), whereas a second target nationality — say, "Swedish" — was always paired with negative words (*pain*, *ugly*, or *bitter*). Thus "Dutch" and "Swedish" served as the *conditioned stimuli*, and the other nationality names were control stimuli paired with emotionally neutral words.

The Staats and Staats study demonstrated significant conditioning of attitudes. When toward the end of the study subjects were asked to rate how they actually felt about the various nationality groups, their attitudes toward the Dutch had become a bit more positive and their attitudes toward Swedes a bit more negative. In a separate group of subjects, the target nationalities were reversed—that is, "Dutch" was paired with negative words and "Swedish" with positive words. These subjects later reported a more negative attitude toward the Dutch and a more positive attitude toward Swedes. Some of the results of this study are presented in Figure 7.5.

An experiment like that of Staats and Staats does not produce a large shift in attitude; no one would end up hating Swedes by participating in such a study. That the study in fact produced significant effects is interesting enough. After all, the experiment was relatively brief and involved mild emotional stimuli. If this experiment can produce mild conditioning effects, imagine what parents can accomplish. They condition their children for years rather than minutes, and they have access to the most potent emotion-eliciting stimuli available — love, physical punishment, and food, to name a few.

Are attitudes that are established through classical conditioning permanent? Can a classically conditioned response be "unlearned," or extinguished? Let's return to Pavlov's dogs. If we cease pairing the conditioned stimulus (the ringing bell) and the unconditioned stimulus (the food), then the conditioned response will fade away. If the sound of the bell no longer signals food but instead occurs at random, then the dogs will eventually stop salivating when they hear the bell. How would such a process of extinction apply to a classically conditioned prejudice? Exposing prejudiced people to the objects of their prejudice in pleasant and nonthreatening circumstances might extinguish their negative feelings and might even condition more positive emotions in their stead. Unfortunately, in real life prejudiced people tend to avoid the people they're prejudiced against, and so they rarely give themselves the opportunity to extinguish their prejudice.

How specific are classically conditioned attitudes? Put another way, when we're classically conditioned, do we show the conditioned response to just the specific conditioned stimulus used during conditioning, or are we also conditioned to similar stimuli? Suppose we condition a subject to salivate whenever we hit "middle C" on a piano. What happens when we hit "D" on the piano, or "E"? Typically, in these kinds of experiments subjects show some degree of *generalization*; that is, they are conditioned most to the conditioned stimulus used in training trials ("middle C"), but they also are somewhat conditioned to similar stimuli ("D" and "E"). The less similar the new stimulus is to the original conditioned stimulus, the smaller the conditioned response subjects will show.

Human beings show a subtle form of generalization referred to as *semantic generalization* (Bem, 1970). That is, people not only show a conditioned response to

FIGURE 7.5   Conditioning of attitudes to nationality names.

Can attitudes be classically conditioned in the laboratory?

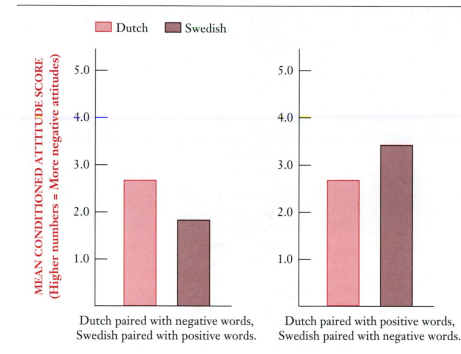

This study used mild emotional stimuli (words such as ugly and happy) to condition attitudes toward nationality names during a relatively short laboratory session. In everyday life powerful emotional stimuli may be paired with conditioned stimuli (the names of nationality and ethnic groups) repeatedly over years, thus leading to much stronger conditioning effects. Staats and Staats argued that classical conditioning took place in their experiment without conscious awareness.

the conditioned stimulus used in training, but also to *semantically related* words and concepts. For example, after being conditioned to salivate in response to the sound of a bell, a person might also salivate to the word *bell*. Or conversely, a person conditioned to salivate to the word *bell* might also salivate in response to the sound of bells.

The occurrence of semantic generalization points to the importance of *language* in the conditioning of human attitudes. For example, one puzzle in research on prejudice has been that people can hold strong prejudices against groups with which they've had no contact. In a famous study of stereotypes, Katz and Braly (1933) found that Princeton students frequently regarded Turks as "treacherous," "dirty," and "ignorant," even though most of them had never met a Turk.

Operant conditioning is generally associated with Harvard psychologist B. F. Skinner. As the text notes, human attitudes, as well as pigeons' responses, can be molded through operant conditioning.

The mechanism of semantic generalization is one way people may acquire prejudice without any contact with the objects of prejudice. If the Princeton students studied by Katz and Braly had heard stories or read newspaper articles that associated the word *Turk* with unpleasant emotions, then conditioned negative emotions to the word *Turk* could easily be generalized to the people referred to by the word. People need only be conditioned to *words*, and then the process of generalization takes over. This is one reason why such bigoted labels as "kike," "nigger," and "wop" help to create and sustain prejudice: They indirectly associate groups of people with negative emotions.

Zanna, Kiesler, and Pilkonis (1970) demonstrated the effects of semantic generalization in a study that conditioned subjects to have negative reactions to the words *light* or *dark* by delivering electric shocks to them whenever these words were presented. Interestingly, subjects showed a conditioned emotional arousal to the words, even in a totally different experimental setting. Furthermore, subjects also showed conditioned emotional arousal to the words *white* and *black*, which are semantically related to *light* and *dark*.

Operant conditioning.   Operant conditioning occurs when rewards and punishments influence *voluntary* behaviors. This kind of learning is closely identified with Harvard psychologist B. F. Skinner, who conducted important research on the effects of *positive reinforcements* (rewards) on behavior (see, for example, Skinner, 1953). A basic principle of operant conditioning is that when a voluntary response is followed by a reinforcer, the probability of future occurrences of that response is increased. From this perspective, attitudes can be viewed as voluntary responses that shift depending on histories of reinforcement. Certainly any verbal statements that express attitudes can be viewed as *operant responses* subject to conditioning (see Figure 7.6).

■■■

Figure 7.6   Operant conditioning of attitudes.

Does operant conditioning explain how we acquire some of our attitudes?

In operant conditioning, a voluntary response that is followed by favorable consequences (reinforcement) tends to be emitted more often.

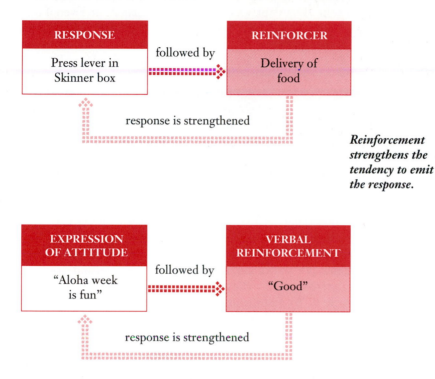

Reinforcement strengthens the tendency to emit the response.

If our expressions of attitudes are reinforced by others, our tendency to express those attitudes may be strengthened.

The operant conditioning approach to attitude formation fits in nicely with Katz's description of the instrumental *function of attitudes — that is, attitudes may help bring us rewards and avoid punishments.*

■■■

Insko (1965) showed that statements of attitude can be operantly conditioned in a study surveying the attitudes of University of Hawaii students toward "Aloha Week," the campus homecoming week. In a telephone survey, students were subtly conditioned with verbal reinforcers; whenever students in one experimental condition said anything favorable about "Aloha Week," the experimenter responded with, "Good." Other subjects were verbally reinforced whenever they made *unfavorable* comments about "Aloha Week." About a week later, the subjects completed another, apparently unrelated, questionnaire assessing their attitudes toward "Aloha Week."

Subjects who had earlier been reinforced for positive statements expressed more positive attitudes toward "Aloha Week" than did students reinforced for negative comments.

Conditioning studies like Insko's have drawn some criticism. One major question is whether conditioning procedures affect deeply held attitudes or merely affect the words we use. Critics have also suggested that many conditioning studies suffer from *demand characteristics* — that subjects often "see through" the purpose of the studies (Page, 1969, 1971, 1974). Despite these criticisms, it seems likely that both operant and classical conditioning play a role in attitude formation. Even if reinforcers do simply mold "surface" behavior, such behaviors may themselves lead us to form certain attitudes. For example, if you constantly observe yourself *saying* bad things about certain groups, you may decide you really don't like them (Bem, 1972).

Modeling and observational learning.   Learning theories propose a third route to acquiring attitudes — through modeling and observational learning. Bandura (1977) has noted that certain forms of learning can take place without classical conditioning or direct reinforcement. For example, children may learn to be aggressive merely by observing their friends fight or by watching violent television shows. In addition to learning aggression, children who watch media violence may develop more tolerant attitudes toward aggression (see Chapter 12 for a thorough discussion of the mass media and aggression). Similarly, children may learn to help others and develop prosocial attitudes by observing positive, helpful models (see Chapter 13).

In our society in which the mass media are so prominent, observational learning may be particularly important in establishing attitudes. In recent years many researchers have noted that TV shows and print media portray men and women quite differently and often stereotypically (Basow, 1986; Bergman, 1974; Sternglanz & Serbin, 1974; Dominick, 1979), and so our attitudes toward men and women may be significantly influenced by observational learning (in Chapter 10 we'll discuss in more detail the social learning of gender-related behaviors and attitudes).

Implications of learning theories.   What do learning theories imply about the formation of attitudes? First, attitudes need not be logical or rational. According to classical conditioning theory, an attitude can at times be something like a phobic response, blindly conditioned into us even when we rationally might wish otherwise. We can sometimes feel prejudice even when we know it is not right or ethical.

Second, our conditioned attitudes need not necessarily be consistent with one another. As we shall see later, personality theories and inference theories of attitude formation assume that people show consistency among their attitudes. But learning theories imply that attitudes may be acquired helter-skelter, depending on our history of conditioning and reinforcement, and on the models we are exposed to.

On a more positive note, learning theories of attitude formation are fairly optimistic about the possibility for creating "good" attitudes in people and removing "bad" attitudes. After all, whatever is learned can be altered through extinction, substitute conditioning, reinforcement, and positive models.

Personality and Attitude Formation

If we do not lift the youth out of the morass of their present-day environment, they will drown in it. . . . This cleansing of our culture must be extended to nearly all fields. Theater, art, literature, cinema, press, posters, and window displays must be cleansed of all manifestations of our rotting world and placed in the service of a moral, political, and cultural idea. Public life must be freed from the stifling perfume of our modern eroticism, just as it must be freed from all unmanly, prudish hypocrisy. . . . The right of personal freedom recedes before the duty to preserve the race.

—— *Mein Kampf*, p. 255

Because it provides a window into a dark and disturbed mind, *Mein Kampf* is a rich source of psychological hypotheses. It is intriguing to note that interspersed among Hitler's vicious pronouncements about race and politics are frequent outbursts concerning sex and gender. He decried "modern eroticism" and worried excessively about prostitution and syphilis. One of his "solutions" to these problems was early marriage, "particularly for the man, as the woman in any case is only the passive part" (p. 251). Among his arsenal of insults, Hitler frequently used "feminine" and "womanish."

These examples suggest that individuals like Hitler may at times form attitudes to serve conscious or unconscious needs in their personalities. Prominent research on the authoritarian personality showed that highly prejudiced people sometimes use their bigoted attitudes to express repressed anger and to guard against feelings of inadequacy and insecurity (Adorno, Frenkl-Brunswick, Levinson, & Sanford, 1950; see Chapter 9 for a more detailed discussion). Furthermore, such people often strongly conform to conventional morality and sex roles. Research on the authoritarian personality helps explain why some people are consistently prejudiced against many different minorities; it is because their prejudice results from their personality dynamics. (Adolf Hitler certainly provides a good example.)

Recent research on the functions of attitudes toward homosexuals provides additional evidence that personality may play a role in attitude formation. Herek (1987) found that subjects who showed negative ego-defensive attitudes toward homosexuals were more likely to have generally defensive personalities and show high conformity to conventional sex roles. By implication, some negative attitudes toward homosexuals may stem from defensiveness, anxiety, and concern about gender.

Religious attitudes may also serve needs in individuals' personalities. Batson and Ventis (1982) reported that people who profess strong devotion to orthodox religious beliefs report relative freedom from worry and guilt. Although they do not prove a cause-effect relationship, these findings suggest that some people may adopt strong religious beliefs to reduce their anxieties.

Although the personality approach has not been dominant in the study of attitude formation, it has nonetheless contributed to our understanding of how certain kinds of attitudes are formed.

Logical Inference Theories

I know people who "read" enormously . . . yet whom I would not describe as "well-read." True, they possess a mass of "knowledge," but their brain is unable to organize and register the material they have taken in. They lack the art of sifting what is valuable for them . . . from that which is without value, of retaining the one forever, and, if possible, not even seeing the rest. . . . For reading is no end in itself, but a means to an end. . . . It is essential that the content of what one reads . . . should not be transmitted to the memory in the

> sequence of the . . . books, but like the stone of a mosaic should fit into the general world picture in its proper place, and thus help to form the general world picture in the mind of the reader.
>
> —— *Mein Kampf*, p. 35

Once attitudes exist for whatever reason, they become the raw material from which people can build new attitudes. In other words, people can infer new attitudes from logically related beliefs and attitudes. This notion is implicit in Katz's suggestion that some attitudes serve a value-expressive and knowledge function.

Attitude and belief systems.   If you contemplate your own beliefs and attitudes, you'll probably conclude that they do not exist in isolation but rather in organized patterns. For example, the highly religious individual holds a systematically organized set of beliefs and attitudes concerning religion, God, sin, morality, and even social issues like abortion, prayer in school, women's rights, and pornography. Much social psychological theory and research has focused on the *organization* of beliefs and attitudes.

As we have seen, social psychologists generally use the term *attitude* to refer to an evaluation or emotional response to some object. A *belief*, on the other hand, refers to cognitive information that need not have an emotional component (see Jones & Gerard, 1967; Rokeach, 1968; Bem, 1970). For example, although you may hold positive attitudes toward the United States, capitalism, and scientific progress, you probably *believe* that the United States is in the northern hemisphere, that capitalism replaced feudalism, and that modern science began in the 1600s. Beliefs and attitudes can often be traced to other beliefs and attitudes (Bem, 1970). For example, perhaps you have a negative attitude toward cigarette smoking. When asked why, you might respond that smoking causes lung cancer and heart disease (a belief), that lung cancer and heart disease are terrible afflictions (attitudes), and finally that because of your religious upbringing you regard cigarette smoking as sinful (a combination of attitudes and beliefs).

Beliefs that are not based on other beliefs are sometimes referred to as *primitive* beliefs. They can be based on direct sensory experience ("I believe that plants are generally green"), or authority figures (your mother tells you that "eating between meals causes people to gain weight"), or simple learning processes (going to the dentist is upsetting because it's classically conditioned to pain). Once we possess primitive beliefs, we can then build "higher-level" beliefs and attitudes through logical inference processes.

In one well-known research study, McGuire (1960) found that changing subjects' *premise beliefs* through persuasive communication ultimately influenced their *conclusion beliefs* as well. In McGuire's study, high school students completed a questionnaire in which they rated how true they believed 48 statements to be. Some of these statements were premises that logically led to other statements. For example, if you believe that "drunk driving causes many deaths of innocent people," "tougher laws have been proven to reduce drunk driving," and "the legislature passes laws that reduce innocent deaths," then logically you should also believe that "The legislature will pass new, tough laws to reduce drunk driving."

Suppose you read an article persuasively arguing that tougher laws *do not* reduce drunk driving or traffic fatalities. The article is so convincing that you change your mind about the truth of the statements that "tougher laws have been proven to reduce drunk driving." McGuire found that over time you will also change your mind about the truth of "the legislature will pass new tough laws to reduce drunk driving." In other words, successfully attacking a premise belief leads ultimately to some change in conclusion beliefs as well. Interestingly, McGuire found that it takes some time for the effects of persuasive messages to "filter through" a subject's belief system. Conclusion beliefs did not shift immediately after subjects heard the persuasive messages but changed significantly after a week had passed.

McGuire's research sought to alter conclusion beliefs by attacking premise beliefs. Rosenburg (1960) tried the reverse — to alter premise beliefs by changing conclusion attitudes. He used a rather unusual technique to change subjects' attitudes — hypnosis. He hypnotized white subjects "to be very much in favor of Negroes moving into white neighborhoods." The intriguing consequence was that subjects shifted those premise beliefs (for example, "Negroes moving into white neighborhoods *will not* lower property values") that were logically related to their hypnotically altered attitude. Rosenburg's results again suggest a kind of logical consistency among beliefs and attitudes. When one attitude changes, logically related beliefs and attitudes may also have to "give" in order to accommodate the initial attitude change.

Sometimes merely having subjects consider and rate their beliefs leads them to shift "spontaneously" so that they become more logically consistent (McGuire, 1960; Henninger & Wyer, 1976). People don't always hold logically consistent beliefs and attitudes. Rather, people are more likely to show logical consistency when their beliefs and attitudes are salient and when they are forced to think about them. Apparently, when forced to notice inconsistencies in their beliefs and attitudes, people will perform some mental work to make them more consistent.

Mathematical models of consistency.   Some researchers have constructed mathematical models of the ways people combine the probabilities of premise beliefs to arrive at conclusion beliefs (McGuire, 1981; Wyer & Hartwick, 1984; Wyer & Carlston, 1979). Suppose you believe that there's a 50 percent probability that some small nation will build its first atom bomb before the end of the century and a 30 percent probability that a nation that has "the bomb" will use it. How likely is it, in your mind, that "some nation will use an atom bomb before the end of the century?"

Research suggests that subjects combine such premise beliefs in ways that can be modeled mathematically (Wyer & Hartwick, 1984). People often reach correct conclusions if they begin with valid premise beliefs. But alas, often they do not. Hitler's outrageous premises would lead to outrageous conclusions even if the intermediate reasoning were correct. Furthermore, the fact that people can reach correct conclusions during an experiment does not mean they always spontaneously infer beliefs in real life. People seem willing to let many of their beliefs "just sit there" without pursuing their logical implications (Bem, 1970).

Social psychologists have also focused considerable attention on mathematical models of how beliefs and attitudes are combined to form other attitudes. A number of theorists have suggested a relatively simple *additive model* of attitude formation (for example, Feather, 1982; Fishbein, 1963; Osgood & Tannenbaum, 1955; Rosenburg, 1956). As an example, Fishbein (1963, Fishbein & Ajzen, 1975) proposed a *value-expectancy model* of attitude formation, which essentially proposes that higher level attitudes are formed from our salient beliefs about an object and from our evaluations of those beliefs.

Suppose you read a detailed magazine article about Horatio Hornblower, who is currently running for the United States Senate in your state. Based on the article,

Inferring Attitudes from Behavior: Self-Perception Theory

In perhaps the most radical inferential theory of attitude formation, Daryl Bem (1965, 1972) argued that people may examine their behavior to infer their attitudes. This proposition may seem counterintuitive at first. Don't people automatically know what their attitudes are? Most of us assume we have "privileged information" about our inner feelings, attitudes, and emotions. We may at times find it difficult to figure out *other* people's feelings, but surely we know our own.

Bem's self-perception theory proposes that just as we must figure out others' attitudes by observing their behavior, so we must sometimes figure out our own attitudes by observing our own behavior (see accompanying figure). How do you know that you're "in love," for example? Maybe you

notice that your heart rate increases whenever your beloved is present and that you break into a cold sweat. Furthermore, you observe that you frequently go on silly errands so you can visit your beloved. And finally, you observe that all you want to talk about with your friends is . . . guess who? When you finally decide you're "in love," it's almost as if you had catalogued your behavior and logically deduced the conclusion.

Self-perception processes may also apply to a more mundane inner state such as hunger (Bem, 1965). Have you ever gone out to eat with a friend and said, "I'm not really hungry. I'll just get something light while you eat." You eat your snack, and then, after your friend leaves most of his dinner, you eat that too, topping it all off with a big dessert. You then con-

clude "Gee, I must have been hungrier than I thought." Notice how well this statement fits in with self-perception theory. In essence, you are saying that you didn't really know how hungry you were until you *observed* yourself eating.

Stated a bit more formally, Bem's self-perception theory argues that to the extent our attitudes are weak or ambiguous, we function as an outside observer, watching our behavior and the situation in which it occurs and then *inferring* our attitudes. We typically infer our attitudes more from behavior that is freely chosen than from behavior that is coerced; if you freely choose to eat spinach, for example, you'll likely conclude that you like spinach, but if your mother forces you to eat spinach, you won't conclude that you have a positive attitude about spinach. Furthermore, we

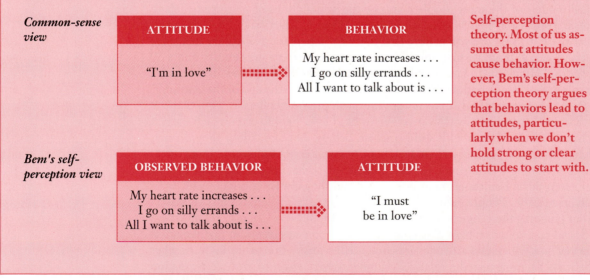

Common-sense view

ATTITUDE
"I'm in love"

BEHAVIOR
My heart rate increases . . . I go on silly errands . . . All I want to talk about is . . .

Bem's self-perception view

OBSERVED BEHAVIOR
My heart rate increases . . . I go on silly errands . . . All I want to talk about is . . .

ATTITUDE
"I must be in love"

Self-perception theory. Most of us assume that attitudes cause behavior. However, Bem's self-perception theory argues that behaviors lead to attitudes, particularly when we don't hold strong or clear attitudes to start with.

you decide that Hornblower is against the Equal Rights Amendment for women (you're 100-percent sure of this), in favor of increased defense spending (you're 100-percent sure of this, too), against leasing National Park land to mineral companies (you're only 50-percent sure of this — the article was a little vague here), and in favor typically infer our attitudes more from statements we make in "truthful" settings (under oath in court) than from statements we make in "untruthful" settings (telling Uncle George how much we like another of his ugly ties). (This discussion is reminiscent of the "discounting principle" in attribution we discussed in Chapter 4: To the extent that obvious external causes for behavior are present, people discount internal causes like attitudes.)

When are self-perception processes most likely to occur? Just as Bem initially theorized, research shows that people infer their attitudes from their behavior particularly when they haven't already given much thought to the topic — that is, when such attitudes are weak or even nonexistent (Fazio, 1987). Chaiken and Baldwin (1981)

demonstrated this in an experiment that manipulated subjects' environmental attitudes by inducing them to endorse either relatively pro-ecology or relatively anti-ecology behavioral statements (such as "I litter," "I carpool," or "I pick up garbage") on a questionnaire. They did this through a clever linguistic device: they inserted either the word "frequently" or "occasionally" into the statements. When the pro-ecology statements contained "occasionally" ("I occasionally pick up garbage"), subjects were more likely to endorse them, but when they contained "frequently" ("I frequently carpool"), subjects were less likely to endorse them.

Intriguingly, subjects induced to endorse many pro-ecology statements later rated their attitude as more pro-environmental, whereas

subjects induced to endorse many anti-ecology statements later rated their attitude as more anti-environmental. This self-perception effect was particularly strong for subjects whose initial environmental attitudes were weak and inconsistent. Most of us think that we say what we believe, but this study suggests that instead we sometimes believe what we say.

Once an individual infers his or her attitude, the attitude then exists in memory and may be accessed without new inferences (Fazio, 1987). Ironically, this implies that when a person doesn't possess an attitude on a certain topic, the act of responding to an attitude scale or opinion poll may create one through self-perception processes (Fazio, Chen, McDonel, & Sherman, 1982).

of prohibiting the legal sale of alcohol (you're 75-percent sure of this). These conclusions constitute your *beliefs* about Horatio Hornblower. As Fishbein (1963) does in his value-expectancy model, we've chosen here to conceptualize beliefs as *subjective probabilities* — that is, as judgments about how sure you are about certain propositions. The final thing we need to know is how you *feel* about each belief you hold about Hornblower; that is, how do you feel about people who oppose the Equal Rights Amendment, and so on?

According to Fishbein's value-expectancy model, your overall attitude is simply the sum of all the products of each of your salient beliefs multiplied by your evaluations of those beliefs. This is expressed concisely by the equation:

$$A = b_1 \times e_1 + b_2 \times e_2 + \ldots + b_n \times e_n$$

where A is your overall attitude, b represents your beliefs about any given issue, e represents your evaluation of those beliefs, and n represents the total number of beliefs under consideration. For your first belief — concerning Hornblower's opposition to the ERA — b_1 (your 100-percent belief that he opposes it) would be multiplied by e_1 (your evaluation of that belief; say, 3 on a scale that ranges from "1 equals hate" to "10 equals love"). The products of each belief and its evaluation are then added to obtain your overall attitude. Beyond all the mathematical particulars, Fishbein is simply arguing that your overall attitude toward Hornblower is

SUMMARY TABLE 7.1   Processes of Attitude Formation

In what ways are attitudes formed?

PROCESS	DESCRIPTION	EXAMPLE
Learning processes Classical conditioning	Emotional reactions to object learned when object is paired with a stimulus that elicits these reactions.	Staats & Staats (1958) study: Attitudes conditioned to nationality names by being paired with positive or negative words.
Operant conditioning	Verbal expressions of attitude strengthened by rewards.	Insko (1965) "Aloha Week" study: Students conditioned to have more or less favorable attitudes toward homecoming week through verbal reinforcement.
Observational learning	Beliefs and attitudes learned by watching others behave.	Learning attitudes toward aggressive behavior by watching aggressive models in violent TV shows.
Personality processes	Attitudes develop to defend individual against anxiety or feelings of insecurity.	Research on authoritarian personality showing that some people vent repressed feelings of anger and insecurity via prejudice against minority groups.
Logical-inference processes	Attitudes logically inferred from other beliefs and attitudes.	Fishbein's (1963) value-expectancy model: Attitudes may be based on other beliefs and evaluations of those beliefs.
Self-perception	Attitudes logically inferred from behavior and its situational context.	Chaiken & Baldwin (1981) study: People with weak environmental attitudes inferred from their attitudes from their questionnaire responses.

Note that attitudes are sometimes formed through thoughtful processes (logical-consistency theories) and sometimes through nonthoughtful processes (classical and operant conditioning). As we will see in Chapter 8, attitudes may also be changed *via both thoughtful and nonthoughtful processes.*

based on *your beliefs* about Hornblower and *your evaluations* of those beliefs. With Fishbein's model, our earlier philosophical discussion of how beliefs and attitudes might be built from premise beliefs and attitudes becomes much more precise and quantifiable; we have moved from a verbal description to a rigorous mathematical model.

Our discussion thus far indicates that attitudes may be formed via a number of processes (an additional and intriguing one is discussed in the box entitled "Inferring Attitudes from Behavior"). Summary Table 7.1 reviews three different routes to attitude formation.

Was there any form of filth or profligacy . . . without at least one Jew involved in it?

If you cut even cautiously into such an abscess, you found, like a maggot in a rotting body, often dazzled by the sudden light — a kike! (p. 57).

Only an adequately large space on this earth assures a nation of freedom of existence (p. 643).

The demand for restoration of the frontiers of 1914 is a political absurdity of such proportions and consequences as to make it seem a crime. . . . They were not the result of a considered political action, but momentary frontiers in a political struggle that was by no means concluded . . . (p. 649).

—— *Mein Kampf*

Reading *Mein Kampf* is a chilling experience, in part because the book presages with great clarity horrors to come during the 1930s and 1940s. In *Mein Kampf* Hitler presented the world with the detailed manifesto of a ruthless madman. His beliefs and attitudes would prove to guide his actions to the bitter end, with tragic consequences for the entire world.

Was Hitler a typical case? In general, do individuals' attitudes predict their behavior? Self-perception theory argues that we sometimes infer attitudes from behavior — that behaviors sometimes "cause" attitudes. Clearly, the opposite causal relation — that attitudes *cause* behavior — seems much more intuitively obvious; in fact, as you'll remember, implicit in most definitions of attitude is the assumption that attitudes mediate behavioral responses. Despite the compelling anecdotal example of Hitler's attitudes in *Mein Kampf*, research studies on the relationship between attitudes and behavior do not unequivocally show a strong relationship between the two. According to the author of one recent review of attitude research, "the low correlations between attitudes and behaviors have been the scandal of the field for half a century" (McGuire, 1985).

Difficulties in Predicting Behavior from Attitudes

A classic study by Richard LaPiere (1934) was one of the first to question how well attitudes predict behavior. LaPiere investigated the correspondence between prejudiced attitudes (as assessed by a questionnaire) and actual discrimination. To test whether words match deeds, LaPiere accompanied a Chinese couple in their travels across the United States; they sought accommodation at 251 restaurants, hotels, and other public establishments. The Chinese couple was refused service only once.

Six months later LaPiere mailed a questionnaire to each establishment. Included in it was the question "Will you accept members of the Chinese race as guests at your establishment?" Out of 128 responses, over 90 percent answered "No." Thus there seemed to be very little correspondence between attitudes, as measured by questionnaires, and actual behavior. The LaPiere study was flawed in at least one important way, however: The people who admitted the Chinese couple to various establishments might not have been the same people who filled out the mailed questionnaires. Clearly, if we want to test the relation between attitudes and behavior, we must measure attitudes and behavior *in the same person.*

You might think that once attitude scaling was developed, dozens of social psychological studies would attempt to predict behaviors from measures of attitudes. How else could attitude scales be validated? The truth is, however, that many early studies did not explicitly assess overt behavior; rather, they more commonly investigated how attitudes differed among *criterion groups* — groups presumed to differ on the attitudes under examination. For example, a scale purporting to measure attitudes toward religion (such as the Thurstone scale in Figure 7.2) might be administered to a group of devout Christians and to a group of atheists. If it showed a significant difference between the two groups, the scale was considered valid.

By the late 1960s, according to a major review by Wicker (1969), fewer than 50 attitude studies had attempted to measure related overt behaviors in the same subjects. In one of those studies, Mann (1959) measured subjects' attitudes toward blacks and then rated the verbally expressed prejudice these subjects showed toward blacks in a group discussion. Surprisingly, he found the correlations between assessed attitudes and verbally expressed prejudice to be quite weak.

These results were not isolated findings. After reviewing all the relevant studies he could find, Wicker (1969) concluded that "it is considerably more likely that attitudes will be unrelated or only slightly related to overt behaviors than that attitudes will be closely related to actions." These measured, academic-sounding words may not seem shocking, but in their way they were a challenge to social psychologists who conducted attitude research. Wicker was saying that based on attitude researchers' own evidence, attitudes make very little difference in people's behavior. The general disillusionment that followed led one well-known attitude theorist to write a paper entitled, "Are Attitudes Necessary?" (Abelson, 1972).

Why was it so difficult to predict concrete behavior from measured attitudes? In the 1970s a number of theorists addressed this question (see Calder & Ross, 1973; Schuman & Johnson, 1976; Fishbein & Ajzen, 1974, 1975). Their discussions produced three possible explanations: variables other than attitudes exert a strong influence on behavior, researchers were not measuring attitudes properly, or researchers were not measuring behavior properly. Let's consider each of these issues in turn.

The effects of other influential variables.   Why should we be disappointed that attitudes don't predict behavior very well? Maybe we are expecting attitudes to explain too much. After all, attitudes are just one of many variables that influence behavior (see Figure 7.7).

Let's return to Mann's study in which measures of prejudice against blacks only weakly predicted subjects' verbal statements of prejudice in a discussion group. Personality variables as well as attitudes may have influenced behavior in that study. For example, if extroverts talk a lot in groups whereas introverts do not, some very prejudiced introverts may not have made prejudiced comments simply because they were too reserved to talk much. Situational pressures may also have weakened the relation between attitudes and behavior (Schuman & Johnson, 1976). For example, perhaps some subjects in Mann's study truly were prejudiced, but because they didn't want to "look bad" in front of other group members, they kept quiet.

Researchers who focus on "other variables" are not saying that attitudes are irrelevant to behavior, but rather that other variables can overwhelm or counteract the effects of attitudes. *Moderator variables* are particularly subtle in that they can influence when attitudes do and do not predict behavior. (This is known as an *interaction effect* between two variables; see Chapter 6.) A number of studies suggest, for example, that when people consciously focus attention on their attitudes, then these attitudes predict their behavior reasonably well, but when their attention is directed externally, attitudes don't predict behavior very well (Carver & Scheier, 1981; see Chapter 6 for a more detailed account of self-focused attention).

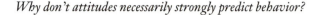

FIGURE 7.7   Beliefs, attitudes, and other explanations of social behavior.

Why don't attitudes necessarily strongly predict behavior?

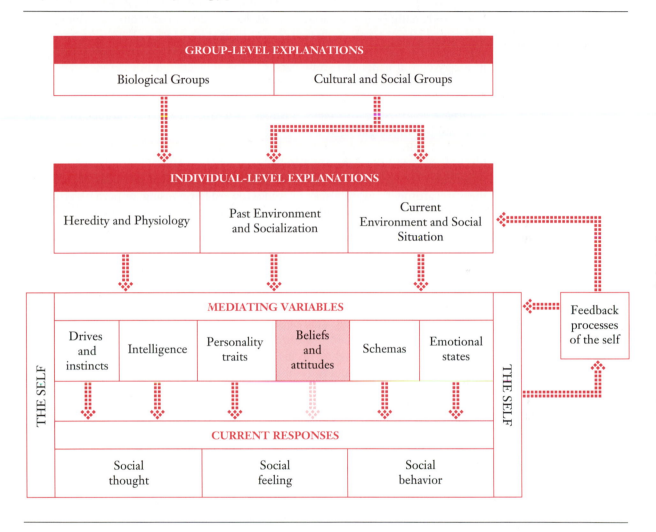

As this diagram illustrates, attitudes are only one of many variables that influence behavior. As discussed in Chapter 1, one explanatory variable (such as attitude) cannot completely explain and predict most complex social behaviors.

Recent research also suggests that some people are more likely than others to behave in a manner that is consistent with their attitudes. For example, Snyder's self-monitoring scale asks people whether they act according to their inner feelings and attitudes or according to situational demands (Snyder, 1979, 1982; see Chapter 6). People who score low on this scale (those who say they act in accordance with internal feelings) sometimes seem to show greater correspondence between their attitudes and their behavior, whereas people who score high on the scale show less correspondence. Thus self-monitoring may *moderate* the relation between attitudes and behavior.

Studies also suggest that attitudes formed through direct experience are more predictive of behavior than are attitudes that are not so formed (Fazio & Zanna, 1981). And finally, recent research suggests that attitudes predict our behavior toward *prototypical* targets particularly well (Lord, Lepper, & Mackie, 1984). For example, subjects in the LaPiere study may well have refused to serve Chinese people dressed in baggy cotton pants and straw hats, but the subjects did not demonstrate their prejudice because the well-dressed Chinese students didn't match their stereotypes.

Improper measures of attitudes.   Fishbein and Ajzen (1975) have argued that many early studies investigating the relation between attitudes and behavior measured attitudes incorrectly. Suppose you want to predict housing discrimination against blacks from measured attitudes. Your subjects will be a random sample of 100 home sellers in your city selected from real estate listings. What attitudes should you measure: attitudes toward blacks, attitudes toward fair housing, or perhaps attitudes toward blacks moving into the neighborhood? Clearly, your choice of attitude can either help or hinder your prediction of behavior.

Improper measures of behavior.   As we saw earlier, social psychologists have devoted enormous attention to developing rigorous multi-item measures of attitudes, but they have often been less careful in developing measures of behavior. We noted earlier that attitude scales possess many items in order to achieve reliability. If single scale items are intrinsically unreliable measures of an attitude, then aren't single behaviors similarly unreliable measures of behavior?

In their influential analysis of the relation between attitudes and behavior, Fishbein and Ajzen (1975; Ajzen & Fishbein, 1980) argue that some behaviors, by definition, are not single acts, but rather *classes of behavior*. "Prejudiced behavior," for example, is not a single act, but rather many acts, including "not selling your house to minorities," "donating money to racist groups," "voting for candidates that foster discrimination," "not hiring minorities," "sending your children to segregated schools," and so on. Perhaps many studies failed to find strong relations between attitudes and behavior because they did not measure behavior properly. The LaPiere study, for example, hoped to assess behavioral prejudice via a single observation of behavior—whether or not the establishment admitted the Chinese couple.

Summing measures of behavior can influence the correlation between attitudes and behavior. To demonstrate this, a study by Fishbein and Ajzen (1974) examined how well religious attitudes predict religious behaviors. This study made use of existing religious attitude scales. In addition to asking subjects to complete attitude scales, Fishbein and Ajzen also asked them to indicate how frequently they engaged in 70 different kinds of "religious behavior." For example, subjects were asked whether they "pray before or after meals," "donate money to religious institutions," "take classes or courses in religion," "attend religious services," and so on.

Fishbein and Ajzen found that religious attitudes correlated quite poorly *with single acts*. In fact, the average correlation coefficient for the association between attitudes and single behaviors was .15. However, when the 70 behaviors were summed to form a composite measure of religious behaviors, the correlation between attitudes and "behavior" rose dramatically (to .71).

▪▪▪▪▪▪▪▪▪▪▪▪▪▪▪▪▪▪▪▪▪▪▪▪

Do religious attitudes predict religious behaviors? As the text notes, attitudes often predict aggregated behaviors better than they predict single behaviors.

▪▪▪▪▪▪▪▪▪▪▪▪▪▪▪▪▪▪▪▪▪▪▪▪

Fishbein and Ajzen's Theory of Reasoned Action

In the 1970s Martin Fishbein and Icek Ajzen developed a model of behavorial prediction that attempts to rectify the shortcomings of earlier research on the relation between attitudes and behavior. This model (see Figure 7.8) argues that there are two major predictors of voluntary behavior: attitudes toward the behavior and subjective norms. In Fishbein and Ajzen's model, *attitudes* refer to evaluative responses or feelings about a behavior; *subjective norms* refer to beliefs about how significant others wish us to behave.

Thus subjective norms constitute another variable that social psychologists must measure in order to adequately predict behavior. Attitudes are "internal" variables, representing our inner sense of right and wrong, good and bad. Subjective norms are our beliefs about "external" influences on our behavior that emanate from important people and groups in our lives. For example, imagine election day is approaching, and you must decide whether to vote for incumbent Senator Horatio Hornblower. If you think that Hornblower is a venal politician, but your mother, best friend, and church urge you to vote for him, then your attitude and subjective norms are probably in conflict.

In Fishbein and Ajzen's model, attitudes and subjective norms combine to influence behavioral intentions, which ultimately determine your behavior. *Behavioral intentions* are simply subjective probabilities of how you intend to behave. Suppose that the day before the election I ask you to rate the likelihood that you will vote for Hornblower. Being somewhat uncertain, you respond "40 percent"—after all, you don't like Hornblower, but all your family members and friends are for him. It is only on election day, when you stand in the voting booth and cast your vote against Hornblower, that we finally know your behavior for certain.

Although Fishbein and Ajzen's model seems fairly straightforward, several subtleties are worth noting. First, Fishbein and Ajzen suggest that social psychologists

FIGURE 7.8   **A schematic diagram of Fishbein and Ajzen's theory of reasoned action.**

What is the relation between attitudes and behavior according to the theory of reasoned action?

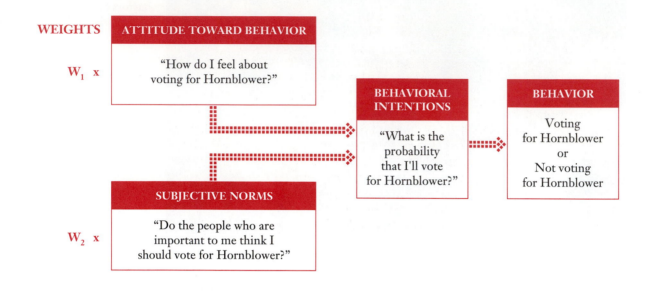

Note in this example that Fishbein and Ajzen's theory is used to predict a single behavior (voting or not voting for Hornblower). As the text notes, however, in many research applications (for example, predicting discriminatory behaviors) it would be more appropriate to obtain summed rather than single measures of behavior.

should generally measure attitudes toward *behavior* rather than attitudes toward *objects*. This may seem like a minor distinction, but actually it can make an important difference in attitude measurement. Your attitude toward *voting for* Senator Horatio Hornblower may not be the same as your attitude toward Hornblower. Maybe your attitude toward Hornblower is mildly negative, but your attitude toward voting for Hornblower is positive because his opponent, Calvin Crackpot, is so completely objectionable to you. Thus Fishbein and Ajzen suggest a subtle, but potentially important, improvement in attitude measurement: Measure *attitude toward behavior* rather than *attitude toward objects* if your goal is to predict behavior.

Another important piece of advice they offer is to make sure that attitudes and behaviors *correspond* in their level of generality (or specificity). In essence, Fishbein and Ajzen argue that attitude measures must be "fine-tuned" to match the behaviors they are to predict. Thus if your goal is to predict housing discrimination against Hispanics, you should probably measure attitudes toward selling or leasing homes to Hispanics rather than, say, attitudes toward Hispanics or attitudes toward minorities.

If you are interested in predicting broad general behaviors (say, prejudice against minorities), then a general prejudice scale may be appropriate. But in that case you will have to use a summed measure of behavior because prejudice does not lead to just a single behavior, but rather to many behaviors. Again, attitudes and behaviors must be measured at the same level of generality.

The weighting of attitudes and subjective norms.   Fishbein and Ajzen argue that attitudes and subjective norms combine to influence our behavioral intentions and ultimately our behavior. The relative importance of these two variables depends on the particular attitude, setting, and subject population. In one study, Fishbein (1966; see Fishbein & Ajzen, 1975) attempted to predict whether or not college students intended to engage in premarital sexual intercourse during a particular semester. He found that by using both attitudes and subjective norms as predictor variables (using a statistical technique called multiple regression), he could predict subjects' behavioral intentions quite well (the correlation between a combination of the two predictors and behavioral intentions was .85). Furthermore, Fishbein found that for male students, subjective norms were more important in predicting intentions, whereas for female students attitudes were more important (see Figure 7.9). In commonsense terms, female students engaged in premarital sex more as a function of their inner sense of right and wrong, whereas males were more influenced by perceived social pressures.

Volition as a variable.   Fishbein and Ajzen named their model a "theory of reasoned action" because it holds that attitudes predict behavior primarily when behavior is conscious and voluntary, and thus "reasoned." Voting is a good example of behavior that can be successfully predicted from attitudes because voting is a voluntary behavior (at least in this country) and because most of us consciously think about our political beliefs and choices.

The model is less successful in predicting behavior that is *not* completely voluntary. For example, Ajzen and Madden (1986) attempted to predict whether a group of upper-division college students would receive "A's" in their classes based on their attitudes toward getting "A's" and their subjective norms. Note that receiving "A's" may not be totally under some students' volitional control; no matter how much students value getting "A's" (attitude) and no matter how much students believe their parents and friends want them to get "A's" (subjective norms), if students lack ability, they may not get "A's." Indeed, Ajzen and Madden found that a weighted combination of attitudes and subjective norms correlated only moderately well with students' grades (correlation coefficient = .39).

To increase the ability to predict behavior that is not entirely under volitional control, Ajzen (1987) recommends adding a third variable—perceived behavioral control—to the theory of reasoned action. That is, social psychologists should measure subjects' attitudes, subjective norms, and their perceived ability to carry out the behavior of interest.

Time as a variable.   Finally, Fishbein and Ajzen (1975) point out that time is a variable of great practical importance in studies that attempt to predict behavior from attitudes. The longer the time interval between measurements of attitude and behavior, the greater the chance that some event will intervene and change attitudes.

FIGURE 7.9   Predicting students' intentions to engage in premarital sexual
intercourse from their attitudes and subjective norms.

Do attitudes and subjective norms predict behavioral intentions?

By combining and weighting information about subjects' attitudes and subjective norms, Fishbein and
Azjen (1975) were able to predict behavioral intentions regarding premarital sex with a high degree of
accuracy. Note, though, that male and female subjects differed significantly in the weighting of these factors.

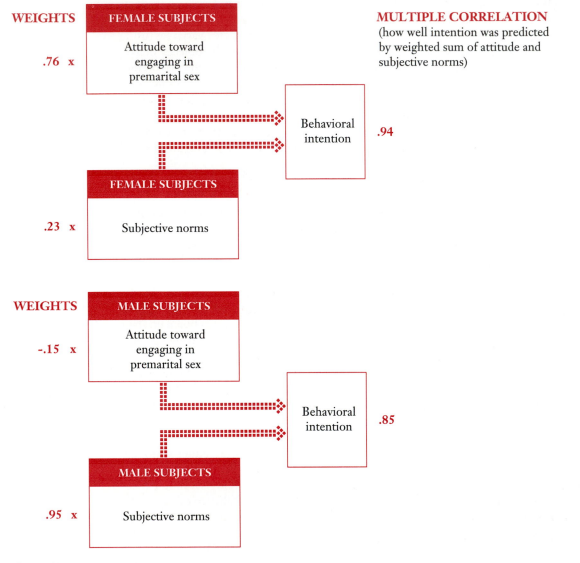

SOURCE: From Fishbein and Ajzen (1975).

Consider this example: In 1972 George McGovern ran as the Democratic presidential candidate against Republican Richard Nixon. A pivotal event in this campaign was the revelation that McGovern's running mate, Senator Thomas Eagleton of Missouri, had suffered from severe depression years earlier and had undergone electric-shock therapy. Suppose your attitude toward voting for McGovern-Eagleton, measured a day before the devastating revelation, was used to predict your vote on Election Day. The prediction might be quite poor (even completely incorrect), not because attitudes don't predict behavior, but because attitudes sometimes change—particularly if a dramatic event intervenes between measurements of attitude and behavior.

Applying Fishbein and Ajzen's model.   Fishbein and Ajzen's model continues to stimulate research studies, but it does not appear to be the final word in predicting behavior from attitudes (for example, Ajzen, 1987; Bentler & Speckart, 1979; Fredericks & Dossett, 1983). One of its major achievements has been to force social psychologists to analyze more carefully what they mean by "attitudes," "behavior," and "other variables." The model proves that when attitudes and behaviors are measured carefully, behavior can be predicted fairly well.

Fishbein and Ajzen's model has been used to predict behavior in a number of applied domains. For example, the theory of reasoned action has served to predict women's choices to work or be homemakers (Sperber, Fishbein, & Ajzen, 1980), to understand and predict family planning decisions (Fishbein, Ajzen, & McArdle, 1980), to analyze consumer attitudes and behavior (Fishbein & Ajzen, 1980), and to predict alcohol abuse and to assess alcohol treatment programs (Fishbein, Ajzen, & McArdle, 1980). One recent study found that high school students' attitudes and subjective norms toward going to college, as assessed from survey data collected in 1955, predicted their level of educational attainment 15 years later moderately well (Harrison, Thompson, & Rodgers, 1985).

Finally, the theory of reasoned action can be used as a framework to analyze the particular beliefs and attitudes that lead to undesirable behaviors (for example, smoking, wasting energy, engaging in dangerous sexual practices); then public education campaigns can be directed at the identified causal beliefs or attitudes (Ajzen & Fishbein, 1980). For example, if research suggests that teenagers generally hold negative attitudes toward smoking ("smoking is dangerous") but strong subjective norms that favor smoking ("all my friends think I should"), then advertising campaigns should be directed at changing teenagers' subjective norms, not their attitudes.

A state which in this age of racial poisoning dedicates itself to the care of its best racial elements must some day become lord of the earth.
—— *Mein Kampf*, p. 688

Beliefs and Attitudes: A Final Comment

We began this chapter with a broad question: Can beliefs and attitudes influence individuals' behavior and even affect world events? The answer is yes. *Mein Kampf* provides a painful reminder of the power of beliefs and attitudes to guide an individual's behavior. Fortunately, the conflagration sparked by Adolf Hitler in 1939 was extinguished by millions of others possessing different, more humane beliefs and attitudes.

During the twentieth century social psychology has made considerable progress in the scientific study of beliefs and attitudes. Sophisticated techniques now exist to measure attitudes, and we understand many of the ways in which attitudes develop and influence behavior. It is up to us to use this scientific knowledge to make beliefs and attitudes more constructive factors in human life.

Summary

1. An attitude is a learned evaluative response, directed at specific objects, which is relatively enduring and influences behavior in a generally motivating way.

2. Attitudes may serve instrumental, ego-defensive, knowledge, and value-expressive functions.

3. Thurstone scales, Likert scales, and semantic differential ratings are three techniques for measuring attitudes through self-report questionnaires.

4. The "bogus pipeline" encourages subjects to respond honestly to self-report attitude scales by informing them (falsely) that their attitudes are being physiologically measured.

5. Attitudes are sometimes assessed with physiological measures such as the Galvanic Skin Response, pupil dilation, and electrical recordings from facial muscles.

6. Learning theories of attitude formation hold that attitudes are learned through the processes of classical conditioning, operant conditioning, and modeling.

7. Personality theories of attitude formation hold that attitudes may develop to serve such needs in an individual's personality as relieving feelings of inferiority or defending against anxiety.

8. Logical inference theories of attitude formation hold that attitudes may be derived from other beliefs and attitudes. Social psychologists have developed mathematical models that describe how people infer conclusion beliefs from premise beliefs and how they infer attitudes from other beliefs and attitudes.

9. Self-perception theory is a radical inferential theory of attitude formation that argues that people infer their attitudes from their behavior and its setting, particularly when attitudes are weak or ambiguous.

10. Research studies often find that attitudes do not predict behavior very well. Three reasons why attitudes may not predict behavior are that variables other than attitudes also influence behavior, attitudes have not been properly measured, and behavior has not been properly measured.

11. Single behaviors are often unreliable measures of behavior, and summed measures of behavior are usually preferable in research on attitudes and behaviors.

12. Fishbein and Ajzen's theory of reasoned action holds that a weighted combination of attitudes (evaluative responses to a target) and subjective norms (beliefs about how significant others think we should behave) predicts behavioral intentions, which ultimately predict behavior.

13. Attitudes best predict behavior when the time interval between measurements of attitude and behavior is brief and when subjects believe that they have voluntary control over the behavior under study.

Glossary

Attitude: A learned evaluative response, directed at specific objects, that is relatively enduring and influences behavior in a general motivating way

Behavioral intention: A concept in Fishbein and Ajzen's theory of reasoned action; a behavioral intention is an individual's subjective probability of behaving in a given way (for example, the probability of voting for a political candidate)

Belief: Cognitive information that need not have an emotional component; in Fishbein's value-expectancy model, a belief is a subjective probability that something is true

Bogus pipeline: A technique to induce subjects to answer self-report attitude questionnaires more honestly by leading them to believe (falsely) that their attitudes are also being measured physiologically

Classical conditioning: The kind of learning that occurs when a person learns an involuntary response (such as salivation or increased heart rate) to a new stimulus (such as a bell); attitudes may be classically conditioned emotional responses

Ego-defensive function: Attitudes serve this function when they help us avoid personality conflicts and anxiety

Generalization: Occurs in classical conditioning when people show a conditioned response not only to a specific stimulus but also to other similar stimuli

Instrumental function: Attitudes serve this function when they help bring us rewards or avoid punishments

Knowledge function: Attitudes serve this function when they help us to order and assimilate information

Likert scales: The most commonly used attitude-scaling technique, Likert scales ask subjects to rate how much they agree or disagree with a number of statements relevant to the attitude; subjects' responses over all the items are then summed

Modeling: The kind of learning that occurs when people observe another's behavior and imitate it; attitudes may be learned through modeling

Moderator variables: Variables that determine when other variables do or do not have an impact; in attitude research, moderator variables determine when attitudes do or do not predict behavior

Operant conditioning: The kind of learning that occurs when voluntary responses are rewarded; attitudes and their verbal expression may sometimes be operantly conditioned responses

Self-perception theory: Holds that particularly when attitudes are weak or ambiguous, people sometimes infer their attitudes from their behavior and the setting in which it occurs

Semantic differential scales: Scales of evaluative meaning (such as "good-bad," "worthy-unworthy") used to measure attitudes; subjects rate the attitude object on these scales and their responses are summed

Semantic generalization: Occurs in human classical conditioning when people show a conditioned response not only to a specific stimulus but also to semantically related words and stimuli

Subjective norms: A concept in Fishbein and Ajzen's theory of reasoned action; subjective norms refer to beliefs about how significant others think we should behave

Theory of reasoned action: Fishbein and Ajzen's theory that a weighted combination of attitudes and subjective norms predict behavioral intentions, which in turn predict voluntary behavior

Thurstone scales: An attitude-scaling technique in which statements are developed that express a range of positive and negative feelings toward the attitude object; subjects then check just those statements with which they agree

Value-expectancy model: A model of attitude formation that holds that an attitude is the sum of salient beliefs about the attitude object multiplied by evaluations of those beliefs; thus, for example, your attitude toward Senator Hornblower is based on beliefs ("he's against the ERA") multiplied by their evaluation ("I don't like people who are against the ERA")

Value-expressive function: Attitudes serve this function when they express deeper values

Friends, Romans, countrymen, lend me your ears;
I come to bury Caesar, not to praise him.
The evil that men do lives after them;
The good is oft interred with their bones.
So let it be with Caesar. The noble Brutus
Hath told you Caesar was ambitious.
If it were so, it was a grievous fault,
And grievously hath Caesar answered it.
Here under the leave of Brutus and the rest
(For Brutus is an honorable man;
So are they all, all honorable men),
Come I to speak in Caesar's funeral. . . .

—— from *Julius Caesar*, Act III, Sc. II
by William Shakespeare

CHAPTER 8

Persuasion and Attitude Change

*I*n one of the most famous persuasive speeches in English literature, Marc Antony deftly turns the Roman plebeians against the assassins of Julius Caesar. His task is formidable, for the crowd has just listened to Brutus — one of the assassins — and is sympathetic to this "noble" man. Through his brilliant words, his innuendo, and his appeals to emotion, Marc Antony completely reverses the crowd's sentiments and incites them to avenge Caesar's death. Was Marc Antony's speech based on sound principles of attitude change? What does scientific research tell us about the nature of persuasion?

Chapter 7 concluded by noting that attitudes can at times usefully predict behavior. Thus it makes practical sense to study attitude change, for when attitudes change, changes in behavior may follow. Marc Antony, after all, was not interested in merely changing the attitudes of the Roman public; he wanted them to attack his enemies, Caesar's assassins. Politicians want to change our attitudes so we will vote for them and support their policies. Companies spend huge amounts of money to change our attitudes so we will buy their products.

A major tradition in attitude change research developed during and after World War II. The results of this research, under the direction of Carl Hovland at Yale University (Hovland, Lumsdaine, & Sheffield, 1949; Hovland, Janis, & Kelley, 1953), suggested that attitudes are learned responses and that persuasion is successful to the extent that people attend to, comprehend, and remember the persuasive message.

A Communication Model of Persuasion: The Yale Research

FIGURE 8.1   **Four factors that influence persuasion.**

What variables in the communication process affect the persuasiveness of messages?

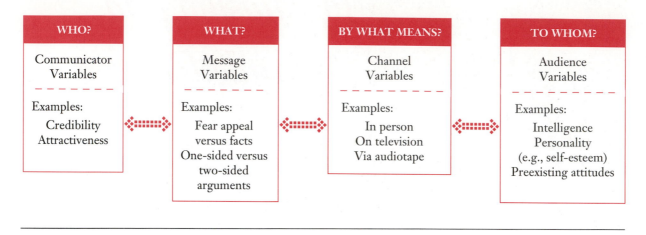

Not only can each type of variable influence persuasion, but, as we shall see, one type of variable may interact with another.

Adopting a communication model developed by Lasswell (1948; Smith, Lasswell, & Casey, 1946), the Yale researchers focused on four factors that influence persuasion: (1) communicator variables, (2) message variables, (3) channel variables, and (4) target or audience variables (see Figure 8.1). Put another way, they studied *who* says *what* by *what means* to *whom*. Let's consider research addressing each of these factors.

Communicator Variables

> . . . he sits high in all the people's hearts,
> And that which would appear offense in us,
> His countenance, like richest alchemy,
> Will change to virtue and to worthiness.
>
> —— *Julius Caesar*, Act I, Sc. III

Marc Antony faced a particularly difficult task in his speech because the crowd has just been convinced of the necessity for Caesar's assassination by Brutus, a highly credible man.

Does a speaker's credibility in fact influence persuasion? In a classic study, Hovland and Weiss (1951) studied the effects of speaker credibility on attitude change. Subjects read an article arguing for the practicality of building nuclear-powered submarines. (Keep in mind this was before such submarines actually existed.) In one experimental condition, the article was attributed to J. Robert Oppenheimer, a famous and respected physicist. In another condition, the article was attributed to

the Soviet newspaper *Pravda*. The researchers presumed, of course, that Oppenheimer was a high-credibility source and *Pravda* a low-credibility source. It probably comes as no surprise that the high-credibility source produced more attitude change as measured immediately after delivery of the persuasive message than did the low-credibility source. Taken together with similar studies on other communicator characteristics (such as trustworthiness, prestige, and attractiveness), this research shows that persuasion may sometimes result from speaker appeal rather than the logic, believability, or rationality of the message itself.

Hovland and Weiss found that the effects of speaker credibility on persuasion are greatest immediately after the message is delivered and fade quickly over time (see Figure 8.2). They also found that although a message attributed to a low-credibility speaker produced little attitude change at first, over time the originally discredited message could lead to significant attitude change. This *sleeper effect* (that is, delayed effectiveness of a persuasive message) was interpreted to result from the fact that subjects eventually dissociate the message from the speaker's low credibility.

Later studies often had difficulty replicating the sleeper effect (Pratkanis, Greenwald, Leippe, & Baumgardner, 1988). For the effect to occur, several conditions must be met (Gruder, Cook, Hennigan, Flay, Alessis, & Halamaj, 1978): (1) the initial discounting cue (such as low credibility) must be potent enough to suppress immediate persuasion, (2) the message must be convincing enough to lead to persuasion in the absence of the discounting cue, and (3) sufficient time must elapse (typically weeks) for the discounting cue to become dissociated from the message.

FIGURE 8.2   The effects of communicator credibility on persuasion.

What are the immediate and long-term effects of communicators' credibility on persuasion?

In the Hovland and Weiss study (1951), differences in communicator credibility produced the greatest difference in persuasive effect immediately after delivery of the message.

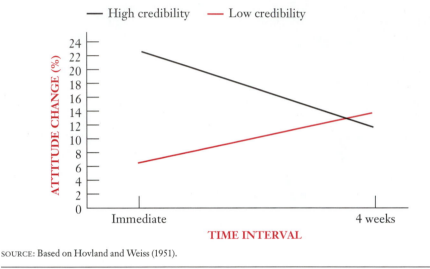

— High credibility   — Low credibility

SOURCE: Based on Hovland and Weiss (1951).

The rising line in the graph shows the sleeper effect. *As the text notes, this effect has not always been found in replications of Hovland and Weiss's study.*

After conducting 16 experiments investigating variables that influence the sleeper effect, Pratkanis, Greenwald, Leippe, and Baumgardner (1988) added two additional qualifications: The sleeper effect occurs particularly when the discounting cue *follows* the persuasive message and when the impact of the discounting cue decays faster than memory for the persuasive message.

Speaker variables (such as credibility, status, and attractiveness) are often used to good effect in advertising. When a "hidden camera" shows "real people" endorsing a product, advertisers are hoping we will view the speakers as unbiased and credible. And, of course, the people who deliver persuasive messages in commercials are often celebrities, frequently highly attractive ones. Sometimes the expertise, credibility, and attractiveness used in TV ads (as in the famous campaign in which football star Joe Namath sold panty hose) have very little to do with the product itself. Recent research supports advertisers' intuitions that speakers perceived to be attractive, credible, expert, trustworthy, and unbiased are indeed more persuasive (Bochner & Insko, 1966; Petty & Cacioppo, 1981; Craig & McCann, 1978; Andreoli & Worchel, 1978; Chaiken, 1979). However, the effects of such speaker variables on persuasion are greatest when the targeted attitudes are not very important to the recipient, and then impact tends to fade quickly (Chaiken, 1987).

You know not what you do. Do not consent
That Antony speak in his funeral.
Know you how much the people may be moved
by that which he will utter?

—— *Julius Caesar*, Act III, Sc. I (Cassius)

Some messages are more persuasive than others, regardless of their source; Marc Antony's speech (see p. 256) is highly persuasive in part because of its content. What characteristics make a message persuasive? Considerable research has focused on: (1) the effectiveness of fear appeals, (2) the use of one-sided vs. two-sided arguments, and (3) the effectiveness of message repetition.

Fear appeals.   Is fear an effective way to change people's attitudes? Will cigarette smokers change their attitudes toward smoking if shown films of lung cancer operations? Will drivers change their attitudes toward using seat belts if shown grisly pictures of traffic accidents?

One early study (Janis & Feshbach, 1953) found that subjects who attended a frightening illustrated lecture on the consequences of poor oral hygiene actually were *less likely* to follow the recommendations contained in the lecture than were subjects who heard a less frightening, factual message. These somewhat surprising findings were questioned by later investigators. Leventhal (1970) found that high-fear messages are effective under certain conditions. First, the message must arouse substantial fear (for example, you must convince a person who doesn't use seat belts that this practice is dangerous). Second, the recipient of the message must be convinced that if the recommendation in the message (to use seat belts) is not followed, fearful outcomes (injuries, death) are quite likely to occur. And finally, the recipient must be convinced that heeding the message's recommendations will indeed eliminate the fearful outcomes (wearing seat belts really does prevent injuries and save lives).

Rogers (1975, 1983) extends this argument by noting four kinds of beliefs that mediate the effects of fear appeals: (1) the subject's belief in the probability of the fearful event ("How likely am I to be in a car accident?"), (2) the subject's belief in the severity of the fearful event ("How likely am I to be severely injured?"), (3) the subject's belief in the effectiveness of the coping response ("Will wearing a seat belt really reduce my chance of injury?"), and (4) the subject's belief in his or her capability of carrying out the coping response ("Well, that's easy enough—all I have to do is buckle my seat belt"). Research suggests that such beliefs do in fact influence the effectiveness of fear appeals (Rogers & Mewborn, 1976), but also suggests that the effectiveness of fear appeals can depend on a host of other variables.

If a persuasive message frightens without providing an easy way to reduce fear, it may be ignored, rejected, or denied by the recipient. For example, Jepson and Chaiken (1986) asked subjects to complete a questionnaire designed to measure how anxious they were about cancer (for example, "How upsetting is it to you when you read or hear something about cancer?"). Subjects then read and evaluated an article advocating regular checkups for cancer. Finally, subjects were asked to list all their thoughts about the article and all the arguments they could recall from the article. Subjects who were highly anxious about cancer listed fewer thoughts, recalled fewer arguments, and ultimately were less persuaded by the article. Highly anxious people may not want to consider carefully the contents of an overly upsetting message.

One-sided versus two-sided messages.   Adolf Hitler cynically wrote in *Mein Kampf* that "all effective propaganda must be limited to a very few points and must harp on these in slogans until the last member of the public understands. . . . As soon as you sacrifice this slogan and try to be many-sided, the effect will piddle away. . . ." (p. 181).

Was he correct? If you attempt to convince an audience, say, to support the construction of nuclear power plants, should you present arguments only in favor of such power plants, or should your presentation be more "balanced"? Hovland, Lumsdaine, and Sheffield (1949) addressed this question in a study during World War II that presented American soldiers with a message arguing that the Pacific war might continue for a long time. Some soldiers heard a one-sided message that stressed only Japan's resources and strengths, whereas other soldiers heard a two-sided message that also provided, and refuted, several arguments for Japan's weakness. This research found no *overall* differences in how much soldiers in the two groups were persuaded. However, it found an intriguing interaction: Soldiers who initially agreed that the Pacific war would be long were more persuaded by one-sided arguments supporting that position, whereas soldiers who initially disagreed with the message were more persuaded by the two-sided arguments.

Later research by Lumsdaine and Janis (1953) again used one-sided and two-sided messages, this time to argue that the Soviet Union would require five years to produce large numbers of atom bombs. (At the time of the study, it was not yet public knowledge that the Soviet Union had the bomb.) One week after the original persuasive message, Hovland and Janis exposed subjects to "counterpropaganda" that argued that the Soviet Union would soon have many atom bombs. As before, two-sided messages did not result initially in more overall persuasion than did one-sided messages; however, intriguingly, two-sided messages did make subjects more resistant to the subsequent "counterpropaganda" (see Figure 8.3).

Message repetition.   Advertisers seem convinced that the more times they repeat a message, the better. (How many times have you heard that Coke is "the real thing" or that phoning a far-off friend or relative is "the next best thing to being there"?) Does repetition enhance persuasion? Two lines of evidence answer this question with a qualified "Yes."

First, many studies show that repeated exposure to a stimulus will, on average, increase our liking for that stimulus (Zajonc, 1968). This *mere exposure effect* occurs for a broad range of stimuli — sounds, abstract symbols, words, and even people. How does this effect relate to attitude change? If you hear the word *Coke* and see pictures of Coke cans thousands of times during your life, your attitude toward Coke may become more positive, and you may be more likely to buy Coca-Cola than a competing brand.

If you feel personally immune to the mere exposure effect in advertising, tally up the number of name-brand products you purchase. Although consumer magazines may tell us that generic products are often as good as name brands, many of us feel safer and more comfortable buying name-brands, even though they are considerably more expensive. This may be due in part to mere exposure.

Mere exposure effects occur particularly for complex stimuli that are not disliked initially. If you are exposed to a very simple stimulus (a beep, for example), you will probably not come to like it more after 200 repetitions, and if you dislike a stimulus to start with (for example, an offensive piece of music), repetition will not necessarily

---

FIGURE 8.3   Effects of one-sided and two-sided messages on resistance to subsequent counterpropaganda.

Which produces greater resistance to counterpropaganda: one-sided or two-sided messages?

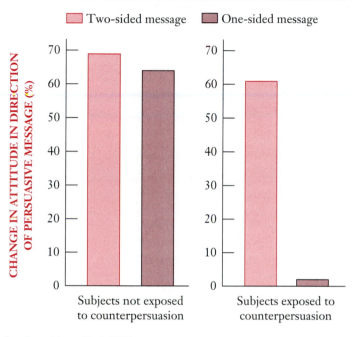

SOURCE: Data from Lumsdaine and Janis (1953).

Given that commercial advertisements often compete against "counterpropaganda" by competitors' ads, this research suggests a potential advantage of two-sided ads over one-sided ads.

---

cause you to like it better. Further, mere exposure increases liking only up to a point—liking will level off, or even decline, after too much exposure (Smith & Dorfman, 1975; Zajonc, Shaver, Tavris, & Kreveld, 1972; Brockner & Swap, 1976; Swap, 1977).

Research on mere exposure effects typically studies how repeated exposure to stimuli (brand names, people, pictures, songs) affects our "gut-liking" for them. Other studies have investigated how repetition of a message's arguments affects comprehension and subsequent persuasion. Here the evidence suggests that *some* repetition can be a good thing. Wilson and Miller (1968), for example, found that presenting legal arguments three times in a jury trial was more effective than a single presentation; such repetition led subjects to remember the arguments better and to agree with them more strongly. Some repetition may make messages more persuasive by helping us to comprehend and retain them.

However, repetition of arguments can be overdone. Some studies have found that whereas many repetitions foster retention of arguments, they can also lead to *reduced* attitude change (Cacioppo & Petty, 1979, 1980; Gorn & Goldberg, 1980). Perhaps people become irritated and bored by too much repetition.

The possibility of excessive repetition illustrates a more general point: An intelligent persuader strives for the optimal, rather than the maximum, use of a persuasion technique (McGuire, 1985). Optimal levels may very well exist for fear-appeals (you don't want to frighten or traumatize recipients *too* much), for pro and con arguments (you don't want to overload recipients with *too* much conflicting information), and for humor (a bit of humor in a persuasive message may make the speaker seem "human" and poised, but too much may make the speaker seem flippant or frivolous).

Channel Variables

Friends, Romans, countrymen, lend me your ears. . . .

—— *Julius Caesar*, Act III, Sc. II

Marc Antony delivers his famous speech in face-to-face contact with his audience. Today, many additional channels of persuasion exist, including newspapers, magazines, radio, television, videos, movies, and computerized mail. Which channel of communication is most persuasive? If you answered, "It depends," then you agree with research findings on this question. There is no single best channel of persuasion; rather, each is suited to different goals and purposes.

Face-to-face persuasion often proves to have more impact than persuasion through the mass media (Berelson, Lazarsfeld, & McPhee, 1954; Katz & Lazarsfeld, 1955). This finding is probably due to several factors. Face-to-face communicators are more salient, personal, and attention-grabbing, and thus they often stimulate more thought and commitment to their persuasive messages. And it is easier to mentally "turn off" a written or mass-media message.

The mass media have a major advantage, however, over face-to-face communication: They can readily reach huge numbers of people. Print media (newspapers, magazines, written briefs) possess the advantage that they are better comprehended, particularly when the persuasive message is complex; however, when messages are simple and relatively easy to comprehend, people seem to yield more to audio or audiovisual messages (Chaiken & Eagly, 1976), perhaps because people think more critically about written material than they do about other kinds of persuasive messages (Maier & Thurber, 1968). At the very least, written material allows the reader to go back and reread information that is missed or misunderstood the first time around.

Because written messages seem to generate more thought, they may be affected less by such "superficial" speaker variables as attractiveness, likability, and credibility. Audio and audiovisual messages, on the other hand, tend to focus more attention on the speaker and thus heighten the impact of speaker variables.

An experiment by Chaiken and Eagly (1983) provides a good illustration of these points. Psychology students at the University of Toronto received a persuasive message prepared by a "college administrator" arguing for higher tuition and reduced student grants. Written, tape-recorded, or videotaped versions of the message were presented to different groups of students. The administrator's likability was varied independently of the channel of communication by attributing to him comments that were either flattering or unflattering to University of Toronto students. After

FIGURE 8.4   Opinion change as a function of communicator
likability and channel of communication.

*Do "superficial" communicator variables have more persuasive
an effect in some channels of communication than in others?*

Chaikin and Eagly (1983) varied both the communicator's
likability and the channel of communication to explore how
these variables interact to affect the persuasiveness of messages.

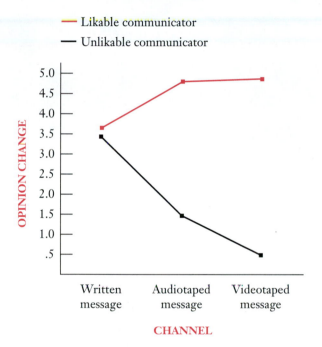

— Likable communicator

— Unlikable communicator

The communicator's likability had the greatest impact on
messages delivered via audiotape or videotape.

SOURCE: Data from Chaiken and Eagly (1983).

receiving the persuasive message, subjects rated their attitudes on the message's
topics and wrote down all their thoughts about both the speaker and the message.

Chaiken and Eagly found that the speaker's persuasiveness depended on both
his likability and the channel of communication (see Figure 8.4). When the communicator was likable, he was more persuasive in audiotapes and videotapes, but
when he was unlikable, he was more persuasive in a written message. Furthermore,
subjects exposed to the audiotapes and videotapes listed more thoughts about the
speaker than did subjects who read the written message. These thoughts tended to
be negative when the speaker was unlikable and positive when he was likable. In

Are you more likely to be persuaded by Jesse Jackson's speech if you see it on TV or read it in a newspaper? According to social psychological research, the answer may depend on how much you like Jackson and how charismatic you find him to be.

other words, audio and visual media tended to pull recipients' thoughts away from the message and focus them more on the speaker and his attributes.

The practical implication of this research is that an attractive, likable, and charismatic speaker is often more persuasive in audio or audiovisual messages, whereas a speaker who is not attractive (but who may be logically convincing) is more persuasive in print messages. A famous political example provides a case in point: Before the first presidential debate of 1960, John Kennedy was the underdog and Richard Nixon the clear front-runner. During the first debate, Kennedy—tanned, calm, and charismatic—was generally perceived to be more persuasive than the more pale, wooden, and perspiring Nixon (Kraus, 1962; White, 1961). However, those who read transcripts of the debate or heard it on radio often perceived Nixon to be the winner. Television—a medium that highlights speaker variables and reduces attention to message contents—favored Kennedy, who went on to win a very narrow victory over Nixon in the 1960 election.

Target or Audience Variables

4. Plebeian: Marked ye his words? He would not take the crown;
   Therefore 'tis certain he was not ambitious.
1. Plebeian: If it be found so, some will dear abide it.
2. Plebeian: Poor soul! his eyes are red as fire with weeping.
3. Plebeian: There's not a nobler man in Rome than Antony.
4. Plebeian: Now mark him. He begins again to speak.

—— *Julius Caesar*, Act III, Sc. II

Marc Antony clearly tailors his speech to his audience. He reminds the crowd that "Caesar brought many captives home to Rome" and helped to fill "the general coffers"; later he informs them that Caesar bequeathed his "private arbors" and "new-planted orchards" to them, the common people.

▪▪

FIGURE 8.5   Items from the "Need for Cognition Scale."

How is the need for cognition measured?

Subjects are asked to respond to the items on scales indicating their "agreement" or "disagreement," or to rate the extent to which the statements are "characteristic" or "uncharacteristic" of them.

1. I would prefer complex to simple problems.
2. I like to have the responsibility of handling a situation that requires a lot of thinking.
3. Thinking is not my idea of fun.
4. I would rather do something that requires little thought than something that is sure to challenge my thinking abilities.
5. I try to anticipate and avoid situations where there is likely chance I will have to think in depth about something.
6. I find satisfaction in deliberating hard and for long hours.
7. I only think as hard as I have to.
8. I prefer to think about small, daily projects to long-term ones.
9. I like tasks that require little thought once I've learned them.
10. The idea of relying on thought to make my way to the top appeals to me.
11. I really enjoy a task that involves coming up with new solutions to problems.
12. Learning new ways to think doesn't excite me very much.
13. I prefer my life to be filled with puzzles that I must solve.
14. The notion of thinking abstractly is appealing to me.
15. I would prefer a task that is intellectual, difficult, and important to one that is somewhat important but does not require much thought.
16. I feel relief rather than satisfaction after completing a task that required a lot of mental effort.
17. It's enough for me that something gets the job done; I don't care how or why it works.
18. I usually end up deliberating about issues even when they do not affect me personally.

Note: Items 3, 4, 5, 7, 8, 9, 12, 16, and 17 are reverse-scored.

SOURCE: From Cacioppo and Petty (1982). Used with permission of John Cacioppo.

▪▪

Must persuasive messages always be tailored to specific audiences? Are there general audience variables that have a consistent effect on persuasion? Research in the Yale tradition investigated a number of audience variables, including intelligence, personality traits (for example, self-esteem), and gender. The results of this research are fairly complex and inconsistent, perhaps because such variables may have opposing effects at different stages of persuasion (McGuire, 1968a, 1968b; Petty & Cacioppo, 1981). For example, intelligence may *increase* audience members' comprehension of a persuasive message but *decrease* the degree to which they yield to the message (presumably because an intelligent person can understand arguments better and also can evaluate those arguments more critically). Indeed, research shows that a highly intelligent person will be persuaded more than will a less intelligent person when the message is complex and sound, but persuaded less when the message is simple (Eagly & Warren, 1976).

In recent years, researchers have studied individual differences that relate directly to a person's tendency to think about arguments in persuasive messages. For example, Cacioppo and Petty (1982) developed a scale to measure an individual's "need for cognition" (see Figure 8.5); people with high scores on this scale like to

━━━

FIGURE 8.6   **Responsiveness to a persuasive message as a function of the quality of arguments and the target's need for cognition.**

How does the need for cognition affect the target's response to a persuasive message?

Cacioppo, Petty, and Morris (1983) presented persuasive messages containing either strong or weak arguments to two groups of women, one with a high need for cognition and one with a low need for cognition.

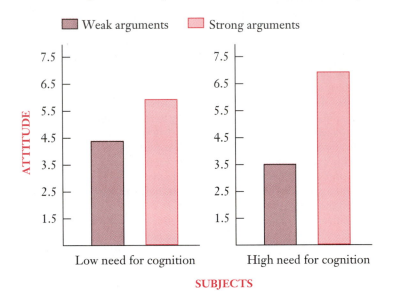

The quality of the arguments had a greater effect on persuasiveness for the women with a high need for cognition.

SOURCE: Data from Cacioppo, Petty, and Morris (1983).

━━━

think and actively strive to understand information, whereas people with low scores use mental shortcuts whenever possible and think only as much as is necessary.

Research suggests that individuals who score differently on the need for cognition scale respond differently to persuasive messages (Petty & Cacioppo, 1986). In one study, female undergraduates measured on need for cognition read a proposal arguing that tuition be raised at their university (Cacioppo, Petty, & Morris, 1983). One group of women read a proposal containing weak arguments; another read one containing strong arguments. The results of this study showed that women with high degrees of need for cognition were more persuaded by strong arguments but less persuaded by weak arguments than were women with low degrees of this need (see Figure 8.6). That is, because they thought a lot about the arguments, women with high needs for cognition were more likely to see the weaknesses of the weak arguments and the strengths of the strong arguments.

The quest for answers to many important questions about persuasion requires that researchers consider a number of variables at once. For example, how much can a speaker disagree with the audience and still retain maximum persuasiveness? At the start of his speech, Marc Antony is careful not to disagree too much with Caesar's assassins: "I speak not to disprove what Brutus spoke, / but here I am to speak what I do know" (*Julius Caesar*, Act III, Sc. I). But as his words begin to change the crowd's sentiments, Antony becomes bolder: "I would ruffle up your spirits, and put a tongue / In every wound of Caesar that should move / The stones of Rome to rise and mutiny" (Act III, Sc. II).

A number of studies indicate that the optimal level of disagreement between speaker and audience depends on the credibility of the speaker (Aronson, Turner, & Carlsmith, 1963; Bochner & Insko, 1966). Such research simultaneously considers three variables: the preexisting attitudes of the audience (an audience variable), the amount the persuasive message disagrees with these attitudes (a message variable), and the speaker's credibility (a speaker variable).

To produce maximum attitude change, a highly credible speaker should disagree with the audience substantially, but a low credibility speaker should disagree with the audience only moderately. A study by Bochner and Insko (1966) provides a good illustration. Subjects read a message arguing that the average person should sleep either 0, 1, 2, 3, 4, 5, 6, 7, or 8 hours a night. This message was attributed to either a Nobel Prize-winning scientist (a high credibility source) or to a Y.M.C.A. director (a low credibility source). As Figure 8.7 shows, as the discrepancy between the amount of sleep advocated by the message and subjects' beliefs (that people require 7 or 8 hours of sleep) grew larger, subjects were more persuaded, up to a point. When the message was too discrepant from subjects' beliefs, however, it became less persuasive. The point at which persuasion declined was higher for the credible sources than for the noncredible source.

Since Cassius first did whet me against Caesar,
I have not slept.
Between the acting of a dreadful thing
And the first motion, all the interim is
Like a phantasma or a hideous dream.
The genius and the mortal instruments
Are then in council, and the state of man,
Like to a little kingdom, suffers then
The nature of an insurrection.

—— *Julius Caesar*, Act II, Sc. I

A second tradition of research on attitude change, quite different and distinct from the Yale research, also emerged in the 1950s. Rather than investigating communication variables, this second tradition was dominated by a specific theory—Leon Festinger's *theory of cognitive dissonance* (Festinger, 1957). Festinger's theory was one of many cognitive consistency theories that emerged in the 1950s (see Chapter 1).

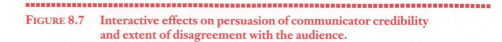

FIGURE 8.7 Interactive effects on persuasion of communicator credibility and extent of disagreement with the audience.

How much should a persuasive message disagree with the audience's beliefs?

Bochner and Insko (1966) investigated the interaction between the communicator's credibility and the extent of disagreement with the audience in determining the persuasiveness of messages.

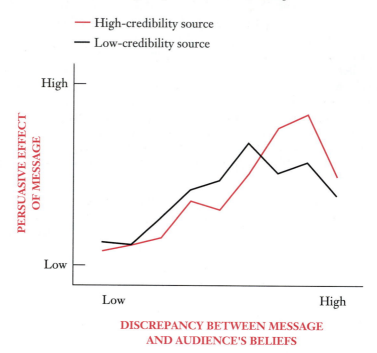

Too much disagreement with an audience backfires, producing less persuasion. But the point at which the "backfire" occurs is higher for a high-credibility communicator.

SOURCE: Adapted from Bochner and Insko (1966). Used with permission of Chester Insko.

As is typical of much of the research in the Yale tradition, this study shows that the effect of one variable (disagreement between message and audience beliefs) depends on another variable (speaker credibility).

The Legacy of the Yale Research

What do studies in the Yale tradition tell us about persuasion? They clearly tell us that it is a complex and multifaceted phenomenon.

If the Yale researchers had hoped for simple answers, then they must have been disappointed by their findings, for they found no unequivocal "laws" of persuasion. The questions posed by the Yale research about the effects of speaker, message, channel, and audience variables often required answers in which "it depends": The effect of speaker credibility depends on the amount of time that passes after the message is delivered; the effectiveness of fear-appeals depends on the level of fear aroused and on the recipient's beliefs about the fearful event; the relative effectiveness of print media and visual media depends on the attractiveness of the speaker and the logic of the message; the effect of audience variables such as intelligence depends on message complexity and quality; and so on.

The many conditions that qualify findings about speaker, message, channel, and audience variables make the practical applications of such findings (to, say, commercial advertising) rather difficult. Furthermore, the complex interactions among variables so often observed in the Yale studies have at times been difficult to replicate. (The "sleeper effect" provides a good example of this difficulty.) Finally, the many complex results compiled by research in the Yale tradition often lack theoretical coherence and meaning.

In recent years a number of theorists have attempted to integrate the findings of the Yale research and the many studies it stimulated into a single theory. Rather than simply cataloging the effects of various speaker, message, channel, and audience variables in isolation, these theorists have focused more on the cognitive processes that lead to persuasion. In general, they have reached a consensus: Some kinds of persuasion are due to quick and "lazy" thought processes, whereas other kinds of persuasion result from more careful and conscientious thought (Chaiken, 1987; Eagly & Chaiken, 1984; Petty & Cacioppo, 1986).

According to this perspective, when people do not think carefully about a message (because they are lazy, distracted, hurried, or simply don't care much about the message), they tend to be influenced more by such "surface" cues as speaker credibility and attractiveness, the sheer number of arguments, and environmental pleasantness. On the other hand, when people think carefully about a message (because they are thoughtful or especially interested in the message), they tend to be influenced more by the quality and content of arguments, and they engage in a process of generating arguments for or against the message.

Many of the Yale studies can be interpreted with respect to these two kinds of thought processes involved in persuasion. For example, research on such speaker variables as credibility and attractiveness often focuses on persuasion that appeals to "lazy" thought processes and is thus quite transient. The repetition of logically compelling arguments is effective to the extent it induces people to understand and think about the arguments. Some channels of persuasion (for example, TV) seem to encourage "lazy" processing based on superficial cues, whereas others (print media) encourage more active and critical thought. Finally, audience variables like intelligence and need for cognition in part influence persuasion through their influence on active, critical thought.

In general, persuasion that results from the stimulation of active thought tends to be more enduring and more likely to produce corresponding behavior change than persuasion that appeals to "lazier" kinds of thought. We shall return to this distinction between "thoughtful persuasion" and "lazy persuasion" at the end of this chapter. As you continue to read about research on attitude change, ask yourself, "Is this an example of 'thoughtful' or 'lazy' attitude change?"

Cigarette smokers may experience dissonance when they try to reconcile negative facts about smoking with their behavior. One way they reduce dissonance is to change their beliefs.

Festinger's Theory of Cognitive Dissonance

The main proposition of Festinger's theory is that when people hold inconsistent beliefs they experience a negative drive state, which Festinger labeled cognitive dissonance. A negative drive state is an unpleasant state of motivational arousal that goads a person to act to reduce the drive state. Thirst, for example, may be viewed as a negative drive state; it is an unpleasant motivational state that goads you to take action (drink something) that will reduce the thirst. Similarly, *dissonance* — the discomfort arising from inconsistent beliefs — is a negative drive state that induces a person to reduce the dissonance. When Brutus decides to join the conspiracy against Julius Caesar, he experiences intense dissonance; he experiences difficulty reconciling his belief that he is a good and decent man with his decision to be a murderer.

How can one reduce dissonance? Festinger suggested two major routes to reduce dissonance: People can either change their behavior, or they can change their beliefs. Brutus, for example, can either renege on his agreement to help kill Caesar, or he can shift his beliefs (which in fact he does by deciding that Caesar is overly ambitious and a threat to the Roman republic).

Consider a more mundane example. Suppose Nancy, a heavy smoker, holds the following beliefs: "Cigarette smoking is dangerous to my health and causes lung cancer, heart disease, and emphysema," "Smoking gives me a hacking cough, yellow teeth, ruins my social life, and annoys my friends," and finally, "I smoke two packs of cigarettes a day." This set of beliefs seems to be logically inconsistent. According to Festinger's theory, Nancy should experience dissonance (unpleasant arousal) upon contemplating her inconsistent beliefs. Because dissonance is a negative drive state, Nancy is motivated to reduce it. One way is to change her behavior — quit smoking — which would eliminate the inconsistency.

But if Nancy is addicted to cigarettes and finds it nearly impossible to give them up, she can reduce dissonance by shifting some of her beliefs. For example, she might say, "Well, I'm not really convinced that smoking is all that unhealthy. I heard that all the evidence is correlational and that there's really no hard cause-effect proof. Besides, look at old Joe down the street — 83 years old, and he's smoked two packs a day for 65 years and is still going strong. I think if you don't stress yourself too much you just don't get heart disease. . . ." Nancy is "squirming out" of some uncomfortable inconsistencies in her beliefs by shifting some of those beliefs. As is diagrammed in Figure 8.8, dissonance theory suggests that we sometimes rationalize our beliefs and attitudes to reduce the discomfort created by their inconsistencies.

FIGURE 8.8   Cognitive dissonance and attitude change.

How does cognitive dissonance theory explain attitude change?

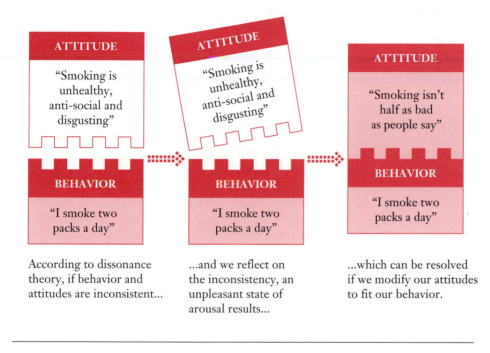

According to dissonance theory, if behavior and attitudes are inconsistent...

...and we reflect on the inconsistency, an unpleasant state of arousal results...

...which can be resolved if we modify our attitudes to fit our behavior.

Note that dissonance theory is a motivational theory of attitude change.

Although dissonance theory discusses the effects of inconsistent *beliefs*, in practice dissonance research almost always investigates inconsistencies between *behavior* and beliefs. Once you behave in a manner that is inconsistent with your beliefs (for example, if I induce you to donate money to a candidate you dislike), you then have a *belief* about your inconsistent behavior. Behavior that is inconsistent with your beliefs necessarily leads to inconsistent beliefs.

When a subject in a dissonance experiment is induced to behave in some way that is inconsistent with his or her beliefs, the experiment is almost always designed so the subject cannot reduce dissonance by changing behavior. In other words, the experiments are contrived to prevent dissonance reduction through behavior change, forcing the subject instead to change beliefs and attitudes. This makes sense, of course, because social psychologists are most interested in dissonance reduction as a process of belief and attitude change.

Note the fundamental difference between dissonance studies and the Yale research: Dissonance studies investigate how an individual's internal inconsistencies generate attitude change, whereas the Yale research investigates how persuasive messages produce attitude change.

The Festinger and Carlsmith (1959) Study

Although Festinger's first systematic exposition of dissonance theory was published in 1957, a convincing experimental demonstration of dissonance effects was not reported until 1959. Festinger and his student, J. Merril Carlsmith, carried out a landmark study characterized by many of the distinctive qualities of later dissonance research — elaborate manipulations, deception of subjects, and relatively simple dependent measures.

Imagine you are a subject in the following experiment: After you arrive at the laboratory, the experimenter asks you to perform two simple motor tasks. The first consists of emptying and refilling a tray with spools, and the second consists of turning 48 pegs stuck into holes a quarter of a turn, over and over. You are asked to perform each of these mindless tasks for half an hour. (The researchers intentionally chose boring and trivial activities.)

After you complete the tasks, the experimenter tells you that the "real" purpose of the study (in fact, a lie) is to investigate the effects of psychological "set" on performance. You are told that some of the subjects are informed that the boring tasks will be "very enjoyable" and "fun," whereas other subjects, like yourself, are told nothing. As a matter of fact, the experimenter continues, the next subject (a young woman waiting in a nearby room) will soon be informed by a research assistant that the tasks are enjoyable and fun.

The experimenter leaves, but soon returns, distraught because his assistant has not yet arrived. Embarrassed, he asks if you would be willing to serve as a research assistant this one time. He might even be able to hire you as a research assistant later in the semester, but for now he'll pay you a fee to convince the new subject how fun and interesting the experiment is. (In other words, he will pay you to *lie* to the subject in the next room.)

Now comes the major manipulation of the experiment. The experimenter offers to pay you either $1 or $20 (depending on which experimental condition you're in) for your "work." You agree and go into the next room where the "subject" (really a confederate) is waiting. You sit down and start talking with her, telling her how fun and interesting the experiment was. The confederate seems surprised and states that a friend who was already in the experiment said it was quite boring. "Boring?" you say. "Oh no, it wasn't boring. It was really quite fun and interesting. There were these little machines, and spools. I'll bet your friend isn't interested in mechanical things. I really thought it was a lot of fun. . . ." You probably breathe a sigh of relief when it's all over, and the experimenter sends you off to a Psychology Department secretary who interviews you, asking how fun and interesting you did in fact find the tasks to be.

Despite the complicated cover story and procedure, the Festinger and Carlsmith study boils down to a fairly simple skeleton: You are asked to perform a boring task, and then you are asked to convince an innocent subject that this boring task was in fact fun, for either $1 or $20. Finally, you are asked to rate how fun and interesting you in fact found the boring tasks to be.

Dissonance theory predicts that subjects paid $1 to lie will show more attitude change than will subjects paid $20. Here is the reasoning: Subjects are forced to confront two inconsistent beliefs: "I think this experiment was really boring" and "I just told that innocent subject that the experiment was fun and interesting." This inconsistency between beliefs and words arouses dissonance, particularly in the subjects given $1. After all, they have little justification for lying—only one measly dollar—whereas the subjects who received $20 had considerable external (economic) incentive to behave inconsistently with their true beliefs.

How could subjects reduce dissonance in this experiment? They couldn't change their behavior, so instead they changed their attitudes. In fact, as dissonance theory predicts, the subjects paid $1 tended to rate the boring task somewhat favorably, whereas both subjects paid $20 and control subjects (who simply performed the boring task and then rated it) found it dull and boring. The results of this study are shown in Figure 8.9.

The results of the Festinger and Carlsmith study are particularly intriguing because they seem to contradict reward theories. Subjects who were paid more showed the least attitude change, whereas subjects who were paid less showed the most attitude change. Conditioning theories seem to predict just the opposite—that subjects who are rewarded most to state an attitudinal position will later espouse that position most strongly (see Chapter 6).

The Psychology of Insufficient Justification

Festinger and Carlsmith were the first of many to investigate the combined effects of counterattitudinal behavior and external incentives on attitude change. Such studies suggest that if people are induced to behave in a way that is inconsistent with their beliefs for little external justification, they will shift their beliefs to be more consistent with their behavior.

In another well-known study on insufficient justification, Cohen (1962) asked students at Yale University to write *counterattitudinal essays* for varying amounts of money. The subject of their essays was a real incident at Yale University: A student demonstration had been broken up by the New Haven police, who were accused of being excessively violent. Student opinion in general was against the police, so Cohen asked his subjects to write essays *in favor* of the police. To make his request plausible, Cohen told subjects that he was conducting research on attitude change and that as part of this research he needed realistic student essays both for and against the New Haven police; because he already had many "anti-police" essays, he needed some "pro-police" essays.

As in the Festinger and Carlsmith study, the major independent variable was monetary incentive. Subjects were offered either 50 cents, $1, $5, or $10 to write their counterattitudinal essay in favor of the police. According to dissonance theory, the inconsistency between subjects' true beliefs and their behavior (writing the counterattitudinal essay) will arouse dissonance, which is presumed to be greatest for subjects paid 50 cents because this condition provides *insufficient justification* for their counterattitudinal behavior. Subjects paid $10 have obvious justification for their inconsistent behavior ("The money justifies my helping the experimenter").

After writing their essays, subjects were asked to rate their actual attitudes toward the New Haven police. Interestingly, the subjects paid 50 cents shifted their attitudes in a direction more favorable to the police, whereas the subjects paid $10

FIGURE 8.9 **Cognitive dissonance and attitude change: The results of the Festinger and Carlsmith study.**

Do we change our attitudes to reduce dissonance?

Festinger and Carlsmith (1959) measured how positively subjects felt about a boring task (attitude) after being induced to tell another person that the task was interesting (behavior).

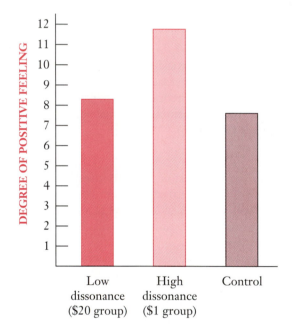

The task was rated most positively by subjects in the high-dissonance condition – those who were paid only a token amount for saying that the task was interesting.

SOURCE: Data from Festinger and Carlsmith (1959).

The Festinger and Carlsmith experiment was the first of many to show that people who behave in ways that are inconsistent with their attitudes for little external justification often shift their attitudes to be more consistent with their behavior.

FIGURE 8.10 **Insufficient justification and attitude change: Results of the Cohen (1962) study.**

When does counterattitudinal behavior lead to dissonance and attitude change?

Cohen (1962) measured attitude change in subjects who had written attitude-inconsistent essays concerning the New Haven police for varying amounts of money.

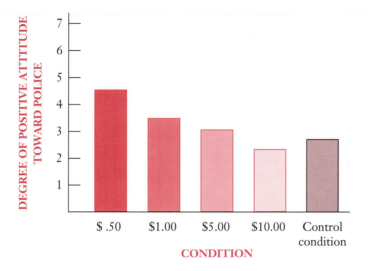

As dissonance theory predicts, the less money subjects were paid, the greater the amount of attitude change.

SOURCE: Adapted from Cohen (1962).

The Cohen study used smaller amounts of money than did the Festinger and Carlsmith study and created four levels of monetary incentive. Still, the basic findings of Festinger and Carlsmith were replicated: Attitude change was greater in the low-incentive conditions.

showed no attitude change; they were still against the police, as were the members of a control group who wrote no essays at all. The subjects paid $1 and $5 showed intermediate amounts of attitude change (see Figure 8.10). Thus in the Cohen study as well, subjects who behaved in attitude-inconsistent ways for small amounts of money showed the largest attitude shifts, whereas subjects who behaved in attitude-inconsistent ways for large amounts of money showed little or no attitude shifts.

As a final example of a study on insufficient justification, let's turn to research by Zimbardo, Weisenberg, Firestone, and Levy (1965) in which subjects were asked to eat grasshoppers. The subjects were military men, and the researchers used a convincing (but deceptive) cover story—namely, that they were investigating the palatability of various nonstandard foods that soldiers might have to eat to survive under difficult circumstances.

Thus an experimenter induced subjects to eat grasshoppers and to rate how palatable they were. In one experimental condition the experimenter was warm and friendly, whereas in the other condition he was cold and arrogant. Now eating a grasshopper seems likely to create dissonance in subjects. (Isn't eating a grasshopper a "counterattitudinal behavior" for you?) When the experimenter was friendly, the subject had some justification: "Oh, I ate the grasshopper because the experimenter was such a nice guy." But when the experimenter was arrogant, the subject had little justification and felt maximum dissonance over his obviously counterattitudinal behavior.

Believe it or not, subjects who interacted with the arrogant experimenter condition rated the grasshopper as being tastier and more palatable than did subjects who interacted with the friendly experimenter. Subjects could not reduce dissonance by changing their behavior—once you've eaten a grasshopper you can't undo it— but they could resolve dissonance by changing their beliefs.

Variations on a Dissonance Theme

Dissonance theory has been applied to a wide variety of topics in social psychology, including prejudice, interpersonal attraction, and group behavior. The following descriptions of a few noteworthy dissonance studies will help provide some sense of how dissonance theory is applied.

Insufficient threat: The "forbidden toy" study.   In the dissonance research described so far, the independent variable was a positive incentive, but studies that instead manipulate *threats or negative incentives* have also been conducted. In a well-known study by Aronson and Carlsmith (1963), for example, young children were individually brought into a playroom, asked to play with five attractive toys, and then asked to rank the toys in order of their preference.

Later, the experimenter placed the child's second-ranked toy on a table, told the child that he was leaving the room for awhile, and stated that the child could play with any of the toys except the one on the table. The experimenter accompanied his request with either a mild threat ("I don't want you to play with the toy on the table. If you played with it, I would be annoyed") or a severe threat ("I don't want you to play with the toy on the table. If you play with it, I would be very angry. I would have to take all of my toys and go home").

Interestingly, children in both the mild-threat and severe-threat conditions *did not* play with the forbidden toy when the experimenter left the room. Afterwards, the children were asked to rank the same toys again to determine whether any attitude change had occurred. As dissonance theory predicts, many of the children in the mild-threat condition *lowered* their ranking of the forbidden toy, whereas none of the children in the severe-threat condition (or in a control condition) showed such a shift in attitude. In essence, the children's dissonant beliefs were: "I really liked the toy on the table, yet I didn't play with it." The stern threat was ample external justification for a child not to play with the desired toy, but the mild threat was an insufficient justification that led the child to experience dissonance. Thus children exposed to a mild threat seem to have resolved their dissonance by devaluing the forbidden toy.

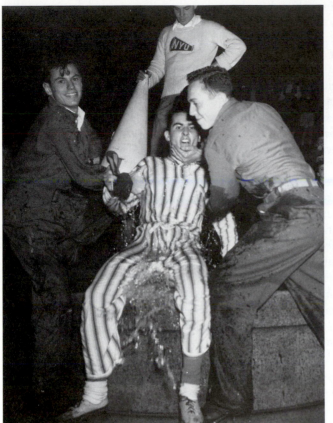

■■■■■■■■■■■■■■■■■■■■■■■■■
A fraternity initiation.
Do severe initiations
to gain admittance to
groups lead us to be
more attracted to the
groups?

Severity of initiation.   Another kind of dissonance study also uses negative incentives, this time to *increase* liking for an activity. The message of research on *severity of initiation* (sometimes called *justification of effort*) is that we may come to like something that we suffer for (Aronson & Mills, 1959; Gerard & Mathewson, 1966).

To illustrate, fraternities commonly put prospective members through unpleasant and embarrassing "hazings" or initiation rites. Dissonance theory predicts that a pledge who is accepted into a fraternity after experiencing a humiliating initiation may very well like the fraternity more as a result of his painful experience.

Aronson and Mills (1959) demonstrated this severity of initiation effect experimentally. College women were invited to participate in a discussion group on the topic of sex. The researchers informed the women that because not all the college students could discuss sex openly, they had developed a screening test to see if the subjects were comfortable with the topic. The "test" was the main manipulation in this experiment. Some subjects participated in a rather mildly worded "test"; each subject read a list of relatively nonthreatening words with sexual meanings, such as "petting" and "prostitute." Other subjects, however, read lists of obscenities and passages from explicit, erotic novels.

After this "initiation," the women listened over earphones to a group discussion of sex. (The researchers explained that people can discuss sex more freely if they don't see one another.) In reality, the subjects heard a tape-recorded discussion that had been constructed by the researchers to be dull, boring, and pointless.

The women in the "severe initiation" condition, who had just experienced considerable discomfort before participating in a group discussion that turned out to be boring, were in a high-dissonance condition. These women could reduce dissonance only by deciding that the discussion group was really interesting and worthwhile (and by rating it accordingly). Women in the "mild initiation" condition, however, rated the discussion group as dull and uninteresting, as did a control group that underwent no initiation at all (see Figure 8.11). This basic finding has been replicated in other studies (Gerard & Mathewson, 1966).

Derogation of the victim.   Dissonance theory makes the unsettling prediction that if we behave badly toward another person, particularly with little justification, then we will shift our beliefs and attitudes to justify our bad behavior; typically, this means that we will come to think more badly of our victim. The application of dissonance theory is fairly straightforward. Most of us consider ourselves to be decent, moral people who would not inflict harm on innocent victims. Thus, if we find ourselves in a situation in which we have harmed an innocent victim, dissonance is aroused. If we can't take back the harmful behavior, the only way to reduce dissonance may be to decide that the victim was "bad" and really deserved ill treatment. Research studies provide convincing evidence that victim derogation actually occurs (for example, Glass, 1964; Davis & Jones, 1960).

Qualifications on Dissonance Theory

Festinger's theory of cognitive dissonance seemed to imply that dissonance occurs whenever a person holds inconsistent beliefs (or behaves in a manner that is inconsistent with his or her beliefs). Research in the 1960s and 1970s, however, suggested that certain special conditions must be met for dissonance to occur and to produce attitude change.

Remember that the typical dissonance study induces subjects to behave in a way that is inconsistent with their beliefs. For dissonance to be maximized and thus lead to attitude change, research subjects must feel that their inconsistent behavior is *freely chosen* and is their personal responsibility, that their behavior is *firmly committed and irrevocable*, and that their behavior has important *consequences* for others. Let's examine the implications of each of these qualifying conditions.

Free choice.   Subjects who behave in ways that are inconsistent with their attitudes experience the most dissonance when they believe they have freely chosen their behavior. For example, suppose I induce you to deliver a speech supporting a political candidate you detest. I can order you to deliver the speech, or I can ask you to deliver the speech while emphasizing that the final choice is your own. If I have ordered you, you very likely will experience less dissonance because you believe you had no choice in the matter.

Linder, Cooper, and Jones (1967) demonstrated the importance of perceived choice in a study that involved counterattitudinal essays. Subjects were asked to write essays advocating that controversial speakers be barred from their university, a topic with which the subjects disagreed. Some subjects were virtually ordered to write their essays, whereas others were *asked* to write their essays and were told that the

FIGURE 8.11   Severity of initiation effects.

Will people come to like a group more if they must suffer for it?

Aronson and Mills (1959) asked female subjects to rate
the interestingness of a boring discussion group after
the subjects had experienced no initiation, a mild initiation,
or a severe initiation in order to participate in the discussion.

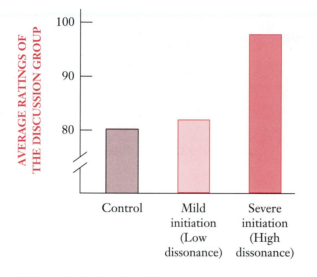

Subjects who had endured the severe initiation rated the
discussion group much more positively than those who
had experienced either mild initiation or no initiation at all.

SOURCE: Data from Aronson and Mills (1959).

*The severity of initiation effects helps explain the function of painful
initiation rites in real-life groups (such as fraternities).*

decision to write the essays was their own. As in the Cohen (1962) study, subjects
were offered either small or large amounts of money to write their counterattitudinal
essays.

In this experiment, the results expected for dissonance studies—that smaller
amounts of money produce larger attitude shifts—occurred only among subjects
given free choice. Among subjects given no choice, the study demonstrated incentive
effects; that is, the larger amount of money produced greater attitude change (see
Figure 8.12).

▪▪▪

FIGURE 8.12   Perceived choice, dissonance, and attitude change.

How does perceived choice to engage in counterattitudinal behavior affect dissonance and attitude change?

Linder, Cooper, and Jones (1967) varied both the incentive offered for counterattitudinal behavior and the subjects' perceived ability to freely choose the behavior.

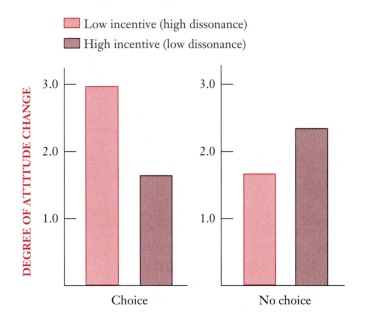

In the choice condition, low-incentive subjects showed greater attitude change than high-incentive subjects, as predicted by dissonance theory. However, in the no-choice condition, <u>incentive effects</u> were observed: low-incentive subjects showed <u>less</u> attitude change than high-incentive subjects.

SOURCE: Data from Linder et al. (1967).

Note that only subjects who perceived themselves as freely choosing their behavior showed dissonance effects. This is one of many studies showing that dissonance effects occur only under certain conditions.

▪▪▪

Commitment and irrevocability.   For counterattitudinal behavior to lead to attitude change, the individual must perceive the behavior to be firmly committed and irrevocable. One well-known study investigating derogation of the victim combined the variables of *choice* and *irrevocability* in one experimental design. Davis and Jones

(1960) asked subjects to serve as the experimenter's accomplices (this was in fact a deceptive cover story) in delivering negative evaluations to another "innocent" subject (actually a confederate). Each subject interacted with the confederate for awhile and then told the confederate that he or she didn't like her. Imagine how uncomfortable that would be for most subjects. This study, of course, sets the stage for subjects to derogate their victim—to decide that the reason they said mean things was because the other subject really *was* unlikable.

Davis and Jones added two additional manipulations to their study. First, they manipulated subjects' perception of choice; they ordered some subjects to deliver the nasty evaluations but only asked others. As a second, independent manipulation, the experimenter told some subjects that they would be able to meet their "victim" after the experiment and "take back" the bad things they said; other subjects were told that they would not meet their victim again and that she would continue to believe the subjects' nasty comments.

Davis and Jones predicted that subjects in the *irrevocable choice* condition would experience the most dissonance because they would feel responsible for their bad behavior and powerless to correct it. Indeed, the greatest attitude change (that is, derogation of the victim) and presumably the highest dissonance arousal occurred for subjects in this condition (see Figure 8.13).

Consequences of behavior.   Counterattitudinal behavior seems to arouse the most dissonance and lead to the most attitude change when we feel that the behavior has real-life consequences. Imagine that I ask you to write an essay advocating higher tuition at your college (presumably a counterattitudinal essay for you). I can manipulate the "consequences" of your writing this essay in the following ways: I can rip up your essay immediately after you write it and say it was just an "exercise"; I can inform you that we will use your essay in an attitude-change study that seeks to change other students' attitudes about raising tuition; or I can inform you that we will use your essay in a statewide publicity campaign to raise college tuition. Wouldn't you experience more dissonance over writing your essay in the "publicity" condition than in the "exercise" condition? The more you perceive your counterattitudinal behavior to have real-life consequences, the more uncomfortable you will feel and thus the more motivated you will be to shift your attitudes to resolve dissonance. Several studies support this general proposition (for example, Cooper & Worchel, 1970; Collins & Hoyt, 1972).

Note that the influence of each of these qualifying variables—choice, responsibility, commitment and irrevocability, and consequences—suggests that dissonance effects may not be nearly so general as originally suggested by Festinger's theory (see Figure 8.14 for a summary). Aronson (1969) offered the general suggestion that counterattitudinal behavior leads to dissonance particularly for those attitudes that are important or central to one's self-concept. Clearly, one direction of dissonance research has been to determine when dissonance effects occur and when they do not.

Soon after Festinger first presented his theory of cognitive dissonance, researchers began to probe its limitations. In the 1960s studies questioning the theoretical assumptions of dissonance theory also began to appear. We'll focus on one alternate explanation to dissonance effects—Daryl Bem's self-perception theory—both because it has been the most significant challenge to dissonance theory and because it

Self-Perception Theory: An Alternate Explanation

FIGURE 8.13   Effects of choice and irrevocability on derogation of the victim.

How do choice and irrevocability of counterattitudinal behavior affect dissonance and attitude change?

Davis and Jones (1960) predicted that subjects who were induced to deliver an undeserved negative evaluation to a "victim" would experience greater dissonance if (a) they believed they had a choice and (b) they saw their behavior as irrevocable.

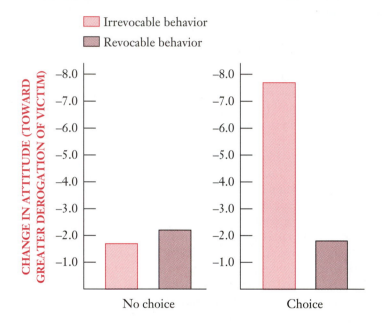

As predicted, the largest attitude change—toward greater derogation of the victim—was shown by subjects in the irrevocable choice condition.

SOURCE: Based on Davis and Jones (1960).

Research on derogation of the victim has important implications in everyday life. For example, people who treat members of certain ethnic groups badly may justify their behavior by derogating their victims. Thus victim derogation may at times foster and perpetuate prejudice.

is an influential theory in its own right, independent of its application to dissonance results (see Chapter 7).

Self-perception theory (Bem, 1967, 1972) is an inferential theory of attitude formation. It argues that when our attitudes are weak or ambiguous, we are in the

•••

FIGURE 8.14   Qualifying conditions affecting the impact of dissonance on attitude change.

When is dissonance likely to produce attitude change?

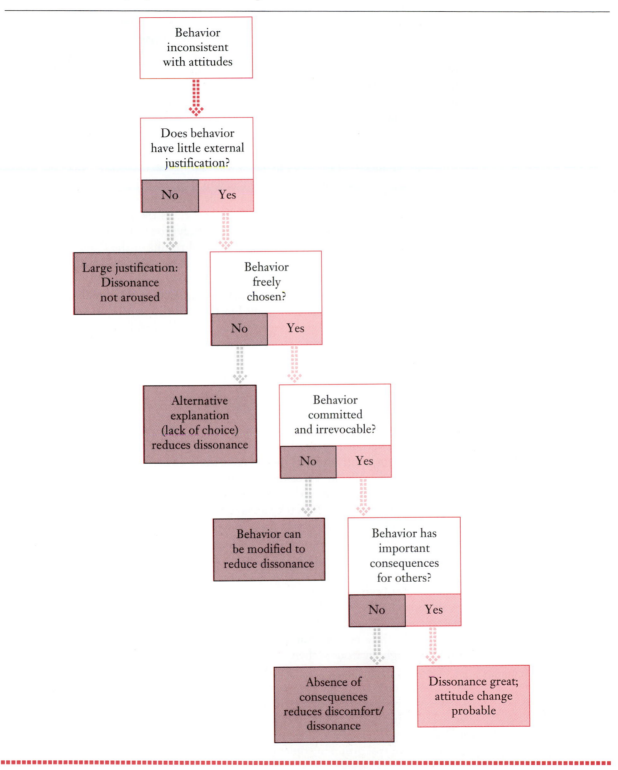

same position as an outside observer; as a result, we infer our attitudes from our behavior and from the setting.

To understand how self-perception theory can explain dissonance effects, let's change the scenario of the Cohen (1962) study a bit. Imagine that you, an outside observer, *watch* one of Cohen's subjects write his essay in favor of the New Haven police. Just to make things a little bit more dramatic, let's say that the subject you observe received either $100 or nothing for writing the essay. Afterward, I ask you to rate what you think the subject's *true attitude* is toward the New Haven police. You probably won't be sure of the paid subject's true attitude—he has such a strong external cause for his behavior that you can discount any attitudinal cause. But, if you watched the subject write his essay for free (no obvious external cause), you'll probably conclude that he really believes what he wrote. (This is an example of the discounting principle in attribution discussed in Chapter 4.)

Bem (1967, 1968) in fact carried out such "interpersonal simulations" of the Cohen study in which outside observers had to guess the attitudes of people described as behaving like subjects in the Cohen study; the attributed attitudes of the outside observers very closely mirrored the actual results of the Cohen study. Bem argued that subjects in Cohen's study "changed" their attitudes through a thought process similar to that of the outside observers.

Thus Bem's self-perception theory makes exactly the same predictions as does dissonance theory for the Cohen study, but for very different reasons. Dissonance theory postulates that an unpleasant state of arousal arises from the inconsistency between subjects' beliefs and behavior, whereas self-perception theory simply postulates that subjects engage in a logical, inferential process that discounts attitudinal causes when strong external causes are present.

Evaluating Dissonance Theory and Self-Perception Theory

Perhaps the critical difference between dissonance theory and self-perception theory is that the first posits a state of arousal, whereas the second does not. Dissonance theory is a "hot, motivational" theory of attitude change, whereas self-perception theory presents a "cold, information-processing" account of the same attitude change. Can we determine which of the two theories is correct? One direct way would be to monitor people as they behave in counterattitudinal ways; if they really are physiologically aroused, this finding would support dissonance theory. Such studies do suggest that subjects who behave in counterattitudinal ways are aroused (Elkin & Leippe, 1986; Higgins, Rhodewalt, & Zanna, 1979; Kiesler & Pallak, 1976; Pallak & Pittman, 1972).

In recent years, another technique has been used to assess the effects of arousal on attitude change in dissonance experiments. If dissonance theory is correct, then subjects' uncomfortable state of arousal leads to attitude change. It then follows that if we can somehow reduce arousal, we should reduce attitude change (and conversely, if we can heighten arousal, then we should increase attitude change).

Cooper, Zanna, and Taves (1978) were able to manipulate subjects' degrees of arousal by using drugs. Subjects were asked to write counterattitudinal essays. Some subjects were given tranquilizers (to reduce or eliminate arousal); other subjects were given an amphetamine (to heighten arousal). A third group of subjects received an inert "drug" (placebo). The attitudes of all the groups were then compared with those of a control group of students who had not written counterattitudinal essays.

FIGURE 8.15   **The effects of drug-induced arousal and calming on attitude change following counterattitudinal behavior.**

Is dissonance an unpleasant state of arousal?

Cooper, Zanna, and Taves (1978) measured attitude change among subjects who committed themselves to write counterattitudinal essays (in favor of Richard Nixon's pardon) after their arousal was manipulated with drugs.

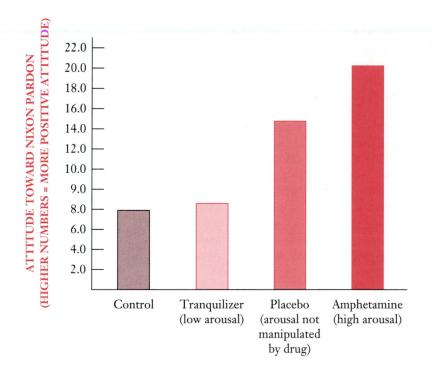

Consistent with dissonance theory, the subjects who experienced the greatest arousal showed the most attitude change.

SOURCE: Data from Cooper, Zanna, and Taves (1978).

Note that subjects in the tranquilizer condition expressed virtually the same attitudes as control subjects who had not written counterattitudinal essays. By implication, the tranquilizer eliminated the unpleasant arousal of dissonance.

Tranquilized subjects showed less attitude change than did placebo subjects, whereas subjects who had taken amphetamines showed greater attitude change (see Figure 8.15). In other words, manipulating arousal with drugs did influence subjects' attitude change, a finding that supports dissonance theory.

Does this mean that self-perception theory is false? Not necessarily. Fazio, Zanna, and Cooper (1977) suggest that dissonance theory may apply particularly to truly *attitude-discrepant* behavior and self-perception theory more to *attitude-congruent* behavior. To demonstrate this, they conducted an experiment in which subjects wrote essays advocating varying degrees of liberal or conservative politics. For some subjects, the political philosophy advocated in their essays was completely unacceptable to them; for others, the advocated position was acceptable, even if not exactly their own. Intriguingly, commitment to write either kind of essay led to attitude change; subjects shifted their attitudes to become more similar to the position advocated in their essays.

Did arousal influence subjects' attitude change? To answer this question, Fazio, Zanna, and Cooper induced some subjects to misattribute their arousal to the experimental setting (see Chapter 4 for a discussion of misattribution research). The researchers reasoned that if subjects could "explain away" their arousal as due to an external cause (rather than to the essay), subjects might not change their attitudes. Intriguingly, misattribution of arousal reduced subjects' attitude change only when subjects had agreed to write essays advocating completely unacceptable philosophical positions.

Fazio, Zanna, and Cooper interpreted these results to imply that dissonance occurred when subjects wrote essays that were highly objectionable, but self-perception processes occurred when subjects wrote mildly attitude-discrepant essays. Thus, under certain conditions attitude-discrepant behavior can stimulate either dissonance or self-perception processes. Dissonance is most likely to occur when such behavior is highly objectionable and when relevant attitudes are strong; self-perception processes are most likely to occur when behavior is not highly discrepant from preexisting attitudes and when relevant attitudes are weak.

Cognitive Responses and Attitude Change

It must be by his death; and for my part,
I know no personal cause to spurn at him,
But for the general. He would be crowned.
How that might change his nature, there's the question.
. . . Crown him that,
And I grant we put a sting in him
That at his will he may do danger with.
The abuse of greatness is when it disjoins
Remorse from power.

—— *Julius Caesar*, Act II, Sc. I

In this soliloquy Brutus is a man debating with himself. He argues back and forth, at some times in favor of Caesar's death, at others appalled by it. At first Brutus joins the conspiracy against Caesar because of the other conspirators' intense persuasion, but eventually his own arguments become paramount in his decision.

How important are self-generated thoughts and arguments in persuasion? Research in the Yale tradition tends to view attitude change as a process in which people attend to, comprehend, and remember a persuasive message; in other words, attitude change is a matter of communication and passive learning. Dissonance theory addresses the logical consistency of beliefs, and its main principle of attitude change is motivational: People strive to reduce an unpleasant state of arousal, often through some process of rationalization. Finally, self-perception theory argues that when we're not sure of our attitudes, we look to our behavior to infer them.

However, none of these three approaches describes attitude change as a process of *active thought* in which people think about persuasive messages, mull them over, relate them to preexisting knowledge, generate counterarguments, and so on. Several recent lines of research have focused on active cognition as an important factor in attitude change. They argue that *cognitive responses* (that is, internal arguments for or against a persuasive message) have a large effect on persuasion (Greenwald, 1968; Petty & Cacioppo, 1981).

Forewarning Effects

A number of studies suggest that warning people ahead of time that they will be the target of attempted persuasion makes them more resistant to persuasion, presumably because it triggers formulation of counterarguments. In one study (Petty & Cacioppo, 1977) college subjects heard a "guest lecturer" advocate that all college freshmen and sophomores be required to live in college dorms (a topic highly relevant to the subjects). Some subjects were told about the topic a few minutes before the lecture, whereas others were simply informed that they would hear a lecture by a counseling-center psychologist. Subjects were asked to list their thoughts in general before hearing the lecture, and afterwards they completed questionnaires that assessed how persuaded they were by the speaker. Interestingly, subjects who were forewarned generated more counterarguments against the message and ultimately disagreed with it to a greater extent than did subjects not forewarned. By implication, subjects' counterargument processes (that is, their internal cognitive responses) led them to reject the message.

Cognitive response theory has been applied to many aspects of persuasion other than forewarning and belief inoculation (see Petty & Cacioppo, 1981; see also pp. 290–291). Let's consider a relatively subtle message variable: the use of rhetorical questions. Suppose incumbent Senator Hornblower is trying to convince you that you're better off now than when he first took office. Will his campaign speech be more persuasive if he ends with a statement ("Clearly, the citizens of this great state are much better off today than six years ago!") or with a question ("Are you better off today than you were six years ago?")?

Cognitive response theory argues that rhetorical questions focus more attention on message arguments and lead to more thought; after all, if someone asks you a concrete question, you are likely to answer it mentally. Thus, if Senator Hornblower's speech is full of weak and specious arguments, it's probably not in his interest to pose a rhetorical question. After all, when you start actually thinking about it, you may decide that you're *not* better off now. On the other hand, if Hornblower's speech is convincing and factually correct, asking the rhetorical question may enhance persuasion. This hypothesis has been supported in empirical research (Petty, Cacioppo, & Heesacker, 1981). Again, notice that the focus of cognitive response theory is on how variables stimulate or inhibit the generation of arguments and counterarguments; that is, the focus is on our cognitive responses to persuasion.

Inoculation: Making People More Resistant to Persuasion

An early study on strategies to make subjects more resistant to persuasion yielded results that fit in nicely with the cognitive response perspective. In this research, McGuire and Papageorgis (1961) attacked subjects' cultural truisms—for example, "you should brush your teeth after every meal" and "mental illness is not contagious." They chose to attack such beliefs because most of us don't think very critically about them and don't have a lot of information with which to defend them.

Before attacking subjects' beliefs, McGuire and Papageorgis exposed subjects to two experimental treatments designed to make them more resistant to persuasion. Some subjects heard a "supportive defense" (that is, arguments in favor of the truisms), whereas other subjects heard an "inoculation defense" (arguments both attacking the truisms and refuting these attacks). Control subjects heard no such arguments at all.

Two days later, subjects heard messages that strongly attacked the truisms. Which subjects turned out to be most resistant to this attack? The "inoculation defense" was clearly superior to the "supportive defense." In fact, the "supportive defense" seemed only marginally better than no preparation at all. Some of the results of this study are presented in the accompanying figure.

To better understand its implications, let's apply this study to a more realistic situation. Imagine that while overseas in the service, you are captured by anti-American terrorists who attempt to indoctrinate you about the "evils of U.S.

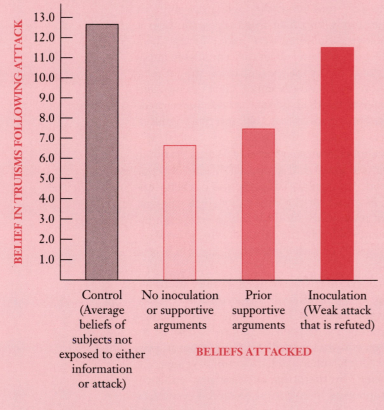

Results of the study by McGuire and Papageorgis (1961). The graph shows the subjects' agreement with the truisms (higher numbers indicate greater agreement). Note that inoculated subjects maintained beliefs almost as strongly as control subjects, who were not exposed to any attacks.

SOURCE: Data from McGuire and Papageorgis (1961).

imperialism." The McGuire and Papageorgis study suggests that you will be *more resistant* to indoctrination if you have previously been exposed to attacks on the American system. If you have lived in a "protected" environment in which you've heard only pro-American positions, you may be more vulnerable to indoctrination.

McGuire (1964) draws an analogy between "inoculation" against persuasive messages and biological inoculation. Just as a person who has not been exposed to certain viruses may not develop antibodies

against them, so a person who has not been exposed to attacks against his or her beliefs may not be able to defend against those attacks.

Consistent with cognitive response theory, McGuire's analysis focuses on the active thought processes that people use when exposed to persuasive messages. Indeed, McGuire (1964) conducted additional research investigating whether belief "inoculation" works better when people *actively* refute the attack on their beliefs or when they *passively* read a refutation prepared for them. Appar-

ently, "passive inoculation" works better if subjects' beliefs are attacked very soon thereafter, whereas "active inoculation" works better when beliefs are attacked sometime later (for example, after a week). The fact that "active inoculation" works better over the long run suggests that people actively think about and generate new arguments over time, and provides additional evidence that persuasion is mediated by an ongoing cognitive process.

Attitudes as Schemas

Attitudes have much in common with schemas (see Chapters 5 and 7), for attitudes are complex knowledge structures used to comprehend and process new information. According to Tesser (1978), our attitudes are not fixed "mental ratings" but are instead more flexible judgments that depend on how and to what extent we process information in our schemas.

For example, what is your attitude toward the "presidency of the United States?" Clearly, most of us possess a fairly complex schema (knowledge structure) about the presidency. If I prime you by mentioning Washington and Lincoln, thus activating components of your schema related to "integrity" and "insightful leadership," your attitude is likely to be favorable. But if I mention Nixon's "Watergate Scandal," Carter's botched rescue mission during the Iranian hostage crisis, and Reagan's "Iran-Contra Affair," then the "corruption" and "incompetence" components of your schema are probably activated. Because your schema about the presidency contains both positive and negative information, one way to "change" your attitude might be to induce you to selectively process the information you have.

You undoubtedly have much more complex, elaborate schemas in some attitude domains than in others. Tesser (1978; Tesser & Leone, 1977) suggests that the mere processing of a highly developed schema often leads to attitude change! If you indeed have a lot of negative information stored in your schema for the presidency, then the more I induce you to think about the presidency, the more polarized and negative will be your attitude.

Evidence for just such an effect was provided by a study by Tesser and Leone (1977), who asked male and female subjects their attitudes on two very different topics: football and fashions. Some subjects were encouraged to think about their

SUMMARY TABLE 8.1   Three Approaches to Understanding Attitude Change

*What are the principal approaches social psychologists have taken
in trying to understand the process of attitude change?*

APPROACH	FOCUS	VARIABLES EMPHASIZED
Analysis of persuasion as a process of communication and learning (the Yale tradition)	How variables in the communication process affect message learning, retention, and persuasion.	Communicator, message, channel, and audience/target variables.
Dissonance theory	Inconsistency of beliefs as a factor that motivates belief and attitude change. (In practice, experiments create inconsistency between behavior and beliefs/attitudes.)	Internal arousal; factors that determine when dissonance does and does not occur, such as degree of external justification for counterattitudinal behavior, choice, irrevocability, and consequences of counterattitudinal behavior; strength and importance of attitudes that are inconsistent with behavior.
Cognitive response analysis	Thought processes involved in responding to persuasive messages; internal arguing and counterarguing.	Factors that increase message-relevant thought (such as high message relevance, high need for cognition) or that decrease such thought (low relevance, low need for cognition).

*The three approaches described here are complementary rather than contradictory; for
example, a cognitive response analysis can help explain* why *communication variables
have the effects they do.*

attitudes (that is, to process information in their schemas), whereas others were distracted from thinking. Tesser and Leone assumed that males had much richer schemas about football and that women had much richer schemas about fashion. Thus, encouraging thought should make men's attitudes toward football more extreme and women's attitudes toward fashion more extreme. These hypotheses were indeed supported by the study's results.

This study also makes an interesting point that extends beyond the specific attitudes studied: Attitude change sometimes results from active and complex processing of "old" information. The cognitive response and information processing approaches to attitude change will undoubtedly continue to be a major topic of research in the years to come. Summary Table 8.1 briefly describes the cognitive response approach to attitude change and compares it with the two other approaches discussed earlier in this chapter: the communication model of persuasion and dissonance theory.

> . . . For this present,
> I would not . . .
> Be any further moved. What you have said
> I will consider; what you have to say
> I will with patience hear. . . .
>
> —— *Julius Caesar*, Act I, Sc. II

Despite their diversity, most of the studies and theoretical approaches presented in this chapter can be classified under one of two main "routes to persuasion" (Petty & Cacioppo, 1981, 1986). The "central route" is followed when the subject consciously deliberates upon the merit, content, and logic of the information contained in a persuasive message. The "peripheral route" is followed when the subject does not carefully reflect upon the content of the message but instead relies upon simple cues (such as who's delivering the message) to accept or reject the message. The peripheral route is the "lazy" route (see Box 1 in this chapter) that people take when they don't much care about the issue. The central route requires more cognitive work; the recipient must attend to the message, analyze its merit, critique it, counterargue, integrate information, and so on. Before he or she will engage in all this work, the recipient must care about the attitude topic.

According to Petty and Cacioppo's (1981, 1986) *elaboration likelihood model*, persuasion critically depends on the degree to which people elaborate (that is, actively, cognitively process) the contents of a persuasive message. The central route to persuasion entails active cognitive elaboration; the peripheral route does not.

We have already surveyed research that illustrates both the central and peripheral routes to persuasion. For example, logical inference theories of attitude formation and change (surveyed in Chapter 7) and cognitive response theory (just described) tend to focus on the thought processes that occur during attitude formation and persuasion, and thus these theories represent the central route to persuasion. Conditioning approaches to attitude formation and change (see Chapter 7) and some of the Yale research (for example, work on speaker credibility) focus more on peripheral cues. Dissonance research, which studies what happens when people consider inconsistencies in their beliefs, represents a kind of central route to persuasion, whereas self-perception theory, by focusing on how people sometimes examine situational cues to infer weak or ambiguous attitudes, represents a more "peripheral" process.

It does not necessarily follow that because a person uses the central route to persuasion, that person's attitude after persuasion is logical and reasonable; rather, it simply means that the person processes information as best he or she can based on the message's arguments and his or her preexisting beliefs and attitudes. Irrational beliefs and attitudes can result from both central and peripheral persuasion, but only central persuasion involves careful thought and deliberation.

The distinction between the central and peripheral routes to persuasion has a number of important implications. First, research suggests that the central route to persuasion leads to more lasting attitudes and attitude changes than does the peripheral route (Chaiken, 1980, 1987; Cialdini, Levy, Herman, Kozlowski, & Petty, 1976; Petty & Cacioppo, 1986). This proposition seems reasonable because "central" attitude change is "hard-won," resulting as it does from considerable thought, and it is thus more likely to be remembered. "Peripheral" persuasion, on the other hand, is based on transient and rather unimportant cues (such as how good you were feeling at the time of persuasion or how attractive the speaker was), and the effects of such cues are likely to wane quickly unless the cues recur.

In Chapter 7 we discussed research on the relation between attitudes and behavior. Such research indicates that attitudes changed or formed via the central route predict behavior better than do attitudes changed or formed via the peripheral route (Pallak, Murroni, & Koch, 1983; Petty, Cacioppo, & Schumann, 1983). This finding may be true for a number of reasons. When you consciously think about and attend to your attitudes, they predict your behavior better than when you do not (see Chapter 6); because "central" attitudes result from conscious thought and deliberation, they may be more available to self-awareness. Furthermore, such attitudes may be easier to recall because they have more cognitive associations. Finally, attitudes formed via the central route may be easier to reconstruct (because they were based on logical thought processes) and less dependent on variable situational cues. All of these arguments suggest that centrally formed attitudes are more mentally available and salient, which helps to explain why such attitudes predict behavior so well.

The distinction between the central and peripheral routes to persuasion can help us to organize and understand many kinds of research on attitude change (see Summary Table 8.2). As an illustration, consider the effects of two message variables on persuasion: the number of arguments and the quality of arguments in a persuasive message. It seems reasonable that the more arguments a message contains, the more persuasive it will be. However, shouldn't persuasiveness also depend on the quality of the arguments? Do ten unconvincing arguments necessarily persuade more than five unconvincing arguments?

If a research subject is following the peripheral route to persuasion and is not carefully attending to the logic of the message's arguments, subjects may indeed be more persuaded by ten bad arguments. That is, if they rely on superficial cues, then the more arguments there are, the more they may be persuaded. If the subjects are following the central route to persuasion and are therefore thinking about the arguments, they will not be taken in by their sheer quantity.

How can we induce a subject to follow the central route in a study? One way is to make the persuasive message highly relevant to the subject. For example, Petty and Cacioppo (1984) asked college students to read an essay supposedly written by the chair of their university's Committee on Academic Policy that recommended that all students be required to pass a difficult comprehensive exam before graduating. (Wouldn't this message catch your attention?) To make this essay highly relevant to some subjects, they were informed that the comprehensive exam, if adopted, would be implemented in the coming year. Subjects in a second, low-relevance condition were informed that the exam would not be implemented for ten years.

In addition to manipulating the relevance of the message, this study also varied the number of arguments in the essay (3 vs. 9) and the quality of these arguments (weak vs. strong). When subjects didn't find the message very relevant—and thus presumably followed the "lazy" peripheral route—they were more persuaded by more arguments, regardless of their quality (see Figure 8.16a). But when subjects found the message highly relevant—and thus followed the central route to persuasion—they were most persuaded by many strong arguments and least persuaded by many weak arguments (Figure 8.16b).

SUMMARY TABLE 8.2 Peripheral Versus Central Routes to Persuasion and Attitude Change

How do the two main routes to persuasion differ?

DESCRIPTION	ASSOCIATED CONCEPTS AND PROCESSES	IMPLICATIONS FOR ATTITUDES AND BEHAVIOR
Peripheral route: Subject relies on superficial cues rather than on actively processing arguments in persuasive message.	Conditioning of attitudes Effect of such communicator variables as credibility and attractiveness Effect of such superficial message characteristics as number of arguments (versus quality of arguments) Self-perception theory (inferring attitudes from behavior)	Attitudes are weaker and less enduring. Attitudes are less likely to predict behavior.
Central route: Subject actively reflects on message content.	Cognitive responses to persuasion Dissonance theory Logical inference theories of attitude formation Effects of message logic and quality of arguments (as opposed to such superficial cues as number of arguments)	Attitudes are stronger and more enduring. Attitudes are more likely to predict behavior.

The distinction between central and peripheral routes to persuasion provides a useful way to conceptualize the many studies that have been conducted on attitude change and persuasion.

The distinction between central and peripheral routes to persuasion undoubtedly will continue to generate new research on the nature of attitude change. You may be tempted at this point to conclude that the central route to persuasion is the truly important one because it results in thoughtful, lasting attitudes that are related to behavior. However, both central and peripheral persuasion play an important role in everyday life. Commercial advertising and sales make heavy use of peripheral cues in persuasion. Even in such socially important and thoughtful settings as the courtroom, jurors may at times yield to peripheral cues (such as the appearance of the defendant or the sheer amount of evidence), rather than following the central route of careful, logical analysis of the evidence. Clearly, a complete understanding of attitude change in real life requires research on both the central and peripheral routes to persuasion.

FIGURE 8.16   **Effects of number and quality of arguments on persuasion
as a function of receiver's involvement in message.**

---

*How does the relevance of a persuasive message affect the
impact of the number and quality of arguments?*

Petty and Cacioppo (1984) varied both subjects' involvement in a persuasive
message and the number and quality of arguments presented.

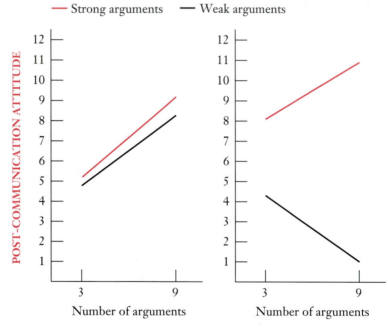

A. LOW INVOLVEMENT   B. HIGH INVOLVEMENT

While the quality of arguments had little effect on persuasion for low-
involvement subjects, high-involvement subjects were far more persuaded
by strong arguments than by weak ones. Indeed, for these subjects,
increasing the number of weak arguments actually reduced persuasion.

SOURCE: Based on Petty and Cacioppo (1984). Used with permission of John
Cacioppo.

---

*This study showed that when the persuasive message was not relevant, subjects followed
the peripheral route to persuasion and were influenced by superficial cues. But when the
message was relevant, subjects followed the central route and thought more carefully
about the quality of arguments.*

Summary

1. The Yale research subscribed to a communication and learning model of persuasion and studied the effects of communicator, message, channel, and audience variables.

2. Highly credible communicators persuade more than noncredible communicators, but this effect fades quickly over time. The sleeper effect occurs when a persuasive message delivered by a low-credibility communicator is more persuasive after time passes.

3. Fear appeals can lead to attitude change if they successfully create fear and include clear recommendations about how recipients can avoid fearful outcomes.

4. A one-sided message is more persuasive to people who already agree with the message, whereas a two-sided message is more persuasive to people who already disagree with the message. A two-sided message leads recipients to resist subsequent "counterpropaganda" better than does a one-sided message.

5. Message repetition can enhance persuasion, in part because of the mere exposure effect, which occurs when people show increased liking for frequently occurring stimuli. Message repetition may also lead recipients to better comprehend and remember persuasive arguments.

6. Face-to-face persuasion is often more effective than media persuasion; however, the mass media can reach a much larger audience. Print media encourage more thoughtful processing of persuasive arguments, whereas audio and visual media shift attention from message content to such speaker attributes as attractiveness and likability.

7. Audience variables such as personality and intelligence have complex effects on persuasion because they may differentially affect comprehension and yielding. Individuals with a high need for cognition are more influenced by message logic and quality than are people with a low need for cognition.

8. Festinger's theory of cognitive dissonance postulates that when people hold logically inconsistent beliefs, they experience a negative state of arousal, called dissonance, which can motivate belief and attitude change.

9. Research on insufficient justification shows that people who behave in attitude-discrepant ways for small incentives are more likely to shift their attitudes to be consistent with their behavior than are people who behave in attitude-discrepant ways for large incentives.

10. In the "forbidden toy" study, children who received a mild threat not to play with a toy were more likely to derogate the toy than were children who received a severe threat. Research on severity of initiation shows that people come to like groups or activities for which they must suffer. Research on derogation of the victim shows that people who harm others for little justification often derogate their victims. All of these findings are consistent with dissonance theory.

11. Counterattitudinal behavior leads to dissonance, particularly when such behavior is freely chosen, firmly committed, irrevocable, and of consequence in real life.

12. Self-perception theory attributes the attitude shift that occurs in dissonance studies to a logical, inferential process, not to a state of arousal.

13. The direct manipulation of arousal (through drugs) or the misattribution of arousal in dissonance experiments affects attitude change. This evidence supports the central assumption of dissonance theory — that arousal plays a role in such attitude change.

14. Self-perception processes are most likely to occur when people engage in mildly attitude-discrepant behavior and when relevant attitudes are weak. Dissonance is most likely to occur when people engage in highly attitude-discrepant behavior and when relevant attitudes are strong.

15. People who are forewarned that they will receive a persuasive message tend to argue mentally against it and thus tend to be less persuaded than are people who are not forewarned.

16. Weakly attacking beliefs can make them more resistant to subsequent stronger attacks.

17. Rhetorical questions stimulate active thought and thus increase persuasion when arguments are convincing, but they decrease persuasion when arguments are not convincing.

18. Attitudes can be viewed as schemas comprising complex information. Actively thinking about an attitude domain can lead to attitude change, particularly if the schema contains predominantly negative or predominantly positive information.

19. The elaboration likelihood model argues that persuasion depends on the degree to which people actively process the contents of a persuasive message. The central route to persuasion is followed when individuals deliberate on the merit and logic of persuasive arguments. The peripheral route is followed when individuals rely upon such superficial cues as speaker characteristics. Both routes are significant in everyday persuasion.

Audience variables: Characteristics of the audience or target of persuasion; examples include intelligence and personality traits

Central route to persuasion: The route followed when subjects consciously deliberate upon the merit, content, and logic of information in a persuasive message

Channel variables: The medium through which a persuasive message is delivered; examples are face-to-face communication, print media, radio, and television

Cognitive dissonance: A negative drive state (an unpleasant state of arousal) that occurs when people hold logically inconsistent beliefs; according to Festinger's theory, dissonance can motivate attitude and belief changes

Cognitive responses: Internal, self-generated arguments for or against a persuasive message

Communicator variables: Characteristics of the person delivering a persuasive message; examples are speaker credibility and attractiveness

Elaboration likelihood model: Petty and Cacioppo's model that holds that persuasion depends on the degree to which people actively cognitively process the contents of a persuasive message

Inoculation: Increasing subjects' resistance to strong persuasive messages by exposing relevant beliefs to earlier weak attacks

Mere exposure effect: The tendency to like stimuli more the more frequently we are exposed to them

Message variables: Characteristics of the content of a persuasive message; examples are the presence or absence of fear appeals and the use of one-sided or two-sided arguments

Peripheral route to persuasion: The route followed when subjects do not carefully reflect on the content of a persuasive message but rather attend to superficial cues, such as speaker credibility or the number of arguments presented

Self-perception theory: When attitudes are weak or ambiguous, people infer their attitudes from their behavior and the setting; self-perception theory serves as an alternate explanation for the findings of dissonance experiments

Sleeper effect: The delayed effectiveness of a persuasive message that is accompanied by a discounting cue (such as low speaker credibility)

He does not see her, because for him there is nothing to see. How can a fifty-two-year-old white immigrant storekeeper . . . *see* a little black girl. Nothing in his life even suggested that the feat was possible, not to say desirable or necessary.

"Yeah?"

She looks up at him and sees the vacuum where curiosity ought to lodge. And something more. The total absence of human recognition — the glazed separateness. She does not know what keeps his glance suspended. Perhaps because he is grown, or a man, and she a little girl. But she has seen interest, disgust, even anger in grown male eyes. Yet this vacuum is not new to her. It has an edge; somewhere in the bottom lid is the distaste. She has seen it lurking in the eyes of all white people. So. The distaste must be for her, her blackness. All things in her are flux and anticipation. But her blackness is static and dread. And it is the blackness that accounts for, that creates, the vacuum edged with distaste in white eyes.

—— from *The Bluest Eye*, by Toni Morrison, p. 42

CHAPTER 9

Prejudice

*T*oni Morrison's haunting novel, *The Bluest Eye*, begins in 1941, in Lorain, Ohio. The central character is Pecola Breedlove, a poor, homely, 11-year-old black girl. Abused by her father, ignored by her mother, and taunted by other children, Pecola is the recipient of an intolerable dose of prejudice. Withdrawing in the face of so much hostility, she dreams of someday having blue eyes. Then, she reasons, things will be better; people will not hate her so.

Perhaps by coincidence, the year that Toni Morrison chose to start the sad tale of Pecola Breedlove also marked the beginning of the Nazis' "final solution" in Europe, in which six million innocent men, women, and children were systematically exterminated simply because they were Jewish. The virulent prejudice that flared in Germany before and during World War II contributed to one of the most horrifying episodes in the twentieth century. But as Morrison's novel reminds us, prejudice has never been limited to just one time or place. In all eras and in all countries it has reared its ugly head and disturbed the peaceful conduct of human affairs.

Precisely for this reason, it is essential to understand prejudice. In his classic social psychological analysis, *The Nature of Prejudice*, Gordon Allport (1954) noted that "it required years of labor and billions of dollars to gain the secret of the atom. It will take a still greater investment to gain the secrets of man's irrational nature. It is easier, someone has said, to smash an atom than a prejudice." Despite the difficulty of the task, social psychologists have striven to understand the nature of prejudice and have worked to reduce its destructive consequences. Social psychological research has addressed some fundamental questions about prejudice: What is its nature? How can it be measured? What are its causes? And how can it be reduced?

In the early 1960s black citizens in the U.S. could not eat in some "white only" restaurants. How much do you think prejudice and discrimination have declined since then?

What Is Prejudice?

A *prejudice* is a negative prejudgment that is often unwarranted and is based on limited, insufficient evidence. As used by social psychologists, prejudice usually refers to one person's prejudgment that is based on another person's membership in a social group. Thus we may hold prejudices about WASPs, blacks, women, Jews, Puerto Ricans, actors, disabled people, professors, or football players.

A prejudice is an *attitude*—an evaluative response directed at some object (see Chapter 7). It is often an overgeneralized attitude that we inflexibly apply to a group or to individual members of a group. Like most attitudes, a prejudice can be considered to have affective, cognitive, and behavioral components (Bagozzi, 1978; Hilgard, 1980).

As noted in Chapter 7, the concept of attitude has often been most centrally defined in terms of its *affective*, or emotional, component. Prejudice is clearly characterized by a host of negative feelings. In the excerpt that begins this chapter, Toni Morrison describes how the white storekeeper regarded Pecola with "distaste." Prejudice often includes stronger emotions as well, including disgust, repulsion, fear, and hatred.

The cognitive component of prejudice embraces the *beliefs* or *stereotypes* we hold about the objects of prejudice. Many people's attitudes toward women, for example, are not just evaluative; they also include beliefs about women—that women are "passive," "emotional," "nurturing," "good cooks," and "bad drivers" (see Chapter 10 for a more complete discussion of stereotypes about women and men). Often, the cognitive component of a prejudiced attitude is richly elaborated and complex. In fact, prejudiced attitudes may have much in common with cognitive *schemas*; that is, they are organized mental categories comprising information about various social objects (Ashmore & Del Boca, 1981; see Chapter 5). Later in this chapter we'll describe the nature and measurement of prejudiced beliefs and stereotypes in much greater detail.

The third component of a prejudiced attitude is behavioral. The term *discrimination* refers to overt acts that treat members of certain groups unfairly. Discriminatory behavior can be as subtle as certain nonverbal behaviors (for example, standing apart, not smiling) or as blatant as unfair housing practices and preferential hiring in business and industry. Prejudiced people often express their negative attitudes through segregation — physical separation from out-group members. The United States legally maintained the unfair doctrine of "separate but equal" until the 1950s. South Africa still enforces apartheid, the institutionalized and legally sanctioned separation of the races.

The most extreme action against the targets of prejudice is physical harm. Allport (1954) described how hostile statements progressed to genocide in one of the most brutal expressions of prejudice in history: Hitler's propaganda "led Germans to avoid their Jewish neighbors and erstwhile friends. This preparation made it easier to enact the Nürnberg laws of discrimination which, in turn, made the subsequent burning of synagogues and street attacks upon Jews seem natural. The final step in the macabre progression was the ovens at Auschwitz" (p. 15).

Analyzing Prejudice

This chapter will bring together ideas that we've examined in previous chapters — social perception and cognition, attribution, attitudes, and attitude change — and will apply them to the serious, real-life issue of prejudice. In addition to drawing upon previous material, we'll explore new ideas and findings as well.

Prejudice can be analyzed in terms of historical causes, sociocultural factors, the social situation, personality, the phenomenology of prejudiced individuals, and the stimulus object (see Figure 9.1). These levels of analysis, formulated by Gordon Allport (1954), begin with broad social causes and progress to more specific individual causes of prejudice. Most of Allport's levels of analysis correspond to explanations of social behavior we discussed in Chapter 1 (again, see Figure 9.1). A concrete example — an analysis of prejudice against blacks in the United States — will make Allport's concepts clearer.

Historical analysis. To understand prejudice against blacks, we first need to understand its historical origins and development. Thus, we might analyze the institution of slavery in the earliest days of colonial America and the differing economies of the North and the South. We might further study the political events leading up to the American Civil War, as well as the Emancipation Proclamation, the Reconstruction period in the postwar South, and the "Jim Crow Laws" that institutionalized various forms of segregation and discrimination.

The 1940s and 1950s marked the beginning of the modern era of race relations in the United States. In the famous 1954 case of *Brown v. the Board of Education*, the U.S. Supreme Court ruled that the "separate but equal" doctrine that had maintained segregation in the public schools since 1896 was no longer tenable. So began the turbulent and as yet unfinished efforts to implement integration in the classroom. (We'll consider the success of these efforts from the vantage point of social psychological research toward the end of this chapter.) The modern civil rights movement in the United States achieved a major legislative success in 1964 with the passage of

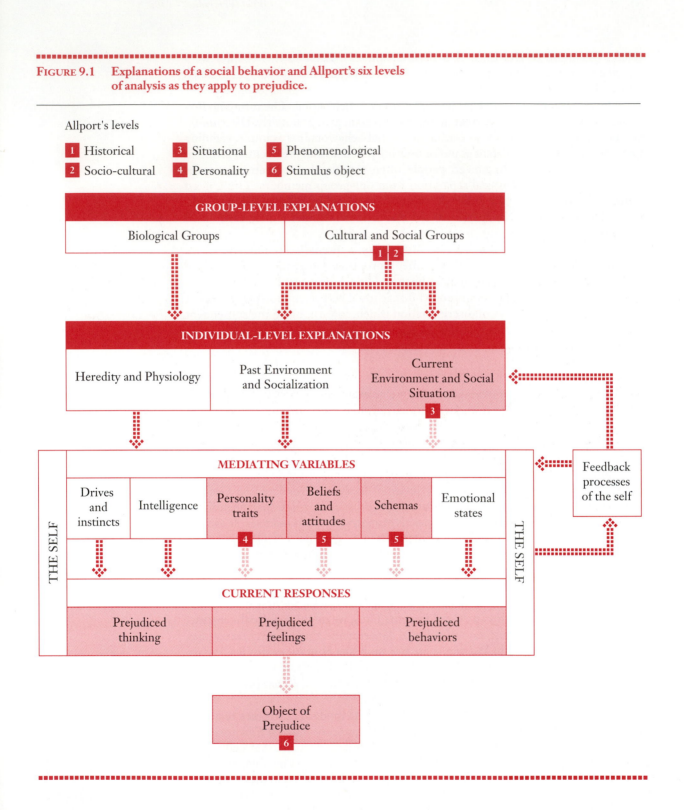

FIGURE 9.1   Explanations of a social behavior and Allport's six levels
of analysis as they apply to prejudice.

Allport's levels

1 Historical   3 Situational   5 Phenomenological
2 Socio-cultural   4 Personality   6 Stimulus object

GROUP-LEVEL EXPLANATIONS

Biological Groups   Cultural and Social Groups
                                          1 2

INDIVIDUAL-LEVEL EXPLANATIONS

Heredity and Physiology | Past Environment and Socialization | Current Environment and Social Situation
                                                              3

THE SELF

MEDIATING VARIABLES

Drives and instincts | Intelligence | Personality traits | Beliefs and attitudes | Schemas | Emotional states
                                      4   5   5

Feedback processes of the self

CURRENT RESPONSES

Prejudiced thinking | Prejudiced feelings | Prejudiced behaviors

THE SELF

Object of Prejudice
6

THE CHINESE QUESTION.—[SEE PAGE 147.]

COLUMBIA.—"HANDS OFF, GENTLEMEN!   AMERICA MEANS FAIR PLAY FOR ALL MEN."

Gordon Allport (1954) noted that throughout U.S. history, blacks, Jews, and Roman Catholics have been the targets of substantial prejudice. However, as these illustrations show, many other groups have been the targets of prejudice as well.

AT BAY: AN INCIDENT OF THE FREIGHT-HANDLERS' STRIKE—
ITALIAN LABORERS ASSAILED BY HOODLUMS.
FROM A SKETCH BY A STAFF ARTIST.—SEE PAGE 375.

the Civil Rights Act banning discrimination based on color, religion, national origin, race, and sex. (See Jones, 1972, for a more complete historical account of prejudice against blacks in the United States.)

Sociocultural factors.   The historical approach tends to study specific instances of prejudice in specific historical periods. In contrast, the sociocultural approach (the second level in Figure 9.1) focuses on more general sociological concepts, such as urbanization, class mobility, and population shifts and density. In the United States, prejudice has often been directed against immigrant urban populations by higher-class, less urban, and more established residents. As blacks and other minorities flocked to America's big cities in the early twentieth century, providing cheap labor to fuel the economy, they often became the targets of cruel stereotypes and prejudice.

The social situation.   Both the historical and sociocultural approaches focus on "group-level explanations"—broad social forces that lead to prejudice. Allport's third level of analysis enters the realm of social psychology by focusing on the individual's immediate social situation as a cause of prejudice. For example, prejudice and discrimination against blacks in the old South was for many simply a matter of *conforming* to group norms and behavior (Pettigrew, 1958, 1980). If you grow up in a bigoted family and society, you are likely to adopt their bigotry through standard processes of social learning and influence. Social psychology has focused considerable attention on the situational level of analysis, and we'll examine research on situational influences on prejudice throughout this chapter.

Personality and prejudice.   Personality analysis, the fourth level in Allport's diagram, focuses on the traits and "character" of the individual as a cause of prejudice. Notable research on the *authoritarian personality* (Adorno, Frenkel-Brunswick, Levinson, & Sanford, 1950), which we'll discuss in greater detail later, suggests that some people may be prejudiced because they were reared by punitive, status-anxious parents and as a result developed defensive, prejudiced personalities. Some Freudian psychologists have argued that prejudiced people often project onto minority group members traits that are problematic in themselves (Ackerman & Johoda, 1950; Bettelheim & Janowitz, 1950). Thus, a white person possessing considerable repressed aggression might consider blacks to be "violent."

The phenomenology of prejudice.   In studying prejudice we must understand the phenomenology of prejudiced individuals—that is, their thought processes and points of view. Put another way, we must study how the prejudiced person "sees the world." Much modern social psychological research, particularly research on stereotypes, is aimed at documenting and accounting for the phenomenology of prejudice. In one of the first studies to measure stereotypes, Katz and Braly (1933) found that a majority of 100 Princeton students believed blacks to be "superstitious" and "lazy." The study of stereotypes often documents what people *believe* to be true of other groups, even though the evidence for these beliefs is weak or lacking. Social psychologists study how stereotypes are formed and sustained, sometimes in the face of nonexistent or contradictory evidence.

The stimulus object.   At Allport's final level of analysis is the "stimulus object." Prejudices and intergroup hostilities may be based at times on real characteristics of the target group; this idea has sometimes been called the "earned reputation theory."

Typically, social psychologists have not been interested in documenting actual group differences. (One interesting exception, discussed in Chapter 10, is research on sex differences.) Although differences among groups exist, we shall see that prejudices and stereotyped beliefs about group differences are typically more abundant and more extreme than the objective evidence can support. As we'll see later in this chapter, people may sometimes form stereotypes based on no supporting evidence, simply as a result of normal thought processes.

The levels of explanation shown in Figure 9.1 are helpful in organizing social psychological research on prejudice. We'll begin our examination of prejudice with a description of the phenomenology of prejudice: What is the nature of stereotypes and prejudiced beliefs? How are they best measured? And what are their consequences in everyday social life? Then we'll turn to the social causes of prejudice: in socialization (child-rearing practices), in social ideologies (for example, political and religious beliefs), in group membership, and in intergroup competition. Finally, we'll consider ways of reducing prejudice.

. . . his mother did not like him to play with niggers. She had explained to him the difference between colored people and niggers. They were easily identifiable. Colored people were neat and quiet; niggers were dirty and loud. He belonged to the former group: he wore white shirts and blue trousers; his hair was cut as close to his scalp as possible to avoid any suggestion of wool, the part was etched into his hair by the barber. In winter his mother put Jergens Lotion on his face to keep the skin from becoming ashen. Even though he was light-skinned, it was possible to ash. The line between colored and nigger was not always clear; subtle and telltale signs threatened to erode it, and the watch had to be constant.

—— *The Bluest Eye*, p. 71

The term *stereotype* was first used in its modern sense by the journalist Walter Lippman (1922). Rather than deal with the complexity of the real world around us, Lippman argued, we create cognitive simplifications—stereotypes—to guide how we perceive people around us and how we process social information.

Measuring Stereotypes

The first attempts to measure stereotypes quantitatively were relatively simple. A classic study by Katz and Braly (1933) set the tone and methodology for much of the subsequent research on stereotypes. In this study, 100 Princeton undergraduates indicated which of 84 traits they felt were "typical" of various groups, including Americans, Japanese, Jews, British, Negroes, and Turks. Most subjects agreed that just a few traits characterized each group; for instance, a majority of subjects' selections for Negroes were accounted for by only five traits, whereas a majority of subjects' selections for Jews were accounted for by only six traits (see Figure 9.2). It is important to note that Katz and Braly assessed stereotypes held by *groups* of people rather than by individuals; certainly, an individual's stereotypes might differ from the consensus of a larger group.

Stereotypes as probabilistic beliefs.

Katz and Braly's method of measuring stereotypes forced subjects to indicate whether all members of a group either possessed or did not possess a given trait. More recently, however, college-student subjects have at times objected to such an all-or-none approach, and they state that they don't subscribe to the notion that all people in a certain group possess given traits (Karlins, Coffman, & Walters, 1969). Although you might believe, for example, that on average women are more "emotional" than men, you probably wouldn't agree that all women are emotional or that all men are unemotional.

Rather than asking subjects whether or not a group possesses a given trait, Brigham (1971) proposed that social psychologists ask subjects *what percentage* of a given group possesses the trait. Thus, to assess your stereotypes about women, I might ask you to check what percentage of women you think are "emotional." But even this strategy has flaws. If you think that 75 percent of all women are "emotional," does this mean you hold strong stereotypes about women? We can't be sure until we know how "emotional" you think people generally are. If you think 75 percent of all people are emotional, then clearly your view of women is no different from your view of anyone else.

··

FIGURE 9.2   Stereotypes about three groups.

──

How did Katz and Braly (1933) measure stereotypes?

──

This table shows the percentages of 100 Princeton students who agreed that Americans, Jews, and Negroes typically show various traits. Note: The traits listed are those that the students believed to be most associated with each group.

GROUP	TRAIT	SUBJECTS ASSOCIATING TRAIT WITH GROUP (%)
Americans	Industrious	48
	Intelligent	47
	Materialistic	33
	Ambitious	33
	Progressive	27
Jews	Shrewd	79
	Mercenary	49
	Industrious	48
	Grasping	34
	Intelligent	29
Negroes	Superstitious	84
	Lazy	75
	Happy-go-lucky	38
	Ignorant	38
	Musical	26

SOURCE: Data from Katz and Braly (1933).

──

Note that Katz and Braly's subjects showed fairly high, but not perfect, consensus about the traits possessed by the three groups. The Katz and Braly technique characterizes a group's, rather than an individual's, stereotypes.

··

The diagnostic ratio approach.   McCauley and Stitt (1978; McCauley, Stitt, & Segal, 1980) offer a remedy to the measurement of stereotypes that is probably the most satisfactory to date. They suggest that besides asking what percentage of a group possesses a given trait, social psychologists must also ask subjects what percentage of *people in general* possess the trait. From these numbers researchers can then compute the *diagnostic ratio* for a given subject by dividing the subject's estimate for the target group by his or her estimate of the percentage of people in general who possess the same trait.

For example, if you think that 75 percent of women are emotional but only 50 percent of people in general are emotional, then your diagnostic ratio for this trait would be $75/50 = 1.5$. If the diagnostic ratio is greater than 1, then the subject believes that the target group possesses the trait to a greater extent than do people

---

FIGURE 9.3   Junior college students' judgments of the percentages of Germans possessing various traits, with computed diagnostic ratios.

How are diagnostic ratios used to measure stereotypes?

McCauley and Stitt (1978) asked students to estimate the percentages of Germans and of people in general who possess various traits. The diagnostic ratio, which indicates how differently Germans are perceived from people in general, is the ratio of the two percentage estimates for a given trait.

TRAIT	PERCENTAGE OF PEOPLE IN GENERAL JUDGED TO HAVE TRAIT	PERCENTAGE OF GERMANS JUDGED TO HAVE TRAIT	DIAGNOSTIC RATIO
Efficient	49.8	63.4	1.27
Extremely nationalistic	35.4	56.3	1.59
Ignorant	34.0	29.2	.66
Impulsive	51.7	41.1	.79
Industrious	59.8	68.2	1.14
Pleasure-loving	82.2	72.8	.89
Scientifically minded	32.6	43.1	1.32
Superstitious	42.1	30.4	.72
Tradition-loving	62.4	57.2	.91

SOURCE: Data from McCauley and Stitt (1978).

Notice that according to the raw percentage ratings, the trait that is attributed to the largest percentage of Germans is "pleasure-loving"; but according to the diagnostic ratio measure, the perceived trait that most distinguishes Germans from people in general is "extremely nationalistic."

---

in general. If the diagnostic ratio equals 1, then the subject sees no difference between the target group and people in general on the trait. And if the diagnostic ratio is less than 1, then the subject considers the target group to possess the trait to a lesser extent than do people in general.

The ratings made by 69 junior college students of the percentages of Germans they felt possessed various traits (from McCauley & Stitt, 1978) are listed in Figure 9.3. Also listed are subjects' estimates of the percentages of people in general who possess these traits and the computed diagnostic ratios. Note that diagnostic ratios can yield quite different information from the percentage ratings. If you looked only at the percentage ratings, you would conclude that the two traits most stereotypically associated with Germans are "pleasure-loving" and "industrious." However, the diagnostic ratios indicate that whereas subjects consider the trait "industrious" to be more characteristic of Germans than of people in general (diagnostic ratio = 1.14), they consider the trait "pleasure-loving" to be *less* characteristic of Germans than of people in general (ratio = .89). The high percentage of "pleasure-loving" Germans is misleading because an even higher percentage of people in general are considered to possess this trait.

For those interested in determining the relative truth or falsity of social stereotypes, diagnostic ratio measures permit a quantitative comparison to normative data.

How Are Stereotypes Wrong?

Social psychologists have long speculated that stereotypes lead to a number of errors in social perception (Allport, 1954; Campbell, 1967). Stereotypes unjustly portray out-groups more negatively than they portray in-groups, exaggerate group differences, and lead people to underestimate (and even ignore) the variability of people within other groups. And stereotypes are often simply factually wrong.

It is important to note that Mc-Cauley and Stitt's (1978) study on the accuracy of stereotypes about blacks focused on characteristics that can be objectively verified. Most studies that assess stereotypes focus on personality and character traits, and it is difficult if not impossible to formulate objective criteria for "superstitiousness" or "cunning" or "materialism." To make such trait attributions even more ambiguous, the same behavior that is viewed positively in the preferred in-group may be viewed negatively in a disliked out-group (Peabody, 1968): "We're thrifty and intelligent, but they're stingy and cunning."

Research supports the hypothesis that stereotypes about out-groups are often more negative than those about in-groups. In Katz and Braly's (1933) classic study, the traits used to characterize various groups were also rated on desirability (see the accompanying table). The traits attributed to Americans were generally positive, whereas those attributed to out-groups (Jews, Chinese, Italians, Negroes, and Turks) were more often undesirable. Ethnocentrism — the belief that one's own group is superior to other groups — is frequently embodied in stereotypes.

Some studies have documented the inaccuracies of specific stereotypes. More than 50 years ago, LaPiere (1936) gathered evidence to test the accuracy of prevailing stereotypes in Fresno County, California, that Armenians were "dishonest" and "deceitful." Objective data showed just the opposite: Armenians tended to have good credit ratings and appeared less frequently in court cases involving unfair business practices than non-Armenians. Sometimes the inaccu-

racy of stereotypes is obvious from their logical inconsistencies. Allport (1954) provides the following conversation as an illustration:

Mr. A.: I say the Jews are too much alone; they stick together, and are clannish.

Mr. B.: But look; in our community there are Cohen and Morris on the Community Chest, several Jews in the Rotary Club and Chamber of Commerce. Many support our community projects. . . .

Mr. A.: That's just what I was saying, they're always pushing and elbowing their way into Christian groups. (p. 195)

Recent research documents a more subtle error fostered by stereotypes: They lead us to view in-groups as more complex and varied than out-groups. The perception of out-groups as uniform, homogeneous, and undifferentiated is expressed by the classic prejudiced statement that "they all look the same to me." In Chapter 5 we saw that people typically possess more complex schemas for in-groups than for out-groups (Lin-

---

For example, McCauley and Stitt (1978) asked a heterogeneous group of Philadelphia high school and college students to estimate the percentages of blacks and of Americans in general who possessed certain characteristics, such as were unemployed, were on welfare, had completed high school, and so on. Surprisingly perhaps, students' stereotypes (expressed as diagnostic ratios) were quite accurate when compared to Census Bureau statistics. Thus stereotypes, when adequately measured, may at times reasonably reflect social reality.

The Formation of Stereotypes

How do people acquire the generalized and often inaccurate beliefs that make up stereotypes? Social psychologists have recently gained considerable insight into the cognitive processes that create and sustain beliefs about social groups. Let's examine several cognitive processes that contribute to the development of stereotypes.

ville, 1982), and we noted how this can lead us to evaluate out-group members more extremely than we evaluate in-group members.

It is not surprising that we often possess more complex knowledge of in-groups than of out-groups; after all, we generally interact with the in-group more, and thus we've learned more about it. Surprisingly, though, the perception that in-groups are more complex and varied than out-groups holds even for an "out-group" that we deal with on a daily basis — the "opposite sex." Park and Rothbart (1982) asked male and female college students to rate what percentages of men and women would endorse various statements, some of which were stereotypically feminine (for example, "I would like to care for a small baby as a way to express my love") and some of which were stereotypically masculine ("I often seek out competitive challenges — whether intellectual or athletic"). Interestingly, women rated men as endorsing more uniformly stereotypical masculine statements than did men themselves, and men

rated women as endorsing more stereotypically feminine statements than did women themselves. In other words, members of each group viewed the other group as more homogeneous and stereotypical than they viewed their own group.

Furthermore, Park and Rothbart's data imply that this illusion of homogeneity in the out-group did *not* result because subjects were trying to make their own group look good at the expense of the other group. Regardless of whether the stereotypical statements were positive or negative, subjects tended to view the out-group more stereotypically. These results are particularly interesting because men and women typically have a great deal of contact with members of the other gender. If the illusion of homogeneity exists in the stereotypes we possess of out-groups we know well and interact with daily, then how much stronger must it be for out-groups with which we don't interact?

The ethnocentrism of stereotypes. Katz and Braly (1933) computed the mean desirability of each of the traits that 100 Princeton students ascribed to ten nationalities or groups. (Desirability ratings were made on a scale from 1 to 10, with higher ratings indicating greater desirability.)

Nationality of Group	Mean Desirability of Traits
Americans	6.77
English	6.26
Germans	6.02
Japanese	5.89
Irish	5.42
Jews	4.96
Chinese	4.52
Italians	4.40
Negroes	3.55
Turks	3.05

SOURCE: Data from Katz and Braly (1933).

Sampling errors and stereotypes.   The human mind strives to categorize the world, to make it more predictable and controllable. Gordon Allport (1954) was one of the first of many social psychologists to note that stereotyping is closely related to other kinds of categorization. If you believe that dogs bite strangers, you will know not to approach strange dogs. Similarly, if you believe that certain groups of people are dishonest, then you will not do business with them. But how do we form these generalizations in the first place? As noted in Chapter 5, we often reach conclusions about various groups based on only a sample of the data available to us. Unfortunately our samples are often biased.

Rothbart (1981) compiled a number of sampling biases that may lead people to develop stereotyped beliefs. To understand these biases, let's use Rothbart's illustration — the common (and certainly false) stereotype that women are "bad drivers." How might you develop such a stereotype in the first place? Unless you simply learn

FIGURE 9.4   **An illustration of sampling bias.**

How might sampling biases contribute to the formation of stereotypes?

The table shows a hypothetical sample of observed good and bad drivers of both genders. The proportion of bad drivers is the same for both genders, but because we tend to notice bad drivers more than good drivers, we may mistakenly conclude that women are poorer drivers then men. Our error lies in sampling data on "bad drivers" only and ignoring data on "good drivers."

SEX	BAD DRIVERS	GOOD DRIVERS	PROPORTION OF BAD DRIVERS
Women	40	80	33%
Men	20	40	33%

it, you would have to reach this conclusion after observing the driving habits of many men and women. Figure 9.4 presents some hypothetical data on the numbers of good and bad drivers you've observed and whether they were women or men. Notice that the proportion of bad female drivers is exactly the same as the proportion of bad male drivers. Still, people can reach the wrong conclusions from such "good" data in a number of ways.

For example, a number of studies (see Kanouse & Hanson, 1971; see Chapter 5) suggest that people disproportionately sample and weight *negative* information in reaching conclusions. Thus we are likely to focus our attention on the "bad drivers" column of the table, and we may conclude from it that there are twice as many bad female drivers as there are bad male drivers.

Memory limitations and stereotypes.   Of course, we rarely (if ever) have an objective tally before us (such as the data in Figure 9.4) when we reach an abstract conclusion about a group of people. Rather, we must retrieve facts from memory, and our memories are often biased by preconceptions (see Chapter 5). If you believe that women are bad drivers, you'll probably find it easier to remember information that is consistent with those beliefs.

Furthermore, Figure 9.4 glosses over the thorny question of how you classify a person's driving as being either "bad" or "good" in the first place. For example, women pay lower auto insurance premiums than do men; so if the criterion for "good" or "bad" is insurance statistics, then women are better drivers than men. Yet, as Chapter 5 documented, social judgments are often quite ambiguous, and preexisting schemas can dramatically influence our perceptions and interpretations of observed behaviors. Thus what reckless male drivers classify as "bad" driving in some women may in fact be sensibly cautious driving.

The discussion of Figure 9.4 assumes that we remember specific instances of people's driving, categorize them as "good" or "bad," and then associate each instance of driving with the driver's gender. However, when exposed to large amounts

FIGURE 9.5   **Stereotypes and memory organization.**

Is memory for a group's behavior organized by people *or by* behaviors?

In this example, if we organized information by people we would remember that there were more good women drivers than bad women drivers. But if we organized information by behaviors we would remember that women displayed more instances of bad driving than good driving. As the text notes, the more memory is loaded (with repeated pieces of information about many people), the more likely we are to organize information by behaviors rather than by people.

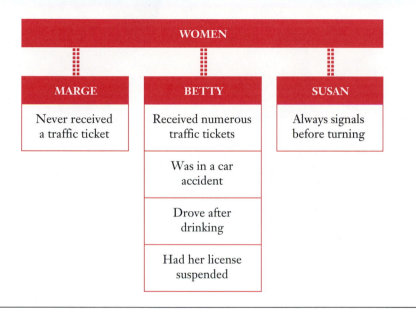

In this example, if we organized information by people, *we would remember that there were more "good" women drivers than "bad" women drivers. But if we organized information by* behaviors, *we would remember that women displayed more instances of bad driving than instances of good driving.*

of redundant information, people may treat repeated instances of a behavior from a single person as independent instances of group behavior (Rothbart, Fulero, Jensen, Howard, & Birrell, 1978).

An examination of Figure 9.5 should make this point clearer. Note that sometimes we observe more than one instance of bad driving in a specific woman ("Betty was in a car accident" and "Betty received numerous traffic tickets"). But overall the figure shows more "good" than "bad" female drivers. If people organize information in their memories with individual women as the units remembered, they will correctly recall that there are more "good" women drivers than "bad" women drivers. But if they remember behavioral units, they will incorrectly perceive that women

Stereotypes as illusory correlations: Here a group of Moslems burn a copy of Salman Rushdie's book *The Satanic Verses*. Rushdie's book was considered blasphemous by religious Moslems, and Rushdie was sentenced to death by Iran's Ayatollah Khomeini. Did the constant barrage of publicity showing a small number of Moslems burning books create a strong belief among many Americans that "Moslems are fanatics"?

show more instances of "bad" driving behavior than those of "good" driving behavior.

Experiments by Rothbart et al. (1978) demonstrated that when subjects' memories were loaded with too much information (64 pairings of people with traits), they lost track of repeated information for specific individuals. On the other hand, when they were not overloaded with information (16 pieces of information about people), subjects could accurately keep track of repetitious information and could organize that information with people as the basic units. Unfortunately, Rothbart's overloaded memory condition is more likely to reflect reality. In the complex social environments of everyday life, we are exposed to a flood of information that competes for limited attention and memory resources.

Stereotypes as illusory correlations.　In Chapter 5 we noted that preexisting associations between pairs of facts or events can lead people falsely to perceive a correlation between those events. If you think women are more likely to be "bad" drivers, you may perceive a correlation between gender and driving aptitude after observing a number of drivers on the road, even when none exists.

We may also perceive an illusory correlation when two events or facts share some distinctive feature, such as frequency of occurrence or perceptual salience. In a study demonstrating this effect, Hamilton and Gifford (1976) asked subjects to

FIGURE 9.6   Illusory correlations and stereotypes.

What leads to illusory correlations?

Hamilton and Gifford (1976) studied illusory correlations that resulted from infrequent bad behaviors in majority and minority groups. Subjects read positive and negative descriptions of members of arbitrarily defined "majority" and "minority" groups. The table shows the number of each type of description read by subjects.

DESCRIPTIONS	GROUP A (MAJORITY)	GROUP B (MINORITY)
Positive	16 Descriptions e.g., "John is honest" and "John's in Group A"	8 Descriptions e.g., "Steve is helpful" and "Steve's in Group B"
Negative	8 Descriptions e.g., "Mike is obnoxious" and "Mike's in Group A"	4 Descriptions e.g., "Tom is a liar" and "Tom's in Group B"

Subjects perceived a correlation between minority-group membership and negative descriptions, even though no such correlation existed (the proportion of negative descriptions was the same for both groups). The key factor seems to be that negative descriptions and minority descriptions shared the characteristic of being *less frequent* and therefore more distinctive, which led subjects to associate them.

SOURCE: Based on Hamilton and Gifford (1976).

Imagine that there is a shoot-out among several students on your college campus. If these students are members of a minority group, will you be likely to associate their group membership with their violence? If these students are not members of a minority group, will you be less likely to associate their group membership with their violence? Conceptualize this "thought experiment" in terms of Hamilton and Gifford's findings.

read statements about both a minority group and a majority group. To prevent subjects' prior knowledge and associations from influencing the results, Hamilton and Gifford labeled the minority group "Group B" and the majority group "Group A." Twice as many statements described majority group members than described minority group members, and about twice as many statements for each group were positive rather than negative, as illustrated in Figure 9.6.

Interestingly, although no correlation between group membership and descriptions existed, subjects perceived such a correlation, overestimating the number of negative statements associated with members of the minority group. According to Hamilton and Gifford's interpretation, events that shared the characteristic of being infrequent (negative descriptions and minority-group membership) became associated in subjects' minds; that is, the *shared distinctiveness* of the events led to an illusory correlation between them.

These findings are quite disturbing; in real life, negative events are rarer than are neutral or positive events (for example, murders are rarer than nonmurders) and, almost by definition, observations of minority members are rarer than observations of majority members. Thus, the cognitive mechanisms that lead to illusory correlations may inevitably place minorities at a disadvantage in terms of how they are portrayed in our stereotypes.

Consequences of Stereotypes

We have learned some of the ways in which we *form* stereotypes, but once they exist, how do they affect our thought processes and behavior? Recent studies suggest that stereotypes may serve as schemas that influence how we process information about members of other groups, how we treat them, and ultimately how they respond to us.

Stereotypes and schematic processing. One recent experiment (Dovidio, Evans, & Tyler, 1986) directly examined the effects of ethnic labels on the *speed* with which we process information about others. Subjects were shown one of three priming words on a computer screen—*white*, *black*, or *house*—and two seconds later were shown an adjective that could apply either to people (for example, *ambitious*) or to a house (for example, *drafty*). Subjects had to answer whether the adjective "could ever be true" of the earlier priming word. For example, could a "white" (person) ever be "ambitious"? Could a "house" be "ambitious"? The subject would signal the answer by pressing the "Yes" or "No" key on the computer keyboard.

Subjects' reaction times in answering these questions were recorded. Interestingly, subjects reacted most quickly to adjectives that were stereotypically related to the primed word. For *white* they responded most quickly to such words as *ambitious* and *conventional*, whereas for *black* they responded to words like *musical* and *lazy*.

The researchers included some adjectives that were fairly positive in tone (for example, *ambitious*, *musical*) and others that were more negative (for example, *conventional*, *lazy*). Disturbingly, subjects responded more quickly to positive traits when *white* was used as the prime and more quickly to negative traits when *black* was the prime, implying a greater association between the negative traits and *black* and between the positive traits and *white*. This study points out the subtle influence of people's racial schemas on how quickly they process social information and on the strength and negativity of their cognitive associations with different races.

Racial slurs and schematic processing. Racial schemas may also influence the broad evaluations we make of people's performances and abilities in everyday life. Greenburg and Pyszczynski (1985) conducted an experiment which showed that an ethnic slur can trigger a destructive chain of schematic processing in those who overhear it. Subjects observed a staged debate between a black confederate and a white confederate on "the value of nuclear energy." (The black debator argued in favor of nuclear energy; the white debator argued against nuclear energy.) In some experimental conditions the black debator presented clearly superior arguments, whereas in other conditions the white debator presented the superior arguments.

After the debators left the room, subjects were asked to evaluate each debator's skill and to rate on a scale which debator had won. Before making these ratings, subjects were exposed to the crucial manipulation of the study: A subject (actually a stooge in the experiment) was overheard making either a racist or a nonracist comment about the black debator. The "nonracist" stooge said, "There's no way the pro debator won the debate." The "racist" stooge said, "There's no way that nigger won the debate."

FIGURE 9.7 The effect of an overheard racist slur on cognitive processes.

Can an overheard racist slur trigger prejudiced thought processes in the listener?

Subjects in the study by Greenburg and Pyszczynski (1985) rated black and white debators after overhearing either a neutral or a racist comment. The graphs show the subjects' evaluations of the losing debator.

Note: Ratings could range from 1 ("very poor") to 21 ("excellent").

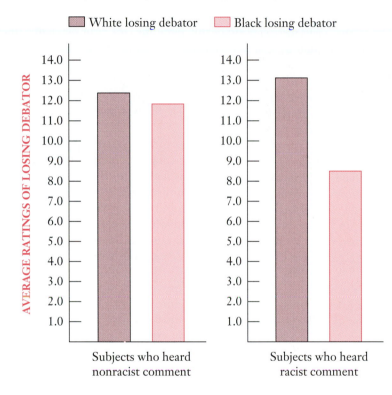

Subjects who overheard the racist slur (right panel) were particularly harsh in their evaluations of the losing black debator.

SOURCE: Data from Greenburg and Pyszczynski (1985).

Many people who consider themselves nonprejudiced tell ethnic jokes. According to this experiment, what are the possible effects of hearing a disparaging ethnic joke?

How did this ethnic slur affect the evaluations? Subjects who overheard the ethnic slur rated the black debator significantly lower, particularly when his arguments were of low quality (see Figure 9.7). Greenburg and Pyszczynski suggest that overhearing derogatory ethnic comments led subjects to use a negative ethnic schema in interpreting and evaluating new information. In the researchers' words, "noxious labels for out-groupers . . . are not merely the symptoms of prejudice but carriers of the disease as well."

The self-perpetuating nature of stereotypes.   Stereotypes are formed and maintained not only by cognitive processes but also by our behavior toward others. The behavioral consequences of stereotypes are particularly insidious in that our behaviors often perpetuate our stereotypes.

The self-perpetuating nature of gender stereotypes was demonstrated convincingly in a clever experiment by Skrypnek and Snyder (1982). Pairs of male and female college students had to decide how to divide a number of experimental tasks between themselves. Some tasks were stereotypically feminine (for example, icing and decorating a cake) and some were stereotypically masculine (for example, fixing a light switch). Subjects could not see each other in this experiment; they sat in different rooms and communicated their task preferences through a system of electric lights. Some male subjects were correctly told that their partner was female, some were given no information about the gender of their partner, and some were falsely told that their partner was another male.

Skrypnek and Snyder computed an index of how stereotypically masculine or feminine were the tasks to which the female subjects finally agreed. Interestingly, when the female subjects had been labeled as females to their male partners, they ended up "choosing" significantly more feminine tasks than when they had been unlabeled or labeled as "male." This "preference" for more feminine tasks remained even in a second stage of the experiment in which the female subjects initiated negotiations. In other words, once a women labeled "female" accepted her role, she tended to persevere in this division of labor, even when she could negotiate otherwise.

In sum, the Skrypnek and Snyder study provides compelling evidence that our stereotypical expectations can influence not only our own behavior but other people's behavior as well. Others may behave in ways that are consistent with our stereotypes because *we induce them to*. If a man expects a woman to perform certain "feminine" tasks, he may influence her in both subtle and not-so-subtle ways to meet his expectations.

The Skrypnek and Snyder study provided an additional disturbing finding: When subjects disagreed in the early stages of negotiation, the males were significantly more likely to compromise—to "give in" to their partner's preferences—when they were led to believe she was male. Apparently, not only did the men expect the women to accept their stereotypical roles; they also expected them to "know their place" as women.

Social Causes of Prejudice

And Pecola is somewhere in that little brown house she and her mother moved to on the edge of town. . . . [She is] plucking her way between the tire rims and the sunflowers, between Coke bottles and milkweed, among all the waste and beauty of the world — which is what she herself was. All of our waste which we dumped on her and which she absorbed. . . . All of us — all who knew her — felt so wholesome after we cleaned ourselves on her. We were so beautiful when we stood astride her ugliness. Her simplicity decorated us, her guilt sanctified us, her pain made us glow with health, her awkwardness made us think we had a sense of humor. Her inarticulateness made us believe we were eloquent. Her poverty kept us generous. Even her waking dreams we used — to silence our own nightmares. And she let us, and thereby deserved our contempt. We honed our egos on her, padded our characters with her frailty, and yawned in the fantasy of our strength.

—— *The Bluest Eye*, p. 159

We have focused up to this point on the phenomenological side of prejudice — stereotyped beliefs and their causes and consequences. However, as we noted earlier in this chapter, this focus constitutes only one level of analysis. Let's turn now to the broader social causes of prejudice. In particular, let's examine socialization and personality, social ideologies, and the organization of people into social groups as causes of prejudice.

The Authoritarian Personality

Are there certain kinds of people who are particularly likely to be prejudiced against many different groups? If so, why are they so prejudiced? Influential research on the *authoritarian personality*, conducted in the 1940s at the University of California, Berkeley, attempted to answer just these questions (Adorno et al., 1950).

As a first step, the researchers developed two questionnaire measures of prejudice: an Anti-Semitism Scale, which assessed attitudes toward Jews, and an Ethnocentrism Scale, which assessed atttitudes toward many different minorities (see Figure 9.8 for sample items). Looking to Nazism as an example, the researchers assumed that prejudice was particularly associated with the political right, and accordingly they developed a scale of economic and political conservatism. Finally, based on the assumption that prejudiced people tend to have defensive personalities, the researchers developed the "F Scale," a test designed to assess fascist (that is, right-wing, totalitarian) personality tendencies (again, see Figure 9.8 for sample items).

After administering the four questionnaire scales to large numbers of volunteer subjects and analyzing their responses, the researchers concluded that prejudiced attitudes are relatively consistent; that is, some subjects tended to be generally prejudiced against many minority groups, whereas others tended to be generally nonprejudiced. Furthermore, prejudiced people tended to be politically and economically more conservative than were nonprejudiced people, and prejudiced people showed more fascist personality characteristics as well.

The researchers next turned to their second question: How does prejudice develop? To obtain an answer, they intensively interviewed 40 prejudiced and 40 nonprejudiced subjects. These interviews pointed to a number of important differences between the two groups. Prejudiced people generally engaged in more rigid, black-and-white kinds of thought than did nonprejudiced people. As you might expect, highly prejudiced subjects tended to focus more on dominance and power in their lives than on warmth and intimacy; they seemed to be concerned with status and "making it." Nonprejudiced subjects, on the other hand, expressed more concern about personal relationships and helping others.

FIGURE 9.8   Sample items from the four scales developed in research on the authoritarian personality. Subjects were asked to rate how much they agreed with each item on a six-point scale ranging from 1 ("strongly disagree") to 6 ("strongly agree").

ITEMS FROM THE ANTI-SEMITISM SCALE

The trouble with letting Jews into a nice neighborhood is that they gradually give it a typical Jewish atmosphere.

I can hardly imagine myself marrying a Jew.

No matter how Americanized a Jew may seem to be, there is always something different and strange, something basically Jewish underneath.

ITEMS FROM THE ETHNOCENTRISM SCALE

Negroes have their rights, but it is best to keep them in their own districts and schools, and to prevent too much contact with whites.

Zootsuiters prove that when people of their type have too much money and freedom, they just take advantage and cause trouble.

America may not be perfect, but the American Way has brought us about as close as human beings can get to a perfect society.

ITEMS FROM THE POLITICAL AND ECONOMIC CONSERVATISM SCALE

The best way to solve social problems is to stick close to the middle of the road, to move slowly, and to avoid extremes.

The only way to provide adequate medical care for the entire population is through some program of socialized medicine.

In general, full economic security is harmful; most men wouldn't work if they didn't need the money for eating and living.

ITEMS FROM THE F SCALE

Obedience and respect for authority are the most important virtues children should learn.

When a person has a worry or problem, it is best for him not to think about it, but to keep busy with more cheerful things.

People can be divided into two distinct classes: the weak and the strong.

The wild sex life of the old Greeks and Romans was tame compared to some of the goings-on in this country, even in places where people might least expect it.

These are all examples of Likert scales (discussed in Chapter 7). Scales such as these may become dated. Do you know what "Zootsuiters" refers to in the second sample item from the Ethnocentrism Scale? Answer: Zootsuiters were Mexican-Americans who were the object of prejudice during the 1940s. They were characterized by their attire — flashy suits and hats. During World War II there were Zootsuit riots in Los Angeles. Because research on the authoritarian personality was conducted in California, its scales addressed some uniquely Californian kinds of prejudice.

●●

Prejudiced subjects tended to describe themselves in positive, glowing terms, whereas nonprejudiced subjects gave comparatively mixed self-portraits. The researchers interpreted this difference to mean that prejudiced people engaged in unrealistic "self-glorification," whereas nonprejudiced people gave more accurate and balanced descriptions of their strengths and weaknesses.

Finally, prejudiced subjects would say nothing overtly bad about their parents. This finding was particularly interesting and ironic because prejudiced subjects consistently described their parents as strict and punitive disciplinarians, whereas nonprejudiced subjects described their parents as more loving and tolerant. Although prejudiced subjects would not explicitly criticize their parents, their interviews often contained indications of deep underlying hostility. The parents of prejudiced subjects, more than those of nonprejudiced subjects, seemed to hold unrealistically high expectations for their children. Their children *had* to be successful.

If prejudiced subjects did not say overtly negative things about themselves or their parents, who then were the targets of their negative feelings? Minority groups, of course. All the hostility and inadequacy they could not express about themselves or their parents was expressed vociferously about "low-class," "stupid," "over-sexed," "immoral," and "dishonest" minorities. From these results, the researchers wove a portrait of the childhood development and resultant personality of the prejudiced person. They used Freudian concepts to explain a syndrome known as the "authoritarian personality."

According to the Berkeley researchers, certain prejudice has its roots in status-anxious, dominating parents who use considerable physical discipline and little love in raising their children. Such children experience feelings of inadequacy in addition to considerable hostility toward their parents. However, because their parents are punitive, they can't express their hostility toward their parents, and because their parents expect them to "make it" and be "perfect," they can't express their insecurities openly. Rather, they repress their aggression and feelings of inadequacy.

Ultimately, such children relieve their repressed hostilities and anxieties through various defense mechanisms — psychological devices they use to express these feelings in disguised ways. For example, they may engage in displacement — a venting of their aggression at safe targets (minority groups) rather than at true targets (mother). Or they may use the common defense mechanism of projection, in which they see all of their own hostilities and shortcomings in others.

Criticisms of the research.   To this day, the research on the authoritarian personality remains the largest single effort aimed at understanding prejudice in terms of child-rearing practices and personality dynamics. Although acknowledged as classic, this research has been criticized on a number of grounds (for example, Christie & Jahoda, 1954; Snyder & Ickes, 1985). Some of this criticism concerns methodological matters. For example, critics have noted flaws in the way questionnaires were developed and in the methods used to conduct and code interviews. Despite these valid concerns, most subsequent research has supported the main conclusions of the original studies on the authoritarian personality (Altemeyer, 1981; Bierly, 1985; Christie & Cook, 1958; Kirscht & Dillehay, 1967; Christie, 1978).

More significantly, criticism has also focused on the researchers' interpretations of their results. Some social psychologists have argued that lack of education, low social class, and low intelligence — not personality — best accounted for prejudice in this research. Indeed, the original authoritarian personality research and subsequent replicating studies have revealed significant correlations between prejudice and such variables as social class, education, and IQ (Hyman & Sheatsley, 1954; Kornhauser et al., 1956).

Such findings have led some psychologists to question the usefulness of Freudian concepts like repression and defense mechanisms in interpreting research on the authoritarian personality. A simpler explanation holds that parents who are authoritarian and strict disciplinarians (often because of their class background, education, and so on) generally produce children who are the same because of social learning and modeling. More generally, critics have held that research on the authoritarian personality focused *too exclusively* on personality as a cause of prejudice.

As you know from Chapter 1, contemporary social psychology tends to focus on the *current situation* as a cause of social behavior, and for this reason research on personality and prejudice is not as actively pursued today. Still, the authoritarian personality remains a plausible explanation for some forms of prejudice.

Social Ideologies and Prejudice

Prejudice, like other attitudes, is generally learned. In Chapter 7 we discussed the roles of classical conditioning, operant conditioning, and modeling in attitude formation. We also described how attitudes may be logically inferred from other beliefs and attitudes. All of this theory and research applies to the topic of prejudice. Inference theories of attitude formation may be particularly relevant to prejudice because prejudice is often linked to broader social ideologies (organized systems of values, beliefs, and attitudes). Research has focused particularly on two ideological domains: political beliefs and religious beliefs.

Political beliefs and prejudice.   Researchers investigating the authoritarian personality assumed that prejudice was associated with the political right. To test this hypothesis, they developed a political and economic conservatism scale based on a traditional view of the political spectrum: conservatism (the political right) advocates personal initiative, free enterprise, and minimal government intervention, whereas liberalism (the political left) advocates social welfare programs and government regulation of business and supports labor unions. The research on the authoritarian personality found a moderately strong correlation between conservatism and prejudice. More recent research also has detected a link between political conservatism and prejudice (Sears, Lau, Tyler, & Allen, 1980; Sniderman & Hagen, 1985). In recent survey research, for example, conservatives tended to oppose racial integration more than did liberals (Kinder & Sears, 1985).

However, a correlation does not necessarily indicate a cause-effect relationship (see Chapter 2). The correlation between political conservatism and prejudice may be mediated by other variables, such as age, education, and religious beliefs. Rokeach (1956, 1960) argued that instead of authoritarian conservatism, dogmatism—subscribing to a rigid, absolute, closed belief system—leads to prejudice. The dogmatic person dislikes out-group members because they disagree with his strong views. According to Rokeach, dogmatism can show itself in members of either the political left (a revolutionary communist) or the political right (a fascist). To test his ideas, Rokeach developed a dogmatism scale.

Dogmatism is related to prejudice (Thompson & Michel, 1972). Although Rokeach hypothesized that dogmatism would be unrelated to political ideology, considerable research suggests it is more characteristic of the political right than of the left (Stone, 1980, 1981). In a particularly realistic study, DiRenzo (1967) administered Rokeach's dogmatism scale to 124 members of the Italian House of Deputies, which comprised many political parties ranging from the neofascist right to the communist left. DiRenzo found that members of right-wing parties had higher dogmatism scores than did members of left-wing parties.

More recent research shows that conservatives (including U.S. senators and Supreme Court justices) show political reasoning that is less cognitively complex than that of liberals (Tetlock, Bernzweig, & Gallant, 1985; Tetlock, Hannum, & Micheletin, 1984). Consistent with early research on the authoritarian personality, this finding suggests that conservatives may engage in more dogmatic political reasoning than do liberals and that by implication such thinking may be conducive to prejudice.

There is yet another possible explanation for the observed relationship between conservatism and prejudice. A number of researchers have noted that an essential component of conservative political ideology is a strong belief in personal responsibility and initiative (Sniderman & Hagen, 1985; Katz & Hass, 1988). To the extent that conservatives believe that "we are what we make of ourselves," they then see disadvantaged people as responsible for their own plights.

Kinder and Sears (1981, 1985) have recently argued that racial attitudes and their links to political attitudes have changed over the past 40 years in the United States. Although racial prejudice has waned (Schuman, Steeh, & Bobo, 1985; Katz & Hass, 1988), racism still remains in disguised forms and is linked in complex ways to traditional American values. Kinder and Sears (1981) call the new variety of prejudice *symbolic racism*:

> This we define as a blend of antiblack affect and the kind of traditional American moral values embodied in the Protestant Ethic. . . . Symbolic racism represents a form of resistance to change in the racial status quo based on moral feelings that blacks violate such traditional American values as individualism and self-reliance, the work ethic, obedience, and discipline. (p. 416)

Symbolic racism is a relatively new concept, and future research will determine whether it truly is a new form of prejudice (Sniderman & Tetlock, 1986; Kinder, 1986).

Religious beliefs and prejudice.   Most religions espouse a version of the "golden rule": Do unto others as you would have them do unto you. Christian denominations frequently emphasize that all of us are "God's children." Thus religious ideology would seem well-suited to reducing prejudice.

Are church members in fact less prejudiced than nonmembers? Unfortunately, systematic research shows that the answer is "No." One recent review categorized 34 studies as showing a positive relationship between church membership and prejudice, but only two showing a negative relationship between them. The authors concluded that ". . . at least for white, middle-class Christians in the United States, religion is not associated with increased love and acceptance but with increased intolerance, prejudice, and bigotry" (Batson & Ventis, 1982, p. 257).

Extending earlier work by Gordon Allport (1959; Allport & Ross, 1967), Batson and Ventis (1982) further argue that there are three different kinds of religiousness, and each relates differently to prejudice. Some individuals are intrinsically religious;

Stigma and Prejudice

. . . she screamed at us, "I am cute! And you ugly! Black and ugly e mos. I am cute!"

. . . We were sinking under the wisdom, accuracy, and relevance of Maureen's last words. If she was cute — and if anything could be believed, she was — then we were not. And what did this mean? We were lesser.

—— The Bluest Eye, p. 61

Prejudice is not only targeted at ethnic, racial, and religious groups but at stigmatized people in general. A *stigma* is a social label or condition that defines a person as "deviant, flawed, limited, spoiled, or generally undesirable" and may be related to "behavior, biography, ancestry, or group membership" (Jones, Farina, Hastorf, Markus, Miller, & Scott, 1984). In our society, people who are disabled, extremely ugly or disfigured, obese, terminally ill, epileptic, mentally ill, or retarded are often stigmatized.

Numerous studies indicate that stigmatizing conditions are perceived to vary systematically in a number of ways (Shears & Jensema, 1969; Tringo, 1970). The following six dimensions are especially important: concealability, course of the stigmatized condition, social disruptiveness, aesthetic qualities, origins, and peril to others (Jones et al., 1984). For example, being a "former mental patient" is often a concealable stigma, and terminal cancer is a stigmatized condition that deteriorates over time. In general, prejudice is greatest against people whose stigmas are obvious and perceived as deteriorating, socially disruptive, unattractive, freely chosen, and dangerous. People with AIDS provide a much-publicized contemporary example (Herek & Glunt, 1988). AIDS is highly stigmatizing because it is perceived as a deteriorating terminal condition that is unattractive and socially disruptive. Furthermore, many perceive AIDS as "freely chosen," associated with other stigmatized conditions (homosexuality, drug addiction), and highly contagious (which it is not).

In a classic analysis, Erving Goffman (1963) argued that stigmas often assume a "master status" — the victim is perceived only in terms of his or her stigma. For example, a college student with AIDS may be described as the "student with AIDS" or simply "the AIDS victim." In *The Bluest Eye* Toni Morrison describes how ugliness becomes a "master status" for each member of the Breedlove family.

. . . they took the ugliness in their hands, threw it as a mantle over them, and went about the world with it. Dealing with it each according to his way. Mrs. Breedlove handled hers as an actor does a prop: for the articulation of character, for support of a role she frequently imagined was hers — martyrdom. Sammy used his as a weapon to cause others pain. He . . . chose his companions on the basis of it: people who could be fascinated, even intimidated by it. And Pecola. She

hid behind hers. Concealed, veiled, eclipsed — peeping out from behind the shroud very seldom . . . (pp. 34–35)

Why are people who possess stigmatized conditions so harshly treated in our society? Goffman (1963) argues that one reason is that they threaten our accustomed social roles and behaviors. Stigmatized people make us uncomfortable, and for this we dislike them. A second possibility is that stigmatized people remind us of our own frailty, vulnerability, and mortality (Berger & Luckmann, 1966; Schutz, 1971); we banish them to banish our own fears and anxieties.

One of the most puzzling and troubling reactions shown by "normal" people to the stigmatized is attributing their condition to some sort of moral or personal failing. Literary critic Susan Sontag (1977) notes how physical illnesses like cancer are often viewed as metaphors for spiritual or moral illness. Melvin Lerner's (1980; Lerner & Miller, 1978) *just world hypothesis* offers a social psychological account of why people sometimes derogate victims of stigmatizing conditions: From our earliest years we are taught that it is a just world in which people get their "just deserts." Thus people who are seriously ill, disfigured, or mentally ill must deserve their conditions. Unfortunately, those people who most need our sympathy, help, and compassion are often unfairly blamed for their unhappy fate.

they view their religion as a central, necessary part of their identity. Others are extrinsically religious; they view religion as a means to other ends (pleasing parents, access to social and business contacts). And finally, some individuals view religion as an existential quest in which they wrestle with the basic questions of life without necessarily arriving at final, dogmatic answers.

Frequency of church attendance has sometimes been taken as a rough indicator of the intrinsic vs. extrinsic orientation; frequently attending individuals are assumed to be more intrinsically religious (Gorsuch & Aleshire, 1974). Among church members, the relatively inactive majority (those who attend church events on average less than once a week) tend to be more prejudiced than the more active minority (Batson & Ventis, 1982), which may imply that intrinsically religious people are less prejudiced than extrinsically religious people.

However, one study found that although intrinsically religious people express less prejudice than do extrinsically religious people on questionnaire scales, they prove to be equally prejudiced when prejudice is measured behaviorally (Batson, Naifeh, & Pate, 1978). The only people with both nonprejudiced attitudes and actions are those with a high degree of quest orientation. Thus the lower prejudice expressed by the intrinsically religious may be more a matter of social desirability than of genuine feeling.

In sum, although some religious beliefs can reduce prejudice, church membership and strong religious beliefs tend to be associated with prejudice. These correlations do not prove a cause-effect relationship, however; the relation between religiousness and prejudice may be mediated by such other variables as age, social class, and educational level (Simpson & Yinger, 1985). And like political beliefs, religious ideologies in part influence prejudice indirectly through their implicit assumptions about free will, personal initiative, and divine providence (Sniderman & Hagen, 1985).

Social Groups and Prejudice

So far we have considered distal social causes of prejudice: the socialization we receive early in life and the political and religious ideologies we learn throughout life. Let's turn now to a more immediate social cause of prejudice: group membership.

As we noted earlier, when we're a member of a group, we often believe that our own group — the in-group — is superior to other groups — out-groups. You can probably think of many reasons for a bias in favor of in-groups. We are typically more similar to in-group members than to out-group members, and considerable research suggests that we like similar people more than we like dissimilar people (Byrne, 1971). We typically engage in more rewarding interaction with in-group members than with out-group members. Finally, we are simply exposed more to people in our own groups than to people in other groups, and mere exposure often leads to liking (Zajonc, 1968; see Chapter 11).

Research on the minimal group.   What would happen if we eliminate all of these reasons for ethnocentrism? Suppose we place you in a room with nine randomly chosen people and arbitrarily — by the flip of a coin — divide the ten people into two groups. Your group has no history of past interaction; it shares no common goals or aspirations. Will you like your group more than you like the other group in this minimal group situation? Many recent studies suggest that, yes, you will like your group more, even if its creation was totally arbitrary. Apparently, when people are placed in groups, some basic cognitive shift takes place that leads them to view their own group as better.

Henri Tajfel (1978, 1982) and his colleagues conducted many studies investigating this effect. For example, Tajfel, Billig, Bundy, and Flament (1971) asked teenage British school boys to participate in a study that seemed, at least on its surface, to deal with visual perception. The boys were shown slides that contained a large number of dots and were asked to quickly estimate the number of dots in each slide. The experimenter told them that some people are "overestimators" who consistently estimate more dots than there really are, whereas others are "underestimators." After the boys had completed the task, the experimenter randomly informed half of them that they were "overestimators" and half that they were "underestimators." Next, the boys played a game in which they assigned points to other boys — points that later could be traded in for money. Interestingly, the boys allocated points so that members of their in-group were rewarded more than members of the out-group. In other words, an "overestimator" rewarded other "overestimators" more in the experimental game.

In some sense, the groups created in this study may not have been totally arbitrary — perhaps the boys in a particular group felt they shared a perceptual trait (being an "overestimator," for example) creating a kind of perceived similarity. To eliminate this possibility, later studies (such as Billig & Tajfel, 1973; Locksley, Ortiz, & Hepburn, 1980) created truly arbitrary minimal groups. Subjects were assigned to groups in an openly random fashion — for example, by the flip of a coin. Yet even when subjects knew that their group had been formed totally by chance, they still showed in-group favoritism.

Tajfel's original study (Tajfel et al., 1971) demonstrated that subjects reward members of their in-group more than they reward members of the out-group. Other research extends this finding by showing that subjects in minimal group situations also rate members of their group as being more attractive and likable (for example, Brewer & Silver, 1978; Locksley, Ortiz, & Hepburn, 1980; Turner, 1978). Such subjects rate work produced by their group as being of higher quality than work produced by the other group (Ferguson & Kelley, 1964), and they also show attributional and memory biases that favor the in-group (Howard & Rothbart, 1980); for example, they remember in-group members' good behaviors better than they remember their bad behaviors. Finally people in minimal groups tend to be more competitive toward the out-group than they would be as individuals (McCullum, Harring, Gilmore, Drenan, Chase, Insko, & Thibaut, 1985). In sum, these results suggest that the mere creation of social groups and the simple perception of being a group member lead us to like our group better, to treat other groups worse, and to behave competitively toward other groups.

Social identity theory.   Why should mere membership in a group lead to consistent in-group favoritism? Tajfel and his colleagues (Tajfel, 1981, 1982; Tajfel & Turner, 1979) proposed a *theory of social identity* that attempts to answer this question.

In essence, social identity theory argues that a person's identity or self-image has two parts, one personal and the other social. Your personal identity contains specific facts about you as an individual: "I'm a straight-A student," "I'm a poor dancer," and "I give money to the American Cancer Society." Your social identity derives from the groups you belong to: "I'm a student at State U," "I'm Catholic," and "I'm Italian." Your self-esteem can be affected by both your personal identity and your social identity. For example, self-esteem related to your personal identity is probably boosted by being a "straight-A student" and diminished by being a "poor dancer." But self-esteem related to your social identities depends on how you evaluate the groups to which you belong. For example, being Italian will boost your self-esteem if you feel positively about Italians, whereas being a student at State U. will lower your self-esteem if you consider it to be a lackluster academic institution.

In-group favoritism and self-esteem.   According to social identity theory, people are motivated to overvalue their own groups because such a valuation boosts their self-esteem. An experiment by Oakes and Turner (1980) supports this hypothesis. Subjects were arbitrarily divided into two groups on the supposed basis of their preference for the paintings of one of two modern artists. (This experimental design is quite similar to that of the "overestimators-underestimators" study described earlier.) As typically occurs in these studies, subjects rewarded members of their in-group more than they rewarded members of the out-group. But these researchers took the study a step further: Subjects completed a self-esteem scale, and the researchers found that subjects who showed in-group favoritism actually reported higher self-esteem than did control subjects.

Out-group derogation and self-esteem.   Meindl and Lerner (1985) demonstrated the relation between self-esteem and group membership in yet another way. They reasoned that subjects whose self-esteem had been artificially lowered might derogate the out-group to bolster their own damaged self-esteem. These researchers induced English-speaking Canadian subjects to suffer the embarrassment of accidentally dropping the experimenter's "important" deck of computer cards on the floor. These subjects were then asked to rate French-speaking Canadians on various traits. Subjects who had suffered this insult to their self-esteems were harsher in their ratings of the out-group than were control subjects.

Social identity theory implies that as our group's fortunes rise and fall in comparison to other groups', so does our own self-esteem. Have you ever noticed, for example, that if your college receives positive publicity—its team wins a big football game or a faculty member wins a prominent award—then you stand a little taller, as if it somehow reflected on you? On the other hand, if the publicity is negative—if, say, a major cheating scandal is disclosed—doesn't your head hang a little lower?

Even if you bear no personal responsibility for either the good behavior or the bad behavior of your group, your self-esteem and identity are still tied to the fortunes of your group. Somehow, the successes and failures of the group "rub off" onto its individual members.

Tajfel's social identity theory points to a fundamental psychological process that leads all of us to perceive our own groups in the best possible light, sometimes at the expense of other groups. We do this for the most selfish of reasons — to make us feel better about ourselves.

Intergroup Competition and Prejudice

Group membership may lead to prejudice in yet another way. When people are split into groups, they often must compete for limited resources. In two innovative field studies Muzafer Sherif (Sherif, Harvey, White, Hood, & Sherif, 1961; Sherif & Sherif, 1953) investigated how group competition leads to the development of prejudice and intergroup hostilities.

Creating prejudice: The Red Devils and the Bull Dogs.   In Sherif's first study, 24 white, lower–middle-class boys from the vicinity of New Haven, Connecticut, were sent to an isolated summer camp in northern Connecticut. On the fourth day of camp, the boys were divided randomly into two groups, the "Red Devils" and the "Bull Dogs." For the next five days, the two groups lived separately, ate at separate tables, and engaged in camp recreational activities separately. Each group established "secret hideaways" and camping spots that were not to be revealed to the other group. Each group developed its own leaders, social structure, and group norms.

After strong feelings of group identification had developed, the staff announced that a series of competitions would take place between the Bull Dogs and the Red Devils. Each group would be awarded points for its performances in various sports events (a daily tug-of-war contest, touch football games, and softball), as well as for their performances in carrying out such camp duties as cleaning their cabins. Each member of the winning group would win an expensive camping knife, a highly desired prize.

The competitions marked the beginning of hostilities between the groups. Boys in both groups showed good sportsmanship toward the opposition during the first few games, but their behavior soon deteriorated into open taunting and jeering. The Bull Dogs eventually won the overall competition and received the coveted camping knives. The Red Devils responded by labeling them as "dirty players" and "cheats." On the evening of the Bull Dogs' victory, the staff held a party for all the boys, but arranged for the Red Devils to arrive first so that they could take the best ice cream and cake. The Bull Dogs, who arrived slightly later, got clearly inferior remains, and they retaliated by calling the Red Devils "low rotten pigs," "dirty pigs," and worse.

Even after the games were over, hostilities continued. One group purposely made messes to increase the work of the other group on K.P. duty. Staff members had to break up food fights that were about to escalate into physical violence, and the two groups waged a "war" with green apples that resulted in two broken windows. This third stage of conflict showed all the hallmarks of prejudice and intergroup hostility: The boys showed a preference for the in-group and disparagement of the out-group, they developed stereotypes of the out-group, and they competed — at times violently — for desirable goods. The mere establishment of groups started a process of in-group identification and attachment; injecting competition produced prejudice and intergroup violence.

Why did competition lead so inexorably to prejudice and conflict in Sherif's field experiment? First, note that when placed in salient, separate groups, the boys developed a strong attraction for their group. Minimal group research suggests that even an arbitrary division into in-group and out-group leads people to prefer the in-group and to reward it preferentially. The subsequent combination of in-group attraction and preference with competition for desirable, limited resources (camping knives, contest points, party food) created the makings of a seemingly inevitable conflict.

Equity theory (Adams, 1965; Hatfield, Walster, & Berscheid, 1978; see Chapters 1 and 11) argues that people strive for a "fair" allocation of resources in social life. For example, if you work for a company, you want to be paid in proportion to the work you do. But what would be an equitable allocation of resources for the Bull Dogs and Red Devils? Of course, the situation was structured by the researchers so that the "winner takes all," necessarily leaving the other group to feel deprived, even cheated. However, even splitting the resources equally between the two groups might not have been enough; after all, if your group is "better" and "more attractive," doesn't it deserve greater rewards? One unfortunate consequence of group membership is that we often overestimate the goods due our group and underestimate what's due other groups.

Defusing intergroup hostility: The Robber's Cave study.

Does the existence of social groups inevitably lead to intergroup hatred, prejudice, and violence? Sherif was interested not only in tracing the development of intergroup conflict, but also in uncovering techniques to reduce it. About ten years after his "Bull Dog/Red Devil" study, he conducted an ambitious replication that went a step further than the earlier research (Sherif, 1966). The subjects this time were 22 white, middle-class boys from Oklahoma City, and the location was an isolated summer camp at Robber's Cave State Park, Oklahoma. These boys were divided into two groups from the very start. For the first week, the two groups—who labeled themselves the "Rattlers" and the "Eagles"—were totally segregated, learning of the other's existence only toward the end of the week.

As in the earlier study, the staff set up a series of competitions between the groups. Again there were desirable rewards for winning—an impressive trophy, medals, and fancy camping knives. Again, as the games progressed, hostilities broke out. After the Rattlers won the first baseball game against the Eagles, the Eagles, eager for revenge, found and burned the Rattlers' banner. When the Rattlers discovered this "desecration," they confronted the Eagles, and a fight would have broken out had the counselors not intervened.

Various assaults and counterassaults followed. After accusing their opponents of cheating in a tug-of-war contest, the Rattlers raided the Eagles' cabin. The following day, the Eagles, carrying sticks and bats, retaliated with a raid of their own. Again, the counselors had to intervene. The Eagles eventually won the overall sports competition and were awarded the trophy and camping knives. The Rattlers later raided the Eagles' cabin and stole the knives, telling their enemies they would have to "crawl on their bellies" to get them back.

Part of Sherif's purpose in this new research was to test the hypothesis that intergroup conflict can be reduced by providing equal-status, noncompetitive contact between the antagonistic groups in their pursuit of a superordinate goal—a higher-order goal that both groups must work together to achieve and that brings rewards to both groups (Deutsch, 1949; Allport, 1954; Amir, 1969, 1976).

SUMMARY TABLE 9.1   Sources of Prejudice

What explanations of prejudice have been emphasized in this chapter?

	SOURCE OF PREJUDICE	EXAMPLE
Group-level explanations	Cultural and social groups	Cultural and social ideologies; political and religious doctrines.
Individual-level explanations	The past environment	Authoritarian personality research on child-rearing practices.
	The current environment and setting	
	Groups and prejudice	Minimal-group research: Mere existence of in-groups and out-groups leads to preferential treatment of the in-group.
		Sherif's studies: Intergroup competition leads to prejudice.
	Situational cues and prejudice	Overhearing ethnic slur can trigger prejudiced thoughts.
Mediating variables	Beliefs, attitudes	Prejudiced beliefs and attitudes learned in many possible ways (see Chapter 7).
		Religious and political beliefs and attitudes.
	Stereotypes, schemas	Learned by observing and remembering social information; can be influenced by sampling errors, memory overload, and illusory correlations.
	Personality	Authoritarianism, dogmatism.
Current responses	Prejudiced thoughts	
	Prejudiced feelings	
	Prejudiced behaviors	Our behaviors may induce others to behave consistently with our stereotypes.

The explanations listed in this table are interdependent. For example, social ideologies may lead to child-rearing practices, which in turn may lead individuals to develop certain personality traits and attitudes. The many sources of prejudice listed here suggest why prejudice is a complex and enduring problem in social interactions.

So the researchers at Robber's Cave created artificial "emergencies" that could be resolved only through cooperation between the two groups. For example, when the summer camp lost its water supply because of a leak in a mile-long pipe, the boys broke into teams to inspect the pipe. And when a truck that would carry the boys to a much-desired campout got stuck in mud, the boys combined forces to pull it out. Pursuing such superordinate goals and introducing noncompetitive activities that included *all* the boys reduced the conflict between the Eagles and Rattlers. By the end of the study, the two groups were working and playing together. Furthermore, boys started to choose friends from both the out-group and in-group. In this limited setting then, with the help of beneficent authorities, groups that had been separated by competitive animosity developed a more peaceful coexistence.

Sherif's studies add intergroup competition to the many factors contributing to prejudice already discussed in this chapter. Summary Table 9.1 reviews these factors and suggests why prejudice remains a stubborn social problem.

Reducing Prejudice: The Intergroup Contact Hypothesis

[Mrs. Breedlove] looked nicer than I had ever seen her, in her white uniform and her hair in a small pompadour.

. . . "I'm gone get the wash. You all stand stock still right here and don't mess up nothing." She disappeared behind a white swinging door. . . .

Another door opened, and in walked a little girl, smaller and younger than all of us. She wore a pink sunback dress. . . . Her hair was corn yellow and bound in a thick ribbon. When she saw us, fear danced across her face for a second. She looked anxiously around the kitchen.

"Where's Polly?" she asked.

The familiar violence rose in me. Her calling Mrs. Breedlove Polly, when even Pecola called her mother Mrs. Breedlove, seemed reason enough to scratch her.

—— *The Bluest Eye*, p. 86

As the Robber's Cave study showed, one way to reduce intergroup prejudices and hostility is to bring people from antagonistic groups together, particularly in pursuit of a common goal. After all, people cannot learn that their stereotypes are in error and that members of other groups are just people like themselves unless they interact with people from those groups. However, as the passage from *The Bluest Eye* vividly illustrates, intergroup contact does not always breed goodwill. When contact is between white master and black servant, or between privileged-majority children and underprivileged-minority children, contact may exacerbate tensions and reinforce stereotypes. What conditions must be met in order for intergroup contact to reduce prejudice?

Drawing upon the work of others (see Miller & Brewer, 1984), Gordon Allport first strongly focused social psychologists' attention on the hypothesis that certain kinds of intergroup contact are necessary to produce beneficial results. Allport concluded that

prejudice . . . may be reduced by equal status contact between majority and minority groups in the pursuit of common goals. The effect is greatly enhanced if this contact is sanctioned by institutional supports (i.e., by law, custom or local atmosphere), and provided it is of a sort that leads to the perception of common interests and common humanity between members of the two groups. (1954, p. 281)

Many studies have examined the validity of Allport's intergroup contact hypothesis over the past 30 years (see, for example, Amir, 1969, 1976; Harding, Proshansky, Kutner, & Chein, 1969; Katz, 1970; Miller & Brewer, 1984). One focus of this research has been to determine *when* intergroup contact leads to greater harmony and less prejudice. Besides the qualifying conditions suggested by Allport, Amir (1969) suggests that intergroup contact is most effective when it's intimate rather than casual, when it's pleasant and noncompetitive, and when it occurs between groups that already possess somewhat favorable attitudes toward each other before contact takes place.

Contact Between Groups in Schools

Can we design programs that facilitate productive contact between real-life social groups, programs that are analogous to the manipulations in the final stages of the Robber's Cave study? Beginning in 1954 with *Brown v. Board of Education*, the United States embarked on a dramatic experiment in social change when it began to desegregate the public schools. Suppose your job was to implement school desegregation. What would be the most effective way to reduce prejudice and foster intergroup harmony?

The list of factors provided by Allport and Amir offers guidance, but it also gives some reasons for pessimism. How does one arrange equal-status, intimate, pleasant contact in the pursuit of common goals between groups that are initially hostile to each other and often come from markedly different socioeconomic backgrounds? Busing disadvantaged urban minority children to a white suburban middle-class school may physically intersperse the children in classrooms and school activities. But almost by definition such busing does not produce "equal-status" contact between white children and minority children; the white children will most likely have a cultural and educational advantage. Can schools foster friendly, intimate contact between such disparate groups? And what common goals can children pursue in school that will foster ties between groups?

Recent summaries of research on school integration have documented mixed results. Since the mid-1950s, when integration was partially implemented in the United States, educational achievement has declined slightly for both blacks and whites (Gerard, 1983; Miller & Brewer, 1984). Of course, declining scholastic performance may not necessarily be related to desegregation. In optimal circumstances, integrated schooling may increase interracial friendships and intergroup relations, but minority students often remain at an educational disadvantage that translates to lower status and power compared to their classmates (Cohen, 1984).

Simply placing students of different races and ethnic groups together in the classroom may not be enough to produce a high-quality integrated educational experience. The dynamics in a typical North American classroom are based on individual achievement and competition among students. In this competitive environment, members of disadvantaged groups often fall further behind and are labeled "unable" by the majority group. One solution suggested by social psychologists is to introduce cooperative learning procedures into the classroom (for example, Aronson, 1978; Chasnoff, 1978; Lyons, 1980; Roy, 1982).

For example, Weigel, Wiser, and Cook (1975) compared the effects of cooperative and traditional teaching techniques in newly desegregated schools. Subjects were junior high and senior high school students who were new to these integrated schools. Approximately 60 percent of the students were white, 20 percent were black,

Do cooperative, integrated classrooms foster positive social interactions among members of different groups?

Weigel, Wiser, and Cook (1975) compared "whole-class" settings, in which students worked as individuals, to cooperative class settings, in which ethnically mixed teams of students worked together. The graph shows the proportion of helping behaviors and behavioral conflicts in the two kinds of classrooms that occurred across ethnic groups.

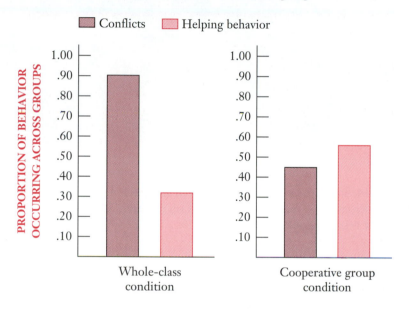

SOURCE: Data from Weigel, Wiser, and Cook (1975).

and 20 percent were Hispanic. In the traditional classrooms, students worked as individuals in whole classes of students; in the cooperative classes, students worked in racially mixed teams of four to six students and cooperated as a group on all assignments. The teachers in this study were ethnically varied, and each teacher taught both traditional and cooperative classes.

The results of this study suggest that *cooperative* ethnic contact indeed has positive effects. Students in the cooperative classes showed significantly less interracial conflict and were significantly more likely to help students of other races (see Figure 9.9). Furthermore, white students in cooperative classrooms were less likely to say that white students possess more desirable traits than do minorities and were more likely to choose nonwhite students as partners in various activities. However, although cooperative classrooms clearly led to greater harmony between groups *in the*

Women join men as workers at a shipbuilding company in Mississippi. Machinist Celia Yanish commented, "It was very rough for a while, but we were determined to stay, and eventually the majority of the men learned to accept us and respect us as co-workers and union sisters."

classroom, students in these classrooms showed no general shifts in their attitudes toward minorities or toward integration and segregation. Other research has produced similar results (Cook, 1984).

The Effect of Contact on Intergroup Attitudes

Thus, the specific experiences of intergroup contact—for example, making friends with a person from a different ethnic group—do not necessarily affect broader attitudes toward the group. Why should this be the case? One possibility is that subjects come to like individuals from other groups with whom they interact, but they don't view these new friends as representative or typical of the larger group.

An experiment by Wilder (1984) attempted to determine when pleasant contact between members of different (and somewhat hostile) groups leads to better feelings between the groups and reduces stereotypes about the out-group. Specifically, Wilder had women students from either Rutgers or Douglas College (both part of the State University of New Jersey) work on various problems (for example, anagrams or riddles) with a female confederate who pretended to be a student from the other college. Pretesting had shown that women from each college had fairly strong and somewhat negative stereotypes about women from the other college. Rutgers women tended to view Douglas women as overly conservative, too concerned with their appearance, and too interested in good grades; Douglas women described Rutgers women as uninterested in scholarship, as "party animals" interested only in having a good time, and as overly liberal.

Some of Wilder's confederates reinforced the stereotype of their supposed school. For example, the confederate labeled as a Douglas student dressed nicely and wore makeup, said she was a home economics major, talked about her conservative

political club, and mentioned that she hoped the experiment would be brief because
she had a lot of studying to do. Other confederates did not reinforce the stereotypes
associated with their supposed school. Wilder manipulated another variable in this
experiment: Sometimes the confederate was pleasant and helpful to the real subject,
and sometimes she was unpleasant and denigrating.

In this experiment, contact with the confederate most influenced subjects' evaluations of the out-group (that is, the other college) when the interaction was pleasant
and the confederate was perceived as *typical* of her college — that is, when she
matched subjects' stereotypes (see Figure 9.10). Although subjects' liking for the
out-group was increased by contact, their stereotypes about the out-group remained
much the same.

This study points to an important bind in which minority group members find
themselves. If they cultivate liking from majority group members, this liking will be
generalized to their group only if they are perceived as typical of their group (that is,
when they show stereotypical traits and characteristics). But that just helps to reinforce those stereotypes, including unflattering ones.

If the minority person doesn't match the majority group's stereotypes and cul-
tivates liking from majority members, then it's easy for members of the majority
group to view him or her as an "exception." Milton (1972) describes an interesting
illustration of this phenomenon in a study that focused on how male police officers
in Washington, D.C., reacted to being assigned female partners. Although most of
these male officers were quite satisfied with their female partner's performance, they
still felt — as strongly as officers with male partners thought — that "it would be a
mistake to hire large numbers of women." Apparently they came to see their partner
as a "good" female exception, but they didn't change their attitudes about women

FIGURE 9.10   Evaluating a group after interacting with one member of the group.

When does interaction with a member of an out-group change our attitudes toward the group?

Wilder (1984) had college women evaluate women from another college (an "out-group") following interaction with a "student" from that college who behaved in either a pleasant or an unpleasant fashion. The student either did or did not match subjects' stereotypes of the out-group. The graph shows the subjects' ratings of the out-group college for each condition (higher numbers represent more positive ratings).

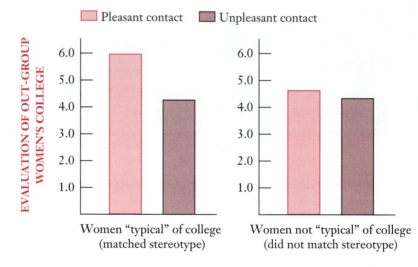

Subjects were more likely to generalize in a positive direction from the experience of one woman's behavior to her college as a whole when she matched their stereotypes about the college.

SOURCE: Data from Wilder (1984).

The Wilder study helps to explain why positive interaction with one member of a minority group may not change our attitudes toward the group. If we view the individual as an "exception" (that is, he or she doesn't match our stereotype of the group), then we won't modify our stereotypes and attitudes.

officers in general. Perhaps if these recalcitrant male officers had been exposed to several "good" female officers, they would have been forced to change their stereotypes and prejudices somewhat more. Apparently, people sometimes deal with the contradictory information they receive through social contact by creating mental "exceptions" and subcategories, rather than by tossing out preexisting stereotypes (see Taylor, 1981).

Considerable (though far from perfect) progress in integrating public facilities, schools, and the workplace has occurred in the United States. Far less satisfactory progress has been made in reducing residential segregation (Hamilton, Carpenter, & Bishop, 1984; Schnare, 1980; Van Valey, Roof, & Wilcox, 1977). One reason for residential segregation may simply be that people prefer to live with "their own kind"; certainly there is abundant social psychological evidence suggesting that similarity leads to attraction (as we shall see in Chapter 11).

The lower economic status of certain minorities — black Americans for example — may also contribute to segregation; minorities simply are less able to afford "mainstream" housing. But this explanation is of limited value because blacks and whites of the same socioeconomic status still tend to live in segregated settings (Bianchi, Farley, & Spain, 1982; Wilson & Taeuber, 1978).

Survey research and opinion polls point clearly to prejudice as a major cause of residential segregation. Although whites have become more tolerant of integration in housing over the past several decades, many still hold reservations. Many whites still strongly prefer to live in all-white neighborhoods, whereas blacks have a much stronger preference for integrated housing (Farley, Schuman, Bianchi, Colasanto, & Hatchett, 1978; Lake, 1981).

In an early and still often-cited study, Deutsch and Collins (1951) investigated the effects of equal-status interracial contact in government housing projects in New York City. Although many psychologists interpret that research to be supportive of the contact hypothesis, others (for example, Cagle, 1973) have argued that enforced residential mixing leads to few actual social contacts between the races. You can live next door to someone and still not talk to him or her.

But is talking really necessary to change attitudes? Hamilton and Bishop (1976) conducted an ambitious field study to see what happens to white residents' attitudes when blacks move into their previously segregated neighborhood. These researchers identified eight middle-class, white neighborhoods around New Haven, Connecticut, in which a black family had recently purchased a home and compared these neighborhoods with a control group of ten comparable neighborhoods into which a white family had just moved.

As you might expect, the arrival of a black family to a formerly all-white neighborhood was a highly salient event. Neighbors continued to describe it to research interviewers as a "change in the nature of the neighborhood" for a year afterwards, whereas the arrivals of white families in control neighborhoods were soon forgotten. Also not surprisingly, the initial comments made by whites about their new black neighbors tended to be unfavorable.

Even though whites did not interact much with their new black neighbors, still their attitudes became less prejudiced and less racist during the following year. Hamilton and Bishop suggest that the whites probably held negative stereotypes about blacks ("They don't take care of their houses") and negative expectations about what would happen to their neighborhood ("Property values will go down"). When their dreaded expectations had not been realized after the first year of "integration," whites' attitudes changed. By the way, Hamilton and Bishop carefully analyzed sales and property assessment data from these neighborhoods and found no evidence for the commonly held belief that the integration of neighborhoods leads to a higher turnover of houses or to reduced property values.

Hamilton and Bishop's study implies that "contact" need not necessarily be intimate, or social, or face-to-face to produce positive results. Particularly if through

Below: The white actors who played "Amos & Andy" portrayed a highly stereotyped image of black Americans; *right:* The cast of "Sesame Street": Does the favorable portrayal of different ethnic groups on TV shows reduce prejudice?

their actions and appearances minority members break commonly held stereotypes of the majority, then the majority's attitudes and beliefs may be altered simply by passive contact — by observing, if not relating to, the minority members. This research points to the general importance of cognitive processes in mediating the effects of intergroup contact (see Rose, 1981). It also suggests that, under certain circumstances, residential integration can help to reduce prejudice.

Vicarious Contact Through the Mass Media

. . . [they] had a loving conversation about how cu-ute Shirley Temple was. I couldn't join them in their adoration because I hated Shirley. Not because she was cute, but because she danced with Bojangles, who was *my* friend, *my* uncle, *my* daddy, and who ought to have been soft-shoeing it and chuckling with me. Instead he was enjoying, sharing, giving a lovely dance thing with one of those little white girls whose socks never slid down under their heels.

—— *The Bluest Eye*, p. 19

You need not physically encounter another group to be in "contact" with that group. For years the mass media have at times intentionally and at times inadvertently fostered stereotypes and intergroup tensions. A study during World War II analyzed how "stock" minority characters were portrayed in the media (Writers' War Board, 1945). Generally, heroes and "good" characters were Anglo-Saxon, whereas menials, servants, and criminals were likely to be minorities. According to this study, the portrayals provided by popular fiction "could easily be used to 'prove' that Negroes are lazy, the Jews wily, the Irish superstitious, and the Italians criminal." This analysis from the 1940s focused considerable attention on radio, the dominant mass medium of the day:

> The broadcasting fraternity has been arguing for years as to whether "Amos 'n' Andy" helps or hurts the Negro race. Some Negroes do, some don't, object to the series. Another continuing argument revolves around "Rochester" on the Jack Benny program. This presentation is good-natured and pictures "Rochester" as quick-witted and wise, yet it is stereotyped on all the usual accounts — addiction to drink, dice, wenching, and razors (qtd. in Allport, 1954, p. 201).

With the advent of television, stereotyping extended to the visual as well as the verbal. Today, stereotyping in the media is less extreme than 40 years ago, but research evidence still accumulates about negative portrayals of various minorities (Berry, 1980; Pierce, 1980) and of women (Basow, 1986).

The mass media have undoubtedly contributed to prejudice in our society. Can they contribute to its reduction as well? The answer seems to be a tentative "Yes." For example, children who watched integrated social interactions on the show "Sesame Street" developed more positive attitudes toward blacks and Hispanics (Bogatz & Ball, 1971). A Canadian replication of this study introduced into "Sesame Street" content that was directly relevant to Canadian minorities — Asians, Indians, and French-Canadians (Gorn, Goldberg, & Kanungo, 1976); again, sympathetic media portrayals led to reduced prejudice. The Canadian preschoolers who viewed "Sesame Street" were more likely to pick nonwhite children as potential playmates than were control children.

An extensive review of research on the effects of TV on racial and ethnic attitudes (Graves, 1980) concludes that positive attitude change is possible, particularly with extensive viewing. "You've got to be taught to hate," states a well-known song lyric from the musical, "South Pacific." Fortunately, with the help of enlightened media programming, people can be taught not to hate as well.

Summary

1. A prejudice is a negative attitude toward a group or toward an individual member of a group. A prejudice is an attitude comprising emotions, beliefs, and behaviors. Prejudice can be analyzed at a number of different levels.

2. Stereotypes are overgeneralized and often inaccurate beliefs we hold about groups or group members. Several different methods have been developed to measure stereotypes.

3. Stereotypes frequently portray out-groups more negatively than they do in-groups and lead people to underestimate the variability of people in out-groups.

4. Stereotypes can result from biased sampling of social information, the processing of complex social information with limited memory resources, and illusory correlations.

5. Stereotypes are like schemas in that they influence how people process social information and how people evaluate members of other groups. Stereotypes often lead to behavior that serves to verify and perpetuate the stereotypes.

6. Research on the authoritarian personality shows that some individuals are consistently prejudiced against many minority groups. Such people report having punitive, status-anxious parents and tend to describe themselves and their parents in an unrealistically positive manner and minorities in an unrealistically negative manner.

7. Research on the authoritarian personality suggests that prejudice results from repressed feelings of anger and insecurity that have their origins in severe treatment by strict parents. Psychologists have criticized the methods and theoretical interpretations of the authoritarian personality researchers.

8. Both political conservatism and religious beliefs are correlated with prejudice in the United States. The factors responsible for these correlations are complex.

9. A stigma is a social label or condition that defines a person as flawed or undesirable. Stigmatizing conditions vary in their concealability, course over time, social disruptiveness, aesthetic qualities, origins, and peril to others. Society often treats stigmatized people harshly.

10. Minimal group research shows that when people are arbitrarily divided into groups, they show bias in favor of their in-group. Tajfel's Social Identity Theory argues that this bias results from people's motivation to boost their self-esteem through a positive social identity.

11. Competition among groups for scarce resources can lead to prejudice. In two studies of school boys at summer camps, Muzafer Sherif found that group competition inevitably led to conflict, prejudice, and stereotypes in the two competing groups. The creation of superordinate goals helped to reduce conflict and prejudice in the second study.

12. The intergroup contact hypothesis holds that certain kinds of contact between groups (for example, contact that is socially supported, equal-status, and in pursuit of common goals) lead to a reduction of prejudice.

13. Competitive classrooms may amplify social inequalities when unequal-status students from different groups are integrated. Cooperative classrooms in which students must work together on projects are more effective in increasing interaction between individuals from different groups. Although contact between different groups can lead to more positive interactions among members of different groups, it does not necessarily lead to changed attitudes toward out-groups.

14. Prejudice is a significant cause of residential segregation. Housing integration can be effective in reducing stereotypes and prejudice.

15. Although the mass media have often perpetuated unflattering stereotypes and prejudice, they can also reduce prejudice through favorable depictions both of minority groups and of interactions among different groups.

Anti-Semitism Scale: A scale developed in research on the authoritarian personality and used to assess attitudes toward Jews

Authoritarian personality: A personality syndrome leading to consistently prejudiced beliefs and attitudes; research on the authoritarian personality suggests that authoritarian people tend to be reared by punitive, status-anxious parents, and as a result they are highly defensive and hold rigid and conventional beliefs

Diagnostic ratio: A method of measuring stereotypes in which subjects are asked to estimate what percentage of people in a group possess a trait and also what percentage of people in general possess the same trait; the diagnostic ratio is the ratio of these two percentage estimates

Discrimination: Overt acts that express prejudice and treat members of a group unfairly compared to members of other groups

Ethnocentrism: The belief that one's own group is superior to other groups

Ethnocentrism Scale: A scale developed in research on the authoritarian personality and used to assess prejudice toward various minority groups and ethnocentric attitudes

F Scale: Also known as the authoritarianism scale; this scale was developed in research on the authoritarian personality and is used to assess people with fascist tendencies; such people, according to scale items, emphasize power, dominance, and toughness in social relationships, derogate tender-mindedness and introspection, and project their own undesirable impulses onto others

Minimal group: An arbitrary group with no social history that is created in the laboratory; research on minimal groups shows that people evaluate in-groups more positively than out-groups, even in such arbitrary groups

Prejudice: A negative prejudgment of a group or group member that is often unwarranted and based on limited, insufficient information; a prejudice can be conceptualized as a negative attitude comprising emotional, cognitive, and behavioral components

Social identity theory: Tajfel's theory that people have both personal and social identities; people are motivated to evaluate in-groups more positively than out-groups in order to enhance their social identities and increase self-esteem

Stigma: A social label or condition that defines a person as flawed or undesirable; terminal diseases, disfigurement, mental illness, and alcoholism are frequently stigmatizing conditions in our society

Superordinate goal: A higher-order goal that can be achieved only if groups cooperate with one another; Sherif argued that intergroup contact in the pursuit of superordinate goals can help to reduce intergroup conflict and prejudice

Symbolic racism: A hypothesized form of racism present today in the United States; symbolic racism consists of prejudice associated with traditional American moral values and the Protestant Ethic

"Tell me, how does the other sex of your race differ from yours?"

He looked startled. . . . "I never thought of that," he said. "You've never seen a woman." He used his Terran-language word, which I knew.

". . . Do they differ much from your sex in mind behavior? Are they like a different species?"

"No. Yes. No, of course not, not really. But the difference is very important. I suppose the most important thing, the heaviest single factor in one's life, is whether one's born male or female. In most societies it determines one's expectations, activities, outlook, ethics, manners — almost everything. Vocabulary. Semiotic usages. Clothing. Even food. Women . . . women tend to eat less. . . . It's extremely hard to separate the innate differences from the learned ones. Even where women participate equally with men in the society, they still after all do all the childbearing, and so most of the child-rearing. . . ."

"Equality is not the general rule then? . . ."

—— from *The Left Hand of Darkness*,
by Ursula K. LeGuin, pp. 234–235

CHAPTER 10

Gender and Social Behavior

*I*t is the distant future. Earth is part of a far-flung association of planets settled by various human races, and the Terran envoy, Genly Ai, must travel to the planet Gethen (also known as "Winter" because of its cold, harsh climate) to negotiate its entry into the organization of civilized worlds. The Gethenians are clearly of human stock, with one major difference: They are hermaphrodites, and thus each Gethenian is capable of either mothering or fathering a child. What is life like on a world with no distinction between "male" and "female"? Try to envision the forms that art, mythology, science, government, warfare, and family life take on the planet Gethen.

In her award-winning novel, *The Left Hand of Darkness*, Ursula K. LeGuin portrays a world without gender, and in so doing she poses a number of profound questions about the planet earth and its people: What *are* the differences between men and women? Is gender "the most important thing" about a person? How does society influence our concept of gender, and conversely, how does gender influence the organization and structure of society? And how would a society of literally androgynous people (that is, people possessing both male and female characteristics) be different from ours?

The British novelist Jane Austen once wrote that history "tells me nothing that does not either vex or weary me. The quarrels of popes and kings, with wars or pestilences, in every page; the men all so good for nothing, and hardly any women at all — it is very tiresome" (*Northanger Abbey*, p. 103). Although it is sometimes tiresome, history

The Changing Roles of Women and Men

can be instructive nonetheless. Let's turn from the fantastical world of Gethen to the more mundane Earth and look briefly at the recent history of women and men, and their changing roles in society.

Throughout much of recorded history the relationship between men and women has been one of accepted inequality. As recently as the nineteenth century, scientists generally held that women were intellectually inferior to men, and some suggested that if women even attempted to think and work like men, they would lose their reproductive capacity (Shields, 1975; Ehrenreich & English, 1979; Cole, 1979; Spence, Deaux, & Helmreich, 1985). Women could not vote, sit on juries, or manage their own financial affairs. They could not even demand legal custody of their children. By law, women were chattel—property—of men.

Barred from most forms of higher education a century ago, women now make up approximately 50 percent of U.S. college students (Social Indicators of Equality for Minorities and Women, 1978; Boudreau, 1986). However, the education that women pursue often differs from that pursued by men. In recent years women have earned over 60 percent of the bachelor's degrees awarded in education, fine arts, foreign languages, and home economics, but less than 20 percent of the degrees in architecture, business, engineering, and the physical sciences (Stockard et al., 1980).

Different educational fields and careers may simply hold different interest for women and men (Eccles, Adler, & Meese, 1984), but because "women's work" is often valued less than "men's work" (Touhey, 1974), the different occupational pursuits of women and men have two important social consequences: They reinforce people's perception that women and men are different, and they often confer lower

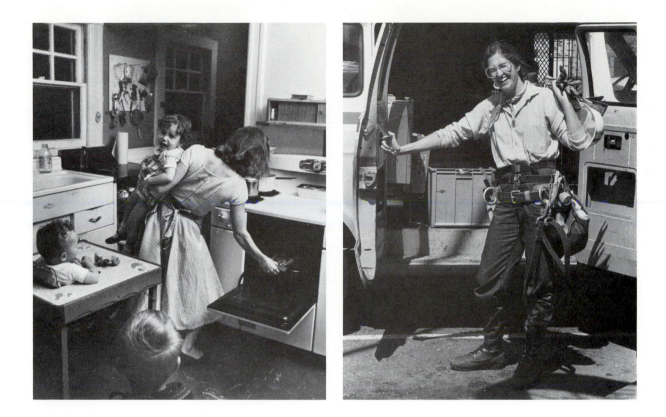

status to women workers. Although its specific definition varies across cultures, women's work almost always is assigned lower status than men's work (Tavris & Wade, 1984). In the Soviet Union, for instance, more women work as physicians, dentists, and pharmacists than in the United States, but these professions do not have nearly as much prestige in the Soviet Union as in the United States (Safilios-Rothschild, 1975).

Employment discrimination based on sex is now illegal in the United States under the Civil Rights Act of 1964, yet women still face discrimination in the workplace. Over the last century, the percentage of women in the U.S. workforce has steadily increased (see Figure 10.1), but women have generally worked in lower-status jobs than men and have received lower wages and fewer opportunities for advancement.

Currently the ratio of the median income of working women to that of men is about .60 (that is, the median income of women is 60 percent of that of men). This ratio varies somewhat depending on the kind of work; it ranges from .51 for sales people and .62 for professional and technical workers up to .71 for service workers (U.S. Department of Labor, 1983). This last statistic is particularly noteworthy because it is difficult to attribute the disparity in the salaries of female and male service workers to differences in education or skill. Perhaps because of the realities of the work world, many women hold lower expectations than do men concerning the pay and prestige of their jobs (Major & Konar, 1984).

While women have participated more and more in the work world, they have also tended to retain primary responsibility for childcare and housekeeping in the

FIGURE 10.1   **Women in the civilian labor force.**

How has the participation of women in the U.S. labor force changed over the last century?

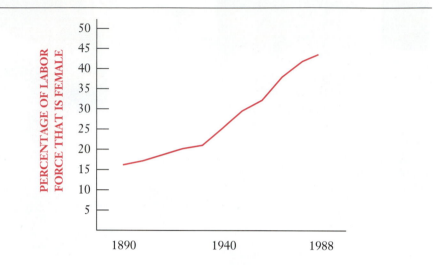

Since 1890 – and especially since World War II – the percentage of U.S. workers who are female has increased dramatically.

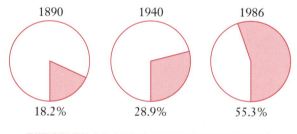

PERCENTAGE OF U.S. WOMEN WHO WORK

And by the end of the 1980s a majority of U.S. women worked.

SOURCE: Data from Lyon (1986); *Employment and Earnings* (February 1989); U.S. Department of Labor, Bureau of Labor Statistics.

Social changes of this magnitude bring with them far-reaching consequences for individuals and for society. In your opinion, how have social beliefs and attitudes about the sexes changed over the past century?

United States (Heiss, 1986). Despite changing attitudes toward sex roles in recent years, men generally have not substantially increased their contributions to housework (Walker & Woods, 1976; Pleck, 1979). Still (perhaps surprisingly), most women are relatively content with their roles as homemakers (Campbell, 1981).

In sum, despite marked changes in the roles of women and men in the twentieth century, gender still has a profound effect on social organization and on individuals' behavior, especially in the domains of work and family.

Some theorists use the word *sex* to refer to the biological status of being male or female and *gender* to refer to social definitions of male and female, including all the nonbiological characteristics that society uses to differentiate men and women (Kessler & McKenna, 1978; Unger, 1979; Deaux, 1985). For most of us, sex is defined primarily by the genitalia — women have vaginas, and men penises. Gender, however, is displayed and defined by a host of cues and behaviors, including styles of dress, nonverbal mannerisms, hobbies and interests, occupations, personality traits, and roles in family life.

Psychological Research on Sex and Gender

Social psychological research on sex and gender has traditionally focused on two main topics: the social perception of men and women, and the existence or nonexistence of sex differences (Unger, 1979; Deaux, 1985). The first kind of research often investigates the stereotypes people hold about men and women, and how people evaluate men and women differently. (For example, are women perceived to be more "emotional" and less "logical" than men? Do managers judge equivalent work performed by women and men differently?) Sex difference research attempts to document the ways in which men and women actually are alike and different in their behavior. (For example, are men on average more aggressive than women? Are women more nonverbally sensitive than men? Do men engage more in task-oriented behaviors in groups, and women more in emotional, friendly behaviors?) We shall consider both of these topics in this chapter.

The topic of behavioral sex differences will lead us naturally to theories of how sex (genes and genitalia) develops into gender (different behaviors and roles for women and men). Finally, we'll turn to newer topics in social psychological research: the nature of masculinity and femininity, and the possibility that individuals can possess both "good" masculine and "good" feminine qualities.

Stereotypes About Women and Men

"...Are they [women] mentally inferior?"

"I don't know. They don't often seem to turn up mathematicians, or composers of music, or inventors, or abstract thinkers. But it isn't that they're stupid. Physically they're less muscular, but a little more durable than men. Psychologically —"

—— *The Left Hand of Darkness*, p. 235

Personality Stereotypes

Strong stereotypes exist about the personality traits possessed by men and women. (See Chapter 9 for a discussion of the definition and measurement of stereotypes.) In one well-known study, Rosenkrantz, Vogel, Bee, Broverman, and Broverman

(1968) asked 80 college women and 74 college men to rate how much "an adult woman" or "an adult man" possessed each of 122 different personality characteristics. The resultant data showed that subjects believed many traits to be more characteristic of one sex or the other (see Figure 10.2).

Statistical analyses of subjects' ratings further indicated the existence of two clusters of traits that subjects thought differentiated women and men (again, see Figure 10.2). One cluster of traits, seen as more typical of men, related to instrumental, goal-oriented behaviors, such as "competitive," "logical," "skilled in business," and "self-confident." The second cluster, seen as more typical of women, dealt with nurturing and expressive behaviors, such as "gentle," "aware of the feelings of others," and "easily expresses tender feelings."

These stereotypes — that men possess instrumental traits and women expressive traits — have been documented in many studies. They are found in people of varying ages (including children as young as age 5 or 6), marital statuses, and educational levels (Broverman, Vogel, Broverman, Clarkson, & Rosenkrantz, 1972; Kohlberg, 1966; Ruble, 1983). They are relatively consistent across cultures (Williams & Best, 1982). And despite changes in women's and men's social roles, they remain largely unchanged in recent years (Ruble, 1983; Martin, 1987).

Do gender stereotypes portray men and women's personalities as "different but equal"? Not necessarily. Subjects often perceive the "male" pole of various trait dimensions to be more desirable (Rosenkrantz et al., 1968). (For example, being "logical" is desirable, but being "illogical" is not. "Logical" is judged to be more characteristic of men and "illogical" more characteristic of women.) Widiger and Settle (1987) have recently argued that the Rosenkrantz study exaggerated the value people attach to "male" traits simply because their list included more positively valued "male" traits than "female" traits. When Williams and Best (1982) assessed the gender stereotypes held by people in many different countries, they found that stereotypically "male" traits were judged to be only slightly more positive than "female" traits, a finding consistent with Widiger and Settle's analysis. However, "male" traits were also judged to be more "active" and "strong" than "female" traits, and strength and activity often have positive connotations.

To study the possibility that "female" and "male" traits are evaluated differently, Broverman and her colleagues (1972) asked groups of clinical psychologists, psychiatrists, and psychiatric social workers to identify those gender-stereotypical traits that were true of a mature, mentally healthy adult man, those that were true of a mature, mentally healthy adult woman, and those that were true of a mature, mentally healthy adult (sex not specified). The results showed that in general "male" traits were judged to indicate mental health more than were "female" traits. Furthermore, the traits used to describe a "healthy man" were like those used to describe a "healthy person," but the traits used to describe a "healthy woman" were less positive.

Broverman and her colleagues (1972) drew the following disturbing conclusions from their data:

> In effect, clinicians are suggesting that healthy women differ from healthy men by being more submissive, less independent, less adventurous, less objective, more easily influenced, less aggressive, less competitive, more excitable in minor crises, more emotional, more conceited about their appearance, and having their feelings more easily hurt.

FIGURE 10.2   Gender stereotypical traits.

What traits have traditionally been associated with women and with men?

The table shows the traits associated with each sex by a sample of college men and women in 1968. The traits are grouped in terms of the rated desirability of being "masculine" or "feminine" on a given trait.

STEREOTYPICAL SEX-ROLE ITEMS *(responses from 74 college men and 80 college women)*

Competency Cluster: Masculine pole is more desirable

Feminine	*Masculine*
Not at all aggressive	Very aggressive
Not at all independent	Very independent
Very emotional	Not at all emotional
Does not hide emotions at all	Almost always hides emotions
Very subjective	Very objective
Very easily influenced	Not at all easily influenced
Very submissive	Very dominant
Dislikes math and science very much	Likes math and science very much
Very excitable in a minor crisis	Not at all excitable in a minor crisis
Very passive	Very active
Not at all competitive	Very competitive
Very illogical	Very logical
Very home oriented	Very worldly
Not at all skilled in business	Very skilled in business
Very sneaky	Very direct
Does not know the way of the world	Knows the way of the world
Feelings easily hurt	Feelings not easily hurt
Not at all adventurous	Very adventurous
Has difficulty making decisions	Can make decisions easily
Cries very easily	Never cries
Almost never acts as a leader	Almost always acts as a leader
Not at all self-confident	Very self-confident
Very uncomfortable about being aggressive	Not at all uncomfortable about being aggressive
Not at all ambitious	Very ambitious
Unable to separate feelings from ideas	Easily able to separate feelings from ideas
Very dependent	Not at all dependent
Very conceited about appearance	Never conceited about appearance
Thinks women are always superior to men	Thinks men are always superior to women
Does not talk freely about sex with men	Talks freely about sex with men

Warmth-Expressive Cluster: Feminine pole is more desirable

Feminine	*Masculine*
Doesn't use harsh language at all	Uses very harsh language
Very talkative	Not at all talkative
Very tactful	Very blunt
Very gentle	Very rough
Very aware of feelings of others	Not at all aware of feelings of others
Very religious	Not at all religious
Very interested in own appearance	Not at all interested in own appearance
Very neat in habits	Very sloppy in habits
Very quiet	Very loud
Very strong need for security	Very little need for security
Enjoys art and literature	Does not enjoy art and literature at all
Easily expresses tender feelings	Does not express tender feelings at all easily

Traits stereotypically perceived to be related to gender fell into two clusters: instrumental traits (such as "dominant," "competitive," or "adventurous"), perceived to be more typical of males, and expressive traits (such as "tactful," "gentle," or "expresses tender feelings"), perceived to be more typical of females.

SOURCE: Rosenkrantz et al. (1968). Used with permission of Donald M. Broverman.

More than two decades have passed since this study was done. Do you think that stereotypes about "female" and "male" traits have changed significantly during that time?

. . . Our hypothesis that a double standard of health exists for men and women was thus confirmed: the general standard of health (adult, sex unspecified) is actually applied to men only, while healthy women are perceived as significantly less healthy by adult standards. (pp. 70–71)

Although clinicians may hold stereotypes about personality differences between men and women, research suggests that such stereotypes do not necessarily lead to different and biased therapeutic treatments for men and women (Smith, 1980). However, mental health professionals may show sex biases in other ways — by interpreting equivalent case information about female and male clients differently and by using different diagnostic categories for women and men (Hare-Musten, 1983; Kaplan, 1983; Widiger & Frances, 1985).

Just as general standards of mental health tend to be the standards for men (but not women), so too the stereotypes of different nationalities tend to be the stereotypes of their men. Eagly and Kite (1987) asked over 300 male and female college students at Purdue University to rate the probability that the people in 28 countries possessed such traits as "honest," "ambitious," "aggressive," "dominant," "kind," and "understanding." A balanced assortment of instrumental and expressive traits was used. One group of students made their ratings for nationalities with sex unspecified (for example, they rated the probability that the "Swiss" are "honest"); other groups rated the men or the women of a given nationality (they rated the probability that "Swiss men" or "Swiss women" are "honest").

Two interesting findings emerged. First, stereotypes of nationality groups in general resembled stereotypes of their men more than those of their women. Second, the ratings of instrumental and expressive traits for the men of various countries were quite variable; by contrast, women were given low ratings on instrumental traits and high ratings on expressive traits, regardless of their nationality (see Figure 10.3). In other words, women of different nationalities tended to be judged more in terms of their gender, whereas men were judged more in terms of their nationality.

Eagly and Kite (1987) explained their findings in terms of the social roles of men and women in most countries:

Because women have considerably less power and status than men do, no doubt their behavior is observed relatively little by foreigners, and the behavior that is observed consists largely of domestic activities and, for some countries, work carried out in low-status, poorly paid occupations. As a result, stereotypes of nationalities are more similar to stereotypes of their men than of their women. (p. 461)

Broader Stereotypes About Gender

Gender stereotypes embrace more than personality traits. To assess people's everyday conceptions of gender, Myers and Gonda (1982) asked over 200 Canadian college students to define the words *masculine* and *feminine*, and they then coded these responses into different content categories. In order of frequency, students most often defined masculinity and femininity in terms of physical appearance and characteristics (for example, "muscular," "wears makeup," or "has a deep voice"), social or biological roles ("bears children," "sexually attractive to men [or women]," "gay" or "not gay"), and biological sex. Personality characteristics were fourth in frequency, accounting for only about 14 percent of subjects' total responses. In a subsequent study Spence and Sawin (1985) asked a group of married men and women in

■■

FIGURE 10.3   Stereotypes of men and women of different countries.

How do gender stereotypes interact with stereotypes of different nationalities?

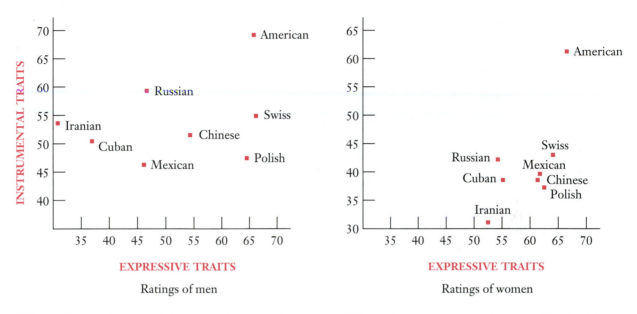

Ratings of men

Ratings of women

When college students rated the men and women of various countries on a number of instrumental and expressive traits, the males were rated quite variably. For example, Iranian males were perceived to be low on expressive traits (not "kind" or "understanding") and moderate on instrumental traits ("dominant," "ambitious"), whereas Polish males were perceived to be high on expressive traits but relatively low on instrumental traits.

Women, however, were rated more uniformly. Except for American women, women from various countries were uniformly perceived to be high on expressive traits but low on instrumental traits. In other words, women tended to be perceived in terms of gender stereotypes, whereas men were perceived in terms of nationality stereotypes.

SOURCE: Eagly and Kite (1987).

Why were American women not rated gender-stereotypically? Eagly's social-role theory provides one possible answer. American college students observe American women in more varied roles, and thus they do not form such strong stereotypes about them. In addition, many of the subjects in this study were American college women. When they rated "American women," they were rating an in-group. Consistent with research discussed in Chapter 9, college subjects in this study showed ethnocentrism: They rated Americans as having better traits than people of other nationalities.

FIGURE 10.4   Components of stereotypes about men and women.

Do gender stereotypes comprise information about personality traits only?

Deaux and Lewis (1983) asked subjects to rate the probability that a member of either sex would display a given trait, behavior, or physical characteristic. The larger the difference in the estimates for men and women on a given item, the more that characteristic was stereotypically perceived to differentiate the two sexes.

CHARACTERISTIC	PROBABILITY JUDGMENT*		CHARACTERISTIC	PROBABILITY JUDGMENT*		CHARACTERISTIC	PROBABILITY JUDGMENT*	
	FOR MEN	FOR WOMEN		FOR MEN	FOR WOMEN		FOR MEN	FOR WOMEN
Trait			*Role Behaviors*			*Physical Characteristics*		
Independent	.78	.58	Financial provider	.83	.47	Muscular	.64	.36
Competitive	.82	.64	Takes initiative with opposite sex	.82	.54	Deep voice	.73	.30
Warm	.66	.77	Takes care of children	.50	.85	Graceful	.45	.68
Emotional	.56	.84	Cooks meals	.42	.83	Small-boned	.39	.62

*Subjects' estimates of the probability that the average person of either sex would possess a characteristic.

Subjects' stereotypes tended to be stronger for role behaviors and physical characteristics than for personality traits.

SOURCE: Based on Deaux and Lewis (1983). Used with permission of Select Press.

The Deaux and Lewis study makes an important point about stereotypes in general: They comprise more than beliefs about personality traits. Social psychological research on stereotypes has often focused on the personality traits attributed to various groups (see Chapter 9); however, studies like Deaux and Lewis's are beginning to investigate broader stereotypes.

Austin, Texas, to describe "masculinity" and "femininity" and to describe what defined their own "manhood" or "womanhood." Again, physical characteristics and social and family roles seemed to define subjects' commonsense notions of gender more than did personality traits.

Kay Deaux (Deaux & Lewis, 1983, 1984; Deaux, 1984) has provided yet additional evidence that gender stereotypes have many components. In one study she asked subjects to rate the probability that men and women display various characteristics; for example, what's the probability that a woman "cooks meals" or is "warm" or is "muscular." Some of the results of this study are presented in Figure 10.4.

Notice that the differences between the subjects' probability judgments for women and for men tend to be larger for physical characteristics and role behaviors than for personality traits. Deaux's research also demonstrated that the different components of gender stereotypes are rather loosely linked; that is, her data showed

When Do Gender Stereotypes Affect Our Evaluations of Specific Individuals?

Broad stereotypes about men and women are common. But do these stereotypes influence our judgments of particular people? And can salient information about individuals override our reliance on stereotypes?

Ann Locksley and her colleagues (1980) conducted an experiment which showed that concrete information about specific women and men seems at times to eliminate the effects of general stereotypes. Specifically, in one experiment both male and female subjects were asked to read descriptions of a college woman and a college man and to estimate on a scale from 0 (never) to 100 (always) how assertive they were. Some subjects received no behavioral information about the woman or man. Other subjects received information that was diagnostic of assertiveness — for example, that in class the student broke into a conversation that was being dominated by another student. Still other subjects received information that was irrelevant to assertiveness — for example, that the student went to get her (or his) hair cut before class.

When subjects received either no behavioral information or information that was irrelevant to assertiveness, they stereotypically judged the woman to be less assertive than the man. However, when provided with information that was diagnostic of assertiveness, gender stereotypes disappeared, and subjects perceived both the woman and the man as assertive (see the accompanying table).

Locksley's results, although intriguing, seem to go against common sense. Don't stereotypes sometimes influence our judgments of others, even when we possess concrete information? In a more careful mathematical analysis, Rasinski, Crocker, and Hastie (1985) examined how individual subjects estimate probabilities (for example, the probability that a person is assertive) based on information about the person's group membership (this person is female) and information about the specific individual (this person breaks into conversations). These researchers found that stereotypes do influence people's judgments of individuals, even when concrete information about the specific individual is present. However, judgments made on the basis of concrete information are less influenced by stereotypes than are judgments based on no concrete information.

Glick, Zion, and Nelson (1988) also provide evidence — this time in the important real-life arena of personnel selection — that gender stereotypes can influence people's judgments of individuals, even in the presence of individuating information. These researchers asked over 200 business professionals in Wisconsin to evaluate a job résumé. Sometimes the applicant's name was "Kate Norriss" and sometimes it was "Ken Norriss." Sometimes the job applicant was described by "feminine" behaviors (for example, had worked as an aerobics instructor and had been captain of the pep squad) and sometimes by "masculine" behaviors (had worked in a sporting goods store and had been captain of the varsity basketball team).

Subjects were asked to rate the applicant's personality and to judge how qualified the applicant was for each of three jobs: sales manager for a heavy machinery company ("masculine" job), administrative assistant at a bank (gender-neutral job), and dental receptionist/secretary ("feminine" job).

Interestingly, the results indicated that concrete information about specific feminine and masculine behaviors, rather than the applicant's sex, determined personality impressions. However, the businesspeople still rated male applicants as more qualified for the "masculine" job and female applicants as more qualified for the "feminine" job, despite the individuating information. Apparently, these businesspeople based their judgments on both gender stereotypes and the individual's characteristics and work experience.

Subjects' judgments of a woman's or a man's assertiveness based on sex and concrete behavioral information. *Note:* **The higher the number in the table, the more assertive the individual was judged to be.**

Kind of Information	Sex of Judged Individual	
	Male	*Female*
Sex only	49.4	46.6
Sex and a behavior unrelated to assertiveness	48.7	44.1
Sex and a behavior diagnostic of assertiveness	67.6	67.3

SOURCE: Data from Locksley et al. (1980).

relatively weak correlations among probability estimates of "male" or "female" physical characteristics, roles, personality traits, and sex (being biologically male or female). Thus people believe that certain behaviors and characteristics tend to correspond with being either male or female, but they do not hold these beliefs in an all-or-nothing fashion.

Gender and the Perception of Ability

We have already seen some evidence that stereotypes of women may at times be more negative than stereotypes of men. These stereotypes also extend to judgments of ability—women are sometimes perceived to be less competent simply because they are women. In a well-known early experiment, Goldberg (1968) asked female subjects to read essays on "masculine" topics (for example, "city planning") and "feminine" topics (for example, "elementary school teaching"); the essays were supposedly written by either female or male authors. The women evaluated articles attributed to male authors more positively than they evaluated those attributed to female authors, even when the topics addressed were "feminine." Thus women seemed to be prejudiced against other women. Although more recent experiments have not always replicated Goldberg's findings (Levenson, Burford, Bonno, & Davis, 1975; Ward, 1981), researchers nonetheless continue to uncover particular circumstances in which women performing work of equal quality to men are judged to be less competent than men. One such circumstance is when women perform "masculine" tasks (Pheterson, Kiesler, & Goldberg, 1971), which is noteworthy because the high-status jobs in most societies are usually considered "masculine."

In addition to sometimes judging women as less competent than men, subjects in experimental studies also *explain* women's work performance differently than they explain men's (see Figure 10.5). Subjects tend to attribute women's success to luck or extremely hard work and to attribute men's success to their ability (Deaux & Emswiller, 1974; Nieva & Guteck, 1981). Thus John gets an "A+" on his chemistry exam because he's smart, but Jane gets an "A+" because she studied hard and had a good day. These differing attributions may result in part from the *assumption* that women are less competent than men.

The tendency to explain women's successes differently from men's sometimes even extends to self-attributions. After examining the results of many studies, Whitley, McHugh, and Frieze (1986) concluded that men explain their own performance relatively more in terms of ability, whereas women explain their performance more in terms of luck.

Sex Differences

Genly Ai, the earth envoy, is the first *man* the Gethenian, Estraven, has ever seen. During an arduous trek across a polar wilderness, Estraven records the following observations about his male companion:

> There is a frailty about him. He is all unprotected, exposed, vulnerable, even to his sexual organ which he must carry always outside himself; but he is strong, unbelievably strong. I am not sure he can keep hauling any longer than I can, but he can haul harder and faster than I—twice as hard. . . . To match his frailty and strength, he has a spirit easy to despair and quick to defiance: a fierce

FIGURE 10.5   Attributions of the work performance of women and men.

Do we tend to explain successes differently for men and women?

Recall from our discussion of attribution (Chapter 4) that one way to analyze our explanations of behavior is to classify them on two dimensions: internal/external and stable/unstable. Research suggests that we tend to show an attributional bias in explaining men's and women's successes: We often attribute men's successes more to ability (a stable, internal explanation) and women's successes more to luck (unstable, external) or effort (unstable, internal). Indeed, women may show this bias in attributions about their own behavior. This difference in our attributions may result from an assumption that women are generally less able than men.

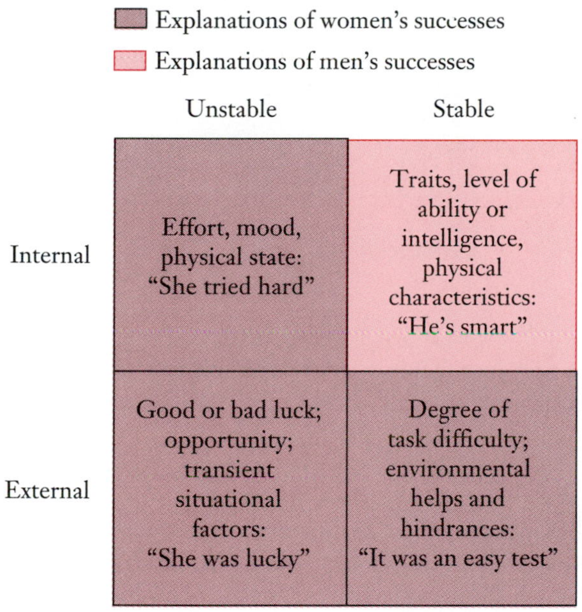

� Explanations of women's successes

▢ Explanations of men's successes

	Unstable	Stable
Internal	Effort, mood, physical state: "She tried hard"	Traits, level of ability or intelligence, physical characteristics: "He's smart"
External	Good or bad luck; opportunity; transient situational factors: "She was lucky"	Degree of task difficulty; environmental helps and hindrances: "It was an easy test"

impatient courage. This slow, hard, crawling work we have been doing these days wears him out in body and will, so that if he were one of my race I should think him a coward, but he is anything but that; he has a ready bravery I have never seen the like of. . . .

. . . By the end of this day . . . scrabbling and squirming . . . up ice-cliffs always to be stopped by a sheer face or overhang, trying farther on and failing again, Ai was exhausted and enraged. He looked ready to cry, but did not. I believe he considers crying either evil or shameful. Even when he was very ill

▪▪▪▪▪▪▪▪▪▪▪▪▪▪▪▪▪▪▪▪▪

Changing images of women in the movies. Mary Pickford, 1920s, and Sigourney Weaver, 1980s.

and weak, the first days of our escape, he hid his face from me when he wept. Reasons personal, racial, social, sexual — how can I guess why Ai must not weep?

—— *The Left Hand of Darkness*, pp. 228–229

The belief that men weep less than women is commonly held. Is it — or any of the stereotypical beliefs we've discussed — based on fact? Even if there are psychological and behavioral differences between women and men, do stereotypes nonetheless exaggerate the magnitude of these differences? Let's turn to these intriguing and difficult questions.

▪▪▪▪▪▪▪▪▪▪▪▪▪▪▪▪▪▪▪▪▪

The Study of Sex Differences

Psychologists have devoted considerable energy to studying and understanding the behavior of men and women (Maccoby & Jacklin, 1974; Deaux, 1985; Eagly, 1987). Research on sex differences clearly has great social relevance, particularly when the roles of women and men are rapidly changing, and such research is often controversial and disputed with great emotion. The study of sex differences may fall prey to two opposite biases (Hare-Musten & Marecek, 1988). The first bias overemphasizes differences, casting females and males as "opposite sexes" with mutually exclusive qualities. The second bias, which is in part a feminist response to sexist traditions in

society and in psychological research, tends to minimize and even ignore sex differences. The truth of the matter of psychological sex differences probably lies somewhere between these two extreme interpretations of the evidence (Eagly, 1987). In order to understand the evidence concerning sex differences, it is important to understand some basic statistical concepts and methods first.

The statistical assessment of group differences.   When groups of people (for example, women and men) are measured on some physical or psychological characteristic (for example, height, aggressiveness, IQ, or amount of eye contact during interaction), these measures can be plotted as frequency distributions. Such distributions show the numbers of people displaying different ranges of scores. When plotted as a graph, they often take the approximate form of a bell-shaped curve called the *normal distribution* (see Figure 10.6). To investigate sex differences, psychologists must compare two distributions, one for women and one for men. Let's illustrate this for a variable that obviously differs between the sexes—height.

The *mean* of a distribution is the arithmetic average of the scores of all the people plotted in the distribution. According to one study (Gillis & Avis, 1980), the mean height of American women is 64 inches (5 feet, 4 inches), and the mean height of American men is 70 inches (5 feet, 10 inches). In a normal distribution, the mean is exactly at the center of the distribution.

━━

FIGURE 10.6   The normal distribution.

What information do the mean and standard deviation provide about the normal distribution?

Some measures (such as height and IQ) obtained from large samples of people approximate a bell-shaped curve called the normal distribution. The mean of a distribution is the arithmetic average of all observed scores. In a normal distribution, the mean is at the center of the distribution. The standard deviation is a conventional measure of the spread of a distribution. In a normal distribution, about two-thirds of all scores are between one standard deviation below and one standard deviation above the mean.

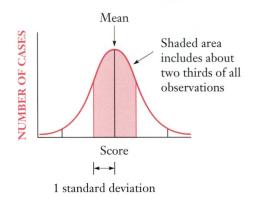

━━

The *standard deviation* is a conventional measure of the spread of a distribution (again, see Figure 10.6). You can roughly think of the standard deviation as being the average distance individuals' scores are from the mean. If most people's scores are close to the mean, the standard deviation is small, whereas if most people's scores are spread out far away from the mean, the standard deviation is large. In the Gillis and Avis (1980) data, the standard deviation of height for each sex is 2.3 inches.

In a normal distribution, a little over two-thirds of all scores fall within one standard deviation above or below the mean (again, see Figure 10.6). Because height is approximately normally distributed, about two-thirds of American women have a height between 61.7 inches and 66.3 inches, and about two-thirds of American men have a height between 67.7 and 72.3 inches. Thus, most men are taller than most women.

Figure 10.7a provides a graphic illustration of the distributions of women's and men's heights, and as you can see, these distributions are quite distinct; they do not overlap very much. To quantify the degree of difference between the two distributions, we compute the difference between the mean height of women and the mean height of men and divide the difference by the standard deviation of these distributions. The resulting number is called *d*, the value of which can be either positive or negative. In our example, *d* is: $(64 - 70)/2.3 = -2.6$. The value of *d* tells how far apart the means of two distributions are, in standard deviation units.

As a general rule of thumb for psychological research, Cohen (1977) suggests that a *d* value of .2 is small, a value of .5 is medium, and a value of .8 is large (enough so to be readily perceived in everyday life). Figure 10.7 shows pairs of distributions with *d* values of .2, .5, and .8, respectively. By Cohen's guidelines, the difference between the mean heights of women and men is enormous ($d = -2.6$).

The *d* statistic allows us to systematically study sex differences. For any study that measures the means and standard deviations of females' and males' scores on a given variable (height, aggression, mathematics ability, and so on), we can compute *d*. But the existence of a sex difference cannot be proven by a single study alone. (See Chapter 2 for a more complete discussion of this issue.) The solution is to average *d* values from many studies addressing the same issue — whether, for example, there are sex differences in aggression.

This is exactly what the statistical technique of *meta-analysis* does (again, see Chapter 2). Meta-analysis accomplishes three main goals: (1) It tells us when a sex difference is consistently found over many studies, (2) it informs us how large the average sex difference is, and (3) it tells us whether sex differences depend on other variables.

For example, in a meta-analysis of 64 studies on sex and aggression, Eagly and Steffen (1986b) computed the average value of *d* to be .40, with men on average being more aggressive than women. Because this difference was relatively consistent across studies, it was quite unlikely to be due to change; thus such a difference is considered highly significant. According to Cohen's (1977) guidelines, this is a small to medium-sized effect. Finally, Eagly and Steffen (1986b) found that *d* values for men's and women's aggression were influenced by other variables; for example, *d* values were higher in studies that measured physical (rather than psychological or verbal) aggression, which implies that men are particularly more *physically* aggressive than women.

The evidence for sex differences.   With these basic tools in mind, let's turn our attention to the research findings on sex differences. Figure 10.8 shows the results of recent meta-analyses that have estimated the size of sex differences for various social behaviors (nonverbal behaviors, aggression, helping behavior, group conformity, behavior in small groups), cognitive abilities, and physical abilities and characteristics.

You might wonder why we are concerned with cognitive abilities (like math or verbal skills) and physical abilities (grip strength) in a social psychology text. There are two reasons. First, such differences may contribute to gender stereotypes and influence the gender roles society creates for women and men. For example, if men are physically stronger than women, this may lead to a stereotype that men are more "forceful" and have "stronger" personalities. Second, the sizes of sex differences in cognitive and physical abilities can be useful in comparing the sizes of sex differences in such social behaviors as aggression, helping behavior, and conformity in groups (Eagly, 1987).

Let's summarize the main findings presented in Figure 10.8. First, the nonverbal behaviors of women and men differ in a number of interesting ways (Hall, 1984).

FIGURE 10.7   Pairs of normal distributions with differing means.

What is the meaning of the d *statistic?*

As explained in the text, the *d* statistic is a measure of the degree of difference between the means of two normal distributions, expressed in standard deviation units.

Panel a shows the distribution of women's and men's heights. The computed value of *d* is very large, indicating that men are noticeably taller than women on average and that the two distributions do not overlap much.

a. *d* = 2.6 (very large)

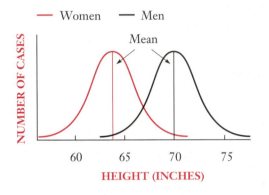

d values of 2.6 are very rare in psychological research. For psychological data, Cohen (1977) describes *d* values of .8 as "large," values of .5 as "medium," and values of .2 as "small."

b. *d* = .8 (large)   **c.** *d* = .5 (medium)   **d.** *d* = .2 (small)

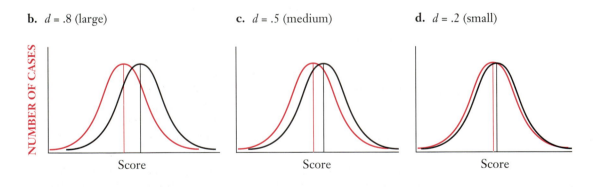

Many of the sex differences in social behavior discussed in this chapter fall in the "small" to "medium" range. As we discuss various sex differences, you may want to refer again to this figure to get an intuitive sense of how big the differences between women and men really are.

   Note: *To simplify the discussion we have assumed that the normal distributions for both men and women have equal standard deviations. However, this assumption is not always warranted. For example, in measures of intellectual abilities, men's scores often have a greater spread (larger standard deviation) than do women's scores — that is, there are more very low-scoring and very high-scoring men than women. However,* d *can still be computed for such distributions.*

FIGURE 10.8   Meta-analyses of sex differences.

What sex differences have been supported by meta-analyses?

This table shows the results of a number of meta-analyses of studies on sex differences. Listed are the mean values of d from all studies that examined a particular variable and the number of studies from which the mean values of d were computed.

BEHAVIOR	SOURCE	MEAN VALUE OF d (POSITIVE VALUES MEAN FEMALES HIGHER)	NUMBER OF STUDIES FROM WHICH d WAS COMPUTED
Social Behaviors			
Nonverbal behaviors	Hall (1984)		
Decoding skill		.43	64
Social smiling		.63	15
Amount of gaze		.68	30
Personal space (distance of approach in natural settings)		−.56	17
Expansiveness of movements		−1.04	6
Filled pauses ("ah's" and "um's" in speech)		−1.19	6
Aggression	Hyde (1986)	−.50 (median d value)	69
Group conformity	Becker (1986)	.28	35
Helping	Eagly & Crowley (1986)		
Overall		−.34	99
When being watched		−.74	16
When not being watched		.02	41
Behavior in small groups	Carli (1982)		
Positive social-emotional behaviors		.59	17
Task-oriented behaviors		−.59	10
Cognitive Abilities			
Verbal	Hyde & Linn (1988)	.11	165
Math	Hyde (1986)	−.43	16
Visual–spatial	Hyde (1986)	−.45	10
Physical Abilities and Characteristics	Thomas & French (1985)		
Throw velocity		−2.18	5
Throw distance		−1.98	11
Grip strength		−.66	4
General motor activity	Gillis & Avis (1980)	−.49	127

Refer to Figure 10.7 to get an intuitive sense of the magnitudes of the d *values listed here. These meta-analyses show that* d *values for social and cognitive variables are generally in the "small" or "medium" range. Among social behaviors, nonverbal behaviors tend to show larger sex differences than other kinds of social behavior (such as aggression, helping behavior, and group conformity).*

Women on average are superior to men in decoding nonverbal cues, particularly facial expressions (see Chapter 3). Women smile more and engage in more eye contact during social interactions than do men. On the other hand, men maintain greater personal space and are more expansive in their body movements and postures. Men make more errors in speech than do women and use more "filled pauses" ("ah's" and "um's") when they talk. As the *d* values in Figure 10.8 indicate, sex differences in nonverbal behaviors are often fairly large.

Smaller sex differences emerge in studies on such social behaviors as aggression, helping behavior, and susceptibility to social influence. On average, men are more aggressive than women (Hyde, 1986; Eagly & Steffen, 1986b); however, as we noted before, this difference is more pronounced for physical than for psychological aggression. On average, men help more in emergencies than do women (Eagly & Crowley, 1986). However, this finding is qualified by the fact that men help more particularly when they are being watched and when the victim is female, which suggests that men may be motivated by the opportunity to display their masculine valor to an audience as much as by the need to be helpful. Finally, women on average are more susceptible than men to social influence in attitude change and conformity studies (Eagly & Carli, 1981; Becker, 1986). This sex difference tends to be strongest in group conformity experiments in which subjects are under the surveillance of other people. In sum, women and men show small to medium differences in aggression, helping behavior, and susceptibility to influence; however, these differences are often moderated by situational factors.

Research on behavior in small groups identifies some moderate to large differences in the behavior of men and women (Carli, 1982). Women on average show more positive social-emotional behaviors (acting friendly, agreeing with others, and offering emotional support); men show more task-oriented behaviors (giving and asking for opinions and trying to solve the group task). These differences may indicate that women are more effective than men in group tasks requiring considerable discussion and negotiation, and that men may be more effective in group tasks requiring focused, task-oriented behavior (Wood, 1987).

Men and women on average display a number of differences in cognitive abilities (Halpern, 1986; Hyde, 1981). For example, men tend to perform better than women on tests of math and visual-spatial ability. These findings must be tempered, however, by the fact that these differences seem in general to be growing smaller in recent years (Rosenthal & Rubin, 1982; Feingold, 1988). Early reviewers noted an overall female superiority in verbal ability (Maccoby & Jacklin, 1974; Hyde, 1981), but the most recent evidence suggests that this difference no longer exists (Hyde & Linn, 1988).

Not surprisingly, women and men display a number of reliable physical differences. Men are stronger than women, particularly at tasks requiring upper body strength (Wardle, Gloss, & Gloss, 1987). Men show higher levels of general motor activity than do women (Eaton & Enns, 1986), and women generally have more flexible joints than men (Percival & Quinkert, 1987).

The Meaning of Sex Differences

What can we make of these findings? Clearly women and men display a number of differences in behavior. However, they are by no means "opposite" sexes; the means of the measures of certain characteristics simply differ between the sexes to various degrees. In general, there is considerable overlap between the distributions of women's and men's social behaviors, and thus sex accounts for only a fraction of the total variance in these measures (Tavris & Wade, 1984; Hyde, 1981).

On the other hand, even if the difference between the *means* of two distributions is relatively small, differences can become quite large at the tails of the distributions. For example, although the mean *d* value for the difference in women's and men's math ability is only − .43, sex differences at the extremes of the distributions are much larger. Five times as many males as females score above 600 on the math part of the Scholastic Aptitude Test, and the ratio of males to females who receive scores above 700 is 17 to 1 (Stanley & Benbrow, 1982). Sex differences of the magnitude presented in Figure 10.8 can have practical consequences (Eagly, 1987; Rosenthal & Rubin, 1982). For example, sex differences in math ability of the magnitude just described could influence the number of men and women who become mathematicians, engineers, and scientists — professions that require math ability in the upper tail of the distribution.

Some of the sex differences listed in Figure 10.8 provide at least partial support for the gender stereotypes we discussed earlier. For example, the behavior of women and men in small groups is consistent with the stereotype that women are more expressive and men more instrumental. Men are somewhat more aggressive than women, as the stereotype holds. However, despite the "kernel of truth" to some gender stereotypes, it is important to emphasize that stereotypes often exaggerate the extent of sex differences (Maccoby & Jacklin, 1974; Martin, 1987).

There is a final important point to note about studies on sex differences: They do not necessarily tell us *why* sex differences exist. Are sex differences biological (that is, genetic and hormonal)? Or are they learned from our culture or from our parents? Are they imposed on us by the structure of society and by social settings? To understand the research findings on sex differences, we must consider theories that attempt to *explain* both sex differences and the development of gender in individuals.

::

Theories of Gender and Sex-Typing

The following must go into my finished Directive: When you meet a Gethenian you cannot and must not . . . cast him in the role of Man or Woman, . . . adopting towards him a corresponding role dependent on your expectations of the patterned or possible interactions between persons of the same or the opposite sex. Our entire pattern of socio-sexual interaction is nonexistent here. They cannot play the game. They do not see one another as men or women. This is almost impossible for our imagination to accept. What is the first question we ask about a newborn baby?

—— *The Left Hand of Darkness*, p. 94

How do people come to behave like men and women? How does biological sex influence personality traits, aggressiveness, conformity, nonverbal behaviors, cognitive abilities, hobbies, and occupational interests? A number of theories have addressed these challenging questions. We'll focus on six approaches: biological theories, Freudian theory, social learning theories, cognitive theories, social role theory, and self-presentation theory. These theories are not necessarily mutually exclusive, however; each may shed a bit of light on the complex topic of gender.

Different theories of gender emphasize different kinds of explanations (see Figure 10.9). For example, biological theories stress biological evolution and the individual's physiology as explanations of sex differences. Freudian theory focuses on the individual's past environment, particularly on emotional relations with parents early in life. Social learning theories emphasize conditioning and modeling as the processes responsible for gender-related behaviors. Cognitive theories focus on how we label ourselves as male or female and on the schemas we hold about gender. Social role theory focuses on the differing status and tasks assigned to men and women in most societies, as well as their psychological consequences. And finally, self-presentation theory holds that we display gender-related behaviors as a kind of impression management (see Chapter 6). Figure 10.9 suggests that many levels of explanation can be applied to gender-related behaviors. Now let's describe each theoretical approach in more detail.

Biological Theories

In describing human sex differences to a Gethenian, Genly Ai notes, "It's extremely hard to separate the innate differences from the learned ones." Biological theories, of course, argue that there are innate differences between women and men. This is obviously true for certain physiological processes. Women produce ova and men produce sperm. Women menstruate and experience cyclical patterns of hormonal activity that men do not. Women give birth and lactate; men do not. Women's bodies produce relatively more estrogen (female hormones) and men's bodies produce relatively more androgens (male hormones), although both women and men produce both kinds of hormones.

Edward O. Wilson, the father of modern sociobiology, argues (1978) that because women were responsible throughout the evolutionary history of our species for bearing, nursing, and caring for children, they evolved to be more nurturing; and because men were responsible for hunting and fighting, they evolved more aggressiveness and better visual-spatial ability. Furthermore, Wilson suggests, women and men have different optimal reproductive strategies; women must guarantee that the relatively few offspring they bear will survive, whereas men, who produce millions of sperm, can father an indefinite number of offspring. As a result, women have evolved to be more sexually coy and desirous of committed relationships, and men have evolved to be more sexually aggressive and promiscuous (see Chapter 11 for a broader discussion of sexual and romantic attraction). Not surprisingly, such speculations are highly controversial (Fausto-Sterling, 1985).

When assessing the role of biological factors, researchers ask four main empirical questions (Maccoby & Jacklin, 1974): (1) Do sex differences occur early in development, before considerable learning has a chance to take place? (If so, the case for biological explanations of sex differences is strengthened.) (2) Do sex differences occur consistently across cultures? (Cross-cultural variability suggests sex differences are learned, whereas cross-cultural universality is consistent with biological causes.) (3) Do sex differences occur consistently across species, particularly species closely related to human beings (other primates, especially apes and monkeys)? (If so, the case for biological causes is strengthened.) And finally, (4) Do physiological variables related to gender (such as sex hormones) have an effect on the behaviors in question? (An affirmative answer provides direct evidence for a biological contribution to sex differences.)

Using these four kinds of evidence, can we make a convincing case that some sex differences result in part from biological factors? Perhaps the strongest case for

What kinds of explanations are offered by different theories of gender?

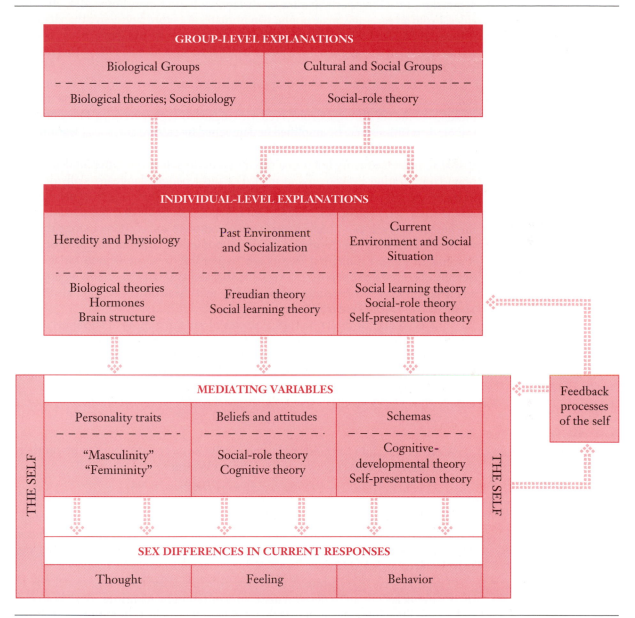

Note that the factors listed in this diagram are not necessarily mutually exclusive. For example, social roles may influence socialization practices, which in turn influence personality traits and schemas. As we discuss different theories of gender, you can refer to this diagram to see where each theory fits into the "big picture."

biological origins of sex differences can be made with respect to aggression (Maccoby & Jacklin, 1974, 1980). Males are more aggressive than females as early as age 2 or 3 and, interestingly, recent evidence suggests that sex differences in aggression *decrease* with age (Hyde, 1986). In a large majority of cultures men are more aggressive than women (D'Andrade, 1966); this difference is reflected in virtually all social indices of aggression, including participation in warfare, violent crimes, homicides, and suicides. From an early age, male nonhuman primates are more aggressive than females (Moyer, 1976). And finally, there is evidence that sex hormones, particularly testosterone, are related to aggression in humans and animals (Olweus, 1986; Moyer, 1976; see Chapter 12).

Does this mean that men are more aggressive than women primarily for biological reasons? Not at all. It merely means that there very likely are biological underpinnings to the sex differences observed with regard to aggressiveness. These biological predispositions may be amplified or dampened by culture and social learning.

Another sex difference that may have a biological underpinning is that of visual-spatial ability. One theory holds that this difference results from different degrees of brain lateralization in women and men. For most people, language skills depend more on the left hemisphere of the brain, whereas visual-spatial skills depend more on the right hemisphere. The lateralization hypothesis holds that the separation of the functions of the two hemispheres is more complete and extreme in men than in women. Even though the evidence for this hypothesis is complex and inconsistent, it seems likely that biological factors are responsible to some degree for the frequently observed sex differences in visual-spatial ability (Halpern, 1986). Again, such a conclusion does not preclude the possibility that these differences are also influenced by cultural and environmental factors.

The evidence for direct biological causes of sex differences in social behaviors other than aggression (such as nonverbal behaviors, helping behavior, and susceptibility to influence) is considerably weaker. As we've already noted, these differences are often strongly influenced by situational factors (the presence or absence of other people, for example), which suggests social rather than biological determinants.

Freudian Theory

> Consider: A child [on Gethen] has no psycho-sexual relationship to his mother and father. There is no myth of Oedipus on Winter.
>
> —— *The Left Hand of Darkness*, p. 94

Until the twentieth century most scholars and laypeople simply assumed that biological differences between women and men explained their behavioral differences. This assumption was radically challenged by Sigmund Freud (1961b, 1961c), the father of psychoanalytic theory.

Freud argued that children's early sexual feelings and their emotional ties to their parents lead them to develop masculine or feminine identities. Both boys and girls begin life with their mother as their primary love object. But after age 3, boys' and girls' development sharply diverges. According to Freudian theory, a particularly critical period occurs for the typical boy between the ages of 3 and 6, when he first experiences genital pleasure. At this point, the boy's love for his mother takes on a sexual tinge and he becomes aware that his father is a major competitor for his mother's affection.

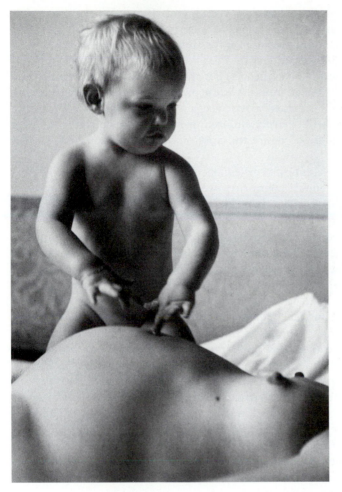

At about this same time, the theory continues, the boy notices the genital differences between men and women and learns that women lack penises. Frightened, the boy assumes that women once possessed penises but somehow lost them, which intensifies the boy's fear of his father and of his own sexual desires, for he reasons that his vengeful father may remove his own penis as punishment for his incestuous desires for his mother. This intense *castration anxiety* leads the boy ultimately to give up his sexual wishes for his mother and to identify with his father. It is as if the boy unconsciously reasons: If I act like Daddy, then someday I will have someone like Mommy.

Freud invented the term *Oedipus complex* to refer to the boy's unconscious feelings of sexual attraction to his mother and his rivalry with his father. This terminology was based on the Greek myth of Oedipus, who unwittingly married his mother and killed his father. According to Freud's theory, the proper resolution of the Oedipus complex occurs when boys identify with their fathers and thus become masculine.

Freud proposed a fundamentally different scenario for girls. They too presumably notice the genital differences between males and females between ages 3 and 6; however, rather than fearing the loss of their genitals, girls unconsciously assume that their penises have already been removed! Freud (1961c) believed that girls naturally valued penises more than vaginas because penises are "strikingly visible and of large proportions, at once recognize[d] as the superior counterpart to their own small and inconspicuous organ . . ." (p. 252).

According to classical Freudian theory, girls are unconsciously forlorn because of their genital "inferiority," and *penis envy* is the prime motivation of the feminine personality. Throughout life, women strive to regain their missing penis by having love relations with men and by having children, particularly male children. Thus Freud explained the "feminine" desire for close emotional relationships and for children.

Freud proposed other significant consequences of women's psychosexual development. Because of their genital "inferiority," women often feel contempt for other women, specifically for their own mothers. For this reason, girls give up their mothers as primary love objects, and instead court their fathers, taking on an "appropriate" male love object. The self-disparagement (due to genital "inferiority") and the desire to please their fathers (and indirectly all males) leads women to be masochistic in their love relationships. Finally, Freud argued that because girls do not experience the wrenching castration anxiety typical of boys, they do not generally resolve their Oedipal stage as strongly as do boys. Thus women end up being more infantile and possessing weaker moral consciences than men.

As you might well guess, feminist scholars have roundly criticized Freudian theory as sexist. Karen Horney (1922), a prominent disciple of Freud, argued that what Freud called "penis envy" was really status envy. Women, particularly in Freud's time, did not long for men's organs but for their power and social prerogatives.

Although most contemporary developmental and social psychologists reject much of Freud's account of how masculinity and femininity develop in children, Freud deserves credit for advancing gender theory in several significant ways. His famous dictum that "anatomy is destiny" did not imply the rigid determinism of biological theories. Rather, Freud argued that genital differences lead to different experiences early in life and that these early experiences lead people to develop "male" or "female" patterns of behavior.

Even though castration anxiety and penis envy may seem far-fetched, the more general Freudian assumptions — that young children form strong emotional attachments to their parents and that these attachments can influence the development of children's gender-related identities and behavior — seem more plausible. Drawing upon Freudian theory, Nancy Chodorow (1978) has argued that because the mother is usually a child's first strong love object, boys and girls indeed develop quite differently. To become masculine, boys must firmly renounce this first identification and even derogate it; in becoming feminine, however, girls can maintain their first primary attachment. Thus, psychological separateness and distance are more a part of men's natures, and connection and intimacy are more a part of women's natures.

Clearly then, some social scientists are still pursuing the implications of Freudian theory.

Social Learning Theories

Whereas biological theories and some aspects of Freudian theory emphasize "innate" differences between men and women, social learning theories as strongly emphasize the learned ones. Walter Mischel (1966, 1970), for example, has argued

■■■■■■■■■■■■■■■■■■■■■■■■
**How do children learn
sex-typed behaviors?**

that differences in women's and men's behavior can be explained by well-understood principles of classical conditioning, operant conditioning, and modeling.

For example, classical conditioning can help explain why "labels like 'sissy,' 'pansy,' 'tough,' or 'sweet' acquire differential value for the sexes" (Mischel, 1966, p. 61). The word *sissy* generally accompanies ridicule in a boy's life and thus becomes a very unpleasant label. A boy will not want to behave like a "sissy" if the very concept is conditioned to create feelings of loathing and revulsion.

Operant conditioning, which occurs when girls' and boys' behaviors are rewarded and punished in systematically different ways, can also lead to sex differences: "Boys and girls discover that the consequences for performing . . . behaviors are affected by their sex, and therefore soon perform them with different frequency" (Mischel, 1966, p. 60). Thus little Joan may receive smiles and praise when she plays with dolls and a toy cooking set, but little John may receive frowns and disapproval for exactly the same behaviors.

Finally, children may acquire sex-typed behaviors through observational learning. Children often learn about "female" and "male" behaviors without being directly rewarded or punished, but rather simply by observing their friends, parents, relatives, and the portrayal of various characters in the mass media. Such models are particularly influential when they have a nurturing relationships with the children, are powerful, and control rewards (Bandura & Huston, 1961; Bandura, Ross, & Ross, 1963a; Mischel & Grusec, 1966). Parents, of course, meet all three of these criteria.

Social learning theory makes an important distinction between the acquisition of behaviors and the performance of those behaviors; people can learn behaviors through observation, but they don't necessarily perform them. For example, most women could convincingly go through the motions of shaving their faces and most men could convincingly go through the motions of shaving their legs, even though they don't usually do so. Thus social learning theory argues that women and men are capable of performing the same behaviors, but they don't because of past conditioning, rewards, punishments, observational learning, and all the situational contingencies that exist in a society that treats women and men differently.

A great deal of research supports social learning theory's basic contention that environmental factors help create and sustain sex differences. For example, a number of studies suggest that parents treat girls and boys differently from birth (Block, 1978; Rubin, Provenzano, & Luria, 1974; Snow, Jacklin, & Maccoby, 1983). Parents provide different toys to their girls and boys (Rheingold & Cook, 1975) and decorate their rooms in dramatically different ways. Parents in essence treat girls as "women-in-training" and boys as "men-in-training." Both peers and parents encourage sex-typed behaviors in children, and they discourage behaviors that are not sex-typed (Fagot, 1977; Pitcher & Schultz, 1983). In one study, when a three-year-old boy stated that he wanted to cook dinner, a female playmate firmly informed him that "daddies don't cook" (Garvey, 1977). In modern industrial society the mass media are also quite important in socializing gender. Television, radio, and the print media often portray women and men in stereotypical ways, and children often view media characters as models for behavior (Basow, 1986).

Cognitive Approaches to Gender

Consider: There is [on Gethen] no division of humanity into strong and weak halves, protective/protected, dominant/submissive, owner/chattel, active/passive. In fact, the whole tendency to dualism that pervades human thinking may be found to be lessened, or changed. . . .

—— *The Left Hand of Darkness*, p. 94

Social learning theories tend to portray the development of sex-typed behaviors as a rather passive process whereby the child develops in such a manner as conditioning and modeling dictate (Maccoby & Jacklin, 1974, 1980; Archer & Lloyd, 1985). Clearly, however, the development of gender identity and sex differences also involves a cognitive process of self-labeling and self-definition. We are not just male or female through what we are conditioned to do; we are also male or female through what we think about ourselves.

In his cognitive-developmental account of sex-typing, Lawrence Kohlberg (1966) proposed that children progress through a number of discrete cognitive stages in becoming psychologically "male" or "female." Drawing upon the work of the Swiss developmental psychologist Jean Piaget, Kohlberg argued that children's conceptions of gender develop in step with their more general levels of cognitive development. For example, most children can correctly identify their gender by age 2 or 3 (Gesell, Halverson, & Amatruda, 1940); this accomplishment requires that they develop stable gender categories. At about the same time children also acquire other kinds of "object constancy" (the knowledge that objects have stable, enduring qualities). According to Kohlberg's analysis, once children develop a stable gender identity ("I am a girl") and stable gender categories ("all people are either female or male"), they begin to identify with others of their own sex ("I am a girl; therefore I like other girls, and girls are good").

Although they are aware of gender as a social category, young children do not think about gender as adults do. For instance, they do not realize that "male" and "female" are defined most fundamentally by genitalia; instead they define gender by its surface manifestations, such as clothing, hair length, and the kinds of games one plays. Three- and four-year-olds will often state that they could be the other sex if they wanted to — all they would have to do is change their clothing, hair style, and toys!

By age 6 or 7, children consistently realize that sex and gender are constant and linked to male and female genital differences. Thus, Kohlberg argued that Freudian accounts of sex-typing, which assume awareness of genital differences between ages 3 and 6, are simply wrong. According to Kohlberg's theory, children older than age 7 continue to develop their concept of gender; for example, they learn diffuse gender stereotypes ("women are gentler than men") and cultural symbols associated with gender ("the moon is a female symbol").

Kohlberg proposed that the act of gender self-categorization ("I'm a girl" or "I'm a boy") leads the child to develop stereotypically female or male behaviors. In Kohlberg's words, ". . . cognitive theory assumes this sequence: 'I am a boy, therefore I want to do boy things, therefore the opportunity to do boy things . . . is rewarding'" (p. 89). Social learning theory, on the other hand, argues for a different sequence: "I want rewards, I am rewarded for doing boy things, therefore I want to be a boy" (Kohlberg, 1966, p. 89). It is not rewards that make the boy masculine, argued Kohlberg; rather, it is identifying oneself as male that makes masculine activities rewarding.

Sandra Bem (1981) has recently extended Kohlberg's cognitive analysis of gender to adults. According to Bem's *gender schema theory*, people learn a complex network of gender-related concepts and symbols from their cultures. For example, "tender" and "petunias" may be seen as feminine, whereas "aggressive" and "jackhammers" are masculine. Once people possess gender schemas, they then perceive their own and others' behavior through the filter of those schemas. (See Chapters 5 and 6 for a more extensive discussion of how schemas affect social perception and self-perception.)

Bem's theory proposes that people who are strongly gender-schematic tend to perceive the world strongly in terms of "male" and "female," and they try to keep their own behavior consistent with stereotypical standards for their sex. People who are not gender-schematic, on the other hand, do not perceive themselves or others primarily in terms of gender; they are less concerned with the "masculinity" or "femininity" of people's behavior. Although there has been considerable debate about the measurement and consequences of gender schemas (Markus, Crane, Bernstein, & Siladi, 1982; Edwards & Spence, 1987; Payne, Conner, & Colletti, 1987), most researchers accept the general proposal that people's cognitive representations of gender can influence their gender-related behaviors and thought processes.

Social Role Theory

Consider: Anyone can turn his hand to anything. This sounds very simple, but its psychological effects are incalculable. The fact that everyone [on Gethen] between seventeen and thirty-five or so is liable to be . . . "tied down to childbearing," implies that no one is quite so thoroughly "tied down" as women, elsewhere, are likely to be — psychologically or physically. Burden and privilege are shared out pretty equally; everyone has the same risk to run or choice to make.

—— *The Left Hand of Darkness*, pp. 93–94

In most cultures, women and men occupy quite different roles (D'Andrade, 1966; Barry, Bacon, & Child, 1957). Women are more responsible for child-rearing and domestic duties; men are more responsible for hunting, fighting, and, in modern industrial society, income-producing work. According to Alice Eagly's (1987) social role analysis of gender, this sex-based division of labor, which occurs in virtually all societies, leads necessarily to sex differences in behavior and to the stereotypical perceptions that women and men are different. Constrained by their social roles to rear children and take care of homes, women show more nurturing behaviors, and people in turn perceive women to be more nurturing. Constrained and guided by their social roles in the competitive world of work, men display more competitive, assertive behaviors, and as a result people perceive men to be more competitive and assertive. However, Eagly contends that these behavioral differences are more a function of roles than of gender.

Eagly's theory does not focus on innate differences between women and men, although it does not deny that such differences may exist. Rather, it stresses the power of social settings to govern social behaviors and affect their perception. Thus in Eagly's theory, settings that make gender roles particularly salient and that assign different status to women and men should create marked differences in the behavior of women and men, whereas settings that do not make gender roles salient and that assign equal status to women and men should lead to similar behaviors.

An experiment by Eagly and Steffen (1986a) provides evidence that social roles, rather than gender *per se*, lead to stereotypical perceptions of men and women. College subjects read descriptions of people (either females or males) engaged in one of three kinds of work: caring for a home and children without outside employment, working part-time outside of the home, or working full-time outside of the home. In a control condition, subjects received no occupational information. In all conditions, subjects were asked to rate the described person on a number of instrumental and expressive traits ("independent," "dominant," "kind," and "warm").

The results (see Figure 10.10) showed that women and men were judged stereotypically when no occupational information was provided; that is, women were perceived as more expressive and men as more instrumental. But when occupational role information was provided, women and men were evaluated by their role, not by their sex. Thus full-time employees, whether male or female, were judged more highly on instrumental traits than on expressive traits, and both male and female homemakers were judged more highly on expressive traits than on instrumental traits. These results imply that when more women are employed full-time and more men participate in childcare and housekeeping, gender stereotypes may fade.

Do men and women actually behave differently because of their social roles? Many sex differences — differences in nonverbal behavior, aggression, helping behavior, and conformity — can be interpreted in terms of women's and men's roles. For example, women, who play the nurturing role in most families, are more sensitive nonverbally, show more affiliative nonverbal behaviors such as smiling, are more expressive, and participate more in the socioeconomical dynamics of group interac-

▪▪

FIGURE 10.10   Social roles and stereotyping.

Do different social roles for men and women lead to gender stereotyping?

Eagly and Steffen (1986a) investigated whether men and women are judged by gender per se or by the social roles they occupy. The table shows how subjects rated the expressive and instrumental characteristics of men and women based on different occupational information.

MEAN RATINGS OF STEREOTYPICAL ATTRIBUTES OF FEMALES AND MALES

Sex of Stimulus Person	Attribute Dimension	No Occupational Description	Occupation of Stimulus Person		
			Full-time Employee	Part-time Employee	Homemaker
Female	Expressive	3.82	3.23	3.66	4.20
	Instrumental	3.06	3.60	2.96	2.88
Male	Expressive	2.99	3.28	3.28	4.11
	Instrumental	3.41	3.40	2.58	2.88

When occupational information was provided, members of both sexes tended to be perceived more in terms of their occupational roles than in terms of their gender.

SOURCE: Adapted from Eagly and Steffen (1986a).

As noted at the start of this chapter, an increasingly large percentage of U.S. women are working. Based on the Eagly and Steffen study, how is this trend likely to change gender stereotypes?

tions. But, argues Eagly, placed in different roles, women may show dramatically different behavior.

Two experiments by John Dovidio and his colleagues (1988) powerfully illustrate how social roles can modify the behavior of men and women. Specifically, these studies measured subjects' patterns of gaze during social interactions. In general, people who possess more power in a relationship gaze at their partner more when they are talking than when they are listening (Ellyson & Dovidio, 1985). Pairs of female and male college students were asked to discuss various hobbies, such as basketball, skiing, and swimming. In the first experiment, the researchers selected topics of discussion to create three different conditions: either the female was more expert on the topic of discussion, or the male was more expert, or neither subject was more expert. The percentage of the time subjects spent gazing at their partner during their conversations was measured both while subjects were speaking and while they were listening.

Who acted more "powerful" in this experiment, women or men? As Figure 10.11 shows, when neither partner possessed expertise and when the man possessed more expertise than the woman, men displayed more "powerful" patterns of gaze. However, when women possessed more expertise, they displayed more powerful patterns of gaze than men.

■■■

FIGURE 10.11   Social roles and patterns of gaze in male-female interactions.

Do social roles lead to behavioral differences in men and women?

Dovidio and his colleagues (1988) had pairs of male and female subjects discuss topics about which one partner or the other (or neither) possessed greater expertise. The researchers measured how much subjects gazed at their partners while speaking and listening.

Condition		Percentage of Time Spent Looking at Partner	
		While Speaking	*While Listening*
Male has expertise	Males	53	54
	Females	40	74
Female has expertise	Males	30	49
	Females	58	56
Neither subject has expertise (control condition)	Males	47	53
	Females	41	77

Males showed more "powerful" patterns of gaze (that is, they gazed *relatively* more while speaking than while listening) when their expertise was greater than or equal to that of their female partners, but females showed more powerful patterns of gaze when they possessed greater expertise.

SOURCE: Data from Dovidio et al. (1988).

■■■

In a second, conceptually similar experiment, Dovidio and his colleagues again asked couples composed of one female and one male to discuss various topics. This time, however, one subject was given the role of rewarding and evaluating the quality of the other's discussion. In a control condition, neither partner evaluated the other. The results: In the control condition and in the "male evaluates female" condition, men showed more "powerful" patterns of gaze than did women. However, when women had the power to evaluate and reward their male partners, they displayed the more powerful pattern of gaze.

The results of these experiments fit nicely with Eagly's (1987) social role theory. In their normal roles women and men often show nonverbal differences consistent with their socially dictated differences in status. But when women's roles give them power, sex differences in nonverbal behavior may disappear and even reverse. Many of the sex differences in nonverbal behavior reported earlier (for example, that women smile more and men take up greater personal space) can be interpreted as resulting from status and power differences between women and men (Henley, 1977).

■■■■■■■■■■■■■■■■■■■■■

Self-Presentation Theory of Gender

The First Mobile, if one is sent, must be warned that unless he is very self-assured, or senile, his pride will suffer. A man wants his virility regarded, a woman wants her femininity appreciated, however indirect and subtle the indications of regard and appreciation. On Winter [Gethen] they will not exist. One is respected and judged only as a human being. It is an appalling experience.

—— *The Left Hand of Darkness*, p. 95

All of the theories we have reviewed so far give gender a kind of phenomenal reality: gender is dictated by biology, by early relations with parents, by conditioning and modeling, by cognitive labeling and schemas, and by social roles. Whatever theory you accept, gender is a real "thing" that people end up with, one way or another, in a fairly fixed form.

More radical views hold that gender is a cultural invention and a social construction (Kessler & McKenna, 1978) and a self-presentation that we enact in certain settings and with certain people (Deaux & Major, 1987). Kay Deaux and Brenda Major (1987) argue that self-presentation research (see Chapter 6) can help us understand gender-related behaviors. We "play" our roles as men and women depending on our own concepts of gender, others' expectations, and the setting in which we happen to be. For example, the same woman may be a no-nonsense, assertive executive at work but quite "feminine" when on a date. Similarly, as we saw in Chapter 6, college women may describe themselves in more stereotypically feminine terms (and even perform more poorly on an intelligence test) when they anticipate meeting a very attractive man who prefers "traditional" women (Zanna & Pack, 1975).

More recently, Mori, Chaiken, and Pliner (1987) have demonstrated that women will change the amount of food they eat depending on the man they're with. Both women and men stereotypically perceive women who eat small amounts of food to be more "feminine," so when a woman wants to present a feminine image she may eat less. Indeed, Mori and her colleagues found that when women participated in a discussion with an "attractive" man (that is, a man who was currently "available" and who possessed interesting hobbies and high academic ambitions), they tended to eat significantly less of the snack mix that "just happened" to be on the table than when they talked with an "unattractive" man.

Another recent study documents yet another self-presentational strategy women use to display their femininity — modifying their voices. Montepare and Vega (1988) recorded college women's phone conversations with either intimate or casual male friends. When women spoke to their boyfriends, their speech displayed significantly more "feminine" cues; their voices were higher in pitch, more "babylike," more pleasant, and more variable in tone. Furthermore, judges rated these women's voices to be significantly more "submissive" and "scatterbrained" when they spoke with their boyfriends. Many of these women were consciously aware of the change; some observed that their voices became more "babylike," "endearing," "girlie," "cutesy," and even "slightly whiny." Clearly, women display different vocal cues depending on the social setting and on the image they want to project. Thus, self-presentation theory suggests that gender displays are quite variable across settings and across social audiences.

Men too may change their display of gender-related behaviors depending on the setting and their social audience. Kite and Deaux (1986) conducted an experiment in which college men interacted with a partner — another man who was described as either heterosexual or homosexual. When men thought they were interacting with a homosexual partner, they discussed their attractions to women more than during their interactions with a heterosexual partner. By implication, some of the men felt the need to display their masculinity in this situation.

What Makes Someone "Female" or "Male" in Everyday Life?

There're only two alternatives in society. You're either a man or a woman. If I don't feel like a woman then it's got to be the other way. . . . Because I don't feel comfortable in the first position, I'm going into the second. I'll give it a try.

—— Robert — a female-to-male transsexual, quoted in Kessler and McKenna (1978, p. 112)

Suzanne Kessler and Wendy McKenna (1978) devised an intriguing exercise called the "Ten Question Gender Game." Here are the rules: Have a partner think of a person, and your job is to guess whether that person is female or male. You can ask your partner ten questions that have "yes" or "no" answers. However, you cannot ask directly, "Is the person female (or male)?" and you cannot ask directly about the person's physical characteristics ("Does the person have a penis?"). What questions would you ask?

And how accurate would you be in determining the target person's sex?

The Ten Question Gender Game poses an intriguing question: What defines a person's "maleness" or "femaleness" in everyday life? A person's gender is usually so obvious to us that we don't think much about how we perceive it. But the attribution of gender may not be quite as clear-cut as you think. Theorists have suggested that gender has a number of components (Kohlberg, 1966; Kessler & McKenna, 1978; Money & Ehrhardt, 1972). (See first table below.) One component is biological sex, which itself is multidimensional, comprising chromosomal sex, hormonal sex, internal and external genitalia, and secondary sex characteristics. A second component is gender identity, a person's sense of being male or female. This is the primary focus of Kohlberg's (1966) cognitive-developmental theory of gender. A

third component is one's focus of erotic interest; heterosexuals are sexually attracted to people of the other sex, homosexuals to people of the same sex. A fourth component of gender concerns social roles and cultural definitions of masculinity and femininity. For example, if you are interested in football and car racing, you show stereotypically masculine interests, whereas if you are interested in cooking and sewing, you show more stereotypically feminine interests.

Because most of us are well-socialized members of our culture, we perceive these four aspects of gender to form a relatively cohesive whole. In fact, however, they are more loosely related than our commonsense notion would suggest. For example, transsexuals are chromosomally and physically one sex but the other sex in terms of their gender identity. As Kessler and McKenna (1978) note, "Pre-operative transsexuals can be men

Four Components of Gender. How Important Is Each Component in Your Conception of "Female" and "Male"?

1	2	3	4
Biological sex	**Gender identify**	**Sexual object choice**	**Gender role**
Chromosomes, hormones, internal and external genitalia	Self-labeling as male or female	Sexual attraction to males, females, or both	Culturally defined "masculine" or "feminine" behaviors

with vaginas or women with penises, and, of course, the bearded lady is still a lady" (p. 2). In other words, gender is not necessarily synonymous with chromosomes, genitals, or secondary sex characteristics (see second table below).

Money and Ehrhardt (1972) describe the case of two identical twin boys, one raised as a boy and the other as a girl. When the boys were circumcised as babies, the electrical cauterizing equipment malfunctioned and burned one boy's penis off. So the parents reared him as a girl. During childhood, this genetic boy came to think of himself (herself?) as a girl and behave quite differently from his (her?) identical twin. (Which theories of gender does this case study support, and which does it argue against?)

Most homosexuals possess firm gender identities and have no desire to be the other sex, although commonly held stereotypes often portray homosexuals as gender "inverts" (Kite & Deaux, 1984). Thus being "male" or "female" is not necessarily determined by who you are sexually attracted to. And most male transvestites (men who dress like women and thus display certain "feminine" behaviors) are clearly biologically male, possess firm male gender identities, and are heterosexual (see figure below). Is a man who loves to dress in ny-

lons and slinky dresses still a man?

By thinking of gender in terms of different components, you can appreciate just how complex it is. Biology, culture, learning, self-concept, sexuality, and personality all come together to produce the extraordinarily complex phenomenon of gender. Perhaps this complicated interplay of factors is one reason why social scientists have been fascinated by the topic. (For a review of theoretical perspectives on sex differences and gender, see Summary Table 10.1.)

Different Combinations of the Four Components of Gender.

	1 **Biological sex**	*2* **Gender identify**	*3* **Sexual object choice**	*4* **Gender role**
Common cultural image of a "female"	Female	Female	Prefers males	Feminine
A male-to-female transsexual	Male	Female	Can vary, but usually prefers males	Usually feminine
A male transvestite	Male	Usually male	Usually prefers females	Can vary, but "feminine" preference for dress
Lesbian (female homosexual)	Female	Female	Prefers females	Variable, can be feminine

SUMMARY TABLE 10.1   Theoretical Perspectives on Sex Differences and Gender

On what variables do different theories of gender focus?

THEORY	MAIN FOCUS
Biological theories	
Sociobiological	Evolutionary pressures on prehistoric women and men.
Physiological	Hormonal and brain differences between the sexes.
Freudian theory	Early emotional and sexual attachments to parents.
Social learning theories	
Classical conditioning	Labels such as "sissy" acquire strong emotional connotations.
Operant conditioning	Different behaviors rewarded and punished for boys and girls.
Observational learning	Children imitate male and female parents, peers, and media models.
Cognitive theories	
Kohlberg's cognitive-developmental theory	Self-labeling as male or female leads to gender-related behaviors.
Gender-schema theory	Gender schemas comprise cultural beliefs about gender; gender-schematic individuals monitor their own and others' behavior with respect to masculinity and femininity.
Social-role theory	Different social roles occupied by men and women lead to gender stereotypes and different behaviors in men and women.
Self-presentation theory	Gender is a social "performance" that varies depending on gender schemas, the setting, and the social audience.

As this table suggests, gender is a complex phenomenon influenced by many different factors.

Masculinity, Femininity, and Androgyny

And I saw then again, and for good, what I had always been afraid to see, and had pretended not to see in him: that he was a woman as well as a man. Any need to explain the sources of that fear vanished with the fear; what I was left with was, at last, acceptance of him as he was. . . . I had not wanted to give my trust, my friendship to a man who was a woman, a woman who was a man.

—— *The Left Hand of Darkness*, p. 248

Whether from biology, early emotional relations with parents, social learning, cognitive self-labeling, or the pervasive impact of social roles, many individuals come to possess gender-related personality traits—that is, internal tendencies to behave in culturally defined "feminine" or "masculine" ways (see Chapter 6 for a broader

DOONESBURY/Garry Trudeau

■■■■■■■■■■■■■■■■■■■■■■■■
**Men and women are
still negotiating their
changing roles.**

discussion of trait theories of personality). According to this trait approach, on average women and men show differences in their degrees of masculinity and femininity. Furthermore, meaningful individual differences exist *within each sex* as well, with some women, for example, being relatively more feminine and others relatively more masculine in their behavior.

The measurement of masculinity-femininity as a personality trait has a long and somewhat controversial history in American psychological research. Lewis Terman (famous for bringing intelligence testing to the United States in the early twentieth century) and Catherine Cox Miles (1936) developed one of the first tests to measure masculinity-femininity, and they conducted research to see whether subjects' masculinity-femininity scores were related to other personality and intellectual traits, and to heterosexual and homosexual behavior. Following Terman and Miles's work, many later personality and vocational-interest inventories included masculinity-femininity scales (Campbell, 1966; Gough, 1964; Hathaway & McKinley, 1943; Strong, 1943). Most of these scales were developed specifically to differentiate women and men (or sometimes, homosexuals and heterosexuals). Thus, for example, an item on a personality inventory would be included on the masculinity-femininity scale if groups of women and men answered the question differently on average.

Early masculinity-femininity tests made two fundamental assumptions: that masculine and feminine behaviors, attitudes, and interests are fairly consistent and cohesive within individuals, and that "masculinity" and "femininity" are opposite ends of a single bipolar dimension (Constantinople, 1973). Furthermore, these early tests tended to promote the implicit value that it is good for people to possess masculinity-femininity scores that are "appropriate" to their sex — that it is desirable for women to be "feminine" and men "masculine."

However, after a half-century of research, many of these early assumptions have proved to be unwarranted (Contantinople, 1973; Reinisch, Rosenblum, & Sanders, 1987). Masculine and feminine attitudes, interests, and traits are not always cohesive (Spence & Sawin, 1985), and the content of masculinity-femininity tests, like the content of gender stereotypes, proves to be multidimensional (Lunneborg, 1972). And finally, "masculinity" is not necessarily always good for men, nor "femininity" always good for women. For example, Maccoby (1966) observed that girls and boys who perform the best intellectually often are *not* extremely sex-typed, and Stein and Bailey (1973) noted that girls with high degrees of stereotypical femininity tend not to strive for achievement as much as less stereotypically feminine girls.

Masculinity and Femininity as Separate Dimensions

With the women's movement of the 1970s came fresh approaches to the measurement of masculinity and femininity. Rejecting the notion that "masculinity" and "femininity" constituted opposite ends of a single dimension, a number of psychologists developed tests that measured masculinity and femininity as separate and independent traits (Bem, 1974; Spence, Helmreich, & Stapp, 1974; Heilbrun, 1976). Typically, these newer tests defined "masculinity" in terms of the instrumental personality traits stereotypically associated with males (for example, "aggressive," "dominant," "strong") and "femininity" in terms of expressive traits associated with women ("compassionate," "tender," and "warm"). Thus, subjects could score high on one scale and low on the other (for example, high on femininity but low on masculinity). But they could also score high on both the masculinity and femininity scales; such subjects are called "androgynous" (see Figure 10.12).

Sandra Bem (1974, 1975; Bem, Martyna, & Watson, 1976), one of the first androgyny researchers, argued that androgyny defined a new standard of mental health and psychological adjustment. Unlike traditionally masculine men and traditionally feminine women, androgynous people are less constrained by limiting sex roles and are more adaptable—they can be warm and nurturing or strong and assertive according to the needs of the situation. In a series of research studies, Bem (1975; Bem et al., 1976) found that androgynous subjects (who typically made up about 20 to 30 percent of the college populations from which they were drawn) were both independent in the face of pressures to conform and nurturing in offering help to troubled peers. Although they were independent in the face of pressures to conform, traditionally masculine men were not nurturing; and although they were nurturing with a troubled peer, traditionally feminine women "caved in" to group pressure. Thus, Bem argued that androgynous people showed both good masculine *and* good feminine behaviors, whereas traditionally masculine and feminine people show competence only in masculine or in feminine domains (Bem & Lenney, 1976).

Since the mid-1970s hundreds of studies have explored the implications of the new masculinity, femininity, and androgyny tests (Cook, 1985). This research provides a somewhat mixed picture. In a comprehensive meta-analysis of studies on masculinity, femininity, and androgyny, Taylor and Hall (1982) found that masculinity scores indeed tend to predict instrumental behaviors and that femininity scores indeed tend to predict expressive behaviors. Although both masculinity and femininity are at times related to indices of mental health and adjustment, the effects for masculinity are more consistent and considerably stronger than are those for femininity (Bassoff & Glass, 1982). Thus, masculine and androgynous people tend to be better adjusted primarily because of their high masculinity scores. This finding does not support Bem's hypothesis that in particular the *combination* of high masculinity and high femininity leads to mental health.

In another recent meta-analysis, Signorella and Jamison (1986) found that high masculinity and low femininity scores tend to be associated with better performance on math and visual-spatial tests. Although these results indicate that masculinity and femininity are related to cognitive performance, clearly they do not indicate that androgyny leads to cognitive superiority, at least in these stereotypically masculine domains. Indeed, a high degree of femininity is associated with poorer performance on these cognitive tests.

When is a high degree of femininity desirable? A number of studies suggest that people who have high degrees of femininity may have more successful and satisfying interpersonal relationships and marriages (Antill, 1983). This conclusion makes

How do traditional masculinity-femininity scales differ from recent scales?

In traditional tests, masculinity–femininity was conceived as a single bipolar dimension. Thus, you could be either feminine or masculine, but not both. Traditional scales often implied the unstated value that it is good for women to be feminine and for men to be masculine.

Masculine   Feminine

Traditional tests

More recently, psychologists have conceptualized masculinity and femininity as two independent dimensions. Masculinity scales measure the degree to which individuals report possessing positive instrumental traits, and femininity scales measure the degree to which individuals report possessing expressive traits. Individuals who have high degrees of both masculinity and femininity are termed "androgynous." Researchers like Sandra Bem have made the value assumption that androgyny is more adaptive than either traditional masculinity or traditional femininity.

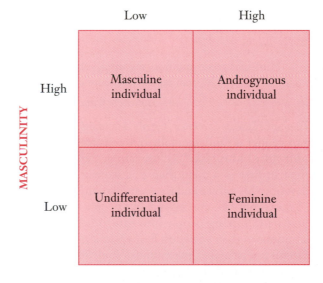

More recent conception

People who score low on both masculinity and femininity are referred to as "undifferentiated." How should we characterize such individuals? One possibility is that they have low self-esteem and thus report possessing few positive traits, whether masculine or feminine. Undifferentiated people are like androgynous people in one important respect, however: They are neither traditionally masculine nor traditionally feminine.

sense, of course, because highly feminine people are more sensitive, nurturing, and warm; that is, they possess just those characteristics needed to be a good partner in a relationship. Spence and Helmreich (1978, 1980) argue that masculinity and femininity scales are in fact instrumentality and expressiveness scales; for this reason, masculinity scales can reasonably well predict behaviors like assertiveness and achievement, and femininity scales can reasonably well predict behaviors like interpersonal warmth and nurturing, but these scales are at best weakly related to other kinds of gender-related behaviors.

Beyond Masculinity, Femininity, and Androgyny

Androgyny clearly was an idea whose time had come in the 1970s, a period in which traditional sex roles were changing rapidly. Androgyny research challenged the traditional assumptions that "masculinity" was the opposite of "femininity," and that men necessarily should be masculine and women feminine. But while challenging traditional notions, the new conceptions of masculinity and femininity once again gave a kind of phenomenal reality and psychological legitimacy to the notion of consistent, internalized, gender-related traits. Sandra Bem (1981) acknowledged in her work on gender schemas that androgyny "is insufficiently radical from a feminist perspective because it continues to presuppose that . . . masculinity and femininity have an independent and palpable reality rather than being themselves cognitive constructs" (p. 363). In Bem's ideal world, "human behaviors and society (would) cease to have gender" (p. 363).

A Final Comment on Gender

> . . . His quiet voice and face, a young, serious face, not a man's face and not a woman's face, a human face, these were a relief to me, familiar, right . . .
>
> —— *The Left Hand of Darkness*, p. 296

In *The Left Hand of Darkness*, Genly Ai comes to grips with a society whose construction of gender is fundamentally different from his own. As an earthling, Ai realizes the difficulty of his task: ". . . my efforts took the form of self-consciously seeing a Gethenian first as a man, then as a woman, forcing him into those categories so irrelevant to his nature and so essential to my own" (p. 12).

Like Genly Ai — and indeed, like people in general — psychologists may at times be guilty of "forcing people into categories" based on the unstated, unconscious assumptions of their societies. Perhaps this is why Bem (1981) argues that we should be careful not to make "masculinity" and "femininity" too real. Still, gender is one of the most fundamental categories that we, as human beings, apply to the social world (Kohlberg, 1966; Kessler & McKenna, 1978). The concept of gender has existed throughout recorded history; its meanings have developed and changed and will undoubtedly continue to change.

Social psychological research helps us to understand our preconceptions about gender, to assess the current behavior of women and men, and to look to new possibilities for women and men in the future. It serves valuable social as well as scientific purposes when it leads us, like Genly Ai, to appreciate the diversity of human beings and to accept people for who they are, regardless of their sex or gender.

1. The roles of women and men have changed substantially in recent years. However, women and men still differ on average with respect to the education and work they pursue, the wages they receive, and the roles they carry out in family life.

2. Common stereotypes hold that expressive traits (such as "warm" and "nurturing") are more characteristic of women and instrumental traits (such as "competitive" and "aggressive") are more characteristic of men.

3. Traits ascribed to men are sometimes more positive than those ascribed to women. General stereotypes of mental health and of nationality groups tend to be those that describe men, not women.

4. Gender stereotypes comprise probabilistic beliefs about the physical traits, social and family roles, sexual behavior, and personality traits of women and men.

5. Work performed by women is sometimes evaluated more negatively and attributed to different causes than is equivalent work performed by men.

6. Judgments of individual women and men based on concrete information tends to be influenced less by gender stereotypes than are judgments based on gender alone. However, concrete information about individuals does not eliminate the influence of gender stereotypes.

7. Meta-analysis is a statistical procedure that enables researchers to combine results of many studies on sex differences. Recent meta-analyses indicate that women and men on average show differences in nonverbal behaviors, aggression, helping behavior, and susceptibility to social influence. Meta-analyses show that in group settings, women engage more in expressive behaviors and men engage more in instrumental behaviors.

8. Biological theories attempt to explain sex differences in terms of evolutionary biology, heredity, and physiology. Such explanations are plausible if sex differences occur early in development, show consistency across cultures, show consistency across species, and relate to sex-linked physiological variables (such as hormones). Sex differences in aggression are probably due in part to biological predispositions.

9. Freudian theory argues that early emotional and sexual attachments to parents lead children to develop masculine or feminine identities.

10. Social learning theories argue that sex differences and gender-related behaviors are learned through processes of classical conditioning, operant conditioning, and observational learning.

11. Kohlberg's cognitive-development theory holds that after labeling themselves as female or male, children strive to behave consistently with their gender identities. Bem's gender schema theory argues that people hold gender schemas that comprise cultural beliefs about gender. Individuals who are gender-schematic hold strong gender schemas and tend to monitor their own and others' behavior in terms of "femininity" and "masculinity."

12. Eagly's social role theory holds that the differing roles assigned to women and men in all societies lead to stereotypical perceptions of women and men and to different behaviors in women and men.

13. Self-presentational theories argue that gender-related behaviors are variably displayed depending on the setting and others' expectations. Both women and men sometimes change their displays of femininity or masculinity depending on their social audience.

14. Gender has a number of components, including biological sex, gender identity, choice of sexual object, and cultural definitions of feminine and masculine behaviors. These four components are not perfectly correlated.

15. Early personality tests conceptualized masculinity-femininity as a single bipolar dimension. More recent conceptions hold that masculinity and femininity are two independent dimensions.

16. Bem argued that people with high degrees of both masculinity and femininity (androgynous people) may be more adaptable and mentally healthy than traditionally masculine or feminine individuals. Research has not consistently supported this hypothesis.

17. Masculinity is positively related to various measures of mental health and to performance on mathematics and visual-spatial tests. Femininity is positively related to success in interpersonal relationships.

Glossary

Androgyny: Possessing both masculine and feminine traits; in terms of current masculinity and femininity scales, an individual is androgynous if he or she reports possessing both instrumental and expressive personality traits

Biological theories: Theories that explain sex differences and gender-related behaviors in terms of evolutionary biology, heredity, and physiology

Cognitive-development theory: Kohlberg's theory that an individual's self-labeling as male or female is critical in the development of gender-related behaviors

Femininity: A personality trait defined in current scales as the degree to which an individual reports possessing expressive personality traits

Freudian theory: Theory originating with Sigmund Freud that focuses on unconscious mental processes and early sexual and emotional development; Freudian theory argues that girls become feminine and boys masculine because of genital differences that lead to different patterns of emotional and sexual development; see *Oedipus complex* and *Penis envy*

Gender: Social definitions of male and female, including all the nonbiological characteristics society uses to differentiate men and women (such as dress, nonverbal behaviors, social roles, occupations, and so on)

Gender identity: An individual's self-definition as male or female

Gender schema theory: Bem's theory that people possess schemas comprising cultural information about gender; those possessing strong gender schemas monitor their own and others' behavior in relation to its "masculinity" and "femininity"

Gender stereotypes: Social beliefs about women's and men's personality traits, abilities, social roles, physical characteristics, and sexual behavior

Masculinity: A personality trait defined in current scales as the degree to which an individual reports possessing instrumental personality traits

Oedipus complex: According to Freudian theory, a young boy's unconscious feelings of sexual attraction to his mother and rivalry with his father; the resolution of the Oedipus complex leads to sex-typing

Penis envy: According to Freudian theory, a major motivation in women's lives; because girls believe they have been castrated and because they unconsciously covet the "superior" male organ, they strive to regain their lost penis, often through having relationships with males or through bearing children

Self-presentation theories: Theories that argue that gender-related behaviors are a social performance that varies depending on the setting and the social audience

Sex: An individual's biological status of being male or female

Social learning theories: Theories that argue that sex differences and gender-related behaviors are the results of classical conditioning, operant conditioning, and observational learning

Social role theory: Eagly's theory that the different roles occupied by women and men lead to differences in the perception of women and men and in the behavior of women and men

"... It's said to be a love match."

"A love match? What antediluvian ideas you have! Who talks about love nowadays?" said the ambassador's wife.

"What can be done? That preposterous old fashion still hasn't died out," said Vronsky.

"So much the worse for those who follow the fashion. The only happy marriages I know are based on reason."

... "But what we call 'marriages based on reason' are those in which both have already sown their wild oats. It's like scarlet fever, it's something you have to go through."

"Then we'll have to find a way to give an inoculation of love, like a vaccination."

... "No, I think, quite seriously, that in order to know what love is you have to make a mistake and then correct it," said Princess Betsy.

"Even after marriage?" said the ambassador's wife archly.

"That's just it," Betsy put in, "you have to make a mistake and correct it. What do you think about all this?" she said to Anna. ...

"I think," said Anna . . . , "I think that — if there are as many minds as there are heads, then there are also just as many kinds of love as there are hearts."

—— from *Anna Karenina*, by Leo Tolstoy, pp. 144–145

CHAPTER 11

Liking, Loving, and Close Relationships

*T*hrough the words of Anna Karenina and her aristocratic friends, Leo Tolstoy pondered the nature of love and intimate relationships over a hundred years ago. Indeed, his novel, *Anna Karenina*, can be seen as a monumental study of the creation and demise of intimate relationships. The central character, Anna, is trapped in a loveless marriage and finds passion for the first time in an adulterous affair with the dashing Count Vronsky. The second main character of the novel, Levin, falls madly in love with Princess Kitty, who first spurns him for Vronsky but later accepts his proposal of marriage after being jilted by Vronsky. Developing these two main plots in counterpoint, Tolstoy offers rich and wise observations about the pathos, problems, and promise of close human relationships. Of course, *Anna Karenina* is but one of hundreds of literary portrayals of attraction in its various forms. What would novelists, dramatists, screenwriters, poets, and composers do without the topics of friendship and love?

And what would our lives be without love and attraction? Individually and as a culture we seem obsessed with interpersonal attraction, its causes, its maintenance, and its significance. From scholarly articles to popular newspaper columns like "Dear Abby," attraction is a topic that attracts us all. Perhaps this profound and enduring interest is well justified, for social life is forever played out against the background of our friendships and loves (Berscheid, 1985). From our conception, through our development in the crucible of family life, to the lifelong support we find in friends, lovers, and spouses, our lives tell the story of relationships between and among people.

387

Trends in the Scientific Study of Attraction

Although most of us think frequently about our attractions to others, social psychologists did not devote much research to this topic until the mid-1960s (Berscheid, 1985; Levinger, 1980), perhaps because they viewed "love" as inaccessible to standard scientific methods. The scientific study of attraction, and particularly of love, has probably been retarded by the cultural attitude that love is mysterious, ineffable, and beyond empirical research. Indeed, some argue that love *should* be protected from the cold scrutiny of scientific inquiry. In 1975, Senator William Proxmire of Wisconsin roundly criticized the funding of research on the causes of romantic love:

> . . . no one — not even the National Science Foundation — can argue that falling in love is a science. . . . I believe that . . . Americans want to leave some things in life a mystery, and right at the top of things we don't want to know is why a man falls in love with a woman and vice versa. . . . (quoted in Walster & Walster, 1978)

Senator Proxmire notwithstanding, this chapter will describe scientific theories and research on why people like and love others. These topics are not frivolous; each of our lives started with an act of attraction, and our happiness at work, at play, and in family life depends on the quality of our friendships and loves.

Certainly, social psychology cannot provide the same kind of information about love that poets and novelists give us. For both practical and theoretical reasons, social psychology has brought certain emphases to the study of liking and loving.

First, social psychology has tended to emphasize *the current situation* as a cause of attraction. Our account of the early stages of attraction will focus on *broad, often external, variables*, such as situationally produced anxiety, proximity, mere exposure, similarity, and physical attractiveness.

Social psychological research has also focused more on *initial and early stages of friendships and romantic attractions* than on their long-term development (Berscheid, 1985; Huston & Levinger, 1978). It is simply more practical to study variables that influence the beginnings of relationships, for beginnings can be created in the laboratory, and mature, intense attractions cannot.

Similarly, social psychology has traditionally focused on *mild attraction* (liking, and particularly liking after first meetings and based on first impressions) rather than on stronger attractions (committed friendships, passionate and romantic love). Again, this focus is partly due to the logistics of conducting research. Mild attraction can be created quickly and investigated in a laboratory experiment, whereas intense attraction requires time to develop and generally is not amenable to experimental investigation.

In the quote that began this chapter, one character suggests that happy marriages are "based on reason." Certainly, sometimes we rationally select our friends and lovers. But do we always? All of us seem to know someone who "fell in love with the wrong person." Sometimes love is blind.

Until relatively recently, social psychologists have emphasized the *cognitive processes that lead to attraction*, in part because of social psychology's general emphasis on cognition (Markus & Zajonc, 1985). Attraction has been related to broader research on beliefs and attitudes (Berscheid, 1985), for we are attracted to people based on the information we have about them. We strive to create consistency among our likes and dislikes (Heider, 1958; Newcomb, 1953). Equity and exchange theories assume that people rationally compute the rewards and costs of relationships in deciding whether or not to pursue them. Attraction as mental calculation has received considerable attention in social psychology; attraction as raw emotion has received less attention (Berscheid, 1983).

Recently, however, social psychologists have expanded their approach to attraction. Research has increasingly focused on romantic and passionate love, and longitudinal studies that follow dating and married couples over long periods of time are becoming more common (Rubin, 1973; Berscheid & Walster, 1974a; Kelley, Berscheid, Christensen, Harvey, Huston, Levinger, McClintock, Peplau, & Peterson, 1983).

Finally, theories of attraction have been formulated to explain causal factors other than broad, situational variables. The findings of sociobiology over the past two decades have increased our appreciation of biological factors in attraction (Buss, 1987, 1988). Close and intimate relationships, a relatively neglected topic in the past, is now the subject of intense theoretical interest (Kelley et al., 1983). And researchers are addressing anew the role of emotion in attraction (Berscheid, 1983). We will describe these new research directions as well as the more traditional approaches in the remainder of this chapter.

The Beginnings of Attraction

Before we ask why people like others, let's consider a more basic question: Why do people simply want to be with others? The word *affiliation* is used by social psychologists to refer to a desire or motivation to be with others, sometimes regardless of one's liking for those others. *Attraction*, on the other hand, refers to a positive attitude or emotion we feel toward others, which presumably leads us to approach them and seek their companionship.

Affiliation and Anxiety: The "Dr. Zilstein Experiment"

In the late 1950s Stanley Schachter (1959) carried out an important program of research that tested a seemingly simple hypothesis — that when people are upset and anxious they are more likely to affiliate with others. (I recall an event that seems to support this hypothesis. As I walked home from school on the day President John F. Kennedy was assassinated in 1963, I saw people standing in groups on the sidewalk, discussing the day's horrifying events. Neighbors who hadn't spoken to one another in days and sometimes months now needed to be with one another.)

It is one thing to observe anecdotally that people want to be with others when they're upset, but it is another thing to demonstrate this proposition in the laboratory. As you know from Chapter 2, experiments have one powerful advantage over correlational studies — they allow us to draw a cause-effect conclusion. Does anxiety *cause* affiliation? To answer this question, Schachter brought female subjects to the laboratory, made them quite anxious, and then gave them the opportunity to wait alone or with others.

Here's how the experiment worked: The subjects were greeted by Dr. Zilstein, the experimenter, who explained that he was studying the effects of electric shocks on people. He informed half of the subjects — those in the low-anxiety condition — that the shock they received would not be painful. He informed the remaining subjects — those in the high-anxiety condition — that they would receive extremely painful electric shocks.

Both groups of subjects were asked to complete a questionnaire while they waited for the experiment to begin. Casually, Dr. Zilstein informed them that they could fill out the questionnaires while sitting alone in a room or while sitting with other subjects, and he asked them to mark on their form where they would like to wait. (The subjects' choice to be alone or with others, of course, was the dependent measure that interested Schachter, and the subjects were not really shocked in this experiment.) Were the high-anxiety subjects more likely than the low-anxiety subjects to choose to wait with others? The data from Schachter's experiment answered this question with a clear "yes" (see Figure 11.1).

Reasons for the anxiety-affiliation relationship.   Why do anxious people seek out others? You can probably think of several plausible reasons. Anxious people may affiliate with others to gain reassurance and reinforcement, or they may be seeking to distract themselves and "take their minds off their problems." Perhaps anxious people want to be with others in order to clarify feelings and compare their reactions to those of others. All of these factors may at times motivate affiliation (Hill, 1987).

The *social comparison* explanation — that we sometimes seek out others so that we can compare ourselves with them — has a distinguished history in social psychology. Leon Festinger's (1954) *social comparison theory* argues that whereas we can objectively know physical reality (for example, how much I weigh), we cannot directly know social reality (how smart I am). To know social reality, we must compare ourselves with others.

Furthermore, Festinger hypothesized that we generally seek to compare ourselves with *similar* others. For example, if you want to know how "smart" you are, shouldn't you compare yourself with other college students rather than with your five-year-old cousin or a Nobel laureate physicist? Indeed, a good time to see social comparison processes in operation is when professors return exams and students eagerly compare scores to see how they stack up against their friends and acquaintances.

Schachter (1959) conducted a clever follow-up experiment to determine whether or not social comparison processes led to affiliation in his Dr. Zilstein study. The new study was similar to the original, with one significant variation — some of the highly anxious subjects were told that they could wait with other subjects; others were informed that they could wait with students waiting to talk to their professors.

This new version of the experiment posed an interesting question: Will anxious subjects wait with just anybody, or only with people who share their predicament? If subjects are merely seeking distraction, then anybody should do; but if they are seeking social comparison, then they must affiliate with other subjects. The results indicated that anxious subjects wanted to wait *only* with other subjects in the shock experiment. Schachter facetiously summarized his results by concluding that whereas his original study supported the old saying that "Misery loves company," the follow-up study amended that to "Misery loves, in particular, miserable company." These results, of course, are consistent with the social comparison explanation for the anxiety-affiliation link. Many subsequent studies have further substantiated the importance of social comparison processes in affiliation (Rofe, 1984; Suls & Miller, 1977).

FIGURE 11.1   Results of Schachter's "Dr. Zilstein study."

Does anxiety cause affiliation?

Schachter (1959) manipulated the anxiety levels of female subjects by leading them to anticipate either painful or innocuous electric shocks. The dependent variable was subjects' choice to wait with others or to wait alone.

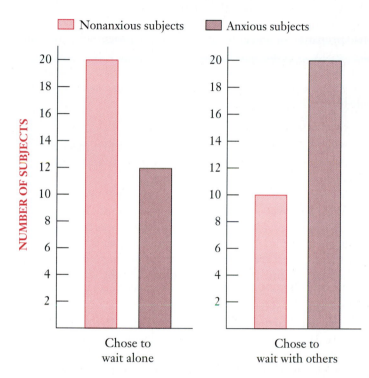

The results supported the hypothesis that anxiety leads to affiliation: Anxious subjects chose to wait with others far more than did nonanxious subjects.

SOURCE: Data from Schachter (1959).

Subsequent research has tried to specify when anxiety does and does not lead to affiliation. One study, for example, suggests that whereas anxiety resulting from fear may lead us to want to be with others, anxiety resulting from social embarrassment may lead us to avoid others (Sarnoff & Zimbardo, 1961).

From Affiliation to Attraction

Often, we seek out others not because we're upset or anxious, but because we're positively attracted. Why do we like some people? What leads us to initiate relationships with some individuals but not with others? Let's seek answers to these questions by turning to several broad variables—proximity, mere exposure, similarity, and physical attractiveness—that influence the early development of friendships and romances.

Proximity: The architecture of attraction.

> The Levins and the Shcherbatskys were two old noble Moscow houses; they had always been on intimate and friendly terms with each other. This relationship had become still stronger during the time Levin had been a student.
> He had prepared for and entered the university together with young Prince Shcherbatsky. . . . During this period Levin spent a great deal of time frequenting the Shcherbatsky house. . . . However strange it might seem, he had fallen in love with the house itself and with the Shcherbatsky family, especially the female half.
>
> —— *Anna Karenina*, p. 22

To become friends or lovers with someone you must first meet that someone. One powerful variable that determines whether you meet someone is *proximity*—the physical or architectural distance that separates you.

A classic study by Festinger, Schachter, and Back (1950) analyzed friendship patterns at Westgate West, a married graduate student housing project at M.I.T. Student families were randomly assigned to available apartments, so almost none of the residents knew one another upon moving in. Later, when residents were asked to list their three closest friends in the housing project, about two-thirds of those friends turned out to live in the same building as the subjects who listed them. Furthermore, of the close friends listed in a subject's own building, about two-thirds lived on the same floor as the nominating subject.

There were five apartments on each of two floors in the typical Westgate building (see Figure 11.2). The Westgate study indicated that people who lived in the middle apartments of their floors (apartments 3 and 8 in Figure 11.2) tended to be nominated as friends more than those who lived in the end apartments, and that those who lived in first-floor apartments near the staircases connecting the two floors (apartments 1 and 5) tended to be nominated more than those who lived farther away from the stairs. Note that middle apartments were both centrally located and in close proximity to neighbors on either side. And apartments near the staircase had less "functional distance" from others in the building; that is, if you lived near the staircase, you would encounter other residents more often because you would "bump into" them as they used the stairs.

Similar studies have investigated friendship patterns in college dormitories. Priest and Sawyer (1967), for example, measured students' friendships in a large University of Chicago dormitory. Neighboring doors in this dorm were only eight feet apart. Yet, on average, students were more likely to be friends with a student who lived one door away than with one who lived two doors away, and so on. Now it's not shocking that large distances make a difference in friendships, but in the Priest and Sawyer study, we're talking about the difference between 8 and 16 feet.

Using a somewhat different methodology, Hays (1985) asked college students to name two other students with whom they thought a friendship might develop during

Varieties of Social Influence

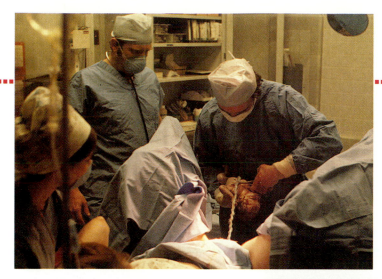

Human beings are social animals. From birth to death we live in a social world. Social influences have a profound impact on what we think, what we feel, and how we behave.

Life begins with the aid of others.

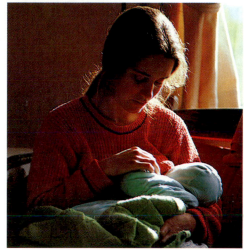

The first strong emotional attachment in life.

Through processes of classical conditioning, operant conditioning, and modeling, children are strongly influenced by their parents.

Early friendships and play prepare children for work and social relationships later in life.

During adolescence people experience "first loves" and gain knowledge about intimate relationships.

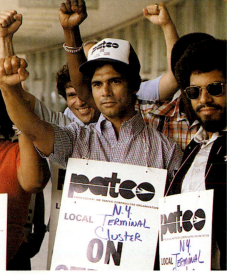

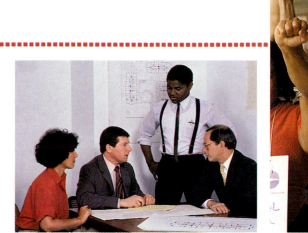

Social relationships play a key role in the world of work. Most people work in groups . . . and both business managers and workers organize into groups to promote their interests.

During adulthood people form long-term, committed relationships.

Friendships are important throughout life.

Nurtured by our parents earlier in life, many of us come to nurture them.

Even in the aftermath of death, people remain social animals. With each new generation, the life cycle of social influence starts once again.

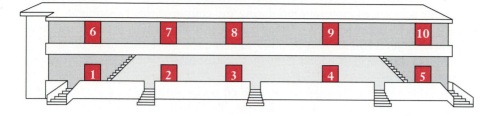

FIGURE 11.2   Schematic diagram of a Westgate West building.

Festinger, Schachter, and Back (1950) studied how the architectural proximity of residents in housing units like this one affected their friendships with other residents.

SOURCE: Adapted from Social Pressures in Informal Groups. © 1950 by Leon Festinger, Stanley Schachter, and Kurt Back. Used with permission of the publishers, Stanford University Press.

the school year. Three months later, subjects rated the intensity of these developing friendships. Hays found a significant negative correlation between the distance separating residences and the rated intensity of friendships. So, the farther away a potential friend lives, the less likely you are to develop a friendship.

Similar results come from studies on noncollege housing projects. In one study (Nahemow & Lawton, 1975), the elderly residents of an urban housing project tended to nominate as their closest friends people who lived in the same building (88 percent of the nominated friends) and people who lived on the same floor (almost 50 percent of the nominated friends).

Proximity affects not only friendships but more intimate relationships as well. In an early sociological study, Bossard (1931) examined 5,000 marriage license applications in Philadelphia and plotted the residences of each applicant on a street map. He too found a clear relationship between proximity and attraction. According to Bossard, the proportion of couples getting married "decreased steadily and markedly as the distance between contracting parties increased." In other words, more couples who lived one block apart got married than couples who lived two blocks apart, and so on. More recent research points to similar conclusions (Katz & Hill, 1958; Ramsoy, 1966; Kerckhoff, 1974).

The research on proximity and attraction makes an important point: To form a relationship with someone you must first come into contact. Your residential, educational, and work settings can have a decisive influence on who you do and don't meet. Parents who send their children to "the right schools" so they will meet and marry "the right people" implicitly acknowledge the role of proximity in attraction.

Mere exposure: I've grown accustomed to your face.   The closer people live, work, or sit to us, the more we see them. Robert Zajonc's research on the *mere exposure effect* (see Chapter 8) shows that, all things being equal, people tend to like stimuli more the more frequently they have been exposed to them. Does this mere exposure phenomenon apply to interpersonal attraction?

In one experiment, Zajonc (1968) found that when subjects were shown photographs of men for various numbers of times, on average they indicated that they liked the men more the more frequently they had seen the photographs. In another study, Saegert, Swap, and Zajonc (1973) had subjects sit next to other subjects on the pretext of participating in an experiment on taste perception. The researchers arranged for subjects to move around during the course of this experiment, so that they sat next to other subjects varying numbers of times. On average, the more frequently subjects had sat next to other subjects, the more they liked them. Thus these results show evidence for a frequency of exposure effect when the stimuli are live human beings.

In yet another study, Segal (1974) studied police cadets who were assigned to their rooms and classroom seats alphabetically. When asked to list their closest friends among other cadets, these subjects were more likely to list someone who was alphabetically similar to them. These results again point to the pervasive effects of mere exposure and proximity. Note that in real life these two variables are often confounded.

Similarity: Birds of a feather.

> Levin was almost the same age as Oblonski, and was on intimate terms with him. . . . Levin had been his comrade and friend since early youth. They were attached to each other in spite of differing characters and tastes, as friends are who meet in early youth. But in spite of this, as often happens between people who have chosen different careers, each of them, even though justifying each other's activity in any argument, despised it at heart. It seemed to each of them that the life he himself was leading was the only real life, while his friend's life was a mere phantom.
>
> —— *Anna Karenina*, p. 18

Many studies suggest that we associate more with others of similar age, socioeconomic status, level of education, political affiliation, attitudes and values, personality traits, religious affiliation, and even physical dimensions like attractiveness and height.

Think of your closest friend. How similar is he or she to you in age? In degree of education? In ethnic background? In values and attitudes? If you are like most people, your best friend is likely more similar to you than not. Researchers at the University of Michigan demonstrated this fact in a survey of 1,000 Detroit-area men who answered questions both about themselves and their three closest friends (Laumann, 1969). Their results showed that friends tended to come from similar social, educational, and religious backgrounds.

Intimate relationships also seem to follow the similarity principle. Sociological and social psychological research indicates that people engage in *assortative mating*; that is, people mate in nonrandom ways, and in particular they seem to match themselves on a variety of dimensions. For example, early research by Burgess and Wallin (1943) demonstrated that engaged couples tended to be similar in age, social class, ethnicity, and religion. More recent research has indicated that engaged and married couples also show matching on intelligence, values, degree of smoking and alcohol consumption, and even physical dimensions like height, weight, lung volume, and—believe it or not—even ear lobe length (Buss, 1985; Osborne, Noble, & Wey, 1978; Vandenberg, 1972). In a study of dating couples, Hill, Rubin, and Peplau (1976) found that couples who stayed together were more similar in age, intelligence, and physical attractiveness than those who broke up.

■■■■■■■■■■■■■■■■■■■■■■
**Does similarity lead
to attraction?**

Virtually all the research just surveyed demonstrates that similarity is correlated with attraction in everyday life, but it doesn't necessarily prove that similarity *leads to* attraction. A study by Theodore Newcomb (1961) was one of the first to clearly demonstrate a causal link between similarity and attraction. Newcomb provided a group of University of Michigan men with free rooms in a local boarding house if they would agree to participate in a study on friendship formation. All of the students were strangers to one another at the start, and thus Newcomb could observe friendships as they developed and probe the causal factors underlying these friendships. Newcomb's data indicated that attitudinal and value similarity predicted who became friends with whom. For example, one group of five friends shared common liberal political views and interests in intellectual and artistic subjects, whereas another group of three friends were all politically conservative engineering students.

In an interesting variation on his boarding house study, Newcomb (1961) intentionally pitted similarity against proximity. He paired as roommates students that he knew to be dissimilar in many ways. For example, an incoming freshman interested in liberal arts and classical music might be paired with an older student who was enrolling in the business school after serving in the military. Surprisingly, roommates were generally strongly attracted to each other, even though they were quite different. Apparently, although we tend to seek out those who are similar to us, we can learn to like dissimilar others if we come in contact with them.

FIGURE 11.3   **Attitude similarity and attraction.**

How does attitude similarity affect attraction?

Byrne and Nelson (1965) asked subjects to rate how much they liked a stranger after learning he agreed with varying proportions of their attitudes expressed on a questionnaire. (Higher numbers indicate greater liking.)

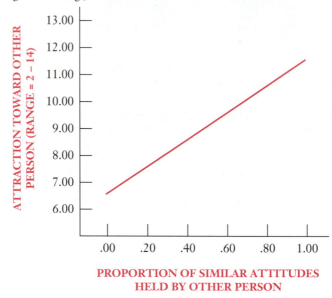

As the graph shows, the greater the proportion of attitudes subjects shared with the stranger, the more subjects liked him.

Because this is an experiment, *it tells us that attitude similarity* causes *attraction.*

In a series of experiments, Byrne and his associates (see Byrne, 1971) have shown that when we think we share similar attitudes with another person, we tend to like him or her more. In these experiments pairs of subjects filled out attitude questionnaires, and each subject was given false information about the other subject's questionnaire responses. The experimenter could thus directly manipulate how much a subject thought the other person agreed with his or her attitudes. Such studies consistently show a strong linear relationship between subjects' perceptions of the proportion of attitudes they share with another subject and their liking for that subject (see Figure 11.3). The causal link between attitudinal similarity and attraction holds across cultures, age groups, and educational and mental health statuses (Byrne, 1971).

Stage Models of Attraction

A number of social psychologists have suggested that friendships and close relationships pass through a series of stages or "filters" (Kerckhoff & Davis, 1962; Levinger & Snoek, 1972; Murstein, 1970). For example, Murstein's (1970) stimulus-value-role model (see the figure) suggests that an intimate relationship starts at a *stimulus stage*, during which each party assesses the other on such externally apparent characteristics as age, appearance, ethnicity, and gender. Typically, we seek others who are similar to us on these dimensions (with the one notable exception of gender in heterosexual attraction). This initial "cut" of the population based on broad demographic and appearance variables can greatly limit our pool of eligibles — that is, the population from which we select potential friends or lovers. The variable of gender in romantic attraction is an obvious example; most people cut their prospects in half on that one criterion alone.

Note that screening people at Murstein's stimulus stage does not require actual interaction. You may be able to tell at a glance that someone is "not right" for you, based on his or her age, appearance, or ethnicity. Murstein's second stage, the value stage, does require interaction, however, because now you seek to learn about the other person's attitudes and values. After several dates with an attractive romantic partner, you may start to learn about your partner's religious values, political attitudes, opinions about family life, leisure activities, career, and so on. In this stage the similarity principle seems to predominate again, for in general people seek others with similar attitudes, values, and interests.

In Murstein's third stage, the role stage, you assess how well your potential partner fits in with the roles you expect each party to take in the relationship. For example, in a traditional marriage, each partner may have expectations about how a "husband" and "wife" are supposed to behave. For instance, the traditional husband is supposed to earn money, mow the lawn, carry out the trash, and physically discipline the children; the traditional wife is supposed to decorate and clean the house, prepare food, and provide emotional support for the family. Note that traditional sex roles are complementary in the sense that they create a division of labor. If the two parties in a marriage don't agree about such roles, they may be in for considerable conflict.

It's worth noting a relatively subtle point here: Although some people may seek out complementary or "opposite" roles in a relationship, their *attitudes* toward such roles are likely to be similar.

An earlier stage model of courtship and attraction (Kerckhoff & Davis, 1962) suggested that in addition to compatible roles, couples seek out complementary personality traits and needs in each other. For example, perhaps a dominant person would be most compatible with a submissive marriage partner. Although this notion that "opposites attract" seems plausible for certain personality traits, it has not generally been supported by research studies (Winch, 1958; Hill, Rubin, & Peplau, 1976; Murstein, 1976; Levinger, 1983).

Stage and filter models of attraction suggest that different variables come into play at different stages of relationships. Probably we should take all such models with a grain of salt (see Levinger, 1983), for they likely assume a universal sequence of development in relationships that is altogether too fixed, linear, and predictable. Still, they serve as prototypes with which to compare the complexity of real relationships, and they suggest testable hypotheses about the kinds of variables that may affect relationships at different times in their life cycles.

Murstein's stimulus-value-role model of attraction. According to Murstein's model, what variables are most important at each stage of a relationship?

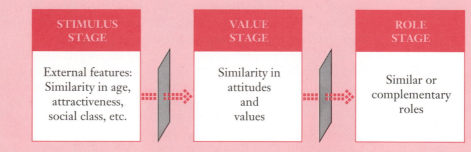

STIMULUS STAGE	VALUE STAGE	ROLE STAGE
External features: Similarity in age, attractiveness, social class, etc.	Similarity in attitudes and values	Similar or complementary roles

Researchers traditionally have assumed that attitudinal similarity causes increased liking, but recently Rosenbaum (1986) has suggested that instead, dissimilarity causes us to be repelled by others. In response, Byrne, Clore, and Smeaton (1986) have suggested that people go through a two-stage process: First we *eliminate* potential friends on the basis of *dissimilarities* and negative characteristics (such as obviously incompatible attitudes, bad breath, or physical unattractiveness), and then we develop relationships from the remaining pool of eligibles on the basis of such positive factors as similar attitudes. None of these recent hypotheses disputes the correlational and experimentally confirmed relationship between similarity and attraction; rather, each seeks to specify further why and how the relationship occurs.

Physical attractiveness.

> The mysterious, delightful Kitty . . . could never love such a plain fellow as he thought himself. . . . A plain, goodhearted fellow . . . might be loved as a friend, he thought, but to be loved the way he loved Kitty, a man had to be handsome. . . .
>
> He had heard that women often loved plain, simple men, but he didn't believe it, since he judged by himself and he himself could only love beautiful, mysterious, and exceptional women.
>
> —— *Anna Karenina*, p. 24

For many years social psychologists ignored the role of physical attractiveness in attraction. After all, when people are surveyed concerning what they look for in dates and mates, physical attractiveness is never at the top of the list (Hill, 1945; Hudson & Henze, 1969; Hudson & Hoyt, 1981; Buss & Barnes, 1986). Subjects typically report that they are more interested in "honesty," "warmth," "dependable character," "emotional stability," and "a sense of humor."

But do people practice what they preach? A study by Walster, Aronson, Abrahams, and Rottman (1966) attempted to answer this question by setting up "computer dates" for over 700 incoming freshmen at the University of Minnesota. These students filled out questionnaires, supposedly so they could be matched up with a "computer date" for a big dance arranged by the researchers. In these questionnaires the researchers assessed subjects' attitudes, personalities, and scholastic aptitudes. They also had student researchers unobtrusively rate each subject's physical attractiveness.

Students were matched randomly with their "computer dates" (with one qualification—the man had to be taller). On the night of the dance, students met their dates and went to the university gymnasium (the site of the dance), where they talked, danced, met other freshmen, and got to know their dates. After a couple of hours, the researchers rounded up all available students during an intermission and asked them to fill out a questionnaire evaluating their dates.

Did scholastic aptitude, attitudes, or personality traits affect students' liking for their dates? Not at all. Did physical attractiveness affect students' liking for their dates? Yes. Only one strongly significant finding emerged from this study: The more physically attractive their dates were, the more students liked them.

These findings unleashed a flood of research on the social implications and consequences of physical attractiveness. A number of replications of the "computer date" study (Brislin & Lewis, 1968; Curran & Lippold, 1975; Tesser & Brodie, 1971) have also indicated that subjects' perceptions of their dates' attractiveness exerts a

■■■■■■■■■■■■■■■■■■■■■■■
**Although physical at-
tractiveness is to some
extent "in the eye of
the beholder," social
psychological research
indicates that people
tend to show high lev-
els of agreement when
rating others' physical
attractiveness.**

"Do you think I'm attractive?"

stronger influence on their attraction to the date than does their perception of any other characteristic. Why does physical attractiveness have such a profound effect on attraction in these studies? One possibility is that these research subjects are quite young and thus have not yet learned to look for "deeper" traits in others. And these studies also focus on first impressions at the very earliest stages of relationships.

In real-life relationships (as opposed to "computer dates"), dating and married couples tend to be matched on attractiveness. Silverman (1971), for example, conducted a field study in which researchers observed couples in natural settings (such as bars and theater lobbies) and rated each partner on physical attractiveness. As suggested by the similarity principle, beautiful women were more likely to be with beautiful men, average-looking women with average-looking men, and homely women with homely men.

McKillip and Riedel (1983) observed both opposite-sex and same-sex pairs of people in real-life settings and rated each member of the pair on attractiveness. The researchers then asked their subjects whether they were friends or lovers, and how strong and committed their relationship was. Interestingly, both friends and lovers tended to be matched on physical attractiveness. Furthermore, close and committed relationships tended to show more matching then did casual relationships.

It probably comes as no surprise to you that physically attractive people are more popular. Walster and her colleagues (1966) found that attractive students had dated more than had less attractive students over a six-month period. Berscheid, Dion, and Walster (1971) extended these results by showing that the correlation between attractiveness and popularity was stronger for females than for males. Perhaps in keeping with traditional sex-role stereotypes, women's popularity is based more on appearance, whereas men may also be popular for wealth, intelligence, or athletic ability. A number of studies indicate that men rate the physical attractiveness of a romantic partner to be more important than do women (Cooms & Kenkel,

1966; Miller & Rivenbark, 1970; Stroebe, Insko, Thompson, & Layton, 1971; Buss & Barnes, 1986).

Does physical attractiveness confer any advantages other than popularity? Dion, Berscheid, and Walster (1972) asked subjects to rate people depicted in photographs on many different traits. (The photographs had been prejudged on attractiveness.) Physically attractive people were not only judged to have more attractive personalities, but better moral characters as well. Furthermore, subjects predicted that the attractive people could expect better job prospects and happier marriages. Apparently, in the minds of many, beautiful is not only popular, it is better as well (Berscheid & Walster, 1974b).

Perhaps there is a kernel of truth to some of these stereotypes about attractive and unattractive people. Analyzing data from national surveys conducted at the University of Michigan, Quinn (1978) found, for example, that the income of good-looking men was on average almost $2,000 higher than that of homely men, whereas the income of good-looking women was more than $1,200 higher than that of homely women. Because these results were based on data collected between 1971 and 1973, the wage differential is probably considerably larger today. Quinn's (1978) survey data also documented that attractive men and women held both more prestigious and better-paying jobs.

To add insult to injury, the work of attractive people is sometimes judged to be of higher quality than equivalent work performed by less attractive people. For example, Landy and Sigall (1974) asked subjects to evaluate an essay that had apparently been written by either a beautiful woman or a homely woman. Some subjects read a well-written essay, others a poorly written essay. The results: Subjects rated the attractive woman's essay as being better, particularly when the essay was of low quality.

Evaluations of children may also be biased by their physical attractiveness. In nursery school, attractive children are more popular with other children (Dion & Berscheid, 1972, 1974), and both teachers and other students base their evaluations of children at least in part on appearance. Clifford and Walster (1973) asked 300 fifth-grade teachers in Missouri to evaluate educational transcripts that included a small photograph of the child. Distressingly, teachers rated attractive children as more intelligent and socially adjusted than unattractive children, even though the transcripts for the attractive and unattractive children were the same. Similarly, Martinek (1981) found that gym teachers expected attractive children to perform better at physical activities.

Attractive people are less likely to get caught and reported as criminals than are unattractive people; if caught they are treated more leniently in the courtroom by juries and judges (Deseran & Chung, 1979; Efran, 1974; Mace, 1972; Steffensmeier & Terry, 1973). However, attractiveness may be a disadvantage to a defendant who is alleged to have used his or her looks for unethical ends — the suave, handsome, confident man who bilks elderly women of their pensions, for example (Sigall & Ostrove, 1975).

Physical attractiveness may even influence mental health. A number of studies suggest that unattractive people are more poorly adjusted in our society and suffer disproportionately from mental illnesses. For example, homely people seem to experience more stress in their lives (Hanseli, Sparacino, & Ronchi, 1982). Hospitalized mental patients prove to be less attractive than control populations, even when judged from photographs taken before their mental disorders developed (Farina, Fischer, Sherman, Smith, Groh, & Nermin, 1977; Napoleon, Chassin, & Young, 1980). Furthermore, unattractive people perceive themselves to be at greater risk of developing mental illness (O'Grady, 1982). Perhaps we should not be surprised by these findings. If unattractive people suffer from lower popularity and negative stereotypes and have less success in work, then clearly they experience more stress and fewer rewards in their lives than do attractive people, and such stresses likely contribute to mental disorders.

Although attractiveness in general brings benefits, extreme attractiveness may carry with it certain penalties as well (Hatfield & Sprecher, 1986). For example, extremely attractive people may have fewer same-sex friends (Krebs & Adinolfi, 1975), and they may suffer from the negative stereotype of being seen as conceited, vain, adulterous, and unsympathetic (Dermer & Thiel, 1975). Finally, very attractive people may at times suffer from a kind of attributional dilemma — they don't know whether others like them for their looks or "for themselves." Perhaps, then, the best of all possible worlds is to be above average in attractiveness, but not *too* attractive.

Although many studies document the advantages of being attractive, it is important to note that most people fall within a range of attractiveness that is compatible with personal happiness and success. Perhaps the people who are treated most harshly are those who are extremely unattractive (Hatfield & Sprecher, 1986; see Chapter 9 for a related discussion of stigma and prejudice).

Theories of Attraction

Why do such variables as proximity, similarity, and physical attractiveness influence attraction? What general theories might help us to organize the varied empirical findings we've presented? Three classes of social psychological theories apply directly to the topic of attraction: learning theories, exchange and equity theories, and cognitive consistency theories.

Learning Theories

Here's a simple proposition: We tend to like people more when they are associated with pleasure, and less when they are associated with pain or costs. For example, all other things being equal, you probably will like an acquaintance who gives you gifts more than you like one who continually tells obnoxious jokes. Thus attraction may be viewed as a kind of classical conditioning (Byrne & Clore, 1970; Lott & Lott, 1974); liking and disliking are in part conditioned emotional responses that occur when people are associated with positive or negative events (Lott & Lott, 1968; Griffit & Veitch, 1971).

Operant conditioning may also play a role in attraction. In general, affiliative behaviors that are rewarded tend to become more frequent, whereas those that are punished tend to extinguish. If you ask someone out on a date and have a wonderful time, you are more likely to ask that person out again. If, however, you suffer through your date's boring conversation and boorish manners, you are less likely to ask him or her out in the future.

We can interpret the effects of proximity, similarity, and physical attractiveness partly in terms of operant and classical conditioning. When we are physically near others, our opportunity for rewarding interactions and pleasant social exchanges with them is increased. When people are similar to us in their attitudes and interests, the likelihood that we have rewarding interaction increases; if chess is your great passion, isn't it rewarding to meet another passionate chess player? Furthermore, people with attitudes similar to our own reward us by validating our opinions and making us feel that we are right (Byrne, 1971). And a good-looking person is reinforcing simply by his or her mere presence — after all, "a thing of beauty is a joy to behold."

The learning perspective implies that if you want a friendship or romance to last, you must continue to reward your partner and ensure that your relationship continues to be associated with positive things. Relationships may indeed begin to fail if we take them for granted and cease providing rewards (praise, candle-lit dinners, fun evenings out, hugs) for our friends and lovers.

Exchange and Equity Theories

Exchange theory and equity theory are in some sense extensions of learning theories. For example, George Homans's (1961, 1974) version of exchange theory applies aspects of Skinner's theory of operant conditioning to human social relations. Homans uses economics terminology, though — we experience rewards, costs, and profits in our relationships. For example, in a love relationship, sex and companionship may be "rewards," periodic fights and the irritating habits of your lover or spouse may be "costs"; and your profits are simply your net rewards minus your net costs.

Exchange theory: the economics of relationships.   Exchange theory makes the plausible assumption that we tend to choose those relationships that are most profitable, and furthermore, that relationships tend to be stable when both parties receive approximately equal profits. For example, "computer date" studies on physical attractiveness show that people prefer the most attractive partner possible (that is, they seek out the most reward and profit they can possibly get), but in everyday life they "settle" for partners with about their own level of attractiveness (for the relationship to endure, both parties must receive about equal profits). When a relationship is unbalanced on one dimension (say, a homely man is married to a beautiful woman), we may automatically assume that the "profits" balance out some other way (perhaps the man is very rich.)

Thibaut and Kelley (1959) complicate the basic assumptions of exchange theory a bit by assuming that in deciding whether to stay in a relationship, we not only assess the costs and rewards of the relationship; we also compare these costs and rewards to a *comparison level* — some standard dictated by social norms and personal expectations. Consider, for example, the following letter to Dear Abby:

> Dear Abby: My wife . . . has recently announced that she has no more interest in sex, and we have stopped all sexual relations. Obviously I am not very pleased with this situation and have conveyed that to her in no uncertain terms. However, she has indicated that that's the way it is — and I had better learn to live with it.

I don't believe my wife is seeing anyone else; she's just decided that she can live without sex. However, I can't. . . .
Frustrated in Downers Grove

Dear Frustrated: If ever a couple needed a therapist, you do. . . .
("Dear Abby," May 6, 1987)

Apparently, "Frustrated" assumes that sex is an expected "reward" in his relationship with his wife. Perhaps he even assumes that all wives "owe" their husbands sexual relations. In this aspect of their relationship, at least, his comparison level — his standard of what's proper and expected — is no longer being met.

Thibaut and Kelley also propose the notion of a *comparison level for alternatives*, in which the level of costs and rewards a person will accept in a relationship is compared to the costs and rewards available in alternative relationships. For example, if "Frustrated" meets a charming, attractive, "available" woman, he may decide to divorce his wife. If no alternative relationships are available to him, though, he may be more likely to stay in his marriage and perhaps take Dear Abby's advice to seek help in improving the profits in his current relationship.

In essence, Thibaut and Kelley's notion of a comparison level for alternatives suggests that we can't consider the costs and rewards of a relationship in isolation; rather, we must consider a relationship in the context of available alternative relationships and their potential costs and rewards as well. Some people remain in "bad" relationships simply because nothing better is available to them and they would rather receive their current inadequate rewards than none at all (Simpson, 1987).

Equity theory: investing in love. Equity theories can be viewed as an extension of exchange theories. These theories (see, Adams, 1963, 1965; Walster, Walster, & Berscheid, 1978) hold that we focus not only on the costs and rewards of a relationship, but also on the *investments* that people bring to the relationship. For example, your current romantic partner may provide you with certain rewards (hugs and companionship) and extract certain costs (work! — you do all the cooking and cleaning). In addition, your partner may bring certain investments to your relationship ($100,000 in the bank and a blue-blood ancestry). We can think of "costs" and "rewards" as consequences that result from the relationship and "investments" as inputs or goods brought to the relationship.

The principle of equity holds that each partner should receive profits from a relationship in proportion to his or her investment. This is obvious in economic transactions: If one partner invests $50,000 in a new company and another invests $25,000, the first partner will certainly expect twice as much return on the investment as the second. Similarly, in friendships and romances, we expect "returns" from a relationship in proportion to our investments (whether in money, time, effort, or valued commodities like physical attractiveness). Thus perhaps your indolent romantic partner believes it's only fair that you do all the housework because he or she is wealthy and thus brings more financial worth to the relationship.

Equity theory further predicts that when relationships are inequitable — when people feel that they are not receiving their "due share" given their investment — the relationship is in trouble. Overbenefited partners tend to feel guilty; under-benefited partners feel angry. Ultimately, something's got to give in the relationship.

Both exchange theories and equity theories can help to explain research findings on similarity in relationships. Almost by definition, relationships in which people are matched on certain characteristics (socioeconomic status, professional accomplishment, attractiveness, intelligence) are more likely to be equitable relationships in which the partners bring equal resources and investments to the relationship and can provide equal rewards and profits to each other.

Cognitive Consistency Theories

A third perspective on attraction holds that our likes and dislikes may sometimes result from our attempts to create consistency among our thoughts and feelings. We've already discussed one famous consistency theory in Chapter 8 — Festinger's theory of cognitive dissonance. This theory hypothesized that people strive for *logical consistency* among their beliefs. *Balance theory* (Heider, 1958; Newcomb, 1953) focuses more on the consistency of our likes and dislikes.

Figure 11.4 illustrates a simple example, the pattern of likes and dislikes among three people — Romeo, Juliet, and Juliet's mother, Mrs. Capulet. Let's look at this situation from the vantage point of Mrs. Capulet, who has just learned about Romeo and Juliet's passionate affair. Mrs. Capulet loves her daughter, Juliet; this is represented as a " + " relationship — a positive attraction — in Figure 11.4. Unfortunately, she also despises Romeo, who is a hated Montague; this is represented in Figure 11.4 as a " − " or negative relationship. Finally, we already know that Romeo and Juliet strongly love each other.

According to balance theory, the pattern of likes and dislikes in Figure 11.4 is unbalanced — that is, a state of tension exists. A simple way to determine whether a triad is balanced is to multiply the three signs algebraically. If the result is negative — as it is for the top triangle in Figure 11.4 — then the triad is unbalanced. If the result is positive, a state of balance exists.

Balance theory argues that people will shift their likes and dislikes to restore balance to an unbalanced triad. For example, Juliet's mother can restore balance to her cognitions in one of three ways. She can persuade Juliet to give up Romeo. If the link between Romeo and Juliet becomes a " −," then balance is restored. Alternatively, she could renounce her daughter and in essence say, "Anyone who could love a despicable Montague can't be a daughter of mine." If the link between mother and daughter becomes a " −," balance is again restored. Finally, Mrs. Capulet could embrace her daughter's choice: "If my daughter loves him, he must be okay." This, of course, is a balanced triad, too.

Balance theory assumes that some patterns of likes and dislikes are more comfortable than others and that we may shift some of our likes to create mental consistency. In a clever experiment, Aronson and Cope (1968) instructed a graduate research assistant to be either nice or obnoxious to individual subjects. Then, in the subject's presence, the graduate student was either praised or chewed out by a professor. As balance theory predicts, subjects tended to either like or dislike the professor so that a balanced triad could result. For example, if the graduate student was obnoxious to the subject (" − " relationship) and the professor chewed out this obnoxious student (a " − " between the student and professor), then the subject would tend to like the professor (a " + " between subject and professor). Although these results may not seem startling, notice that subjects are basing their like or dislike for the professor only on the professor's relationship with a third party and not on any direct interaction.

How does balance theory explain patterns of likes and dislikes?

According to balance theory, the perceived pattern of likes and dislikes among three people can be either cognitively harmonious (balanced) or unharmonious (unbalanced). In the diagrams below, "+" indicates liking and "−" disliking. A triad is unbalanced if the algebraic product of the three signs is negative (or, equivalently, when there is an odd number of negative signs in the triad).

The diagrams below show one unbalanced and three balanced patterns of likes and dislikes among Romeo, Juliet, and Mrs. Capulet (Juliet's mother).

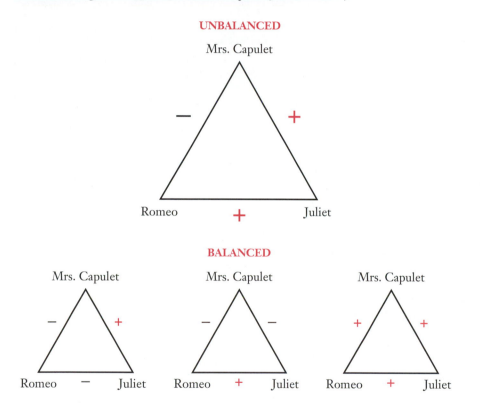

Balance theory argues that unbalanced patterns of likes and dislikes are uncomfortable and thus unstable. Thus, we would expect the unbalanced pattern in the top diagram to shift to one of the three more stable, balanced configurations below it.

Clearly, the examples given here describe simple cases. In real life, balance processes may involve more than just three people, and our likes and dislikes actually vary in degree rather than being simply a "plus" or a "minus."

■■■■■■■■■■■■■■■■■■■■■■■■■
Are there as many kinds of love as there are hearts? Clockwise from top left: *A Czechoslovakian wedding procession; the bond between mother and child; attachment between pet and pet owner; a gay couple.*

Such balance processes can be seen in real life. For example, suppose you have a bitter breakup with a former spouse or lover. Both of you consider Tom a good friend. Isn't it difficult to remain friends with Tom when he still associates with your "ex"? You may decide, in keeping with balance theory, that anyone who is a friend of your disgusting "ex" can't be friends with you. Or you may try to convince Tom that your "ex" isn't worth knowing. When one major relationship changes in our lives, we often have to shift others to provide consistency to the total configuration of relationships.

Balance theory can also help explain empirical data on attraction. For example, balance theory predicts that we will be most comfortable in relationships when we hold attitudes similar to those of our partner. For example, if you and your best friend hold similar, positive attitudes toward the current president of the United States (all pluses in the balance diagram), then your likes are in balance. But if you admire the president and your best friend hates him, then a state of unbalance exists.

Note that we have now provided three useful explanations for similarity effects in attraction: (1) Similarity in others is rewarding, (2) similarity in relationships fosters equality and equity in social relations, and (3) attitudinal similarity with friends and romantic relations leads to cognitive balance. One reason the similarity

principle is so robust in research on attraction is that this effect is very likely affected by multiple factors; that is, several causal processes impel us to like similar others more than we like dissimilar others.

▪▪▪

Love

Was Anna Karenina correct when she said, ". . . if there are as many minds as there are heads, then there are also just as many kinds of love as there are hearts"? How many kinds of love are there? And is this a question science can answer?

Love in its various forms — passionate love, romantic love, and maternal love — is not necessarily just a stronger form of liking. Loving may be qualitatively different from liking in several ways. First, romantic, passionate, and maternal love very likely have biological underpinnings and evolutionary histories that distinguish them from liking; passionate love is clearly related to reproduction. Love may be more "emotional" and less "cognitive" than liking. Berscheid and Walster (1974a) speculate that passionate love may entail more illusion and fantasy than does mere liking. The love object is idealized, and love may be a kind of obsession. Finally, the time courses of love and liking may be quite different — rapturous love may explode and then die quickly, whereas a good friendship may be rather more a steady flame.

Because love is inherently complex, we'll inspect it from various perspectives. First we'll examine its biological evolution and cultural history, and then we'll turn to recent social psychological research.

The Sociobiological Perspective

As human beings we take love for granted. We don't necessarily take for granted the love we give and receive in our own lives, but we do take for granted the human need and propensity for love. We simply know people seek out *pair-bonding* — intense emotional attachments with others. Music, art, literature, and drama treat love as a central human experience, and individually many of us feel our most profound emotions in the realm of love.

The evolutionary origins of love.

Why do human beings love? Let's pose this question in biological rather than literary or philosophical terms. Perhaps human love evolved from maternal love in birds and mammals (Mellen, 1981). Clearly, such love, as well as the love of offspring for their mothers, serves a biological purpose: The nurturing and protection evoked by such love ensure the survival of the species and the transmission of genes from one generation to the next.

What event in the evolution of the human species prompted the development of intense emotional bonds between people? To answer this question, sociobiologists (see, Buss, 1987; Dawkins, 1976; Mellen, 1981; Symons, 1979) look back hundreds of thousands of years to our hominid ancestors. Human evolution was characterized by a huge increase in brain size that enabled our species to develop and use tools, to hunt with foresight, and to invent language and culture.

However, as human brain size increased, childbirth became more difficult because the newborn's head was larger. As an evolutionary adaptation to this, human infants were born at a more immature stage of growth (so mothers would not have to bear a fully developed head). These more helpless infants had to be cared for over an extended period. The advent of language and culture further extended the time needed to train and socialize the young.

A strong family unit evolved to care for and educate children. According to some sociobiological theories, romantic love and intense pair-bonding serve the evolutionary purpose of binding together family units to nurture helpless infants.

Are we different from other species?

Some sociobiological speculation focuses on the unique characteristics of human love and sexuality — that is, on the ways in which we differ from our closest animal relatives. For example, chimpanzees and gorillas do not display the kind of intense pair-bonding that humans do (Mellen, 1981). Jane Goodall (1971), who observed chimpanzees in the wild, reported that chimps are quite promiscuous; a female in heat will mate with many males in succession. Occasionally a male and a female will form a "consort pair" and go off by themselves for a time, but this is typically brief and exceptional behavior. In chimpanzee society, males have little or no involvement in rearing the young, and the period of infant helplessness is considerably shorter than it is for humans.

Clearly, humans seem more attached and faithful than chimps in their mating behavior. Again, sociobiologists contend that this more committed pair-bonding in humans originates in the need for a tightly bonded family unit that will take care of the young for many years.

Sex differences in love and sexuality.   Sociobiologists offer many other speculations. For example, some argue (Dawkins, 1976; Mellen, 1981; Symons, 1979) that male and female sexuality has evolved differently in humans because males and females have different optimal evolutionary strategies. According to one recent view (Dawkins, 1976), the "goal" of evolution is to maximize transmission of an individual's genes to future generations. Because females must gestate, nurse, and care for the young, they must guarantee (not in a personal sense, but in evolutionary terms) that their young survive until they are reproductively mature. Males, on the other hand, produce abundant sperm (not a single egg each month, as human females do), and thus males are not constrained by the biological burden of bearing, nursing, and caring for the young.

Thus, according to the sociobiological argument, men have evolved to be more interested in sex, more promiscuous, and less desirous of emotional commitment and "pair-bonding." Men must "sow their wild oats" to maximize the transmission of their genes. Indeed, surveys since the time of Kinsey and his colleagues (1948, 1953) suggest that men are more sexually active and open to casual sex than are women. But because of their intense biological commitment to the care of their offspring, women seek commitment and a mate who can provide continuing resources for those offspring. Indeed, survey research shows that women more than men prefer mates who can "bring home the bacon" — that is, provide good earning potential and higher educational and occupational status (Berscheid & Walster, 1974a; Buss, 1985; Langhorne & Secord, 1955).

Because a woman must be young, healthy, and strong to bear and raise children, men have evolved to prefer youth and beauty in a mate. (Beauty indirectly indicates youth, health, and good physical condition.) Survey research suggests that men do in fact give higher priority to beauty in a mate than do women (Buss, 1988; Buss & Barnes, 1986). Because a man must have power and possessions to provide adequately for children, women have evolved to be more attracted to maturity, power, and status in men. In keeping with this sociobiological speculation, Sadalla, Kenrick, and Vershure (1987) recently found that nonverbal dominance in videotaped males made them significantly more sexually attractive to female subjects, but this characteristic did not make videotaped females any more attractive to males. Dominance can be viewed as an indication of power and status.

Much of sociobiological theory remains speculative. However, sociobiology reminds us that love and sex serve biological as well as social purposes, and that a complete understanding of human love requires examination of our biological past as well as of the current social setting.

▪▪▪▪▪▪▪▪▪▪▪▪▪▪▪▪▪▪▪▪▪▪▪▪▪▪

The History of Love in Western Culture

Love is in some regards a cultural invention. As sociobiological theory suggests, intense emotional attractions and pair-bonding between people may well be a nearly universal human experience. But the particular form these attractions take, the ethical and moral context in which they're held, and their relation to romantic attraction, marriage, and family vary enormously across cultures. Let's look briefly at the history of romantic love in Western civilization by focusing on two fundamental topics: the ethical status of love in various Western civilizations and the relation between love and marriage. (For extended discussions of these and related issues, see Bullough, 1976; De Riencourt, 1974; Hunt, 1959; Murstein, 1974.)

We look to the ancient Greeks for the origin of Western conceptions of love, for theirs was perhaps the first society to idealize romantic love, to hold it in high ethical esteem, and thus to view love as a noble and highly desirable goal in life. To this day we use classical Greek images and mythology (Cupid, the Roman god of love, derives from the earlier Greek god, Eros), and we use Greek terminology to describe kinds of love ("erotic," "platonic").

The kinds of love idealized in ancient Greece were quite different from those idealized in modern America, however. Women in ancient Greece generally had low status. Marriage was often viewed with distaste and was disdained by Greek men; to reproduce and produce legal heirs was a "duty" one performed for the state. Even Plato, who in *The Republic* argued for equality between the sexes, wrote that "a woman is inferior to a man."

Clearly, then, the typical Greek man did not idealize or romantically love his wife in the modern sense. Who then did he love? There seems to have been two possibilities: another male in a homosexual relationship or a courtesan, who was typically more educated, elegant, and desirable than his wife. (The Greeks had a complex caste system of prostitution; the "pornae," or common prostitutes, were not idealized or viewed as love objects, but the "heterae," the most refined courtesans, were.) Greek love, although idealized and socially supported, did not take place in the context of marriage or family.

Women had higher status in imperial Rome than they had in ancient Greece. The Romans idealized love less and practiced sex with more license than did the ancient Greeks. In many ways, Roman society had a contemporary flavor: divorce, abortion, and contraception were practiced; extramarital sex was quite common. As Hunt (1959) describes it,

> . . . Roman love as it emerged in the second and first centuries B.C. involved a variety of possible unions, all of them outside of marriage. The only illegal one was adultery, but up-to-date Romans favored it above all others, regarding it much as modern man regards cheating on his income-tax return — a zestful wrong-doing that involves no sense of wrong or sin. . . . (p. 67)

Romantic liaisons in Rome were promiscuous, but they were not characterized by emotional commitment or idealization. Love was not necessarily attached to marriage.

Very early Christianity adopted Roman mores and was fairly tolerant of sexuality in various forms. However, as the Roman Empire crumbled and the Church became the central social and moral institution of Europe, a much sterner attitude toward love and sex emerged. Christianity idealized chastity rather than sexual love. Because of its ties to "original sin," sex was considered to be corrupting. The writings of Saint Augustine in the early fifth century A.D. defined the new Christian abhorrence of sex, even in marriage: ". . . marriage and continence are two goods," he wrote, "the second of which is better." Sex was tolerated in marriage, but in no other relationship. Romantic and sexual love, even in marriage, were not held in high ethical esteem.

Common attitudes toward love and sexuality did not recover from the blow dealt by Augustine and other Christian theologians until the period of *courtly love* in Europe during the twelfth century. The Hollywood and literary images we have of this period are replete with daring knights in armor performing valiant deeds for

their high-born ladies. Indeed, the art of courtly love (see Capellanus, 1969) prescribed that knights perform excruciatingly difficult deeds to gain even a glimpse of
their lady loves. However, courtly love was a dalliance available only to the nobility;
the peasants and serfs of medieval Europe married for practical economic reasons,
not for something as frivolous as love. Even among the nobility, courtly love was
conducted outside of marriage; the lady love was typically of higher status than the
knight who admired her. Courtly love was so idealized that it rarely led to physical
intimacy, let alone sexual intercourse; the lady was worshipped from afar. Such
"romantic love" is strange indeed to our current perspective.

The Sex Ratio Hypothesis

Marcia Guttentag and Paul Secord (1983) have offered a startlingly simple explanation for historical variations in attitudes toward love and marriage. The critical variable, according to these researchers, is the ratio of men to women in a particular society. Even though most of us take it for granted that there are about equal numbers of men and women in most societies, this is not necessarily true. Variations in birth rates, death rates, and immigration and emigration patterns for men and women can lead to large inequalities in their relative numbers.

Guttentag and Secord define the sex ratio as the ratio of men to women in a given society. What happens when this ratio is high (that is, when there are more men than women)? Guttentag and Secord hypothesize that

in such societies, young adult women would be highly valued. The manner in which they would be valued would depend on the society. Most often, single women would be valued for their beauty and glamour, and married

women as wives and mothers. Men would want to possess a wife and would be willing to make and keep a commitment to remain with her. But in some societies, this might be carried to an extreme, and scarce women might be valued as chattels and/or possessions.

. . . [W]omen would be valued as romantic love objects. . . . (pp. 19–20)

However, when the sex ratio is low:

More men and women would remain single or, if they married, would be more apt to get divorced. . . . The divorce rate would be high, but the remarriage rate would be high for men only.

. . . Sexual relationships outside of marriage would be accepted. . . . Women would not expect to have the same man remain with them throughout their childbearing years. Brief liaisons would be usual. . . . [M]en would have opportunities to move successively from woman to woman or to maintain multiple relationships with different women. . . . The outstanding characteristic of

times when women were in oversupply would be that men would not remain committed to the same woman. . . . The culture would not emphasize love and commitment, and a lower value would be placed on marriage and the family. (pp. 20–21)

To test these hypotheses, Guttentag and Secord analyzed historical sex ratio data from a number of countries during different historical periods, including ancient Greece, medieval Europe, and the United States during a number of historical periods. In general, they found that high sex ratios were related to the idealization of women, marriage, and romantic love, and low sex ratios were related to both decreased idealization of women and love and to increased sexual license.

According to Guttentag and Secord, there were more men than women in the United States until about 1940, but since then the sex ratio has continued to decrease fairly steadily (see the accompanying figure). Thus they argue that the dramatic changes in sexual and

Western civilization since the Renaissance has gone through repetitive cycles: Sometimes love and sex are valued and idealized, sometimes not; sometimes love occurs primarily within marriage, sometimes not. The people of some historical periods took a cynical and licentious attitude toward love and sex (for example, those of the Enlightenment or of Restoration England), and others had a more idealized and repressed view (those of the Victorian period). Whatever the historical reasons for these fluctuations, they make clear the notion that the form of romantic love and its relationship to marriage are culturally and historically variable.

The Social Psychology of Love

The sociobiological and cultural/historical perspectives on love complement rather than compete with social psychological perspectives. Psychological influences on love, after all, occur within a broader biological and cultural context. Let's turn now romantic mores occurring in the United States since World War II have been due in part to changes in the sex ratio.

Guttentag and Secord present their intriguing hypotheses and data in a book entitled *Too Many Women*? You might wonder why the book wasn't entitled *Too Many Men*? Guttentag and Secord argue that because men possess greater power than women in most socie- ties (see Chapter 10), women be- come defined as a "commodity" that is either in oversupply or un- dersupply in the "marketplace" of romantic relationships.

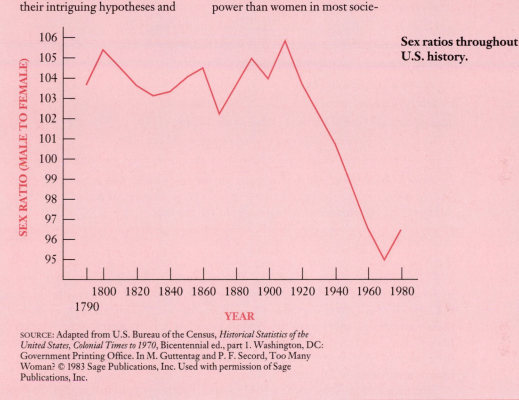

Sex ratios throughout U.S. history.

SOURCE: Adapted from U.S. Bureau of the Census, *Historical Statistics of the United States, Colonial Times to 1970*, Bicentennial ed., part 1. Washington, DC: Government Printing Office. In M. Guttentag and P. F. Secord, Too Many Woman? © 1983 Sage Publications, Inc. Used with permission of Sage Publications, Inc.

to a couple of psychological questions: How can we empirically measure love? And how do we know when we're in love?

Three ways of defining love.   In a line of poetry so often repeated that it has become a cliché, Elizabeth Barrett Browning asked, "How do I love thee? Let me count the ways." How do social psychologists count the ways of love? Do we have acceptable operational definitions of so elusive a concept?

After combing through the philosophical and scientific literature on love, Rubin (1970, 1973, 1974) developed questionnaire scales to measure liking and loving. In Rubin's conceptualization, liking and loving were related, yet somewhat different kinds of attraction: Liking for another person entails respecting the person's abilities, judgment, and attitudes, whereas loving entails feelings of intimacy, caring, and preoccupation. Figure 11.5 lists a few items from Rubin's liking and loving scales.

FIGURE 11.5   Rubin's love and liking scales.

What kinds of attraction are measured by Rubin's love and liking scales?

Rubin developed two scales to measure different kinds of attraction. The love scale assesses feelings of intimacy, possessiveness, and preoccupation toward another, whereas the liking scale assesses feelings of respect and perceived similarity with another.

ITEMS FROM THE LOVE SCALE

I feel that I can confide in _____ about virtually everything.

If I could never be with _____, I would feel miserable.

It would be hard for me to get along without _____.

ITEMS FROM THE LIKING SCALE

I would highly recommend _____ for a responsible job.

_____ is one of the most likable people I know.

_____ is the sort of person whom I myself would like to be.

Love and liking, as measured by these scales, are not independent; that is, your feelings of love for others tend to be correlated with your feelings of liking. As the text notes, both love and liking help to predict the course of romantic relationships.

In one study, Rubin asked 182 student couples (dating or engaged, but not married) to rate both their partners and a close same-sex friend on his liking and loving scales. The resulting data indicated that subjects' liking and loving scores for their romantic partners were moderately correlated. Not surprisingly, subjects reported that they loved their romantic partners considerably more than they loved their friends. Subjects did not report nearly as great a difference in their liking for friends and romantic partners.

Rubin asked his subjects how likely it was that they would marry their romantic partners. Both liking and loving scores were correlated with this response, but the correlation with loving was stronger. Six months later Rubin's subjects were mailed questionnaires that asked what had happened in their relationships. The results: Both liking and loving scores somewhat predicted the courses of these romantic relationships (that is, whether the relationships broke apart, got weaker, or intensified); these scores better predicted the relationships of students who described themselves as being "romantic" than those of students who described themselves as "nonromantic."

Rubin developed a single-score measure of romantic love, but other researchers have tried to break love into parts or types. For example, Sternberg (1986; Sternberg & Grajek, 1984) has characterized love relationships along three dimensions: intimacy (can you talk with and confide in your partner?), passion (do you feel sexually attracted and "in love"?), and commitment (do you intend to remain in your relationship?). (See Figure 11.6.) Rubin's love scale seems to assess intimacy and passion, but not commitment.

FIGURE 11.6   Sternberg's love components.

What are the three main dimensions of love?

According to Sternberg's analysis, love can be analyzed in terms of three components: passion, intimacy, and commitment. Love may contain high degrees of one, two, or all three components.

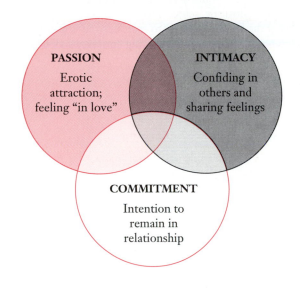

Note that different combinations of Sternberg's three components are possible. For example, you can feel intimacy and commitment, but not passion, as in a "companionate" marriage that is almost like a good, solid friendship. Or, you can feel passion, but neither intimacy nor commitment, in a quick, volatile affair; as Frank Sinatra once sang, "It was just one of those things." Some relationships possess commitment, but neither intimacy nor passion; marriages that grow cold and distant but stay intact for financial reasons or "for the children" fit this category. Of course, the ideal romantic relationship has high degrees of all three dimensions, but such "consummate loves" may be difficult to achieve and more difficult still to sustain.

Drawing on the work of sociologist J. A. Lee (1973), Hendrick and Hendrick (1986) have developed questionnaire scales that assess three primary "styles" of love — Eros (passionate, erotic, intensely felt emotional love), Ludus (game-playing love with little commitment), and Storge (friendship love) — as well as three secondary "styles" of love — Mania (obsessive, possessive love), Pragma (practical, "shopping-list" love), and Agape (altruistic, selfless love). See Figure 11.7 for sample items from Hendrick and Hendrick's scales.

FIGURE 11.7   Hendrick and Hendrick's love style scales.

What are the six "styles" of love assessed by Hendrick and Hendrick's scales?

Drawing upon the work of Lee (1974), Hendrick and Hendrick (1986) developed scales to assess six different "styles" of love. According to Lee's analysis, the three primary "styles" of love are Eros (passionate, erotic love), Ludus (game-playing, uncommitted love), and Storge (friendship love). Three secondary "styles" are Mania (possessive and obsessive love), Pragma (practical, "shopping-list" love), and Agape (altruistic, selfless love). A "secondary style" is supposed to combine aspects of the "primary styles" to each side but is also supposed to be qualitatively different from its two neighboring "primary styles."

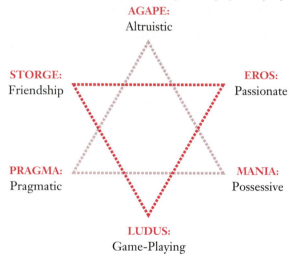

AGAPE:
Altruistic

STORGE: **EROS:**
Friendship   Passionate

PRAGMA: **MANIA:**
Pragmatic   Possessive

LUDUS:
Game-Playing

Following are some of Hendrick and Hendrick's scale items that operationally define each of Lee's styles. Which style or styles do you think characterize you? You might test yourself by thinking of a current or past relationship and rating your agreement or disagreement with each of the items shown. Do you tend to agree most with the items for any particular style?

SOURCE: Adapted from John Alan Lee, "color circle for love," *The Colors of Love*, 1973.

Clearly, Hendrick and Hendrick's love "styles" can be conceptualized, at least in part, in terms of Sternberg's three dimensions. For example, Eros has high degrees of the passion dimension; Ludus is low on commitment and intimacy, and perhaps moderately passionate; and Storge has high degrees of commitment and intimacy but not of passion.

Empirical data suggest that on average men and women differ somewhat in their love "styles" (Hendrick & Hendrick, 1986). Men take a more playful, uncommitted attitude toward love, whereas women regard love more like friendship and base it more on practical considerations. Note that these findings are consistent with sociobiological speculations.

▪▪▪

Items from Hendrick and Hendrick's Scale on Styles of Love

EROS

1. My lover and I have the right physical "chemistry" between us.
2. Our lovemaking is very intense and satisfying.
3. My lover fits my ideal standards of physical beauty/handsomeness.

LUDUS

4. I try to keep my lover a little uncertain about my commitment to him/her.
5. I have sometimes had to keep two of my lovers from finding out about each other.
6. I enjoy playing the "game of love" with a number of different partners.

STORGE

7. Genuine love first requires *caring* for a while.
8. The best kind of love grows out of a long friendship.
9. Love is really a deep friendship, not a mysterious, mystical emotion.

PRAGMA

10. I consider what a person is going to become in life before I commit myself to him/her.
11. A main consideration in choosing a lover is how he/she reflects on my family.
12. One consideration in choosing a partner is how he/she will reflect on my career.

MANIA

13. Sometimes I get so excited about being in love that I can't sleep.
14. When my lover doesn't pay attention to me, I feel sick all over.
15. If my lover ignores me for a while, I sometimes do stupid things to get his/her attention back.

AGAPE

16. I cannot be happy unless I place my lover's happiness before my own.
17. I am usually willing to sacrifice my own wishes to let my lover achieve his/hers.
18. I would endure all things for the sake of my lover.

SOURCE: Adapted from Hendrick and Hendrick (1986). Used with permission of the authors.

▪▪▪

Consistent with the similarity principle, Hendrick, Hendrick, and Adler (1988) report that college-student couples tend to be matched on their love "styles." By implication, partners who hold very different definitions of romantic love may experience conflict and thus be less likely to maintain their relationships. Hendrick, Hendrick, and Adler also report that their subjects' love "styles" were related to their satisfaction with their relationship. For both men and women, Eros tended to positively correlate and Ludus to negatively correlate with relationship satisfaction; apparently, erotic attraction helps (and game-playing hurts) the perceived quality of a relationship. For women, Storge (friendship love) was also correlated with satisfaction.

This relationship seems to be high on commitment but low on intimacy and passion.

How Do You Know You're in Love?

Levin got up and saw Kitty to the door.

Everything had been said in their conversation. . . . [S]he loved him and would tell her father and mother.

. . . [N]ever again did he see what he saw then. He was moved in particular by two children going to school, some silvery gray pigeons that flew down from the rooftop to the pavement, and some little loaves of bread. . . . The loaves, pigeons, and two little boys seemed unearthly. It all happened at the same time: a little boy ran over to a pigeon, glancing over at Levin with a smile; the pigeon flapped its wings and fluttered, gleaming in the sunshine . . . while the smell of freshly baked bread was wafted out of a little window as the loaves were put out. All this together was so extraordinarily wonderful that Levin burst out laughing and crying for joy.

—— *Anna Karenina*, pp. 430–431

Passionate love is a strong emotion. In Chapter 4 we discussed Schachter and Singer's two-component theory of emotion, which proposes two conditions that are necessary to feel any intense emotion: You must experience physiological arousal, and you must cognitively label that arousal as being due to some emotion. The label that results from the cognitive labeling process is often influenced by your situation and by cultural conventions.

Berscheid and Walster (1974a; Walster & Berscheid, 1971) applied this two-component theory of emotion to passionate love. The application is straightforward: To experience passionate love, you must experience physiological arousal and you must label your arousal as being due to love. According to this theory, if you can unobtrusively increase a person's arousal in the presence of a potential romantic partner, you may increase his or her feelings of love and attraction because the arousal would be misattributed as being due to the love object.

In his *Ars Amatoria* ("The Art of Loving"), the canny Roman, Ovid, gave advice on the art of seduction that is consistent with the two-component theory. Take your targets of seduction, he said, to the gladiatorial combats to increase their passion and attraction to you. Because it is physically arousing to see bloody combat, Ovid seems to suggest that part of this arousal may be attributed to the person next to you (if that person is an appropriate love object). If this suggestion seems improbable to you, note that many of the places people go on dates — amusement parks, horror and adventure movies, rock concerts, and sporting events — have the net effect of arousing them.

Does some of the "rush" of arousal spark romance? A number of studies suggest that it is possible. For example, the arousal triggered by viewing erotica, performing exercise, or being threatened with painful electric shocks often leads subjects to report more attraction to potential romantic partners in the laboratory (see Carducci, Cozby, & Ward, 1978; Dermer & Pyszczynski, 1978; Stephan, Berscheid, & Walster, 1971; White, Fishbein, & Rutstein, 1981; White & Knight, 1984).

In one clever study (Dutton & Aron, 1974), an attractive female experimenter approached men as they crossed either a high, rickety suspension bridge or a low, nonfrightening bridge. The woman introduced herself as a psychology researcher and asked the men to make up stories for a psychology study. She gave the subjects her name and phone number and told them to call her if they wanted more information about the study. The results: The men interviewed on the high, rickety bridge included more sexual imagery in their stories than did men interviewed on the low bridge, and they were significantly more likely to call the attractive woman. Apparently, arousal can heighten attraction. Or, in the words of Walster and Berscheid (1971), "Adrenaline makes the heart grow fonder."

Kenrick and Cialdini (1977) argue that rather than supporting the two-component theory, studies like the rickety-bridge experiment work because of reinforcement effects; the presence of others in an anxiety-producing situation is rewarding

SUMMARY TABLE 11.1   Theories and Research on Attraction and Their Relation to the Explanations of Social Behavior

What kinds of explanations do different theories of attraction emphasize?

	THEORETICAL APPROACHES	TYPE OF EXPLANATION	VARIABLES/ISSUES STUDIED
Group Level	Historical/cultural approach	Cultural norms Social groups	Comparison of love across cultures and historical periods; sex ratios
	Sociobiology	Biological evolution Biological groups	Physiology; species differences and similarities; sex differences
Individual Level	Learning theories	Environmental (past and current environments)	Rewards, punishments, conditioned emotions; can be used to explain effects of proximity, similarity, and physical attractiveness
Mediating Variables	Exchange and equity theories	Cognitive tallies of costs and rewards (also social norms)	Give-and-take in relationships; longevity of relationships; satisfaction with relationships; help explain similarity effects
	Social comparison theory	Affiliation resulting from desire to compare self with others	Affiliation resulting from situationally induced anxiety
	Schachter-Singer theory of emotion	Cognitive labeling and physiological arousal	Extraneous arousal intensifies feelings of passionate love
	Balance theory	Cognitive consistency processes	Patterns of likes and dislikes among several people/objects; effect of attitude similarity
	Love styles, components, and scales	Love as an attitude or personality trait	Effects of love on relationship satisfaction and duration; the subjective experience of love

As the table makes clear, liking and loving are complex behaviors that are influenced by biological, cultural, environmental, cognitive, and emotional variables.

and reduces anxiety. (Recall Schachter's experiments on anxiety and affiliation.) This analysis seems more plausible for arousal created through negative emotions (fear of the rickety bridge or of electric shocks) than for neutral or positive arousal (from exercise or viewing erotica).

Male subjects in the rickety-bridge study may have been particularly likely to misattribute their arousal to attraction because they did not want to admit that they were frightened, particularly in the presence of an attractive woman. If you were a typical male who had to choose between "My heart's pounding because I'm frightened" or "My heart's pounding because I'm attracted to this woman," which would you choose?

The two-component theory offers insight into a perplexing feature of passionate love — it can be heightened by strong negative emotions. Have you ever experienced a painful "lover's quarrel" that then seemed to heighten the passion of "making up"? The arousal of anger can contribute to the emotional fervor of passion, an observation that is also in keeping with the two-component theory.

Clearly, attraction, liking, and love have been approached at several levels of explanation, ranging from broad biological and social forces to the highly specific individual-level factors in the two-component theory of emotion. Summary Table 11.1 presents an overview of the theory and research we have presented on this endlessly fascinating subject.

The Life Cycle of Close Relationships

Relationships have beginnings, middles, and alas, ends. Recently social psychologists have begun to analyze the life cycle of intimate relationships. Levinger (1980, 1983) has described five possible stages in the development of a close relationship: (1) initial attraction, (2) buildup, (3) continuation and consolidation, (4) deterioration and decline, and (5) ending (see Figure 11.8). Clearly, all relationships do not necessarily go through all stages. Let's consider each stage briefly in turn.

Initial Attraction and Beginnings

As we've already seen, proximity influences the beginnings of many relationships, and we generally seek out others who are similar to us in age, attractiveness, socioeconomic status, and attitudes. Clearly, we tend to be most responsive to those who seem attracted to us (Huston & Levinger, 1978). Most basic of all, beginnings occur when we are actively seeking a relationship: A happily married person may not necessarily view another person as a potential new romantic partner, but a searching single person undoubtedly will.

Erotic and passionate love may provide a strong source of attraction in the beginnings of romantic relationships. Unfortunately, research and theory on the nature of human emotion suggest that these intense feelings are unlikely to persist at their initial peak levels (Berscheid, 1983; Solomon & Corbit, 1974).

Altman and Taylor's (1973) *social penetration theory* describes the beginning and intensification of a close relationship in terms of increasing levels of self-disclosure (that is, the revealing of important information about one's self) and of social exchange (the exchange of social goods and rewards). The closer our relationship is with another, the more we tend to know about that person. Indeed, research suggests that dating and married couples who confide in each other generally have happier and more lasting relationships (Adams & Shea, 1981). Both close friendships and romantic relationships are fostered by the intimate exchange of information (Hays, 1985).

FIGURE 11.8   The life cycle of a relationship.

What are Levinger's five stages in the life cycle of a close relationship?

Levinger (1980,1983) describes five stages in the life cycle of a relationship. As the relationship moves through the stages, it is affected by different variables and characterized by different degrees and kinds of emotion.

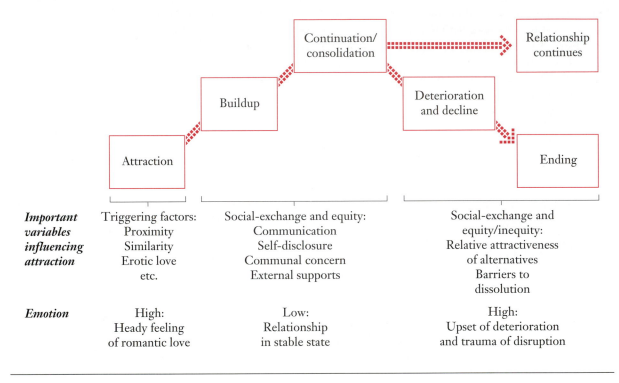

| | *Important variables influencing attraction* | Triggering factors:
Proximity
Similarity
Erotic love
etc. | Social-exchange and equity:
Communication
Self-disclosure
Communal concern
External supports | Social-exchange and equity/inequity:
Relative attractiveness of alternatives
Barriers to dissolution |

Important variables influencing attraction

Triggering factors:
Proximity
Similarity
Erotic love
etc.

Social-exchange and equity:
Communication
Self-disclosure
Communal concern
External supports

Social-exchange and equity/inequity:
Relative attractiveness of alternatives
Barriers to dissolution

Emotion

High:
Heady feeling of romantic love

Low:
Relationship in stable state

High:
Upset of deterioration and trauma of disruption

Real relationships are often more variable than this diagram might suggest. Sometimes relationships enter the "deterioration" stage but then revive and cycle back to "buildup" or "continuation." Not all relationships progress through all five stages.

Self-disclosure, a gradually unfolding process in close relationships, is characterized by mutual and reciprocal exchanges (Cozby, 1973; Taylor, De Soto, & Lieb, 1979). The process is complicated by people's tendencies, particularly early in a relationship, to provide false or limited information about themselves. As Lederer and Jackson (1968) state in *The Mirages of Marriage*, "During the wooing, both people constantly attempt to be as attractive as possible; each tries to exhibit only those parts of himself which will please and capture the other" (p. 246). Even though social penetration theory suggests a definite linear increase in intimacy, real relationships may follow a more variable, cyclical pattern of self-disclosure (Altman, Vinsel, & Brown, 1981).

Although physical appearance, demographic characteristics, and the heady excitement of romantic love may provide the initial impetus to close relationships, subsequent progress likely depends more on processes of social exchange (recall our earlier discussion of exchange and equity theories). As noted before, in close relationships we exchange information about ourselves; we also exchange goods, pleasures, and alas, unpleasantness.

Rusbult (1980) asked over 100 students at the University of North Carolina to rate the "rewards" and "costs" of their current or previous romantic relationships. Some of the rewards subjects rated were physical attractiveness of their partner, similarity of attitudes with partner, pleasantness of partner's personality, partner's sense of humor, and sexual satisfaction. Some of the rated costs were time constraints created by the relationship, monetary costs, embarrassing behaviors of partner, conflict with partner, and partner's lack of faithfulness. Using an exchange theory model, Rusbult was very well able to predict both subjects' satisfaction with and their commitment to their relationships.

Interestingly, Rusbult's data suggested that rewards were more predictive of satisfaction and commitment than were costs. This finding may reflect the fact that as close relationships develop, costs almost necessarily increase (Hays, 1985; Braiker & Kelley, 1979; Eidelson, 1980; Huston & Burgess, 1979). In *Anna Karenina*, Levin comes to this realization after finally marrying his beloved Kitty: "Another disenchantment . . . was their quarreling. Levin had never been able to imagine that between him and his wife there could be anything but a tender, respectful, and loving relationship; and suddenly, even at the very beginning, they had a quarrel . . ." (p. 514). Besides being a source of love and comfort, close relationships are also a source of anger, conflict, and even physical violence (Gelles & Straus, 1979; Straus & Hotaling, 1980; Straus, Gelles, & Steinmetz, 1980).

Building a Relationship

Many relationships reach a stable "middle age" in which the partners have worked out a mutually agreed-upon pattern of social exchange and relationship norms. In such mature relationships the partners have meshed their lives together smoothly, with innumerable points of connection. Despite these many close ties, however, the partners may display little overt emotion. In essence emotion may be dampened by the very success of the relationship (Berscheid, 1983).

According to one recent theory (Mandler, 1975), such emotions as elation, fright, upset, and anger typically accompany a violation of expectations and a disruption of the normal course of life, as occurs, for example, when you learn that your spouse or lover has been unfaithful. Thus there may be some truth to the notion that people tend to take relationships for granted once they settle into a stable state. The closeness and latent emotional ties of a mature relationship may be apparent only when the relationship breaks up (through death or departure of one member) and when the remaining partner is traumatized by the disruption.

Continuation and Consolidation

Communication in relationships. Consistent with popular wisdom, communication between partners helps to maintain relationships. Gottman (1979) reports that in successful marriages spouses listen to each other and often validate each other's points of view. Couples in unsuccessful marriages are more likely to engage in "cross complaining," venting their ire without really listening to or acknowledging what their spouse is saying. Continuing marriages may not always be rapturously passionate, but the partners are more likely to talk and listen to each other.

Communal vs. exchange relationships.   Partners should *not* necessarily talk about the precise rewards and punishments in their relationship as if they were reviewing a bank account statement. Clark and Mills (1979; Mills & Clark, 1982; Clark, Mills, & Powell, 1986) distinguish between exchange relations and communal relations. *Exchange relations* (such as a business transaction) are characterized by a careful tally of costs and an expectation of constant reciprocity. On the other hand, *communal relations* (the "give and take" in good marriages) are characterized by concern with the partner's well-being and with giving according to the partner's need, not according to rigid standards of reciprocity. If partners in intimate relationships too explicitly calculate their exchanges, the relationship may be in danger (Levinger, 1980). Nit-picking over what we give and get in a relationship probably means we are unhappy about what we're getting.

External supports.   Not surprisingly, external factors and a positive social environment can foster the continuance of relationships. Marriages tend to last longer when there is adequate monetary income and joint property, and supportive family and friends (Levinger, 1976). Low income and unstable jobs contribute to rockier marriages (Jaffe & Kanter, 1976). Even if "love conquers all," it still helps to have money in the bank and good friends.

Deterioration and Decline

Never before had a quarrel lasted a whole day. This was the first time, and it was not a quarrel — it was a manifest admission that the estrangement was complete. How was it possible for him to look at her as he had? . . . To look at her, to see that her heart was torn with despair, and then to go out in silence with that calmly indifferent expression? Not only had he cooled off to her, he hated her, because he loved some other woman — that was clear.

—— *Anna Karenina*, p. 797

Not all relationships decline and dissolve; yet it may be unrealistic to expect that the rewards and pleasures of a close relationship will continue to grow forever. Research suggests that on average marital satisfaction tends to decline somewhat over time (Blood & Blood, 1978). Perhaps this is to be expected based on external factors alone. As relationships continue and we get older, we may learn that not all of our youthful ambitions will be fulfilled, and the intense passions of romantic love and sexual excitement fade somewhat.

Still, the fading of romantic love into companionate love — a love based on intimacy, affection, and mutual interdependence, rather than on intense passion — does not necessarily signal the end of a relationship. Why do some relationships stay warm and caring, whereas others degenerate into bitter acrimony and painful separations?

Alternatives and barriers.   Drawing from exchange theory, Levinger (1976) noted three broad factors that influence the likelihood that a relationship will end: (1) the attractiveness of the relationship itself, which is positively related to its rewards and negatively related to its costs, (2) the attractiveness of alternate relationships, and (3) the "barriers" to ending the relationship (for example, costs like lawyers' fees, alimony payments, family disapproval, and emotional upset).

The divorce rate in the United States has increased sharply throughout much of this century—19 percent of marriages commencing in 1929 ended in divorce, 27 percent in 1950, 34 percent in 1960, and approximately 50 percent from the mid-1970s to the present (Weed, 1980). Perhaps this increase can be attributed in part to changing patterns of rewards, costs, and barriers. For example, divorce has become less stigmatized. In the 1960s Nelson Rockefeller could be discounted as a presidential candidate because of his divorce, but in the 1980s Ronald Reagan was enthusiastically elected by conservative voters who were apparently unconcerned about his earlier divorce. Furthermore, women have become less economically dependent on marriage (see Chapter 10). Berscheid and Campbell (1981) argue that once the costs and barriers to divorce declined, more people divorced, which added to the pool of people available for alternate relationships, which in turn further encouraged divorce. With fewer social, legal, and economic constraints to stay married, a person today may stay in relationship more because of "the sweetness of its contents" (Berscheid, 1985).

Equity and inequity in relationships.   Equity theory (see Walster, Walster, & Berscheid, 1978; Hatfield, Utne, & Traupman, 1979) adds an additional factor to the "economics" of breakups: Partners in close relationships not only compare their rewards and costs to the costs and rewards available in alternate relationships, but they also attend to their investments. When inequity exists—that is, when the ratios of profits to investments are unequal for the partners—the relationship suffers.

To illustrate, Hatfield, Walster, and Traupman (1978) asked over 500 college men and women to rate their perceptions of the equity in their romantic relationships. Did they feel they were getting more than their fair share in the relationship, less than their share, or was the "give and take" equitable? Interestingly, both subjects who felt overbenefited and subjects who felt underbenefited predicted that their relationships were less likely to last than equitable relationships. Consistent with equity theory, overbenefited subjects felt guilty, whereas underbenefited subjects felt angry. Indeed, when contacted three months later, students in inequitable relationships were more likely to report that they had broken up.

Extending equity theory to the relationships of married couples, Hatfield, Traupman, and Walster (1978) asked 2,000 married subjects to rate the degree to which they felt overbenefited or underbenefited in their relationships. One interesting finding was that subjects who felt underbenefited engaged sooner and more frequently in extramarital affairs. Apparently, when you're not getting what you think you should from your spouse, you are more likely to look outside the relationship for additional rewards. These discontented spouses may also have been seeking to punish their spouses with the extramarital affairs in order to create additional "costs" for them in the marriage. This possibility is also perfectly in keeping with equity theory—to "balance the score" (create equity), you may adjust either your partner's costs or your own rewards, or both.

Negotiating bad times.   Once problems exist in a relationship, what can be done to rectify them? Rusbult and Zembrodt (1983) asked 50 undergraduates to describe

FIGURE 11.9 **Rusbult and Zembrodt's typology of responses to dissatisfaction in relationships.**

What are the four common ways of dealing with dissatisfaction in relationships?

Rusbult and Zembrodt (1983) asked college students to describe how they behaved when they were dissatisfied with a romantic relationship. They found that most responses could be classified into four categories: voice, loyalty, neglect, and exit. Two main dimensions underly these categories: how active or passive the response was and how destructive or constructive the response was.

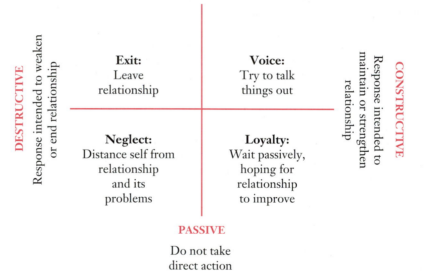

how they dealt with dissatisfactions in their romantic relationships. Sophisticated statistical analyses indicated that virtually all of their responses fell into one of four categories: "voice" (actively talking and discussing problems), "loyalty" (passively waiting for things to improve), "neglect" (distancing one's self from the relationship and allowing it to decline), or "exit" (leaving the relationship). These four modes vary on two dimensions: how active-passive they are and how constructive-destructive they are (see Figure 11.9).

Subsequent research suggests that people's style of dealing with dissatisfaction relates to levels of happiness and distress in their real-life relationships as well (Rusbult, Johnson, & Morrow, 1986). For example, subjects reported being less content with their relationships when their partners engaged in "exit" or "neglect," the two destructive modes. It remains to be seen whether Rusbult and Zembrodt's four modes of dealing with dissatisfaction are causes as well as symptoms of distressed relationships.

"I came to tell you that I'm leaving for Moscow tomorrow and shall not be returning to this house; you will be informed of my decision by a lawyer to whom I shall entrust a suit for divorce. My son will go to my sister's," said Karenin.

"You want Seryozha in order to hurt me," she said. . . . "You don't love him. . . . Leave me Seryozha!"

"Yes, I've even lost my love for my son because he's associated with my loathing for you. But I shall take him all the same. . . ."

—— *Anna Karenina*, p. 391

Divorce was uncommon in Russia a century ago. Today, more and more Americans seem to believe that "exit" is an acceptable response to a troubled marriage. A 1974 Roper poll reported that 60 percent of all those surveyed felt that divorce was an acceptable solution to a "bad marriage" (Roper Organization, 1974). The figure is likely to be higher today. Many polls and social surveys estimate that approximately half of all U.S. marriages that begin today will end in divorce (*Newsweek*, June 13, 1987).

Breakups are rarely mutually desired (Burgess & Wallin, 1953), and often one party in a marriage or relationship plans for and emotionally "works through" the breakup more than does the other (Levinger, 1983; Vaughan, 1986). After reviewing research on this topic, Bloom, White, and Asher (1979) concluded that men seem to suffer more disruption from breakups than do women. Rubin, Peplau, and Hill (1981) drew a similar conclusion, and furthermore they observed that "boyfriends" in relationships were more insensitive than "girlfriends" to relationship problems and were less likely to foresee a breakup. Perhaps on average women ponder and evaluate their relationships more than do men.

Research on the end of marriages tends to be anecdotal and scanty (see Burgess & Wallin, 1953; Waller, 1930; Weiss, 1975). Some studies focus on the explanations subjects give for their breakups (Fletcher, 1983; Fletcher, Fincham, Cramer, & Heron, 1987); however, it is unclear what relation subjects' verbal accounts bear to the actual causes of breakups (Levinger, 1983). One thing is certain, however: Despite the continual demise of some relationships, close relationships survive. Most who divorce eventually remarry. As Woody Allen states at the end of the movie, *Annie Hall*:

. . . I thought of that old joke: . . . this guy goes to a psychiatrist and says, "Doc, my brother's crazy. He think he's a chicken."

And the doctor says, "Well, why don't you turn him in?"

The guy says, "I would but I need the eggs."

Well, I guess that's pretty much now how I feel about relationships. They're totally irrational and crazy and absurd, but I guess we keep going through it because most of us need the eggs.

—— from *Annie Hall*, 1977

Summary

1. Social psychological research on attraction has traditionally emphasized external variables, mild forms of attraction, early stages of attraction, and cognitive rather than emotional processes. In recent years, such research has also addressed sociobiological theory and intimate, long-term relationships.

2. People often seek affiliation when they are anxious, so that they can compare their feelings with those of others.

3. We are more likely to become friends and romantic partners with people who live or work near us. The effects of proximity are due in part to the mere exposure effect—we like stimuli the more frequently we're exposed to them.

4. Friends and romantic partners tend to be similar on a host of dimensions. Attitudinal similarity leads to attraction.

5. Stage models of attraction are used to specify the variables that most influence the different stages of relationships. Murstein describes three stages in close relationships: a stimulus stage, a value stage, and a role stage.

6. Physical attractiveness has a broad impact on attraction. In general, attractive people are more popular and are judged to have better traits than unattractive people.

7. Learning theories argue that attraction can be understood in terms of operant and classical conditioning.

8. Exchange and equity theories offer an economic analysis of attraction in terms of "costs," "rewards," "profits," and "investments." People tend to prefer the most profitable relationships. Stable relationships tend to provide partners with nearly equal profits.

9. Balance theory analyzes attraction in terms of our desire to maintain cognitively harmonious patterns of likes and dislikes.

10. Sociobiological theory argues that romantic love originated evolutionarily as a means of binding the human family unit together and thus providing care for helpless infants.

11. Historical analyses of love indicate that different cultures and historical eras vary in the degree to which they idealize romantic love and incorporate romantic love into marriage.

12. The sex ratio hypothesis holds that when men are more numerous than women, women and romantic love are valued, but when women are more numerous than men, women and romantic love are devalued.

13. Rubin developed liking and loving scales that help predict the course of romantic relationships.

14. Sternberg argues that love consists of varying degrees of three components: intimacy, passion, and commitment.

15. Hendrick and Hendrick developed scales to measure six "styles" of romantic love: Eros, Storge, Ludus, Pragma, Mania, and Agape.

16. Schachter and Singer's two-component theory of emotion implies that extraneous arousal can sometimes intensify feelings of passionate attraction.

17. Levinger described five stages in the development of close relationships: initial attraction, buildup, continuation and consolidation, deterioration and decline, and ending.

18. The first stages of close relationships are characterized by increased self-disclosure and social exchange.

19. In exchange relationships, partners carefully tally costs and rewards and expect exact reciprocity. In communal relationships, people do not tally exact costs and rewards and instead give resources more in response to the partner's needs.

20. Rewards, costs, and barriers help predict whether relationships will end. Equitable relationships are more likely to survive than inequitable relationships.

21. Rusbult and Zembrodt identified four kinds of behavior that people use to deal with dissatisfaction in relationships: voice, loyalty, neglect, and exit.

Glossary

Affiliation: Choosing to be with others; the desire or motivation to be with others

Assortative mating: Nonrandom mating, usually occurring because people tend to mate with partners who are similar to them

Attraction: A positive attitude or emotion felt toward another person

Balance theory: A cognitive consistency theory that argues that people strive for a cognitively harmonious pattern in their likes and dislikes

Comparison level: In Kelley and Thibaut's version of exchange theory, a comparison level is a standard of expected costs and rewards in a relationship; such a standard is dictated by social norms or personal expectations

Comparison level for alternative: In Kelley and Thibaut's version of exchange theory, the level of costs and rewards a person will accept in a relationship based on alternative relationships that are available

Communal relationships: Relationships characterized by concern with the partner's well-being, in which costs and rewards are not exactly tallied

Equity theory: An economic theory of attraction that focuses on rewards, costs, profits, and investments in relationships; stable relationships tend to be equitable — both partners have the same ratio of profits to investments; equity theory differs from exchange theory in that the former incorporates the concept of "investment"

Exchange relationships: Relationships characterized by a careful tally of rewards and costs; exact reciprocity is expected

Exchange theory: An economic theory of attraction that focuses on rewards, costs, and profits in relationships; people are hypothesized to prefer maximally profitable relationships, and relationships endure to the extent that both parties receive equal profits

Learning theories: Theories that explain attraction in terms of operant and classical conditioning

Mere exposure effect: The tendency to like stimuli more the more frequently we've been exposed to them; partly accounts for proximity effects in attraction

Proximity: Physical distance from another person, often determined by architectural and residential arrangements

Sex ratio: The ratio of men to women in a society; the sex ratio hypothesis holds that high sex ratios lead societies to idealize women and love, whereas low sex ratios lead societies to devalue women and love

Similarity principle: People are more frequently friends and romantic partners with people who are similar to them on demographic, intellectual, personality, and physical characteristics

Social comparison theory: Festinger's theory that people desire to compare themselves with similar others in order to know their own social feelings and attributes

Social penetration theory: Altman and Taylor's theory that describes the development of close relationships in terms of increasing self-disclosure and social exchange

Sociobiology: A theoretical perspective that explains attraction and love in terms of evolutionary biology

Stimulus-value-role model: Murstein's model that holds that people in relationships progress through three stages in which they focus respectively on the surface attributes of their partner, shared attitudes and values, and relationship roles

"Ow! Stop it! You're hurting!"

The butt end of a spear fell on his back. . . .

"Hold him!"

They got his arms and legs. Ralph, carried away by a sudden thick excitement, grabbed Eric's spear and jabbed at Robert with it.

"Kill him! Kill him!"

All at once, Robert was screaming and struggling with the strength of frenzy. Jack had him by the hair and was brandishing his knife. Behind him was Roger, fighting to get close. The chant rose ritually, as at the last moment of a dance or a hunt.

"Kill the pig! Cut his throat! Kill the pig! Bash him in!"

Ralph too was fighting to get near, to get a handful of that brown, vulnerable flesh. The desire to squeeze and hurt was overmastering.

—— from *Lord of the Flies*, by William Golding, p. 104

CHAPTER 12

Aggression

A plane full of British schoolboys is shot down over a small tropical island during a raging world war. The plane crash-lands, and no adult survives. The boys, however, are unhurt, apart from civilization and far-removed from the conventional rules and authorities that have governed their lives. They try to organize, to find food and water. What then?

Here is one possibility: While waiting to be rescued, they form a simple, cooperative, and uncorrupted society. Working together, they hunt and fish. They build shelters and care for one another. Separated from the "evil" influences of human social institutions, they find natural peace and harmony in their new simple life.

There is another, darker possibility, though: Even on this untainted tropical island, the boys fall prey to an innate human tendency to violence. Some of the boys compete for leadership. They form factions and start fighting with one another. Eventually, like savages, they go to war against one another.

Which ending do *you* think is more likely: peace or violence? In his chilling allegorical novel *Lord of the Flies* (1954), William Golding takes the pessimistic view. The boys on his island begin by establishing a democratic rule of law, but their society degenerates into violence, and finally, into open warfare. Golding sees in human beings an innate depravity that leads us inevitably to do violence against one another.

Is Golding's pessimism warranted? Is aggression part of human nature? Even a cursory survey of human history provides abundant evidence of human aggressiveness. Ashley Montagu (1976), a noted anthropologist, describes one researcher's attempt to tabulate the number of wars in recorded history. The result: 14,531 wars, or an average of 2.6 wars every year, occurred. Since this tally was computed in the early 1960s, the world has seen war in Vietnam, genocide in Cambodia, several wars

■■■■■■■■■■■■■■■■■■■■■■■■■■

In *Lord of the Flies* a group of British school boys stranded on a tropical island descend from civilized behavior . . . into savagery.

in the Middle East, the Soviet invasion of Afghanistan followed by a bloody guerrilla insurgency, a British skirmish with Argentina over the Falkland Islands, revolutions and guerrilla wars in Central America, prolonged conflict between Iran and Iraq, horrible fighting in Ethiopia and South Africa . . . and the list goes on.

War is institutionalized aggression conducted by groups, usually nation-states. A glance through the daily newspaper, however, shows that individuals too behave quite violently. Throughout the 1980s violent crime (murder, rape, robbery, and aggravated assault) in the United States increased at a faster rate than did the general population. From 1977 to 1986 the number of violent crimes increased from a little over a million to a staggering 1,488,140, including over 20,000 homicides and over 90,000 forcible rapes each year (The World Almanac, 1988).

Aggression intrudes even into intimate family relationships. According to the American Humane Association, more than one million cases of child abuse and neglect are reported each year in the United States. In a major survey of family violence, Straus, Gelles, and Steinmetz (1980) compiled a host of disturbing results: Seventy-one percent of the parents surveyed reported that they slapped or spanked their children; 20 percent hit their children with such objects as sticks, switches, and straps; and 3 percent kicked, bit, or punched their children. Mothers and fathers hit each other as well. The researchers note that "if you are married, the chances are almost one out of three that your husband or wife will hit you" (p. 32). In 4 percent of the marriages surveyed, spouses reported attacking each other with knives or guns! Spouse-beating occurred in all social classes, religions, and ethnic groups. Apparently, many people interpret a marriage license as a "hitting license" (Straus et al., 1980).

Statistics on wars, violent crimes, and family violence all point to the fundamental questions we will consider in this chapter: Why are people so aggressive? Is aggression a natural behavior for human beings? Or is it learned — from our culture, from the mass media, and from other people? What conditions lead people to do violence against others, and what conditions reduce violence?

Although most of us think we know aggression when we see it, a closer analysis shows that our commonsense notion of aggression is somewhat ambiguous. For example, which of the following behaviors are examples of aggression (see Johnson, 1972)?

A cat kills a mouse.

A hunter kills an animal.

A doctor gives an inoculation to a screaming child.

A tennis player smashes his racket after missing a volley.

A boxer gives his opponent a bloody nose.

A Boy Scout tries to assist an old lady but trips her by mistake.

A woman nags and criticizes her husband.

A firing squad executes a prisoner.

A man commits suicide.

The president asks Congress for more money for the Department of Defense.

These examples vary in several ways. Sometimes a living being is harmed (killing a person or animal, punching someone), sometimes not (smashing a tennis racket). Sometimes the harm is intentional (hunting), sometimes not (the accidental tripping). Sometimes the harm is physical (shooting, punching), sometimes psychological (nagging and criticizing). Sometimes harm is directed at another (punching someone) and sometimes at oneself (suicide). Finally, sometimes harm is done out of emotion or anger (the frustrated tennis player), sometimes for monetary reward (the professional boxer), and sometimes because it is "part of the job" (the firing squad). People may even inflict pain (the doctor giving a shot) in the best interests of the person being hurt.

Here's a general working definition (see Johnson, 1972; Baron, 1977; Krebs & Miller, 1985): *Aggression is behavior directed against another living being that is intended to harm or injure*. This definition rules out some of the previous examples as being truly aggressive (for example, the doctor administering a shot). Our definition applies primarily to human behavior because the intentionality of animal behavior is difficult, if not impossible, to determine. And our definition allows for the possibility of psychological as well as physical injury, although we shall focus primarily on physical aggressiveness in this chapter.

Social psychologists distinguish between two main kinds of human aggression: hostile aggression and instrumental aggression (Buss, 1961, 1971; Feshbach, 1970; Baron, 1977; Zillman, 1979). *Hostile aggression* is generally provoked by pain or upset; it is emotional, and its primary purpose is to do harm. For example, Straus, Gelles, and Steinmetz (1980) describe a husband who punches his wife after she yells at him, "You're a bust, you're a failure, I want you out of here, I can always get men who'll work, good men, not scum like you" (p. 37). It seems likely that this husband was furious when he punched his wife and fully intended to harm her.

Instrumental aggression, however, is not necessarily caused by anger or emotion. Its goal is to gain some desired rewards like money or valuable goods. For example, the Mafia hit man who assassinates for money is engaging in instrumental aggression. Some robbers assault their victims to gain money, not to do harm. In the words of one New York mugger, "We ain't into the kill thing. Anybody on that junk is workin' out of the fruit and nuts bag. We just want the money, like anybody else" (Stevens, 1971). A child who hits another child to obtain a desired toy or a presidential candidate who spreads damaging gossip about an opponent may also be practicing instrumental aggression.

Why is it important to distinguish between hostile and instrumental aggression? One reason is that people hit, punch, shoot, and kill for different reasons. Hostile aggression may be triggered by painful stimuli (such as insults and frustration) and made more likely by anything that increases emotional arousal. In addition, hostile impulses may be turned into deadly behaviors by the presence of environmental cues or stimuli (like a weapon). Instrumental aggression, on the other hand, may be controlled more by environmental rewards and histories of social learning.

Hostile and instrumental aggression may also be reduced in different ways. For example, hostile aggression may be reduced if we can somehow distract the person in a passionate rage. We might be more likely to reduce instrumental aggression by changing the rewards and punishments that sustain or inhibit the aggressive behavior.

▪▪▪▪▪▪▪▪▪▪▪▪▪▪▪▪▪▪▪▪▪▪▪▪▪

Measuring Aggression

Research studies measure aggression in many different ways (Baron, 1977; Bertilson, 1983; Krebs & Miller, 1985). Early studies (Davitz, 1952; Doob & Sears, 1939; McClelland & Apicella, 1945) tended to use verbal measures. After some sort of provocation, subjects were asked to rate another person on some characteristics, and if the ratings were negative, subjects were presumed to be showing "aggressive" behavior. One problem with verbal ratings, however, is that they may have no real consequences for the target of aggression. To remedy this, experimenters sometimes lead subjects to believe that their ratings may actually hurt another person. For example, in one clever study (Worchel, 1974) an experimenter frustrated a group of subjects by reneging on a promise to give them some prizes. Subjects then had the opportunity to rate the experimenter's competence in the belief that their ratings would influence the decision to rehire that researcher.

More recent studies tend to use behavioral measures of aggression. One popular laboratory device—the "aggression machine"—was developed by Arnold Buss in the early 1960s (Buss, 1961). Under the guise of studying the effects of punishment on learning, subjects were given the opportunity to deliver electric shocks to a "learner." The number, intensity, and duration of shocks serve as measures of aggression. (This should remind you a bit of Milgram's obedience paradigm; see Chapter 2.) Other behavioral measures of aggression include observed violence during play (Bandura, Ross, & Ross, 1963b; Liebert & Baron, 1972) and simulated aggression, such as throwing sponge-rubber bricks and shooting rubber bands at people (Diener, 1976; Diener, Doneen, & Endresen, 1975) or playing war games (Zillman, Johnson, & Day, 1974).

Questions have sometimes been raised about the validity of various experimental measures of aggression (Krebs & Miller, 1985). How well do such measures reflect aggression in everyday life? Berkowitz and Donnerstein's (1982) review of the research indicates that there is a significant relationship between lab measures and real-life aggressiveness. In social psychological research on aggression, the findings are most convincing when they hold for many different kinds of measured aggression (Bertilson, 1983; see our discussion of operational definitions and conceptual replications in Chapter 2).

Factors That Influence Human Aggression

Human aggression is complex and influenced by many different factors, and theorists have attempted to explain it at many different levels (see Figure 12.1). At the "group level" of explanation, biological groups (for example, species) and cultural groups influence aggression. At the "individual level," the individual's heredity and physiology (hormone levels, biological sex, brain function), the past environment (did you watch a lot of violent TV shows as a child?), and the current environment (are you currently hot, in pain, and surrounded by an aggressive mob?) influence aggression. At the third level of explanation are "mediating variables" — hypothetical processes within people — that influence aggression, such as instincts, emotions, arousal, attributions, schemas, and personality traits.

The levels of explanation portrayed in Figure 12.1 provide us a way of conceptualizing theories and research on aggression, and they suggest that there is no single "cause" of human aggression. With this in mind, we can consider a number of broad factors that influence human aggression.

Biological Groups, Instincts, and Aggression

Is aggression instinctive? Sigmund Freud (1930) argued that people are often motivated by primitive, biologically-based, aggressive impulses. More recently, the European ethologist Konrad Lorenz (1966) also proposed that people, like other animals, possess innate aggressive impulses. Lorenz further argued that most animals have evolved inhibitory mechanisms to control aggression among members of their own species, but that cultural evolution has outpaced the evolution of human inhibitions. In Lorenz's (1966) words: "The invention of artificial weapons upset the equilibrium of killing potential and social inhibitions; . . . man's position was very nearly that of a dove which, by some unusual trick of nature, has suddenly acquired the beak of a raven" (p. 34). Submachine guns, hand grenades, napalm bombs, and nuclear warheads are fearsome beaks indeed!

Both Freud and Lorenz argued that aggressive energy or impulses build up and must somehow be vented. Freud (1930), particularly toward the end of his life, was quite pessimistic about the possibilities for peace. He felt there would always be wars and conflict. Lorenz (1966), slightly more optimistic, proposed that athletic contests and other kinds of staged aggression could perhaps provide "safety valves" that would allow humanity's inevitable aggressive impulses to be expressed without bloodshed.

Aside from being pessimistic, simple instinct theories of human aggression are often scientifically unsatisfying because their explanation is circular: Why are people aggressive? Because of their aggressive instincts. How do we know people possess aggressive instincts? Because they are aggressive. When instinct theories are specific enough to provide testable hypotheses, they may simply prove to be wrong. For

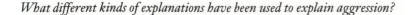

FIGURE 12.1   Levels of explanation applied to aggression.

What different kinds of explanations have been used to explain aggression?

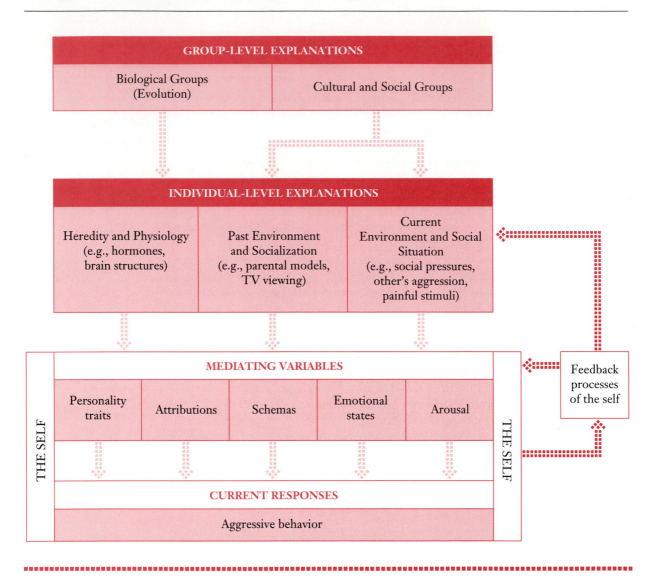

example, the "catharsis hypothesis" — the notion that by "venting" their aggressions, people display less aggression later on — is consistent with the writings of both Freud and Lorenz as well as with many people's commonsense notions. Yet, as we shall see, it is not always consistent with the research evidence.

Instinct theories of aggression sometimes suggest that biological factors strictly determine and inevitably lead to aggressive behavior (Montagu, 1976). In fact, however, biological factors create in people and animals a predisposition to be aggressive in certain situations. As Edward O. Wilson (1975), the father of modern sociobiology, notes, "Aggression evolves not as a continuous biological process, like the beat of a heart, but as a contingency plan of the animal's endocrine and nervous system, programmed to be summoned up in time of stress" (p. 248). Aggression exists as a potential, but not an inevitable behavior.

Aggressive behavior may sometimes help individual animals and species to survive (Maynard-Smith, 1974). For example, an aggressive animal may get more food by fighting off competitors, mate successfully by fighting off sexual rivals, and guarantee its survival and that of its offspring by fighting off predators. But aggression also has substantial costs. If you fight too much, a rested rival or predator may pounce on you when you're weak and defeat you. Moreover, if you lose the fight, you may be injured or killed. Because of these potent costs, Maynard-Smith (1974) argues, many species fight if they must but bluff or flee if they can. Within social species, aggression is used to compete—not to kill—and to enforce the social "law and order" of dominance hierarchies (Montagu, 1976).

Krebs and Miller (1985) summarize the evolutionary view of aggressive behavior succinctly:

> Because of its potentially high costs, aggressive behavior should be employed mainly in circumstances where other methods of satisfying needs are not available (e.g., in overcrowded situations, when there are insufficient resources) and/or when the potential gains of aggression are great. Because of the potential costs to individuals in most social species of the injury and death of an ingroup cohort, ingroup aggression should be more constrained than outgroup aggression. (p. 10)

Cultural Influences on Aggression

Instinct theories often propose universal aggressive impulses for all people. However, anthropologists, who focus on social groups and their cultures as explanations of aggression, note that levels of aggression vary considerably across cultures. As Montagu (1976) observes, "When aggressive behavior is strongly discouraged, as among the Hutterites and Amish, the Hopi and Zuni Indians, it is practically unknown." Yet many societies, including our own, show high levels of aggressive behavior. Eibl-Eibesfeldt (1979) catalogs the atrocities committed by warring Pygmy tribes, the !Kung Bushmen of southwest Africa, and the Aranda tribes of central Australia. What determines whether a particular culture is violent or peaceful? Eibl-Eibesfeldt (1979) believes that it may depend on the availability of the resources necessary for survival:

> Wars are fought for hunting grounds, pasture land, and arable land, and if in earlier times, climatic alterations made a group's living area inhospitable, it was actually compelled to find new territory by force of arms. The drying up of the Central Asian steppes set the Mongol peoples in motion, and their warlike expeditions took them all the way to Europe. Their clash with the Teutonic peoples in turn forced the latter to migrate. . . .
>
> . . . War is a means that aids groups to compete for the wealth essential to life (land, mineral resources, etc.). . . .
>
> . . . If one asks whether modern war still performs functions I have described, the answer is yes. . . . (pp. 185–186)

Individual Differences in Aggression

Even though psychologists don't ignore the influence of biological evolution and cultural norms on aggression, they tend to be more interested in explaining why people within a given society vary in their levels of aggressiveness. Why do some people hit their spouses, whereas others do not? Why are some children aggressive bullies and others peaceful? Many answers have been proposed, including personality traits, physiological factors (such as individual differences in brain structures and hormones), and learning from the individual's family, friends, and the mass media.

Aggressiveness as a trait.   In *Lord of the Flies*, some of Golding's characters are clearly more violent than others. Piggy, the "intellectual," is quite timid and nonviolent. Ralph, the original leader of the boys, is strong but aggressive only when provoked. Jack, his rival, is more violent, particularly when his ego is threatened. And Roger, Jack's ally, seems to be a natural sadist who enjoys inflicting pain on both animals and people.

Was Golding's intuition correct? Does aggressiveness vary in different people, and is it a trait that is stable over time? Research indicates that an individual's general level of aggressiveness is relatively consistent and stable over time. Olweus (1979) summarized the results of 16 studies on the temporal consistency of aggression, including classics by Kagan and Moss (1962) and Block (1971), and found that aggressiveness is almost as stable a characteristic as intelligence (see Figure 12.2). Not surprisingly, aggressiveness is more stable over shorter, rather than longer, periods of time. Thus a child's aggressiveness at age 5 is more consistent with his aggressiveness at age 6 than with that at age 10. Furthermore, aggressiveness may express itself differently at different ages (Caspi, 1987). For example, an aggressive individual might bite playmates as a child but abuse his or her spouse as an adult.

Part of the stability of general aggressiveness may be due to genetic and biological factors. In a recent study, Rushton and his colleagues (1986) studied the self-reported aggressiveness of 573 pairs of adult British twins in order to estimate the heritability of aggressiveness. The correlation between the aggressiveness of identical twins was .40, whereas the corresponding correlation for fraternal twins was only .04, clearly indicating a genetic component to the trait. Statistical analyses indicated that over 50 percent of the variability in these subjects' self-reported aggression was due to hereditary factors.

Animal studies also demonstrate the possibility of genetic influences on aggression. Birds, rats, and dogs can be bred for aggressiveness (Moyer, 1976). In one controlled study, Lagerspetz (1964) reared six generations of mice, allowing only the most aggressive and least aggressive males to reproduce each generation. By the sixth generation, the most aggressive of the "peaceful" mice was less aggressive than the least aggressive of the "violent" mice.

Physiology and aggression.   How are aggressive tendencies linked to heredity and physiology? Research has focused on several distinct biological factors. First, aggression is influenced by specific structures in the brain: regions of the temporal lobe (the sides of the cortex, or surface, of the brain) and of the limbic system (a crescent-shaped array of structures deep inside the brain). Clinical evidence suggests that tumors or infectious diseases in these areas can trigger aggression (Moyer, 1976). Brain injuries before or during birth may also contribute to later aggression (Mednick, Brennan, & Kandel, 1988).

▪▪

FIGURE 12.2   The stability of aggressiveness over time.

Is the trait of aggressiveness stable over time?

Olweus (1979) used the results from 16 studies to examine the consistency of individuals' aggressiveness over time. As the graph shows, aggressiveness is quite stable over short periods of time; when subjects' aggressiveness is measured a year apart, the two measures correlate almost .8.

Individuals' measures of aggressiveness correlate significantly even when measures are obtained more than 20 years apart.

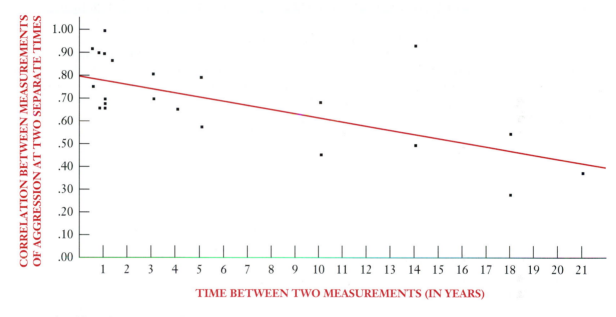

SOURCE: Adapted from Olweus (1979). Used with permission of Dan Olweus.

Olweus notes that aggression is almost as stable as intelligence over time.

▪▪

One man with a tumor in the temporal lobe attempted to kill his wife and daughter with a butcher knife (Sweet, Ervin, & Mark, 1969). After surgery to re-move the tumor, his aggressiveness subsided. The much-publicized case of Charles Whitman ended much more tragically. After seeing a psychiatrist and complaining of excruciating headaches and uncontrollable violent impulses in 1966, Whitman shot his wife and mother, climbed atop a tower at the University of Texas, and shot another 38 people, killing 14. Whitman was killed by the police, and an autopsy revealed a malignant tumor the size of a walnut in the temporal lobe of his brain (Johnson, 1972).

Body chemistry too can influence aggression. In particular, some studies suggest a relationship between the sex hormone testosterone and aggression (Olweus, 1986), which may partly account for the well-documented finding that men and boys are more aggressive than women and girls (Maccoby & Jacklin, 1974, 1980) and that these sex differences occur across cultures and across species of primates. As noted in Chapter 10, men are more aggressive than women, particularly when the kind of aggression measured produces pain and injury rather than psychological harm (Eagly & Steffen, 1986b).

Differences in aggression among individuals of the same sex may also be partly a function of testosterone levels. For example, Swedish teenage boys with higher testosterone levels were more likely to respond to provocations with both verbal and physical aggressiveness (Olweus, 1986). However, although sex hormones may influence aggression in human beings, it is important to emphasize that physiology *is not* destiny. Hormones (and brain structures) may predispose people to aggression in certain situations, but they do not rigidly determine aggression (Mazur, 1983).

Like naturally occurring hormones, some drugs can influence human aggression. Anecdotal evidence suggests that anabolic steroids (which are closely related to testosterone) can increase aggressiveness. Alcohol, perhaps in part because it tends to reduce inhibitions, tends to increase subjects' aggressiveness in experimental studies (Shuntich & Taylor, 1972; Taylor & Gammon, 1975; Taylor, Vardaris, Rawitch, Gammon, Cranston, & Lubetkin, 1976). Marijuana does not increase, and in certain circumstances may even reduce, aggression (Taylor et al., 1976; Myerscough & Taylor, 1985). Even though they increase general arousal, amphetamines do not seem to have any systematic effect on aggression (Taylor, 1986).

The Environment, Internal Psychological Processes, and Aggression

Biological evolution, cultural norms, and individuals' physiology and heredity all play roles in the complex story of human aggression. However, social psychologists usually concentrate more on environmental and psychological influences on aggression. What environmental stimuli most commonly lead to aggression? And how do they have their effects?

Aggression as a response to aggression. Perhaps the most obvious environmental cause of aggression is being attacked by another. Indeed, research consistently shows that people respond to attacks with counterattacks, often in a matched, reciprocal fashion (Borden, Bowen, & Taylor, 1971; Dengerink & Myers, 1977; Ohbuchi & Kambara, 1985). The principle that aggression begets aggression is basic to most social psychological experiments on aggression. Social psychologists frequently have confederates attack experimental subjects verbally or with electric shocks and then allow the subjects to retaliate against their attackers.

The reasons why attacks elicit counterattacks are many: Principles of equity and exchange (see Chapters 1 and 11) demand that we "give" as we "get" in social relationships. Furthermore, when we are attacked, we become angry and aroused, and this state generates hostile aggression. And finally, when we are attacked, we are often in pain.

Physical pain and aggression. In bullfighting, men called *banderilleros* thrust decorated barbs, called *banderillas*, into the shoulders and neck of the bull before the matador enters the arena. The bull—bleeding, goaded, and enraged—becomes all

the more ferocious. The bullfight makes use of a basic psychological principle: Pain incites aggression.

Ulrich and Azrin (1962) were the first psychologists to systematically study the nature and limits of this phenomenon. Specifically, they observed that when two rats were shocked in a small box with an electrified floor, the animals would rear up on their hind legs and fight with each other by "boxing" and biting. Pain also leads to aggression in many other animals, including monkeys, cats, opossums, racoons, roosters, alligators, and snakes (Azrin, 1967; Moyer, 1976).

Ulrich and Azrin (1962) initially referred to the relationship between pain and aggression as automatic and "reflexive." Even animals that have been reared in total social isolation will attack in response to pain (Hutchinson, 1983), suggesting that the pain-aggression link does not have to be learned. However, pain does not inevitably lead to aggression. Many animals will try to escape rather than fight after receiving shocks. Pain incites aggression particularly when the animals are confined to a small space and cannot escape (Azrin, Hutchinson, & Hake, 1966).

Although the basic link between pain and aggression may not be a learned one, learning can greatly modify pain-induced aggression. For example, Ader (1975) noted that animals that were low in dominance hierarchies show less aggression when in pain, perhaps because they have learned to inhibit their aggression when around more dominant animals. Furthermore, the effects of pain on aggression critically depend on reinforcement. When pain-induced aggression is rewarded with a decrease in pain, fighting becomes more likely after pain (Azrin, 1967); conversely, when pain-induced aggression is punished with greater pain, fighting becomes less likely.

Hutchinson (1983) posed an interesting question about the "fighting" that follows pain: Is it truly aggressive, intended to injure another animal, or is it "defensive" behavior designed to reduce or escape from pain? The answer may very well be "Both" (Berkowitz, 1983a). Azrin, Hutchinson, and McLaughlin (1965) found that shocked monkeys would actually learn to pull a chain in order to obtain something to attack. In other words, a pained animal finds fighting rewarding.

Does pain lead to aggression in human beings as well as in animals? Research suggests that in this regard people are like animals. People become more hostile and aggressive when exposed to such unpleasant stimuli as bad smells (Rotton, Barry, Frey, & Soler, 1978), cigarette smoke (Jones & Bogat, 1978), and "disgusting" pornography (White, 1979). For obvious ethical reasons, social psychologists cannot expose human subjects to painful electric shocks to see whether they will attack another person. Berkowitz, Cochran, and Embree (1981) did, however, conduct a somewhat milder experiment.

Under the guise of studying "the effects of discomfort on performance in a . . . work setting," they asked female subjects to place their hands in a tank of either comfortably warm or painfully cold water while "supervising" another woman working in a nearby cubicle. Subjects could deliver either rewards or punishments to the "worker" as part of their supervision. Some subjects were told that the punishments "hurt" the worker and interfered with her performance; others were told that appropriately delivered punishments would "help" the worker's performance. The results: The women in pain were least rewarding and most punitive, particularly when they thought their punishments would hurt. Thus people too seem motivated to hurt others when they're in pain.

Heat and aggression.
One common kind of "pain"—namely, unpleasant heat—seems to have a pervasive impact on human aggression. Experimental studies suggest that, within limits, people become more aggressive as temperatures increase; this relationship sometimes breaks down when heat becomes so oppressive that people don't have the energy to be aggressive (Baron & Bell, 1975; Bell & Baron, 1976).

Correlational studies also indicate that hot people are often "hot under the collar." Carlsmith and Anderson (1979) reported a significant relationship between temperature and the number of riots occurring in the United States in the late 1960s and early 1970s. Other studies have shown that the number of violent crimes in Chicago and Houston (Anderson & Anderson, 1984) and in Des Moines and Indianapolis (Cotton, 1986) increases as temperatures rise. Hot cities have higher rates of violent crimes than do more temperate cities (Anderson, 1987), and high humidity adds to the impact of heat on crime (Harries & Stadler, 1988). Family violence also tends to increase as temperatures rise (Rotton & Frey, 1985), and violent crimes are more influenced by heat than are nonviolent crimes (Anderson, 1987).

Frustration and aggression.

> Numberless and inexpressible frustrations combined to make his rage elemental and awe-inspiring.
>
> —— *Lord of the Flies*, p. 67

Clearly, physical pain and discomfort encourage aggression. Does psychological pain also lead to aggression? One kind of psychological pain—frustration—has long been studied as a likely cause of aggression. You can probably think of many instances in life when frustration seems to lead to aggression. A vending machine gobbles up your money without delivering the goods; you kick the machine. A woman compet-

▪▪▪▪▪▪▪▪▪▪▪▪▪▪▪▪▪▪▪▪▪▪▪▪▪

**Does frustration lead
to aggression?**

ing in a golf tournament putts a "sure one" only to have the ball roll up to the hole and stop right before falling in; she swears and throws her club down in disgust. You learn that you failed an exam you thought you "aced," and you snap at your friend when he asks how you did. In the late summer of 1987, southern California was plagued with a rash of freeway shootings — a number of motorists literally pulled out guns and shot at other drivers "apparently out of frustration with the area's growing gridlock" (*Newsweek*, August 10, 1987).

Psychologists concur that frustration can contribute to aggression. In their classic book *Frustration and Aggression*, Dollard, Doob, Miller, Mowrer, and Sears (1939) argued an even stronger position: that frustration always leads to aggression, and aggression is always caused by frustration. According to their definition, frustration is "interference with the occurrence of [a] . . . goal-response. . . ." Thus if your goal is to drink a glass of water after an hour of sweaty exercise, anything that interferes with your drink is frustrating. If you are very hungry, the phone call that interrupts your dinner is frustrating. And if you are sexually aroused, whatever prevents sexual activity is frustrating.

Do frustrations in fact lead to aggression? Early research findings suggested that they do, at least at times. In one classic study, Barker, Dembo, and Lewin (1941) allowed children into a room that contained many desirable toys. Some children

Frustration and Societal Aggression

Can the frustration-aggression hypothesis shed any light on the causes of such societal upheavals as the French Revolution of 1789 or the American race riots of the mid- to late-1960s? Perhaps bad economic times or governmental oppression led to "frustration," which then exploded into violence.

Some historians have argued that frustrated optimism, rather than abject pessimism, produces revolutions. For example, the famous French political writer, Alexis de Tocqueville (1856), observed in his analysis of the French Revolution that:

. . . *the French found their condition the more unsupportable in proportion to its improvement. . . . Revolutions are not always brought about by a gradual decline from bad to worse. Nations that have endured patiently and almost unconsciously the most overwhelming oppression often burst into rebellion against the yoke the moment it begins to grow lighter. . . . Evils which are patiently endured when they seem inevitable become in-tolerable when once the idea of escape from them is suggested. (p. 214)*

Political scientist James Davies (1972), looking at several historical examples, including the French Revolution, proposed a "J-curve" theory of social revolutions (see the accompanying figure). "Revolutions are most likely to occur when a prolonged period of objective economic and social development is followed by a short period of sharp reversal" (Davies, 1972, p. 68); that is, social frustration occurs particularly when people expect improving conditions but actually experience worsening conditions.

Do research findings support Davies's hypothesis? In a study of 84 nations, Feierabend and Feierabend (1972) found a clear relationship between political instability (strikes, riots, revolts) and economic frustration. "Frustrated countries" were defined as those that both suffered from poor economic conditions (such as low GNP, inadequate food supplies, insufficient numbers of telephones and doctors) and were well acquainted with the higher living standards of industrial, urbanized countries. Furthermore, Feierabend and Feierabend found that nations with highly oppressive or nonoppressive governments were more stable than nations with moderately oppressive governments. Thus, de Tocqueville's observation that revolutions are born more of a "ray of hope" than of absolute hopelessness may be correct.

Both Feierabend and Feierabend's research and Davies's "J-curve" theory suggest that frustration may result from *relative deprivation*—the gap between expectations and reality. Poor countries exposed to modern standards of living are more "frustrated" than are poor countries isolated from the modern world. And deprived people who have experienced some recent progress are more frustrated than people who have experienced only poverty and oppression.

were permitted to play with the toys, whereas other children were allowed to "look but not touch" and were thus frustrated. In subsequent play activities, the frustrated children proved to be more aggressive and destructive.

Some studies have linked frustration to hostile prejudice. For example, Hovland and Sears (1940) found a significant correlation between the lynching of blacks in the South and the price of cotton between 1882 and 1930, and this finding has been replicated in more sophisticated recent statistical analyses (Hepworth & West, 1988). Presumably, the frustration of hard economic times led white southerners to violence against vulnerable blacks. Miller and Bugelski (1948) found that men who were prevented at the last minute from enjoying an entertaining "night on the town" expressed more negative attitudes toward various minority groups.

Contrary to the original frustration-aggression hypothesis, however, frustration does not inevitably lead to aggression. Many studies demonstrate that our thought

The term *relative deprivation* first appeared in studies on the job satisfaction of American soldiers during World War II (Merton & Kitt, 1950; Stouffer, Suchman, De-Vinney, Star, & Williams, 1949). Ironically, these studies showed that soldiers who received quick promotions were unsatisfied if they perceived that everyone else was getting even quicker promotions, whereas soldiers who got few promotions were satisfied if they felt that others were not being promoted any faster. Thus, frustration and contentment are relative, not absolute. A poor person feels rich if he's eating while everyone else is starving. A corporate tycoon may feel "frustrated" if he earns $100,000 a year when all his friends at the country club earn at least twice as much.

Relative deprivation is frequently cited to help explain the U.S. race riots of the 1960s (Jones, 1972). Consistent with de Tocqueville's observations, these riots occurred during a time of both generally improving conditions and rising expectations for blacks. However, conditions had improved more rapidly for whites, as blacks could see in the mass media. Thus the deprivation of blacks relative to their rising expectations and relative to society at large provided one of the ingredients needed for explosive social violence.

Davies's "J-curve" theory of violent social revolution. According to Davies's "J-curve" theory, social revolutions are most likely to occur when a period of prolonged economic development is followed by a short period of sharp economic reversal. This combination of events creates an intolerable gap between people's expectations and actual economic conditions.

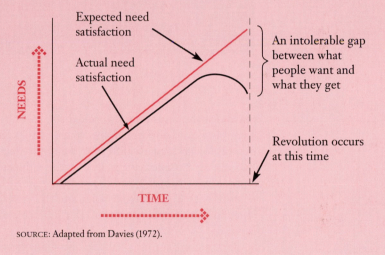

SOURCE: Adapted from Davies (1972).

processes mediate this relationship. Baron (1977) argued that arbitrary and strong frustrations in particular goad people to aggression, whereas mild frustrations or frustrations that exist for a "good reason" are less likely to provoke aggression. If you are stopped behind a car at an intersection when the light turns green, yet can't move because the driver in front of you is combing his hair, you will probably feel angry, and perhaps you'll honk in frustration. But if you're stuck at the intersection because the driver in front of you had a heart attack and is being carried off by paramedics, you probably will not feel hostility. You are frustrated, but there is a good reason for your delay.

Kulik and Brown (1979) have clearly demonstrated how cognitive attributions may affect the relationship between frustration and aggression. They asked 60 Harvard undergraduates to solicit charitable donations by telephone. Some subjects were led to expect general success by being told that 60–65 percent of the people called

Economic frustration and social violence. In 1989 Venezuela's troubled economy triggered violent riots.

would donate, and others were led to expect little success (that only 10–15 percent of people would donate). Subjects actually spoke to a confederate, who refused their request for money in different ways. In one condition the confederate refused abruptly and unpleasantly, telling the subject that charities were a "rip-off." In another condition, he told the subject that he was sympathetic to charities but had recently been laid off from work and thus couldn't afford to make a donation now. Thus, in the second condition, the subject was frustrated by a refusal that seemed justified.

Upon completing a call, subjects' anger was measured by recording how hard they slammed down the phone. In addition, subjects' verbal aggression during a call and their choice of sending mild or critical follow-up letters to the people they solicited were assessed. As you can guess, subjects showed more anger and aggression when their frustration was unexpected and arbitrary. Thus the effects of frustration depend on our cognitive expectancies and how reasonable the frustration seems to be (see also Burnstein & Worchel, 1962; Worchel, 1974).

So the original strong version of the frustration-aggression hypothesis turns out to be false—frustration does not always and inevitably lead to aggression. The converse hypothesis—that aggression always presupposes frustration—is false as well. Physical pain as well as frustration can lead to aggression. And as we shall see later, aggression does not have to be elicited by either pain or frustration; it can also be a learned response.

Where does 50 years of research leave the original frustration-aggression hypothesis? Much reduced and qualified, to be sure. Leonard Berkowitz (1978, 1983b, 1988) argues that frustration leads to aggression insofar as it makes people angry, and that frustration incites aggression because it is a kind of pain—psychological pain. A profoundly frustrating experience may be similar to a sharp jolt of electricity: Both can make us "mad," and if the occasion is right, we may strike out at another person.

Arousal and aggression.   Frustration may influence aggression simply because it leads to general arousal, which then "energizes" aggressive behavior, particularly in a person who has already learned to respond in aggressive ways (Bandura, 1973). Classic learning theories suggest that anything that increases general arousal or "drive" increases the probability of dominant responses. If aggressive responses are dominant (that is, well learned), then general arousal will increase aggression (Berkowitz, 1983b; Zillman, 1988).

Schachter and Singer's (1962) two-component theory of emotion (see Chapter 4 for details) also suggests that general arousal can influence aggression. As you'll recall, this theory proposes that a person is more likely to experience a strong emotion when physiologically aroused in a setting that induces the individual to attribute that arousal to an emotion. The Schachter-Singer theory thus has an interesting implication for human aggression: Anything that increases unexplained physiological arousal may contribute to hostile aggression. For example, fear, sexual excitement, or even physical exercise may facilitate aggression, particularly if the aroused person attributes his arousal to anger (Zillman, 1983).

Research has supported this link between arousal and aggression. Zillman (1971) found that after being insulted by a confederate, subjects were more aggressive if they had just watched a sexually arousing film than if they had watched a non-arousing film. Presumably, subjects mistakenly interpreted their sexual arousal as being due to anger. In a similar experiment, Geen, Rokosky, and Pigg (1972) asked male subjects to read a sexually explicit passage from the novel *Rabbit, Run* by John Updike. While they read, a confederate "distracted" them with electric shocks. Some subjects were told that their arousal was due to reading the sexual passage, others that it was caused by the shocks, and yet others that it was caused by a pill they had taken. The results: Subjects who attributed their arousal to the shocks were more aggressive when shocking the confederate in retaliation than were subjects who attributed their arousal to the sexual passage or to the pill. Other studies have also confirmed that sexual arousal can contribute to aggression (Donnerstein, Donnerstein, & Evans, 1975; Zillman, Hoyt, & Day, 1974).

Zillman (1983) argued that the relationship between arousal and aggression is multifaceted. Sometimes sexual arousal, exercise, or fear can contribute to aggression, particularly if the decay of arousal is slow and the person misattributes the arousal to anger. Clearly, people experience arousal in many painful or frustrating situations, which may contribute to aggressive responses. The Schachter-Singer theory suggests that the effects of moderately intense, unexplained arousal on aggression may be mediated by cognitive interpretations and attributions. Arousal may also energize dominant responses, triggering aggression in people who already have strong aggressive tendencies (Berkowitz, 1983b). When arousal is very intense, people may lose cognitive control of their behavior and engage in truly impulsive, angry aggression. Passion killings are sometimes the product of such intense arousal.

▪▪▪▪▪▪▪▪▪▪▪▪▪▪▪▪▪▪▪▪▪▪▪

Social Learning and Aggression

Roger stooped, picked up a stone, aimed, and threw it at Henry — threw it to miss. The stone . . . bounced five yards to Henry's right and fell in the water. Roger gathered a handful of stones and began to throw them. Yet there was a

**Is aggression innate
or learned?**

space round Henry, perhaps six yards in diameter, into which he dare not throw. Here, invisible yet strong, was the taboo of the old life. Round the squatting child was the protection of parents and school and policemen and the law. Roger's arm was conditioned by a civilization that knew nothing of him and was in ruins.

—— *Lord of the Flies*, p. 56

Are people "conditioned" to be aggressive or nonaggressive? If so, how? In his influential social learning analysis of aggression, Albert Bandura (1973) argues that people may learn to be aggressive (or nonaggressive) through both instrumental conditioning and observational learning.

The basic principle of instrumental conditioning is straightforward when applied to aggression: The probability of the occurrence of aggressive behaviors that are rewarded increases. The effects of instrumental conditioning on aggression have been demonstrated in both animals and people. For example, peaceful rats can be taught to attack other rats if they are deprived of water and rewarded with a drink for attacking (Ulrich, Johnson, Richardson, & Wolff, 1963). The positive reinforcement of food and the negative reinforcement of terminating painful shocks can also be potent rewards for aggressive behaviors in animals (Hutchinson, 1972; Scott, 1973).

The rewards that affect human aggression are even more numerous. Human behavior is influenced both by such primary (unlearned) reinforcers as food, drink, and sex and by such secondary (learned) reinforcers as money, material goods, and social status. Studies indicate that when aggression brings people money, material goods, candy, or social approval, it is more likely to occur in the future (Buss, 1971; Gaebelein, 1973; Walters & Brown, 1963). In a telling field study, Patterson, Littman, and Bricker (1967) observed children's attempts to retaliate in response to other children's aggression. When children succeeded (for example, by regaining an expropriated toy), they subsequently tended to be more aggressive. Apparently, if you fight and win, you're more likely to fight again.

Of course, people do not learn to aggress merely by "trying out" violent behaviors in a trial-and-error fashion, hoping for rewards. Rather, they often learn by observing others and imitating their behavior. The importance of observational learning is central to Bandura's (1973) analysis: Not only can people become aggressive just by watching others, they can also learn through observation when aggression is rewarded and when it is punished. Aggressive models may also reduce our learned inhibitions by showing that it is acceptable to behave in violent ways in the current setting.

In a classic series of experiments, Bandura, Ross, and Ross (1961, 1963b) demonstrated that children can learn to behave aggressively simply by watching aggressive models. In one experiment, nursery-school children were taken to a room containing a number of toys, including a "Bobo doll," a large inflated clown weighted on the bottom so that whenever it was knocked down it popped back upright. Some children observed an adult punch and kick the Bobo doll while yelling statements like, "Sock him in the nose . . ." and "Hit him down." Other children watched the adult play peacefully. Later, the children were allowed to play freely with the toys, and their behavior was recorded by hidden observers. Children exposed to aggressive models were significantly more aggressive, often in ways that exactly imitated the adults. Boys tended to imitate adults' aggression more than did girls, and both boys and girls tended to imitate male models more than female models. Furthermore, the children imitated aggressive models more when the models' aggression was rewarded and less when it was punished (Bandura, 1965).

In such Bobo-doll studies, children do not always exactly imitate the aggression observed; sometimes they aggress in novel ways. Thus, watching models does not merely teach children specific aggressive behaviors; it may release their inhibitions against aggression in general. Furthermore children have been observed performing aggressive acts they learned in Bobo-doll experiments as much as eight months later (Hicks, 1965, 1968), and their learned behavior is sometimes directed against real people as well (Hanratty, O'Neal, & Sulzer, 1972).

The mass media and aggression.

The mass media and aggression.   Bandura's analysis implies that besides learning aggressive behavior by directly observing others, people may also learn such behavior by watching violence in TV shows, videos, and movies. It also implies that people may become less inhibited after viewing media violence.

Imitative violence occurs in real-life as well as in Bobo-doll experiments. For example, recent research shows that suicide rates increase significantly after highly publicized suicides and that people who attempt an imitative suicide are often similar in some way to the person described in the publicized suicide (Bollen & Phillips, 1982). Auto fatalities also increase after publicized suicides (Phillips, 1979), suggesting that some "auto accidents" are really suicides. The Los Angeles freeway shootings described earlier provide yet another recent illustration of "copycat" violence. Although fostered by frustration, the shootings were propagated through media coverage and subsequent imitation.

In a careful analysis Phillips (1983) found that homicide rates increased by more than 12 percent on average following heavyweight championship prize fights; this increase tended to be greater following highly publicized fights. These findings are significant because they suggest that media violence not only triggers direct imitation, but may instigate unrelated kinds of aggression as well.

Social psychologists speculate that media violence can desensitize viewers so that they become less upset by actual violence. Both children (Cline, Croft, & Courrier, 1973) and adults (Thomas, 1982) who view violent television programming seem to experience less physical arousal when they subsequently behave aggressively. In addition, watching excessive media violence may influence viewers' long-term attitudes and values about aggression and about the general levels of violence in society (Gerbner, Gross, Signorielli, & Morgan, 1980). Compared with people who watch little television, heavy viewers of TV overestimate the prevalence of violence in society, the percentage of people employed in law enforcement, and the possibility that violence will affect them.

Violent TV may instigate aggression in still another way. Drawing upon recent research on memory, Leonard Berkowitz (1984) has proposed that viewing TV violence primes aggressive ideas and thoughts, which then facilitate aggressive behaviors. For example, in one experiment subjects viewed film of either a brutal prizefight or a footrace (Berkowitz, 1965). Later they were given the opportunity to shock another student who was described as either a "college boxer" or a "speech major." The results were clear: Subjects who saw the boxing movie were more aggressive toward the "boxer" than toward the "speech major." Boxing had become a cue (something like a conditioned stimulus) to aggression for these people.

Weapons may also serve as conditioned cues to aggression. In a classic and controversial experiment, Berkowitz and LePage (1967) showed that after receiving shocks from a peer (actually a confederate), subjects responded more punitively when a gun, as opposed to badminton rackets, was lying on a nearby table. Berkowitz (1968) noted, "Guns not only permit violence, they can stimulate it as well. The finger pulls the trigger, but the trigger may also be pulling the finger." Even though other researchers have not always replicated this "weapons effect" or have attributed it to demand characteristics (that is, they contend that the subjects "saw through" the purpose of the study; see Page & Scheidt, 1971), the effect seems to be real (Frodi, 1975; Leyens & Parke, 1975; Turner & Layton, 1976; Berkowitz, 1983b). In a society like ours, in which weapons are freely available and continually shown in the mass media, these findings are troubling. They imply that TV may increase the degree to which weapons serve as aggressive cues by constantly associating weapons with vivid portrayals of justified violence. And they also suggest that TV may instigate real-life aggression by constantly providing people with these cues to aggression in the comfort of their living rooms.

The learning of novel cues from violent TV, as well as the power of these cues to trigger real-life aggression, can be seen in a carefully controlled experiment by Josephson (1987), who showed violent and nonviolent TV programs to 396 second- and third-grade Canadian boys. In the violent program, a SWAT (Special Weapons and Tactics) police team killed or knocked unconscious a group of snipers who had murdered a police officer in cold blood. The SWAT officers communicated throughout the TV segment with walkie-talkies. The nonviolent TV show portrayed a police officer coaching a boys' motorbike racing team.

After viewing the TV shows, the boys played a game of floor hockey in a gymnasium. But before they played, each boy was asked by the experimenter to give a pregame interview "like they do on the radio." The interview was conducted with either a tape recorder and microphone or with a walkie-talkie. Observers then rated the boys' verbal and physical aggression during the hockey game. In this ingenious experiment, Josephson found that boys who watched the violent TV show were more aggressive, particularly those who were interviewed with a walkie-talkie. The walkie-talkie, which had played a critical role in the violent TV show, served as an "aggressive cue."

The effects of TV violence on children.   Josephson's experiment is one of many that focuses on the effects of TV on children. Children may be particularly susceptible to the influences of violent programming, for they lack a mature understanding of what they see on TV and may in general be more easily influenced than adults (Liebert & Sprafkin, 1988). Clearly, the effect of TV on children is a topic of great social import, and both national commissions (National Commission on the Causes and Prevention of Violence, 1969) and Surgeon General's reports (Cisin, Coffin, Janis, Klapper, Mendelsohn, Omwake, Pinderhughes, Pool, Siegel, Wallace, Watson, & Wiebe, 1972) have focused on the potentially negative effects of violent TV on children.

To assess these effects, we must first answer a preliminary question: How violent is the content of TV programming? Since the late 1960s George Gerbner and his colleagues at the University of Pennsylvania have conducted careful content analyses of the violence contained in primetime and weekend daytime television (Gerbner, Gross, Signorielli, & Morgan, 1986). Their data show that U.S. TV programming is very violent and that the level of violence has remained relatively constant over the past 20 years (see Figure 12.3). Particularly distressing are the data for violence in cartoons, which are directed primarily at children. According to Gerbner, the typical TV cartoon portrays an aggressive act on average once every three minutes.

And children watch this violence. By the mid-1980s the average U.S. household had a TV set turned on more than seven hours a day (Steinberg, 1985). Infants less than one year old are exposed to more than one hour of TV each day (Hollenbeck & Slaby, 1979); by early adolescence children view almost four hours daily (Liebert & Sprafkin, 1988). Similar patterns of childhood TV viewing are found in other developed countries as well (Murray, 1980).

Does watching all this TV violence actually influence children's behavior? Many experimental and correlational studies suggest that it does. First, laboratory experiments show that immediately after viewing violent TV shows, children often behave and play more aggressively (Liebert & Baron, 1972; Steuer, Applefield, & Smith, 1971) and choose aggressive solutions to social problems (Leifer & Roberts, 1972).

In a set of three carefully conducted field experiments in the United States and Belgium, Parke, Berkowitz, Leyens, West, and Sebastian (1977) found that viewing violent films significantly increased the aggressiveness of juvenile delinquents living in minimum security institutions. In the Belgian experiment, boys living in different "cottages" (that is, residences) saw either violent or nonviolent movies each night for a week. Observers periodically rated different aspects of the boys' aggressiveness—for example, their physical threats (fist waving), physical attacks (hitting, slapping, kicking), verbal aggression (cursing, insulting), and noninterpersonal physical aggression (hitting or breaking an object). These observations were made during a "baseline" period (the week before the boys saw the films) and also during the week

FIGURE 12.3   Percentage of TV programs containing violence, 1967–1985.

How violent is TV programming in the United States?

Gerbner, Gross, Signorielli, and Morgan (1986) measured the percentage of TV programs containing violence over an extended period; the graph shows what they found.

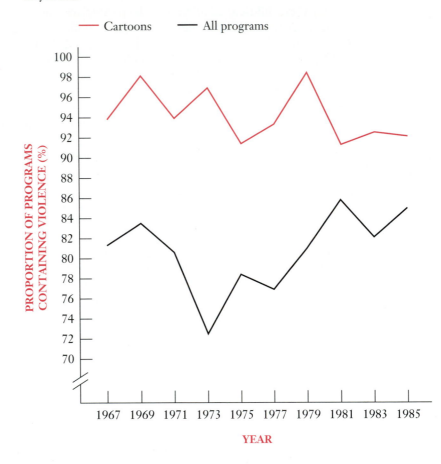

The high level of violence documented in cartoons is particularly disturbing because these programs are targeted at young children, who may be more impressionable than older children or adults.

of watching films. Each boy's reputed aggressiveness was also assessed. The results, shown in Figure 12.4, suggest that viewing aggressive movies particularly increased the physical aggressiveness of the boys who were the most aggressive to start with.

▪▪▪

FIGURE 12.4   Violent behaviors of juvenile-delinquent boys after exposure to violent or nonviolent movies.

Does watching violent movies increase observed aggression in a natural setting?

Parke and his colleagues (1977) observed the naturally occurring aggressive behaviors of institutionalized delinquent boys living in four separate cottages after they viewed either violent or nonviolent movies every day for a week. Based on observations collected during a baseline period before the movies were shown, the researchers classified the boys in each cottage as having either generally low or high degrees of aggressiveness.

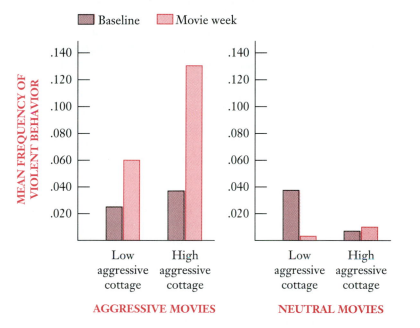

The results showed that boys who viewed violent movies tended to become more aggressive, and this effect was most pronounced for boys who were highly aggressive to start with.

SOURCE: Adapted from Parke et al. (1977). Used with permission.

This study makes the important point that not all children are affected equally by violent TV and movies.

▪▪▪

Correlational studies also suggest a relationship between real-life TV viewing and aggression in children. In one recent large-scale research effort, Huesmann, Lagerspetz, and Eron (1984; Eron & Huesmann, 1986) studied 1,505 children in the

United States, Finland, Poland, and Australia. All of these related studies found significant correlations — with correlation coefficients generally ranging from .2 to .3 — between the amount of violent TV children watch and their aggression as rated by peers. These correlations, although not strong, were quite consistent across studies.

The relationship between violent TV viewing and aggression seems particularly strong for boys who strongly identify with the violent characters they see on TV, for girls who prefer "masculine" activities, and for children in general who are not socially or intellectually skilled (Eron & Huesmann, 1986). Complex statistical analyses by Huesmann and his colleagues (1984) suggest a reciprocal relationship between TV viewing and aggression; that is, violent TV increases aggressiveness, and aggressiveness also leads to increased viewing of violent TV. Thus, for some children at least, viewing violence and aggressiveness seem to feed on each other.

Using data that had been collected over a period of 22 years, Huesmann and his colleagues (Huesmann, 1986; Huesmann et al., 1984) found a distinct relationship between subjects' viewing of violent TV at age 8 and their aggressiveness and level of criminal behavior at age 30 (see Figure 12.5). Drawing upon these same data, Eron (1987) reported a significant correlation of .41 between amount of violent TV viewed at age 8 and a composite index of aggressive behaviors at age 30.

In a fascinating quasi-experimental study of TV viewing and aggression, Joy, Kimball, and Zabrack (1986) measured children's physical and verbal aggressiveness in three similar Canadian towns. Why these particular towns? One had no television reception until 1974 (it was nicknamed "Notel" by the researchers). The second town received broadcasts only from the Canadian Broadcasting Network (nickname: "Unitel"). And the third town received both CBC broadcasts and those from the three commercial U.S. television networks (nickname: "Multitel"). The mean increase in children's aggressiveness was measured in Notel, Unitel, and Multitel during the same time period — when TV was introduced to Notel. The results (see Figure 12.6) plainly indicated that children in Notel showed larger increases in their mean levels of aggressiveness than did children in the other two towns, presumably because TV had been introduced to their community.

Dozens of studies have investigated the relationship between TV violence and children's aggressiveness. Although some social psychologists (see Freedman, 1984) have questioned the evidence, the preponderance of research documents a relationship between TV viewing and aggression in children (Dorr & Kovaric, 1980; Friedrich-Cofer & Huston, 1986; Hearold, 1986). In a comprehensive meta-analysis of 230 studies, Hearold (1986) found consistent evidence that TV violence is related to children's aggressiveness. In addition, she observed the following trends: The effects of viewing violent TV tend to increase with age for boys but decrease for girls; TV violence encourages real-life violence, particularly when it is realistic and portrayed as justified; and finally, children need not be aroused to be affected by TV violence. But as research on frustration and arousal suggests, these variables can heighten the effects of media violence on children's aggressiveness.

Media sex and aggression.   There is a final way in which the mass media may influence aggression — through their sexual content. The effects of media "obscenity" and "pornography" have been the topic of two controversial government commission reports (Report of the Commission on Obscenity and Pornography, 1970; Attorney General's Commission on Pornography, 1986) and remain a subject

---

**FIGURE 12.5   Seriousness of criminal acts before age 30 as a function
of frequency of TV viewing at age 8.**

Is viewing violent TV in childhood associated with criminal behavior in adulthood?

In a longitudinal study conducted with several other researchers, Eron (1987) reported
that TV viewing at age 8 was related to criminal acts committed up to the age of 30.

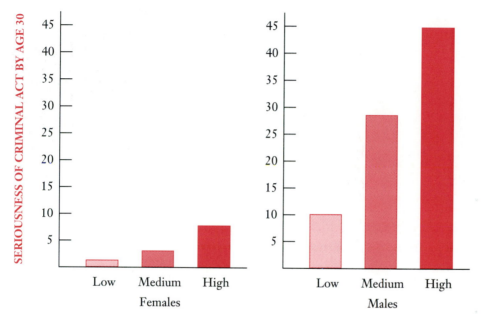

FREQUENCY OF TV VIEWING AT AGE 8

SOURCE: From Eron (1987). Used with permission of Leonard Eron.

---

*Eron (1987) argued that specific programs viewed in childhood do not directly influence
aggression during adulthood. Rather, TV viewing exerts its effects indirectly by changing
attitudes and by teaching people aggressive behaviors and aggressive styles of social
interaction.*

---

of intense debate among both government officials and scholars (Einsiedel,
1988; Koop, 1987; Wilcox, 1987; Linz, Donnerstein, & Penrod, 1987; Linz &
Donnerstein, 1988). What does social psychological research tell us about this provocative topic? Might there be a link between portrayals of sex and aggression? What
kinds of "pornography" are most likely to foster aggression? And what kinds of
aggression are most stimulated by "pornography"?

FIGURE 12.6   Increase in children's aggressiveness following introduction of television to a Canadian town.

Does the introduction of television increase aggressiveness in children?

Joy, Kimball, and Zabrack (1986) observed children's aggressiveness in three Canadian towns: "Notel," "Unitel," and "Multitel." Notel had no television reception before 1974. Unitel received one Canadian network, and Multitel received one Canadian and three U.S. networks. The researchers measured schoolchildren's aggressiveness in all three towns one year before Notel acquired TV reception and one year thereafter.

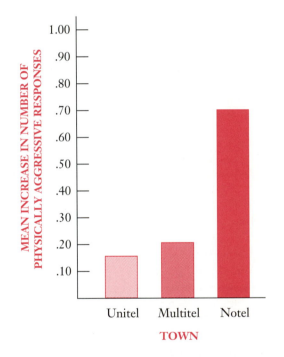

As the graph shows, children's aggression increased more in Notel than in the two other towns. Furthermore, the increase was statistically significant in Notel but not in the other towns.

SOURCE: Based on data from Joy et al. (1986).

These results were particularly interesting because they were true for both boys and girls, for children who initially had either low or high degrees of aggressiveness, and for children who watched varying amounts of TV. This research is a good example of a quasi-experimental study.

Since Sigmund Freud's (1953) seminal *Three Essays on Sexuality*, psychologists have speculated that there may be some link between sexual and aggressive drives. In Freudian psychology, sex and aggression are the two major "instincts" of human motivation, and they often get tangled together in complex ways. The sexual "perversions" of sadism and masochism represent blendings of violence with sexuality (Carson, Butcher, & Coleman, 1988).

With an explicit nod to Freudian assumptions, William Golding wrote a pivotal scene in *Lord of the Flies* that linked sex and aggression. Hunting for meat on their tropical island, the stranded boys corner and kill a wild pig, and this act of sexually tinged violence seems to clear the way for later aggression:

> . . . the sow fell and the hunters hurled themselves at her. This dreadful eruption from an unknown world made her frantic; she squealed and bucked and the air was full of sweat and noise and blood and terror. Roger ran round the heap, prodding with his spear whenever pigflesh appeared. Jack was on top of the sow, stabbing downward with his knife. Roger found lodgment for his point and began to push till he was leaning with his whole weight. The spear moved forward inch by inch, and the terrified squealing became a high-pitched scream. Then Jack found the throat and the hot blood spouted over his hands. The sow collapsed under them and they were heavy and fulfilled upon her.
> (p. 188)

One doesn't need to be a Freudian psychologist, however, to postulate some link between sexual arousal and aggression. We've already noted that any kind of arousal can contribute to angry aggression (Zillman, 1983), and sexual excitement is certainly a kind of arousal. In addition, social learning theory suggests that viewers of violent pornography may learn new forms of sexual aggression from it (Byrne & Kelley, 1984), that they may become "desensitized" to sexual violence, and that they may (falsely) learn that others derive sexual pleasure from aggression. Finally, the constant combination of sex and aggression in the mass media may lead people to cognitively associate the two, as well as classically condition sexual arousal to aggressive cues and aggressive behavior to sexual arousal (Malamuth, 1984).

Does recent research provide any support for these social psychological perspectives on media sex and aggression? Unfortunately, yes. A number of recent experimental studies suggest that violent pornography can increase aggression, particularly by males against females. In one experiment (Donnerstein, 1980), 120 male subjects were angered by either a male or a female confederate. Subjects then viewed either an erotic film (a couple having intercourse), an aggressive-erotic film (a man with a gun breaks into a woman's home and forces her to have sexual intercourse), or a neutral film (a talk-show interview). Finally, the subjects participated in a separate "learning experiment" in which they could deliver electric shocks to the confederate who had earlier angered them.

The results of this experiment are disturbing: Subjects who had viewed the "aggressive-erotic" film were most aggressive, particularly against females (see Figure 12.7). In a related set of experiments, Donnerstein and Berkowitz (1981) found again that "aggressive-erotic" films increased males' aggression against females but not against males. Furthermore, they found that when "aggressive-erotic" films suggested that the depicted women enjoyed forced sex, even nonangered men increased their aggressiveness against women.

FIGURE 12.7   Effect of aggressive-erotic films on aggression.

Does viewing violent pornography increase aggression?

Donnerstein (1980) showed male subjects either a neutral film, an erotic film, or an aggressive-erotic film. Subjects then participated in a "learning experiment" in which they could shock a male or female confederate who had earlier angered them.

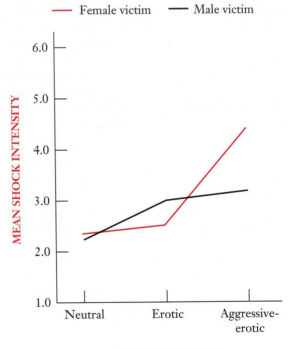

The data showed that viewing aggressive-erotic films increased aggression, particularly against a female confederate.

SOURCE: Adapted from Donnerstein (1980). Used with permission of Edward Donnerstein.

Violent pornography may not only stimulate aggression against women; it may also modify the viewer's long-term beliefs and attitudes as well. In one study, Malamuth and Check (1981) showed men at the University of Manitoba either nonsexual movies or movies in which a man sexually overpowered a woman. A week later, in a seemingly separate study, the men completed a questionnaire that assessed their attitudes toward women and toward rape. The men who had viewed sexually violent movies expressed a greater tolerance toward rape and greater agreement that women enjoy rape. In a replication, Malamuth and Check (1985) found that viewing sexually violent movies increased false beliefs about rape, particularly in men who already possessed negative, aggressive attitudes toward women. Sometimes sexually explicit movies do not even have to contain violence to foster "rape myths" and change sexual attitudes; however, the combination of aggression and sex in movies seems most potent in producing antisocial attitudes and behaviors (Donnerstein, 1984).

Correlational as well as experimental studies point to a link between pornography and aggression against women. Although some early studies suggested that liberalized laws against sexually explicit movies and publications had neutral or even positive consequences, more recent evidence points to a link between access to pornography and aggressive crimes (Ben-Veniste, 1971; Byrne & Kelley, 1984; Court, 1984; Kutchinsky, 1973). For example, in recent times the crime of forced rape has become more common in societies and communities with liberal pornography laws. Court (1984) reports an interesting analysis of reported rapes in Hawaii between 1961 and 1977. When legal restraints were imposed against free access to pornography from 1974 to 1976, rape rates decreased (see Figure 12.8). Court (1984) argues against assuming a direct cause-effect link between pornography and crimes like rape, however. Rather, he hypothesizes that complex social trends are leading to higher rates of rape, and these trends are exacerbated by easily accessible scenes of sexual violence in the mass media and in pornography.

Indeed, the production and distribution of pornographic materials have increased in the past two decades (Williams, 1979; Lederer, 1980; McCarthy, 1980). As of 1980, in the United States alone the sale of erotically explicit magazines was a business earning $4 billion annually (Lederer, 1980). And although it is difficult to define precisely any trends in the content of pornographic materials, pornography seems to have become more violent in the past two decades, particularly in the late 1970s (Linz, Donnerstein, & Penrod, 1987). With the advent of home video recorders, erotically explicit films are available to a larger audience than ever before.

Sexual violence.   Research on pornography relates to a much larger social issue, the incidence of sexual violence in general. One recent survey of 500 women in Albuquerque, New Mexico (DiVasto, Kaufman, Rosner, Jackson, Christy, Pearson, & Burgett, 1984) found that 14 percent had been victims of attempted rape, and 10 percent had been victims of actual rape. In general, "invasive" sexual assaults (undesired fondling, attempted rape, and rape) were carried out by acquaintances, friends, and relatives, whereas "noninvasive" assaults (obscene phone calls, offenses by "flashers" and "Peeping Toms") were perpetrated by strangers.

A study by Sigelman, Berry, and Wiles (1984) underlines the finding that violence, including sexual violence, can occur even in close relationships. Over 500 college students were surveyed to assess violence in their heterosexual relationships. Over half the men and women reported committing some violent act against their partner, such as throwing something, pushing, or slapping. Two questions in the survey assessed sexual violence: How often have you "used strong physical force to try to engage in a sex act against other's will," and how often have you "used violence

FIGURE 12.8   Pornography restrictions and reported rape rates in Hawaii.

Is the availability of pornography associated with sexual violence?

Court (1984) plotted reported rape rates in Hawaii before and after pornography was legally restricted. The data indicate that restrained access to pornography may have reduced rape rates.

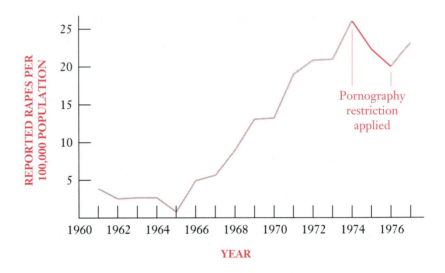

SOURCE: Adapted from Court (1984). Used with permission.

Court (1984) cautions against interpreting these data in simple cause-effect terms. Because the decline in rape rates between 1974 and 1976 may have been due to random fluctuations or factors unrelated to legal restrictions, firm conclusions must await additional studies.

to try to engage in a sex act against other's will"? Almost 12 percent of male respondents, and under 2 percent of female respondents, acknowledged engaging in such sexual coercion.

In an attempt to identify potential rapists, Malamuth (1981) asked college men to rate their likelihood of raping a woman if they could be absolutely assured that they would not be apprehended or punished. Disturbingly, 35 percent admitted to some possibility of committing such a rape, whereas the remaining 65 percent responded that it "was not at all likely." In a separate survey, Rapaport and Burkhart (1984) found that 15 percent of 201 college men surveyed reported "having forced intercourse at least once or twice." Rapaport and Burkhart's subjects completed a battery of personality and attitude measures, and the sexually coercive males were characterized as irresponsible, lacking in social conscience, and possessing negative

:::

SUMMARY TABLE 12.1   Explanations of Aggression

:::

How have social scientists sought to explain human aggression?

	LEVEL OF EXPLANATION	THEORIES	VARIABLES/PROCESSES STUDIED
Group level	Biological group	Instinct theories	Biological evolution
	Social groups		Social norms, cross-cultural variations
Individual level	Heredity and physiology		Brain structures, hormones, sex differences, heritability
	Past environment	Social learning theory	Classical conditioning, operant conditioning, observational learning; media effects
	Current environment	Frustration-aggression hypothesis	Modeling effects; media effects; pain, heat, situationally produced frustration
		Aggressive cues	"Weapons effect"; violent pornography; media effects
Mediating variables	Personality traits		Stability of aggressiveness over time
	Emotional arousal	Schachter-Singer theory	Effects of extraneous arousal, sexual arousal
		Drive theory (learning theory)	Effects of arousal on learned aggressive responses
	Attitudes		Effects of pornography on attitudes toward women and toward rape; media effects

and aggressive attitudes toward women. Malamuth, Check, and Briere (1986) recently extended these findings: They identified men who reported experiencing no, moderate, or high sexual arousal to the use of force. Men who were aroused by force tended to be more accepting of violence against women and dominance over women; however, the groups did not differ in their sex drive or degree of sexual inhibition.

These data seem consistent with feminist analyses of sexual violence against women (Brownmiller, 1975; Dworkin, 1987; Groth & Birnbaum, 1979): Rape and sexual violence are acts of power and dominance as well as sexual acts.

Clearly, ferreting out the causes not only of sexual violence but of aggression in general is an important task for students of human social behavior. Summary Table 12.1 reviews the explanations of aggression we have discussed. We turn next to a practical question: How can aggression be reduced?

Reducing Aggression

"We saw your smoke. What have you been doing? Having a war or something?"

Ralph nodded. . . .

"Nobody killed, I hope? Any dead bodies?"

"Only two. And they've gone."

The officer leaned down and looked closely at Ralph.

"Two? Killed?"

Ralph nodded again. Behind him, the whole island was shuddering with flame. The officer knew, as a rule, when people were telling the truth. He whistled softly. . . .

"I should have thought," said the officer, . . . "I should have thought that a pack of British boys — you're all British, aren't you? — would have been able to put up a better show than that — I mean — "

"It was like that at first," said Ralph, "before things — "

—— *Lord of the Flies*, pp. 183–184

Lord of the Flies ends with a scene of brilliant irony, when a British naval ship, attracted by the smoke of warfare, rescues the fighting boys. Golding wrote his own commentary about this ending:

> . . . adult life appears, dignified and capable, but in reality enmeshed in the same evil as the symbolic life of the children on the island. The officer, having interrupted a man-hunt, prepares to take the children off the island in a cruiser which will presently be hunting its enemy in the same implacable way. And who will rescue the adult and his cruiser? (Notes on *Lord of the Flies*, 1954, p. 186)

Who indeed? Why are so many human enterprises tainted with violence? Perhaps more to the point, how can we control and prevent aggression? Many techniques have been proposed (Baron, 1983; Center for Research on Aggression, 1983). Let's focus here on five strategies studied by social psychologists: (1) venting aggression to reduce subsequent aggression (also known as "catharsis"), (2) punishing aggression, (3) creating responses that are incompatible with aggression, (4) providing social restraints, and (5) using cognitive strategies to deal with aggression.

Catharsis

The concept of catharsis originated with Aristotle (*Poetics*, Book 6), who argued that by viewing powerful emotional events in the theater, people could purge themselves of these emotions. More than 2,000 years later, Sigmund Freud extended the notion of catharsis to aggression. He postulated that aggressive acts could sometimes "drain off" aggressive impulses. But Freud was doubtful, at least in his early writings, whether symbolic aggression could lead to catharsis: "The reaction of an injured person to a trauma has really only . . . a 'cathartic' effect if it is expressed in an adequate reaction like revenge" (Breuer & Freud, 1961, p. 5).

The notion of catharsis seems consistent with common sense. People often say they need to "let off steam" or "get something off their chest." Numerous studies

▪▪▪▪▪▪▪▪▪▪▪▪▪▪▪▪▪▪▪▪▪▪▪▪▪▪

Do sports and vigorous exercise serve to "vent" aggressive impulses?

have looked for catharsis effects, but in general such studies offer little support for the proposition that catharsis can serve as a general technique for controlling aggression (Quanty, 1976; Geen & Quanty, 1977). Let's summarize some of the evidence.

Experimental subjects sometimes show reductions in the physiological arousal caused by anger (for example, raised blood pressure) if given the opportunity to shock the person who angered them (Hokanson, 1961; Hokanson & Shetler, 1961; Hokanson & Burgess, 1962). For example, in one study Hokanson and Burgess (1962) allowed subjects to vent their aggressive feelings toward a tormentor in one of three ways — through physical aggression, verbal aggression, or fantasy aggression (by writing aggressive stories). Only physical aggression successfully reduced physiological arousal (thus providing some support for Breuer and Freud's insight that only true revenge is really satisfying).

Of course, reduced arousal does not necessarily mean reduced aggression. Other studies have investigated the value of catharsis in actually reducing behavioral aggression. In general, this research indicates that physically "letting off steam" through sports or exercise does not serve the function of catharsis. For example, Patterson (1974) found that, if anything, high-school football players were *more* aggressive after a season of football than before it. Apparently, playing football encouraged aggression rather than serving to "vent" it. In a laboratory study on the cathartic value of physical violence, Ryan (1970) allowed some angered subjects to pound a rubber mallet before shocking the confederate who had angered them. This physical activity did nothing to "vent" their subsequent aggression.

Verbal aggressiveness, like general physical activity, does not consistently reduce subsequent aggression in experimental studies; it may even increase aggression under certain circumstances (Rothaus & Worchel, 1964; Wheeler & Caggiula, 1966).

Focusing on some real-life consequences of verbal "catharsis," Straus (1974) studied the relationship between the verbal "venting" of aggression and actual aggression between spouses. The results: Verbal aggression encouraged rather than discouraged physical aggression. These findings were replicated in a subsequent study of 2,143 couples by Straus, Gelles, and Steinmetz (1980). These authors concluded that "for those who engage in little or no verbal aggression, there is little or no physical violence (less than half of 1 percent)." On the other hand, ". . . a clear majority of the top quarter [of married couples] who express conflict through verbal blasts were violent" (p. 169).

Does direct physical aggression serve a cathartic function? A number of experiments suggest that people who are given an opportunity to aggress directly against someone who has angered them may actually become *more* aggressive subsequently and derogate as well as punish their victim (Buss, 1966; Geen, 1968; Geen, Stonner, & Shope, 1975; Berkowitz & Geen, 1966, 1967; Ebbesen, Duncan, & Konecni, 1975). Perhaps the Roman, Tacitus, was right when he wrote, "It is part of human nature to hate the man you have hurt." This effect—that aggressive behavior leads to further aggression—might be a result of a number of psychological processes. When people aggress against someone, their aggression is "disinhibited." Furthermore, upon aggressing successfully against a tormentor, people learn that their aggression will not be punished and may feel the "positive reinforcement" of revenge. Finally, dissonance theory (see Chapter 8) predicts that after behaving aggressively, people need to justify their bad behavior and may do so by derogating their victim. Derogation may then lead to a vicious cycle of further aggression.

This research does not imply that you should bottle up your hostilities and aggressive feelings, however. The venting of inhibited feelings may be satisfying and even therapeutic (Feshbach, 1984). Catharsis is simply not a consistently effective method of reducing human aggression.

Punishing Aggression

Punishment—delivering an aversive stimulus after an undesired behavior—is one of the most common means that societies and individuals use to control aggression (Blanchard & Blanchard, 1986). Legal systems punish violent criminals by throwing them into jail. Athletic teams punish overly violent players by suspending them. And parents punish aggressive children by spanking them.

Sometimes, punishment works. The famous behaviorist B. F. Skinner (1938) argued that punishment only temporarily suppresses a behavior. For example, a boy who is punished by his mother for hitting his little brother may be temporarily aroused by the punishment and desist from hitting, for a while at least. But later, when his arousal dies down, he may return to his violent behavior, particularly if his mother is not around.

Punishment may be particularly tricky as a method of controlling aggression because punishment is itself a kind of aggression. As we already know, aggression often instigates counteraggression. Furthermore, an aggressive punisher may serve as a model of aggression. In particular, parental violence and punitiveness often seem to encourage rather than discourage aggression in children (Sears, Maccoby, & Levin, 1957; Olweus, 1980; Stevenson-Hinde, Hinde, & Simpson, 1986).

Undoubtedly punishment works best to control instrumental rather than hostile aggression. Someone who commits a "crime of passion" may aggress despite threats of the most terrible punishment (such as the death penalty). Finally, it is important to note that even though punishment may help to suppress aggressive behaviors, it does not serve to substitute aggression with more positive or productive kinds of social behavior; at best punishment is a partial solution.

Still, punishment may at times be a necessary response to human aggression. When is punishment most likely to be effective? Research suggests the following rules of thumb (Baron, 1983): To be effective, punishment should be relatively strong; it should be applied quickly and consistently after the undesired aggressive behavior; and finally (even though this may seem obvious, it is a principle often violated by parents) punishment should be clearly contingent upon the "bad" aggressive behavior. Patterson (1983) described a "nattering" style of parental punishment, characterized by parents' verbally nagging and fussing at their children without really focusing on specific bad behaviors. Such nattering is the ideal way *not* to punish.

If punishment (or the threat of punishment) is consistent, clear, and strong, it can be effective in reducing violence. This phenomenon is well illustrated by a recent study on how punishment can be used to reduce family violence. To appreciate this study, you must realize that the police have traditionally been quite reluctant to intrude into cases of domestic violence (Roy, 1977; Langley & Levy, 1977), and as a result spouse-abusers often think they won't be "caught," arrested, or punished. Sherman and Berk (1984) describe a program conducted by the Minneapolis police department to test three techniques of dealing with domestic violence: (1) counseling both parties involved in the violent episode, (2) separating the combatants for several hours, thus allowing the situation some time to "cool off," or (3) arresting the violent party. Arrest was most effective in reducing subsequent violence, producing a 10-percent rate of recidivism compared to 19 percent and 24 percent in the first two groups. Thus the threat of tough punishment can have an effect on violence. The threat, of course, must be enforced consistently.

Creating Responses Incompatible with Aggression

Have you ever felt like "throttling" someone, when a quick-thinking friend cracked a joke and suddenly eased the tension? Somehow, laughter seemed incompatible with aggression. In general, any response that is incompatible with aggression — for example, humor, empathy, or mild sexual arousal — may serve to reduce aggression (Baron, 1983; Ramirez, Bryant, & Zillman, 1983).

Baron (1976) demonstrated the ability of incompatible responses to defuse hostility in a clever field experiment. Male motorists were frustrated at an intersection when the driver in front of them (actually a confederate) failed to drive on when the traffic light changed from red to green. Hidden observers recorded whether the frustrated drivers honked their horns, made hand gestures, or yelled out angry comments. While the drivers were stopped at the intersection, Baron arranged for three different kinds of distraction to occur: In a "humor" condition, a woman dressed as a clown crossed the street in front of the subject's car; in an "empathy" condition, a woman on crutches crossed the street; and in a "sexual arousal" condition, a scantily clad woman crossed the street. This experiment also included two control conditions: Either no one crossed the street or a "normal," conservatively dressed woman crossed the street. Subjects in the "humor," "empathy," and "sexual arousal" conditions all showed less angry horn-honking than did control subjects.

Predicting and Reducing Family Violence

Elizabeth Steinberg was buried last week in a white coffin lined with pink satin. She was mourned by hundreds of New Yorkers . . . who lined up in the morning cold outside a Greenwich Village funeral home. They had read the shocking accounts of the six-year-old girl's death. Law-enforcement officials allege she was savagely beaten by 46-year-old Joel Steinberg, a lawyer who claimed to be her adoptive father. . . . The tragedy seemed incomprehensible: How could such a horrible thing happen? More important, who could have saved the child?

Elizabeth's legacy may be that her death has once again focused national attention on the problem of child abuse. It is growing at an alarming rate. . . .

—— Newsweek, Nov. 23, 1987, p. 70

In the 1980s the topic of family violence came out of the closet onto the front pages. The statistics were disturbing: From the mid-1970s to the mid-1980s official reports of child abuse in the United States rose over 200 percent. Officially, over 1,000 children died of child abuse in 1986. Because such deaths are often misreported as "accidents" or "crib deaths" and because much child abuse is never officially reported, experts believe the true incidence is much higher than the official statistics suggest (Keller & Erne, 1983).

Child abuse is not the only kind of violence to occur commonly in American families. Spouses frequently beat, and sometimes kill, each other. Indeed, over 30 percent of all murders are perpetrated by family members against one another (Curtis, 1974; Bohannan, 1960; Straus, Gelles, & Steinmetz, 1980). Women are particularly victimized: About 1,700 American women die annually from marital violence (Steinmetz, 1980).

What can be done to prevent family violence? Goldstein (1983) describes three levels of treatment: Primary prevention techniques are designed to prevent family violence before it starts; secondary prevention focuses on early identification of family violence and on trying to "nip it in the bud"; and tertiary prevention is designed to treat recurring, problematic family violence. Let's outline how each strategy works.

Primary prevention relies partly on public education (Gelles, 1982). First, the topic of family violence must be brought into the open. Primary prevention also relies on the enactment of appropriate laws. For example, one proposed legislative reform is to make spouse abuse a "criminal" rather than a "civil" offense, thus simultane-

Factors that predict spouse abuse. Straus, Gelles, and Steinmetz (1980) identified 25 factors that distinguish spouse abusers from nonabusers. By adding up these factors in a given family, the researchers computed an index that predicted spouse abuse quite well.

Checklist of Factors Predicting Spouse Abuse

CHARACTERISTICS IMPORTANT FOR BOTH WIFE-BEATING AND HUSBAND-BEATING

1. Husband employed part time or unemployed
2. Family income under $6,000
3. Husband a manual worker
4. Husband very worried about economic security
5. Wife very dissatisfied with standard of living
6. Two or more children
7. Disagreement over children
8. Grew up in family in which father hit mother
9. Married less than ten years
10. Age thirty or under
11. Non-white racial group
12. Above average score on Marital Conflict Index
13. Very high score on Stress Index
14. Wife dominant in family decisions
15. Husband was verbally aggressive to wife
16. Wife was verbally aggressive to husband
17. Gets drunk but is not alcoholic
18. Lived in neighborhood less than two years
19. No participation in organized religion

CHARACTERISTICS IMPORTANT FOR WIFE-BEATING

20. Husband dominant in family decisions
21. Wife is full-time housewife
22. Wife very worried about economic security

CHARACTERISTICS IMPORTANT FOR HUSBAND-BEATING

23. Wife was physically punished at age thirteen plus by father
24. Wife grew up in family in which mother hit father
25. Wife is a manual worker

SOURCE: Adapted from *Behind Closed Doors: Violence in the American Family,* by Murray A. Straus, Richard J. Gelles, and Suzanne K. Steinmetz. © 1980 by Richard J. Gelles and Murray A. Straus. Used with permission.

ously increasing legal punishments and social awareness of the problem (Gelles, 1982; Straus, 1980).

Is it possible to identify people who are likely to become abusive parents or spouses? In a study of over 2,000 married couples, Straus, Gelles, and Steinmetz (1980) identified 25 characteristics that predicted wife-beating or husband-beating. Using these 25 items as a checklist, the researchers assigned each couple a score from 0 to 25, depending on how many of the 25 characteristics were true of the couple. The checklist and how well it predicted spouse abuse is shown in the first figure. The same researchers also developed a checklist to predict child abuse. This list of 16 family characteristics and its relation to child abuse is shown in the second figure.

The checklists for both spouse abuse and child abuse point to

Joel Steinberg and Hedda Nussbaum — the "parents" of Elizabeth Steinberg. As this photo suggests, Joel Steinberg battered his common-law wife as well as his adopted daughter.

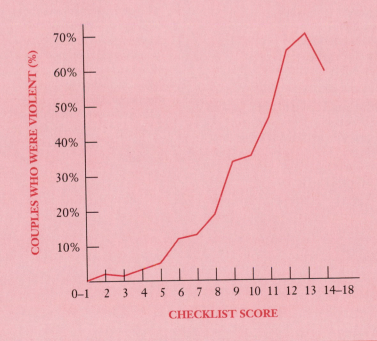

some important contributors to family violence — economic deprivation, large families, drunkenness, stress, and a prior history of family violence. Thus, one goal of "primary prevention" is to alleviate some of these social and economic causes of family abuse through adequate day care, family planning resources, alcohol treatment facilities, and so on.

Once family violence occurs, secondary prevention becomes important. Family violence must be detected to be stopped. Elizabeth Steinberg, the six-year-old New York girl beaten to death by her adoptive father, "slipped through the cracks" of society. Neither her neighbors nor her teacher re-

ported her abuse to proper authorities. Secondary prevention is in part a matter of public education. All concerned citizens must learn that domestic violence is their business and must be reported to the authorities. Hospital staffs, police, and mental-health clinic personnel should be educated to screen people for evidence of family violence. Helping services and governmental agencies have traditionally regarded the family as "off limits" when investigating and reporting violence.

Tertiary treatment programs deal with ongoing, entrenched patterns of family violence. They involve a complex mix of psychological treatment, legal policy, and social

welfare. For example, chronically abused women may be helped by psychotherapy designed to boost self-esteem and remove their feelings of helplessness (Lieberkneckt, 1978; Hilberman, 1980). Legal policy can address spouse abuse by clearly defining it as a punishable offense and by instituting "dispute centers" to mediate cases of family violence (Dellapa, 1977). In intractable cases, social welfare systems must exist to allow victims to escape from abuse. For example, shelters for abused women provide them with an immediate safe haven, as well as with physical, economic, and psychological support (Goldstein, 1983; Straus, Gelles, & Steinmetz, 1980).

Factors that predict child abuse. Straus, Gelles, and Steinmetz (1980) also identified 16 factors that distinguish parents who abuse their children from those who do not. A summed index computed from these factors predicted child abuse quite well.

Checklist of Factors Predicting Child Abuse

IMPORTANT FOR CHILD ABUSE BY EITHER PARENT

1. Was verbally aggressive to the child (insulted, smashed things, etc.)
2. Above average conflict between husband and wife
3. Husband was physically violent to wife

IMPORTANT FOR ABUSE BY MOTHERS

4. Husband was verbally aggressive to wife
5. Husband a manual worker
6. Husband dissatisfied with standard of living
7. Wife a manual worker
8. Wife age thirty or under
9. Wife was physically punished at age thirteen plus by father

IMPORTANT FOR ABUSE BY FATHERS

10. Two or more children at home
11. Wife is a full-time housewife
12. Married less than ten years
13. Lived in neighborhood less than two years
14. No participation by father in organized groups
15. Husband was physically punished at age thirteen plus by mother
16. Grew up in family where mother hit father

Elizabeth Steinberg—
one of the many
victims of family
violence.

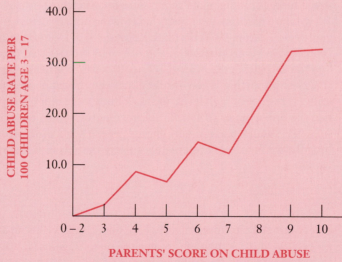

CHILD ABUSE RATE PER
100 CHILDREN AGE 3 – 17

40.0

30.0

20.0

10.0

0 – 2   3   4   5   6   7   8   9   10

PARENTS' SCORE ON CHILD ABUSE
"PREDICTION" CHECKLIST

SUMMARY TABLE 12.2   Techniques for Reducing Aggression

What techniques are effective in reducing aggression?

TECHNIQUE	WHEN IS IT EFFECTIVE?
Catharsis (venting aggression through fantasy, exercise, verbal aggression, or physical aggression)	Inconsistently effective; sometimes effective when aggression is targeted directly at tormentor
Punishment (aversive stimulus delivered after an aggressive behavior)	Must be consistent and contingent on aggressive behavior; most effective in reducing instrumental rather than hostile aggression
Incompatible responses (humor, empathy, or mild sexual arousal)	Documented for aggression in response to mild frustration
Social restraints and modeling (presence of nonaggressive models)	Requires proper social environment; modeling often is strongest when the model is powerful and attractive
Cognitive strategies (analyzing why TV is unrealistic; developing stress-management and communication skills)	Can help to mitigate effects of other variables, such as TV violence and frustration

Providing Social Restraints

Aggression is a social behavior, subject to social influences. We already know that social models can instigate aggression; fortunately, they can also reduce it.

Many experiments suggest that viewing nonaggressive models makes people less aggressive (Baron, 1971; Baron & Kepner, 1970; Donnerstein & Donnerstein, 1976). Nonaggressive people can play more than the positive (but passive) role of being "good examples"; they can also openly censure others' aggressive behavior. Baron (1972) showed that when insulted subjects heard a peer (actually a confederate) criticize the use of high levels of shock, they were much less punitive when they later had the opportunity to shock their tormentor. Thus, to reduce individuals' aggression, we should place them among people who disapprove of aggression. More broadly, we must work to create a society that disapproves of, rather than glorifies, violence.

Cognitive Strategies for Controlling Aggression

The ability to think separates humans from other animals. At our best, we can use that ability to help control aggression. Given that we live in a world full of aggressive models, we must somehow "inoculate" people against the abundant cues to aggression that surround them. Huesmann and his colleagues (1983) tried to reduce the impact of violent TV programming on first- and third-grade children by having the children write papers about "How television is not like real life," "Why it is bad to imitate TV violence," and "Why it is bad for a kid to watch too much TV." A week after writing their essays, the children were videotaped reading them and answering questions about the same topics in a "talk-show" format.

This brief procedure turned out to have a lasting effect on the children: It significantly changed their attitudes about TV violence, and most importantly, it reduced their levels of aggression two years later! Certainly, this experiment suggests

that it is possible to mitigate the effects of violent TV programming with simple educational programs. Other cognitive skills that may be taught to reduce aggression are negotiation skills (Toch, 1985), effective strategies of interpersonal communication (Baron, 1983), and mental strategies to deal with stress and frustration (Goldstein, Spratfkin, & Gershaw, 1976). These and other techniques for reducing aggression are reviewed in Summary Table 12.2.

A Concluding Word on Controlling Aggression

In 1929, Mahatma Gandhi asserted, "Nonviolence is the first article of my faith. It is also the last article of my creed." Unfortunately, the world has since witnessed millions of violent deaths.

To control aggression, we must first, as individuals and as a society, want to control aggression. Over the past 50 years social psychology has made impressive progress in understanding the factors that both incite and reduce aggression. Still, aggression remains a central problem of our society, and indeed of human existence. Keniston (1968) has argued that as sex was the central issue of the Victorian era, violence is the central issue of the current era. As more and more powerful weapons are developed, the possibilities for human aggression become ever more ominous. John F. Kennedy stated it simply in an address to the United Nations: "Mankind must put an end to war or war will put an end to mankind." We must also put an end to violent crime, family violence, and sexual abuse as well.

Undoubtedly the world will witness yet more violence and wars. And thus there is one grand war yet to be fought and won. It is a war we must all wage—a war against aggression itself (Goldstein & Keller, 1983).

Summary

1. Aggression is behavior directed against another living being that is intended to harm or injure. Social psychologists distinguish between hostile aggression — which is emotional and provoked by pain or upset — and instrumental aggression, which is unemotional and performed to gain rewards.

2. Freud and Lorenz argued that aggression is an instinct that must be vented. Evolutionary theory suggests that although aggression has survival value, it occurs only under certain circumstances.

3. Aggression is cross-culturally variable. It may occur particularly among groups competing for scarce resources.

4. Aggressiveness is a trait that is relatively stable over time and is in part due to hereditary factors.

5. Aggression is influenced by specific brain structures and may be influenced by testosterone, alcohol, and marijuana.

6. Aggression often elicits counteraggression.

7. Pain frequently incites aggression. Although unlearned, the link between pain and aggression can be influenced by learning.

8. People tend to be more aggressive in hot environments.

9. The original frustration-aggression hypothesis held that frustration always leads to aggression and that aggression is always the result of frustration. Research suggests that arbitrary, strong frustrations without reasonable explanations particularly incite aggression. Aggression can occur without frustration.

10. Frustration can contribute to social upheavals. The "J-curve" theory holds that violent social revolutions are most likely to occur when a prolonged period of economic development is followed by a period of sharp economic reversal. Research suggests that economic frustration is more a function of relative deprivation than absolute deprivation.

11. Arousal contributes to aggression in several ways: It can energize dominant learned aggressive responses; it can heighten anger through misattribution; and at high levels, it can reduce cognitive controls on behavior. Arousal created by exercise or by viewing erotica can increase subsequent angry aggression.

12. Aggression can be learned through operant conditioning and observational learning. Experimental and correlational studies document imitative aggression. Stimuli (like weapons) frequently associated with aggression may become learned aggressive cues.

13. Experimental, quasi-experimental, and correlational studies suggest a relationship between viewing violent TV and aggression in children.

14. Viewing violent pornography can increase aggression, particularly by males against females, and it can lead men to hold negative attitudes toward women and to endorse rape myths.

15. Catharsis — the venting of aggressive impulses through fantasy, physical exercise, verbal aggression, or physical aggression — does not consistently reduce subsequent aggression.

16. Family violence is a serious problem in the United States. Primary, secondary, and tertiary prevention programs can help reduce such violence.

17. Incompatible responses such as humor, empathy, or mild sexual arousal can sometimes reduce aggression.

18. Nonaggressive models lead observers to be less aggressive.

19. Thinking about the bad effects of TV viewing, as well as certain communication skills and mental strategies for coping with stress and frustration, can help reduce aggression.

Glossary

Aggression: Behavior directed against another living being that is intended to harm or injure

Catharsis: The venting of aggressive impulses through fantasy, exercise, verbal aggression, or physical aggression

Frustration: According to the early research on the frustration-aggression hypothesis, an interference with the occurrence of a goal-response

Frustration-aggression hypothesis: The hypothesis that frustration leads to aggression and that all aggression is caused by frustration

Hostile aggression: Emotional, angry aggression often provoked by pain or frustration

Incompatible responses: Responses — such as humor, empathy, or mild sexual arousal — that are incompatible with aggression

Instrumental aggression: Nonemotional aggression performed to gain a reward

J-curve theory: Davies's theory that violent social revolutions are most likely to occur when a prolonged period of economic development is followed by a short period of sharp economic reversal

Relative deprivation: The gap between reality and expectations of social standards; frustration may be more a function of relative deprivation rather than of absolute deprivation

Weapons effect: The effect documented in some experiments that weapons may serve as "aggressive cues" and thus may increase aggression by their mere presence

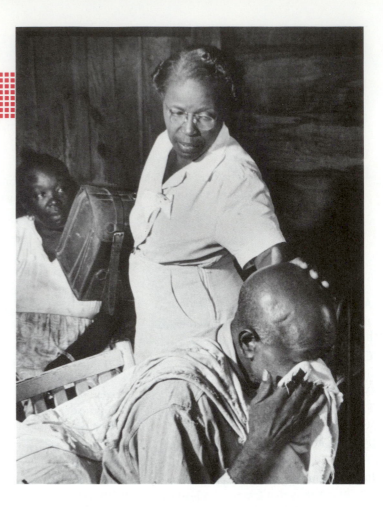

"... Once upon a time there lived a very nasty, horrible old woman. When she died, she didn't leave behind her one single good deed. So the devils got hold of her and tossed her into the flaming lake. Meantime, her guardian angel stood there, trying hard to think of one good deed of hers that he could mention to God in order to save her. Then he remembered and said to God: 'Once,' he said, 'she pulled up an onion in her garden and gave it to a beggar woman.' So God said to him: 'Take that onion, hold it out to her over the lake, let her hold on to it, and try to pull herself out. If she does, let her enter heaven; if the onion breaks, the old woman will just have to stay where she is.' So the angel hurried to the woman, held out the onion to her, and told her to take hold of it and pull. Then he himself began to pull her out very carefully and she was almost entirely out of the lake when the other sinners saw she was being pulled out and grabbed on to her so that they'd be pulled out of the flames too. But when she saw them, that wicked, horrible woman started kicking them, saying: 'I'm being pulled out, not you, for it's my onion, not yours!' As soon as she said that, the onion snapped and the woman fell back into the flaming lake, where she's still burning to this day. ..."

—— from *The Brothers Karamazov*, by Fyodor Dostoevsky, pp. 426–427

CHAPTER 13

Altruism and Prosocial Behavior

Dostoevsky's tale of one onion is wonderfully ironic. An old woman performs only a single good deed during her life—giving an onion to a beggar. When this minuscule act of kindness is later used to justify her release from hell, the old woman's unwillingness to help others—this time, to escape from hell—leads to her eternal damnation. Dostoevsky's parable is more than a sly analysis of one person's selfishness to the bitter end. It poses a number of questions that strike to the core of Western moral thought: Are people naturally selfish and evil, or is compassion also a part of human nature? When are we likely to help, and who are we most likely to help? Are some kinds of people more likely than others to be "good Samaritans" who aid others in need?

Dostoevsky, a novelist of penetrating psychological insight, believed that human beings have profound possibilities for both helping and hurting. In *The Brothers Karamazov* he analyzes the personalities of three brothers, each of whom seems to represent a different side of human nature. Dmitry, the eldest, is impulsive and emotional—a man of action. Ivan, the second brother, is cold and logical—a man of thought. And Alyosha, the youngest, is a religious mystic—a man of the spirit. Alyosha seems to be the true altruist in *The Brothers Karamazov*, repeatedly performing good deeds for others at no personal gain. As we shall see, helping, like the brothers Karamazov, can at times be impulsive, at times calculated, and, sometimes perhaps, truly altruistic.

477

Emergency intervention. This lineworker gives mouth-to-mouth resuscitation to a colleague shocked unconscious by a live electric wire. Because of his quick action, his co-worker lived.

Defining and Measuring Prosocial Behavior

Prosocial behavior is behavior that intentionally helps or benefits another person (Bar-Tal, 1976). In a sense, prosocial behavior is the opposite of aggression, which is intentional harm or injury of another (Krebs & Miller, 1985). Consider the following dramatic example:

> . . . [four-year-old] Michelle [DeJesus] wriggled her hand free from her mother's [and] hopped toward the edge to look for the [subway] train — but slipped and fell onto the tracks. The screams and shouts for help began: "There's a girl on the tracks!" "Somebody get her!" "Save her!"
>
> . . . Fifteen seconds passed. The crowd felt a gush of wind caused by [an] oncoming train, then heard the first distant grumble as it barreled . . . toward them. Down on the tracks, Michelle began to rouse. Her eyes tightly closed, she cried, "Mommy! Mommy!"
>
> The shouts for somebody to save the little girl kept up, but nobody moved. Ten seconds more ticked by. . . . Then Everett [Sanderson] . . . asked himself, "What if it was my child down there?" And in a jumble of gallantry and foolhardiness, he jumped down to the tracks and started running. (Young, 1977, pp. 92–93)

Defying death, Sanderson threw Michelle to bystanders at the side of the subway platform and then was pulled from the tracks himself only a second before the train rushed by. Everett Sanderson's rescue of Michelle DeJesus illustrates one particular kind of prosocial behavior: *emergency intervention* — a quick response to sudden events that endanger another and that may sometimes place the helper in considerable danger (Latané & Darley, 1970; Piliavin, Dovidio, Gaertner, & Clark, 1981).

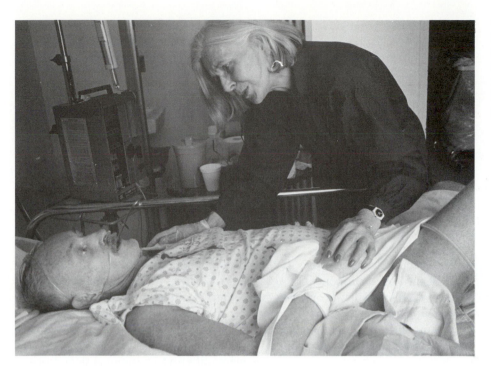

Rescuing a girl who falls onto subway tracks, rushing into a burning house to save a trapped person, and giving immediate first aid to the bloody victim of an automobile accident are all emergency interventions.

Donating blood regularly to the Red Cross, giving solace to a depressed friend, sharing food and belongings with others, and giving money to charities are also examples of prosocial behavior. Although they don't require split-second decisions in the heat of a crisis, such generous acts are still very important in everyday life. In fact, such mundane forms of prosocial behavior are probably much more important to the maintenance of human society than more dramatic emergency interventions.

Clearly, helping comes in many forms. In the previous chapter we distinguished between two kinds of aggression, hostile and instrumental. Hostile aggression is more impulsive and emotional, whereas instrumental aggression is influenced by rewards, punishments, and "rational" considerations. A similar distinction can be made for prosocial behavior: One kind is triggered by quick, nonrational, emotional arousal in response to emergencies; the other kind is influenced more by the potential helper's analysis of the costs and benefits of helping (Piliavin et al., 1981).

Based on evidence from 26 different studies, Jane Piliavin and her colleagues (1981) concluded that impulsive helping is most likely to occur when (1) the emergency is quite clear, (2) the emergency occurs in a real-life (as opposed to a laboratory) setting, and (3) the helper has some prior relationship with the victim (for example, the victim needing help is a family member or friend). The case of Everett Sanderson, who saved Michelle DeJesus from almost certain death, meets the first two criteria, but not the third — Everett faced a clear, real-life emergency, but he had no prior relationship with Michelle.

Sanderson's rescue may have seemed particularly impressive to you precisely because he was a stranger to little Michelle. There was "nothing in it for him" to rescue the girl, except great personal danger. The word *altruism* refers to helping another person for no reward, and even at some cost to oneself (Krebs & Miller, 1985; Batson, 1987).

Philosophers have argued for centuries about whether or not people are ever truly altruistic (Rushton & Sorrentino, 1981). Their debate is complicated by the fact that although people sometimes aid others for no apparent external gain (such as money, rewards, or social esteem), they may still be motivated by internal rewards and punishments (self-esteem, or avoidance of guilt or of unpleasant arousal). Batson (1987) has labeled altruism that is motivated by such internal rewards and punishments as "pseudoaltruism" because the good acts are done to increase the individual's pleasure or to reduce his or her pain. According to Batson, pure altruism must be motivated by an honest concern for another's well-being, not by any sort of self-reward or by avoidance of self-punishment. Later in this chapter, we'll describe some intriguing recent research that attempts to demonstrate the existence of pure altruism in humans.

Even if pure altruism exists, it constitutes only one kind of prosocial behavior. Peter Blau (1964), a proponent of a cost-reward analysis of helping behaviors, notes somewhat cynically that people who help others "without a thought of reward and even without expecting gratitude . . . are virtually saints, and saints are rare" (p. 16). Interestingly, the one brother in *The Brothers Karamazov* who is portrayed as altruistic is the mystic, saint-like Alyosha.

Just as research on aggression uses many different operational definitions of aggression, so research on prosocial behavior uses many measures of altruism and helping. Indeed, operational definitions of prosocial behavior seem to be even more varied than those of aggression (Krebs & Miller, 1985). To list just a few examples, various studies have measured whether subjects mail lost letters (Hornstein, Masor, Sole, & Heilman, 1971), give money to people in need (Bickman & Kamzan, 1973; Latané, 1970), donate to the Salvation Army (Bryan & Test, 1967), donate a kidney to a person suffering from kidney failure (Fellner & Marshall, 1981), aid people who drop their groceries (Tipton & Browning, 1972), stop or call the police to help motorists with flat tires (Bryan & Test, 1967; Penner, Dertke, & Achenbach, 1973), intervene in a fight between a man and a woman (Shotland & Straw, 1976), and help a man who suffers an apparent heart attack (Staub, 1974).

The helping behaviors just listed vary in a number of ways. Sometimes they are in response to emergencies (intervening in a fight), and sometimes not (donating money). Sometimes they entail considerable costs (donating a kidney), and sometimes not (mailing a lost letter). Sometimes the recipient knows he or she is being helped (aiding a person who drops groceries), and sometimes not (calling the police to aid a motorist). Note that studies on prosocial behavior tend to use behavioral rather than subjective measures.

▪▪

Major Approaches to the Study of Prosocial Behavior

Prosocial behavior, like aggression, can be analyzed at many different levels (see Figure 13.1). Group-level explanations analyze prosocial behavior in terms of biological evolution and cultural norms. Individual-level explanations focus on the individual's heredity and physiology (Is altruism heritable?), the past environment (Does

FIGURE 13.1   Levels of explanation applied to altruism and prosocial behavior.

*What different kinds of explanations have been used
to explain altruism and prosocial behavior?*

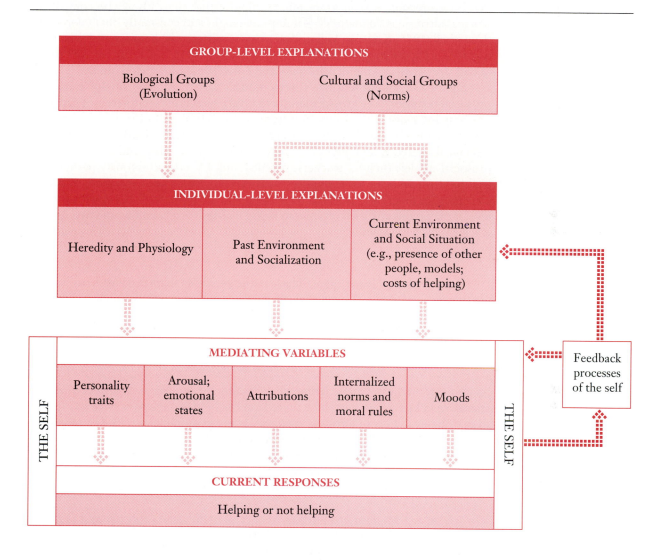

parental rearing influence children's prosocial behavior? Does TV viewing affect
altruism?), and the current environment (Does helping in an emergency depend on
the clarity of the situation, the number of other people around, and the presence of
helpful models?). Mediating variables — the third level of explanation — include internal psychological states and processes that are presumed to influence helping,

such as personality traits, arousal and emotions, guilt, moods, internalized social rules and norms, cognitive calculations of risk and reward, and attributions.

Unlike research on aggression, research on prosocial behavior has focused primarily on cognitive calculations and decisions. Perhaps this is because social psychologists have implicitly assumed an "original sin" model of human behavior; that is, aggression is seen as an innate impulse that must always be controlled, whereas altruism is "unnatural" — it must be taught and constantly "hammered in" (Campbell, 1975; Krebs & Miller, 1985). Stated differently, helping others is often regarded as something we may "reason ourselves into" based on considerations of costs, rewards, and moral principles, and not as something that is innate.

Figure 13.1 should sensitize you to the fact that there is no single "cause" of prosocial behavior. The arrows indicate that variables at different levels of explanation may influence one another. For example, biological evolution may support the development of certain cultural norms and influence individuals' physiology. An individual's heredity and physiology may influence personality, and so on. Viewing prosocial models (helpful teachers, parents, and TV characters) may particularly lead to prosocial behavior in children with certain genetic predispositions and personalities. In describing research on helping and altruism, we'll begin with group-level explanations and then proceed to individual-level explanations and psychological mediating variables.

Sociobiological Theory and Prosocial Behavior

"I must admit," Ivan began, "I have never been able to understand how it was possible to love one's neighbors. And I mean precisely one's neighbors, because I can conceive of loving those who are far away. . . ."

". . . and there are masses of people just like me. The question is, then, whether this is because people are bad or because that is their nature. . . ."

—— *The Brothers Karamazov*, p. 284

As we noted in the previous chapter, the evolution of aggressive behaviors is understandable in Darwinian terms, for aggression can help animals to survive and reproduce. The evolution of altruism, however, is more problematic. In *The Descent of Man* (1871), Charles Darwin first noted a paradox: An animal that behaves in a truly altruistic, self-sacrificing way fosters others' survival at its own expense. But the whole "goal" of Darwinian evolution is survival and reproduction. Altruistic self-sacrifice thus seems to be an evolutionary dead end.

Kin selection.   Modern evolutionary theory partially solves this paradox through the notion of kin selection (Hamilton, 1964). Whereas classical Darwinian theory focused on individual and species survival, modern evolutionary theory focuses more on gene survival (Dawkins, 1976; Ridley & Dawkins, 1981): An animal is evolutionarily successful if it passes its genes on to future generations. This can occur in two ways: if the animal produces offspring or if its genetic relatives (for example, brothers or sisters) produce offspring. Thus natural selection should favor animals who show "altruism" toward genetically related individuals.

Pure, self-sacrificing altruism occurs most dramatically in social insects, such as bees. Because of the peculiarities of bee reproduction (the father drone bee always contributes the same chromosomes to all daughters), worker bees share three-fourths of their genes with their sisters (unlike human siblings who on average share one-half of their genes). Furthermore, worker bees are sterile and thus cannot pass on their genes through individual reproduction. Thus, a worker bee ensures the survival of her genes by ensuring the survival of her sisters. Indeed, worker bees readily sacrifice their lives to protect other bees in their hive (Ridley & Dawkins, 1981).

Reciprocal altruism.   Another proposed route for the development of seemingly altruistic behaviors is *reciprocal altruism* — that is, behavior that benefits another with the proviso that the other is expected to return the favor. The "cost" of giving up some resources for the benefit of another is more than offset, in terms of evolutionary fitness, by the later reciprocated favor. Biologist Robert Trivers (1971) offers the following as examples of reciprocal altruism in animals: (1) symbiotic cleaning, in which large fish allow certain species of small fish to swim in their mouths without eating them because the small fish clean them of parasites and (2) birds' warning calls that inform other birds of danger but at the same time place the warning bird in danger by drawing attention to it.

In reciprocal altruism, if one animal helps another but is not "returned the favor," then it may not help again. Mathematical modeling studies (for example, Axelrod & Hamilton, 1981) demonstrate that in particular, a very simple strategy of reciprocal altruism called "tit for tat" is particularly stable and adaptive. This strategy has just two rules: (1) In a relationship with another, always begin with a cooperative "altruistic" response, and (2) in all subsequent interactions, behave as your partner did last — that is, if he was most recently altruistic, be altruistic in return, but if he was selfish, be selfish in return.

The "tit-for-tat" strategy has several noteworthy features (Trivers, 1983). It is "eternally optimistic" in that it always starts with altruism and returns to altruism whenever the partner does. It has a very "short memory" and is ever-ready to "turn over a new leaf," and thus it is not vindictive — if your partner has "cheated" in the past and behaved selfishly, you reciprocate altruism as soon as your partner "reforms" and shows altruism. Finally, this "tit-for-tat" strategy shows a no-nonsense approach to cheaters — as soon as your partner is selfish, you are selfish in return. There is no self-sacrificing "turning the other cheek."

Reciprocal altruism is most likely to evolve in species in which individuals repeatedly interact and thus have the opportunity to reciprocate altruism (Trivers, 1971, 1983). The conditions that foster repeated, mutually beneficial interaction include: (1) a long lifespan, (2) animals living in close proximity (for example, in social groups), (3) mutual dependence, whereby survival depends on the help of others, (4) a long period of parental care, and (5) the absence of rigid dominance hierarchies, which guarantees that "altruistic" coalitions of individuals confer power to those individuals. The animals that most possess these characteristics are higher mammals, such as dolphins, nonhuman primates, and, of course, human beings.

A number of studies have shown evidence of altruism in nonhuman primates. Nissen and Crawford (1936) conducted a fascinating early demonstration. Two hungry chimpanzees were placed in adjacent cages, and one of the chimps was given a small piece of food. The food-bearing chimp would often share, sometimes without being "asked" and sometimes after the other chimp begged. In both cases, chimps sacrificed a desired good to "help" another. Interestingly, more sharing occurred when the chimps were "friends" rather than strangers. This makes good biological sense, for acquaintanceship increases the probability of reciprocity.

■■■■■■■■■■■■■■■■■■■
**Four adult chimpan-
zees share foliage. In
the wild, chimps most
often share the meat of
freshly captured prey.
Is this an example of
pure or reciprocal
altruism?**

Helping behaviors have also been observed in whales and dolphins (Conner &
Norriss, 1982). According to Trivers (1983),

> . . . This help comes in three forms: standing by, assistance, and support.
> Standing by occurs when an animal stays with another animal in distress but
> does not offer obvious aid. Often an individual will remain in a dangerous
> situation far longer than it would if there were no one in distress. Assistance
> includes approaching an injured comrade and showing excited behavior, such
> as swimming between the captor and its prey, biting or attacking capture ves-
> sels, and pushing an injured individual away from a would-be captor. . . . Sup-
> port occurs when one or more animals maintain a distressed animal at the
> surface of the water — either right-side up or upside-down — and presses up-
> ward, leaving this position only long enough to breathe, but keeping the
> stricken animal at the surface.
> . . . There is no doubt that whales and dolphins understand when another
> cetacean is being captured. They will often bite restraining lines of harpooned
> animals during capture, propel injured animals away from captors, and even
> attack the captors. (pp. 53–54)

Higher mammals not only show helpful behaviors; they also show signs of
experiencing empathy for others in distress. The anecdotal evidence just presented
for chimpanzees, dolphins, and whales provides some evidence of this. In a series of
more controlled experiments, Masserman, Wechkin, and Terris (1964) designed an
apparatus in which monkeys could receive food by pulling either of two chains.
However, whereas both chains delivered food, one also delivered a shock to another

monkey. Interestingly, the monkeys learned to avoid pulling the chain that shocked another monkey, even though this response led to a reward. Apparently, the cries of pain from the other monkey were distressing, and the chain-pulling monkey experienced a kind of empathy for its suffering companion.

Our mention of empathy in higher mammals suggests an important point: The effects of biological evolution on helping must eventually be embodied in psychological dispositions and processes; that is, altruism toward kin and reciprocal altruism may show themselves in individuals in terms of feelings of "love" and "loyalty" toward family and in-group and feelings of friendship and empathy toward people who do us favors. In other words, evolutionary principles may complement rather than contradict psychological findings (Rushton, 1988).

Note that evolutionary theories of altruism may account for a weak form of altruism (doing something positive for another when there's "something in it for you"—either fostering your genes' survival or promoting later reciprocity). However, evolutionary theories do not predict pure altruism (doing something positive for a stranger in a truly self-sacrificing manner). Campbell (1975, 1983) has argued that biological evolution can never lead to pure altruism in humans, and even though weak altruism may have evolved in people, selfishness, cheating, and aggression have also evolved as competing behavioral tendencies. Thus pure selfless altruism must result from learned cultural belief systems; in Campbell's view, fostering altruism and tempering innate self-seeking tendencies are some of the major functions of religious and moral traditions.

▪▪▪▪▪▪▪▪▪▪▪▪▪▪▪▪▪▪▪▪
Cultural Norms of Prosocial Behavior

There will be moments when you will feel perplexed, especially in the presence of human sin. You will ask yourself: "Must I combat it by force or try to overcome it by humble love?" Always choose humble love, always. Once you have chosen it, you will always have what you need to conquer the whole world. Loving humility is a powerful force, the most powerful, and there is nothing in the world to approach it.

—— *The Brothers Karamazov*, p. 386

Most of the world's great religious and moral traditions have taught the virtues of love, kindness, compassion, and altruism. People do not always live up to these ideals, but still such rules provide a standard of behavior to counteract more "sinful" tendencies (Campbell, 1975, 1983).

Social norms. The concept of a norm has been used by anthropologists and sociologists to describe the prescriptive rules society has developed to guide social conduct. A *norm* is "a statement made by members of a group, not necessarily all of them, that its members ought to behave in a certain way in certain circumstances" (Homans, 1961, p. 40). A norm embodies both a standard of conduct and some cultural consensus that people ought to behave according to the standard (Eagly, 1987).

What are the most prominent norms governing prosocial behavior? The *norm of reciprocity* is a nearly universal norm prescribing that people should help and not hurt those who have helped them (Gouldner, 1960). Stated a bit more informally, this norm holds that "I'll scratch your back if you'll scratch mine." This principle seems to hold for politicians, friends, lovers, and business partners, and social psychology experiments support its existence. For example, Wilke and Lanzetta (1970) asked subjects to play a "trucking game" in which they had to transport goods across a simulated highway. When a subject's partner (actually a confederate) did a "favor" and helped a subject to transport his goods, the subject tended to reciprocate the favor in a carefully graded way—the bigger the original favor, the bigger the returned favor.

It is interesting to note the congruence between the norm of reciprocity and the sociobiological notion of reciprocal altruism. Apparently reciprocity is a powerfully adaptive behavior that occurs in both biological and cultural evolution.

Another rule guiding prosocial behavior—the *norm of equity*—is in some sense an elaboration of the norm of reciprocity. It holds that people should receive "goods" from a relationship in proportion to what they invest in the relationship (Walster, Walster, & Berscheid, 1978). Whereas the norm of reciprocity dictates an equal exchange of favors, the norm of equity holds that what one gets in a relationship should be proportional to what one puts into it (see Chapter 11 for a more complete discussion of equity theory). For example, in a marriage, two people may not exactly reciprocate services and favors because one partner brings a higher "investment" to the relationship (greater beauty, wealth, or social status). The norm of equity helps to define what people perceive to be just and unjust prosocial exchanges in their relationships.

Although they regulate the degree to which we engage in prosocial behavior with others, neither reciprocity nor equity promotes pure altruism. Both require that you "get" something in return for what you give.

The *norm of social responsibility* (Berkowitz, 1972) is a more purely altruistic principle of social behavior that prescribes that a person should give aid to dependent others who need assistance. The aid should be proportional to the need of the dependent person. Imagine, for example, that a mother wins a lottery and decides to set up trust funds for her two children. One child is handicapped, the other is not. The norm of social responsibility would hold that more money be set aside for the handicapped child, who is more dependent on the parent. Experiments show that people often, but not always, aid dependent others in need, even when their aid is anonymous (Berkowitz, 1972; Berkowitz & Daniels, 1963). Sometimes, then, people do give aid without expecting something back from the recipient.

Norms of prosocial behavior, like prosocial evolutionary strategies, presumably developed because they aid individual and group survival. The norms of reciprocity, equity, and social responsibility lead to mutually rewarding social relationships, guard against "cheaters," protect the weakest members of society, and prevent, through agreed-upon rules, the violence unleashed by unbridled self-seeking. Unfortunately, these norms of prosocial behavior may apply most strongly to relatives and members of in-groups and less to "outsiders" (Krebs & Miller, 1985). Again, we see a convergence between social norms and biological evolution, both of which promote altruism primarily toward kin and in-group members—people with whom one repeatedly interacts.

In discussing the cultural basis of altruism, Ronald Cohen (1978) presents a compelling example of how prosocial norms apply primarily to insiders:

> In Africa I soon learned that feeling for others was not always considered a profitable or even a proper way to behave. Upon expressing my concern over

the fate and feelings of a newcomer to my little village, the leaders of the town said "Why are you doing all this: after all, this is just a person!" The implication was very clear. In their culture, relationships, especially kinship and hierarchical (patron-client) relations, are the most important things in life. A mere individual outside such relations — as this man was — is of no importance, nor is his fate, whatever it might be. (p. 95)

The limitations of normative approaches.   Although cultural norms undoubtedly influence prosocial behavior, they rarely lead to exact predictions of helping behavior in specific situations. Latané and Darley (1970) argue that so many norms of prosocial behavior have been proposed that none is very powerful as an explanation. Like naive instinct theories, normative theories of prosocial behavior may become circular (Krebs, 1970): Why did Joe give money to the beggar? Because of the norm of social responsibility. How do we know there is a norm of social responsibility? Because people like Joe donate money to dependent people.

Various norms may contradict one another. For example, the norm of reciprocity might suggest that you won't give money to a beggar, who has never done anything for you; however, the norm of social responsibility clearly requires you to give, particularly if the beggar is somehow dependent on you. Some people may internalize cultural norms more strongly than others, and thus individual differences may affect when norms are and are not obeyed. Finally, as we shall see in the rest of this chapter, situational variables may be very important in determining when people do and do not behave consistently with learned norms. All of this is not to say that the normative approach is false; rather, it is incomplete.

The Psychology of Prosocial Behavior

... I want to make it clear that young Alyosha was in no sense a fanatic. ... Let me tell you my opinion of him right from the start: he was just a boy who very early in life had come to love his fellow men and if he chose to enter a monastery, it was simply because at one point that course had caught his imagination and he had become convinced that it was the ideal way to escape from the darkness of the wicked world, a way that would lead him toward light and love.

—— *The Brothers Karamazov*, p. 20

A complete understanding of prosocial behavior requires that we consider environmental and psychological variables (designated individual-level and mediating variables in Figure 13.1), as well as biological and cultural variables. Earlier we distinguished between prosocial behavior in general and the more specific kind of helping that occurs during emergencies. Let's first describe the factors that contribute to prosocial behavior in general, and then we'll turn to the interesting special case of emergency intervention.

Is There a Prosocial Personality?

In Chapter 6 we discussed a general issue: whether people possess traits and thus behave consistently across situations. Now let's pose a question specifically about prosocial behavior: Do some people possess a trait of altruism and thus show

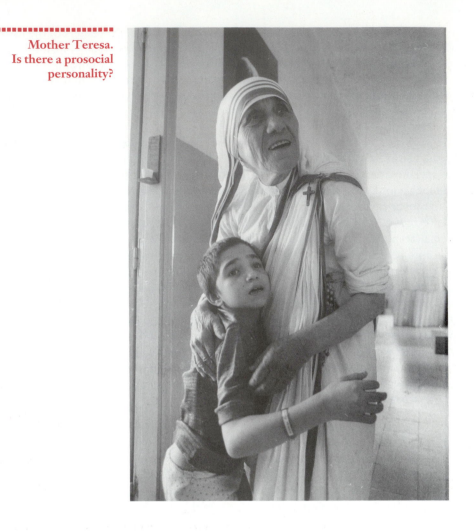

Mother Teresa. Is there a prosocial personality?

prosocial behaviors consistently across situations? Our common sense tells us they do — think, for example, of Mother Teresa or Albert Schweitzer.

Surprisingly, early research suggested that people show little consistency in their prosocial behaviors. As part of their classic research, Hartshorne and May (1928, 1929; Hartshorne, May, & Shuttleworth, 1930; see Chapter 6) devised 33 different behavioral measures of altruism, self-control, honesty, and cheating, and administered them to over 10,000 elementary and high school students. Measures of altruism included students' votes to divide class money among themselves or to donate it to charity, students' decisions to give away items in a gift pencil case to needy children, and students' efforts to find stories and pictures to donate to children in hospitals. In general, such single measures of altruism neither correlated strongly with one another (the average intercorrelation coefficient was .23) nor with other measures of "morality." Hartshorne and May interpreted these results to mean that altruism and morality are not "unified character traits." Many contemporary researchers have echoed this conclusion (Krebs, 1978; Gergen, Gergen, & Meter, 1972; Mussen & Eisenberg-Berg, 1977).

However, as we noted in Chapter 6, we now know that single measures of behavior tend to be quite unreliable (Epstein, 1979, 1980). When Hartshorne and May's measures of altruism are combined into a composite score, they correlate .61 with measures of the children's reputation of altruism among teachers and classmates (Rushton, 1981b). This clearly suggests a more stable trait of altruism than Hartshorne and May saw in their data. Other more recent studies have shown evidence for moderate consistency in children's altruism (Krebs & Sturrup, 1974; Strayer, Wareing, & Rushton, 1979). Furthermore, self-report measures of altruism show considerable heritability (for example, the altruism of identical twins is more similar than that of fraternal twins), again suggesting the existence of a trait (Rushton, Fulker, Neale, Nias, & Eysenck, 1986).

If some people indeed display relatively consistent altruistic behaviors, what are these people like? Research suggests that altruistic people are empathetic, particularly as adults, and able to analyze situations from the emotional and moral perspectives of other people (Underwood & Moore, 1982; Batson, Bolen, Cross, & Neuringer-Benefield, 1986). They possess more strongly internalized norms of prosocial behavior and show advanced kinds of moral reasoning (Blasi, 1980; Staub, 1974; Eisenberg-Berg, 1979; Krebs & Rosenwald, 1977), and they tend not to have high degrees of stereotypical masculinity (Tice & Baumeister, 1985; Siem & Spence, 1986).

Gender may also be related to prosocial behavior. As we noted in Chapter 10, on average women help less than men in experimental studies on emergency interventions (Eagly & Crowley, 1986); however, these sex differences occur particularly in studies in which the helping act is perceived as somewhat dangerous, there is an audience watching, and the victim is a woman. Eagly (1987) argues that when studies focus more on nurturing, nonheroic kinds of helping (for example, caring for friends or giving to charity), then women — consistent with their sex-role socialization — will prove to be more helpful than men.

The development of prosocial behavior.   How do some people come to be more helpful than others? Developmental psychologists have identified a number of factors that lead to the development of prosocial behaviors in children. (Such factors would fit in the box labeled "past environment" in Figure 13.1.) The development of empathy and altruism in children is fostered by a loving, caring relationship with a primary care-giver, who may or may not be the mother (Sroufe, 1978). London (1970) studied heroic Christians who risked their lives to rescue Jews during World War II and found that typically such altruists had very close relationships with at least one parent who was strongly committed to humanitarian causes.

Clearly, adult models of altruism contribute to the development of altruism in children (Yarrow, Scott, & Waxler, 1973), and not surprisingly, what adults do is more important than what they say in fostering children's prosocial behavior (Bryan, 1972). Rewards and praise can help to mold prosocial behavior in children (Mussen & Eisenberg-Berg, 1977), and importantly, children become more helpful when they are placed in the role of helper (Staub, 1975, 1979). Finally, general psychological health and security contribute to prosocial behavior: Children who are optimistic and who possess good self-esteem tend to behave more helpfully than depressed and insecure children (Mussen & Eisenberg-Berg, 1977). The short recipe then for producing a prosocial child seems to be love, a prosocial environment, and giving the child responsibility for caring for others (such as siblings, classmates, and pets).

Does Prosocial Television Programming Lead to Prosocial Behavior in Children?

We know from the previous chapter that viewing violent television is linked to aggression in children. Can prosocial content in television programs encourage prosocial behaviors in children? The answer provided by many research studies seems to be an encouraging "Yes." For example, after children view videotapes of generous models (such as people who donate their winnings to charity), they are significantly more likely to be generous themselves in similar situations (Bryan, 1975; Elliot & Vasta, 1970; Rushton & Owen, 1975). Television models can also lead children to be more friendly and less prejudiced and to engage in constructive forms of self-control (Rushton, 1981a). Let's illustrate the prosocial potential of TV with several carefully conducted studies.

Sprafkin, Liebert, and Poulos (1975) carried out a particularly realistic experiment using real TV shows. Children in the experimental group viewed an episode of "Lassie" — a popular TV show about a collie — in which a child

risked his life to rescue Lassie's pup from a mine shaft. Children in two control groups saw either a "neutral" Lassie episode or an episode of the situation comedy "The Brady Bunch" (neither of which contained examples of prosocial behavior). Later, the children were given the choice of earning points for prizes or working to help animals in need. Children who had watched the prosocial episode of "Lassie" were significantly more willing to give up prizes in order to work for the welfare of animals (see the accompanying figure).

Children's willingness to cooperate can also be influenced by television. In one study, Baran, Chase, and Courtright (1979) showed second- and third-grade children either an episode of "The Waltons" portraying a cooperative solution to a conflict, a control video that did not portray cooperation, or no TV program at all. When they later played with other children in a game, the children who had viewed the cooperative TV show were significantly more

cooperative than children in the other two groups.

Some studies have tried to tailor video examples to the prosocial behavior being studied. For example, Moriarity and McCabe (1977) studied over 200 Canadian children who participated in team sports (baseball, lacrosse, and ice hockey). Children viewed videotaped examples of their particular sport that illustrated either prosocial behaviors (such as helping others or apologizing for a misdeed), antisocial acts (aggression), or neutral behaviors. Viewing prosocial examples increased the prosocial behavior of most of the children, but intriguingly, antisocial examples had no effect on the children's behavior.

The finding that prosocial television may have a greater impact on behavior than antisocial television is not limited to just the Moriarity and McCabe study. Susan Hearold (1986) analyzed almost 200 published tests of the effects of prosocial TV on children's behavior. Her combined results show that

The Psychology of Emergency Intervention

People often perform quite heroic deeds:

One spring evening, Mr. James Harris was riding in the subway in New York when he observed an attempted robbery at knifepoint. He disarmed the man and prevented the crime from being carried through to its conclusion. Scott Spink, 5 years old, threw a rope to his friend Nicholle, also 5, and pulled her to safety when she fell into a creek in which they were fishing. Rebecca Griggs and her sister Shirley Bowland let the air out of the tires of two bankrobbers' getaway car, then chased and caught one of the men and tied him up with his own belt. Late one night Don and Arlene Matzkin and Angela McGhee heard screams outside their house in Philadelphia. Don jumped from his chair and ran out, followed by the two women, finding a neighbor who had just been prosocial TV programming has a highly significant effect in fostering prosocial behaviors in children and that furthermore, the effect of prosocial TV on prosocial behavior was about twice as large as the effect of antisocial TV on antisocial behavior. Based on her analysis, Hearold (1986) concluded:

Many organizations and groups have chosen to work for the removal of sex and violence in televised programs. It is a defensive position: eliminate the negative. Alternatively, I would recommend accentuating the positive; apply money and effort to creating new entertainment programs with prosocial themes, especially for children (to whom the empirical evidence most clearly applies). Although fewer studies exist on prosocial themes, the effect size is so much larger, holds up better under more stringent experimental conditions, and is consistently higher for boys and girls, that the potential for prosocial effects overrides the smaller but persistent effects of antisocial programs. (p. 116)

Viewing prosocial behavior in TV shows leads children to behave in prosocial ways. In this study, first-grade children who had viewed the prosocial episode of "Lassie" were significantly more likely to engage in helping behavior than those who had watched TV programs that did not contain examples of prosocial behavior.

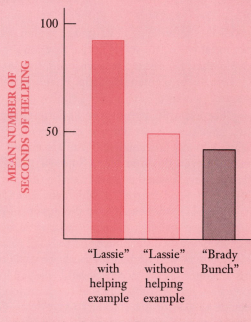

SOURCE: Based on data from Sprafkin, Liebert, and Poulos (1975).

stabbed. Eleanor Harden, a 22-year-old clerk typist, jumped into a freezing river and pulled out a 75-year-old woman whose car had plunged into 12 feet of water. (Piliavin, Dovidio, Gaertner, & Clark, 1981, p. 1)

Lest these examples make you feel complacent about the strength of human virtue, however, consider in contrast one of the most infamous stories of nonintervention in recent history:

Kitty Genovese is set upon by a maniac as she returns home from work at 3 a.m. Thirty-eight of her neighbors in Kew Gardens come to their windows when she cries out in terror; none come to her assistance even though her stalker takes over half an hour to murder her. No one even so much as calls the police. She dies. (Latané & Darley, 1970, p. 1)

The behavior of Kitty Genovese's New York City neighbors in 1964 became the subject of impassioned newspaper articles and editorials, magazine stories, an off-Broadway play, religious discourse, innumerable everyday conversations, and a series of famous social psychology experiments (Latané & Darley, 1970). Why were her neighbors so callous and uncaring? Was it the apathy of big-city living? More broadly, why do people sometimes immediately help in emergencies, and sometimes not at all? Before jumping to conclusions about the Kitty Genovese case, let's first analyze the social psychology of emergency situations.

Latané and Darley's cognitive model.   In their influential book *The Unresponsive Bystander: Why Doesn't He Help?* (1970), Bibb Latané and John Darley portray emergency intervention as a five-stage decision process (see Figure 13.2). To intervene, a potential helper must: (1) notice that something is wrong, (2) decide that it's a true emergency, (3) assume responsibility for the problem, (4) decide how to help, and (5) actually implement the help. Helping can be "short-circuited" at any of the five stages.

For example, if you lived in Kitty Genovese's apartment building, you would first have to hear her screams and become aware of the emergency. If your TV was playing loudly and you lived in an apartment far from the murder, you may not have reached even this first stage. Suppose you did hear the screams. Then you would have to decide whether it was a real emergency. You might decide, for example, that it was a "lovers' quarrel" in which you shouldn't get involved.

Suppose you actually see the attack and know it's murderous. Now you must assume responsibility to help. Perhaps you falsely assume that one of your neighbors has already called the police and thus fail to act yourself. If you do assume responsibility, you now must decide exactly what to do. Should you rush out and try to chase off a dangerous murderer? Should you yell from your window? Should you call the police? Clearly, some kinds of intervention are riskier than others. Suppose you decide to go outside and try to save Kitty Genovese. Now you must think about implementing your decision: How should you approach the murderer? Should you bring a weapon with you?

In an emergency situation, potential helpers must make all these decisions in a split second. Emergencies are typically events with which we have little experience. (How many times in your life have you had to intervene in a murder?) We're often not sure what constitutes correct action. What determines, in such difficult situations, when people do and do not help?

The bystander effect.   The murder of Kitty Genovese seemed particularly horrifying and senseless because it took place while 38 neighbors watched. Surely one of them should have helped. After all, there's safety in numbers, right? Maybe not. In a series of ground-breaking experiments, Latané and Darley (1970) demonstrated a surprisingly robust phenomenon termed the *bystander effect*: The presence of other bystanders often inhibits people from helping in emergencies.

In one experiment, Latané and Darley (1968) asked some Columbia University students to sit alone in a room while they completed a questionnaire on "the problems of urban life." Soon after beginning, each subject suddenly witnessed an "emergency": smoke began pouring into the room from a small vent in the wall. Within four minutes, half of the subjects took some action concerning the smoke (for example, reported it to someone), and three-fourths of them took action within six

▪▪▪

FIGURE 13.2   Latané and Darley's decision model of emergency intervention (1970).

What are the cognitive steps an individual must progress through before offering help in an emergency?

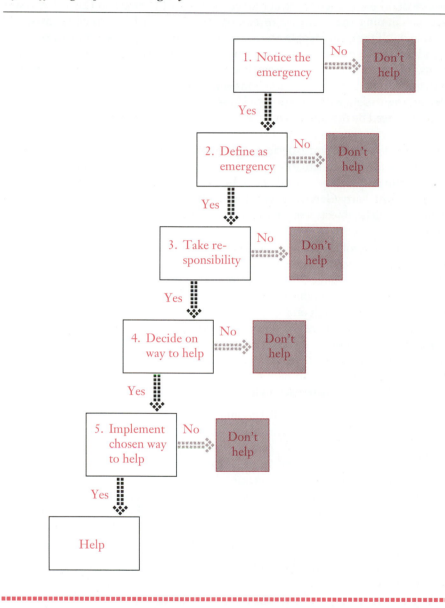

▪▪▪

minutes, at which time the experiment ended. In a second experimental condition, groups of three subjects were sitting in the room when smoke began to pour in. Only 1 out of 24 subjects took action within the first four minutes, and only three reported the smoke within the entire duration of the experiment. In still a third condition, two confederates joined the one real subject in the smoke-filled room. The confederates were instructed not to respond to the smoke. If the subject asked them any questions, they said "I dunno" and continued filling in their questionnaires. In this condition, only 1 of 10 subjects reported the smoke (see Figure 13.3).

Why were subjects in a group so much less likely to respond to the smoke? The presence of others seemed to affect the second stage of Latané and Darley's decision process — defining the event as an emergency. These subjects seemed to say to themselves, "If the other people aren't worried, then perhaps it's not really serious."

Indeed, in the group conditions, subjects came up with many ingenious explanations for the smoke — that it was air-conditioning vapor, simulated smog, even "truth gas." Apparently, in an ambiguous emergency situation people look to others to decide how to define the situation and how to respond. Afterwards, subjects denied being influenced by the other people in the room, but the data told quite a different story.

The smoke-filled room experiment differs in two important ways from the Kitty Genovese incident: The situation was not clearly an emergency, and there was no human victim desperately in need of aid. In an attempt to more closely approach the dynamics of the Kitty Genovese case, Latané and Darley (1970) created a dramatic situation in which subjects believed they were witnessing a student's severe epileptic seizure.

Subjects were told that they would be participating in a discussion of "personal problems faced by normal college students." To ensure anonymity, students would sit in separate rooms and communicate via microphones. Each person would have two minutes to speak; then his microphone would automatically switch off and the next student's would switch on.

In one condition, subjects talked with another student seated in a nearby room. The student spoke about his difficulties adjusting to college life, and then, with some embarrassment, confided that he sometimes suffered from seizures, particularly when stressed. The conversation switched back and forth, and then, while speaking, the other student actually seemed to have an epileptic seizure. He gasped:

> I-er-um-I think I-I need-er-if-if could-er-er-somebody er-er-er-er-er-er-er-give me a little-er-give me a little help here because-er-I-er-I'm-er-er-h-h-having a-a-a real problem-er-right now and I-er-if somebody could help me out it would-it would-er-er s-s-sure be-sure be good . . . because-er-there-er-er-ag cause I-er-I-uh-I've got a-a one of the-er-sei — er-er-things coming on and-and-and I could really-er-use some help so if somebody would-er-give me a little h-help-uh-er-er-er-er c-ould somebody-er-er-help-er-uh-uh-uh (choking sounds). . . . I'm gonna die-er-er-I'm . . . gonna die-er-help-er-er-seizure-er (chokes, then quiet). (Latané & Darley, 1970, pp. 95–96)

Clearly, the speaker was in trouble and needed immediate help. Did subjects help? How quickly?

As you may already suspect, subjects in this experiment were really listening to a tape recording of a simulated seizure. Latané and Darley systematically varied the size of the discussion groups — sometimes a subject thought only he or she and the seizure victim were having a discussion; sometimes a subject thought there was one other participant; and sometimes a subject thought there were four others. Just as in the smoke-filled room study, the number of other bystanders dramatically affected subjects' helping behavior. Again, the results showed that the presence of more people led to less helping (see Figure 13.4).

FIGURE 13.3   Cumulative percentages of subjects responding
in different conditions to smoke pouring into the room.

What effect does the presence of other people have on our response to a possible emergency?

In this study by Latané and Darley (1970) subjects sat in a
room either alone, with two other subjects, or with two
passive confederates. As they completed questionnaires,
smoke began pouring into the room through an air vent.
The researchers measured how quickly subjects sought help
or reported the emergency.

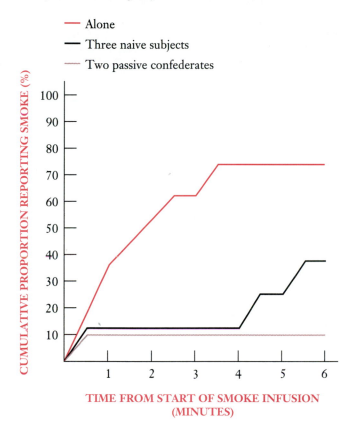

As the graph shows, single subjects were much more likely
to seek help, and they responded to the possible emergency
more quickly.

SOURCE: Adapted from Latané and Darley, *The Unresponsive Bystander.* © 1970.
Used with permission of Prentice-Hall, Inc.

Note the strength of the bystander effect in this study:
Only a minority of subjects sought help when others were present.

■■■

FIGURE 13.4   Cumulative percentages of subjects responding
               to an epileptic seizure under different conditions.

*Does the bystander effect occur in an unambiguous emergency
involving a suffering human victim?*

Latané and Darley (1970) had subjects communicate via a
microphone with another student in a nearby room. Subjects
believed there were no, one, or four other people listening in
on the conversation. Partway through the experiment, the
other student seemed to experience an epileptic seizure. The
researchers observed how quickly subjects helped the victim.

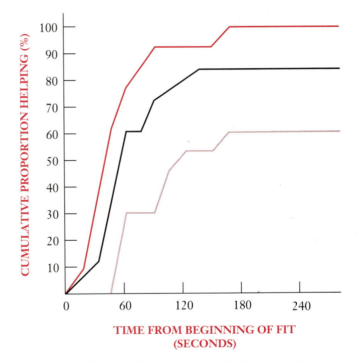

— Subject and victim

— Subject, victim, and stranger

— Subject, victim, and 4 strangers

As the graph shows, subjects were more likely to help the
victim of the seizure when they were the only person participating in the conversation. All subjects who believed that they
were alone when they heard the seizure aided the victim within
three minutes; however, not all subjects in the other two conditions aided the victim.

SOURCE: Adapted from Latané and Darley, *The Unresponsive Bystander.* © 1970.
Used with permission of Prentice-Hall, Inc.

*As the text notes, all subjects in this experiment tended to be quite upset
by the emergency, so subjects' inaction could not be explained as being due to apathy.*

■■■

Because the emergency in the epileptic seizure study was unambiguous, the presence of other people could not be influencing subjects' definition of the situation. Indeed, most seemed to grasp the problem immediately. Some subjects gasped to themselves, "My God, he's having a fit!"

Latané and Darley argued that under these circumstances the presence of other people influenced the third stage of the decision process: The presence of others in the emergency situation led to a *diffusion of responsibility* whereby each person felt less personally responsible for dealing with the emergency.

It is important to note that whether they were alone or in groups, subjects in the epileptic seizure study were not apathetic. Both those who helped and those who failed to help seemed upset. Indeed, subjects who did not intervene often seemed more aroused, showing physical signs of nervousness (trembling hands and sweaty palms). Their inaction can partly be explained by the notion of diffusion of responsibility and partly by subjects' fear of appearing foolish or overly emotional in the eyes of those present.

The epileptic seizure study says something potentially quite important about the Kitty Genovese case: People may have been frozen into inaction *because of* their awareness of other bystanders. Kitty's neighbors may have been victims of social influence more than of "bystander apathy." One practical moral of Latané and Darley's research is "Never assume others have responded to an emergency; always act as if you were the only person present."

The bystander effect turns out to be remarkably robust. By the early 1980s over 50 studies had investigated the effects of bystanders on helping, and a clear majority showed that people help more when alone than when with others (Latané, Nida, & Wilson, 1981). Thus the social setting can have a profound effect on individuals' behavior in emergencies.

Emotional arousal and perceived cost as factors.

Latané and Darley's decision model focuses largely on cognitive processes. Piliavin, Dovidio, Gaertner, and Clark (1981) formulated another model that in some ways extends and complements Latané and Darley's model (see Figure 13.5). One central feature added to this newer, fairly complex, model is bystanders' arousal during an emergency. (We already have some evidence of subjects' upset from the epileptic seizure study.) Piliavin and her colleagues (1981) argued that there is a strong emotional as well as cognitive component to helping in emergencies.

Many research studies support the notion that emergencies are physiologically arousing. For example, in one series of studies, subjects watched a TV screen as a woman in the next room climbed onto a chair to set up a projection screen (Byeff, 1970; Piliavin, Piliavin, & Trudell, 1974; both cited in Piliavin et al., 1981). Suddenly, the woman appeared to fall over, out of the range of the TV camera, and subjects heard a loud crashing sound. Exposure to this emergency increased subjects' heart rates and galvanic skin responses (a measure of skin conductivity and thus of perspiration).

In experiments in which subjects must face an emergency, there is often a correlation between subjects' degree of arousal and their degree of helping. For example, in one study (Gaertner & Dovidio, 1977) women overheard a female victim scream when a stack of chairs apparently fell on top of her. The correlation between subjects' heart rate increase and the amount of time they waited before intervening was $-.58$. That is, the more physiologically aroused the women were by the accident, the more quickly they helped the victim.

*What factors lead individuals to intervene in emergencies,
and what are the causal links among factors?*

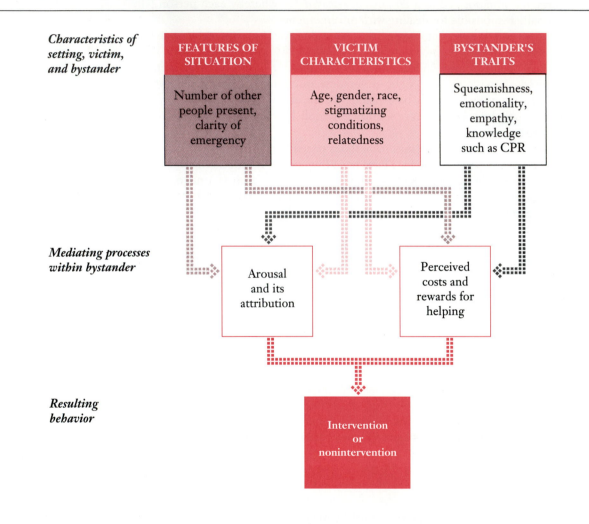

*Characteristics of
setting, victim,
and bystander*

**FEATURES OF
SITUATION**

Number of other
people present,
clarity of
emergency

**VICTIM
CHARACTERISTICS**

Age, gender, race,
stigmatizing
conditions,
relatedness

**BYSTANDER'S
TRAITS**

Squeamishness,
emotionality,
empathy,
knowledge
such as CPR

*Mediating processes
within bystander*

Arousal
and its
attribution

Perceived
costs and
rewards for
helping

*Resulting
behavior*

**Intervention
or
nonintervention**

*The version of Piliavin, Dovidio, Gaertner, and Clark's model presented here, although
somewhat simplified, still suggests the complexity of factors influencing emergency interventions. Imagine that while walking across campus you see a student collapse. You are likely to
experience more arousal if the emergency is unambiguous (the student is bleeding profusely),
the victim is a friend, and you are empathetic and squeamish. The more bystanders are
present, the less aroused you may be and the less costly you may perceive nonintervention to
be. Your squeamishness increases your arousal, but it also increases the costs of aiding a
bleeding victim. Thus, whether you help is determined by a complex interplay of factors.*

▪▪▪

FIGURE 13.6   Piliavin and Piliavin's (1972) cost analysis of emergency intervention.

How do perceived costs for helping and not helping affect our willingness to intervene in an emergency?

Piliavin and Piliavin (1972) propose that a moderately aroused bystander to an emergency assesses the costs of helping and not helping before deciding whether to intervene. The table below predicts what a bystander is most likely to do in an emergency when the costs for helping are low or high and the costs for not helping are low or high.

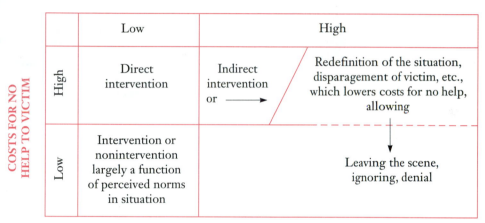

COSTS FOR DIRECT HELP TO VICTIM

		Low	High	
COSTS FOR NO HELP TO VICTIM	High	Direct intervention	Indirect intervention or ⟶	Redefinition of the situation, disparagement of victim, etc., which lowers costs for no help, allowing
	Low	Intervention or nonintervention largely a function of perceived norms in situation		Leaving the scene, ignoring, denial

SOURCE: Adapted from Piliavin and Piliavin (1972). Used with permission of Jane Piliavin.

▪▪▪

Sometimes, though, it is easier for people to avoid an emergency situation than it is to help. What determines when arousal leads a person to help and when it leads him or her to flee? According to Piliavin and Piliavin (1972), the answer involves a cost analysis of the situation. Figure 13.6 presents four possible emergency situations defined by two cost factors: the cost for not helping the victim and the cost for directly helping.

To make this a bit clearer, imagine you watch as a man slips and falls into a river. If you know that this man is frail and can't swim and that the water is ice-cold, then the costs of not helping are very high — he'll probably drown, and you'll experience terrible guilt as well as social censure. If the man is an expert swimmer and the water warm, the costs of not helping are much lower. The costs of directly helping may also vary: If there's a rope and a life preserver on the river bank, you have a low-cost means of helping available. On the other hand, if the water is icy, the river currents treacherous, and you must dive in to rescue the man, then direct intervention is costly indeed.

Now look again at the cost analysis presented in Figure 13.6. If the costs of not helping are high (the drowning man will die) and the costs of helping are low (you

The bystander effect: Did the presence of many people increase or decrease the chances that this man would receive help?

can throw him a life preserver), then you will probably help. If the costs of not helping are low (the man is a good swimmer and the water warm) and the costs of helping are also low (you can throw the life preserver), then your helping will depend on situationally appropriate norms. For example, if the man is your employee, you might help because of the norms of reciprocity or social responsibility.

If the costs of not helping are high (the man will die) and the costs of helping are also high (you have to dive into treacherous, icy water), you face a dilemma. You might choose some "indirect intervention" (for example, calling the police), or you might engage in cognitive defenses that redefine the situation or disparage the victim ("The man's a member of the Polar Bear Club and knows how to swim in icy water," or "He's a worthless drug addict who deserves to die"). Finally, if the costs for not helping are low (the man can swim and somebody else seems about to help, so the man probably won't die) and the costs for helping are high (treacherous, icy water), you may decide simply to leave the scene.

A number of studies support the general notion that costs affect helping. For example, in one experiment Piliavin and Piliavin (1972) had confederates—men walking with canes—collapse on Philadelphia subways. Sometimes the victim had fake blood trickling from his mouth after falling (which presumably increased the costs of helping because most people find blood repellent); other times he did not. The unbloodied victim was helped more often and more quickly than the bloody victim. In one trial two teenage girls saw the victim collapse and got up to help him. Upon seeing the blood, one girl said, "Oh, he's bleeding!" And both girls promptly sat down.

In another study, subjects witnessed a realistic fight between a man and a woman on an elevator (Shotland & Straw, 1976). In one experimental condition the woman and man were perceived as strangers (the woman screamed, "Get away from me. I don't know you"); in the other condition they were portrayed as married ("Get away

A man without legs is ignored by passers-by. When will people help others? When won't they?

from me. I don't know why I ever married you"). Thirteen of 20 subjects — well over half — intervened in the "stranger" fight, whereas only four of 20 intervened in the "married" fight.

Shotland and Straw interpreted this large difference in terms of perceived costs. Indeed, subjects who were shown videotapes of the fights perceived the woman in the "stranger" fight to be in greater danger (thus there was higher cost for not helping), and they also perceived that if they intervened, the combatants were more likely to turn on them in the "married" fight (higher cost for helping) than in the "stranger" fight. Thus the costs for not helping and the costs for helping were quite different for the two kinds of fights.

The principle that higher costs mean less help applies to all kinds of helping, not just emergency interventions. Allen (1968, cited in Latané & Darley, 1970) illustrated this in a clever experiment in which a bewildered-looking man on a New York subway asked a man reading a body-building magazine whether the subway was going "uptown" or "downtown." (Both of these participants were confederates.) The body-builder then responded with the wrong answer. In this "control" situation 50 percent of bystanders on the subway intervened and corrected the mistaken information.

Then Allen modified the experimental conditions to dramatically increase the perceived costs of helping. A minute before the bewildered rider asked for directions, another subway passenger (again, a confederate) stumbled over the body-builder's legs. In one condition the body-builder shouted threats at the stumbler, and in another he made embarrassing comments about the stumbler. Would you contradict the body-builder now when he gives incorrect directions to the hapless man? Figure 13.7 shows that few people did.

If the costs of helping are *too* great, people may reduce their arousal by actually fleeing. In one study, residents of Cambridge, Massachusetts, witnessed either an

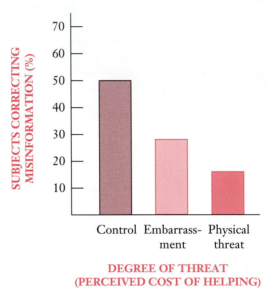

FIGURE 13.7   Helping a subway rider given wrong information, as a function of costs.

Do costs affect helping in nonemergency settings?

Allen (1968) observed how often bystanders in a subway corrected wrong information given by a confederate who, moments earlier, had either threatened another passenger, embarrassed another passenger, or, in the control condition, not interacted with another passenger.

SUBJECTS CORRECTING MISINFORMATION (%)

DEGREE OF THREAT
(PERCEIVED COST OF HELPING)

The results clearly showed that the more threatening the confederate had been, the less willing bystanders were to "cross his path" and correct the false information. Thus, the more costly helping seems to be, the less likely we are to offer it.

apparent knee injury (a man grabs his knee and falls to the ground) or a heart attack (a man grabs his chest and falls to the ground) as they walked down the street. Surprisingly, subjects helped the "knee injury" victim more than they helped the "heart attack" victim (Staub, 1974). Perhaps the costs of dealing with the heart attack victim were simply too great for many people — "I don't know what to do. He may die while I'm there. What if somebody sues me?" Some people actively tried to avoid or escape the situation by averting their gaze or crossing to the other side of the street. Seeing someone suffer is painful, so if helping is too costly we may assume a "see no evil" stance.

Misattribution of arousal.   There is another way in which cognitions can mediate the impact of arousal on helping—namely, through attributions. As we discussed in Chapter 4, people sometimes misattribute the causes of their emotional arousal, particularly if the source of their arousal is somewhat ambiguous in the first place (Nisbett & Schachter, 1966).

Gaertner and Dovidio (1977) conducted an experiment in which some subjects were led to misattribute their arousal during an emergency. Subjects were falsely told that they were participating in a study on how ESP is affected by specific drugs. They were then given a pill (actually a placebo) and informed that the drug might have some side effects. Half the subjects were told it might increase their heart rate, whereas the other half were told it might give them a dull headache.

While participating in the "ESP experiment," subjects heard the sounds of a woman moving around in the next room and then what sounded like a stack of chairs falling on her. To vary the ambiguity of this emergency, sometimes the victim screamed and sometimes she did not. The researchers measured how quickly subjects ran to her aid (see Figure 13.8). In the ambiguous emergency (without screams), subjects helped less when they could "explain away" their arousal as being due to the pill they had taken recently. This study provides additional evidence that arousal plays a role in motivating helping.

Pure altruism: Fact or fantasy?   Thus far our social psychological analysis of helping has not included the possibility of pure altruism. People help because they're aroused and upset, and they strive to reduce their arousal. Sometimes they accomplish this by helping others, sometimes by fleeing. In general, people seem to help because it allows them to avoid costs and gain rewards (whether external or internal). And sometimes people help others to display their virtue and heroism to a public audience. But none of this is pure altruism.

Recently, C. Daniel Batson (1987; also see Hoffman, 1976) has argued that indeed people sometimes show true altruistic concern for others. In essence, Batson proposes that a person can experience two kinds of upset upon witnessing a suffering victim—personal distress (general, unpleasant arousal that the person wants to reduce however possible) and empathy (compassion, sympathetic concern). Personal distress can be reduced by fleeing from a victim, but true empathy will not be satisfied by flight.

This distinction between an uncaring, egocentric arousal and a more caring, loving concern is illustrated well by a disturbing scene in the documentary film, "Shoah," which features interviews of people who participated in and survived the Nazi holocaust. An elderly German woman recounts her memories of a small Polish town in which Jews were herded together in a church and then forced into vans, where they were gassed with automotive exhaust. She protests that she suffered too; she had to listen to the screams of dying men, women, and children. If she could have escaped from those screams, she implies, everything would have been fine. Clearly, this woman experienced "personal distress," but not "empathy."

Is it possible to distinguish empathy from personal distress in an experiment? Batson and his colleagues (1981) devised a clever situation to do just that. Female subjects were asked to watch a college woman named Elaine over closed-circuit TV as she received electric shocks in a learning experiment. (Actually, subjects watched a prepared videotape.) As the experiment progressed, Elaine seemed to show extreme distress in response to the shocks. When the experimenter paused to check on her,

FIGURE 13.8   Misattribution of arousal and speed of helping
in ambiguous or unambiguous emergencies.

How do attributions of arousal affect our behavior in emergency situations?

In Gaertner and Dovidio's (1977) experiment, subjects sat in a room and heard what sounded like a stack of chairs falling on a woman in the next room. Sometimes the emergency was unambiguous (the woman screamed), and sometimes it was ambiguous (no scream). Subjects had earlier taken a pill (a placebo); some were told that it might increase their heart rate, and some were not. Gaertner and Dovidio measured how quickly subjects responded to the possible emergency in the next room.

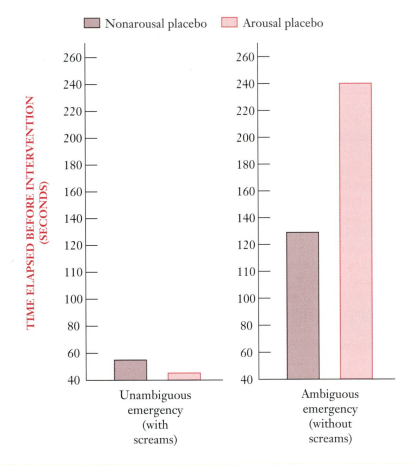

Overall, subjects responded more slowly to the ambiguous emergency. Furthermore, subjects exposed to the ambiguous emergency responded even less quickly when they could misattribute their arousal to the pill.

SOURCE: Data from Gaertner and Dovidio (1977).

Elaine explained that as a child she had fallen against an electric fence, which had left her very sensitive to electric shocks. The researcher then proposed a solution: Perhaps the subject watching Elaine over closed-circuit TV would consent to changing places with her. The experimenter then entered the subject's room and asked her if she were willing to trade places with Elaine. Subjects who agreed to changing places were showing altruism toward Elaine, at some cost to themselves (they would now have to receive the electric shocks).

Batson and his colleagues (1981) assumed that all subjects would feel personal distress in this experiment; they experimentally manipulated the degree of "empathy" subjects would feel for Elaine. Some subjects learned that they and Elaine had answered an attitude and interest questionnaire quite similarly; this was the "high-empathy" group. Others (the "low-empathy" group) learned that they and Elaine had answered dissimilarly. The ease with which subjects could escape from Elaine's suffering was also manipulated: Some subjects (in the "easy-escape" condition) were told they would no longer have to watch Elaine, whereas others (in the "difficult-escape" condition) were told they must continue to watch. (The four experimental conditions are shown in Figure 13.9.)

Subjects who knew they would have to keep watching Elaine should have been motivated to help by personal distress, but subjects who knew they would no longer have to watch did not have that motivation. However, the subjects who felt empathy for Elaine would still have reason to help, for they were honestly concerned with her well-being. Only members of the "easy-escape, low-empathy" group had no motivation to help and thus were not expected to be very altruistic. This is exactly what the data showed (see Figure 13.9).

In a replication of the "Elaine study," Batson and his colleagues (1988) told subjects that before they could receive shocks in Elaine's place, they had to take a qualifying test that assessed their "numeric recall" ability. Intriguingly, highly empathetic subjects (as assessed by a self-report questionnaire) earned the highest scores on this test, particularly when they were informed that the score needed to qualify was quite high. Remember, a high score would qualify them to receive shocks in Elaine's place, and they could easily avoid getting these shocks by simply reducing their effort on the test.

Thus, empathetic people sometimes help even when they can conveniently escape another's suffering and can provide a reasonable excuse for not helping. Such people help because they are genuinely concerned about another. Although Batson (1987) believes that people can be motivated by pure altruism, he also notes that such "emotion may be a fragile flower, easily crushed by overriding egoistic concerns" (p. 109).

▪▪▪▪▪▪▪▪▪▪▪▪▪▪▪▪▪▪▪▪▪▪▪▪▪

Guilt, Moods, and Helping

"And what other ordeals do you have in your world . . . ?" Ivan asked with peculiar eagerness.

"What ordeals? Ah, I wish you hadn't asked me that. Before, we had all kinds, but nowadays they are mostly of a moral nature, like a guilty conscience and all that sort of nonsense. . . . Of course, the principal beneficiaries are those who have no conscience at all and so obviously cannot be tormented by guilt. On the other hand, the decent ones, who still have a conscience and a sense of honor, suffer the most. . . . The good old hell fire was much better . . ."

—— *The Brothers Karamazov*, pp. 774–775

FIGURE 13.9   **Willingness to help a suffering victim as a function
of empathy and ability to escape.**

Do people ever show pure altruism?

Batson and his colleagues (1981) gave subjects the opportunity to
receive shocks in place of a woman who feared receiving shocks.
Some subjects believed they would continue to view the woman as
she received her shocks ("difficult-escape" condition), and others
believed they would not have to view her ("easy-escape" condition).
Some subjects were led to believe they shared similar values and
interests with the woman ("high-empathy" condition) and others that
they did not ("low-empathy" condition). The researchers assessed
the proportion of subjects in each condition who "altruistically"
volunteered to receive shocks in place of the frightened woman.

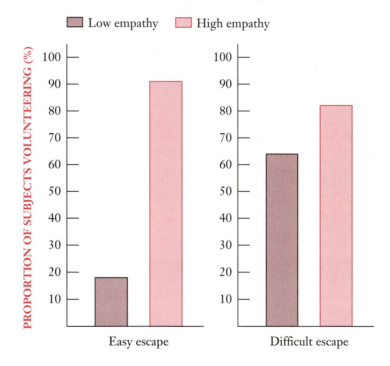

Subjects who had to continue viewing the woman ("difficult-escape"
condition) were likely to volunteer to substitute for her. Presumably,
this was the only way they could reduce their arousal. In the "easy-
escape" condition, only the "high-empathy" subjects were likely to
volunteer to receive shocks in place of the woman. Because these
subjects could escape from viewing the woman's suffering, they
presumably volunteered not simply to reduce their arousal, but also
because of honest concern about the woman's well-being.

SOURCE: Data from Batson et al. (1981).

"I find there's a lot of pressure to be good."

The hallucinated devil in Ivan Karamazov's nightmare makes a telling point: Sometimes people behave "morally" because of external rewards and punishments (such as the threat of "hell fire") and sometimes because of internal emotional states (such as a "guilty conscience"). Let's turn to research on the effects of guilt and other temporary emotional states on helping.

Guilt.   According to *The American Heritage Dictionary*, guilt is "remorseful awareness of having done something wrong." This definition implies two things: Guilt occurs when we believe we have committed a moral transgression, and it is unpleasant. Equity theory provides one analysis (Walster, Walster, & Berscheid, 1978): Guilt occurs when we "give" too little and "get" too much in a relationship. Imagine, for example, that you are married to an ideal spouse who showers you with love, attention, and material gifts. If you are lazy, indifferent, and not "giving" in return, you may very well feel guilty. We may also feel guilty when we lie, unfairly criticize, or accidentally injure others — that is, when we break rules of conventional morality.

Social psychology experiments repeatedly demonstrate that guilt can motivate helping: Once people have been induced to do something wrong (such as break an experimenter's apparatus, cheat on an experimental task, break a rule, or lie), they are significantly more willing to help the experimenter, and others as well (Carlsmith & Gross, 1969; Wallace & Sadalla, 1966; McMillen, 1971; Silverman, Rivera, & Tedeschi, 1979; Katzev, Edelsack, Steinmetz, Walker, & Wright, 1978).

For example, in one clever experiment (Regan, Williams, & Sparling, 1972) a confederate approached individual women at a shopping center and asked them to take a picture of him with his camera. Unfortunately for these helpful women, the camera was designed to break. In the "guilt" condition of the experiment, the confederate suggested that it was the woman's fault that the camera broke, whereas in a "nonguilt" condition the confederate reassured the woman that she was not to blame, that the camera frequently "acted up." A little while later the same women encountered another confederate whose grocery bag had ripped open, scattering candy on the ground. Fifty-five percent of the guilty subjects helped, but only 15 percent of the nonguilty subjects helped.

In a conceptually similar study (Katzev et al., 1978), experimenters reprimanded some visitors to the Portland Zoo who, in violation of posted rules, fed food to the bears. To arouse guilt, they scolded, "Hey, don't feed unauthorized food to the animals. Don't you know it could hurt them?" Later, subjects passed a confederate who had dropped his belongings on the ground. Fifty-eight percent of the reprimanded subjects offered help, as compared to under a third of nonreprimanded transgressors.

These two studies suggest some important points about guilt and helping. First, people seem to feel particularly guilty about a "bad" act when they are forced to assume responsibility for it: The people who fed the bears but weren't scolded clearly did not feel as guilty as the scolded people. Second, people may relieve their guilt by aiding someone who is not the original victim of their transgression.

Doing good for people who are not the victims of your wrongdoing is somewhat puzzling from the perspective of equity theory, for such helping does not "balance the scales" unbalanced by the original transgression; it does not right the original wrong or recompense the original victim. Of course, some people may believe in divine scales of equity that need to be balanced and may hold that God records all our sinful and virtuous deeds, justly rewarding or punishing us in an afterlife (Lerner & Meindl, 1981).

Sadly, it may be impossible for us to make direct amends for our wrongdoings in every case. Sometimes a transgression cannot be undone (murdering someone or "cheating" on a spouse), and sometimes our victims are no longer available to receive compensation (your victim moves to a faraway city). If a transgression is major, even doing good deeds for others may not fully relieve guilt.

Thus many societies have devised ways for dealing with unbearable guilt. The ancient Hebrews practiced a ritual whereby people could symbolically lay their sins upon a "scapegoat," an animal which was then released into the wilderness, carrying the community's transgressions with it. Confessions too provide a way to vent guilty feelings. Interestingly, experimental studies suggest that confessing a wrongdoing in fact reduces guilt, for people who have just confessed help less than those who haven't. In a clever field study, Harris, Benson, and Hall (1975) showed that people leaving a Catholic church, presumably after confession, showed less helping than did people entering the church.

Bad moods and helping.   Do negative moods other than guilt affect helping? Suppose you're sad because of a tragic accident you just saw on the nightly news, or depressed because you just failed an exam. Are you more or less likely to be helpful after such an event?

The research evidence is mixed. Hornstein and his colleagues (1975) had subjects listen to either an uplifting or a depressing news story on the radio and then participate in a game in which they could either cooperate or compete with others.

Subjects exposed to depressing news tended to be more competitive and less cooperative. Further research has suggested that bad news leads to less helping because it leads subjects to see people in general as bad and undeserving of help (Holloway, Tucker, & Hornstein, 1977; Veitch, DeWood, & Bosko, 1977). Sadness too can depress helping; studies have found that saddened subjects are less helpful than control subjects (Moore, Underwood, & Rosenhan, 1973; Weyant, 1978).

To complicate the research picture, however, other studies have shown that negative moods can sometimes increase helping. For example, Isen and her colleagues (1973) observed that subjects led to believe that they had failed at an experimental task helped more than did control subjects.

When do negative moods increase helping and when do they decrease helping? One possibility is that individuals are more likely to be helpful after negative or embarrassing experiences when they are being observed by others; they then behave in helpful, "altruistic" ways to repair their damaged public image. A study by Kenrick, Baumann, and Cialdini (1979) showed this effect clearly. School children in grades 1 through 3 were first put in a bad mood (by being asked to reminisce about a sad experience) and were then given an opportunity to help other children. Sometimes, an adult was present and sometimes not. The children put in a bad mood were more helpful than control children only when the adult was present. Thus they seemed to behave helpfully to receive public admiration and reinforcement.

Adults may differ from children in that they internalize the reward of doing good deeds (Cialdini, Darby, & Vincent, 1973; Cialdini, Schaller, Houlihan, Arps, Fultz, & Beaman, 1987); thus adults in a negative mood may help specifically to boost their mood (not just to appear good to others). To test this hypothesis Cialdini and Kenrick (1976) created sad or neutral moods in school children from three different age groups — grades 1–3, grades 5–7, and grades 10–12. As part of the experiment, children had the opportunity to share coupons, which they could trade for prizes, with other students. The results (see Figure 13.10) clearly showed that a sad mood increased the generosity of older but not of younger students.

Thus Cialdini and his colleagues argue that adults in a bad mood most often help others for a self-serving reason — to improve their own mood. This negative-mood–relief model may help to explain the relationships between guilt and helping, and between empathy-produced sadness and helping (Cialdini et al., 1987). It implies that if sad people get a mood boost from another source (such as hearing a funny story or finding some money), then they will have no need to help another person. Sadly, a number of experiments (Cialdini et al., 1973; Cunningham, Steinberg, & Greu, 1980) support this hypothesis. Thus, a sad person may be a rainy-day helper (if he can thereby boost his morale) but a fair-weather nonhelper.

Good moods and helping.   Although the research on bad moods and helping has some subtle twists, the research on good moods and helping is much more clear-cut: Good moods consistently lead to more helping and prosocial behavior. For example, the happiness created when subjects learn they've succeeded at a task (Isen, 1970), received small gifts of money or food (Isen & Levin, 1972), remembered happy events in their lives (Moore et al., 1973), and experienced nice weather (Cunningham, 1979) leads to greater helping.

Why do positive moods lead to helping? One possibility is that positive moods stimulate positive thoughts in general (Isen, 1987); if other people are seen as "nice," "honest," and "decent," then clearly they deserve to be helped. Another possibility

FIGURE 13.10   Helping behavior as a function of age and negative or neutral moods.

Do we help others to improve our own mood?

Cialdini and Kenrick (1976) induced students in three different age groups to experience either negative or neutral moods. Students were then given the opportunity to share valuable coupons with other students.

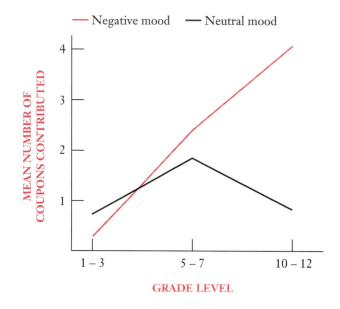

A negative mood led to increased sharing in older but not younger children.

SOURCE: Adapted from Cialdini and Kenrick (1976). Used with permission of Robert Cialdini.

By implication, older children and adults have internalized social rules about the virtue of prosocial behavior, and so engaging in helpful behavior is internally rewarding. According to Cialdini and Kenrick, adults may help others when in a negative mood to obtain a self-reward and thereby boost their morale. This is a subtly selfish motivation to help.

is that happy people are not as self-focused as sad people (see Chapter 6), and the more you focus your attention on others, the more you should be sensitive to their needs (McMillen, Sander, & Solomon, 1977).

Unfortunately, the "warm glow" that leads people to help more after a happy event may be quite transient. In one study by Alice Isen and her colleagues (1976), subjects who had just received a free gift (stationery) received a phone call from a confederate, who said that she had reached the wrong number and had just spent her last dime at a payphone. The confederate asked whether the subject would help her

▪▪

SUMMARY TABLE 13.1   Explanations of Helping Behavior

How have social scientists explained altruism and prosocial behavior?

	KIND OF EXPLANATION	VARIABLES/PROCESSES STUDIED	RESEARCH QUESTIONS AND TOPICS
Group-level explanations	Biological groups	Biological evolution	Kin selection, reciprocal altruism
	Cultural groups	Cultural norms	Norms of reciprocity, equity, and social responsibility
Individual-level explanations	Past environment	Modeling, learning	Development of prosocial behavior; media effects
	Current environment	Modeling	Effect of prosocial models; media effects
		Bystander effect	Effect of presence of other bystanders
Mediating variables	Cognitive processes and decision making	Latané and Darley's five-stage model	When will people help in emergencies?
		Piliavin and Piliavin's cost analysis	
	Others	Personality traits	Consistency of altruistic behavior across settings
		Arousal and emotion misattribution	When does emotional arousal lead to helping?
		Guilt	When and why does guilt motivate helping?
		Bad moods	When and why do bad moods motivate helping?
		Good moods	Why do good moods motivate helping? How long does the effect last?
		Empathy	Do people ever show pure altruism?

out by making a phone call for her. Subjects experiencing the "warm glow" of recently receiving a free gift were quite helpful — 60–100 percent of subjects in two separate studies made the requested call when asked to do so in the first few minutes after receiving their gift. But this helpfulness faded quickly; when subjects were called 20 minutes after receiving their gift, under 20 percent complied with the request.

The different explanations of helping behavior that we have discussed are reviewed in Summary Table 13.1.

Receiving Help: A Mixed Blessing?

A major assumption made in this chapter has been that giving help is good. But is it good to receive help? A number of social psychological theories predict that receiving help can be a source of pain as well as pleasure.

For example, equity and exchange theories (Adams, 1965; Walster et al., 1978) propose that people want a fair "give and take" in their relationships. Thus, if someone helps you too much, you may feel indebted to him or her, which is clearly uncomfortable. As the Roman historian Tacitus noted, "Benefits are only acceptable so far as they seem capable of being requited; beyond that point, they excite hatred instead of gratitude."

Sometimes people give aid in order to exert control over others. For example, parents may give an allowance so that they can then threaten their disobedient child with cutting it off. And a nation may give "foreign aid" to other nations with the ulterior motive of influencing their policies and extracting favors in return (Gergen & Gergen, 1971). Reactance theory (Brehm, 1966; Brehm & Brehm, 1981) states that people are unhappy whenever they believe their freedom of choice is being limited by others. Thus if help is seen as an attempt to influence behavior, people may very well dislike it.

Finally, receiving aid from others may be unpleasant because it signals some inadequacy on the part of the recipient and thus threatens self-esteem (Fisher, Nadler, & Whitcher-Alagner, 1982). People often believe, for example, that students require help in their studies only when they aren't "getting it" on their own; that workers require help at work when they are not performing adequately; and that people require therapeutic help only when their lives and relationships are not functioning properly. To some people, accepting help is an admission of failure, particularly if others do not also seem to need such help (Tessler & Schwartz, 1972; Gross, Wallson, & Piliavin, 1979).

Although it might seem consistent with common sense that people most appreciate help when they are most in need of it, research does not support this "obvious" conclusion (Calhoun, Dawes, & Lewis, 1972; Franklin, 1975; Morse & Gergen, 1971). People may reject sorely needed help for several reasons: It may be viewed as particularly obligating (your helper can later say, "You ingrate, I helped you when you were at rock bottom!"); it may very strongly restrict the recipient's freedom of choice ("I have no choice—I must go on welfare and put up with all their demeaning rules and regulations"); and finally, it may be particularly damaging to self-esteem ("I'm accepting this help because I'm really desperate").

What kinds of people find aid most threatening? Men often feel less comfortable receiving help than women do (Hoffman, 1972; Gourash, 1978). In a related vein, stereotypically feminine people are more likely to be comfortable seeking help, whereas stereotypically masculine people are likely to be less comfortable under such circumstances (DePaulo, 1978; see Chapter 10 for a broader discussion of femininity and masculinity).

Cultural rules also play a role in reactions to receiving help. Fisher, DePaulo, and Nadler (1981) noted that "people in Western cultures are taught that independence is a virtue and that dependence is shameful" (p. 418). Communal societies seem to encourage both offering and receiving help more than do individualistic societies. In one illustrative study (Nadler, 1986), kibbutz (Israeli collective-farm) dwellers reported that they would be more willing to seek help (for example, in schoolwork) than did Israeli city dwellers. When given an intellectual task, kibbutz dwellers in fact sought more aid when it was presented as a group task, and city dwellers sought more aid when it was an individual task; this pattern was particularly pronounced for male subjects. Thus situational variables in conjunction with culturally learned rules can influence when people seek help.

In sum, although it may be godly to give, it is often uncomfortable to receive. The discomfort caused by receiving aid depends on the recipient's ability to reciprocate, the "strings attached" to aid, how much aid is needed, and the recipient's cultural background, gender, and personality. One final note: Offering help in an emergency is unlikely to trigger resentment. It is help offered in the normal "give and take" of everyday life that is most problematic.

"... Let us first of all be kind and then honest. ..."

"You know, boys," Alyosha said, "you needn't be afraid of life! Life is so good when you do something that is good and just."

—— *The Brothers Karamazov*, p. 936

In the last pages of *The Brothers Karamazov*, the spiritual, altruistic Alyosha counsels a group of Russian schoolboys to do good deeds. He wants to encourage prosocial behavior in his charges.

This chapter has described numerous factors that influence helping and altruism, and of course, all of these factors may have consequences for increasing or decreasing prosocial behavior. Let's conclude by considering four common techniques to increase helping behavior: (1) moral exhortation (verbally urging others to help and to live according to moral principles), (2) providing prosocial models, (3) heightening feelings of responsibility for people needing help, and (4) individuating and personalizing those needing help.

Exhortation

Moralists of all persuasions (including Alyosha Karamazov) have reminded people to show compassion for others and to love their neighbors. Unfortunately, however, simple exhortation — as in parental lectures and religious sermons — is not a particularly powerful way to foster prosocial behaviors. After all, exhortation is aimed at reminding people of norms of prosocial behavior. But social psychological research shows that helping is often influenced more by features of the social situation (the number of bystanders present, the costs of helping, or the ease of escape from a suffering victim) than by social norms.

A dramatic experiment by John Darley and C. Daniel Batson (1973) powerfully demonstrated how situational pressures can overwhelm salient moral principles. Forty students at Princeton's Theological Seminary were subjects in a study that supposedly dealt with "the vocational careers of seminary students." The seminary students were asked to deliver a talk in a nearby university building to assess "how well they could think on their feet." Half of the students were asked to speak about "jobs in which seminary students would be most effective." The others were asked to talk about the parable of the Good Samaritan.

Here is the parable:

A man was going down from Jerusalem to Jericho, and he fell among robbers, who stripped him and beat him, and departed, leaving him half dead. Now by chance a priest was going down the road; and when he saw him he passed by on the other side. So likewise a Levite, when he came to the place and saw him, passed by on the other side. But a Samaritan, as he journeyed, came to where he was; and when he saw him, he had compassion, and went to him and bound his wounds, pouring on oil and wine; then he set him on his own beast and brought him to an inn, and took care of him. And the next day he took out two dennarii and gave them to the innkeeper, saying, "Take care of him; and whatever more you spend, I will repay you when I come back." Which of these three, do you think proved neighbor to him who fell among the robbers? He said, "The one who showed mercy on him." And Jesus said, . . . "Go and do likewise." (Luke 10: 29–37)

Darley and Batson also manipulated how rushed subjects were. In a "high-hurry" condition, the students were told, "Oh, you're late. They were expecting you a few minutes ago. You'd better get moving." In an "intermediate-hurry" condition, subjects were told, "The assistant is ready for you, so please go over," whereas in a "low-hurry" condition, subjects were informed, "It'll be a few minutes before they're ready for you, but you might as well head on over."

On the way to the appointment, each seminary student passed an alley in which a confederate was sitting, slumped over, with his eyes closed. The instant the student passed by, the confederate coughed twice, groaned, and kept his head down. Clearly he needed help!

Were students assigned to talk about the Good Samaritan more likely to help than the others? This result would make sense. After all, these students were preparing to discuss one of the most famous of all biblical injunctions to help a victim in need, so helping should have been highly salient to them. Yet the topic of students' talks did not significantly influence whether or not they helped the man in distress. The hurry manipulation, however, was highly significant: 63 percent of the low-hurry students, 45 percent of the intermediate-hurry students, and only 10 percent of the high-hurry students helped the distressed man. Overall, only 40 percent of the seminary students offered any kind of aid to the victim.

The irony of these results was not lost on Darley and Batson (1973):

A person not in a hurry may stop and offer help to a person in distress. A person in a hurry is likely to keep going. . . . He is likely to keep going even if he is hurrying to speak on the parable of the Good Samaritan, thus inadvertently confirming the point of the parable. (Indeed, on several occasions, a seminary student going to give his talk on the parable of the Good Samaritan literally stepped over the victim as he hurried on his way!) (p. 107)

It is easy to view these students as hypocrites who did not practice what they preached, but this interpretation is too simplistic. Some of the hurried subjects did not seem even to notice the victim because their attention was focused so narrowly on their immediate goal. Those who did notice the victim were placed in a conflict: Whom should they help, the rushed experimenter or the possibly sick victim? Darley and Batson noted that "Conflict, rather than callousness, can explain their failure to stop."

The Darley and Batson study is relevant to a broader finding: People in cities often help less than people in rural areas (Korte, 1981). City dwellers are often more rushed than their rural counterparts, and they suffer from sensory overload because so many things are happening at once in the city (Milgram, 1970). Thus people in cities, like Darley and Batson's "high-hurry" subjects, rush to their appointments, narrow the focus of their attention, and are sometimes oblivious to people who need help.

The Good Samaritan study suggests that reminding people of their moral principles may have only limited effects on their helping behavior. If seminary students (who should be exquisitely sensitive to moral issues) do not necessarily help a victim when rushing to deliver a talk on the Good Samaritan, how will the rest of us fare under the influence of their moral exhortations?

■■■■■■■■■■■■■■■■■■■■■■■
Modeling

When discussing developmental influences on prosocial behavior, we noted that parents' behavior may be more important than their "lectures" in fostering their children's prosocial behavior. Research on TV and prosocial behavior underscores the power that prosocial models can have in influencing children's behavior.

Modeling can foster helping behavior in adults as well. In one experiment (Bryan & Test, 1967), an undergraduate woman stood next to a Ford Mustang with a flat tire in a residential area of Los Angeles. Passing motorists who had seen a man helping another woman change a tire a quarter of a mile back on the road were almost twice as likely to stop and help as motorists who did not previously observe helping. Similarly, more people donated to a Salvation Army solicitor after observing another person (actually a confederate) donate money (Bryan & Test, 1967).

Just as aggressive behavior can be discouraged by nonaggressive models, prosocial behavior can be encouraged by prosocial models. In particular, research suggests that prosocial models who are warm and nurturing and who are perceived as similar to the observer are most effective in fostering imitative prosocial behaviors (Yarrow et al., 1973; Rushton, 1980). On a personal level, your helping behavior can encourage helping among your family, friends, and colleagues.

Assuming Responsibility

"... know ... that every one of us is answerable for everyone else and for everything. I don't know how to explain it to you, but I feel it so strongly that it hurts."

—— *The Brothers Karamazov*, p. 347

How can we encourage people to be responsible for others' well-being? We already know that the presence of other bystanders during an emergency can lead to a diffusion of responsibility whereby each individual no longer feels as responsible for intervening. Does the presence of others inevitably decrease helping?

No, not when the other people are friends! Latané and Darley (1970) replicated their epileptic seizure study so that some subjects participated in the "group discussion" with a stranger and the seizure victim and others with a friend and the victim. Intriguingly, subjects did not show a diffusion of responsibility when with a friend. This finding has been replicated in more recent studies as well (Rutkowski, Gruder, & Romer, 1983; Yinon, Sharon, Gonen, & Adam, 1982). Latané and Darley (1970) speculate that diffusion of responsibility does not occur among friends because they regard themselves as a unit — as "we," not as "me and a stranger."

Friends may be less inhibited in scrutinizing each other's nonverbal cues during an emergency and thus may perceive that their fellow bystander is upset. Darley, Teger, and Lewis (1973) showed that people sitting face-to-face respond to emergencies more quickly than people sitting back-to-back. This implies that nonverbal cues are important in triggering emergency intervention in groups.

Friends can also anticipate discussing the emergency later and thus being accountable to one another for their behavior. You cannot be anonymous in a group of friends; your identity, and your response to the crisis, is known. The effects of bystanders' knowing one another is yet another explanation for the observed differences between city and country dwellers: In small towns the bystanders to emergencies are likely to know one another; in big cities they are likely to be strangers.

On a practical level, these research findings suggest that becoming acquainted with the people around you will foster prosocial behavior. Meet your neighbors and work colleagues — people who know one another tend to take responsibility more readily for others in emergencies.

Another remarkably easy way to encourage people to be responsible for others is simply to assign them responsibility. In one study, Staub (1970) explicitly told individual kindergarten children that he was leaving them "in charge." When these children heard another person in distress in the next room, they were more likely to intervene. Adults also help more when assigned responsibility. For example, Moriarity (1975) staged thefts of radios and suitcases in public places. Sometimes bystanders had been asked by a confederate to "keep an eye" on their belongings, sometimes not. When assigned responsibility, subjects intervened in the "theft" in virtually every case; when not assigned responsibility, only about a third of the bystanders intervened.

Thus, to encourage prosocial behavior in friends, colleagues, workers, students, and children, it helps to assign them responsibility for behaving in prosocial ways.

Humanizing the Victim Who Needs Help

In many experiments on bystander intervention, the victim is a nameless person who falls off a chair, or collapses, or suffers an epileptic seizure. Certainly, it seems more likely that we would help a friend or a relative than a stranger.

Interestingly, social psychological research shows that even a trivial acquaintance with a "victim" increases helping behavior. For example, in yet another version of their epileptic seizure study, Latané and Darley (1970) had some subjects meet the "epileptic victim" in the hallway and strike up a brief conversation before the experiment began. Later, in six-person discussion groups, only 31 percent of subjects responded to the epileptic seizure if they had not previously met the victim; however, 75 percent responded if they had previously conversed with the victim face-to-face. Some subjects reported that after meeting the victim they visualized him suffering his seizure, and this spurred them to action. In addition, after talking with the victim, not only did subjects know him, but he knew them; thus subjects may have felt more personally accountable and responsible for his fate.

Subsequent studies have confirmed the finding that a brief interaction that reduces the victim's anonymity can greatly increase the incidence of helping behavior. For example, receiving a warm smile or holding a trivial conversation (". . . aren't you Suzie Spear's sister?") increases subjects' willingness to help a stranger (Solomon, Solomon, Arnone, Maur, Reda, & Rother, 1981).

All of this research makes an important point: Flesh-and-blood people — people we have seen and talked with — evoke our sympathy more than do abstract strangers. Thus the ties of acquaintance and friendship facilitate helping in two ways: Bystanders who are friends are more likely to help, and bystanders acquainted with victims are also more likely to help.

Education About Helping

Now that you've read this chapter, you can use your knowledge to become a more helpful person. For example, because you know that the presence of many bystanders leads to reduced helping, you can consciously decide to help, even when others are present. Just last year I had occasion to ponder Latané and Darley's notable research on the bystander effect. As I exited from a busy freeway in southern California, I saw a tractor-trailer that had toppled off the exit ramp, apparently after driving too quickly around a tight curve. My immediate thought was, "Surely someone has already reported this to the police." I thought about the bystander effect and then drove to a pay phone and reported the accident.

Research by Beaman and his colleagues (1978) shows that people like you and me who have learned about the bystander effect are more likely to help in emergencies. In other words, because of our cognitive and intellectual capacities, we can sometimes "stand above" social influences and act according to our informed social conscience rather than in response to blind social pressures. Thus, our knowledge about helping and altruism can help us to help more often, and we can more closely approach Dostoevsky's ideal whereby "every one of us is answerable for everyone else."

Summary

1. Prosocial behavior is behavior that people engage in to intentionally help or benefit another. Altruism is help offered to another for no external reward, and even at some cost.

2. Theories of biological evolution suggest that pure altruism cannot result from natural selection. However, altruism to kin is adaptive because it fosters the

survival of one's own genes; reciprocal altruism is adaptive, particularly in social species, because it fosters individual and group survival.

3. Norms of prosocial behavior are prescriptive social rules that govern when help should be offered to others. The norms of reciprocity, equity, and social responsibility help enforce and regulate prosocial behavior.

4. Although Hartshorne and May's early studies suggested that altruistic behaviors in children are not consistent across settings, recent studies show evidence for moderate consistency.

5. Children who observe prosocial adult models, who are placed in the role of helper, and who are psychologically secure are more likely to show prosocial behaviors.

6. Viewing prosocial TV programming increases prosocial behavior in children.

7. Latané and Darley describe emergency intervention as a five-stage decision process in which a potential helper must notice the situation requiring intervention, define it as an emergency, assume responsibility, decide how to help, and actually intervene.

8. Many studies document the bystander effect, which occurs when the presence of other bystanders inhibits people from helping in emergencies. This effect results in part from a diffusion of responsibility that occurs when people in groups feel less personally responsible for helping than they would if alone.

9. Emergencies are physiologically arousing. Highly aroused bystanders are sometimes more likely to help in an emergency; however, if the costs of helping are too high, they may also flee the scene of the emergency.

10. People who misattribute their arousal during an ambiguous emergency are less likely to help.

11. Helping can be motivated both by personal distress (general unpleasant arousal) and by empathy (compassionate concern). Experiments demonstrate the presence of empathy when subjects help a suffering victim even when they could escape from observing the suffering.

12. Guilt — unpleasant feelings of remorse following moral transgressions — motivates prosocial behavior particularly when people assume responsibility for their transgressions. Guilt can motivate an individual to help someone who was not the original victim of the individual's transgression.

13. People experiencing negative moods help particularly when they are observed by others and when their helping leads to a more positive mood.

14. People experiencing good moods are more likely to help, but the prosocial consequences of good moods tend to be short-lived.

15. Receiving help can be uncomfortable when it makes the recipient feel indebted, restricts freedom, or lowers self-esteem. Gender, personality characteristics, and cultural norms influence an individual's willingness to receive help.

16. Exhortation has limited effectiveness in encouraging prosocial behavior.

17. Prosocial models foster helping in both children and adults.

18. The bystander effect is less likely to occur when groups of friends witness an emergency and when people in groups can monitor one another's nonverbal cues.

19. People are more likely to help in emergencies when they are acquainted with victims.

20. People can use their knowledge about research on prosocial behavior to be more helpful.

Altruism: Helping another for no reward, and even at some cost

Bystander effect: The tendency for individuals to help less during emergencies when in the presence of others

Diffusion of responsibility: The tendency for individuals to feel less personally responsible for helping when in the presence of others; one explanation for the bystander effect

Emergency intervention: Quick helping in response to sudden events that endanger another and that sometimes places the helper in danger

Guilt: A negative emotion that occurs when an individual believes he or she has committed a moral transgression; guilt can motivate helping

Kin selection: According to modern evolutionary theory, the process by which natural selection favors animals that promote the survival of genetically related individuals; such "altruism" helps ensure that the individual's genes will be propagated to future generations

Norm of equity: A social norm that prescribes that people should receive goods in a relationship in proportion to their investment

Norm of reciprocity: A social norm that prescribes that people should help and not hurt those who have helped them; that is, people should give as they get in social relationships

Norm of social responsibility: A social norm that prescribes that people give aid to a dependent person in proportion to his or her need

Prosocial behavior: Behavior that intentionally helps or benefits another person

Reciprocal altruism: Mutually beneficial behavior between two members of the same or different species; biological evolution can lead to reciprocal altruism because the "cost" of helping another is more than offset by the evolutionary benefits of the reciprocated help

Tit for tat: A strategy of reciprocal altruism in which a partner in a relationship starts with an altruistic response and in all subsequent interactions reciprocates the partner's preceding response (that is, selfishness is matched with selfishness, and altruism with altruism); tit for tat is a highly stable and adaptive strategy of reciprocal altruism

Moonie wedding: Over 4,000 members of the Church of Unification (Reverend Moon's sect) show absolute conformity during a mass wedding. Reverend Moon decided who would marry whom.

. . . He wondered again for whom he was writing this diary. For the future, for the past — for an age that might be imaginary. And in front of him there lay not death but annihilation. The diary would be reduced to ashes and himself to vapor. Only the Thought Police would read what he had written, before they wiped it out of existence and out of memory. . . .

 . . . He went back to the table, dipped his pen, and wrote:

To the future or to the past, to a time when thought is free, when men are different from one another and do not live alone — to a time when truth exists and what is done cannot be undone:

From the age of uniformity, from the age of solitude, from the age of Big Brother, from the age of doublethink — greetings!

—— from *1984*, by George Orwell, pp. 28–29

CHAPTER 14

Conformity, Compliance, and Obedience

Welcome to the world of *1984*: The Americas and England are governed ruthlessly by the Party under the iron rule of Big Brother. Not only is it a crime to oppose the Party; it is a crime even to think bad thoughts about the Party. The Thought Police constantly search for dissidents guilty of "thoughtcrime" and "vaporize" them.

The homes of all Party members have "telescreens" that broadcast a constant barrage of state propaganda and contain cameras and microphones that permit constant surveillance. Big Brother's eyes watch you always—from the ever-present telescreens, from posters, and from coins. You can have no private opinions. The Party brutally enforces absolute conformity. Children regularly spy on their parents and turn them in to the Thought Police. Periodically, in a mass exercise of hysteria called the "Two Minutes Hate," the Party whips citizens into a frenzy of patriotic fervor against internal and external enemies.

In *1984*, citizens practice "doublethink"—they believe official Party "facts" that go against their senses, and they readily accept contradictory pieces of information. Indeed, doublethink is basic to governmental institutions in *1984:* The Ministry of Love tortures nonconformists into absolute submission; the Ministry of Peace engages in continual warfare against other countries; and, most horrible of all, the Ministry of Truth constantly rewrites history, editing out all facts that prove embarrassing to the Party.

George Orwell's *1984* is a profoundly disturbing account of powerful forms of social influence designed to control people's behavior and thought completely. It is also the story of one rebellious man—Winston Smith—who engages in "thoughtcrime" when he tries to oppose the power of the Party and the tyranny of Big Brother. With the words that open this chapter, Smith takes his first steps toward independence—he starts to write a forbidden diary.

Innocuous and danger-ous forms of social in-fluence: *right:* A Boy Scout attempting to sell candy; *opposite:* Nazi youth march-ing in unison.

Kinds of Social Influence

In the nightmarish world of *1984* people conform completely, obey absolutely, and comply with every demand made by the Party and Big Brother. But social influence occurs not only in the imaginary world of *1984*; it occurs in our world, too. Social psychologists have extensively studied the three kinds of social influence so prevalent in *1984: conformity, compliance,* and *obedience.* People *conform* when they maintain or change their behavior to be consistent with group standards; they *comply* when they accede to a request made by another; and they *obey* when they follow a direct command, typically from someone perceived to be a legitimate authority.

Conformity, compliance, and obedience are commonplace. You change your style of dress to be more like that of your friends. (This is conformity.) A Girl Scout comes to your door and asks you to donate $10 to Girl Scout summer camp. You refuse. Then she asks if you will buy a box of Girl Scout cookies instead. You do (first noncompliance, then compliance). The notorious Nazi war criminal, Adolf Eich-mann, sends hundreds of thousands of innocent men, women, and children to exter-mination camps after being ordered to do so by his superiors (obedience). You accompany your friend to church for Sunday services; when the whole congregation rises to its feet, you do too, even though you're not sure why everyone is rising (conformity). Your roommate asks for a loan of $20; you reluctantly hand it over (compliance). After waiting in line for half an hour at the Department of Motor Vehicles to register your car, the clerk tells you that you're in the wrong line and you must go wait in another long line; you go quietly (obedience).

As these examples suggest, social influence can affect things as trivial as our style of dress and events as profound as the Nazi holocaust. Social psychologists have striven to answer some basic questions about the nature of social influence: When will people conform, comply, and obey, and when won't they? What psychological processes account for different kinds of social influence? Are individuals always at

the mercy of social pressures, or can they sometimes fight back? How powerful are social influences: Is the grim world of *1984* just a novelist's fantasy, or can social pressures so totally control individuals' behavior?

> "It's the one thing they can't do. They can make you say anything — *anything* — but they can't make you believe it. They can't get inside of you."
>
> —— *1984*, p. 167

Levels of Social Influence

Sometimes people go along with others just on the surface, and sometimes they are truly converted to others' beliefs. In an early analysis, Herbert Kelman (1958) identified three different levels of social influence: (1) We may publicly comply with others in order to gain rewards or avoid punishments while refusing to change our private opinions; (2) we may behave like others because we're attracted to them and continue to be influenced as long as our attraction lasts; and (3) we may behave and think like others when we are logically convinced by their arguments and opinions. In essence, Kelman argued that some kinds of social influence (public compliance) are shallow and temporary, whereas other kinds (rational persuasion) are deeper and more enduring.

In Orwell's *1984*, the Party was not satisfied simply to gain citizens' public compliance and surface conformity; it demanded their private conversion as well. It was not enough that people obeyed Big Brother; they had to love him as well. In the sections that follow, you will discover that the distinction between public and private influence is quite important in recent theory and research. As we discuss research on conformity, compliance, and obedience, ask yourself, "Is it only subjects' public behavior that changes, or their inner beliefs as well?"

Conformity

. . . It was as though some huge force were pressing down upon you — something that penetrated inside your skull, battering against your brain, frightening you out of your beliefs, persuading you, almost, to deny the evidence of your senses. . . .

—— *1984*, p. 80

We all behave like others at times. We dress like our friends, pray like members of our congregation, and frequently vote for the same political candidates as our family members. We often *conform* — we behave in a manner that is consistent with group standards because of real or implied pressures from the group. What is the nature of conformity, and why and when does it occur?

Research on Conformity

Modern experimental research on conformity began with classic studies by Muzafer Sherif (1935) and Solomon Asch (1951, 1955, 1956).

Sherif and the autokinetic effect.

Sherif (1935) conducted a series of laboratory studies to document how social pressures influence ambiguous perceptual judgments. In these studies Sherif made use of a perceptual illusion called the autokinetic effect: When people view a single stationary point of light in the dark, the light appears to move.

In one experiment Sherif placed groups of three subjects together in a dark room and asked them to estimate the distance a point of light appeared to move. Each subject initially offered a different estimate — perhaps the first subject reported eight inches of movement; the second, two inches of movement; and the third, one inch. Sherif's experiments showed conclusively that when subjects announced their estimates to the group, their judgments tended to converge over successive trials (see Figure 14.1).

When asked, most of Sherif's subjects vehemently denied that they had been influenced by other subjects' judgments, but the data clearly told another story. Sherif proposed that groups create their own norms, or standards; when faced by ambiguous realities, they converge on a reality defined by the group.

Subjects in autokinetic studies seem to experience private conversion to (as well as public compliance with) the group norm; they come to believe the group consensus. For example, subjects who changed their estimates of the amount of light movement after hearing others' judgments continued to be influenced by the group norm as much as a year later, even in the absence of the original group (Rohrer, Baron, Hoffman, & Swander, 1954).

Jacobs and Campbell (1961) extended the autokinetic paradigm a step further by exposing single subjects to three confederates who made extreme judgments (that the light moved 16 inches). Despite the extremity of the confederates' estimates (control subjects not exposed to confederates tended to estimate about four inches of movement), the subjects strongly conformed, making judgments almost as extreme as those of the three confederates. Next, Jacobs and Campbell created successive "generations" of four-person groups. They removed one confederate from the group, substituted another naive subject, and again had subjects estimate the movement of the light for 30 trials. Then they removed yet another confederate and added another naive subject. This process continued until the group was composed of naive

▪▪

FIGURE 14.1   Results for one group of subjects in Sherif's (1935) autokinetic studies.

Do ambiguous perceptual judgments announced in a group tend to converge?

Subjects in Sherif's autokinetic studies estimated how far a point of light appeared to move.

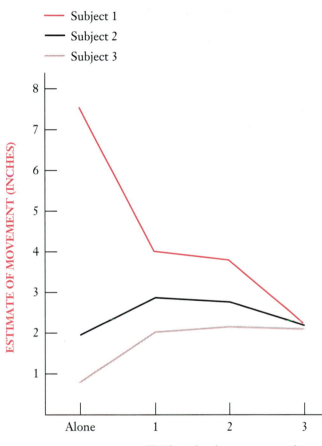

When subjects announced their estimates to one another, their estimates tended to converge over successive trials.

SOURCE: Data from Sherif (1935).

subjects only. The extreme group norm created by the confederates at the start continued to influence the judgment of successive generations of groups, and that influence subsided after multiple "generations" (see Figure 14.2). Do you think this effect occurs outside the laboratory—that we conform to norms that originated in previous times and that have now outlived their usefulness or validity?

▪▪▪

FIGURE 14.2   Transmission of an arbitrary norm across "generations" of subjects.

Do norms persist within groups, even when the individuals responsible for the norms are no longer group members?

In this autokinetic study, the "norms" established by confederates'extreme judgments affected successive "generations" of subjects. In the first "generation," a group consisting of three confederates and one naive subject made judgments for 30 trials. In each succeeding generation, one group member was replaced by a new member. By the fourth generation, groups consisted entirely of naive subjects.

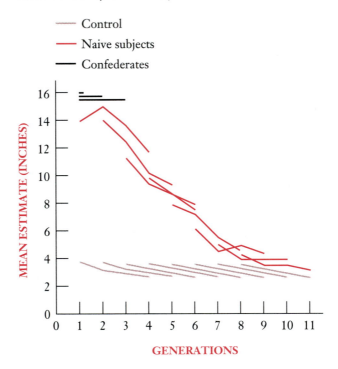

As the graph shows, the extreme norms created by confederates persisted for a number of generations after confederates had been removed from the groups.

SOURCE: Jacobs and Campbell (1961).

▪▪▪

Asch's minority of one against a unanimous majority.   Sherif's research showed that when asked to make ambiguous perceptual judgments, people conform to emerging social norms. Almost 20 years after Sherif's studies, Solomon Asch (1951, 1956) reasoned that if subjects were required to make a more obvious perceptual

FIGURE 14.3   **An example of the stimulus lines used in Asch's classic conformity experiments (1955). Subjects were asked to judge which of the three lines of obviously unequal length (shown in the right panel) were equal in length to the standard line (shown in the left panel).**

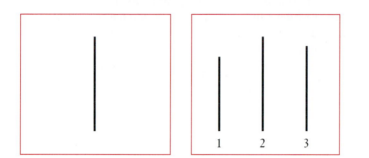

SOURCE: Asch (1955).

judgment, they would conform less than did Sherif's subjects. After all, if you see white, you're not going to say "black" just because everyone else says "black," are you? To test this hypothesis, Asch created an experimental situation that set the standard for most subsequent conformity research.

Imagine that you are the subject in this experiment. You come to a room with seven to nine other subjects (actually they are confederates, but you don't realize this). The experimenter informs you that this is a study on visual perception. Specifically, your job is to examine three lines of different lengths drawn on a large white card and judge which of the three is equal in length to a standard line drawn on another card. You will make such judgments 18 times during the experiment. Figure 14.3 shows a sample of the experimental stimuli.

The experiment begins uneventfully, with subjects announcing their answers aloud to the rest of the group. You are the next-to-last person in a row of seated subjects, so most subjects answer before you. The correct answers are quite obvious (again, see Figure 14.3), and on the first two trials all subjects give the correct answers.

On the third trial, however, the first subject gives an obviously incorrect answer. Perhaps you smile to yourself and think, "This guy must have been out partying last night." But then, the second subject also gives the same incorrect answer. Is it possible, two partiers in the same group? The third and fourth subjects also give the same incorrect answer. Now you begin to feel nervous. What's wrong? Why is everyone else seeing the lines differently from you? The correct answer seems obvious, yet, the fifth, sixth, and seventh subjects give the same wrong answer. Finally, it's your turn, and you face quite a dilemma: Do you state the answer that your senses tell you is obviously correct, or do you "cave in" to the unanimous majority that offers what seems to be an incorrect answer?

In Asch's experiment, confederates unanimously gave incorrect answers on 12 of the 18 trials. Of 123 subjects, 94 (that is, 75 percent) conformed at least once on such a "critical trial." And on average, subjects conformed on more than four of the 12 critical trials (that is, more than one-third of the time). Thus, even when the "truth" was absolutely clear, subjects would often conform to a mistaken but unanimous majority.

Asch (1955) commented upon these results with obvious distress:

> That we have found the tendency to conformity in our society so strong that reasonably intelligent and well-meaning young people are willing to call white black is a matter of concern. It raises questions about our ways of education and about the values that guide our conduct. (p. 34)

Compare Asch's concerns with this chilling passage from *1984*:

> . . . society rests ultimately on the belief that Big Brother is omnipotent and that the Party is infallible. But since in reality Big Brother is not omnipotent and the Party is not infallible, there is need for an unwearying, moment-to-moment flexibility in the treatment of facts. The key word here is *black-white*. . . . Applied to a Party member, it means a loyal willingness to say that black is white when Party discipline demands this. But it means also the ability to *believe* that black is white, and more, to *know* that black is white, and to forget that one has ever believed the contrary. (p. 213)

Did Asch's subjects actually come to believe the incorrect answers they stated in conformity with the majority? In general, no. Asch found that if subjects could write their judgments rather than publicly announce them, conformity declined to about a third of the level observed in his original study. (In this variation Asch arranged for subjects to arrive "late" at the ongoing experiment and told them to join in by writing their judgments rather than by publicly announcing them to the rest of the group.) Thus subjects' conformity in the original experiment was mostly public compliance.

In subsequent interviews most of Asch's subjects stated that they did not believe their conforming responses. Why then did they go along with an obviously incorrect majority? One subject answered, "They might think I was peculiar." Another said, "Mob psychology builds up on you." A third noted, "I think a majority is usually right." And one subject even offered, "When in Rome, do as the Romans do."

Two themes seem to emerge in the statements made by Asch's subjects. First, they felt pressured by the group; they didn't want to "stick out" and risk ridicule or rejection by the group. Second, they sometimes looked to the group for correct information—". . . a majority is usually right." Morton Deutsch and Harold Gerard (1955) labeled these two kinds of pressure normative and informational social influence. *Normative social influence* occurs when people conform to gain rewards and avoid punishments from the group, whereas *informational social influence* occurs when people look to the group to gain accurate information. It seems likely that conformity in Sherif's autokinetic studies was due more to informational social influence (subjects looked to the group to define ambiguous reality), whereas conformity in Asch's studies was due more to normative social pressures (subjects didn't want the group to think them "weird"). Recent experiments (such as Insko, Drenan, Solomon, Smith, & Wade, 1983; Insko, Smith, Alicke, Wade, & Taylor, 1985) support the notion that people conform to groups both to be liked (normative social influence) and to be correct (informational social influence).

In one variation of his classic experiment, Asch (1952) showed that his subjects had valid reason to fear ridicule if they didn't conform to the group. This time he placed one confederate among a group of naive subjects in his line-judgment task. On critical trials the sole confederate was instructed to give obviously incorrect answers. The majority responded by laughing at this "deviate." Clearly, it's not much fun to be a nonconformist in a group; you may indeed be ridiculed. (You might be wondering at this point how Asch's original confederates treated subjects on the critical conformity trials. They were instructed not to stare at subjects or to make any comments. There was no overt ridicule or pressure on Asch's subjects, which makes the high levels of observed conformity even more startling.)

Do groups exert pressures other than ridicule on nonconformists? The answer is clearly, "Yes." In a classic experiment by Stanley Schachter (1951), groups of five to seven college men convened to discuss the case of "Johnny Rocco," a juvenile delinquent who was awaiting sentence for a minor crime. The men were asked, in essence, to decide what society should do with Johnny. Should they punish him severely? Send him to reform school? Send him to a foster home? Three confederates were planted in each discussion group. One — the "deviate," or nonconformist — always championed an extreme point of view that differed from that of the rest of the group. The second confederate — the "mode" — always agreed with the majority; he was the "yes man" of the group. A third confederate — the "slider" — started out disagreeing with the group, but then slid into agreement. Schachter measured the amount of group communication directed at each confederate and how much the group liked each.

In general, Schachter's experiment showed that the discussion group liked the mode and the slider, but not the deviate. Furthermore, the group initially directed much more of its discussion at the deviate than at either the mode or the slider. Apparently, when faced with a nonconformist, the group tried hard to persuade him to agree. When it became clear, however, that he was not going to yield, the group often reduced its attempts to communicate with him, particularly when the group was cohesive (that is, when group members were attracted to one another) and highly involved in the discussion.

The two kinds of normative social influence that occurred in the Johnny Rocco study — direct persuasive communication, followed by rejection — occur in everyday life as well. In 1984 a small church in Oklahoma concluded that one of its members, Nurse Marian Guinn, was engaging in extramarital sex. To bring Marian back into the fold, church elders visited her and tried to persuade her to give up her "sinful" behavior. When she refused, the church publicly announced her sin to the congregation and moved to "withdraw fellowship" from Marian — that is, to excommunicate her and have all church members shun her (*Newsweek*, February 27, 1984; *Time*, March 26, 1984). Like the groups in Schachter's Johnny Rocco study, this church dealt with a nonconformist first by directly pressuring her and then by rejecting her. Faced with such pressures, perhaps it is not surprising that people do often conform to standards set by churches, families, and cliques of friends.

People do not always conform. A significant number of Asch's subjects successfully resisted a unanimous majority. And as we already know, when subjects could record their answers privately rather than announce them publicly, conformity decreased substantially. Thus conformity must partly be a function of people and partly a function of the setting of social influence (see Chapter 6). Research has focused on two main kinds of "person" variables that influence conformity: personality traits and gender. And research has identified a host of important situational factors that

Factors That Influence Conformity

influence conformity, including the size of the influencing group, the attractiveness and cohesiveness of the group, the subject's status in the group, the presence of other nonconformers, and the subject's degree of public commitment to his or her answer in the face of pressures to conform. Let's look more closely at these factors.

Personality.   Common sense suggests that some people are naturally inclined to conform and that others are naturally independent. Is there in fact a conforming personality? Asch (1956) speculated that people who feel inadequate and who possess low self-worth might be particularly compliant in conformity studies; however, he offered no empirical evidence for this speculation. Other psychologists modified Asch's procedures to examine the role personality plays in conformity. For example, Richard Crutchfield (1955) automated Asch's experimental procedure so that it was unnecessary to use confederates. Subjects made judgments at a control panel, which also supposedly displayed the responses of other subjects. Subjects sat in individual cubicles, and the experimenter controlled the responses that appeared on subjects' control panels. In his streamlined version of the Asch paradigm, Crutchfield found, among other things, that subjects who scored high on intellectual competence and ego strength tended to conform less, whereas subjects who scored high on authoritarianism (see Chapter 9) tended to conform more.

Although specific traits do at times correlate with conformity, these correlations are often weak and vary from study to study. Furthermore, an individual's level of conformity is often quite inconsistent across settings (McGuire, 1968a). To complicate matters further, different personality traits may predict different kinds of conformity.

For example, McDavid and Sistrunk (1964) gave subjects several personality inventories and then asked them to make perceptual judgments (such as picking which of a pair of projected circles of light was larger) that were either very clear-cut (as in Asch's studies) or quite difficult to judge (as in Sherif's studies). On critical trials, subjects faced a unanimous majority of other subjects, and the researchers observed how much subjects conformed.

These researchers found that different personality traits correlated with conformity, depending on the sex of the subjects and the ambiguity of their judgments. For example, conformity on clear-cut judgments seemed more related to subjects' timidity, dominance, and need for approval, whereas conformity on ambiguous judgments was more a function of their degree of trust, degree of suspiciousness and cynicism, and sex-role-related traits. Thus there probably is no single kind of conforming personality and no small set of traits that consistently predicts all kinds of conformity for all people.

Gender.   Crutchfield's (1955) studies were the first of many to show that women on average conform more than men. Recent meta-analyses provide support for the existence of on average a difference in conformity between women and men; however, such differences vary considerably across studies (Becker, 1986; Eagly & Carli, 1981; Eagly, 1987; see Chapter 10).

Why do women sometimes conform more than men? Sistrunk and McDavid (1971) argue that traditional conformity studies are biased in favor of finding more conformity in women because they often entail judgment tasks that are subtly biased in favor of men. Indeed, when Sistrunk and McDavid studied conformity on opinion items, they found that men conformed *more* than women on such "feminine" topics as fashion, home economics, and family care.

Alice Eagly's (1987; see Chapter 10) social-role theory of sex differences holds that women conform more than men because of the different and often lower-status roles they occupy (for example, secretary rather than boss). Women also frequently occupy nurturing roles (for example, mother, nurse, elementary school teacher), and deference and maintenance of group solidarity are integral to such roles. Eagly argues that women's sex-roles should be particularly salient in public group settings, and indeed research suggests that observed sex differences in social influence are strongest when women are in groups and are observed by others (Eagly, 1987; Eagly & Chrvala, 1986). If Eagly's theory is correct, then we should expect sex differences in conformity to decrease as women attain higher social status and as sex-roles change.

Group size.   Since Asch's classic studies, social psychologists have devoted considerable attention to situational factors that influence conformity. Perhaps the most obvious of these is group size. Doesn't it make intuitive sense that the larger the group that pressures you, the more you will conform?

Unfortunately, commonsense notions are not always supported by data. In his original studies, Asch (1955) varied the number of unanimous confederates from one to 15 people (see Figure 14.4). Surprisingly, he found that conformity approached its peak level in a group of three or four individuals. Conformity actually seemed to decline slightly for the largest groups, a finding that has sometimes been replicated by others (for example, Rosenberg, 1961).

One reason that conformity (at least as measured in experiments) may not increase much when pressuring groups are larger than four people is that some subjects may grow suspicious of the unexpected unanimity they observe in the large groups (Insko et al., 1985). Another reason is that subjects often do not consider members of unanimous groups to be independent. They assume that people who announce their judgments after hearing others are being influenced by the previously announced judgments. Indeed, some of Asch's (1956) subjects stated this hypothesis in their interviews: "I thought the mob were following the first man. . . . Yes, people tend to follow the leader."

An experiment by Wilder (1977) clearly demonstrated that a group produces more conformity when its members' judgments are perceived to be independent. After subjects heard tape recordings of four people stating strong opinions about a lawsuit, they were asked to give their own opinions about the suit. Some subjects heard all four people in a single discussion; others heard two separate discussions involving two people each. Although the opinions expressed were the same in each case, the subjects exposed to the two separate groups were influenced more than were subjects exposed to one group of four.

In recent years social psychologists have attempted to construct precise mathematical models to describe the amount of social influence (for example, pressure to conformity) that groups of varying sizes exert on target groups of varying sizes (Latané, 1981; Latané & Wolf, 1981; Tanford & Penrod, 1984). Tanford and Penrod's *Social Influence Model* (1984), for example, holds that a family of curves best depicts the relation between group size and social influence (see Figure 14.5).

There are three important implications of these curves: (1) Initially, social influence increases rapidly with each additional member of the influencing group, but it levels off after a point. (The top curve in Figure 14.5 is analogous to Asch's experiments in which one target is influenced by unanimous groups of different sizes. This curve approximates Asch's results very well: Influence increases as groups increase in

FIGURE 14.4   Results of Asch's studies of group size and conformity.

Does conformity increase with group size?

Asch (1955) measured the percent of conforming responses subjects made when faced with unanimous disagreement from groups of various sizes.

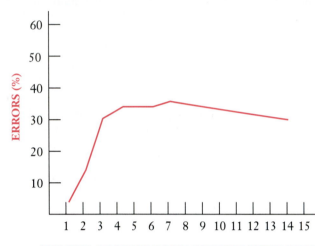

NUMBER OF PEOPLE DISAGREEING WITH SUBJECT

Instead of increasing steadily with group size, conformity reached close to its maximum level when the group consisted of four people.

SOURCE: Adapted from S. E. Asch, "Opinions and Social Pressure," *Scientific American*. Copyright © 1955 Scientific American, Inc. All rights reserved. Used with permission.

size to about four people and then levels off.) (2) As the target group gets larger, the curves get flatter; in other words, each additional member of the influencing group adds less and less to the group's total impact on the target of influence. And (3) there is a maximum level of social influence that can be exerted by a given group; that is, influence does not increase indefinitely as group size increases.

The Social Influence Model proves to be very good at accounting for observed data in many different kinds of studies. For example, Tanford and Penrod (1984) compared predictions made by a computer simulation based on their model with data from classic conformity studies, including Asch's, and their predictions agreed with the results of these studies quite accurately. It is important to note that the Social Influence Model mathematically describes *how* variables are related, but does not say *why* they are related.

Group attractiveness and cohesiveness.   In general people conform more to groups to which they are highly attracted (Festinger, Schachter, & Back, 1950; Lott & Lott, 1961; Sakurai, 1975). Groups are termed *cohesive* when all members on average are

▪▪▪

FIGURE 14.5   Predictions of the Social Influence Model.

*How are the size of influencing groups and the size of target
groups related to social influence?*

Tanford and Penrod's Social Influence Model (1984) is an attempt to
mathematically describe the amount of social influence that occurs when
groups of various sizes influence target groups of various sizes. The numbers within the graph indicate the number of people in each target group.

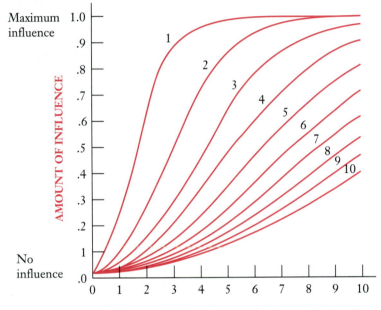

NUMBER OF PEOPLE IN INFLUENCING GROUP

According to Tanford and Penrod's mathematical model, when influencing groups are small, additional members increase the groups' social
influence more than when groups are large (the curves rise steeply at
first and then "flatten out").   Furthermore, social influence does not
increase indefinitely as the size of the influencing group increases (no
curve reaches a value greater than 1.0).

SOURCE: Tanford and Penrod (1984). Used with permission of Sarah Tanford.

*As the text notes, the Social Influence Model describes how group size relates to social
influence, but it does not explain the psychological processes that account for the relationship.
As we shall see later, the Social Influence Model has been used to describe how minorities
influence majorities as well as how majorities influence minorities (as in Asch's
experiments).*

▪▪▪

highly attracted to the group, and, not surprisingly, cohesive groups tend to produce greater pressures to conform than do noncohesive groups (Schachter, 1951; Forsyth, 1983).

Theodore Newcomb (1943) conducted a classic study that demonstrated the power of cohesive groups to influence members' opinions. Newcomb's subjects were women attending Bennington College, a small liberal arts school in Vermont; they tended to come from wealthy, politically conservative families. Upon arriving at Bennington, freshmen left their old social groups (families, neighborhoods, and school friends) and came into contact with new groups (upperclassmen, faculty) who were much more politically and economically liberal than the freshmen. Newcomb found that, in general, students' attitudes became more liberal during each succeeding year at Bennington (see Figure 14.6).

Many of Newcomb's subjects experienced a clash between the norms of their old and new groups. One woman expressed her conflict quite eloquently in an essay she wrote about visiting home:

> . . . I don't want to go home this vacation — there's no one I want to see for more than 5 minutes.
>
> An increasing crescendo of scattered remarks of my friends mounts up in my mind and culminates in a dissonant, minor chord. What is the matter with these dissatisfied, bewildered, cynical girls? It's a simple answer, yet dishearteningly complex. Bennington is their trouble. . . . We went to Bennington, and our friends went to Vassar, Yale, Sarah Lawrence, Harvard, finishing school, St. Paul's-to-broker's-office. They came home changed, a little. A slightly smarter jargon, unerring taste in clothes and Things To Do, and one and all, victrola records of the conventional ideas. We came home, some of us, talking a new language, some cobwebs swept out, a new direction opening up ahead, we were dying to travel. Liberal, we thought we were. "What the hell's happened to You? Become a Parlor Pink?" "Well, hardly, ha, ha." It was a little bewildering. (Newcomb, 1943, p. 11)

Presumably, new Bennington freshmen were highly attracted to the high-status members of their new community—namely, the faculty and upperclassmen, and thus they conformed to the standards of these groups. Students who got most involved in academics, student government, and extracurricular activities tended to show the greatest attitude change, whereas those who did not integrate into the new community and who held on to their old family ties and friends were least likely to change. Moreover, the conformity that many Bennington students showed to their new community turned out not be mere public compliance; it developed into permanent attitude change. After interviewing many of his subjects some 20 years later, Newcomb (1963) found that women who had become more liberal during their years at Bennington remained so decades after leaving college.

Status in the group.   The Bennington College study shows that we conform more to groups to which we are attracted. But do we conform more to groups that are attracted to us? How does our status in a group influence our conformity to the group?

To answer these questions, James Dittes and Harold Kelley (1956) conducted a two-stage experiment. First, subjects participated in group discussions and were asked to rate everyone else in the group on their "desirability" and contribution to

░░

FIGURE 14.6   **Results of Newcomb's (1943) study of changes
in Bennington students' attitudes.**

Do we conform more when we are attracted to a group?

Newcomb (1943) measured changes in the political and economic
attitudes of five separate entering classes during the years they
spent at Bennington College, where the faculty and upperclassmen tended to be more liberal (progressive) than themselves.
(Note: Lower scores on the graph indicate greater liberalism.)

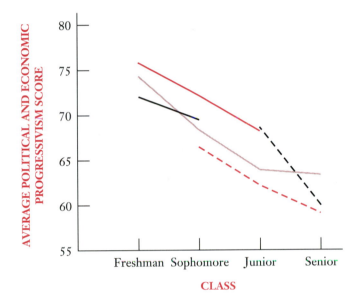

All five classes showed a marked tendency to become more
liberal after exposure to the Bennington College environment.

SOURCE: Adapted from Theodore M. Newcomb, *Personality and Change*, 1957 Reissue. Copyright © 1957 by Holt,
Rinehart and Winston, Inc. Used with permission of publisher.

*The Bennington College study provides a good illustration of the sociological concept of a
"reference group" — a group that is particularly important to us and against which we
compare ourselves. The Bennington College study suggests that we conform more to reference groups than to nonreference groups.*

░░

the group. Subjects were allowed to see how others had rated them (actually they
were given fake rating slips filled in by the experimenters). In this way Dittes and
Kelley created four groups of subjects: those who learned that other members of
their group rated them as high, average, low, or very low in desirability.

●●

FIGURE 14.7   **Conformity as a function of acceptance by a group.**

How does our status within a group affect our tendency to conform?

To see how conformity changes with our perceptions of our status in a group, Dittes and Kelly (1956) measured the conformity of subjects who were told that their discussion group had rated them either high, average, low, or very low in "desirability."

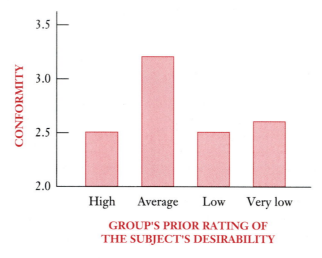

Conformity was greatest among subjects who believed that the group had rated them average in desirability.

SOURCE: Data from Dittes and Kelley (1956).

●●

These subjects then participated in a study similar to Asch's, with this difference: The people who appeared to disagree with them on perceptual judgments were the members of their earlier discussion group. In which condition did subjects conform most? Those subjects who believed that the pressuring group had earlier rated them as average in desirability tended to conform most (see Figure 14.7).

Dittes and Kelley reasoned that these subjects conformed most because they believed they could improve their status in the group by conforming to group norms. High-status people felt secure in their position and were thus not as compelled to conform (Hollander, 1958), whereas low-status people felt rejected by the group and were thus no longer attracted to it.

Harvey and Consalvi (1960) corroborated Dittes and Kelley's findings in a more realistic setting. To investigate the effects of actual status on conformity, they studied friendship cliques in a school for delinquent boys. Placing these cliques in a conformity experiment, Harvey and Consalvi observed that second-status boys (as measured by the boys' own ratings) conformed more than top-status boys or low-status boys.

Observations from everyday life also suggest that high-status people (such as movie stars) and low-status people (minority out-groups) often conform less to social conventions than do average- or marginal-status people (the middle class). Thus conformity depends not only on how much you like the group, but also on how much the group likes you.

Social support: the presence of other nonconformists.   Being a subject in Asch's experiment must have been a very lonely experience. Do you think that Asch's subjects would have conformed less in the presence of others who broke away from the majority?

Again, we can look back to Asch's (1956) seminal studies for relevant data. Asch sometimes instructed one confederate to give the correct answer and thus dissent from the majority. The effect of this one dissenting opinion on subjects was remarkable: Their conformity dropped to one-fourth the level shown by subjects faced with a unanimous majority. This dramatic reduction in conformity was likely due to decreases in both normative and informational social pressure: Subjects observed that nothing terrible happened to the dissenting confederate and thus also felt more secure in rebelling against the group; furthermore, they probably felt more doubt about the accuracy of the majority. Subjects reported feeling a bond of attachment to their partner in nonconformity, so they probably experienced social influence emanating from their new "friend" as well as from the disagreeing majority.

George Orwell clearly recognized the freeing power of social support. In *1984* Winston Smith meets a partner in "thoughtcrime," a woman named Julia, and this emboldens him to resist further the influence of the Party and Big Brother. Totalitarian governments have always intuitively understood the import of Asch's results: Allowing one dissident to break from a controlling, powerful group permits others to follow suit. So, of course, such governments choose to squelch all dissent—to enforce absolute conformity.

Does a nonconformist always reduce others' conformity, or are there some limits to this phenomenon? For example, must a dissenting confederate give the correct answer to reduce subjects' conformity, or is any disagreeing response sufficient? Asch (1956) found that even when the dissenting confederate gave objectively incorrect answers that were worse than the majority's answers, subjects still showed significantly reduced conformity.

Unfortunately, allies in nonconformity serve to reduce conformity only as long as they continue to deviate from the majority. Asch (1955) found that if the dissenting confederate "returned to the fold" and began agreeing again with the majority, subjects' levels of conformity went up almost to the levels observed in his original experiments.

The effect of a nonconforming ally depends on whether subjects make perceptual judgments (as in Asch's studies) or ratings of opinion (Allen, 1975). Asch's findings—that the presence of any other nonconformist in the group reduces a subject's conformity—are accurate for perceptual judgments. However, on matters of opinion ("How strongly do you believe there should be government-subsidized health insurance?"), social support reduces conformity only when the nonconformist agrees with your opinion, not when he or she expresses an opinion even more extreme than that of the majority (Allen & Levine, 1968, 1969).

Will a nonconformist reduce your conformity if you are prejudiced against the nonconformist? Sometimes. Malof and Lott (1962) found that racially prejudiced

FIGURE 14.8   Conformity as a function of commitment to one's own judgment.

Do we conform less when we have made a commitment to a nonconforming response?

Deutsch and Gerard (1955) explored the effects of commitment on conformity by creating four levels of commitment before subjects were exposed to opposing views expressed by confederates.

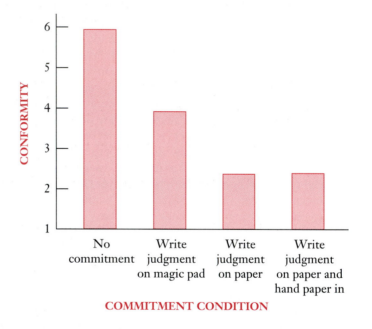

Subjects who had committed themselves by writing down their initial judgments before being exposed to a disagreeing majority showed a greater tendency to "stick to their guns" in the face of group pressure.

SOURCE: Data from Deutsch and Gerard (1955).

white subjects showed reduced conformity to a white majority on perceptual judgments, regardless of whether the nonconformist was black or white. However, social support from a member of a disliked out-group seems to be less successful in reducing conformity on statements of opinion (Boyanowsky & Allen, 1973).

Commitment and conformity.

The first step had been a secret, involuntary thought; the second had been the opening of the diary. He had moved from thoughts to words, and now from words to actions.

—— *1984*, p. 160

<table>
<tr><td colspan="3">SUMMARY TABLE 14.1   Variables That Affect Conformity</td></tr>
</table>

What variables affect our tendency to conform?

	VARIABLE	EFFECT
Person characteristics	Personality traits	May weakly correlate with conformity, but relationships vary depending on type of conformity
	Gender	On average, women conform slightly more than men, but this difference is variable across studies
Situational factors	Public versus private response	Subjects conform more when they must publicly announce responses
	Group size	Increased group size leads to increased conformity as groups increase from one to four members, then conformity levels off; larger groups may lead to greater conformity if group members are perceived to be independent of one another
	Group attractiveness	Subjects conform more to attractive groups than to unattractive groups
	Acceptance by group/status in group	Average- and marginal-status group members conform more than high- or low-status members
	Social support	The presence of a nonconformist in a group reduces conformity
	Commitment	A written commitment to a judgment leads subjects to conform less when faced by an opposing majority

The more that people commit themselves to a nonconforming response, the more they will stick to it in the face of group pressure. A clever experiment by Deutsch and Gerard (1955) clearly demonstrated this phenomenon. Subjects were asked to write down certain perceptual judgments before seeing confederates' judgments on a control panel. Subjects then made their "official" judgment by pressing a button on their control panel. In one condition subjects wrote and signed their names to their initial judgments, expecting that they would later hand them in to the experimenter; in a second condition subjects wrote their judgments on pieces of paper but were not required to turn them in; in a third condition subjects wrote their initial judgments on a "magic writing pad" that was erased after each judgment trial; and in a fourth (control) condition subjects did not write their judgments and thus made no commitment to their initial opinions.

The results: Subjects showed the most conformity in the "no written commitment" condition, intermediate conformity in the "magic pad" condition, and the least conformity in the two "write down on paper" conditions (see Figure 14.8). George Orwell was correct — there is a link "from words to actions." Writing down or publicly expressing our dissent strengthens us in resisting pressures from a disagreeing majority (Kiesler, 1971; Kerr & MacCoun, 1985). This as well as other factors influencing conformity are reviewed in Summary Table 14.1.

What Is Conformity — A Closer Look

Asch devised a simple and widely used operational definition of conformity. First, create a judgment task with an obviously correct answer, and on critical trials expose subjects to a unanimous disagreeing group. Then observe whether the subject changes his or her answer to be consistent with the group. Conformity consists of *changing* one's response *to be like* the group's.

Later theorists have noted that Asch's operational definition, although meaningful and intuitively appealing, is incomplete (Willis, 1965; Willis & Levine, 1976; Nail, 1986; Nail & Willis, 1988). For example, Asch did not address the possibility that after experiencing group pressure, subjects might shift their judgments to be *less* like the group's. Such *anticonformity,* although not apparent in Asch's

studies, has been documented in some studies when subjects are alienated from the group (for example, Frager, 1970) or feel that their freedom of choice is being unduly restricted (Brehm & Brehm, 1981).

Asch's definition of conformity also ignored the possibility that one may originally agree with the group and that maintaining that agreement is also a kind of conformity. In other words, conformity can consist either of *movement* toward the group or maintenance of *congruence* with the group. Common stereotypes of conformity — for example, behavior in oppressive small towns where everyone thinks the same, dresses the same, and decorates his or her house the same — typically portray conformity as congruence more than movement.

To describe more completely the

different varieties of conformity, Richard Willis (1965; Willis & Levine, 1976) devised a *diamond model* (so named because of its shape in graphic representations). A version of this model as elaborated by Paul Nail (1986; Nail & Willis, 1988) is shown in the accompanying graph. In the diamond model two dimensions are required to describe all possible conforming or nonconforming responses to social influence: the subject's degree of movement and the subject's degree of congruence with the group.

Movement is the amount a subject changes his or her judgment after social influence. Movement (plotted on the horizontal axis of the graph) is the proportion of trials in which a subject changes his or her position; thus it ranges from 0 (movement in no trials) to 1

The diamond model of social influence. This graph assumes the group agrees with subject's initial judgments on half of the trials and disagrees on the other half.

SOURCE: Based on Nail and Willis (1988).

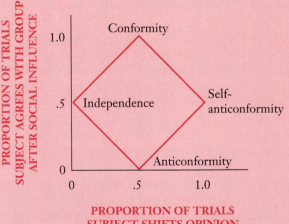

(movement in all trials). In Asch's studies, if a subject never changed his judgment to be like the group's on critical trials, he then showed zero movement; if he conformed in six out of 12 trials, he showed movement of .5; if he conformed on all trials, he showed the maximum possible movement, which corresponds to a value of 1.

Congruence, the second dimension of the diamond model, refers to agreement between the subject and the group after social influence. The vertical axis of the graph represents the proportion of trials in which a subject ends up in agreement with the group. In Asch's studies, if a subject conformed on none of the critical trials he would show zero congruence with the group; if he conformed on half of the trials, he would show .5 congruence; and if he conformed on all trials, he would show perfect (1) congruence. Interestingly, on noncritical trials — when both subjects and confederates gave correct answers — subjects also showed perfect congruence with the group.

The diamond model encompasses all the possible responses to social influence. Each corner of the diamond in the graph represents a pure style of response. Imagine you are in a study that first measures your opinions on ten topics and then exposes you to a group that expresses its unanimous opinions on these same ten topics. On five of the topics, the group agrees with your opinions; on the other five, it disagrees. How might you respond to the group?

You could conform completely (the upper corner of the diamond in the graph). In other words, whenever the group agrees with you, you maintain your opinion, but whenever the group disagrees with you, you change your opinion. The net result: You always end up in congruence with the group (1 on the vertical axis) and you change your opinion half the time (.5 on the horizontal axis).

You could anticonform (the bottom corner of the diamond). Now, whenever the group agrees with your original opinion, you *change* your opinion. If the group disagrees with you, however, you maintain your initial opinion. In other words, when the group "zigs," you "zag." You always end up in disagreement with the group (0 on the vertical axis), and you change your opinion half of the time (.5 on the horizontal axis).

But there are two more possibilities. You could simply be independent of the group's opinions (the left-hand corner of the diamond). That is, you always maintain your initial opinion, regardless of what the group thinks. Thus you never show a change in your opinions (0 on the horizontal "movement" axis), and you agree with the group half of the time, when they just happen to have the same opinions you do (.5 on the vertical axis).

Finally, you could be independent of the group, but always change your mind from your initial opinion (the right-hand corner of the diamond). Nail (1986) calls this strange response style "self-anticonformity." For example, if you decide when taking true-false tests in subjects you're weak in that "my first guesses are usually wrong" and then consistently change your answers, you would be engaging in self-anticonformity. Although it is a theoretical possibility, self-anticonformity is undoubtedly a rare response style.

Nail (1986; Nail & Willis, 1988) argues that to understand completely the causes and correlates of conformity, social psychologists must separately measure movement and congruence, and determine whether subjects display conformity, anticonformity, independence, or self-anticonformity. For example, personality variables may correlate differently with these four different kinds of responses to social influence.

The diamond model demonstrates how scientific concepts develop over time. Furthermore, it illustrates that precise, scientific definitions of psychological phenomena like conformity may be more complex than our everyday definitions.

Minority influence.   Traditional conformity research has studied social influence in one direction only — from the group to the individual. Indeed, it could not be otherwise in Asch's studies, for the unanimous group that faced individual subjects was not a real group, but rather a group of confederates instructed to display artificially rigid judgments.

In real groups, however, minorities and majorities interact with and exert mutual influence on each other. History is full of examples in which dedicated and persuasive minorities, sometimes consisting of single individuals, have influenced powerful, entrenched majorities. Such scientific geniuses as Copernicus, Galileo, and Darwin endured scathing attacks from the orthodox majority, but their ideas eventually prevailed. Such artistic geniuses as composer Ludwig van Beethoven, painter Vincent Van Gogh, and playwright Anton Chekhov were first scorned as wildly eccentric and untalented, and later were imitated by the majority. And civil rights activists, from the suffragists to Martin Luther King, Jr., faced vilification by the majority, followed eventually by mainstream acceptance of their ideas.

Do laboratory experiments support the observation that minorities can at times influence a strong majority? Beginning in the late 1960s the French social psychologists Serge Moscovici (Moscovici, 1976) conducted a series of experiments that proved that minorities can have a surprisingly potent impact on majority judgments and opinions. For example, in a kind of "reverse-Asch" experiment, Moscovici, Lage, and Naffrechoux (1969) asked groups of subjects to judge whether the color of projected blue slides was either green or blue. Each group consisted of two confederates and four real subjects. The confederates were instructed to label slides consistently as green. The subjects in the majority, faced by a consistently disagreeing minority, labeled the blue slides green over 8 percent of the time; furthermore, almost a third of the subjects reported after the judgment trials that they had seen a "green" slide at least once during the experiment.

When is a minority most likely to influence a majority? Studies show that minorities must consistently state their dissenting opinions if they are to budge the majority (Moscovici & Personnaz, 1980; Mugny, 1982; Maass & Clark, 1984). Consistent minorities are perceived to be more confident and committed to their position than are inconsistent minorities (Bray, Johnson, & Chilstrom, 1982; Nemeth & Wachtler, 1973, 1974). At the same time, the minority must not be overly rigid and dogmatically repetitious in stating its dissenting opinion (Nemeth, Swedlund, & Kanki, 1974). Thus a minority must remain logically and intellectually consistent but vary the way it phrases and negotiates its position (Mugny, 1975).

Minorities may have the greatest influence when their positions reinforce prevailing cultural norms and trends (Paicheler, 1976, 1977; Maass, Clark, & Haverhorn, 1982). For example, civil rights activists of the 1960s were in accord with the prevailing liberal political climate of the time, and leaders of the women's movement during the 1970s voiced opinions reinforced by larger, societal changes in women's roles.

Finally, research suggests that *double minorities* — minority groups that not only differ in their opinions but also in other obvious ways from the majority — have less impact on majorities than do *single minorities*. For example, Maass and Clark (1982) showed that a minority, believed to be gay, that argued in favor of gay rights was less successful in changing the heterosexual majority's views than was a heterosexual minority arguing the same position. Perhaps double minorities are less persuasive because they are perceived to have less credibility and more of a vested interest in their positions (Maass & Clark, 1984).

▪▪▪▪▪▪▪▪▪▪▪▪▪▪▪▪▪▪▪▪▪▪▪▪▪▪

**When do minorities
succeed in changing
the views of majorities?**

Consistent with Schachter's "Johnny Rocco study," studies on minority influence often find that dissenting minorities are disliked and even abused (Nemeth & Wachtler, 1974), but intriguingly, such minorities still frequently influence the majority. How? Majority members often don't want to be associated with the disliked minority and thus will not publicly go along with minority opinions. But privately they are often persuaded — if the minority presents persuasive arguments (Nemeth & Wachtler, 1973, 1974; Moscovici, 1980).

Another experiment by Anne Maass and Russell Clark (1983) demonstrated clearly that minority influence can produce private acceptance while failing to elicit public compliance. Over 400 University of Florida undergraduates read a discussion on gay rights written by five college-age women. In one condition the majority (four out of five women) was in favor of gay rights, and the minority opposed it. In a second condition, the majority was opposed to gay rights and the minority in favor of it. And finally, in a control condition subjects read no group discussion.

Subjects then expressed their attitudes toward gay rights: Half the subjects were asked to publicly express their attitudes in questionnaires that would be read by other students, whereas the other half privately expressed their attitudes in a questionnaire that would remain anonymous. The results of this study are shown in Figure 14.9. Note that when expressing their attitudes privately, subjects were more influenced by the minority, but when expressing their attitudes publicly, they were more influenced by the majority. (Recall that Asch's data were consistent with these findings, for they showed that majorities pressured subjects into public compliance, but not private acceptance.)

Theorists have debated whether minority influence results from the same or from different processes that produce majority influence (Mackie, 1987; Maass, West, & Cialdini, 1987). Tanford and Penrod's Social Influence Model (described earlier; see Figure 14.5) describes minority influence with the same kinds of mathematical functions used to describe majority influence, and it predicts that minorities

FIGURE 14.9 **Minority influence on public versus private attitudes.**

Are minorities more likely to influence private attitudes, whereas majorities are more likely to influence public attitudes?

Maass and Clark (1983) had subjects read a transcript of a discussion in which the majority either favored or opposed gay rights. In a control condition, subjects read no transcript. Subjects then rated their attitude toward gay rights on either a "private" questionnaire or on a questionnaire that would be seen by other students in a future discussion group. (Higher scores on the graph = greater opposition to gay rights.)

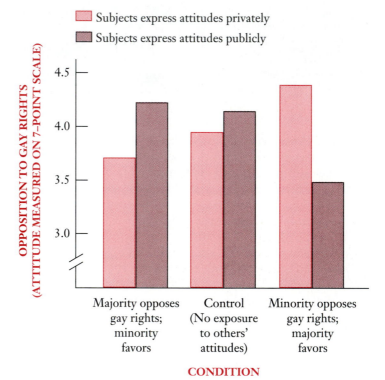

The results showed that minority opinions had a greater impact on subjects' privately expressed attitudes, whereas majority opinions had a greater impact on publicly expressed attitudes.

SOURCE: Data from Maass and Clark (1983).

have less impact on groups than do majorities simply because of their numerical inferiority. Undoubtedly, both minorities and majorities can exert normative and informational social influence to varying degrees.

Still, a number of studies suggest that minority influence is sometimes qualitatively different from majority influence. As already noted, minority influence often leads more to private conversion, whereas majority influence leads more to public compliance. Group members probably attend more to a lone dissenter than to a unanimous majority and may perceive his or her motives differently than they perceive those of a unanimous majority (Maass, West, & Cialdini, 1987). For example, a lone dissenter may be perceived as a courageous and committed (but possibly wrong) individual, whereas a unanimous group may be perceived as conforming "sheep."

Nemeth (1986) argued that minorities are more likely to produce private conversion in part because a consistent, disagreeing minority leads individuals in the majority to question their pat assumptions and rethink issues. Sometimes dissenting minorities — even when they fail to win the majority over to their position — provide the majority with a wider range of acceptable positions. Majorities, even when they provide normative social pressure to conform, don't necessarily foster careful thought. Nemeth believes that groups facing minority dissent often produce more creative and thoughtful judgments than do more uniform and homogeneous groups. Thus, even though they sometimes create tension and stress, disagreeing minorities may also serve to increase the ultimate quality of the group's decisions and judgments.

▪▪

Compliance

There was a knocking at the door.

> Already! He sat as still as a mouse, in the futile hope that whoever it was might go away after a single attempt. But no, the knocking was repeated. The worst thing of all would be to delay. His heart was thumping like a drum. . . .
>
> As he put his hand to the doorknob Winston saw that he had left the diary open on the table. DOWN WITH BIG BROTHER was written all over it, in letters almost big enough to be legible across the room. It was an inconceivably stupid thing to have done. . . .
>
> He drew in his breath and opened the door. Instantly a warm wave of relief flowed through him. A colorless, crushed-looking woman, with wispy hair and a lined face was standing outside.
>
> "Oh, comrade," she began in a dreary, whining sort of voice, "I thought I heard you come in. Do you think you could come across and have a look at our kitchen sink? It's got blocked up and — "
>
> . . . Winston followed her down the passage.
>
> —— *1984*, p. 21

Winston Smith happily complied with his neighbor's request, for he had imagined that it was the Thought Police knocking on his door. And so he agreed to remove a gob of hair from her clogged pipes.

Compliance — acceding to a request made by another person — is an everyday occurrence. We comply with friends who ask us for loans, with lovers who ask us to give up our "bad" habits, and with solicitors who ask for charitable donations. Sales staffs, proselytizing religious sects, and self-help "therapy" groups seeking new, paying members have developed clever strategies to gain our compliance (Cialdini, 1988). Why do such strategies work? When do they work? Are they based on valid psychological research? In a world full of requests, it is valuable indeed to understand the nature of compliance.

We will focus on four common strategies used to gain compliance: (1) associating a request with positive situations or moods, (2) using the norm of reciprocity to gain compliance—that is, making a request after doing a favor, (3) creating commitment, often by getting a person to agree first either to a smaller initial request or under false conditions, and (4) using psychological reactance, or "reverse psychology," to gain compliance. Let's briefly look at each of these important strategies.

Positive Moods and Compliance

Because of his elation at not facing the Thought Police, Winston Smith was probably particularly susceptible to his neighbor's request for help. Psychological research supports the notion that positive moods aid us in gaining others' compliance. For example, using the "luncheon technique," Razran (1938, 1940) found that it's easier to gain subjects' compliance and agreement while they are eating. No wonder businesspeople choose to "wine and dine" prospective clients (Janis, Kaye, & Kirschner, 1965).

Perhaps the most direct way to "soften someone up" before making a request is to say nice things about him or her. Such *ingratiation* is a standard strategy to gain influence with another person. Although you might think that people would be suspicious of praise preceding a request, research suggests that we often like people who say nice things about us regardless of their apparent motives (Byrne, Rasche, & Kelley, 1974; Jones, 1964; Jones & Wortman, 1973). Flattery doesn't even have to be true to increase our liking for and subsequent compliance with the flatterer (Drachman, de Carufel, & Insko, 1978).

Cialdini (1988) describes a master of ingratiation, Joe Girard, who was named by the *Guinness Book of World Records* as the world's "greatest car salesman." What was his secret to success? In part, it was simply flattering his customers and getting them to like him:

> He did something that, on the face of it, seems foolish and costly. Each month he sent every one of his more than 13,000 former customers a holiday greeting card containing a printed message. The holiday greeting card changed from month to month (Happy New Year, Happy Valentine's Day, Happy Thanksgiving, and so on), but the message printed on the face of the card never varied. It read, "I like you." (Cialdini, 1988, p. 166)

Reciprocity and Compliance

The norm of reciprocity holds that we should return favors in social relations (Gouldner, 1960; see Chapters 11 and 13 for additional discussions.) Perhaps the success of Joe Girard's greeting cards is partly based on the norm of reciprocity; people want to "repay" the kindness of Joe's cards, so they buy their cars from him.

But wait a minute, you may be thinking, something seems out of balance here: The cost of a sales commission on a car sale is not at all equivalent to the cost of a few cards! Indeed, this is exactly how the clever salesperson or solicitor makes use of

A member of the Hare Krishna sect solicits donations by first giving "free" gifts. This strategy makes use of the norm of reciprocity.

the principle of reciprocity to our disadvantage: He does us a small favor and then asks a large favor in return. It seems ridiculous that people should succumb to such a strategy, but the norm of reciprocity is so strong that it often works.

Laboratory research clearly demonstrates that doing a small favor can indeed pave the way to reciprocal compliance. In one study (Regan, 1971), college subjects worked on a task with another student (actually a confederate). During a rest period, the confederate stepped out for a few minutes and then returned either with a cola for the subject or with nothing. Later on, the confederate asked the subject if he would buy some 25-cent raffle tickets. The results: Subjects who had been given the "free" cola bought an average of two tickets, whereas control subjects (those who got no cola) bought only one. Because colas were worth a dime when this study was carried out, the sale of one extra ticket was a good return (25 cents) on an investment of a dime.

Reciprocity is a strategy of compliance that has been used to good effect by the Hare Krishna sect (Cialdini, 1988). Throughout the 1970s, Hare Krishna members — with their bells, shaved heads, and strange Eastern garb — approached passersby in airports and other public places, and without a word gave them a "gift," often a flower. If the hapless victim tried to return the flower, the Hare Krishna member would refuse to take back his "gift," and then he would ask for a donation. This simple ploy was often successful because the norm of reciprocity that we must repay a "gift" with a "gift" is so strong. (Incidentally, most people so solicited immediately threw out their unwanted "gift" flower. The practical Hare Krishnas collected these discarded flowers to use as "gifts" for their next targets.)

Reciprocity is a commonly used sales strategy. Food companies hire personnel to give away "free samples" in supermarkets, hoping for a purchase in return.

■■■■■■■■■■■■■■■■■■■■■■
The "door-in-the-face" technique: Follow an outrageously large request with one that is more reasonable.

Realtors and insurance agents give us "free" bottle-openers, pads of paper, and refrigerator magnets, hoping we will keep them in mind when we purchase a home or insurance. And resort developers inform us that we have won "free" appliances—all we have to do is pick them up in person and listen to their sales pitch. Research on reciprocity suggests that "free" gifts are often far from free.

The reciprocity principle helps to explain the effectiveness of the *door-in-the-face technique*, which consists of following an outrageously large request that the target is almost certain to reject with a smaller, more reasonable request. (The "door-in-the-face" technique takes its name from the solicitor who makes a large request, gets the door slammed in his or her face, and then comes back with a more modest request.) A study by Cialdini and his colleagues (1975) provides a dramatic illustration of the phenomenon. College students were asked to commit themselves to spend two hours a week as counselors to juvenile delinquents for at least two years. Not surprisingly, they refused to make this enormous commitment. Then, the same students were asked for a smaller favor: Would they then instead help chaperone a group of juvenile delinquents during a day's trip to the zoo? Fifty percent of the subjects agreed to this smaller request, compared with 17 percent of a control group who had not first been approached with the larger request.

Why did subjects comply so frequently after having turned down the larger initial request? The person making the request made a "concession" by reducing his request, and the norm of reciprocity holds that subjects should "repay" his concession with a concession of their own—compliance with the smaller request. The door-in-the-face technique is a method whereby the requestor creates a kind of fake debt and then immediately cashes in on it.

The *that's-not-all technique* also makes use of the norm of reciprocity to induce compliance (Burger, 1986). Here a subject is offered a product (for example, a cupcake at a bake sale) at a high price ($1), and before he or she has time to respond the salesperson "sweetens" the deal by lowering the price (say, to 75 cents) or by throwing in something extra (say, two cookies). Interestingly, significantly more subjects will accept this "sweetened" deal than will subjects offered the better deal initially. In part this effect seems due to subjects' reciprocating the "concession" made by the salesperson. (Note that one way the door-in-the-face technique differs from the that's-not-all technique is that the subject is given the opportunity to refuse the initial outrageous request in the first method, but he or she is not given time to refuse the initial deal in the second method.)

In our discussion of conformity, we noted that committing people to their judgments can help them resist pressures to conform. However, commitment has the potential to entrap us as well. Two important strategies of gaining compliance rely on committing people (at times unfairly) to a course of action: the "foot-in-the-door" and the "low-ball" techniques.

How does each of these work? The basic principle of the *foot-in-the-door technique* is simple: Follow a small initial request with a much larger second request. Jonathan Freedman and Scott Fraser (1966) conducted the first study that demonstrated just how powerful the foot-in-the-door technique can be. Posing as representatives of the "Community Committee for Traffic Safety," experimenters asked homeowners in Palo Alto, California, if they would display in their window a small three-inch-square sign that read "Be a safe driver." Two weeks later, a different experimenter returned with a much larger request: Would the homeowners allow a large, rather unattractive "Drive carefully" sign to be placed in their front lawn? Surprisingly, 76 percent of subjects who had earlier agreed to display the window sign complied, compared with 17 percent of a control group of homeowners who had not been exposed to the initial request.

Why does complying with a small initial request so increase the odds that subjects will comply with a much larger second request? Freedman and Fraser found evidence for the effect even when a different person made the second request. Even more startling, they found evidence for the foot-in-the-door effect even when the topics of the signs were different for the first and second requests (for example, subjects might be asked initially to display a "Be a safe driver" sign and then a "Keep California beautiful" sign).

After complying with a small initial request, people feel committed to their behavior and even come to change their perceptions of themselves (DeJong, 1979; DeJong & Musilli, 1982). For example, after displaying a "Be a safe driver" sign in your window, you might decide that you are committed to the cause of traffic safety, and you might even conclude that you are a helpful, civic-minded person. Research shows that a small initial commitment, such as signing a petition (for example, to provide facilities for the mentally handicapped), can significantly increase the probability that you will later donate money to the same cause (Schwarzwald, Bizman, & Raz, 1983).

The *low-ball technique* also uses initial commitment to increase subsequent compliance; the person making the request gets you to comply under very favorable conditions and then reneges on some of these conditions once you make the commitment. For example, a car salesperson may offer you a great deal on your dream car, with lots of options thrown in. You agree to the purchase. Then the salesperson contacts you and says she was mistaken; some of the options are not really included in the quoted price. Do you back out of the deal now, or do you grit your teeth and stick to your initial commitment to buy? Surprisingly, many proceed with the deal.

Cialdini and his colleagues (1978) demonstrated the power of the low-ball in a simple study. A woman called up introductory psychology students to schedule them for an experiment. Unfortunately, there was one relatively undesirable feature about this experiment—it was scheduled for 7:00 in the morning. In one experimental condition (the low-ball condition), the woman informed subjects that the experiment was at 7 A.M. *after* they had already agreed to participate. In the control condition, subjects were informed of the 7 A.M. time before they were asked to participate.

More subjects agreed to be in the experiment in the low-ball condition (56 percent) than in the control condition (31 percent). Furthermore, significantly more of the low-ball subjects (53 percent) actually showed up, bleary-eyed, to their 7 A.M. appointment than did control subjects (24 percent).

The low-ball can be used for more important purposes than getting college students out of bed early in the morning. A study by Pallak, Cook, and Sullivan (1980) induced Iowa residents to conserve energy through a clever application of the low-ball strategy. Specifically, consumers were induced to reduce their use of natural gas during the winter with the promise that, if successful, their names would be published in a newspaper article praising energy-conserving citizens. Subjects reduced their gas consumption by over 12 percent. Then the researchers told the homeowners that the newspaper article would not be published. Once the "reason" for their initial compliance had disappeared, did the homeowners return immediately to their energy-wasteful ways? Not at all. Rather, they reduced gas consumption even more! The low-ball got each of them to make an initial commitment, but then those commitments took on a life of their own. As a matter of fact, removing the "prop" of their initial reason seemed to induce subjects to justify their acts of conservation with new reasons (for example, "I am a civic-minded, energy-conserving citizen").

Psychological Reactance and Compliance

Sometimes people get us to do something by telling us we cannot or may not be able to do it. A realtor tells a wishy-washy customer that someone else has just made an offer on a house, and the formerly undecided customer immediately makes a higher counteroffer. A salesperson tells a shopper there is "just one left," and the customer buys it at once. A woman tells her unwilling-to-make-a-commitment boyfriend that she's found a new boyfriend and wants to end their relationship; he immediately proposes marriage to her.

Why does taking something away get us to act? The theory of *psychological reactance* (Brehm, 1966; Brehm & Brehm, 1981) argues that when people feel that their freedom of choice is threatened, they experience unpleasant arousal (that is, reactance), which motivates them to restore their freedom. If someone takes away your freedom to buy a house, how can you restore that freedom? Obviously, you must buy the house.

In *1984* Winston Smith seems to experience psychological reactance. Chafing against the horrible restrictions to personal freedom imposed by the Party and Big

▪▪

SUMMARY TABLE 14.2   Strategies for Gaining Compliance

What strategies make us more likely to comply with others' requests?

STRATEGY	PRINCIPLE	EXAMPLE
Positive moods	Make request in a setting that creates positive mood in target	Make request during a delicious dinner at a pleasant restaurant
Ingratiation	Say flattering things to target	Praise target's intelligence, appearance, or personality; then make request
Favors	Do small favor for target (makes use of norm of reciprocity)	Buy target a soft drink, then try to sell product
Door-in-the-face	Follow a very large request that the target is likely to refuse with a smaller, more reasonable request (makes use of reciprocity)	Ask target to volunteer for two years of charity work; after he or she refuses, ask target to volunteer to work for one weekend
That's-not-all	Offer a product for a high price, and before target has chance to refuse, lower price slightly or "throw in" something extra (makes use of reciprocity)	Offer to sell a cupcake for $1, then quickly lower price to 75 cents or throw in "extra" cookies
Foot-in-the-door	Follow small initial request with a much larger second request (makes use of commitment and self-perception processes)	Ask target to sign a petition endorsing a charity; come back later and ask for a large donation to the charity
Low-ball	Get target to commit to comply under very favorable terms, then later renege on some of the terms (makes use of commitment)	Car salesperson gets customer to agree to car purchase with many options "thrown in," and then later informs customer that not all options are included
Reactance	Get target to comply by threatening his or her freedom of choice, sometimes by creating an illusion of scarcity	Salesperson informs customer that product is "the last one," and after it's sold the customer will be unable to purchase it

Brother, Winston decides that he wants to rebel against all the Party's rules and regulations. College students also seem to react against legal restrictions by desiring to engage in the forbidden activities. For example, underage students find a book more attractive when it is labeled as "restricted to those 21 years and over" (Zellinger, Fromkin, Speller, & Kohm, 1974). Studies like this suggest that censorship may sometimes backfire insofar as it makes the banned material even more attractive to many people. Want to sell a book? Tell people they *can't* buy it.

Summary Table 14.2 reviews the compliance strategies we have discussed — information you may find highly practical. After all, forewarned is forearmed.

Brainwashing — The Ultimate in Social Influence?

. . . O'Brien watched him, . . . four fingers still extended. He drew back the lever. This time the pain was only slightly eased.

"How many fingers, Winston?"

"Four."

The needle went up to sixty.

"How many fingers, Winston?"

"Four! Four! What else can I say? Four!"

The needle must have risen again. . . .

"How many fingers, Winston?"

"Four! Stop it, stop it! How can you go on? Four! Four!"

"How many fingers, Winston?"

"Five! Five! Five!"

"No, Winston, that is no use. You are lying. You still think there are four. How many fingers, please?"

"Four! Five! Four! Anything you like. Only stop it, stop the pain!"

—— *1984, p. 253*

Winston Smith eventually falls into the hands of the Thought Police. Imprisoned in the "Ministry of Love," he undergoes an excruciating and degrading process of brainwashing. In the grim world of Big Brother, no technique of influence is forbidden — grinding indoctrination, starvation, mind-altering drugs, or physical torture.

Of course, no social psychologist could conduct ethically acceptable experiments on brainwashing techniques. However, psychologists have studied people who have been the unfortunate victims of "brainwashing" — for example, American soldiers captured by the Communist Chinese during the Korean War (Schein, 1956) and political prisoners detained in Nazi concentration camps (Bettelheim, 1943). Although the Nazis often used physical torture, the Communist Chinese relied more on "psychological" methods of brainwashing. What were these methods? It may surprise you to learn that we've touched on some of them — albeit in much milder forms — already in this chapter.

For example, the Chinese used the techniques of ingratiation and associating themselves with positive, rewarding events. After capturing American soldiers, the Chinese reminded them how fortunate they were to be captives of the "friendly" Chinese rather than of the "brutal" North Koreans. Although conditions were generally bleak, men who cooperated with the Chinese did receive special favors — small items of clothing, hot tea, fresh fruit. It was made clear, however, that these favors would go only to those who "learned the truth." What was the "truth"? — that South Korea started the war and that the United States was an imperialistic aggressor in a civil war. By offering rewards to collaborators, the Chinese destroyed solidarity among the soldiers by breaking up groups of friends, removing social supports, and making prisoners suspicious that others were collaborators.

It might seem strange to you that abused people could ever come to identify with and believe their oppressors, but this has been documented in certain cases. For example, Bruno Bettelheim (1943) noted that inmates in Nazi con-

Obedience

"You are prepared to cheat, to forge, to blackmail, to corrupt the minds of children, to distribute habit-forming drugs, to encourage prostitution, to disseminate venereal diseases — to do anything which is likely to cause demoralization and weaken the power of the Party?"

"Yes."

"If, for example, it would somehow serve our interests to throw sulphuric acid in a child's face — are you prepared to do that?"

"Yes. . . ."

centration camps sometimes "identified with the aggressor," even to the point of imitating their SS guards. In a powerful passage in *1984*, George Orwell similarly portrays a strange attachment between Winston Smith and his torturer, O'Brien:

. . . he was shaking uncontrollably, his teeth were chattering, the tears rolling down his cheeks. For a moment he clung to O'Brien like a baby, curiously comforted by the heavy arm round his shoulders. He had the feeling that O'Brien was his protector, that the pain was something that came from outside, from some other source, and that it was O'Brien who would save him from it. (p. 254)

The Chinese also made good use of the foot-in-the-door technique. They conducted grueling, repetitious interviews with prisoners. If a prisoner ever admitted something negative about the United States, he was asked to elaborate on the "errors" of his country, and he was reminded repeatedly of his critical statement in future interrogations.

Sometimes prisoners were asked to "copy" noncontroversial answers provided by the Chinese to interview questions — a seemingly harmless concession. Then these were shown to other soldiers, who believed them to be voluntary collaborations. The camps in which prisoners lived had elaborate sets of rules that were so complex that the men could not help but violate some of them. When the inevitable violation occurred, prisoners had to write out confessions to their misdeeds, and this provided an initial foot-in-the-door to extract confessions for larger misdeeds.

The Chinese also made clever use of the principle of committing people to positions contrary to their beliefs. For example, the Chinese offered highly desired prizes, like cigarettes, for prisoners' essays dealing with certain political topics. Writing an essay seemed to prisoners a harmless way to obtain some of the small pleasures of life. But then the "winning" essays — typically se-

lected because they supported some Communist dogma — were published in the camp newspaper. In writing these essays, many prisoners ended up making larger (and more public) commitments than they had bargained on.

Despite their total control of prisoners' lives and their patient and interminable indoctrination sessions, the Chinese generally seemed not to be highly successful in "brainwashing" a majority of American prisoners of war (Schein, 1956). We should not take great satisfaction in this, however, for the Chinese attempts at brainwashing suffered from one major limitation: The Chinese often lacked a good command of the English language, and thus the prisoners of war could often rebel with subtle kinds of linguistic sarcasm that was unintelligible to the Chinese.

How about Winston Smith? Did he succumb to O'Brien's brainwashing? To find out, you must read *1984*.

"You are prepared to commit suicide, if and when we order you to do so?"
"Yes."

—— *1984*, p. 173

If Winston Smith's glib agreement to perform outrageously immoral acts upon command strikes you as a bit melodramatic, then consider this painful truth: Horrible forms of obedience occur in fact as well as in fiction. During World War II obedient Germans sent millions of men, women, and children to their deaths in extermination camps. In 1978, over 900 devoted followers of the Reverend Jim Jones obeyed his command to commit mass suicide by drinking cyanide-laced punch. And during the My Lai massacre in Vietnam, American soldiers obeyed commands to kill innocent civilians. Mike Wallace of CBS News obtained the following grim testimony from one participant:

Q. Started pushing them off into the ravine?
A. Off into the ravine. . . . And we started shooting them. . . .
Q. Again — men, women, and children?
A. Men, women, and children.
Q. And babies?
A. And babies. And so we started shooting them. . . .
Q. Why did you do it?
A. Why did I do it? Because I felt like I was ordered to do it. . . . (quoted in Milgram, 1974, p. 185)

The Nature of Obedience

How does obedience differ from conformity and compliance? For one thing, the social pressures to obey are more out in the open; pressures to conform are often "beneath the surface." In Asch's studies, for example, confederates exerted no overt pressure on subjects. Pressures to comply are more obvious — someone makes a direct request. Pressures to obey are most obvious; they occur when someone, typically a legitimate authority, commands us to do something. Obedience also differs from compliance and conformity in that the social influence almost always comes from a "higher-up" — someone who occupies a position of higher status or authority.

Why did people obey in Nazi Germany, at the Jonestown mass suicide, and at the My Lai massacre? Could average people obey in such horrible ways, if placed in the right situation? When are people most likely and least likely to obey?

These are exactly the questions addressed by Stanley Milgram (1974) in an extraordinary series of experiments, some of which we already examined in Chapter 2. In the guise of conducting a learning experiment, an experimenter asked subjects to deliver increasingly severe and painful electric shocks to an innocent victim strapped into a chair in the next room. The experimenter repeatedly ordered the subject to continue, and as the shocks increased from 15 volts up to the maximum possible of 450 volts, the victim showed increasing evidence of pain; he screamed in anguish and called out repeatedly, "Let me out of here." In one particularly dramatic version of the study, the victim stated that he suffered from a "heart condition." In all these experiments the "victim" was in fact a confederate, and his highly convincing screams and protests were tape recordings.

The basic finding of Milgram's study was that 26 out of 40 subjects (65 percent) obeyed the experimenter completely and delivered shocks of up to 450 volts to the screaming, protesting victim. Milgram (1974) summed up the moral import of his findings succinctly:

The results . . . are . . . disturbing. They raise the possibility that human nature, or — more specifically — the kind of character produced in American democratic society, cannot be counted on to insulate its citizens from brutality and inhumane treatment at the direction of malevolent authority. A substantial proportion of people do what they are told to do, irrespective of the content of

▪▪▪▪▪▪▪▪▪▪▪▪▪▪▪▪▪▪▪▪▪▪▪▪▪

The mass suicide at Jonestown. When are people most likely to obey destructive and immoral commands?

the act and without limitations of conscience, so long as they perceive that the command comes from a legitimate authority. (p. 189)

Milgram was not satisfied simply to demonstrate obedience in his laboratory; he also wanted to understand the factors that influence obedience. One of these factors was the proximity of the victim: When the victim was in the next room, 63 percent of the subjects obeyed completely; when the victim sat in the same room as the subject, obedience declined to 40 percent; and if the subject was required to touch the victim (in order to force his hand down onto the shock plate), obedience declined still more — to 30 percent. Milgram found an inverse relationship between obedience and the proximity of the authority figure — the greater the distance between authority and subject, the less the obedience. For example, when the experimenter was out of the room and gave his commands by telephone, obedience went down to 21 percent.

Milgram investigated a number of other factors that influence obedience in his experiments. Among the most important were the institutional setting of the experiment, the presence of social pressures to obey or rebel, and the roles occupied by the people who gave orders and who were victims. Let's briefly consider each of these variables.

Institutional setting and obedience.   Milgram's initial studies were conducted in a well-equipped laboratory at Yale University. Subjects, who were solicited by newspaper ads from the local community, often regarded Yale and its faculty with great respect. Thus perhaps part of the high obedience Milgram observed was due to the prestige of the institution conducting the research.

FIGURE 14.10 **Adding conformity pressures to the Milgram obedience paradigm: a schematic representation of the experiment's physical setup. In this variation of his obedience studies, Milgram added two more "teachers" (actually confederates) who either obeyed or rebelled against the experimenter. Milgram wanted to see what effect the other teachers' behavior had on subjects' obedience.**

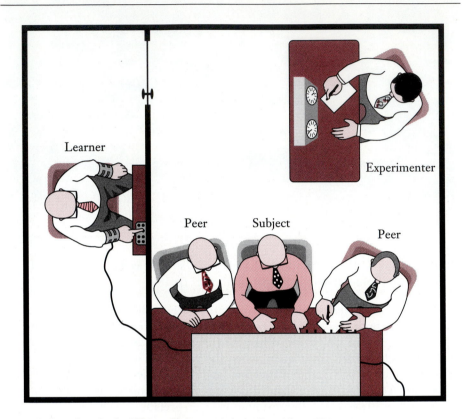

SOURCE: Redrawn from Stanley Milgram, *Obedience to Authority*. Copyright © 1974 by Stanley Milgram. Reprinted by permission of Harper & Row, Publisher, Inc.

To test this possibility, Milgram moved his study to a run-down office building in a nearby industrial city—Bridgeport, Connecticut. The study was now totally divorced from Yale University; however, the procedures were the same. Did obedience go down markedly? No. It declined slightly, to 48 percent.

Social pressures and obedience. In a fascinating set of experimental variations, Milgram combined conformity pressures with pressures to obey. Now the subject was one of three teachers: one teacher's job was to read the words the victim was to learn, another teacher recorded whether or not the learner gave correct answers, and the third teacher delivered shocks to the learner when he answered incorrectly. In fact the first two teachers were confederates; the teacher delivering shocks was the real subject. Figure 14.10 presents a schematic layout of this study.

Milgram created two dramatically different situations. In one, the two teachers who were confederates rebelled against the experimenter, whereas in the other they complied completely and without protest. In the first instance, one teacher stopped obeying when shocks reached 150 volts. Despite the experimenter's orders to continue, this teacher left his seat in protest and sat on the other side of the room. The experimenter then ordered the second teacher to take over the first teacher's responsibilities. The experiment continued with just two teachers until shocks reached 210 volts, at which point the second teacher also rebelled. Now the experimenter ordered the third teacher (the actual subject) to take over the responsibilities of the two rebelling teachers.

Upon seeing two peers protest against the shock procedures and rebel against the experimenter, what percentage of subjects continued in the study and proceeded to 450 volts? Only 10 percent obeyed fully. How about in the condition in which the other teachers meekly complied without protest? In that case 93 percent of the subjects obeyed fully. Clearly, conformity pressures had an extraordinary impact on subjects' behavior in Milgram's obedience experiments. Indeed, the difference between a 10 percent and 93 percent obedience level is virtually the most powerful effect possible. What factor was most successful in influencing obedience? Ironically, another variety of social influence—namely, conformity pressures. In a sense, Milgram was fighting fire with fire.

These experiments suggest that people in groups may at times possess greater resources to resist unjust authority than do individuals, at least when they can look to others to support their rebellion. Gamson, Fireman, and Rytina (1982) provided additional evidence that social support can foster rebellion. These researchers had groups of subjects come to a hotel in southeastern Michigan to participate in a study on "community standards." Specifically, subjects were videotaped as they discussed their opinions about a court case in which a big oil company was attempting to oust a gas station manager who spoke out against the company's practice of fixing high oil prices. The oil company claimed it was firing the manager because of his "moral turpitude" in living with a woman out of wedlock.

As the study progressed, it became increasingly clear to subjects that their job in this "study" was to express false opinions, which would be videotaped and then used to help the oil company in its court case. Unlike subjects in Milgram's studies, most subjects rebelled and successfully resisted pressures to comply with the experiment's "authorities." Why were these subjects successful in rebelling? One critical factor was that they were in groups, and during periodic "rest breaks" they could talk to one another.

By communicating with one another—by expressing their upset and defining the situation as unjust—groups of subjects could mobilize their resources. Often, one "trigger person" who was particularly outraged began the rebellion, and then others followed suit. Once some members of the group rebelled, conformity pressures induced other members to join in. The Gamson, Fireman, and Rytina study and the "peer rebellion" version of the Milgram study demonstrate that there may be safety in numbers when we oppose unjust authority.

The role of the person giving and receiving commands.   Milgram (1974) summarized his many experiments in a book entitled *Obedience to Authority*. The title makes an important point: We do not obey just any person, but rather someone whom we perceive to be a legitimate authority. This point is underscored by several intriguing variations of the Milgram study.

In one version, the *learner* ordered the subject to deliver increasingly severe shocks and the *experimenter* received these shocks. How did this strange state of affairs come to be? After the experimenter initially described the study, the learner stated that he was afraid of shocks and reluctant to participate. He then offered a solution—why didn't the experimenter go through the procedure first as the "learner," and if that worked out, then he would participate. The experimenter agreed and the experiment proceeded, this time with the learner (actually a confederate) ordering the subject to deliver increasingly severe shocks to the strapped-in experimenter.

As the shock levels increased, the experimenter began to cry out in pain and protest, just as the victim did in other versions of the experiment. He demanded to be released. What happened next? Did the subject obey the confederate goading him on, or did he comply with the experimenter? In fact, no subject completely obeyed the confederate in this version of the study. Indeed, no one exceeded 150 volts, the point at which the experimenter first started protesting.

In another strange permutation of roles, Milgram created a situation in which the *victim* demanded to be shocked while the experimenter suggested terminating the experiment. Here's specifically what happened: The experiment began as usual, and when the shocks reached 150 volts, the learner began to cry out in pain. The experimenter stated that this learner's reaction seemed to be more severe than usual and that they should stop the study. The learner, overhearing this comment from the next room, insisted that they continue with the experiment; to stop would be an affront to his manliness. He was certain he could stand the pain.

Whom did the subject obey, the experimenter or the learner? Again, no subject proceeded past 150 volts in this version of the study, and thus everyone obeyed the experimenter, not the learner. Although this may not surprise you, there is an important lesson to draw from this variation: The power in Milgram's obedience experiment lay with the experimenter, not with the victim. When the experimenter ordered subjects to deliver shocks, there seemed to be almost nothing the victim could say to get subjects to stop. Conversely, when the experimenter ordered subjects to stop shocking, there was nothing the victim could say to get subjects to continue.

■■■■■■■■■■■■■■■■■■■■■■■

The Milgram Studies in Perspective

Milgram's obedience studies are among the most famous in social psychology. In the words of social psychologist Arthur Miller (1986), "It would not be hyperbole . . . to say that the obedience experiments have sent shock waves throughout the academic world and beyond. . . ." Milgram's research has been attacked for the stresses it created in its subjects (Baumrind, 1964), discussed in numerous magazine and newspaper articles, and even dramatized as a television movie. Milgram's studies seem more than just academic investigations of social behavior; they make powerful statements about "human nature" and the human capacity for evil.

How are we to interpret the high levels of obedience in Milgram's studies? Were his subjects sadists? The answer here seems clearly to be, "No." Most subjects in Milgram's experiments were quite upset over their victim's suffering, even to the point of showing such physical symptoms as choking, sweating, and hysterical laughter. And yet they still complied with the experimenter's orders. Milgram conducted one version of his study in which subjects were free to choose their own levels of shock; only two subjects exceeded 150 volts. Thus, although there may be a small minority of sadistic people, sadism is not an adequate explanation for most subjects' behavior.

Milgram (1974) offered several explanations for the high level of obedience in his studies. Consistent with the foot-in-the-door phenomenon, subjects complied first at low levels of shock and then gradually proceeded to higher, more painful levels. Subjects seemed to be restricted by social norms to treat authority figures with politeness and deference. (Think, for example, how you generally talk to such authorities as bosses, clergy, and police officers.) Milgram demonstrated that obedience is not something rare and peculiar; rather, it is part of the fabric of everyday social life. In organized social groups (families, businesses, the military, religions) people occupy positions within authority hierarchies, and they learn to give up their freedom of choice to "legitimate" authorities — parents, bosses, generals, religious leaders. A problem occurs — as Milgram's studies dramatically illustrate — when legitimate authorities ask us to do immoral things.

Milgram's findings are dramatic in part because they are so unexpected. Most of us seem to expect subjects' ethics, conscience, and compassion to be stronger — and the influence of the authority figure to be weaker — than demonstrated in Milgram's experiments. Milgram underscored the counterintuitive quality of his findings by asking both naive college students and professional psychiatrists to predict how subjects would behave in his obedience paradigm. Both groups grossly underestimated the actual levels of obedience observed.

Just as some people do not conform in conformity studies, some people do not obey in obedience studies. The existence of the 65 percent of subjects who obeyed completely in the basic Milgram study should not blind us to the 35 percent who disobeyed. How were these subjects different? Milgram (1974) investigated the effects on obedience of a number of "person variables" (such as personality, gender, religion, and social class), and in general he did not find strong effects. There was some tendency for people with high degrees of authoritarianism to be more obedient, but the relation between personality traits and obedience typically was weak. Milgram found that women obeyed as much as men in his paradigm. There was a tendency for Roman Catholics to obey more than Protestants and Jews, and for uneducated and lower-class people to obey more than educated and higher-class people, but again these effects were weak and inconsistent across studies.

Milgram (1974) concluded that "often, it is not so much the kind of person a man is as the kind of situation in which he finds himself that determines how he will act." According to Milgram, the individual differences that occur in obedience are not well understood.

Obedience Studies Since Milgram's

In science it is important to replicate findings, and a number of replications of Milgram's studies have been published. Some of these document obedience across cultures. For example, Mantell (1971) found that when a group of West German subjects were placed in the Milgram paradigm, 85 percent obeyed completely. Shanab and Yahya (1977) reported a 63 percent level of obedience among Jordanian teenage students. (In this study, the experimenter ordering subjects to deliver shocks was a woman.) In a somewhat modified version of the Milgram study, Kilham and Mann (1974) reported high levels of obedience — up to 68 percent — among Australian subjects.

SUMMARY TABLE 14.3   Variables That Affect Obedience

SUMMARY TABLE 14.3   Variables That Affect Obedience

What factors make us more or less likely to engage in destructive obedience?

VARIABLE	EFFECT
Proximity to victim	Subjects obey less the closer they are to a suffering victim
Proximity to authority	Subjects obey less the farther away is the authority who gives commands
Institutional setting	Conducting Milgram's obedience experiments in a run-down office building in Bridgeport, Connecticut, rather than at Yale University, reduced obedience only slightly
Conformity pressures	Obedient peers increase subjects' obedience; rebellious peers greatly reduce obedience
Role of person giving commands	People obey others most when others are perceived to be legitimate authorities; in Milgram's studies, subjects generally obeyed the experimenter but did not obey other subjects
Personality traits	In Milgram's studies, assessed traits correlated weakly with obedience
Gender	Milgram found no difference between men and women in their average levels of obedience
Cultural differences	Cross-cultural replications show some variation across cultures, but obedience in Milgram-type studies tends to be high regardless of culture

Other studies have documented destructive obedience in naturalistic settings and in situations that possessed a high degree of realism. For example, one study showed that nurses will deliver dangerous levels of medication if ordered to do so by a doctor (Hofling, Brotzman, Dalrymple, Graves, & Pierce, 1966). And Sheridan and King (1972) conducted a dramatic study in which subjects delivered *real* electric shocks to yelping puppies; their subjects obeyed at even higher levels than did Milgram's. In sum, destructive obedience is a real phenomenon occurring in many different places and settings. For a review of the factors that affect obedience behavior, see Summary Table 14.3.

Resisting Social Influence

The clever thing was to break the rules and stay alive all the same. He wondered vaguely how many others . . . there might be in the younger generation — people who had grown up . . . knowing nothing else, accepting the Party as something unalterable, like the sky, not rebelling against its authority but simply evading it, as a rabbit dodges a dog.

—— *1984*, p. 133

When Winston Smith decided to rebel—to stop conforming to the Party and obeying Big Brother—he faced the prospect of brainwashing, torture, and death. Although most of us don't face such horrible possibilities, we still often find it difficult to resist social pressures. Surely one of the most troubling aspects of Milgram's obedience studies is that subjects who were distraught over their "immoral" behavior and were not under any direct, physical duress still could not muster the psychological resources needed to rebel against an unjust authority.

You probably would not want to act like the majority of Milgram's subjects. How can you help to ensure that you will not? Perhaps unknowingly you've already taken a first step, for research suggests that people who learn about psychology experiments may change their behavior in analogous real-life settings (Sherman, 1980); by implication, knowing about obedience experiments may make you more resistant to unjust authority in real-life settings. Clearly, the first step to resisting unfair social pressures is to think about them, question them, and sometimes challenge them. Obedience should never be blind; it should always be thoughtful. In *1984* the Party repeats one slogan over and over: "Ignorance is strength." But the truth is, ignorance is ignorance; and in particular, ignorance of social psychological research may make you *weaker* in the face of social influence (which, of course, is just what the Party in *1984* would want).

If you think carefully about the research described in this chapter, it will provide you with many possibilities for resisting social influence. For example, research on both conformity and obedience demonstrates that social support can help us to resist social pressures. Let's translate this to a practical example: You are about to go to a car dealer, and you're afraid that you may be overwhelmed by a smooth-talking salesperson. One solution is to take along a friend or family member who can support you against the salesperson.

Cialdini (1988) noted that most of the common strategies used to gain compliance suggest corresponding strategies of defense. For example, if you are aware of the "luncheon technique" — that people are more compliant when eating and feeling good—then make it a rule of thumb never to make a major decision over lunch. Tell the person plying you with food and pleasure that you must "sleep on it."

Don't be captured by the low-ball or the foot-in-the-door if you don't want to be. A good strategy here is to ask yourself the explicit question, "Would I agree to do this if I hadn't made my initial commitment?" For example, a car dealer uses the low-ball to induce you to agree to buy a car and then later tells you that some of the options aren't really included. Now ask yourself, "Would I have agreed to purchase this car in the first place if these options were not included?" If your answer is "No," smile politely at the dealer and walk away, regardless of your prior commitment.

If a salesperson uses psychological reactance to corral you, ask yourself, "Is the commodity really scarce?" Is your freedom really limited? So what if someone has made an offer on this particular house — there are thousands of other houses to be bought. Don't let someone else create illusions of scarcity.

Above all, be aware of the power of social influence. We have seen in this chapter that people will say things they don't believe, agree to give away their hard-earned money, and even torture innocent human beings — all because of pressures from other people. By being informed and constantly aware of the power of social influence, we can resist it when it is unjust. And in the process, we can help guarantee that the world of *1984* never becomes a reality.

Summary

1. Individuals conform when they maintain or change their behavior to be consistent with group standards, comply when they accede to a request made by another, and obey when they follow a direct command, typically from someone perceived to be a legitimate authority.

2. Kelman described three levels of social influence: (1) when an individual complies on the surface to gain rewards or avoid punishments, (2) when an individual behaves like others because he or she is attracted to them, and (3) when an individual behaves like others because he or she is rationally persuaded by them.

3. Sherif's autokinetic studies showed that subjects who made ambiguous perceptual judgments in a group setting were influenced by other group members' judgments. This influence extended to private beliefs as well as public statements.

4. In a relatively simple task that required subjects to judge the lengths of lines, Solomon Asch found that 75 percent of his subjects conformed at least once to a unanimous but incorrect majority. Conformity was substantially lower if subjects could write rather than publicly announce their answers.

5. People sometimes conform because of normative social pressures — rewards and punishments delivered by groups to foster conforming behavior and discourage nonconforming behavior. Direct pressure and rejection are two powerful forms of normative social pressure exerted by groups. In addition, people sometimes conform because of informational social influence; that is, they look to the group as a source of accurate information.

6. A number of personality traits correlate weakly with conformity. However, research suggests there is no single kind of conforming personality or set of traits that predicts all kinds of conformity.

7. Conformity tends to increase as the pressuring groups increase in size to four people, and then remains relatively stable. Larger groups tend to produce greater conformity than smaller groups when group members are perceived to be independent. The Social Influence Model provides a precise mathematical description of the amount of social influence that pressuring groups of varying sizes exert on target groups of varying sizes.

8. In general, people conform more to groups to which they are attracted. Newcomb's Bennington College study demonstrated that college women changed

their attitudes to be more similar to those of attractive upperclassmen and faculty members.

9. People of average or marginal status in a group tend to conform more to the group's standards than do high- or low-status people.

10. Subjects conform substantially more to a unanimous group than to a group containing one other nonconformist.

11. The more individuals commit themselves to a response (for example, by writing it down) before announcing it to a disagreeing group, the less likely they are to conform to the group.

12. Conformity sometimes consists of changing behavior to be like a group's, and sometimes it consists of maintaining behavior to be like a group's. The diamond model describes all possible responses to social influence in terms of two dimensions: movement (changing behavior after social influence) and congruence (whether behavior is like or unlike the group's after influence).

13. Minority influence occurs when disagreeing minorities influence the behavior of the majority. Minorities are most likely to influence majorities when they consistently argue their position, when their views are consistent with prevailing cultural trends, and when they are single rather than double minorities.

14. Minority influence is more likely to produce private conversion, whereas majority influence is more likely to produce public compliance. Furthermore, minority influence sometimes leads groups to think more about the topics of disagreement and arrive at more creative and thoughtful judgments.

15. People are more likely to comply with requests when they are in pleasant surroundings or the target of ingratiation.

16. Doing small favors for people makes them more likely to comply with later requests. This finding is consistent with the norm of reciprocity.

17. The door-in-the-face technique consists of following a very large request that the target is likely to reject with a smaller, more reasonable request. This technique substantially increases the likelihood that the target will comply with the second request. The that's-not-all technique increases compliance by offering a target a product for a high price and then reducing the price slightly or adding something extra to the deal before the target has time to refuse.

18. The foot-in-the-door technique consists of following a small initial request with a much larger second request. This technique substantially increases the likelihood that the target will comply with the second request.

19. The low-ball technique consists of committing the target to comply with a request that has favorable conditions and then reneging on some of the conditions. This technique increases the likelihood that the target will agree to the less favorable terms.

20. People experience psychological reactance — a state of unpleasant arousal — when they believe that their freedom of choice is threatened. Consistent with reactance theory, people sometimes can be induced to engage in a behavior by informing them that they cannot.

21. "Brainwashing" often makes use of standard processes of influence in settings in which indoctrinators have complete control over their targets' environment.

22. Stanley Milgram found that a majority of subjects obeyed an experimenter's command to deliver highly painful electric shocks to an innocent victim. Obedience declined the closer the victim was to subjects and the farther the experimenter was from subjects.

23. Obedience in Milgram's study was not strongly influenced by the institutional setting. Rebellious peers greatly reduced subjects' obedience in Milgram's experiments, whereas compliant peers increased obedience.

24. Subjects in Milgram's studies obeyed the experimenter but not other subjects. In general, people obey only those they perceive to be legitimate authorities.

25. Knowledge about social influence can help us to resist unjust influence in everyday life.

Glossary

Autokinetic effect: A perceptual illusion that occurs when a stationary point of light in a dark room appears to move; Sherif asked subjects in groups to estimate the movement of such lights and thus used the autokinetic effect as a means to study conformity

Cohesiveness: The degree to which group members, on average, are attracted to the group

Compliance: Acceding to a request made by another

Conformity: Maintaining or changing behavior to be consistent with group standards

Diamond model: A model that tries to specify all possible responses to social influence; the diamond model uses two dimensions to describe an individual's response to social influence: movement (whether the individual changes his or her opinion after influence) and congruence (whether the individual agrees or disagrees with the group's position after influence)

Door-in-the-face technique: The strategy of following a very large request that the target is likely to reject with a smaller, more reasonable request; a strategy to gain compliance

Foot-in-the-door technique: The strategy of following a small initial request with a much larger second request; a strategy to gain compliance

Informational social influence: Occurs when people look to the group to gain accurate information

Ingratiation: The strategy of saying pleasant things to another in order to gain compliance

Low-ball technique: A strategy of getting a target to agree to a request under favorable terms and then reneging on some of the terms once the commitment is made; a technique of gaining compliance

Minority influence: The influence exerted on majorities by disagreeing minorities

Normative social influence: Occurs when people conform to gain rewards or avoid punishments delivered by a group

Obedience: Following a direct command, typically from someone perceived to be a legitimate authority

Reactance: Negative arousal experienced when people feel that their freedom of choice is threatened; reactance can be used as a strategy to gain compliance — people are induced to engage in the desired behavior by informing them that they may not be able to

That's-not-all technique: The strategy of offering a product at a high price and improving the deal (by lowering the price or adding an additional product) before the target has a chance to refuse; a strategy to gain compliance

HAWTHORNE'S VOICE: Now, Martha Corey, there is abundant evidence in our hands to show that you have given yourself to the reading of fortunes. Do you deny it?

MARTHA COREY'S VOICE: I am innocent to a witch. I know not what a witch is.

HAWTHORNE'S VOICE: How do you know, then, that you are not a witch?

MARTHA COREY'S VOICE: If I were, I would know it.

HAWTHORNE'S VOICE: Why do you hurt these children?

MARTHA COREY'S VOICE: I do not hurt them. I scorn it!

GILES'S VOICE, *roaring:* I have evidence for the court!

Voices of townspeople rise in excitement.

DANFORTH'S VOICE: Remove that man, Marshal!

GILES'S VOICE: You're hearing lies, lies!

A roaring goes up from the people.

—— from *The Crucible*, Act III, by Arthur Miller

CHAPTER 15

Groups

*I*t is 1692, and the citizens of Salem, Massachusetts, are about to descend into hysteria and send dozens of innocent people to the gallows for the crime of witchcraft.

In his dramatization of the Salem witch trials, playwright Arthur Miller shows us social groups at their most destructive and capricious. Cliques of girls succumb to hysterical contagion and make false accusations against their neighbors. Warring factions of townspeople exact personal vengeance against their enemies through false testimony, and the legal system — composed of groups of judges and citizens — falls prey to the collective frenzy.

But Miller also portrays the constructive side of groups in *The Crucible* and reminds us that human life is a drama that is always played out in the context of groups — families, work teams, religious congregations, and friends. Groups nurture us, socialize us, teach us, defend us, and govern us. Miller notes in his commentary on the play that the Puritans of Salem could not have survived the hostile wilderness of Massachusetts without organizing into groups:

> . . . Massachusetts tried to kill off the Puritans, but they combined; they set up a communal society which, in the beginning, was little more than an armed camp with an autocratic and very devoted leadership. It was, however, an autocracy by consent, for they were united from top to bottom by a commonly held ideology whose perpetuation was the reason and justification for all their sufferings. So their self-denial, their purposefulness, their suspicion of all vain pursuits, their hard-handed justice, were altogether perfect instruments for the conquest of this space so antagonistic to man. (p. 140)

Thus in Salem we see both the best and the worst possibilities of groups: achievement, defense, and security on the one hand, and collective illusions, oppression, and violence on the other.

The Crucible indirectly poses a number of basic questions about people in groups: How do groups affect individuals' work and thought? What is the nature of leadership, and how do leaders influence the behavior of groups? Why do some groups (such as mobs and, of course, the witch-hunting tribunals of Puritan Salem) behave in uninhibited and destructive ways? When do groups lead their members to cooperate, and when do they lead them to compete?

Social psychological theories and research can help us to answer these questions, and in the process they can help us to understand better how the Salem witch trials came to pass.

What Is a Group?

A *group* is a collection of individuals who interact and communicate with one another over a period of time. Various theorists have noted the following important characteristics of people in groups: (1) They frequently interact (Lewin, 1948), often in a face-to-face manner (Homans, 1950); (2) they typically share *norms* (prescribed standards of behavior) and occupy agreed-upon, interdependent roles (Newcomb, 1951); and (3) they usually perceive themselves to be part of a collective with the same goals, and they often act similarly to others in the group (Deutsch, 1968; Merton, 1957).

Social groups in Puritan Salem possessed all the characteristics just listed. The people of Salem frequently interacted with one another; indeed, Salem in the late

HUMAN NATURE: GOOD OR EVIL?

Philosophers and theologians have long speculated about the nature of "human nature." Are we innately good, neutral, or evil?

The Judeo-Christian tradition views men and women as innately disposed to evil because of original sin. Masaccio, *The Expulsion from Paradise*, fresco, 1427. In previous eras as well as today, some have explained human evil in terms of diabolical forces. Martin Schongauer, *The Tribulations of St. Anthony*, engraving, c. 1480-90. Buchenwald concentration camp. The devastation and suffering caused by World War II led social psychologists to study many of the evil sides of social behavior — prejudice, aggression, propaganda, and intergroup conflict.

Certainly, human social behavior has a dark side.

Violence during
elections in Panama.
White supremacists.
Riots at a Belgian
soccer match.

In the summer of
1989, Chinese stu-
dents peacefully
demonstrated in
Beijing for democatic
reforms, and were
met by a brutal gov-
ernment crackdown.

But throughout this book we discuss many kinds of good social behavior as well. . . .

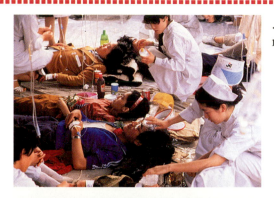

. . . including the kind of altruism displayed by these medical workers tending to injured Chinese students.

People receive love and support from social groups such as the family and from friends. At the AIDS Names Project — which commemorates people who have died from AIDS — a man is consoled by his friend.

While many forms of evil involve large groups of people, so do many forms of good. For example, collective action can effectively oppose social injustices, and groups often can perform constructive tasks that individuals cannot.

A barn-raising in Ohio, c. 1880. A woman's suffrage parade in Washington, D.C., March, 1913. Civil rights marchers in Selma, Alabama, March, 1965.

Are we good, or are we evil? Social psychology tends to take an environmental position: to a great extent we are what the social setting makes us.

Conducting both process and outcome studies, social psychologists have intensively studied how juries arrive at their verdicts.

"I still say you never can tell which way a jury will go."

1600s was little more than a village by modern standards. The citizens of Salem shared rigid norms that defined acceptable behavior and moral propriety, and they certainly felt themselves to be part of a collective community, in part because they had fled from common oppression and faced common dangers. As Arthur Miller notes, ". . . danger was still a possibility, and in unity lay the best promise of safety. . . . The edge of the wilderness was close by" (p. 139).

Studying Group Behavior

Social scientists have used many different research strategies to study behavior in groups (Cartwright & Zander, 1968; Forsyth, 1983). A number of classic studies have observed real-life groups. For example, Whyte (1943) described the social organization of young men who congregated on a street corner in a slum neighborhood of Boston. To study extreme beliefs in groups, Festinger, Schachter, and Back (1950) infiltrated a doomsday sect predicting the imminent end of the world, and Kerckhoff and Back (1968) investigated (after the fact) how and why a group of Southern textile workers succumbed to an outbreak of hysteria-induced illness.

More commonly, social psychologists have studied group outcomes and group processes in the laboratory. *Group outcomes* refer to the final products of group activities — for example, the verdict of a jury, the ideas produced by a "brainstorming" session, or the performance of a relay-racing team. *Group processes* refer to the ongoing communications and interactions among group members that lead to group outcomes — for example, who says what to whom over time in a jury and how this communication process leads to the final verdict.

FIGURE 15.1   **The twelve content categories of Interaction Process Analysis. Bales (1970) developed the IPA categories to classify the behavior of participants in groups.**

General Kinds of Group Behaviors	Specific IPA Content Categories
A. Positive (and mixed) actions	1. Seems friendly 2. Dramatizes 3. Agrees
B. Attempted answers	4. Gives suggestion 5. Gives opinion 6. Gives information
C. Questions	7. Asks for information 8. Asks for opinion 9. Asks for suggestion
D. Negative (and mixed) actions	10. Disagrees 11. Shows tension 12. Seems unfriendly

SOURCE: Bales (1970). Used with permission of Robert Bales.

Dimensions of Group Behavior

A number of studies suggest that there are a small number of fundamentally important dimensions of group behavior (Schutz, 1958; Triandis, 1978; Wish, Deutsch, & Kaplan, 1976). Beginning in the late 1940s, Harvard social psychologist Robert Bales conducted a well-known series of process studies in which he convened groups of subjects (usually seated around a large conference table) to discuss and resolve human-relations problems. Subjects might role-play, for example, that they were engaging in contract negotiations for a company. Based on his observations, Bales (1950, 1970) devised a content-analysis system called *Interaction Process Analysis* (IPA) that classified each group member's statements and behaviors into one of twelve content categories (see Figure 15.1). Some of the IPA content categories focused on emotional behaviors (for example, "agrees"), whereas others focused on informational, task-oriented behaviors ("asks for information").

Bales quantified each group member's behavior using IPA and also asked group members to rate one another on their likability and their contributions to the group. Factor analyses of these data suggested the existence of three main dimensions of group behavior: general activity, likability, and task ability. The activity dimension refers to the general quantity of a group member's participation in the group. For example, a person who rates high in activity talks a lot, makes numerous suggestions, and participates frequently in group discussion. Likability refers to a member's role in the social and emotional life of the group. A person with a high degree of likability engages in many positive socioemotional behaviors and is rated as likable by other members of the group. Finally, task ability refers to a member's task-oriented behaviors within the group. A person rated high in task ability contributes to achieving the group's goal and is rated as intelligent and productive by other members of the group.

Bales's research pointed to two fundamental functions of groups and group behavior: getting work done and dealing with emotional and social relationships. There are many obvious examples of the task-oriented, "work" functions of groups. Juries strive to achieve reasoned verdicts, teams of engineers design new products, and legislatures attempt to enact wise and just laws. There are also many examples of the socioemotional functions of groups: Religious groups provide people with values and a sense of belonging to a larger unit, families nurture and support their members, and therapy groups use intimate emotional communication to foster positive changes in members. (Bales, by the way, first started developing his IPA system while attempting to study the dynamics of Alcoholics Anonymous meetings.) To get work done, groups must often first address social and emotional relations within the group. Legislators, for example, frequently argue and debate, then mend fences and compromise to pass legislation.

Playwright Arthur Miller clearly perceived both the task-oriented and socioemotional functions of groups in Puritan Salem: "Massachusetts tried to kill off the Puritans, but they combined; they set up a communal society. . . . The people of Salem developed a theocracy . . . to prevent any kind of disunity that might open it to destruction by material or ideological enemies" (pp. 140–141). Miller implied that groups in Salem served two main functions: They grew food, built houses, and fought off Indians; and they also enforced ideology, mediated disputes, and promoted cohesiveness.

Groups at Work

When a new farmhouse was built, friends assembled to "raise the roof," and there would be special foods cooked and probably some potent cider passed around. . . . Probably more than the creed, hard work kept the morals of the place from spoiling, for the people were forced to fight the land like heroes for every grain of corn, and no man had very much time for fooling around.

—— *The Crucible*, p. 138

Many animal species show organization into social groups. From an evolutionary perspective, these groups make good sense, for they promote collective defense and allow animals to achieve goals that are impossible to achieve as individuals (Forsyth, 1983). A troop of baboons can fight off predators better than an individual; a pack of wolves can track and hunt prey better than a lone wolf; and a group of people can send a rocket to the moon, whereas an individual certainly cannot. As Miller's quote suggests, the people of Salem realized the power of groups to accomplish large tasks. So have social psychologists, who have studied groups at work for almost 100 years.

Social Facilitation

Let's start with a basic question: How does the presence of other people affect an individual's work performance? In one of the first social psychology experiments ever published in the United States, Norman Triplett (1897) observed that children,

Social groups occur in many species other than *Homo Sapiens*. Thus, social groups must contribute to evolutionary fitness.

when instructed to wind fishing reels as fast as they could, performed faster in groups than when alone. In other words, Triplett found evidence for a *social facilitation effect*: People perform a task faster or better when with others. After Triplett's research, other experiments demonstrated social-facilitation effects in other domains — for example, when subjects perform simple clerical tasks or such simple motor tasks as tracking a moving spot with their finger (Allport, 1920; Dashiell, 1930; Travis, 1925; Zajonc, 1965). Animals as well often show increased performance when in the presence of other members of their species and when performing the same behavior: Ants work harder at building nests in the presence of other working ants (Chen, 1937), and rats eat more heartily when in the presence of other eating rats (Harlow, 1932).

Although a number of early studies clearly demonstrated social facilitation, other studies found just the opposite — that the presence of others sometimes slows down or undermines performance. For example, the presence of other people makes it more difficult for subjects to learn the solution to a maze (Husband, 1931; Pessin & Husband, 1933) and to solve complex problems (Allport, 1920). Because the early studies on social facilitation were inconsistent and contradictory, research on the topic largely died out by World War II.

After some 30 years of neglect, social psychologist Robert Zajonc (1965) revived interest in the topic by offering a surprisingly simple and elegant explanation for the contradictions of the earlier studies. Zajonc expressed his explanation in the theoretical language of Hullian learning theory (see Hull, 1943), but we can state it in more everyday language: The presence of others is arousing, and this arousal facilitates dominant, well-learned habits but inhibits nondominant, poorly learned habits.

To understand the implications of Zajonc's theory of social facilitation better, consider the following question: Does the presence of other people help or hurt the quality of a musical performance — for example, a piano recital? Zajonc's answer is: It depends on how well the artist has learned the material. A brilliant virtuoso pianist may be spurred to greater heights of excellence by an audience, whereas a novice

FIGURE 15.2   Zajonc's theory of social facilitation.

How does the presence of others affect our performance on tasks?

Zajonc's (1965) theory of social facilitation argues that the presence of other people increases arousal, which then facilitates dominant, well-learned habits but inhibits nondominant, poorly learned habits.

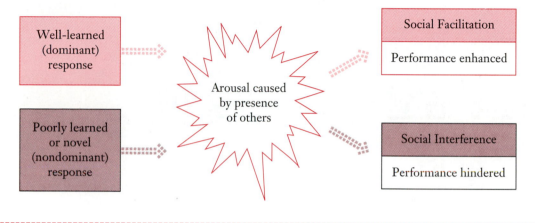

may find her fingers twisted by stage fright. Or consider this personally relevant example: When taking an important exam, would you perform better sitting in a classroom full of other students (as is typically the case) or sitting alone? According to Zajonc, if you know the material extremely well, you will perform better in the more arousing group setting, but if you know the material marginally, then you will perform better in the less arousing, solitary setting (see Figure 15.2).

In *The Crucible*, Arthur Miller described Giles Corey, who could not say his prayers when his wife was around: "I tried and tried and could not. . . . And then she closes her book and walks out of the house, and suddenly—mark this—I could pray again!" Tragically, Giles's observation contributed to the charges that his wife was a witch. Miller noted with irony, "that she stopped his prayer is very probable, but he forgot to say that he'd only recently learned his prayers, and it didn't take much to make him stumble over them" (p. 174). In Zajonc's terminology, saying prayers was a nondominant, poorly learned habit for Giles, and thus the presence of others interfered with his performance.

Many studies offer support for Zajonc's theory (Bond & Titus, 1983; Guerin, 1986; Zajonc, 1980). For example, the presence of others facilitated college students learning a simple maze but interfered with their learning a complex maze (Hunt & Hillery, 1973). Similar effects have been observed in cockroaches! In a clever experiment, Zajonc, Heingartner, and Herman (1969) had roaches escape from a bright light by running through either an easy maze (in which roaches had to run straight ahead to the goal box) or a difficult maze (roaches had to turn right to get to the goal box; see Figure 15.3). Intriguingly, when cockroaches ran in groups or in the presence of "spectator" cockroaches housed in plexiglass "audience" boxes, the sprinting

FIGURE 15.3   **Two mazes used in experiments on social facilitation in cockroaches (Zajonc et al., 1969). Compared with roaches running alone, roaches running in groups or in the presence of "spectator" roaches ran faster in the easy maze and slower in the difficult maze — a cockroach equivalent of the paradoxical effects of others' presence on human performance.**

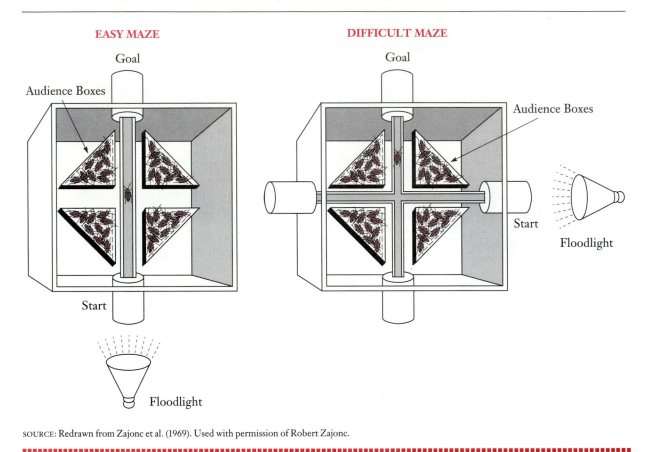

SOURCE: Redrawn from Zajonc et al. (1969). Used with permission of Robert Zajonc.

cockroaches performed as predicted by Zajonc's theory: Compared with roaches running alone, roaches running in the presence of others ran faster in the easy maze but slower in the difficult maze.

The cockroach study makes an important point. Psychologists and lay people are tempted to attribute social facilitation effects solely to competitive feelings or to worrying that others are evaluating one's performance. Zajonc's theory holds that the *mere presence* of others is arousing and that this arousal has automatic effects on performance that are independent of competitive feelings or evaluation anxiety. Because it is unlikely that cockroaches possess complex cognitions of any sort, the cockroach experiment suggests that Zajonc's arousal theory is a viable explanation for occurrences of social facilitation in both higher and lower animals.

The mere presence of others proves at times to be arousing to people as well as cockroaches. In one experiment, Markus (1978) had college students remove their shoes and then put on unfamiliar socks, tennis shoes, and a lab coat. Later in the same experiment, subjects removed these novel items of clothing and put their own shoes back on. Some subjects were alone while undressing and dressing, others were in the presence of someone who watched them, and still others were in the presence of a person who was repairing a machine and had his back to them. Interestingly, the presence of either a watchful or an inattentive person increased the speed of well-learned habits (putting on one's own shoes) but decreased the speed of novel, poorly learned habits (putting on the strange lab coat). Thus the presence of another person can lead to social facilitation effects even when the other person cannot evaluate (or even see) the behavior of the subject.

In a conceptually similar experiment, Schmitt and his colleagues (1986) asked college students to type their names into a computer either forward (easy task) or backward (difficult, unfamiliar task). Subjects were either alone, in the presence of the observing experimenter, or in the presence of another subject who was wearing a blindfold and earphones. Consistent with Zajonc's theory, the presence of others — even the blindfolded person who could not evaluate the subjects — speeded subjects' performance on the easy task but slowed their performance on the difficult task (see Figure 15.4).

Why is the mere presence of others arousing? One possibility is that others' presence may place us "on guard," for we never are quite sure what other people will do (Zajonc, 1980). There are other possibilities as well. People, unlike cockroaches, do sometimes experience evaluation apprehension and competitive feelings in the presence of others, particularly when they are observing us and when there are normative or "right" ways to perform a task (Guerin, 1986). Worringham and Messick (1983) found that joggers in Santa Barbara, California, ran faster when watched by a woman seated on a bench than when they were alone or in the presence of a woman with her back turned to them. Note that jogging is not simply a well-learned, dominant habit; it is also a behavior that is evaluated according to normative standards: Vigorous jogging is "better" than slothful jogging.

Many careful experiments suggest that a number of psychological processes contribute to human social facilitation. Zajonc's theory that the mere presence of others is arousing holds, particularly in settings when the other people present are strangers (Zajonc, 1980; Guerin, 1986). As we just noted, people may also experience learned evaluation apprehension in the presence of others, particularly when there are clear normative standards of how the behavior should be performed (Cottrell, Wack, Seberak, & Rittle, 1968; Guerin, 1986). Finally, the presence of others may influence performance because it is cognitively distracting (Baron, 1986). Imagine trying to type a term paper with ten people standing around watching you! Rallying our mental resources in the face of distraction may facilitate easy tasks, but the distraction may be simply too great when we work on difficult tasks requiring complex thought; then the presence of others will interfere with performance.

Whereas many theories of social facilitation agree that the presence of other people is arousing, they sometimes disagree in their explanations of the nature of the arousal; each theory may provide a partial explanation for social facilitation effects.

When a new farmhouse was built, friends assembled to "raise the roof."
—— *The Crucible*, p. 138

Individual Versus Group Performance

It seems obvious that 20 people can build a house better than one person. Is this a general principle? Do groups always outperform individuals? Before jumping to a

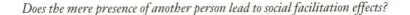

Does the mere presence of another person lead to social facilitation effects?

Schmitt et al. (1986) asked college students to type their
names either forward (easy task) or backward (difficult
task). Subjects were either alone, in the presence of a
watching experimenter, or in the presence of another
subject who was wearing a blindfold and earphones.

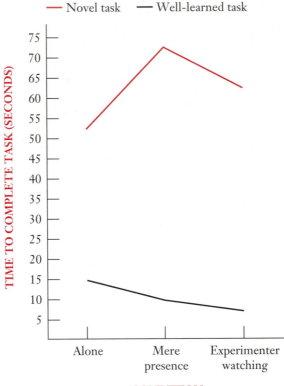

Interestingly, subjects showed social facilitation effects
(that is, less time taken on the easy task, more time taken on
the difficult task) even when the person present could not
see them, which suggests that the mere presence of another
person is somewhat arousing.

SOURCE: Data from Schmitt et al. (1986).

■■■■■■■■■■■■■■■■■■■■■■■■

**Groups at work: Farm
workers move a piece
of heavy equipment.**

quick conclusion, consider this example: A head engineer at a computer company
wants to develop a new piece of circuitry. She can either assign this task to a "brainstorming group" of staff engineers or break up the task among several individual
engineers. Which strategy is more likely to produce the best product?

Here's another example: Imagine that your social psychology professor gives
your class two test options. Students can take their exams either individually (as you
probably do in your current class) or communally — that is, the class as a whole can
discuss each question and then vote on the correct answers. Would the average
student working alone score better or worse than the class as a whole in the communal version of the test? Here's a more difficult question: Would the *best* student
working alone score better or worse than the class as a whole in the communal
version of the test?

What is the relationship between a group's performance and the performance
of individual members in the group? Social facilitation research investigates how the
presence of others influences performance; in such studies, subjects do not *interact*
with the other people present. When people work together on tasks, what happens
to individual performance? Does interaction in groups help or hinder work? Are
"two heads better than one"? Always? Sometimes?

Steiner's analysis of group tasks.   In an influential analysis of work groups, Ivan
Steiner (1972, 1976) proposed a comprehensive classification of group tasks. Steiner
identified four important kinds of group tasks: additive tasks, conjunctive tasks,
disjunctive tasks, and divisible tasks (see Figure 15.5).

In an *additive task* people pool their identical efforts together in order to produce
a summed group product (hence the term *additive*). A tug-of-war team provides a

▪▪

FIGURE 15.5   Four kinds of group tasks identified by Steiner (1972, 1976).

What are common kinds of group tasks, and how do they differ from one another?

KIND OF TASK	DESCRIPTION	EXAMPLES
Additive	Group members pool or add their efforts	Tug-of-war Crop harvesters
Conjunctive	Group members separately perform same subtask(s)	Relay race Bowling team Mountain-climbing team
Disjunctive	Group members collaborate to arrive at an "either/or," "yes/no" decision	Quiz game team Jury
Divisible	Group members perform subcomponents of task; a true division of labor	Football team Baseball team NASA

Steiner argued that the relationship between individual members' performance and overall group performance is different for the four kinds of group tasks listed here.

▪▪

good example, for team members pool their individual tugs together to produce a group tug. In general, Steiner argued that additive groups outperform individuals. For example, a team of people generally beats an individual in a tug-of-war. Other examples of additive groups support this general conclusion. For example, on average a group of soldiers will beat an opposing individual soldier, and larger additive groups (1,000 soldiers) generally outperform smaller additive groups (100 soldiers).

In *conjunctive groups* individual members of the group perform the same subtask, but they don't literally add their efforts together. Examples of conjunctive groups are relay-racing, bowling, and mountain-climbing teams. Note that in a relay-racing team each member separately performs the same subtasks — running as fast as possible and passing the baton smoothly to the next runner. How does individual performance relate to group performance in a conjunctive group? Steiner argued that in general conjunctive groups perform as well as their *weakest* members. For example, if three members of a relay team run superbly but the fourth runner trips and falls, the team will probably lose. The nature of conjunctive groups is captured by the saying that "a chain is as strong as its weakest link."

The opposite is true of disjunctive groups — their performance is more a function of their ablest members. A *disjunctive group* must answer a "yes-no" or "either-or" question based on group deliberation. The communal social psychology test described earlier is a good example. Team quiz games in general are examples of disjunctive tasks. Note that in a quiz game, if one member of the group knows the correct answer, then the group has the possibility of answering the question correctly.

Of course, it is also possible that an ignorant majority may vote down the one knowledgeable member of the group (Hill, 1982).

Finally, in a *divisible group* members perform different subcomponents of the task. Baseball, football, and basketball teams are all divisible groups because different players have different positions or roles in the team. Clearly, in our bureaucratic-industrial society, divisible groups are very common. Assembly lines are based on a division of labor in which each worker performs a separate component of the manufacturing task. When corporations execute major projects (such as designing a new rocket for NASA, developing a new computer, introducing design changes for the next model-year of cars), they divide the task into pieces. The relationship between individual performance and group performance is quite complex in large divisible tasks. Indeed, modern management theory attempts to systematically analyze complicated divisible tasks (like designing a new rocket) in order to uncover the "weakest link" in the task and streamline the group effort.

Social loafing.   Steiner's classification system can help us understand the social psychology of work groups. Let's return to the tug-of-war (a simple additive task). We noted earlier that additive groups generally outperform individuals and that larger additive groups generally outperform smaller additive groups. But is there a literal addition of effort in additive groups? Do four people tend to pull in a tug-of-war four times as hard as the average individual?

The answer to this question is clearly no. In a much-cited early study, the French agricultural engineer Max Ringelmann (1913; see Kravitz & Martin, 1986) first asked male subjects either working alone or in groups of varying sizes to pull on a rope as hard as they could and then measured their effort with a dynamometer (a force meter). Ringelman found that as the number of workers increased, the average force contributed by each worker decreased (see Figure 15.6). Why? There are two possibilities (Latané, Williams, & Harkins, 1979): Subjects did not coordinate their pulling in an optimal fashion and subjects showed *social loafing* — that is, they actually exerted less individual effort when in groups (this last possibility is similar to the notion of "diffusion of responsibility" discussed in Chapter 13).

Experiments have found evidence for both phenomena in additive groups. In one study, Latané, Williams, and Harkins (1979) blindfolded college subjects and placed headphones producing static-like noise over their ears. Subjects were then asked to yell as loudly as they could. Sometimes subjects were alone and sometimes they combined their yells in groups of two or six people. In addition, some subjects were falsely led to believe that they were in groups of two or six people when in fact they were alone. (This deception was possible because subjects wore blindfolds and earphones.) The results of the experiment demonstrated that solo subjects tended to yell louder than individual subjects in groups; furthermore, actual groups showed lower overall performance than the summed performance of "pseudogroups" of solo people (who believed themselves to be in groups; see Figure 15.7).

What are the implications of these results? That actual groups performed more poorly than pseudogroups illustrates that group yelling suffered from problems of coordination — everyone in the real groups didn't yell most loudly at the same optimal instant. That individual effort in both pseudogroups and actual groups was lower than the individual effort of solo individuals demonstrates social loafing effects — people simply tended to "goof off" in the real or perceived group situations.

FIGURE 15.6   **The Ringelmann effect.**

Is an additive group's effort equal to the sum of individual members' efforts?

Ringelmann (1913) asked individual students and groups of students to pull a rope as hard as they could.

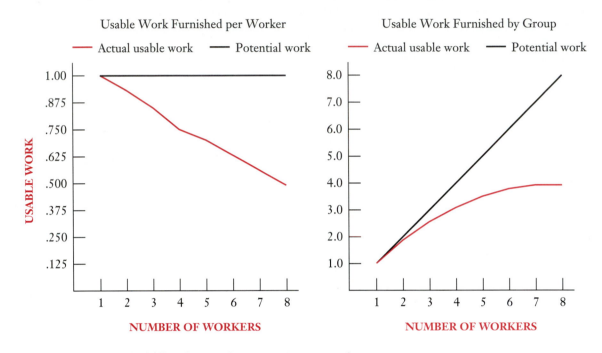

He found that individual effort decreased as group size increased.

SOURCE: Data from Ringelmann (1913).

Social loafing is caused by a number of factors. Often individuals' efforts are anonymous in additive group settings. Because it is the group's and not the individual's production that is measured, the individual can be a "free rider" with impunity (Sweeney, 1973; Harkins, 1987). Second, people in groups may assume that others will slack off, and then consistent with exchange and equity theories they slack off in return (Jackson & Harkins, 1985; see Chapters 1 and 11). Finally, it may be the case that when people perform in additive groups, they are not as aroused and motivated as people who perform as individuals (Jackson & Williams, 1985).

This last point may seem to contradict social facilitation research. Please note, however, that social loafing studies differ from social facilitation studies in the following important way: Subjects pool their efforts together in social loafing studies but not in social facilitation studies. Thus subjects can "hide in the crowd" in social loafing studies but not in social facilitation studies. The presence of others may *reduce* people's arousal and evaluation apprehension in social loafing studies but

FIGURE 15.7   Social loafing and loss of coordination in additive groups.

Does average individual effort decrease in additive groups?

Latané, Williams, and Harkins (1979) asked students wearing blindfolds and earphones to yell as loudly as they could. Sometimes subjects were alone, sometimes they were in groups, and sometimes they were in "pseudogroups," that is, they thought they were in groups when in fact they were alone. The researchers measured how loudly subjects yelled.

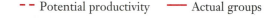

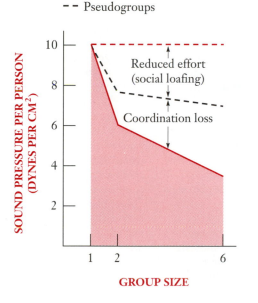

The results showed that on average solitary individuals yelled louder than individuals in groups. Furthermore, the efforts of individuals in "pseudogroups" surpassed the average effort per individual in actual groups. Thus, the total performance of additive groups suffers from both "social loafing" and a lack of coordination among individual members.

SOURCE: Adapted from Latané, Williams, and Harkins (1979). Used with permission of Bibb Latané.

heighten these same variables in social facilitation studies (Harkins, 1987; Harkins & Szymanski, 1987).

Social loafing is clearly a phenomenon that can sap the productivity of real-life additive work groups. One way to reduce social loafing is to inform participants in additive tasks that their individual performances, as well as the entire group's output, are being evaluated. In the galley ships of ancient Rome, slaves worked together in

Brainstorming as a Means of Enhancing Group Creativity

Social facilitation research shows that the presence of others may interfere with individuals' performance on complex or difficult tasks. And social loafing research shows that additive groups foster a loss of individual productivity. Thus both kinds of research portray groups as interfering with individual performance. Do groups ever improve the quality of individual members' work?

Alex Osborn (1957) argued that groups can foster *creativity* in their members: "The average person can think up twice as many ideas when working with a group than when working alone" (p. 229). Osborn coined the term *brainstorming* to describe what he considered to be the optimal procedure for stimulating creativity in groups. In brainstorming groups people are instructed to: (1) express any idea that comes to mind, regardless of how strange or ridiculous it seems, (2) refrain from critically evaluating their own or others' ideas at first, (3) generate as many ideas as they can, and (4) build upon and extend others' ideas.

Although Osborn's brainstorming technique seems a plausible way to foster creativity in groups, studies generally have not shown that brainstorming groups are more creative, either in the quantity or quality of their ideas, than equivalent numbers of separate individuals working on the same task (Lamm & Trommsdorff, 1973; Diehl & Stroebe, 1987). Indeed, in one of the first careful studies of brainstorming, Taylor, Berry, and Block (1958) found evidence that was almost exactly opposite to Osborn's prediction: Nominal groups (that is, groups of isolated individ-

uals pooled together for the sake of statistical comparison) produced nearly twice as many ideas as brainstorming groups of an equivalent size. Despite the weak research evidence for its effectiveness, brainstorming remains a popular technique for fostering creativity (Ulschak, Nathanson, & Gillan, 1981).

Why didn't the technique of brainstorming live up to Osborn's expectations? Diehl and Stroebe (1987) suggested three problems that may reduce creativity in brainstorming groups: (1) Members may suffer from social loafing, (2) despite explicit instructions not to evaluate ideas, group members may still suffer from evaluation apprehension in brainstorming groups, and (3) group settings may sometimes block the production of ideas — for example, one person on the verge of formulating a novel idea may be interrupted by another group member and lose his or her train of thought. In a careful set of experiments, Diehl and Stroebe found some evidence for all three processes in brainstorming groups. However, the third process — production blocking — seemed to be the most important barrier to creativity.

Where do brainstorming groups fit into Steiner's analysis of group tasks? Effective brainstorming probably constitutes both an additive and a disjunctive task. Group members clearly pool their efforts by producing as many novel ideas as they can, but at some point group members must also critically evaluate ideas, pursuing those with promise and rejecting those that are too outlandish.

Research on the limitations of

brainstorming suggests some new techniques that may increase creativity in groups. The *nominal group technique* (Delbecq, Van de Ven, & Gustafson, 1975), for example, attempts to combine individual and group creativity into a single process. First, a group discussion leader presents and defines a problem. Second, group members silently generate as many ideas as they can and write them down on paper. Third, each member describes his or her ideas for the group, and the group poses questions but does not criticise or evaluate the ideas. Fourth, members write down and rank what they think are the five best ideas generated by the group. Finally, these votes are then tallied and presented to the group; at this point another cycle of group discussion may ensue.

Note that because group members work individually during the first stage and because each must present his or her ideas to the group, social loafing is minimized. Because members write down their ideas, production blocking is reduced. Finally, nonevaluative group discussion and anonymous balloting to identify several good ideas help to reduce evaluation anxiety and avoid placing individuals "on the spot." There may be a price to pay for the Nominal Group Technique, however: It is highly structured, and thus it may not produce the freewheeling discussion found in more traditional brainstorming groups.

the grueling additive task of pulling the ship's oars. To maintain the slaves' individual efforts, taskmasters constantly monitored their performance and brutally punished slackers. In modern work settings no one would tolerate such a cruel solution to the problem of social loafing; however, managers can periodically evaluate individual workers' performances in group tasks and inform them of the results. One recent experiment suggests that simply having subjects compare their individual outputs to normative standards — that is, to engage in self-evaluation — can eliminate social loafing (Szymanski & Harkins, 1987). Thus individual evaluation — either by oneself or by others — is one way to reduce social loafing.

HALE: Excellency, I have signed seventy-two death warrants; I am a minister of the Lord, and I dare not take a life without there be proof so immaculate no slightest qualm of conscience may doubt it.
DANFORTH: Mr. Hale, you surely do not doubt my justice.
HALE: I have this morning signed away the soul of Rebecca Nurse. Your Honor, I'll not conceal it, my hand shakes yet as with a wound!
—— *The Crucible*, p. 231

Work groups must often make decisions. Juries and courts decide who is guilty and who is innocent. The Congress of the United States decides when to declare war on another nation. The Department of Energy decides when a nuclear reactor is safe to operate. And NASA decides when to give the "go ahead" to manned space launches.

Often groups make wise decisions: Few would argue, for example, with the U.S. Congress's decision to declare war against the Axis powers in World War II. Unfortunately, groups sometimes arrive at stupid and destructive decisions: The courts of Puritan Salem condemned innocent people to death for witchcraft. The Department of Energy operated a nuclear reactor at Fernald, Ohio, for many years with the clear knowledge that it was contaminating the nearby countryside with radioactive wastes (*Time*, October 31, 1988). And on a fateful January day in 1986, NASA decided to launch the space shuttle *Challenger* despite engineers' serious reservations about the design of its solid rocket boosters (*Time*, March 10, 1986). Seventy-three seconds after launch, the flight ended in disaster when the *Challenger* exploded.

Group polarization.　In order to prevent bad group decisions, we must first understand how groups affect decision making. Let's begin with a question that has been the subject of an enormous amount of social psychological research: Do groups tend to make riskier or more conservative decisions than individuals? In the 1950s the sociological literature suggested that groups exert a stultifying, conservative influence on decision making (see, for example, Whyte, 1956).

In one of the first experiments to address this issue, M.I.T. graduate student James Stoner (1961) presented subjects with hypothetical "choice dilemmas." Here's a shortened version: Mr. Jones is an engineer who has two job offers — one is an average-paying position with a big company offering good benefits and security; the other is a highly creative position in a new, high-risk company. If the new company succeeds, Jones will make a fortune; however, there is a significant chance that the new company will fail, and then Jones will be out of a job. How good must the odds be that the small, risky company will succeed before you would recommend that Jones accept its job offer — 1 in 10, 3 in 10, 5 in 10, . . . 10 in 10?

Stoner had subjects respond to his choice dilemmas first as individuals; then they discussed their responses in a group; and finally, they again responded to the choice dilemmas as individuals. In general, subjects' responses tended more toward riskier choices after group discussion, and this phenomenon was soon dubbed "the risky shift." Stoner's finding was replicated by other researchers, even in situations that presented subjects with real rather than hypothetical risks (Bem, Wallach, & Kogan, 1965; Wallach, Kogan, & Bem, 1962).

Although group discussion tended to produce riskier decisions on most choice dilemma items, there were a small number of items that showed more conservative decisions as well (Wallach, Kogan, & Bem, 1962). Indeed, dozens of studies since the early 1960s indicate that the "risky shift" was a misnomer — group discussion in fact leads to *more extreme* decisions, not necessarily riskier decisions, and today this phenomenon is referred to as *group polarization* (Moscovici & Zavalloni, 1969; Myers & Lamm, 1976). What determines the direction of group polarization? The general principle seems to be that after group discussion, members tend to shift in the direction of the average initial position of the group. In other words, if the group on average responds to a choice dilemma with risky responses, then group discussion will tend to polarize responses to be even riskier, but if the group on average responds initially with conservative responses, then group discussion will polarize responses to be more conservative.

Group polarization applies not only to decisions of risk, but also to judgments and attitudes in general. For example, Moscovici and Zavalloni (1969) found that after group discussions, French students expressed more positive attitudes toward General Charles de Gaulle (to whom they were positive to begin with) but more negative attitudes toward Americans (to whom they were somewhat negative to begin with). Other research suggests that group discussions may lead unprejudiced people to become less prejudiced and prejudiced people to become more so (Myers & Bishop, 1970). Group discussion in juries tends to lead members to arrive at more extreme opinions and verdicts after deliberation (Isozaki, 1984).

Why does group polarization occur? Social psychological research has converged on two processes: informational influence and social comparison processes. *Informational influence* occurs when people learn new information and hear new persuasive arguments during the course of group discussion (Burnstein & Vinokur, 1973, 1977). *Social comparison processes* occur when people learn the group's consensus during discussion. Assuming that the group is likely to be "correct" and experiencing social pressures from the group to conform (see Chapter 14), members shift in the direction of the group norm. (The informational influence and social comparison explanations of group polarization are clearly related to the concepts of informational and normative social influence discussed in Chapter 14.)

Experiments clearly indicate that both informational influence and social comparison processes contribute to group polarization (Isenberg, 1986). For example, when people hear novel arguments without learning the specific positions of other members in the group, they still show polarization effects (Burnstein & Vinokur, 1973, 1977), and this evidence supports the informational explanation. On the other hand, when people learn others' positions but don't hear their supporting arguments, they also show polarization effects; this evidence supports the social comparison explanation (Sanders & Baron, 1977; Goethals & Zanna, 1979). In real-life groups, informational influence and social comparison processes frequently go hand in hand and may even facilitate each other. Although the effects of informational influence prove to be larger than those for social comparison processes in experimental studies (Isenberg, 1986), this finding may simply indicate that experimental studies do not create social comparison processes that are as powerful as those that can occur in real-life groups, which are often highly cohesive, attractive to members, and engaged in long-term patterns of interaction.

Is group polarization good or bad? Like most things, it depends. On the positive side, group polarization can lead to group consensus, cohesiveness, and group action. On the negative side, it can exaggerate ill-considered judgments and decisions. Jury decisions provide a good real-life example of group polarization. Often the best predictor of a jury's ultimate verdict is the majority's consensus at the time of the jury's first polling (Kerr, 1981). Juries tend to achieve greater consensus over time because the minority tends to join the majority (and thus moves in the direction of the average group judgment). Intriguingly, polarization is most likely to occur in juries when their judgments concern values and opinions (for example, what are fair punitive damages in a libel suit?) rather than factual questions (did the defendant commit the murder?), and juries are more likely to show polarization when they are required to reach unanimous decisions (Kaplan & Miller, 1987).

Group polarization seems to occur most strongly in groups that have a strong "in-group" feeling (Mackie, 1986), perhaps because people in such groups falsely perceive opinion in their group to be more consistent and extreme than it really is; the result is the creation of social comparison processes that strongly push group members toward polarization. The groups of Puritan Salem, of course, were in-groups of the strongest sort.

••••••••••••••••••••••••••

Groupthink

> Aye, it is a proper court they have now. They've sent four judges out of Boston . . . weighty magistrates of the General Court, and at the head sits the Deputy Governor of the Province.
>
> . . . There be fourteen people in the jail now. . . .
>
> . . . The Deputy Governor promise hangin' if they'll not confess. . . . The town's gone wild, I think.
>
> —— *The Crucible*, p. 186

Is group polarization sufficient to explain the irrational behavior of the Salem witch hunters? Although it contributed to the general hysteria, group polarization is certainly only a partial explanation. What else might account for the poor decisions made by the Salem witch tribunals? More generally, what leads groups of intelligent men and women to make obviously foolish and even disastrous decisions sometimes? To answer such questions, Yale social psychologist Irving Janis (1972, 1985) analyzed a series of famous, ill-fated group decisions, and in the process he discerned a general syndrome of biased decision making in cohesive groups, which he termed *groupthink*:

> I use the term "groupthink" as a quick and easy way to refer to a mode of thinking that people engage in when they are deeply involved in a cohesive in-group, when the members' strivings for unanimity override their motivation to realistically appraise alternative courses of action. "Groupthink" is a term of the same order as the words in the newspeak vocabulary George Orwell presents in his dismaying *1984*—a vocabulary with terms such as "doublethink"

This group possesses one of the factors that contribute to group-think: an authoritarian leader who doesn't tolerate dissent.

and "crimethink." By putting groupthink with those Orwellian words, I realize that groupthink takes on an invidious connotation. The invidiousness is intentional: Groupthink refers to a deterioration of mental efficiency, reality testing, and moral judgment that results from in-group pressures. (Janis, 1972, p. 9)

We've already mentioned some likely examples of groupthink: the deliberations at the Salem witch trials, the Department of Energy's decision to continue operating the Fernald reactor, and NASA's catastrophic decision to launch the space shuttle *Challenger.*

Janis adds to this list a number of famous historical episodes. In 1938, despite ominous signs of Germany's rapid preparation for war, British Prime Minister Neville Chamberlain and his inner circle of advisers decided to appease Adolf Hitler at Munich, thus setting the stage for World War II and providing Germany with the necessary time to become almost invincible. In 1961, President John F. Kennedy approved his advisors' plan to help a group of Cuban exiles invade Cuba. The result was the Bay of Pigs fiasco, in which all the invaders were captured or killed by Castro's forces and the United States was humiliated. Throughout the mid-1960s President Lyndon Johnson met regularly with his "Tuesday lunch group" of trusted, close advisors to discuss the growing U.S. involvement in southeast Asia. Despite discouraging intelligence reports and pleas from war-weary citizens and skeptical allies to disengage, Johnson and his advisors continued to escalate the war, with disastrous consequences for both Vietnam and the United States.

Janis saw commonalities among all these foreign-policy blunders: Cohesive, intelligent groups of advisors developed an unrealistic consensus and protected their leaders from any contradictory information. According to Janis (1985), groups are most susceptible to groupthink when they are isolated, cohesive, and homogeneous, and when the leader signals his preferences and discourages argumentation within the group. Stressful circumstances — recent failures, moral dilemmas, and a seeming lack of viable alternatives — also foster the development of groupthink.

Virtually all of these contributing factors were present in Puritan Salem. Decision-making groups were extraordinarily isolated, cohesive, and homogeneous. The

▪▪▪

Figure 15.8   The stages of groupthink.

According to Janis's model, what are the causes and consequences of groupthink?

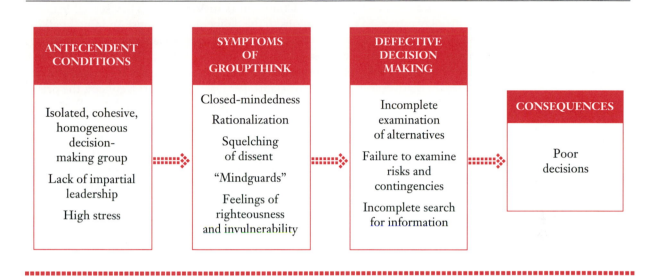

religious and secular leaders of the witch hunt constantly asked witnesses leading questions and expressed their firm conviction that witchcraft was afoot in Salem. And finally, because of factionalism Salem was a highly stressed community at the time of the witch hunts.

Once groupthink develops, it is characterized by a number of symptoms. The cohesive in-group overestimates its power and moral authority, stereotypes its opposition, rationalizes its poor decisions, and then squelches all dissent by creating an illusion of unanimity. Often the group develops "mindguards" whose job is to protect the group from unwelcome (but realistic) information that might cast doubts on its decisions. Figure 15.8 presents an overview of Janis's description of groupthink.

The Salem witch tribunals as portrayed in *The Crucible* have many of the symptoms of groupthink. The in-group's assumption of authority and moral virtue is captured succinctly by Judge Danforth's smug statement, "You surely do not doubt my justice" (p. 231). When Danforth later in fact begins to doubt his justice, he rationalizes the court's decision and squelches dissent:

> Twelve are already executed; the names of these seven are given out, and the village expects to see them die this morning. Postponement now speaks a floundering on my part; reprieve or pardon must cast doubt upon the guilt of them that died till now. While I speak God's law, I will not crack its voice with whimpering. (p. 260)

During the court hearings, when townspeople present evidence casting doubt upon the charges of witchcraft, the paranoid Reverend Parris serves as a mindguard by attempting to deflect all compromising evidence from the court: "Your Excellency, this is a trick to blind the court!" (p. 239). Parris and his zealous followers stereotype their opponents as sinners corrupted by Satan.

The symptoms of groupthink can be seen as well in the foreign policy disasters Janis analyzed. The advisors of Neville Chamberlain, John Kennedy, and Lyndon Johnson all saw themselves as a moral, righteous elite facing despicable foes (Hitler's Germany, Castro's Cuba, and the Communists in Vietnam). They served leaders who strongly expressed their opinions to the deliberating groups. And finally, all of these advisory groups suffered from a suppression of reasonable dissent. Theodore Sorenson, one of Kennedy's close advisors during the ill-fated Bay of Pigs invasion, noted, "No strong voice of opposition was raised in any of the key meetings, and no realistic alternatives were presented" (Janis, 1972, p. 39). Robert Kennedy, the president's brother, served as a mindguard when he told one dissenter, "The President has made his mind up. Don't push it any further" (p. 42).

How can groups guard against groupthink? Janis (1985) offers a number of prescriptions. The group leader should strive to be impartial and to foster an atmosphere of open inquiry and debate. Group members should be encouraged to express doubts and criticisms as well as support for group plans. "Outside experts" should be brought into the group to challenge it and give it fresh perspectives. Finally, after arriving at a consensus, the group should schedule a "second chance" meeting in which members can express lingering doubts or reservations.

Janis's account of groupthink is based on anecdotal historical analysis more than on laboratory experimentation. Janis (1985) argued for the value of a kind of "psychological autopsy" in which the processes leading to bad decisions in real-life groups are dissected after the fact. Experimental evidence for Janis's hypotheses has been mixed (for example, see Callaway, Marriott, & Esser, 1985; Courtright, 1978). Still, the concept of groupthink provides a compelling portrait of bad decision making in cohesive groups and suggests a number of useful research hypotheses.

Leadership in Groups

Enter Deputy Governor Danforth. . . . On his appearance, silence falls. Danforth is a grave man in his sixties, of some humor and sophistication that do not, however, interfere with an exact loyalty to his position and his cause.

—— *The Crucible*, p. 217

Janis's account of groupthink introduces an important new factor into our discussion of groups—namely, leaders. Groupthink, according to Janis, is caused both by characteristics of the group (cohesiveness, homogeneity) and by characteristics of the leader (expression of strong opinions, intolerance of dissent). To understand fully the nature of group processes, we must address the nature of leadership.

What Is Leadership?

Leaders are members of groups who are particularly influential and who act to guide, direct, and motivate the group to achieve its goals (Hollander, 1985). Leadership is in part determined by the leader's characteristics (such as intelligence, skill), the group's thoughts and feelings (the members' attraction to and respect for the leader), the nature of the group (a ballet corps, a jury, a corporate board), and the group setting (a besieged, highly stressed group).

Research on leadership began in earnest during the period immediately following World War II, and this early research suggested that leaders engage in two main kinds of behavior (Halpin & Winer, 1952; Kerr, Schriesheim, Murphy, & Stogdill, 1974; Bales, 1958): *task-oriented* behaviors that direct the group's work toward achieving the group's goals and *socioemotional* behaviors that foster positive relations and emotions in the group and that promote group cohesiveness. (These two kinds of leadership behavior closely correspond to two of the three main dimensions of group behavior — task ability and likability — discussed earlier.) A leader who excels at task-oriented but not socioemotional skills is often referred to as a *task specialist* (Bales, 1958), whereas a leader who excels at socioemotional but not task-oriented skills is often referred to as a *socioemotional leader* (Bales, 1958) or a *maintenance specialist* (Thibaut & Kelley, 1959). Great leaders may be those who excel in both domains (Borgatta, Couch, & Bales, 1954).

Theories of Leadership

Social psychologists have applied three different approaches to the study of leadership: (1) the trait approach, which attempts to identify the personal characteristics that distinguish leaders from nonleaders; (2) the situational approach, which examines how social settings foster or inhibit the development of leadership; and (3) the interactional (contingency) approach, which analyzes leadership as a function of both personal and situational factors.

The trait approach to leadership.

The "great man/great woman" theory of leadership holds that leaders are born, not made. The obvious question implied by this approach is: What are the traits that make a person a "natural leader"? Research attempting to answer this question has had a mixed record of success.

One of the most consistent research findings is a small but significant relationship between intelligence and leadership (Mann, 1959; Stogdill, 1974). Managerial leaders and the leaders of small laboratory groups tend to be somewhat more intelligent than the average group member, but intriguingly, they also tend not to be the most intelligent member of the group. Apparently, many groups appreciate being led by people who are smarter than they are, but not too much smarter. Gibb (1968) noted that although research consistently indicates that intelligence in fact contributes to leadership skill, "the crowd prefers to be ill-governed by people it can understand" (p. 218). Specific, task-relevant skills also contribute to leadership (Goldman & Fraas, 1965; Stogdill, 1974). For example, the "majority whip" of the Senate is a more effective leader if he knows the byzantine procedural rules of the Senate, and the head of an engineering team is more effective when she is an expert at the engineering tasks facing her group.

A number of personality and intellectual traits correlate to some degree with leadership. Stogdill (1974) noted that leaders tend on average to be more energetic, self-confident, and sociable than nonleaders. Leaders also seem to have higher needs for achievement and for affiliation than do nonleaders (Sorrentino & Field, 1986). Physical and demographic characteristics may also correlate with leadership: On average, leaders tend to be taller than nonleaders, but, of course, there are notable

Einstein possessed "expert power" when he advised Franklin D. Roosevelt to proceed with the development of the atom bomb.

exceptions (for example, Napoleon). Leaders in bureaucratic groups (such as business and government organizations) tend to be older than nonleaders, in part because greater knowledge and experience accrue with age but also because a leader must "work his way up" in most organizations, and this takes time.

The personal characteristics that contribute to leadership may be inherited and ascribed as well as innate. For example, the kings and queens of old Europe were not necessarily leaders because of their intelligence or special skills; rather, they were leaders by virtue of their hereditary status. Inherited wealth may also confer leadership on some individuals. Leaders must possess power, which can derive from a number of different sources.

In an influential analysis, French and Raven (1959) described five different kinds of power—reward power, coercive power, legitimate power, referent power, and expert power—and this classification can be applied to the topic of leadership. A leader possesses *reward power* when he or she controls desired goods and resources. For example, a boss can use potential pay raises as a means of influencing employees' behavior. *Coercive power* makes use of threats and punishment—a boss threatens to fire an employee who doesn't "shape up." A leader exerts *legitimate power* when he or she is perceived to possess legitimate authority in some domain. For example, Catholics perceive the pope to be a legitimate authority on church doctrine; at work, bosses are often perceived as legitimate authorities. A leader possesses *referent power* when followers are attracted to him. John F. Kennedy was a charismatic president who possessed referent power for many Americans. Finally, a leader has *expert power* by virtue of special knowledge or skills. Albert Einstein possessed clear expert power when he advised President Franklin D. Roosevelt to proceed with the development of the atom bomb.

The situational approach to leadership.   The great British Prime Minister Winston Churchill showed little promise in his early career, and yet during World War II he emerged as one of the world's great leaders. Was Churchill great because of his personal traits, or did the dire circumstances facing England during World War II force him to "rise to the task"?

A number of researchers have noted that strong leaders are more likely to arise when groups face crisis and stress (Mulder & Stemerding, 1963; Helmreich & Collins, 1967). Winston Churchill took command during England's "darkest hour,"and his archenemy, Adolf Hitler, rose to power in a period when Germany suffered from economic disaster and recent military humiliation. Minor situational factors can also foster the development of leadership. For example, in a series of studies on jury deliberations, Strodtbeck and his colleagues (Strodtbeck, James, & Hawkins, 1958; Strodtbeck & Hook, 1961) observed that members who sat at the ends of tables during deliberation were significantly more likely to be selected as jury foremen.

A number of studies suggest that the more frequently people talk and participate in a group, the more likely they are to be perceived as leaders (Bales, 1958; Gintner & Lindskold, 1975; Stein & Heller, 1979). Of course, participation may partly be a function of stable traits like sociability, but it may also be influenced by situational factors. In one study, for example, when quiet subjects were placed in groups that agreed with them and supported their positions, they began to show more participation and "leadership behaviors" (Pepinsky, Hemphill, & Shevitz, 1958). In other studies, participants in group discussions watched a light that signalled whenever the experimenter deemed that they made "good contributions" to the group. Actually, the signal had no relation to the quality of their statements. Not surprisingly, subjects who saw the light go on a lot began to speak more. More surprisingly, these artificially encouraged participants were then more likely to be perceived as leaders by others in the group (Bavelas, Hastorf, Gross, & Kite, 1965; Zdep & Oakes, 1967). Thus leaders can at times be "manufactured" by situational reinforcements.

Fiedler's contingency approach to leadership.   What makes a leader effective? It probably comes as no surprise to you that leadership effectiveness is in part a function of the leader's characteristics and is in part a function of the leadership setting. In his *contingency model of leadership*, Fred Fiedler (1978; Fiedler & Garcia, 1987) attempted to specify which characteristics of the leader and which characteristics of the situation are critically important in determining leadership effectiveness.

In keeping with earlier research, Fiedler argued that there are two main kinds of leaders—those who are more task-oriented and those who focus more on the emotional relationships in the group. To identify these two kinds of leaders, Fiedler developed a questionnaire called the *Least Preferred Coworker Scale*, which asks leaders to rate and evaluate the person in their group who they like least. According to Fiedler, leaders who describe their least preferred coworker in quite negative terms tend to be task-oriented leaders, whereas those who describe their least preferred coworker in more positive terms tend to be socioemotional leaders.

Who is the more effective, the task-oriented or the socioemotional leader? According to Fiedler's contingency model, it depends on the nature of the leadership situation. In particular, Fiedler poses three main questions to assess how favorable a given leadership setting is: (1) How good are the leader's relations with group members? (2) How clearly defined are the goals and tasks of the group? And (3) How much legitimate authority does the leader possess over the group?

Some situations can be favorable on all three dimensions—the leader has good relations with the group, a clear goal to pursue, and considerable legitimate authority. Some situations are unfavorable on all three dimensions—the leader has poor relations with the group, unclear goals, and little legitimate authority. And, of course, there are intermediate situations, which are moderately favorable or unfavorable. The contingency model proposes that task-oriented leaders are most effective in very favorable or in very unfavorable settings, whereas socioemotional leaders are more effective in intermediate conditions (see Figure 15.9).

According to Fiedler, in very positive situations the leader doesn't have to worry about morale or whether group members will follow instructions, and thus the task-oriented leader is most effective at focusing on the task at hand. In very negative situations, morale and group relations are so bad that they will not be easily improved; again the leader is best served by being task-oriented and by "trying to pick up the pieces" as best he or she can. In moderately good or bad situations, however, the leader has most to gain by improving morale and personal relations, and thus the socioemotional leader is uniquely effective.

Many studies have tested Fiedler's contingency model in both real-life and laboratory settings, and in general they support the general predictions of the model (Strube & Garcia, 1981; Peters, Hartke, & Pohlmann, 1985; Fiedler & Garcia, 1987). Figure 15.10 presents the median correlations between the Least Preferred Coworker (LPC) Scale and leadership effectiveness from nine different studies. Higher LPC scores are possessed by more relationship-motivated leaders and lower scores by more task-motivated leaders, and thus Fiedler's model predicts that LPC scores should positively correlate with leadership effectiveness in moderately favorable

FIGURE 15.9   Fiedler's contingency model of leadership effectiveness.

When are task-oriented or socioemotional leaders most effective?

According to Fiedler's (1978) contingency model of leadership, leadership effectiveness depends both on the leader's style of leadership and the favorableness of the leadership setting: Task-oriented leaders tend to be most effective in very favorable or very unfavorable leadership settings, whereas socioemotional leaders tend to be most effective in moderately favorable leadership settings.

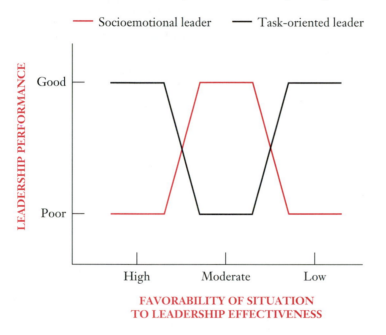

SOURCE: Adapted from Fiedler (1978). Used with permission of Fred Fiedler.

settings but should negatively correlate with effectiveness in very favorable or very unfavorable settings. The correlations in Figure 15.10 tend to support these predictions.

The Good and Bad of Groups

To this point we have focused primarily on groups at work. Let's now consider the broader effects of groups on social behavior: Are people more likely to behave in evil, antisocial ways in groups? Is behavior more emotional and volatile in group settings? Do group settings encourage the spread of rumors, hysterical emotions,

::

FIGURE 15.10   Results of research on Fiedler's contingency model.

*What is the relationship between leadership style and
leadership effectiveness in different leadership settings?*

The graph below shows median correlations from nine studies
between leaders' Least Preferred Coworker Scale scores and
their measured leadership effectiveness. As Fiedler's model
predicts, these correlations show that socioemotional leaders
(who tend to score high on the LPC Scale) tend to be more
effective in moderately favorable leadership settings, whereas
task-oriented leaders (who tend to score low on the LPC Scale)
tend to be more effective in leadership settings that are either
low or high on favorability.

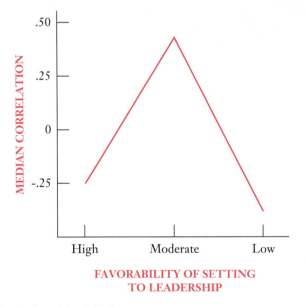

SOURCE: Data from Fiedler and Garcia (1987).

::

fears, and panic? And finally, do groups tend to encourage cooperation or competition among members?

Deindividuation

DANFORTH, *to Mary Warren:* Why does she see this vision?
MARY WARREN: She sees nothin'!
ABIGAIL, *now staring full front as though hypnotized, and mimicking the exact tone
of Mary Warren's cry:* She sees nothin'!
MARY WARREN, *pleading:* Abby, you mustn't!
ABIGAIL AND ALL THE GIRLS, *all transfixed:* Abby, you mustn't!
MARY WARREN, *to all the girls:* I'm here, I'm here!

Is behavior more emotional and volatile in group settings?

GIRLS: I'm here, I'm here!
DANFORTH, *horrified:* Mary Warren! Draw back your spirit out of them!
MARY WARREN: Mr. Danforth!
GIRLS, *cutting her off:* Mr. Danforth!
DANFORTH: Have you compacted with the Devil? Have you?
MARY WARREN: Never, never!
GIRLS: Never, never!

—— *The Crucible*, p. 247

In the previous section we discussed how leadership can be most effective in directing and motivating group members to achieve group goals. However, there is a darker side to leadership. To perceive it, you need only contemplate such figures as Adolf Hitler, Joseph Stalin, Charles Manson, and the Reverend Jim Jones. Sigmund Freud (1922) argued that groups sometimes engage in destructive, irrational activities because of their attachments to the group leader. According to Freud, the leader is a kind of love object to followers, and when groups adulate and idealize their leaders, they substitute the leader's wishes for their own superego (that is, for their conscience and moral principles). If you substitute the wishes of an Adolf Hitler or a Charles Manson for your own conscience, you are in deep trouble indeed.

Freud drew heavily upon an earlier work by Gustave Le Bon (1896), entitled *The Crowd*, which attempted to analyze processes that lead to mob behavior. Le Bon argued that in crowds people are more likely to engage in antisocial behaviors because they are anonymous and feel invulnerable. Le Bon wrote that an individual in a crowd "descends several rungs in the ladder of civilization" (p. 36). People in crowds show "impulsiveness, irritability, incapacity to reason," and "exaggeration of sentiments" (p. 40), and they suffer from behavioral contagion and suggestibility comparable to that experienced during hypnosis. Both Freud and Le Bon tended to be quite pessimistic about the effects of crowds on individuals' behavior.

Deindividuated subjects in Zimbardo's (1970) experiment. These subjects delivered longer electric shocks to an innocent victim than did nondisguised subjects wearing name tags.

Social psychologists Leon Festinger, Albert Pepitone, and Theodore Newcomb (1952) offered a somewhat different account of the effects of groups on individuals' behavior. They argued that people in groups seem to experience *deindividuation* — that is, they feel themselves to be "submerged in the group" and lose their personal identity.

Why does such deindividuation occur? Philip Zimbardo (1970) proposed that arousal, feelings of anonymity, and diffusion of responsibility foster deindividuation in group settings. Furthermore, novel environments that produce sensory overload (for example, riots, casinos, Mardi Gras) and drug-induced alterations in consciousness may also contribute to deindividuation. Once in a state of deindividuation, an individual shows little self-observation, little consistency with internal standards, and lowered inhibitions. As a result, he or she may engage in repetitive, impulsive, emotional, and at times destructive behaviors.

According to Zimbardo, deindividuation is not a single process; rather, it is an altered subjective state with multiple causes and multiple consequences. Some group settings (those that are arousing, full of distracting stimuli, and in which people cannot be easily identified) are more conducive to deindividuation than others.

Research supports the hypotheses that group settings and anonymity affect individuals' willingness to engage in antisocial behaviors. For example, Zimbardo (1970) found that women dressed in white laboratory coats and hoods delivered longer shocks to victims in an experiment than did subjects wearing normal clothes and ID tags displaying their names. Thus, anonymity contributed to uninhibited aggression. Watson (1973) compiled anthropological data from many cultures across the world and found a strong correlation between the degree to which societies disguise their warriors before they go into battle (for example, by using war paint or masks) and the brutality of their warfare (torturing captives and mutilating victims). These data also suggest a link between anonymity and antisocial behavior.

In a clever experiment, Diener and his colleagues (1976) simultaneously examined the effects of disguise, anonymity, and group membership on antisocial behavior

FIGURE 15.11   Effects of group membership and deindividuation on children's likelihood of stealing.

Does being an anonymous member of a group increase our willingness to engage in antisocial behavior?

Diener and his colleagues (1976) gave trick-or-treaters the opportunity to steal candy and coins. Some children were alone and others were in groups. In addition, some children were identified by name (nonanonymous) and others were not (anonymous).

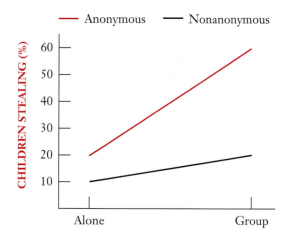

Children were significantly more likely to steal when in groups and when anonymous.

SOURCE: Adapted from Diener et al. (1976). Used with permission of Edward Diener.

in trick-or-treating children. The experimenters (women giving out candy in 27 different homes in Seattle, Washington) either identified children by asking for their names and addresses or let them remain anonymous. Some children naturally arrived in groups; others were alone. Leaving the room to "return to work," experimenters left subjects standing next to a table with a bowl of candy and a bowl of coins after telling them to take one piece of candy each before they left. A hidden observer watched and recorded whether or not the children stole extra candy or any coins. The results showed that many children did steal, particularly when they were in groups and were not identified by name (see Figure 15.11).

Deindividuation may be particularly potent in "total institutions," such as mental hospitals, prisons, and concentration camps, which remove people from the moorings of their normal identities and strip them of their individuality. In a simulation of a prison environment, Zimbardo and his colleagues (Zimbardo, 1972) assigned one group of college males to be prisoners and another group to be guards in a jail constructed in the basement of Stanford University's Psychology

Mass Psychogenic Illness

ABIGAIL, with hushed trepidation: *How is Ruth sick?*

MERCY: *It's weirdish, I know not — she seems to walk like a dead one since last night.*

ABIGAIL — she turns at once and goes to Betty, and now, with fear in her voice: *Betty?* Betty doesn't move. She shakes her. *Now stop this! Betty! Sit up now!* Betty doesn't stir. Mercy comes over.

MERCY: *Have you tried beatin' her? I gave Ruth a good one and it waked her for a minute. Here, let me have her.*

—— The Crucible, p. 151

In *The Crucible*, Abigail and other girls enlist the slave, Tituba, to conjure spirits. Together, they chant, drink the blood of a chicken, and dance in the woods, when suddenly they are discovered by Reverend Parris. Two of the girls immediately fall into a trance-like illness. What was the nature of the girls' disorder — demonic possession? More likely, they suffered from a *mass psychogenic illness* — an illness of psychological origin that occurs in group settings due to hysterical contagion (Colligan, Pennebaker, & Murphy, 1982).

In one of the first systematic studies of such an illness, Kerckhoff and Back (1968) traveled to a Southern textile factory where a group of female workers had earlier developed a strange malady; the case is well summarized by an early news report:

Officials of Montana Mills shut down their Strongsville plant this afternoon because of a mysterious illness.

According to a report just in from Strongsville General Hospital, at least ten women and one man were admitted for treatment. Reports describe symptoms as severe nausea and a breaking out over the body.

Indications are that some kind of insect was in a shipment of cloth that arrived from England at the plant today. And at the moment the bug is blamed for the outbreak of sickness (Kerckhoff, 1982, p. 6).

Over the 11-day course of the "epidemic," 62 factory workers (59 women and 3 men) were treated for the "mysterious illness," and neither doctors nor factory officials could find any infectious agent or diagnose any known disease. The malady disappeared as quickly as it had appeared, and investigators began to suspect psychological rather than physical causes.

Kerckhoff and Back's careful research discovered some clear patterns to the sickness. The women who fell ill tended to be highly stressed and did not want to continue working at their tedious factory jobs. Furthermore, they tended to deny their stress and were thus more likely to attribute it to an external source, such as some infectious bug. Finally, most of the women who became sick worked during the same shift and in the same area of the plant, and the "disease" typically progressed through social networks. For ex-

Department. Both prisoners and guards were deindividuated in many ways: The prisoners wore dress-like uniforms and nylon stocking caps (to simulate having their heads shaved), and they were assigned serial numbers to be used in place of their names. Guards wore deindividuating khaki uniforms, billy clubs, and reflective sunglasses that masked their expressions and identities.

Although Zimbardo's prison was to be a "simulation," both prisoners and guards quickly began to act as if the situation were real. The guards created brutal punishments for prisoners who broke the "prison rules." In response, the prisoners staged a "revolt" that was subsequently crushed by the guards. The guards then increased their surveillance and abuse of the prisoners, and within days some prisoners suffered breakdowns and others became docile and apathetic. Many subjects in the prison simulation showed some of the hallmarks of deindividuation — a lowered sense of personal identity, an altered state of subjective consciousness, and a host of disinhibited antisocial behaviors.

ample, when one woman fell ill, her close friends and work associates were often the next to fall ill.

Since Kerckhoff and Back's seminal study, additional cases of mass psychogenic illness have been reported and analyzed. Colligan and Murphy (1982) reviewed reports of 23 separate instances of hysterical illnesses in work settings involving over 1,000 individuals. Their findings reinforce Kerckhoff and Back's conclusions. Eighty-nine percent of affected individuals were women. In general, people who succumbed to outbreaks of psychogenic illness worked in boring, repetitive, and stressful jobs. (This, by the way, may in part explain why more women than men seem to experience such illness — women may more often find themselves in boring, "dead end" jobs.) Finally, psychogenic illnesses were most likely to occur in work settings characterized by poor management-labor relations.

A number of social psychological processes help to explain mass psychogenic illnesses. The Schachter and Singer two-component theory of emotion (see Chapter 4) holds that both physiological arousal and social comparison processes are important determinants of emotional experience. In general, factory workers who fall prey to mass psychogenic illnesses are highly stressed and aroused, and illness gives them a concrete cognitive label for their stress. Furthermore, "sick" people can legitimately leave the stressful setting.

As we already know, anonymous, stressful group settings can foster deindividuation, and this can lead people to behave in uninhibited ways. In addition, people in groups may suffer from behavioral contagion (Wheeler, 1966), which occurs particularly when individuals want to engage in some behavior (such as become sick and leave an unpleasant job) but experience restraining inhibitions. When other people engage in the suppressed

behavior, they thereby release observers' inhibitions.

Were the girls in Salem, who claimed to be under the spell of witchcraft, really suffering from mass psychogenic illness? We'll never know for sure. But it certainly seems that the right ingredients were present: The girls were highly stressed, they had been performing a deindividuating ritual prior to their discovery, and they constituted a close-knit group of friends. Witchcraft and demonic possession were real possibilities to the superstitious Puritans of Salem, and this provided the girls with a ready cognitive explanation for their arousal and upset. The Salem witch hysteria underscores an important point: Mass psychogenic illnesses can have serious real-life consequences.

One can see parallels between the Zimbardo prison simulation and the deindividuation that occurs in many real-life institutions. For example, the military shaves the heads of new recruits and issues them serial numbers, "dog tags," and standard uniforms. In basic training, soldiers live in groups in a novel environment and are frequently highly stressed and aroused. Separated from their normal social supports, soldiers are drilled to follow commands rather than inner moral standards. The "good soldier" submerges himself in the group and becomes a kind of professional aggression machine.

Deindividuation and self-awareness.   What is deindividuation like to the person experiencing it? Drawing on recent research on self-awareness, Edward Diener (1980; Diener, Lusk, DeFour, & Flax, 1980) argued that deindividuation is due in part to shifts in individuals' attention. In arousing, overstimulating group settings people pay attention to the dramatic events around them, not to their inner values,

FIGURE 15.12   **The subjective experience of deindividuation.**

*What aspects of subjective experience distinguish
deindividuated people from individuated people?*

In the study by Prentice-Dunn and Rogers (1980), deindividuated and individuated subjects rated their subjective experiences during the experiment on a number of questionnaire items. Two clusters of questionnaire items distinguished deindividuated subjects from individuated subjects. One assessed "altered experience," the other "self-awareness." The table shows these two kinds of questionnaire items.

FACTOR 1 (ALTERED EXPERIENCE)	FACTOR 2 (SELF-AWARENESS)
Thinking was somewhat altered	Felt self-conscious
Emotions were different from normal	Heightened sense of individual identity
Felt aroused	Felt inhibited
Responsibility was shared	I had responsibility for harm doing
Time seemed to go quickly	Concerned with what experimenter thought of me
Thoughts were concentrated on the moment	Concerned with what victim thought of me
Session was enjoyable	Concerned with what other group members thought of me
Willing to volunteer for similar study	
Liked other group members	
Feeling of togetherness among group members	

SOURCE: Prentice-Dunn and Rogers (1980). Used with permission of Steven Prentice-Dunn.

standards, and attitudes. Thus deindividuated people do not engage in self-directed attention (see Chapter 6), and thus they are less likely to behave in a manner that is consistent with their internal standards.

To investigate the subjective state of deindividuated subjects, Prentice-Dunn and Rogers (1980) asked groups of college men to deliver electric shocks to an innocent victim as part of a "biofeedback" experiment. In a condition designed to create deindividuation, subjects sat in a dimly lit room and heard arousing background noise. Furthermore, these deindividuated subjects were not addressed by name, and they were told that the levels of shock they delivered would not be measured. Conditions were just the opposite for individuated subjects: They sat in a brightly lit, quiet room, wore name tags, and learned that the intensities of their shocks would be measured. Consistent with earlier studies, deindividuated subjects delivered more intense shocks to their victims than did individuated subjects.

Prentice-Dunn and Rogers then asked their subjects to fill out a 19-item questionnaire asking them to report on their thoughts and experiences during the experiment. A factor-analysis of these items indicated that deindividuated subjects differed from individuated subjects on two main dimensions: altered experience and self-awareness (see Figure 15.12 for examples of each kind of item). Interestingly, both altered experience and degree of self-awareness correlated significantly with the intensity of electric shocks that subjects delivered to their victims. This and other

studies (for example, Diener, 1979) suggest that deindividuation is in part a function of reduced self-awareness.

From the perspective of self-awareness theory, deindividuation is neither intrinsically good nor bad; rather, it leads to a relaxation of normal standards, rules, and values. Although most social psychological research has focused on antisocial consequences of deindividuation, there is at least one exception to this rule. Gergen, Gergen, and Barton (1973) asked groups of college men and women to interact together in an "environmental chamber," a small padded room. Their instructions were quite vague: "You will be left in the chamber for no more than an hour with some other people. There are no rules . . . as to what you should do together." Subjects were informed that after the experiment they would not interact with the others any more and that they would leave the experiment alone.

We've left out a central fact, however: In one experimental condition the room was brightly lit; in the other it was dark. Subjects in the dark room were deindividuated because they were anonymous, probably aroused, and in an undefined and somewhat mysterious environment. Half of the subjects in the dark room hugged another person, whereas no one hugged in the lit room. Eighty-nine percent of the subjects in the dark room intentionally touched others, whereas none did in the lit room. Subjects in the dark room reported the experience to be fun and sensuous, and many volunteered to return for a repeat experience.

By implication, deindividuation can be freeing when one's inhibitions are painful and limiting. Perhaps this is why we sometimes seek out deindividuating settings — for example, the masked, chaotic, crowded (and fun) setting of Mardi Gras. Sometimes being somewhat anonymous in a novel setting (for example, being a new student, away from home for the first time, or at a large university) can be a liberating experience.

Competition and Cooperation in Groups

DANFORTH: Your husband — did he indeed turn from you?
ELIZABETH, *in agony:* My husband — is a goodly man, sir.
DANFORTH: Then he did not turn from you.
ELIZABETH, *starting to glance at Proctor [her husband]:* He —
DANFORTH, *reaches out and holds her face, then:* Look at me! To your knowledge, has John Proctor ever committed the crime of lechery? *In a crisis of indecision she cannot speak.* Answer my question! Is your husband a lecher!
ELIZABETH, *faintly:* No, sir.
DANFORTH: Remove her, Marshal.
PROCTOR: Elizabeth, tell the truth!
DANFORTH: She has spoken. Remove her.
PROCTOR, *crying out:* Elizabeth, I have confessed it!
ELIZABETH: Oh, God! *The door closes behind her.*

—— *The Crucible*, pp. 244–245

In one of the most painful scenes in *The Crucible*, Elizabeth Proctor faces a horrible dilemma: Her husband John has tried to discredit Abigail — the woman who is accusing Elizabeth and others of witchcraft — by informing the court that he had an illicit affair with her. Proctor tells the court that his wife can vouch for the truth of his charge. Judge Danforth then calls in Elizabeth to corroborate her husband's accusation. Not knowing that he has already confessed to "lechery," she must decide between two agonizing alternatives — exposing the immorality of a vicious witness at the cost of ruining her husband's reputation or protecting her husband at the cost of continuing the madness of the witch trials. Elizabeth's tragedy is that in choosing to "cooperate" with her husband, she actually betrays both him and a community caught in an hysterical witch hunt.

▪▪▪▪▪▪▪▪▪▪▪▪▪▪▪▪▪▪▪▪▪▪▪▪

Cooperation and Competition in Experimental Games

To better understand conflicts like that faced by Elizabeth Proctor, social psychologists have appealed to mathematical game theory, which analyzes patterns of costs and rewards in different kinds of interpersonal dilemmas (Rapoport, 1967). Experiments have often focused on the smallest groups possible, namely dyads (two people only). In order to understand cooperation and competition in groups, let's turn to research on two classic experimental dilemmas: the Prisoner's Dilemma and the Commons Dilemma.

The Prisoner's Dilemma.   The Prisoner's Dilemma takes its name from the following scenario (Luce & Raiffa, 1957): A district attorney tries to develop a case against two suspects accused of robbing a bank. The suspects are arrested for a minor offense, and the evidence implicating them in the bank robbery is weak. The district attorney therefore devises a devious method to extract a confession from one or both suspects: He takes each suspect to a separate room and tells him that he can either confess or not confess to the bank robbery. If one suspect "turns state evidence" (that is, informs on his partner) and the other does not, then the helpful informer will be freed, whereas his partner in crime will be sentenced to 15 years in jail. If both suspects refuse to confess, then each one will receive a one-year sentence for the lesser crime. Finally, if both suspects confess, then they will both receive ten years in

■■■

FIGURE 15.13   **The original Prisoner's Dilemma: Two suspects are tempted by the cost/reward matrix to confess and inform on each other.**

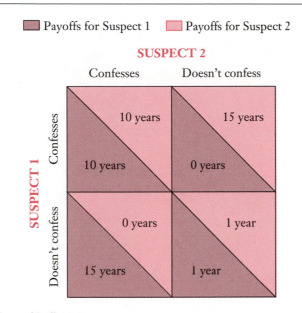

■ Payoffs for Suspect 1   ■ Payoffs for Suspect 2

SUSPECT 2

	Confesses	Doesn't confess
Confesses	10 years / 10 years	15 years / 0 years
Doesn't confess	0 years / 15 years	1 year / 1 year

SUSPECT 1

SOURCE: Based on Luce and Raiffa (1957).

■■■

prison. The reward and cost matrix of this unfortunate situation (for the suspects, at least) is shown in Figure 15.13.

The Prisoner's Dilemma is a dilemma precisely because it sorely tempts each suspect to inform on the other. Both can minimize their *combined* time in prison by not confessing. But this strategy requires each to trust the other. If one suspect cooperates but the other confesses, then the unfortunate "sucker" goes to jail for 15 years and his devious partner gets off free.

In laboratory experiments, the Prisoner's Dilemma translates to a game in which subjects can choose one of two moves — one cooperative and the other competitive. The combined moves of both players determine each player's rewards or costs. Figure 15.14 illustrates one of many possible Prisoner's Dilemma payoff matrices. Note that for a single trial in the Prisoner's Dilemma, the competitive move is the most rational in the following sense: Your average expected outcome (assuming complete uncertainty as to how your partner will behave) is more positive when you compete than when you cooperate. For example, in Figure 15.13, a suspect's average prison term is five years if he confesses and eight years if he doesn't, whereas in Figure 15.14, a player receives on average 25 cents when she competes but loses on average 25 cents when she cooperates.

The picture becomes more complicated, however, when subjects play several trials of the Prisoner's Dilemma game. Then, if a competitive partner victimizes a cooperative player, the cooperative player can switch to a competitive move on her next trial. Research on the Prisoner's Dilemma shows that when one partner behaves competitively, trust is substantially reduced, and the game often degenerates into

FIGURE 15.14   The Prisoner's Dilemma as an experimental game.

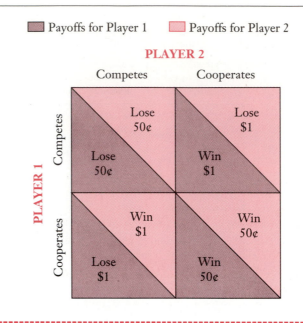

■ Payoffs for Player 1   ■ Payoffs for Player 2

PLAYER 2

	Competes	Cooperates
Competes	Lose 50¢ / Lose 50¢	Lose $1 / Win $1
Cooperates	Win $1 / Lose $1	Win 50¢ / Win 50¢

mutual competition (Brickman, Becker, & Castle, 1979; Deutsch, 1973).

Conversely, subjects will often reciprocate a partner's cooperative behavior with cooperative choices of their own (Black & Higbee, 1973). Thus to some degree, cooperation fosters reciprocal cooperation and competition fosters reciprocal competition (Rubin & Brown, 1975). One important qualification needs to be added to this general finding, however: When one party in the Prisoner's Dilemma behaves in an unconditionally and unilaterally cooperative fashion, the other will often exploit him and choose competitive moves (Shure, Meeker, & Hansford, 1965; Reychler, 1979). The reward structure of the Prisoner's Dilemma tempts subjects paired with overly cooperative partners to earn high rewards by defecting to the competitive response.

Experimental studies have repeatedly found that the simple strategy of "tit for tat" is most consistently effective in getting a partner to cooperate (Rubin & Brown, 1975; McClintock & Liebrand, 1988; see Chapter 13 for a discussion of tit-for-tat behavior in relation to reciprocal altruism). Tit-for-tat behavior consists of starting with cooperation and thereafter consistently responding to your partner's competitive or cooperative move by making the same move. Why does this strategy lead to cooperation? Axelrod (1984) explains:

> What accounts for TIT-FOR-TAT's robust success is its combination of being nice, retaliatory, forgiving and clear. Its niceness prevents it from getting into unnecessary trouble. Its retaliation discourages the other side from persisting whenever defection is tried. Its forgiveness helps to restore mutual coopera-

tion. And its clarity makes it intelligible to the other player, thereby eliciting long-term cooperation. (p. 54)

The Prisoner's Dilemma parallels many real-life group situations. For example, in trade relations between, say, the United States and Japan, each country can choose either cooperative policies (low tariffs, a free market for the other country's products) or competitive policies (high tariffs, restricted markets). If both countries cooperate, then both economies may prosper moderately. If one cooperates and the other competes, then the competitor has a large economic advantage and the cooperator suffers. If both countries compete, each will suffer economically.

Different players approach the Prisoner's Dilemma and other experimental games with different motives (McClintock & Van Avermaet, 1982; Knight & Dubro, 1984). For example, some people tend to be *cooperators* who strive to maximize the joint profits of both players. Others are *competitors* who want to maximize the difference between their own profits and those of their partner. And finally, some are *individualists* who strive to maximize their own profits without regard for how their partner is doing. Knight and Dubro (1984) offer some evidence that men are more likely to be competitors and that women are more likely to be cooperators.

Games like the Prisoner's Dilemma can be generalized to include more than two people and can be played by groups rather than by individuals. McCallum and her colleagues (1985) had subjects play the Prisoner's Dilemma either as individuals or as two-person teams. Subjects were significantly less cooperative when playing in groups and were more likely to show motivations typical of competitors—that is, they preferred to maximize the difference in rewards between their group and the other group. Apparently it is more difficult for groups than for individuals to cooperate, perhaps in part because of the tendency for groups to develop ethnocentric attitudes and to derogate out-groups (Insko & Schopler, 1987; see Chapter 9).

The Commons Dilemma.

The Commons Dilemma.   In a classic paper, Garret Hardin (1968) described what he termed the "tragedy of the commons." Imagine a village with a communal piece of land—the commons—available to all local shepherds. Further, imagine that the commons is large enough to support 50 sheep; more than that will overgraze the commons and reduce it to barren land. If 50 shepherds graze one animal each on the land, all is well. But suppose one shepherd decides to graze two sheep and thus reap more profit from the commons. Not to be outdone, others also graze more sheep. The net result: A barren commons that can support no sheep. By pursuing individual profit, the shepherds instead achieve collective disaster.

The parable of the commons applies to any situation in which a group of people uses a finite resource with a fixed rate of replacement. Some obvious examples are when lumber companies deforest land, when nations "harvest" whales, when farmers pump out underground water for irrigation, and when people consume electricity on a hot summer's day. The tragedy of the commons is that its reward structure creates a *social trap*—a situation in which seemingly rational behavior leading to short-term gains for individuals results ultimately in collective ruin. The individual is always tempted to increase his consumption of the communal resource, but if he does his decision often spurs others to do the same. And the downward spiral of group behavior begins and ultimately results in decimation of the resource.

The Commons Dilemma shares a number of features with the Prisoner's Dilemma. Both situations tempt participants to make competitive, exploitative responses. Both constitute what game theorists term "nonzero-sum" games; that is,

▪▪▪▪▪▪▪▪▪▪▪▪▪▪▪▪▪▪▪▪▪▪

Depletion of the Earth's forests. Social psychological research on the Commons Dilemma may help us to manage real-life resources more wisely.

the profits and losses of all participants *do not* necessarily add up to zero. In the commons, everyone can lose if resources are exploited, whereas everyone can win if resources are conserved wisely. (The game of poker, on the other hand, is generally a zero-sum game in which one player's win is necessarily another player's loss.) Finally, in both the Prisoner's Dilemma and the Commons Dilemma, one participant's competition tends to spur others to compete as well, often to everyone's detriment.

The Commons Dilemma, like the Prisoner's Dilemma, can be simulated in laboratory games. For example, Edney (1979) had college-student subjects gather around a bowl containing ten metal nuts. Students were told that they could remove as many nuts as they wished and that every ten seconds the number of nuts remaining in the bowl would be doubled. The object of the game was for each subject to accumulate as many nuts as possible. Do you think these students devised a fair and rational strategy to "harvest" nuts without depleting them? Unfortunately, no. Most of Edney's groups didn't even make it past the first ten-second replacement period—everyone simply lunged and grabbed as many nuts as he or she could.

Some situational factors seem to exacerbate the tragedy of the commons. Komorita and Lapworth (1982) found that both the number of people in a group and the number of subgroups in a group were positively related to exploitation of the commons. Whale hunting provides a good example here. The more people there are who hunt whales and the more subgroups of people (for example, nations) there are who hunt whales, the more we can expect overhunting. Large numbers of people seem more likely to exploit common resources in part because they feel anonymous and believe that their individual use makes little difference to the total resource; the existence of subgroups leads to greater exploitation of the commons by fostering feelings of in-group–out-group competition.

There are ways to avoid the tragedy of the commons. In some experiments subjects have resisted the temptation to gobble up resources competitively through rational communication and regulation of the resources (Messick, Wilke, Brewer, Krammer, Zemke, & Lui, 1983; Samuelson, Messick, Rutte, & Wilke, 1984). Clearly, this is a technique that is sometimes used to regulate real resources. The federal government may carefully regulate the lumber harvest in federal forests, and the electric company may seek volunteers to reduce electricity consumption during peak periods of power use. Brewer and Kramer (1986) reported that subjects show greater restraint in exploiting the commons when they are made to identify with other members of their group. In this age of shrinking forests, fossil-fuel supplies, and basic resources like clean air and water, the challenge we all face in preserving "the commons" for future generations is not simply to identify with our immediate groups, but to identify with our entire planet as well.

Groups: A Final Word

We began this chapter with a small group of people in a courtroom in Salem, Massachusetts. We ended by considering a much larger group—humanity on the finite planet Earth. Clearly, human groups hold both promise and peril. As we have seen repeatedly, groups profoundly affect our work, our decisions, our morality, our health—and even our future survival on this planet.

The word *crucible* has two meanings: a vessel in which substances are strengthened through exposure to great heat, and a severe test or trial. In Miller's play, the Salem witch hunt was the crucible, strengthening some characters and testing all with terrible ordeals. In this chapter, *the group* constitutes the crucible of human social life, full of possibilities for both good and bad.

Summary

1. A group is a collection of individuals who interact and communicate with one another over time.

2. Three main dimensions of group behavior are general activity, likability, and task ability.

3. The mere presence of other people can affect the speed and quality of an individual's task performance. Zajonc's theory of social facilitation holds that the presence of others is arousing and that this arousal facilitates dominant, well-learned habits but interferes with nondominant, poorly learned habits. Evaluation apprehension and cognitive distraction also contribute to social facilitation in humans.

4. Group tasks may be additive, conjunctive, disjunctive, or divisible. In additive tasks, group members pool their efforts or production. In conjunctive tasks, all members perform the same subtasks. In disjunctive tasks, groups must make either-or, right-wrong decisions. In divisible groups, tasks are divided into different subtasks.

5. Individuals in additive groups sometimes show social loafing — that is, they exert less individual effort when in groups than when alone. Social loafing is reduced when individual performance is evaluated by oneself or by others.

6. Brainstorming — a technique to encourage the uninhibited expression of creative ideas in group settings — often is ineffective because of social loafing, evaluation apprehension, and production blocking; thus it does not necessarily increase creativity in group members.

7. Group polarization occurs when group discussion leads group members to make more extreme decisions or to hold more extreme attitudes. Group polarization results both from informational influence in groups and from social comparison processes.

8. Groupthink refers to a syndrome of bad decision making that occurs in stressed, cohesive groups directed by leaders who are intolerant of dissent.

9. Leaders are members of groups who are particularly influential and who act to guide, direct, and motivate the group to achieve its goals. Leaders often engage in task-oriented behaviors (which direct the group's work) and socioemotional behaviors (which foster positive group relations and cohesiveness).

10. Intelligence and various personality traits are weakly correlated with leadership.

11. French and Raven described five different kinds of power: reward power, coercive power, legitimate power, referent power, and expert power. Each may contribute to a leader's power and effectiveness.

12. Strong leaders are more likely to emerge when groups are stressed. Situational factors such as seating arrangements and reinforcements for group participation can influence who becomes the leader of a group.

13. Fiedler's contingency model holds that leadership effectiveness depends both on leadership style and the leadership setting. According to the model, the favorableness of a leadership setting is a function of the positiveness of leader-group relations, the clarity of group goals, and the leader's degree of legitimate power. The model hypothesizes that task-oriented leaders tend to be more effective than socioemotional leaders in very favorable or very unfavorable settings, whereas socioemotional leaders tend to be more effective than task-oriented leaders in moderately favorable settings.

14. People are deindividuated when they lose their personal identity and become "submerged in the group." According to Zimbardo, arousal, anonymity, sensory overload, and drug-induced alterations in consciousness can all contribute to deindividuation, which then leads to lowered inhibitions and behavior that is not consistent with internal standards. Consistent with deindividuation theory, research suggests that anonymity in group settings can foster antisocial behavior.

15. Deindividuation is due in part to reduced self-awareness. Deindividuated people report experiencing reduced self-awareness and an altered state of consciousness.

16. Mass psychogenic illness is an illness of psychological origin that occurs in group settings and is due to hysterical contagion. Such illness occurs most frequently among stressed workers performing tedious jobs, and it seems to result from mislabeled arousal, behavioral contagion, and deindividuation.

17. In the Prisoner's Dilemma two players simultaneously choose either coopera-

tive or competitive "moves." The reward structure of the Prisoner's Dilemma tempts each player to choose the competitive response, which rewards the player and simultaneously hurts the other player. Players often reciprocate competitive or cooperative responses in repeated trials of the Prisoner's Dilemma game. Groups playing the Prisoner's Dilemma tend to be more competitive than individual players.

18. The Commons Dilemma refers to any situation in which a group of people uses a finite resource with a fixed rate of replacement. The reward structure of the Commons Dilemma creates a social trap in which seemingly rational individual behavior leads to collective ruin. People tend to exploit the commons more when in large groups that are divided into many subgroups. Rational communication and regulation of resources can help to prevent the tragedy of the commons.

Glossary

Activity: A major dimension of group behavior; *activity* refers to the individual's general level of participation in group discussions and activities

Additive task: A task, such as a tug-of-war, in which individuals pool their identical efforts together

Brainstorming: A technique to foster creativity in groups; individuals are asked to express any idea that comes to mind, to refrain from evaluating their own or others' ideas, and to build upon one another's ideas

Commons Dilemma: A situation in which a group of people use a finite resource that has a fixed rate of replacement; in such a situation individuals are tempted to seek short-term gains that lead to long-term collective ruin; see *social trap*

Competitors: People who strive to maximize the difference between their own profits and those of their partner in games such as the Prisoner's Dilemma

Conjunctive task: A task, such as mountain-climbing, in which individuals all perform the same subtask; a group engaged in a conjunctive task tends to be as effective as its weakest members

Contingency model of leadership: Fiedler's model that holds that leadership effectiveness is a function of the leader's style of leadership and the leadership setting; task-oriented leaders are hypothesized to be more effective in very favorable or very unfavorable leadership settings, whereas socioemotional leaders are more effective in moderately favorable leadership settings

Cooperators: People who strive to maximize the joint profits of themselves and their partner in games such as the Prisoner's Dilemma

Deindividuation: A disinhibited state that occurs when people lose their individual identities in group settings; arousal, anonymity, and sensory overload can foster deindividuation; lowered inhibitions and behavior that is inconsistent with internal standards can result from deindividuation

Disjunctive task: A task, such as a group quiz game, in which the group must arrive at a yes-no, either-or decision or answer; the disjunctive group tends to be as effective as its strongest members

Divisible task: A task, such as manufacturing an appliance, in which different group members perform different subtasks

Group: A collection of individuals who interact and communicate with one another over a period of time

Group polarization: Occurs when group discussion leads group members to make more extreme decisions or to arrive at more extreme judgments

Groupthink: A syndrome of bad decision making in cohesive groups; according to Janis, groupthink occurs in stressed, cohesive groups directed by leaders who are intolerant of dissent

Individualists: People who strive to maximize their own profits without regard for how their partner is doing in games such as the Prisoner's Dilemma

Informational influence: One explanation for group polarization; when people learn new information and arguments from a group discussion, they may then change their judgments or decisions

Interaction Process Analysis: A content-analysis system developed by Robert Bales to code behavior in groups; IPA focuses on socioemotional and task-oriented behaviors that are both positive and negative

Leaders: Members of groups who are particularly influential and who act to guide, direct, and motivate the group to achieve its goals

Least Preferred Coworker Scale: Fiedler's scale to assess leadership style; it asks leaders to rate and evaluate the member of their group that they like least; leaders who rate their least-preferred coworker negatively tend to be task-oriented leaders, whereas those who rate their least-preferred coworker positively tend to be socioemotional leaders

Likability: A major dimension of group behavior; it refers to the degree to which an individual engages in positive or negative socioemotional behaviors

Mass psychogenic illness: An illness of psychological origin that occurs in group settings due to hysterical contagion

Nominal group technique: A technique to foster both individual and group creativity; individual group members first silently generate ideas and write them down and then discuss them in the group; the group finally selects the best ideas

Prisoner's Dilemma: A game in which each of two players simultaneously chooses either a competitive or a cooperative response; the reward matrix of the Prisoner's Dilemma is structured so that if both players cooperate, then each receives a modest reward; if both compete, each pays a modest penalty; and if one player competes and the other cooperates, the competitor receives a large reward and the cooperator pays a large penalty

Social comparison processes: Such processes help to explain group polarization; social comparison occurs when group discussion leads members to become aware of group norms, and members then shift their decisions or judgments because of this knowledge

Social facilitation: Occurs when an individual performs a task faster or better in the presence of others than when alone

Social loafing: Occurs when individuals exert less effort working on a task in a group than when alone; tends to occur in additive tasks in which individual performance is not being monitored

Social trap: A situation in which seemingly rational behavior leading to short-term gains for individuals results ultimately in collective ruin; see *Commons Dilemma*

Socioemotional leader: A leader who excels at socioemotional but not task-oriented skills; also known as a maintenance specialist

Task ability: A major dimension of group behavior; it refers to the degree to which an individual engages in behaviors directed at achieving the group's goal or task

Task specialist: A leader who excels at task-oriented but not socioemotional skills

Tit for tat: The strategy that is most successful in eliciting cooperation from a partner in repeated trials of the Prisoner's Dilemma game; tit for tat consists of starting with cooperation and thereafter always responding to your partner's cooperative or competitive move with the same move

     (PANGLOSS *sings*)
Wherefore and hence, therefore and ergo —
     (CHORUS *sings*)
Wherefore and hence, therefore and ergo —
     (PANGLOSS *sings*)
All's for the best in this best of all possible worlds.
     (CHORUS *sings*)
All's for the best in this best of all possible worlds.
     (PANGLOSS *sings*)
Any questions?
Ask without fear.
     (*Touches his head*)
I've all the answers here.

> —— lyrics from "The Best of All Possible Worlds," by Richard Wilbur, from the operetta *Candide* (1957, pp. 5, 6), based on Voltaire's satire

CHAPTER 16

Applying Social Psychology

*V*oltaire's wickedly satirical novel *Candide* (1759) portrays the incredible mishaps of its young protagonist and contrasts them with the hopelessly optimistic philosophy of his teacher, Dr. Pangloss. After witnessing the apparent murder of his fiancée by invading soldiers, Candide flees from his native land, Westphalia. Wandering across Europe and South America, he experiences — among other disasters — a terrible earthquake in Portugal, persecution at the hands of the Inquisition, beatings, starvation, and theft. Despite his misery and suffering, Candide is repeatedly assured by Dr. Pangloss that this is "the best of all possible worlds."

Because of Voltaire's satire, the word *Panglossian* has come to refer to naive and unrealistic optimism. After reading this book, you may find it difficult to be Panglossian, for you have learned about the complex causes of many enduring social problems, including prejudice (Chapter 9); aggression (Chapter 12); destructive forms of conformity, compliance, and obedience (Chapter 14); and antisocial behavior in groups (Chapter 15).

Precisely because we *do not* live in the best of all possible worlds, social psychologists study social problems and attempt to contribute to their solution. In this final chapter we turn to the practice of applied social psychology. Unlike Dr. Pangloss, we cannot claim to have "all the answers here," but social psychology does have some of the answers. And even when no answers currently exist, social psychological theories and research methods can help to find them.

Social psychologists apply their knowledge to real-life problems in three different ways (see Helmreich, 1975; Hornstein, 1975; Rodin, 1985). First, they attempt to answer important social questions. Second, social psychologists use their theories **613**

Dr. Pangloss lectures to his students about "the best of all possible worlds" in a scene from the operetta *Candide*.

and research findings to design programs to solve or alleviate social problems. And finally, because of their expertise in conducting social research, social psychologists are frequently asked to assess the effectiveness of programs designed to solve social problems (this is referred to as *evaluation research*). Let's briefly illustrate these three ways of applying social psychology with examples from previous chapters.

Answering Social Questions

Social psychology provides important information to society and to policy makers. For example, in Chapter 12 we examined research on the relationship between TV viewing and aggression. Although social psychologists cannot answer the value questions that enter into public policy (for example, how should society balance the potentially destructive consequences of violent TV programming against freedom of speech and freedom of the press?), they can provide the data needed for a reasoned debate. Social psychologists have helped to document the relationship between viewing violent TV and aggression, and they have identified variables that moderate the relationship.

Designing Social Interventions

Social psychological theory and research can be used to design effective programs that may alleviate social problems. In Chapter 4 we described how an attributional analysis of depression led to new forms of therapy for treating depression. In Chapter 9 we described Muzafer Sherif's classic research on reducing boys' intergroup hostilities by creating superordinate goals for antagonistic groups. In Chapter 12 we described an educational program to reduce the impact of violent TV on children's behavior. And in Chapter 15, we suggested strategies that can help prevent groups from making extreme and ill-considered decisions.

Social psychological research helps society assess the outcomes of social policies. In Chapter 9 we discussed the intergroup contact hypothesis and the effects of school integration on children. The research showed that classroom integration can foster positive interactions between groups, particularly in cooperative rather than competitive classrooms.

Evaluating Social Programs

In Chapter 12 we examined the effectiveness of police interventions in cases of family violence. Here, social psychological research helped to assess whether the social policy of arresting violent family members reduced subsequent violence, and how effective this policy was as compared with that of other procedures such as "cooling-off periods."

As these examples make clear, we have discussed applied social psychology throughout this book. Here we'll extend the discussion to focus on an active new research area in social psychology—health psychology. We'll use health psychology to illustrate the three ways to apply social psychology. First, we'll look at research that attempts to answer a number of important questions about social factors in health. For example, does stress lead to illness? If so, can social support mitigate some of the negative effects of stress? Then we turn to research that attempts to design and evaluate psychological programs to improve health. For example, can social psychological research help society formulate policies to improve conditions in medical institutions (such as hospitals and convalescent homes for the elderly)?

Social Psychological Factors in Health

Candide was flogged. . . .

    . . . stunned, stupefied, despairing, bleeding, trembling, [he] said to himself: — If this is the best of all possible worlds, what are the others like? . . .

    He was being led away, barely able to stand, lectured, lashed, absolved, and blessed, when an old woman approached and said, — My son, be of good cheer and follow me.

    . . . Candide was of very bad cheer, but he followed the old woman to a shanty; she gave him a jar of ointment to rub himself, left him food and drink; she showed him a tidy little bed; next to it was a suit of clothing.

    — Eat, drink, sleep, she said. . . . I will be back tomorrow.

    Candide, still completely astonished by everything he had seen and suffered, and even more by the old woman's kindness, offered to kiss her hand.

              —— *Candide*, by Voltaire (1966), pp. 12–13

The world is full of stresses. Some of us withstand them and stay healthy and optimistic, others succumb to them, grow ill, and despair. After his brutal beating by the Inquisition (a decidedly stressful event), Candide was wounded and helpless. It was only with the help of another person that he returned to good health.

Stress, Social Support, and Illness

How much do social factors influence our health? Because other people may be sources of both stress and support, it seems reasonable that others can contribute to both illness and health. Does stress in fact lead to illness? And can the support of

▪▪▪▪▪▪▪▪▪▪▪▪▪▪▪▪▪▪▪▪▪▪▪▪▪
Positive as well as negative events may sometimes be stressful. Holmes and Rahe's list of stressful life events includes: "change in residence"; and . . . "Christmas."

others buffer us against stress and thereby foster health? Recently, social psychologists have become interested in such questions (Rodin & Salovey, 1989).

Stress and health.   When confronted with threatening physical or emotional stimuli, the body responds by mobilizing its resources. The sympathetic nervous system—which prepares the body for emergencies and for quick action—becomes aroused. Heart rate, blood pressure, and respiration increase, and blood is diverted away from the internal, digestive organs to the voluntary skeletal muscles (Selye, 1956, 1976). In such a state of preparedness, the body is ready for either "fight or flight." Although such arousal is frequently a temporary response to a temporary crisis, it can become chronic if an individual is exposed to repeated or unrelenting stressors. When the body is constantly mobilized, it begins to exhaust its resources. Continuous arousal can lead to stress-related maladies such as ulcers, colitis, asthma, high blood pressure, and reduced immunity to infectious diseases (Selye, 1956, 1976).

Stress depends on our subjective perceptions of events as well as on objective threats; according to one definition, a situation is stressful when it "is appraised by the person as taxing or exceeding his or her resources and endangering his or her well-being" (Lazarus & Folkman, 1984, p. 19). For example, one student may perceive final exams as exciting and challenging, whereas another may perceive them as highly threatening and thus regard them as a source of considerable stress.

In an early attempt to measure stress, Holmes and Rahe (1967) compiled a list of 43 positive and negative events that may require major readjustments in people's

lives. Preliminary research suggested that these events tended to precede the onset of disease in a sample of 5,000 patients. Holmes and Rahe asked their subjects to rate how much readjustment each event required. Then, based on these ratings, they assigned a numerical rating of stressfulness to each event. The investigators assessed stress by asking respondents to indicate which of the listed events had occurred over a specified period of time (for example, over the last six months) and then summing the point values of all those events checked by the subjects; the result was the Schedule of Recent Life Experiences (see Figure 16.1).

Some later researchers have argued for assessing positive and negative life events separately (see Dohrenwend, Krasnoff, Askenasy, & Dohrenwend, 1978, 1982). Others have proposed using individual subjects' ratings of how stressful they perceive particular events to be, rather than employing normative ratings made by others (Sarason, Johnson, & Siegel, 1978; Sarason & Sarason, 1984).

Recently researchers have also noted that minor as well as major stresses may affect health. Lazarus and his colleagues (Lazarus, DeLongis, Folkman, & Gruen, 1985; Kanner, Coyne, Schaefer, & Lazarus, 1981) developed a Hassles Scale: a list of 117 everyday occurrences that people frequently find to be annoying, irritating, or frustrating (such as, "rising prices of common goods," "too many things to do," "taxes," and concerns about "physical appearance"). A factor analysis of the Hassles Scale revealed that the scale assesses eight main areas of stress in everyday life (see Figure 16.2).

Do stresses and everyday hassles influence health? The answer, distilled from many studies, seems to be a tentative "Yes" — stress is correlated with physical and

FIGURE 16.1   The Schedule of Recent Life Experiences.

How is stress measured?

Holmes and Rahe (1967) compiled a list of positive and negative events that require people to make major readjustments in their lives. They then developed a scale — the Social Readjustment Rating Scale — to measure how stressful each event is perceived to be. The life events and their mean stress ratings are listed here.

RANK	LIFE EVENT	MEAN VALUE	RANK	LIFE EVENT	MEAN VALUE
1	Death of spouse	100	23	Son or daughter leaving home	29
2	Divorce	73	24	Trouble with in-laws	29
3	Marital separation	65	25	Outstanding personal achievement	28
4	Jail term	63	26	Wife begin or stop work	26
5	Death of close family member	63	27	Begin or end school	26
6	Personal injury or illness	53	28	Change in living conditions	25
7	Marriage	50	29	Revision of personal habits	24
8	Fired at work	47	30	Trouble with boss	23
9	Marital reconciliation	45	31	Change in work hours or conditions	20
10	Retirement	45	32	Change in residence	20
11	Change in health of family member	44	33	Change in schools	20
12	Pregnancy	40	34	Change in recreation	19
13	Sex difficulties	39	35	Change in church activities	19
14	Gain of new family member	39	36	Change in social activities	18
15	Business readjustment	39	37	Mortgage or loan less than $10,000	17
16	Change in financial state	38	38	Change in sleeping habits	16
17	Death of close friend	37	39	Change in number of family get-togethers	15
18	Change to different line of work	36	40	Change in eating habits	15
19	Change in number of arguments with spouse	35	41	Vacation	13
20	Mortgage over $10,000	31	42	Christmas	12
21	Foreclosure of mortgage or loan	30	43	Minor violations of the law	11
22	Change in responsibilities at work	29			

SOURCE: From Holmes and Rahe (1967). Used with permission of Pergamon Press, Inc. and Thomas Holmes.

psychological illness. However, the relationship tends to be relatively weak, with correlation coefficients in the range of .2 to .3 (Kobasa, 1982; Rabkin & Struening, 1976; Rahe, 1984; Tausig, 1982; Zegans, 1982). The negative effects of stress on health tend to subside when the stress subsides; the elevated risk of illness generally does not last more than a year or two after elevated stress levels (Rahe, 1984).

Typically, studies on the relationship between stress and health ask subjects to report the number of stressful events they have recently experienced. In retrospective studies, subjects are asked at the *same* time to report on recent illnesses or symptoms of illness; then the stress score and the illness score are correlated. In

FIGURE 16.2   **Eight factors and sample items from the Hassles Scale.**

FACTOR	SAMPLE ITEMS
Household hassles	Preparing meals Home maintenance
Health hassles	Physical illness Side effects of medication
Time pressure hassles	Too many things to do Not enough time to do the things you need to do
Inner concern hassles	Being lonely Concerns about inner conflicts
Environmental hassles	Noise Crime
Financial hassles	Financial responsibility Concerns about owing money
Work hassles	Job dissatisfaction Problems getting along with fellow workers
Future security hassles	Concerns about retirement Property, investments, or taxes

SOURCE: Adapted from Lazarus, DeLongis, Folkman, and Gruen (1985). Used with permission of Richard Lazarus.

prospective studies, subjects' stress scores are correlated with illness assessed at some *later* time to determine whether stress predicts future illness. Retrospective studies may suffer from the problem that current stress levels lead to biased memories and reports of illness. For example, if you are now under great stress you may recall an earlier illness as more severe than it actually was. Moreover, some subjects report high levels of both stress and illness because they have a general tendency to experience negative feelings and report negative experiences (Watson & Pennebaker, 1989).

Despite these and other methodological problems and interpretive ambiguities, many studies suggest that stress and illness are related (Maddi, Bartone, & Puccetti, 1987). Stress-related diseases include heart disease (Rahe & Lind, 1971), difficulties during pregnancy and birth (Gorsuch & Key, 1974), childhood illnesses (Bedell, Giordani, Amour, Tavormina, & Boll, 1977; Weigel, Wertlieb, & Feldstein, 1989), asthma (Elliott & Eisdorfer, 1982), and rheumatoid arthritis (Weiner, 1977).

How does stress lead to illness? Experimental studies on animals show that stress suppresses the immune system (Laudenslager, Ryan, Drugan, Hyson, & Maier,

1983). This may help explain why stress influences the development of a number of diseases, including possibly cancer (Justice, 1985). Correlational studies on humans also suggest a link between stress and immunity. For example, stressful marriages lead not only to psychological distress in women but also to depressed immune functions (Kiecolt-Glaser, Fisher, Ogrocki, Stout, Speicher, & Glaser, 1987). Through its effects on the immune system, stress can activate latent viral diseases such as herpes (Goldmeier & Johnson, 1982). One recent study demonstrated that the levels of antibodies in college students saliva were lower during final exam week than they were during either the preceding or following weeks (Jemmott & Magloire, 1988).

The relatively weak correlations between stress and illness should not be interpreted to mean that stress is unimportant in the development of illness. Clearly, illness is a function of many factors, including socioeconomic status, knowledge (do you know the "warning signs" of cancer?), habits (diet, smoking, sexual behavior), exposure to environmental hazards, and infectious agents, as well as stress. Even a modest correlation between stress and illness can have social significance when viewed in the context of populations of millions of people.

Social support and health.   Perhaps the relationship between stress and health is weak because other variables influence either the strength of the relationship or whether the relationship even occurs at all. (As we noted in Chapter 6, variables that influence the relationship between two other variables are termed *moderator variables*.) One variable that may possibly moderate the effects of stress on illness is social support (Cohen & Syme, 1985a; Coyne & DeLongis, 1986; Schradle & Dougher, 1985; Wallston, Alagna, DeVellis, & DeVellis, 1983).

Social support has been defined as "the comfort, assistance, and/or information one receives through formal or informal contacts with individuals or groups" (Wallston, Alagna, DeVellis, & DeVellis, 1983, p. 369), or even more simply as "resources provided by other people" (Cohen & Syme, 1985b, p. 4). Such resources come in many forms. Cohen and McKay (1984) distinguish among three broad varieties: tangible support, cognitive and informational support, and emotional support.

Imagine, for instance, that you contract a severe case of influenza and are bedridden for several days. If your best friend runs errands for you and prepares your meals, he or she is providing tangible support. If your friend informs you what to expect during the course of your illness ("You'll feel extremely weak for several days and have a high fever. . . ."), he or she is providing informational support. Finally, if your friend informs you that he or she is concerned about you and that all your friends wish you a speedy recovery, he or she is offering emotional support. Tangible support reduces your stress by reducing your need to attend to the chores and responsibilities of everyday life. Cognitive support reduces stress by providing clarity and knowledge about your situation (what social psychologists term social comparison information—see Chapters 11 and 15). Finally, emotional support fosters your well-being by boosting your self-esteem and informing you that you are loved, valued, and part of a caring social network.

Social support has been measured in many different ways (House & Kahn, 1985). Epidemiological studies (that is, studies of disease patterns in large populations) sometimes rely on self-reports about specific social relationships ("Are you married or single?") as broad measures of social support. Social network measures assess the number and interconnectedness of social supports ("How many friends do you have? Are they a tightly knit, cohesive group?"). Finally, a number of self-report questionnaires ask respondents about the kinds and degree of social support they receive (Cohen, Mermelstein, Kamarck, & Hoberman, 1984; Barrera, Sandler, & Ramsay, 1981; Sarason, Levine, Basham, & Sarason, 1983; Turner, 1981). Such questionnaires might ask you to list to whom you turn for consolation when you are very upset and to rate how satisfied you feel with the support you receive from each of those people.

Social support may foster health directly; that is, people with high levels of support simply may be healthier on average than people with lower levels of support. Or, more subtly, social support may buffer the effects of stress on health; for example, high levels of social support may have little influence on the health of nonstressed people but may serve to reduce illness in highly stressed individuals. Research has documented both effects.

Epidemiological studies show that people integrated into social networks show significantly lower mortality rates than do more socially isolated people (Berkman & Breslow, 1983; Berkman & Syme, 1979; House, Robbins, & Metzner, 1982; Schradle & Dougher, 1985). In a careful study of 4,725 residents of Alameda County, California, Berkman and Syme (1979) constructed an index of social support from four measures of social contact — marital status, amount of contact with close friends and relatives, church membership, and membership in formal and informal groups. Based on this social network index, subjects were divided into four groups ranging from those with the most numerous social ties to those with the fewest social ties. Over a nine-year period, Berkman and Syme found that on average the people with the fewest social ties died at rates that were two to four times higher than those for people with the most social ties (see Figure 16.3). Furthermore, the degree of social contact was related to deaths from many different causes, including heart disease, stroke, cancer, accident, and suicide (Berkman, 1985). In fact, as assessed in the Alameda County study, social isolation is a larger risk factor for death than is cigarette smoking (Rogot, 1974).

Like all correlational studies, epidemiological studies on social support and mortality are causally ambiguous (see Chapter 2). Why is social support related to death rates? One possibility is that concerned friends and loved ones may lead us to seek medical care and to practice preventive and therapeutic health-related behaviors, such as eating and sleeping properly (Berkman & Syme, 1979). Social support may help people to refrain from unhealthy behaviors, such as drug and alcohol abuse. Lack of social support may lead to psychological states (such as depression) that foster poor health. Finally, both social support and health may be a function of other variables. For example, socially isolated people may tend to be socially unskilled or maladjusted (Monroe & Steiner, 1986) or poor and underprivileged (Jenkins, 1982), and such people may lack the resources to develop social supports, even when they need and desire them.

Social psychologists have been extremely interested in the possibility that social support may buffer individuals against the negative effects of stress (Cassel, 1976; Zegans, 1982). In a comprehensive review, Cohen and Wills (1985) noted that such buffering effects are found particularly in studies that measure perceived informational and emotional support; that is, having someone to talk to, boost your morale,

FIGURE 16.3   Social support and mortality in Alameda County, California, 1965–1974.

Is social support related to mortality?

This graph displays findings from Berkman and Syme's (1974) study of social support and death rates.

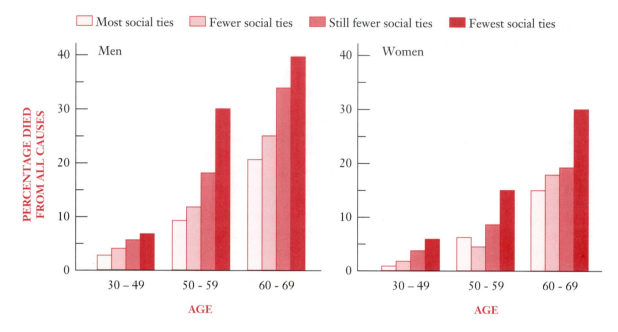

The level of social support was clearly related to death rates for both men and women. Evidently, social isolation is hazardous to your health.

SOURCE: Adapted from Berkman and Syme (1979). Used with permission.

The relation between social isolation and mortality was present for virtually all causes of death. This study conceptualized social support as the degree to which individuals were involved in social relationships — marriages, friendships, church groups, and so on.

and provide you with useful information is particularly valuable when you are highly stressed. On the other hand, belonging to social networks (families, church groups, friendship networks) has direct positive health effects. Whether you are stressed or not, your health is likely to be better if you are part of a group that provides you with feelings of well-being and secure attachment.

Social support may have different effects at different stages of illness (Wallston, Alagna, DeVellis, & DeVellis, 1983). For example, the stress-buffering hypothesis holds that social support may influence the *development* of illness and protect against the negative effects of stress. Once ill, people with high levels of social support often recover faster and with fewer complications than do people with poorer levels of social support (Wallston, Alagna, DeVellis, & DeVellis, 1983); thus social support shows a direct rather than a buffering effect on recovery. To illustrate, one recent study found that married men recovered more quickly from coronary bypass surgery and took less pain medication when visited frequently by their wives (Kulik & Mahler, in press). For chronically ill persons, social support may influence adherence to medical programs and regimens — taking drugs regularly, watching diet, and seeking regular medical checkups (Porter, 1969; Caplan, Robinson, French, Caldwell, & Shinn, 1976). Thus social support may reduce decline and neglect in existing cases of illness.

■■■■■■■■■■■■■■■■■■■■■■■■■

Personality, Health, and Illness

CANDIDE: We will survive.

MARTIN: Why do you wish to survive?

CANDIDE: Because I am convinced that there is as much good as there is evil in the world, and I am determined to find the good in others and in myself —

MARTIN: As much good as there is evil. In a world where men march across continents to kill each other without even asking why. Where the scientist strives to prolong life and at the same minute invents weapons to wipe it out. Where children are taught the rules of charity and kindness until they grow to the age where they would be considered insane if they put the rules into practice. Where half the world starves and the other half diets. . . .

CANDIDE: Yes, much of what you say is true, and many of my dreams have faded. But I still believe in the essential goodness of the human heart —

—— *Candide* (1957), pp. 110–111

Are some people healthier than others because of their personality characteristics? Popular wisdom holds that some people have a stronger "will to live" than others do. Even in such overwhelmingly stressful environments as concentration camps, some individuals survive. What distinguishes survivors from nonsurvivors in both everyday life and in highly stressful circumstances? Is psychological and physical health in part a function of personal feelings of worth and control? Of optimism? Of general hardiness?

Feelings of control.   In Chapter 4 we discussed attribution theories, which try to predict when people will make internal and external attributions. The attributions we make about our own behavior depend not just on objective information but also on our personality characteristics and emotional states. Depressed people tend to explain their failures as being due to stable, internal causes ("I'm stupid and worthless") and their successes as being due to uncontrollable, unstable, external causes ("I was lucky"). Depressed people also tend to assess the amount of control they have over events more accurately than do nondepressed people, who often hold the benign illusion that they have more control over events in their lives than they in fact do (Taylor & Brown, 1988).

The tendency to believe that we have control over events versus the tendency to believe that we are victims of circumstance can be conceptualized as a personality

Stress is a function of cognitive appraisals as well as of the objective situation.

trait, as a stable attributional style. In 1966, Julian Rotter developed a Locus of Control Scale to assess individuals' perception of the degree to which internal or external factors control events in their lives. Since then, locus of control has become one of the most studied personality traits in social psychology (Strickland, 1989).

Rotter's scale presents respondents with pairs of statements and asks them to check the statement in each pair with which they agree most. Here are three such pairs:

> a. It is impossible for me to believe that chance or luck plays an important role in my life.
> b. Many times I feel that I have little influence over the things that happen to me.
>
> a. In the long run people get the respect they deserve in this world.
> b. Unfortunately, an individual's worth often passes unrecognized no matter how hard he tries.
>
> a. In my case getting what I want has little or nothing to do with luck.
> b. Many times we might just as well decide what to do by flipping a coin.
> (1966, pp. 11–12)

A person with an internal locus of control (one who explains his or her behavior as being due to controllable internal factors) tends to choose response *a* on these items, whereas an individual with an external locus of control (one who explains his or her behavior as being due to uncontrollable external factors) tends to choose response *b*. Individuals with an internal locus of control tend to take more responsibility for their behavior and assume a more active role in planning their behavior and changing situations they don't like than people with an external locus of control (Lefcourt, 1984; Phares, 1976; Rotter, 1975).

The Locus of Control Scale has a number of different components (Collins, 1974; Reid & Ware, 1974), so later researchers have developed scales tailored to specific domains, including health-related behaviors (Wallston, Wallston, Kaplan, & Maides, 1976; Wallston, Wallston, & DeVellis, 1978). The Health Locus of Control Scale (Wallston et al., 1976) asks respondents to rate how strongly they agree or disagree with such items as: "If I take care of myself, I can avoid illness," "Good health is largely a matter of good fortune," "People who never get sick are just plain lucky," and, "I am directly responsible for my health." In other words, the Health Locus of Control Scale asks people to rate how much control they feel over their own health.

Does locus of control correlate with health and health-related behaviors? It seems reasonable to predict that a person with an internal locus of control will take more responsibility for his or her health and take action to prevent or remedy ill-health. Despite the obviousness of this prediction, research suggests a more complex and inconsistent relationship (Wallston & Wallston, 1982). Sometimes individuals with an internal locus of control engage more in preventive behaviors and seek out more health-related information than do individuals with an external locus of control, but sometimes they do not.

In some health settings an internal locus of control may be a liability. For example, if a sick individual with an internal locus of control decides he can "cure himself" and so fails to seek medical attention quickly enough, he may endanger his health. In some situations it may be most adaptive to relinquish control, at least temporarily (Taylor, 1979). For example, if you are seriously ill and in an intensive care unit, you might best conserve your strength and mental resources by entrusting your care to competent health professionals rather than worrying about the details of every medical procedure.

Hardiness.   Even though a sense of personal control may not consistently lead to healthy behavior, it may buffer you against the deleterious effects of stress. Suzanne Kobasa (1979, 1982; Kobasa, Maddi, & Kahn, 1982) argues that a sense of personal control is one component of what she termed the *hardy* personality. Two other components are a sense of commitment (a sense of personal meaning and involvement in life) and a sense of challenge (a desire for growth and change and an openness to new experiences). Hardy individuals negotiate stress well, according to Kobasa, because they believe they have the resources they need to deal with stressful events, they do not become helpless and hopeless in the face of stress, and they thrive on change and challenge. In a sense, they approach stressful situations with zest rather than dread.

In one study on hardiness, 259 managers at a large utility company periodically completed stress, health, and personality questionnaires over a five-year period (Kobasa, Maddi, & Kahn, 1982). Personal control was assessed by Rotter's Locus of Control Scale and a scale of powerlessness. Commitment was assessed by an alienation scale (sample item: "Life is empty and has no meaning in it for me"). Challenge was assessed with a need for security scale (sample item: "I don't like situations that are uncertain"). Subjects' scores on these three components of hardiness were combined, and subjects were then divided into groups that had high degrees (above the median) or low degrees (below the median) of hardiness. Subjects were independently divided into groups that had high or low degrees of stress.

Kobasa, Maddi, and Kahn found that managers who were highly stressed and had low degrees of hardiness experienced the most illness (see Figure 16.4). As you might expect, stress also contributed independently to illness, with highly stressed managers reporting more illness than less stressed managers reported. And hardiness independently affected the frequency of illness; hardy subjects on average reported less illness than nonhardy subjects reported.

Later studies have not always corroborated Kobasa's findings. For example, one study of college women found that hardiness offered protection against stress only when combined with social support (Ganellen & Blaney, 1984). Kobasa and Puccetti (1983) also reported that hardy people benefit from social support but that nonhardy

FIGURE 16.4   Self-reported illness as a function of hardiness and stress levels.

Does hardiness buffer the effects of high levels of stress on illness?

Kobasa, Maddi, and Kahn (1982) assessed hardiness, self-reported stress, and subsequent illness in a group of utility company managers. (The numbers displayed in this graph represent tallies of subjects' self-reported illnesses and physical symptoms.)

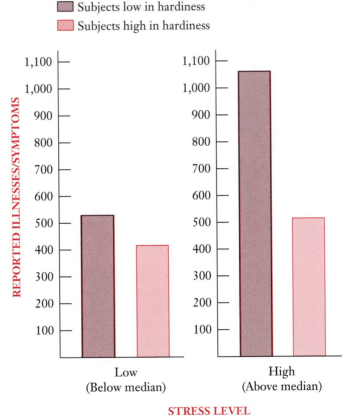

Highly stressed managers reported more illness than less stressed managers, and hardy managers reported less illness than nonhardy managers. Most interesting, however, was the finding that the relationship between stress and illness was much stronger for non-hardy than hardy managers.

SOURCE: Data from Kobasa, Maddi, and Kahn (1982).

people do not. In a study of 82 female secretaries, Schmied and Lawler (1986) found that hardiness did not buffer the effects of stress on health. Perhaps this study failed to replicate Kobasa's earlier research partly because it used female rather than male subjects. Males (particularly the managers, executives, and lawyers who served as subjects in Kobasa's studies) are socialized to view control, commitment, and challenge differently than are females. Unlike Schmied and Lawler, Rhodewalt and Zone (1989) found that hardiness buffered the effects of stress on self-reported illness and depression in 212 women. Their data suggested that these effects were due to the tendency of nonhardy women to appraise stressful events much more negatively than did hardy women.

Researchers have recently examined more closely what "hardiness" entails. Some argue that nonhardy people are in fact people who experience negative emotions in general (Allred & Smith, 1989; Funk & Houston, 1987). Furthermore, because hardiness comprises three components, it may be that one, two, or all three components produce hardiness effects and interactions in studies (Carver, 1989; Hull, Van Treuren, & Virnelli, 1987). After reviewing a number of hardiness studies, Hull, Van Treuren, and Virnelli (1987) argued that the control and commitment components of hardiness, not the challenge component, relate significantly to measures of illness and health. Furthermore, they argue that lack of control and lack of commitment influence health because they themselves are stressful, and they only sometimes buffer the effects of other kinds of stress.

Optimism.

"— Oh Pangloss!" cried Candide, "you had no notion of these abominations! I'm through, I must give up your optimism after all."

"What's optimism? . . ."

"Alas," said Candide, "it is a mania for saying things are well when one is in hell."

—— *Candide* (1966), pp. 41–42

Social support, a sense of personal control, and hardiness may all have their effects in part because they correlate with or foster a sense of well-being — a sense of optimism about life. Scheier and Carver (1985) developed a Life Orientation Test that directly assesses optimism — the degree to which individuals have a general expectancy that successes and positive events will occur. Some sample items are: "In unusual times, I usually expect the best" and "I hardly ever expect things to go my way." (Pangloss's continual comment that this is the best of all possible worlds could be an item on an optimism scale.) Scheier and Carver note that individuals with high degrees of optimism report less physical illness and greater physical well-being. Furthermore, optimists seem to cope with stress differently from pessimists (Scheier, Weintraub, & Carver, 1986). Optimists are more likely to try to take action, seek social support, and interpret stressful events as "growth experiences," whereas pessimists are more likely to focus on their feelings of stress and deny or distance themselves from their problems.

Optimism and pessimism may relate to a broader syndrome of general negative emotionality (Smith, Pope, Rhodewalt, & Poulton, 1989; Watson & Pennebaker, 1989); that is, optimistic people in general do not suffer from negative, anxious

FIGURE 16.5   Social psychological variables, stress, and health.

How do social-psychological variables influence stress and its effects on health and illness?

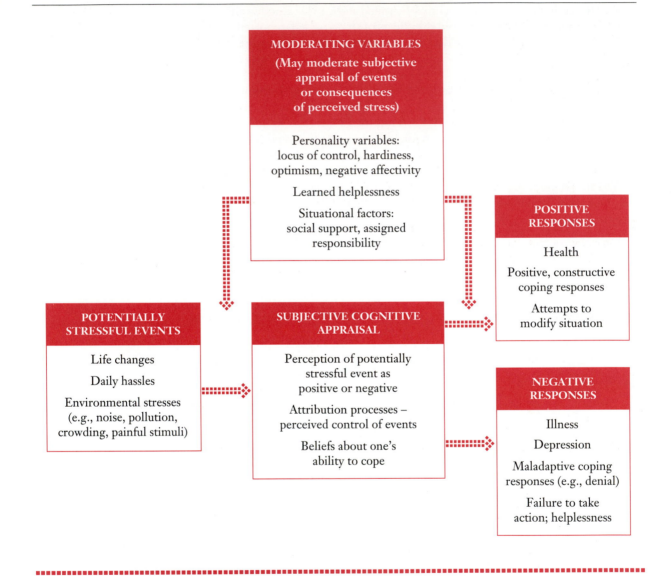

feelings, and pessimistic people do. Negative emotionality may correlate with a number of different kinds of illness (Friedman & Booth-Kewley, 1987b).

Clearly there are many psychological variables that may influence how people perceive and react to potentially stressful events (see Figure 16.5).

The Type A Personality and Coronary Heart Disease

Coronary heart disease is the leading cause of death in the United States, accounting for over one-third of all deaths (U.S. Department of Health and Human Services, 1984). Considerable research has focused on identifying medical risk factors that increase the likelihood of heart disease (such as high cholesterol levels, high blood pressure, a high-fat diet, smoking, and lack of exercise), but these factors are only partially successful in predicting who does and who does not develop heart disease (Keys, Aravnis, Blackburn, Van Buchem, Buzina, Djordjevic, Fidanza, Kavonen, Menotti, Pudov, & Taylor, 1972).

In the 1950s researchers began to study psychological factors that may contribute to heart disease. Cardiologists Meyer Friedman and Ray Rosenman (1959) described the Type A behavior pattern, which they argued was conducive to heart disease. Type A behaviors are "characterized by intense ambition, competitive 'drive,' constant preoccupation with occupational 'deadlines' and a sense of time urgency" (p. 1295). People who show Type A behavior are impatient, are often hostile, and frequently try to engage in more than one activity at the same time (for example, eating and working, or driving and talking on the car phone). People who show the contrasting Type B behavior are characterized by lower degrees of urgency, impatience, and incessant goal seeking.

To assess people showing Type A and Type B behaviors (whom for simplicity we will label Type A's and Type B's), Friedman, Rosen-

man, and their colleagues (1968) developed the Structured Interview—a technique in which a trained interviewer asks subjects questions designed to elicit Type A responses and then codes these responses for both verbal and non-verbal content. The 26 questions of the Structured Interview address three main themes: the subject's drive and ambition ("Would you describe yourself as a hard-driving, ambitious type of person in accomplishing the things you want, or would you describe yourself as a relatively relaxed and easy-going person?"); the subject's competitive, aggressive, and hostile feelings ("What irritates you most about your work, or the people with whom you work?"); and the subject's sense of urgency ("Do you have the feeling that time is passing too rapidly for you to accomplish all the things you think you should get done in one day?").

In the Structured Interview, interviewers intentionally interrupt or challenge subjects during their responses to designated questions in order to elicit Type A behaviors. According to Friedman and Rosenman, categorizing people as Type A or Type B depends as much on *how* they answer (for example, are their answers loud and abrupt, and do they interrupt the interviewer?) as on the content of their responses. Indeed, a number of studies suggest that subjects' voice quality alone during the interviews is sufficient to classify subjects as Type A or Type B (Glass, Ross, Isecke, & Rosenman, 1982; Schucker & Jacobs, 1977).

Early research using the Structured Interview suggested that

Type A subjects suffered about twice the rate of fatal heart attacks as Type B subjects (Brand, Rosenman, Sholtz, & Friedman, 1976; Rosenman, Brand, Sholtz, & Friedman, 1976), an effect that was independent of other risk factors such as smoking, diet, and blood pressure. These findings have been replicated in other studies (Haynes, Feinleib, & Eaker, 1983).

Because the Structured Interview is a laborious way to classify subjects, questionnaire measures of Type A and Type B behavior have also been developed. Perhaps the best known is the Jenkins Activity Survey, a self-report scale with the same kind of content as the Structured Interview, including items assessing hard-driving competitiveness, speed, and impatience. Many studies show a relation between scores on the Jenkins Activity Survey and heart disease (the average correlation coefficient is approximately .10), but in general the Structured Interview is a better predictor of heart disease (average correlation coefficient of .20; Friedman & Booth-Kewley, 1987a). The Structured Interview and the Jenkins Activity Survey seem to measure somewhat different constructs (Matthews, Krantz, Dembroski, & MacDougall, 1982).

Why does Type A behavior elevate one's risk for heart disease? One possibility is that Type A's possess considerable self-induced stress and respond readily to stressful settings with physiological arousal (Krantz, Arabian, Davia, & Parker, 1982; Matthews, 1982). Type A behavior in adults may be determined in part by temperamental factors that are present

The Type A Personality and Coronary Heart Disease (Continued)

early in life (MacEvoy, Lambert, Karlberg, Karlberg, Klackenberg-Larsson, & Klackenberg, 1988).

Interestingly, Type A behavior is linked not only to coronary heart disease but also to headaches, gastrointestinal disorders, respiratory disease, and sleep disorders (Woods, Morgan, Day, Jefferson, & Harris, 1984; Woods & Burns, 1984). These findings are consistent with the view that Type A behavior may be associated in general with arousal and stress.

Although Type A behavior has received the greatest share of research attention, other personality traits are also related to heart disease (Friedman & Booth-Kewley, 1987b). Anxiety, depression, anger and hostility, and even extrover-

sion show a relation with heart disease that is comparable in magnitude to the relation between Type A behavior and heart disease. One thread that seems to tie all these traits together is their link to stress and autonomic arousal. Rhodewalt and Smith (in press) suggest that hostility is the component of Type A behavior that is most linked to heart disease.

Recent reviews indicate that although Type A people are at greater risk for experiencing a first heart attack, they are not necessarily at greater risk for experiencing the recurrence of heart attacks (Matthews, 1988; Ragland & Brand, 1988). Perhaps the hostile, competitive, and urgent emotional style of the Type A person primes

the conditions that trigger a heart attack, but after surviving such an attack Type A's may ambitiously take on the challenge of "reforming" themselves and moderating their Type A behaviors.

Friedman and Ulmer (1984) reported encouraging preliminary findings suggesting that it is possible to teach Type A's who have experienced heart attacks various techniques to modify their urgent, competitive, and emotionally arousing behaviors and thereby reduce their future risk of heart attack. These findings have been replicated in other studies (Gill, Price, Friedman, Thoresen, Powell, Ulmer, Brown, & Drews, 1985). Future research will undoubtedly pursue this possibility.

Using Social Psychology to Make People Healthier

(CANDIDE *sings*)
They bathe each dawn in a golden lake.
Emeralds hang upon a vine.
All is there for all to take,
Food and God and books and wine.

They have no words for fear and greed,
For lies and war, revenge and rage.
They live and dance and think and read.
They live in peace, and die of age.

—— lyrics from "Eldorado," by Lillian Hellman,
Candide (1957), p. 100

All societies have a vision of utopia, a place where people live in health and harmony. Traveling by boat across South America, Candide is swept by a swift river current through an underground chasm and finally deposited in Eldorado, the fabled land of gold. There he experiences, for a time, happiness in a nation of peace and plenty, a land where people live more than a hundred years and then "die of age," not of illness.

Of course, Eldorado, like all utopian visions, is a fantasy. But such visions serve a purpose, for they encourage us to examine the imperfections of this world and to work to remedy them. In the previous section we documented some links between social settings and personality and people's health. Let's turn now to social psychological research that actively evaluates and designs techniques intended to improve health. Such research is part of social psychology's contribution to the quest for a better world.

▪▪▪▪▪▪▪▪▪▪▪▪▪▪▪▪▪▪▪▪▪▪▪▪▪▪

Personal Control and Health

Both Rotter's concept of locus of control and Kobasa's construct of hardiness view personal control as a personality characteristic. But control is also a function of situations.

Many studies suggest that controllable situations are less stressful than uncontrollable ones. For example, Suls and Mullen (1981) asked subjects to check whether they perceived the stressful events listed in Holmes and Rahe's Schedule of Recent Life Experiences to be controllable or uncontrollable. They found that life changes perceived to be uncontrollable were related to illness, whereas those perceived to be controllable were not. Stern, McCants, and Pettine (1982) report similar results.

Experiments have shown that noxious stimuli, such as loud noises or electric shocks, are less stressful and easier to tolerate when subjects feel they can control them — for example, by pressing a button to stop them (Glass & Singer, 1972; Kanfer & Seider, 1973; Sherrod, Hage, Halpern, & Moore, 1977). Furthermore, subjects can work better in the presence of unpleasant stimuli when they think they can control their occurrence (Glass & Singer, 1972). Interestingly, in such experiments subjects often do not press the button to terminate the stressful stimulus (usually because the experimenter asks them to try to tolerate the stimulus as much as they can), but the mere knowledge that they can "turn off" unpleasant noise or shocks seems to reduce anxiety and upset.

Research on the stressful effects of crowding also suggests the importance of perceived control. Although the relation between physical crowding and stress is complex (Epstein, 1982), many studies show that crowding is less stressful when people can exercise some control over it (Baron & Rodin, 1978; Rodin & Baum, 1978; Sherrod, 1974). For example, Baum and Valins (1977) found that college students randomly assigned to live in dorm rooms on long, crowded corridors and who had to share facilities with many other students tended to be more socially detached, apathetic, and unassertive than students assigned to live in less crowded suites on shorter corridors. Being with other people can be aversive if you have no control over when and where you interact with them.

People who feel they have no control over important events in their lives may show a maladaptive style of behavior termed *learned helplessness* (Seligman, 1975; Abramson, Garbner, & Seligman, 1980). Seligman (1975) first observed learned helplessness in dogs he trained to avoid painful shocks by jumping over a hurdle from one side of a box to the other. In these experiments, an audible tone sounded, and several seconds later, a shock was delivered to the dog's feet through an electric grid on the floor of the box. Dogs readily learned to jump the hurdle to escape such shocks. Indeed, after a number of learning trials dogs would jump as soon as they heard the signaling tone and thereby entirely avoid receiving shocks.

Some of the dogs in Seligman's experiment, however, had previously been exposed to unavoidable shocks. They had been restrained in a harness, and every time they heard the tone, they received a shock from which they could not escape. Later, when they were unrestrained, these dogs did not learn to jump the hurdle to escape

Does Charlie Brown suffer from learned helplessness?

from shocks. Instead, they crouched in their boxes, whining and yelping, without trying to escape. In essence, the dogs had learned to be helpless.

Learned helplessness applies to people as well as to dogs. In one experiment, Hiroto and Seligman (1975) found that students exposed to uncontrollable noise later failed to discover that they could control the noise by moving a switch in their experimental apparatus. In contrast, subjects who had been exposed earlier either to no noise or to controllable noise quickly discovered how to control the noise.

Human beings, unlike dogs, reinforce their helplessness with maladaptive cognitions. Abramson, Garbner, and Seligman (1980) described learned helplessness in humans in attributional terms. When people are exposed to uncontrollable aversive events, they develop maladaptive styles of attribution that lead them to generalize their helplessness and attribute it to internal traits. Helpless people tend to consider their inability to control unpleasant circumstances to be due to stable internal factors ("I'm an incapable, incompetent person"). After repeatedly experiencing their inability to control events, helpless people may develop global negative attributions. (This account is reminiscent of the attributional account of depression presented in Chapter 4. Indeed, learned helplessness provides one theoretical model for the development of depression.)

Helplessness in the Elderly

People living in "total institutions" — mental hospitals, prisons, the military — often experience greatly reduced personal control. Although we don't usually think of hospitals as "total institutions," they too deprive their charges of control (Taylor, 1979; Schulz & Aderman, 1973). When an individual checks into a hospital, his or her status is often reduced from that of a competent, mature adult to that of a childlike, passive "thing" who strips upon command, lies in bed, and allows appropriate authorities to poke, prod, and puncture as they see fit. The patient eats whatever the hospital deigns to serve, according to the hospital's schedule. The patient must sleep and awaken according to an institutional regime and is sometimes roused from a deep sleep in order to be subjected to some arbitrary medical procedure. In other words, hospitals intentionally and unintentionally encourage helplessness by taking control away from the patient.

The confiscation of control is perhaps nowhere more apparent than in "homes" for the elderly. Nursing homes, by virtue of their medical mission, treat their clients with the authoritarian directiveness of medical settings in general. Because of stereotypes about the elderly, they often also assume that their clients are incapable of caring for themselves and making reasonable decisions. Thus patients in nursing homes face a kind of double jeopardy. By assuming complete control, nursing homes frequently encourage the elderly to become helpless, hopeless, and mindless; the elderly person need not actively think, make decisions, or choose rewarding activities. Cognitive and emotional involvement in life atrophies (Langer, 1981).

Ellen Langer and Judith Rodin (1976) demonstrated how small degrees of control can dramatically influence the well-being of the institutionalized elderly. Residents on two separate floors of a nursing home in Connecticut were selected to be subjects in an experiment on the effects of personal control and responsibility on health. The residents of each floor were roughly equivalent in physical health and socioeconomic status before the experiment began. The experimental manipulation was relatively simple: The residents of one floor were assigned responsibility for everyday aspects of their lives, whereas the residents of the other floor were informed that the staff would take care of their needs.

Specifically, here is what the nursing-home administrator told residents who were assigned responsibility:

> I brought you together today to give you some information about Arden House [the nursing home]. I was surprised to learn that many of you don't know about the things that are available to you and more important, that many of you don't realize the influence you have over your own lives here. Take a minute to think of the decisions you can and should be making. For example, you have the responsibility of caring for yourselves, of deciding whether or not you want to make this a home you can be proud of and happy in. You should be deciding how you want your room to be arranged — whether you want it to be as it is or whether you want the staff to help you rearrange the furniture. You should be deciding how you want to spend your time, for example, whether you want to be visiting your friends who live on this floor . . . whether you want to visit in your room or your friend's room, in the lounge, the dining room, etc., or whether you want to be watching television, listening to the radio, writing, reading, or planning social events. In other words, it's your life and you can make of it whatever you want.
>
> This brings me to another point. If you are unsatisfied with anything here, you have the influence to change it. It's your responsibility to make your complaints known, to tell us what you would like to change, to tell us what you would like. . . . (pp. 193–194)

After the talk, each resident was given a present from the nursing home — a potted plant — and was informed that the plant was "yours to keep and take care of as you'd like."

In contrast, here is what residents on the other floor were told by the administrator:

> I brought you together today to give you some information about Arden House. I was surprised to learn that many of you don't know about the things that are available to you; that many of you don't realize all you're allowed to do here. Take a minute to think of all the options that we've provided you with in order for your life to be fuller and more interesting. For example, you're permitted to visit people on the other floors and to use the lounge on this floor for visiting as well as the dining room or your own rooms. We want your rooms to be as nice as they can be, and we've tried to make them that way for you. We want you to be happy here. We feel that it's our responsibility to make this a home you can be proud of and happy in, and we want to do all we can to help you.

Medical Practice as a Social Psychological Process

Scarcely was Candide in his hotel, when he came down with a mild illness caused by exhaustion. . . . Martin said: — I remember that I too was ill on my first trip to Paris; I was very poor; and as I had neither friends, pious ladies, nor doctors, I got well.

However, as a result of medicines and bleedings, Candide's illness became serious.

—— Candide *(1966), p. 48*

Medical "science" in Voltaire's day often did more harm than good. Medical science in the twentieth century, on the other hand, has made truly revolutionary advances and can successfully treat many diseases. The modern physician uses a complex array of technologies, drugs, and procedures. As effective treatments have become available for many illnesses, doctors have begun to regard themselves more as applied scientists and less as psychological resources to patients.

However, advances in medical science and technology should not blind us to the fact that the doctor, the patient, and the doctor-patient relationship are subject to psychological influences. Social psychological theory and research can help us to understand both the in-terpersonal dynamics of patient-physician interactions and the thought processes of the participants (Mentzer & Snyder, 1982). Such factors can have a substantial impact on medical care and its outcomes.

The first step a patient takes in seeking medical care is to visit the doctor. As we know from Chapter 13, some people (women, feminine people, people from certain cultural backgrounds) are more willing to seek and accept help than others, and this extends to seeking medical care (Kirscht, 1983).

After taking this first step the patient must provide information to the physician. Diagnostic interviews sometimes require that patients reveal personal and potentially embarrassing information, for example, information about sexual behaviors and bowel functions. The social psychology of self-disclosure is relevant here (Chaiken, Derlega, & Miller, 1976; Cozby, 1973; see Chapter 11). For example, people generally disclose intimate information about themselves more in relationships they perceive to be reciprocal, and this principle applies to doctor-patient relationships as well (Davis, 1968). A cold, impersonal, "nongiving" physician is not likely to elicit as accurate and complete information from patients as would a warm, personal, and more interactive physician.

Communication between patient and doctor may be further impeded by the fact that each uses a different vocabulary to describe the same events. Doctors often confuse their patients by using technical jargon (Svarstad, 1976). The following patient describes her misunderstanding quite vividly:

When my first child was born, the doctor kept coming in every day and asking, "Have you voided?" So I'd say, "No." So in comes the nurse with some paraphernalia that was scary. So I said, "What the devil are you going to do?" And she said, "I'm going to catheterize you, you haven't voided." Well, of course, I knew what catheterization was. I said, "You are going to play hell. I've peed every day since I've been here." . . . Why didn't he just ask me if I'd peed? I'd have told him. (from Samora, Saunders, & Larson, 1961)

Sometimes patients may not be able to verbalize their symptoms and bodily sensations very accurately (Pennebaker, 1984). As sug-

This brings me to another point. If you have any complaints or suggestions about anything, let [nurse's name] know what they are. Let us know how we can best help you. (p. 194)

These patients were also given plants, but they were told that "the nurses will water them and care for them for you."

Both speeches provided much the same information and expressed the staff's desire to make residents happy and comfortable. However, in many ways, the speech delivered to the subjects assigned responsibility informed them that they needed to gested by Schachter and Singer's arousal-labeling theory of emotion (see Chapter 4), people often seek to label bodily sensations based on social information. Sometimes biased or defensive labeling ("I have indigestion," rather than "I'm suffering from a heart attack") can lead to dangerous delays in seeking medical attention (Janis & Rodin, 1979; Cacioppo, Andersen, Turnquist, & Petty, 1986). People strive to attribute the causes of their illnesses to themselves or to external factors (Taylor, Lichtman, & Wood, 1984; see Chapter 4). Such attributions can sometimes be self-defeating and blaming ("I am responsible for my cancer") and can help to foster helplessness and depression rather than positive coping behaviors.

Attributions may affect medical care in other ways. As we know from Chapter 4, people tend to attribute their own behavior more to situational causes and others' behavior more to dispositional causes (Jones & Nisbett, 1972). This pervasive bias can set the stage for serious misunderstandings between medical personnel and patients. For example, a patient in a hospital may attribute his complaints to the environment ("Nobody ever tells me what's going on, and the nurses don't respond when I page them"), whereas the staff may explain the patient's behavior dispositionally ("He's neurotic and a trouble maker"). Conversely, the doctor may explain his own abrupt behavior with a patient externally ("I'm harried and late for my next call"), whereas the patient may explain the doctor's behavior dispositionally ("He's cold and unconcerned").

We know from Chapters 3 and 5 that people frequently suffer from a number of biases in perceiving others. Doctors and patients are no exception. For example, physicians may suffer from primacy effects and schematic processing of information (see Chapters 3 and 5) so that a preliminary diagnosis systematically distorts their perception of later information (Schiffman, Cohen, Nowik, & Selinger, 1978). People's many shortcomings in processing information can affect medical diagnoses. For example, the physician may ask questions unintentionally designed to verify his or her diagnosis (Mentzer & Snyder, 1982; see Chapter 5), may apply inappropriate decision rules in combining information in arriving at a diagnosis (Chapter 5), and may not adequately take into account baserate information in making diagnoses (Chapters 4 and 5).

Doctors often are unsuccessful in inducing patients to comply with their recommendations — to take drugs regularly, change dietary habits, and exercise, for example (DiNicola & DiMatteo, 1982). The social psychology of compliance and obedience is relevant here (see Chapter 14). Patients with high levels of social support seem more likely to comply with medical advice (Doherty, Schrott, Metcalf, & Iasiello-Vailas, 1983; Sherwood, 1983), which suggests that social influences exert an important effect on compliance and noncompliance with medical recommendations. It also suggests that doctors should give information to friends and families of patients as well as to the patients themselves.

---

make decisions and actively participate in nursing-home events, whereas the speech delivered to the subjects who were not assigned responsibility suggested that they were passive and that the staff would make decisions.

The results of these instructions were dramatic. During the three weeks that followed the speeches, self-report questionnaires indicated that residents who had been assigned personal responsibility were significantly happier and more active than residents not assigned responsibility. Nurses' ratings corroborated these self-reports: Nurses reported that residents who had been assigned responsibility showed greater improvement in their rated well-being and activity than those not assigned responsibility. Furthermore, the residents assigned responsibility spent more time visiting each other and talking to staff members; they also participated more in scheduled activities, such as attending movies.

The most dramatic results of the assignment of responsibility were revealed in a follow-up study that assessed residents 18 months later (Rodin & Langer, 1977). Seven of the 47 residents (15 percent) assigned responsibility had died, whereas 13 of 44 residents (30 percent) not assigned responsibility had died, a statistically significant difference. (The death rate for the entire nursing home during the same period was 25 percent.) Rodin and Langer (1977) noted that assigning personal responsibility to residents may have had a particularly large effect in this nursing home because the staff there was highly responsive to residents' concerns and requests. In other words, residents were reinforced for assuming responsibility for themselves. In nursing homes with less enlightened staffs, however, patients induced to exert control over their lives might learn helplessness and hopelessness instead. A number of nursing homes have responded to research like Langer and Rodin's by assigning more responsibilities to residents (Hall, 1984).

Rodin and Langer's study poses an interesting ethical question: Once research has demonstrated that manipulating perceived control in nursing homes can affect residents' death rates, is it then ethically acceptable to conduct replications to further investigate variables that influence perceived control and health in nursing homes? How would you feel about conducting a study in which some of your subjects might be more likely to die than others because of your experimental manipulations? Few would deny that such research is socially important, but does this importance justify a procedure that literally can mean life or death for some subjects? (See Chapter 2 for a broader discussion of ethical issues in social psychological research.)

The ethical issues in such research are highlighted by another study conducted at about the same time as Langer and Rodin's. Schulz (1976) arranged for some Duke University students to individually visit over a period of two months 42 elderly people living in a local, church-affiliated retirement home. Students visited according to one of three schedules: Some students visited only when the elderly person wanted a visit, and the duration of the visit was determined by the elderly person; some students visited the elderly person at times specified by the student; and some students would randomly "drop in" to visit the elderly person. Each subject received the same total number of visits. Residents in these three conditions were compared with a group of residents who received no visits at all from students.

Clearly, the elderly residents had the most control over the visits in the first experimental condition and the least control in the third condition. The elderly subjects were interviewed after the last visits and were rated on their degree of general activity and their physical health. In general, residents were happier and more active when they could control and predict the visits by students, and were less so when students just "dropped in" (see Figure 16.6).

Unfortunately, a follow-up study showed that the residents who had originally most benefited from the students' visits (those in the controllable and predictable visit conditions) experienced the steepest decline in their well-being after the students' visits ceased and tended to experience higher mortality rates (Schulz & Hanusa, 1978; again, see Figure 16.6). Again these results can be interpreted in terms of perceived control. Unlike subjects in Rodin and Langer's study, who could continue to exercise responsibility and control over their environment throughout the follow-up period, subjects in Schulz's study lost control when the students' visits

FIGURE 16.6   The effect of predictable and unpredictable student visits
on the health status of retirement-home residents.

Does the perceived control of pleasant events enhance physical health?

In this study Duke University students visited residents of a
retirement home. Some students visited only if and when
residents wanted them to visit (controllable visits). Some
students arranged their visits ahead of time (predictable visits).
Some students dropped in unannounced (random "drop in").
The health of residents receiving visits was compared with that
of a group of residents receiving no visits.

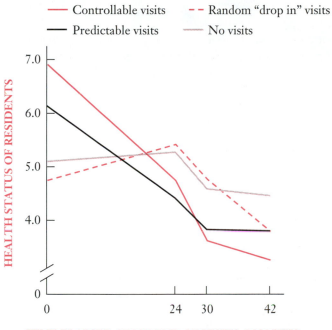

TIME ELAPSED SINCE END OF VISITS (MONTHS)

Student visits, particularly those that were controllable and
predictable, improved the health status of these elderly people.
Unfortunately, after students stopped their visits, those
residents who originally showed the most improvement
subsequently showed the steepest decline in health status.

SOURCE: Adapted from Schulz and Hanusa (1978). Used with permission of
Richard Schulz.

*Studies like this pose serious ethical questions. Should social psychologists conduct
experiments that may affect the health and even mortality of subjects?*

■■■■■■■■■■■■■■■■■■■■■■■■■
Predictable and controllable social interactions foster health among the elderly.

ceased. Perhaps these elderly people felt heightened sadness and loneliness when they realized that the pleasant (and for some, predictable and controllable) companionship of their student visitors was over.

Studies like these show that relatively minor changes in the routines of homes for the elderly can have a large impact on the quality of residents' lives. In both noninstitutionalized and institutionalized settings, the elderly can benefit from possessing more control in their lives. Kastenbaum (1982) noted that many elderly people voluntarily enter institutions rather than stay at home because they fear being alone if an emergency occurs. One procedure that allows the elderly to remain at home, maintain personal control, and avoid the fear of being alone in an emergency is to provide them with emergency alarms that can be used to signal for help 24 hours a day. Here again, a relatively simple intervention can have dramatic positive effects and can be cost-effective when compared with institutionalization.

■■■■■■■■■■■■■■■■■■■■■■■■■
The Age of Prevention

The very success of modern medicine has paradoxically led to new medical problems. The conquest of many infectious diseases, improved hygiene, and readily available medical care have led to a steady increase throughout this century in the lifespan of the average American. However, as a result more and more people live to an advanced age and ultimately suffer from such degenerative diseases as cancer, heart disease, and stroke. Recent technological advances in medicine have saved many lives, but they have also dramatically increased the cost of health care and made medical procedures seem frightening and alienating.

The successes of modern medicine have guaranteed that psychology will play a large role in health care in the future. The Center for Disease Control (1980) has estimated that about half of all deaths in the United States can be attributed to "chosen" behaviors — smoking, diet, alcohol and drug abuse, and stressful activities.

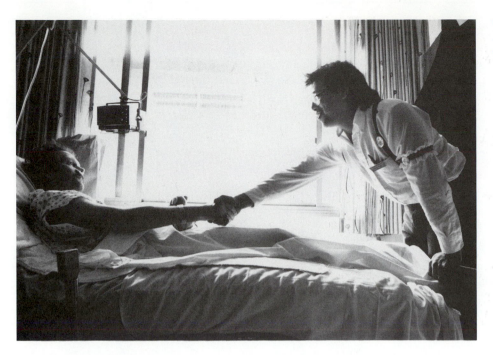

Doll and Peto (1981) noted that the two leading causes of fatal cancers are tobacco use (30 percent) and dietary habits (35 percent). In other words, many serious illnesses and deaths could be avoided if people would simply change their behavior.

Unfortunately, "simply" isn't so simple. People smoke, eat fatty foods, and drink alcoholic beverages because such activities are pleasurable. To practice preventive medicine, individuals must forgo short-term pleasures in the pursuit of long-term health. Inducing people to engage in preventive behaviors is a complex matter that involves research on beliefs and attitudes (Chapter 7), persuasion (Chapter 8), and social influences on behavior (Chapter 14). In other words, preventive medicine is very much in the domain of social psychology.

In the 1980s the world faced a dramatic new health challenge—AIDS (acquired immune deficiency syndrome), a viral disease transmitted primarily via sexual contact and intravenous drug use. In a century marked by the conquest of many infectious diseases, AIDS serves as a reminder that modern medicine is not omnipotent and that health is a function of behavior as well as of medical technology. The battle against AIDS will depend on psychological as well as medical research (Morin, 1988), and social psychologists will contribute their particular expertise about beliefs and attitudes, persuasion, attraction, and social influences on behavior.

Cultivating Our Garden

. . . and Pangloss sometimes used to say to Candide:—All events are linked together in the best of all possible worlds. . . .
— That is very well put, said Candide, but we must cultivate our garden.
—— *Candide* (1966), p. 77

FIGURE 16.7   Levels of explanation, health, and illness.

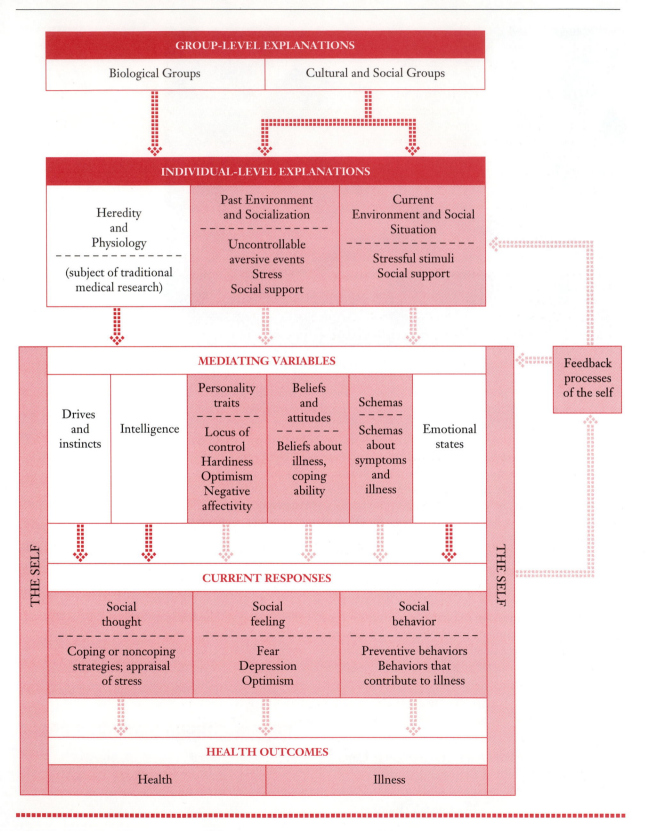

At the end of *Candide*, all the main characters come to a simple but profound conclusion: Happiness is not to be found in vain illusions or in aimlessly roaming the four corners of the earth; rather, happiness lies in plain work — in tilling our own garden.

This final chapter has given you a brief account of social psychological research on health. Its primary goal has been to illustrate various ways of applying social psychology. We discussed both research that tries to answer real-life questions (Does social support influence health?) and research that studies applied interventions and their effectiveness (Does giving control to the elderly in nursing homes improve their health and well-being?). Figure 16.7 summarizes the many psychological factors that may influence health and illness.

You may have noticed a recurring theme in this chapter — that of personal control. People are happier and healthier when they believe that they are in control of their lives. Perhaps this principle applies to social psychologists as well. Applied social psychology represents an attempt to control our social environment in constructive ways. It is an optimistic endeavor because it assumes that by applying the results of scientific research we can change our world for the better.

Applied social psychologists tend to be a hardy lot: They firmly believe they can make a difference in the world; they are committed to their field; and they experience a continual sense of challenge in pursuing practical applications of social psychological theory and research. They cultivate their garden by applying social psychology.

Summary

1. Applied social psychology attempts to answer social questions, evaluate social programs, and design social interventions.

2. There is a small but consistent relationship between assessed stress and illness. Research studies measure stress by having people complete self-report questionnaires that assess major life changes and everyday hassles.

3. Social support is the comfort, assistance, and/or information one receives from others. Social support may be tangible, informational, or emotional.

4. People integrated into social networks show significantly lower mortality rates than people who are socially isolated.

5. Informational and emotional support from others sometimes serves to buffer individuals against the negative effects of stress on health.

6. Rotter's Locus of Control Scale measures individuals' tendency to believe they have control over events in their lives versus the tendency to believe they are the victims of luck or external circumstances. The Health Locus of Control Scale assesses the degree to which people feel in control of their own health. Locus of control measures are related to health behaviors in complex ways.

7. Kobasa hypothesized that hardy individuals — those who possess a sense of personal control, commitment, and challenge in life — negotiate stress more successfully than do nonhardy individuals. A number of studies suggest that stress leads to less illness in hardy individuals than in nonhardy individuals.

8. Optimistic individuals possess a general expectancy that successes and positive events will occur in their lives. Such people report less physical illness and negotiate stress more adaptively than pessimistic individuals. Optimism and pessimism may be related to a broader syndrome of negative emotionality.

9. Type A behavior, characterized by intense ambition, competitiveness, hurry, and hostility, is related to coronary heart disease. The Type A behavior pattern is best assessed by the Structured Interview.

10. In general, people perceive uncontrollable life changes to be more stressful than controllable changes. Furthermore, people find noxious stimuli less stressful and are able to work more effectively in the presence of noxious stimuli when they believe they can exert control over these stimuli.

11. When animals and people are repeatedly exposed to uncontrollable aversive events, they often show learned helplessness — a behavioral syndrome in which they do not even attempt to escape from aversive stimuli or exert control over their environment. Learned helplessness in humans is reinforced by maladaptive attributions in which helpless individuals tend to explain aversive events in terms of their own stable internal characteristics.

12. Institutions such as hospitals and nursing homes take personal control away from their clients and frequently foster a sense of helplessness. Experiments show that giving the institutionalized elderly responsibility for and control of everyday aspects of their lives enhances their well-being and health.

13. Social psychological processes affect doctor-patient interactions. Social psychological theory and research can help us to understand and improve diagnostic interviews, doctor-patient communication, and patients' adherence to medical advice.

14. The successes of modern medicine guarantee that social psychology will play an important role in future medical practice and research. The successful practice of preventive medicine requires research on beliefs and attitudes, persuasion, social cognition, and social influence.

15. Applied social psychology is an optimistic endeavor because it assumes that social psychological research can contribute to a better world.

Glossary

Applied social psychology: Social psychological theory and research that attempts to answer social questions, evaluate social programs, or design social interventions

Evaluation research: Research that measures the effectiveness of a social program or applied intervention

Hardiness: Kobasa's personality construct that comprises three components — a sense of control, commitment, and challenge in life; Kobasa hypothesized that hardiness buffers stressed individuals against illness

Health locus of control: The degree to which individuals feel in control of their health

Learned helplessness: A behavioral syndrome, first described by Seligman, characterized by a failure to avoid aversive stimuli or to try to modify one's environment; learned helplessness results from repeatedly experiencing uncontrollable aversive events; in humans it is bolstered by maladaptive attributions whereby the helpless individual explains negative events in terms of his or her stable internal traits

Locus of control: Rotter's construct assessing the degree to which individuals believe they have control over events in their lives versus the degree to which they believe they are victims of luck or external circumstances

Optimism: The degree to which individuals have a general expectation that successes and positive events will occur; optimism is related to reports of less illness and to more adaptive coping with stress

Personal control: Individuals' perception that they are able to control aspects of their environment

Preventive medicine: Medical practices designed to modify individuals' behavior to prevent the development of illness rather than to treat illness once it occurs

Social support: The comfort, assistance, and/or information one receives from others; such support may be tangible, informational, or emotional

Stress: External stimuli and the appraisal of external stimuli that lead to chronic arousal of the autonomic nervous system; major life changes and daily hassles are two common sources of stress

Type A behavior pattern: A style of behavior characterized by extreme ambition, competitiveness, hurry, and hostility; Type A behavior is associated with coronary heart disease

Abelson, R. P. (1972). Are attitudes necessary? In B. T. King & E. McGinnies (Eds.), *Attitudes, conflicts, and social change.* New York: Academic Press.

Abelson, R. P. & Levi, A. (1985). Decision making and decision theory. In G. Lindzey & E. Aronson (Eds.), *Handbook of social psychology* (Vol. 1, 3rd ed.). New York: Random House.

Abramson, L. Y., Garbner, J., & Seligman, M. E. P. (1980). Learned helplessness in humans: An attributional analysis. In J. Garbner & M. E. P. Seligman (Eds.), *Human helplessness: Theory and applications.* New York: Academic Press.

Abramson, L. Y., Seligman, M. E. P., & Teasdale, J. D. (1978). Learned helplessness in humans: Critique and reformulation. *Journal of Abnormal Psychology, 87,* 49–74.

Ackerman, N. W. & Jahoda, M. (1950). *Anti-semitism and emotional disorder.* New York: Harper.

Adair, J. G., Dushenko, T. W., & Lindsay, R. C. L. (1985). Ethical regulations and their impact on research practice. *American Psychologist, 40,* 59–72.

Adams, G. R. & Shea, J. A. (1981). Talking and loving: A cross-lagged panel investigation. *Basic and Applied Social Psychology, 2,* 81–88.

Adams, J. S. (1963). Toward an understanding of inequity. *Journal of Abnormal and Social Psychology, 67,* 422–436.

Adams, J. S. (1965). Inequity in social exchange. In L. Berkowitz (Ed.), *Advances in experimental social psychology* (Vol. 2). New York: Academic Press.

Ader, R. (1975). Competitive and noncompetitive rearing and shock-elicited aggression in the rat. *Animal Learning and Behavior, 3,* 337–339.

Adorno, T. W., Frenkel-Brunswick, E., Levinson, D. J., & Sanford, R. N. (1950). *The authoritarian personality.* New York: Harper.

Ajzen, I. (1987). Attitudes, traits, and actions: Dispositional prediction of behavior in personality and social psychology. In L. Berkowitz (Ed.), *Advances in experimental social psychology* (Vol. 20). San Diego: Academic Press.

Ajzen, I. & Fishbein, M. (1980). *Understanding attitudes and predicting social behavior.* Englewood Cliffs, NJ: Prentice-Hall.

Ajzen, I. & Madden, T. (1986). Prediction of goal-directed behavior: Attitudes, intentions, and perceived behavioral control. *Journal of Experimental Social Psychology, 22,* 453–474.

Albright, L., Kenny, D. A., & Malloy, T. E. (1988). Consensus in personality judgments at zero acquaintance. *Journal of Personality and Social Psychology, 55,* 387–395.

Allen, H. (1968). Unpublished doctoral dissertation, New York University.

Allen, V. L. (1975). Social support for nonconformity. In L. Berkowitz (Ed.), *Advances in experimental social psychology* (Vol. 8). New York: Academic Press.

Allen, V. L. & Levine, J. M. (1968). Social support, dissent, and conformity. *Sociometry, 31,* 138–149.

Allen, V. L. & Levine, J. M. (1969). Consensus and conformity. *Journal of Experimental Psychology, 5,* 389–399.

Alloy, L. B. & Abramson, L. Y. (1979). Judgment of contingency in depressed and nondepressed students: Sadder but wiser? *Journal of Experimental Psychology, General, 108,* 441–485.

Allport, F. H. (1920). The influence of the group upon association and thought. *Journal of Experimental Psychology, 3,* 159–182.

Allport, G. W. (1935). Attitudes. In C. M. Murchison (Ed.), *Handbook of social psychology.* Worcester, MA: Clark University Press.

Allport, G. W. (1937). *Personality: A psychological interpretation.* New York: Holt, Rinehart & Winston.

Allport, G. W. (1950). *The individual and his religion: A psychological interpretation.* New York: Macmillan.

Allport, G. W. (1954). *The nature of prejudice.* Cambridge, MA: Addison-Wesley.

Allport, G. W. (1961). *Pattern and growth in personality.* New York: Holt, Rinehart & Winston.

Allport, G. W. (1985). The historical background of social psychology. In G. Lindzey & E. Aronson (Eds.), *Handbook of social psychology* (Vol. 1). New York: Random House.

Allport, G. W. & Odbert, H. S. (1936). Trait-names: A psycho-lexical study. *Psychological Monographs: General and Applied, 47* (1, Whole No. 211).

Allport, G. W. & Postman, L. (1965). *The psychology of rumor.* New York: Russell & Russell. (Originally published 1947.)

Allport, G. W. & Ross, J. M. (1967). Personal religious orientation and prejudice. *Journal of Personality and Social Psychology, 5,* 432–443.

References

Allred, K. D. & Smith, T. W. (1989). The hardy personality: Cognitive and physiological responses to evaluative threat. *Journal of Personality and Social Psychology, 56,* 257–266.

Altemeyer, B. (1981). *Right-wing authoritarianism.* Winnipeg: The University of Manitoba Press.

Altman, I. & Taylor, D. A. (1973). *Social penetration: The development of interpersonal relationships.* New York: Holt, Rinehart & Winston.

Altman, I., Vinsel, A., & Brown, B. A. (1981). Dialectic conceptions in social psychology: An application to social penetration and privacy regulation. In L. Berkowitz (Ed.), *Advances in experimental social psychology* (Vol. 14). New York: Academic Press.

American Psychiatric Association. (1987). *Diagnostic and statistical manual of mental disorders* (3rd ed., revised). Washington, DC: Author.

American Psychological Association Ad Hoc Committee on Ethical Standards. (1982). *Ethical principles in the conduct of research with human participants.* Washington, DC: American Psychological Association.

Amir, Y. (1969). Contact hypothesis in ethnic relations. *Psychological Bulletin, 71,* 319–342.

Amir, Y. (1976). The role of intergroup contact in change of prejudice and ethnic relations. In P. Katz (Ed.), *Towards the elimination of racism.* New York: Pergamon Press.

Anastase, A. (1976). *Psychological testing* (4th ed.). New York: Macmillan.

Anderson, C. A. (1983). Abstract and concrete data in the perseverance of social theories: When weak data lead to unshakable beliefs. *Journal of Experimental Social Psychology, 19,* 93–108.

Anderson, C. A. (1987). Temperature and aggression: Effects on quarterly, yearly, and city rates of violent and nonviolent crime. *Journal of Personality and Social Psychology, 52,* 1161–1173.

Anderson, C. A. & Anderson, D. C. (1984). Ambient temperature and violent crime: Tests of the linear and curvilinear hypotheses. *Journal of Personality and Social Psychology, 46,* 91–97.

Anderson, C. A., Lepper, M. R., & Ross, L. (1980). Perseverance of social theories: The role of explanation in the persistence of discredited information. *Journal of Personality and Social Psychology, 39,* 1037–1049.

Anderson, J. R. (1980). *Cognitive psychology and its implications.* San Francisco: Freeman.

Anderson, N. H. (1974). Cognitive algebra: Integration theory applied to social attribution. In L. Berkowitz (Ed.), *Advances in experimental social psychology* (Vol. 7). New York: Academic Press.

Anderson, N. H. & Hubert, S. (1963). Effect of concomitant verbal recall on order effects in personality impression formation. *Journal of Verbal Learning and Verbal Behavior, 2,* 379–391.

Andreoli, V. & Worchel, S. (1978). Effects of media, communicator, and position of message on attitude change. *Public Opinion Quarterly, 42,* 59–70.

Antill, J. T. (1983). Sex role complementarity versus similarity in married couples. *Journal of Personality and Social Psychology, 45,* 145–155.

Archer, J. & Lloyd, B. (1985). *Sex and gender.* Cambridge, England: Cambridge University Press.

Arkin, R. M. & Baumgardner, A. H. (1985). Self-handicapping. In J. H. Harvey & C. Weary (Eds.), *Attribution: Basic issues and applications.* New York: Academic Press.

Aronson, E. (1969). The theory of cognitive dissonance: A current perspective. In L. Berkowitz (Ed.), *Advances in experimental social psychology* (Vol. 4). New York: Academic Press.

Aronson, E. (1978). *The jigsaw classroom.* Beverly Hills, CA: Sage.

Aronson, E., Brewer, M., & Carlsmith, J. M. (1985). Experimentation in social psychology. In G. Lindzey & E. Aronson (Eds.), *Handbook of social psychology* (Vol. 1). New York: Random House.

Aronson, E. & Carlsmith, J. M. (1963). Effect of severity of threat on the devaluation of forbidden behavior. *Journal of Abnormal and Social Psychology, 66,* 584–588.

Aronson, E. & Carlsmith, J. M. (1968). Experimentation in social psychology. In G. Lindzey & E. Aronson (Eds.), *Handbook of social psychology* (Vol. 2) (2nd ed.). Reading, MA: Addison-Wesley.

Aronson, E. & Cope, B. (1968). My enemy's enemy is my friend. *Journal of Personality and Social Psychology, 8,* 8–12.

Aronson, E. & Mills, J. (1959). The effects of severity of initiation on liking for a group. *Journal of Abnormal and Social Psychology, 59,* 177–181.

Aronson, E., Turner, J. A., & Carlsmith, J. M. (1963). Communicator credibility and communication discrepancy as determinants of opinion change. *Journal of Abnormal and Social Psychology, 67,* 31–36.

Asch, S. E. (1946). Forming impressions of personality. *Journal of Abnormal and Social Psychology, 41,* 258–290.

Asch, S. E. (1951). Effects of group pressure upon the modification and distortion of judgments. In H. Guetzkow (Ed.), *Groups, leadership, and men.* Pittsburgh, Carnegie Press.

Asch, S. E. (1952). *Social Psychology.* New York: Prentice-Hall.

Asch, S. E. (1955, November). Opinions and social pressure. *Scientific American,* 31–35.

Asch, S. E. (1956). Studies of independence and conformity: I. A minority of one against a unanimous majority. *Psychological Monographs, 70(9)* (Whole No. 416).

Ashmore, R. D. & Del Boca, F. K. (1981). Conceptual approaches to stereotypes and stereotyping. In D. L. Hamilton (Ed.), *Cognitive processes in stereotyping and intergroup behavior.* Hillsdale, NJ: Erlbaum.

Attorney General's Commission on Pornography. (1986). Washington, DC: United States Department of Justice.

Austen, J. (1957). *Northanger Abbey.* Linden: The Zodiac Press. (Originally published 1818.)

Axelrod, R. (1984). *The evolution of cooperation.* New York: Basic Books.

Axelrod, R. & Hamilton, W. D. (1981). The evolution of cooperation. *Science, 211,* 1390–1396.

Azrin, N. H. (1967, May). Pain and aggression. *Psychology Today,* 27–33.

Azrin, N. H., Hutchinson, R. R., & Hake, D. F. (1966). Extinction-induced aggression. *Journal of the Experimental Analysis of Behavior, 9,* 191–204.

Azrin, N. H., Hutchinson, R. R., & McLaughlin, R. (1965). The opportunity for aggression as an operant reinforcer during aversive stimulation. *Journal of the Experimental Analysis of Behavior, 8,* 171–180.

Babad, E. Y., Inbar, J., & Rosenthal, R. (1982). Pygmaleon, Galatea, and the Golem: Investigations of biased and unbiased teachers. *Journal of Educational Psychology, 74,* 459–474.

Bagozzi, R. P. (1978). The construct validity of the affective, behavioral and cognitive components of attitude by analysis of covariance structure. *Multivariate Behavioral Research, 13,* 9–31.

Bales, R. F. (1950). *Interaction process analysis: A method for the study of small groups.* Reading, MA: Addison-Wesley.

Bales, R. F. (1958). Task roles and social roles in problem-solving groups. In E. E. Maccoby, T. M. Newcomb, & E. L. Hartley (Eds.), *Readings in social psychology.* New York: Rinehart & Winston.

Bales, R. F. (1970). *Personality and interpersonal behavior.* New York: Holt, Rinehart & Winston.

Bandura, A. (1965). Influence of model's reinforcement contingencies on the acquisition of imitative responses. *Journal of Personality and Social Psychology, 1,* 589–595.

Bandura, A. (1986). *Social foundations of thought and action: A social cognitive theory.* Englewood Cliffs, NJ: Prentice-Hall.

Bandura, A. (1973). *Aggression: A social learning analysis.* Englewood Cliffs, NJ: Prentice-Hall.

Bandura, A. (1977). *Social learning theory.* Englewood Cliffs, NJ: Prentice-Hall.

Bandura, A. & Huston, A. C. (1961). Identification as a process of incidental learning. *Journal of Abnormal and Social Psychology, 63,* 311–318.

Bandura, A., Ross, D., & Ross, S. A. (1961). Transmission of aggression through imitation of aggressive models. *Journal of Abnormal and Social Psychology, 63,* 575–582.

Bandura, A., Ross, D., & Ross, S. A. (1963a). A comparative test of the status envy, social power and secondary reinforcement theories of identificatory learning. *Journal of Abnormal and Social Psychology, 67,* 527–534.

Bandura, A., Ross, D., & Ross, S. A. (1963b). Vicarious reinforcement and imitative learning. *Journal of Abnormal and Social Psychology, 67,* 601–607.

Baran, S. J., Chase, L. J., & Courtright, J. A. (1979). Television drama as a facilitator of prosocial behavior: "The Waltons." *Journal of Broadcasting, 23(3),* 277–284.

Bar-Hillel, M. & Fischoff, B. (1981). When do base rates affect predictions? *Journal of Personality and Social Psychology, 41,* 671–680.

Barker, R. G., Dembo, T., & Lewin, K. (1941). Frustration and regression: An experiment with young children. *University of Iowa Studies in Child Welfare, 18(1).*

Baron, R. A. (1971). Reducing the influence of an aggressive model: The restraining effects of discrepant modeling cues. *Journal of Personality and Social Psychology, 20,* 240–245.

Baron, R. A. (1972). Reducing the influence of an aggressive model: The restraining effects of peer censure. *Journal of Personality and Social Psychology, 8,* 266–275.

Baron, R. A. (1976). The reduction of human aggression: A field study of the influence of incompatible reactions. *Journal of Applied Social Psychology, 6,* 260–274.

Baron, R. A. (1977). *Human aggression.* New York: Plenum.

Baron, R. A. (1983). The control of human aggression: An optimistic perspective. *Journal of Social and Clinical Psychology, 1,* 97–119.

Baron, R. A. & Bell, P. A. (1975). Aggression and heat: Mediating effects of prior provocation and exposure to an aggressive model. *Journal of Personality and Social Psychology, 31,* 825–832.

Baron, R. A. & Kepner, C. R. (1970). Model's behavior and attraction toward the model as determinants of adult aggressive behavior. *Journal of Personality and Social Psychology, 14,* 335–344.

Baron, R. S. (1986). Distraction-conflict theory: Progress and problems. In L. Berkowitz (Ed.), *Advances in experimental social psychology.* Orlando, FL: Academic Press.

Baron, R. S. & Rodin, J. (1978). Perceived control and crowding stress. In A. Baum, J. Singer, & S. Valins (Eds.), *Advances in environmental psychology* (Vol. 1). Hillsdale, NJ: Erlbaum.

Barrera, M., Sandler, I., & Ramsay, T. (1981). Preliminary development of a scale of social support: Studies on college students. *American Journal of Community Psychology, 9,* 434–447.

Barry, H., Bacon, M. K., & Child, E. L. (1957). A cross-cultural survey of same sex differences in socialization. *Journal of Abnormal and Social Psychology, 55,* 327–332.

Bar-Tal, D. (1976). *Prosocial behavior: Theory and research.* Washington, DC: Hemisphere.

Bartlett, F. C. (1932). *Remembering: A study in experimental and social psychology.* Cambridge, England: Cambridge University Press.

Basow, S. A. (1986). *Gender stereotypes: Traditions and alternatives* (2nd ed.). Monterey, CA: Brooks/Cole.

Bassoff, E. S. & Glass, G. V. (1982). The relationship between sex roles and mental health: A meta-analysis of twenty-six studies. *Counseling Psychologist, 10,* 105–112.

Batson, C. D. (1987). Prosocial motivation: Is it ever truly altruistic? In L. Berkowitz (Ed.), *Advances in experimental social psychology* (Vol. 20). San Diego: Academic Press.

Batson, C. D., Bolen, M. H., Cross, J. A., & Neuringer-Benefield, H. E. (1986). Where is the altruism in the altruistic personality? *Journal of Personality and Social Psychology, 50,* 212–220.

Batson, C. D., Duncan, B. D., Ackerman, P., Buckley, T., & Birch, K. (1981). Is empathic emotion a source of altruistic motivation? *Journal of Personality and Social Psychology, 40,* 290–302.

Batson, C. D., Dyck, J. L., Brandt, J. R., Batson, J. G., Powell, A. L., McMaster, M. R., & Griffitt, C. (1988). Five studies testing two new egoistic alternatives to the empathy-altruism hypothesis. *Journal of Personality and Social Psychology, 55,* 52–77.

Batson, C. D., Jones, C. H., & Cochran, P. J. (1979). Attributional bias in counselors' diagnoses: The effects of resources. *Journal of Applied Social Psychology, 9,* 377–393.

Batson, C. D., Naifeh, S. J., & Pate, S. (1978). Social desirability, religious orientation, and racial prejudice. *Journal for the Scientific Study of Religion, 17,* 31–41.

Batson, C. D. & Ventis, W. L. (1982). *The religious experience: A social psychological perspective.* New York: Oxford University Press.

Baum, A. & Valins, S. (1977). *Architecture and social behavior: Psychological studies of social density.* Hillsdale, NJ: Erlbaum.

Baumeister, R. F. (Ed.). (1986). *Public self and private self.* New York: Springer-Verlag.

Baumeister, R. F. & Darley, J. M. (1982). Reducing the biasing effects of perpetrator attractiveness in jury simulation. *Personality and Social Psychology Bulletin, 8,* 286–292.

Baumrind, D. (1964). Some thoughts on the ethics of research: After reading Milgram's "Behavioral study of obedience." *American Psychologist, 19,* 421–423.

Bavelas, A., Hastorf, A. H., Gross, A. E., & Kite, W. R. (1965). Experiments on the alteration of group structure. *Journal of Experimental Social Psychology, 1,* 55–70.

Bazerman, M. H., Magliozzi, T., & Neale, M. A. (1985). Integrative bargaining in a competitive market. *Organizational Behavior and Human Decision Processes, 35,* 294–313.

Beaman, A. L., Barnes, P. J., Klentz, B., & McQuirk, B. (1978). Increasing helping rates through information dissemination: Teaching pays. *Personality and Social Psychology Bulletin, 4,* 406–411.

Beaman, A. L., Klentz, B., Diener, E., & Svanum, S. (1979). Objective self-awareness and transgression in children: A field study. *Journal of Personality and Social Psychology, 37,* 1835–1846.

Beck, A. T. (1976). *Cognitive therapy and the emotional disorders.* New York: International Universities Press.

Becker, B. J. (1986). Influence again: Another look at studies of gender differences in social influence. In J. S. Hyde & M. C. Linn (Eds.), *The psychology of gender: Advances through meta-analysis.* Baltimore: Johns Hopkins University Press.

Bedell, J. R., Giordani, B., Amour, J. L., Tavormina, J., & Boll, T. (1977). Life stress and the psychology and medical adjustment of chronically ill children. *Journal of Psychosomatic Research, 21,* 237–243.

Begam, R. (1977). Voir dire: The attorney's job. *Trial, 13,* 3.

Bell, P. A. & Baron, R. A. (1976). Aggression and heat: The mediating role of negative affect. *Journal of Applied Social Psychology, 6,* 18–30.

Belleza, F. S. & Bower, G. H. (1981). Person stereotypes and memory for people. *Journal of Personality and Social Psychology, 41,* 856–865.

Belmore, S. M. (1987). Determinants of attention during impression formation. *Journal of Experimental Psychology: Learning, Memory and Cognition, 13,* 480–489.

Bem, D. J. (1965). An experimental analysis of self-persuasion. *Journal of Experimental Social Psychology, 1,* 199–218.

Bem, D. J. (1967). Self-perception: An alternative interpretation of cognitive dissonance phenomena. *Psychological Review, 74,* 183–200.

Bem, D. J. (1968). The epistemological status of interpersonal simulations: A reply to Jones, Linder, Kiesler, Zanna, and Brehm. *Journal of Experimental Social Psychology, 4,* 270–274.

Bem, D. J. (1970). *Beliefs, attitudes, and human affairs.* Monterey, CA: Brooks/Cole.

Bem, D. J. (1972). Self perception theory. In L. Berkowitz (Ed.), *Advances in experimental social psychology* (Vol. 6). New York: Academic Press.

Bem, D. J. (1983). Toward a response style theory of persons in situations. In M. M. Page (Ed.), *Personality — Current theory and research: Nebraska symposium on motivation 1982.*

Bem, D. J. & Allen, A. (1974). On predicting some of the people some of the time: The search for cross-situational consistencies in behavior. *Psychological Review, 81,* 506–520.

Bem, D. J., Wallach, M. A., & Kogan, N. (1965). Group decision making under risk of aversive consequences. *Journal of Personality and Social Psychology, 1,* 453–460.

Bem, S. L. (1974). The measurement of psychological androgyny. *Journal of Consulting and Clinical Psychology, 42,* 155–162.

Bem, S. L. (1975). Sex role adaptability: One consequence of psychological androgyny. *Journal of Personality and Social Psychology, 31,* 634–643.

Bem, S. L. (1981). Gender schema theory: A cognitive account of sex typing. *Psychological Review, 88,* 354–364.

Bem, S. L. & Lenney, E. (1976). Sex typing and the avoidance of cross-sex behavior. *Journal of Personality and Social Psychology, 33,* 48–54.

Bem, S. L., Martyna, W., & Watson, C. (1976). Sex typing and androgyny: Further explorations of the expressive domain. *Journal of Personality and Social Psychology, 34,* 1016–1023.

Bentler, P. M. & Speckart, G. (1979). Models of attitude-behavior relations. *Psychological Review, 86,* 452–464.

Ben-Veniste, R. (1971). Pornography and sex-crime: The Danish experience. *Technical reports of the committee on obscenity and pornography* (Vol. 8). Washington, DC: U.S. Government Printing Office.

Berelson, B., Lazarsfeld, P. L., & McPhee, W. N. (1954). *Voting.* Chicago: University of Chicago Press.

Berger, C. R. (1980). Power and the family. In M. E. Roloff & G. E. Miller (Eds.), *Persuasion: New directions in theory and research.* Beverly Hills, CA: Sage.

Berger, D. L. & Luckmann, T. (1966). *The social construction of reality: A treatise in the sociology of knowledge.* New York: Doubleday.

Berglas, S. & Jones, E. E. (1978). Drug choice as a self-handicapping strategy in response to noncontingent success. *Journal of Personality and Social Psychology, 36,* 405–417.

Bergman, J. (1974). Are little girls being harmed by Sesame Street? In J. Staceyu (Ed.), *And Jill came tumbling after: Sexism in American education.* New York: Dell.

Berkman, L. (1985). The relationship of social networks and social support to morbidity and mortality. In S. Cohen & S. L. Syme (Eds.), *Social support and health.* Orlando, FL: Academic Press.

Berkman, L. & Breslow, L. (1983). *Health and ways of living: Findings from the Alameda County study.* New York: Oxford University Press.

Berkman, L. & Syme, S. L. (1979). Social networks, host resistance, and mortality: A nine-year follow-up of Alameda County residents. *American Journal of Epidemiology, 109,* 186–204.

Berkowitz, L. (1965). Some aspects of observed aggression. *Journal of Personality and Social Psychology, 2,* 359–369.

Berkowitz, L. (1968, May). Impulse, aggression, and the gun. *Psychology Today,* 18–22.

Berkowitz, L. (1972). Social norms, feelings and other factors affecting helping behavior and altruism. In L. Berkowitz (Ed.), *Advances in experimental social psychology* (Vol. 6). New York: Academic Press.

Berkowitz, L. (1978). Whatever happened to the frustration-aggression hypothesis? *American Behavioral Scientist, 21,* 691–708.

Berkowitz, L. (1983a). Aversively stimulated aggression: Some parallels and differences in research with animals and humans. *American Psychologist, 38,* 1135–1144.

Berkowitz, L. (1983b). The experience of anger as a parallel process in the display of impulsive, "angry" aggression. In R. G. Geen & E. I. Donnerstein (Eds.), *Aggression: Theoretical and empirical reviews* (Vol. 1). New York: Academic Press.

Berkowitz, L. (1984). Some effects of thoughts on anti- and pro-social influences of media events: A cognitive-neoassociation analysis. *Psychological Bulletin, 95,* 410–427.

Berkowitz, L. (1988). Frustrations, appraisals, and aversively stimulated aggression. *Aggressive Behavior, 14,* 3–11.

Berkowitz, L., Cochran, S., & Embree, M. (1981). Physical pain and the goal of aversively stimulated aggression. *Journal of Personality and Social Psychology, 40,* 687–700.

Berkowitz, L. & Daniels, L. R. (1963). Responsibility and dependency. *Journal of Abnormal and Social Psychology, 66,* 429–436.

Berkowitz, L. & Donnerstein, E. (1982). External validity is more than skin deep: Some answers to criticisms of laboratory experiments (with special reference to research on aggression). *American Psychologist, 37,* 245–257.

Berkowitz, L. & Geen, R. G. (1966). Film violence and the cue properties of available targets. *Journal of Personality and Social Psychology, 3,* 525–530.

Berkowitz, L. & Geen, R. G. (1967). Stimulus qualities of the target of aggression: A further study. *Journal of Personality and Social Psychology, 5,* 364–368.

Berkowitz, L. & LePage, A. (1967). Weapons as aggression-eliciting stimuli. *Journal of Personality and Social Psychology, 7,* 202–207.

Bermant, G. (1977). Conduct of the voir dire examination: Practices and opinions of federal district judges. Washington, DC: Federal Judicial Center.

Berry, D. S. & McArthur, L. Z. (1986). Perceiving character in faces: The impact of age-related craniofacial changes in social perception. *Psychological Bulletin, 100,* 3–18.

Berry, G. L. (1980). Television and Afro-Americans: Past legacy and present portrayals. In S. B. Withey & R. P. Abeles (Eds.), *Television and social behavior: Beyond violence and children.* Hillsdale, NJ: Erlbaum.

Berscheid, E. (1983). Emotion. In H. H. Kelley, E. Berscheid, A. Christensen, J. H. Harvey, T. L. Huston, G. Levinger, E. McClintock, L. A. Peplau, & D. R. Petersen (Eds.), *Close relationships.* New York: Freeman.

Berscheid, E. (1985). Interpersonal attraction. In G. Lindzey & E. Aronson, (Eds.), *Handbook of social psychology* (Vol. II). New York: Random House.

Berscheid, E. & Campbell, B. (1981). The changing longevity of heterosexual close relationships: A commentary and forecast. In M. Lerner (Ed.), *The justice motive in times of scarcity and change.* New York: Plenum.

Berscheid, E., Dion, K., & Walster, E. (1971). Physical attractiveness and dating choice: A test of the matching hypothesis. *Journal of Experimental Social Psychology, 7,* 173–189.

Berscheid, E. & Walster, E. (1974a). A little bit about love. In T. L. Huston (Ed.), *Foundations of interpersonal attraction.* New York: Academic Press.

Berscheid, E. & Walster, E. (1974b). Physical attractiveness. In L. Berkowitz (Ed.), *Advances in experimental social psychology.* New York: Academic Press.

Bertenthal, B. I. & Fisher, K. W. (1978). Development of self-recognition in the infant. *Developmental Psychology, 14,* 44–50.

Bertilson, H. S. (1983). Methodology in the study of aggression. In R. G. Geen & E. I. Donnerstein (Eds.), *Aggression: Theoretical and empirical reviews* (Vol. 1). New York: Academic Press.

Bettelheim, B. (1943). Individual and mass behavior in extreme situations. *Journal of Abnormal and Social Psychology, 38,* 417–452.

Bettelheim, B. & Janowitz, M. (1950). *Dynamics of prejudice: A psychological and sociological study of veterans.* New York: Harper & Row.

Bianchi, S. M., Farley, R., & Spain, D. (1982). Racial inequalities in housing: An examination of recent trends. *Demography, 19,* 37–51.

Bickman, L. & Kamzan, N. (1973). The effects of race and need on helping behavior. *Journal of Social Psychology, 98,* 73–77.

Bierly, M. M. (1985). Prejudice toward contemporary outgroups as a generalized attitude. *Journal of Applied Social Psychology, 15,* 189–199.

Billig, M. & Tajfel, H. (1973). Social categorization and similarity in intergroup behavior. *European Journal of Social Psychology, 3,* 27–52.

Black, T. E. & Higbee, K. L. (1973). Effects of power, threat, and sex on exploitation. *Journal of Personality and Social Psychology, 27,* 382–388.

Blanchard, D. C. & Blanchard, R. J. (1986). Punishment and aggression: A critical reexamination. In R. J. Blanchard & D. C. Blanchard (Eds.), *Advances in the study of aggression.* Orlando, FL: Academic Press.

Blasi, A. (1980). Bridging moral cognition and moral action: A critical review of the literature. *Psychological Bulletin, 88,* 1–45.

Blau, P. M. (1964). *Exchange and power in social life.* New York: Wiley.

Block, J. (1971). *Lives through time.* Berkeley, CA: Bancroft Books.

Block, J. H. (1978). Another look at sex differentiation in the socialization behaviors of mothers and daughters. In J. Sherman and F. Denmark (Eds.), *Psychology of women: Future directions of research.* New York: Psychological Dimensions.

Block, J., Weiss, D. S., & Thorne, A. (1979). How relevant is a semantic similarity interpretation of personality ratings? *Journal of Personality and Social Psychology, 37,* 1055–1074.

Blood, R. O. & Blood, M. (1978). *Marriage* (3rd ed.). New York: Free Press.

Bloom, B. L., White, S. W., & Asher, S. J. (1979). Marital disruption as a stressful life event. In G. Levinger & O. C. Moles (Eds.), *Divorce and separation.* New York: Basic Books.

Bochner, S. & Insko, C. A. (1966). Communicator discrepancy, source credibility, and opinion change. *Journal of Personality and Social Psychology, 4,* 614–621.

Bogatz, G. A. & Ball, S. J. (1971). *The second year of Sesame Street: A continuing evaluation.* 2 Vols. Princeton, NJ: Educational Testing Service.

Bohannan, P. (1960). *African homicide and suicide.* New York: Atheneum.

Bollen, K. A. & Phillips, D. P. (1982). Imitative suicides: A national study of the effects of television news stories. *American Sociological Review, 47,* 802–809.

Bond, C. F., Jr. & Titus, L. J. (1983). Social facilitation: A meta-analysis of 241 studies. *Psychological Bulletin, 94,* 265–292.

Borden, R. J., Bowen, R., & Taylor, S. P. (1971). Shock setting as a function of physical attack and extrinsic reward. *Perceptual and Motor Skills, 33,* 563–568.

Borgatta, E. F., Couch, A. A., & Bales, R. F. (1954). Some findings relevant to the great man theory of leadership. *American Sociological Review, 19,* 755–759.

Bossard, J. H. S. (1931). Residential propinquity as a factor in marriage selection. *American Journal of Sociology, 38,* 219–224.

Boudreau, F. A. (1986). Education. In F. A. Boudreau, R. S. Sennott, & M. Wilson (Eds.), *Sex roles and social patterns.* New York: Praeger.

Bower, G. H., Black, J. B., & Turner, T. J. (1979). Scripts in memory for text. *Cognitive Psychology, 11,* 177–220.

Bowers, K. S. (1973). Situationism in psychology: An analysis and a critique. *Psychological Review, 80,* 307–336.

Boyanowsky, E. O. & Allen, V. L. (1973). Ingroup norms and self-identity as determinants of discriminatory behavior. *Journal of Personality and Social Psychology, 25,* 408–418.

Bradshaw, J. L. (1969). The information conveyed by varying dimensions of features in human outline faces. *Perception and Psychophysics, 6,* 5–9.

Braiker, H. B. & Kelley, H. H. (1979). Conflict in the development of close relationships. In R. L. Burgess & T. L. Huston (Eds.), *Social exchange in developing relationships.* New York: Academic Press.

Brand, R. J., Rosenman, R. H., Sholtz, R. I., & Friedman, M. (1976). Multivariate prediction of coronary heart disease in the Western Collaborative Group Study compared to the findings of the Framingham Study. *Circulation, 53,* 938–955.

Bransford, J. D. & Johnson, M. K. (1972). Contextual prerequisites for understanding: Some investigations of comprehension and recall. *Journal of Verbal Learning and Behavior, 11,* 717–726.

Bray, R. M., Johnson, D., & Chilstrom, J. T. (1982). Social influence by group members with minority opinions: A comparison of Hollander and Moscovici. *Journal of Personality and Social Psychology, 43,* 78–88.

Brehm, J. (1966). *A theory of psychological reactance.* New York: Academic Press.

Brehm, S. S. & Brehm, J. W. (1981). *Psychological reactance.* New York: Academic Press.

Breuer, J. & Freud, S. (1961). *Studies in hysteria.* Boston: Beacon Press.

Brewer, M. B., Dull, V., & Lui, L. (1981). Perceptions of the elderly: Stereotypes as prototypes. *Journal of Personality and Social Psychology, 41,* 656–670.

Brewer, M. B. & Kramer, R. K. (1986). Choice behavior in social dilemmas: Effects of social identity, group size, and decision framing. *Journal of Personality and Social Psychology, 50,* 543–549.

Brewer, M. B. & Silver, M. (1978). Ingroup bias as a function of task characteristics. *European Journal of Social Psychology, 8,* 393–400.

Brickman, P., Becker, L. J., & Castle, S. (1979). Making trust easier and harder through forms of sequential interaction. *Journal of Personality and Social Psychology, 37,* 515–521.

Brigham, J. C. (1971). Ethnic stereotypes. *Psychological Bulletin, 76,* 15–38.

Brislin, R. W. & Lewis, S. A. (1968). Dating and physical attractiveness: A replication. *Psychological Reports, 22,* 976.

Brockner, J. & Swap, W. C. (1976). Effects of repeated exposure on self-disclosure and interpersonal attraction. *Journal of Personality and Social Psychology, 33,* 531–540.

Broverman, I. K., Vogel, S. R., Broverman, D. M., Clarkson, F. E., & Rosenkrantz, P. S. (1972). Sex-role stereotypes: A current appraisal. *Journal of Social Issues, 28(2),* 59–79.

Brown, G. W. & Harris, T. (1978). *Social origins of depression: A study of psychiatric disorder in women.* New York: Free Press.

Brown, P., Keenan, J. M., & Potts, G. R. (1986). The self-reference effect with imagery encoding. *Journal of Personality and Social Psychology, 51,* 897–906.

Brownmiller, S. (1975). *Against our will: Men, women and rape.* New York: Simon & Schuster.

Bryan, J. H. (1972). Why children help: A review. *Journal of Social Issues, 28(3),* 87–104.

Bryan, J. H. (1975). Children's cooperation and helping behaviors. In E. M. Hetherington (Ed.), *Review of child development research* (Vol. 5). Chicago: University of Chicago Press.

Bryan, J. H. & Test, M. J. (1967). Models and helping: Naturalistic studies in aiding behavior. *Journal of Personality and Social Psychology, 6,* 400–407.

Bullough, V. (1976). *Sexual variance in society and history.* New York: Wiley.

Burger, J. M. (1986). Increasing compliance by improving the deal: The that's-not-all technique. *Journal of Personality and Social Psychology, 51,* 277–283.

Burgess, E. W. & Wallin, P. (1953). *Engagement and marriage.* Philadelphia: Lippincott.

Burgess, E. W. & Wallin, P. W. (1943). Homogamy in social characteristics. *American Journal of Sociology, 49,* 109–124.

Burnham, J. C. (1968). Historical background for the study of personality. In E. F. Borgatta & W. W. Lambert (Eds.), *Handbook of personality theory and research.* Chicago: Rand McNally.

Burnstein, E. & Vinokur, A. (1973). Testing two classes of theories about group-induced shifts in individual choice. *Journal of Experimental Social Psychology, 9,* 123–137.

Burnstein, E. & Vinokur, A. (1977). Persuasive arguments and social comparison as determinants of attitude polarization. *Journal of Experimental Social Psychology, 13,* 315–332.

Burnstein E. & Worchel, P. (1962). Arbitrariness of frustration and its consequences for aggression in a social setting. *Journal of Personality, 30,* 528–540.

Buss, A. H. (1961). *The psychology of aggression.* New York: Wiley.

Buss, A. H. (1966). Instrumentality of aggression, feedback, and frustration as determinants of physical aggression. *Journal of Personality and Social Psychology, 3,* 153–162.

Buss, A. H. (1971). Aggression pays. In J. L. Singer (Ed.), *The control of aggression and violence.* New York: Academic Press.

Buss, D. M. (1985). Human mate selection. *American Scientist, 73,* 47–51.

Buss, D. M. (1987). Sex differences in human mate selection criteria: An evolutionary perspective. In C. Crawford, M. Smith, & D. Krebs (Eds.), *Sociobiology and psychology: Ideas, issues, and application.* Hillsdale, NJ: Erlbaum.

Buss, D. M. (1988). The evolution of human intrasexual competition: Tactics of mate selection. *Journal of Personality and Social Psychology, 54,* 616–628.

Buss, D. M. & Barnes, M. (1986). Preferences in human mate selection. *Journal of Personality and Social Psychology, 50,* 559–570.

Buss, D. M. & Craik, K. H. (1980). The frequency concept of disposition: Dominance and prototypically dominant acts. *Journal of Personality, 48,* 379–392.

Byeff, P. (1970). *Helping behavior in audio and audio-video conditions.* Senior honors thesis, University of Pennsylvania, Philadelphia.

Byrne, D. (1971). *The attraction paradigm.* New York: Academic Press.

Byrne, D. & Clore, G. L. (1970). A reinforcement model of evaluative responses. *Personality: An International Journal, 1,* 102–128.

Byrne, D., Clore, G. L., & Smeaton, G. (1986). The attraction hypothesis: Do similar attitudes affect anything? *Journal of Personality and Social Psychology, 51,* 1167–1170.

Byrne, D. & Kelley, K. (1984). Introduction: Pornography and sex research. In N. M. Malamuth & E. Donnerstein (Eds.), *Pornography and sexual aggression.* Orlando, FL: Academic Press.

Byrne, D. & Nelson, D. (1965). Attraction as a linear proportion of positive reinforcements. *Journal of Personality and Social Psychology, 1,* 659–663.

Byrne, D., Rasche, L., & Kelley, K. (1974). When "I like you" indicates disagreement. *Journal of Research in Personality, 8,* 207–217.

Cacioppo, J. T., Andersen, B. L., Turnquist, D. C., & Petty, R. E. (1986). Psychophysiological comparison processes. In B. L. Andersen (Ed.), *Women with cancer: Psychological perspectives.* New York: Springer-Verlag.

Cacioppo, J. T. & Petty, R. E. (1979). Effects of message repetition and position on cognitive responses, recall, and persuasion. *Journal of Personality and Social Psychology, 37,* 97–109.

Cacioppo, J. T. & Petty, R. E. (1980). Persuasiveness of commercials is affected by exposure frequency and communicator cogency: A theoretical and empirical analysis. In J. H. Leigh & C. R. Martin (Eds.), *Current issues and research in advertising.* Ann Arbor: University of Michigan Press.

Cacioppo, J. T. & Petty, R. E. (1982). The need for cognition. *Journal of Personality and Social Psychology, 42,* 116–131.

Cacioppo, J. T. & Petty, R. E. (1987). Stalking rudimentary processes of social influence: A psychophysiological approach. In M. P. Zanna, J. M. Olson, & C. P. Herman (Eds.), *Social influence: The Ontario symposium* (Vol. 5). Hillsdale, NJ: Erlbaum.

Cacioppo, J. T., Petty, R. E., Losch, M. E., & Kim, H. S. (1986). Electromyographic activity over facial muscle regions can differentiate the valence and intensity of affective reactions. *Journal of Personality and Social Psychology, 50,* 260–268.

Cacioppo, J. T., Petty, R. E., & Morris, K. (1983). Effects of need for cognition on message evaluation, recall, and persuasion. *Journal of Personality and Social Psychology, 45,* 805–818.

Cagle, L. T. (1973). Interracial housing: A reassessment of the equal-status contact hypothesis. *Sociology and Social Research, 57,* 342–355.

Calder, B. J. & Ross, M. (1973). *Attitudes and behavior.* Morristown, NJ: General Learning Press.

Caldwell, D. F. & O'Reilly, C. A. (1982). Boundary spanning and individual performance: The impact of self-monitoring. *Journal of Applied Psychology, 67,* 124–127.

Calhoun, L. G., Dawes, A. S., & Lewis, P. M. (1972). Correlates of attitudes toward help-seeking in outpatients. *Journal of Consulting and Clinical Psychology, 38,* 153.

Callaway, M. R., Marriott, R. G., & Esser, J. K. (1985). Effects of dominance on group decision making: Toward a stress-reduction explanation of groupthink. *Journal of Personality and Social Psychology, 49,* 949–952.

Campbell, A. (1981). *The sense of well-being in America.* New York: McGraw-Hill.

Campbell, D. F. (1966). *Revised manual for Strong Vocational Interest Blank.* Stanford, CA: Stanford University Press.

Campbell, D. T. (1967). Stereotypes and the perception of group differences. *American Psychologist, 22,* 817–829.

Campbell, D. T. (1975). On the conflict between biological and social evolution and moral tradition. *American Psychologist, 30,* 1103–1126.

Campbell, D. T. (1983). The two distinct routes beyond kin selection to ultrasociality: Implications for the humanities and social sciences. In D. L. Bridgeman (Ed.), *The nature of prosocial development.* New York: Academic Press.

Campbell, D. T. & Fiske, D. (1959). Convergent and discriminant validation by the multitrait-multimethod matrix. *Psychological Bulletin, 56,* 81–105.

Campbell, D. T. & Stanley, J. C. (1963). Experimental and quasi-experimental designs for research. In N. L. Gage (Ed.), *Handbook of research in teaching.* Skokie, IL: Rand McNally.

Campbell, D. T. & Stanley, J. C. (1966). *Experimental and quasi-experimental designs in research.* Skokie, IL: Rand McNally.

Campbell, J. D. (1986). Similarity and uniqueness: The effects of attribute type, relevance, and individual differences in self-esteem and depression. *Journal of Personality and Social Psychology, 50,* 281–294.

Candide: A comic operetta based on Voltaire's satire. (1957). Book by Lillian Hellman, lyrics by Richard Wilbur, other lyrics by John Latouche and Dorothy Parker. New York: Random House.

Cantor, N. & Kihlstrom, J. F. (1987). *Personality and social intelligence.* Englewood Cliffs, NJ: Prentice-Hall.

Cantor, N. & Mischel, W. (1977). Traits as prototypes: Effects on recognition memory. *Journal of Personality and Social Psychology, 35,* 38–48.

Capellanus, A. (1969). *The art of courtly love.* J. Parry (Trans.). New York: Norton.

Caplan, N. & Nelson, S. D. (1973). On being useful: The nature and consequences of psychological research on social problems. *American Psychologist, 28,* 199–211.

Caplan, R. D., Robinson, E. A. R., French, J. R. P., Jr., Caldwell, J. R., & Shinn, M. (1976). *Adherence to medical regimens: Pilot experiments in patient education and social support.* University of Michigan Research Center for Group Dynamics, Institute for Social Research, Ann Arbor, MI.

Carducci, B. J., Cozby, P. C., & Ward, C. D. (1978). Sexual arousal and interpersonal evaluations. *Journal of Experimental Social Psychology, 14,* 449–457.

Carli, L. L. (1982). *Are women more social and men more task oriented? A meta-analytic review of sex differences in group interaction, reward allocation, coalition formation, and cooperation in the Prisoner's Dilemma Game.* Unpublished manuscript, University of Massachusetts, Amherst.

Carlsmith, J. M. & Anderson, C. A. (1979). Ambient temperature and the occurrence of collective violence: A new analysis. *Journal of Personality and Social Psychology, 37,* 337–344.

Carlsmith, J. M., Ellsworth, P. C., & Aronson, E. (1976). *Methods of research in social psychology.* Reading, MA: Addison-Wesley.

Carlsmith, J. M. & Gross, A. E. (1969). Some effects of guilt on compliance. *Journal of Personality and Social Psychology, 11,* 232–239.

Carson, R. C., Butcher, J. N., & Coleman, J. C. (1988). *Abnormal psychology and modern life* (8th ed.). Glenview, IL: Scott, Foresman.

Cartwright, D. & Zander, A. (1968). Issues and basic assumptions. In D. Cartwright & A. Zander (Eds.), *Group dynamics: Research and theory* (3rd ed.). New York: Harper & Row.

Carver, C. S. (1975). Physical aggression as a function of objective self-awareness and attitudes toward punishment. *Journal of Experimental Social Psychology, 11,* 510–519.

Carver, C. S. (1989). How should multifaceted personality constructs be tested? Issues illustrated by self-monitoring, attributional style, and hardiness. *Journal of Personality and Social Psychology, 56,* 577–585.

Carver, C. S., DeGregorio, E., & Gillis, R. (1980). Ego-defensive attribution among two categories of observers. *Personality and Social Psychology Bulletin, 6,* 44–50.

Carver, C. S. & Scheier, M. F. (1981). *Attention and self-regulation: A control theory approach to human behavior.* New York: Springer-Verlag.

Caspi, A. (1987). Personality in the life course. *Journal of Personality and Social Psychology, 53,* 1203–1213.

Cassel, J. C. (1976). The contribution of the social environment to host resistance. *American Journal of Epidemiology, 104,* 107–123.

Cattell, R. B. (1965). *The scientific analysis of personality.* Baltimore: Penguin Books.

Center for Research on Aggression. (1983). *Prevention and control of aggression.* New York: Pergamon Press.

Center for Disease Control. (1980). *Ten leading causes of death in the United States.* Washington, DC: U.S. Government Printing Office.

Chaikin, A. L., Derlega, V. J., & Miller, S. J. (1976). Effects of room environment on self-disclosure in a counseling analogue. *Journal of Counseling Psychology, 23,* 479–481.

Chaiken, S. (1979). Communicator physical attractiveness and persuasion. *Journal of Personality and Social Psychology, 37,* 1387–1397.

Chaiken, S. (1980). Heuristic versus systematic information processing and the use of source versus message cues in persuasion. *Journal of Personality and Social Psychology, 39,* 752–766.

Chaiken, S. (1987). The heuristic model of persuasion. In M. P. Zanna, J. M. Olson, & C. P. Herman (Eds.), *Social influence: The Ontario symposium* (Vol 5). Hillsdale, NJ: Erlbaum.

Chaiken, S. & Baldwin, M. W. (1981). Affective-cognitive consistency and the effect of salient behavioral information on the self-perception of attitudes. *Journal of Personality and Social Psychology, 41,* 1–12.

Chaiken, S. & Eagly, A. H. (1976). Communication modality as a determinant of message persuasiveness and message comprehensibility. *Journal of Personality and Social Psychology, 34,* 605–614.

Chaiken, S. & Eagly, A. H. (1983). Communication modality as a determinant of persuasion: The role of communicator salience. *Journal of Personality and Social Psychology, 45,* 241–256.

Chapman, L. J. & Chapman, J. P. (1967). Genesis of popular but erroneous diagnostic observations. *Journal of Abnormal Psychology, 72,* 193–204.

Chapman, L. J. & Chapman, J. P. (1969). Illusory correlation as an obstacle to the use of valid psychodiagnostic signs. *Journal of Abnormal Psychology, 14,* 271–280.

Chapman, L. J. & Chapman, J. P. (1982). Test results are what you think they are. In D. Kahneman, P. Slovic, & A. Tversky (Eds.), *Judgment under uncertainty: Heuristics and biases.* New York: Cambridge University Press.

Chase W. G. & Simon, H. A. (1973). Perception and chess. *Cognitive Psychology, 4,* 55–81.

Chasnoff, R. (Ed.). (1978). *Structuring cooperative learning in the classroom: The 1979 handbook.* Minneapolis, MN: Cooperative Network.

Chen, S. C. (1937). Social modification of the activity of ants on nest-building. *Physiological Zoology, 10,* 420–436.

Chodorow, N. (1978). *The reproduction of mothering.* Berkeley: University of California Press.

Christie, R. (1978). Reconsideration: The authoritarian personality. *Human Nature.*

Christie, R. & Cook, P. (1958). A guide to the published literature relating to the authoritarian personality through 1956. *Journal of Psychology, 45,* 171–199.

Christie, R. & Jahoda, M. (Eds.). (1954). *Studies in the scope and method of "the authoritarian personality."* New York: Free Press.

Cialdini, R. B. (1988). *Influence: Science and practice* (2nd ed.). Glenview, IL: Scott, Foresman/Little, Brown.

Cialdini, R. B., Borden, R. J., Thorne, A., Walker, M. R., Freeman, S., & Sloan, L. R. (1976). Basking in reflected glory: Three (football) field studies. *Journal of Personality and Social Psychology, 34,* 366–375.

Cialdini, R. B., Cacioppo, J. R., Bassett, R., & Miller, J. A. (1978). Low-ball procedure for producing compliance: Commitment then cost. *Journal of Personality and Social Psychology, 36,* 463–476.

Cialdini, R. B., Darby, B. L., & Vincent, J. E. (1973). Transgression and altruism: A case for hedonism. *Journal of Experimental Social Psychology, 9,* 502–516.

Cialdini, R. B. & Kenrick, D. T. (1976). Altruism as hedonism: A social developmental perspective on the relationship of negative mood state and helping. *Journal of Personality and Social Psychology, 34,* 907–914.

Cialdini, R. B., Levy, A., Herman, P., Kozlowski, L., & Petty, R. (1976). Elastic shifts of opinion: Determinants of direction and durability. *Journal of Personality and Social Psychology, 34,* 663–672.

Cialdini, R. B., Schaller, M., Houlihan, D., Arps, K., Fultz, J., & Beaman, A. L. (1987). Empathy-based helping: Is it selflessly or selfishly motivated? *Journal of Personality and Social Psychology, 52,* 749–758.

Cialdini, R. B., Vincent, J. E., Lewis, S. K., Catalan, J., Wheeler, D., & Darby, B. L. (1975). Reciprocal concessions procedure for inducing compliance: The door-in-the-face technique. *Journal of Personality and Social Psychology, 31,* 206–215.

Cisin, I. H., Coffin, T. E., Janis, I. L., Klapper, J. T., Mendelsohn, H., Omwake, E., Pinderhughes, C. A., Pool, I. de Sola, Siegel, A. E., Wallace, A. F. C., Watson, A. S., & Wiebe, G. D. (1972). *Television and growing up: The impact of televised violence.* Washington, DC: U.S. Government Printing Office.

Clark, L. F. & Woll, S. B. (1981). Stereotype biases: A reconstructive analysis of their role in reconstructive memory. *Journal of Personality and Social Psychology, 41,* 1064–1072.

Clark, M. S. & Mills, J. (1979). Interpersonal attraction in exchange and communal relationships. *Journal of Personality and Social Psychology, 37,* 12–27.

Clark, M. S., Mills, J., & Powell, M. C. (1986). Keeping track of needs in communal and exchange relationships. *Journal of Personality and Social Psychology, 51,* 333–338.

Clifford, M. M. & Walster, E. (1973). The effect of physical attractiveness on teacher expectation. *Sociology of Education, 46,* 248–258.

Cline, V. B., Croft, R. G., & Courrier, S. (1973). Desensitization of children to television violence. *Journal of Personality and Social Psychology, 27,* 360–365.

Cline, V. B. & Richards, J. M. (1960). Accuracy of interpersonal perception—a general trait? *Journal of Abnormal and Social Psychology, 60,* 1–7.

Cohen, A. (1962). An experiment on small rewards for discrepant compliance and attitude change. In J. W. Brehm & A. R. Cohen (Eds.),

Explorations in cognitive dissonance. New York: Wiley.

Cohen, C. E. (1981). Person categories and social perception: Testing some boundaries of the processing effects of prior knowledge. *Journal of Personality and Social Psychology, 40,* 441–452.

Cohen, C. E. & Ebbesen, E. B. (1979). Observational goals and schema activation: A theoretical framework for behavior perception. *Journal of Experimental Social Psychology, 15,* 305–329.

Cohen, E. G. (1984). The desegregated school: Problems in status, power and interethnic climate. In N. Miller & M. B. Brewer (Eds.), *Groups in contact: The psychology of desegregation.* New York: Academic Press.

Cohen, J. (1977). *Statistical power analysis for the behavioral sciences.* New York: Academic Press.

Cohen, R. (1978). Altruism: Human, cultural, or what? In L. Wispe (Ed.), *Altruism, sympathy, and helping: Psychological and sociological principles.* New York: Academic Press.

Cohen, S. & McKay, G. (1984). Social support, stress, and the buffer hypothesis: A theoretical analysis. In A. Baum, S. E. Taylor, & J. E. Singer (Eds.), *Handbook of psychology and health* (Vol. IV): *Social psychological aspects of health.* Hillsdale, NJ: Erlbaum.

Cohen, S., Mermelstein, R., Kamarck, T., & Hoberman, H. (1984). Measuring the functional components of social support. In I. Sarason (Ed.), *Social support: Theory, research and application.* The Hague, Netherlands: Marine Niijhoff.

Cohen, S. & Syme, S. L. (Eds.). (1985a). *Social support and health.* Orlando, FL: Academic Press.

Cohen, S. & Syme, S. L. (1985b). Issues in the study and application of social support. In S. Cohen & S. L. Syme (Eds.), *Social support and health.* Orlando, FL: Academic Press.

Cohen, S. & Wills, T. A. (1985). Stress, social support, and the buffering hypothesis. *Psychological Bulletin, 98,* 310–357.

Cole, J. R. (1979). *Fair science: Women in the scientific community.* New York: Free Press.

Colligan, M. J. & Murphy, L. R. (1982). A review of mass psychogenic illness in work settings. In M. J. Colligan, J. W. Pennebaker, & L. R. Murphy (Eds.), *Mass psychogenic illness: A social psychological analysis.* Hillsdale, NJ: Erlbaum.

Colligan, M. J., Pennebaker, J. W., & Murphy, L. R. (Eds.). (1982). *Mass psychogenic illness: A social psychological analysis.* Hillsdale, NJ: Erlbaum.

Collins, B. E. (1974). Four components of the Rotter internal-external scale: Belief in a difficult world, a just world, a predictable world, and a politically responsive world. *Journal of Personality and Social Psychology, 29,* 381–391.

Collins, B. E. & Hoyt, M. G. (1972). Personal responsibility for consequences: An integration and extension of the "forced compliance" literature. *Journal of Experimental Social Psychology, 8,* 558–593.

Conley, J. J. (1985). Longitudinal stability of personality traits: A multitrait-multimethod-multioccasion analysis. *Journal of Personality and Social Psychology, 49,* 1266–1282.

Conner, R. C. & Norriss, K. S. (1982). Are dolphins reciprocal altruists? *American Naturalist, 119,* 358–374.

Constantinople, A. (1973). Masculinity-femininity: An exception to a famous dictum? *Psychological Bulletin, 80,* 389–407.

Cook, E. P. (1985). *Psychological androgyny.* New York: Pergamon Press.

Cook, S. W. (1984). Cooperative interaction in multiethnic contexts. In N. Miller & M. B. Brewer (Eds.), *Groups in contact: The psychology of desegregation.* New York: Academic Press.

Cook, T. D. & Campbell, D. T. (Eds.). (1979). *The design and analysis of quasi-experiments for field settings.* Chicago: Rand McNally.

Cooley, C. H. (1902). *Human nature and the social order.* New York: Scribner.

Cooms, R. H. & Kenkel, W. F. (1966). Sex differences in dating aspirations and satisfaction with computer-selected partners. *Journal of Marriage and the Family, 28,* 62–66.

Cooper, J. & Worchel, S. (1970). Role of undesired consequences in arousing cognitive dissonance. *Journal of Personality and Social Psychology, 16,* 199–206.

Cooper, J., Zanna, M. P., & Taves, P. A. (1978). Arousal as a necessary condition for attitude change following induced compliance. *Journal of Personality and Social Psychology, 36,* 1101–1106.

Cotton, J. L. (1986). Ambient temperature and violent crime. *Journal of applied social psychology, 16,* 786–801.

Cottrell, N. B., Wack, D. L., Seberak, G. J., & Rittle, R. M. (1968). Social facilitation of dominant responses by the presence of an audience and the mere presence of others. *Journal of Personality and Social Psychology, 9,* 245–250.

Court, J. H. (1984). Sex and violence: A ripple effect. In N. M. Malamuth & E. Donnerstein (Eds.), *Pornography and sexual aggression.* Orlando, FL: Academic Press.

Courtright, J. A. (1978). A laboratory investigation of groupthink. *Communications Monographs, 43,* 229–246.

Coyne, J. C. & DeLongis, A. (1986). Going beyond social support: The role of social relationships in adaptation. *Journal of Consulting and Clinical Psychology, 54,* 454–460.

Coyne, J. C. & Gotlieb, I. H. (1983). The role of cognition in depression: A critical appraisal. *Psychological Bulletin, 94,* 472–505.

Cozby, P. C. (1973). Self-disclosure: A literature review. *Psychological Bulletin, 79,* 73–91.

Craig, C. S. & McCann, J. M. (1978). Item non-response in mail surveys: Extent and correlates. *Journal of Marketing Research, 15,* 285–289.

Crano, W. D. & Brewer, M. B. (1986). *Principles and methods of social research.* Boston: Allyn and Bacon.

Crawford, C., Smith, M., & Krebs, D. (Eds.) (1986). *Sociobiology and psychology: Ideas, issues, and applications.* Hillsdale, NJ: Erlbaum.

Crocker, J. & Weber, R. (1983). Cognitive structure and stereotype change. In R. P. Bagozzi & A. M. Tybout (Eds.), *Advances in consumer research* (Vol. 10). Ann Arbor, MI: Association for Consumer Research.

Cronbach, L. J. (1955). Processes affecting scores on "understanding of others" and "assumed similarity." *Psychological Bulletin, 52,* 177–193.

Cronbach, L. J. (1984). *Essentials of psychological testing.* New York: Harper & Row.

Crow, W. J. & Hammond, K. R. (1957). The generality of accuracy and response in interpersonal perception. *Journal of Abnormal and Social Psychology, 54,* 384–390.

Crutchfield, R. A. (1955). Conformity and character. *American Psychologist, 10,* 191–198.

Cunningham, M. R. (1979). Weather, mood, and helping behavior: Quasi-experiments with the sunshine Samaritan: *Journal of Personality and Social Psychology, 37,* 1947–1956.

Cunningham, M. R., Steinberg, J., & Greu, R. (1980). Wanting to and having to help: Separate motivation for positive mood and guilt-induced helping. *Journal of Personality and Social Psychology, 38,* 181–192.

Curran, J. P. & Lippold, S. (1975). The effects of physical attractiveness and attitude similarity on attraction in dating dyads. *Journal of Personality, 43,* 528–539.

Curtis, L. (1974). *Criminal violence: National patterns and behavior.* Lexington, MA: Lexington Books.

Curtis, R. C. & Miller, K. (1986). Believing another likes or dislikes you: Behaviors making the beliefs come true. *Journal of Personality and Social Psychology, 51,* 284–290.

D'Andrade, R. (1966). Sex differences and cultural institutions. In E. E. Maccoby (Ed.), *The development of sex differences.* Stanford, CA: Stanford University Press.

Danheiser, P. R. & Graziano, W. G. (1982). Self-monitoring and cooperation as a self-presentational strategy. *Journal of Personality and Social Psychology, 42,* 497–505.

Darley, J. M. & Batson, C. D. (1973). From Jerusalem to Jericho: A study of situational and dispositional variables in helping behavior. *Journal of Personality and Social Psychology, 27,* 100–108.

Darley, J. M. & Latané, B. (1968). Bystander intervention in emergencies: Diffusion of responsibility. *Journal of Personality and Social Psychology, 8,* 377–383.

Darley, J. M., Teger, A. I., & Lewis, L. D. (1973). Do groups always inhibit individuals' response to potential emergencies? *Journal of Personality and Social Psychology, 26,* 395–399.

Darwin, C. (1859). *The origin of the species.* London: John Murray.

Darwin, C. (1871). *The descent of man.* London: John Murray.

Darwin, C. (1872). *The expression of emotions in man and animals*. London: John Murray.

Dashiell, J. F. (1930). An experimental analysis of some group effects. *Journal of Abnormal and Social Psychology, 25*, 190–199.

Davies, J. C. (1972). Toward a theory of revolution. In I. K. Feierabend & R. L. Feierabend (Eds.), *Anger, violence, and politics: Theories and research*. Englewood Cliffs, NJ: Prentice-Hall.

Davis, K. E. & Jones, E. E. (1960). Changes in interpersonal perception as a means of reducing cognitive dissonance. *Journal of Abnormal and Social Psychology, 61*, 402–410.

Davis, M. S. (1968). Variations in patients' compliance with doctors' advice: An empirical analysis of patterns of communication. *American Journal of Public Health, 58*, 274–288.

Davitz, J. R. (1952). The effects of previous training on post frustration behavior. *Journal of Abnormal and Social Psychology, 47*, 309–315.

Dawes, R. M. (1976). Shallow psychology. In J. Carroll & J. Payne, (Eds.), *Cognition and social behavior*. Hillsdale, NJ: Erlbaum.

Dawes, R. M. (1980). You can't systematize human judgment: Dyslexia. In R. A. Shweder (Ed.), *New directions for methodology of social and behavioral science* (Vol. 4). San Francisco: Jossey-Bass.

Dawes, R. M. (1988). *Rational choice in an uncertain world*. San Diego: Harcourt Brace Jovanovich.

Dawes, R. M. & Corrigan, B. (1974). Linear models in decision making. *Psychological Bulletin, 81*, 95–106.

Dawkins, R. (1976). *The selfish gene*. New York: Oxford University Press.

Deaux, K. (1984). From individual differences to social categories: Analysis of a decade's research on gender. *American Psychologist, 39*, 105–116.

Deaux, K. (1985). Sex and gender. In M. R. Rosenzweig & L. W. Porter (Eds.), *Annual review of psychology* (Vol. 36). Palo Alto, CA: Annual Reviews.

Deaux, K. & Emswiller, T. (1974). Explanation for successful performance on sex-linked tasks: What is skill for the male is luck for the female. *Journal of Personality and Social Psychology, 29*, 80–85.

Deaux, K. & Lewis, L. L. (1983). Assessment of gender stereotypes: Methodology and components. *Psychological Documents, 13*, 25. (Ms. No. 2583.)

Deaux, K. & Lewis, L. L. (1984). The structure of gender stereotypes: Interrelationships among components and gender label. *Journal of Personality and Social Psychology, 46*, 991–1004.

Deaux, K. & Major, B. (1987). Putting gender into context: An interactive model of gender-related behavior. *Psychological Review, 94*, 369–389.

Deci, E. L. (1975). *Intrinsic motivation*. New York: Plenum.

Deci, E. L. & Ryan, R. M. (1980). The empirical exploration of intrinsic motivational processes. In L. Berkowitz (Ed.), *Advances in experimental social psychology* (Vol. 13). New York: Academic Press.

Deci, E. L. & Ryan, R. M. (1985). *Intrinsic motivation and self-determination in human behavior*. New York: Plenum.

DeJong, W. (1979). An examination of the self-perception mediation of the foot-in-the-door effect. *Journal of Personality and Social Psychology, 37*, 2221–2239.

DeJong, W. & Musilli, L. (1982). External pressure to comply: Handicapped versus nonhandicapped requesters and the foot-in-the-door phenomenon. *Personality and Social Psychology Bulletin, 8*, 522–527.

Delbecq, A. L., Van de Ven, A. H., & Gustafson, D. H. (1975). *Group techniques for program planning*. Glenview, IL: Scott, Foresman.

Dellapa, F. (1977). Mediation and the community dispute center. In M. Roy (Ed.), *Battered women: A psycho-sociological study of domestic violence*. New York: Van Nostrand Reinhold.

Dengerink, H. A. & Myers, J. D. (1977). The effects of failure and depression on subsequent aggression. *Journal of Personality and Social Psychology, 35*, 88–96.

DePaulo, B. M. (1978). Accepting help from teachers—When the teachers are children. *Human Relations, 31*, 459–474.

DePaulo, B. M., Kenny, D. A., Hoover, C. W., Webb, W., & Oliver, P. V. (1987). Accuracy of person perception: Do people know what kinds of impressions they convey? *Journal of Personality and Social Psychology, 52*, 303–315.

DePaulo, B. M., Lassiter, G. D., & Stone, J. H. (1982). Attentional determinants of success at detecting deception and truth. *Personality and Social Psychology Bulletin, 8*, 273–279.

DePaulo, B. M. & Pfeifer, R. L. (1986). On-the-job experience and skill at detecting deception. *Journal of Applied Social Psychology, 16*, 249–267.

DePaulo, B. M. & Rosenthal, R. (1979). Telling lies. *Journal of Personality and Social Psychology, 37*, 1713–1722.

DePaulo, B. M., Stone, J., & Lassiter, G. D. (1985). Deceiving and detecting deceit. In B. R. Schlenker (Ed.), *The self and social life*. New York: McGraw-Hill.

De Riencourt, A. (1974). *Sex and power in history*. New York: McKay.

Dermer, M. & Pyszczynski, T. A. (1978). Effects of erotica upon men's loving and liking responses for women they love. *Journal of Personality and Social Psychology, 36*, 1302–1309.

Dermer, M. & Thiel, D. L. (1975). When beauty may fail. *Journal of Personality and Social Psychology, 31*, 1168–1176.

Deseran, F. A. & Chung, C. S. (1979). Appearance, role-taking, and reactions to deviance: Some experimental findings. *Social Psychology Quarterly, 42*, 426–430.

de Tocqueville, A. (1856). *The old regime and the French Revolution*. New York: Harper Brothers. (The Stuart Gilbert translation, Garden City, NY: Doubleday, 1955.)

Deutsch, M. (1949). The directions of behavior: A field-theoretical approach to the understanding of inconsistencies. *Journal of Social Issues, 5*, 45.

Deutsch, M. (1968). The effects of cooperation and competition upon group process. In D. Cartwright & A. Zander (Eds.), *Group dynamics: Research and theory* (3rd ed.). New York: Harper & Row.

Deutsch, M. (1973). *The resolution of conflict*. New Haven, CT: Yale University Press.

Deutsch, M. & Collins, M. E. (1951). *Interracial housing: A psychological evaluation of a social experiment*. Minneapolis: University of Minnesota Press.

Deutsch, M. & Gerard, H. B. (1955). A study of normative and informational social influences upon individual judgment. *Journal of Abnormal and Social Psychology, 51*, 629–636.

Dibiase, W. & Hjelle, L. (1968). Body-image stereotypes and body-type preferences among male college students. *Perception and Motor Skills, 27*, 1143–1146.

Dickey, R. V. & Knower, F. H. (1941). A note on some ethnological differences in recognition of simulated expressions of the emotions. *American Journal of Sociology, 47*, 190–193.

Diehl, M. & Stroebe, W. (1987). Productivity loss in brainstorming groups: Toward the solution of a riddle. *Journal of Personality and Social Psychology, 53*, 497–509.

Diener, E. (1976). Effects of prior destructive behavior, anonymity, and group presence on deindividuation and aggression. *Journal of Personality and Social Psychology, 33*, 497–507.

Diener, E. (1979). Deindividuation, self-awareness, and disinhibition. *Journal of Personality and Social Psychology, 37*, 1160–1171.

Diener, E. (1980). Deindividuation: The absence of self-awareness and self-regulation in group members. In P. B. Paulus (Ed.), *Psychology of group influence*. Hillsdale, NJ: Erlbaum.

Diener, E., Doneen, J., & Endresen, K. (1975). Effects of altered responsibility, cognitive set, and modeling on physical aggressiveness and deindividuation. *Journal of Personality and Social Psychology, 31*, 328–337.

Diener, E., Fraser, S. C., Beaman, A. L., & Kelem, R. T. (1976). Effects of deindividuating variables on stealing by Halloween trick-or-treaters. *Journal of Personality and Social Psychology, 33*, 178–183.

Diener, E., Lusk, R., DeFour, D., & Flax, R. (1980). Deindividuation: Effects of group size, density, number of observers, and group member similarity on self-consciousness, and disinhibited behaviors. *Journal of Personality and Social Psychology, 39*, 449–459.

Diener, E. & Wallbom, M. C. (1976). Effects of self-awareness on antinormative behavior. *Journal of Research in Personality, 10*, 107–111.

DiNicola, D. D. & Di Matteo, M. R. (1982). *Achieving patient compliance: The psychology of the medical practitioner's role*. New York: Pergamon Press.

Dion, K. K. & Berscheid, E. (1972). *Physical attractiveness and social perception of peers in preschool children.* Unpublished manuscript.

Dion, K. K. & Berscheid, E. (1974). Physical attractiveness and peer perception among children. *Sociometry, 37,* 1–12.

Dion, K. K., Berscheid, E., & Walster, E. (1972). What is beautiful is good. *Journal of Personality and Social Psychology, 24,* 285–290.

DiRenzo, G. J. (1967). *Personality, power, and politics.* Notre Dame, IN: University of Indiana Press.

Dittes, J. E. & Kelley, H. H. (1956). Effects of different conditions of acceptance upon conformity to group norms. *Journal of Abnormal and Social Psychology, 53,* 100–107.

DiVasto, P. V., Kaufman, A., Rosner, L., Jackson, R., Christy, J., Pearson, S., & Burgett, T. (1984). The prevalence of sexually stressful events among females in the general population. *Archives of Sexual Behavior, 13,* 59–67.

Doherty, W. J., Schrott, H. G., Metcalf, L., & Iasiello-Vailas, L. (1983). Effects of spouse support and health beliefs on medication adherence. *Journal of Family Practice, 17,* 837–841.

Dohrenwend, B. S., Krasnoff, L., Askenasy, A. R., & Dohrenwend, B. P. (1978). Exemplification of a method for scaling life events: The PERI life events scale. *Journal of Health and Social Behavior, 19,* 205–229.

Dohrenwend, B. S., Krasnoff, L., Askenasy, A. R., & Dohrenwend, B. P. (1982). The psychiatric epidemiology research interview life events scale. In L. Goldberger & S. Breznitz (Eds.), *Handbook of stress: Theoretical and clinical aspects.* New York: Free Press.

Doll, R. & Peto, R. (1981). *The causes of cancer.* New York: Oxford University Press.

Dollard, J., Doob, J., Miller, N., Mowrer, O., & Sears, R. (1939). *Frustration and aggression.* New Haven, CT: Yale University Press.

Dominick, J. R. (1979). The portrayal of women in prime time, 1953–1977. *Sex Roles, 5,* 405–411.

Donnerstein, E. (1980). Aggressive erotica and violence against women. *Journal of Personality and Social Psychology, 39,* 269–277.

Donnerstein, E. (1984). Pornography: Its effect on violence against women. In N. M. Malamuth & E. Donnerstein (Eds.), *Pornography and sexual aggression.* Orlando, FL: Academic Press.

Donnerstein, E. & Berkowitz, L. (1981). Victims' reactions in aggressive erotic films as a factor in violence against women. *Journal of Personality and Social Psychology, 41,* 710–724.

Donnerstein, E. & Donnerstein, M. (1976). Research on the control of interracial aggression. In R. G. Geen & E. C. O'Neal (Eds.), *Perspectives on aggression.* New York: Academic Press.

Donnerstein, E., Donnerstein, M., & Evans, R. (1975). Erotic stimuli and aggression: Facilitation or inhibition. *Journal of Personality and Social Psychology, 32,* 237–244.

Doob, L. W. & Sears, R. R. (1939). Factors determining substitute behavior and the overt expression of aggression. *Journal of Abnormal and Social Psychology, 34,* 293–313.

Dornbusch, S. M., Hastorf, A. H., Richardson, S. A., Muzzy, R. E., & Vreeland, R. S. (1965). The perceiver and the perceived: Their relative influence on categories of interpersonal perception. *Journal of Personality and Social Psychology, 1,* 434–440.

Dorr, A. & Kovaric, P. (1980). Some of the people some of the time—But which people? Televised violence and its effects. In E. L. Palmer & A. Dorr (Eds.), *Children and the faces of television: Teaching, violence, and selling.* New York: Academic Press.

Dostoevsky, F. (1970). *The brothers Karamazov.* Toronto: Bantam Books. (Originally published 1880.)

Dovidio, J. F., Ellysen, S. L., Keating, C. F., Heltman, K., & Brown, C. E. (1988). The relationship of social power to visual displays of dominance between men and women. *Journal of Personality and Social Psychology, 54,* 233–242.

Dovidio, J. F., Evans, N., & Tyler, R. B. (1986). Racial stereotypes: The contents of their cognitive representations. *Journal of Experimental Social Psychology, 22,* 22–37.

Doyle, A. C. (1955). *A treasury of Sherlock Holmes.* New York: Doubleday.

Drachman, D., de Carufel, A., & Insko, C. A. (1978). The extra credit effect in interpersonal attraction. *Journal of Experimental Social Psychology, 14,* 458–465.

Dudycha, G. J. (1936). An objective study of punctuality in relation to personality and achievement. *Archives of Psychology, 204,* 1–319.

Duncan, B. L. (1976). Differential social perception and attribution of intergroup violence: Testing the lower limits of stereotyping of blacks. *Journal of Personality and Social Psychology, 34,* 590–598.

Dutton, D. G. & Aron, A. P. (1974). Some evidence for heightened sexual attraction under conditions of high anxiety. *Journal of Personality and Social Psychology, 30,* 510–517.

Duval, S. & Wicklund, R. A. (1972). *A theory of objective self-awareness.* New York: Academic Press.

Dworkin, A. (1987). *Intercourse.* New York: Free Press.

Dymond, R. (1949). A scale for the measurement of empathic ability. *Journal of Consulting Psychology, 13,* 127–133.

Dymond, R. (1950). Personality and empathy. *Journal of Consulting Psychology, 14,* 343–350.

Eagly, A. H. (1978). Sex differences in influencibility. *Psychological Bulletin, 85,* 86–116.

Eagly, A. H. (1987). *Sex differences in social behavior: A social role interpretation.* Hillsdale, NJ: Erlbaum.

Eagly, A. H. & Carli, L. L. (1981). Sex of researchers and sex-typed communications as determinants of sex differences in influence-ability: A meta-analysis of social influence studies. *Psychological Bulletin, 90,* 1–20.

Eagly, A. H. & Chaiken, S. (1984). Cognitive theories of persuasion. In L. Berkowitz (Ed.), *Advances in experimental social psychology* (Vol. 17). New York: Academic Press.

Eagly, A. H. & Chrvala, C. (1986). Sex differences in conformity: Status and gender-role interpretations. *Psychology of Women Quarterly, 10,* 203–220.

Eagly, A. H. & Crowley, M. (1986). Gender and helping behavior: A meta-analytic review of the social psychological literature. *Psychological Bulletin, 100,* 283–308.

Eagly, A. H. & Kite, M. E. (1987). Are stereotypes of nationalities applied to both women and men? *Journal of Personality and Social Psychology, 53,* 457–462.

Eagley, A. H. & Steffen, V. J. (1986a). Gender stereotypes, occupational roles, and beliefs about part-time employees. *Psychology of Women Quarterly, 10,* 252–262.

Eagly, A. H. & Steffen, V. J. (1986b). Gender and aggressive behavior: A meta-analytic review of the social psychological literature. *Psychological Bulletin, 100,* 309–330.

Eagly, A. H. & Warren, R. (1976). Intelligence, comprehension, and opinion change. *Journal of Personality, 44,* 226–242.

Eaton, W. O. & Enns, L. R. (1986). Sex differences in human motor activity level. *Psychological Bulletin, 100,* 19–28.

Ebbesen, E. G., Duncan, B., & Konecni, V. J. (1975). Effects of content of verbal aggression on future verbal aggression: A field experiment. *Journal of Experimental Social Psychology, 11,* 192–204.

Eccles (Parsons), J., Adler, T., & Meece, J. L. (1984). Sex differences in achievement: A test of alternate theories. *Journal of Personality and Social Psychology, 46,* 26–43.

Eder, R. A., Gerlach, S. G., & Perlmutter, M. (1987). In search of children's selves: Development of the specific and general components of the self-concept. *Child Development, 58,* 1044–1050.

Edney, J. H. (1979). The nuts game: A concise commons dilemma analog. *Environmental Psychology and Nonverbal Behavior, 3,* 252–254.

Edwards, V. J. & Spence, J. T. (1987). Gender-related traits, stereotypes, and schemata. *Journal of Personality and Social Psychology, 53,* 146–154.

Efran, M. G. (1974). The effect of physical appearance in the judgment of guilt, interpersonal attraction, and severity of recommended punishment. *Journal of Research in Personality, 8,* 45–54.

Ehrenreich, B. & English, D. (1979). *For her own good: 150 years of experts' advice to women.* Garden City, NY: Anchor/Doubleday.

Eibl-Eibesfeldt, I. (1979). *The biology of peace and war: Man, animals, and aggression.* New York: Viking Press.

Eidelson, R. J. (1980). Interpersonal satisfaction and level of involvement: A curvilinear relationship. *Journal of Personality and Social Psychology, 39,* 460–470.

Einhorn, H. J. & Hogarth, R. M. (1986). Judging probable cause. *Psychological Bulletin, 99,* 3–19.

Einsiedel, E. F. (1988). Uneasy bedfellows: Social science and pornography. *Journal of Communication, 38,* 107–121.

Eisenberg-Berg, N. (1979). Relationship of prosocial moral reasoning to altruism, political liberalism, and intelligence. *Developmental Psychology, 15,* 87–89.

Ekman, P. (1972). Universals and cultural differences in facial expressions of emotion. In J. Cole (Ed.), *Nebraska symposium on motivation* (Vol. 19). Lincoln: University of Nebraska Press.

Ekman, P. (1985). *Telling lies.* New York: Norton.

Ekman, P. & Friesen, W. V. (1969a). Nonverbal leakage and clues to deception. *Psychiatry, 32,* 88–106.

Ekman, P. & Friesen, W. V. (1969b). The repertoire of nonverbal behavior: Categories, origins, usage, and coding. *Semiotica, 1,* 124–129.

Ekman, P. & Friesen, W. V. (1971). Constants across cultures in the face and emotion. *Journal of Personality and Social Psychology, 17,* 124–129.

Ekman, P. & Friesen, W. V. (1974). Detecting deception from the body or face. *Journal of Personality and Social Psychology, 29,* 288–298.

Ekman, P. & Friesen, W. V. (1975). *Unmasking the face.* Englewood Cliffs, NJ: Prentice-Hall.

Ekman, P. & Friesen, W. V. (1982). Measuring facial movement with the Facial Action Coding System. In P. Ekman (Ed.), *Emotion in the human face.* Cambridge, England: Cambridge University Press.

Ekman, P., Friesen, W. V., & Ancoli, S. (1980). Facial signs of emotional experience. *Journal of Personality and Social Psychology, 39,* 1125–1134.

Ekman, P., Friesen, W. V., & Ellsworth, P. (1972). *Emotion in the human face.* New York: Pergamon Press.

Ekman, P., Friesen, W. V., & Ellsworth, P. (1982a). What are the similarities and differences in facial behavior across cultures? In P. Ekman (Ed.), *Emotion in the human face* (2nd ed.). Cambridge, England: Cambridge University Press.

Ekman, P., Friesen, W. V., & Ellsworth, P. (1982b). Does the face provide accurate information? In P. Ekman (Ed.), *Emotion in the human face* (2nd ed.). Cambridge, England: Cambridge University Press.

Ekman, P., Friesen, W. V., & O'Sullivan, M. (1988). Smiles when lying. *Journal of Personality and Social Psychology, 54,* 414–420.

Ekman, P., Friesen, W. V., O'Sullivan, M., Chan, A., Diacoyanni-Tarlatzis, I., Heider, K., Krause, R., LeCompte, W. A., Pitcairn, T., Ricci-Bitti, P. E., Scherer, K., Tomita, M., &

Tzavaras, A. (1987). Universals and cultural differences in the judgments of facial expressions of emotion. *Journal of Personality and Social Psychology, 53,* 712–717.

Ekman, P., Friesen, W. V., O'Sullivan, M., & Scherer, K. (1980). Relative importance of face, body, and speech in judgments of personality and affect. *Journal of Personality and Social Psychology, 38,* 270–277.

Ekman, P., Friesen, W. V., & Tompkins, S. S. (1971). Facial affect scoring technique (FAST): A first validity study. *Semiotica, 3,* 37–58.

Ekman, P., Hagar, J. C., & Friesen, W. V. (1981). The symmetry of emotion and deliberate facial action. *Psychophysiology, 18,* 101–106.

Elkin, R. A. & Leippe, M. R. (1986). Physiological arousal, dissonance, and attitude change: Evidence for a dissonance-arousal link and a "don't remind me" effect. *Journal of Personality and Social Psychology, 51,* 55–65.

Elliot, R. & Vasta, R. (1970). The modeling of sharing: Effects associated with vicarious reinforcement, symbolization, age, and generalization. *Journal of Experimental Child Psychology, 10,* 8–15.

Elliott, G. R. & Eisdorfer, C. (Eds.). (1982). *Stress and human health: Analysis and implications of research.* New York: Springer-Verlag.

Ellsworth, P. C. & Carlsmith, J. M. (1968). Effects of eye contact and verbal content on affective response to a dyadic interaction. *Journal of Personality and Social Psychology, 10,* 15–20.

Ellyson, S. L. & Dovidio, J. F. (1985). *Power, performance, and nonverbal behavior.* New York: Springer-Verlag.

Endler, N. S. (1981). Persons, situations, and their interactions. In A. I. Rabin (Ed.), *Further explorations in personality.* New York: Wiley.

Endler, N. S. (1983). Interactionism: A personality model, but not yet a theory. In M. M. Page (Ed.), *Personality—Current theory and research: Nebraska symposium on motivation 1982.*

Endler, N. S. & Hunt, J. McV. (1966). Sources of behavioral variance as measured by the S-R inventory of anxiousness. *Psychological Bulletin, 65,* 336–346.

Endler, N. S. & Hunt, J. McV. (1969). Generalizability of contributions from sources of variance in the S-R inventory of anxiousness. *Journal of Personality, 37,* 1–24.

Epstein, S. (1973). The self-concept revisited: Or a theory of a theory. *American Psychologist, 28,* 404–416.

Epstein, S. (1979). The stability of behavior: I. On predicting most of the people most of the time. *Journal of Personality and Social Psychology, 37,* 1097–1126.

Epstein S. (1980). The stability of behavior. II: Implications for psychological research. *American Psychologist, 35,* 790–806.

Epstein, S. (1983). A research paradigm for the study of personality and emotions. In M. M. Page (Ed.), *Personality—Current theory and research: Nebraska symposium on motivation 1982.*

Epstein, S. & O'Brien, E. J. (1985). The person-situation debate in historical and current perspective. *Psychological Bulletin, 98,* 513–537.

Epstein, Y. M. (1982). Crowding, stress, and human behavior. In G. W. Evans (Ed.), *Environmental stress.* Cambridge: Cambridge University Press.

Eron, L. D. (1987). The development of aggressive behavior from the perspective of a developing behaviorism. *American Psychologist, 42,* 435–442.

Eron, L. D. & Huesmann, L. R. (1986). The role of television in the development of prosocial and antisocial behavior. In D. Olweus, J. Block, & M. Radke-Yarrow (Eds.), *Development of antisocial and prosocial behavior: Research, theories, and issues.* Orlando, FL: Academic Press.

Exline, R. (1972). Visual interaction: The glances of power and preference. In J. Cole (Ed.), *Nebraska symposium on motivation, 1971.* Lincoln: University of Nebraska Press.

Eysenck, H. J. (1952). *The scientific study of personality.* London: Routledge & Kegan Paul.

Fagot, B. I. (1977). Consequences of moderate cross-gender behavior in pre-school children. *Child Development, 48,* 902–907.

Farina, A., Fischer, E., Sherman, S., Smith, W., Groh, T., & Nermin, P. (1977). Physical attractiveness and mental illness. *Journal of Abnormal Psychology, 86,* 510–517.

Farley, R., Schuman, H., Bianchi, S., Colasanto, D., & Hatchett, S. (1978). "Chocolate city, vanilla suburbs": Will the trend toward racially separate communities continue? *Social Science Research, 7,* 319–344.

Fausto-Sterling, A. (1985). *Myths of gender: Biological theories about women and men.* New York: Basic Books.

Fazio, R. H. (1987). Self-perception theory: A current perspective. In M. Zanna, J. M. Olson, & C. P. Herman (Eds.), *Social influence: The Ontario symposium* (Vol. 3). Hillsdale, NJ: Erlbaum.

Fazio, R. H., Chen, J., McDonel, E. C., & Sherman, S. J. (1982). Attitude accessibility, attitude-behavior consistency, and the strength of the object-evaluation association. *Journal of Experimental Social Psychology, 18,* 339–357.

Fazio, R. H. & Zanna, M. P. (1981). Direct experience and attitude-behavior consistency. In L. Berkowitz (Ed.), *Advances in experimental social psychology* (Vol. 14). New York: Academic Press.

Fazio, R. H., Zanna, M. P., & Cooper, J. (1977). Dissonance and self-perception: An integrative view of each theory's proper domain of application. *Journal of Experimental Social Psychology, 13,* 464–479.

Feather, N. T. (1982). *Expectations and actions: Expectancy-value models in psychology.* Hillsdale, NJ: Erlbaum.

Feierabend, I. & Feierabend, R. (1972). Systematic conditions of political aggression: An application of frustration-aggression theory. In I. K. Feierabend, R. L. Feierabend, & T. R.

Gurr (Eds.), *Anger, violence, and politics.* Englewood Cliffs, NJ: Prentice-Hall.

Feingold, A. (1988). Cognitive gender differences are disappearing. *American psychologist, 43,* 95–103.

Fellner, C. H. & Marshall, J. R. (1981). Kidney donors revisited. In J. P. Rushton & R. M. Sorrentino (Eds.), *Altruism and helping behavior: Social, personality, and developmental perspectives.* Hillsdale, NJ: Erlbaum.

Fenigstein, A., Scheier, M. R., & Buss, A. H. (1975). Public and private self-consciousness: Assessment and theory. *Journal of Consulting and Clinical Psychology, 43,* 522–527.

Ferguson, C. K. & Kelley, H. H. (1964). Significant factors in overevaluation of own-group's product. *Journal of Abnormal and Social Psychology, 69,* 223–228.

Feshbach, S. (1970). Aggression. In P. H. Mussen (Ed.), *Carmichael's manual of child psychology.* New York: Wiley.

Feshbach, S. (1984). The catharsis hypothesis, aggressive drive, and the reduction of aggression. *Aggressive Behavior, 10,* 91–101.

Festinger, L. (1954). A theory of social comparison processes. *Human Relations, 7,* 117–140.

Festinger, L. (1957). *A theory of cognitive dissonance.* Evanston, IL: Row, Peterson.

Festinger, L. & Carlsmith, J. M. (1959). Cognitive consequences of forced compliance. *Journal of Abnormal and Social Psychology, 58,* 203–210.

Festinger, L., Pepitone, A., & Newcomb, T. (1952). Some consequences of deindividuation in a group. *Journal of Abnormal and Social Psychology, 47,* 382–389.

Festinger, L., Rieken, H. W., & Schachter, S. (1956). *When prophecy fails.* Minneapolis: University of Minnesota Press.

Festinger, L., Schachter, S., & Back, K. (1950). *Social pressures in informal groups: A study of human factors in housing.* New York: Harper & Brothers.

Fiedler, F. E. (1978). Contingency model and the leadership process. In L. Berkowitz (Ed.), *Advances in experimental social psychology.* New York: Academic Press.

Fiedler, F. E. & Garcia, J. E. (1987). *Leadership: Cognitive resources and performance.* New York: Wiley.

Fishbein, M. (1963). An investigation of the relationship between beliefs about an object and the attitude towards that object. *Human Relations, 16,* 233–239.

Fishbein, M. (1966). *Sexual behavior and propositional control.* Paper presented at annual meeting of the Psychonomic Society.

Fishbein, M. & Ajzen, I. (1974). Attitudes towards objects as predictors of single and multiple behavioral criteria. *Psychological Review, 81,* 59–74.

Fishbein, M. & Ajzen, I. (1975). *Belief, attitude, intention and behavior: An introduction to theory and research.* Reading, MA: Addison-Wesley.

Fishbein, M. & Ajzen, I. (1980). Predicting and understanding consumer behavior: Attitude-behavior correspondence. In I. Ajzen & M. Fishbein (Eds.), *Understanding attitudes and predicting social behavior.* Englewood Cliffs, NJ: Prentice-Hall.

Fishbein, M., Ajzen, I., & McArdle, J. (1980). Changing the behavior of alcoholics: Effects of persuasive communication. In I. Ajzen & M. Fishbein (Eds.), *Understanding attitudes and predicting social behavior.* Englewood Cliffs, NJ: Prentice-Hall.

Fishbein, M., Jaccard, J. J., Davidson, A. B., Ajzen, I., & Loken, B. (1980). Predicting and understanding family planning behaviors: Beliefs, attitudes, and intentions. In I. Ajzen & M. Fishbein (Eds.), *Understanding attitudes and predicting social behavior.* Englewood Cliffs, NJ: Prentice-Hall.

Fisher, J. D., DePaulo, B. M., & Nadler, A. (1981). Extending altruism beyond the altruistic act: The mixed effects of aid on the recipient. In J. P. Rushton & R. M. Sorrentino (Eds.), *Altruism and helping behavior: Social, personality, and developmental perspectives.* Hillsdale, NJ: Erlbaum.

Fisher, J. D., Nadler, A., & Whitcher-Alagner, S. (1982). Recipient reactions to aid. *Psychological Bulletin, 91,* 27–54.

Fiske, S. T., Kinder, D. R., & Larter, W. M. (1983). The novice and expert: Knowledge based strategies in political cognition. *Journal of Experimental Social Psychology, 19,* 381–400.

Fiske, S. T. & Taylor, S. E. (1984). *Social cognition.* Reading, MA: Addison-Wesley.

Fletcher, G. J. O. (1983). The analysis of verbal explanations for marital separation: Implications for attribution theory. *Journal of Applied Social Psychology, 13,* 245–258.

Fletcher, G. J. O., Fincham, F. D., Cramer, L., & Heron, N. (1987). The role of attributions in the development of dating relationships. *Journal of Personality and Social Psychology, 53,* 481–489.

Foa, U. G. (1961). Convergences in the analysis of the structure in interpersonal behavior. *Psychological Review, 68,* 341–352.

Forsterling, F. (1985). Attributional retraining: A review. *Psychological Bulletin, 98,* 495–512.

Forsyth, D. R. (1983). *An introduction to group dynamics.* Monterey, CA: Brooks/Cole.

Frager, R. (1970). Conformity and anticonformity in Japan. *Journal of Personality and Social Psychology, 15,* 203–210.

Frank, L. K. (1957). Tactile communication. *Genetic Psychology Monographs, 56,* 209–255.

Franklin, B. J. (1975). Need, receipt or denial of aid, and attitudes toward the benefactor. *Journal of Social Psychology, 97,* 261–266.

Fredericks, A. J. & Dossett, D. L. (1983). Attitude-behavior relations: A comparison of the Fishbein-Ajzen and the Bentler-Speckart models. *Journal of Personality and Social Psychology, 45,* 501–512.

Freedman, J. L. (1984). Effect of television violence on aggressiveness. *Psychological Bulletin, 92,* 227–246.

Freedman, J. L. & Fraser, S. C. (1966). Compliance without pressure: The foot-in-the-door technique. *Journal of Personality and Social Psychology, 4,* 195–203.

French, J. R. P., Jr. & Raven, B. (1959). The bases of social power. In D. Cartwright (Ed.), *Studies in social power.* Ann Arbor, MI: Institute for Social Research.

Freud, S. (1922). *Group psychology and the analysis of the ego.* London: Hogarth Press.

Freud, S. (1953). Three essays on sexuality. In *The standard edition of the complete psychological works* (Vol. VII). London: Hogarth Press.

Freud, S. (1961a). *Civilization and its discontents.* New York: Norton. (Originally published 1930.)

Freud, S. (1961b). *The dissolution of the Oedipus complex* (Vol. 19, standard ed.). London: Hogarth Press. (Originally published 1924.)

Freud, S. (1961c). *Some psychical consequences of the anatomical distinction between the sexes* (Vol. 19, standard ed.). London: Hogarth Press. (Originally published 1925.)

Friedman, H. S. & Booth-Kewley, S. (1987a). Personality, Type A behavior, and coronary heart disease: The role of emotional expression. *Journal of Personality and Social Psychology, 53,* 783–792.

Friedman, H. S. & Booth-Kewley, S. (1987b). The "disease-prone personality": A meta-analytic view of the construct. *American Psychologist, 42,* 539–555.

Friedman, M. & Rosenman, R. H. (1959). Association of specific overt behavior pattern with blood and cardiovascular findings—blood cholesterol level, blood clotting time, incidence of arcus senilis and clinical coronary artery disease. *Journal of the American Medical Association, 169,* 1286–1296.

Friedman, M., Rosenman, R. H., Straus, R., Wurm, M., & Kositchek, R. (1968). The relationship of behavior pattern A to the state of the coronary vasculature: A study of fifty-one autopsy subjects. *American Journal of Medicine, 44,* 525–537.

Friedman, M. & Ulmer, D. (1984). *Treating type A behavior and your heart.* New York: Knopf.

Friedrich-Cofer, L. & Huston, A. C. (1986). Television violence and aggression: The debate continues. *Psychological Bulletin, 100,* 364–371.

Frodi, A. (1975). The effect of exposure to weapons on aggressive behavior from a cross-cultural perspective. *International Journal of Psychology, 10,* 283–292.

Funder D. C. (1987). Errors and mistakes: Evaluating the accuracy of social judgment. *Psychological Bulletin, 101,* 75–90.

Funder, D. C. & Harris, M. J. (1986). On the several facets of personality assessment: The case of social acuity. *Journal of Personality, 54,* 528–550.

Funk, S. C. & Houston, B. K. (1987). A critical analysis of the hardness scale's validity and utility. *Journal of Personality and Social Psychology, 53,* 572–578.

Gaebelein, J. W. (1973). Third-party instigation of aggression: An experimental approach. *Journal of Personality and Social Psychology, 27,* 389–395.

Gaertner, S. L. & Dovidio, J. F. (1977). The subtlety of white racism, arousal, and helping behavior. *Journal of Personality and Social Psychology, 35,* 691–707.

Gallup, G. G. (1977). Self-recognition in primates: A comparative approach to the bidirectional properties of consciousness. *American Psychologist, 32,* 329–338.

Gallup, G. G. & Suarez, S. D. (1986). Self-awareness and the emergence of mind in humans and other primates. In J. Suls & A. G. Greenwald (Eds.), *Psychological perspectives on the self* (Vol. 3). Hillsdale, NJ: Erlbaum.

Gamsom, W. A., Fireman, B., & Rytina, S. (1982). *Encounters with unjust authority.* Homewood, IL: Dorsey Press.

Ganellen, R. J. & Blaney, P. H. (1984). Hardiness and social support as moderators of the effects of life stress. *Journal of Personality and Social Psychology, 47,* 156–163.

Garvey, C. (1977). *Play.* Cambridge, MA: Harvard University Press.

Geen, R. G. (1968). Effects of frustration, attack, and prior training on aggressiveness upon aggressive behavior. *Journal of Personality and Social Psychology, 9,* 316–321.

Geen, R. G. & Quanty, M. B. (1977). The catharsis of aggression: An evaluation of a hypothesis. In L. Berkowitz (Ed.), *Advances in experimental social psychology* (Vol. 10). New York: Academic Press.

Geen, R. G., Rokosky, J. J., & Pigg, R. (1972). Awareness of arousal and its relation to aggression. *British Journal of Social and Clinical Psychology, 11,* 115–121.

Geen, R. G., Stonner, D., & Shope, G. L. (1975). The facilitation of aggression by aggression: Evidence against the catharsis hypothesis. *Journal of Personality and Social Psychology, 31,* 721–726.

Gelles, R. J. (1982). Domestic criminal violence. In M. E. Wolfgang & N. A. Weiner (Eds.), *Criminal violence.* Beverly Hills, CA: Sage.

Gelles, R. J. & Straus, M. A. (1979). Violence in the American family. *Journal of Social Issues, 35,* 15–39.

Gerard, H. B. (1983). School desegregation: The social science role. *American Psychologist, 38,* 869–877.

Gerard, H. B. & Mathewson, G. C. (1966). The effects of severity of initiation on liking for a group: A replication. *Journal of Experimental Social Psychology, 2,* 278–287.

Gerbner, G., Gross, L., Signorielli, N., & Morgan, M. (1980). Television violence, victimization, and power. *American Behavioral Scientist, 23,* 705–716.

Gerbner, G., Gross, L., Signorielli, N., & Morgan, M. (1986). *Television's mean world: Violence profile No. 14–15.* Philadelphia: University of Pennsylvania, Annenberg School of Communications.

Gergen, K. J. (1971). *The concept of self.* New York: Holt, Rinehart & Winston.

Gergen, K. J. (1973). Social psychology as history. *Journal of Personality and Social Psychology, 26,* 309–320.

Gergen, K. J. (1978). Experimentation in social psychology: A reappraisal. *European Journal of Social Psychology, 36,* 1344–1360.

Gergen, K. J. & Gergen, M. M. (1971). International assistance from a psychological perspective. In *The yearbook of international affairs* (Vol. 25). London: London Institute of World Affairs.

Gergen, K. J. & Gergen, M. M. (1983). Narratives of the self. In T. R. Sarbin & K. E. Scheive (Eds.), *Studies in social identity.* New York: Praeger.

Gergen, K. J. & Gergen, M. M. (1988). Narrative and the self as relationship. In L. Berkowitz (Ed.), *Advances in experimental social psychology* (Vol. 21). San Diego: Academic Press.

Gergen, K. J., Gergen, M. M., & Barton, W. H. (1973). Deviance in the dark. *Psychology Today, 10,* 129–130.

Gergen, K. J., Gergen, M. M., & Meter, K. (1972). Individual orientations to prosocial behavior. *Journal of Social Issues, 8,* 105–130.

Gesell, A. L., Halverson, H. M., & Amatruda, C. (1940). *The first five years of life: A guide to the study of the preschool child.* New York: Harper.

Gibb, C. A. (1968). Leadership. In G. Lindzey & E. Aronson (Eds.), *Handbook of social psychology* (2nd ed., Vol. 4). Reading, MA: Addison-Wesley.

Gibbons, F. X. (1978). Sexual standards and reactions to pornography: Enhancing behavioral consistency through self-focused attention. *Journal of Personality and Social Psychology, 36,* 976–987.

Gibbons, F. X. & Kassin, S. M. (1987). Information consistency and perceptual set: Overcoming the mental retardation "schema." *Journal of Applied Social Psychology, 17,* 810–827.

Gill, J. J., Price, V. A., Friedman, M., Thoresen, C. E., Powell, L. H., Ulmer, D., Brown, B., & Drews, F. R. (1985). Reduction of type A behavior in healthy middle-aged American military officers. *American Heart Journal, 110,* 503–514.

Gillis, J. S. & Avis, W. E. (1980). The male-taller norm in mate selection. *Personality and Social Psychology Bulletin, 6,* 396–401.

Gilmore, R. & Duck, S. (1980). *The development of social psychology.* London: Academic Press.

Ginosar, Z. & Trope, Y. (1980). The effects of base rates and individuating information on judgments about another person. *Journal of Experimental Social Psychology, 16,* 228–242.

Gintner, G. & Lindskold, S. (1975). Rate of participation and expertise as factors influencing leader choice. *Journal of Personality and Social Psychology, 32,* 1085–1089.

Glass, D. (1964). Changes in liking as a means of reducing cognitive discrepancies between self-esteem and aggression. *Journal of Personality, 32,* 531–549.

Glass, D. C., Ross, D. T., Isecke, W., & Rosenman, R. H. (1982). Relative importance of speech characteristics and content of answers in the assessment of behavior pattern A by the structured interview. *Basic and Applied Social Psychology, 3,* 161–168.

Glass, D. C. & Singer, J. E. (1972). *Urban stress: Experiments on noise and social stressors.* New York: Academic Press.

Glass, G. V., McGraw, B., & Smith, M. L. (1981). Meta-analysis in social research. Beverly Hills, CA: Sage.

Glick, P., Zion, C., & Nelson, C. (1988). What mediates sex discrimination in hiring? *Journal of Personality and Social Psychology, 55,* 178–186.

Goethals, G. P. & Zanna, M. P. (1979). The role of social comparison in choice shifts. *Journal of Personality and Social Psychology, 37,* 1469–1476.

Goffman, E. (1959). *The presentation of self in everyday life.* Garden City, NY: Doubleday (Anchor Books).

Goffman, E. (1963). *Stigma: Notes on the management of spoiled identity.* Englewood Cliffs, NJ: Prentice-Hall.

Goffman, E. (1967). *Interaction ritual.* Garden City, NY: Doubleday.

Goldberg, L. R. (1978). Differential attribution of trait-descriptive terms to oneself as compared to well-liked, neutral, and disliked others: A psychometric analysis. *Journal of Personality and Social Psychology, 36,* 1012–1028.

Goldberg, L. R. (1981). Language and individual differences: The search for universals and personality lexicons. In L. Wheeler (Ed.), *Review of personality and social psychology* (Vol. 2). Beverly Hills, CA: Sage.

Goldberg, P. (1968). Are women prejudicial against women? *Transaction, 5,* 28–30.

Golding, W. (1954). *Lord of the Flies.* New York: Wideview/Perigee.

Goldman, M. & Fraas, L. A. (1965). The effects of leader selection on group performance. *Sociometry, 28,* 82–88.

Goldmeier, D. & Johnson, A. (1982). Does psychiatric illness affect the recurrence rate of genital herpes? *British Journal of Venereal Diseases, 58,* 40–43.

Goldstein, A. P. & Keller, H. R. (1983). Aggression prevention and control: Multitargeted, multichannel, multiprocess, multidisciplinary. In *Prevention and control of aggression.* New York: Pergamon Press.

Goldstein, A. P., Spratfkin, R. P., & Gershaw, N. J. (1976). *Skill training for community living.* New York: Pergamon Press.

Goldstein, D. (1983). Spouse abuse. In *Prevention and control of aggression.* New York: Pergamon Press.

Goodall, J. (1971). *In the shadow of man.* Boston: Houghton Mifflin.

Gordon, C. (1968). Self-conceptions: Configurations of content. In C. Gordon & K. J. Gergen (Eds.), *The self in social interaction* (Vol. 1). New York: Wiley.

Gorn, G. G. & Goldberg, M. E. (1980). Children's responses to repetitive TV commercials. *Journal of Consumer Research, 6*, 421–424.

Gorn, G. J., Goldberg, M. E., & Kanungo, R. N. (1976). The role of educational television in changing the intergroup attitudes of children. *Child Development, 47*, 277–280.

Gorsuch, R. L. & Aleshire, D. (1974). Christian faith and ethnic prejudice: A review and interpretation of research. *Journal for the Scientific Study of Religion, 13*, 281–307.

Gorsuch, R. L. & Key, M. K. (1974). Abnormalities of pregnancy as a function of anxiety and life stress. *Psychosomatic Medicine, 36*, 352.

Gottman, J. M. (1979). *Marital interaction: Experimental investigations.* New York: Academic Press.

Gough, H. G. (1964). *California psychological inventory: Manual.* Palo Alto, CA: Consulting Psychologists Press.

Gouldner, A. W. (1960). The norm of reciprocity: A preliminary statement. *American Sociological Review, 25*, 161–178.

Gourash, N. (1978). Help-seeking: A review of the literature. *American Journal of Community Psychology, 6*, 413–424.

Graesser, A., Woll, S. B., Kowalski, D. J., & Smith, D. A. (1980). Memory for typical and atypical actions in scripted activities. *Journal of Experimental Psychology: Human Learning and Memory, 6*, 503–515.

Graves, S. B. (1980). Psychological effects of black portrayals on television. In S. B. Withey & R. P. Abeles (Eds.), *Television and social behavior: Beyond violence and television.* Hillsdale, NJ: Erlbaum.

Greenberg, J., Pyszczynski, T., & Solomon, S. (1982). The self-serving attributional bias: Beyond self-presentation. *Journal of Experimental Social Psychology, 18*, 56–67.

Greenburg, J. & Pyszczynski, T. (1985). The effect of an overheard ethnic slur on evaluations of the target: How to spread a social disease. *Journal of Experimental Social Psychology, 21*, 61–72.

Greenwald, A. G. (1968). Cognitive learning, cognitive responses to persuasion, and attitude change. In A. G. Greenwald, T. C. Brock, & T. M. Ostrom (Eds.), *Psychological foundation of attitudes.* New York: Academic Press.

Greenwald, A. G. (1980). The totalitarian ego: Fabrication and revision of personal history. *American Psychologist, 35*, 602–618.

Greenwald, A. G. (1982). Is anyone in charge? Personalysis versus the principle of personal unity. In J. Suls (Ed.), *Psychological perspective on the self* (Vol. 1). Hillsdale, NJ: Erlbaum.

Griffit, W. & Veitch, R. (1971). Hot and crowded: Influences of population density and temperature on interpersonal affective behavior. *Journal of Personality and Social Psychology, 17*, 92–98.

Gross, A. E. & Fleming, I. (1982). Twenty years of deception in social psychology. *Personality and Social Psychology Bulletin, 8*, 107–112.

Gross, A. E., Wallson, B. S., & Piliavin, I. (1979). Reactance attribution, equity and the help recipient. *Journal of Applied Social Psychology, 9*, 297–313.

Groth, A. N. & Birnbaum, H. J. (1979). *Men who rape: The psychology of the offender.* New York: Plenum.

Gruder, C. L., Cook, T. D., Hennigan, K. M., Flay, B. R., Alessis, C., & Halamaj, J. (1978). Empirical tests of the absolute sleeper effect predicted from the discounting cue hypothesis. *Journal of Personality and Social Psychology, 36*, 1061–1074.

Guerin, B. (1986). Mere presence effects on humans: A review. *Journal of Personality and Social Psychology, 22*, 38–77.

Guttentag, M. & Secord, P. F. (1983). *Too many women? The sex ratio question.* Beverly Hills, CA: Sage.

Hall, E. (1984, December). A sense of control. *Psychology Today*, 38–45.

Hall, E. T. (1966). *The hidden dimension.* New York: Doubleday.

Hall, J. A. (1984). *Nonverbal sex differences: Communication accuracy and expressive style.* Baltimore: Johns Hopkins University Press.

Halleck, S. L. (1971). *The politics of therapy.* New York: Harper.

Halpern, D. F. (1986). *Sex differences in cognitive abilities.* Hillsdale, NJ: Erlbaum.

Halpin, A. W. & Winer, B. J. (1952). *The leadership behavior of the airplane commander.* Columbus: Ohio State University Research Foundation.

Hamill, R., Wilson, T. D., & Nisbett, R. E. (1980). Insensitivity to sample bias: Generalizing from atypical cases. *Journal of Personality and Social Psychology, 39*, 578–589.

Hamilton, D. L. (1981). Stereotyping and intergroup behavior: Some thoughts on the cognitive approach. *Cognitive processes in stereotyping and intergroup behavior.* Hillsdale, NJ: Erlbaum.

Hamilton, D. L., & Bishop, G. D. (1976). Attitudinal and behavioral effects of initial integration of white suburban neighborhoods. *Journal of Social Issues, 32*, 47–67.

Hamilton, D. L., Carpenter, S., & Bishop, G. D. (1984). Desegregation of suburban neighborhoods. In N. Miller & M. B. Brewer (Eds.), *Groups in contact: The psychology of desegregation.* New York: Academic Press.

Hamilton, D. L. & Gifford, R. K. (1976). Illusory correlation in interpersonal perception: A cognitive basis of stereotypic judgments. *Journal of Experimental Social Psychology, 12*, 392–407.

Hamilton, W. D. (1964). The genetical evolution of social behavior. *Journal of Theoretical Biology, 7*, 1–52.

Hanratty, M. A., O'Neil, E., & Sulzer, J. L. (1972). The effect of frustration upon imitation of aggression. *Journal of Personality and Social Psychology, 21*, 30–34.

Hanseli, S., Sparacino, J., & Ronchi, D. (1982). Physical attractiveness and blood pressure: Sex and age differences. *Personality and Social Psychology Bulletin, 8*, 113–121.

Hardin, G. (1968). The tragedy of the commons. *Science, 162*, 1243–1248.

Harding, J., Proshansky, H., Kutner, B., & Chein, J. (1969). Prejudice and ethnic relations. In G. Lindzey & E. Aronson (Eds.), *Handbook of social psychology* (Vol. 5). Reading, MA: Addison-Wesley.

Hare-Musten, R. T. (1983). An appraisal of the relationship between women and psychotherapy: 80 years after the case of Dora. *American Psychologist, 38*, 593–601.

Hare-Musten, R. T. & Marecek, J. (1988). The meaning of difference: Gender theory, post modernism, and psychology. *American Psychologist, 43*, 455–464.

Harkins, S. G. (1987). Social loafing and social facilitation. *Journal of Personality and Social Psychology, 23*, 1–18.

Harkins, S. G. & Szymanski, K. (1987). Social loafing and social facilitation: New wine in old bottles. In C. Hendrick (Ed.), *Group processes and intergroup relations: Review of personality and social psychology* (Vol. 9), Newbury Park, CA: Sage.

Harlow, H. F. (1932). Social facilitation of feeding in the albino rat. *Journal of Genetic Psychology, 41*, 211–221.

Harries, K. D. & Stadler, S. J. (1988). Heat and violence: New findings from Dallas field data, 1980–1981. *Journal of Applied Social Psychology, 18*, 129–138.

Harris, M. B., Benson, S. M., & Hall, C. L. (1975). The effects of confession on altruism. *Journal of Social Psychology, 96*, 187–192.

Harrison, W., Thompson, V. D., & Rodgers, J. L. (1985). Robustness and sufficiency of the theory of reasoned action in longitudinal prediction. *Basic and Applied Social Psychology, 6*, 25–40.

Hart, D. & Damon, W. (1986). Developmental trends in self-understanding. *Social Cognition, 4*, 388–407.

Hartshorne, H. & May, M. A. (1928). *Studies in the nature of character* (Vol. I), *Studies in deceit.* New York: Macmillan.

Hartshorne, H. & May, M. A. (1929). *Studies in the nature of character* (Vol. II), *Studies in service and self-control.* New York: Macmillan.

Hartshorne, H., May, M. A., & Shuttleworth, F. K. (1930). *Studies in the nature of character* (Vol. III), *Studies in the organization of character.* New York: Macmillan.

Harvey, J. H. & Consalvi, C. (1960). Status and conformity to pressure in informal groups. *Journal of Abnormal and Social Psychology, 60*, 182–187.

Hastie, R. (1981). Schematic principles in human memory. In E. T. Higgins, C. Herman, & M. Zanna (Eds.), *Social cognition: The Ontario symposium on personality and social psychology.* (Vol. 1). Hillsdale, NJ: Erlbaum.

Hatfield, E. & Sprecher, S. (1986). *Mirror, mirror . . . The importance of looks in everyday life.* Albany, NY: University of New York Press.

Hatfield, E., Traupman, J., & Walster, G. W. (1978). Equity and extramarital sexuality. *Archives of Sexual Behavior, 7,* 127–142.

Hatfield, E., Utne, M. K., & Traupman, J. (1979). Equity theory and intimate relationships. In R. L. Burgess & T. L. Huston (Eds.), *Social exchange in developing relationships.* New York: Academic Press.

Hatfield, E., Walster, G. W., & Berscheid, E. (1978). *Equity: Theory and research.* Boston: Allyn & Bacon.

Hatfield, E., Walster, G. W., & Traupman, J. (1978). Equity and premarital sex. *Journal of Personality and Social Psychology, 37,* 82–92.

Hathaway, S. R. & McKinley, J. C. (1943). *The Minnesota multiphasic personality inventory.* New York: Psychological Corporation.

Haynes, S. G., Feinleib, M., & Eaker, E. D. (1983). Type A behavior and the ten-year incidence of coronary heart disease in the Framingham heart study. In R. H. Rosenman (Ed.), *Psychosomatic risk factors and coronary heart disease.* Berne, Switzerland: Huber.

Hays, R. B. (1985). A longitudinal study of friendship development. *Journal of Personality and Social Psychology, 48,* 909–924.

Hearold, S. (1986). *A synthesis of 1043 effects of television on social behavior.* In G. Comstock (Ed.), *Public communications and behavior* (Vol. 1). New York: Academic Press.

Heider, F. (1946). Attitudes and cognitive organization. *Journal of Psychology, 21,* 107–112.

Heider, F. (1958). *The psychology of interpersonal relations.* New York: Wiley.

Heilbrun, A. B. (1976). Measurement of masculine and feminine sex role identities as independent dimensions. *Journal of Consulting and Clinical Psychology, 44,* 183–190.

Heiss, J. (1986). Family roles and behavior. In F. A. Boudreau, R. S. Sennott, & M. Wilson (Eds.), *Sex roles and social patterns.* New York: Praeger.

Helmreich, R. L. (1975). Applied social psychology: The unfulfilled promise. *Personality and Social Psychology Bulletin, 1,* 548–560.

Helmreich, R. L. & Collins, B. E. (1967). Situational determinants of affiliative preference under stress. *Journal of Personality and Social Psychology, 6,* 79–85.

Hendrick, C. & Hendrick, S. (1986). A theory and method of love. *Journal of Personality and Social Psychology, 50,* 392–402.

Hendrick, C., Hendrick, S., & Adler, N. L. (1988). Romantic relationships: Love, satisfaction, and staying together. *Journal of Personality and Social Psychology, 54,* 980–988.

Henley, N. M. (1977). *Body politics: Power, sex, and nonverbal communication.* Englewood Cliffs, NJ: Prentice-Hall.

Hennigan, K. M., Del Rosario, M. L., Heath, L., Cook, T. D., Wharton, J. D., & Calder, B. J. (1982). Impact of television on crime in the United States: Empirical findings and theoretical implications. *Journal of Personality and Social Psychology, 42,* 461–477.

Henninger, M. & Wyer, R. S. (1976). The recognition and elimination of inconsistencies among syllogistically related beliefs: Some new light on the "Socratic effect." *Journal of Personality and Social Psychology, 34,* 680–693.

Hepworth, J. T. & West, S. G. (1988). Lynchings and the economy: A time-series reanalysis of Hovland and Sears (1940). *Journal of Personality and Social Psychology, 55,* 239–247.

Herek, G. M. (1986). The instrumentality of attitudes: Toward a neofunctional theory. *Journal of Social Issues, 42,* 99–114.

Herek, G. M. (1987). Can functions be measured? A new perspective on the functional approach to attitudes. *Social Psychology Quarterly, 50,* 285–303.

Herek, G. M. & Glunt, E. K. (1988). An epidemic of stigma: Public reaction to AIDS. *American Psychologist, 43,* 886–891.

Hess, E. H. (1975). *The tell-tale eye.* Cincinnati: Van Nostrand.

Hesse, Hermann (1963). *Steppenwolf.* New York: Holt, Rinehart & Winston. (Originally published 1929.)

Hicks, D. J. (1965). Imitation and retention of film-mediated aggressive peer and adult models. *Journal of Personality and Social Psychology, 2,* 97–100.

Hicks, D. J. (1968). Short- and long-term retention of affectively varied modeled behavior. *Psychonomic Science, 11,* 369–370.

Higbee, K. L., Millard, R. J., & Folkman, J. R. (1982). Social psychology research during the 1970's: Predominance of experimentation and college students. *Personality and Social Psychology Bulletin, 8,* 180–183.

Higgins, E. T. (1987). Self-discrepancy: A theory relating self and affect. *Psychological Review, 94,* 319–340.

Higgins, E. T. & King, G. A. (1981). Accessibility of social constructs: Information-processing consequences of individual and contextual variability. In N. Cantor & J. F. Kihlstrom (Eds.), *Personality, cognition, and social interaction.* Hillsdale, NJ: Erlbaum.

Higgins, E. T., Klein, R., & Strauman, T. (1985). Self-concept discrepancy theory: A psychological model for distinguishing among different aspects of depression and anxiety. *Social Cognition, 3,* 51–76.

Higgins, E. T., Rhodewalt, F., & Zanna, M. P. (1979). Dissonance reduction: Its nature, persistence, and reinstatement. *Journal of Experimental Social Psychology, 5,* 16–34.

Higgins, E. T., Rholes, W. S., & Jones, C. R. (1977). Category accessibility and impression formation. *Journal of Experimental Social Psychology, 13,* 141–154.

Hilberman, E. (1980). Overview: The "wife-beater's wife" reconsidered. *American Journal of Psychiatry, 137,* 1336–1346.

Hilgard, E. R. (1980). The trilogy of mind: Cognition, affection, and conation. *Journal of the History of Behavioral Science. 16,* 107–117.

Hill, C. H. (1987). Affiliation motivation: People who need people . . . but in different ways.

Journal of Personality and Social Psychology, 52, 1008–1018.

Hill, C., Rubin, Z., & Peplau, L. A. (1976). Breakups before marriage: The end of 103 affairs. *Journal of Social Issues, 32,* 147–167.

Hill, G. W. (1982). Group versus individual performance: Are N + 1 heads better than one? *Psychological Bulletin, 91,* 517–539.

Hill, R. (1945). Campus values in mate selection. *Journal of Home Economics, 37.*

Hiroto, D. S. & Seligman, M. E. P. (1975). Generality of learned helplessness in man. *Journal of Personality and Social Psychology, 31,* 311–327.

Hitler, A. (1962). *Mein Kampf.* Boston: Houghton Mifflin. (Originally published 1925.)

Hoch, S. J. (1987). Perceived consensus and predictive accuracy: The pros and cons of projection. *The Journal of Personality and Social Psychology, 53,* 221–234.

Hoffman, L. W. (1972). Early childhood experiences and women's achievement motives. *Journal of Social Issues, 28,* 157–176.

Hoffman, M. L. (1976). Empathy, role taking, guilt, and the development of altruistic motives. In T. Lickona (Ed.), *Moral development and behavior.* New York: Holt, Rinehart & Winston.

Hoffman, S. A. (1988, February). The doctor as dramatist. *Newsweek,* 10.

Hofling, C. K., Brotzman, E., Dalrymple, S., Graves, N., & Pierce, C. (1966). An experimental study of nurse-physician relations. *Journal of Nervous and Mental Disease, 143,* 171–180.

Hogan, R. (1983). A socioanalytic theory of personality. In M. M. Page (Ed.), *Personality—Current theory and research: Nebraska symposium on motivation 1982.*

Hokanson, J. E. (1961). The effects of frustration and anxiety on overt aggression. *Journal of Abnormal and Social Psychology, 62,* 346–351.

Hokanson, J. E. & Burgess, M. M. (1962). The effects of status, type of frustration, and aggression on vascular processes. *Journal of Abnormal and Social Psychology, 65,* 232–237.

Hokanson, J. E. & Shetler, S. (1961). The effect of overt aggression on physiological arousal. *Journal of Abnormal and Social Psychology, 63,* 446–448.

Hollander, E. P. (1958). Conformity, status, and idiosyncratic credits. *Psychological review, 65,* 117–127.

Hollander, E. P. (1985). Leadership and power. In G. Lindzey & E. Aronson (Eds.), *Handbook of social psychology* (Vol. II). New York: Random House.

Hollenbeck, A. R. & Slaby, R. G. (1979). Infant visual and vocal responses to television. *Child Development, 50,* 41–42.

Holloway, S., Tucker, L., & Hornstein, H. A. (1977). The effects of social and nonsocial information on interpersonal behavior of males: The news makes news. *Journal of Personality and Social Psychology, 35,* 514–522.

Holmes, T. H. & Rahe, R. H. (1967). The social readjustment rating scale. *Journal of Psychosomatic Research, 11,* 213–218.

Homans, G. C. (1950). *The human group.* New York: Harcourt, Brace & World.

Homans, G. C. (1961). *Social behavior: Its elementary forms.* New York: Harcourt, Brace & World.

Homans, G. C. (1974). *Social behavior: Its elementary forms* (rev. ed.). New York: Harcourt Brace Jovanovich.

Horney, K. (1973). On the genesis of the castration complex in women. In J. B. Miller (Ed.), *Psychoanalysis and women.* New York: Brunner/Mazel.

Hornstein, H. A. (1975). Social psychology as social intervention. In M. Deutsch & H. A. Hornstein (Eds.), *Applying social psychology: Implication for research, practice, and training.* Hillsdale, NJ: Erlbaum.

Hornstein, H. A., Lakind, E., Frankel, G., & Manne, S. (1975). Effects of knowledge about remote social events on prosocial behavior, social conception, and mood. *Journal of Personality and Social Psychology, 32,* 1038–1046.

Hornstein, H. A., Masor, H. N., Sole, K., & Keilman, M. (1971). Effects of sentiment and completion of a helping act on observer helping: A case for socially mediated Ziegarnik effects. *Journal of Personality and Social Psychology, 17,* 107–112.

House, J., Robbins, C., & Metzner, H. (1982). The association of social relationships and activities with mortality: Prospective evidence from the Tecumseh community health study. *American Journal of Epidemiology, 116,* 123–140.

House, J. S. & Kahn, R. L. (1985). Measures and concepts of social support. In S. Cohen & S. L. Syme (Eds.), *Social support and health.* Orlando, FL: Academic Press.

Hovland, C. I., Janis, I. L., & Kelley, H. H. (1953). *Communication and persuasion.* New Haven, CT: Yale University Press.

Hovland, C. I., Lumsdaine, A. A., & Sheffield, F. D. (1949). *Studies in social psychology in World War II* (Vol. 3), *Experiments on mass communications.* Princeton, NJ: Princeton University Press.

Hovland, C. I. & Sears, R. R. (1940). Minor studies in aggression: VI. Correlation of lynchings with economic indices. *Journal of Personality, 9,* 301–310.

Hovland, C. I. & Weiss, W. (1951). The influences of source credibility on communication effectiveness. *Public Opinion Quarterly, 15,* 635–650.

Howard, J. & Rothbart M. (1980). Social categorization and memory for in-group and out-group behavior. *Journal of Personality and Social Psychology, 38,* 301–310.

Hudson, J. W. & Henze, L. F. (1969). Campus values in mate selection: A replication. *Journal of Marriage and the Family, 31,* 772–775.

Hudson, J. W. & Hoyt, L. L. (1981). Personal

characteristics important in mate preference among college students. *Social Behavior and Personality, 9,* 93–96.

Huesmann, L. R. (1986). Psychological processes promoting the relation between exposure to media violence and aggressive behavior by the viewer. *Journal of Social Issues, 42,* 125–139.

Huesmann, L. R., Eron, L. D., Klein, R., Brice, P., & Fischer, P. (1983). Mitigating the imitation of aggressive behaviors by changing children's attitudes about media violence. *Journal of Personality and Social Psychology, 44,* 899–910.

Huesmann, L. R., Eron, L. D., Lefkowitz, M. M., & Walder, L. O. (1984). The stability of aggression over time and generations. *Developmental Psychology, 20* 1120–1134.

Huesmann, L. R., Lagerspetz, K., & Eron, L. D. (1984). Intervening variables in the TV violence-aggression relations: Evidence from two countries. *Developmental Psychology, 20,* 746–775.

Hull, C. L. (1943). *Principles of behavior.* New York: Appleton-Century-Crofts.

Hull, J. G. (1981). A self-awareness model of the causes and effects of alcohol consumption. *Journal of Abnormal Psychology, 90,* 586–600.

Hull, J. G., Van Treuren, R. R., & Virnelli, S. (1987). Hardiness and health: A critique and alternative approach. *Journal of Personality and Social Psychology, 53,* 518–530.

Hull, J. G., Young, D. Y., & Jouriles, E. (1986). Applications of the self-awareness model of alcohol consumption: Predicting patterns of use and abuse. *Journal of Personality and Social Psychology, 51,* 760–796.

Hunt, M. (1959). *The natural history of love.* New York: Knopf.

Hunt, P. J. & Hillery, J. M. (1973). Social facilitation in a location setting: An examination of the effects over learning trials. *Journal of Personality and Social Psychology, 9,* 563–571.

Husband, R. W. (1931). Analysis of methods in human maze learning. *Journal of Genetic Psychology, 39,* 258–277.

Huston, T. L. & Burgess, R. L. (1979). Social exchange in developing relationships: An overview. In R. L. Burgess & T. L. Huston (Eds.), *Social exchange in developing relationships.* New York: Academic Press.

Huston, T. L. & Levinger, G. (1978). Interpersonal attraction and relationships. *Annual Review of Psychology, 29,* 115–156.

Hutchinson, R. R. (1972). The environmental causes of aggression. In J. K. Cole & D. D. Jensen (Eds.), *Nebraska symposium on motivation.* Lincoln: University of Nebraska Press.

Hutchinson, R. R. (1983). The pain-aggression relationship and its expression in naturalistic settings. *Aggressive Behavior, 9,* 229–242.

Hyde, J. S. (1981). How large are cognitive gender differences? A meta-analysis using ω^2 and d. *American Psychologist, 36,* 892–901.

Hyde, J. S. (1986). Gender differences in aggression. In J. S. Hyde & M. C. Linn (Eds.), *The psychology of gender: Advances through meta-*

analysis. Baltimore: Johns Hopkins University Press.

Hyde, J. S. & Linn, M. C. (1988). Gender differences in verbal ability: A meta-analysis. *Psychological Bulletin, 104,* 53–69.

Hyman, H. H. & Sheatsley, P. B. (1954). "The authoritarian personality" — A methodological critique. In R. Christie & M. Jahoda (Eds.), *Studies in the scope and method of "the authoritarian personality."* New York: Free Press.

Ingram, R. E. & Smith, T. S. (1984). Depression and internal versus external locus of attention. *Cognitive Therapy and Research, 8,* 139–152.

Insko, C. A. (1965). Verbal reinforcement of attitude. *Journal of Personality and Social Psychology, 21,* 621–623.

Insko, C. A., Drenan, S., Solomon, M. R., Smith, R., & Wade, T. J. (1983). Conformity as a function of the consistency of positive self-evaluation with being liked and being right. *Journal of Experimental Social Psychology, 19,* 341–358.

Insko, C. A. & Schopler, J. (1987). Categorization, competition, and collectivity. In C. Hendrick (Ed.), *Group processes: Review of personality and social psychology* (Vol. 8). Newbury Park, CA: Sage.

Insko, C. A., Smith, R. H., Alicke, M. D., Wade, J., & Taylor, S. (1985). Conformity and group size: The concern with being right and the concern with being liked. *Personality and Social Psychology Bulletin, 11,* 41–50.

Isen, A. M. (1970). Success, failure, attention and reaction to others: The warm glow of success. *Journal of Personality and Social Psychology, 15,* 294–301.

Isen, A. M. (1987). Positive affect, cognitive processes, and social behavior. In L. Berkowitz (Ed.), *Advances in experimental social psychology* (Vol. 20). San Diego: Academic Press.

Isen, A. M., Clark, M., & Schwartz, M. (1976). Duration of the effect of mood on helping: "Footprints on the sands of time." *Journal of Personality and Social Psychology, 34,* 385–393.

Isen, A. M., Horn, N., & Rosenhan, D. L. (1973). Effects of success and failure on children's generosity. *Journal of Personality and Social Psychology, 27,* 239–247.

Isen, A. M. & Levin, P. F. (1972). Effect of feeling good on helping: Cookies and kindness. *Journal of Personality and Social Psychology, 21,* 384–388.

Isenberg, D. J. (1986). Group polarization: A critical review and meta-analysis. *Journal of Personality and Social Psychology, 50,* 1141–1151.

Isozaki, M. (1984). The effect of discussion on polarization of judgments. *Japanese Psychological Research, 26,* 187–193.

Izard, C. E. (1969). The emotions and emotion constructs in personality and culture research. In R. B. Cattell (Ed.), *Handbook of modern personality theory.* Chicago: Aldine.

Jaccard, J. J. (1974). Predicting social behavior from personality traits. *Journal of Research in Personality, 7,* 358–367.

Jackson, J. & Harkins, S. (1985). Equity in effort: An explanation of the social loafing effects. *Journal of Personality and Social Psychology, 49,* 1119–1206.

Jackson, J. & Williams, K. (1985). Social loafing on difficult tasks: Working collectively can improve performance. *Journal of Personality and Social Psychology, 49,* 937–942.

Jacobs, R. C. & Campbell, D. T. (1961). The perpetuation of an arbitrary tradition through several generations of a laboratory microculture. *Journal of Abnormal and Social Psychology, 62,* 649–658.

Jaffe, D. T. & Kanter, R. M. (1976). Couple strains in communal households: A four-factor model of the separation process. *Journal of Social Issues, 32,* 169–191.

James, William (1890). *The principles of psychology* (Vols. 1 and 2). New York: Henry Holt & Co.

Jamieson, D. W., Lydon, J. E., & Zanna, M. P. (1987). Attitude and activity preference similarity: Differential bases of interpersonal attraction for low and high self-monitors. *Journal of Personality and Social Psychology, 53,* 1052, 1060.

Janis, I. L. (1972). *Victims of groupthink.* Boston: Houghton Mifflin.

Janis, I. L. (1985). Sources of error in strategic decision making. In J. M. Pennings (Ed.), *Organizational strategy and change.* San Francisco: Jossey-Bass.

Janis, I. L. & Feshbach, S. (1953). Effects of fear-arousing communications. *Journal of Abnormal and Social Psychology, 48,* 78–92.

Janis, I. L., Kaye, D., & Kirschner, P. (1965). Facilitating effects of "eating-while-reading" on responsiveness to persuasive communications. *Journal of Personality and Social Psychology, 1,* 181–186.

Janis, I. L. & Rodin, J. (1979). Attribution, control, and decision making: Social psychology and health care. In *Health psychology—A handbook.* San Francisco: Jossey-Bass.

Jemmott, J. B., III & Magloire, K. (1988). Academic stress, social support, and secretory immunoglobulin A. *Journal of Personality and Social Psychology, 55,* 803–810.

Jenkins, C. D. (1982). Overview: Behavioral perspectives on health risks among the disadvantaged. In D. L. Parron, F. Solomon, & C. D. Jenkins (Eds.), *Behavior, health risks, and social disadvantage.* Washington, DC: Academy Press.

Jennings, D. L., Lepper, M. R., & Ross, L. (1981). Persistence of impressions of personal persuasiveness: Perseverance of erroneous self-assessments outside the debriefing paradigm. *Personality and Social Psychology Bulletin, 7,* 257–263.

Jepson, C. & Chaiken, S. (1986). *The effect of anxiety on the systematic processing of persuasive communications.* Paper presented at the annual meeting of the American Psychological Association, Washington, DC.

Jessop, D. J. (1982). Topic variation in levels of agreement between parents and adolescents. *Public Opinion Quarterly, 46,* 538–559.

Johnson, R. N. (1972). *Aggression in man and animals.* Philadelphia: Saunders.

Jones, E. E. (1964). *Ingratiation.* New York: Appleton-Century-Crofts.

Jones, E. E. (1979). The rocky road from acts to dispositions. *American Psychologist, 34,* 107–117.

Jones, E. E. (1985). Major developments in social psychology during the past five decades. In G. Lindzey & E. Aronson (Eds.), *Handbook of social psychology* (3rd. ed., Vol. 1). New York: Random House.

Jones, E. E., Bell, L., & Aronson, E. (1972). The reciprocation of attraction from similar and dissimilar others. In C. McClintock (Ed.), *Experimental social psychology.* New York: Holt, Rinehart & Winston.

Jones, E. E. & Berglas, S. (1978). Control of attributions about the self through self-handicapping strategies: The appeal of alcohol and the role of under-achievement. *Personality and Social Psychology Bulletin, 4,* 200–206.

Jones, E. E. & Davis, K. E. (1965). From acts to dispositions: The attribution process in person perception. In L. Berkowitz (Ed.), *Advances in experimental social psychology* (Vol. 2). New York: Academic Press.

Jones, E. E., Davis, K. E., & Gergen, K. J. (1961). Role playing variations and their informational value for person perception. *Journal of Abnormal and Social Psychology, 63,* 302–310.

Jones, E. E., Farina, A., Hastorf, A. H., Markus, H., Miller, D. T., & Scott, R. A. (1984). *Social stigma: The psychology of marked relationships.* New York: Freeman.

Jones, E. E. & Gerard, H. B. (1967). *Foundations of social psychology.* New York: Wiley.

Jones, E. E. & Goethals, G. R. (1972). Order effects in impression formation: Attribution context and the nature of the entity. In E. E. Jones, D. E. Kanouse, H. H. Kelley, R. E. Nisbett, S. Valines, & B. Weiner (Eds.), *Attribution: Perceiving the causes of behavior.* Morristown, NJ: General Learning Press.

Jones, E. E. & Harris, V. A. (1967). The attribution of attitudes. *Journal of Experimental Social Psychology, 13,* 1–24.

Jones, E. E. & McGillis, D. (1976). Correspondent inferences and the attribution cube: A comparative reappraisal. In J. H. Harvey, W. J. Ickes, & R. F. Kidd (Eds.), *New directions in attribution research* (Vol. 1). Hillsdale, NJ: Erlbaum.

Jones, E. E. & Nisbett, R. E. (1972). The actor and observer: Divergent perception of the causes of behavior. In E. Jones, D. Kanouse, H. Kelley, R. Nisbett, S. Valins, & B. Weiner (Eds.), *Attribution: Perceiving the causes of behavior.* Morristown, NJ: General Learning Press.

Jones, E. E. & Pittman, T. S. (1982). Toward a general theory of strategic self-presentation. In J. Suls (Ed.), *Psychological perspectives on the self* (Vol. 1). Hillsdale, NJ: Erlbaum.

Jones, E. E., Rock, L., Shaver, K. G., Goethals, G. R., & Ward, L. M. (1968). Pattern of performance and ability attribution: An unexpected primacy effect. *Journal of Personality and Social Psychology, 10,* 317–340.

Jones, E. E. & Sigal, H. (1971). The bogus pipeline: A new paradigm for measuring affect and attitudes. *Psychological Bulletin, 76,* 349–364.

Jones, E. E. & Wortman, C. (1973). *Ingratiation: An attributional approach.* Morristown, NJ: General Learning Press.

Jones, J. M. (1972). *Prejudice and racism.* Reading, MA: Addison-Wesley.

Jones, J. W. & Bogat, G. A. (1978). Air pollution and human aggression. *Psychological Reports, 43,* 721–722.

Jones, S. C. (1973). Self and interpersonal evaluations: Esteem theories vs. consistency theories. *Psychological Bulletin, 79,* 185–199.

Josephson, W. L. (1987). Television violence and children's aggression: Testing the priming, social script, and disinhibition predictions. *Journal of Personality and Social Psychology, 53,* 882–890.

Jourard, S. & Rubin, J. (1968). Self-disclosure and touching: A study of two modes of interpersonal encounter and their inter-relation. *Journal of Humanistic Psychology, 8,* 39–48.

Joy, L. A., Kimball, M. M., & Zabrack, M. L. (1986). Television and children's aggressive behavior. In T. M. Williams (Ed.), *The impact of television: A natural experiment in three communities.* Orlando, FL: Academic Press.

Judd, C. M. & Kulik, J. A. (1980). Schematic effects of social attitudes on information processing and recall. *Journal of Personality and Social Psychology, 38,* 569–578.

Justice, A. (1985). Review of the effects of stress on cancer in laboratory animals: Importance of time of stress application and type of tumor. *Psychological Bulletin, 98,* 108–138.

Kagan, J. & Moss, H. A. (1962). *Birth to maturity.* New York: Wiley.

Kahneman, D. & Tversky, A. (1973). On the psychology of prediction. *Psychological Review, 80,* 237–251.

Kahneman, D. & Tversky, A. (1979). Prospect theory: An analysis of decision under risk. *Econometrica, 47,* 263–291.

Kahneman, D. & Tversky, A. (1984). Choices, values, and frames. *American Psychologist, 39,* 341–350.

Kanfer, F. & Seider, M. L. (1973). Self-control: Factors enhancing tolerance of noxious stimulation. *Journal of Personality and Social Psychology, 25,* 381.

Kanner, A. D., Coyne, J. C., Schaefer, C., & Lazarus, R. S. (1981). Daily hassles and uplifts versus major life events. *Journal of Behavioral Medicine, 4,* 1–39.

Kanouse, D. E. & Hanson, L. R., Jr. (1972). Negativity in evaluations. In E. E. Jones, D. E. Kanouse, H. H. Kelley, R. E. Nisbett, S. Valins, & B. Weiner (Eds.), *Attribution: Perceiving the causes of behavior.* Morristown, NJ: General Learning Press.

Kaplan, H. (1983). A woman's view of DSM-III. *American Psychologist, 38,* 786–792.

Kaplan, M. R. & Miller, C. E. (1987). Group decision making and normative versus informational influence: Effects of type of issue and assigned decision rule. *Journal of Personality and Social Psychology, 53,* 306–313.

Karaz, V. & Perlman, D. (1975). Attribution at the wire: Consistency and outcome finish strong. *Journal of Experimental Social Psychology, 11,* 470–477.

Karlins, M., Coffman, T. L., & Walters, G. (1969). On the fading of social stereotypes: Studies in three generations of college students. *Journal of Personality and Social Psychology, 13,* 1–16.

Kassin, S. M. & Wrightsman, L. S. (1988). *The American jury on trial: Psychological perspectives.* New York: Hemisphere.

Kastenbaum, R. (1982). Healthy, wealthy, and wise? Health care provision for elderly from a psychological perspective. In G. S. Sanders & J. Suls (Eds.), *Social psychology of health and illness.* Hillsdale, NJ: Erlbaum.

Katsev, R., Edelsack, L., Steinmetz, G., Walker, T., & Wright, R. J. (1978). The effect of reprimanding transgressions on subsequent helping behavior: Two field experiments. *Personality and Social Psychology Bulletin, 4,* 326–329.

Katz, A. M. & Hill, R. (1958). Residential propinquity and family living. *Marriage and Family Living, 20,* 27–34.

Katz, D. (1960). The functional approach to the study of attitudes. *Public Opinion Quarterly, 24,* 163–204.

Katz, D. & Braly, K. W. (1933). Racial stereotypes of 100 college students. *Journal of Abnormal and Social Psychology, 28,* 280–290.

Katz, E. & Lazarsfeld, P. F. (1955). *Personal influence.* Glencoe, IL: Free Press.

Katz, I. (1970). Experimental studies of Negro-white relationships. In L. Berkowitz (Ed.), *Advances in experimental social psychology* (Vol. 5). New York: Academic Press.

Katz, I. & Hass, R. G. (1988). Racial ambivalence and American value conflict: Correlational and priming studies of dual cognitive structures. *Journal of Personality and Social Psychology, 55,* 893–905.

Keenan, J. M. & Baillet, S. D. (1980). Memory for personally and socially significant events. In R. S. Nickerson (Ed.), *Attention on performance III.* Hillsdale, NJ: Erlbaum.

Keller, H. R. & Erne, D. E. (1983). Child abuse: Toward a comprehensive model. In *Prevention and control of aggression.* New York: Pergamon Press.

Kelley, H. H. (1967). Attribution theory in social psychology. In D. L. Vine (Ed.), *Nebraska symposium on motivation.* Lincoln: University of Nebraska Press.

Kelley, H. H. (1972). Causal schemata and the attribution process. In E. Jones, D. Kanouse, H. Kelley, R. Nisbett, S. Valins, & B. Weiner (Eds.), *Attribution: Perceiving the causes of behavior.* Morristown, NJ: General Learning Press.

Kelley, H. H., Berscheid, E., Christensen, A., Harvey, J. H., Huston, T. L., Levinger, G., McClintock, E., Peplau, L. A., & Peterson, D. R. (1983). *Close relationships.* New York: Freeman.

Kelly, G. A. (1955). *The psychology of personal constructs* (Vols. 1 and 2). New York: Norton.

Kelman, H. C. (1958). Compliance, identification, and internalization: Three processes of attitude change. *Journal of Conflict Resolution. 2,* 51–60.

Keniston, K. (1968). *Young radicals: Notes on committed youth.* New York: Harcourt, Brace & World.

Kenny, D. A. & Albright, L. (1987). Accuracy in interpersonal perception: A social relations analysis. *Psychological Bulletin, 102,* 390–402.

Kenny, D. A. & La Voie, L. (1984). The social relations model. In L. Berkowitz (Ed.), *Advances in experimental social psychology* (Vol. 18). Orlando, FL: Academic Press.

Kenrick, D. T., Baumann, D. J., & Cialdini, R. B. (1979). A step in the socialization of altruism as hedonism: Effects of negative mood on children's generosity under public and private conditions. *Journal of Personality and Social Psychology, 37,* 756–768.

Kenrick, D. T. & Cialdini, R. B. (1977). Romantic attraction: Misattribution vs. reinforcement explanations. *Journal of Personality and Social Psychology, 35,* 381–391.

Kenrick, D. T. & Funder, D. C. (1988). Profiting from controversy: Lessons from the person-situation debate. *American Psychologist, 43,* 23–34.

Kenrick, D. T. & Stringfield, D. O. (1980). Personality traits and the eye of the beholder: Crossing some traditional philosophical boundaries in the search for consistency in all of the people. *Psychological Review, 87,* 88–104.

Kerckhoff, A. C. (1974). The social context of interpersonal attraction. In T. L. Huston (Ed.), *Foundations of interpersonal attraction.* New York: Academic Press.

Kerckhoff, A. C. (1982). Analyzing a case of mass psychogenic illness. In M. J. Colligan, J. W. Pennebaker, & L. R. Murphy (Eds.), *Mass psychogenic illness: A social psychological analysis.* Hillsdale, NJ: Erlbaum.

Kerckhoff, A. C. & Back, K. W. (1968). *The June bug: A study of hysterical contagion.* New York: Appleton-Century-Crofts.

Kerckhoff, A. C. & Davis, K. E. (1962). Value consensus and need complementarity in mate selection. *American Sociological Review, 27,* 295–303.

Kerr, N. L. (1981). Social transition schemes: Charting the group's road to agreement. *Journal of Personality and Social Psychology, 41,* 684–702.

Kerr, N. L. & MacCoun, R. J. (1985). The effects of jury size and polling method on the process and product of jury deliberation. *Journal of Personality and Social Psychology, 48,* 349–363.

Kerr, S., Schriesheim, C. A., Murphy, C. J., & Stogdill, R. M. (1974). Toward a contingency theory of leadership based upon the consideration and initiating structure literature. *Organizational Behavior and Human Performance, 12,* 62–82.

Kessler, S. J. & McKenna, W. (1978). *Gender: An ethnomethodological approach.* New York: Wiley.

Keys, A., Aravnis, C., Blackburn, H., Van Buchem, F. S. P., Buzina, R., Djordjevic, B. S., Fidanza, F., Kavonen, M. J., Menotti, A., Pudov, V., & Taylor, H. L. (1972). Probability of middle-aged men developing coronary heart disease in 5 years. *Circulation, 45,* 815–828.

Kiecolt-Glaser, J. K., Fisher, L., Ogrocki, P., Stout, J. C., Speicher, C. E., & Glaser, R. (1987). Marital quality, marital disruption, and immune function. *Psychosomatic Medicine, 49,* 13–34.

Kiesler, C. A. (1971). *The psychology of commitments: Experiments linking behavior to belief.* New York: Academic Press.

Kiesler, C. A. & Pallak, M. S. (1976). Arousal properties of dissonance reduction. *Psychological Bulletin, 83,* 1014–1025.

Kihlstrom, J. F. & Cantor, N. (1984). Mental representations of the self. In L. Berkowitz (Ed.), *Advances in experimental social psychology* (Vol. 17). New York: Academic Press.

Kihlstrom, J. F., Cantor, N., Albright, J. S., Chew, B. R., Klein, S. B., & Niedenthal, P. M. (1988). Information processing and the study of self. In L. Berkowitz (Ed.), *Advances in experimental social psychology* (Vol. 21). New York: Academic Press.

Kilham, W. & Mann, L. (1974). Level of destructive obedience as a function of transmitter and executant roles in the Milgram obedience paradigm. *Journal of Personality and Social Psychology, 29,* 696–702.

Kinder, D. R. (1986). The continuing American dilemma: White resistance to racial change 40 years after Myrdal. *Journal of Social Issues, 42,* 151–172.

Kinder, D. R. & Sears, D. O. (1981). Prejudice and politics: Symbolic racism versus racial threats to the good life. *Journal of Personality and Social Psychology, 40,* 414–431.

Kinder, D. R. & Sears, D. O. (1985). White opposition to busing: On conceptualizing and operationalizing group conflict. *Journal of Personality and Social Psychology, 48,* 1141–1147.

Kinsey, A., Pomeroy, W. B., & Martin, C. E. (1948). *Sexual behavior in the human male.* Philadelphia: Saunders.

Kinsey, A., Pomeroy, W. B., Martin, C. E., & Gebhard, P. H. (1953). *Sexual behavior in the human female.* Philadelphia: Saunders.

Kirscht, J. P. (1983). Preventive health behavior: A review of research and issues. *Health Psychology, 2,* 277–301.

Kirscht, J. P. & Dillehay, R. C. (1967). *Dimensions of authoritarianism: A review of research and theory.* Lexington: University of Kentucky Press.

Kite, M. E. & Deaux, K. (1984). Gender belief systems: Homosexuality and the implicit inversion theory. *Psychology of Women Quarterly, 11*, 83–96.

Kite, M. E. & Deaux, K. (1986). Attitudes toward homosexuality: Assessment and behavioral consequences. *Basic and Applied Social Psychology, 7*, 137–162.

Klein, S. B. & Loftus, J. (1988). The nature of self-referent encoding: The contributions of elaborative and organizational processes. *Journal of Personality and Social Psychology, 55*, 5–11.

Knight, G. P. & Dubro A. F. (1984). Cooperative, competitive, and individualistic social values: An individualized regression and clustering approach. *Journal of Personality and Social Psychology, 46*, 98–105.

Kobasa, S. C. (1979). Stressful life events, personality and health: An inquiry into hardiness. *Journal of Personality and Social Psychology, 37*, 1–11.

Kobasa, S. C. (1982). The hardy personality: Toward a social psychology of stress and health. In G. S. Sanders & J. Suls (Eds.), *Social psychology of health and illness.* Hillsdale, NJ: Erlbaum.

Kobasa, S. C., Maddi, S. R., & Kahn, S. (1982). Hardiness and health: A prospective study. *Journal of Personality and Social Psychology, 42*, 168–177.

Kobasa, S. C. O. & Puccetti, M. D. (1983). Personality and social resources in stress resistance. *Journal of Personality and Social Psychology, 45*, 839–850.

Kohlberg, L. (1966). A cognitive-developmental analysis of children's sex role concepts and attitudes. In E. E. Maccoby (Ed.), *The development of sex differences.* Stanford, CA: Stanford University Press.

Komorita, S. S. & Lapworth, C. W. (1982). Cooperative choice among individuals versus groups in a N-person dilemma situation. *Journal of Personality and Social Psychology, 42*, 487–496.

Koop, C. E. (1987). Report of the surgeon general's workshop on pornography and public health. *American Psychologist, 42*, 944–945.

Kornhauser, A., Sheppard, H. L., & Mayer, A. J. (1956). *When Labor Votes.* New York: University Books.

Korte, C. (1981). Constraints on helping in an urban environment. In J. P. Rushton & R. M. Sorrentino (Eds.), *Altruism and helping behavior: Social, personality, and developmental perspectives.* Hillsdale, NJ: Erlbaum.

Krantz, D. S., Arabian, J. M., Davia, J. E., & Parker, J. S. (1982). Type A behavior and coronary artery bypass surgery: Intraoperative blood pressure and perioperative complications. *Psychosomatic Medicine, 44*, 273–284.

Kraus, S. (1962). *The great debates: Background, perspective, effects.* Bloomington, IN: Indiana University Press.

Kraut, R. E. (1980) Humans as lie-detectors: Some second thoughts. *Journal of Communication, 30*, 209–216.

Kraut, R. E. & Poe, D. (1980). Behavioral roots of person perception: The deception judgments of customs inspectors and laymen. *The Journal of Personality and Social Psychology, 39*, 784–798.

Kravitz, D. A. & Martin, B. (1986). Ringelmann rediscovered: The original article. *Journal of Personality and Social Psychology, 50*, 936–941.

Krebs, D. & Adinolfi, A. A. (1975). Physical attractiveness, social relations, and personality style. *Journal of Personality and Social Psychology, 31*, 245–253.

Krebs, D. L. (1970). Altruism—An examination of the concept and a review of the literature. *Psychological Bulletin, 73*, 258–302.

Krebs, D. L. (1978). A cognitive-developmental approach to altruism. In L. Wispe (Ed.), *Altruism, sympathy, and helping: Psychological and sociological principles.* New York: Academic Press.

Krebs, D. L. & Miller, D. T. (1985). Altruism and aggression. In G. Lindzey & E. Aronson (Eds.), *Handbook of social psychology* (Vol. II, 3rd ed.). New York: Random House.

Krebs, D. L. & Rosenwald, A. (1977). Moral reasoning and moral behavior in conventional adults. *Merrill-Palmer Quarterly of Behavior Development, 23*, 77–88.

Krebs, D. L. & Sturrup, B. (1974). Role-taking ability and altruistic behavior in elementary school children. *Personality and Social Psychology Bulletin, 1*, 401–407.

Kruglanski, A. W. (1970). Attributing trustworthiness in supervisor-worker relations. *Journal of Experimental Social Psychology, 6*, 214–232.

Kruglanski, A. W. & Freund, T. (1983). The freezing and unfreezing of lay inferences: Effects of impressional primacy, ethnic stereotyping, and numerical anchoring. *Journal of Experimental Social Psychology, 19*, 448–468.

Kruglanski, A. W., Hamel, I. Z., Maides, S. A., & Schwartz, J. M. (1978). Attribution theory as a special case of lay epistemology. In J. H. Harvey, W. Ickes, & R. F. Kidd (Eds.), *New directions in attribution research* (Vol. 2). Hillsdale, NJ: Erlbaum.

Kulik, J. A. & Brown, R. (1979). Frustration, attribution of blame, and aggression. *Journal of Experimental Social Psychology, 15*, 183–194.

Kulik, J. A. & Mahler, H. I. M. (in press). Social support and recovery from surgery. *Health Psychology.*

Kutchinsky, B. (1973). Eroticism without censorship. *International Journal of Criminology and Penology, 1*, 217–225.

Lagerspetz, K. (1964). Studies of the aggressive behavior of mice. *Annales Academiae Scientiarum Fennicae, Series B, 131*, 1–131.

Lake, R. W. (1981). *The new suburbanites: Race and housing in the suburbs.* New Brunswick, NJ: Center for Urban Policy Research.

Lamm, H. & Trommsdorff, G. (1973). Group versus individual performance on tasks requiring ideational proficiency (brainstorming): A review. *European Journal of Social Psychology, 3*, 361–388.

Landis, C. (1924). Studies of emotional reactions: II. General behavior and facial expression. *Journal of Comparative Psychology, 4*, 447–509.

Landis, C. (1929). The interpretation of facial expression in emotion. *Journal of General Psychology, 2*, 59–72.

Landy, D. & Sigall, H. (1974). Beauty is talent: Task evaluation as a function of the performer's physical attractiveness. *Journal of Personality and Social Psychology, 29*, 299–304.

Langer, E. (1981). Old age: An artifact? In S. Kiesler & J. McGaugh (Eds.), *Biology, behavior, and aging.* New York: Academic Press.

Langer, E. & Rodin, J. (1976). The effects of choice and enhanced personal responsibility for the aged: A field experiment in an institutional setting. *Journal of Personality and Social Psychology, 34*, 191–198.

Langer, E. J. (1978). Rethinking the role of thought in social interaction. In J. H. Harvey, W. J. Ickes, & R. F. Kidd (Eds.), *New directions in attribution research* (Vol. 2). Hillsdale, NJ: Erlbaum.

Langer, E. J. & Abelson, R. P. (1974). A patient by any other name: Clinical group differences in labeling bias. *Journal of Consulting and Clinical Psychology, 42*, 4–9.

Langhorne, M. C. & Secord, P. F. (1955). Variations in marital needs with age, sex, marital status, and regional composition. *Journal of Social Psychology, 41*, 19–37.

Langley, R. & Levy, R. C. (1977). *Wife beating: The silent crisis.* New York: Dutton.

LaPiere, R. T. (1934). Attitudes vs. actions. *Social Forces, 13*, 230–237.

LaPiere, R. T. (1936). Type-rationalization of group antipathy. *Social Forces, 15*, 232–237.

Lasswell, H. D. (1948). The structure and function of communication in society. In L. Bryson (Ed.), *Communication of ideas.* New York: Harper.

Latané, B. (1970). Field studies in altruistic compliance. *Representative Research in Social Psychology, 1*, 49–61.

Latané, B. (1981). The psychology of social impact. *American Psychologist, 36*, 343–356.

Latané, B. & Darley, J. M. (1968). Group inhibition of bystander intervention. *Journal of Personality and Social Psychology, 10*, 215–221.

Latané, B. & Darley, J. M. (1970). *The unresponsive bystander: Why doesn't he help?* New York: Appleton-Century-Crofts.

Latané, B., Nida, S. A., & Wilson, D. W. (1981). The effects of group size on helping behavior. In J. P. Rushton & R. M. Sorrentino (Eds.), *Altruism and helping behavior: Social, personality, and developmental perspectives.* Hillsdale, NJ: Erlbaum.

Latané, B., Williams, K., & Harkins, S. (1979). Many hands make light the work: The causes and consequences of social loafing. *Journal of Personality and Social Psychology, 37*, 822–832.

Latané, B. & Wolf, S. (1981). The social impact of majorities and minorities. *Psychological Review, 88*, 438–453.

Laudenslager, M. L., Ryan, S. M., Drugan, R. C., Hyson, R. L., & Maier, S. F. (1983). Coping and immunosuppression: Inescapable but not escapable shock suppresses lymphocyte proliferation. *Science, 221*, 568–570.

Laumann, E. O. (1969). Friends of urban men: An assessment of accuracy in reporting their socioeconomic attributes, mutual choice, and attitude development. *Sociometry, 32*, 54–69.

Layden, M. A. (1982). Attributional therapy. In C. Anataki & C. Brewin (Eds.), *Attributions and psychological change: Applications of attributional theories to clinical and educational practice*. London: Academic Press.

Lazarus, R. S., DeLongis, A., Folkman, S., & Gruen, R. (1985). Stress and adaptational outcomes: The problem of confounded measures. *American Psychologist, 40*, 770–779.

Lazarus, R. S. & Folkman, S. (1984). *Stress, appraisal, and coping*. New York: Springer-Verlag.

Le Bon, G. (1896). *The crowd: A study of the popular mind*. New York: Macmillan.

Lederer, L. (1980). *Take back the night: Women on pornography*. New York: Morrow.

Lederer, W. J. & Jackson, D. D. (1968). *The mirages of marriage*. New York: Norton.

Lee, A. M. (1946). The press in control of intergroup tensions. *The Annals of the American Academy of Political and Social Science, 244*, 144–151.

Lee, J. A. (1973). *The colors of love: An exploration of the ways of loving*. Don Mills, Ontario: New Press.

Lefcourt, H. M. (1984). *Research with the locus of control construct* (Vol. 3): *Extensions and limitations*. New York: Academic Press.

Lefkowitz, M. M., Eron, L. D., Walder, L. O., & Huesmann, L. R. (1972). Television violence and child aggression: A followup study. In G. A. Comstack and E. A. Rubinstein (Eds.), *Television and social behavior* (Vol. III): *Television and adolescent aggressiveness*. Washington, DC: U.S. Government Printing Office.

LeGuin, U. K. (1969). *The left hand of darkness*. New York: Ace Books.

Leifer, A. D. & Roberts, D. F. (1972). Children's response to television violence. In J. P. Murray, E. A. Rubinstein, & G. A. Comstock (Eds.), *Television and social behavior* (Vol. 2): *Television and social learning*. Washington, DC: U.S. Government Printing Office.

Lepper, M. R. & Greene, D. (Eds.). (1978). *The hidden costs of rewards: New perspectives in the psychology of human motivation*. Hillsdale, NJ: Erlbaum.

Lepper, M. R., Greene, D., & Nisbett, R. E. (1973). Undermining children's intrinsic interest with external rewards: A test of the overjustification hypothesis. *Journal of Personality and Social Psychology, 28*, 129–137.

Lerner, M. J. (1980). *The belief in a just world: A fundamental delusion*. New York: Plenum.

Lerner, M. J. & Meindl, J. R. (1981). Justice and altruism. In J. P. Rushton & R. M. Sorrentino (Eds.), *Altruism and helping behavior: Social, personality and developmental perspectives*. Hillsdale, NJ: Erlbaum.

Lerner, M. J. & Miller, D. T. (1978). Just world research and the attribution process: Looking back and ahead. *Psychological Bulletin, 85*, 1030–1051.

Levenson, H., Burford, B., Bonno, B., & Davis, L. (1975). Are women still prejudicial against women? *Journal of Psychology, 59*, 67–71.

Leventhal, H. (1970). Findings and theory in the study of fear communication. In L. Berkowitz (Ed.), *Advances in experimental social psychology* (Vol. 5). New York: Academic Press.

Levinger, G. (1976). A social psychological perspective on marital dissolution. *Journal of Social Issues, 32*, 21–47.

Levinger, G. (1980). Toward the analysis of close relationships. *Journal of Experimental Social Psychology, 16*, 510–544.

Levinger, G. (1983). Development and change. In H. H. Kelley, E. Berscheid, A. Christensen, J. H. Harvey, T. L. Huston, G. Levinger, E. McClintock, L. A. Peplau, & D. R. Peterson (Eds.), *Close relationships*. New York: Freeman.

Levin, I. P., Schnittjer, S. K., & Thee, S. L. (1988). Information framing effects in social and personal decisions. *Journal of Experimental Social Psychology, 24*, 520–529.

Lewin, K. (1935). *A dynamic theory of personality*. New York: McGraw-Hill.

Lewin, K. (1936). *Principles of topological psychology*. New York: McGraw-Hill.

Lewin, K. (1948). *Resolving social conflicts: Selected papers on group dynamics*. New York: Harper.

Lewinsohn, P. M., Hoberman, H., Teri, L., & Hautziner, M. (1985). An integrative theory of depression. In S. Reiss & R. Bootzin (Eds.), *Theoretical issues in behavior therapy*. New York: Academic Press.

Lewis, M. (1986). Origins of self-knowledge and individual differences in early self-recognition. In J. Suls & A. G. Greenwald (Eds.), *Psychological perspective on the self* (Vol. 3). Hillsdale, NJ: Erlbaum.

Lewis, M. & Brooks, H. (1978). Self-knowledge and emotional development. In M. Lewis & L. Rosenblum (Eds.), *The development of affect*. New York: Plenum.

Leyens, J. P. & Parke, R. D. (1975). Aggressive slides can induce a weapons effect. *European Journal of Social Psychology, 5*, 229–236.

Lieberknecht, K. (1978). Helping the battered wife. *American Journal of Nursing, 4*, 654–656.

Liebert, R. M. & Baron, R. A. (1972). Some immediate effects of televised violence on children's behavior. *Developmental Psychology, 6*, 469–475.

Liebert, R. M. & Spiegler, M. D. (1987). *Personality: Strategies and issues*. Chicago: Dorsey Press.

Liebert, R. M. & Sprafkin, J. (1988). *The early window: Effects of television on children and youth* (3rd ed.). New York: Pergamon Press.

Likert, R. (1932). A technique for the measurement of attitudes. *Archives of Psychology*, No. 140.

Linder, D. E., Cooper, J., & Jones, E. E. (1967).

Decision freedom as a determinant of the role of incentive magnitude in attitude change. *Journal of Personality and Social Psychology, 6*, 245–254.

Lingle, J. H., Geva, N., Ostrom, T. M., Leippe, M. R., & Baumgardner, M. H. (1979). Thematic effects of person judgments on impression organization. *Journal of Personality and Social Psychology, 37*, 674–687.

Lingle, J. H. & Ostrom, T. M. (1979). Retrieval selectivity on memory-based judgments. *Journal of Personality and Social Psychology, 37*, 180–194.

Linton, M. (1978). Real world memory after six years: An in vivo study of very long term memory. In M. Gruenberg, P. Morris, & R. Sykes (Eds.), *Practical aspects of memory*. New York: Academic Press.

Linville, P. W. (1982a). The complexity-extremity effect and age-based stereotyping. *Journal of Personality and Social Psychology, 42*, 193–211.

Linville, P. W. (1982b). Affective consequences of complexity regarding the self and others. In M. S. Clark & S. T. Fiske (Eds.), *Affect and cognition: The 17th annual Carnegie symposium on cognition*. Hillsdale, NJ: Erlbaum.

Linville, P. W. (1985). Self-complexity and affective extremity: Don't put all of your eggs in one cognitive basket. *Social Cognition, 3*, 94–120.

Linville, P. W. (1987). Self-complexity as a cognitive buffer against stress-related illness and depression. *Journal of Personality and Social Psychology, 52*, 663–676.

Linville, P. W. & Jones, E. E. (1980). Polarized appraisals of out-group members. *Journal of Personality and Social Psychology, 38*, 689–703.

Linville, R. (1982). Consequences of complexity regarding the self and others. In M. S. Clark & S. T. Fiske (Eds.), *Affect and cognition: The 17th annual Carnegie symposium on cognition*. Hillsdale, NJ: Erlbaum.

Linz, D. & Donnerstein, E. (1988). The methods and merits of pornography research. *Journal of Communication, 38*, 180–192.

Linz, D., Donnerstein, E., & Penrod, S. (1987). The findings and recommendations of the attorney general's commission on pornography: Do the psychological "facts" fit the political fury? *American Psychologist, 42*, 946–953.

Lippa, R. (1976). Expressive control and the leakage of dispositional introversion-extraversion during role-played teaching. *Journal of Personality, 44*, 541–559.

Lippa, R. (1978). Expressive control, expressive consistency, and the correspondence between expressive behavior and personality. *Journal of Personality, 46*, 438–461.

Lippa, R. (1983). Expressive behavior. In L. Wheeler & P. Shaver (Eds.), *Review of personality and social psychology*. Beverly Hills, CA: Sage.

Lippman, W. (1922). *Public opinion*. New York: Harcourt Brace Jovanovich.

Lively, W. J. & Bromly, D. B. (1973). *Person perception in childhood and adolescence*. New York: Wiley.

Locksley, A., Borgida, E., Brekke, N., & Hepburn, C. (1980). Sex stereotypes and social judgment. *Journal of Personality and Social Psychology, 39,* 821–831.

Locksley, A., Ortiz, V., & Hepburn, C. (1980). Social categorization and discriminatory behavior: Extinguishing the minimal intergroup discrimination effect. *Journal of Personality and Social Psychology, 39,* 773–783.

Loftus, E. F. & Palmer, J. C. (1974). Reconstruction of automobile destruction: An example of the interaction between language and memory. *Journal of Verbal Learning and Verbal Behavior, 13,* 585–589.

London, H. & Nisbett, R. (1974). Elements of Schachter's cognitive theory of emotional states. In H. London & R. E. Nisbett (Eds.), *Thought and feeling.* Chicago: Aldine.

London, P. (1970). The rescuers: Motivational hypotheses about Christians who saved Jews from the Nazis. In J. Macaulay & L. Berkowitz (Eds.), *Altruism and helping behavior.* New York: Academic Press.

Lord, C. G. (1980). Schemas and images as memory aids: Two modes of processing social information. *Journal of Personality and Social Psychology, 38,* 257–269.

Lord, C. G., Lepper, M. R., & Mackie, D. (1984). Attitude prototypes as determinants of attitude-behavior consistency. *Journal of Personality and Social Psychology, 46,* 1254–1266.

Lord, C. G., Ross, L., & Lepper, M. R. (1979). Biased assimilation and attitude polarization: The effects of prior theories on subsequently considered evidence. *Journal of Personality and Social Psychology, 37,* 2098–2109.

Lorenz, K. (1966). *On aggression.* New York: Harcourt, Brace & World.

Lott, A. & Lott, B. (1961). Group cohesiveness, communication level, and conformity. *Journal of Abnormal and Social Psychology, 62,* 408–412.

Lott, A. & Lott, B. (1968). A learning theory approach to interpersonal attitudes. In A. G. Greenwald, T. C. Brock, & T. M. Ostrom (Eds.), *Psychological foundations of attitudes.* New York: Academic Press.

Lott, A. & Lott, B. (1974). The role of reward in the formation of positive interpersonal attitudes. In T. L. Huston (Ed.), *Foundations of interpersonal attraction.* New York: Academic Press.

Lott, B. & Lott, A. J. (1985). Learning theory in contemporary social psychology. In G. Lindzey and E. Aronson (Eds.), *Handbook of social psychology* (Vol. 1). New York: Random House.

Luce, R. D. & Raiffa, H. (1957). *Games and decisions.* New York: Wiley.

Luchins, A. S. (1957). Primacy-recency in impression formation. In C. Hovland (Ed.), *The order of presentation in persuasion.* New Haven, CT: Yale University Press.

Lumsdaine, A. A. & Janis, I. L. (1953). Resistance to "counterpropaganda" produced by one-sided and two-sided "propaganda" presentation. *Public Opinion Quarterly, 17,* 311–318.

Lunneborg, P. W. (1972). Dimensionality of MF. *Journal of Clinical Psychology, 28,* 313–317.

Lyon, E. (1986). The economics of gender. In F. A. Boudreau, R. S. Sennott, & M. Wilson (Eds.), *Sex roles and social patterns.* New York: Praeger.

Lyons, V. (Ed.). (1980). *Structuring cooperative learning in the classroom: The 1980 handbook.* Minneapolis, MN: Cooperative Network.

Maass, A. & Clark, R. D., III (1982). *Minority influence theory: Is it applicable only to majorities?* Paper presented at the 33rd Congress of the German Psychological Association, Mainz, West Germany.

Maass, A. & Clark, R. D., III (1983). Internalization versus compliance: Differential processes underlying minority influence and conformity. *European Journal of Social Psychology, 13,* 45–55.

Maass, A. & Clark, R. D., III (1984). Hidden impact of minorities: Fifteen years of minority influence research. *Psychological Bulletin, 95,* 428–450.

Maass, A., Clark, R. D., III, & Haverhorn, G. (1982). The effects of differential ascribed category membership and norms on minority influence. *European Journal of Social Psychology, 12,* 89–104.

Maass, A., West, S. G., & Cialdini, R. B. (1987). Minority influence and conversion. In C. Hendrick, (Ed.), *Group processes: Review of personality and social psychology* (Vol. 8). Newbury Park, CA: Sage.

McArthur, L. Z. (1972). The how and the what of why: Some determinants and consequences of causal attribution. *Journal of Personality and Social Psychology, 22,* 171–193.

McCallum, D. M., Harring, K. Gilmore, J. P., Insko, C. A., & Thibaut, J. (1985). Competition and cooperation between groups and between individuals. *Journal of Experimental Social Psychology, 21,* 301–320.

McCarthy, S. J. (1980). Pornography, rape and the cult of the macho. *The Humanist, 56,* 11–20.

McCauley, C., & Stitt, C. L. (1978). An individual and quantitative measure of stereotypes. *Journal of Personality and Social Psychology, 36,* 929–940.

McCauley, C., Stitt, C. L., & Segal, M. (1980). Stereotyping: From prejudice to prediction. *Psychological Bulletin, 87,* 195–208.

McClelland, D. C. & Apicella, F. S. (1945). A functional classification of verbal reactions to experimentally induced failure. *Journal of Abnormal and Social Psychology, 46,* 376–390.

McClintock, C. G. & Liebrand, W. B. (1988). Role of interdependence structure, individual value orientation, and another's strategy in social decision making: A transformational analysis. *Journal of Personality and Social Psychology, 55,* 396–409.

McClintock, C. G. & Van Avermaet (1982). Social values and rules of fairness: A theoretical perspective. In V. J. Derlega & J. Grzelak

(Eds.), *Cooperation and helping behavior: Theories and research.* New York: Academic Press.

McCloskey, M. E. & Glucksberg, S. (1978). Natural categories: Well-defined or fuzzy sets? *Memory and Cognition, 6,* 462–472.

Maccoby, E. E. (1966). Sex differences in intellectual functioning. In E. E. Maccoby (Ed.), *The development of sex differences.* Stanford, CA: Stanford University Press.

Maccoby, E. E. & Jacklin, C. N. (1974). *The psychology of sex differences.* Stanford, CA: Stanford University Press.

Maccoby, E. E. & Jacklin, C. N. (1980). Sex differences in aggression. A rejoinder and reprise. *Child Development, 51,* 954–980.

McCrae, R. R. & Costa, P. T., Jr. (1985). Updating Norman's "adequate taxonomy": Intelligence and personality dimensions in natural language and in questionnaires. *Journal of Personality and Social Psychology, 49,* 710–721.

McCrae, R. R. & Costa, P. T., Jr. (1987). Validation of the five-factor model of personality across instruments and observers. *Journal of Personality and Social Psychology, 52,* 81–90.

McCullum, D. M., Harring, K., Gilmore, R., Drenan, S., Chase, J. P., Insko, D., & Thibaut, J. (1985). Competition and cooperation between groups and between individuals. *Journal of Experimental Social Psychology, 21* 301–320.

McDavid, J. W. & Sistrunk, F. (1964). Personality correlates of two kinds of conformity behavior. *Journal of Personality, 32,* 421–435.

Mace, K. C. (1972). The "over-bluff" shoplifter: Who gets caught? *Journal of Forensic Psychology, 4,* 26–30.

MacEvoy, B., Lambert, W. W., Karlberg, P., Karlberg, J., Klackenberg-Larsson, I., & Klackenberg, G. (1988). Early affective antecedents of adult Type A behavior. *Journal of Personality and Social Psychology, 54,* 108–116.

McGuire, W. J. (1960). A syllogistic analysis of cognitive relationships. In M. J. Rosenburg & C. I. Hovland (Eds.), *Attitude organization and change.* New Haven, CT: Yale University Press.

McGuire, W. J. (1964). Inducing resistance to persuasion: Some contemporary approaches. In L. Berkowitz (Ed.), *Advances in experimental social psychology* (Vol. 1). New York: Academic Press.

McGuire, W. J. (1968a). Personality and susceptibility to social influence. In E. F. Borgatta & W. W. Lambert, (Eds.), *Handbook of personality theory and research.* Chicago: Rand McNally.

McGuire, W. J. (1968b). Personality and attitude change: An information-processing theory. In A. G. Greenwald, T. C. Brock, & T. M. Ostrom (Eds.), *Psychological foundations of attitudes.* New York: Academic Press.

McGuire, W. J. (1981). The probabilological model of cognitive structure. In R. E. Petty, T. M. Ostrom, & T. C. Brock (Eds.), *Cognitive responses in persuasion.* Hillsdale, NJ: Erlbaum.

McGuire, W. J. (1985). Attitudes and attitude change. In G. Lindzey & E. Aronson (Eds.),

Handbook of social psychology (Vol. 2). New York: Random House.

McGuire, W. J. & McGuire, C. V. (1982). Significant others in self-space: Sex differences and developmental trends in the social self. In J. Suls (Ed.), *Psychological perspectives on the self.* Hillsdale, NJ: Erlbaum.

McGuire, W. J. & McGuire, C. V. (1988). Content and process in the experience of self. In L. Berkowitz (Ed.), *Advances in experimental social psychology* (Vol. 21). San Diego: Academic Press.

McGuire, W. J., McGuire, C. V., Child, P., & Fujioka, T. (1978). Salience of ethnicity in the spontaneous self-concept as a function of one's ethnic distinctiveness in the social environment. *Journal of Personality and Social Psychology, 36,* 511–520.

McGuire, W. J. & Padawer-Singer, A. (1976). Trait salience in the spontaneous self-concept. *Journal of Personality and Social Psychology, 33,* 743–754.

McGuire, W. J. & Papageorgis, D. (1961). The relative efficacy of various types of prior belief-defense in producing immunity against persuasion. *Journal of Abnormal and Social Psychology, 62,* 327–337.

Mackie, D. M. (1986). Social identification effects in group polarization. *Journal of Personality and Social Psychology, 50,* 720–728.

Mackie, D. M. (1987). Systematic and nonsystematic processing of majority and minority persuasive communications. *Journal of Personality and Social Psychology, 53,* 41–52.

McKillip, J. & Riedel, S. L. (1983). External validity of matching on physical attractiveness for same and opposite sex couples. *Journal of Applied Social Psychology, 13,* 328–337.

McLeod, J. M., Atkin, C. K., & Chaffee, S. H. (1972a). Adolescents, parents, and television use: Adolescent self-report measures from Maryland and Wisconsin samples. In G. A. Comstock & E. A. Rubinstein (Eds.), *Television and social behavior* (Vol. III), *Television and adolescent aggressiveness.* Washington, DC: U.S. Government Printing Office.

McLeod, J. M., Atkin, C. K., & Chaffee, S. H. (1972b). Adolescents, parents, and television use: Self-report and other-report measures from the Wisconsin sample. In G. A. Comstock & E. A. Rubinstein (Eds.), *Television and social behavior* (Vol. III), *Television and adolescent aggressiveness.* Washington, DC: U.S. Government Printing Office.

McMillen, D. L. (1971). Transgression, self-image, and compliant behavior. *Journal of Personality and Social Psychology, 20,* 176–179.

McMillen, D. L., Sander, D. V., & Solomon, G. S. (1977). Self-esteem, attentiveness, and helping behavior. *Personality and Social Psychology Bulletin, 3,* 257–261.

McNemar, Q. (1946). Opinion-attitude methodology. *Psychological Bulletin, 43,* 289–374.

Maddi, S. R. (1976). *Personality theories: A comparative analysis* (3rd ed.). Chicago: Dorsey Press.

Maddi, S. R., Bartone, P. T., & Puccetti, M. C. (1987). Stressful events are indeed a factor in physical illness: Reply to Schroeder & Costa (1984). *Journal of Personality and Social Psychology, 52,* 833–843.

Mahl, G. F. (1968). Gestures and body movements in interviews. In J. M. Shlien (Ed.), *Research in psychotherapy.* Washington, DC: American Psychological Association.

Maier, N. R. & Thurber, J. A. (1968). Accuracy of judgments of deception when an interview is watched, heard, and read. *Personal Psychology, 21,* 23–30.

Major, B. (1980). Information acquisition and attribution processes. *Journal of Personality and Social Psychology, 39,* 1010–1024.

Major, B. & Konar, E. (1984). An investigation of sex differences in pay expectations and their possible causes. *Academy of Management Journal, 27,* 777–792.

Malamuth, N. M. (1981). Rape fantasies as a function of exposure to violent sexual stimuli. *Archives of Sexual Behavior, 10,* 33–47.

Malamuth, N. M. (1984). Aggression against women: Cultural and individual causes. In N. M. Malamuth & E. Donnerstein (Eds.), *Pornography and sexual aggression.* Orlando, FL: Academic Press.

Malamuth, N. M. & Check, J. V. P. (1981). The effects of media exposure on acceptance of violence against women: A field experiment. *Journal of Research in Personality, 15,* 436–446.

Malamuth, N. M. & Check, J. V. P. (1985). The effects of aggressive pornography on beliefs in rape myths: Individual differences. *Journal of Research in Personality, 19,* 299–320.

Malamuth, N. M., Check, J. V. P., & Briere, J. (1986). Sexual arousal to aggression: Ideological, aggressive, and sexual correlates. *Journal of Personality and Social Psychology, 50,* 330–340.

Malof, M. & Lott, A. J. (1962). Ethnocentrism and the acceptance of Negro support in a group pressure situation. *Journal of Abnormal and Social Psychology, 65,* 254–258.

Mandler, G. (1975). *Mind and emotion.* New York: Wiley.

Mann, J. H. (1959). The relationship between cognitive, affective, and behavioral aspects of racial prejudice. *Journal of Social Psychology, 49,* 223–228.

Mann, R. D. (1959). A review of the relationships between personality and performance in small groups. *Psychological Bulletin, 56,* 241–270.

Mantell, D. M. (1971). The potential for violence in Germany. *Journal of Social Issues, 27,* 101–112.

Markus, H. (1977). Self-schemas and processing information about the self. *Journal of Personality and Social Psychology, 35,* 63–78.

Markus, H. (1978). The effect of mere presence on social facilitation: An unobtrusive test. *Journal of Experimental Social Psychology, 14,* 389–397.

Markus, H., Crane, M., Bernstein, S., & Siladi, M. (1982). Self-schemas and gender. *Journal of Personality and Social Psychology, 42,* 38–50.

Markus, H. & Nurius, P. (1986). Possible selves. *American Psychologist, 41,* 954–969.

Markus, H. & Sentis, K. (1982). The self in social information processing. In J. Suls (Ed.), *Social psychological perspectives on the self.* Hillsdale, NJ: Erlbaum.

Markus, H. & Smith, J. (1981). The influence of self-schemata on the perception of others. In N. Cantor & J. Kihlstrom (Eds.), *Personality, cognition, and social interaction.* Hillsdale, NJ: Erlbaum.

Markus, H., Smith, J., & Moreland, R. L. (1985). Role of the self-concept in the perception of others. *Journal of Personality and Social Psychology, 49,* 1494–1512.

Markus, H. & Zajonc, R. B. (1985). The cognitive perspective in social psychology. In G. Lindzey & E. Aronson (Eds.), *Handbook of social psychology* (Vol. 1). New York: Random House.

Marshall, G. & Zimbardo, P. G. (1979). Affective consequences of inadequately explained physiological arousal. *Journal of Personality and Social Psychology, 37,* 970–988.

Martin, C. L. (1987). A ratio measure of sex stereotyping. *Journal of Personality and Social Psychology, 52,* 489–499.

Martinek, T. J. (1981). Physical attractiveness: Effects on teacher expectations and dyadic interactions in elementary age children. *Journal of Sports Psychology, 3,* 196–205.

Maslach, C. (1979). Negative emotional biasing of unexplained arousal. *Journal of Personality and Social Psychology, 37,* 953–969.

Masserman, J. H., Wechkin, S., & Terris, W. (1964). Altruistic behavior in rhesus monkeys. *American Journal of Psychiatry, 121,* 584–585.

Matthews, K. A. (1982). Psychological perspectives on the type A behavior pattern. *Psychological Bulletin, 91,* 293–323.

Matthews, K. A. (1988). Coronary heart disease and type A behaviors: Update on and alternative to Booth-Kewley and Friedman (1987) quantitative review. *Psychological Bulletin, 104,* 373–380.

Matthews, K. A., Krantz, D. S., Dembroski, T. M., & MacDougall, J. A. (1982). The unique and common variance in the structured interview and the Jenkins activity survey measures of the type A behavior pattern. *Journal of Personality and Social Psychology, 42,* 303–313.

Maynard-Smith, J. (1974). The theory of games and the evolution of animal conflict. *Journal of Theoretical Biology, 47,* 209–221.

Mazur, A. (1983). Physiology, dominance and aggression in humans. In *Prevention and control of aggression.* New York: Pergamon Press.

Mead, G. H. (1934). *Mind, self, and society.* Chicago: University of Chicago Press.

Mead, M. (1935). *Sex and temperament.* New York: Morrow.

Mednick, S. A., Brennan, P., & Kandel, E. (1988). Predisposition to violence. *Aggressive Behavior, 14,* 25–33.

Meehl, P. E. (1954). *Clinical vs. statistical prediction: A theoretical analysis and a review of the evidence.* Minneapolis: University of Minnesota Press.

Mehrabian, A. & Wiener, M. (1967). Decoding of inconsistent communication. *Journal of Personality and Social Psychology, 6,* 108–114.

Meindl, J. R. & Lerner, M. J. (1985). Exacerbation of extreme responses to an out-group. *Journal of Personality and Social Psychology, 47,* 71–84.

Mellen, S. L. W. (1981). *The evolution of love.* San Francisco: Freeman.

Mentzer, S. J. & Snyder, M. L. (1982). The doctor and the patient: A psychological perspective. In G. S. Sanders & G. Suls (Eds.), *Social psychology of health and illness.* Hillsdale, NJ: Erlbaum.

Merton, R. K. (1948). The self-fulfilling prophecy. *Antioch Review, 8,* 193–210.

Merton, R. K. (1957). *Social theory and social structure.* Glencoe, IL: Free Press.

Merton, R. K. & Kitt, A. A. (1950). Contributions to the theory of reference group behavior. In R. K. Merton & P. F. Lazarsfeld (Eds.), *Continuities in social research: Studies in the scope and method of the American soldier.* Glencoe, IL: Free Press.

Messick, D. M., Wilke, H., Brewer, M. B., Krammer, R. M., Zemke, P. E., & Lui, L. (1983). Individual adaptations and structural change as solutions to social dilemmas. *Journal of Personality and Social Psychology, 44,* 294–309.

Meyer, P. (1970). If Hitler asked you to electrocute a stranger, would you? . . . What if Mr. Milgram asked you? *Esquire,* 72–73.

Milgram, S. (1963). Behavioral study of obedience. *Journal of Abnormal and Social Psychology, 67,* 371–378.

Milgram, S. (1964). Issues in the study of obedience: A reply to Baumrind. *American Psychologist, 19,* 848–852.

Milgram, S. (1970). The experience of living in cities. *Science, 167,* 1461–1468.

Milgram, S. (1974). *Obedience to authority: An experimental view.* New York: Harper & Row.

Miller, A. (1971). The Crucible. In H. Clurman (Ed.), *The portable Arthur Miller.* New York: Viking Press.

Miller, A. G. (1986). *The obedience experiments: A case study of controversy in social science.* New York: Praeger.

Miller, D. T. (1978). What constitutes a self-serving attributional bias? A reply to Bradley. *Journal of Personality and Social Psychology, 36,* 1211–1223.

Miller, D. T. & Ross, M. (1975). Self-serving biases in the attribution of causality: Fact or fiction? *Psychological Bulletin, 82,* 213–225.

Miller, G. A., Galanter, E., & Pribram, K. H. (1960). *Plans and the structure of behavior.* New York: Holt, Rinehart & Winston.

Miller, H. L. & Rivenbark, W. H., III (1970). Sexual differences in physical attractiveness as a determinant of heterosexual liking. *Psychological Reports, 27,* 701–702.

Miller, N. & Brewer, M. B. (1984). The social psychology of desegregation: An introduction. In N. Miller & M. B. Brewer (Eds.), *Groups in contact: The psychology of desegregation.* New York: Academic Press.

Miller, N. E. & Bugelski, R. (1948). The influence of frustrations imposed by the in-group on attitude expressed toward out-group. *Journal of Psychology, 25,* 437–442.

Miller, N. E. & Dollard, J. (1941). *Social learning and imitation.* New Haven, CT: Yale University Press.

Mills, J. & Clark, M. S. (1982). Communal and exchange relationships. In L. Wheeler (Ed.), *Review of personality and social psychology* (Vol. 3). Beverly Hills, CA: Sage.

Milton, C. (1972). *Women in policing.* Washington, DC: Police Foundation.

Mischel, W. (1966). A social learning view of sex differences. In E. E. Maccoby (Ed.), *The development of sex differences.* Stanford, CA: Stanford University Press.

Mischel, W. (1968). *Personality and assessment.* New York: Wiley.

Mischel, W. (1970). Sex-typing and socialization. In P. H. Mussen (Ed.), *Carmichael's manual of child psychology* (Vol. 2). New York: Wiley.

Mischel, W. (1973). Toward a cognitive social learning reconceptualization of personality. *Psychological Review, 80,* 252–283.

Mischel, W. (1977). The interaction of person and situation. In D. Magnusson & N. S. Endler (Eds.), *Personality at the crossroads: Current issues in interactional psychology.* Hillsdale, NJ: Erlbaum.

Mischel, W. (1982). *A cognitive-social learning approach to assessment.* New York: Guilford.

Mischel, W., Ebbesen, E. B., & Zeiss, A. R. (1973). Selective attention to the self: Situational and dispositional determinants. *Journal of Personality and Social Psychology, 27,* 129–142.

Mischel, W. & Grusec, J. (1966). Determinants of the rehearsal and transmission of neutral and aversive behavior. *Journal of Personality and Social Psychology, 3,* 197–205.

Mischel, W. & Peake, P. K. (1982). Beyond *deja vu* in the search for cross-situational consistency. *Psychological Review, 89,* 730–755.

Mischel, W. & Peake, P. K. (1983). Analyzing the construction of consistency in personality. In M. M. Page (Ed.), *Personality—Current theory and research: Nebraska symposium on motivation 1982.*

Money, J. & Ehrhardt, A. A. (1972). *Man and woman, boy and girl.* Baltimore: Johns Hopkins University Press.

Monroe, S. M. & Steiner, S. C. (1986). Social support and psychopathology: Interrelationships with preexisting disorder, stress, and personality. *Journal of Abnormal Psychology, 95,* 29–39.

Monson, T. C., Hesley, J. W., & Chernick, L. (1981). Specifying when personality can and cannot predict behavior: An alternative to abandoning the attempt to predict single-act

criteria. *Journal of Personality and Social Psychology, 43,* 385–399.

Montagu, A. (1976). *The nature of human aggression.* New York: Oxford University Press.

Montemayor, R. & Eisen, M. (1977). The development of self-conceptions from childhood to adolescence. *Developmental Psychology, 13,* 314–319.

Montepare, J. M. & Vega, C. (1988). Women's vocal reactions to intimate and casual male friends. *Personality and Social Psychology Bulletin, 14,* 103–113.

Mook, D. G. (1983). In defense of external invalidity. *American Psychologist, 38,* 379–387.

Moore, B. S., Underwood, B., & Rosenhan, D. L. (1973). Affect and altruism. *Developmental Psychology, 8,* 99–104.

Mori, D., Chaiken, S., & Pliner, P. (1987). "Eating lightly" and the self-presentation of femininity. *Journal of Personality and Social Psychology, 53,* 693–702.

Moriarity, D. & McCabe, A. E. (1977). Studies of television and youth sport. In *Ontario royal commission on violence in the communications industry report* (Vol. 5): *Learning from the media.* (Research Reports.) Toronto: Queen's Printer for Ontario.

Moriarity, T. (1975). Crime, commitment and the responsive bystander: Two field experiments. *Journal of Personality and Social Psychology, 31,* 370–376.

Morin, S. F. (1988). AIDS: The challenge to psychology. *American Psychologist, 43,* 838–842.

Morrison, T. (1970). *The bluest eye.* New York: Washington Square.

Morse, S. J. & Gergen, J. J. (1971). Material aid and social attraction. *Journal of Applied Social Psychology, 2,* 34–46.

Moscovici, S. (1976). *Social influence and social change.* London: Academic Press.

Moscovici, S. (1980). Toward a theory of conversion behavior. In L. Berkowitz (Ed.), *Advances in experimental social psychology* (Vol. 13). New York: Academic Press.

Moscovici, S., Lage, E., & Naffrechoux, M. (1969). Influence of a consistent minority on the response of a majority in a color perception task. *Sociometry, 32,* 365–379.

Moscovici, S. & Personnaz, B. (1980). Studies in social influence: V. Minority influence and conversion behavior in a perceptual task. *Journal of Experimental Social Psychology, 16,* 270–282.

Moscovici, S. & Zavalloni, M. (1969). The group as a polarizer of attitudes. *Journal of Personality and Social Psychology, 12,* 125–135.

Moyer, K. E. (1976). *The psychology of aggression.* New York: Harper & Row.

Mugny, G. (1975). Negotiations, image of other and the process of minority influence. *European Journal of Social Psychology, 5,* 204–229.

Mugny, G. (1982). *The power of minorities.* London: Academic Press.

Mulder, M. & Stemerding, A. (1963). Threat, attraction to group, and need for strong leadership. *Human Relations, 16,* 317–334.

Mullen, B., Atkins, J. L., Champion, D. S., Edwards, C., Hardy, D., Story, J. E., & Vanderklok, M. (1985). The false consensus effect: A meta-analysis of 115 hypothesis tests. *Journal of Experimental Social Psychology, 21*,262–283.

Murphy, G. & Likert, R. (1938). *Public opinion and the individual: A psychological study of student attitudes on public questions, with a retest five years later.* New York: Harper.

Murray, H. A. (1933). The effect of fear upon estimates of the maliciousness of other personalities. *Journal of Social Psychology, 4*, 310–329.

Murray, H. A. (1962). *Explorations in personality.* New York: Science Editions.

Murray, J. B. (1980). *Television and youth: 25 years of research and controversy.* Boys Town, NE: Boys Town Center for the Study of Youth Development.

Murstein, B. I. (1970). Stimulus-value-role: A theory of marital choice. *Journal of Marriage and Family, 32*, 465–481.

Murstein, B. I. (1974). *Love, sex, and marriage through the ages.* New York: Springer.

Murstein, B. I. (1976). *Who will marry whom? Theories and research in marital choice.* New York: Springer.

Mussen, P. & Eisenberg-Berg, N. (1977). *Roots of caring, sharing, and helping: The development of prosocial behavior in children.* San Francisco: Freeman.

Myers, A. M. & Gonda, G. (1982). Utility of the masculinity-femininity construct: Comparison of traditional and androgyny approaches. *Journal of Personality and Social Psychology, 43*, 514–522.

Myers, D. G. & Bishop, G. D. (1970). Discussion effects on racial attitudes. *Science, 169*, 778–789.

Myers, D. G. & Lamm, H. (1976). The group polarization phenomenon. *Psychological Bulletin, 83*, 602–627.

Myers, M. (1979). Rule departures and making law: Juries and their verdicts. *Law and Society Review, 13*, 781–797.

Myerscough, R. & Taylor, S. (1985). The effects of marihuana on physical aggression. *Journal of Personality and Social Psychology, 49*, 1541–1546.

Nadler, A. (1986). Help seeking as a cultural phenomenon: Differences between city and kibbutz dwellers. *Journal of Personality and Social Psychology, 51*, 976–982.

Nahemow, L. & Lawton, M. P. (1975). Similarity and propinquity in friendship formation. *Journal of Personality and Social Psychology, 32*, 205–213.

Nail, P. R. (1986). Toward an integration of some models and theories of social response. *Psychological Bulletin, 100*, 190–206.

Nail, P. R. & Willis, R. H. (1988). *An analysis and reformulation of the diamond model of social response.* Unpublished manuscript.

Napoleon, T., Chassin, L., & Young, R. D. (1980). A replication and extension of physical attractiveness and mental illness. *Journal of Abnormal Psychology, 89*, 250–253.

National Commission on the Causes and Prevention of Violence. (1969). *Commission statement on violence in television entertainment programs.*

Nemeth, C. (1986). Differential contributions of majority and minority influence. *Psychological Review, 93*, 23–32.

Nemeth, C., Swedlund, M., & Kanki, B. (1974). Patterning of the minority's responses and their influence on the majority. *European Journal of Social Psychology, 4*, 53–64.

Nemeth, C. & Wachtler, J. (1973). Consistency and modification of judgment. *Journal of Experimental Social Psychology, 9*, 65–79.

Nemeth, C. & Wachtler, J. (1974). Creating the perceptions of consistency and confidence: A necessary condition for minority influence. *Sociometry, 37*, 529–540.

Newcomb, T. M. (1929). Consistency of certain extrovert-introvert behavior patterns in 51 problem boys. New York: Columbia University Teachers College, Bureau of Publication.

Newcomb, T. M. (1943). *Personality and social change.* New York: Dryden Press.

Newcomb, T. M. (1951). Social psychological theory. In J. H. Roher & M. Sherif (Eds.), *Social psychology at the crossroads.* New York: Harper.

Newcomb, T. M. (1953). An approach to the study of communicative acts. *Psychological Review, 60*, 393–404.

Newcomb, T. M. (1961). *The acquaintance process.* New York: Holt, Rinehart & Winston.

Newcomb, T. M. (1963). Persistence and regression of changed attitudes: A long range study. *Journal of Social Issues, 19*, 3–14.

Newsweek (1984, February 27). Suing over a scarlet letter, 46.

Newsweek (1987, June 13). The divorce game: Slippery numbers, 55.

Newsweek (1987, August 10). Gunplay on the freeway, 18.

Newsweek (1987, November 23). How to protect abused children, 70–71.

Newton, D. (1974). Dispositional inferences from effects of actions: Effects chosen and effects forgone. *Journal of Experimental Social Psychology, 10*, 489–496.

Nieva, V. F. & Guteck, B. A. (1981). Sex effects in evaluation. *The Academy of Management Review, 5*, 267–276.

Nisbett, R. E., Caputo, C., Legant, P., & Marecek, J. (1973). Behavior as seen by the actor and as seen by the observer. *Journal of Personality and Social Psychology, 27*, 154–164.

Nisbett, R. E. & Ross, L. (1980). *Human inference: Strategies and shortcomings of social judgment.* Englewood Cliffs, NJ: Prentice-Hall.

Nisbett, R. E. & Schachter, S. (1966). Cognitive manipulation of pain. *Journal of Experimental Social Psychology, 2*, 227–236.

Nisbett, R. E., Zuckier, H., & Lemley, R. E. (1981). The dilution effect: Nondiagnostic information weakens the implications of diagnostic information. *Cognitive Psychology, 13*, 248–277.

Nissen, H. W. & Crawford, M. P. (1936). A preliminary study of food-sharing behavior in young chimpanzees. *Journal of Comparative Psychology, 22*, 383–419.

Norman, W. T. (1963). Toward an adequate taxonomy of personality attributes: Replicated factor structure in peer nomination personality ratings. *Journal of Abnormal and Social Psychology, 66*, 574–583.

Oakes, P. J. & Turner, J. C. (1980). Social categorization and intergroup behavior: Does minimal intergroup discrimination make social identity more positive? *European Journal of Social Psychology, 10*, 295–301.

O'Grady, K. E. (1982). Sex, physical attractiveness, and perceived risk for mental illness. *Journal of Personality and Social Psychology, 43*, 1064–1071.

Ohbuchi, K. & Kambara, T. (1985). Attacker's intent and awareness of outcome, impression management, and retaliation. *Journal of Experimental Social Psychology, 21*, 321–330.

Olson, J. M. (1988). Misattribution, preparatory information, and speech anxiety. *Journal of Personality and Social Psychology, 54*, 758–767.

Olweus, D. (1979). Stability of aggressive reaction patterns in males: A review. *Psychological Bulletin, 86*, 852–875.

Olweus, D. (1980). Familial and temperamental determinants of aggressive behavior in adolescent boys: A causal analysis. *Developmental Psychology, 16*, 644–666.

Olweus, D. (1986). Aggression and hormones: Behavioral relationships with testosterone and adrenaline. In D. Olweus, J. Block, & M. Radke-Yarrow (Eds.), *Development of antisocial and prosocial behaviors: Research, theories, and issues.* Orlando, FL: Academic Press.

Orne, M. (1962). On the social psychology of the psychology experiment. *American Psychologist, 17*, 776–783.

Orwell, G. (1977). *1984.* New York: Harcourt Brace Jovanovich. (Originally published 1949.)

Osborn, A. F. (1957). *Applied imagination.* New York: Scribner.

Osborne, R. T., Noble, C. E., & Wey, N. J. (Eds.). (1978). *Human variation: Biopsychology of age, race, and sex.* New York: Academic Press.

Osgood, C. E., Luria, Z., Jeans, R. E., & Smith, S. W. (1976). The three faces of Evelyn: A case report. *Journal of Abnormal Psychology, 85*, 249–270.

Osgood, C. E., Suci, G., & Tannenbaum, P. H. (1957). *The measurement of meaning.* Urbana: University of Illinois Press.

Osgood, C. E. & Tannenbaum, P. H. (1955). The principle of congruity in the prediction of attitude change. *Psychological Review, 62*, 42–55.

Oskamp, S. (1977). *Attitudes and opinions.* Englewood Cliffs, NJ: Prentice-Hall.

Page, M. M. (1969). Social psychology of a classical conditioning of attitudes experiment. *Journal of Personality and Social Psychology, 11*, 177–186.

Page, M. M. (1971). Postexperimental assessment of awareness in attitude conditioning. *Educational and Psychological Measurement, 31,* 891–906.

Page, M. M. (1974). Demand characteristics and the classical conditioning of attitudes experiment. *Journal of Personality and Social Psychology, 30,* 468–476.

Page, M. & Scheidt, R. (1971). The elusive weapons effect: Demand awareness evaluation and slightly sophisticated subjects. *Journal of Personality and Social Psychology, 20,* 304–318.

Paicheler, G. (1976). Norms and attitude change: I. Polarization and styles of behavior. *European Journal of Social Psychology, 6,* 405–427.

Paicheler, G. (1977). Norms and attitude change: II. The phenomenon of bipolarization. *European Journal of Social Psychology, 7,* 5–14.

Pallak, M. & Pittman, T. S. (1972). General motivational effects of dissonance arousal. *Journal of Personality and Social Psychology, 21,* 349–358.

Pallak, M. S., Cook, D. A., & Sullivan, J. J. (1980). Commitment and energy conservation. In L. Bickman (Ed.), *Applied social psychology annual* (Vol. 1). Beverly Hills, CA: Sage.

Pallak, S. R., Murroni, E., & Koch, J. (1983). Communicator attractiveness and expertise, emotional versus rational appeals, and persuasion. *Social Cognition, 2,* 122–141.

Park, B. (1986). A method for studying the development of impressions of real people. *Journal of Personality and Social Psychology, 51,* 907–917.

Park, B. & Rothbart, M. (1982). Perception of out-group homogeneity and levels of social categorization: Memory for the subordinate attributes of in-group and out-group members. *Journal of Personality and Social Psychology, 42,* 1051–1068.

Parke, R. D., Berkowitz, L., Leyens, J. P., West, S. G., & Sebastian, J. (1977). Some effects of violent and nonviolent movies on the behavior of juvenile delinquents. In L. Berkowitz (Ed.), *Advances in experimental social psychology* (Vol. 10). New York: Academic Press.

Parkinson, M. G. (1979). *Language behavior and courtroom success.* Paper presented at meeting of the British Psychological Society, University of Bristol, England.

Passini, F. T. & Norman, W. T. (1966). A universal conception of personality structure? *Journal of Personality and Social Psychology, 4,* 44–49.

Patterson, A. H. (1974). Hostility catharsis: A naturalistic quasi-experiment. Paper presented at the annual meeting of the American Psychological Association.

Patterson, G. R. (1983). *Coercive family process: A social learning approach* (Vol. 3). Eugene, OR: Castalia.

Patterson, G. R., Littman, R. A., & Bricker, W. (1967). Assertive behavior in children: A step toward a theory of aggression. *Monographs for the Society for Research in Child Development, 32(5)* (Serial No. 113).

Payne, T. J., Connor, J. M., & Colletti, G. (1987). Gender-based schematic processing:

An empirical investigation and reevaluation. *Journal of Personality and Social Psychology, 52,* 937–945.

Peabody, D. (1968). Group judgments in the Philippines: Evaluative and descriptive aspects. *Journal of Personality and Social Psychology, 12,* 296–300.

Pennebacker, J. W. (1984). Accuracy of symptom perception. In A. Baum, S. E. Taylor, and J. E. Singer (Eds.), *Handbook of psychology and health* (Vol. IV): *Social psychological aspects of health.* Hillsdale, NJ: Erlbaum.

Penner, L. A., Dertke, M. C., & Achenbach, C. J. (1973). The "flash" system: A field study of altruism. *Journal of Applied Social Psychology, 3,* 362–370.

Pepinsky, P. N., Hemphill, J. K., & Shevitz, R. N. (1958). Attempts to lead, group productivity, and morale under conditions of acceptance and rejection. *Journal of Abnormal and Social Psychology, 57,* 47–54.

Percival, L. & Quinkert, K. (1987). Anthropometric factors. In M. A. Baker (Ed.), *Sex differences in human performance.* Chichester, England: Wiley.

Pessin, J. & Husband, R. W. (1933). Effects of social stimulation on human maze learning. *Journal of Abnormal and Social Psychology, 28,* 148–154.

Peters, L. H., Hartke, D. D., & Pohlmann, J. R. (1985). Fiedler's contingency theory of leadership: An application of the meta-analysis procedures of Schmidt and Hunter. *Psychological Bulletin, 97,* 274–285.

Peterson, D. R. (1968). *The clinical study of social behavior.* New York: Appleton-Century-Crofts.

Pettigrew, T. F. (1958). Personality and sociocultural factors in intergroup attitudes: A cross-national comparison. *Journal of Conflict Resolution, 2,* 29–42.

Pettigrew, T. F. (1979). The ultimate attribution error: Extending Allport's cognitive analysis of prejudice. *Personality and Social Psychology Bulletin, 5,* 461–476.

Pettigrew, T. F. (1980). Prejudice. In *Harvard encyclopedia of American ethnic groups.* Cambridge, MA: Harvard University Press.

Petty, R. E. & Cacioppo, J. T. (1977). Effects of forewarning of persuasive intent and involvement on cognitive responses and persuasion. *Personality and Social Psychology Bulletin, 5,* 173–176.

Petty, R. E. & Cacioppo, J. T. (1981). *Attitudes and persuasion: Classic and contemporary approaches.* Dubuque, IA: Brown.

Petty, R. E. & Cacioppo, J. T. (1984). The effects of involvement on responses to argument quantity and quality: Central and peripheral routes to persuasion. *Journal of Personality and Social Psychology, 46,* 69–81.

Petty, R. E. & Cacioppo, J. T. (1986). *Communication and persuasion: Central and peripheral routes to attitude change.* New York: Springer-Verlag.

Petty, R. E., Cacioppo, J. T., & Heesacker, M.

(1981). The use of rhetorical questions in persuasion: A cognitive response analysis. *Journal of Personality and Social Psychology, 40,* 432–440.

Petty, R. E., Cacioppo, J. T., & Schumann, D. (1983). Central and peripheral routes to advertising effectiveness: The moderating role of involvement. *Journal of Consumer Research, 10,* 134–148.

Phares, E. J. (1976). *Locus of control in personality.* Morristown, NJ: General Learning Press.

Pheterson, G. I., Kiesler, S. B., & Goldberg, P. A. (1971). Evaluation of the performances of women as a function of their sex, achievement, and personal history. *Journal of Personality and Social Psychology, 19,* 114–118.

Phillips, D. P. (1979). Suicide, motor vehicle fatalities, and the mass media: Evidence toward a theory of suggestion. *American Journal of Sociology, 84,* 1150–1174.

Phillips, D. P. (1983). The impact of mass media violence on U.S. homicides. *American Sociological Review, 48,* 560–568.

Piaget, J. (1966). *Judgment and reasoning in the child.* Totowa, NJ: Littlefield, Adams. (Originally published 1924.)

Pierce, C. M. (1980). Social trace contaminants: Subtle indicators of racism in T.V. In S. B. Withey & R. P. Abeles (Eds.), *Television and social behavior: Beyond violence and children.* Hillsdale, NJ: Erlbaum.

Piliavin, I. M., Rodin, J., & Piliavin, J. A. (1969). Good Samaritanism: An underground phenomenon? *Journal of Personality and Social Psychology, 13,* 289–299.

Piliavin, J. A., Dovidio, J. F., Gaertner, S. L., & Clark, R. D. (1981). *Emergency intervention.* New York: Academic Press.

Piliavin, J. A. & Piliavin, I. M. (1972). The effect of blood on reactions to a victim. *Journal of Personality and Social Psychology, 23,* 253–261.

Piliavin, J. A., Piliavin, I. M., & Trudell, B. (1974). *Incidental arousal, helping, and diffusion of responsibility.* Unpublished study, University of Wisconsin, Madison.

Pitcher, E. G. & Schultz, L. H. (1983). *Boys and girls at play: The development of sex roles.* New York: Praeger.

Pleck, J. (1979). Men's family work: Three perspectives and some new data. *Family Coordinator, 28,* 481–488.

Poppleton, P. K. & Pilkington, G. W. (1964). A comparison of four methods of scoring an attitude scale in relation to its reliability and validity. *British Journal of Social and Clinical Psychology, 3,* 36–39.

Porier, G. W. & Lott, A. J. (1967). Galvanic skin responses and prejudice. *Journal of Personality and Social Psychology, 5,* 253–259.

Porter, A. M. W. (1969). Drug defaulting in a general practice. *British Medical Journal, 1,* 218–222.

Powell, S. R. & Juhnke, R. G. (1983). Statistical models of implicit personality theory: A comparison. *Journal of Personality and Social Psychology, 44,* 911–922.

Pratkanis, A. R., Greenwald, A. G., Leippe, M. R., & Baumgardner, M. H. (1988). In search of reliable persuasion effects: III. The sleeper effect is dead. Long live the sleeper effect. *Journal of Personality and Social Psychology, 54*, 203–218.

Prentice-Dunn, S. & Rogers, R. W. (1980). Effects of deindividuating situation cues and aggressive models on subjective deindividuation and aggression. *Journal of Personality and Social Psychology, 39*, 104–113.

Priest, R. F. & Sawyer, J. (1967). Proximity and peership: Bases of balance in interpersonal attraction. *American Journal of Sociology, 72*, 633–649.

Pryor, J. B., Gibbons, F. X., Wicklund, R. A., Fazio, R. A., & Hood, R. (1977). Self-focused attention and self-report validity. *Journal of Personality, 45*, 513–527.

Pyszczynski, T. (1982). Cognitive strategies for coping with uncertain outcomes. *Journal of Research in Personality, 16*, 386–399.

Pyszczynski, T. & Greenberg, J. (1985). Depression and preference for self-focusing stimuli following success and failure. *Journal of Personality and Social Psychology, 49*, 1066–1075.

Pyszczynski, T. & Greenberg, J. (1987). Self-regulatory perseveration and the depressive self-focusing style: A self-awareness theory of reactive depression. *Psychological Bulletin, 102*, 122–138.

Quanty, M. B. (1976). Aggression catharsis: Experimental investigations and implications. In R. G. Geen & E. C. O'Neal (Eds.), *Perspectives on aggression*. New York: Academic Press.

Quinn, R. P. (1978). *Physical deviance and occupational mistreatment: The short, the fat, and the ugly*. Master's thesis, University of Michigan Survey Research Center, Ann Arbor.

Rabkin, J. G. & Struening, E. L. (1976). Life events, stress, and illness. *Science, 194*, 1013–1020.

Ragland, D. R. & Brand, R. J. (1988). Type A behavior and mortality from coronary heart disease. *New England Journal of Medicine, 318*, 65–69.

Rahe, R. H. (1984). Developments in life change measurement: Subjective life change unit scaling. In B. S. Dohrenwend & B. P. Dohrenwend (Eds.), *Stressful life events and their contexts*. New Brunswick, NJ: Rutgers University Press.

Rahe, R. H. & Lind, E. (1971). Psychosocial factors and sudden cardiac death: A pilot study. *Journal of Psychosomatic Research, 15*, 19–24.

Ramirez, J., Bryant, J., & Zillman, D. (1983). Effects of erotica on retaliatory behavior as a function of level of prior provocation. *Journal of Personality and Social Psychology, 43*, 971–978.

Ramsoy, N. R. (1966). Assortative mating and the structure of cities. *American Journal of Sociology, 31*, 773–786.

Rapaport, K. & Burkhart, B. R. (1984). Personality and attitudinal characteristics of sexually coercive college males. *Journal of Abnormal Psychology, 93*, 216–221.

Rasinski, K. A., Crocker, J., & Hastie, R. (1985). Another look at sex stereotypes and social judgments: An analysis of the social perceiver's use of subjective probabilities. *Journal of Personality and Social Psychology, 49*, 317–326.

Razran, G. H. S. (1938). Conditioning away social bias by the luncheon technique. *Psychological Bulletin, 35*, 693.

Razran, G. H. S. (1940). Conditioned response changes in rating and appraising sociopolitical slogans. *Psychological Bulletin, 37*, 481.

Regan, D. R., Williams, M., & Sparling, S. (1972). Voluntary expiation of guilt: A field experiment. *Journal of Personality and Social Psychology, 24*, 42–45.

Regan, D. T. (1971). Effects of a favor and liking on compliance. *Journal of Experimental Social Psychology, 7*, 627–639.

Reid, D. & Ware, E. E. (1974). Multidimensionality of internal versus external control: Addition of a third dimension and non-distinction of self versus others. *Canadian Journal of Behavioral Science, 6*, 131–142.

Reinisch, J. M., Rosenblum, L. A., & Sanders, S. A. (Eds.). (1987). *Masculinity/femininity: Basic perspectives*. New York: Oxford University Press.

Reisenzein, R. (1983). The Schachter theory of emotion: Two decades later. *Psychological Bulletin, 94*, 239–264.

Report of the Commission on Obscenity and Pornography. (1970). Washington, DC: U.S. Government Printing Office.

Rheingold, H. & Cook, K. (1975). The contents of boys' and girls' rooms as an index of parents' behavior. *Child Development, 4*, 459–463.

Rhodewalt, F. & Smith, T. W. (in press). Type A behavior, coronary proneness, and coronary heart disease: Current issues for research and intervention. In C. R. Snyder & D. F. Forsyth (Eds.), *Handbook of social and clinical psychology: The health perspective*. New York: Pergamon Press.

Rhodewalt, F. & Zone, J. B. (1989). Appraisal of life change, depression, and illness in hardy and nonhardy women. *Journal of Personality and Social Psychology, 56*, 81–88.

Ridley, M. & Dawkins, R. (1981). The natural selection of altruism. In J. P. Rushton & R. M. Sorrentino (Eds.), *Altruism and helping behavior: Social, personality, and developmental perspectives*. Hillsdale, NJ: Erlbaum.

Ringelmann, M. (1913). Research on animate sources of power: The world of man. *Annales de l'institute national agronomique*, 2e serie — tome XII, 1–40.

Rodin, J. (1985). The application of social psychology. In G. Lindzey and E. Aronson (Eds.), *Handbook of social psychology* (3rd. ed., Vol. 2). New York: Random House.

Rodin, J. & Baum, A. (1978). Crowding and helplessness: Potential consequences of density and loss of control. In A. Baum & Y. M. Epstein (Eds.), *Human response to crowding*. Hillsdale, NJ: Erlbaum.

Rodin, J. & Langer, E. (1977). Long-term effect of a control-relevant intervention. *Journal of Personality and Social Psychology, 35*, 897–902.

Rodin, J. & Salovey, P. (1989). Health psychology. In M. R. Rosenzweig & L. W. Porter (Eds.), *Annual review of psychology, 40*, 533–579.

Rofe, Y. (1984). Stress and affiliation: Activity theory. *Psychological Review, 91*, 235–250.

Rogers, R. W. (1975). A protection motivation theory of fear appeals and attitude change. *Journal of Psychology, 91*, 93–114.

Rogers, R. W. (1983). Cognitive and physiological processes in fear appeals and attitude change: A revised theory of protection motivation. In J. Cacioppo & R. Petty (Eds.), *Social psychophysiology*. New York: Guilford.

Rogers, R. W. & Mewborn, R. (1976). Fear appeals and attitude change: Effects of a threat's noxiousness, probability of occurrence, and the efficiency of coping response. *Journal of Personality and Social Psychology, 34*, 54–61.

Rogers, T. B., Kuiper, N. A., & Kirker, W. S. (1977). Self-reference and the encoding of personal information. *Journal of Personality and Social Psychology, 35*, 677–688.

Rogot, E. (1974). Smoking and mortality among U.S. veterans. *Journal of Chronic Diseases, 27*, 189–203.

Rohrer, J. H., Baron, S. H., Hoffman, E. L., & Swander, D. V. (1954). The stability of autokinetic judgments. *Journal of Abnormal and Social Psychology, 49*, 595–597.

Rokeach, M. (1956). Political and religious dogmatism: An alternative to the authoritarian personality. *Psychological Monographs, 70(18)* (Whole No. 425).

Rokeach, M. (1960). *The open and closed mind*. New York: Basic Books.

Rokeach, M. (1968). *Beliefs, attitudes, and values: A theory of organization and change*. San Francisco: Jossey-Bass.

Roper Organization. (1974). *The Virginia Slims opinion poll* (Vol. 3). New York: Author.

Rosch, E. (1978). Principles of categorization. In E. Rosch & B. B. Lloyd (Eds.), *Cognition and categorization*. Hillsdale, NJ: Erlbaum.

Rosch, E., Mervis, C. B., Gray, W., Johnson, D., & Boyes-Braem, P. (1976). Basic objects in natural categories. *Cognitive Psychology, 8*, 382–439.

Rose, T. L. (1981). Cognitive and dyadic processes in intergroup contact. In D. L. Hamilton (Ed.), *Cognitive processes in stereotyping and intergroup behavior*. Hillsdale, NJ: Erlbaum.

Rosenbaum, M. E. (1980). Cooperation and competition. In P. B. Paulus (Ed.), *The psychology of group influence*. Hillsdale, NJ: Erlbaum.

Rosenbaum, M. E. (1986). The repulsion hypothesis: On the nondevelopment of relationships. *Journal of Personality and Social Psychology, 51*, 1156–1166.

Rosenberg, L. A. (1961). Group size, prior experience, and conformity. *Journal of Abnormal and Social Psychology, 63*, 436–437.

Rosenburg, M. J. (1956). Cognitive structure and attitudinal affect. *Journal of Abnormal and Social Psychology, 53*, 367–372.

Rosenburg, M. J. (1960). Cognitive reorganization in response to the hypnotic reversal of attitudinal affect. *Journal of Personality, 28,* 39–63.

Rosenburg, S., Nelson, C., & Vivekanathan, P. S. (1968). A multidimensional approach to the structure of personality impressions. *Journal of Personality and Social Psychology, 9,* 283–294.

Rosenkrantz, P., Vogel, S., Bee, H., Broverman, I., & Broverman, D. M. (1968). Sex-role stereotypes and self-concepts in college students. *Journal of Consulting and Clinical Psychology, 32,* 286–295.

Rosenman, R. H. Brand, R. J., Sholtz, R. I. & Friedman, M. (1976). Multivariate prediction of coronary heart disease during 8.5 year follow-up in the Western Collaborative Group Study. *American Journal of Cardiology, 37,* 903–910.

Rosenthal, R. (1966). *Experimenter effects in behavioral research.* New York: Appleton-Century-Crofts.

Rosenthal, R. (1984). *Meta-analytic procedures for social research.* Beverly Hills, CA: Sage.

Rosenthal, R. & Fode, K. L. (1963). Three experiments in experimenter bias. *Psychological Reports, 12,* 491–511.

Rosenthal, R., Hall, J. A., DiMatteo, M. R., Rogers, P. L., & Archer, D. (1979). *Sensitivity to nonverbal communication: The PONS test.* Baltimore: Johns Hopkins University Press.

Rosenthal, R. & Jacobson, L. (1968). *Pygmalion in the classroom: Teacher expectation and pupils' intellectual development.* New York: Holt, Rinehart & Winston.

Rosenthal, R. & Rubin, D. D. (1982). Further meta-analytic procedures for assessing cognitive gender differences. *Journal of Educational Psychology, 74,* 708–712.

Ross, L. (1977). The intuitive psychologist and his shortcomings: Distortions in the attribution process. In L. Berkowitz (Ed.), *Advances in experimental social psychology* (Vol. 10). New York: Academic Press.

Ross, L., Amabile, T. M., & Steinmetz, J. L. (1977). Social roles, social control, and biases in social perception processes. *Journal of Personality and Social Psychology, 35,* 485–494.

Ross, L. D. & Anderson, C. A. (1982). Shortcomings in the attributions process: On the origins and maintenance of erroneous social assessments. In D. Kahneman, P. Slovic, & A. Tversky (Eds.), *Judgment under uncertainty: Heuristics and biases.* New York: Cambridge University Press.

Ross, L. D., Lepper, M. R., & Hubbard, M. (1975). Perseverance in self-perception and social perception: Biased attributional processes in the debriefing paradigm. *Journal of Personality and Social Psychology, 32,* 880–892.

Ross, L., Greene, D., & House, P. (1977). The "false consensus effect": An egocentric bias in social perception and attribution processes. *Journal of Experimental Social Psychology, 13,* 279–301.

Ross, M. & Fletcher, G. J. O. (1985). Attribution and social perception. In G. Lindzey & E. Aronson (Eds.), *Handbook of social psychology* (Vol. 11). New York: Random House.

Roth, D. L., Snyder, C. R., & Pace, L. M. (1986). Dimensions of favorable self-presentation. *Journal of Personality and Social Psychology, 51,* 867–874.

Rothaus, P. & Worchel, P. (1964). Ego-support communication, catharsis, and hostility. *Journal of Personality, 32,* 296–312.

Rothbart, M. (1981). Memory processes and social beliefs. In D. L. Hamilton (Ed.), *Cognitive processes in stereotyping and intergroup behavior.* Hillsdale, NJ: Erlbaum.

Rothbart, M., Fulero, S., Jensen, C., Howard, J., & Birrell, P. (1978). From individual to group impressions: Availability heuristics in stereotype formation. *Journal of Experimental Social Psychology, 14,* 237–255.

Rotter, J. B. (1954). *Social learning and clinical psychology.* Englewood Cliffs, NJ: Prentice-Hall.

Rotter, J. B. (1966). Generalized expectancies for internal versus external control of reinforcement. *Psychological Monographs, 80* (Whole No. 609).

Rotter, J. B. (1975). Some problems and misconceptions related to the construct of internal versus external control of reinforcement. *Journal of Consulting and Clinical Psychology, 40,* 313–321.

Rotton, J., Barry, T., Frey, J., & Soler, E. (1978). Air pollution and interpersonal attraction. *Journal of Applied Social Psychology, 8,* 57–71.

Rotton, J. & Frey, J. (1985). Air pollution, weather, and violent crimes: Concomitant time-series analysis of archival data. *Journal of Personality and Social Psychology, 49,* 1207–1220.

Roy, M. (1977). *Battered women: A psychosociological study of domestic violence.* New York: Van Nostrand Reinhold.

Roy, P. (Ed.). (1982). *Structuring cooperative learning in the classroom: The 1982 handbook.* Minneapolis, MN: Interaction Books.

Rubin, J. Z. & Brown, B. R. (1975). *The social psychology of bargaining and negotiation.* New York: Academic Press.

Rubin, J. Z., Provenzano, F. J., & Luria, Z. (1974). The eye of the beholder: Parents' views on the sex of newborns. *American Journal of Orthopsychiatry, 44,* 512–519.

Rubin, Z. (1970). Measurement of romantic love. *Journal of Personality and Social Psychology, 16,* 265–273.

Rubin, Z. (1973). *Liking and loving: An invitation to social psychology.* New York: Holt, Rinehart & Winston.

Rubin, Z. (1974). From liking to loving: Patterns of attraction in dating relationships. In T. L. Huston (Ed.), *Foundations of interpersonal attraction.* New York: Academic Press.

Rubin, Z., Peplau, L. A., & Hill, C. T. (1981). Loving and leaving: Sex differences in romantic attachments. *Sex Roles, 7,* 821–835.

Ruble, D. N. & Feldman, N. S. (1976). Order of consensus, distinctiveness, and consistency information and causal attribution. *Journal of Personality and Social Psychology, 34,* 930–937.

Ruble, T. L. (1983). Sex stereotypes: Issues of change in the 1970s. *Sex Roles, 9,* 397–402.

Rusbult, C. E. (1980). Commitment and satisfaction in romantic associations: A test of the investment model. *Journal of Experimental Social Psychology, 16,* 172–186.

Rusbult, C. E., Johnson, D. J., & Morrow, G. D. (1986). Impact of couple patterns of problem solving in distress and nondistress in dating relationships. *Journal of Personality and Social Psychology, 50,* 744–753.

Rusbult, C. E. & Zembrodt, I. M. (1983). Response to dissatisfaction in romantic involvements: A multidimensional scaling analysis. *Journal of Experimental Social Psychology, 19,* 274–293.

Rushton, J. P. (1980). *Altruism, socialization, and society.* Englewood Cliffs, NJ: Prentice-Hall.

Rushton, J. P. (1981a). Television as a socializer. In J. P. Rushton & R. M. Sorrentino (Eds.), *Altruism and helping behavior: Social, personality, and developmental perspectives.* Hillsdale, NJ: Erlbaum.

Rushton, J. P. (1981b). The altruistic personality. In J. P. Rushton & R. M. Sorrentino (Eds.), *Altruism and helping behavior: Social, personality, and developmental perspectives.* Hillsdale, NJ: Erlbaum.

Rushton, J. P. (1988). Epigenic rules in moral development: Distal-proximal approaches to altruism and aggression. *Aggressive Behavior, 14,* 35–50.

Rushton, J. P., Fulker, D. W., Neale, M. C., Nias, D. K. B., & Eysenck, H. J. (1986). Altruism and aggression: The heritability of individual differences. *Journal of Personality and Social Psychology, 50,* 1192–1198.

Rushton, J. P. & Owen, D. (1975). Immediate and delayed effects of TV modeling and preaching on children's generosity. *British Journal of Social and Clinical Psychology, 14,* 309–310.

Rushton, J. P. & Sorrentino, R. M. (1981). Altruism and helping behavior: An historical perspective. In J. P. Rushton & R. M. Sorrentino (Eds.), *Altruism and helping behavior: Social, personality, and developmental perspectives.* Hillsdale, NJ: Erlbaum.

Rutkowski, G. K., Gruder, C. L., & Romer, D. (1983). Group cohesiveness, social norms, and bystander intervention. *Journal of Personality and Social Psychology, 44,* 545–552.

Ryan, E. D. (1970). The cathartic effect of vigorous motor activity on aggressive behavior. *Research Quarterly, 41,* 542–551.

Sadalla, E. K., Kenrick, D. T., & Vershure, B. (1987). Dominance and heterosexual attraction. *Journal of Personality and Social Psychology, 52,* 730–738.

Saegart, S., Swap, W., & Zajonc, R. B. (1973). Exposure, context, and interpersonal attraction. *Journal of Personality and Social Psychology, 25,* 234–242.

Safilios-Rothschild C. (1975). A cross-cultural examination of women's marital, educational, and occupational options. In M. T. S. Mednick, S. S. Tangri, & L. W. Hoffman (Eds.), *Women and achievement: Social and motivational analyses.* Washington, DC: Hemisphere.

Sagar, H. A. & Schofield, J. W. (1980). Racial and behavioral cues in black and white children's perceptions of ambiguously aggressive cues. *Journal of Personality and Social Psychology, 39,* 590–598.

Sakurai, M. M. (1975). Small group cohesiveness and detrimental conformity. *Sociometry, 38,* 340–357.

Samora, J., Saunders, L., & Larson, R. F. (1961). Medical vocabulary knowledge among hospital patients. *Journal of Health and Social Behavior, 2,* 83–89.

Sampson, E. E. (1977). Psychology and the American ideal. *Journal of Personality and Social Psychology, 35,* 767–782.

Samuelson, C. D., Messick, D. M., Rutte, C. G., & Wilke, H. (1984). Individual and structural solutions to resource dilemmas in two cultures. *Journal of Personality and Social Psychology, 47,* 94–104.

Sanders, G. S. & Baron, R. S. (1977). Is social comparison irrelevant for producing choice shifts? *Journal of Experimental Social Psychology, 13,* 303–314.

Sarason, I. G., Johnson, J. H., & Siegel, J. M. (1978). Assessing the impact of life changes: Development of the life experiences survey. *Journal of Consulting and Clinical Psychology, 46,* 932–946.

Sarason, I. G., Levine, H. M., Basham, R. B., & Sarason, B. R. (1983). Assessing social support: The social support questionnaire. *Journal of Personality and Social Psychology, 14,* 127–139.

Sarason, I. G. & Sarason, B. R. (1984). Life changes, moderators of stress, and health. In A. Baum, S. E. Taylor, & J. E. Singer (Eds.), *Handbook of psychology and health* (Vol. IV): *Social psychological aspects of health.* Hillsdale, NJ: Erlbaum.

Sarnoff, I. & Zimbardo, P. G. (1961). Anxiety, fear and social affiliation. *Journal of Abnormal and Social Psychology, 62,* 356–363.

Sawyer, J. (1966). Measurement and prediction, clinical and statistical. *Psychological Bulletin, 66,* 178–200.

Schachter, S. (1951). Deviation, rejection, and communication. *Journal of Abnormal and Social Psychology, 46,* 190–207.

Schachter, S. (1959). *The psychology of affiliation.* Stanford, CA: Stanford University Press.

Schachter, S. & Singer, J. (1962). Cognitive, social and physiological determinants of emotional state. *Psychological Review, 69,* 379–399.

Schank, R. C. & Abelson, R. P. (1977). *Scripts, plans, goals, and understanding.* Hillsdale, NJ: Erlbaum.

Scheier, M. F., Buss, A. H., & Buss, D. M. (1978). Self-consciousness, self-reports of aggressiveness, and aggression. *Journal of Research in Personality, 12,* 133–140.

Scheier, M. F. & Carver, C. (1977). Self-focused attention and the experience of emotion: Attraction, repulsion, elation and depression. *Journal of Personality and Social Psychology, 35,* 625–636.

Scheier, M. F. & Carver, C. S. (1985). Optimism, coping, and health: Assessment and implications of generalized outcome expectancies. *Health Psychology, 4,* 219–247.

Scheier, M. F., Carver, C. S., & Gibbons, F. X. (1979). Self-directed attention, awareness of bodily states, and suggestibility. *Journal of Personality and Social Psychology, 37,* 1576–1588.

Scheier, M. F., Carver, C. S., & Gibbons, F. X. (1981). Self-focused attention and reactions to fear. *Journal of Research in Personality, 15,* 1–15.

Scheier, M. F., Weintraub, J. K., & Carver, C. S. (1986). Coping with stress: Divergent strategies of optimists and pessimists. *Journal of Personality and Social Psychology, 51,* 1257–1264.

Schein, E. H. (1956). The Chinese indoctrination program for prisoners of war: A study of attempted "brainwashing." *Psychiatry, 19,* 149–172.

Schiffman, A., Cohen, S., Nlowik, R., & Selinger, D.(1978). Initial diagnostic hypotheses: Factors which may distort physicians' judgment. *Organizational Behavior and Human Performance, 21,* 305–315.

Schlenker, B. R. (1980). *Impression management: The self-concept, social identity, and interpersonal relations.* Monterey, CA: Brooks/Cole.

Schlenker, B. R. (1985). *The self and social life.* New York: McGraw-Hill.

Schmied, L. A. & Lawler, K. A. (1986). Hardiness, type A behavior, and the stress-illness relation in working women. *Journal of Personality and Social Psychology, 51,* 1218–1223.

Schmitt, B. H., Gilovich, T., Goore, N., & Joseph L. (1986). Mere exposure and social facilitation: One more time. *Journal of Experimental Social Psychology, 22,* 242–248.

Schmitt, J. P. (1983). Focus of attention in the treatment of depression. *Psychotherapy: Theory, Research, and Practice, 20,* 457–463.

Schnare, A. B. (1980). Trends in residential segregation by race: 1960–1970. *Journal of Urban Economics, 7,* 293–301.

Schneider, D. J., Hastorf, A., & Ellsworth, P. C. (1979). *Person Perception* (2nd ed.). Reading, MA: Addison-Wesley.

Schradle, S. B. & Dougher, M. J. (1985). Social support as a mediator of stress: Theoretical and empirical issues. *Clinical Psychology Review, 5,* 641–661.

Schrauger, J. S. (1975). Responses to evaluation as a function of initial self-perceptions. *Psychological Bulletin, 82,* 581–596.

Schucker, B. & Jacobs, D. R. (1977). Assessment of behavior pattern A by voice characteristics. *Psychosomatic Medicine, 39,* 219–228.

Schul, Y. & Burnstein, E. (1985). The informational basis of social judgments: Using past impression rather than the trait description in forming a new impression. *Journal of Experimental Social Psychology, 21,* 421–439.

Schulz, R. (1976). Effects of control and predictability on the physical well-being of the institutionalized aged. *Journal of Personality and Social Psychology, 33,* 563–573.

Schulz, R. & Aderman, D. (1973). Effect of residential change on the temporal distance of death of terminal cancer patients. *Omega: Journal of Death and Dying, 4,* 157–162.

Schulz, R. & Hanusa, B. H. (1978). Long-term effects of control and predictability enhancing interventions: Findings and ethical issues. *Journal of Personality and Social Psychology, 36,* 1194–1201.

Schuman, H. & Johnson, M. P. (1976). Attitudes and behavior. *Annual Review of Sociology, 2,* 161–207.

Schuman, H., Steeh, C., & Bobo, L. (1985). *Racial attitudes in America.* Cambridge, MA: Harvard University Press.

Schutz, A. (1971). *Collected papers* (Vol. 1): *The problem of social reality.* The Hague, Netherlands: Martinus Nijhoff.

Schutz, W. C. (1958). *FIRO: A three-dimensional theory of interpersonal behavior.* New York: Rinehart & Co.

Schwartz, B. (1978). *Psychology of learning and behavior.* New York: Norton.

Schwarzwald, J., Bizman, A., & Raz, M. (1983). The foot-in-the-door paradigm: Effects of second request size on donation probability and donor generosity. *Personality and Social Psychology Bulletin, 9,* 443–450.

Scott, J. P. (1973). Hostility and aggression. In B. Wolman (Ed.), *Handbook of general psychology.* Englewood Cliffs, NJ: Prentice-Hall.

Sears, D. O. (1975). Political socialization. In F. I. Greensteing & N. W. Polsby (Eds.), *Handbook of political science* (Vol. 2). Reading, MA: Addison-Wesley.

Sears, D. O. (1986). College sophomores in the laboratory: Influences of a narrow data base on social psychology's view of human nature. *Journal of Personality and Social Psychology, 5,* 515–530.

Sears, D. O., Lau, R. R., Tyler, T. R., & Allen, H. M., Jr. (1980). Self-interest vs. symbolic politics in policy attitudes and presidential voting. *American Political Science Review, 74,* 670–684.

Sears, R. R., Maccoby, E., & Levin, H. (1957). *Patterns of child rearing.* Evanston, IL: Row, Peterson.

Secord, P. F., Dukes, W. F., & Bevan, W. (1954). Personalities in face: I. An experiment in social perceiving. *Genetic Psychology Monographs, 49,* 231–279.

Segal, M. W. (1974). Alphabet and attraction: An unobtrusive measure of the effect of propinquity in a field study. *Journal of Personality and Social Psychology, 30,* 654–657.

Seligman, M. E. P. (1975). *Helplessness.* San Francisco: Freeman.

Selye, H. (1956). *The stress of life.* New York: McGraw-Hill.

Selye, H. (1976). *Stress in health and disease.* Reading, MA: Butterworths.

Shakespeare, W. (1960). *The tragedy of Julius Caesar.* New York: Washington Square Press.

Shanab, M. E. & Yahya, K. A. (1977). A behavioral study of obedience in children. *Journal of Personality and Social Psychology, 35,* 530–536.

Shaw, M. E. & Costanzo, P. R. (1970). *Theories of social psychology.* New York: McGraw-Hill.

Shears, L. M. & Jensema, D. J. (1969). Social acceptability of anomalous persons. *Exceptional Children, 36,* 91–96.

Sheridan, C. L. & King, R. G. (1972). Obedience to authority with an authentic victim. *Proceedings of the American Psychological Association,* 165–166.

Sherif, M. (1935). A study of some social factors in perception. *Archives of Psychology, 27,* 1–60.

Sherif, M. (1966). *Group conflict and cooperation: Their social psychology.* London: Routledge & Kegan Paul.

Sherif, M., Harvey, O. J., White, B. J., Hood, W. R., & Sherif, C. W. (1961). *Intergroup conflict and cooperation: The Robbers Cave experiment.* Norman: University of Oklahoma Book Exchange.

Sherif, M. & Sherif, C. W. (1953). *Groups in harmony and tension: An integration of studies on intergroup relations.* New York: Octagon Books.

Sherman, L. W. & Berk, R. A. (1984). The specific deterrent effects of arrest on domestic assault. *American Sociological Review, 49,* 261–272.

Sherman, S. J. (1980). On the self-erasing nature of errors of prediction. *Journal of Personality and Social Psychology, 39,* 211–221.

Sherman, S. J., Judd, C. M., & Park, B. (1989). Social cognition. In M. R. Rosenzweig & L. W. Porter (Eds.), *Annual review of psychology* (Vol. 40). Palo Alto, CA: Annual Reviews Inc.

Sherrod, D. (1974). Crowding, perceived control, and behavioral effects. *Journal of Applied Social Psychology, 4,* 171–186.

Sherrod, D. R., Hage, J. M., Halpern, P. L., & Moore, B. S. (1977). Effects of personal causation and perceived control on responses to an aversive environment: The more control the better. *Journal of Experimental Social Psychology, 13,* 14–27.

Sherwood, R. J. (1983). Compliance behavior of hemodialysis patients and the role of the family. *Family Systems Medicine, 1,* 60–72.

Shields, S. A. (1975). Functionalism, Darwinism, and the psychology of women: A study in social myth. *American Psychologist, 30,* 739–754.

Shotland, R. L. & Straw, M. K. (1976). Bystander response to an assault: When a man attacks a woman. *Journal of Personality and Social Psychology, 34,* 990–999.

Shuntich, R. & Taylor, S. (1972). The effects of alcohol on human physical aggression. *Journal of Experimental Research in Personality, 6,* 34–38.

Shure, G. H., Meeker, R. J., & Hansford, E. A. (1965). The effectiveness of pacifist strategies in bargaining games. *Journal of Conflict Resolution, 9,* 106–117.

Shweder, R. A. (1982). Fact and artifact in trait perception: the systematic distortion hypothesis. In B. A. Maher (Ed.), *Progress in experimental personality research* (Vol. 11). New York: Academic Press.

Siem, F. M. & Spence, J. T. (1986). Gender-related traits and helping behavior. *Journal of Personality and Social Psychology, 51,* 615–621.

Sigall, H. & Ostrove, N. (1975). Beautiful but dangerous: Effects of offender attractiveness and nature of the crime on juridic judgment. *Journal of Personality and Social Psychology, 31,* 410–414.

Sigelman, C. K., Berry, C. J., & Wiles, K. A. (1984). Violence in college students' dating relationships. *Journal of Applied Social Psychology, 5,* 530–548.

Signorella, M. L. & Jamison, W. (1986). Masculinity, femininity, androgyny, and cognitive performance: A metaanalysis. *Psychological Bulletin, 100,* 207–228.

Silverman, I. (1971). Physical attractiveness. *Sexual Behavior,* September, 22–25.

Silverman, L. J., Rivera, A. N., & Tedeschi, J. T. (1979). Transgression-compliance: Guilt, negative affect, or impression management? *Journal of Social Psychology, 108,* 57–62.

Simpson, G. E. & Yinger, J. M. (1985). *Racial and cultural minorities: An analysis of prejudice and discrimination.* New York: Plenum.

Simpson, J. A. (1987). The dissolution of romantic relationships: Factors involved in relationship stability and emotional distress. *Journal of Personality and Social Psychology, 53,* 683–692.

Sistrunk, F. & McDavid, J. W. (1971). Sex variable in conformity behavior. *Journal of Personality and Social Psychology, 17,* 200–207.

Skinner, B. F. (1938). *The behavior of organisms.* New York: Appleton-Century.

Skinner, B. F. (1953). *Science and human behavior.* New York: Macmillan.

Skowronski, J. J. & Carlston, D. E. (1987). Social judgment and social memory: The role of cue diagnosticity in negativity, positivity, and extremity biases. *Journal of Personality and Social Psychology, 52,* 689–699.

Skrypnek, B. J. & Snyder, M. (1982). On the self-perpetuating nature of stereotypes about women and men. *Journal of Experimental Social Psychology, 18,* 277–291.

Slovic, P., Fischoff, B., & Lichtenstein, S. (1977). Behavioral decision theory. *Annual Review of Psychology, 28,* 1–39.

Smith, B. L., Lasswell, H. D., & Casey, R. D. (1946). *Propaganda, communication, and public opinion.* Princeton, NJ: Princeton University Press.

Smith, G. F. & Dorfman, D. D. (1975). The effect of stimulus uncertainty on the relationship between frequency of exposure and liking. *Journal of Personality and Social Psychology, 31,* 150–155.

Smith, M. L. (1980). Sex bias in counseling and psychotherapy. *Psychological Bulletin, 57,* 392–407.

Smith, T. W., Ingram, R. E., & Roth, D. L. (1985). Self-focused attention and depression: Self-evaluation, affect, and life stress. *Motivation and Emotion, 9,* 323–331.

Smith, T. W., Pope, M. K., Rhodewalt, F., & Poulton, J. L. (1989). Optimism, neuroticism, coping, and symptom reports: An alternative interpretation of the Life Orientation Test. *Journal of Personality and Social Psychology, 56,* 640–648.

Sniderman, P. M. & Hagen, M. (1985). *Race and inequality.* New York: Chatham House.

Sniderman, P. M. & Tetlock, P. E. (1986). Symbolic racism: Problems of motive attribution in political analysis. *Journal of Social Issues, 42,* 129–150.

Snow, M. E., Jacklin, C. N., & Maccoby, E. E. (1983). Sex-of-child differences in father-child interaction at one year of age. *Child Development, 54,* 227–232.

Snyder, M. (1974). The self-monitoring of expressive behavior. *Journal of Personality and Social Psychology, 30,* 526–537.

Snyder, M. (1979). Self-monitoring processes. In L. Berkowitz (Ed.), *Advances in experimental social psychology* (Vol. 12). New York: Academic Press.

Snyder, M. (1981). On the self-perpetuating nature of social stereotype. In D. L. Hamilton (Ed.), *Cognitive processes in stereotyping and intergroup behavior.* Hillsdale, NJ: Erlbaum.

Snyder, M. (1982). When believing means doing: Creating links between attitudes and behavior. In M. P. Zanna, E. T. Higgins, & C. P. Herman (Eds.), *Consistency in social behavior* (Vol. 2). Hillsdale, NJ: Erlbaum.

Snyder, M. (1987). *Public appearances/Private realities.* New York: Freeman.

Snyder, M., Berscheid, E., & Glick, P. (1985). Focusing on the exterior and the interior: Two investigations of the initiation of personal relationships. *Journal of Personality and Social Psychology, 48,* 1427–1439.

Snyder, M., Berscheid, E., & Matwychuk, A. (1988). Orientations toward personnel selection: Differential reliance on appearance and personality. *Journal of Personality and Social Psychology, 54,* 972–979.

Snyder, M. & Campbell, B. H. (1980). Testing hypotheses about other people: The role of the hypothesis. *Personality and Social Psychology Bulletin, 6,* 421–426.

Snyder, M. & DeBono, K. G. (1985). Appeals to images and claims about quality: Understanding the psychology of advertising. *Journal of Personality and Social Psychology, 49,* 586–597.

Snyder, M. & DeBono, K. G. (1987). A functional approach to attitudes and persuasion. In M. P. Zanna, J. M. Olson, & C. P. Herman (Eds.), *Social influence: The Ontario symposium* (Vol 5). Hillsdale, NJ: Erlbaum.

Snyder, M. & Gangestad, S. (1982) Choosing social situations: Two investigations of self-monitoring processes. *Journal of Personality and Social Psychology, 43,* 123–135.

Snyder, M., Gangestad, S., & Simpson, J. A. (1983). Choosing friends as activity partners: The role of self-monitoring. *Journal of Personality and Social Psychology, 45,* 1061–1072.

Snyder, M. & Ickes, W. (1985). Personality and social behavior. In G. Lindzey & E. Aronson (Eds.), *Handbook of social psychology* (3rd ed.). New York: Random House.

Snyder, M. & Monson, T. C. (1975). Persons, situations, and the control of social behavior. *Journal of Personality and Social Psychology, 32,* 637–644.

Snyder, M. & Simpson, J. A. (1984). Self-monitoring and dating relationships. *Journal of Personality and Social Psychology, 47,* 1281–1291.

Snyder, M. & Swann, W. B. (1978). Hypothesis-testing processes in social interaction. *Journal of Personality and Social Psychology, 36,* 1202–1212.

Snyder, M. & Swann, W. B., Jr. (1976). When actions reflect attitudes: The politics of impression management. *Journal of Personality and Social Psychology, 34,* 1034–1042.

Snyder, M. & Tanke, E. D. (1976). Behavior and attitude: Some people are more consistent than others. *Journal of Personality and Social Psychology, 44,* 510–517.

Snyder, M., Tanke, E. D., & Berscheid, E. (1977). Social perception and interpersonal behavior: On the self-fulfilling nature of social stereotypes. *Journal of Personality and Social Psychology, 35,* 656–666.

Snyder, M. & Uranowitz, S. W. (1978). Reconstructing the past: Some cognitive consequences of person perception. *Journal of Personality and Social Psychology, 36,* 941–950.

Social indicators of equality for minorities and women (1978). A report of the United States Commission on Civil Rights.

Sohl, R. & Carr, A. (Eds.). (1970) *The gospel according to zen: Beyond the death of God.* New York: Mentor.

Solomon, H., Solomon, L. Z., Arnone, M. M., Maur, B. J., Reda, R. M., & Rother, E. O. (1981). Anonymity and helping. *Journal of Social Psychology, 113,* 37–43.

Solomon, R. L. & Corbit, J. D. (1974). An opponent-process theory of motivation: I. Temporal dynamics of affect. *Psychological Review, 81,* 119–145.

Sontag, S. (1977). *Illness as metaphor.* New York: Farrar, Straus & Giroux.

Sorrentino, R. M. & Field, N. (1986). Emergent leadership over time: The functional value of positive motivation. *Journal of Personality and Social Psychology, 50,* 1091–1099.

Spence, J. T., Deaux, K. & Helmreich, R. L. (1985). Sex roles in contemporary American society. In G. Lindzey & E. Aronson (Eds.), *Handbook of social psychology* (Vol. II). New York: Random House.

Spence, J. T. & Helmreich, R. L. (1978). *Masculinity and femininity: The psychological dimensions, correlates, and antecedents.* Austin: University of Texas Press.

Spence, J. T. & Helmreich, R. L.(1980). Masculine instrumentality and feminine expressiveness: Their relationships with sex role attitudes and behaviors. *Psychology of Women Quarterly, 5,* 147–163.

Spence, J. T., Helmreich, R. L., & Stapp, J. (1974). The personal attributes questionnaire: A measure of sex role stereotypes and masculinity-femininity. *JSAS Catalog of Selected Documents in Psychology, 4,* 43. (MS No. 617.)

Spence, J. T. & Sawin, L. L. (1985). Images of masculinity and femininity: A reconceptualization. In V. E. O'Leary, R. K. Unger, & B. S. Wallston (Eds.), *Women, gender, and social psychology.* Hillsdale, NJ: Erlbaum.

Sperber, B. M., Fishbein, M., & Ajzen, I. (1980). Predicting and understanding women's occupational orientations: Factors underlying choice intentions. In I. Ajzen & M. Fishbein (Eds.), *Understanding attitudes and predicting social behavior.* Englewood Cliffs, NJ: Prentice-Hall.

Sprafkin, J. N., Liebert, R. M., & Poulos, R. W. (1975). Effects of a prosocial televised example on children's helping. *Journal of Experimental Child Psychology, 20,* 119–126.

Sroufe, A. L. (1978). Attachment and the roots of human competence. *Human nature, 1(10),* 50–57.

Staats, A. W. & Staats, C. K. (1958). Attitudes established by classical conditioning. *Journal of Abnormal and Social Psychology, 57,* 37–40.

Stanley, J. C. & Benbrow, C. P. (1982). Huge sex ratios at upper end. *American Psychologist, 37,* 972.

Stapp, J. & Fulcher, R. (1981). The employment of APA members. *American Psychologist, 36,* 1263–1314.

Staub, E. (1970). The effect of focusing responsibility on children on their attempts to help. *Developmental Psychology, 2,* 152–154.

Staub, E. (1974). Helping a distressed person: Social, personality, and stimulus determinants. In L. Berkowitz (Ed.), *Advances in experimental social psychology,* (Vol. 7). New York: Academic Press.

Staub, E. (1975). To rear a prosocial child: Reasoning, learning by doing, and learning by teaching others. In D. Palma & J. Folly (Eds.), *Moral development: Current theory and research.* Hillsdale, NJ: Erlbaum.

Staub, E. (1979). *Positive social behavior and morality* (Vol. 2): *Socialization and development.* New York: Academic Press.

Steffensmeier, D. J. & Terry, R. M. (1973). Deviance and respectability: An observational study of reactions to shoplifting. *Social Forces, 51,* 417–426.

Stein, A. H. & Bailey, M. N. (1973). The socialization of achievement orientation in females. *Psychological Bulletin, 80,* 345–366.

Stein, R. T. & Heller, T. (1979). An empirical analysis of the correlations between leadership, status and participation rates reported in the literature. *Journal of Personality and Social Psychology, 37,* 1993–2002.

Steinberg, C. (1985). *TV facts.* New York: Facts on File Publications.

Steiner, I. D. (1972). *Group process and productivity.* New York: Academic Press.

Steiner, I. D. (1976). Task-performing groups. In J. W. Thibaut, J. T. Spence, & R. C. Carson (Eds.), *Contemporary topics in social psychology.* Morristown, NJ: General Learning Press.

Steinmetz, S. K. (1980). Women and violence: Victims and perpetrators. *American Journal of Psychotherapy, 3,* 334–349.

Stephan, W. G., Berscheid, E., & Walster, E. (1971). Sexual arousal and heterosexual perception. *Journal of Personality and Social Psychology, 20,* 93–101.

Stern, G. S., McCants, T. R., & Pettine, P. W. (1982). Stress and illness: Controllable and uncontrollable life events' relative contributions. *Personality and Social Psychology Bulletin, 8,* 140–145.

Sternberg, R. (1986). A triangular theory of love. *Psychological Review, 93,* 119–135.

Sternburg, R. J. & Grajek, S. (1984). The nature of love. *Journal of Personality and Social Psychology, 47,* 312–329.

Sternglanz, S. H. & Serbin, L. A. (1974). Sex role stereotyping in children's TV programs. *Developmental Psychology, 10,* 710–715.

Steuer, F. B., Applefield, J. M., & Smith, R. (1971). Televised aggression and the interpersonal aggression of preschool children. *Journal of Experimental Child Psychology, 11,* 442–447.

Stevens, S. (1971, November 28). The "rat packs" of New York. *The New York Times.*

Stevenson-Hinde, J., Hinde, R. A., & Simpson, A. E. (1986). Behavior at home and friendly or hostile behavior in preschool. In D. Olweus, J. Block, & M. Radke-Yarrow (Eds.), *Development of antisocial and prosocial behavior: Research, theories, and issues.* Orlando, FL: Academic Press.

Stewart, J. E., II. (1980). Defendant's attractiveness as a factor in the outcome of criminal trials: An observational study. *Journal of Applied Social Psychology, 10,* 348–361.

Stogdill, R. M. (1974). *Handbook of leadership.* New York: Free Press.

Stone, W. F. (1980). The myth of left-wing authoritarianism. *Political Psychology,* 3–19.

Stone, W. F. (1981). Political psychology: A Whig history. In S. L. Long (Ed.), *The handbook of political behavior* (Vol. 1). New York: Plenum.

Stoner, J. A. F. (1961). *A comparison of individual and group decisions involving risk.* Unpublished master's thesis, Massachusetts Institute of Technology, Cambridge, MA.

Storms, M. D. (1973). Videotape and the attribution process: Reversing actors and observer's points of view. *Journal of Personality and Social Psychology, 27,* 165–175.

Stouffer, S. A., Suchman, E. A., DeVinney, L. C., Star, S. A., & Williams, R. M., Jr. (1949). *The American soldier: Adjustment during army life* (Vol. 1). Princeton, NJ: Princeton University Press.

Strauman, T. J. & Higgins, E. T. (1987). Automatic activation of self-discrepancies and emotional syndromes: When cognitive structures influence affect. *Journal of Personality and Social Psychology, 53*, 1004–1014.

Straus, M. A. (1974). Leveling, civility, and violence in the family. *Journal of Marriage and the Family, 36*, 12–29.

Straus, M. A. (1980). The marriage license as a hitting license: Evidence from popular culture, law and social science. In M. Straus & G. Hotaling (Eds.), *The social causes of husband-wife violence*. Minneapolis: University of Minnesota Press.

Straus, M. A., Gelles, R. J., & Steinmetz, S. K. (1980). *Behind closed doors: Violence in the American family*. Garden City, NY: Anchor Books.

Straus, M. A. & Hotaling, G. T. (Eds.). (1980). *The social causes of husband-wife violence*. Minneapolis: University of Minnesota Press.

Strayer, F. F., Wareing, S., & Rushton, J. P. (1979). Social constraints on naturally occurring preschool altruism. *Ethology and Sociobiology, 1*, 3–11.

Strickland, B. R. (1989). Internal-external control expectancies: From contingency to creativity. *American Psychologist, 44*, 1–12.

Strickland, L. H. (1958). Surveillance and trust. *Journal of Personality, 26*, 200–215.

Strodtbeck, F. L. & Hook, L. H. (1961). The social dimensions of a twelve-man jury table. *Sociometry, 24*, 397–415.

Strodtbeck, F. L., James, R. M., & Hawkins, C. (1958). Social status in jury deliberations. In E. E. Maccoby, T. M. Newcomb, & E. L. Hartley (Eds.), *Readings in social psychology* (3rd ed.). New York: Holt.

Stogdill, R. M. (1974). *Handbook of leadership*. New York: Free Press.

Stroebe, W., Insko, C. A., Thompson, V. D., & Layton, B. D. (1971). Effects of physical attractiveness, attitude similarity, and sex on various aspects of interpersonal attraction. *Journal of Personality and Social Psychology, 18*, 79–91.

Strong, E. K. (1943). *Vocational interests of men and women*. Stanford, CA: Stanford University Press.

Strube, M. J. & Garcia, J. E. (1981). A meta-analytic investigation of Fiedler's contingency model of leadership effectiveness. *Psychological Bulletin, 90*, 307–321.

Suls, J. & Greenwald, A. G. (Eds.). (1986). *Psychological perspectives on the self* (Vol. 3). Hillsdale, NJ: Erlbaum.

Suls, J. M. & Miller, R. L. (Eds.). (1977). *Social comparison processes: Theoretical and empirical perspective*. Washington, DC: Halsted-Wiley.

Suls, J. & Mullen, B. (1981). Life events, perceived control and illness: The role of uncertainty. *Journal of Human Stress, 7*, 30–34.

Sutherland, E. H. & Cressey, D. R. (1966). *Principles of criminology* (7th ed.). Philadelphia: Lippincott.

Svarstad, B. L. (1976). Physician-patient communication and patient conformity with medi-

cal advice. In D. Mechanic (Ed.), *The growth of bureaucratic medicine: An inquiry into the dynamics of patient behavior and the organization of medical care*. New York: Wiley.

Swann, W. B., Jr., Griffin, J. J., Jr., Predmore, S. C., & Gaines, B. (1987). The cognitive-affective crossfire: When self-consistency confronts self-enhancement. *Journal of Personality and Social Psychology, 52*, 881–889.

Swann, W. B., Jr. & Pelham, B. W. (1987). *The social construction of identity: Self-verification through friends and intimate selection*. Unpublished manuscript.

Swann, W. B., Jr. & Read, S. J. (1981). Self-verification processes: How we sustain our self-conceptions. *Journal of Experimental Social Psychology, 17*, 351–372.

Swap, W. C. (1977). Interpersonal attraction and repeated exposure to rewarders and punishers. *Personality and Social Psychology Bulletin, 3*, 248–251.

Sweeney, J. (1973). An experimental investigation of the free rider problem. *Social Science Research, 2*, 277–292.

Sweet, W. H., Ervin, F., & Mark, V. H. (1969). The relationship of violent behavior to focal cerebral disease. In S. Garattini & E. B. Sigg (Eds.), *Aggressive behavior*. New York: Wiley.

Symons, D. (1979). *The evolution of human sexuality*. New York: Oxford University Press.

Szymanski, D. & Harkins, S. G. (1987). Social loafing and self-evaluation with a social standard. *Journal of Personality and Social Psychology, 5*, 871–897.

Taft, R. (1955). The ability to judge people. *Psychological Bulletin, 52*, 1–23.

Tajfel, H. (Ed.). (1978). *Differentiation between social groups*. New York: Academic Press.

Tajfel, H. (1981). *Human groups and social categories*. Cambridge, England: Cambridge University Press.

Tajfel, H. (1982). *Social identity and intergroup relations*. Cambridge, England: Cambridge University Press.

Tajfel, H., Billig, M. G., Bundy, R. P., & Flament, C. (1971). Social categorization and intergroup behavior. *European Journal of Social Psychology, 1*, 149–178.

Tajfel, H. & Turner, J. C. (1979). An integrative theory of social conflict. In W. Austin & S. Worchel (Eds.), *The social psychology of intergroup relations*. Monterey, CA: Brooks/Cole.

Tanford, S. & Penrod, S. (1984). Social influence model: A formal integration of research on majority and minority influence processes. *Psychological Bulletin, 95*, 189–225.

Tausig, H. L. (1982). Measuring life events. *Journal of Health and Social Behavior, 23*, 52–64.

Tavris, C. & Wade, C. (1984). *The longest war: Sex differences in perspective*. New York: Harcourt Brace Jovanovich.

Taylor, D. W., Berry, P. C., & Block, C. H. (1958). Does group participation when using brainstorming facilitate or inhibit creative thinking? *Administrative Science Quarterly, 3*, 23–47.

Taylor, J. A. (1953). A personality scale of manifest anxiety. *Journal of Abnormal and Social Psychology, 48*, 285–290.

Taylor, M. C. & Hall, J. A. (1982). Psychological androgyny: Theories, methods, and conclusions. *Psychological Bulletin, 92*, 347–366.

Taylor, R. B., De Soto, C. B., & Lieb, R. (1979). Sharing secrets: Disclosure and discretion in dyads and triads. *Journal of Personality and Social Psychology, 37*, 1196–1203.

Taylor, S. E. (1979). Hospital patient behavior: Reactance, helplessness, or control? *Journal of Social Issues, 35*, 156–184.

Taylor, S. E. (1981). A categorizing approach to stereotyping. In D. Hamilton (Ed.), *Cognitive processes in stereotyping and intergroup behavior*. Hillsdale, NJ: Erlbaum.

Taylor, S. E. (1981). The interface of cognitive and social psychology. In J. Harvey (Ed.), *Cognition, social behavior, and the environment*. Hillsdale, NJ: Erlbaum.

Taylor, S. E. & Brown, J. D. (1988). Illusion and well-being: A social psychological perspective on mental health. *Psychological Bulletin, 103*, 193–210.

Taylor, S. E. & Crocker, J. (1981). Schematic bases of social information processing. In E. T. Higgins, C. Herman, & M. Zanna (Eds.), *Social cognition: The Ontario symposium on personality and social psychology*. Hillsdale, NJ: Erlbaum.

Taylor, S. E. & Fiske, S. T. (1975). Point of view and perception of causality. *Journal of Personality and Social Psychology, 32*, 439–445.

Taylor, S. E. & Fiske, S. T. (1978). Salience, attention, and attribution: Top of the head phenomena. In L. Berkowitz (Ed.), *Advances in experimental social psychology* (Vol. 11). New York: Academic Press.

Taylor, S. E., Lichtman, R. R., & Wood, J. V. (1984). Attributions, beliefs about control, and adjustment to breast cancer. *Journal of Personality and Social Psychology, 46*, 489–502.

Taylor, S. E. & Thompson, S. C. (1982). Stalking the elusive "vividness effect." *Psychological Review, 89*, 155–181.

Taylor, S. & Gammon, C. (1975). Effects of type and dose of alcohol on human physical aggression. *Journal of Personality and Social Psychology, 32*, 169–175.

Taylor, S., Vardaris, R., Rawitch, A., Gammon, C., Cranston, J., & Lubetkin, A. (1976). The effects of alcohol and delta-atetrahydrocannabinol on human physical aggression. *Aggressive Behavior, 2*, 153–161.

Taylor, S. P. (1986). The regulation of aggressive behavior. In R. J. Blanchard & D. C. Blanchard (Eds.), *Advances in the study of aggression*. Orlando, FL: Academic Press.

Terman, L. M. & Miles, C. C. (1936). *Sex and personality: Studies in masculinity and femininity*. New York: Russell & Russell.

Tesser, A. (1978). Self-generated attitude change. In L. Berkowitz (Ed.), *Advances in experimental social psychology* (Vol. 11). New York: Academic Press.

Tesser, A. (1986). Some effects of self-evaluation maintenance on cognition and action. In R. M. Sorrentino & E. T. Higgins (Eds.), *The handbook of motivation and cognition: Foundations of social behavior.* New York: Guilford.

Tesser, A. & Brodie, M. (1971). A note on the evaluation of a computer date. *Psychonomic Science, 23,* 300.

Tesser, A., Campbell, J., & Smith, M. (1984). Friendship choice and performance: Self evaluation maintenance in children. *Journal of Personality and Social Psychology, 46,* 561–574.

Tesser, A. & Leone, C. (1977). Cognitive schemas and thought as determinants of attitude change. *Journal of Experimental Social Psychology, 13,* 340–356.

Tesser, A. & Moore, J. (1986). Convergence of public and private aspects of self. In R. F. Baumeister (Ed.), *Public self and private self.* New York: Springer-Verlag.

Tesser, A. & Rosen, S. (1975). The reluctance to transmit bad news. In L. Berkowitz (Ed.), *Advances in experimental social psychology* (Vol. 8). New York: Academic Press.

Tessler, R. C. & Schwartz, S. H. (1972). Help seeking, self-esteem, and achievement motivation: An attributional analysis. *Journal of Personality and Social Psychology, 21,* 318–326.

Tetlock, P. E., Bernzweig, J., & Gallant, J. L. (1985). Supreme court decision making: Cognitive style as a predictor of ideological consistency of voting. *Journal of Personality and Social Psychology, 48,* 1227–1239.

Tetlock, P. E., Hannum, K. A., & Micheletti, P. M. (1984). Stability and change in the complexity of senatorial debate: Testing the cognitive versus rhetorical style hypotheses. *Journal of Personality and Social Psychology, 46,* 979–990.

The Man of La Mancha (1966). Music by Mitch Leigh. Musical play by Dale Wasserman. Lyrics by Joe Darion. New York: Random House.

The World Almanac. (1988). New York: Pharos Books.

Thibaut, J. W. & Kelley, H. H. (1959). *The social psychology of groups.* New York: Wiley.

Thibaut, J. W. & Rieken, W. H. (1955). Some determinants and consequences of the perception of social causality. *Journal of Personality, 24,* 114–133.

Thomas, J. R. & French, K. E. (1985). Gender differences across age in motor performance: A meta-analysis. *Psychological Bulletin, 98,* 260–282.

Thomas, M. H. (1982). Physiological arousal, exposure to a relatively lengthy aggressive film, and aggressive behavior. *Journal of Research in Personality, 16,* 72–81.

Thompson, R. C. & Michel, J. B. (1972). Measuring authoritarianism: A comparison of the F and D scales. *Journal of Personality, 40,* 180–190.

Thoreau, H. D., 27 June 1840. *The writings of Henry David Thoreau, Journal I, 1837–1846.* Boston: Houghton Mifflin.

Thurstone, L. L. (1928). Attitudes can be measured. *American Journal of Sociology, 33,* 529–554.

Thurstone, L. L. & Chave, E. J. (1929). *The measurement of attitude.* Chicago: University of Chicago Press.

Tice, D. M. & Baumeister, R. F. (1985). Masculinity inhibits helping in emergencies: Personality does predict the bystander effect. *Journal of Personality and Social Psychology, 49,* 420–428.

Time (1984, March 26). Marian and the elders. *123,* 70.

Time (1986, March 10). "A serious deficiency": The Rogers commission faults NASA's "flawed" decision making process. *127(10),* 38–42.

Time (1988, Oct. 31). "They lied to us": Unsafe, aging U.S. weapons plants are stirring fear and disillusion. *132(18),* 60–65.

Tipton, R. M. & Browning, S. (1972). The influence of age and obesity on helping behavior. *British Journal of Social and Clinical Psychology, 11,* 404–406.

Toch, H. (1985). The catalytic situation in the violence equation. *Journal of Applied Social Psychology, 15,* 105–123.

Tolstoy, L. (1981). *Anna Karenina.* New York: Bantam Books. (Originally published 1876.)

Touhey, J. C. (1974). Effects of additional women professionals in ratings of occupational prestige and desirability. *Journal of Personality and Social Psychology, 29,* 86–89.

Travis, L. E. (1925). The effect of a small audience upon eye-hand coordination. *Journal of Abnormal and Social Psychology, 20,* 142–146.

Triandis, H. C. (1977). *Interpersonal behavior.* Monterey, CA: Brooks/Cole.

Triandis, H. C. (1978). Some universals of social behavior. *Personality and Social Psychology Bulletin, 4,* 1–16.

Tringo, J. L. (1970). The hierarchy of preference toward disability groups. *Journal of Special Education, 4,* 295–306.

Triplett, N. (1897). The dynamogenic factors in pacemaking and competition. *American Journal of Psychology, 9,* 507–533.

Trivers, R. L. (1971). The evolution of reciprocal altruism. *Quarterly Review of Biology, 46,* 35–57.

Trivers, R. L. (1983). The evolution of cooperation. In D. L. Bridgeman (Ed.), *The nature of prosocial development.* New York: Academic Press.

Tunnell, G. (1980). Intraindividual consistency in personality assessment: The effects of self-monitoring. *Journal of Personality, 48,* 220–232.

Turner, C. W. & Layton, J. F. (1976). Verbal imagery and connotation as memory induced mediators of aggressive behavior. *Journal of Personality and Social Psychology, 33,* 755–763.

Turner, J. C. (1978). Social categorization and social discrimination in the minimal group situation. In H. Tajfel (Ed.), *Differentiation between social groups.* London: Academic Press.

Turner, R. J. (1981). Social support as a contingency in psychological well-being. *Journal of Personality and Social Psychology, 22,* 357–367.

Tversky, A. & Kahneman, D. (1973). Availability: A heuristic for judging frequency and probability. *Cognitive Psychology, 5,* 207–232.

Tversky, A. & Kahneman, D. (1974). Judgment under uncertainty: Heuristics and biases. *Science, 185,* 1124–1131.

Tversky, A. & Kahneman, D. (1981). The framing of decisions and the psychology of choice. *Science, 211,* 453–458.

Tversky, A. & Kahneman, D. (1982). Judgments of and by representativeness. In D. Kahneman, P. Slovic, & A. Tversky (Eds.), *Judgment under uncertainty: Heuristics and biases.* New York: Cambridge University Press.

Ulrich, R. & Azrin, N. H. (1962). Reflexive fighting in response to aversive stimulation. *Journal of the Experimental Analysis of Behavior, 5,* 511–520.

Ulrich, R. E., Johnson, M., Richardson, J., & Wolff, P. (1963). The operant conditioning of fighting behavior in rats. *Psychological Record, 13,* 465–470.

Ulschak, P. L., Nathanson, L., & Gillan, P. G. (1981). *Small group problem solving.* Reading, MA: Addison-Wesley.

Underwood, B. & Moore, B. (1982). Perspective-taking and altruism. *Psychological Bulletin, 91,* 143–173.

Unger, R. K. (1979). Toward a redefinition of sex and gender. *American Psychologist, 34,* 1085–1094.

United Nations: Demographic Yearbook (1986). New York: United Nations.

U.S. Department of Health and Human Services. (1984). *Annual summary of births, deaths, marriages, and divorces: United States, 1983.* (DHHS Publication No. PHS 84-1120). Washington, DC: U.S. Government Printing Office.

U.S. Department of Labor, Women's Bureau (1983). *Times of change: 1983 handbook on women workers.*

Vandenberg, S. G. (1972). Assortative mating, or who marries whom? *Behavior Genetics, 2,* 127–158.

Van Der Pligt, J. & Eiser, J. R. (1983). Actors' and observers' attributions, self-serving bias, and positivity. *European Journal of Social Psychology, 13,* 95–104.

Van Valey, T. L., Roof, W. C., & Wilcox, J. E. (1977). Trends in residential segregation: 1960–1970. *American Journal of Sociology, 82,* 826–844.

Vaughan, D. (1986). *Uncoupling.* New York: Vintage Books.

Veitch, R., DeWood, R., & Bosko, K. (1977). Radio news broadcasts: Their effect on interpersonal helping. *Sociometry, 40,* 383–386.

Vernon, P. E. (1964). *Personality assessment: A critical survey.* New York: Wiley.

Voltaire. (1966). *Candide or optimism* (Robert M. Adams, Trans. and Ed.). New York: Norton. (Originally published 1759.)

Walker, K. E. & Woods, M. E. (1976). *Time use: A measure of household production of goods and services.* Washington, DC: American Home Economics Association.

Wallace, J. & Sadalla, E. (1966). Behavioral consequences of transgressions: II. The effects of social recognition. *Journal of Experimental Research in Personality, 1,* 187–194.

Wallach, M. A., Kogan, N., & Bem, D. J. (1962). Group influence on individual risk taking. *Journal of Abnormal and Social Psychology, 65,* 75–86.

Waller, W. (1930, 1967). *The old love and the new: Divorce and readjustment.* Carbondale: Southern Illinois University Press.

Wallston, B. S., Alagna, S. W., DeVellis, B. M., & DeVellis, R. F. (1983). Social support and physical health. *Health Psychology, 2,* 367–391.

Wallston, B. S., Wallston, K. A., Kaplan, G. D., & Maides, S. A. (1976). Development and validation of the health locus of control (HLC) scale. *Journal of consulting and clinical psychology, 44,* 580–585.

Wallston, K. A. & Wallston, B. S. (1982). Who is responsible for your health? The construct of health locus of control. In G. S. Sanders & J. Suls (Eds.), *Social psychology of health and illness.* Hillsdale, NJ: Erlbaum.

Wallston, K. A., Wallston, B. S. & DeVellis, R. (1978). Development of the multi-dimensional health locus of control (MHLC) scales. *Health Education Monographs, 6,* 161–170.

Walster, E. (1965). The effect of self-esteem on romantic liking. *Journal of Experimental Social Psychology, 1,* 184–197.

Walster, E., Aronson, E., Abrahams, D., & Rottman, L. (1966). Importance of physical attractiveness in dating behavior. *Journal of Personality and Social Psychology, 4,* 508–516.

Walster, E. & Berscheid, E. (1971). Adrenaline makes the heart grow fonder. *Psychology Today, 5,* 46–50.

Walster, E. & Walster, G. W. (1978). *A new look at love.* Reading, MA: Addison-Wesley.

Walster, E., Walster, G. W., & Berscheid, E. (1978). *Equity: Theory and research.* Boston: Allyn & Bacon.

Walters, R. H. & Brown, M. (1963). Studies of reinforcement of aggression: III. Transfer of responses to an interpersonal situation. *Child Development, 34,* 536–571.

Ward, C. (1981). Prejudice against women: Who, when, and why? *Sex Roles, 7,* 163–171.

Wardle, M. G., Gloss, M. R., & Gloss, D. S. III. (1987). Response differences. In M. A. Baker (Ed.), *Sex differences in human performance.* Chichester, England: Wiley.

Watson, D. (1982). The actor and the observer: How are their perceptions of causality divergent? *Psychological Bulletin, 92,* 682–700.

Watson, D. & Pennebaker, J. W. (1989). Health complaints, stress, and distress: Exploring the central role of negative affectivity. *Psychological Review, 96,* 234–254.

Watson, R. I., Jr. (1973). Investigation into deindividuation using a cross-cultural survey technique. *Journal of Personality and Social Psychology, 25,* 342–345.

Webb, E. J., Campbell, D. T., Schwartz, R. D., Sechrest, L., & Grove, J. (1981). *Nonreactive measures in the social sciences.* Boston: Houghton Mifflin.

Weber, R. & Crocker, J. (1983). Cognitive processes in the revision of stereotypic beliefs. *Journal of Personality and Social Psychology, 45,* 961–977.

Weed, J. A. (1980). National estimates of marriage dissolution and survival. *Vital and Health Statistics,* series 3, no. 19.

Wegner, D. M. & Vallacher, R. R. (Eds.). (1980). *The self in social psychology.* New York: Oxford University Press.

Weigel, C. Wertlieb, D., & Feldstein, M. (1989). Perceptions of control, competence, and contingency as influences on the stress-behavior symptom relation in school-age children. *Journal of Personality and Social Psychology, 56,* 456–464.

Weigel, R., Wiser, P., & Cook, S. (1975). The impact of cooperative learning experiences on cross-ethnic relations and attitudes. *Journal of Social Issues, 31,* 219–243.

Weiner, B. (1985). "Spontaneous" causal thinking. *Psychological Bulletin, 97,* 74–84.

Weiner, B., Frieze, I., Kukla, A., Reed, L., Rest, S., & Rosenbaum, R. M. (1972). Perceiving the causes of success and failure. In E. Jones, D. Kanouse, H. Kelley, R. Nisbett, S. Valins, & B. Weiner (Eds.), *Attribution: Perceiving the causes of behavior.* Morristown, NJ: General Learning Press.

Weiner, H. (1977). *Psychobiology and human disease.* New York: American Elsevier.

Weiss, R. S. (1975). *Marital separation.* New York: Basic Books.

West, S. G., Gunn, S. P., & Chernicky, P. (1975). Ubiquitous Watergate: An attributional analysis. *Journal of Personality and Social Psychology, 32,* 55–65.

Weyant, J. M. (1978). Effects of mood states, costs, and benefits on helping. *Journal of Personality and Social Psychology, 36,* 1169–1176.

Wheeler, L. (1966). Toward a theory of behavioral contagion. *Psychological Review, 73,* 179–192.

Wheeler, L. & Caggiula, A. R. (1966). The contagion of aggression. *Journal of Experimental Social Psychology, 2,* 1–10.

White, G. L., Fishbein, S., & Rutsein, J. (1981). Passionate love and the misattribution of arousal. *Journal of Personality and Social Psychology, 41,* 56–62.

White, G. L. & Knight, T. D. (1984). Misattribution of arousal and attraction: Effects of salience of explanations for arousal. *Journal of Experimental Social Psychology, 20,* 55–64.

White, J. D. & Carlston, D. E. (1983). Consequences of schemata for attention, impressions, and recall in complex social interactions. *Journal of Personality and Social Psychology, 45,* 538–549.

White, L. A. (1979). Erotica and aggression: The influence of sexual arousal, positive affect, and negative affect on aggressive behavior. *Journal of Personality and Social Psychology, 37,* 591–601.

White, T. H. (1961) *The making of the president, 1960.* New York: Atheneum.

Whitley, B. E., Jr., McHugh, M. C., & Frieze, I. H. (1986). Assessing the theoretical models of sex differences in causal attribution. In J. S. Hyde & M. C. Linn (Eds.), *The psychology of gender: Advances through meta-analysis.* Baltimore: Johns Hopkins University Press.

Whyte, W. H. (1943). *Street corner society.* Chicago: University of Chicago Press.

Whyte, W. H. (1956). *The organization man.* New York: Simon & Schuster.

Wicker, A. W. (1969). Attitudes vs. action: The relation of verbal and overt behavioral responses to attitude objects. *Journal of Social Issues, 25(4),* 41–78.

Wicklund, R. A. (1982). How society uses self-awareness. In J. Suls (Ed.), *Psychological perspectives on the self* (Vol. 1). Hillsdale, NJ: Erlbaum.

Widiger, T. A. & Frances, A. (1985). Axis II personality disorders: Diagnostic and treatment issues. *Hospital and Community Psychiatry, 36,* 619–627.

Widiger, T. A. & Settle, S. A. (1987). Broverman et al. revisited: An artificial sex bias. *Journal of Personality and Social Psychology, 53,* 463–469.

Wiener, N. (1948). *Cybernetics: Control and communication in the animal and the machine.* Cambridge, MA: MIT Press.

Wiggins, J. S. (1973). *Personality and prediction: Principles of personality assessment.* Reading, MA: Addison-Wesley.

Wilcox, B. L. (1987). Pornography, social science, and politics: When research and ideology collide. *American Psychologist, 42,* 941–943.

Wilde, Oscar (1974). *The picture of Dorian Gray.* London: Oxford University Press. (Originally published 1891.)

Wilder, D. A. (1977). Perception of groups, size of opposition, and social influence. *Journal of Experimental Social Psychology, 13,* 253–268.

Wilder, D. A. (1984). Intergroup contact: The typical member and the exception to the rule. *Journal of Experimental Social Psychology, 20,* 177–194.

Wilke, H. & Lanzetta, J. T. (1970). The obligation to help: The effects of amount of prior help on subsequent helping behavior. *Journal of Experimental Social Psychology, 6,* 488–493.

Williams, B. (1979). *Report of the committee on obscenity and film censorship.* London: Her Majesty's Stationery Office.

Williams, J. E. & Best, D. L. (1982). *Measuring sex stereotypes: A thirty-nation study.* Beverly Hills, CA: Sage.

Willis, R. H. (1965). Conformity, independence, and anticonformity. *Human Relations, 18,* 373–388.

Willis, R. H. & Levine, J. M. (1976). Interpersonal influence and conformity. In B. Seidenberg & A. Snadowski (Eds.), *Social psychology: An introduction.* New York: Free Press.

Wilson, E. O. (1975). *Sociobiology: The new synthesis.* Cambridge, MA: Belknap Press.

Wilson, E. O. (1978). *On human nature.* Cambridge, MA: Harvard University Press.

Wilson, F. D. & Taeuber, K. E. (1978). Residential and school desegregation: Some tests of the association. In F. D. Bean & W. P. Frisbie (Eds.), *The demography of racial and ethnic groups.* New York: Academic Press.

Wilson, G. (1977). Introversion/extraversion. In T. Blass (Ed.), *Personality variables in social behavior.* Hillsdale, NJ: Erlbaum.

Wilson, T. D., Hull, J. B., & Johnson, J. (1981). Awareness and self-perception: Verbal reports on internal states. *Journal of Personality and Social Psychology, 40,* 53–71.

Wilson, T. D. & Linville, P. W. (1982). Improving the academic performance of college freshmen: Attribution therapy revisited. *Journal of Personality and Social Psychology, 42,* 367–376.

Wilson, T. D. & Linville, P. W. (1985). Improving the performance of college freshmen with attributional techniques. *Journal of Personality and Social Psychology, 49,* 287–293.

Wilson, W. & Miller, H. (1968). Repetition, order of presentation, and timing of arguments as determinants of opinion change. *Journal of Personality and Social Psychology, 9,* 184–188.

Wimer, S. & Kelley, H. H. (1982). An investigation of the dimensions of causal attribution. *Journal of Personality and Social Psychology, 43,* 1129–1162.

Winch, R. (1958). *Mate-selection: A study of complementary needs.* New York: Harper.

Wish, M., Deutsch, M., & Kaplan, S. J. (1976). Perceived dimensions of interpersonal relations. *Journal of Personality and Social Psychology, 33,* 409–420.

Wishner, J. (1960). Reanalysis of "Impression of personality." *Psychological Review, 67,* 96–112.

Wood, W. (1987). Meta-analytic review of sex differences in group performance. *Psychological Bulletin, 102,* 53–71.

Woods, P. J. & Burns, J. (1984). Type A behavior and illness in general. *Journal of Behavioral Medicine, 7,* 411–415.

Woods, P. J., Morgan, B. T., Day, B. W., Jefferson, W., & Harris (1984). Findings on a relationship between type A behavior and headaches. *Journal of Behavioral Medicine, 7,* 277–286.

Worchel, S. (1974). The effects of three types of arbitrary thwarting on the instigation to aggression. *Journal of Personality, 42,* 301–318.

Worringham, D. J. & Messick, D. M. (1983). Social facilitation of running: An unobtrusive study. *Journal of Social Psychology, 121,* 23–29.

Wright, J. C. & Dawson, V. L. (1988). Person perception and the bounded rationality of social judgment. *Journal of Personality and Social Psychology, 55,* 780–794.

Wright, J. C. & Mischel, W. (1987). A conditional approach to dispositional constructs: The local predictability of social behavior. *Journal of Personality and Social Psychology, 53,* 1159–1177.

Wyer, R. S. & Srull, T. K. (1980). The processing of social stimulus information: A conceptual integration. In R. Hastie, T. M. Ostrom, E. B. Ebbesen, R. S. Wyer, D. Hamilton, & D. E. Carlston (Eds.), *The cognitive basis of social perception.* Hillsdale, NJ: Erlbaum.

Wyer, R. S., Srull, T. K., & Gordon, S. E. (1984). The effects of predicting a person's behavior on subsequent trait judgments. *Journal of Experimental Social Psychology, 20,* 29–46.

Wyer, R. S., Jr. & Carlston, D. E. (1979). *Social cognition, inference, and attribution.* Hillsdale, NJ: Erlbaum.

Wyer, R. S., Jr. & Hartwick, J. (1984). The recall and use of belief statements as bases for judgments: Some determinants and implications. *Journal of Experimental Social Psychology, 20,* 65–85.

Yarrow, M. R., Scott, P. M., & Waxler, C. Z. (1973). Learning concern for others. *Developmental Psychology, 8,* 240–260.

Yinon, Y., Sharon, I., Gonen, Y. & Adam, R. (1982). Escape from responsibility and help in emergencies among persons alone or within groups. *European Journal of Social Psychology, 12,* 301–305.

Young, W. R. (1977, February). There's a girl on the tracks! *Reader's Digest,* 91–95.

Zajonc, R. B. (1965). Social facilitation. *Science, 149,* 269–274.

Zajonc, R. B. (1968). Attitudinal effects of mere exposure. *Journal of Personality and Social Psychology,* Monograph Supplement 9, 1–27.

Zajonc, R. B. (1980). Compresence. In P. B. Paulus, (Ed.), *Psychology of group influence.* Hillsdale, NJ: Erlbaum.

Zajonc, R. B., Heingartner, A., & Herman, E. M. (1969). Social enhancement and impairment of performance in the cockroach. *Journal of Personality and Social Psychology, 13,* 83–92.

Zajonc, R. B., Shaver, P., Tavris, C., & Kreveld, D. V. (1972). Exposure, satiation, and stimulus discriminability. *Journal of Personality and Social Psychology, 21,* 270–280.

Zanna, M. P. & Hamilton, D. L. (1972). Attribute dimension and patterns of trait inferences. *Psychonomic Science, 27,* 353–354.

Zanna, M. P. & Hamilton, D. L. (1977) Further evidence for meaning change in impression formation. *Journal of Experimental Social Psychology, 13,* 224–238.

Zanna, M. P., Kiesler, C. A., & Pilkonis, P. A. (1970). Positive and negative attitudinal affect established by classical conditioning. *Journal of Personality and Social Psychology, 13,* 224–238.

Zanna, M. P. & Pack, S. J. (1975). On the self-fulfilling nature of apparent sex differences in behavior. *Journal of Experimental Social Psychology, 11,* 583–591.

Zdep, S. M. & Oakes, W. I. (1967). Reinforcement of leadership behavior in group discussion. *Journal of Experimental Social Psychology, 3,* 310–320.

Zegans, L. S. (1982). Stress and the development of somatic disorders. In L. Goldberger & S. Breznitz (Eds.), *Handbook of stress: Theoretical and clinical aspects.* New York: Free Press.

Zeisel, H. & Diamond, S. (1978). The effect of peremptory challenges on jury and verdict: An experiment in a federal district court. *Stanford Law Review, 30,* 491–531.

Zillman, D. (1971). Excitation transfer in communication-mediated aggressive behavior. *Journal of Experimental Social Psychology, 7,* 417–434.

Zillman, D. (1979). *Hostility and aggression.* Hillsdale, NJ: Erlbaum.

Zillman, D. (1983). Arousal and aggression. In R. G. Geen & E. Donnerstein (Eds.), *Aggression: Theoretical and empirical reviews.* New York: Academic Press.

Zillman, D. (1988) Cognition-excitation interdependencies in aggressive behavior. *Aggressive Behavior, 14,* 51–64.

Zillman, D. & Bryant, J. (1974). Effect of residual excitation on the emotional response to provocation and delayed aggressive behavior. *Journal of Personality and Social Psychology, 30,* 782–791.

Zillman, D., Hoyt, J. L., & Day, K. D. (1974). Strength and duration of aggressive, violent, and erotic communications on subsequent behavior. *Communication Research, 1,* 286–306.

Zillman, D., Johnson, R. C., & Day, K. D. (1974). Attribution of apparent arousal and proficiency of recovery from sympathetic activation affecting activation transfer to aggressive behavior. *Journal of Experimental Social Psychology, 10,* 503–515.

Zellinger, D. A., Fromkin, H. L., Speller, D. E., & Kohm, C. A. (1974). A commodity theory analysis of the effects of age restrictions on pornographic materials (Paper No. 440). Lafayette, IN: Purdue University Institute for Research in the Behavioral, Economic, and Management Sciences.

Zimbardo, P. G. (1970). The human choice: individuation, reason, and order versus deindividuation, impulse, and chaos. In W. J. Arnold & D. Levine (Eds.), *Nebraska symposium on motivation, 1969.* Lincoln: University of Nebraska Press.

Zimbardo, P. G. (1972, April). Psychology of imprisonment. *Transaction/Society,* 4–8.

Zimbardo, P. G., Weisenberg, M., Firestone, I., & Levy, B. (1965). Communicator effectiveness in producing public conformity and private attitude change. *Journal of Personality, 33,* 233–255.

Zuckerman, M. (1978). Actions and occurrences in Kelley's cube. *Journal of Personality and Social Psychology, 36,* 647–656.

Zuckerman, M., DePaulo, B. M., & Rosenthal, R. (1981). Verbal and nonverbal communication in deception. In L. Berkowitz (Ed.), *Advances in experimental social psychology* (Vol. 14). New York: Academic Press.

Zuckerman, M., Koestner, R., DeBoy, T., Garcia, T., Maresca, B. C., & Sartoris, J. M. (1988). To predict some of the people some of the time: A reexamination of the moderator variable approach in personality theory. *Journal of Personality and Social Psychology, 54,* 1006–1019.

Zuckier, H. (1982) The role of the correlation and the dispersion of predictor variables in the use of nondiagnostic information. *Journal of Personality and Social Psychology, 43,* 1163–1175.

Abelson, R. P., 117, 142, 159, 244
Abrahams, D., 398, 399
Abramson, L. Y., 128, 211, 631, 632
Achenbach, C. J., 480
Ackerman, N. W., 306
Ackerman, P., 503, 505, 506
Adair, J. B., 49
Adam, R., 516
Adams, G. R., 421
Adams, J. S., 16, 329, 403, 512
Ader, R., 443
Aderman, D., 632
Adinolfi, A. A., 401
Adler, N. L., 417
Adler, T., 344
Adorno, T. W., 9, 237, 306, 319
Ajzen, I., 221, 226, 229, 239, 244, 246, 249, 250, 251
Alagner, S. W., 620, 622, 623
Albright, J. S., 197, 198
Albright, L., 75, 76
Aleshire, D., 325
Alessis, C., 259
Alicke, M. D., 528, 531
Allen, H., 501, 502
Allen, H. M., Jr., 322
Allen, V. L., 537, 538
Alloy, L. B., 128
Allport, F. H., 570
Allport, G. W., 6, 9, 11, 143, 173, 174, 175, 221, 301, 303, 305, 310, 311, 323, 329, 331, 339
Allred, K. D., 627
Altemeyer, B., 321
Altman, I., 421, 422
Amabile, T. M., 117, 118
Amatruda, C., 370
Amir, Y., 329, 332
Amour, J. L., 619
Anastase, A., 176
Ancoli, S., 84
Anderson, B. L., 635
Anderson, C. A., 154, 444
Anderson, D. C., 444
Anderson, J. R., 141, 142
Anderson, N. H., 137, 138
Andreoli, V., 260
Antill, J. T., 380
Apicella, F. S., 436
Applefield, J. M., 453
Arabian, J. M., 629
Aravnis, C., 629
Archer, D., 85
Archer, J., 370
Arkin, R. M., 126
Arnone, M. M., 517
Aron, A. P., 419
Aronson, E., 27, 33, 40, 47, 229, 269, 278, 279, 281, 283, 285, 332, 398, 399, 404

Arps, K., 509
Asch, S. E., 135, 137, 524, 526, 527, 528, 530, 531, 532, 537
Asher, S. J., 427
Ashmore, R. D., 303
Askenasy, A. R., 617
Atkins, J. L., 75
Avis, W. E., 357, 358, 361
Axelrod, R., 483, 604
Azrin, N. H., 442, 443, 444

Babad, E. Y., 63
Back, K., 392, 393, 532, 569
Back, K. W., 569, 598
Bacon, M. K., 372
Bagozzi, R. P., 302
Baillet, S. D., 198
Baldwin, M. W., 241, 242
Bales, R. F., 589, 591
Ball, S. J., 339
Bandura, A., 173, 176, 236, 369, 436, 449, 450, 451
Bar-Hillel, M., 160
Bar-Tal, D., 478
Baran, S. J., 490
Barker, R. G., 445
Barnes, M., 398, 400, 409
Barnes, P. J., 517
Baron, R. A., 31, 32, 48, 435, 436, 444, 447, 453, 463, 467, 472, 473
Baron, R. S., 584, 631
Baron, S. H., 524
Barrera, M., 621
Barry, H., 372
Barry, T., 444
Bartlett, F. C., 140
Barton, W. H., 601
Bartone, P. T., 619
Basham, R. B., 621
Basow, S. A., 236, 339, 370
Bassett, R., 549
Bassoff, E. S., 380
Batson, C. D., 117, 237, 323, 325, 480, 489, 500, 503, 505, 506, 513, 514
Batson, J. G., 505
Baum, A., 631
Baumann, D. J., 509
Baumeister, R. F., 71, 206, 489
Baumgardner, A. H., 126
Baumgardner, M. H., 259, 260
Baumrind, D., 50, 558
Bavelas, A., 590
Bazerman, M. H., 165
Beaman, A. L., 202, 509, 517, 596, 597
Beck, A. T., 211
Becker, B. J., 361, 362, 530
Becker, L. J., 604
Bedell, J. R., 619

Bee, H., 347–348, 349
Begam, R., 70
Bell, L., 229
Bell, P. A., 444
Belleza, F. S., 148
Belmore, S. M., 138
Bem, D. J., 178, 221, 232, 236, 238, 239, 240, 284, 286, 584
Bem, S. L., 142, 182, 371, 380, 382
Ben-Veniste, R., 461
Benbrow, C. P., 363
Benson, S. M., 508
Bentler, P. M., 251
Berelson, B., 264
Berger, C. R., 223
Berger, D. L., 324
Berglas, S., 124, 125
Bergman, J., 236
Berk, R. A., 467
Berkman, L., 621, 622
Berkowitz, L., 436, 444, 448, 449, 452, 453, 455, 459, 466, 486
Bermant, G., 70
Bernstein, S., 195, 371
Bernzweig, J., 323
Berry, C. J., 461
Berry, D. S., 65, 71
Berry, G. L., 339
Berry, P. C., 582
Berscheid, E., 16, 26, 65, 151, 186, 329, 387, 388, 389, 399, 400, 403, 407, 409, 418, 419, 421, 423, 425, 486, 507, 512
Bertenthal, B. I., 190
Bertilson, H. S., 436, 438
Best, D. L., 348
Bettelheim, B., 306, 552
Bevan, W., 65
Bianchi, S. M., 337
Bickman, L., 480
Bierly, M. M., 321
Billig, M. G., 326
Birch, K., 503, 505, 506
Birnbaum, H. J., 463
Birrell, P., 313, 314
Bishop, G. D., 337, 584
Bizman, A., 549
Black, J. B., 142
Black, T. E., 604
Blackburn, H., 629
Blanchard, D. C., 466
Blanchard, R. J., 466
Blaney, P. H., 625
Blasi, A., 489
Blau, P. M., 480
Block, C. H., 582
Block, J., 78, 440
Block, J. H., 370
Blood, M., 424
Blood, R. O., 424
Bloom, B. L., 427
Bobo, L., 323
Bochner, S., 260, 269, 270
Bogat, G. A., 444
Bogatz, G. A., 339

Bohannan, P., 468
Bolen, M. H., 489
Boll, T., 619
Bollen, K. A., 451
Bond, C. F., Jr., 573
Bonno, B., 354
Booth-Kewley, S., 628, 629, 630
Borden, R. J., 209, 442
Borgatta, E. F., 589
Bosko, K., 509
Bossard, J. H. S., 393
Boudreau, F. A., 344
Bowen, R., 442
Bower, G. H., 142, 148
Bowers, K. S., 179
Boyanowsky, E. O., 538
Boyes-Braem, P., 141
Bradshaw, J. L., 65
Braly, K. W., 233, 306, 307, 308, 310, 311
Brand, R. J., 629, 630
Brandt, J. R., 505
Bransford, J. D., 141
Bray, R. M., 542
Brehm, J. W., 512, 540, 550
Brehm, S. S., 512, 540, 552
Brennan, P., 440
Breslow, L., 621
Breuer, J., 464
Brewer, M. B., 27, 33, 144, 228, 326, 331, 332, 607
Brice, P., 472
Bricker, W., 450–451
Brickman, P., 604
Briere, J., 463
Brigham, J. C., 66, 307
Brislin, R. W., 398
Brockner, J., 263
Brodie, M., 398
Bromly, D. B., 193
Brooks, H., 190
Brotzman, E., 41, 560
Broverman, D. M., 66, 347–348, 349
Broverman, I. K., 66, 347–348, 349
Brown, B., 630
Brown, B. A., 422
Brown, B. R., 604
Brown, G. W., 211
Brown, J. D., 623
Brown, M., 450
Brown, P., 198
Brown, R., 447
Browning, S., 480
Brownmiller, S., 462
Bryan, J. H., 480, 489, 490, 515
Bryant, J., 101, 467
Buckley, T., 503, 505, 506
Bugelski, R., 446
Bullough, V., 410
Bundy, R. P., 326
Burford, B., 354
Burger, J. M., 548
Burgess, E. W., 394, 427

Burgess, M. M., 465
Burgess, R. L., 423
Burgett, T., 461
Burkhart, B. R., 462
Burnham, J. C., 173
Burns, J., 630
Burnstein, E., 150, 448, 584
Buss, A. H., 204, 435, 436, 450, 466
Buss, D. M., 178, 204, 389, 394, 398, 400, 408, 409
Butcher, J. N., 459
Buzina, R., 629
Byeff, P., 497
Byrne, D., 325, 396, 398, 401, 402, 459, 461, 546

Cacioppo, J. T., 221, 229, 260, 264, 267, 268, 289, 293, 294, 296, 271, 635
Caggiula, A. R., 465
Cagle, L. T., 337
Calder, B. J., 36, 244
Caldwell, D. F., 186
Caldwell, J. R., 623
Calhoun, L. G., 512
Callaway, M. R., 588
Campbell, A., 346
Campbell, B., 425
Campbell, B. H., 152
Campbell, D. F., 379
Campbell, D. T., 29, 36, 39, 49, 480, 485, 524, 526
Campbell, J., 209
Campbell, J. D., 75
Cantor, N., 142, 173, 191, 197, 198
Capellanus, A., 411
Caplan, N., 117
Caplan, R. D., 623
Caputo, C., 118, 119, 120
Carducci, B. J., 419
Carli, L. L., 361, 362, 530
Carlsmith, J. M., 27, 33, 40, 47, 68, 269, 276, 278, 444, 507
Carlston, D. E., 138, 144, 239
Carpenter, S., 337
Carson, R. C., 459
Cartwright, D., 569
Carver, C. S., 10, 124, 203, 204, 205, 206, 244, 627
Casey, R. D., 258
Caspi, A., 440
Cassel, J. C., 621
Castle, S., 604
Catalan, J., 548
Cattell, R. B., 173, 175
Chaiken, S., 241, 242, 260, 261, 264, 265, 271, 293, 375
Chaikin, A. L., 634
Champion, D. S., 75
Chan, A., 81
Chapman, J. P., 155
Chapman, L. J., 155
Chase, J. P., 326
Chase, L. J., 490
Chase, W. G., 196
Chasnoff, R., 332

Chassin, L., 401
Chave, E. J., 223, 225
Check, J. V. P., 460, 461, 463
Chein, J., 332
Chen, J., 241
Chen, S. C., 570
Chernick, L., 182
Chernicky, P., 119
Chew, B. R., 197, 198
Child, E. L., 372
Child, P., 152, 193
Chilstrom, J. T., 542
Chodorow, N., 368
Christensen, A., 389
Christie, R., 321
Christy, J., 461
Chrvala, C., 531
Chung, C. S., 400
Cialdini, R. B., 209, 293, 419, 509, 510, 543, 545, 546, 547, 548, 549, 561
Cisin, I. H., 453
Clark, L. F., 148
Clark, M., 510
Clark, M. S., 424
Clark, R. D., 478, 479, 491, 497, 498
Clark, R. D., III, 542, 543, 544
Clarkson, F. E., 66, 348
Clifford, M. M., 400
Cline, V. B., 75, 452
Clore, G. L., 398, 401
Cochran, P. J., 117
Cochran, S., 444
Coffin, T. E., 453
Coffman, T. L., 307
Cohen, A., 275, 277, 281, 286
Cohen, C. E., 144, 145
Cohen, E. G., 332
Cohen, J., 359
Cohen, R., 486
Cohen, S., 620, 621, 635
Colasanto, D., 337
Cole, J. R., 344
Coleman, J. C., 459
Colletti, G., 371
Colligan, M. J., 598, 599
Collins, B. E., 283, 591, 624
Collins, M. E., 337
Conley, J. J., 78
Conner, R. C., 484
Connor, J. M., 371
Consalvi, C., 536
Constantinople, A., 379
Cook, D. A., 550
Cook, E. P., 380
Cook, K., 370
Cook, P., 321
Cook, S. W., 332, 333, 334
Cook, T. D., 36, 39, 259
Cooley, C. H., 191
Cooms, R. H., 399–400
Cooper, J., 280, 282, 283, 286, 287, 288
Cope, B., 404
Corbit, J. D., 421

Corrigan, B., 159
Costa, P. T., Jr., 78, 175
Costanzo, P. R., 13, 26
Cotton, J. L., 444
Cottrell, N. B., 575
Couch, A. A., 589
Courrier, S., 452
Court, J. H., 461, 462
Courtright, J. A., 490, 588
Coyne, J. C., 128, 617, 620
Cozby, P. C., 419, 422
Craig, C. S., 260
Craik, K. H., 178
Cramer, L., 427
Crane, M., 195, 371
Crano, W. D., 228
Cranston, J., 442
Crawford, M. P., 483
Cressey, D. R., 70
Crocker, J., 9, 142, 153, 353
Croft, R. G., 452
Cronbach, L. J., 74, 75, 176
Cross, J. A., 489
Crow, W. J., 74
Crowley, M., 361, 362, 489
Crutchfield, R. A., 530
Cunningham, M. R., 509
Curran, J. P., 398
Curtis, L., 468
Curtis, R. C., 63

Dalrymple, S., 41, 560
Damon, W., 194
D'Andrade, R., 366, 372
Danheiser, P. R., 189
Daniels, L. R., 486
Darby, B. L., 509, 548
Darley, J. M., 37, 71, 478, 487, 491, 492, 493, 494, 495, 496, 501, 513, 514, 516, 517
Darwin, C. R., 78, 482
Dashiell, J. F., 572
Davia, J. E., 629
Davies, J. C., 446, 447
Davis, K. E., 15, 103, 105, 280, 282–283, 284, 397
Davis, L., 354
Davis, M. S., 634
Davitz, J. R., 436
Dawes, A. S., 512
Dawes, R. M., 159, 167
Dawkins, R., 408. 409, 482, 483
Dawson, V. L., 76
Day, B. W., 630
Day, K. D., 436, 449
Deaux, K., 182, 226, 227, 228, 344, 347, 352, 354, 356, 375, 377
DeBono, K. G., 186
DeBoy, T., 178
de Carufel, A., 546
Deci, E. L., 112, 113
DeFour, D., 599
DeGregorio, E., 124
DeJong, W., 549
Delbecq, A. L., 580
Del Boca, F. K., 303

Dellapa, F., 470
DeLongis, A., 617, 619, 620
Del Rosario, M. L., 36
Dembo, T., 445
Dembroski, T. M., 629
Dengerink, H. A., 442
DePaulo, B. M., 75, 86, 87, 89, 90, 92, 512
De Riencourt, A., 410
Derlega, V. J., 634
Dermer, M., 401, 419
Dertke, M. C., 480
Deseran, F. A., 400
De Soto, C. B., 422
de Tocqueville, A., 446
Deutsch, M., 329, 337, 528, 538, 539, 568, 570, 604
DeVellis, B. M., 620, 622, 623
DeVellis, R. F., 620, 622, 623, 624
DeVinney, L. C., 447
DeWood, R., 509
Diacoyanni-Tarlatzis, I., 81
Diamond, S., 70
Dibiase, W., 65
Dickey, R. V., 81
Diehl, M., 582
Diener, E., 202, 436, 596, 597, 599, 601
Dillehay, R. C., 321
Di Matteo, M. R., 85, 635
DiNicola, D. D., 635
Dion, K. K., 65, 399, 400
DiRenzo, G. J., 323
Dittes, J. E., 534, 536
DiVasto, P. V., 461
Djordjevic, B. S., 629
Doherty, W. J., 635
Dohrenwend, B. P., 617
Dohrenwend, B. S., 617
Doll, R., 639
Dollard, J., 8, 176, 445
Dominick, J. R., 236
Doneen, J., 436
Donnerstein, E., 436, 449, 457, 459, 460, 461, 472
Donnerstein, M., 449, 472
Doob, J., 8, 445
Doob, L. W., 436
Dorfman, D. D., 263
Dornbusch, S. M., 76
Dorr, A., 456
Dossett, D. L., 251
Dougher, M. J., 620, 621
Dovidio, J. F., 316, 373, 374, 478, 479, 491, 497, 498, 503, 504
Drachman, D., 546
Drenan, S., 326, 528
Drews, F. R., 630
Drugan, R. C., 619–620
Dubro, A. F., 605
Duck, S., 39
Dudycha, G. J., 178
Dukes, W. F., 65
Dull, V., 144
Duncan, B., 466

Duncan, B. D., 503, 505, 506
Duncan, B. L., 144, 146
Dushenko, T. W., 49
Dutton, D. G., 419
Duval, S., 191, 201, 202, 203, 206
Dworkin, A., 463
Dyck, J. L., 505
Dymond, R., 74

Eagly, A. H., 8, 43, 264, 265, 267, 271, 350, 351, 356, 357, 359, 361, 362, 363, 372, 373, 374, 442, 485, 489, 530, 531
Eaker, E. D., 629
Eaton, W. O., 362
Ebbesen, E. B., 200
Ebbesen, E. G., 144, 466
Eccles, (Parsons), J., 344
Edelsack, L., 507, 508
Eder, R. A., 194
Edney, J. H., 606
Edwards, C., 75
Edwards, V. J., 371
Efran, M. G., 400
Ehrenreich, B., 344
Ehrhardt, A. A., 376, 377
Eibl-Eibesfeldt, I., 439
Eidelson, R. J., 423
Einhorn, H. J., 107
Einsiedel, E. F., 457
Eisdorfer, C., 619
Eisen, M., 193
Eisenberg-Berg, N., 488, 489
Eiser, J. R., 124
Ekman, P., 67, 80, 81, 82, 83, 84, 86, 87, 88, 90, 91
Elkin, R. A., 286
Elliot, R., 490
Elliott, G. R., 619
Ellsworth, P. C., 40, 47, 63, 68, 80, 81, 83
Ellyson, S. L., 373
Embree, M., 444
Emswiller, T., 354
Endler, N. S., 179
Endresen, K., 436
English, D., 344
Enns, L. R., 362
Epstein, S., 178, 489
Epstein, Y. M., 631
Erne, D. E., 468
Eron, L. D., 34, 44, 455, 456, 457, 472
Ervin, F., 441
Esser, J. K., 588
Evans, N., 316, 373, 374
Evans, R., 449
Exline, R., 68
Eysenck, H. J., 173, 175, 440, 489

Fagot, B. I., 370
Farina, A., 324, 401
Farley, R., 337
Fausto-Sterling, A., 364
Fazio, R. A., 203
Fazio, R. H., 241, 246, 288

Feather, N. T., 239
Feierabend, I., 446
Feierabend, R., 446
Feingold, A., 362
Feinleib, M., 629
Feldman, N. S., 111
Feldstein, M., 619
Fellner, C. H., 480
Fenigstein, A., 204
Ferguson, C. K., 326
Feshbach, S., 261, 435, 466
Festinger, L., 13, 26, 269, 276, 390, 392, 393, 532, 569, 596
Fidanza, F., 629
Fiedler, F. E., 590, 591, 592
Field, N., 589
Fincham, F. D., 427
Fireman, B., 557
Firestone, I., 277
Fischer, E., 401
Fischer, P., 472
Fischoff, B., 162
Fishbein, M., 221, 226, 229, 239, 241, 242, 244, 246, 249, 250, 251
Fishbein, S., 419
Fisher, J. D., 512
Fisher, K. W., 190
Fisher, L., 620
Fiske, D., 29
Fiske, S. T., 121, 123, 139, 140, 148
Flament, C., 326
Flax, R., 599
Flay, B. R., 259
Fleming, I., 49
Fletcher, G. J. O., 98, 427
Foa, U. G., 68
Fode, K. L., 47
Folkman, J. R., 39
Folkman, S., 616, 617, 619
Forsterling, F., 101, 128
Forsyth, D. R., 534, 569, 571
Fraas, L. A., 589
Frager, R., 540
Frances, A., 350
Frank, L. K., 69
Frankel, G., 508
Franklin, B. J., 512
Fraser, S. C., 549, 596, 597
Fredericks, A. J., 251
Freedman, J. L., 43, 456, 549
Freeman, S., 209
French, J. R. P., Jr., 590, 623
French, K. E., 361
Frenkel-Brunswick, E., 9, 237, 306, 319
Freud, S., 191, 366, 368, 437, 444, 459, 595
Freund, T., 73, 144
Frey, J., 444
Friedman, H. S., 628, 629, 630
Friedman, M., 629, 630
Friedrich-Coffer, L., 43, 456
Friesen, W. V., 67, 80, 81, 82, 83, 84, 86, 87, 88, 90, 91

Frieze, I., 91, 98
Frieze, I. H., 354
Frodi, A., 452
Fromkin, H. L., 553
Fujioka, T., 152, 193
Fulcher, R., 19
Fulero, S., 313, 314
Fulker, D. W., 440, 489
Fultz, J., 509
Funder, D. C., 75, 76, 85, 179
Funk, S. C., 627

Gaebelein, J. W., 450
Gaertner, S. L., 478, 479, 491, 497, 498, 503, 504
Gaines, B., 201
Galanter, E., 204
Gallant, J. L., 323
Gallup, G. G., 190
Gammon, C., 442
Gamson, W. A., 557
Ganellen, R. J., 625
Gangestad, S., 186
Garacia, J. E., 592
Garbner, J., 631, 632
Garcia, T., 178
Garvey, C., 370
Gebhard, P. H., 409
Geen, R. G., 449, 464, 466
Gelles, R. J., 423, 434, 435, 466, 468, 469, 470
Gerard, H. B., 238, 279, 280, 332, 528, 538, 539
Gerbner, G., 452, 453, 454
Gergen, J. J., 512
Gergen, K. J., 17, 39, 105, 190, 198, 489, 512, 601
Gergen, M. M., 198, 489, 512, 601
Gerlach, S. G., 194
Gershaw, N. J., 473
Gesell, A. L., 370
Geva, N., 150
Gibb, C. A., 589
Gibbons, F. X., 144, 203, 204
Gifford, R. K., 314, 316
Gill, J. J., 630
Gillan, P. G., 582
Gillis, J. S., 357, 358, 361
Gillis, R., 124
Gilmore, J. P., 605
Gilmore, R., 39, 326
Gilovich, T., 575, 576
Ginosar, Z., 160
Gintner, G., 591
Giordani, B., 619
Glaser, R., 620
Glass, D., 280
Glass, D. C., 629, 631
Glass, G. V., 43, 380
Glick, P., 186, 353
Gloss, D. S., III, 362
Gloss, M. R., 362
Glucksberg, S., 141
Glunt, E. K., 324
Goethals, G. P., 584

Goethals, G. R., 72, 138
Goffman, E., 69, 207, 324
Goldberg, L. R., 78, 120
Goldberg, M. E., 264, 339
Goldberg, P. A., 354
Goldman, M., 589
Goldmeier, D., 620
Goldstein, A. P., 473
Goldstein, D., 470
Gonda, G., 350
Gonen, Y., 516
Goodall, J., 408
Goore, N., 575, 576
Gordon, C., 194
Gordon, S. E., 150
Gorn, G. G., 264
Gorn, G. J., 339
Gorsuch, R. L., 325, 619
Gotlieb, I. H., 128
Gottman, J. M., 423
Gough, H. G., 379
Gouldner, A. W., 16, 485, 546
Gourash, N., 512
Graesser, A., 148
Grajek, S., 414
Graves, N., 41, 560
Graves, S. B., 339
Gray, W., 141
Graziano, W. G., 189
Greenberg, J., 124, 210, 211, 212, 316, 318
Greene, D., 75, 112, 113
Greenwald, A. G., 172, 198, 200, 259, 260, 289
Greu, R., 509
Griffin, J. J., Jr., 201
Griffit, W., 401
Griffitt, C., 505
Groh, T., 401
Gross, A. E., 49, 507, 512, 592
Gross, L., 452, 453, 454
Groth, A. N., 463
Grove, J., 49
Gruder, C. L., 259, 516
Grusec, J., 369
Guerin, B., 573, 575
Gunn, S. P., 119
Gustafson, D. H., 580
Guteck, B. A., 354
Guttentag, M., 412, 413

Hagar, J. C., 84
Hage, J. M., 631
Hagen, M., 322, 323, 325
Hake, D. F., 443
Halamaj, J., 259
Hall, C. L., 508
Hall, E., 86, 359, 361, 636
Hall, E. T., 68
Hall, J. A., 85, 380
Hall, J. H., 86, 359, 361, 636
Halleck, S. L., 117
Halpern, D. F., 362, 366
Halpern, P. L., 631
Halpin, A. W., 589

Halverson, H. M., 370
Hamel, I. Z., 160
Hamill, R., 158, 160
Hamilton, D. L., 136, 138, 162, 314, 316, 337
Hamilton, W. D., 482, 483
Hammond, K. R., 74
Hannum, K. A., 323
Hanratty, M. A., 451
Hanseli, S., 400
Hansford, E. A., 604
Hanson, L. R., 312
Hanson, L. R., Jr., 137
Hanusa, B. H., 636, 637
Hardin, G., 605
Harding, J., 332
Hardy, D., 75
Hare-Musten, R. T., 350, 356
Harkins, S. G., 579, 580, 581, 583
Harlow, H. F., 572
Harries, K. D., 444
Harring, K., 326, 605
Harris, 630
Harris, M. B., 508
Harris, M. J., 85
Harris, T., 211
Harris, V. A., 114, 115
Harrison, W., 251
Hart, D., 194
Hartke, D. D., 592
Hartshorne, H., 178, 488
Hartwick, J., 239
Harvey, J. H., 389, 536
Harvey, O. J., 328
Hass, R. G., 323
Hastie, R., 9, 141, 148, 353
Hastorf, A., 63
Hastorf, A. H., 76, 324, 592
Hatchett, S., 337
Hatfield, E., 26, 40, 65, 329, 425
Hathaway, S. R., 379
Hautziner, M., 128, 210
Haverhorn, G., 542
Hawkins, C., 591
Haynes, S. G., 629
Hays, R. B., 392, 421, 423
Hearold, S., 456, 490, 491
Heath, L., 36
Heesacker, M., 289
Heider, F., 13, 15, 98, 100, 102, 388, 404
Heider, K., 81
Heilbrun, A. B., 380
Heingartner, A., 573, 574
Heiss, J., 346
Heller, T., 591
Helmreich, R. L., 344, 380, 382, 591, 613
Hemphill, J. K., 591
Hendrick, C., 417
Hendrick, S., 417
Henley, N. M., 374
Hennigan, K. M., 36, 259
Henninger, M., 239
Henze, L. F., 398

Hepburn, C., 326, 353
Hepworth, J. T., 446
Herek, G. M., 223, 224, 237, 324
Herman, E. M., 573, 574
Herman, P., 293
Heron, N., 427
Hesley, J. W., 182
Hess, E. H., 229
Hicks, D. J., 451
Higbee, K. L., 39, 604
Higgins, E. T., 152, 153, 206, 286
Hilberman, E., 470
Hilgard, E. R., 302
Hill, C., 394, 397
Hill, C. H., 390
Hill, C. T., 427
Hill, G. W., 579
Hill, R., 393, 398
Hillery, J. M., 573
Hinde, R. A., 466
Hiroto, D. S., 632
Hjelle, L., 65
Hoberman, H., 128, 210, 621
Hoch, S. J., 75
Hoffman, E. L., 524
Hoffman, L. W., 512
Hoffman, M. L., 503
Hoffman, S. A., 208
Hofling, C. K., 41, 560
Hogan, R., 175
Hogarth, R. M., 107
Hokanson, J. E., 465
Hollander, E. P., 536, 586
Hollenbeck, A. R., 453
Holloway, S., 509
Holmes, T. H., 616, 618
Homans, G. C., 16, 402, 485, 568
Hood, R., 203
Hood, W. R., 328
Hook, L. H., 591
Hoover, C. W., 75
Horn, N., 509
Horney, K., 368
Hornstein, H. A., 508, 509, 613
Hotaling, G. T., 423
Houlihan, D., 509
House, J. S., 620, 621
House, P., 75
Houston, B. K., 627
Hovland, C. I., 8, 219, 257, 258, 260, 262, 446
Howard, J., 313, 314, 326
Hoyt, J. L., 449
Hoyt, L. L., 398
Hoyt, M. G., 283
Hubbard, M., 54, 154
Hubert, S., 138
Hudson, J. W., 398
Huesmann, L. R., 34, 44, 455, 456, 457, 472
Hull, C. L., 572
Hull, J. B., 112
Hull, J. G., 204, 627
Hunt, J. McV., 179
Hunt, M., 410

Hunt, P. J., 573
Husband, R. W., 572
Huston, A. C., 43, 369, 456
Huston, T. L., 388, 389, 421, 423
Hutchinson, R. R., 443, 444, 450
Hyde, J. S., 361, 362, 363, 366
Hyman, H. H., 322
Hyson, R. L., 619–620

Iasiello-Vailas, L., 635
Ickes, W., 172, 179, 182, 321
Inbar, J., 63
Ingram, R. E., 211
Insko, C. A., 235, 242, 260, 269, 270, 400, 528, 531, 546, 605
Insko, D., 326
Isecke, W., 629
Isen, A. M., 509, 510
Isenberg, D. J., 584, 585
Isozaki, M., 584
Izard, C. E., 81

Jaccard, J. J., 178
Jacklin, C. N., 356, 362, 363, 364, 366, 370, 442
Jackson, D. D., 422
Jackson, J., 580
Jackson, R., 461
Jacobs, D. R., 629
Jacobs, R. C., 524, 526
Jacobson, L., 62–63, 151
Jaffe, D. T., 424
Jahoda, M., 306, 321
James, R. M., 591
James, W., 10, 191, 206
Jamieson, D. W., 186
Jamison, W., 380
Janis, I. L., 219, 257, 261, 262, 263, 453, 546, 585, 586, 588, 635
Janowitz, M., 306
Jeans, R. E., 210
Jefferson, W., 630
Jemmott, J. B., III, 620
Jenkins, C. D., 621
Jennings, D. L., 54
Jensema, D. J., 324
Jensen, C., 313, 314
Jepson, C., 261
Jessop, D. J., 223
Johnson, A., 620
Johnson, D., 141, 542
Johnson, D. J., 426
Johnson, J., 112
Johnson, J. H., 617
Johnson, M., 450
Johnson, M. K., 141
Johnson, M. P., 244
Johnson, R. C., 436
Johnson, R. N., 435, 441
Jones, C. H., 115, 118
Jones, C. R., 153
Jones, E. E., 11, 15, 17, 72, 103, 105, 114, 115, 116, 117, 118, 119, 120, 124, 125, 138, 148, 149, 150, 209, 226, 229, 238, 280, 282–283, 284, 324, 546, 635

Jones, J. M., 305, 447
Jones, J. W., 444
Jones, S. C., 200
Joseph, L., 575, 576
Josephson, W. L., 452
Jourard, S., 69
Jouriles, E., 204
Joy, L. A., 456, 458
Judd, C. M., 133, 148, 223
Juhnke, R. G., 78
Justice, A., 620

Kagan, J., 440
Kahn, R. L., 620
Kahn, S., 625, 626
Kahneman, D., 157, 161, 162, 163, 164
Kamarck, T., 621
Kambara, T., 442
Kamzan, N., 480
Kandel, E., 440
Kanfer, F., 631
Kanki, B., 542
Kanner, A. D., 617
Kanouse, D. E., 137, 312
Kanter, R. M., 424
Kanungo, R. N., 339
Kaplan, G. D., 624
Kaplan, H., 350
Kaplan, M. R., 585
Kaplan, S. J., 570
Karaz, V., 111
Karlberg, J., 630
Karlberg, P., 630
Karlins, M., 307
Kassin, S. M., 70, 71, 144
Kastenbaum, R., 638
Katsev, R., 507, 508
Katz, A. M., 393
Katz, D., 222, 230, 233, 306, 307, 308, 310, 311
Katz, E., 264
Katz, I., 323, 332
Kaufman, A., 461
Kavonen, M. J., 629
Kaye, D., 546
Keenan, J. M., 198
Keilman, M., 480
Kelem, R. T., 596, 597
Keller, H. R., 468, 473
Kelley, H. H., 15, 16, 98, 103, 107, 111, 219, 257, 326, 389, 402, 423, 468, 534, 536, 589
Kelley, K., 459, 461, 546
Kelly, G. A., 173
Kelman, H. C., 523
Keniston, K., 473
Kenkel, W. F., 399–400
Kenny, D. A., 75, 76
Kenrick, D. T., 178, 179, 409, 419, 509, 510
Kepner, C. R., 472
Kerckhoff, A. C., 393, 397, 569, 598
Kerr, N. L., 539, 585

Kerr, S., 589
Kessler, S. J., 347, 375, 376, 382
Key, M. K., 619
Keys, A., 629
Kiecolt-Glaser, J. K., 620
Kiesler, C. A., 234, 286, 539
Kiesler, S. B., 354
Kihlstrom, J. F., 173, 191, 197, 198
Kilham, W., 559
Kim, H. S., 229
Kimball, M. M., 456, 458
Kinder, D. R., 148, 323
King, G. A., 153
King, R. G., 560
Kinsey, A., 409
Kirker, W. S., 198, 199
Kirschner, P., 546
Kirscht, J. P., 321, 634
Kite, M. E., 226, 227, 228, 350, 351,
   375, 377
Kite, W. R., 592
Kitt, A. A., 447
Klackenberg, G., 630
Klackenberg-Larsson, I., 630
Klapper, J. T., 453
Klein, R., 206, 472
Klein, S. B., 197, 198
Klentz, B., 202, 517
Knight, G. P., 605
Knight, T. D., 419
Knower, F. H., 81
Kobasa, S. C., 618, 625, 626
Kobasa, S. C. O., 625
Koch, J., 294
Koestner, R., 178
Kogan, N., 584
Kohlberg, L., 348, 370, 371, 376,
   382
Kohm, C. A., 553
Komorita, S. S., 606
Konar, E., 345
Konecni, V. J., 466
Koop, C. E., 457
Kornhauser, A., 322
Korte, C., 514
Kositchek, R., 629
Kovaric, P., 456
Kowalski, D. J., 148
Kozlowski, L., 293
Kramer, R. K., 607
Krammer, R. M., 607
Krantz, D. S., 629
Krasnoff, L., 617
Kraus, S., 266
Krause, R., 81
Kraut, R. E., 87, 92
Kravitz, D. A., 579
Krebs, D., 401
Krebs, D. L., 435, 436, 439, 478,
   480, 482, 486, 487, 488, 489
Kreveld, D. V., 263
Kruglanski, A. W., 73, 112, 144, 160
Kuiper, N. A., 198, 199
Kukla, A., 91, 98
Kulik, J. A., 148, 223, 447, 623

Kutchinsky, B., 461
Kutner, B., 332

Lage, E., 542
Lagerspetz, K., 440, 455
Lake, R. W., 337
Lakind, E., 508
Lambert, W. W., 630
Lamm, H., 582, 584
Landis, C., 80
Landy, D., 400
Langer, E., 633, 636
Langer, E. J., 117, 204
Langhorne, M. C., 409
Langley, R., 467
Lanzetta, J. T., 486
LaPiere, R. T., 243, 310
Lapworth, C. W., 606
Larson, R. F., 634
Larter, W. M., 148
Lassiter, G. D., 86, 87, 89, 90, 92
Lasswell, H. D., 258
Latané, B., 37, 478, 480, 487, 491,
   492, 493, 494, 495, 496, 497,
   501, 516, 517, 531, 579, 581
Lau, R. R., 322
Laudenslager, M. L., 619–620
Laumann, E. O., 394
La Voie, L., 76
Lawler, K. A., 627
Lawton, M. P., 393
Layden, M. A., 128
Layton, B. D., 400
Layton, J. F., 452
Lazarsfeld, P. F., 264
Lazarsfeld, P. L., 264
Lazarus, R. S., 616, 617, 619
Leary, T., 68
Le Bon, G., 595
LeCompte, W. A., 81
Lederer, L., 461
Lederer, W. J., 422
Lee, J. A., 415, 417
Lefcourt, H. M., 624
Lefkowitz, M. M., 34, 44, 456
Legant, P., 118, 119, 120
Leifer, A. D., 453
Leippe, M. R., 150, 259, 260, 286
Lemley, R. E., 163
Lenney, E., 182, 380
Leone, C., 291
LePage, A., 452
Lepper, M. R., 54, 112, 113, 144, 154,
   246
Lerner, M. J., 324, 327, 508
Levenson, H., 354
Leventhal, H., 261
Levi, A., 159
Levin, H., 466
Levin, I. P., 164
Levin, P. F., 509
Levine, H. M., 621
Levine, J. M., 537, 540
Levinger, G., 388, 389, 397, 421, 422,
   424, 427

Levinson, D. J., 9, 237, 306, 319
Levy, A., 293
Levy, B., 277
Levy, R. C., 467
Lewin, K., 179, 445, 568
Lewinsohn, P. M., 128, 210
Lewis, L. D., 516
Lewis, L. L., 352
Lewis, M., 190
Lewis, P. M., 512
Lewis, S. A., 398
Lewis, S. K., 548
Leyens, J. P., 452, 453, 455
Lichtenstein, S., 162
Lichtman, R. R., 635
Lieb, R., 422
Lieberkneckt, K., 470
Liebert, R. M., 31, 32, 48, 175, 436,
   453, 490, 491
Liebrand, W. B., 604
Likert, R., 219, 224, 226
Lind, E., 619
Linder, D. E., 280, 282
Lindsay, R. C. L., 49
Lindskold, S., 591
Lingle, J. H., 150
Linn, M. C., 361, 362
Linton, M., 198
Linville, P. W., 129, 148, 149, 150,
   210, 213, 310–311
Linz, D., 457, 461
Lippa, R., 66, 189
Lippman, W., 307
Lippold, S., 398
Littman, R. A., 450–451
Livesly, W. J., 193
Lloyd, B., 370
Locksley, A., 326, 353
Loftus, E. F., 151
Loftus, J., 190
London, H., 100
London, P., 489
Lord, C. G., 144, 198, 246
Lorenz, K., 437
Losch, M. E., 229
Lott, A. J., 13, 229, 401, 532, 537
Lott, B. E., 13, 401, 532
Lubetkin, A., 442
Luce, R. D., 602
Luchins, A. S., 71
Luckmann, T., 324
Lui, L., 144, 607
Lumsdaine, A. A., 219, 257, 262, 263
Lunneborg, P. W., 379
Luria, Z., 210, 370
Lusk, R., 599
Lydon, J. E., 186
Lyon, E., 346
Lyons, V., 332

Maass, A., 542, 543, 544, 545
McArdle, J., 251
McArthur, L. Z., 65, 71, 110, 160
McCabe, A. E., 490
McCallum, D. M., 605

McCann, J. M., 260
McCants, T. R., 631
McCarthy, S. J., 461
McCauley, C., 308. 309, 310
McClelland, D. C., 436
McClintock, C. G., 604, 605
McClintock, E., 389
McCloskey, M. E., 141
Maccoby, E., 466
Maccoby, E. E., 356, 362, 363, 364,
   366, 370, 379, 442
MacCoun, R. J., 539
McCrae, R. R., 78, 175
McCullum, D. M., 326
McDavid, J. W., 530
McDonel, E. C., 241
MacDougall, J. A., 629
Mace, K. C., 400
MacEvoy, B., 630
McGillis, D., 105
McGraw, B., 43
McGuire, C. V., 152, 193
McGuire, W. J., 9, 152, 193, 220,
   221, 238, 239, 243, 264, 267,
   290, 530
McHugh, M. C., 354
McKay, G., 620
McKenna, W., 347, 375, 376, 382
Mackie, D., 246
Mackie, D. M., 543, 583
McKillip, J., 399
McKinly, J. C., 379
McLaughlin, R., 444
McMaster, M. R., 505
McMillen, D. L., 507, 510
McNemar, Q., 226
McPhee, W. N., 264
McQuirk, B., 517
Madden, T., 249
Maddi, S. R., 175, 619, 625, 626
Magliozzi, T., 165
Magloire, K., 620
Mahl, G. F., 68
Mahler, H. I. M., 623
Maides, S. A., 160, 624
Maier, S. F., 619–620
Maier, N. R., 264
Major, B., 160, 182, 345, 375
Malamuth, N. M., 459, 460, 461,
   462, 463
Malloy, T. E., 76
Malof, M., 537
Mandler, G., 9, 423
Mann, J. H., 244, 589
Mann, L., 559
Manne, S., 508
Mantell, D. M., 559
Marecek, J., 118, 119, 120, 356
Maresca, B. C., 178
Mark, V. H., 441
Markus, H., 15, 133, 142, 194, 195,
   196, 197, 198, 324, 371, 388, 574
Marriott, R. G., 588
Marshall, G., 101
Marshall, J. R., 480

Martin, B., 579
Martin, C. E., 409
Martin, C. L., 348, 363
Martinek, T. J., 400
Martyna, W., 380
Maslach, C., 101
Masor, H. N., 480
Masserman, J. H., 484
Mathewson, G. C., 279, 280
Matthews, K. A., 629, 630
Matwychuk, A., 186
Maur, B. J., 517
May, M. A., 178, 488
Mayer, A. J., 322
Maynard-Smith, J., 439
Mazur, A., 442
Mead, G. H., 191
Mead, M., 6
Mednick, S. A., 440
Meece, J. L., 344
Meehl, P. E., 159
Meeker, R. J., 604
Mehrabian, A., 66
Meindl, J. R., 327, 508
Mellen, S. L. W., 408, 409
Mendelsohn, H., 453
Menotti, A., 629
Mentzer, S. J., 634, 635
Mermelstein, R., 621
Merton, R. K., 151, 447, 568
Mervis, C. B., 141
Messick, D. M., 575, 607
Metcalf, L., 635
Meter, K., 489
Metzner, H., 621
Mewborn, R., 261
Michel, J. B., 322
Micheletti, P. M., 323
Miles, C. C., 379
Milgram, S., 22, 24, 25, 27, 47, 49,
    50, 55, 117, 514, 554, 555, 556,
    557, 559
Millard, R. J., 39
Miller, A. G., 41, 50, 51, 558
Miller, C. E., 585
Miller, D. T., 124, 324, 435, 436,
    439, 478, 480, 482, 486
Miller, G. A., 204
Miller, H., 263
Miller, H. L., 400
Miller, J. A., 549
Miller, K., 63
Miller, N., 8, 331, 332, 445
Miller, N. E., 176, 442
Miller, R. L., 390
Miller, S. J., 634
Mills, J., 279, 281, 424
Milton, C., 335
Mischel, W., 142, 173, 174, 176, 177,
    178, 179, 182, 200, 368, 369
Money, J., 376, 377
Monroe, S. M., 621
Monson, T. C., 182, 187, 189
Montagu, A., 433, 438, 439
Montemayor, R., 193

Montepare, J. M., 375
Mook, D. G., 40
Moore, B., 489
Moore, B. S., 509, 631
Moore, J., 209
Moreland, R. L., 196, 197
Morgan, B. T., 630
Morgan, M., 452, 453, 454
Mori, D., 375
Moriarity, D., 490
Moriarity, T., 516
Morin, S. F., 639
Morris, K., 268
Morrow, G. D., 426
Morse, S. J., 512
Moscovici, S., 542, 543, 582
Moss, H. A., 440
Mowrer, O., 8, 445
Moyer, K. E., 366, 440, 443
Mugny, G., 542
Mulder, M., 589
Mullen, B., 75, 631
Murphy, C. J., 589
Murphy, G., 224, 226
Murphy, L. R., 598, 599
Murray, H. A., 153, 173
Murray, J. B., 453
Murroni, E., 294
Murstein, B. I., 397, 410
Musilli, L., 549
Mussen, P., 488, 489
Muzzy, R. E., 76
Myers, A. M., 350
Myers, D. G., 584
Myers, J. D., 442
Myers, M., 70
Myerscough, R., 442

Nadler, A., 512
Naffrechoux, M., 542
Nahemow, L., 393
Naifeh, S. J., 325
Nail, P. R., 540, 541
Napoleon, T., 401
Nathanson, L., 582
Neale, M. A., 165
Neale, M. C., 440, 489
Nelson, C., 78, 79, 353
Nelson, D., 396
Nelson, S. D., 117
Nemeth, C., 542, 543, 545
Nermin, P., 401
Neuringer-Benefield, H. E., 489
Newcomb, T., 596
Newcomb, T. M., 13, 178, 388, 395,
    404, 534, 535, 568
Newtson, D., 106
Nias, D. K. B., 440, 489
Nida, S. A., 497
Niedenthal, P. M., 197, 198
Nieva, V. F., 354
Nisbett, R. E., 100, 112, 113, 118, 120,
    121, 157, 158, 160, 163, 503, 635
Nissen, H. W., 483
Nlowik, R., 635

Noble, C. E., 394
Norman, W. T., 78
Norriss, K. S., 484
Nurius, P., 198

Oakes, P. J., 327
Oakes, W. I., 592
O'Brien, E. J., 178
Odbert, H. S., 175
O'Grady, K. E., 401
Ogrocki, P., 620
Ohbuchi, K., 442
Oliver, P. V., 75
Olson, J. M., 101
Olweus, D., 366, 440, 441, 442, 466
Omwake, E., 453
O'Neil, E., 451
O'Reilly, C. A., 186
Orne, M., 48
Ortiz, V., 326, 353
Osborn, A. F., 582
Osborne, R. T., 394
Osgood, C. E., 210, 226, 239
Oskamp, S., 221
Ostrom, T. M., 150
Ostrove, N., 400
O'Sullivan, M., 81, 86, 90, 91
Owen, D., 490

Pace, L. M., 200
Pack, S. J., 209, 375
Padawer-Singer, A., 152, 193
Page, M., 452
Page, M. M., 236
Paicheler, G., 542
Pallak, M. S., 286, 550
Pallak, S. R., 294
Palmer, J. C., 151
Papageorgis, D., 290
Park, B., 62, 77, 133, 311
Parke, R. D., 452, 453, 455
Parker, J. S., 629
Parkinson, M. G., 71
Passini, F. T., 78
Pate, S., 325
Patterson, A. H., 465
Patterson, G. R., 450–451, 467
Payne, T. J., 371
Peabody, D., 310
Peake, P. K., 174, 177, 178, 179
Pearson, K., 461
Pelham, B. W., 200
Pennebacker, J. W., 598, 599, 619,
    627, 634
Penner, L. A., 480
Penrod, S., 457, 461, 531, 532, 533
Pepinsky, P. N., 591
Pepitone, A., 596
Peplau, L. A., 394, 397, 389, 427
Percival, L., 362
Perlman, D., 111
Perlmutter, M., 194
Personnaz, B., 542
Pessin, J., 572
Peters, L. H., 592
Peterson, D. R., 177, 389

Peto, R., 639
Pettigrew, T. F., 117, 306
Pettine, P. W., 631
Petty, R. E., 221, 229, 260, 264, 267,
    268, 271, 289, 293, 294, 296,
    635
Pfeifer, R. L., 92
Phares, E. J., 624
Pheterson, G. I., 354
Phillips, D. P., 451
Piaget, J., 191
Pierce, C. M., 41, 339, 560
Pigg, R., 449
Piliavin, I. M., 38, 497, 499, 500, 512
Piliavin, J. A., 38, 478, 479, 491, 497,
    498, 499, 500
Pilkington, G. W., 226
Pilkonis, P. A., 234
Pinderhughes, C. A., 453
Pitcairn, T., 81
Pitcher, E. G., 370
Pittman, T. S., 209, 286
Pleck, J., 346
Pliner, P., 375
Poe, D., 92
Pohlmann, J. R., 592
Pomeroy, W. B., 409
Pool, I de Sola,, 453
Pope, M. K., 627
Poppleton, P. K., 226
Porier, G. W., 229
Porter, A. M. W., 623
Postman, L., 143
Potts, G. R., 198
Poulos, R. W., 490, 491
Poulton, J. L., 627
Powell, A. L., 505
Powell, L. H., 630
Powell, M. C., 424
Powell, S. R., 78
Pratkanis, A. R., 259, 260
Predmore, S. C., 201
Prentice-Dunn, S., 600
Pribram, K. H., 204
Price, V. A., 630
Priest, R. F., 392
Proshansky, H., 332
Provenzano, F. J., 370
Pryor, J. B., 203
Puccetti, M. C., 619
Puccetti, M. D., 625
Pudov, V., 629
Pyszczynski, T., 124, 210, 211, 212,
    316, 318, 419

Quanty, M. B., 464, 465
Quinkert, K., 362
Quinn, R. P., 400

Rabkin, J. G., 618
Ragland, D. R., 630
Rahe, R. H., 616, 618, 619
Raiffa, H., 602
Ramirez, J., 467
Ramsay, T., 621
Ramsoy, N. R., 393

Rapaport, K., 462
Rasche, L., 546
Rasinski, K. A., 353
Raven, B., 590
Rawitch, A., 442
Raz, M., 549
Razran, G. H. S., 546
Read, S. J., 199, 201, 211
Reda, R. M., 517
Reed, L., 91, 98
Regan, D. R., 507
Regan, D. T., 547
Reid, D., 624
Reinisch, J. M., 379
Reisenzein, R., 101
Rest, S., 91, 98
Rheingold, H., 370
Rhodewalt, F., 286, 627, 630
Rholes, W. S., 153
Ricci-Bitti, P. E., 81
Richards, J. M., 75
Richardson, J., 450
Richardson, S. A., 76
Ridley, M., 482, 483
Riedel, S. L., 399
Rieken, W. H., 112
Ringelmann, M., 579, 580
Rittle, R. M., 575
Rivenbark, W. H., III, 400
Rivera, A. N., 507
Robbins, C., 621
Roberts, D. F., 453
Robinson, E. A. R., 623
Rock, L., 72
Rodgers, J. L., 251
Rodin, J., 19, 38, 55, 613, 631, 633, 635, 636
Rofe, Y., 390
Rogers, P. L., 85
Rogers, R. W., 261, 600
Rogers, T. B., 198, 199
Rogot, E., 621
Rohrer, J. H., 524
Rokeach, M., 238, 322
Rokosky, J. J., 449
Romer, D., 516
Ronchi, D., 400
Roof, W. C., 337
Rosch, E., 141
Rose, T. L., 338
Rosen, S., 209
Rosenbaum, M. E., 398, 604
Rosenbaum, R. M., 91, 98
Rosenberg, L. A., 531
Rosenblum, L. A., 379
Rosenburg, M. J., 239
Rosenburg, S., 78, 79
Rosenhan, D. L., 509
Rosenkrantz, P., 347–348, 349
Rosenkrantz, P. S., 66, 348
Rosenman, R. H., 629
Rosenthal, R., 43, 47, 62–63, 85, 86, 90, 151, 362, 363
Rosenwald, A., 489
Rosner, L., 461

Ross, D., 369, 436, 451
Ross, D. T., 629
Ross, J. M., 323
Ross, L., 54, 75, 100, 116, 117, 118, 144, 154, 158, 160
Ross, M., 98, 124, 244
Ross, S. A., 369, 436, 451
Roth, D. L., 200, 211
Rothaus, P., 465
Rothbart, M., 311, 313, 314, 326
Rother, E. O., 517
Rotter, J. B., 9, 173, 176, 624
Rottman, L., 398, 399
Rotton, J., 444
Roy, M., 467
Roy, P., 332
Rubin, D. D., 362, 363
Rubin, J., 69
Rubin, J. Z., 370, 604
Rubin, Z., 29, 68, 389, 394, 397, 413, 427
Ruble, D. N., 111
Ruble, T. L., 348
Rusbult, C. E., 423, 425, 426, 440, 480, 485, 489, 490, 515
Rushton, J. P., 489
Rutkowski, G. K., 516
Rutsein, J., 419
Rutte, C. G., 607
Ryan, E. D., 465
Ryan, R. M., 112, 113
Ryan, S. M., 619–620
Rytina, S., 557

Sadalla, E., 507
Sadalla, E. K., 409
Saegart, S., 394
Safilios-Rothschild, C., 345
Sagar, H. A., 145
Sakruai, M. M., 532
Samora, J., 634
Sampson, E. E., 17
Samuelson, C. D., 607
Sander, D. V., 510
Sanders, G. S., 584
Sanders, S. A., 379
Sandler, I., 621
Sanford, R. N., 9, 237, 306, 319
Sarason, B. R., 617, 621
Sarason, I. G., 617, 621
Sarnoff, I., 391
Sartoris, J. M., 180
Saunders, L., 634
Sawin, L. L., 350, 359
Sawyer, J., 159, 392
Schachter, S., 100, 389, 390, 391, 392, 393, 449, 503, 529, 532, 534, 569
Schaefer, C., 617
Schaller, M., 509
Schank, R. C., 142
Scheidt, R., 452
Scheier, M. F., 10, 204, 205, 206, 244, 627
Scheier, M. R., 204

Schein, E. H., 552, 553
Scherer, K., 81, 86
Schiffman, A., 635
Schlenker, B. R., 194, 206, 209
Schmied, L. A., 627
Schmitt, B. H., 575, 576
Schmitt, J. P., 211
Schnare, A. B., 337
Schneider, D. J., 63
Schnittjer, S. K., 164
Schofield, J. W., 145
Schopler, J., 605
Schradle, S. B., 620, 621
Schrauger, J. S., 200, 201
Schriesheim, C. A., 589
Schrott, H. G., 635
Schucker, B., 629
Schul, Y., 150
Schultz, L. H., 370
Schulz, R., 632, 636, 637
Schuman, H., 244, 323, 337
Schumann, D., 294
Schutz, A., 324
Schutz, W. C., 570
Schwartz, B., 230
Schwartz, J. M., 160
Schwartz, M., 510
Schwartz, R. D., 49
Schwartz, S. H., 512
Schwarzwald, J., 549
Scott, J. P., 450
Scott, P. M., 489, 515
Scott, R. A., 324
Sears, D. O., 223, 322, 323
Sears, R., 8, 445, 446
Sears, R. R., 436, 466
Sebastian, J., 453, 455
Seberak, G. J., 575
Sechrest, L., 49
Secord, P. F., 65, 409, 412, 413
Segal, M., 308
Segal, M. W., 394
Seider, M. L., 631
Seligman, M. E. P., 128, 211, 631, 632
Selinger, D., 635
Selye, H., 626
Sentis, K., 142
Serbin, L. A., 236
Settle, S. A., 348
Shanab, M. E., 559
Sharon, I., 516
Shaver, K. G., 72
Shaver, P., 263
Shaw, M. E., 13, 26
Shea, J. A., 421
Shears, L. M., 324
Sheatsley, P. B., 322
Sheffield, F. D., 219, 257, 262
Sheppard, H. L., 322
Sheridan, C. L., 560
Sherif, C. W., 328
Sherif, M., 328, 329, 524, 525
Sherman, L. W., 467
Sherman, S., 401
Sherman, S. J., 133, 241, 561, 635

Sherrod, D. R., 631
Shetler, S., 465
Shevitz, R. N., 591
Shields, S. A., 344
Shinn, M., 623
Sholtz, R. I., 629
Shope, G. L., 466
Shotland, R. L., 480, 500
Shuntich, R., 442
Shure, G. H., 604
Shuttleworth, F. K., 178, 488
Shweder, R. A., 78
Siegel, A. E., 453
Siegel, J. M., 617
Siem, F. M., 489
Sigal, H., 226
Sigall, H., 400
Sigelman, C. K., 461
Signorella, M. L., 380
Signorielli, N., 452, 453, 454
Siladi, M., 195, 371
Silver, M., 326
Silverman, I., 399
Silverman, L. J., 507
Simon, H. A., 196
Simpson, A. E., 466
Simpson, G. E., 325
Simpson, J. A., 186, 403
Singer, J., 100, 449
Singer, J. E., 631
Sistrunk, F., 530
Skinner, B. F., 234, 466
Skowronski, J. J., 138
Skrypnek, B. J., 318
Slaby, R. G., 453
Sloan, L. R., 209
Slovic, P., 160
Smeaton, G., 398
Smith, B. L., 258
Smith, D. A., 148
Smith, G. F., 263
Smith, J., 142, 196, 197
Smith, M. L., 43, 209, 350
Smith, R. H., 453, 528, 531
Smith, S. W., 210
Smith, T. S., 211
Smith, T. W., 211, 627, 630
Smith, W., 401
Sniderman, P. M., 322, 323, 325
Snow, M. E., 370
Snyder, C. R., 200
Snyder, M., 9, 150, 152, 172, 179, 182, 183, 184, 185, 186, 187, 189, 245, 318, 321
Snyder, M. L., 634, 635
Sole, K., 480
Soler, E., 444
Soloman, S., 124
Solomon, G. S., 510
Solomon, H., 517
Solomon, L. Z., 517
Solomon, M. R., 528
Solomon, R. L., 421
Sontag, S., 324
Sorrentino, R. M., 480, 589

Spain, D., 337
Sparacino, J., 400
Sparling, S., 507
Speckart, G., 251
Speicher, C. E., 620
Speller, D. E., 553
Spence, J. T., 344, 350, 371, 379, 380, 382, 489
Sperber, B. M., 251
Spiegler, M. D., 175
Sprafkin, J. N., 453, 490, 491
Spratfkin, R. P., 473
Sprecher, S., 65, 401
Sroufe, A. L., 489
Srull, T. K., 150, 153
Staats, A. W., 232, 242
Staats, C. K., 232, 242
Stadler, S. J., 444
Stanley, J. C., 36, 39, 363
Stapp, J., 19, 380
Star, S. A., 447
Staub, E., 480, 489, 502, 516
Steeh, C., 323
Steffen, V. J., 8, 43, 359, 362, 372, 373, 442
Steffensmeier, D. J., 400
Stein, R. T., 591
Steinberg, C., 453
Steinberg, J., 509
Steiner, I. D., 577, 578
Steiner, S. C., 621
Steinmetz, G., 507, 508
Steinmetz, J. L., 117, 118
Steinmetz, S. K., 423, 434, 435, 466, 468, 469, 470
Stemerding, A., 589
Stephan, W. G., 419
Stern, G. S., 631
Sternburg, R. J., 414
Sternglanz, S. H., 236
Steuer, F. B., 453
Stevens, S., 436
Stevenson-Hinde, J., 466
Stewart, J. E., II, 71
Stitt, C. L., 308, 309, 310
Stogdill, R. M., 589
Stone, J. H., 86, 87, 89, 90, 92
Stone, W. F., 323
Stoner, J. A. F., 583
Stonner, D., 466
Storms, M. D., 121
Story, J. E., 75
Stouffer, S. A., 447
Stout, J. C., 620
Strauman, T. J., 206
Straus, M. A., 423, 434, 435, 466, 468, 469, 470
Straus, R., 629
Straw, M. K., 480, 500
Strayer, F. F., 489
Strickland, B. R., 624
Strickland, L. H., 112
Stringfield, D. O., 178
Strodtbeck, F. L., 591
Stroebe, W., 400, 582

Strong, E. K., 379
Strube, M. J., 592
Struening, E. L., 618
Sturrup, B., 489
Suarez, S. D., 190
Suchman, E. A., 447
Suci, G., 226
Sullivan, J. J., 550
Suls, J., 172, 631
Suls, J. M., 390
Sulzer, J. L., 451
Sutherland, E. H., 70
Svanum, S., 202
Svarstad, B. L., 634
Swander, D. V., 524
Swann, W. B., 151
Swann, W. B., Jr., 189, 199, 200, 201, 211
Swap, W., 394
Swap, W. C., 263
Swedlund, M., 542
Sweeney, J., 580
Sweet, W. H., 441
Syme, S. L., 620, 621, 622
Symons, D., 408, 409
Szymanski, D., 583
Szymanski, K., 581

Taeuber, K. E., 337
Taft, R., 74
Tajfel, H., 326
Tanford, S., 531, 532, 533
Tanke, E. D., 151, 189
Tannenbaum, P. H., 226, 239
Tausig, H. L., 618
Taves, P. A., 286, 287
Tavormina, J., 619
Tavris, C., 263, 345, 363
Taylor, D. A., 421
Taylor, D. W., 582
Taylor, H. L., 629
Taylor, J. A., 27
Taylor, M. C., 380
Taylor, R. B., 422
Taylor, S., 442, 528, 531
Taylor, S. E., 9, 121, 123, 139, 140, 142, 160, 336, 623, 625, 632, 635
Taylor, S. P., 442
Tedeschi, J. T., 507
Teger, A. I., 516
Teri, L., 128, 210
Terman, L. M., 379
Terris, W., 484
Terry, R. M., 400
Tesser, A., 209, 223, 291, 398
Tessler, R. C., 512
Test, M. J., 480, 515
Tetlock, P. E., 323
Thee, S. L., 164
Thibaut, J., 326, 605
Thibaut, J. W., 16, 112, 402, 589
Thiel, D. L., 401
Thomas, J. R., 361
Thomas, M. H., 452

Thompson, R. C., 322
Thompson, S. C., 160
Thompson, V. D., 251, 400
Thoresen, C. E., 630
Thorne, A., 78, 209
Thurber, J. A., 264
Thurstone, L. L., 219, 223, 225
Tice, D. M., 489
Tipton, R. M., 480
Titus, L. J., 573
Toch, H., 473
Tomita, M., 81
Tompkins, S. S., 83
Touhey, J. C., 344
Traupman, J., 425
Travis, L. E., 572
Triandis, H. C., 68, 570
Tringo, J. L., 324
Triplett, N., 26, 571
Trivers, R. L., 483, 484
Trommsdorff, G., 582
Trope, Y., 160
Tucker, L., 509
Tunnell, G., 189
Turner, C. W., 452
Turner, J. A., 269
Turner, J. C., 326, 327
Turner, R. J., 621
Turner, T. J., 142
Turnquist, D. C., 635
Tversky, A., 157, 161, 162, 163, 164, 165
Tyler, R. B., 316, 373, 374
Tyler, T. R., 322
Tzavaras, A., 81

Ulmer, D., 630
Ulrich, R., 442
Ulrich, R. E., 450
Ulschak, P. L., 582
Underwood, B., 489, 509
Unger, R. K., 347
Uranowitz, S. W., 148
Utne, M. K., 425

Valins, S., 631
Vallacher, R. R., 11
Van Avermaet, E., 605
Van Buchem, F. S. P., 629
Vandenberg, S. G., 394
Vanderklok, M., 75
Van Der Pligt, J., 124
Van de Ven, A. H., 580
Van Treuren, R. R., 627
Van Valey, T. L., 337
Vardaris, R., 442
Vasta, R., 490
Vaughan, D., 427
Vega, C., 375
Veitch, R., 401, 509
Ventis, W. L., 237, 323, 325
Vernon, P. E., 177
Vershure, B., 409
Vincent, J. E., 509, 548
Vinokur, A., 584
Vinsel, A., 422

Virnelli, S., 627
Vivekanathan, P. S., 78, 79
Vogel, S. R., 66, 347–348, 349
Vreeland, R. S., 76

Wachtler, J., 542, 543
Wack, D. L., 575
Wade, C., 345, 363
Wade, J., 528, 531
Wade, T. J., 528
Walder, L. O., 34, 44, 456
Walker, K. E., 346
Walker, M. R., 209
Walker, T., 507, 508
Wallace, A. F. C., 453
Wallace, J., 507
Wallach, M. A., 584
Wallbom, M. C., 202
Waller, W., 427
Wallin, P., 427
Wallin, P. W., 394
Wallson, B. S., 512
Wallston, B. S., 620, 622, 623, 624, 625
Wallston, K. A., 624, 625
Walster, E., 16, 54, 65, 154, 388, 389, 398, 399, 400, 403, 407, 409, 418, 419, 425, 486, 507, 512
Walster, G. W., 16, 26, 329, 388, 403, 425, 486, 507, 512
Walters, G., 307
Walters, R. H., 450
Ward, C., 354
Ward, C. D., 419
Ward, L. M., 72
Wardle, M. G., 362
Ware, E. E., 624
Wareing, S., 489
Warren, R., 267
Watson, A. S., 453
Watson, C., 380
Watson, D., 119, 619, 627
Watson, R. I., Jr., 596
Waxler, C. Z., 489, 515
Webb, E. J., 49
Webb, W., 75
Weber, R., 153
Wechkin, S., 484
Weed, J. A., 425
Wegner, D. M., 11
Weigel, C., 619
Weigel, R., 332, 333
Weiner, B., 91, 98, 104
Weiner, H., 619
Weintraub, J. K., 627
Weisenberg, M., 277
Weiss, D. S., 78
Weiss, R. S., 427
Weiss, W., 258, 260
Wertlieb, D., 619
West, S. G., 119, 446, 453, 455, 543, 545
Wey, N. J., 394
Weyant, J. M., 509
Wharton, J. D., 36

Wheeler, D., 548
Wheeler, L., 465, 599
Whitcher-Alagner, S., 512
White, B. J., 328
White, G. L., 419
White, J. D., 144
White, L. A., 444
White, S. W., 427
White, T. H., 69, 266
Whitley, B. E., Jr., 354
Whyte, W. H., 569, 583
Wicker, A. W., 244
Wicklund, R. A., 191, 201, 202, 203, 206
Widiger, T. A., 348, 350
Wiebe, G. D., 453
Wiener, M., 66
Wiener, N., 204
Wiggins, J. S., 159
Wilcox, B. L., 457
Wilcox, J. E., 337
Wilder, D. A., 334, 336, 531
Wiles, K. A., 461

Wilke, H., 486, 607
Williams, B., 461
Williams, J. E., 348
Williams, K., 579, 580, 581
Williams, M., 507
Williams, R. M., Jr., 447
Willis, R. H., 540, 541
Wills, T. A., 621
Wilson, D. W., 497
Wilson, E. O., 364, 439
Wilson, F. D., 337
Wilson, G., 176
Wilson, T. D., 112, 129, 158
Wilson, W., 263
Wimer, S., 98
Winch, R., 397
Winer, B. J., 589
Wiser, P., 332, 333
Wish, M., 570
Wishner, J., 136
Wolf, S., 531
Wolff, P., 450
Woll, S. B., 148

Wood, J. V., 635
Wood, W., 362
Woods, M. E., 346
Woods, P. J., 630
Worchel, P., 448, 465
Worchel, S., 260, 283, 436, 448
Worringham, D. J., 575
Wortman, C., 209, 546
Wright, J. C., 76, 177
Wright, R. J., 507, 508
Wrightsman, L. S., 70, 71
Wurm, M., 629
Wyer, R. S., 150, 153, 239
Wyer, R. S., Jr., 239

Yahya, K. A., 559
Yarrow, M. R., 489, 515
Yinger, J. M., 325
Yinon, Y., 516
Young, D. Y., 204
Young, R. D., 401
Young, W. R., 478

Zabrack, M. L., 456, 458

Zajonc, R. B., 15, 133, 142, 262, 263, 325, 388, 393, 394, 572, 573, 574, 575
Zander, A., 569
Zanna, M. P., 136, 138, 186, 209, 234, 246, 286, 287, 288, 375, 584
Zavalloni, M., 582
Zdep, S. M., 592
Zegans, L. S., 618, 621
Zeisel, H., 70
Zeiss, A. R., 200
Zellinger, D. A., 553
Zembrodt, I. M., 425, 426
Zemke, P. E., 607
Zillman, D., 101, 435, 436, 449, 459, 461, 467
Zimbardo, P. G., 101, 277, 391, 596, 597
Zion, C., 353
Zone, J. B., 627
Zuckerman, M., 86, 90, 111, 178
Zuckier, H., 163

Subject Index   *References to figures, tables, and photographs are printed in italic type*

Ability
   direct judgments about, 72–73
   gender and perceptions of, 354, *355*
Academic performance, attribution theory applied to improving, 128–129
Accuracy of direct judgments, 73–93
   deceptive smiles and, 90–91
   detecting deception, 86–93
   on emotions, 78–86
   on personality, 73–78
Activity in groups, 570
Actor-observer effect, 118–121, *127*
   reasons for, 119–120, 121
   research on, 118, 119
Adaptors, nonverbal behavior, 68
Additive group tasks, 577–578
   social loafing and, 580, *581*
Additive model of attitude formation, 239
Affect displays, 67
Affiliation, 389
   relationship to anxiety, 389–390, *391*
   transition to attraction, 392–401
Aggregate behaviors, 178
Aggression, 433–475
   factors influencing, 437–462, *463*
      biology and instincts, 437–439
      cultural influences, 439
      environment and internal psychology, 442–449
      frustration and societal aggression, 446–447

   individual differences, 440–442
   social learning, 449–463
   in families (*see* Family violence)
   hostile vs. instrumental, 435–436, 479
   in human history, 433–435
   levels of explanation for human, 6–9, *438*, *463*
   mass media and, 8, 451–453
      effect of TV violence on children, 31–36, 39, 43, 452, 453–456, *457*, *458*, 472–473
      sex and sexual violence, 456–463
   measuring, 436–437
   predicting/reducing family violence, 468–471
   reducing, 464–473
      catharsis, 464–466
      controlling with cognitive strategies, 472–473
      fostering responses incompatible with aggression, 467
      punishment, 466–467
      social restraints, 472
      technique summary, *472*
   sex differences in, 359, 362, 442
   in children, TV violence and, 456, *457*
   stability of, *441*
   summary, 463, 472, 474–475
AIDS (acquired immune deficiency syndrome), *479*, 324, 639

Air travel, *161*
Allport's analysis of prejudice, 303–306
Altruism, 37–38
   defined, 480
   "pure," 503, 505, *506*
   reciprocal, 483–485
American Psychiatric Association, 210
American Psychological Association, ethical guidelines of, *52*
American Psychological Association Ad Hoc Committee on Ethical Standards, 52
Americans, stereotypes about, 307, *308*
Amish culture, 439
Amos & Andy (television), *338*
Anderson's weighted averaging model of impression formation, 137–139
Androgyny, 378–382
Animals
   altruism in, 483–485
   self-awareness in, *190*
Anti-Semitism Scale, 319, *320*
Anxiety
   affiliation and, 389–390, *391*
   operational definitions of, 27, 29
Applied social psychology, 17–20, 613–643
   attribution theories applied, 126–129
   health psychology factors, 615–629

   levels of explanation for health and illness, *640*, 641
   personality and health/illness, 623–628
   stress, social support, and illness, 615–623
   Type A personality and heart disease, 629–630
   variables affecting, *628*
   improving health with, 630–639
      helplessness in the elderly, 632–638
      personal control, 631–632
      prevention in health care, 638–639
   introduction to, 613–614
      answering social questions, 614
      designing social interventions, 614
      evaluating social programs, 615
   linking theory to reality, 17–19
   medical practices, 634–635
   social psychology as a profession, 19–20
   summary, 641–642
Arguments, persuasiveness of
   quality of, *268*
   receiver's involvement in message, *296*
Armenia, Soviet Union
   hostility between peoples of Azerbaijan and, 6–9
   human responses to earthquake in, 3–6, 18

Arousal
  aggression and, 449, 459, 465
  emergency intervention and,
      497–502
  misattribution and, 503, *504*
  love and, 418–421
Asch, Solomon
  conformity to social norms model,
      526–529, 537
  Gestalt model of impression
      formation, 135–136, *137*
  group size and conformity studies,
      531, *532*
  operational definition of
      conformity, 540
Assortative mating, 394
Attitude(s), 7, 9, 219–255
  attraction and similarities in, *396*
  behavior and, 243–252
      improper measures of, 246
      inferring attitudes from
          behavior, 240–241
      problems of predicting behavior
          from attitudes, 243–246
      theory of reasoned action,
          247–251
      vs. belief, 238
  characteristics of, 221–222
  comment on, 251–252
  effect of contact on intergroup,
      334–336
  formation of, 229–242
      learning theories on, 230–236
      logical inference theories on,
          237–242
      personality and, 236–237
  functional approach to, 222–223,
      224
  measurement of, 223–229
      Likert scales, 224, 226, *227*
      scale development, 228
      semantic differential scales, 226
      Thurston scales, 223–224, *225*
      validity of scales, 226, 229
  prejudicial (*see* Prejudice)
  public vs. private, 523
  minority influence on, 543, *544*
  as schema, 291–292
  summary, *242*, 252–253
Attitude change, 257–299
  cognitive responses and, 288–292
      attitudes as schemas, 291–292
      forewarning effects, 289
  communication model of
      persuasion affecting,
      257–269
      channel variables, 264–266
      communicator variables,
          258–260
      legacy of, 271
      message variables, 261–264
      target (audience) variables,
          266–268
      variable interaction, 269
  dissonance theory and research
      on, 269–288

cognitive dissonance, 272–274
  evaluating, 286–288
  Festinger and Carlsmith study,
      274–275
  insufficient justification,
      275–278
  qualifications on, 280–283
  self-perception theory as
      alternate to, 283–286
  variations on, 278–280
elaboration likelihood model
    of persuasion affecting,
    293–296
innoculation against persuasion
    and, 290–291
summary, *292, 295*, 297–298
Attorney General's Commission on
    Pornography, 458
Attraction
  affiliation as precursor to,
      389–391
  defined, 389
  as first phase of the relationship
      cycle, 421–422
  love and (*see* Love)
  stage models of, 397
  theories of, 401–408
      cognitive consistency, 404–407
      exchange and equity, 402–404
      learning, 401–402
      summary, *420*
  transition from affiliation to,
      392–401
      mere exposure, 393–394
      physical attractiveness, 398–401
      proximity, 392–393
      similarity, 394–398
  trends in research on, 388–389
Attribution, 97–130
  applying theories of, 126–129
      improving academic
          performance, 128–129
      treating depressions, 128
  emotion and, 100–101
  errors and biases in, 116–126
      actor-observer effect, 118–121
      fundamental attribution error,
          116–117
      ignoring social roles, 117–118
      motivational biases, 122–126
      salience effects, 121
  frustration, aggression, and,
      447–448
  internal and external causes,
      98–103
      preference for internal
          explanations, 100–103
  in medical care, 635
  as research topic, 63, *64*
  summary of theory and research
      on, *127*, 130
  theories of, *14*, 15, 97, 103–116
      causal schemas, 111–116
      correspondent inferences,
          103–107
      cube model, 107–111

Audience variables influencing
    persuasion, 266–268
Authoritarian personality, prejudice
    and, 306, 319–322
Authority figures, obedience to,
    558–559
Autokinetic effect, 524, *525, 526*
Availability heuristic, 160–162
Azerbaijan, Soviet Union, hostility
    between peoples of Armenia
    and, 6–9
Balance theory, 13, 15
  attractions and, 404, *405*, 406
Baserate information,
    underutilization of, 158, 160
Behavior(s). *See also* Social behavior
  aggregate, 178
  attitudes and, 221, 229, 243–251
      improper measures of, 246
      inferring attitudes from
          behavior, 240–241
      problems of predicting behavior
          from attitudes, 243–246
      theory of reasoned action,
          247–251
  classes of, 246
  common/noncommon effects of,
      106
  consensus and consistency of, 107
  covariation principle of, 107–108
  dispositional causes of, 98, *99*
  external reasons (*see* External
      explanations for behavior)
  internal reasons (*see* Internal
      explanations for behavior)
  nonverbal (*see* Nonverbal
      behaviors)
  stable/unstable dimensions to, 98,
      99
  summed, 178
  voluntary, operant conditioning
      of, 234–236
Behavioral intentions, 247
Belief(s)
  vs. attitude, 238
  attitude formation and, 238–239
  mathematical models of
      consistency in, 239–242
  prejudice and, 322–325
  stereotypes as probabilistic beliefs,
      307
Bennington College study on
    conformity, 534, *535*
Bias in attribution, 122–126, *127*
Bias in social psychology research,
    47–49
  in experimenters, 47–48
  related in sex differences, 356–357
  in subjects, 48–49
Biology
  aggression and, 437, 440–442
  prosocial behavior and, 482–485
  sex differences and, 364–366
Blacks
  analysis of prejudice toward,
      303–306

stereotypes about, 307, *308*
Bobo doll study, 451
Bogus pipeline method, 226
Brainstorming, enhancing group
    creativity with, 582
Brainwashing, 552–553
Brown v. the Board of Education, 303,
    332
Bullfighting, 442, *443*
Bystander intervention, 37–39,
    492–497, *500*, 517
Carlsmith, J. Merril, study with
    Festinger on dissonance and
    attitude change, 274–275, *276*
Castration anxiety, 367
Category-based expectancies, 105
Catharsis, reducing aggression
    through, 464–466
Causal agents, people perceived as,
    62
Causal schemas of attribution,
    111–116, *127*
Cause-effect relationships
  correlation studies and, *34, 35*
  experiments and, *30, 32, 34*
Center for Research on Aggression,
    464
Centers for Disease Control, 638
Central route to persuasion, 293–295
Challenge, sense of, in hardy
    personalities, 625
Change, self's resistance to, 198–200
Channel variables influencing
    persuasion, 264–266
Children
  abuse of, 434, 468, 470, *471*
  development of prosocial behavior
      in, 489, 490–491, 515
  impact of television violence on
      children's aggression, 31–35,
      36, 39, 43, 452, 453–456,
      457, 458, 472–473
  learned aggression in, 451
China
  brainwashing techniques during
      Korean War, 552, 553
  student uprising of 1989, *104*
Churchill, Winston, *67*, 591
Church of Unification, *520*
Cigarette smoking and dissonance,
    272
Civil Rights Act, 303
Civil rights movement, *18*, 303
Classical conditioning
  attitudes, 230–234
  sex differences, 369
Coercive power, leadership's, 590
Cognitive complexity and
    depression, 213
Cognitive-consistency theories, 13,
    14, 15
  attraction and, 404–407
  relationship to equity and
      exchange theories, 16–17

Cognitive-development theory, Kohlberg's, 370–371
Cognitive dissonance. *See* Dissonance theory
Cognitive information-processing theories, *14*, 15. *See also* Social cognition
Cognitive responses and attitude change, 288–292
 attitudes as schemas, 291–292
 effects of forewarning, 289
Cohesiveness in groups and conformity, 532, 534
Committment
 attitude change and, 282–283, *284*
 conformity and, 538, *539*
 hardy personalities and, 625
Common effects of behaviors, 106
Commons, tragedy of the, 605, 606–607
Commons Dilemma experimental game, 605–607
Communal vs. exchange relationships, 424
Communication in relationships, 423–424
Communication model of persuasion, 257–269, 271
Communication variables influencing persuasion, 258–260
Comparison level, 402–403
Comparison level for alternatives, 403
Competition in groups, 602–607
Competitors, 605
Compliance, 522, 545–551
 commitment and, 549–550
 positive moods and, 546
 psychological reactance and, 550–551
 reciprocity and, 546–548
 strategies for gaining, 548–550, *551*
Computer date study, 398–399
Conceptual replication, 41
Conclusion beliefs, 238–239
Conditioned stimulus/response, 230, *231*
Conditioning
 aggression and, 450–451
 attitude formation and, 230–236
 sex differences and, 369
Conformity, 522
 definitions and models of, 540–541
 factors influencing, 529–545
 commitment and, 538–539
 gender, 530–531
 group attractiveness and cohesiveness, 532–534, *535*
 group size, 531–532, *533*
 minority influence, 542–545
 personality, 530
 social support, 537–538

status in the group, 534–537
 summary, *538*
 pressures of, on obedience, 556–557
 research on, 524–529
 autokinetic effect, 524–526
 minority of one against unanimous majority, 526–529, 537
Conjunctive group tasks, 578
Consensus of behavior, 107
Consequences of behavior in dissonance theory and attitude change, 283, *285*
Consistency of behavior, 107
Consistency of beliefs, 239–242
Construct validity, 176
Consumer behavior and self-monitoring, 186
Contingency model of leadership, 592, *593*, *594*
Control, feelings of, and health, 623–625
 fostering, 631–632
Control group, 31, *32*
Control model of self, 204, *205*
Cooperation in groups, 602–607
Cooperators, 605
Coronary heart disease and Type A personality, 629–630
Correlation(s), illusory
 in social perception, 155
 stereotypes and, 314, *315*, 316
Correlational coefficients, 44–47
Correlational studies, 29, 33–36, *37*
 causation and, *34*, 35
 correlational coefficients in, 44–47
 differing magnitudes of correlations, *46*
 positive, negative, and zero correlation, *45*
 vs. experiments, 33, *34*
Correspondent inferences, theory of, 103–107, *127*
Cost factors and emergency intervention, 407–502
 analysis, *499*
 model of, *498*
 nonemergency settings, *502*
Courtly love, 410–411
Courtrooms, first impressions in, 70–71
Covariation principle of behavior, 107–108
Creativity in groups, brainstorming and, *582*
Credibility of communicators on persuasion, 260, *261*, 264, *265*, 266
Crime, impact of TV violence on, 456, *457*
Criterion groups, 244
Crowding, control over, and stress, 631

Cube model of attribution, Kelley's, 107–111, *127*
Culture
 aggression and, 439
 gender stereotypes and, 350, 352, 354
 love in western, 409–412
 prejudice and, 305
 prosocial behavior and norms of, 485–487
 reactions to receiving help and, 512
 universality of facial expressions in different, 81–83, *84*
Davie's "J-curve" theory of violent social revolutions, 446–447
Death rates
 among elderly persons with little or no control, 636
 relationship to social support, 621, *622*
Debriefing of subjects in social psychology studies, 54–55
Deception
 detecting, 86–93
 actual vs. perceived, 88–89
 nonverbal cues, 87, *88*, 89
 in real-life situations, 89, 92–93
 in smiles, 90–91
 vocal cues, 87
 in social psychology research, 52
Decision making
 combining information and making social inferences, 159
 framing effects in, 163–166
 in groups, 583–585
 biased, 585–588
Deindividuation, 566, 594–601
 antisocial behavior and, 596, *597*
 in institutions, 597–598
 mass psychogenic illness and, 598–599
 self-awareness and subjective experience of, 599–601
Demand characteristics, 48
Dependent variable, 30
Depression
 attribution theory and treatment for, 126–128
 breaking cycles of, 211, *212*
 cognitive complexity and, 213
 self-awareness and, 210–211
Depressive realism, 128
Derogation of the victim, dissonance theory and, 280
 effects of choice and irrevocability on, *284*
Diagnostic ratio approach to prejudice measurement, 308, *309*, 310
Diamond model of social influence, *540*, 541
Differential accuracy, 75
Diffusion of responsbility, 497, 579
Dilemmas, understanding group cooperation and competition

through experimental, 602–607
Dilution effect, 163
Direct judgments, 65–93
 accuracy of, 73–93
 based on gender roles, 353
 first impressions, 65–73
 postscript on, 93
 as research topic, 63, *64*
Discounting principle in attribution, 111–112, *127*
 failure of, 114–116
Discriminant validity, 176
Disjunctive group tasks, 578–579
Display rules on emotions, 81
Dispositional causes for behavior, 98, *99*
Dissonance theory, 13–14, 26, 269–288
 evaluating, 286–288
 Festinger and Carlsmith study, 274–275, *276*
 Festinger's theory of, 269, 272, *273*, 274
 psychology of insufficient justification, 275–278
 qualifications on dissonance theory, 280–283
 self-perception theory as alternate to, 283–286
 variations on dissonance theory, 278–280
Distinctiveness of behavior, 107
Divisible group tasks, 579
Divorce, 425, 427
Doctor-patient relationship, 634–635
Dogmatism, 322–323
Domestic violence. *See* Family violence
Door-in-the-face reciprocity technique, 548, *551*
Double minorities, 542
Drugs and aggression, 442
d statistic, 359, *360*

Earned reputation theory, 306
Earthquake disaster, human responses to, 3–6, 18
Ecological crisis and commons dilemma, *606*
Education about helping, 517
Ego-defensive function of attitudes, 222, 223
Einstein, Albert, *590*
Elaboration likelihood model of persuasion, 293–296
Elderly, helplessness and health among, 632–638
 death rates, 636
 perceived sense of control and, 636, *637*
Emblems, 67
Emergency intervention, 478–479, 490–495
 altruism and, 503, 505

Emergency intervention (*continued*)
  bystander effect, 37–39, 492–497, 517
    diffusion of responsibility, 497
  emotional arousal
    misattribution of, 503, *504*
    and perceived cost as factors in, 497–502
  Kitty Genovese case and failure of, 491–492
  Latané and Darley's cognitive model, 492, *493*, 494, *495*, *496*, 497, 517
  sex differences in, 362, 489
Emotion(s). *See also* Arousal
  aggression and, 444–449
  attractions and (*see* Attraction)
  attribution and, 100–101
  direct judgments about, 78–86
    cross-cultural universality on, 81–83, *84*
    Darwin's work on, 78–81
    facial scoring systems, 83–86
    recent research on, 81
  elements of, in prejudice (*see* Prejudice)
  of passionate love, 418–421
  prosocial behavior and
    arousal, 497–502
    guilt, 507–508
    moods, 508–511
  social behavior and, 7, 9, 10
Empathy, 74
  vs. personal distress, 503, 505, *506*
Experimental games, 602–607
  Commons Dilemma, 605–607
  Prisoner's Dilemma, 602–605
Environmental factors and social behavior, 8
  aggression and, 442–444
  impact of institutional setting on obedience, 555–556
  impact of institutional setting on the elderly, 632–638
Errors in attribution, 116–126, *127*
  actor-observer effect, 118–122
  fundamental, 116–118
  motivational biases and, 122–126
  salience effects, 121
Equity/inequity in relationships, 425
Equity theory, *14*, 16–17, 26
  applied to relationships, 425
  on attractions, 389–390, 403–404
  impact of receiving help as understood by, 512
  intergroup competition and, 329
Ethics in social psychology research, 49–55
  health care and, 636–638
  measures to reduce problems of, 52–55
  Milgram studies on obedience, 50–51
  problems of, 50–52
Ethnic stereotypes, first impressions and, 66

Ethnocentrism Scale, 319, *320*
Evaluation research, 614
Event schemas (scripts), 142
  race and, 144–145, *146*
Evolution, human
  love and, 408
  prosocial behavior, 482–483
Exact replication, 40–41
Exchange theory, *14*, 16–17
  on attractions, 388–389, 402–403
  impact of receiving help as understood by, 512
Exchange vs. communal relationships, 424
Exhortation, encouraging helping behavior through, 513–515
Experiment(s), 29, 30–33, 37
  bias in, 47–49
  control groups, 31
  vs. correlational studies, 33, *34*
  independent/dependent variables, 30
  Liebert and Baron's design for, 31, *32*, 39, 43, 48
  random assignment in, 30–31, 33
  realism in, 40
  schematic diagram of, *30*
Experimental realism, 40
Experimental setting, bias in, 49
Experimenter(s)
  bias of, in research studies, 48–49
  in Milgram obedience studies, 558
Expert power, leadership's, 590
Expression of Emotion in Man and Animals, The (Darwin), *80*
Expressive traits attributed to women, 348, *349*
External explanations for behavior, 98, *99*
  cube model of attribution and, 108, 110
External validity, 39
Eye contact, 68–70

Facial Action Coding System (FACS), 83–85, 90, *91*
Facial Affect Scoring Technique (FAST), 83, *85*
Facial expressions
  cross-cultural universality in interpreting, 81–83, *84*
  Darwin's work on, 78–79, *80*
  research on accuracy in interpreting, 78–81
  scoring systems for interpreting, 83–86
Family violence, 434, 468–471
  factors predicting child abuse, 470, *471*
  factors predicting spouse abuse, 468, *469*
  reducing by punishment, 467
Fear appeals in persuasion, 261
Features of schemas, 141–142
Feedback in control model of the self, 204, *205*

Femininity, 350, 378–382
  as a dimension separate from masculinity, 380, 382
  traditional/current conceptions of, *381*
Festinger, Leon, his cognitive dissonance theory, 269, 272–274
  study with Carlsmith based on, 274–275, *276*
Field studies vs. laboratory studies, 36–39
Films, aggressive-erotic, and aggression, 459, *460*
First impressions of people, 65–73. *See also* Impression formation
  in courtrooms, 70–71
  nonverbal behaviors, 66–70
  physical characteristics, 65–66
  power of, 70–73
Fishbein and Ajzen's theory of reasoned action, 247–251
Foot-in-the-door reciprocity technique, 549, *551*, 559
Forewarning effects on attitude change, 289
Framing effects in decision making, 163–166
Fraternity initiation, *279*
Free choice, dissonance theory and, 280–281, *282*
French Revolution, 446–447
Freud, Sigmund, theories of aggression, 437, 459
  sex differences, 366–368
Friendships, 388. *See also* Attraction
  proximity and, 392–393
  similarity and, 395
Frustration and aggression, 444–449
  in social revolutions, 446–447
F Scale, 319, *320*
Fundamental attribution error, 116–117, *127*
  ignoring the power of social roles as a, 117–118

Galvanic Skin Response, 29, 229
Gandhi, Mahatma, 473
Gender, 343–385
  changing roles of the sexes, 343–347
  defined, 347
  as defined in everyday life, 376–377
  first impressions and, 66
  masculinity, femininity, and androgyny, 378–382
    conceptions of, *381*
    dimensions of, 380, 382
  psychological research on, 347
  self-perpetuating stereotypes of, 318
  sex differences, 354–363 (*see also* Sex differences)
  stereotypes based on, 347–354
    broad cultural, 350, 352, 354

    evaluations of individuals and, 353
    perception of ability and, 354
    personality, 347–350
    summary, *378*, 383–384
  theories of sex-typing and, 363–378
    biological, 364–366
    cognitive, 370–371
    Freudian, 366–368
    self-presentation, 374–375
    social learning, 368–370
    social role, 371–374
Gender-schema theory, 371
Generalization in classical conditioning, 232–234
Gestalt model of impression formation, Asch's, 135–136, *137*
Gevinger's life cycle of a relationship, *422*
Good Samaritan parable, 513–514
Group(s), 567–611
  competition and cooperation in, 602–607
  conformity to, 524–529, 540–541
    attractiveness and cohesiveness of groups, 532, 534, *535*
    size of groups and, 531, *532*, *533*
    status in the group, 534–535, *536*, 537
  control (experimental), 31, *32*
  criterion, 244
  decision making in, 583–585
  defined, 568–569
  enhancing creativity of, through brainstorming, 582
  explanations for social behavior linked to, 6, 7
  in-group/out-group schemas, 148, *149*, 150, 310–311, 327–328
  leadership in, 588–593
    defining, 588–589
    theories of, 589–593
  mass psychogenic illness in, 598–599
  outcomes and processes, 569
  positive and negative aspects of, 593–601
    deindividuation, *566*, 594–601
  prejudice and, 305–306, 325–331
  research on, 569–571
  summary of, 607–609
  workings of, 571–588
    groupthink decision making, 585–588
    individual vs. group performance, 575–583
    social facilitation, 571–575
Group polarization, 583–585
Group tasks, Steiner's analysis of, 577, *578*, 579
Groupthink, 585–588
  foreign policy errors and, 586, 588

Groupthink (*continued*)
  Salem witchcraft trials as an
    example of, 585, 586–588
  stages of, *587*
Guilt and prosocial behavior,
    507–508

Hardiness, personality type and
    health, 625–627
Hare Krishna sect, 547
Hassles Scale, stress measurement
    with, 617, *619*
Health Locus of Control Scale,
    624–625
Health psychology
  applying, to improve health,
    630–639
    helplessness in the elderly,
      632–638
    personal control, 631–632
    prevention, 638–639
  factors in
    personality, health, and illness,
      623–628
    stress, support, and illness,
      615–623
    type A personality and heart
      disease, 629–630
    variables in, *628*
  medical practice and, 634–635
Heat and aggression, 444
Hedonic relevance principle,
    106–107
Helping behavior. *See* Prosocial
    behavior
Helplessness
  in elderly individuals, 632–638
  learned, 631–632
Hendrick and Hendrick's love style
    scales, 416–417
Heredity and physiology, and social
    behavior, 7, 8
Heuristics and social inference,
    160–163
  availability heuristic, 160–162
  representativeness heuristic,
    162–163
Historical factors in prejudice, 303,
    305
Homicides, 451–452
Homosexuality, attitudes toward,
    223, *224, 227*, 237, 543, *544*
Hopi culture, 439
Hostile aggression, 435, 479
Hutterite culture, 439

"I" self concept
  vs. "me" self concept, 191
  self-awareness in, 201–206
Ideologies and prejudice, 322–325
Illness and health. *See* Health
    psychology
Illustrators, nonverbal behavior, 67
Impression formation, 134–139, *165.*
    See also First impressions of
    people

Anderson's weighted averaging
    model of, 137–139
  Asch's Gestalt model of, 135–136,
    137
Impression management, 207–210
Independent variable, 30
Individual, effect of crowds on. *See*
    Deindividuation
Individual vs. group performance,
    575–583
  creativity and, 582
  social loafing, 579–583
  Steiner's analysis of group tasks,
    577–579
Individualists, 605
Inference, social, 134, 156–166
  attitude formation and, 237–242
  decision making and, 159
  effects of sampling errors on,
    157–160
  framing effects in decision
    making, 163–166
  heuristics as a shortcut to,
    160–163
  influence of schemas on, 148–151
  underutilization of baserate
    information and, 160
Inferential statistics, 43
Influences on social behavior, 6
Informational social influence, 528
  group polarization and, 584
Informed consent in social
    psychological studies, 53–54
Ingratiation, 546
In-group/out-group schemas, 148,
    149, 150, 310–311
  in-group favoritism and self-
    esteem, 327
  out-group derogation and self-
    esteem, 327–328
  prosocial norms and, 486–487
Insects, social facilitation among,
    572, 573, *574*
Instincts and aggression, 437–439
Institutional setting
  learned helplessness and, 632–638
  obedience and, 555–556
Instrumental aggression, 435–436
Instrumental conditioning and
    aggression, 450–451
Instrumental function of attitudes,
    222–223
Instrumental traits attributed to
    men, 348, *349*
Insufficient justification, psychology
    of, 275–278
Insufficient threat and dissonance
    research, 278
Intelligence and leadership, 589
Interaction effect between variables,
    244
  persuasion variables, 269, *270*
Interaction Process Analysis (IPA),
    12 content categories of, *570*
Intergroup competition and
    prejudice, 328–329

creating prejudice, 328–329
  defusing hostility through contact,
    329–339
Internal explanations for behavior,
    98–103
  cube model of attribution and,
    108, 110
  human preference for, 100–103
  personality and, 173, *174,* 175–176
    self-awareness, 202–204
    self-discrepancy, 206
    self-monitoring, 183–188
Internal validity, 39
Intrinsic motivation and attribution,
    112–114
Invasion of privacy in social
    psychology research, 50–51
Investments in relationships,
    403–404

Jackson, Jesse, *266*
"J-curve" theory of violent social
    revolution, 446–*447*
Jenkins Activity Survey, 629
Jews, stereotypes about and
    prejudice toward, 229, 230,
    307, *308,* 319, *320*
John Paul II, Pope, *591*
Johnson, Lyndon, *96*
Jones, Jim, and mass suicide, 553,
    555
Jones and Davis's correspondent
    inferences theory, 103–107
Jury, first impressions of defendants
    by, 70–71
Justification of effort and dissonance
    research, 279–281
Just world hypothesis, 324
Juvenile delinquents, impact of TV
    violence on aggression in,
    453–454, *455*

Kelley's cube model of attribution,
    107–111
Kin selection, 482–483
Knowledge function of attitudes,
    222, 223

Labor, sex-based division of, 372
Laboratory studies vs. field studies,
    36–39
Labor force, women in, *346*
La Guardia, Fiorello, *187*
Language
  role in attitude formation,
    233–234
  stereotype formation and,
    316–318
Latané and Darley's cognitive model
    of emergency intervention
    behavior, 492, *493,* 494, *495,*
    496, 497, 517
Leadership, 588–593
  defined, 588–589
    task-oriented vs.
      socioemotional, 589
  theories of, 589–593

contingency approach,
    592–593
  situational approach, 591–592
  trait approach, 589–590
Learned helplessness, 631–632
Learners in Milgram's obedience
    studies, 558
Learning. *See* Social learning
    theories
Least Preferred Coworker Scale,
    Fiedler's, 592, *594*
Legitimate power, leadership's, 590
Levels of explanation for behavior, 7,
    9–10
  aggression, *438*
  attitudes/beliefs and, *245*
  gender and sex-related
    differences, *365*
  health and illness, *640*
  personality and, *174*
  prejudice, *304*
  prosocial behavior, *481*
  self and, *192*
Liebert and Baron's design for
    experiments on aggression,
    31, *32,* 39, 43, 48
Life Orientation Test, 627
Likability in groups, 570
Likert scales (summated rating
    scales) on attitudes, 224, 226,
    227, 320
Linear model of decision making,
    159
Locus of Control Scale, Rotter's, 624
Logical inference theories on
    attitude formation, 237–242
Lord of the Flies (film), *434*
Love, 388, 389, 407–421
  assortative mating, 394
  determining if you are in, 418–421
  history of, in western culture,
    409–412
  operational definition of
    romantic, 29
  proximity and, 393
  sex ratio hypothesis on, 412–413
  social psychology of, 412–417
    Hendrick and Hendrick's love
      style scales, *416–417*
    Rubin's loving and living scales,
      414
    Sternberg's love components,
      415
  sociobiological perspectives on,
    408–409
    evolutionary origins, 408
    sex differences in, 409
    species differences, 408–409
Low-ball reciprocity technique,
    549–550, *551*

Maintenance specialist, 589
Manson, Charles, *18*
Masculinity, 350, 378–382
  as a dimension separate from
    femininity, 380, 382

Masculinity (*continued*)
traditional/current conceptions
of, *381*
Mass media
aggression and, 8, 451–453
effect of TV violence on
children, 31–36, 39, 43, 452,
453–456, *457, 458,* 472–473
media sex, 456–461
sexual violence, 461–463
gender socialization by, 370
persuasiveness of, 264–266
vicarious contact with groups via,
338–339
"Me" self concept
vs. "I" self concept, 191
self-knowledge and schemas as,
194–201
Mean, statistical, 44, 357, 359, *360*
Media. *See* Mass media
Median, statistical, 44
Mediating variables in social
behavior, 7, 8
Medicine
practice of, as a social
psychological process,
634–635
social psychology and
preventative, 638–639
Memory
inferences based on, 150–151
influence of schemas on, 145–148
stereotypes and organization of,
312, *313,* 314
Men
aggression in, 442
changing roles of, 343–347
differences between women and,
354–363
masculinity concept, 350,
378–382
sex ratio, 412–413
stereotypes about, 347–355,
372–373
affecting evaluations of
individuals, 353
broad cultural, 350, 352, 354
components of, *352, 378*
in different countries, 351
perception of ability and, 354,
355
personality traits, 347–350
Mental health
attribution theory and treatment
for depression, 128
physical attractiveness and,
400–401
self and, 210–213
Mere exposure effect, 262
impact on attractions, 393–394
Mere presence of others, social
facilitation theory and,
574–575, *576*
Message variables influencing
persuasion, 261–264

Meta-analysis, 43
applied to sex differences, 359,
361
Middle, statistical, 44
Mild attraction, 288
Milgram, Stanley, obedience studies,
23–25, 27, 554–555
avoidance of bias in, 47–48, 49
ethics of, 50–51
institutional setting and, 555–556
replication of, 41, *42,* 43
role of command givers and
receivers, 557–558
significance of, 558–559
social pressures and, *556–557*
studies after, 559–560
Minimal groups, research on,
325–326
Minority influence on conformity,
542–545
public vs. private attitudes and,
543, *544*
Modeling
attitude formation, 236
prosocial behavior, 515
sex differences, 369
Moderator variables
acting on attitudes as predictors of
behavior, 244–246
personality/self and, 179–184, 204
social support as, on health,
620–623
Montana Mills, psychogenic illness
at, 598–599
Moods and helping behavior
bad or neutral moods, 508–509,
510
good moods, 509–511
positive, and compliance, 546
Mother-infant bonding, 366, *367*
Mother Teresa, *488*
Motivation factors in attribution
biases concerning, 122–126, *127*
intrinsic motivation, 112–114
Mundane realism, 40
Murstein's stage model of attraction,
397
My Lai massacre, Vietnam, 554

National Commission on the Causes
and Prevention of Violence,
453
Nationality names, conditioning of
attitudes to, *233*
Nazi Party, 218, 219, 522, *523*
Need for cognition scale, *267*
Newsweek, 427, 445, 468, 529
Nominal group technique, 582
Noncommon effects of behaviors,
106
Nonlinear decision rules, 159
Nonreactive measures, 49
Nonverbal behaviors, 66–70
detecting deception in, 87, *88, 89*
kinds of, 67–68
power and preference, 68–70

significance of, in creating first
impressions, 66–67
Norm(s), 485–487
in groups, 568
prosocial behavior and, 485–487
studies on conformity to, 524–529
minority of one against
unanimous majority,
526–529
transmission of arbitrary, across
generations, 524–525, *526*
Normal distribution, statistical, 357,
358
d statistic as difference between
means of, 359, *360*
Normative social influence, 528
Norm of equity, 486
Norm of reciprocity, 16, 485–486
Norm of social responsibility, 486
North, Oliver, *102*
Nussbaum, Hedda, child abuse case,
448–471

Obedience, 522, 552–560
Milgram studies on, 23–25, 27,
554–555
avoidance of bias in, 47–48, 49
ethics of, 50–51
institutional setting and,
555–556
replication of, 41, *42,* 43
role of command givers and
receivers, 557–568
significance of, 558–559
social pressures and, 556–557
nature of, 554–558
institutional setting, 555–556
role of command givers and
receivers, 557–558
social pressures, 556–557
post-Milgram studies, 559–560
variables affecting, *560*
Object constancy, 370–371
Object perception, 61, 62–63
Observational learning and attitude
formation, 236
Occupations, schemas about, 145,
147
Oedipus complex, 367
Olivier, Laurence, *173*
One-sided vs. two-sided persuasive
messages, 262, *263*
Operant conditioning
attitudes, 234–236
attraction, 401
sex differences, 369
Operant responses, 234, *235*
Operational definitions in social
psychology, 27–29
Optimism, 613
health and, 627–628
Overjustification effect, 112–114

Pain and aggression, 442–444
Panglossian optimism, 613
Past environment, individual's, 7, 8

Peer influence. *See* Social influence
Peer review in social psychological
research, 52–53
Penis envy, 367–368
Perception
autokinetic effect, 524, *525, 526*
illusory correlations in social, 155
influence of schemas on, 143–145
Peripheral route to persuasion,
293–295
Perseverance effect of schemas,
153–154
Persona, 172–173
Personal distress vs. empathy, 503,
505, *506*
Personalism principle, 106–107
Personality, 171–217
attitude formation and, 236–237
conformity and, 530
definition of, 172–173
direct judgments about, accuracy
of, 73–78
dimensions of perceived
personality and, 76–78, *79*
early research and statistical
measures on, 74–75
later research on, 75–76
direct judgments about, primacy
effect and, 71–72
effect on health and illness,
623–628
feelings of control, 623–625
hardiness, 625–627
optimism, 627–628
Type A personality and heart
disease, 629–630
gender and, 347–350, 379
prejudice and authoritarian, 306,
319–322
of prosocial behavior, 487–490
development, 489
television programming,
490–491
self and, 189–213 (*see also* Self)
social behavior and theories of, 7,
8, 172–188
internal processes and
mediating variables in, 173,
174
research on, 177–188
social learning theories of,
176–177, 183–188
trait theories of, 175–188, *189*
(*see also* Personality trait(s))
summary, *189,* 213–215
Personality tests, 175–176
Personality trait(s)
aggressiveness as, 440
behavior attributed to, 116–117,
121
gender-based stereotypes on,
347–348, *349,* 350, *351*
impression formation and central,
136, *137,* 138, *139*
leadership and, 589–590

Personality trait(s) (*continued*)
  personality theories based on, 175–188, *189*
  schematic people vs. aschematic people in judging whether traits are self-descriptive, 194, *195*
Personal space, 68–69
Person perception, 61–94. *See also* Relationship(s)
  accuracy of direct judgments, 73–93
  attribution (*see* Attribution)
  first impressions, 65–73
  nature of, 61–62
  object perception vs., 62–63
  prejudice in (*see* Prejudice)
  research topics in, 63–65
  social cognition (*see* Social cognition)
  two main dimensions of, 78, *79*
Person schema, 142
Persuasion
  central vs. peripheral routes to, 293–295
  communication model of, *258*
    channel variables, 264–266
    communicator variables, 258–260
    interactions among, 269, *270*
    lazy vs. thoughtful persuasion, 271
    legacy of, 271
    message variables, 261–264
    target (audience) variables, 266–268
  conformity to, 529
  elaboration likelihood model of, 293–296
Phenomenology of prejudice, 306
Physical and psychological discomfort in research study subjects, 50, 51
Physical attractiveness, 398–401
Physical characteristics, direct judgments of people based on, 65–66
Physiology and aggression, 440–442
Pickford, Mary, *356*
Polarization in groups and decision making, 583–585
Political and economic conservatism scale, 319, *320*
Political beliefs and prejudice, 322–323
Pornography, impact on aggression, 456–461
  sexual violence and, 459, *460*, 461, *462*, 463
Positive reinforcements (rewards), 234–236
Power, inferences of, from nonverbal behavior, 68–70
Precipitating situations, 182
Predictive validity, 176

Preference, inferences of, from nonverbal behavior, 68–70
Prejudice, 237, 301–341
  analyzing, 303–306
  components of, 302–303
  prediction of behavior based on prejudiced attitudes, 243–244, 246
  reducing (intergroup contact hypothesis), 331–339
    effect of contact on, 334–336
    residential contact, 337–338
    school contact between groups, 332–333
    vicarious contact through the media, 338–339
  semantic generalization and aquisition of, 234
  social cause of, 318–331
    authoritarian personality as, 319–322
    intergroup competition as, 328–331
    social groups as, 325–328
    social ideologies as, 322–325
  stereotypes and, 307–318
    consequences of, 316–318
    formation of, 310–316
    measurement of, 307–310
    stigma and, 324
  summary, *330*, 339–340
Premise beliefs, 238–239
Primacy effect
  ability judgments and, 72–73
  personality judgments and, 71–72
Priming effects of schema, 152–153
Prisoner's Dilemma experimental game, 602–605
Private self-consciousness scale, 204
Private self vs. public self, 206
Probabilistic beliefs, stereotypes as, 307
Probability, 43–44
Profile of Nonverbal Sensitivity (PONS), 85–86
Prosocial behavior, 477–519
  approaches to the study of, 480–488
    cultural norms, 485–487
    levels of explanation, *481*
    sociobiological theories, 482–485
  defining and measuring, 478–480
  encouraging, 513–517
    assuming responsibility, 516
    education and, 517
    exhortation, 513–515
    humanizing victims, 516–517
    modeling, 515
  impact of receiving help, 512
  psychology of, 487–511
    emergency intervention, 490–505
    guilt, moods, and helping, 505–511
    personality, 487–490

  summary, *511*
  television programming and, 490–491
  sex differences in, 362, 489
  summary, 517–519
Prospect theory, 164–166
Prototypes
  personality traits, 178
  schemas and, 142
Proximity, relationship to attraction, 392–393
Psychoanalytic theory applied to sex differences, 366–368
Psychogenic illness and deindividuation, 598–599
Psychological reactance theory and compliance, 550–551
Public self
  vs. private self, 206
  self-presentational strategies for, 207–210
Punishment, controlling aggression with, 466–467

Quasi-experimental studies, 36, *37*

Race, schemas about, 143–146, *147*
  in-group/out-group and, 148, *149*, 150, 310–311
  prejudice about (*see* Prejudice)
Racial slurs and stereotype formation, 316, *317*, 318
Racism, symbolic, 323
Random assignment, 30–31, 33
  absent in quasi-experimental studies, 36
Random sampling, 30–31
Rape, media sex, pornography and, 459, 460–461, *462*, 463
Reactance and compliance, 550–551
Realism in social psychology experiments, 40
Real-life situations. *See* Situation(s)
Reasoned action, theory of, 247–251
Recency effect, 72
Reciprocal altruism, 483–485
Reciprocity and compliance, 546–548
Reference groups, 535
Referent power, leadership's, 590
Reflected glory, self-presentation through, 209
Regulators, nonverbal behavior, 68
Relationship(s), 387–431
  attraction
    beginnings of, 389–401
    stage models of, 397
    theories of, 401–408
    trends in the study of, 388–389
  life cycle of close, *422*
    building stage, 423
    continuation and consolidation, 423–424
    deterioration and decline, 424–427
    endings of, 427
    initial attraction, 421–422

  love, 407–421
    passionate, 418–421
    social psychology of, 412–417
    sociobiological perspective on, 408–409
    in western culture, 409–412
    summary, *420*, 428–429

Relative deprivation in frustration and aggression, 446–447
Relevance of social psychological research, 55
Reliability of research measures, 29, 176
  attitude scales, 228
  test-retest, 176
Religion
  attitudes about, *225*, 237
  prejudice based on, 323, 325
Repetition of persuasive messages, 262–264
Replication in social psychology studies, 39–43
Report of the Commission on Obscenity and Pornography, 456
Representativeness heuristic, 162–163
Research in social psychology, 23–57
  ethics in, 49–55
    health care, 636–638
    measures to reduce problems, 52–55
    problems, 50–52
  evaluation, 614
  issues in, 25–49
    bias, 47–49
    generalizing from study results, 36–43
    kinds of studies, 29–36
    operational definitions, 27–29
    realism in experiments, 40
    reliability and validity of measures, 29
    statistics, 43–47
    theories, 26–27
  role of theory in focusing and directing, 13
  social relevance of, 55
  summary, *37*, 55–57
  theory, hypothesis, and, *28*
Residential contact, reducing prejudice through, 337–338
Response sets, 74
Responsibility, assumption of, 516
Reward power, leadership's, 590
Rewards and attribution, 112–114
Ringelmann effect, *580*
Robber's Cave study, 329–331
Role-schemas, 142
Roper Organization, 427
Rubin's loving and liking scales, *414*
Rusbult and Zembrodt's study on dissatisfaction in relationships, 425, *426*
Rushdie, Salman, *314*

Salem witchcraft hysteria as group behavior, 566–569, 585, 586–588, 598–599
Salience effects in attribution, 121, *127*
Sampling
  errors in, effects on inferences, 157–158, 160
  errors in, effects on stereotypes, 311–312
  random, 30–31
Satanic Verses, The (Rushdie), *314*
Schedule of Recent Life Experiences, stress measurement with, 617, *618*
Schema(s), 9, 134, 139–155, *164*
  attitudes as, 291–292
  causal, of attribution, 111–116
  effects of, on social cognition, 142–153
  gender and sex-typing, 371
  illusory correlations in, 155
  influence on perception, 143, 144, 145
  kinds of, in social cognition, 142
  nature of schemas, 141–142
  persistence of, 153–154
  prejudice and, 302–303, 316–318
  self (*see* Self-schemas)
Schools, reducing prejudice by integrating groups in, 332–333
Scripts (event schemas), 142
Self, 189–213. See also Personality
  awareness theory, 201–206
  classic views of, 190–194
  knowledge and schema about one's, 194–201
  mental health and, 210–213
  monitoring, 184–188
  public and private, 206–210
  role of, in social psychology, 7, 10–11
  summary, *207*, 213–215
Self-awareness theory, 201–206
  consequences of self-directed attention, 202, *203*
  control model of self, 204, *205*
  internal standards and self-awareness, 202–204
  self-discrepancy, 206
Self-concept. See also Self-schemas
  aspects of child's, 194
  pragmatic vs. principled, 184
Self development, 191–194
Self disclosure in relationships, 422, 634
Self-discrepancy, 206
Self-enhancement vs. self-verification, 200–201
Self-esteem
  impact of help on, 512
  in-group favoritism/out-group derogation and, 327–328
Self-fulfilling prophecy, 151

Self-handicapping strategies in attribution, 124–*126*, *127*
Self-monitoring of personality traits, 184–188
  in everyday life, 186
  as a moderator variable, *184*
  responsiveness to social setting and, *188*
  Snyder's scale to determine, *185*
Self-perception theory, 240–241
  as alternative to dissonance theory in attitude change, 283–288
Self-presentation theory
  attributions and, 124
  gender and sex-typing based on, 374–375
Self-reference effect, 198, *199*
Self-schemas, 142, 194–195
  "chunking" of schema-relevant information, *197*
  complexity of, 197–198
    effect on depression, 213
  schematic people as experts on the self, 195–197
  schematic people vs. aschematic people in judging if traits are self-descriptive, 194, *195*
  self reference effect, 198, *199*
  self's resistance to change, 198–200
  self-verification vs. self-enhancement, 200–201
Self-serving biases in attribution, 122–124, *127*
Self-verification, 199–200, *201*
  vs. self-enhancement, 200–201
Semantic differential scales on attitudes, 226
Semantic generalization, 232–234
Sesame Street (television), *338*
Severity of initiation and dissonance research, 279–280, *281*
Sex
  mass media, and aggression linked to, 456–462
  predicting behavior regarding premarital, from attitudes, *250*
Sex(es). See also Gender
  defined, 347
  research based on gender and, 347, 356–362
Sex differences, 354–363
  aggression and, 359, 362, 442
    in children, TV violence and, 456, *457*
  conformity and, 530–531
  in everyday life, 376–377
  in love and sexuality, 409
  meaning of, 362–363
  prosocial behavior and, 362, 489
  reactions to receiving help and, 512
  study of, 356–362
    evidence for sex differences, 359, *361*, 362

statistical assessment, 357, *358*, 359, *360*
theories of, 363–375
  biological, 364–366
  cognitive approaches, 370–371
  Freudian, 366–368
  levels of explanation, *365*
  social learning, 368–370
  social role, 371–374, 531
Sex ratio and love, 412–413
Sexual identity, schemas about, 150
Sexual violence and pornography, 459, *460*, 461, *462*, 463
Sherif, Muzafer, autokinetic effect in conformity studies, 524–526
Significance levels in social psychology studies, 43–44
Similarity, relationship to attraction, 394–398
  in attitudes, *396*
Single minorities, 542
Situation(s)
  applying social psychology to, 17–19 (*see also* Applied social psychology)
  attributions based on, 117, *120*
  detecting deception in real-life, 89, 92–93
  gender definitions in everyday, 376–377
  leadership development in stressful, 591–592
  personality and social behavior linked to, 179–183
  precipitating, 182
  self-monitoring in everyday, 186
  self-presentation, 374–375
  social behavior and individual's current, 7, 8
Skinner, B. F., and operant conditioning, 234–236
Sleeper effect in persuasive messages, 259, 271
Smiles, detecting deceptive, 90–91
Social behavior
  aggressive (*see* Aggression)
  attitudes affecting (*see* Attitude(s); Attitude change)
  emphasis on, by social psychology, 10
  explanations of, by social psychology, 6–10
    levels of explanation, 7, 9–10
    responses to be explained, 10
  gender and (*see* Gender)
  influence(s) on, 6 (*see also* Social influence)
    schemas as, 151–152
  intimate (*see* Relationship(s))
  personality and (*see* Personality; Self)
  prejudicial (*see* Prejudice)
  prosocial (*see* Prosocial behavior)
  understanding individuals' (*see* Attribution; Direct judgments; Social cognition)

Social cognition, 133–169
  attractions and, 388–389
  conclusions on, 166–167
  gender and sex typing, 370–371
  impression formation, 134–139
    Gestalt model, 135–137
    weighted averaging model, 137–139
  prosocial behavior and, 492–497
  reducing aggression through strategies based on, 472–473
  as research topic, 63, *64*, 65, *164*
  schemas and, 139–155
    effects of, 142–143
    illusory correlations, 155
    influence of, on perception, 144
    kinds of, 142
    nature of, 141–142
    persistence of, 153–154
  social inference and decision making, 156–166
    effects of sampling errors, 157–158, 160
    framing effects, 163–166
    heuristics, 160–163
    underutilization of baserate information, 160
  summary, 167–168
Social comparison processes and group polarization, 584–585
Social comparison theory on anxiety-affiliation relationships, 390
Social desirability principle, 104–106
  impression formation and, 137–138
Social facilitation, 26, 571–575
  effect of, *572*
  among insects, *572*, 573, *574*
  mere presence of others and, 574, 575, *576*
  Zajonc's theory of, 572, *573*, 574
Social feedback and the self, 191
Social identity theory, 326–327
Social influence, 521–565. See also Persuasion
  brainwashing, 552–553
  compliance, 522, 545–551
    commitment and, 549–550
    positive moods and, 546
    psychological reactance and, 550–551
    reciprocity and, 546–548
    strategies for gaining, *551*
  conformity, 522, 524–545
    definitions and models of, 540–541
    factors influencing, 529–545
    research on, 524–529
    variables affecting, *538*
  diamond model of, 540–541
  levels of, 523
  normative vs. informational, 528
  obedience, 522, 552–560

Social influence (*continued*)
Milgram studies, 23–25, 27, 41, *42*, 43, 47–48, 49, 50–51, 554–555, 558–559
nature of, 554–558
post-Milgram studies, 559–560
variables affecting, *560*
resisting, 560–562
summary, 562–564
Social Influence Model, 531, 532, *533*
Social interventions, designing, 614
Social learning theories, 13, *14*
on aggression, 449–463
mass media sex, 456–461
mass media violence, 451–456
sexual violence, 461–463
on attitude formation, 222, 230–236
on attraction, 401–402
on gender and sex differences, 368–370
on personality, 177–178
self-monitoring as, 183–188
vs. trait theories, *180–181*
relationship to equity and exchange theories, 16
Social loafing, 579–583
loss of coordination in additive groups and, *581*
Ringelmann effect, *580*
Social norms. *See* Norm(s)
Social penetration theory, 421
Social programs, evaluating, 615
Social psychologists, *19–20*
Social psychology, 3–20
application of, 17–20 (*see also* Applied social psychology)
human responses to disaster and, 3–6, 18
nature of, 6–11
explanations of social behavior, 6–10
role of the self, 10–11
study of social behavior, 10
overview, *12*
relationship of, to other sciences, 11, 26
research (*see* Research in social psychology)
theories in, 11–17
four theoretical perspectives, 13–17
functions of, 11–13
Social questions, role of social psychology in, 614
Social relations model of accuracy in personality judgment, 76
Social restraints on aggression, 472
Social revolution and aggression, 446–447
Social role(s)
gender and sex stereotypes, 351, 371–374, 531
ignoring the power of, as an attribution error, 117–118

Social support
conformity/nonconformity and, 537
health and, 620–623
Social traps, 605
Sociobiological theory
attraction and love explained by, 408–409
prosocial behavior, 482–485
Socioemotional leadership, 589
effectiveness of, 592, *593, 594*
Sports and catharsis, 465
Spouse abuse, 434, 468, *469*
Stable causes for behavior, 98, *99*
Standard deviation, statistical, 358
Standardization, avoiding bias through, 47–48
Statistical measures in social psychology research, 43–47
on accuracy of personality judgments, 74–75, 76
correlational coefficients, 44–47
d statistic, 359, *360*
mean, median, and middle, 44, 357
meta-analysis, 43, 359, *361*
normal distribution, 357, *358*
on sex differences, 357–359
significant levels, 43–44
standard deviation, 358
Status in a group and conformity, 534–537
Steinberg, Joel, child abuse case, 468–471
Steiner's analysis of group tasks, 577–579
Stereotype(s), 306–318
accuracy/inaccuracy of, 75, 310–311
consequences of, 316–318
formation of, 310–316
gender, 347–354, 372, *373*
measuring, 307–310
on physical attractiveness, 400
self-perpetuating nature of, 318
Sternberg's love components, *415*
Stigma and prejudice, 324
Stimulus object of prejudice, 306
Stimulus-value-role model of relationships, 397
Stress, impact on health, 615–620
diseases, 619–620
measurement of
with Hassles Scale, 617, *619*
with Schedule of Recent Life Experiences, 617, *618*
personal hardiness and, 625, *626*, 627
Subject bias in research studies, 48–49
Subjective norms, 247
weighing of, vs. weighing of attitudes, 249
Subjective reports, 27
Suicide, 451

mass, by followers of Jim Jones, 553
Summated rating scales (Likert scales) on attitudes, 224, 226, 227, *320*
Summed behaviors, 178
Superordinate goal, 329–331
Supports, external, for relationships, 424
Swaggart, Jimmy, *208*
Symbolic racism, 323
Systemic replication, 41, *42*

Target-based expectancies, 105
Target variables influencing persuasion, 266–268
Task ability in groups, 570–571
Task-oriented leadership, 589
effectiveness of, 592, *593, 594*
Task specialist, 589
Taylor Manifest Anxiety Scale, 27
Television
impact of prosocial programming on children, 490–491
impact of violence in, 451
on children's aggression, 31–35, 36, 39, 43, 452, 453–456, *457, 458*, 472–473
percentage of programs containing violence, years 1967–1985, *454*
vicarious contact with other groups through, *338*
Ten Question Gender Game, 376–377
Testosterone and aggression, 442
Test-retest reliability, 29
That's-not-all reciprocity technique, 548–549, *551*
Theories in social psychology, 11–17, 26–27
four classes of, 13–17
functions of, 11–13
relationship of, to research, *28*
role of, in focusing research, 13
summary of, *14*
Threats and dissonance research, 278
Thurston scales on attitudes, 223–224, *225*
Time, 529, 583
Time as a variable in predicting behavior from attitudes, 249
Tit-for-tat strategy, 483, 604–605
Touching, 69–70
Tragedy of the commons, 605, 606–607
Traits. *See* Personality trait(s)
Type A personality and coronary heart disease, 629–630

Unconditioned stimulus/response, 230, *231*
United Nations: Demographic Yearbook, 7
United States Commission on Civil Rights, 344

U.S. Department of Health and Human Services, 629
U.S. Department of Labor, Women's Bureau, 345
Unobtrusive measures, 49
Unstable causes for behavior, 98, *99*

Validity of research measures, 29
in attitude scales, 226, 228, 229
construct, 176
discriminant, 176
internal and external, 39
predictive, 176
Value-expectancy model of attitude formation, 239–242
Value-expressive function of attitudes, 222, 223
Variables
in aggression, *438*
in attitudes and beliefs, 244, *245*, 246
in attraction, 388
in conformity, 529–545
confounded, 39
correlational coefficients, 44–47
dependent and independent, 30
in gender and sex differences, 364, *365*
in health psychology, *628, 640*
interaction effect between, 244
moderator (*see* Moderator variables)
obedience, *560*
in personality theories, *174*, 179–184, 204
in persuasion, 258–268
possible causal relationships among correlated, *35*
in prejudice, *304*
in prosocial behavior, *481*
in social behavior, 7
in study of the self, *192*
time as, 249
volition as, 249
Verbal aggression and catharsis, 466–467
Victims
dissonance theory and derogation of, 280, *284*
humanizing to encourage prosocial behavior, 516–517
in Milgram obedience studies, 558
Violence. *See* Aggression; Family violence
Vocal cues of deception, 87
Volition
dissonance theory, attitude change, and, 280–281, *282*
as a variable in predicting behavior from attitudes, 249

War, 435–436
Weapons effect on aggression, 452
Weaver, Sigourney, *357*
Weighted averaging model
of decision making, 159
of impression formation, 137–139

Women
    changing film images of, *356, 357*
    changing roles of, *334, 335,*
        343–347
    differences between men and,
        354–363
    femininity concept in, 350
    in the labor force, *346*
    sex ratio, 412–413
    stereotypes about, 347–355,
        372–373

affecting evaluations of
    individuals, 353
broad cultural, 350, 352, 354
components of, *352, 377*
in different countries, *351*
perception of ability and, 354,
    355

personality traits, 347–350
World Almanac, The, 434

Yale communication model of
    persuasion, 257–269, 271

Zuni culture, 439

Acknowledgments

Quotation Credits **Chapter 2** Stanley Milgram, *Obedience to Authority*. Copyright © 1974 by Stanley Milgram. Reprinted by permission of Harper & Row, Publishers, Inc. **Chapter 4** Dale Wasserman and Joe Darion, *Man of La Mancha: A Musical Play*. Dialogue copyright © 1966 by Dale Wasserman. Lyrics copyright © 1965 by Andrew Scott, Inc./Helena Music Corp.; international copyright secured; all rights reserved; sole selling agent is Cherry Lane Music Company, Inc. Quotations from the dialogue are reprinted by permission of Dale Wasserman. Quotations from the lyrics are reprinted by permission of Cherry Lane Music Company, Inc. **Chapter 6** Hermann Hesse, *Steppenwolf*. Translated by Basil Creighton. Copyright 1929 by Henry Holt and Company and renewed 1957 by Basil Creighton. Quotations are reprinted by permission of Henry Holt and Company, Inc. Stephen A. Hoffmann, "The Doctor as Dramatist," *Newsweek*, February 1, 1988, p. 10. The quotation from this article is reprinted by permission of Stephen A. Hoffmann. **Chapter 7** Adolf Hitler, *Mein Kampf*. Translated by Ralph Manheim. Copyright 1943 and copyright © renewed 1971 by Houghton Mifflin Company. Quotations are reprinted by permission of Houghton Mifflin Company. **Chapter 9** Toni Morrison, *The Bluest Eye*. Copyright © 1970 by Toni Morrison. Quotations are reprinted by permission of Henry Holt and Company, Inc. **Chapter 10** Ursula K. LeGuin, *The Left Hand of Darkness*. Copyright 1969 by Ursula LeGuin. Quotations are reprinted by permission of The Berkley Publishing Group. **Chapter 11** Abigail Van Buren, *Dear Abby* column, May 6, 1987. Copyright 1987 Universal Press Syndicate. All rights reserved. A portion of the column is reprinted by permission of Universal Press Syndicate. **Chapter 12** William Golding, *The Lord of the Flies*. Copyright © 1954 by William Golding. Quotations are reprinted by permission of The Putnam Publishing Group. **Chapter 14** George Orwell, *1984*. Copyright 1946 Harcourt Brace Jovanovich, Inc. Copyright renewed © 1977 Sonia Brownell Orwell. Reprinted by permission of Harcourt Brace Jovanovich, Inc. **Chapter 15** Arthur Miller, "The Crucible," *Collected Plays, Volume I*. Copyright © 1957, renewed © 1985 by Arthur Miller. All rights reserved. Quotations are reprinted by permission of Viking Penguin, a division of Penguin Books USA, Inc.

Photo Credits p. 2 Steve Raymer © National Geographic Society. p. 5 Sovfoto. p. 16 Peanuts © Charles M. Schulz. Reprinted by permission of UFS, Inc. p. 18 top left: National Archives; top right: UPI/Bettmann Newsphotos; bottom: Bruce Davidson/Magnum. p. 22 Ken Heyman. p. 25 both: Copyright 1965 by Stanley Milgram. From the film *Obedience*, distributed by the New York University Film Library and the Pennsylvania State University, PCR. p. 31 Gale Zucker/Stock, Boston. p. 38 Hazel Hankin/Stock, Boston. p. 41 Copyright 1965 by Stanley Milgram. From the film *Obedience*, distributed by the New York University Film Library and the Pennsylvania State University, PCR. p. 53 © 1988 by Sidney Harris/American Scientist Magazine. p. 60 Henri Cartier-Bresson/Magnum. p. 67 Popperfoto. p. 69 Peter Menzel/Stock, Boston. p. 79 Ken Heyman. p. 80 Office of Special Collections, The New York Public Library. p. 82 Ken Heyman. p. 83 Courtesy Paul Ekman, Human Interaction Laboratory, University of California, San Francisco. p. 85 Courtesy Paul Ekman, Human Interaction Laboratory, University of California, San Francisco. p. 86 Rose Is Rose. Reprinted by Permission of UFS, Inc. p. 91 Courtesy Paul Ekman, Human Interaction Laboratory, University of California, San Francisco. p. 96 Courtesy Lyndon Baines Johnson Library, Austin, Texas. p. 98 Peanuts © Charles M. Schulz. Reprinted by permission of UFS, Inc. p. 102 AP/Wide World Photos. p. 104 UPI/Bettmann Newsphotos. p. 105 Ken Miller, *Kim's Mohawk*, © 1987. p. 110 Performing Arts Research Center, The New York Public Library. p. 122 Ken Miller, *Early Punks, Cole Street*, © 1983. p. 132 Robert Doisneau/Photo Researchers. p. 135 Esther Bubley/University of Louisville Photographic Archives. p. 140 Springer/Bettmann Film Archive. p. 154 Jane Scherr/Jeroboam. p. 157 Calvin and Hobbes © 1989 Universal Press Syndicate. Reprinted with permission. All rights reserved. p. 161 Reprinted with permission of The San Francisco Examiner © 1989 The San Francisco Examiner. p. 170 Springer/Bettmann Film Archive. p. 173 Culver Pictures. p. 187 AP/Wide World Photos. p. 190 Frans de Waal, Wisconsin Regional Primate Research Center. p. 193 Marvin. Reprinted with special permission of NAS, Inc. p. 196 Michael Grecco/Stock, Boston. p. 208 UPI/Bettmann Newsphotos. p. 218 Bill Aron/Jeroboam. p. 220 The Bettmann Archive. p. 222 Elizabeth Mangelsdorf/San Francisco Examiner. p. 234 Ken Heyman. p. 247 Henri Cartier-Bresson/Magnum. p. 256 Sovfoto. p. 259 The Museum of Modern Art/Film Stills Archive. p. 266 Bob Daemmrich/Stock, Boston. p. 272 Doonesbury © 1989 Universal Press Syndicate. G. B. Trudeau. Reprinted with permission. All rights reserved. p. 279 UPI/Bettmann Newsphotos. p. 300 Arthur Siegel/Library of Congress. p. 302 Bruce Davidson/Magnum. p. 305 Prints Old & Rare, San Francisco. p. 314 Derek Hudson/Sygma. p. 327 Bloom County by Berke Breathed © 1989 Washington Post Writers Group. Reprinted with permission. p. 334 National Archives. p. 335 Hazel Hankin/Stock, Boston. p. 338 left: Culver Pictures; right: © 1989 Children's Television Workshop; Sesame Street Muppet Characters © Muppets, Inc. p. 342 Ken Heyman. p. 344 National Archives. p. 345 left: Elliot Erwitt/Magnum; right: Hazel Hankin/Stock, Boston. p. 356 Culver Pictures. p. 357 The Museum of Modern Art/Film Stills Archive. p. 367 Ken Heyman. p. 369 Patricia Hollander Gross/Stock, Boston. p. 379 Doonesbury © 1986 Universal Press Syndicate. G. B. Trudeau. Reprinted with permission. All rights reserved. p. 386 Elliot Erwitt/Magnum. p. 395 Ken Miller, *Marisa & Paul (The Kiss)* © 1985. p. 399 © 1978 Edward Koren. p. 406 top: Cornell Capa/Magnum; bottom: © Sage Sohier, *Lloyd and Joel*. p. 407 top: Elizabeth Crews; bottom: Elliot Erwitt/Magnum. p. 411 Library of Congress. p. 418 Bizarro © Dan Piraro. Reprinted by permission of Chronicle Features, San Francisco. p. 419 Brassaï, *The Kiss*, 1935–37, © G. Brassaï 1989. p. 432 Lois Greenfield/Stock, Boston. p. 434 both: The Museum of Modern Art/Film Stills Archive. p. 443 Stephen J. Potter/Stock, Boston. p. 445 UPI/Bettmann Newsphotos. p. 448 Sygma. p. 450 Doonesbury © 1987 Universal Press Syndicate. G. B. Trudeau. Reprinted with permission. All rights reserved. p. 465 Peanuts © Charles M. Schulz. Reprinted by Permission of UFS, Inc. p. 469 Ari Mintz/Newsday. p. 471 Newsday. p. 473 Margaret Bourke-White, Life Magazine © Time Inc. p. 476 W. Eugene Smith/Black Star. p. 478 AP/Wide World Photos. p. 479 Sibylla Herbrich. p. 484 Frans de Waal, Wisconsin Regional Primate Research Center. p. 488 Arnaud de Wildenberg/Sygma. p. 500 Ellis Herwig/Stock, Boston. p. 501 Copyright © The Estate of Garry Winogrand. Courtesy Fraenkel Gallery, San Francisco. p. 507 Drawing by Weber; © 1984 The New Yorker Magazine, Inc. p. 515 Elizabeth Crews. p. 520 Diego Goldberg/Sygma. p. 522 Tom

Cheek/Stock, Boston. p. 523 AP/Wide World Photos. p. 543 David Robert Austen/Stock, Boston. p. 547 Owen Franken/Stock, Boston. p. 548 Foxtrot © 1989 Universal Press Syndicate. Reprinted with permission. All rights reserved. p. 550 Calvin and Hobbes © 1986 Universal Press Syndicate. Reprinted with permission. All rights reserved. p. 555 Philippe Ledru/Sygma. p. 566 David Powers/Stock, Boston. p. 568 Fred Fehl. p. 569 Drawing by Modell; © 1989 The New Yorker Magazine, Inc. p. 572 Carson Baldwin, Jr./Animals, Animals. p. 577 George W. Gardner/Stock, Boston. p. 586 Bizarro © Dan Piraro. Reprinted by Permission of Chronicle Features, San Francisco. p. 590 AP/Wide World Photos. p. 591 Giansanti/Sygma. p. 595 Hulton Picture Library/ The Bettmann Archive. p. 596 Philip Zimbardo, Stanford University. p. 601 The Museum of Modern Art/Film Stills Archive. p. 606 George Bellerose/ Stock, Boston. p. 612 George Gardner/The Image Works. p. 614 Martha Swope Associates/Carol Rosegg. p. 616 Jean-Claude Lejeune/Stock, Boston. p. 617 Jerry Howard/Stock, Boston. p. 624 Frank & Ernest. Reprinted by permission of NEA, Inc. p. 632 Peanuts © Charles M. Schulz. Reprinted by permission of UFS, Inc. p. 638 Elizabeth Crews/Stock, Boston. p. 639 Annie Wells.

Insert 1: Explanations of Social Behavior First page, top to bottom: S. Hrdy/Anthro-Photo (monkeys); Napoleon Chagnon/Anthro-Photo (Yanomamo parade). Second page, top to bottom: Charlie Cole/Picture Group (Hells Angels); Cary Wolinsky/Stock, Boston (Amish); Bob Daemmrich/Stock, Boston (wrestlers). Third page, top to bottom: Jeffrey W. Myers/Stock, Boston (children with guns); Jean-Claude Lejeune/Stock, Boston (childrens' soccer teams); Bill Gallery/Stock, Boston (highway gridlock). Fourth page, clockwise from top: AP/Wide World Photos (lynching); AP/Wide World Photos (M. L. King); AP/Wide World Photos (Hitler). **Insert 2: Applying Social Psychology** First page, clockwise from top: UPI/Bettmann Newsphotos (desegregation/ troops); J. P. Laffont/Sygma (Tokyo crowd scene); Stacy Pick/Stock, Boston (courtroom); Billy E. Barnes/Stock, Boston (two women at computer). Second page, clockwise from top: Kevin Horan/Stock, Boston (classroom); Bob Daemmrich/Stock, Boston (Customs stop); Lawrence Migdale/Stock, Boston (men in office). Third page, clockwise from top: Richard Pasley/Stock, Boston (therapy); Courtesy San Francisco AIDS Foundation ("Don't Share"); Courtesy American Cancer Society ("Smoking Pollutes"). Fourth page, left to right: Richard Pasley/Stock, Boston (three elderly women); Donald Dietz/Stock, Boston (recycling). **Insert 3: Varieties of Social Influence** First page, clockwise from top: James Holland/Stock, Boston (birth); Robert V. Eckert Jr./ Stock, Boston (breastfeeding); Bill Gallery/Stock, Boston (father and son). Second page, clockwise from top left: Bob Daemmrich/Stock, Boston (tug-of-war); Jerry Howard/Stock, Boston (Girl Scouts); Youth Services Section, Los Angeles City Schools (child in wheelchair with bat); Ellis Herwig/Stock, Boston (prom); Rick Smolan/Stock, Boston (Asian couple). Third page, clockwise from top right: Michael Grecco/Stock, Boston (strikers); Bill Gallery/ Stock, Boston (middle-aged couple); Bob Daemmrich/Stock, Boston (shuffleboard). Fourth page, top to bottom: Rick Browne/Stock, Boston (elderly mother/daughter); John Coletti/Stock, Boston (cemetery scene). **Insert 4: Human Nature: Good or Evil?** First page, clockwise from top left: Scala/Art Resource (Masaccio); National Gallery of Art, Washington, D.C., (Schongauer engraving); Margaret Bourke-White, Life Magazine © Time Inc. (Buchenwald prisoners). Second page, clockwise from top left: Ron Haviv/Agence France-Presse (Panama beating); AP/Wide World Photos (White supremacists); S. Franklin/Sygma (Belgian soccer riots); Peter Turnley/Black Star (Chinese tanks); Peter Turnley/Black Star (Chinese student demonstrations). Third page, clockwise from top left: Peter Turnley/Black Star (medical workers, aftermath of Beijing massacre); Jose Carrillo/Stock, Boston (Sequoia trees); Marcel Miranda/The Names Project (Names Project quilt). Fourth page, clockwise from top left: The Massillon Museum, Massillon, Ohio (barn raising); The Bettmann Archive (suffragettes); James H. Karales (Selma march).